HISTORIC DOCUMENTS CUMULATIVE INDEX 1972–2005

CQ Press

A Division of Congressional Quarterly Inc.
Washington, D.C.

Carolyn McGovern wrote the first edition of the *Historic Documents Index.*
Victoria Agee was the indexer on this volume.
Sally Ryman was the editor on this volume.

CQ Press
1255 22nd Street, NW, Suite 400
Washington, DC 20037

Phone: 202-729-1900; toll-free, 1-866-4CQ-PRESS (1-866-427-7737)

Web: www.cqpress.com

Cover design: McGaughy Design, Centerville, Virginia
Cover photos: AP Images

∞ The paper used in this publication exceeds the requirements of the American National Standard for Information Sciences—Permanence of Paper for Printed Library Materials, ANSI Z39.48-1992.

Printed and bound in the United States of America

10 09 08 07 06 1 2 3 4 5

The Library of Congress cataloged the first issue of *Historic Documents* as follows:

Historic documents. 1972–
Washington. Congressional Quarterly Inc.

1. United States — Politics and government — 1945– — Yearbooks.
2. World politics — 1945– — Yearbooks. I. Congressional Quarterly Inc.

E839.5H57 917.3'03'9205 72-97888

ISBN 0-87289-327-8
ISSN 0892-080X

EXPLANATORY NOTE

This cumulative index covers all documents presented in the thirty-four volumes of *Historic Documents,* from 1972 through 2005.

Each index entry gives the year, shown in bold, of every *Historic Documents* volume that contains information on that subject, followed by the page numbers. Cross-references account for alternative names of commissions, committees, countries, and treaties and help the reader locate people, places, concepts, and events.

Members of Congress are identified by their party and state. The dates in parentheses after the names of former members indicate the years of their congressional service; no distinction is made between House and Senate service. Dates of service are not given for former members who became president.

If the name of a Supreme Court case is not known, the list under the *Supreme Court opinions* heading may jog the memory. Alternatively, the main issue in the case may be found under *Supreme Court,* under a particular justice's name, or under the listing for the issue itself.

American domestic and foreign affairs can be found under the appropriate subject headings. Supreme Court cases involving the United States as a party are listed under the opposing party's name.

Names of Chinese leaders are listed for the most part as they are in the text of *Historic Documents,* which took into account the change made by the Chinese government in 1979. However, leaders who became known by their old-style names are listed under their traditional names—for instance, Mao Tse-tung, Lin Piao.

The following list identifies a number of abbreviations that are frequently used in the subentries of this index:

ABA, American Bar Association
ABM, Anti-Ballistic Missile Treaty
ACLU, American Civil Liberties Union
AID, Agency for International Development
AIDS, acquired immune deficiency syndrome
AIG, American International Group
AIM, American Indian Movement
ALS, amyotrophic lateral sclerosis (*aka* Lou Gehrig's disease)
AMA, American Medical Association
ANC, African National Congress
AT&T, American Telephone & Telegraph Co.
ATF, Bureau of Alcohol, Tobacco, Firearms, and Explosives
AWACS, Advanced Warning and Control System
BCCI, Bank of Credit and Commerce International
BIA, Bureau of Indian Affairs
CAFTA, Central American Free Trade Agreement
CASA, National Center on Addiction and Substance Abuse
CBO, Congressional Budget Office
CBS, Columbia Broadcasting System
CDC, Centers for Disease Control and Prevention
CDF, Children's Defense Fund

Explanatory Note

CEA, Council of Economic Advisers
CETA, Comprehensive Employment and Training Act
CFCs, chlorofluorocarbons
CFTC, Commodity Futures Trading Commission
CIA, Central Intelligence Agency
CLC, Cost of Living Council
CRP, Committee for the Re-election of the President
CSCE, Conference on Security and Cooperation in Europe
DMZ, Demilitarized Zone
DOD, Department of Defense
EC, European Community
EEOC, Equal Employment Opportunity Commission
EPA, Environmental Protection Agency
ERA, Equal Rights Amendment
EU, European Union
FAA, Federal Aviation Administration
FAO, Food and Agriculture Organization
FBI, Federal Bureau of Investigation
FCC, Federal Communications Commission
FDA, Food and Drug Administration
FDIC, Federal Deposit Insurance Corporation
FEA, Federal Energy Administration
FEC, Federal Election Commission
Fed, Federal Reserve Board
FEMA, Federal Emergency Management Agency
FOIA, Freedom of Information Act
FTC, Federal Trade Commission
GAO, General Accounting Office; Government Accountability Office
GATT, General Agreement on Tariffs and Trade
HEW, Health, Education, and Welfare Department
HHS, Health and Human Services Department
HIV, human immunodeficiency virus
HUD, Housing and Urban Development Department
IAEA, International Atomic Energy Agency
ICC, International Criminal Court
ICJ, International Court of Justice
ILO, International Labor Organization
IMF, International Monetary Fund
INF, Intermediate-range Nuclear Force Treaty
INS, Immigration and Naturalization Service
IOM, Institute of Medicine
IRA, Irish Republican Army
IRS, Internal Revenue Service
ITT, International Telephone and Telegraph Corp.
MIA, missing in action
NAACP, National Association for the Advancement of Colored People
NAFTA, North American Free Trade Agreement
NASA, National Aeronautics and Space Administration
NATO, North Atlantic Treaty Organization
NCAQ, National Commission on Air Quality
NCES, National Center for Education Statistics
NEPAD, New Partnership for Africa's Development
NIH, National Institutes of Health
NRA, National Rifle Association
NSA, National Security Agency
NSC, National Security Council
OECD, Organization for Economic Cooperation and Development
OEO, Office of Economic Opportunity
OMB, Office of Management and Budget
OPEC, Organization of the Petroleum Exporting Countries
OSHA, Occupational Safety and Health Administration
PACs, political action committees
PATCO, Professional Air Traffic Controllers Organization
PBBs, polybrominated biphenyls
PBGC, Pension Benefit Guaranty Corporation
PLO, Palestine Liberation Organization
POWs, prisoners of war
PRC, People's Republic of China
PRG, Provisional Revolutionary Government (Vietnam)
RICO, Racketeer Influenced and Corrupt Organizations Act
SALT, Strategic Arms Limitation Talks/Treaty
SARS, severe acute respiratory syndrome
SDI, Strategic Defense Initiative
SEC, Securities and Exchange Commission
SLA, Symbionese Liberation Army
SST, supersonic transport
START, Strategic Arms Reduction Talks/Treaty
UAW, United Auto Workers
UFW, United Farm Workers
UMW, United Mine Workers
UN, United Nations
UNSC, United Nations Security Council
VA, Veterans Administration
VAT, value-added tax
WHO, World Health Organization
WMO, World Meteorological Organization
WTO, World Trade Organization

Cumulative Index, 1972–2005

The years in boldface type in the entries indicate which volume is being cited.

A

A. G. Edwards, welfare-to-work program, **1997** 622
AAA. *See* American Automobile Association
AAAS. *See* American Association for the Advancement of Science
Aaron, Hank
  on racial reconciliation, **2000** 35
  on steroid policy for baseball, **2005** 216, 217
AARP (*formerly* American Association of Retired Persons)
  See also American Association of Retired Persons
  eminent domain, **2005** 364
  health care benefits for retirees ruling, **2005** 489
  Medicare reform legislation, **2003** 1120
  obesity and aging, **2002** 626
  prescription drug importation, **2004** 984
  Social Security reform, **2005** 113, 114
Aarvik, Egil, on Nobel Peace Prize, **1984** 1027; **1985** 781; **1986** 1075
AAUW. *See* American Association of University Women
ABA. *See* American Bankers Association; American Bar Association
Abacha, Sani
  coup in Nigeria, **1999** 274
  death of, **1998** 220; **1999** 274; **2000** 64
  executions of dissidents in Nigeria, **1995** 696-697
Abashidze, Aslan
  confrontation with Saakashvili and withdrawal to Russia, **2004** 75
  Georgian parliamentary elections, **2003** 1041; **2004** 72
Abbas, Mahmoud (*aka* Abu Mazen)
  Israeli-Palestinian peace accord, **1993** 747, 751, 761, 765
  Palestinian Authority prime minister appointment, **2003** 193
  Palestinian leader, successor to Arafat, **2004** 301, 806, 808-809
  peace negotiations and cease-fire agreement, **2005** 529-530
  peace talks with Sharon, **2005** 28, 29-30
  presidential election, **2005** 27-40, 271
  presidential speech, **2005** 35-40
  resignation, **2003** 197, 1201
  "roadmap" to Middle East peace, **2003** 194-197
Abbas, Maldom Bada, human rights report, **1993** 560
Abbasi, Feroz, Guantanamo Bay detainee, **2002** 833, 837-841
ABC. *See* American Broadcasting Co.
Abdel-Mehdi, Adel, on Saddam Hussein, **2003** 1192
Abdul-Aziz, Fahd ibn (king of Saudi Arabia), **1992** 225-248
Abdullah, Abdullah, Afghan foreign minister, **2004** 916, 918
Abdullah, Georges Ibrahim, in French prison for terrorism, **1986** 831, 838
Abdullah, Omar, Kashmir elections, **2002** 330
Abdullah bin Abdul Aziz (crown prince of Saudi Arabia)
  address to the nation, **2003** 235-236
  Group of Eight (G-8) meeting, declined attending, **2004** 629
  Israeli-Palestinian peace initiatives, **2002** 370-372
  Middle East Initiative, response to, **2004** 628
  political reform, **2004** 521
  Qaddafi assassination attempt, **2004** 168, 172
  al Qaeda terrorists, limited amnesty of, **2004** 519
  Saudi Arabia local elections, **2005** 272
  Saudi Arabia municipal elections, **2003** 960
  Syrian troop withdrawal from Lebanon, **2005** 688
  terrorist bombings
    linked to Zionists, **2004** 518
    in Riyadh, **2003** 227-244
  terrorists in Saudi Arabia, crackdown on, **2004** 517
Abdullah ibn Hussein (king of Jordan), **1988** 580-581
Abdullah II (king of Jordan)
  political reforms, **2003** 961
  state visit of John Paul II, **2000** 79
  on terrorist bombings in Amman, **2005** 400-401
Abel, Gene, **1992** 509
Abel, I. W., steel agreement, **1973** 437-438
Abilio Soares, Jose Osorio, East Timor war criminal, **2002** 260
Abington Township School District v. Schempp, **1985** 379, 386, 390, 395; **1992** 559, 561, 562; **1995** 547

Abiola, Moshood K. O., Yoruba leader imprisonment and death, **1999** 273-274
Abizaid, John
attacks of regime loyalists in Iraq, **2003** 942-943
Iraq insurgency assessment, **2005** 660-661
Abkhazia, rebel region of Georgia, **2003** 1046; **2004** 75-76
ABM Treaty. *See* Anti-Ballistic Missile (ABM) Treaty
Abortion
abortion rights upheld, Supreme Court on, **1992** 589-613
American Party platform on, **1972** 617
by amniocentesis, state restrictions on, **1976** 483-484, 487-488
antiabortion demonstrations, **1992** 250, 591; **1998** 809-814; **2000** 429-446
protesters and RICO law, Supreme Court on, **1994** 26-33
violence and deaths, **2003** 999-1000
as birth control means, **1972** 301, 309-310
Catholic Church
John Paul II on respect for life, **1988** 171
opposition to, **1998** 811-812
Catholic teaching on, **1979** 725, 729, 758; **1980** 873, 876, 880; **1982** 837-838; **1983** 93-94, 100, 242; **1985** 363, 373; **1987** 701, 709, 712; **1993** 843-850; **1995** 145-146, 149-151, 153-155, 157-158, 161
clinic blockades, Supreme Court on, **1993** 93-112; **1994** 311-326
clinic bombings, **1985** 54; **2005** 820
constitutional right to, **1973** 101-114; **1983** 543-576; **1986** 559-580
Court division on, **1981** 576
Democratic Party platform on, **1976** 545, 562; **1980** 713, 727, 741, 770; **1984** 550, 608; **1992** 696-697; **1996** 623-624, 639; **2000** 615
in developing countries
health services and, **1987** 440, 446, 457
population programs, **1987** 440, 454-455, 457
developments in, **2005** 819-820
Dole position on, **1996** 496
in Eastern Europe, **1994** 428
family clinics advice on, Supreme court on, **1991** 257-273
federal or public funding for, **1977** 407-426, 861-863, 865-866; **1980** 515-535, 713, 727, 741, 770; **1985** 53-56
Bush administration opposition to, **2002** 223
fetal pain studies, **2005** 818
fetal research, HEW regulations on, **1975** 543-555
as galvanizing issue, **1988** 722-723, 736-738, 766-767; **1989** 366-369
incidence of, **2003** 996-997
informed consent, **2005** 818-819
Irish case, **1992** 249-254
Mexico City policy (overseas counseling funding), **2001** 127-131
Moral Majority on, **1983** 818
"morning-after pill" (Plan B) controversy, **2000** 429, 781-786; **2001** 128; **2003** 997, 998-999; **2005** 814-831
organized religion's influence in politics, in Reagan-Anderson debate and, **1980** 849, 864-866
overseas programs, federal funding for, **2001** 127-131; **2002** 223; **2005** 52
parental notification or consent for, **1976** 483-487; **1983** 269, 271-273, 543-576; **1989** 369; **1990** 387-407; **2005** 817-818
partial birth abortion
federal ban on, **2003** 995-1000
Supreme Court on, **2000** 429-446; **2005** 818
population programs
in developing countries, **1987** 440, 454-455, 457
and liberalization of laws on, **1972** 301, 307-310
premature babies, saving the life of, HHS enforcement, **2005** 819-820
prenatal diagnosis, Vatican on, **1987** 273-274
presidential campaigns, Nader presidential campaign and, **2000** 898
presidential views
Bush position on, **1988** 610, 617
Carter position on, **1976** 812
Ford position on, **1976** 812
Reagan position on, **1983** 273, 756; **1985** 107, 114; **1986** 40, 45; **1988** 58, 65
Quayle's "Murphy Brown" speech, **1992** 444-445
Republican Party platform on, **1976** 618, 636; **1980** 569, 583, 619; **1984** 662-663, 706, 715; **1988** 615-617, 642-643; **1992** 799-800, 817; **1996** 496-497, 518-519; **2000** 509-510, 513
right-to-life demonstration, **1985** 53-56
spousal notification, Supreme Court on, **2005** 563
spouse's consent for, state laws on, **1976** 483-487
state restrictions on, **1973** 101-114; **1986** 559-580; **1989** 365-389
Florida bill defeated, **1990** 217
Idaho bill defeated, **1990** 215-219
Supreme Court appointments
Bork's judicial views, **1987** 718-719
Bush (George H. W.) appointments, **1990** 616-617
Bush (George W.) nominations, **2005** 560-561, 563
Foster nomination, **1995** 61-62
O'Connor position on, **1981** 578, 582-585
Souter confirmation hearings, **1990** 624-627
Thomas confirmation hearings, **1991** 551, 559-561, 563-565, 570-571
Supreme Court rulings on, **2005** 554
teenage pregnancy and, **1986** 1058, 1061-1064
UN population conference, **1994** 352-353; **1995** 583
vice-presidential debate on, **1992** 991-994
Abraham, Lorraine, **1987** 374
Abraham, Spencer
energy secretary confirmation, **2001** 97
massive power blackout, **2003** 1018-1024
Abraham Lincoln Opportunity Foundation (ALOF), **1997** 6-7
Abrahamson, James A.
resignation from SDI program, **1988** 326
on SDI concept, **1984** 259
Abram, Morris B., on life-sustaining measures, **1983** 279, 281, 318
Abramoff, Jack, lobbyist corruption scandal, **2005** 631, 633, 635
Abrams, Creighton W., **1973** 730

Abrams, Elliott
human rights appointment of, **1981** 780-781, 784
human rights policy, **1982** 108; **1984** 155; **1985** 145
Iran-contra affair, **1991** 430-431, 619; **1992** 1073-1079
Iran-contra conviction, **1994** 12
Iran-contra testimony, **1994** 13, 18-19
WHO infant formula code, **1981** 447-448
Abrams, Floyd, **1984** 299
Arthur Ashe aids status, media handling of, **1992** 336
campaign finance reform, **2003** 1156
Abrams, Kathryn, **1993** 941
Abrecht, Gary I., on shooting of fellow Capitol police officers, **1998** 516-517
Abromowitz, Morton I., U.S.-North Korean relations, **2001** 269
Abscam investigation, **1980** 899-906; **1981** 673-679
Abu Ghrai prison abuse scandal
anti-American sentiments and, **2004** 629; **2005** 580
cases and trials of U.S. soldiers, **2005** 911-913
comparison with abuses in U.S. Prisons, **2004** 764
Justice Department on, **2004** 336-347, 375
U.S. Army report on, **2004** 207-234
videotapes and photographs of abuses, **2004** 881; **2005** 905, 920
worldwide criticism of, **2005** 450
Abu Mazen (*nom de guerre*). *See* Abbas, Mahmoud
Abu Nidal (Sabry al-Banna)
and hijacking of Egyptian airliner, **1985** 468
Libyan connections of, **1986** 348
Saddam Hussein support for, **2003** 137
Abu Rudeis oil fields, return of to Egypt, **1975** 573, 583
Abu Sayyaf (Father of the Sword) guerillas, **2001** 105-106; **2004** 536
Abubakar, Abdulsalami
Nigerian president, **1999** 274
Zimbabwe elections, **2002** 135
Abzug, Bella S. (D-N.Y.)
Nixon inaugural, **1973** 81
U.S. monitoring of cable traffic, **1975** 711
at women's conference, **1977** 862
Academic achievement. *See* Educational achievement
Academic freedom
See also Students' rights
at Catholic universities, **1986** 758-760, 764
teaching of creation science, **1987** 566, 568-571
Accutane, drug safety of, **2004** 853
ACDA. *See* Arms Control and Disarmament Agency
Ace Ltd., lawsuit, **2004** 418
Acebes, Angel, Madrid terrorist bombings investigation, **2004** 106, 108
Aceh Freedom Movement, **2001** 566
Acevedo v. Nassau County, NY, **1992** 468
Acheson, Dean, role in NATO, **1999** 121
Achille Lauro, hijacking of, **1985** 463, 467; **1986** 349
Achmalensee, Richard L., new CEA member, **1990** 82
Acid rain
causes and effects, **1983** 197-210
Clean Air Act amendments and, **1990** 715-720
controls on coal burning, **1981** 277
funding to combat, **1984** 100
ACIR. *See* Advisory Commission on Intergovernmental Relations
Ackerman, Gary (D-N.Y.), mad cow disease, **2003** 1238
Ackerman, T. P., on nuclear winter, **1983** 857, 860-870; **1985** 542
Ackroyd, Frederick W., **1972** 837
ACLF. *See* American Constitutional Law Foundation
ACLU. *See* American Civil Liberties Union
Acquired immunodeficiency syndrome. *See* AIDS (acquired immunodeficiency syndrome)
ACS. *See* American Cancer Society
Act of Paris. *See* Vietnam war, Paris peace accords
Activase, FDA approval of, **1987** 876, 879
Acupuncture, NIH panel on, **1997** 749-759
ADA. *See* Americans with Disabilities Act
Adamec, Ladislav, **1989** 637
Adams, Brock (D-Wash.)
on air traffic control changes, **1978** 793
on Ford budget, **1976** 40
resignation from Transportation Department, **1979** 561
Adams, Gerry (Sinn Féin leader)
call for IRA end to violence, **2005** 509
IRA disarmament issue, **2001** 760; **2005** 508
Northern Ireland assembly and, **2001** 759
Northern Ireland peace process, **1993** 925; **1999** 755, 758-759
on Omagh bombing, **1998** 206
visa for U.S. visit, **1994** 449, 454; **1995** 728; **1998** 204
visit to Great Britain, **1998** 204
Adams, John
at first presidential inaugural, **1989** 124
on Vatican diplomatic relations, **1984** 19
Adams, John Quincy, **2000** 519
Adams, Robert McCormick, on Native American skeletal remains, **1989** 539-543
Adams, Samuel A., Westmoreland libel suit against CBS, **1983** 402-403; **1985** 159, 162, 164
Adams v. Richardson, **1995** 245
Adamson, Richard, obesity and diet, **2003** 484
Adamson, Terrence B., **1978** 58-60
Adarand Constructors, Inc. v. Peña, **1995** 307-326, 371, 485-486; **1997** 190, 191, 193, 194; **1998** 855-856; **2003** 370
Addiction Treatment Providers, National Association of, **1988** 279
Addington, David S., White House chief of staff appointment, **2005** 705
Addington v. Texas, **1979** 335-344
al-Adel, Saif, terrorist arrested in Iran, **2003** 1056
Adelphia Communications Corp., corporate scandal, **2002** 392, 399; **2003** 332, 339; **2004** 415, 422
Adenauer, Konrad, **1990** 107
Adhe, Brig Malek, United States v., **1993** 435
Adjibade, Tiamiou, **1975** 646
Adkins, Terrence, **1989** 699
Admadinejad, Mahmoud, UN General Assembly speech, **2005** 593, 595, 596-603
Administration on Aging, mental health disorders, **2001** 577-578

Administrative Conference of the United States, on IRS operations, **1975** 829-859
Administrative Procedures Act, **1992** 457-458; **1993** 381-383
 and drug testing of employees, **1986** 841
Admiralty Island National Monument, **1978** 732
Adolescents. *See* Teenagers; Youth
Adoption
 Jessica DeBoer case, **1993** 515-529
 Republican platform on, **1988** 635-636
 teenage pregnancy and, **1986** 1058, 1060-1061
Adoption Assistance and Child Welfare Act (1980), **1989** 671-672
ADRDA. *See* Alzheimer's Disease and Related Disorders Association
Adult theaters, and city zoning ordinance, **1986** 131-144
Advanced Cell Technology (Worcester, Mass.)
 human embryo clones for stem cell research, **2001** 541; **2002** 513, 517; **2004** 158
 South Korean stem cell research scandal impact on, **2005** 320, 322
Advani, L. K.
 attack on Indian parliament, **2001** 963-970
 India elections, **2004** 350
Advertising
 alcoholic beverages and marketing to youth, **2002** 178
 consumers and TV advertising, **1982** 366
 distilled spirits, on television, **1996** 770-775
 by lawyers, state bar rules on, **1982** 65-71
 obesity in children, media role in, **2004** 653-654, 660; **2005** 7
 prescription drug prices, **1976** 351-363
 prescription drugs
  benefit for seniors, HHS ad campaign controversy, **2004** 577
  direct marketing to consumer, **2004** 852, 855
  GAO report on, **2002** 945-958
 tobacco companies, FTC report on, **2003** 265
 tobacco products, **1996** 590-591, 596-598; **1997** 38, 332, 334, 336-337
  effect on young people, **1994** 172-184
  restrictions on, **1972** 46; **1973** 64; **1988** 310-312, 314-315
 weight-loss products, FTC on, **2002** 624-632
Advertising Council, adult attitudes toward children, **1997** 424, 426; **1999** 386
Advisory Commission on Intergovernmental Relations (ACIR)
 on Proposition 13 effects, **1978** 398
 unfunded mandates legislation, **1995** 142-143
 on value-added tax to fund education, **1972** 221
Advisory Committee on Human Radiation Experiments, radiation tests on citizens, **1994** 55, 60
Advisory Committee on Religious Freedom Abroad, **1998** 19-29
Adzharia, "autonomous" region of Georgia, **2003** 1041, 1046
AEA. *See* American Economic Association
AEC. *See* Atomic Energy Commission
Aerojet-General Corp., in EPA Superfund investigation, **1982** 966; **1983** 750
Aerosol propellants, proposed ban on, **1975** 437-453
AFDC. *See* Aid to Families with Dependent Children
Afewerki, Isaias, Eritrean president, **2000** 754
Affirmative action
 ban, federal appeals court panel on, **1997** 183-194
 Bush (George H. W.) on Job Rights Bill, **1991** 759-765
 Bush (George W.) administration, **2002** 973-974
 California legislation, **1996** 759-763
 Clinton endorsement of, **1995** 483-496, 574-575; **1997** 315
 Clinton presidential debate on, **1996** 728
 Democratic platform on, **1980** 740; **1984** 550-551, 606
 Dole opposition to, **1995** 483-484, 574-575
 enforcement of
  in Carter administration, **1981** 59
  in Reagan administration, **1983** 51-52, 756, 913-917; **1987** 43-45, 48, 58; **1988** 189-190
 federal government plans, **1995** 307-326
 labor union's discriminatory practices, **1986** 651-667
 minority broadcasters, **1990** 419-435
 minority firefighters and past discrimination, **1986** 652-653, 667-678
 in public schools, **1998** 855-868
 reverse discrimination in medical school admissions, **1978** 467-492
 seniority
  and layoffs of new minority workers, **1984** 365-385
  and reverse discrimination, **1979** 493-507
 set-aside programs for broadcasting, **1990** 419-435
 sex discrimination in workplace, **1985** 789-790, 796
 student success stories, **1997** 321
 Supreme Court on, **2003** 358-386; **2005** 554
 tenure review disclosure, **1990** 23-34
 University of Michigan, Supreme Court case, **2002** 970, 973-974
Afghanistan
 Afghanistan army, creation of, **2003** 1094
 agreement on, U.S. and Soviet role in, **1988** 356, 358, 361
 child soldiers, **2002** 918, 925
 conflict in
  continuing after agreement, **1989** 607
  superpower support for, **1979** 967-980; **1985** 708, 715, 716; **1988** 616, 675
 constitution, **2003** 1097-1098
 detainees
  See also Guantanamo Bay detainees
  deaths of investigated, **2004** 216-217
  as "enemy combatants" and rights under Geneva Conventions, **2004** 212-213, 336-337
  military tribunals, **2005** 446-447
  release of, **2005** 976
  treatment of, **2005** 976-977
 economic sanctions against, **1999** 524, 525-526; **2000** 280
 economic situation, **2005** 982-983
 education, **2005** 982, 986-987
 elections
  kidnapping of UN election workers, **2004** 917

legitimacy of, **2005** 275
parliamentary and presidential elections, **2004** 914-917
parliamentary elections, **2005** 970-973
presidential elections, **2003** 1098
foreign policy and international relations, **2005** 983-984, 987-988
human rights in, **1986** 919-936; **1988** 884, 889; **1999** 531-534; **2005** 982
human trafficking, **2002** 341
humanitarian aid, **1999** 526-527; **2002** 15-32
hunger in, **2003** 756
interim government, **2001** 880-891
International Security Assistance Force (ISAF), **2003** 1093-1094; **2004** 138, 913
Karzai presidential inauguration, **2004** 912-922
Karzai speech to parliament, **2005** 970-989
land mine casualties, **1995** 47, 48
Mujaheddin guerrillas, and peace agreements, **1988** 257-259
narcotics trade, **2003** 1101; **2004** 919; **2005** 978-979, 985
NATO peacekeeping mission, **2003** 1093-1094; **2004** 138, 913
opium growing in, **1972** 646, 648-649
Pakistani agreements with on peace and refugees, **1988** 257-264
political situation
UN report on, **2002** 15-32
UN secretary general on, **1999** 524-535; **2003** 1089-1109
reconstruction efforts, **2003** 1099-1101; **2004** 912, 918; **2005** 977-978
Bush state of the Union address on, **2004** 23
UN postwar reconstruction fund, **2001** 741, 880, 884
refugees, **1981** 179, 190; **1986** 919-926, 936
and displaced persons, **2003** 1098-1099; **2004** 918; **2005** 978
UN report on, **1991** 673
security situation, **2004** 912-914; **2005** 974-976, 981-982, 987
Soviet admission of law violation in, **1989** 400
Soviet call for cease-fire in, **1988** 928-929, 935
Soviet propaganda about, Project Truth on, **1981** 763
terrorism, campaign against, **2005** 985
terrorist attacks, **2003** 1053; **2004** 535
terrorist sanctuary, **2000** 280
UN peacekeeping forces, **2001** 690-691, 882-883; **2003** 1091, 1092
UN postwar reconstruction fund, **2001** 741, 880, 884
U.S. agreements, **1988** 257-266
U.S. aid to, **1979** 968
U.S. air strikes against terrorists, **1998** 555, 586-591
U.S. relations, anti-U.S. sentiment, **2005** 977
war in
Arab public opinion, **2002** 488
Bush and Blair on start of, **2001** 686-697
Bush State of the Union address, **2002** 39-40
Operation Avalanche (children killed by U.S. troops), **2003** 1092
Pakistan support of U.S., **2001** 615, 626, 627, 632-636; **2002** 40, 165
U.S. base "Camp Stronghold Freedom" in Uzbekistan, **2005** 429
violence in, **2004** 535
war on terrorism, **2005** 985
warlords and militia, **2003** 1095
Afghanistan, Soviet intervention in
atrocities committed, **1986** 919-936
Brezhnev on, **1980** 5, 9-12
Carter on, **1980** 27-33, 40, 84, 86-87
counter-revolutionary forces in, Brezhnev on, **1981** 225-226, 230-231, 237
Democratic platform on, **1980** 713, 758, 759-760
economic summit on, **1980** 503-506; **1981** 593-594
and human rights, **1980** 189-190, 195; **1981** 179-180, 189-190; **1982** 107, 109-111; **1983** 183-185; **1986** 919-936
invasion, **1979** 965-983
Islamic countries on, **1980** 3-15
military strength of Soviets in, **1981** 189, 719-720
Sakharov protest of, **1986** 1091-1092
and SALT II, **1979** 418; **1985** 751
and U.S. defense posture, **1980** 110, 113, 123, 125, 127
U.S. response to, **1980** 115, 477, 481, 777, 791; **1986** 268
use of chemical warfare, **1981** 681-682, 684-689; **1982** 235-236, 248-250, 254-255
Afghanistan, Soviet occupation of, **1984** 146, 289, 291, 811, 813, 817, 828
Afghanistan, Soviet withdrawal from, **1986** 147, 166; **1987** 991, 993, 999, 1005; **1990** 207, 210, 211
agreement on, **1988** 66, 257-266
economic summit on, **1987** 528; **1988** 393-394
AFL-CIO. *See* American Federation of Labor-Congress of Industrial Organizations
Africa
See also names of specific countries
AIDS, spread of, **1999** 489-498, 587-588
AIDS programs, Millennium Challenge Account, **2003** 453-454, 766
Carter visits in, **1978** 270-271, 281-290
Catholic rites in, **1980** 968; **1985** 500, 502-504
Central African refugee crisis, **1996** 809-815
Clinton state visit, **1998** 159-168, 221; **1999** 54, 428; **2000** 64-65
conflicts in, **2002** 447
Clinton comments on, **2000** 71-72
Soviet and Cuban involvement in, **1978** 224-225, 239, 271, 374
UN Secretary General on, **1998** 220-232
debt-relief program, **2000** 64, 69, 412, 450, 475, 479; **2005** 406-408
Democratic Party platform, **1996** 645
economic aid, G-8 meeting on, **2005** 405-427
economic development, **1997** 352-355; **2001** 504-515; **2002** 449
U.S. promotion of, **1973** 515, 526
economic situation, **2001** 669
elections, **2003** 451

Africa *Continued*
foreign domination of, Carter on, **1978** 271, 282-286
HIV/AIDS
incidence of, **2005** 53-54
UN envoy on, **2003** 780-790
infant deaths in, UNICEF on, **1981** 911-912
John Paul II's trips to, **1980** 968; **1985** 499-514
land mine problem, **1995** 47-49, 50-51
majority rule in, and U.S. efforts, **1977** 190, 192-193, 738, 743; **1981** 86, 96-97
Multilateral Debt Relief Initiative, **2005** 407
New African Initiative, **2001** 504-515; **2002** 447
New Partnership for African Development (NEPAD), **2002** 446-466; **2003** 766; **2005** 405-406
oil embargo effects on, and Arab promise of assistance, **1974** 256
OPEC production quotas and oil quality from, **1982** 980
peacekeeping mission of UN High Commissioner for Refugees, **1999** 428-438
population growth, **1984** 522, 526, 531, 542; **1999** 587-588
and food supply, **1987** 447-448, 453, 456
reform in, UN secretary general on, **2003** 450-469
Republican Party platform, **1996** 543-544
sex trade and human trafficking, **2004** 131
special needs of, **2000** 709-710
sub-Saharan
child labor rate, **2002** 222
desertification in, **1987** 447
famine in, **1984** 973-983, 990; **1985** 28, 33, 350, 353-354; **1986** 442
HIV/AIDS pandemic, **1998** 882-884; **1999** 489; **2002** 470; **2004** 429
poverty in, **1992** 642
U.S. defense policy, **1993** 712-713
U.S. economic aid, **2002** 449
U.S. policy, **1976** 287-295; **1979** 647, 650-651; **1984** 641, 714-715; **1998** 159-168; **1999** 54; **2000** 63-73
Africa, National Summit on (Wash., D.C.), **2000** 63
African Americans
See also Apartheid system; Blacks; Civil rights; Discrimination, race; Equal opportunity; Minorities; Race relations
AIDS incidence in women, **2004** 433
and cocaine penalties sentencing, **1997** 245-247, 252
mental health, surgeon general's report on, **2001** 584-585
obesity of black women, **2002** 625
population in U.S., **2003** 349
poverty rates, **1999** 390; **2000** 53; **2002** 55
teenage birth rates, **1998** 261-262
uninsured, **2001** 12
African Development Bank, **1974** 256, 285; **2005** 407
African National Congress (ANC)
antiapartheid agenda and, **1991** 54-55; **1992** 284; **1993** 878
Constitution of South Africa, **1984** 1027; **1996** 250
De Klerk-Mandela recipients of Nobel Peace Prize, **1993** 877-884
history of underground movement, **1993** 878
human rights abuses, **1998** 755-758
lifting ban on, **1989** 546, 547; **1990** 66-69
Mandela as nonviolent leader of, **1985** 533; **1993** 877, 878
Mandela presidential inauguration, **1994** 247-251
Mandela's release from prison, **1990** 65-68; **1992** 284; **1993** 878-879
De Klerk address to South African parliament, **1990** 68-72
De Klerk announcement of, **1990** 72
Mandela's address to U.S. Congress, **1990** 76-80
Mandela's speech in Cape Town, **1990** 72-76
Mbeki presidential inauguration, **1999** 297-303
MK-Spear of the Nation (ANC military wing), proposed dissolution of, **1992** 289-290
plenary meeting in South Africa, **1991** 55
Sisulu release from prison, **1989** 140, 546; **1990** 65
South African Truth and Reconciliation Commission report findings, **1998** 755-758, 769-771
U.S.-South African relations, **1998** 164
violent activities of ("mass action" campaign), **1984** 167, 1034; **1986** 372, 582-583, 588-589; **1990** 140; **1992** 285-286
African Nuclear Weapon Free Zone Treaty, **1995** 236, 237
African Trade and Development Act, **1998** 45; **1999** 54
African Union (AU)
debt relief program, **2005** 408
economic development proposals, **2001** 504-515
establishment of, **2001** 504, 506; **2003** 1226
Ivory Coast peace plans, **2005** 805
Sudan peacekeeping mission, **2004** 588, 592, 594, 595; **2005** 518-519
summit meeting (Mozambique), Annan address, **2003** 450-469
Afrikaans language, compulsory use of abolished, **1976** 678-679
Afrikaner Resistance Movement, **1992** 289
AFSCE. *See* American Federation of State, County, and Municipal Employees
AFT. *See* American Federation of Teachers
Agca, Mehmet Ali, **1981** 427; **2000** 77
Age discrimination. *See* Discrimination, age
Age Discrimination Act (1975), **1992** 195
Age Discrimination and Employment Act (1967), **1985** 397-407
Aged. *See* Senior citizens
Agee, Philip, passport revocation for CIA exposé, **1981** 541-555
Agency for Health Care Policy and Research (AHCPR), end-of-life care, **1997** 328, 329
Agency for International Development (AID)
Atwood resignation, **1999** 700
on carbon dioxide gas eruption in Cameroon, **1987** 61-77
economic assistance to Central America, **1984** 36
food production assistance, **1974** 284
Palestinian aid, **2002** 936
population assistance, **1987** 456, 458
resignations in protest against infant formula industry, **1981** 448-449
Sudan genocidal war, **2004** 591
Sudanese relief workers killed, **2003** 835

support for expansion of, **1981** 14
tsunami disaster aid, **2004** 992
Turkey earthquake relief, **1999** 467, 469-471
Agenda for Civil Justice Reform in America, **1992** 107
Agent Orange, **1989** 25
Aggett, Neil, **1982** 797-798
Agha Shahi, **1980** 4
Aging. *See* Senior citizens
Agnew, Spiro T.
attacks on news media, **1973** 899; **1992** 444
charges against, Nixon on, **1973** 746-747, 750; **1977** 323, 353-354
FBI surveillance of, **1975** 881-882
on McGovern's economic program, **1972** 738
on Nixon and Watergate, **1973** 499
nomination acceptance speech, **1972** 711-716
on peace demonstrations, **1984** 349-350
resignation of, **1973** 827-838, 969; **1974** 696, 987
and transfer of power, **1985** 492
Agnos, Art, **1989** 305-306
Agostini v. Felton, **1997** 361-381
Agrava, Corazon J., on B. Aquino assassination, **1984** 915, 926-929
Agricultural development
modernization, and women's workload, **1975** 507-508, 510-513, 518-521
U.S. aid for, **1976** 293; **1981** 14, 19-20
world aid for developing countries, **1974** 939-944, 948-950; **1975** 602
World Bank project in Indonesia, **1986** 860
Agricultural Development, International Fund for, establishment of, **1974** 940-942, 949-950
Agricultural exports
See also Grain sales; Trade, exports and imports
controls, presidential authority over, **1973** 577, 580-581, 709
growth in, Carter on, **1979** 102; **1981** 63-64
opening foreign markets to U.S., Nixon on, **1973** 380, 388
reduction of barriers to, **1979** 66-67; **1983** 78, 84, 86, 112
subsidies for, Reagan effort to end worldwide, **1988** 393, 396
U.S. to Japan, **1983** 894; **1985** 320
Agricultural policy
AIDS epidemic impact on, **2000** 419-420
and biotechnology, **1986** 287-306
commodity price supports, **1995** 70-71; **1996** 199-200
Democratic platform on, **1984** 589-591; **1988** 564-565; **1992** 692; **1996** 648
as election issue, **1988** 751-752, 775, 812-813
exemption from U.S. price controls, **1973** 577, 580, 583, 704-705, 709-710, 712
farm bill, **1996** 199-203, 696
reform of
Carter proposals for, **1980** 84-85, 96
Reagan and advisers on, **1987** 117, 119, 124-127, 140-141
Republican platform on, **1980** 603-608; **1984** 673-679; **1988** 660-664; **1992** 828-829; **1996** 537-538
sustainable development, **2002** 593-604; **2004** 929
trade with China, **2004** 946
Agricultural Science and Technology, Council on, on animal rights, **1988** 348
Agricultural subsidies
in developed countries, opposition from developing countries, **2003** 8, 14, 743
economic summit (Houston), **1990** 469, 471-473, 480
Reagan on elimination of, **1987** 526; **1988** 393, 396
trade barriers and subsidies, **2005** 409-412
U.S. farm bill and, **2002** 450
U.S.-European Community dispute over, **1990** 480; **1992** 639
Agriculture
See also Farms; Food production; Food safety
and biotechnology, **1986** 287-306
Chinese, sideline production allowed by PRC constitution, **1975** 44, 47
farm labor
California law on, **1975** 377-399
dignity of, John Paul II on, **1981** 714
hiring of temporary residents, **1986** 964-965, 968-969
farmer protection, Carter program for, **1978** 14, 23-25
food aid to Soviet Union, **1990** 807-814
grains agreement with Soviet Union, **1990** 337
Houston economic summit, **1990** 469, 471-473, 480
income transfers in, **1986** 59-61, 67-68, 83-85
Mount St. Helens eruption and, **1980** 814, 817-819
natural resources essential for, **1980** 666-670, 682, 686-689
nuclear war effects on, **1983** 859, 878-879; **1985** 541-543, 552-553
poor harvests
in developing countries, **1972** 859, 865-866
and food prices, **1974** 118, 421
global economic impact of, **1975** 195-197
poverty summit on, **1981** 769, 777
research, U.S.-Soviet agreements on, **1972** 806, 808; **1973** 588, 608
research and trade, U.S.-Polish agreement on, **1974** 884-885
research assistance to farms, **1986** 288, 298-300, 303-306
rising costs of inputs, **1980** 679-680, 688
Soviet
Gorbachev's reform program, **1989** 145-152
personal incentives in, **1987** 858, 861, 863-864
Soviet-U.S., and trade as element in foreign policy, **1982** 823-835
water rights and conservation, **1982** 689-701
Agriculture Department (USDA)
See also Food safety
biotechnology in agriculture, secretary Glickman on, **1999** 401-411
biotechnology in farming, **1986** 287-306
chemicals in food, **1994** 379-386
dietary guidelines, **1996** 3-16; **2001** 936
on drought, **1988** 863
farm bill, secretary Glickman on, **1996** 199-203
fire-management policy of, **1988** 941-946
food guide pyramid, **1992** 397-400; **2005** 8-9
food safety, **1997** 690-698

Agriculture Department (USDA) *Continued*
enforcement, **2001** 700-701
recalls, **2002** 579, 581-582
foreign loan program, **1990** 808
genetically engineered foods, **1992** 470
Healthy Lunch Pilot Program, in schools, **2004** 656
meat inspection rules, **1996** 414-417
milk price supports decision, **1974** 4, 6-15
National Residue Program (NRP), **1994** 379-386
nutrition studies, **1992** 397-404
secretary Espy's resignation, **1994** 403-408
trans fatty acid study, **1992** 399, 403-404
university laboratory security, **2003** 902
wildfire prevention guidelines, **2000** 712-722
Aguilar v. Felton, **1985** 433-436, 449-461, 480, 487; **1997** 361-381
Aguilera, Davy, **1993** 825
AHA. *See* American Heart Association; American Hospital Association
Ahadi, Anwar ul-Haq, Afghanistan finance minister appointment, **2004** 917
Ahern, Bertie
EU British rebate controversy, **2005** 343
EU membership expansion, remarks on, **2004** 198, 202-204
IRA peace process, **2005** 509, 511
Northern Ireland peace agreement, **1998** 203-219; **1999** 753
Ahmadinejad, Mahmoud
anti-Israel rhetoric, **2005** 591
hostage taking, U.S. embassy (Tehran) and, **2005** 591
Iranian presidential elections, **2005** 589-590, 778
Ahmed, Rabei Osman el Sayed, terrorist bombings in Madrid, **2004** 110
Ahtisaari, Martti
Jenin "massacre" investigations, **2002** 934
UN postwar Iraq report, **1991** 165-174
UN special envoy to Kosovo, **2005** 856
AID. *See* Agency for International Development
Aid to Families with Dependent Children (AFDC)
black recipients, overrepresentation of, **1983** 43, 53
and Carter's welfare plan, **1977** 552, 555, 560
cutbacks in, **1982** 145, 150; **1987** 149, 162-163
elimination of, **1996** 452; **1997** 618; **1998** 357; **1999** 261
homeless report, **1994** 258-259
management of, Nixon on, **1973** 304, 310-311
minimum benefit for, in Carter welfare reform, **1979** 390-391, 394
shortcomings of, **1985** 200-201, 204
state aid for poor report, **1991** 827-830
state responsibility for, **1982** 74, 81; **1988** 848-849
welfare reform legislation, **1988** 847-848
AIDS (acquired immunodeficiency syndrome)
See also United Nations Programme on HIV/AIDS (UNAIDS)
adolescent cases, **1993** 448
AIDS-related complex, symptoms of, **1986** 891
blacks in U.S. and, **1987** 44, 55-58
Arthur Ashe's AIDS announcement, **1992** 335-338
Magic Johnson, resignation from AIDS Commission, **1992** 710-711, 891-893
Magic Johnson, retirement from basketball, **1991** 747-749; **1992** 335, 340
causes of, **2000** 414-415; **2004** 929-930
Durban Declaration on, **2000** 415
Maathai controversial statements on, **2004** 929-930
children with, **1999** 386-387
confidentiality of patient information, **1987** 829-830
crisis, future projections, **2001** 319
Democratic convention, Glaser speech at, **1992** 669, 783
Democratic Party platform on, **1984** 612; **1992** 694
discrimination against victims of, **1986** 888-889, 898; **1987** 817-818, 821, 828-829; **1988** 439-441; **1989** 306
domestic partner rights, **1989** 305, 307
drug abusers and, **1988** 416, 421, 431, 435-436
drugs for treatment of, **1987** 327-330
education about, **1986** 887, 889, 893-895, 897-898, 906; **1992** 146, 147
AMA recommendations on, **1987** 817-818, 822-824, 827
federal program for, **1987** 319-326
in schools, **1988** 416, 433-434
federal spending on, **1983** 533, 539-541; **1986** 887-888, 897-901, 908; **1988** 150, 155
global HIV/AIDS epidemic, **1986** 887, 889-892; **2002** 469-482
UN report on, **1998** 878-889; **2000** 410-428
Haitian refugee detention camp closing, **1993** 371-383
health care financing, **1988** 443-445
health care providers and, **1988** 424-425, 442-443
high-risk groups, **1983** 533-534, 536-537; **1985** 734-737
counseling for, **1987** 822-824
education of, **1987** 319-320, 323, 325-326
Haitian refugees, **1993** 371-383; **1993** 414-415
HIV among Haitian refugees, **1993** 414-415
HIV-infected speakers at political conventions, **1992** 709-715, 783, 891-893
homeless persons and, **1994** 255-256, 262
homosexuals
discrimination against, **1983** 534-535
march on Washington, **1993** 329-331
pastoral care of, **1986** 910, 915
incidence of
in African nations, **1999** 428, 489-498; **2000** 32, 63, 70-71
in Angola, **2002** 156
in Asia, **2005** 54-55
in China, **2001** 438, 440; **2002** 331, 470-471, 855; **2003** 1175
in United States, **2003** 781; **2004** 433; **2005** 55
U.S. modeling of AIDS and HIV infection, **1988** 418-419
worldwide incidence, **2002** 470-471; **2003** 781; **2005** 53-54
Zimbabwe pandemic, **2002** 136-137; **2003** 1112
International AIDS Conference (Bangkok), **2004** 432, 433-441

job discrimination and, **1987** 246-247
John Paul II on, **1987** 699, 701
Millennium Challenge Account, **2003** 453-454, 766
minorities and, **1993** 447-448; **1996** 447-448
National Commission on AIDS report, **1993** 447-457
national policy on, AMA recommendations on, **1987** 817-818, 821-832
patient care, **1986** 899-901; **1988** 420-424
physical and psychological effects of, **1983** 534
political consequences of, **1985** 735-736, 746-747
political issue of, **1988** 730-731
presidential commission on, **1988** 415-446
presidential debates on, **1992** 924-926
prevention and treatment, **1988** 420-424; **2002** 472-473
ABC principles (abstain, be faithful, use a condom), **2004** 431; **2005** 52
antiretroviral (ARV) drug therapy, **2003** 785-786; **2004** 431-432; **2005** 50-63
control of, **1983** 534, 538; **1987** 817-832; **1995** 65; **1997** 81-93
funding and AIDS drugs, **2004** 431-433
with tenofovir, **2005** 55-56
rape victims and, **1992** 387, 391-393
Republican Party platform on, **1988** 615, 617, 638; **1992** 811-812
research, **1983** 537-538, 541; **1986** 887, 901-905, 907-908; **1987** 320, 327; **1988** 425-431
AMA recommendations on, **1987** 817, 818, 821, 828, 830-831
Clinton comments on, **1993** 329-330; **1995** 428, 433, 434-435; **1997** 38, 761; **2000** 32, 70-71
federal programs, **1996** 156-166
government support for, **1985** 733; **1986** 887-888, 897, 904, 906; **1988** 150, 155
Helms opposition to, **1995** 428, 433, 459
programs needed, **1997** 91-92
on "triple therapy," **1997** 81-82
in Russia, **2001** 255, 439; **2002** 471; **2004** 429, 430; **2005** 54
symptoms of, **1985** 734
testing, **1986** 889, 890, 895-897
AMA recommendations on, **1987** 817, 818, 824-828
and confidentiality, **1988** 433, 441
legislation on, **1987** 320
for pregnant women, **1995** 441-452
voluntary, **1988** 416, 432-433
transmission of, **1985** 734-746; **1986** 888-892, 894-895; **1987** 319, 323-325
criminal penalties for, **1988** 416, 442
sexually transmitted diseases and, **1987** 819-820
unsafe sex risks of high school students, **1992** 339-343
tuberculosis infection and, **1992** 1008, 1010-1011; **1993** 857-858
UN General Assembly Declaration on, **2001** 438-455
U.S. policy
Bush AIDS initiative, **2003** 21-22, 29, 453-454, 780, 781-783; **2005** 51-53, 55-56
Bush AIDS relief, emergency program, **2004** 429-441; **2005** 51-53
drug patent rules and, **2003** 742
UV radiation and, **1992** 77
vaccine research, **1987** 328
ethical issues, **1987** 352; **1988** 427-429
warning to third parties, **1987** 818, 831-832
women and, **1993** 654
women's rights and, **2000** 326; **2004** 430-431
workplace and, **1985** 733-747; **1988** 437-439
World AIDS Day (December 1), **2004** 430; **2005** 51
AIG. *See* American International Group
Aigen, Betsy, **1988** 73
AIM. *See* American Indian Movement
Air Force (U.S.)
readiness, **1994** 531
Roswell incident, **1997** 395-405
slang dictionary for returning POWs, **1973** 246-253
Air Force Academy (U.S.)
hazing and other practices, **1992** 481-487
sexual misconduct allegations, **2003** 791-807
Air Line Pilots Association (ALPA), **1988** 269
Air pollution and air quality
acid rain causes and effects, U.S. and Canadian studies of, **1983** 197-210
atmospheric pollution, from nuclear war, **1983** 858, 860-878
biological and genetic consequences of, U.S.-Soviet agreement to share information on, **1972** 806, 810-811
chemicals in cities, linked to lung cancer, **1972** 775-781
Clean Air Act "new source review" dispute, **2002** 895-897, 902-905; **2003** 173-190; **2004** 664-674; **2005** 100
Clear Skies Initiative, **2002** 229, 299, 894, 898-899; **2003** 27, 179-180; **2004** 666-667; **2005** 79, 83, 95, 98-99
diesel engine pollution controls, **2004** 668
from fossil fuels, **1972** 689; **1980** 690-691
from fuel alternatives to oil, **1980** 666, 669, 690
greenhouse gas emissions reduction, **2004** 832
health effects research, Nixon proposal, **1972** 150
mercury emissions regulations, **2004** 667, 842; **2005** 95-110
oil refineries, air pollution requirements, **2004** 667-668
particle pollution, EPA regulations, **2005** 101
power plant regulations, **2001** 215-216, 218
reduction in pollution, as Clean Air Act succeeds, NCAQ on, **1981** 275-295
regulations
cost-benefit analysis, **1987** 123
costs of, **1981** 275-295
relaxation of during coal miners' strike, **1978** 112, 115
research, U.S.-Soviet agreement on, **1972** 805-807
smog and ozone level reductions, **2004** 668
smoke in atmosphere, from nuclear war, **1985** 542, 545-548
soot (fine-particle air pollution) regulations, **2004** 668
stationary source enforcement and bubble concept, **1984** 427-437

Air pollution and air quality *Continued*
sulfur emissions
control of, **1972** 149; **1973** 217
U.S.-Canadian acid rain studies, **1983** 197-210
tests in New York, **2003** 174
from tobacco smoke, **1972** 45-47, 53-54
Air traffic control system
air traffic control security and, **2003** 729, 732
changes in, FAA on, **1978** 793-807
equipment and procedure changes, FAA on, **1978** 793-807
modernization of, **1988** 150, 156
privatization in, **1988** 233
safety of, **1986** 253-266; **1988** 267-272, 274-276
Air traffic controllers
drug testing of, **1986** 254-255, 839
strike by, **1981** 621-629; **1986** 253-260
training of, **1986** 254-256, 258-259, 263-264
workload of, **1986** 253-266
Air travel. *See* Airline industry; Aviation safety
Airborne Warning and Control Systems (AWACS). *See* Airplanes, AWACS
Airline Deregulation Act (1978), **1988** 268-269, 272-273
Airline industry
See also Air traffic control system; Air traffic controllers; Aviation safety; Aviation security
air controllers strike, effect on, **1981** 622
bankruptcies, **2002** 53; **2005** 486
deregulation of
business effects of, **1988** 118, 144-148
Carter on, **1978** 32, 689-690; **1979** 24, 30; **1980** 948; **1981** 59
economic report on, **1986** 60, 85-87
impact on air traffic, **1986** 253
safety effects of, **1988** 268-270, 272-275
drug smuggling, **1992** 209-210
Polish service in U.S., suspension of, **1981** 884, 895-896
relationship with FAA, **1988** 268, 270
smoking bans on flights, **1986** 1080-1081
Soviet in U.S., suspended for Polish martial law, **1981** 884
SST ban in U.S., **1973** 235-244
underfunded pension plans, **2003** 708, 709; **2005** 197-211
U.S.-Cuban antihijacking agreement, **1973** 265-268
U.S.-downing of Iranian airliner, **1973** 265-268; **1988** 703-717
U.S.-PRC agreement on, **1980** 829, 832, 836-842
U.S.-Soviet agreement on, **1973** 589, 607
U.S.-Soviet resumption of service
agreement on, **1987** 993, 1000
Geneva summit discussions of, **1985** 750, 755, 759
West German-Soviet agreements on mutual landing rights, **1973** 557-558, 560
Airline safety. *See* Aviation safety; Aviation security
Airplane crashes. *See* Aviation safety
Airplanes
See also Aviation safety; Bombers
AWACS radar planes, in drug interdiction, **1990** 116
AWACS sold to Saudis by U.S., **1981** 787-788, 793-798
Boeing 737 mechanical problems, **1999** 115-116
Concorde, opposition to overflight of U.S., **1976** 331, 342-343
DC-10 safety and maintenance, **1979** 949-963
Enola Gay (B-29 bomber), in Smithsonian exhibit, **1995** 55-58
ocean dumping from, international agreements on, **1972** 173-177, 907-919
SST ban in U.S., **1973** 235-244
Airport security. *See* Aviation security
Akayesu, Jean-Paul, genocide trials, **1998** 616
Akayev, Askar, ousted president of Kyrgyzstan, **2005** 433-435
Ake v. Oklahoma, **1985** 207-219
Akhromeyev, Sergei F.
congressional testimony by, **1989** 439-444
at Iceland summit, **1986** 876
Akihito (Emperor of Japan), and death of Hirohito, **1989** 99, 102
Akinola, Peter (bishop), homosexuality, Anglican Church ordinances on, **2005** 865
Akron v. Akron Center for Reproductive Health, Inc., **1983** 543-564; **1990** 400, 401, 402; **1992** 597, 601, 605-606
ALA. *See* American Library Association
A.L.A. Schechter Poultry Corp. v. United States, **1995** 187, 192
Alabama
Hunt ethics law conviction, **1993** 303-305
law on alimony for men, **1979** 193-195, 198-200, 205-206
law on silent prayer in schools, **1985** 379-395
secular humanism in schools, **1987** 598-599
Alan Guttmacher Institute, abortion incidence, **2003** 996
Alaska
Aleut native wartime relocation, **1983** 212, 228; **1988** 287, 291-292
Arctic National Wildlife Refuge, oil exploration, **2001** 335-336; **2003** 182, 1017; **2004** 670; **2005** 783-784
environmental preservation in, **1972** 802; **1978** 731-740
Exxon Valdez oil spill, **1991** 641-648
congressional hearing on, **1989** 225-237
report, **1990** 513-530
subsistence fishing and hunting by natives, **1978** 732, 734-735
Tongass National Forest, protection of roadless lands, **1999** 593-594; **2001** 216-217; **2002** 899; **2004** 669
windfall profits tax on oil and, **1983** 517-519
Alaska Native Claims and Settlement Act (1971), **1978** 732-733
Alaska oil pipeline
alternative Canadian land route for, **1972** 272, 280-282
construction of, **1972** 271-272; **1973** 472-473, 914
economic and security aspects of, **1972** 271-277

environmental impact of, **1972** 271, 277-280
Alaska Statehood Act (1959), **1978** 732
Albania
Albanian Muslim guerrillas in the Balkans, **2001** 554-555
career and death of Hoxha, **1985** 325-331
health problems, **1994** 415-430
human trafficking, **2002** 342
NATO membership candidacy, **2004** 136
political situation, **1997** 360
U.S. relations, **1985** 325-328
Warsaw Pact withdrawal, **1991** 399
Albemarle Paper Co. v. Moody, **1998** 450
Alberswerth, David, national energy policy, **2001** 337
Albert, Carl A. (D-Okla.)
Agnew's request for House investigation, **1973** 828, 832-834
on congressional power, **1973** 4
on congressional-executive cooperation, **1972** 74
on economic and energy crises, **1975** 15-18, 32-41
on inflation summit, **1974** 861-866
Korean influence-buying investigation, **1978** 846, 863, 892, 894, 897-900
on Nixon's social program cutbacks, **1973** 171
in presidential succession, **1973** 827
on White House tapes, **1973** 697; **1974** 674
Albert, Speer, on Turkey's supply of chromite to Nazi Germany, **1998** 292
Alberts, Bruce, NAS global climate change statement, **2005** 921
Alberts, Louw, **1975** 363
Albright, David, Libya nuclear weapons program, **2004** 170
Albright, Madeleine K.
Africa, economic assistance, **1999** 430
Armenia-Azerbaijan relations, **1999** 640
chemical weapons treaty, **1997** 195-201
Congo conflict, **2000** 72; **2001** 159
Congo visit, **1997** 880-885
Cuba, U.S. sanctions against, **1998** 32
diplomatic posts evaluation, **1999** 690-692
Iran
regret for 1953 coup, **2001** 795
U.S. relations, **1998** 689-690
Iraq
UN weapons inspection, **1998** 936
U.S. sanctions against, **1997** 770
war in, **2002** 614
Kosovo peace negotiations, **1999** 135
land mines, **1997** 847
Middle East
Camp David Summit, **2000** 496
Israel-Palestinian peace talks in Paris, **2000** 932
Israel-Palestinian talks, **1999** 891-892, 894
NATO
future of, **1998** 912-919
membership ceremony, **1999** 121, 127-133
North Korea state visit, **1999** 571-572; **2000** 359, 679, 866-872; **2001** 268
nuclear weapons test moratorium, **1999** 603
Panama Canal transfer ceremony, absence from, **1999** 852-853
religious freedom, **1997** 563; **1998** 19, 21, 23
Rwanda genocidal war, **1999** 861; **2000** 453
terrorism, **1998** 587
United Nations
secretary candidates, **1996** 825
U.S. role, **1993** 815
U.S. embassy bombings, **1998** 558, 560-561; **1999** 307
Vietnam, U.S. consulate in, **1997** 489-492; **1999** 475-479; **2000** 913
on Zaire leader Kabila, **1998** 161
Albright, Robert, desegregation at Mississippi colleges, **1992** 577
Albuquerque Tribune, human radiation test investigations, **1993** 987-988
Alcoa Inc., "new source" review, **2003** 177
Alcohol Abuse and Alcoholism, National Advisory Council on, college drinking report, **2002** 175-192
Alcohol Abuse and Alcoholism, National Institute on, **2002** 176
Alcohol Marketing and Youth, Center on, **2002** 178
Alcohol, Tobacco, and Firearms (ATF) Bureau
ballistic "fingerprinting," **2002** 961
guns, estimates of number of, **1995** 466-467
National Tracing Center, **1995** 469
WACO compound incident, **1993** 293, 296, 819-840; **1999** 480
Alcohol use
See also Alcoholism
beer advertising, **1994** 173-174
cancer risk and, **1982** 163, 508, 516
college drinking, national task force on, **2002** 175-192
dietary guidelines on, **2005** 13
and disease among minorities, **1985** 685-687, 690, 698-702
federal survey results, **1996** 577-578; **1999** 460, 462
health benefits of drinking, **1996** 3-4, 16
liquor advertising on television, **1996** 770-775
marketing to youth, **2002** 178
national drug policy on, **1973** 394, 396-397, 401-403, 405
operation of oil tanker and, **1989** 225-226, 232-234, 238-239
in public schools, **1975** 213, 219
standards of conduct for government officials, **1989** 106, 109-112, 118-119
teenage drinking, **2002** 175-176, 178
Alcoholism
See also Alcohol use; Substance abuse
in African American communities, **1983** 43
causes and treatments, **1972** 193-200; **1983** 335-354
as disease or willful misconduct, **1988** 277-285
new definition of, **1992** 849-852
occupational programs for, **1978** 649
in Soviet Union, **1987** 86
Alcorn State University (Mississippi), **1992** 576, 578-587
Alden v. Maine, **1999** 334-349
Aldridge, Edward C. "Pete", Jr., on Bush space program, **2004** 11
Alekseyeva, Yelizaveta, **1981** 747-749
Alencar, José
Brazilian economic recovery, **2003** 5

Alencar, José *Continued*
Brazilian vice presidential candidate, **2002** 777; **2003** 9
Aleut natives, reparations for wartime relocation, **1983** 212, 228; **1988** 287, 291-292
Alexander, Bill (D-Ark.), **1982** 181
Alexander, Donald C.
on IRS investigation of tax shelters, **1975** 830
on Nixon's tax deduction, **1974** 239
Alexander, Duane, child health care, **1997** 425
Alexander, Ferris J., Jr., **1993** 432, 438-446
Alexander, Fritz, **1990** 268-273
Alexander, Jane, future of the arts, **1997** 700
Alexander, Kent B., **1996** 447
Alexander, Lamar
college athletics reform, **1991** 129-130
diversity in schools, **1991** 331-332
international math and science test, **1992** 86-88
national education strategy, **1991** 219; **1992** 221
national standards for education testing, **1992** 46
Alexander v. United States, **1993** 432, 437, 438-446
Alexandre, Boniface, Haiti interim president, **2004** 96
Alfonsín, Raúl
Argentine "dirty war" trials, **2003** 828
Argentine disappeared persons, reports on, **1983** 455-457; **1984** 789-791
Argentine president resignation, **2002** 83
court-martial of Argentine juntas, **1983** 456-457
election of, **1983** 456-457; **1984** 157-158, 797
human rights in Argentina, **1983** 463-465; **1984** 789-793; **1985** 148-149
Alfred P. Sloan Foundation, DNA "fingerprint" study, **1992** 366
Algeria
chemical weapons treaty, **1993** 72
Egyptian relations with, **1977** 829; **1978** 607
intermediary between Iran and U.S., **1980** 999-1007; **1981** 146
on lifting oil embargo against U.S., **1974** 221
on oil-consuming countries' cooperation, **1974** 124
and OPEC oil prices, **1979** 251, 254; **1980** 995; **1981** 799; **1982** 980
at poverty summit, **1981** 770
on raw materials of developing countries, **1974** 255-264
role in Israeli-Lebanese security agreement, **1983** 472-473
terrorist organizations, **1999** 499
Ali, Ahmed Abu, U.S. detainee, **2005** 914
Ali, Muhammad, **1984** 1020
Ali Megrahi, Abdel Basset, Lockerbie case conviction, **2003** 1223
Alia, Ramiz, **1985** 325, 327-328
Aliens, illegal. *See* Immigrants and immigration
Alimony payments, to needy husbands, **1979** 193-206
Alioto, Joseph, **1977** 802-805
Alireza, Ali A., **1976** 938
Alison, Graham T., Russian nuclear weapons panel, **2001** 19
Alito, Samuel A., Jr.
abortion issue, **2005** 815
Supreme Court confirmation, **2005** 79, 551, 558, 563, 815
Aliyev, Heydar, **1999** 640
All Writs Act (1789), **1977** 883-891
Allard, Wayne (R-Colo.), sexual misconduct at Air Force Academy, **2003** 792
Allawi, Ayad
coup attempt (1996), **2004** 401
Iraq elections, **2005** 943, 944
Iraq interim prime minister, **2004** 401; **2005** 941, 944
Iraqi security challenges, **2004** 874-884
speech to Congress, **2005** 89
Allbaugh, Joseph, relationship with Michael Brown, **2005** 569
Allchin, James, **1999** 656
Allegheny County v. Greater Pittsburgh ACLU, **1992** 556, 559; **1995** 399, 401, 402
Allen, Ernie, on sex offenders, **1997** 384
Allen, George (R-Va.)
and balanced budgets, **1995** 11
lynchings, Senate apology for, **2005** 357
Allen, Henry, **1993** 959
Allen, James B. (D-Ala.), **1977** 96-97
Allen, Lew, Jr., **1987** 30
Allen, Paul, **1999** 655
Allen, Richard V., **1982** 562
FBI investigation of, **1981** 847-854
"October Surprise" report, **1993** 11
Allen, Thad, Hurricane Katrina rescue operations, **2005** 568
Allen, Tom (D-Maine), prescription drug benefit reform, **2000** 133
Allen v. Illinois, **1997** 393
Allen v. State Board of Elections, **1993** 466
Allende Gossens, Salvador
CIA campaign against, **1974** 805; **1975** 403, 873-875, 884-910
on exploitation of developing countries, **1972** 329-336
government of, Nixon view of, **1977** 323, 351-352
military coup against, CIA involvement in, **1975** 710, 715-716, 763-770, 780
on multinational corporations, **1972** 396
president of Chile, **2005** 771
on U.S. economic retaliation, **1972** 67
Alley, Wayne, **1997** 624
Alliance Capital Management, mutual funds scandal, **2003** 696
Alliance for Progress, **1975** 884
Alliance for Responsible CFC Policy
on CFC reductions, **1988** 223
on ozone treaty, **1987** 748
Alliance for Schools That Work, **1994** 412-414
Allon, Yigal, **1976** 192-193
Almatov, Zokrijon, Uzbekistan interior minister, **2005** 433
ALOF. *See* Abraham Lincoln Opportunity Foundation
ALPA. *See* Air Line Pilots Association
Altenburg, John, military tribunals, **2003** 113
Alternative medicine, for hormone replacement therapy, **2002** 506-507
Altman, Drew E., managed cared, **1997** 788
Altman, Robert, BCCI banking scandal, **1991** 621-636
Alvarez, Aida, welfare system, **1997** 620

Alwyn, Patricio, **1990** 187-193
Alyeska Pipeline Service Company, oil spill cleanup, **1989** 226-227, 234-236; **1990** 514, 529
Alzheimer's disease
care and services, federal policies on, **1987** 391-406
drug therapy, **2004** 855
Reagan as victim of, **2001** 541
Reagan letter announcing, **1994** 498-500
research on, **1987** 405-406
Alzheimer's Disease and Related Disorders Association (ADRDA), **1987** 391, 396, 399, 405
AMA. *See* American Medical Association
Ambassadorial appointments, link to campaign contributions, **1974** 604
Amberg, Claus von, **1980** 389
Ambrose, Stephen E., **1989** 17
Ambuhl, Megan M., Abu Ghraib prison abuse conviction, **2004** 215
Amendments to the Constitution. *See under* Constitutional amendments (U.S.)
America 2000 education plan, **1992** 45, 101, 106, 143, 144, 449
Bush statement on, **1991** 219-226
America 2000 Excellence in Education Act, **1992** 107-108
America Coming Together, **2004** 777
America Online (AOL)
indecent materials restrictions, **1997** 444
merger with Time Warner, **2000** 1034-1046
America Reads Challenge, **1997** 35, 64-65; **1998** 77, 88
American Academy of Neurology, **1990** 376
American Academy of Pediatrics, **1983** 282-283
infants and whole cow's milk, **1992** 401
soft drinks in school ban, **2004** 655
student drug testing, **2002** 427
American Airlines, flight 191 crash investigation, **1979** 949-963
American Anthropological Association, on return of skeletal remains, **1989** 541
American Assembly on the United States and the United Nations, **1972** 337, 340-342
American Association for the Advancement of Science (AAAS), **1992** 135; **2002** 745
American Association of Colleges for Teacher Education, **1992** 144
American Association of Museums, on Native American skeletal remains, **1989** 539-540
American Association of Pediatrics, **1986** 542
American Association of Retired Persons (AARP)
See also under its later name AARP
on for-profit hospitals, **1986** 489
grandparents' rights, **2000** 268
health care, **1997** 790
prescription drug benefit reform, **2000** 133
American Association of Tissue Banks, **1989** 553
American Association of University Women (AAUW)
schools shortchanging girls report, **1992** 141-154
sexual harassment in public schools, **1993** 353-361
American Automobile Association (AAA), aggressive driving, **1997** 551
American Bankers Association (ABA)
Burns speech on international monetary reform, **1972** 413
Volcker speech on Fed action on inflation, **1979** 772-773, 778-780
American Bar Association (ABA)
Blackman speech on Watergate, **1973** 723-727
on Bork Supreme Court nomination, **1987** 724-726
on brain-death statutes, **1983** 282, 290-291
Burger speech on criminal justice system, **1981** 191-196, 434
Burger speech on state of judiciary, **1972** 639-643
Carter criticism of, **1978** 328, 335
domestic violence report, **1994** 63
enemy combatant procedures, **2003** 112, 113
on flag protection amendment, **1989** 345
independent counsel legislation, **1999** 168
on insanity defense, **1983** 27, 40
justices' speeches on Court workload, **1982** 705-706, 712-718
on legal professionalism, **1986** 767-778
Meese speech on Court, **1985** 479
Reagan speech on terrorism, **1985** 463-477
Roberts Supreme Court nomination, **2005** 562
on tort reform, **1987** 165-181
American Bar Foundation, on legal rights of embryos, **1989** 552
American Broadcasting Co. (ABC), Sakharov interview, **1986** 1093-1095
American Campaign Academy, **1997** 10, 15
American Cancer Society (ACS)
dietary guidelines, **1996** 3, 5
"Great American Weigh In," **2003** 480
involuntary smoking, **1986** 1080, 1084
thyroid cancer and radiation, **1997** 591
value of mammograms, **1997** 144, 145
weight-related deaths, **2005** 6
American Center for Law and Justice, **2005** 817
American Citizens' Television (ACTV), **1997** 7
American Civil Liberties Union (ACLU)
abortion rights, **2003** 998
Abu Ghraib prison scandal, **2004** 214; **2005** 912
affirmative action, **1996** 761-762
affirmative action and seniority, **1984** 367
aviation security and CAPPS II program, **2003** 722
Bork nomination, **1987** 719
California gubernatorial recall election, **2003** 1008
campaign finance reform, **2003** 1158
child pornography and "community standards," **2002** 290
civil rights Court rulings, **1989** 324
creation science, **1982** 5; **1987** 566
death penalty, **1983** 711; **1987** 463
domestic partners' rights, **1989** 307
domestic security investigations, **1972** 486; **1983** 258
draft discrimination against men, **1981** 523
draft evader pardon, **1974** 820; **1977** 96
drug abuse legislation, **2005** 679
drug testing, **1986** 180-181
of students, **1995** 341
faith-based initiatives, **2001** 134
flag protection amendment, **1989** 345
gay rights, **1996** 286
on gay rights to march in parade, **1995** 327-335

American Civil Liberties Union (ACLU) *Continued*
Guantanamo Bay detainees abuses, **2004** 342; **2005** 449
on hate crimes, **1992** 545
indigents' right to psychiatric aid, **1985** 209
intelligent design, **2005** 1012
Internet and free speech, **1997** 444-458
Internet pornography ban, **1996** 354-355
Internet pornography filters, **2003** 388
IRS political investigations, **1975** 830
as issue in presidential debates, **1988** 722, 732-734, 760
juvenile curfew laws, **1996** 327
medical records privacy, **2001** 487
parental leave, **1987** 19
political asylum, **1987** 255
press freedoms, **1979** 513; **1988** 38-39
on prison inmates beaten by guards, **1992** 176-177
prisoners' rights, **1984** 479-480
public display of Nativity scene, **1984** 218
on race-based redistricting ruling, **1995** 372
right to die issue, **1990** 373
school prayer and, **1984** 243, 244; **1992** 555
school vouchers, **1997** 364
student drug testing, **2002** 424
tax exemptions for discriminatory schools, **1983** 491
Ten Commandments display case, **2005** 376-389
terrorist suspects interrogation abuses, **2004** 380
terrorist suspects watch list, **2003** 158
unreasonable searches, **2001** 409; **2003** 611-612
USA Patriot Act, legal challenge to, **2003** 611
American Coalition of Life Activists, "wanted" posters for abortion doctors, **2003** 999
American College of Cardiology, **1987** 779
American College of Obstetricians and Gynecologists
morning-after pill for unintended pregnancies, **2003** 999
partial birth abortion ban, **2003** 998
American College Testing, desegregation in Mississippi colleges, **1992** 575-587
American Congress of American Indians, **1989** 539
American Conservative Union, **2003** 722
American Constitutional Law Foundation (ACLF), **1999** 5-14
American Convention on Human Rights, **1980** 191, 193
American Council of Life Insurance, on sex bias in pension plans, **1983** 693-694
American Council on Education (ACE)
teacher quality, **1999** 64, 66
tenure review disclosure, **1990** 24-25
American Cyanimid Co., and EPA regulation of chemical discharge, **1977** 131-141
American Economic Association (AEA), Burns speech on inflation, **1972** 961-970
American Enterprise Institute for Public Policy, **1983** 786
China AIDS projections, **2002** 470-471
independent counsel report, **1999** 168
American Family Association, **1990** 511
American Federation of Labor-Congress of Industrial Organizations (AFL-CIO)
affirmative action, **1979** 495
bankruptcy and labor, **1984** 183
Bork nomination, **1987** 719
Califano speech on workplace health, **1978** 633-641
campaign finance reform, **2003** 1158
Clinton endorsement, **1992** 345
coal strike settlement, **1990** 20
Kirkland retirement, **1995** 680-681
labor movement advances, **1999** 630-638
lifting of wage and price controls, **1973** 45
NAFTA opposition, **1993** 954
national health plan and, **1978** 545
Panama Canal treaties, **1977** 592, 593
Pittston coal strike settlement, **1990** 19-22
prescription drug benefit reform, **2000** 134
smoking in workplace, **1985** 810; **1986** 1080
Social Security reform, **2005** 113
split by several unions, **2005** 485-497
support for Polish Solidarity and Walesa, **1983** 925-926; **1989** 524, 538
Sweeney's election remarks, **1995** 680-685
union membership, **1985** 417
United Farm Workers and, **1975** 377-379
American Federation of State, County, and Municipal Employees (AFSCME), **2005** 488
on privatization, **1988** 231
on Proposition 13 in California, **1978** 398-399
American Federation of Teachers (AFT)
affirmative action and seniority, **1984** 367
and Education Department, **1979** 159
education reform, **1986** 459; **1988** 299; **1989** 563
school violence, **1975** 208, 213
science education, **1988** 379
American Finance Association, Burns speech on inflation, **1972** 961-970
American Forest and Paper Association, **1999** 595
American Foundation for AIDS research, **1986** 889
American Geographical Society, **1988** 832
American Health Care Association, nursing home care, **2002** 119, 131
American Heart Association (AHA)
body mass index (BMI) data, **2004** 652
childhood obesity prevention programs, **2005** 6
on cholesterol education, **1987** 779
dietary guidelines, **1996** 3, 5
on involuntary smoking, **1986** 1080
obesity studies, **2004** 652-653
American Hospital Association (AHA)
hospital occupancy rate, **1988** 334
patient safety, **1999** 782
patient's bill of rights, **1973** 39-42
severely handicapped infants, treatment of, **1986** 541-558
American Immigration Lawyers' Association, **1987** 255
American Independent Party, **1972** 615
American Indian Movement (AIM), occupation of Wounded Knee, **1973** 531-535
American Indians. *See* Native Americans
American Indians Against Desecration, **1989** 541
American International Group (AIG)
lawsuit, **2004** 418

SEC investigation, **2004** 418
American Iron and Steel Institute v. Natural Resources Defense Council, **1984** 427-437
American Israel Public Affairs Committee, Baker speech on Middle East peace requirements, **1989** 289-296
American Jewish Commission, on role of U.S. Jews in holocaust, **1981** 382; **1983** 143-161
American Jewish Committee, Mondale speech on U.S. commitment to Israel, **1978** 127-128, 131-134
American Jewish Congress
hate crimes, **1992** 545
on role of U.S. Jews in holocaust, **1983** 145
school vouchers, opposition to, **2002** 409-410
on UN vote on Israeli settlements, **1980** 238
American Journal of Public Health, beer advertising, **1994** 173-174
American Judicature Society, Stevens speech on Court workload, **1982** 705, 707-712
American Law Institute, **1990** 311
American Legion
Dole speech on social issues, **1995** 573-580
on draft evader pardon, **1977** 96
on Panama Canal treaties, **1977** 593
American Library Association (ALA)
FBI access to patron records, **2002** 563
Internet pornography ban, **1996** 354-355
Internet pornography filters in public libraries, Supreme Court on, **2003** 387-400
USA Patriot Act, opposition to, **2003** 609-610
American Library Association v. United States, **2002** 288, 291-297; **2003** 393-400
American Life League, **1994** 313
American Lung Association, **1986** 1080
American Meat Institute, **1982** 507
American Medical Association (AMA)
AIDS management, **1987** 817-832
AIDS testing, **1988** 416
alcoholism as disease, **1988** 277-279
antismoking campaign, **1994** 207
assaults against women, **1992** 607
boxing ban, **1984** 1019-1021
brain-death statutes, **1983** 282, 290-291
Carter criticism of, **1978** 328, 337
cholesterol education, **1987** 779
contagious disease and job discrimination, **1987** 245, 250
domestic violence, **1994** 63
end-of-life care education and practice reform, **1996** 329
euthanasia, **1990** 376
gun violence report, **1992** 493-498
health care reform, opposition to, **1993** 782
labor unions for medical profession, **1999** 633
medical records privacy, **1997** 583
and national health insurance, **1978** 544
patient's bill of rights, **1973** 40
physician-assisted suicide
doctor/patient privilege, **1999** 442
opposition to, **1994** 501-502; **1996** 124; **1997** 460
prescription drug importation, **2004** 984
treatment of handicapped infants, **1986** 542-544
weight-related deaths, **2005** 6
American National Red Cross v. S.G., **1992** 462
American Newspaper Publishers Association (ANPA)
on confidentiality of news sources, **1972** 508
on FOIA restrictions, **1981** 395
on press access to pretrial hearings, **1979** 513
on press freedom, **1979** 287
American Newspaper Publishers Association v. National Citizens Committee for Broadcasting, **1978** 419-432
American Opportunities Workshop (AOW), **1997** 6-7
American Pain Society, **1997** 328
American Party platform, **1972** 615-625
American PEN, on Rushdie death threat, **1989** 96
American Petroleum Institute, on federal control of offshore oil, **1975** 168
American Physical Society (APS), **1992** 379
American Psychiatric Association (APA)
on insanity defense, **1982** 534; **1983** 25-40; **1985** 209
on psychiatric testimony, **1981** 432-433; **1983** 710, 720
American Psychoanalytic Association, medical records privacy, **2001** 487
American Psychological Association (APA)
children and television advertising, **2004** 654
television violence, **1993** 488
American Public Health Association, prison occupancy standard, **1981** 477
American Public Welfare Association, on welfare reform, **1988** 850
American Red Cross
See also International Committee of the Red Cross
disaster relief, **1984** 974
efforts in hurricane and earthquake disasters, **1989** 667-670
holocaust victims, **1993** 310
American Servicemembers Protection Act (2002), **2002** 608; **2003** 101
American Society of Health-System Pharmacists, flu vaccine price gouging, **2004** 641
American Society of Newspaper Editors (ASNE)
broadcast license renewal, **1973** 57
confidentiality of news sources, **1972** 507
Fallaci speech on U.S. in European affairs, **1973** 488, 495-498
Kissinger speech on Vietnam, **1975** 252-262
right to reply, **1974** 524
American Society of Plastic and Reconstructive Surgery, **1993** 369
American Telephone & Telegraph Co. (AT&T), deregulation and antitrust settlement, **1982** 17-33; **2000** 308; **2002** 797
American Textile Manufacturers Institute v. Donovan, **1981** 491-505
American University, study of Nixon administration's relations with press, **1973** 630-637
American Values, **2005** 112
Americans for Gun Safety, **2002** 962
Americans for Tax Reform, **1998** 894; **2003** 722
Americans United for Separation of Church and State, **1984** 243; **2001** 134, 423; **2002** 407; **2005** 379

Americans United for Separation of Church and State *Continued*
 intelligent design case, **2005** 1012-1013
Americans with Disabilities Act (ADA, 1990)
 and AIDS discrimination, **1998** 378-392
 definition of disability, Supreme Court on, **1999** 317-332; **2002** 3-4
 disabilities in the workplace, Supreme Court on, **2002** 3-14
 and EEOC guidelines on mental disabilities, **1997** 127-141
 Oregon health plan, **1992** 742-745
 Republican Party platform on, **1992** 818
America's Cup race, court rulings on, **1989** 183-193; **1990** 267-273
America's Private Investment Companies, **2000** 49
Americas Watch
 on human rights in Nicaragua, **1985** 255, 258-260
 on State Department human rights reports, **1983** 182; **1984** 156; **1985** 146
AmeriCorps
 Bush state of the Union address, **2002** 37, 44
 church volunteers and, **1997** 244
 Clinton administration support for, **1995** 34, 82, 438; **1997** 35, 40; **1999** 56; **2000** 34
 program expansion, **1997** 239
 program objectives, **1997** 243
 rebuilding burnt churches, **1997** 311-312
 training for private sector jobs, **1997** 621
 volunteers helping flood victims, **1997** 243
Ames, Aldrich, espionage case, **1994** 475-497; **1995** 532-533; **1996** 794; **2001** 150-151
Ames, Rosario, **1994** 476, 483
Amin, Hafizullah, execution of, **1979** 965, 969-970, 974, 976; **1980** 190
Amin, Hussam Muhammad, Iraq weapons inspections, **2002** 718
Amin, Idi
 attacks in UN on Israel, Moynihan on, **1975** 645-646, 649
 death in exile, **2003** 470
 and Entebbe hostages, **1976** 518
 human rights abuses in Uganda, **2001** 505; **2003** 470-471
 on human rights in Uganda, **1977** 143-148
 ousted from Uganda, **2003** 470
Amir, Yigal, assassin of Yitzhak Rabin, **1995** 689
Amish, religious freedom issues, **1997** 407
Amnesty
 for illegal aliens, **1981** 265-266; **1986** 964-966
 for military draft evaders
  Democratic platform on, **1972** 528, 576
  Ford on, **1974** 768, 813, 819-831; **1976** 701-703
  Nixon on, **1972** 12-13, 722; **1973** 193-194, 197-198
Amnesty International
 Argentina's disappeared persons, **1983** 455-456, 463-465
 Chinese political repression, **2005** 619
 death penalty opponent, **2005** 179
 genocide and, **2004** 118
 Guantanamo Bay detentions, **2002** 831; **2005** 449
 Haiti human rights abuses, **2004** 98; **2005** 332-333
 human rights report, **1988** 883-889; **1989** 597-609; **1990** 129-130, 132-142; **1993** 559-578
 Indigenous Americans abuses report, **1992** 897-905
 Israeli war crimes, demolition of Palestinian homes, **2004** 310
 South African political prisoners, **1982** 798
 State Department report, source for, **1977** 3-6, 9, 11, 18, 22
 Sudan conflict, **2004** 590
 U.S. detention policies, **2004** 208, 214, 216
Amniocentesis, state restrictions on, **1976** 483-484, 487-488
Amoco Cadiz oil spill (1978), **1989** 229
Amorim, Celso, WTO trade talk negotiations, **2003** 741
Amrozi, and Bali terrorist bombing, **2002** 706
Amtrak
 GAO testimony on, **1994** 197-204
 privatization of, **1988** 150, 235
 train accident in Arizona desert, **1995** 178
 train accident in Silver Spring, Maryland, **1996** 189-190
Ana de los Angeles Monteaguedo, beatification of, **1985** 58
Anand, K. S., abortion and fetal pain research, **2005** 818
al-Anbar, Abdul Amir, **1987** 610
ANC. *See* African National Congress
Ancess, Jacqueline, **1992** 625
Andean Pact countries
 condemnation of Castro, **1980** 338
 political and economic cooperation of, **1979** 717, 719
Anderson, Gerald, Roswell incident, **1997** 401
Anderson, Jack
 CIA activities, **1975** 402-403
 documents on U.S. position in Indo-Pakistani conflict, **1972** 23
 on ITT antitrust settlement, **1972** 395-396; **1974** 4
 Johnson's mood on leaving office, **1972** 789
 Kissinger Vietnam study (1969), **1972** 361
 libel action against, **1986** 357-358
 and publication of Pentagon Papers, **1972** 491
Anderson, Jeffrey, on sexual abuse, **1993** 408
Anderson, John B. (R-Ill.)
 debate with Reagan, **1980** 847-869
 on Nixon impeachment, **1974** 674
 on Nixon income taxes, **1974** 236
 on Nixon resignation, **1974** 302
 presidential candidacy of, **1980** 772, 919
Anderson, Michael P., *Columbia* astronaut, **2003** 633
Anderson, Terry, **1991** 751, 755, 756-758; **1993** 83
Anderson, Thomas J.
 equal time demands of, **1976** 695
 as vice-presidential candidate, **1972** 615
Anderson, Warren M., on Bhopal accident, **1984** 1024; **1985** 296-297
Anderson, Wendell R. (D-Minn.), **1976** 544
Anderson v. Liberty Lobby, **1986** 357-358
Andover Foundation for Archaeological Research, **1992** 135, 137

Andreotti, Giulio, **1977** 367; **1990** 467; **1992** 638
Andres Pérez, Carlos
on Central American peace, **1989** 163
on Panama Canal treaties, **1978** 270
on Venezuela's debt reduction, **1989** 138
Andrews, David, U.S. bombing of Chinese embassy, **1999** 307
Andrews, Lori, **1989** 552
Andropov, Yuri V.
on arms control, **1982** 983-988; **1983** 793-794
career of, **1982** 871-872
death of, **1984** 145-154; **1985** 271
on U.S. space defense program, **1983** 306
Andrus, Cecil D.
abortion bill veto, **1990** 215, 217-219
on Alaska federal lands, **1978** 732-734
appointment to secretary of interior, **1976** 878
Andujar, Joaquin, **1986** 170
Angelou, Maya
Clinton inauguration, **1993** 131
at Million Man March, **1995** 656
Angleton, James, CIA counterintelligence, **1994** 480-481
Anglican Church, Lambeth Conference, on women as bishops, **1989** 51, 54
Anglican Consultative Council, gay ordinances splitting the church, **2005** 865
Angola
AIDS pandemic, **2002** 156
civil war
accord on, **1988** 947-950
Brezhnev on, **1976** 144, 146-147
cease-fire agreement, **2002** 151-164, 447
Soviet and Cuban involvement in, **1976** 287, 346; **1985** 708, 715-716
U.S. involvement, **1976** 15, 25, 27, 33; **1988** 616, 675
conflict in, **1999** 431
Cuban withdrawal from, **1988** 356, 947-950
economic sanctions against Rhodesia, lifting of, **1979** 941
land mine problem, **1995** 48-49
Lusaka accord, **2002** 154-155, 163-164
Namibia peace accord, **1988** 947-949
Namibian independence, **1990** 200
as oil supplier, **1981** 800
Peace Accord, **1991** 287-300
presidential and legislative elections, **2002** 153
on Rhodesian settlement plan, **1976** 721-722, 728-729; **1978** 150
UN peacekeeping mission, **2003** 450
UN report on refugees, **1991** 672
UN role in, **1995** 355
Angrisani, Bob, **1985** 305
Aniakchak National Monument, **1978** 731, 735-736
Animal rights, Swedish law on, in farming, **1988** 347-351
Anker, Irving, **1975** 208
Annan, Kofi
Afghanistan
creation of an army, **2002** 19
humanitarian aid, **1999** 526-527; **2001** 883-884
political situation, **2003** 1089-1109
UN peace negotiations, **1999** 525
UN peacekeeping forces, **2002** 18; **2004** 913
Africa
conflicts in, **1998** 220-232; **2001** 505-506; **2002** 447
economic development plan, **2002** 450, 451
reform in, **2003** 450-469
UN assistance, **1999** 429
AIDS
epidemic, **2005** 50
global fund to fight, **2001** 439; **2002** 473
global involvement in prevention of, **2002** 476; **2003** 780
Angola
assassination of, rewards offered for, **2004** 536
children as victims of war, **2002** 156
general elections, **2002** 155
peacekeeping forces, **2002** 153
Burundi
humanitarian aid, **2003** 926
peacekeeping mission, **2003** 925
children
child soldiers report, **2002** 916-926
UN special session on, **2002** 221, 223
Congo
political situation, **2004** 505-516
progress toward democracy, **2005** 1027-1035
Congo war, **1999** 645-653; **2000** 978-987; **2001** 160, 164-166; **2002** 548-550
humanitarian situation, **2002** 552-553
UN peacekeeping mission, **2003** 289, 293-294
Cyprus, peace negotiations, **2004** 977
East Timor independence, **2001** 593-599; **2002** 256, 259, 261-262; **2004** 757
Eritrea-Ethiopia war, **2000** 753-761
foreign development assistance, **2005** 408
global economy, **1999** 393
Haiti
human rights abuses, **2004** 98
political situation, **2000** 952-960; **2001** 396
UN Stabilization Mission, **2005** 329-337
India, nuclear testing, **1998** 327
Indonesia, human rights, **1999** 513
International Criminal Court (ICC), **2002** 605-611; **2003** 99-104
Iraq
human rights, **2000** 583
UN mission, **2003** 810, 939-940, 945
UN multilateral action, **2002** 616
UN multinational force authorized, **2003** 945
UN security "dysfunctional," **2003** 939
UN weapons inspections for disarmament of, **1998** 935, 936; **2002** 716
Iraq War, U.S.-led invasion "illegal," **2004** 890
Israel
Israeli-Palestinian violence, **2002** 927-941
security wall controversy, **2003** 1209-1210
West Bank settlements, **2004** 310
Ivory Coast
elections, **2005** 805
peace negotiations, **2004** 820
UN peacekeeping mission, **2003** 240

Annan, Kofi *Continued*
  Kosovo
    conflict, **1998** 830, 831; **1999** 288
    elections, **2001** 819
    Kosovo Assembly, role of, **2003** 1139
    Lebanon-Syria relations, **2004** 560, 561
    UN policy toward, **2004** 952
  Lebanon, Hariri assassination, UN investigation, **2005** 691-692
  Liberia
    civil war, **2002** 251
    UN humanitarian aid, **2003** 770
    UN peacekeeping forces, **2003** 767, 772-773; **2005** 801
  Middle East peace process, **2002** 375, 377; **2003** 1203, 1209-1210
  Millennium Development Goals, **2003** 756; **2004** 888
  Nobel Peace Prize recipient, **2001** 517, 899-906
  nuclear nonproliferation, **2000** 204
  Pakistan, earthquake relief efforts, **2005** 478-479
  Rwanda genocidal war, **1998** 222; **1999** 860; **2000** 449, 452-453; **2004** 115-121
  Sierra Leone
    elections, **2002** 248
    UN peacekeeping mission, **2002** 250
  small arms trade, **2001** 516
  Srebrenica massacre, UN response, **1999** 735, 737, 741; **2001** 899
  state of the world report ("We the Peoples"), **2000** 700-701
  Sudan
    genocidal war, **2004** 116, 591, 592, 593, 595; **2005** 515, 526
    peace negotiations, **2005** 521
    rape victims, **2005** 518
  tsunami relief effort, **2004** 994, 995; **2005** 992
  UN peacekeeping mission reforms, **2000** 642
  UN reform efforts, **2000** 179-181; **2003** 808-816; **2004** 887-911; **2005** 228-245, 408
  UN secretary general, **1997** 152-153
  UN secretary general appointment, **1996** 824-827
  war crimes tribunals, **2003** 1073
  women's rights, **2000** 326
  worldwide population growth, **1999** 585
Annan, Kojo (son of Kofi Annan), UN oil-for-food program scandal, **2004** 892; **2005** 235
Annas, George, human cloning, **2002** 516
Annunzio, Frank (D-Ill.), BCCI banking scandal, **1991** 632
ANPA. *See* American Newspaper Publishers Association
Anpilov, Viktor, **1993** 770
Anrig, Gregory, international math and science test, **1992** 86
Ansar al-Islam (Islamic group), **2004** 539
Antall, Jozsef, **1991** 400
Antarctica
  ozone layer depletion over, **1987** 745-746, 756-764; **1988** 222-228
  world park in, **1972** 797
Anthony, Beryl F., Jr. (D-Ark.)
  Bush's no-tax pledge, **1990** 409, 413
  on Foster suicide, **1993** 533
Anthrax mailings in U.S., **2001** 3, 130, 360, 615, 665, 672, 674-676; **2003** 904; **2004** 442-443
Anthrax vaccine, **2004** 442, 446
Anti-Ballistic Missile (ABM) Treaty, **2000** 203, 205-206, 677-678, 680; **2001** 281-282, 516, 893-894, 927-934; **2002** 276, 1026-1027
  achievements of, **1978** 550, 556-557, 563
  compliance with
    former defense officials on, **1986** 781-782, 785-788
    Nitze on, **1978** 576
    and SDI, **1983** 306; **1984** 258-259, 262, 265; **1986** 877-880, 884-885; **1988** 325, 327-330
  ratification debate, **1979** 413
  reinterpretation of by Reagan administration, **1987** 289-317
  signing of, **1972** 431-436, 452-458
  strategic balance in, **1972** 768-769, 774
Anti-Defamation League
  B'nai B'rith
    on affirmative action ruling, **1978** 470
    on discrimination in Medal of Honor award, **1989** 697, 700
  church arson prevention, **1997** 311
  hate crimes, **1992** 545
  lynching, opposition to, **2005** 356
Anti-Deficiency Act (1950), **1974** 591; **1975** 136; **1981** 832
Anti-Drug Abuse Act (1988)
  and drug sentencing, **1997** 248-250
  and military interception of drugs, **1989** 500
Anti-Personnel Landmine Ban Treaty, **1998** 541
Antipoverty programs, transfer of to Cabinet departments, Nixon on, **1973** 304, 311-312
Antiquities Act (1906)
  national monument designations, Clinton administration and, **2001** 217
  preservation of Alaskan lands under, **1978** 731-735
Antiretroviral (ARV) drug therapy, **2005** 50-63
Anti-Semitism
  See also Jews
  in Argentina, **1981** 180, 184
  Austrian election and, **1986** 745, 749-750
  Holocaust as myth and, **1981** 382, 385-387
  Shostakovich on, **1981** 376, 378
  U.S., Begin on, **1981** 901, 906-907
  U.S. Medal of Honor award and, **1989** 697-700
  Walesa's apology to Israel for, **1991** 253-256
Anti-Terrorism. *See* Counterterrorism; Terrorism
Anti-Terrorism Act (1987), and closing of PLO observer mission to UN, **1988** 479-485
Anti-Terrorism and Effective Death Penalty Act, **2000** 991-992
Anti-Torture Act (1994), **2004** 338, 341
Antitrust
  Aramco investigation by Justice Department, **1983** 921-924
  AT&T settlement, **1982** 17-33; **2000** 308; **2002** 797
  Hughes case, **1973** 976
  immunity of cities in regulating business, **1982** 35-49

intra-enterprise conspiracy doctrine, **1984** 413-426
ITT settlement with Justice Department, and political contributions, **1972** 395-405; **1974** 3-5, 16-20, 407-410; **1975** 654, 656, 666
Microsoft Corp. breakup ruling, **2000** 308-324
Microsoft Corp. case, **1999** 654-689; **2000** 105-130, 302-303
Microsoft Corp. settlement, **2001** 775-792; **2002** 797-817
Antitrust Procedures and Penalties Act (Tunney Act), **1982** 20
Antiwar movement, Kent State University, **1990** 289-294
Anxiety disorders, among U.S. adults, **1984** 833-834, 836-838, 840
ANZUS (Australia-New Zealand-U.S.) defense alliance, collapse of, **1985** 633
Aoun, Michel
leader of mass protest against Syria, **2004** 562
Lebanese presidential candidate, **2005** 689
APA. *See* American Psychiatric Association; American Psychological Association
Apartheid system
Botha's reaffirmation of, **1985** 515-527
Commonwealth of Nations on, **1986** 581-590
and constitutional changes, **1983** 890
De Klerk and repeal of apartheid system laws, **1991** 53-65
human rights in South Africa and, **1984** 167-168; **1985** 146-147, 155-156; **1989** 602-603
Immorality Act, **1984** 1033
movement toward reform, **1989** 545, 547, 550
in Namibian interim government proposal, **1976** 612
Nobel Peace Prize awarded on ending of, **1993** 877-884
pass laws, **1984** 1034; **1986** 369-381
Population Registration Act, **1984** 1032
Prohibition of Mixed Marriages Act, **1984** 1032-1033
protests against, black leaders on, **1976** 677-680
social effects of, **1984** 1027-1037
South African Truth and Reconciliation Commission report, **1998** 755-758
South Africa's Constitution, **1992** 283-292
UN arms embargo against South Africa and, **1977** 823-825
U.S. policy on, **1985** 531-536; **1986** 99, 101; **1987** 190, 193
women's conference condemnation of, **1975** 507, 509, 521
APEC Forum. *See* Asia-Pacific Economic Cooperation (APEC) Forum
Apfel, Kenneth S., Social Security reform, **1998** 98
Apodaca v. Oregon, **1972** 423, 426-429
Apollo space craft, **2003** 632
Appalachian Regional Commission, **1981** 641
Apparel industry, code of conduct to end sweatshops, **1997** 206-211
Appel, Judy, student drug testing, **2002** 427
Apple, R. W., Jr.
on issue of morality, **1997** 21
role of NATO, **1990** 457
Applewhite, Marshall Herff, Heaven's Gate cult leader, **1997** 122-124
Apprendi v. New Jersey, **2002** 357; **2004** 358, 360; **2005** 680
APS. *See* American Physical Society
Aqaba pipeline, and Meese investigation, **1988** 497-498, 510-516
Aqil, Aqeel Abdulazziz, financing of al Qaeda terrorist activities, **2004** 521
al-Aqsa Martyrs Brigade, **2002** 930-931; **2003** 196; **2005** 33
Aquino, Benigno S., Jr.
assassination of, **1983** 893; **1984** 166-167, 925-932; **1986** 98, 111, 307-308; **1987** 843
trial of, **1977** 23
Aquino, Corazon
cease-fire agreement with communist insurgents, **1986** 1037-1039
coup attempt against, **1987** 843-850
election and new government of, **1986** 307-314
and human rights, **1987** 190-191, 201-202
leadership of, **1987** 843-854
ouster of Marcos, **1986** 98, 307-309
Philippine presidential election, **2001** 103
Pope John Paul II support for, **2005** 293
suit for return of Philippines assets, **1988** 868
Arab and Political Prisoners, Committee for Solidarity with, **1986** 831
Arab Fund for Economic and Social Development, **2002** 484
Arab League
Arab world development, UN report on, **2002** 484
condemnation of Sadat by, **1977** 829
on economic cooperation with EC, **1974** 185
on Egypt, relations with, **1979** 224, 226; **1987** 869-871, 874
Fez peace proposal of, **1982** 754
on Iran-Iraq war, **1987** 869-873
Iraqi invasion of Kuwait, **1990** 558
on Moynihan's attack on OAU, **1975** 646
Saudi peace initiatives, **2002** 371
on Saudi peace plan, **1981** 631, 633
Arab states
See also Middle East
boycott of U.S. firms trading with Israel, **1976** 734, 742, 755-756
Bush Middle East Initiative, **2003** 957-959; **2004** 628-629
consensus among, Nasser efforts for, **1981** 733
EC proposal on cooperation with, **1974** 185-188, 530
Egyptian relations with, **1974** 436; **1981** 745-746
Egyptian-Israeli agreements, **1974** 436; **1975** 575
elections, **2005** 270-272
human development index, **2002** 484
human rights conferences in, **1981** 182
in ILO, **1983** 969
intellectual freedom, UN report on, **2003** 955-978
on Israeli raid on Iraq, **1981** 507
Israeli relations with, **1989** 289-290, 294-295
nationalism, and Palestinian homeland, **1988** 581-582
peace negotiations, Arab-Israeli war, **1973** 932

Arab states *Continued*
on PLO departure from Lebanon, **1982** 743
promoting democracy in
Bush administration, **2004** 628-629; **2005** 42-43, 164, 269-270
UN Development Programme report on, **2005** 269-289
Sadat assassination, reaction to, **1981** 734
UN human development reports on the Arab world, **2002** 483-502; **2003** 489-502, 956-957; **2004** 628; **2005** 269-289
UN Zionism resolution, **1975** 825-826
U.S. relations, improvement in, **1974** 449-471
U.S. sales of warplanes to, **1978** 125-134
U.S. television broadcasts (Al Hurra), **2005** 581
Arab-American Institute, **1989** 58
Arab-Israeli conflict
Arab League on, **1987** 870, 873-874
Labor Party victory and, **1992** 655-665
roots of, **1974** 926-933; **1988** 579-582
violence on the Temple Mount, **1990** 695-711
Arab-Israeli war (October war, 1973)
See also Middle East, peace process
cease-fire negotiations, U.S. and Soviet roles in, **1973** 881-896
Egyptian-Israeli disengagement agreement, **1974** 29-32
Egyptian-U.S. relations, **1976** 171-172
Israeli-Egyptian cease-fire, **1973** 931-937
Israeli-Syrian disengagement of forces, **1974** 435-439
military alert during, **1973** 881-882, 887-889, 892-893, 898-900
OPEC embargo on oil shipments to supporters of Israel, **1975** 3
threat of superpower confrontation, Nixon on, **1977** 322, 338-339
U.S. airlift to Israel, **1977** 338-339
Arab-Israeli war (Six-day war, 1967)
See also Israel, occupied territories
Egyptian defeat and reliance on Soviet aid, **1976** 169
Israeli occupation of Sinai, **1979** 225
territories seized by Israel in, **1976** 191-196
Arad, Moshe, **1989** 317
Arafat, Yasir
on Camp David accords, **1978** 606
Camp David peace negotiations, **2000** 475, 494-507; **2001** 360, 361
"captive" in Palestinian territory, **2002** 932
checkered *kaffiyeh* headdress as signature of, **2005** 28
death of, **2004** 301, 308, 629, 806-817; **2005** 27, 271
denial of U.S. visa, **1988** 907
funeral of, **2004** 808
on Israeli-Egyptian Sinai disengagement, **1974** 31
Israeli-Palestinian peace accord, **1993** 747, 749, 767-768; **1996** 337
Jackson and Fauntroy meeting with, **1979** 649
Middle East peace process, **2001** 363
Namibian independence, **1990** 199
new Palestinian leadership and, **2002** 369-381; **2003** 192-193
Nobel Peace Prize recipient, **2003** 1130
Palestinian Authority and, **2002** 927, 932-933
PLO faction opposed to, **1985** 468
recognition of Israel, **1989** 291
role in Israeli-Lebanese security agreement, **1983** 473
on Saudi peace plan, **1981** 633
Sharon policy toward, **2004** 301
state visit of John Paul II, **2000** 79-80
terrorist bombings and, **2001** 363-365, 367
UN speech on Zionism and Palestinian rights, **1974** 919-937
U.S. talks with PLO, conditions for, **1988** 905-908
West Bank agreement, **1995** 622-624, 626-628
Wye River peace agreement, **1998** 742-745, 751-753; **1999** 891-892
Aramco, Justice Department antitrust probe of, **1983** 921-924
Aramony, William, spending habits as United Way's president, **1992** 303-311
Arar, Maher, wrongful detention case, **2005** 914
Arbour, Louise
Kosovo human rights investigations, **1999** 290, 803
Sudan sexual violence, UN report on, **2005** 515
Arby's Restaurant, smoking ban, **1994** 596
Arcara v. Cloud Books, Inc., **1993** 442-443
Archer, Bill (R-Texas)
House Speaker elections, **1998** 802
IRS reform, **1997** 663
on Social Security and budget surplus, **1999** 43
U.S.-China trade relations, **2000** 220
Archer Daniels Midland Co. (ADM), "new source" review, **2003** 177
Archives of General Psychiatry, on mental disorders among U.S. adults, **1984** 833-843
Archives of Internal Medicine, cholesterol studies, **1992** 398
Arctic Climate Impact Assessment (ACIM), **2004** 827-840
Arctic ecology, U.S.-Soviet agreement on study of, **1972** 806, 812
Arctic National Wildlife Refuge (Alaska), oil exploration, **1989** 230; **2001** 331, 335-336; **2003** 182, 1017; **2004** 670; **2005** 79, 783-784
ARENA (Nationalist Republican Alliance) Party, **1992** 23-32
Arens, Moshe, **1981** 632-633
Argant, Robert-Jean, on violence in Haiti, **2005** 331
Argentina
aid to Nazi Germany, **1997** 259, 262, 263; **1998** 291, 292
allied relations and negotiations with, **1998** 295-298
bombings in Jewish community, **2003** 828-829
China trade relations, **2004** 938
and Contadora Group, **1987** 638
debt crisis in, **1982** 972; **1984** 796-797
disappeared persons, **1983** 455-467; **1984** 789-793
dissenters, "dirty war" against, **2003** 828-829
economic debt crisis, **2002** 80-91, 691, 693; **2003** 6, 754-755
economic growth, **2005** 768-769
economic recovery, President Kirchner on, **2003** 824-834

Falklands (Malvinas) war, **1982** 283-304; **1983** 3-23
German assets, **1997** 267
human rights in, **1980** 191, 195-196; **1981** 180, 184; **1982** 109, 111; **1983** 185-187; **1984** 155-158; **1985** 148-149; **1988** 98-100
and U.S. aid, **1977** 3, 5-8
John Paul II's visit to, **1982** 410
military coup (1976), **1983** 7-8
nuclear nonproliferation supporter, **2004** 325
presidential elections, **2003** 824-826
smoking in the Americas, **1992** 269
Argentine Republic v. Amerada Hess Shipping Corp., **1992** 462
Argersinger v. Hamlin, **1979** 208-214
Argov, Shlomo, **1982** 741
Arias, Arnulfo, president of Panama, **1999** 851
Arias Calderon, Ricardo, election of, **1989** 702, 706
Arias Sánchez, Oscar
Central American peace plan, **1987** 637-648; **1988** 241-242, 243
El Salvador settlement, **1992** 24
Nicaraguan president's inaugural, **1990** 259, 266
Nobel Peace Prize, **1987** 1007-1011
Tela accord, **1989** 161, 163, 168, 172
Aristide, Jean-Bertrand
elections and coup attempt, **2001** 395-396; **2005** 329-330
Haitian Refugees, **1992** 454; **1993** 413
letter of agreement to Clinton, **2000** 959-960; **2001** 396
ousting and forced exile, **2004** 94-96; **2005** 329
re-election as Haitian president, **2000** 952-956; **2001** 395
return to Haiti, **1994** 436-444
Arizona
See also University of Arizona
drug use survey, **1999** 464
impeachment of Mecham, **1988** 249-256
medical use of marijuana, **1996** 755-756
reversal of ERA approval, **1981** 924-938; **1982** 612
Arizona (USS), memorial ceremony on fiftieth anniversary, **1991** 779-781
Arizona v. Fulminante, **1991** 175-184
Arizona v. Robertson, **1990** 789, 791; **2000** 393
Arizona Governing Committee for Tax Deferred Annuity and Deferred Compensation Plans v. Norris, **1983** 691-705; **1990** 429
Arizonans for Official English v. Arizona, **1997** 189
Arkansas v. Sanders, **1991** 382
Arkansas Ed. Television Communication v. Forbes, **2003** 395
Arkansas Writers' Project, Inc. v. Ragland, **1991** 262, 819-822
Arkin, William M., on "smart" weapons, **1997** 494-495
Arlidge, Edward C. "Pete," on Pentagon "data mining" system, **2002** 560-561
Arline, Gene, contagious disease and job discrimination, **1987** 245-249
Arlington Heights v. Metropolitan Housing Development Corp., **1976** 225; **1977** 35-44; **1993** 467
Arlington National Cemetery
Tomb of the Unknowns, disinterment remarks, **1998** 281-283
Vietnam unknown serviceman, **1984** 347-348
Armacost, Michael H., **1988** 82
Armed forces or Armed services. *See* Conventional forces in Europe; Military personnel; Military services
Armenia
Alma-Ata Declaration, **1991** 804-806
Commonwealth Pact, **1991** 803-804
earthquake relilef, **1988** 928
Elena Bonner on, **1990** 212-213
European Security Summit, **1994** 584
human trafficking, **2002** 342
relations with Azerbaijan, **1999** 640-641
shootings in parliament, **1999** 639-642
Soviet Union restructuring plans, **1991** 532-541
Armey, Dick (R-Texas)
Chinese nuclear-espionage matter, **1999** 237-238
gift limits to members of Congress, **1995** 701
Gingrich ethics violations, **1997** 5
health care reform, **1997** 791
homeland security plan, congressional committee on, **2002** 533, 564
legal immigration, **1995** 565
Republican senior leader, **1998** 952
retirement, **2002** 822; **2005** 632
Armitage, Richard
commission on terrorist attacks testimony, **2004** 453
India-Pakistan relations, **2002** 328-329
Iran-contra affair and, **1994** 19
Sri Lanka humanitarian aid, **2002** 95
state visit to Saudi Arabia, bombings during, **2003** 230
Armor, David J., **1987** 672
Arms control
See also Strategic Arms Reduction Treaty (START)
ABM treaty reinterpretation, effect on, **1987** 290, 292, 310-311, 315-317
Andropov proposal on missile reductions in Europe, **1982** 983-988
Brezhnev proposals, **1976** 144, 149-151; **1982** 225-243
Bush proposals
on chemical weapons, **1990** 648-649
for conventional arms cuts, **1990** 57
Bush-Gorbachev summit, **1990** 332, 346-350
Bush-Yeltsin Summit Meetings (Washington), **1992** 519-529
Carter farewell address on, **1981** 32, 34
Carter proposals at UN, **1977** 737-745
conventional forces in Europe treaty, **1990** 727, 729-732
Democratic platform on, **1980** 713, 759-760; **1984** 628-630
economic summits, London, **1992** 520
Geneva summit progress in, **1985** 749-754, 757-758
German agreement, **1990** 604
Gorbachev on Soviet goals in, **1989** 400, 403-405
Gorbachev proposals, **1986** 9-20, 164-166; **1988** 927, 931-932, 937-940; **1992** 434, 436, 436-437
Iceland summit discussions, **1986** 875-885

Arms control *Continued*
John Paul II on at Hiroshima, **1981** 204, 209
Malta summit progress on, **1989** 643, 645, 648, 652-654
Middle East weapon-free zone, Israel proposal for, **1981** 514-515, 748
Moscow summit progress in, **1988** 353-355, 357-358, 367-370, 372-373
and national security policy, Nixon on, **1973** 515, 519, 521, 525, 527-528
NATO military doctrine, **1990** 456, 459-460, 462, 463-464
non-nuclear weapons in Europe, **1990** 728-729, 739-740
nuclear disarmament, European support for, **1981** 718
in presidential debates, **1984** 847, 880-882, 895-896, 899-900
Reagan administration efforts, Clark letter to bishops on, **1982** 886-887, 897-901
Reagan at UN on, **1985** 708-709, 712-715, 718
Reagan on nuclear weapons reduction (START proposal), **1982** 385-393
as reinforcement of nuclear deterrence, **1982** 313-315
Republican Party platform on, **1984** 719-720; **1992** 836-837
Shevardnadze statements, **1990** 640-641, 811-812
Soviet propaganda on U.S. policy, **1981** 754, 758-759
Soviet-German treaty, **1990** 610
State of the Union address, **1990** 57; **1992** 60
strategy for, former defense officials on, **1986** 781-783, 789-790
zero-option nuclear force reduction in Europe, Reagan proposals, **1981** 823-830; **1983** 792, 796
Arms control agreements
See also Anti-Ballistic Missile (ABM) Treaty; Intermediate-range Nuclear Force (INF) Treaty; Strategic Arms Limitation Talks/Treaty (SALT)
Democratic platform on, **1976** 546, 585-588
Fissile Material Cut-Off Treaty, **2004** 327
negotiating from strength, **1972** 651, 660, 665-666, 723
Reagan on desire for, **1986** 40, 46-47
Soviet violations of, Reagan on, **1983** 791-792
U.S.-Russian nuclear arms control treaty, **2002** 275-286
U.S.-Russian relations, **2000** 205-206
verification of, **1983** 78, 88-89; **1986** 11, 14-15
weapons of mass destruction, Group of Eight (G-8) agreement, **2002** 437-445
Arms Control and Disarmament Agency (ACDA), on chemical weapons ban, **1989** 28
Arms control talks
See also Strategic Defense Initiative (SDI)
Geneva
discussed at Iceland summit, **1986** 879, 881, 883
effect of Washington summit on, **1987** 991, 995-997, 1006
resumption of, **1984** 811-813, 817-820, 822-825; **1986** 9-10, 16
MX missile as bargaining tool, **1982** 903-918; **1983** 365-374
nuclear weapons limitation, Brezhnev on, **1981** 237-238
Reagan assurances to Japan on, **1983** 894, 901-902, 905
and Reagan defense buildup, **1985** 106-107, 114-115
SALT II progress, Carter on, **1978** 9, 16, 49
Soviet conditions for, Chernenko on, **1984** 917-923
space weapons as threat to, **1984** 258-260, 813, 824
Arms Export Control Act (1976), **1987** 30
Israeli violation of in raid on Iraq, **1981** 508
and U.S. arms sales to Iran, **1987** 227-230, 905, 914, 927
Arms race
curbing
Carter on, **1977** 90, 92, 190-194
Gromyko on, **1984** 824-827
Democratic platform on, **1984** 627, 630
European communist parties on, **1976** 433, 436-437, 440, 445
review of nuclear nonproliferation treaty, **1975** 361-363, 370, 496
Sakharov on, **1981** 748
Arms sales
See also under Iran; Israel; Saudi Arabia
to developing countries, **1976** 583, 588; **1977** 251, 265, 267
to drug traffickers, **1989** 514
restraint in, Carter on, **1976** 733-734; **1977** 738-739, 742; **1978** 105-109
Soviet to Egypt, cancellation of, **1976** 169-170, 172-174
to Uganda, Amin on, **1977** 146
UN embargo on to South Africa, **1977** 823-825
U.S. credits for, Nixon administration on, **1974** 278-279, 285
U.S. to Egypt, **1976** 169-172; **1978** 106
U.S. to Middle East, Carter and Ford debate on, **1976** 733-734, 743-744
U.S. to Taiwan, continuation after withdrawal of recognition, **1978** 783
Armstrong, Eugene "Jack," hostage killed in Iraq, **2004** 876
Armstrong, Lance, allegations of steroid use, **2005** 217-218
Armstrong, Neil K.
on *Challenger* commission, **1986** 517
on *Columbia* space shuttle, **1981** 419
Armstrong, Robert, Kennedy assassination anniversary, **1993** 962-963
Armstrong, William L. (R-Colo.), **1988** 849, 852
Army (U.S.)
abuses of Iraqi prisoners, **2004** 207-234
and Barbie affair, **1983** 738-747
Calley case, pretrial publicity and witnesses for, **1974** 857-859
expanding, **2004** 786
extremist activity in, task force on, **1996** 178-185
first Muslim chaplain, **1993** 973-975
on Medal of Honor investigation, **1989** 697-700

national guard forces, preparedness, **2004** 784-793
No Gun Ri (Korea) incident, **2001** 33-51
sexual harassment in the military, **1997** 654-660
Army Corps of Engineers (U.S.), and control of water projects, **1978** 385, 387, 389
Arnaout, Enaam, indictment of, **2002** 1018
Arnold, Jim, on moon ice findings, **1998** 116, 119
Aronovitz, Leslie G., nursing home abuse, **2002** 119, 122-132
Arrests, without warrant in suspects' homes, **1980** 281-297
Arrhenius, Svante, **1988** 862
Arroyo, Gloria Macapagal, Philippine presidential inauguration, **2001** 102-108
Arrupe, Pedro, on papal order on Drinan, **1980** 412, 415-416
Arson, **1999** 622; **2000** 860
FBI crime report, **2001** 756-757; **2004** 769; **2005** 684
Arthur Andersen & Co., Enron bankruptcy, **2001** 861; **2002** 54, 391, 396-397, 1033, 1036; **2003** 333, 347
Article 19 (anticensorship organization), and death threat against Rushdie, **1989** 96
Articles of Confederation, and signing of U.S. Constitution, **1987** 766-767, 769, 772
Articles of the Constitution. *See under* Constitution (U.S.)
Artificial insemination, Vatican on, **1987** 267-269, 277-283
Arts and humanities
cultural centers agreement (Soviet-U.S.), **1990** 340
decency in the arts, Supreme Court on, **1998** 405-418
NEA report on future of, **1997** 699-710
Arum Shinrikyo (terrorist group), **1999** 502, 503; **2000** 278, 282
ARV therapy. *See* Antiretroviral (ARV) drug therapy
Asbestos exposure
federal regulations on, **1978** 634, 637-638, 644-646
and smoking, **1985** 811, 813-814, 818
ASCD. *See* Association for Supervision and Curriculum Development
Aschkenasy, Ernest, acoustical analysis of Kennedy assassination, **1978** 910; **1979** 594, 602
ASEAN. *See* Association of Southeast Asian Nations
Ash, Roy L., **1975** 84
Ashcroft, John (attorney general)
abortion rights opponent, **2001** 127-128; **2003** 1003-1004
affirmative action, **2002** 974
anthrax attacks investigations, **2004** 443
attorney general confirmation, **2000** 1028
bioterrorism attacks, **2001** 676
CIA leak case recusal, **2005** 701
confirmation as attorney general, **2001** 97, 127, 128, 378
crime rate, **2003** 981
Cuban trade sanctions, **2000** 268
death penalty, **2002** 355
death penalty and minorities, **2001** 390-391
FBI internal security review, **2001** 154
FBI investigations without restrictions, **2002** 562-563
Foreign Terrorist Tracking Task Force, **2001** 765-766
Guantanamo Bay detentions, **2002** 830, 833; **2003** 108
gun control
background checks, **2001** 725; **2003** 158
opposition to, **2001** 518
right to bear arms, **2001** 722, 724; **2002** 959, 960
Hanssen espionage case, **2001** 152, 157
immigrant screening, **2002** 842-849
INS reorganization, **2001** 764, 767
Iraq-Niger uranium sales case recusal, **2003** 21
Khobar Towers bombing indictment, **2001** 807
Microsoft antitrust case, **2001** 779
physician-assisted suicide, **2001** 290, 292-293, 326
pledge of allegiance unconstitutional, **2002** 382
racial profiling, **2001** 179
resignation as attorney general, **2004** 778; **2005** 45
Satcher nomination opponent, **2001** 458
sentencing laws, **2003** 982; **2004** 359
sentencing of repeat offenders, **2003** 979-980
terrorist suspect cases, secret electronic surveillance and wiretaps, **2002** 562
terrorist threat, news conference on, **2004** 268-279
tobacco company lawsuit, opposition to, **2001** 222, 225; **2003** 261, 263
torture in terrorism interrogations, **2004** 341
USA Patriot Act, speeches on, **2003** 607-611, 613-619
war on terrorism, **2001** 642
Ashcroft, John (Missouri governor)
Commission on America's Urban Families chairman, **1992** 67
Kerner Commission member, **1988** 187
Ashcroft v. American Civil Liberties Union, **2002** 290-291
Ashcroft v. Planned Parenthood Association of Kansas City, Missouri, **1983** 545, 565-572
Ashdown, Paddy
Bosnia war criminals, **2004** 953-954
Bosnian economic reform, **2003** 462; **2005** 852
Kardzvic war crimes, **2003** 461; **2004** 953
Ashe, Arthur, Jr., AIDS announcement, **1992** 335-338
Asia
See also Southeast Asia
AIDS epidemic, **2005** 54-55
China's role in, **2003** 1178-1179
Democratic Party platform, **1996** 644-645
economic recovery, **2003** 68-69
financial crisis, **1997** 832-843; **1998** 532, 602, 722-734, 923; **1999** 87; **2000** 45, 476, 701; **2002** 82; **2004** 938
impact on Indonesia, **2002** 707
Northeast Asia weapons development, **1996** 216-217
Republican Party platform, **1996** 544
SARS (severe acute respiratory syndrome) outbreak, **2003** 68-69, 121-134, 754, 757; **2004** 924
sex trade and human trafficking, **2004** 123-124, 128-129
South Asia economic situation, **2000** 1050

Asia *Continued*
subcontinent of, economic development in, U.S. promotion of, **1973** 515, 526
U.S. alliances in, Carter on, **1981** 93-96
U.S. defense policy, **1993** 712
Asian Americans
and California's English-only law, **1986** 959, 961
dietary health risks, **1992** 402
health of, **1985** 685-688, 693-698, 701-702, 705-706
mental health, surgeon general's report on, **2001** 586-587
Asian Development Bank, U.S. aid requested for by Nixon, **1974** 285
Asia-Pacific Economic Cooperation (APEC) Forum, **1995** 74; **2001** 741, 895; **2004** 938; **2005** 608
Asia-Pacific Partnership for Clean Development and Climate, **2005** 921
Asiedu, Manfo Kwaku, London terrorist bombing suspect, **2005** 397
Askew, Reubin, on busing and equal educational opportunity, **1972** 201-206
ASNE. *See* American Society of Newspaper Editors
Aspin, Les
defense secretary resignation, **1993** 695; **1994** 23
on Gulf War Syndrome, **1994** 268
Iraq war resolution, **1991** 4
Middle East oil interests, **1990** 535
military base closings, **1993** 501-502
military homosexual ban guidelines, **1993** 154, 155, 162-164
national security needs, **1993** 695-715
Rubitsky denied medal of honor, **1989** 699
Soviet relations, **1989** 298
women in combat, easing ban on, **1993** 333-336
al-Assad, Bashar (Syrian president)
Iraq, UN resolution on disarmament of, **2002** 716-717
Israeli-Syrian peace negotiations, **2004** 559
Israel-Syria peace negotiations, **2000** 495
Lebanon relations, **2004** 558, 561
political situation, **2003** 961; **2004** 558, 561-562
terrorist attacks on U.S., **2001** 625
terrorist bombings in Lebanon, linked to associates of, **2005** 686
al-Assad, Hafez (Syrian president), **1999** 362, 364; **2000** 494-495
Arab relations, **1987** 869-871
Beirut hijacking negotiations, **1985** 465
death of, **2004** 558
on Egyptian-Israeli peace initiatives, **1975** 575; **1977** 829
Israeli-Syrian cease-fire, **1973** 932
Israeli-Syrian disengagement, **1974** 435-436
Assad, Maher (brother of Bashar Assad), Hariri assassination, UN investigation, **2005** 691
Assassinations
attempted
John Paul II, **1981** 427-430
Reagan, Ronald, **1981** 351-367
Wallace, George, **1975** 156
Djindjic, Zoran (prime minister of Serbia), **2003** 57-60; **2004** 955
Evers, Medgar (civil rights leader), **1995** 456
Faisal (king of Saudi Arabia), **2003** 228
Gandhi, Rajiv (prime minister of India), **2002** 93, 94; **2004** 348
Habyarimana, Juvenal (president of Rwanda), **1994** 541; **1998** 614; **1999** 863; **2000** 452, 455
Hariri, Rafiq (prime minister of Lebanon), **2005** 80-81, 271, 272, 686-696
Kabila, Laurent (Congolese leader), **2001** 159-161; **2002** 548; **2003** 289
Kadyrov, Akhmad (president of Chechnya), **2004** 565
Kennedy, John F. (president of United States), **1997** 104; **1999** 422
materials declassified, **1992** 3, 10
thirtieth anniversary, **1993** 959-963
Kennedy, Robert F. (U.S. presidential candidate), **1999** 422
Kennedy and King, investigations of, **1975** 409, 436; **1979** 593-622
Malcolm X (civil rights leader), **1995** 657
Mustafa, Abu Ali (PFLP leader), **2001** 364
Mustafa, Xhemail (political aid in Kosovo), **2000** 146
Ndadaye, Melchoir (president of Burundi), **2003** 923
Ntaryamira, Cyprien (president of Burundi), **1999** 863; **2000** 452
political
CIA involvement in, **1976** 236
authorization of, **1975** 775-795
legislation recommended to prohibit, **1975** 711, 797-799; **1976** 117, 119, 251
Rockefeller commission on, **1975** 401-403
Senate investigation of, **1975** 709-799
standby capability for, **1975** 756-759, 783, 791-792
prohibition of, Democratic platform on, **1976** 546, 587
by U.S. intelligence agencies, rules prohibiting, **1976** 126-127, 129, 139, 236; **1981** 868; **1984** 904
Qadir, Haji Abdul (vice president of Afghanistan), **2002** 18
Rabin, Yitzhak (prime minister of Israel), **1995** 622, 689-695; **1996** 337; **1998** 742; **1999** 890; **2004** 307, 309; **2005** 531
Rantisi, Abdel Aziz (Hamas leader), **2004** 302
Romero, Oscar A., in El Salvador, **1980** 412-413; **1992** 23; **1993** 239, 242-243
al-Sadat, Anwar (Egyptian leader), **2005** 164
al-Sadr, Ayatollah Mohammed Sadeq (Shiite cleric in Iraq), **1999** 145
Salinas de Gortari, Carlos (president of Mexico), **1994** 563-564
Sarkisian, Vazgen (prime minister of Armenia), **1999** 639
as terrorist act, international increase in, **1981** 461, 465, 468, 470
Tolbert, William, Jr. (president of Liberia), **2003** 768
U.S. presidents, history of, **1981** 353
Uwilingiyimana, Agathe (prime minister of Uganda), **1998** 614

Yassin, Sheikh Ahmed (Hamas leader), **2004** 301, 302, 810
Zeevi, Rehavam (minister of tourism in Israel), **2001** 364
Assayed, Tamil (Chechen rebel leader), assassination of Akhmad Kadyrov, **2004** 565
Asset forfeiture
drug trafficking, **1990** 122
international efforts, **1992** 212
Associated Milk Producers, Inc. (AMPI), dairy price supports, Nixon campaign contributions and, **1974** 8-9, 11-13, 604-605, 616; **1975** 663, 666-667
Associated Press
CIA manual and, **1984** 903, 906
Kissinger speech on Atlantic alliance, **1973** 487-495
Associated Press v. NLRB, **1991** 328
Associated Press v. U.S., **1990** 426
Associated Press Managing Editors Association, Nixon press conference on Watergate, **1973** 947-964
Association for Supervision and Curriculum Development (ASCD), on teaching about religion, **1987** 597-608
Association of American Colleges
curriculum of undergraduate colleges, **1985** 127-144
state of humanities, **1988** 518
Association of American Publishers
on Court's obscenity standards, **1973** 612
educational testing standards, **1992** 47
Association of Southeast Asian Nations (ASEAN)
Cambodian censure, **1997** 640
on Chinese invasion of Vietnam, **1979** 184-185
future of, **1997** 643-644
Reagan meeting with, **1986** 438
Astin, Alexander W., **1991** 310
AstraZeneca, Crestor advertisements, **2004** 855
Astroline Communications Co. v. Shurbuerg Broadcasting of Hartford, Inc., **1990** 419-435
Astronomy
See also Hubble space telescope
age of the universe, **1994** 458-462; **1996** 265-269; **2002** 213
birth of stars, **1995** 288-293
Hubble space telescope, **1995** 288-293; **1996** 265-269; **1998** 115; **2002** 212-218; **2003** 304, 306; **2004** 7
multiplanet solar system, discovery of, **1999** 173-178
Near Infrared Camera and Multi-Object Spectrometer (NICMOS), **2002** 212-218
planets, discovery of, **2001** 146-147
Quaoar (subplanet) discovery, **2004** 7
Sedna (planetoid) discovery, **2004** 7
Aswan Dam (Egypt), **1976** 169
Asylum, political
See also Immigrants and immigration; Refugees
defectors to U.S., CIA handling of, **1975** 427-428
for Elian Gonzalez, **2000** 265-276
eligibility for, and fear of persecution in homeland, **1987** 253-265
Mariel boatlift of Cuban refugees, **1980** 337-350
U.S. policy, **1998** 26-28
U.S.-Cuban antihijacking agreement, **1973** 265-266, 268
women, new U.S. rules on, **1995** 276-280
AT&T (American Telephone & Telegraph Co.), antitrust settlement, **1982** 17-33; **2000** 308; **2002** 797
Atatürk, Kemal, **1980** 808
Atef, Muhammad
death of, **2004** 537
al Qaeda security chief, **1998** 555; **2001** 692
ATF. *See* Alcohol, Tobacco, and Firearms (ATF) Bureau
Athletics
college, and academic career of black athletes, **1989** 213-223
Knight report on reforming college athletics, **1991** 129-142
sex discrimination in school programs, HEW rules prohibiting, **1974** 507-511
Athy, Andrew, Russian nuclear weapons panel, **2001** 19
Atkins, Daryl "James," death penalty case, **2001** 388; **2005** 178-179
Atkins, Humphrey, **1981** 404-409
Atkins v. Virginia, **2002** 353-368; **2005** 178-179, 187, 188, 190, 193
Atlanta (Georgia), riot of Cuban detainees, **1987** 929-932, 936-937
Atlantic Monthly
libel and disclosure of editorial process, **1979** 286, 289
Stockman on supply-side economics in, **1981** 642
Atlantic Ocean, federal control of offshore resources, **1975** 167, 169-175
Atlantis (space shuttle), **1995** 419-421
Atmosphere, nuclear war effects on, **1983** 858-878
Atomic bombs, *Enola Gay* exhibit (Smithsonian Institution), **1995** 55-58
Atomic Energy Act, **1997** 107; **1999** 241
and U.S.-PRC nuclear accord, **1984** 288
Atomic Energy Commission (AEC)
human radiation experiments, **1993** 987-995
power plant licenses during energy crisis, **1973** 914, 917
review of federal research and development, **1973** 467, 476
Atomic Energy Suppliers, Conference of, **1977** 273
ATSA. *See* Aviation and Transportation Security Act
Atta, Mohammed
hijacker's visa status, **2002** 843-844
meeting with Iraqi officials, **2003** 46-47
September 11 terrorist hijacker, **2001** 619; **2002** 617
Attica Prison (New York), inmate uprising, **1972** 783-788
Attorney general
See also Ashcroft, John; Reno, Janet
approval of wiretaps and electronic surveillance, **1974** 391-405
authority of under intelligence restrictions, **1981** 866
Baird nomination withdrawal, **1991** 135-139; **1993** 135-137
Clinton nominations, **1991** 135-139
granting of political asylum, **1987** 254-265

Attorney general *Continued*
report on reducing crime, **1993** 376-377
separation of from election campaigns, **1975** 654, 672-673, 678
Attorney General's Task Force on Violent Crime
insanity defense legislation, **1983** 30
report, **1981** 647-670
Attorneys. *See* Lawyers
Attorneys general, tobacco settlement, **1998** 842-854
Atwater v. City of Lago Vista, **2001** 407-408
Atwood, J. Brian
resignation from AID, **1999** 700
Russian nuclear weapons panel, **2001** 19
UN peacekeeping reform panel, **2000** 643
AU. *See* African Union
Aubrac, Raymond, **1972** 491, 495-496
AuCoin, Les (D-Ore.), **1982** 908
Augustine, Norman R., **1990** 754, 755
Auletta, Ken, Microsoft antitrust case, **2001** 776
Aurillac, Michel, **1986** 831
Auschwitz. *See* Nazi concentration camps
Austin, Hudson, **1983** 848-849
Austin, Lambert, NASA resignation, **2003** 634
Austin v. United States, **1993** 431-438, 440
Australia
and ANZUS pact, **1985** 633
global warming policy, **2002** 303-304
Iraq War "coalition" ally, **2003** 138
Skylab's breakup over, **1979** 553-555, 558
U.S. arms sales to, **1978** 106, 108-109
Austria
election of Waldheim, **1986** 743-750
EU membership, **2004** 197
euro currency, **1998** 271
John Paul II's visit, **1988** 405-414
Nixon trip to, **1974** 449-450
poverty summit participant, **1981** 770
Author's Guild, death threat against Rushdie, **1989** 96
Automobile industry
See also Automobiles
Chrysler loan guarantee, **1979** 693-695
economic situation, **2005** 137, 139
federal loan guarantee for Chrysler, **1979** 693-712
impacts of oil embargo and inflation on, **1974** 420, 422
"junk bond" credit ratings, **2005** 200
U.S.-Japan relations, **1992** 11, 12, 15, 20
wage and benefit concessions, **2005** 486
Automobile safety
aggressive driving, **1997** 550-561
air bag regulations, **1996** 801-806; **1997** 774-779
environmental and safety regulations, cost of, **1979** 694, 697-698, 703, 711
Firestone tire recall, **2000** 688-699
Automobile Workers v. Johnson Controls, Inc., **1991** 143-153; **1993** 945
Automobiles
electric automobiles, **1996** 17-20
emissions
and lung cancer in cities, **1972** 777
standards for, **1979** 694, 697-698; **1981** 280, 287-288
fuel efficiency of
affected by emissions regulation, **1975** 193
Carter on, **1976** 708; **1977** 278, 284, 287
Democratic platform on, **1976** 545, 575
FEA on, **1974** 910, 915
Ford program on, **1975** 91
industry agreement to strive for, **1975** 17, 29
restriction of, in national parks, **1972** 795-796, 800-801
search of, constitutionality of, **1982** 425-446
Aventis Pasteur
bird flu vaccine research, **2004** 925-926
flu vaccine supplier, **2004** 639, 640, 644
Avian influenza (bird flu)
bird flu in Texas, **2004** 924
outbreaks, **2004** 923, 924-925; **2005** 747-749
pandemic, U.S. government plan, **2005** 747-764
Aviation and Transportation Security Act (ATSA, 2001), **2003** 726, 728; **2004** 147
Aviation safety
See also Aviation security
air accidents, **2000** 490-491
Air France flight 4590 crash (Concorde plane), **2000** 488-493
air traffic control system, **1997** 114-115, 119-120
airline safety enforcement, GAO report on, **1998** 169-179
Alaska Airlines flight 261 crash, **2000** 490
American Airlines flight 191 crash, **1979** 949-963
Boeing 737 mechanical problems, **1999** 115-116
Brown, Ron, mission crash, **1996** 204-209
commuter airline recommendations, **1994** 535-540
Egyptair flight 990 crash, **1999** 113
FAA and airline safety inspections, **1996** 237-246; **1997** 115; **1999** 113-114
French UTA airliner bombing, **2003** 1224
GAO reports on, **1997** 113-121; **2001** 650-659
Gulf Air flight 072 crash, **2000** 490
Kennedy, John F., Jr. crash, **1999** 422-427
Korean Air 747 near miss, **2000** 491
near-collissions, **1978** 793-796, 805-806; **2000** 491-492
NTSB commuter safety recommendations, **1994** 535-540
Pan Am flight 103 (Lockerbie, Scotland) bombing, **2003** 1218, 1223-1224; **2004** 171
Russian airliners bombings, **2004** 566
Singapore Airlines flight 006 crash, **2000** 490-491
Soviet downing of Korean airliner, **1983** 775-783
Swiss Air Flight 111 fire, **1998** 171
terrorism aboard, U.S.-sponsored UN proposals on, **1972** 752, 754-757, 762
and terrorism report, presidential commission on, **1990** 301-310
TWA flight 800 crash, **1996** 231, 233, 237, 662-663; **1997** 116, 780-786; **1998** 171-172; **2000** 491
United Airlines crash, **1999** 116
U.S. Airways crash (North Carolina), **2003** 485
USAir crash (Pennsylvania), **1999** 116
ValuJet flight 592 crash, **1996** 237-240; **1997** 113, 116; **1998** 172
weight limits for passengers/baggage, **2003** 485
White House Commission recommendations, **1997** 116-119

Year 2000 (Y2K) conversion, **1998** 548, 549
Aviation Safety Commission, recommendations of, **1988** 267-276
Aviation security
See also Aviation safety
air cargo security, **2004** 153
air marshal program, **2004** 145-146, 151
air traffic control security, **2003** 729, 732
airport personnel screening, **2003** 725
airport screening, **2002** 531-532; **2003** 218
baggage and cargo screening, **2003** 721-723, 732-733
cargo screening, and "known shipper program," **2003** 723
color-coded threat alerts systems, **2004** 268-269
Computer Assisted Passenger Prescreening System (CAPPS II) program, **2003** 722, 726-727, 731; **2004** 144-145, 148-149
costs and funding of, **2003** 724-725, 736-737
economic summit on terrorism and, **1987** 529-530
Federal Aviation Administration role in, **2003** 546
Federal aviation security, GAO report on, **2001** 650-659; **2003** 720-739; **2004** 142-154
general aviation security, **2003** 723-724, 733-734
Man-Portable Anti-aircraft Defense Systems (MANPADS), **2004** 152
missiles and lasers threat, **2004** 146-147, 152
national commission on September 11 recommendations, **2005** 899
national commission terrorist attack report, **2004** 469
passenger screening, **2003** 720-722; **2004** 142-145; **2005** 896
perimeter of airport, **2003** 723-724, 734-735; **2004** 152-153
requirements, GAO report on, **1996** 662-671
Transportation Department investigations of, **1999** 114-115
Transportation Security Administration (TSA), **2002** 530, 740, 746-747; **2003** 720, 726; **2005** 896
Transportation Workers Identification Card (TWIC) program, **2003** 726, 730-731
White House Commission recommendations, **1997** 115, 120-121
Aviation Security Advisory Committee, **1996** 664-665
"Axis of evil," Bush State of the Union address, **2002** 33-34, 40-41, 56, 612, 614, 635, 732; **2003** 19, 875, 1025, 1219; **2004** 867; **2005** 579
Axworthy, Lloyd, Rwandan genocide, **2000** 449-450
Ayalon, Ami, Middle East peace plans ("People's Voice"), **2003** 1203
Aylwin, Patricio, **1990** 187-193
Ayotte v. Planned Parenthood of Northern New England, **2005** 818
Ayres, Richard E., on NCAQ clean air report, **1981** 277, 288-292
Azcona Hoyo, José
signing of Tela accord, **1989** 161, 172
and U.S. support for Nicaraguan contras, **1987** 639
Azerbaijan
Alma-Ata Declaration, **1991** 804-806
Commonwealth Pact, **1991** 803-804
European Security Summit, **1994** 584
financial aid restrictions lifted, **2001** 628
relations with Armenia, **1999** 640; **2001** 628
Soviet Union restructuring plan, **1991** 532-533
Aziz, Abdul, al Qaeda official captured, **2001** 692
Aziz, Nayef bin Abdel (Saudi Arabian prince), Khobar Towers bombing, **2001** 807
Aziz, Shaukat (Pakistan prime minister)
elected as prime minister, **2004** 1011
India relations, **2004** 353
Aziz, Tariq, **1993** 15-16
UN weapons inspections, **1997** 768-769
Aznar, José María
Spanish elections, **2004** 108
terrorist bombings in Madrid, **2004** 105, 107, 110, 111, 112-114
AZT (azidothymidine)
FDA approval of, **1987** 327-330
therapeutic use with pregnant women, **1995** 441-452
Azurdy Arrieta, Gabriela, at UN special session on children, **2002** 221

B

Baade, Walter, age of universe, **1994** 461-462
Baali, Abdallah, Lebanon-Syria relations, **2004** 560
Bab el Mandeb, Strait of, ending of Egyptian blockade of, **1973** 931; **1974** 30; **1975** 573, 584
Babayan, Richard, **1993** 10
Babb, Eugene, on WHO infant formula code, **1981** 448-449
Babbitt, Bruce
on endangered species, **1995** 360
forests and national fire plan, **2000** 712-722
logging policy, **1993** 498-499
prescribed fires moratorium, **2000** 713
Supreme Court candidate, **1993** 393, 396
Babbitt v. Sweet Home Chapter of Communities for a Greater Oregon, **1995** 359-368
Baby Jane Doe case (1982),and treatment of severely handicapped infants, **1983** 282-283, 283; **1986** 541-558
Baby M case, legality of surrogate mother contracts, **1987** 373-387; **1988** 71-79
Bacanovic, Peter E., Martha Stewart insider trading scandal, **2004** 420-421
Bach, Gavriel, Demjanjuk war crime acquittal, **1993** 621-622
Bachelet, Michelle, Chile presidential elections, **2005** 771
Bacon, Kenneth H., on "smart" weapons, **1997** 494
Bacteria, patenting of, **1980** 493-502
Bacteriological (Biological) and Toxic Weapons, Convention on Prohibition and Destruction of (1972), **1972** 323-328; **1981** 682, 685-686; **1998** 50; **2001** 676-677
Bacteriological (Biological) weapons, Geneva Protocol on prohibition of use of (1925), **1972** 323-324; **1981** 682, 685-686
al-Badawi, Jamal, **2000** 863
Badr Organization for Reconstruction and Development, **2005** 663-664, 673
Bagenstos, Sam, on disability rights, **2002** 4

Bagley, Bruce M., **1992** 203
Bahrain
human trafficking, **2002** 342
non-NATO ally designation, **2001** 628
oil production by, **1980** 996
Bail, excessive, and protection of society, **1987** 492, 496, 500-507
Bail Reform Act (1966),changes in proposed by violent crime task force, **1981** 647-648, 658-661
Bail Reform Act (1984),and preventive detention, **1987** 491-508
Bailey, Doug, presidential debate, **1992** 908
Bailey, Sue, Firestone tire recall, **2000** 692, 693-696
Baillie, Fred, weapons materials security, **2003** 902
Bailweg, Lawrence F., **1997** 661-662
Baird, Zoë, attorney general nomination withdrawal, **1993** 135-137
Bakayoko, Soumaila, Ivory Coast rebel commander, **2003** 240
Baker, Charles Henri, Haiti presidential candidate, **2005** 330
Baker, David, Palestinian Authority, **2002** 933
Baker, Dusty, **1986** 171
Baker, Howard H., Jr. (R-Tenn.)
on CIA role in Watergate, **1974** 605
on Nixon pardon, **1974** 813
post-Congressional years
appointment as chief of staff, **1987** 207-208
on independent counsel legislation, **1999** 167-168
National Commission on the Separation of Powers co-chair, **1998** 908
Russian nuclear weapons panel (Baker-Cutler panel), **2001** 17-22
security lapses at Los Alamos National Laboratory, **2000** 745
tobacco industry lobbyist, **1997** 335
Reagan budget cuts, **1983** 103
Reagan letter to on Saudi AWACS sale, **1981** 793-796
on Reagan State of the Union, **1982** 74; **1983** 79, 80; **1984** 84
on SALT II, **1979** 418
on school prayer, **1984** 242, 244
Stockholm environment conference, **1972** 476
Volcker reappointment, **1983** 596
Watergate committee opening statement, **1973** 549-550, 554-556
on White House tapes, **1973** 698, 860-861, 870
Baker, James A., III
Angola Peace Accord, **1991** 288
Bush's Chief of Staff, **1992** 295
Cambodia settlement, **1991** 691
Central American peace, bipartisan accord on, **1989** 163-164
chemical weapons treaty, **1997** 201
Czechoslovakian policy, **1990** 15
debt relief plan, **1985** 643-652; **1988** 392-393; **1989** 137-138, 140
at economic summits, **1985** 348; **1989** 414
Georgian free parliamentary elections negotiations, **2003** 1040, 1045
German reunification, **1989** 627, 634; **1990** 600
Glaspie-Hussein pre-war meeting, **1991** 155
Gorbachev on, **1992** 435-436
gun violence report, **1992** 494
at Hirohito's funeral, **1989** 100
international monetary system, **1985** 623; **1986** 41, 45
meetings with European leaders on Iraq War, **2003** 41, 948
Middle East peace process, **1989** 289-296; **1991** 122, 125, 719
Namibian independence, **1990** 200
on NATO reorganization, **1989** 646
Persian Gulf war
congressional testimony, **1990** 779-782
Geneva talks, **1991** 15-16
peaceful solution to, **1990** 767-768
UN remarks, **1990** 768, 769-771
Princeton speech on end of Cold War, **1991** 791-803
Rabin's election in Israel, **1992** 656-657
Russian aid, **1992** 257
secretary of state appointment, **1988** 892, 895, 902
Soviet Union
chemical weapons negotiations, **1989** 26
collapse of, **1991** 787
food aid to, **1990** 809-814
Shevardnadze resignation, **1990** 827
trade agreement, **1990** 332
START meeting with Shevardnadze, **1989** 645
and stock market crash, **1987** 833, 837
war powers debate, **1990** 665-667
Baker, James Jay, NRA executive director, right to bear arms, **2001** 724
Baker, Pauline
South African constitution, **1993** 1005
on South African sanctions, **1990** 67
Baker, Russell T., investigation of political dismissal, **1978** 52, 55-56, 63-64
Baker v. Carr, **1972** 935, 937-938; **1990** 616; **1993** 91
Baker v. Los Angeles Examiner, **1991** 322
Bakhtiar, Shahpur, U.S. support for, **1978** 699-702; **1979** 868, 874
Bakiyev, Kurmanbek, Kyrgyzstan presidential elections, **2005** 434-436
Bakke, Allan, affirmative action in medical school admissions, **1978** 467-492
Bakke case. *See University of California Regents v. Bakke*
al-Bakr, Ahmed Hassan, leader of Iraq ousted by Saddam, **2003** 1190
Balaguer, Joaquin, Columbus Memorial Lighthouse, **1992** 899-900
Balance of payments
See also Budget deficit; Trade deficit
developing countries' deficits
and IMF assistance, **1976** 4, 6
Kissinger proposal for, **1976** 300, 304-305, 313-314
impact of oil price rise on, **1974** 75-76, 121-122
industrialized countries' deficits, economic summit on short-term aid, **1976** 427, 429-430
U.S. deficits, impact on international monetary stability, **1973** 385, 389
U.S. gains in, OECD on inflation's effect on, **1973** 683, 691-692

world deficits, and international monetary reform proposals, **1972** 815-826
Balanced budget
bipartisan agreement, **1997** 602-610; **1998** 801
Carter administration
plan, **1976** 597, 602, 694-695, 699-700
revised plan, **1980** 109-111, 118-121, 243-244, 254-257
Clinton administration plan, **1996** 53; **1997** 29, 33; **1998** 40, 42-43
Democratic Party platform, **1996** 627-628
Ford administration plan for, **1976** 41, 672, 694, 698, 706; **1977** 57, 60-61
government shutdown, **1995** 737-745; **1996** 53; **1997** 33, 231, 603; **1998** 501, 800
price controls, in Nixon's economic stabilization program, **1973** 706, 711-712
Republican Party platform, **1996** 505-506
Balanced Budget Act (1997), **1998** 88-89
Balanced budget amendment
bipartisan issue, **1995** 10-11; **1998** 801
Bush on, **1989** 74
Clinton and Republican impasse, **1995** 737-745; **1997** 3
Clinton response, **1995** 32-33; **1996** 24; **1997** 30
Clinton's line-item veto, **1997** 611
Dole support for, **1995** 575
Reagan on, **1984** 82, 89, 101, 105; **1985** 39, 44, 85-86; **1986** 40, 44; **1987** 106, 111, 122; **1988** 58, 61, 63, 161; **1989** 11
Republican leaders and, **1996** 696
Republican platform, **1984** 662, 669
Senate response to, **1995** 165, 169
signing ceremony, **1997** 602-610
Balanced Budget and Emergency Deficit Control Act (1985)
Bush economic report and, **1990** 84, 89
Bush tax program and, **1990** 410
effect on African Americans, **1987** 44, 52-55
health care program cuts, **1987** 152
meeting targets of, **1987** 3-5, 7, 15, 121-122, 133; **1989** 71-72, 74, 83-84
passage of, **1985** 803-808
pressures of, **1986** 40, 43-44
Reagan budget prepared under, **1986** 49-58
Reagan economic report on, **1986** 66, 69, 74, 76
role of comptroller general, **1986** 705-730
sequester order, Reagan on, **1987** 836, 838
Balasingham, Anton, Sir Lanka cease-fire negotiations, **2002** 95
Baldrige v. Shapiro, **1982** 171-178
Baldus, David C., study on race and death penalty, **1987** 464-475
Balfour Declaration (1917), **1974** 927-928; **1977** 838, 844-845
Bali, terrorist bombings, **2002** 702-712, 1014, 1016; **2003** 1052; **2004** 754-756; **2005** 399-400
Baliles, Gerald L., unpopularity in coal region, **1990** 43
Balkans
EU membership issue, **2004** 199-200
political situation, GAO report on, **2000** 141-157
Balkenende, Jan Peter, EU membership invitation, **2004** 976, 978-980
Ball, Robert M., Social Security investments, **1998** 101
Ballistic Missile Defense System (BMDS). *See* Missile systems
Ballmer, Steven
diversity in the workplace, **2005** 869
Internet viruses and worms, **2003** 391-392
Ballot initiatives, Supreme Court on, **1999** 3-14
Baltic states
boundaries and Soviet domination of, Helsinki Final Act on, **1975** 481, 488, 559-560, 562-563
freedom statements of, and Soviet reaction, **1989** 469-475
Lithuanian independence, **1990** 183-186
nonrecognition of Soviet republics, **1989** 471
Soviet Union restructuring plans and, **1991** 532-533
U.S. diplomatic relations, **1991** 545-549
Baltimore (Maryland)
bicentennial of Catholic diocese, **1989** 619-623
school privatization, **1994** 410
school uniform policy, **1996** 91
Balucci, Muktar. *See* Mohammed, Khalid Sheikh
Bamford, James, U.S. intelligence programs, **2001** 153
Banana, Canaan, at Zimbabwe independence, **1980** 317, 334-335
Bandar bin Sultan Abdul Aziz (prince of Saudi Arabia), **1990** 656
Lockerbie case agreement, **2003** 1223
Bandaranaike, S. W., **1987** 616
Bandelier National Monument (New Mexico), **1995** 124
Bandur, Mate, Bosnia-Herzegovina constitutional reform, **2005** 858-859
Bangladesh
conflict in, U.S. position on, **1972** 23-39
economic aid to, Democratic platform on, **1972** 580
human trafficking, **2004** 125
independence of, **1972** 163-165; **1977** 538
Islamic conference on Afghanistan, **1980** 3
population of, **1984** 522, 525-526, 531, 533-534; **1987** 445, 449
poverty summit participant, **1981** 770
Bangura, Pallo, Sierra Leone presidential candidate, **2002** 248-249
Bank Insurance Fund, **1990** 817
Bank of America, mutual funds scandal, **2004** 419
Bank of Credit and Commerce International (BCCI), **1991** 621-636
Bank One, affirmative action, **2003** 362
Bankruptcy
See also Bethlehem Steel; Enron Corporation; United Airlines; U.S. Airways; WorldCom
Bridgeport (Conn.), city filing for, **1991** 303-307
courts
constitutionality of, **1982** 597-610
reform of, **1984** 183-184
labor contracts and, **1984** 181-199
labor unions and, **2005** 486
underfunded corporate pension plans, PBGC director testimony on, **2005** 197-211
Banks, Delma, murder conviction appeal, **2004** 795
Banks, Dennis, **1973** 532

Banks, Dennis, **2004** 795-796
Banks and banking
See also Financial institutions; Savings and loan institutions
BCCI scandal, **1991** 621-636
commercial firms and, **1991** 74
competition in, and utilization of savings, **1974** 86-87
deregulation in, **1986** 59-61, 67, 90-91
failure of banks
and drain deposit insurance funds, **1990** 815-823
and rescue by FDIC, **1988** 913-914
FOIA exemption for, **1981** 394
Japanese economic crisis, **1998** 534-535
Lance's practices as bank director, **1977** 625-675
mutual funds scandal, **2003** 698-699
robbery statistics, **2003** 991-992
Y2K conversion compliance, **1998** 546, 548
Banny, Charles Konan, Ivory Coast prime minister, **2005** 805
Bantam Books, Inc. v. Sullivan, **1993** 444
Banzhaf, John
restaurant obesity lawsuits, **2003** 484
teenage smoking, **2004** 281
Baradei, Mohammed. *See* ElBaradei, Mohammed
Barak, Aharon, and Palestinian refugee camp massacre inquiry, **1982** 783; **1983** 163
Barak, Ehud
Camp David peace negotiations, **2000** 475, 494-507; **2001** 360, 361; **2003** 1204
Israel prime minister on new government programs, **1999** 359-367
Israeli elections, **2000** 931, 935
Israel-Syria peace negotiations, **1999** 890, 891, 896
and Marc Rich presidential pardon, **2001** 90, 91
state visit of John Paul II, **2000** 79
Baran, Jan, lawyer for Gingrich ethics case, **1997** 4
Barayagwiza, Jean-Bosco
Rwanda genocide war crimes conviction, **2003** 1073, 1075-1088
Rwanda genocide war crimes indictment, **1999** 866
Barayev, Mosvar, death of Chechen guerilla commander, **2002** 764
Barbados, on Caribbean Basin Initiative, **1982** 181
Barber, Anthony, on international monetary reform, **1972** 817
Barber, James David, **1990** 295-299
Barber, Lord, of Wentbridge, study group on South Africa, **1986** 582
Barber, Red, on boxing, **1984** 1019
Barbie, Klaus
trial of, **1987** 517-524
U.S. contacts with, **1983** 737-747; **1985** 409, 414
Barbour, Haley
formerly RNC Republican chairman and lobbyist, **2002** 895
as Mississipi governor, hurricane disaster response, **2005** 540, 570-571
tobacco industry lobbyist, **1997** 335
Barclay v. Florida, **1983** 710; **1993** 388
Barco Vargas, Virgilio
on drug cartel war, **1989** 499-501, 511-515
drug summit at Cartagena, **1990** 115-126; **1992** 204
Barger, James E., acoustical analysis of Kennedy assassination, **1979** 594, 602-603
Barghouti, Marwan, jailed Palestinian leader, **2004** 809; **2005** 28, 33, 271
Barghouti, Mustafa
Palestinian leader, **2004** 808-809
Palestinian presidential campaign, **2005** 28
Barkdale, James, on Microsoft Corp. antitrust case, **1999** 656, 659
Barker, Bernard L.
Ellsberg break-in, **1974** 205-210, 411-417, 661-662, 666-668
Watergate break-in, **1973** 414-415, 419-423; **1974** 159-163
Watergate committee testimony, **1973** 550
Barker, United States v., **1990** 494, 499-501
Barnes, Fred, at Reagan-Mondale debates, **1984** 848, 855-857, 865-867
Barnes, Michael D. (D-Md.)
on Caribbean Basin Initiative, **1982** 181
on Democratic platform, **1988** 558
on U.S. Central American policy, **1983** 441; **1984** 33, 905; **1993** 238
Barnes v. Gorman, **2002** 7
Barney, Daniel R., **1973** 21
Barnier, Michel, Syrian troop withdrawal from Lebanon, **2005** 688
Baron, David, Afghanistan security forces, **2003** 1094
Baron, Frederick B., **1978** 60
Barr, Bob (R-Ga.) , House Judiciary Committee impeachment inquiry, **1998** 709-710
Barr, Michael L. , on aviation accidents, **1999** 424
Barr, William P.
Clinton's Passport Search, **1992** 1047
Sessions investigation, **1993** 609-610
Violent Crime Reports, **1993** 376-377
Barr Laboratories, morning-after pill (Plan B), **2003** 998; **2005** 815-816
Barre, Raymond, **1979** 253
euro currency proposal, **1998** 272
Barrett, Thomas M. (D-Wis.) , House Judiciary Committee impeachment inquiry, **1998** 711
Barroso, José Manuel
EU constitution ratification process, **2005** 341-342
European Commission cabinet slate, **2004** 202
European Commission president election, **2004** 201-202
Barrow, Nita, **1986** 582
Barry, Marion S.
on CDF's infant mortality report, **1987** 149
entrapment of, **1992** 313
as figurehead, **1996** 784
as mayor of Washington, **1995** 498
at Million Man March, **1995** 656
as "race-hustling poverty pimp," **1997** 31
sentencing of, **1990** 707-711
Barry, Peter, **1985** 726
Barshefsky, Charlene, U.S-China bilateral trade agreement, **1999** 724, 726, 728-734
Barth, James R., **1990** 816
Bartholdi, Auguste, **1986** 699

Bartle, Harvey, III, libraries and pornography, **2002** 288
Barton, Joe L. (R-Texas) , stem cell research supporter, **2005** 318
Barzani, Massoud, Iraq situation report, **1996** 680-686
Barzel, Rainer, **1972** 898
Barzun, Jacques, multicultural education, **1991** 344-345
Basayev, Shamil (Chechen rebel)
  Beslan school crisis, **2004** 567-568; **2005** 304
  as Chechnya deputy prime minister, **2005** 304
  terrorist attacks and, **2005** 304-305
Base Realignment and Closure, Commission on, **1988** 951-954
Baseball, major league
  cancellation of the season, **1994** 360-362
  McGwire home run record, **1998** 626-631
  penalties for drug use in, **1986** 169-175
  Ripken on breaking Gehrig's consecutive game record, **1995** 588-590; **1998** 628-629
  Rose, Pete
    banning of, **1989** 477-484
    sentencing of, **1990** 483-487
  Sosa home run record, **1998** 626-627, 626-628
  Steinbrenner removal, **1990** 483-485, 487-490
  steroid policy, **2005** 213-217
  steroids and performance-enhancing drugs, **2004** 29; **2005** 212-227
  suspensions, **2005** 215-216
    Schott suspended for racist remarks, **1993** 167-170
  Vincent resignation as commissioner, **1992** 855-858
  World Series, interrupted by earthquake, **1989** 669
Basel Convention on Control of Transboundary Movements of Hazardous Wastes, **1989** 153-160
Basescu, Traian, Romanian presidential candidate, **2004** 199
Bashir, Abu Bakar
  arrested as bombing suspect, **2002** 705-706
  Islamic extremist leader, acquitted and new trial conviction, **2004** 756; **2005** 400
  al-Bashir, Omar Hassan
  Sudan conflict in Darfur, **2004** 589, 590, 592
  Sudan peace negotiations, **2003** 837, 841; **2005** 520
  U.S. air strike in Sudan, **1998** 587
Basic educational opportunity grants (BEOGs), and *Grove City* opinion, **1984** 201, 204-213
Basketball, Magic Johnson's retirement, **1991** 747-749; **1992** 335, 340
Basle Accords (1988), **1992** 115
Basnan, Osama, connections to terrorist networks, **2003** 232
Basque movement
  independence from Spain, **2004** 105
  Madrid terrorist bombing suspects, **2004** 105-108
  nationalists, and Spanish constitution, **1978** 809, 811
Bass, United States v. , **1995** 189
Bates, Tom, California term limits, **1997** 887
Batista de Araujo, Brazilian economic situation, **2003** 6
Batson, Neal, Enron bankruptcy, **2003** 336
Batson v. Kentucky, **1986** 409-433
Battelle Columbus Laboratories, **1975** 545
Battle, Parris C. , on math and science testing, **1992** 88
Baucus, Max (D-Mont.), Clean Air Act revisions, **1990** 717
Bauer, Gary
  constitutional amendments on same-sex marriages, **2004** 40
  mandatory testing for AIDS, **1987** 818-819
  same-sex marriages, **1999** 899
  Social Security reform, **2005** 112
Baxter, Harold, mutual funds scandal, **2003** 696
Baxter, William F., **1983** 921
Baxter Healthcare, manufacturer of breast implants, **1995** 516
Bay Area Laboratory Cooperative (BALCO) **2005** 213
Bay Area Rapid Transit (BART) system, Y2K-related problems, **2000** 9
Bayh, Birch (D-Ind.)
  on Kleindienst confirmation, **1972** 396, 404-406
  on school vandalism, **1975** 207
  and Twenty-fifth Amendment, **1985** 493
Bayh, Evan (D-Ind.) , tax subsidies for vaccine producers, **2004** 644
Baykal, Deniz, Turkey political situation, **2002** 907
al-Bayoumi, Omar, contact with September 11 hijackers, **2003** 232
Bazargan, Mehdi, **1979** 869, 878
Bazell, W. W., Roswell incident, **1997** 395
Bazelon, David L., **1973** 842
Bazemore v. Friday, **1992** 582
BBC (British Broadcasting Corporation)
  on British Intelligence failures, **2004** 718
  film on Hirohito, **1989** 100
BCCI. *See* Bank of Credit and Commerce International
BCOA. *See* Bituminous Coal Operators Association
Beagle 2 surface-rover to Mars fails, **2003** 302-303; **2004** 3, 4
Beal v. Doe, **1977** 407-419
Beales, Howard, weight loss advertising, **2002** 628
Beall, George, charges against Agnew, **1973** 828-832
Beame, Abraham D.
  New York City blackout, **1977** 546-547
  New York City's fiscal crisis, **1975** 862, 866-867; **1976** 864; **1977** 567-568, 573, 575-576
Beard, Dita Davis, on ITT antitrust settlement and political contributions, **1972** 395-398, 403-405; **1974** 4
Beasley, Michele, on political asylum for women, **1995** 277
Beatrix (queen of the Netherlands)
  coronation of, **1980** 387-390, 392-397
  at International Criminal Court opening ceremony, **2003** 100
Beauharnais v. Illinois, **1992** 546
Becharof National Monument, **1978** 732, 739-740
Beck, Allen
  incarceration rates increasing, **2003** 981
  mental illness of prisoners, **1999** 840
  prison population, **2002** 786
Beck, George, **1993** 304
Beck, Harry F., Union Political Activity, **1992** 345-347

Beck v. Alabama, **1993** 150
Beckel, Bob, presidential debate, **1992** 909
Becker, Edward R., libraries and pornography, **2002** 288
Becker, Jo, Convention on the Rights of the Child, **2002** 224
Becker, Judith, **1992** 509
Becker, Lance, heart attack incidence and care, racial differences, **1993** 671-675
Beckman, John C., space mission failures, **1999** 715
Beckwith, Bryon De La, Medgar Evers trial conviction, **2002** 239; **2005** 353
Becton, Julius W., Jr., new superintendent of D.C. schools, **1996** 785
Bedell, Susanna, on cardiopulmonary resuscitation, **1984** 276, 281-285
Beer v. U.S., **1993** 472
Beeson, Ann E.
  child pornography on the Internet, **2002** 291
  USA Patriot Act, **2003** 612
Beggs, James M., **1984** 82
Begin, Menachem
  on annexation of Golan Heights, **1981** 899-907
  on bombing of Iraqi nuclear plant, **1983** 834
  Camp David accords, **1978** 605-608, 618-619; **1979** 223-224
  and Lebanon invasion, **1982** 742; **1983** 833
  Middle East peace agreement on Sinai peninsula, **1998** 744
  Nobel Peace Prize recipient, **1978** 607, 628-632; **1983** 834; **2002** 981; **2003** 1131
  Palestinian refugee camp massacre, **1982** 781-783, 793-795; **1983** 163-165, 173-174
  on Reagan peace plan, **1982** 753
  resignation of, **1983** 831, 834
  on Sadat's visit to Jerusalem, **1977** 827-829, 841-847
  on Saudi peace plan, **1981** 632
  U.S. support for, **1978** 276
  on U.S.-Soviet declaration on peace conference, **1977** 738
  visit to Ismailia (Egypt), **1977** 827, 829, 847-855; **1978** 607-608, 621-622
Begleiter, Ralph, pictures of flag-draped coffins, **2005** 648-649
Beijing summit, Nixon-Chou En-lai, **1972** 183-192
Beijing University, Mondale speech at, **1979** 669-670, 673
Beilin, Yossi, Middle East peace negotiations, **2003** 198, 1203-1204, 1205
Beirut (Lebanon)
  bombing of Marine headquarters (1983), **1983** 933-966; **1984** 886, 935; **1985** 464; **2004** 319
  terrorist attack on U.S. embassy (1983),**1983** 934, 940; **1984** 886, 935; **2004** 319
  TWA hijacking in, **1985** 463-466, 469, 474
Belarus
  Commonwealth Pact, **1991** 787-791
  human trafficking, **2002** 342
  merger with Russia, Putin proposal, **2005** 301
  nuclear weapons, dismantling of, **2001** 18; **2004** 169
  nuclear weapons nonproliferation, **1996** 220, 221
Belgium
  Carter visit, **1977** 897
  euro currency, **1998** 271
  John Paul II visit, **1985** 363, 365, 374-376
  war on terrorism, support for U.S., **2001** 627
Belin, David W., **1979** 596
Belize
  land use and forestry practices, **2001** 113
  smoking in the Americas, **1992** 269
  U.S. economic aid to, **1984** 32
Bell, Griffin B.
  on affirmative action ruling, **1978** 470
  attorney general appointment, **1976** 878-879
  attorney general resignation, **1979** 561
  Bush role in Iran-contra affair, **1994** 9
  Carter warehouse investigation, **1979** 802
  delay of King FBI report, **1977** 114
  FOIA guidelines from, **1981** 393
  National Commission on the Separation of Powers, **1998** 908, 910
  political dismissal of U.S. attorney, **1978** 51-55, 59-64
  on violent crime task force, **1981** 647-670
Bell, Robert G., defense policy, **1997** 814
Bell, Terrel H.
  and Carnegie report on urban schools, **1988** 197
  on competence of adult Americans, **1975** 691
  education report, **1990** 154
Bell v. Hood, **1992** 192, 196, 198
Bell v. Ohio, **1978** 495-498, 511-514
Bell v. Wolfish, **1992** 178
Bell Laboratories, effect of AT&T divestiture on, **1982** 19
Bellahouel, Mohamed Kamel, September 11 detainee, **2003** 316
Bellamy, Carol
  HIV/AIDS pandemic in Africa, **1999** 489-498
  sexual exploitation of children, **2001** 955-962
  vaccination of children, **1999** 387
  on worldwide poverty, **1999** 585
Bellmon, Henry (R-Okla.), **1976** 40; **1979** 11
Belloti v. Baird, **1990** 388, 392, 395, 397, 400-402, 405-406
Belo, Carlos Ximenes (bishop), East Timor independence, **1999** 513, 515
Belt, Bradley D.
  Pension Benefit Guaranty Corp., financial condition, **2004** 734-745
  underfunded corporate pension plans, **2005** 197-211
Bemba, Jean-Pierre
  human rights violations, **2003** 290
  vice president of Congo, **2003** 290, 291
Benecchi, Valdo, on ecumenism, **2000** 81
Benedick, Richard E., **1987** 748
Benedict XVI (pope)
  funeral mass for Pope John Paul II, **2005** 290-298
  homosexuality, Catholic Church position on, **2005** 864
  selection as new pope, **2005** 294-295
Ben-Eliezer, Benjamin, as Israeli defense minister, **2002** 937
Benevolence International Foundation, **2002** 1018

Benitez, Jose Federico, assassination of, **1994** 564
Benjamin, Burton, on Westmoreland suit against CBS, **1983** 402-412
Benjamin, Joel, chess champion, **1997** 274
Bennett, Charles (NASA scientist), on "Big Bang" theory, **1992** 382
Bennett, Charles Edward (D-Fla.), Gulf of Tonkin resolution, **1991** 5
Bennett, Robert F. (R-Utah)
  Clinton censure resolution, **1999** 21
  Clinton impeachment trial, **1999** 21, 29
  medical records security, **1997** 583
Bennett, Robert S. (Washington attorney)
  child sexual abuse of priests, **2004** 84, 86
  presidential immunity case, **1997** 290
  Schott suspension for racist remarks, **1993** 168
Bennett, Robert T. (Ohio Republican Party chairman), presidential campaign, and gay marriage issue, **2004** 41
Bennett, William J. (education secretary)
  AIDS education, **1987** 319-320
  college education, **1985** 129; **1986** 940
  as drug czar, **1989** 499-500, 503
  education summit, **1989** 563
  elementary education, **1986** 803-817
  humanities education, **1984** 997-1003; **1987** 682
  progress and goals in education, **1988** 297-306
  school prayer amendment, **1985** 381
  school-based family planning clinics, **1986** 1058
  teaching and learning research, **1986** 217
  teaching profession, **1986** 459
Benoit, Gary, **1976** 596
Benshoof, Janet, **1988** 38-39
Benson, Arthur A., III, **1990** 228
Benton Foundation
  "digital divide" issue, **2002** 69
  public access to communications media, **1999** 371
Bentsen, Lloyd (D-Texas)
  budget compromise, **1990** 411
  campaign fund raising by, **1988** 800-801, 809, 816-817
  Clinton economic team member, **1992** 1021
  deficit reduction, **2000** 22
  differences with Dukakis, **1988** 750-751, 801, 803, 807-808, 826-827
  economic summits, Tokyo, **1993** 541
  election results, **1988** 891, 892, 894
  Joint Economic Committee report, **1979** 215; **1980** 209
  and Tower nomination, **1989** 105
  vice-presidential debate, **1988** 799-829
  vice-presidential nomination, **1988** 533, 535, 542-546
  welfare reform, **1988** 848-849, 852
Ben-Veniste, Richard, **1974** 24
  national commission on terrorist attacks hearings, **2004** 454
Benz, Jeffrey G., **1999** 109
Beregovoy, Pierre, **1985** 624
Bereuter, Doug (R-Neb.)
  U.S.-China trade relations, **2000** 216
  U.S.-Iranian policy, **2002** 34
Berezovksy, Boris
  Russian entrepreneur, **2001** 256
  Russian entrepreneur, or "oligarch," **2000** 173
Berg, Alfred, on depression, **2002** 266
Berg, Nicholas, hostage killed in Iraq, **2004** 876
Berg, Paul, **1975** 320
Bergalis, Kimberly, **1992** 709
Berge, Gunnar, Carter as Nobel Peace Prize recipient, **2002** 982
Bergen, Candice, Quayle's "Murphy Brown" Speech, **1992** 443-452
Bergen-Belsen. *See* Nazi concentration camps
Berger, Joel, **1983** 711
Berger, Marilyn, **1976** 774
Berger, Samuel R. "Sandy"
  Chinese nuclear-espionage matter, **1999** 237-238
  commission on terrorist attacks testimony, **2004** 453
  on Russian nuclear weapons, **1997** 515
Bergier, Jean-François, **1998** 293
Bergland, Bob (D-Minn.)
  Alaska federal lands, **1978** 733-734
  appointment to agriculture secretary, **1976** 878
Bergna and Brown v. Stanford Daily, **1978** 355-372
Bergsten, C. Fred, U.S. trade deficits, **2004** 239
Bergstrom, Charles, **1984** 243
Bering Land Bridge National Monument, **1978** 731, 737
Berk, Richard A., **1983** 358
Berkemer v. McCarty, **2000** 394
Berkowitz, David, **1991** 813-825
Berlin, East, European communists' meeting in, **1976** 433-461
Berlin, Fred, on sex offenders, **1997** 384-385
Berlin, West
  discothèque bombing, **1986** 350, 439, 833
  four-power agreement on (1971),**1972** 449; **1973** 558, 605; **1974** 801
    signing of final protocol, **1972** 467-470
  traffic to and from, **1974** 802; **1976** 349
  West German-Soviet agreement on, **1973** 558
Berlin Airlift (1948), **1986** 793, 796
Berlin Press Association, Haig speech on Soviet chemical warfare, **1981** 681-694
Berlin Wall
  anniversary of, **1986** 791-792, 794-799
  construction of (1961),**1972** 467; **1986** 791-799
  fall of, **2004** 198, 319
  and four-power Berlin agreement, **1972** 467
  opening and dismantling of, **1989** 625-630
  Reagan at, **1987** 526
Berliner, Don, Roswell incident, **1997** 400
Berliner, Lucy, Rape in America Report, **1992** 386
Berlinguer, Enrico, on Italian Communist Party, **1976** 434, 455-457
Berlusconi, Silvio (Italian prime minister)
  demonstration against terrorists in Spain, **2004** 107
  elections, **2004** 201; **2005** 409
  European Commission cabinet appointments controversy, **2004** 202
  meeting with Qaddafi, **2004** 168
Berman, Howard L. (D-Calif.)
  Clinton's passport search, **1992** 1047

Berman, Howard L. (D-Calif.) *Continued*
House Judiciary Committee impeachment inquiry, **1998** 703-704
Berman, Jay, **1990** 509
Berman v. Parker, **2005** 368-371, 373-375
Bermúdez, Enrique, **1987** 639; **1988** 243
Bermúdez, Morales, **1977** 17-18
Bernabo, Chris, **1983** 199
Bernadotte, Folke, **1983** 832
Bernal, Richard L., WTO trade talks collapse, **2003** 740
Bernanke, Ben S., Federal Reserve Board chairman confirmation hearings, **2005** 142
Bernardin, Cardinal Joseph
and bishops' letter on nuclear war, **1982** 886
on compassion for AIDS victims, **1986** 910
sexual abuse of children by priests, **1992** 507-518
on Vatican on bioethics, **1987** 269
Bernardino, Joseph P., Enron Corp. audits, **2001** 861
Bernhard (king of the Netherlands), **1980** 389
Bernstein, Jared, **1993** 271
Bernstein, Robert L., **1973** 613
Berra, Dale, **1986** 170
Berri, Nabih, **1985** 465
Lebanon speaker of parliament, **2005** 690
Berrick, Cathleen A., airport passenger screening, **2004** 143
Berry, Mary Frances, **1983** 915
on economic status of blacks, **1989** 447
on higher education for blacks, **1983** 43, 50
Berry, Steven K., Clinton's passport search, **1992** 1046
Berthelot, Rene, and European Commission scandal, **1999** 156
Bertini, Catherine
Afghanistan humanitarian aid, **2001** 884
Palestinian humanitarian aid, **2002** 935
UN undersecretary resignation, **2005** 236
Bertolini, Michael, **1989** 478-479
Bertrand v. Sava, **1992** 460
Berwick, Donald M., **1999** 781
Bessette, Lauren, death of, **1999** 422
Bessmertnykh, Alexander, **1991** 288
Best, Judah, **1973** 828-829, 832
Betancourt, Ingrid, kidnapping of Colombian presidential candidate, **2002** 571; **2003** 427
Betancur, Belisario, **1986** 639; **1993** 237
Bethe, Hans, **1984** 257
Bethel School District v. Fraser, **1986** 731-742
Bethlehem Steel
bankruptcy and pension plans, **2005** 198, 199, 209
Los Angeles riots and, **1992** 409
Bextra, drug safety studies, **2004** 852-853
Bhagwati, P. N., **2000** 450
Bhopal (India), toxic gas poisoning at, **1984** 1023-1026; **1985** 295-302
Bhutto, Benazir, former Pakistan prime minister, **1999** 624; **2002** 167, 169
Bhutto, Zulfikar Ali, arrest and trial of, **1977** 537-538
BIA. *See* Bureau of Indian Affairs
Biafra, independence movement, **1995** 697
Biaggi, Mario (D-N.Y.), **1988** 498-499
Biaggi, Richard, **1988** 498
Bias, Len, death from cocaine, **1986** 181, 839
Bible reading, in schools, **1987** 597-598, 602-605
Bicentennial celebrations
Baltimore Catholic diocese, **1989** 619-623
Congress, **1989** 123-133
Constitution of the U.S., **1987** 107-108, 113-115, 765-766, 765-775, 771-775
Declaration of Independence, **1976** 331-343, 509-516, 537-542
U.S. Capitol, **1993** 893-904
Biden, Joseph R., Jr. (D-Del.)
AIDS prevention programs, **2002** 474
antidrug program, **1989** 501, 508-511
arms control proposal, **1989** 298
"Big Bang" theory, **1992** 379-383
Bork nomination, **1987** 719
Casey investigation, **1981** 855
chemical weapons treaty, **1997** 196
flag burning and protection of, **1989** 345; **1990** 358
on Foster, surgeon general nomination, **1995** 62
on Freeh, FBI director nomination, **1993** 611
Glaspie-Hussein pre-war meeting, **1991** 1161
nuclear test ban treaty, **1999** 604, 609
Rehnquist appointment, **1986** 592
Souter nomination, **1990** 618, 622-625
Thomas confirmation hearings, **1991** 557-561, 575-576, 582-583, 592-595, 615-616
U.S.-British extradition treaty, **1986** 752
war powers debate, **1990** 671-673
Biggs, John H., accounting board nomination, **2002** 1033
Bigone, Reynaldo, **1982** 287
on Argentina's disappeared persons, **1983** 455-467
Bijur, Peter I., statement on racial slurs of Texaco executives, **1996** 764-769
Biko, Stephen, **1982** 798
Bilingual education
California initiative, **1998** 313-319
and California's English-only law, **1986** 960-961
debate on, **1988** 208
Bill and Melinda Gates Foundation, HIV/AIDS prevention programs, **2002** 472
Bill of attainder
custody of Nixon papers and tapes, **1977** 465-467, 482-486, 492-493, 507-510
student aid and draft registration, **1984** 493-501
Bill of Rights. *See under* Constitution (U.S.)
Billington, James H., Thurgood Marshall's papers, release of, **1993** 339-345
Bin Laden, Osama
See also al Qaeda terrorist network
Afghanistan harboring of, **2000** 280
Afghanistan resistance, **2002** 16
assassination attempts, **2001** 806-807
at-large status, **2003** 1050; **2004** 18, 534, 1012; **2005** 970
British report on, **2001** 802-818
embassy bombings, **1998** 555-558; **1999** 53, 525, 691; **2000** 277
linked to, **2001** 803-804
head of al Qaeda terrorist network, **2002** 20, 740; **2003** 228
as inspiration for terrorists, **2005** 401
planning attacks on U.S., **2004** 454

Russian nuclear weapons acquisitions and, **2001** 17, 22
September 11 terrorist attacks
indictment for, **2001** 620
involvement in, **2001** 3, 614, 617, 626, 686, 802-818; **2003** 546, 550-575
Sudan expels, **2001** 688, 803; **2003** 840
survives U.S. air strikes, **1998** 586; **2001** 688
U.S. forces in Saudi Arabia, opposition to, **2003** 233
U.S. relations, **2002** 487-488
USS *Cole* bombing, involvement in, **2000** 861, 863; **2001** 3, 6-7, 805
videotapes/audiotapes for broadcast, **2001** 805-806; **2003** 1054; **2004** 272, 519, 520, 536-537
whereabouts unknown, **2002** 1015-1017; **2003** 1054-1055
al-Zarqawi loyalty to, **2004** 877
Binalshibh, Ramzi
al Qaeda leader captured, **2002** 1016
September 11 terrorist attacks, **2001** 620
Binder, Alan B., on moon ice findings, **1998** 114, 116, 119
Bingaman, Jeff (D-N.M.)
energy prices and oil company profits, congressional hearings on, **2005** 786-787
on judicial impeachment, **1986** 850, 853-856; **1989** 585, 588
nuclear weapons policy, **2002** 278
Bioethics
See also Physician-assisted suicide
cloning research, **1997** 212-220; **2000** 669
president's council on, **2002** 512-529; **2004** 157-167
"culture of life"
politics of, **2005** 157-159
John Paul II's statements on, **2005** 293
euthanasia, Catholic teaching on, **1995** 146, 155-158
genetic testing in the workplace, **1998** 63-72
genetically engineered foods, **1992** 469-473
human genetics research, **2000** 400-401
life-sustaining measures
commission report, **1983** 279-303
in Quinlan case, **1975** 805-806, 815-820; **1976** 197-206, 212-217
Schiavo end-of-life care case, **2005** 154-163, 376
moral theology, Pope's encyclical on, **1993** 843-850
parental decisions on treatment for handicapped infants, **1986** 541-558
pharmacists' right to refuse filling prescriptions, **2005** 817
reproductive technologies, Vatican on, **1987** 267-287
sex selection technique, **1998** 65-66
stem cell research, **2000** 667-673; **2001** 539-546; **2004** 157, 843
alternative sources of, President's Council on Bioethics on, **2005** 317-328
Catholic Church opposition to, **2005** 317
South Korean cloning from human embryos scandal, **2005** 317, 320-322
Biogenics Corp., on chromosome damage at Love Canal, **1980** 446, 452-454
Biological diversity
effect of nuclear war on, **1985** 542-543, 550-554
genetically altered foods, **1992** 469-473; **1999** 401-411
Biological weapons
See also Bioterrorism; Terrorism; Weapons of mass destruction (WMD)
Bush administration policy, **2001** 516
Clinton administration policy, **1998** 49-50
Clinton's UN address, **1993** 811-812
Cuban development of, **2002** 223
economic summits, London, **1991** 451-456
Gulf War syndrome, **1994** 264-275, **1997** 740-745
Iraq threat, **2003** 876-877; **2004** 715-716, 730-733; **2005** 249-250
Iraq warfare research, **1991** 193
terrorist threat preparedness, **2005** 894
UN weapons inspection in Iraq, **1997** 768; **1998** 934-944
worldwide proliferation of, **1996** 210-230
Biological Weapons Convention (1972)
effectiveness and enforcement of, **1998** 50
enforcement procedures, **1998** 50; **2001** 676-677
prohibition destruction of, **1972** 323-328
Soviet violations of, **1981** 682, 685-686
Biomedical Corporation of Canada, flu vaccine supplier, **2004** 645
Biomedical research
See also Medical research
Alzheimer's disease, **1987** 405-406
federal regulations on, **1987** 362, 367-372
"hot labs" with dangerous pathogens, **2004** 446-447
human tissues and cells, ownership of, **1987** 351-372
security issues, **2004** 443, 446-447
Biotechnology
agricultural impacts of, **1986** 287-306
in agriculture, secretary Glickman on, **1999** 401-411
Earth Summit (Rio), **1992** 499-506
federal safety regulation, **1986** 289
genetically engineered foods, **1992** 469-473; **1999** 401-411
interferon approval, **1986** 481-485
ownership of human tissues and cells, **1987** 351-372
Scope document, **1992** 471
Bioterrorism
anthrax threat, **2001** 3, 130, 360, 615, 672, 674-676; **2003** 904; **2004** 442-443
Bush executive order, **2004** 445
hospital preparedness, **2003** 904
preparations against
GAO report on, **2001** 672-685; **2004** 444
U.S. vulnerability, **2004** 443-444
Project BioShield Act (2004),**2003** 30; **2004** 442-449
ricin poison discovery, Senate Office Building, **2004** 268, 442-443
Bipartisan Campaign Reform Act (2002), **2003** 1155-1156, 1158-1159
Birch, Elizabeth
Clinton and gay rights, **1997** 760, 762
same-sex marriages, **1996** 689

Bird flu. *See* Avian influenza (bird flu)
Birkenau. *See* Nazi concentration camps
Birth control
See also Abortion; Contraception; Family planning
abstinence programs, **2001** 128, 457, 458; **2004** 21, 29
Catholic Church on, **2005** 293
condemnation of, by John Paul II, **1982** 837-838; **1985** 500, 501
campaigns against birth, **1988** 170
in India, 1986.25-26, **1986** 36
dispute between Vatican and Dutch Catholics, **1985** 363-364
"morning after" emergency contraception pill, FDA rulings, **2003** 998-999; **2005** 814-831
Birth defects, children of Persian Gulf War veterans, **2001** 909-910
Birth rates
See also Teenagers, pregnancy
and Social Security's financial condition, **1975** 115-116, 125-126
for teenagers, **1998** 261-262
of women in developing countries, **1984** 527, 534, 536
Bishara, Abdullah Yacoub, at Young's meeting with PLO UN observer, **1979** 647-648, 655-656
Bishop, Kathleen, **1988** 290
Bishop, Maurice, **1983** 847-848
Bissell, John W., secret domestic detentions, **2002** 835
Bitburg (West Germany), Reagan visit, **1985** 347, 357-362; **1986** 1076; **1989** 488
Bittman, Robert, Lewinsky scandal investigations, **1998** 567, 569-576
Bituminous Coal Operators Association (BCOA), coal miners' strike, **1978** 111-113, 118, 122
Bituminous Contractors, Association of, coal miners' strike, **1978** 112
Biunno, Vincent P., **1982** 20
Bizimungu, Pasteur, Rwandan Hutu president, **2000** 454; **2003** 1069-1070
BJS. *See* Bureau of Justice Statistics
Black, Cofer, on attacking al Qaeda, **2004** 37
Black, Conrad M., Hollinger International, corporate scandal, **2004** 423-424
Black, Creed C., **1991** 129
Black, Ed, Microsoft antitrust case, **2001** 779-780
Black, Hugo, **1981** 170
Black Panther group, **2002** 563
Black Panther Party, confidentiality of news sources in, **1972** 507, 512-513
Blackburn, Elizabeth, dismissal from President's Council on Bioethics, **2004** 159, 843
Blackburn, George L., overweight children, **2002** 625
Blackburn v. Alabama, **1991** 179
Blackley, Ronald, **1994** 403
Blackmun, Harry A.
abortion
consent requirements and method restrictions, **1976** 483-488
legalization of, **1993** 339
parental consent for teenage, **1990** 387-407
public funding for, **1977** 408, 414, 418-419, 425, 428
right to, **1973** 102-114; **1983** 544, 565-566, 569-572; **1986** 559, 561-569
state restrictions on, **1989** 367, 379-387
women's right to choose, **1992** 589-609, 611
abortion clinics
advice issue, **1991** 258-259, 266-272
blockades, **1993** 93, 101-102
protests, **1994** 312-320
advertising prescription drug prices, **1976** 351-360
affirmative action, **1986** 654
job program, **1979** 494, 500-501
medical school admission, **1978** 468-469, 471, 478, 489-490
promotion opportunities for women, **1987** 332-333
age discrimination, **1983** 232
alcoholism and veterans' benefits, **1988** 279, 284-285
alimony for men, **1979** 200
antitrust immunity of cities, **1982** 35
asset forfeiture
drug trafficking, **1993** 432-438
pornography seized, **1993** 432, 440-446
bankruptcy law, **1982** 597-610; **1984** 182, 193
broadcast of offensive material, **1978** 515, 517, 525
child pornography, **1982** 677; **1990** 239-245
entrapment in case of, **1992** 313-322
church and state separation, church objection to liquor license, **1982** 956
clean air regulations, **1984** 427
coastal property rights, **1992** 616
coerced confessions, **1991** 175-176
compensation law, **1991** 815, 823
congressional immunity, **1979** 467
corporate free speech in referendum campaigns, **1978** 307
Court workload, **1975** 461, 462
creation science, **1987** 566
deaf parochial student, **1993** 400, 403-406
death penalty
constitutionality of, **1972** 499, 504-505
constitutionality of state laws, **1976** 489-490
and *habeas corpus* appeals, **1983** 709, 710, 719-723
mandatory for murder of police officer, **1977** 397, 400-401
mitigating factors, **1978** 508, 514; **1982** 51, 60
mother's request for stay against defendant's wishes, **1976** 923
racial discrimination, **1987** 463, 473
for rape, **1977** 517
renunciation of, **1994** 161-171
state's misuse of, **1980** 455, 457
discrimination compensation, **1984** 366-367, 376-385; **1989** 322, 331
education for alien children, **1982** 490
election campaign financing, **1976** 110
exclusionary rule, **1984** 507-508, 514-515
federal and state powers, **1985** 168, 170-182
flag burning and free speech, **1989** 343; **1990** 357-362
freedom of residential signs, **1994** 290-297
gay rights to march, **1995** 327-335

Haitian refugees returned, **1993** 414, 421
hate crimes, **1992** 544-551; **1993** 385-389
historic preservation and property takings, **1978** 453
home video taping, **1984** 54-55, 56, 69-80
impeachment, Senate's authority to remove judge, **1993** 82-91
intra-enterprise conspiracy doctrine, **1984** 414
job discrimination
  fetal protection, **1991** 144, 146-150
  involving African Americans, **1993** 424, 424-430
  parental leave and employment discrimination, **1987** 17
  proof of, **1989** 322, 328-329
  suit against member of Congress, **1979** 399
judicial immunity, **1978** 260
jury selection, gender discrimination, **1994** 223, 227-231
jury trials, split verdicts in, **1972** 423
labor union members' freedom to resign, **1985** 415, 416-417, 424-429
legislative intent, **1993** 250-253
legislative veto, **1983** 619
libel from misquotation, **1991** 329
libel of private and public persons, **1986** 355, 357, 364
military draft, sex discrimination in, **1981** 521
minimum wage, **1976** 378, 385
minority set-aside programs, **1980** 539-540, 558; **1990** 419-428
Miranda warnings
  and definition of interrogation, **1980** 431
  rule affirmed, **1990** 785-790
NAACP boycott, **1982** 656
Nativity scenes, public display of, **1984** 219, 231, 239
Nixon papers and tapes, **1977** 487-488
Noriega phone calls dispute, **1990** 721-724
obscenity, legal tests for, **1987** 479
parental rights in child custody, **1982** 260-271
parties' right to open political primaries, **1986** 1065
passport revocation, **1981** 541
patenting of living organisms, **1980** 493
political asylum, **1987** 253, 255
political firings from public jobs, **1980** 259
pregnancy coverage in company disability plans, **1976** 892
presidential immunity, **1982** 539, 552
press
  access to pretrial hearings, **1979** 511, 513, 525-533
  confidentiality of sources, **1972** 507
  gag orders and right to fair trial, **1976** 464
  libel of public figure, **1979** 285
  newsroom searches, **1978** 355
preventive detention, **1987** 491
prison crowding, **1981** 478, 484
prisoners' rights
  appeals, **1991** 205, 215-218
  appeals from death row, **1993** 142, 149-152
  inmates beaten by guards, **1992** 176-182
  in searches, **1984** 480, 481, 485
public lands and developers, **1994** 299, 306-309
reapportionment, and one-man, one-vote rule, **1973** 278
redistricting
  gerrymandering in, **1986** 618
  race-based redistricting, **1993** 461, 474-481
  racial criteria in, **1977** 152
right to counsel, **1977** 219, 234; **1979** 213-214, 297
right to die, **1990** 375, 382-386
schools
  book banning, **1982** 578
  desegregation, **1991** 24, 29-33
  desegregation and restrictions on busing, **1982** 620, 643
  operation of, judicial intervention in, **1975** 68, 75
  prayer in, **1992** 553-562
  public aid to private schools, **1977** 431-440; **1985** 433
  use of school facilities by religious groups, **1993** 363-369
search and seizure, of automobile, **1978** 753; **1982** 425
sentencing
  double jeopardy and, **1980** 977-986
  excessive prison sentences, **1983** 659
  murder case sentencing, **1991** 391-395
separation of powers, Balanced Budget Act and, **1986** 707, 708, 728-730
sex bias
  in pension plans, **1978** 293-294, 305-306; **1983** 691-692, 701-704
  in Social Security survivors' benefits, **1977** 170, 177
  in statutory rape laws, **1981** 340, 345
sexual harassment, monetary damages for, **1992** 188-197
snail darter protection from dam project, **1978** 434, 446
sodomy and privacy right, **1986** 601-603, 608-614
student newspaper censorship, **1988** 38, 45
students' rights
  and corporal punishment, **1977** 293
  in searches, **1985** 14
suspects' rights and public safety, **1984** 388
tax increase for school desegregation, **1990** 227-228, 229-232
tenure review disclosure, **1990** 23-34
tobacco-related ills, damages for, **1992** 564-573
treatment of severely handicapped infants, **1986** 543, 545
treaty termination, **1979** 918, 933, 937
tuition tax credit, **1983** 676, 684-688
uncompensated takings, **1987** 541
unitary taxation, **1983** 645
U.S. Capitol bicentennial, **1993** 893, 898-899
utilities regulation, **1982** 448-460
warrants for OSHA safety inspections, **1978** 340, 346
water rights, **1982** 689
Watergate and government ethics, **1973** 723-727
wiretapping authorization by attorney general, **1974** 392, 399
worker's health protection, **1981** 492

Blacks
See also Affirmative action; African Americans; Apartheid system; Civil rights; Discrimination, race; Equal opportunity; Minorities; Race relations
affirmative action and seniority system, **1984** 365-385
alcoholism effects on, **1983** 344-345
apology for racism to, **1995** 336-338
Army's first Muslim chaplain, **1993** 973-975
college careers of athletes, **1989** 213-223
college enrollment, **1997** 186
condition of in America, Urban League on, **1983** 41-55; **1985** 27-37; **1987** 43-60
De Klerk and Mandela on South African changes, **1990** 65-80
death penalty, **1990** 313-314
Democratic Party commitment to, **1984** 550-551
dietary health risks, **1992** 402
discrimination against
past, Marshall on, **1978** 469-470, 487-489
in private school admissions, **1976** 391-404
economic status of, **1983** 41-55, 766; **1989** 445-459
educational opportunities, **1992** 629-632
employment disparities among, **1982** 919-944
employment for high school graduates, **1992** 624
family summit, **1985** 28, 33, 36
founding of Liberia, **1980** 275, 276
girls in classroom, **1992** 142, 145, 146
guns as cause of death, **1992** 493-495
health problems of, **1985** 685-689, 693-697, 699, 702-706
heart attack incidence and care, **1993** 671-675
infant mortality among, **1987** 147-151, 154, 156
interracial contact in schools, **1975** 613-614, 618-624, 631-632
job discrimination, **1993** 423-430
King holiday designation, **1983** 883-888
labor market, **1999** 101-102
majority rule in Rhodesia, internal agreement for, **1978** 149-155
minority broadcasting set-aside programs, **1990** 419-435
poverty and unemployment among, in U.S. cities, **1988** 185-194
Quayle on black underclass, **1992** 447-448
race-based redistricting, **1993** 459-481; **1995** 369-384
reaction against apartheid policies, **1976** 677-680
reverse discrimination in firing employees, **1976** 405-411
in school majority, and continued balance in desegregation plans, **1976** 413-423
self-help for in U.S., **1985** 28, 30, 32-34
South African constitutional changes, **1983** 889-892
Stuart murder hoax, **1990** 35-40
and U.S. foreign policy, Young's impact on, **1979** 647-649
Virginia's first black governor, **1990** 41-47
vote for in South Africa, **1989** 545, 550
Blackwater Security Consulting, Iraq insurgent attacks on, **2004** 880
Blackwell, Ron, wage and benefit concessions, **2005** 486
Blagojevich, Rod (Illinois governor)
death penalty legislation, **2004** 798-799
filling prescriptions, pharmacy requirements, **2005** 817
Blah, Moses, Liberian president appointment, **2003** 771-772
Blair, Dennis C.
American spy plane incident, **2001** 249
U.S. mission to Philippines, **2001** 106
Blair, Steven N.
on exercise, **1993** 626; **1996** 419
on physical fitness and health, **1989** 613-617
Blair, Tony (British prime minister)
Afghanistan war against Taliban regime, **2001** 686-697
Africa debt relief program, **2005** 407
African economic development, **2001** 504; **2002** 449-450; **2005** 405-406
climate change, G-8 declaration on, **2005** 920-921
on death of Diana (princess of Wales), **1997** 647, 649
at economic summit (Denver), **1997** 342
EU British rebate controversy, **2005** 343-344
EU constitution, **2005** 341-342
EU Parliament address, **2005** 346-350
euro currency in Britain, **1999** 76
European Commission reforms, **1999** 157
greenhouse gas emissions, **1997** 481
Hong Kong transfer ceremony, **1997** 502
Human Genome Project, **2000** 397, 403-405
inaugural election as prime minister, **1997** 277-283
IRA peace process, **2005** 509-511
Iraq
interim government, news conference on, **2004** 402, 410, 411
support for "regime change" in, **2002** 614, 714; **2003** 40
weapons of mass destruction, prewar intelligence, **2003** 874, 883-884
Iraq War
British prewar intelligence failures, **2004** 718-719
capture of Saddam Hussein, **2003** 1221
support for, **2003** 42, 44, 48, 49-51, 136, 138
Labor Party elections, **2005** 394
Libya relations, **2003** 1219, 1221
Middle East
meeting with Qaddafi, **2004** 168
state visit, **2004** 810
Middle East peace process, **2003** 194, 1204
Northern Ireland peace agreement, **1998** 203-219; **1999** 753-754
September 11 attacks on U.S., report on, **2001** 802-818
terrorist bombings in London, **2005** 393-404
Turkey, EU membership supporter, **2004** 976
war on terrorism, support for, **2001** 625, 626, 630-631
Zimbabwe suspension from British Commonwealth, **2003** 1115
Blakely, Ralph Howard, Jr., sentencing case, **2004** 360
Blakely v. Washington, **2004** 358-374; **2005** 680
Blakey, Deborah Layton, on People's Temple, **1979** 348-349, 351, 371

Blakey, G. Robert, **1978** 912
Blanchard, James G. (Michigan governor)
  education goals, **1990** 154
  Michigan's abortion legislation, **1990** 217
Blanck, Maj. Gen. Ronald, on Gulf War syndrome, **1994** 268
Blanco, Kathleen Babineaux (Louisiana governor), hurricane disaster response, **2005** 540, 568
Blandon, Jose, **1990** 722
Blanton, Thomas E., church bombing trial (Birmingham, 1963) conviction, **2002** 241
Blanton, Thomas L. (D-Texas), House censure of, **1979** 623; **1980** 486
Blassie, Michael J., disinterment from Tomb of the Unknowns, **1998** 281-282
Blendon, Robert J., child heath care survey, **1997** 425
Bliley, Thomas J., Jr. (R-Va.), on tobacco regulations, **1995** 672
Blix, Hans
  Iraq weapons inspections, **2000** 585; **2002** 718; **2003** 45-46, 878-880; **2004** 711-712
  Nobel Prize nomination, **2004** 929
BLM. *See* Bureau of Land Management
Bloch, Felix S., espionage investigations, **2001** 151, 155
Blocher, Christoph, **1997** 259
Block grants
  See also Community development, block grants for; Revenue sharing
  Bush support for, **1991** 69
  consolidation of social programs
    in Ford budget, **1976** 38, 43
    in Reagan budget, **1981** 217, 219, 334-335, 641, 644-645; **1984** 100, 107
  for food aid, **1984** 4-5, 15
Block v. Rutherford, **1984** 481, 488-491
Bloodworth-Thomason, Linda, **1992** 669
Bloom, Allan, **1988** 518
Bloom, Philip H., Iraq reconstruction no-bid contracts, **2005** 723
Bloomberg, Michael R., NYC response to terrorist threat alerts, **2004** 271
Bloomer, Arthur W., **1978** 654
Bloomer, Phil, WTO trade talks collapse, **2003** 744
Bloomfield, Lincoln, small arms trade, **2001** 518
BLS. *See* Bureau of Labor Statistics
Blue, Vida, **1986** 171
Blum, Yehuda Z.
  Israeli raid on Iraq, **1981** 508-515
  Young's meeting with PLO observer, **1979** 648, 653, 655
Blumenthal, David, **1986** 274
Blumenthal, Sidney, and Clinton impeachment trial, **1999** 17
Blumenthal, W. Michael
  New York City's fiscal crisis, **1977** 568-569
  Peking mission of, **1979** 185
  resignation from Treasury, **1979** 561
  strengthening the dollar, **1978** 685, 698
Blumstein, Alfred
  on carjackings, **1999** 616
  crime reports, **1996** 732-734; **1999** 615; **2000** 853
  on homicide rate, **1995** 710
  on juvenile curfew laws, **1996** 327
Blunt, Anthony, as Soviet spy, **1979** 905-914
Blunt, Roy (R-Mo.), House majority leader, **2005** 634
Blynn, Barry, school vouchers, **2002** 407
BMW of North America, Inc. v. Ira Gore, Jr., **1996** 274-283
Bo Yibo, U.S.-PRC commercial agreements, **1980** 829-834
Board of Education v. Allen, **1993** 405
Board of Education v. Dowell, **1991** 23-33
Board of Education of Central School District No. 1 v. Ball, **1995** 395
Board of Education of Independent School District No. 92 of Pottawatomie County v. Earls, **2002** 424-436
Board of Education of Kiryas Joel School v. Grumet, **1997** 362, 366
Board of Education of Westside Community Schools (Dist. 66) v. Mergens, **1995** 392-393, 398
Boaz, David, on computer access, **1999** 370
Bobbe's Private School, racial discrimination in admission, **1976** 392-395
Bobbitt, Lorena, domestic violence case, **1994** 62-63
Bobko, Karol, **1974** 883
Bobovikov, Ratmir S., on Soviet elections, **1989** 174, 178-179
Bodie, Zvi, pension fund accounting practices, **2004** 738
Bodman, Samuel W.
  as Energy Department secretary, **2005** 45
  energy prices and Hurricanes Rita and Katrina, **2005** 780
Body mass index (BMI), **2001** 936; **2004** 652
Boehlert, Sherwood (R-N.Y.), Gingrich resignation, **1998** 802
Boehner, John (R-Ohio)
  education reform, **2002** 42
  pension legislation, **2004** 737
Boeing, pension fund accounting practices, **2004** 738
Boerma, A. H., on agricultural production in developing countries, **1972** 859-860, 865-866
Boesky, Ivan F., insider trading case, **1987** 883; **1990** 252, 254-255
Boff, Leonardo
  and liberation theology, **1986** 317
  Vatican disciplining of, **1986** 757
Boggs, Lindy (D-La.), **1989** 125-126
Bogle, John, corporate scandals, **2003** 696-697
Boies, David, Westmoreland libel suit against CBS, **1985** 159, 164
Bok, Derek C.
  on legal system, **1983** 391-400
  on Solzhenitsyn, **1978** 405
Bokat, Stephen
  disability, definition of, **1999** 319
  on sexual harassment liability, **1998** 440
Boland, Edward P. (D-Mass.)
  on aid to contras, **1983** 441-442
  on CIA manual, **1984** 905
Boland amendment
  application of to NSC, **1987** 218, 892, 898, 919, 926-927

Boland amendment *Continued*
diversion of funds in circumvention of, **1986** 1013; **1987** 892, 896, 898, 900, 904-905, 907; **1994** 16
legislative history of, **1987** 920-921, 925-927
Bolick, Clint
school vouchers, **2002** 409
Thomas Supreme Court nomination, **1992** 34
Bolivia
Barbie's residence in, **1983** 737-738
drug control measures, **1992** 216-217
drug summit, **1990** 115-126; **1992** 201-221
essential drug chemicals agreement, **1990** 126-128
human rights in, **1981** 180, 185
Morales presidential election, **2005** 765, 769-770
nationalization of property by, **1972** 67
presidential elections, **2005** 769
smoking report, **1992** 267-275
U.S. support to drug enforcement, **1986** 181-182; **1989** 500-501, 505
Bolling v. Sharpe, **1990** 430; **1995** 313
Bolt, Beranek and Newman, acoustical analysis of Kennedy assassination, **1979** 594, 602-603
Bolten, Joshua B., video news releases (VNRs), **2005** 647
Bolton, John R.
congressional testimony on UN, **1990** 630-635
India-U.S. relations, **2005** 465
Iran nuclear weapons program, **2004** 868
national security strategy, **2002** 634
nuclear nonproliferation, **2004** 325
small arms trade, **2001** 517-518
UN ambassador appointment controversy, **2005** 236-237
Bombers
B-1 bomber
cancellation of, **1977** 529-533; **1978** 571-572
Ford support for, **1977** 46, 55
production of, **1977** 256, 261
B-2 Stealth bombers
in Reagan budget, **1983** 102
Soviet general on, **1989** 440
B-29 bomber, *Enola Gay* in Smithsonian exhibit, **1995** 55-58
B-52 bomber, **1978** 555; **1981** 90
SALT II provision on, **1978** 566-567; **1979** 413, 421-423, 453
Soviet Backfire
and achieving strategic balance in SALT II, **1978** 571-573
in SALT II negotiations, **1977** 243-250, 253, 258, 261; **1978** 550, 556, 564
U.S. report on, **1981** 720-721
Bombings. *See under* Suicide bombings; Terrorism
Bond, Christopher S. (R-Mo.), **1990** 228
Bond, Kit, pledge of allegiance unconstitutional, **2002** 382
Bond, Langhorne M., on air traffic control changes, **1978** 793-794
Bondevik, Kjell Magne, Iraq, UN actions against, **2002** 616
Bonds, Barry, steroid use in baseball, **2005** 213
Bonior, David (D-Mich.)
and Gingrich ethics violation complaint, **1995** 748, 751; **1996** 839
minority whip, **2001** 549
Bonn Declaration (1978),and terrorism in civil aviation, **1987** 529-530
Bonner, Yelena G.
acceptance of Sakharov's Nobel Peace Prize, **1975** 915-917
exile of, **1980** 103-104, 106
hunger strike of, **1981** 747-749
pardon of, **1986** 1091, 1092
permission to travel, **1985** 782; **1986** 111-112
release from exile, **1987** 190, 202
remarks on Gorbachev's aims, **1990** 207-213
return to Moscow, **1986** 822
Bonnichsen, Rob, **1992** 136
Bono (U2 rock band lead singer), antipoverty campaign, **2005** 406, 409
Bono, Mary (R-Calif.), House Judiciary Committee impeachment inquiry, **1998** 713
Bono, Sonny (R-Calif.), death of, **1998** 41
Booh, Jacques-Roger, **1999** 862
Booker, Freddie, sentencing of, **2004** 361
Boone v. Lightner, **1993** 252, 255, 257
Boorstin, Daniel J., **1987** 682
Boos v. Barry, **1990** 360
Boot, Max, UN Security Council membership reform, **2004** 889
Booth, Arch, **1973** 46
Booth v. Maryland, **1991** 382-396
Border security. *See under* National security; Terrorism
Borders, William A., Jr., in impeachment case, **1989** 584, 588-589
Boren, David L. (D-Okla.)
chemical weapons treaty, **1997** 201
CIA reforms, **1992** 5, 10
Gates confirmation hearings, **1991** 652
as president of University of Oklahoma, **2001** 19
Russian nuclear weapons panel, **2001** 19
Borge, Tomás, **1987** 641
Borges, Francisco, NAACP treasurer, **1995** 454
Borges, Julio, Venezuela political situation, **2004** 551
Borja Cevallos, Rodrigo, **1992** 201
Bork, Robert H.
appointment of second Watergate prosecutor, **1973** 898, 901
on civil rights, **1987** 718-719, 732-734
confirmation battle of, **1987** 717-744
on the Constitution, **1987** 720, 726-729, 734-738, 742-743
on executive power, **1987** 738-739
firing of Cox, **1973** 859, 862, 876-878; **1975** 660-662; **1987** 718, 720, 725, 739-740; **1998** 906
on judicial role, **1987** 718-723, 744
on precedent and original intent, **1987** 729-731
on privacy right, **1987** 718, 720, 731-732
Supreme Court confirmation nomination, **2005** 558-559
Supreme Court nomination rejection, **1990** 616; **1991** 551; **1998** 696

Bose Corp. v. Consumers Union of the United States, **1984** 299-312
Boskin, Michael J.
CEA report, **1989** 4; **1992** 98-99
North American Free Trade Agreement, **1992** 760
presidential relations, **1990** 81-82
Bosnia
civil war, **1993** 543; **1995** 717-718; **1998** 827; **2000** 142-143
Clinton's UN address, **1993** 805, 813
constitutional reform, **2005** 853, 858-859
Dayton peace agreement, **1999** 735-736; **2000** 142-143; **2002** 717; **2003** 461, 463; **2004** 953
tenth anniversary, **2005** 851-853, 859-862
economic summits, Tokyo, **1993** 541, 543
elections, **1996** 817-818; **2001** 822-823; **2003** 461-462
European Security Summit, **1994** 584-587
European Union Force (EUFOR) peacekeeping mission, **2003** 463; **2004** 138, 197, 954; **2005** 852-853
European Union membership, **2005** 851
human rights report, **1993** 561-564
human trafficking, **2002** 335-336
Izetbegovic attack on Western nations, **1994** 584-585
NATO membership, **2005** 851
NATO peacekeeping mission, **1997** 342; **1998** 49; **1999** 120-121, 286, 735-737; **2001** 823; **2003** 463; **2004** 197, 954; **2005** 852
political situation, **1996** 816-823; **2000** 141-157; **2004** 952-955; **2005** 852-853
rape of women and children, **2001** 957
Republican Party platform, **1996** 540
Senate Yugoslav "Ethnic Cleansing" report, **1992** 771-779
UN membership, for Yugoslavia, **1992** 875-878
UN peacekeeping mission, **1995** 717-726; **1996** 818-819; **1997** 151, 154, 155; **2000** 643; **2003** 460-469, 811; **2004** 785, 953, 954
UN resolutions
on Bosnian relief, **1992** 765-769
on Serb aggression, **1994** 550-554
UN role in, **1995** 351
U.S. peacekeeping mission, **1995** 717-726
Bosnia-Herzegovina
conflict, **2004** 952-953
constitutional reform, **2005** 858-859
history of, **2003** 56
human trafficking, **2002** 343
Boston (Massachusetts), sexual abuse by priest claims, **2004** 87
Boswell, Thomas
baseball season cancellation, **1994** 360
on college athletics, **1991** 131
Schott suspension, **1993** 168
Bosworth, Barry, on deficit reduction, **1993** 183
Bosworth, Dale, roadless initiative for national forest preservation, **2001** 216
Bot, Bernard, EU constitution debate, **2005** 340
Botha, Pieter W.
Commonwealth study group meeting with, **1986** 582, 588
constitution changes, **1983** 889-891; **1984** 1027
election defeat by de Klerk, **1990** 65
ending of pass laws, **1986** 370
reaffirmation of apartheid, **1985** 515-527, 531-533
repressive government in South Africa, **1998** 756-757, 762-763
resignation of, **1989** 546
state of emergency, **1986** 99, 371-372
stroke, **1993** 879
Botha, Pik, **1985** 533
Botha, Roelof F., **1977** 824
Botswana
Clinton state visit, **1998** 159
dependence on South Africa, **1986** 582-583, 585
economic sanctions against Rhodesia, lifting of, **1979** 941
HIV/AIDS victims, **2004** 429
life expectancy, **2002** 470
Rhodesian settlement plans, **1976** 721-722, 728-729; **1978** 150
U.S. aid to and consultation with, **1976** 288, 292
World Bank project in, **1986** 860
Bouchard, Lucien, Quebec independence, **1998** 592-595
Boucher, Richard (State Department spokesman)
Georgia (country) political situation, **2003** 1045
Lebanon, Syrian troop withdrawal from, **2004** 560
North Korean nuclear weapons program, **2002** 733, 737-738
Sudan peace negotiations, **2003** 841
U.S. sanctions against China, **2000** 219
U.S.-Cuba relations, **2004** 248-249
Boucher, Rick (D-Va.), House Judiciary Committee Clinton impeachment inquiry, **1998** 704-705
Boucher, Robert A., El Salvador violence report, **1993** 239
Bouie v. City of Columbia, **1990** 243
Boumediene, Houari
oil-consuming countries' cooperation, **1974** 124
raw materials of developing countries, **1974** 255-264
Bourassa, Robert, **1976** 855, 858; **1990** 367-368, 369
Bourget, Didier, UN peacekeeping mission sexual abuses, **2005** 1030
Bout, Victor, Congo resource exploitation, **2002** 551
Bouteflika, Abdelazia
African economic development plan, **2002** 450
on emergence of third world, **1974** 833-839
Boutros-Ghali, Boutros
Bosnian conflict, **1999** 738
Bosnian relief resolution, **1992** 765-766
chemical weapons treaty, **1993** 72; **1996** 740-743
Clinton's UN address, **1993** 815
Earth Summit (Rio), **1992** 502, 503
El Salvador violence report, **1993** 240
International Olympics Committee investigations, **1999** 109
Rwanda genocidal war, **1999** 861-862; **2000** 452
Rwandan refugee camps, **1994** 541-549
Somalian relief, **1992** 1069, 1071
UN fiftieth anniversary remarks, **1995** 350, 352-353
UN secretary general
final statements as, **1996** 824-825, 827-830

Boutros-Ghali, Boutros *Continued*
relations with Congress, **1997** 152-153
UN summit on poverty, **1995** 136
Bovine spongiform encephalopathy (BSE), **2000** 880-992
Bowen, Otis R.
AIDS education, **1987** 319-320
catastrophic illness coverage, **1986** 1025-1035
interferon, **1986** 481, 483-484
Bowen, Stewart W., Jr., Iraq reconstruction, **2005** 717-733
Bowen v. American Hospital Association, **1986** 541-558
Bowen v. Kendrick, **1993** 401
Bowers, Sam, civil rights workers murders conviction, **2005** 354-355
Bowers v. Hardwick, **1986** 601-614; **1996** 285; **2003** 402-404, 407-413
Bowles, Camilla Parker, **1997** 648
Bowles, Erskine, balanced budget agreement, **1997** 604
Bowman, Frank O., III, sentencing guidelines, **2004** 361
Bowman, Isaiah, **1988** 832
Bowman, James, Sr., discrimination in jury selection, **1994** 225-236
Bowsher, Charles A.
Grace commission proposals, **1984** 169
savings and loan bailout, **1990** 817
savings and loan crisis, **1988** 914
Bowsher v. Synar, **1986** 705-730
Boxer, Barbara (D-Calif.)
military base closings, **1995** 409
partial birth abortion ban opponent, **2003** 997
Boxing, AMA call for ban on, **1984** 1019-1021
Boy Scouts of America, homosexual leaders' dismissal, **1999** 901; **2000** 158, 159-160
Boyce, Ralph, Indonesia relations **2002** 704
Boycotts
against Nestlé for infant formula marketing, **1981** 448
California labor law on, **1975** 387-391
as ERA strategy to combat discrimination, **1982** 614-615
by NAACP, damages arising from, **1982** 655-674
of table grapes and lettuce by UFW, **1975** 378
Boyd, Gerald G., nuclear weapons plants, **1994** 340
Boyd, Graham, student drug testing, **2002** 424
Boyd, James, **1972** 396
Boyd, Kenneth Lee, death penalty execution, **2005** 179
Boyd, Ralph F., Jr.
affirmative action, **2002** 974
UN conference against racism, **2001** 605-606
Boyer, Ernest L.
undergraduate colleges, **1986** 939-958
urban school crisis, **1988** 197
Boyle, Andrew, on Soviet spies in British intelligence, **1979** 905-906, 909
Boyle, Dan, Enron Corp. scandal, **2004** 416-417
Boyle, J. Patrick, food safety and beef, **2002** 582
Boyle, Joseph R., **1984** 1019
Boynton, William, water on Mars, **2002** 215
BP America, oil company profits, congressional hearings on, **2005** 781
Bradburn, Norman M., international math and science test, **1992** 87
Brademas, John (D-Ind.)
on Nixon budget, **1974** 98
status of the arts, **1997** 700
Braden, Mark, **1986** 1067
Bradford, David F., CEA report, **1992** 99
Bradley, Bill (D-N.J.)
college sports, **1989** 216
at Democratic national convention, **2000** 612
Gates confirmation, opposition to, **1991** 652
LAPD abuse investigation, **1991** 403-404
presidential campaign, **2000** 619
Reagan's State of the Union, **1983** 79
retirement from Senate, **1995** 558-562
smoking as an addiction, **1988** 310
on tax credit, **1993** 184
Bradley, Tom, Los Angeles riots, **1992** 408-429
Bradley v. School Board of Richmond, Virginia, **1972** 15-21
Brady, James S.
at Democratic Party convention, **1996** 601
on release of American hostages from Iran, **1981** 137
signing of Brady bill, **1993** 965-969
wounded in Reagan assassination attempt, **1981** 351-352; **1991** 185, 188; **1995** 463-464
Brady, Nicholas F.
bank failures, **1990** 815, 818-823
in budget negotiation, **1989** 72
economic summits, Munich, **1992** 638-639
food aid to Soviets, **1990** 809, 810
plan for world debt relief, **1989** 137-144
as secretary of the Treasury, **1988** 892
on stock market crash commission, **1988** 9
Brady, Sarah, Brady gun control bill, **1993** 965-968; **1995** 463
Brady v. Maryland, **1991** 208-209
Brady commission
appointment of, **1987** 834-835
stock market crash causes, **1988** 9-25
stock market crash chronology, **1988** 17-25
stock market regulation, **1988** 9, 11, 14-16, 29-34
Brady gun control bill
passage of, **1991** 186-187
proposal to repeal, **1995** 463
Reagan support for, **1991** 188
Republican opposition to, **1996** 601
signing of, **1993** 965-969
Bragdon v. Abbott, **1998** 378-392
Brahimi, Lakhdar
Afghanistan UN Mission, **2001** 881; **2003** 1096
assassination of, rewards offered for, **2004** 536
Iraqi interim government, representing UN on, **2004** 400, 401, 890
on Taliban regime "defeat," **2003** 1090
UN peacekeeping mission reforms, **2000** 643, 644-647
Brainwashing and interrogation techniques, CIA project on, **1985** 334, 336
Bram v. U.S., **1991** 179

Branch v. Texas, **1972** 499-505
Branch Davidians
  Waco Cult compound attack, **1993** 293-301
  Waco investigations, **1993** 819-840
Brandeis, Louis D.
  on government, **1997** 626, 627
  on state legislative experimentation, **1981** 164
  on the Supreme Court, **1993** 395
Brandt, Edward N., Jr., **1982** 164
Brandt, Willy
  economic aid for developing countries, **1981** 770
  relations with East Germany, **1972** 898
  Soviet-West German agreements, **1973** 557-562
  West German policy, **1990** 107-108
Branham, Lynn S., sex offenders legislation, **1997** 382
Branscomb, Lewis, **1986** 457, 459
Branstad, Terry E. (R-Iowa)
  education goals, **1990** 54, 154-165
  at education summit, **1989** 562
  on Midwest floods, **1993** 484-486
Brant, Peter N., insider trading case, **1987** 882, 885-886
Branti v. Finkel, **1980** 259-271
Branzburg, Paul M., confidentiality of news sources, **1972** 507-510
Branzburg v. Hayes, **1972** 507-517; **1990** 28, 34; **1998** 401
Brassard, Jacques, Quebec independence, **1998** 594
Bray, Linda L., **1989** 704
Bray v. Alexandria Women's Health Clinic, **1993** 93-112
Brazil
  activist Catholic clergy in, **1980** 967-970; **1986** 317
  AIDS prevention and treatment programs, **2002** 475; **2003** 785
  China trade relations, **2004** 938
  Contadora Group, **1987** 638
  debt crisis, **2002** 691, 693, 774-775
    and export income, **1982** 972
    foreign debt, **1985** 6
  Earth Summit (Rio), **1992** 499-506
  economic conditions, **1998** 76, 722; **1999** 87; **2003** 3-7, 754-755
  election in, **1985** 3-12
  foreign policy, **2003** 14-16
  human rights in, **1984** 155; **1990** 138
    and Carter visit, **1978** 269-270, 272-274, 279-280
  land reform, **2003** 5, 11
  land use and forestry practices, **2001** 113
  Lula da Silva presidential inauguration speech, **2003** 3-17
  Mengele discovered living in, **1985** 409-413
  minimum wage, **2003** 5
  National Council for Economic and Social Development, **2003** 4, 12
  nuclear nonproliferation supporter, **2004** 325
  nuclear technology from West Germany, **1975** 363
  population problems in, **1987** 445, 446
  poverty summit participant, **1981** 770
  presidential election, **2002** 774-783
  rainforest issue, **1990** 468
  smoking in the Americas, **1992** 269
  student test scores, **1992** 90, 92, 94, 95
  UNSC membership proposal, **2003** 811
  U.S. relations, **2003** 7-8, 15; **2005** 765-776
  WTO trade negotiations, **2003** 741
  Zero Hunger (*Fome Zero*) campaign, **2003** 4, 5, 10-11
Breast cancer. *See* Cancer, breast
Breastfeeding
  breast-milk survey, for PBB contamination, **1978** 653-658
  and family planning in developing countries, **1987** 441, 452, 458, 461
Breaux, John (D-La.)
  on Clinton State of the Union address, **1995** 26
  on Hurricane Andrew, **1992** 534
  nursing home abuse, **2002** 120
  nursing homes, deaths of residents, **2002** 118
  response to Clinton State of the Union address, **1995** 26
  Social Security reform, **2005** 84
  universal health insurance, **2003** 849
Breeden, Richard, corporate scandals, **2002** 393; **2003** 334; **2004** 417
Breitel, Charles D., **1976** 863
Breitenstein, A. G., medical records privacy, **1997** 582
Bremer, L. Paul, III
  assassination of, rewards offered for, **2004** 536
  capture of Saddam Hussein, **2003** 1189, 1192, 1197-1198
  as head of Coalition Provisional Authority, **2004** 400-402; **2005** 941
  postwar Iraq operations, **2003** 935-936, 945-946, 948, 949; **2005** 722
  terrorist threat in U.S., **2000** 277-278
  troop strength in Iraq, **2004** 676
  UN relations, **2004** 890
Brendle, Bryan, mercury emissions regulations, **2005** 99
Brennan, William J.
  abortion
    parental consent for teenage, **1990** 387-407
    and privacy right, **1973** 102
    public funding of, **1977** 408-409, 414-416, 418, 425-430; **1980** 515-516, 525-528
    right to, **1983** 544, 565-566, 569-572; **1986** 559
    state restrictions on, **1989** 367, 379
  affirmative action
    discrimination by labor union, **1986** 654-667
    job program, **1979** 494-500
    medical school admissions, **1978** 468-469, 471, 478-485
    promotion of minorities, **1986** 668-676
    promotion opportunities for women, **1987** 332-333, 335-344
  age discrimination, **1983** 232, 233
  alcoholism and veterans' benefits, **1988** 279, 284
  alimony for men, **1979** 193-200
  antitrust immunity of cities, **1982** 35, 37-43
  auto search and seizure, **1978** 754, 761; **1982** 425, 439
  bankruptcy law, **1982** 597-610; **1984** 182-184, 193-199
  broadcast of offensive material, **1978** 515, 517, 526-530

Brennan, William J. *Continued*
child pornography, **1982** 677; **1990** 240, 245-249
church and state separation, church's objection to liquor license, **1982** 955-961
class action suits, **1974** 428, 432
clean air regulations, **1984** 427
compensation for discrimination, **1984** 366-367, 376
congressional immunity, **1979** 467, 469, 478-479, 481, 491
contagious disease and job discrimination, **1987** 246-250
corporate free speech in referendum campaigns, **1978** 307, 318
Court workload, **1982** 706, 718-719
covert entry for electronic surveillance, **1979** 269, 271, 278-279
creation science teaching, **1987** 566-572
death penalty
constitutionality of state laws, **1976** 489-490, 921
as cruel and unusual, **1972** 499, 501; **1980** 455, 457, 462; **1982** 51
ex post facto, **1977** 519
mandatory, for murder of police officer, **1977** 397
racial discrimination in, **1987** 463, 465, 473-476
for rape, **1977** 517, 525
and summary procedures, **1983** 709, 710, 719-723
disruptive handicapped students, **1988** 47-56
education for alien children, **1982** 489-501
electronic surveillance, **1977** 884, 891
equal contractual opportunities, **1989** 323
exclusionary rule, **1984** 506-508, 516-519
on flag burning and free speech, **1989** 343-344, 346-350; **1990** 357-362
historic preservation and property takings, **1978** 453-461
home video taping, **1984** 53-54
immunity of municipalities, **1980** 299-308
intra-enterprise conspiracy doctrine, **1984** 414, 422
job discrimination
proof of, **1989** 322, 328
suit against member of Congress, **1979** 399-408
jurors opposed to death penalty, **1986** 454
jury size and unanimous verdict, **1979** 264, 268
jury trials, split verdicts in, **1972** 423
labor union members' freedom to resign, **1985** 415, 424
legislative veto, **1983** 619
libel
of private and public persons, **1986** 355, 357-358, 364
suit against magazine, jurisdiction for, **1984** 248, 252-253
Meese criticism of Court, **1985** 479, 653-666
military draft, sex discrimination in, **1981** 521, 523, 532-540
on minimum wage laws, **1976** 378, 385-388
minority set-aside programs, **1980** 539-540, 558; **1990** 419-428
Miranda warnings, **1984** 388, 395; **1985** 225-226, 236-250
and definition of interrogation, **1980** 431, 433, 439
pre-Miranda right to counsel, **1974** 482-483
NAACP boycott, **1982** 656
Nixon papers and tapes, **1977** 466-487
obscenity standards, **1973** 612, 622-628; **1974** 516, 519-520, 522; **1987** 479
PAC spending limits, **1985** 279-280, 290
parental leave
and employment discrimination, **1987** 17
seniority rights after, **1977** 872, 877
parental rights in child custody, **1982** 260
passport revocation, **1981** 541-542, 552
patenting of living organisms, **1980** 494, 500-502
political asylum, **1987** 253
political firings from public jobs, **1980** 259
political primaries, open, **1986** 1065
praised by Bush, **1990** 616
pregnancy coverage in companies, **1976** 892, 900-905
presidential immunity, **1982** 539, 552
press
access to pretrial hearings, **1979** 317-318, 511, 513, 525
confidentiality of sources, **1972** 508
criticism of Court and editorial privilege, **1979** 311-318
gag orders and right to fair trial, **1976** 464, 473-478
libel of public figure, **1979** 285, 287-288, 298-306
preventive detention, **1987** 491-493, 502
prison crowding, **1981** 478, 484
prisoners' rights in searches, **1984** 480-481, 485, 491
public aid for private schools, **1977** 431-432, 441; **1985** 433-434, 436-448, 450-452
public broadcasting editorials, **1984** 449-461
public display of Nativity scene, **1984** 217, 219, 231-239
race discrimination
settlements, **1989** 322, 331
state and local government liability for, **1989** 323
rape laws, sex discrimination in, **1981** 340, 346
reapportionment and one-man, one-vote rule, **1973** 278, 284-289
redistricting, **1983** 599-609
and gerrymandering, **1986** 618
racial criteria in, **1977** 152, 159-163
resignation, **1990** 217, 615
retirement, **1991** 175
right of reply by political candidate, **1974** 524, 527
right to counsel, **1977** 220; **1979** 207-208, 211-213
right to life, **1990** 375, 382-386
school book banning, **1982** 567-578
school desegregation
busing restrictions, **1982** 620, 643
cross-district remedies for, **1974** 639, 649, 651
plan's continued balance, **1976** 414, 421
remedies for, **1977** 447, 455-457
school financing based on property tax, **1973** 363
search and seizure, and *habeas corpus* claim, **1976** 522-523, 532-535
secrecy of CIA sources, **1985** 333, 342
segregation remedies, public housing in suburbs, **1976** 233

seniority systems and job discrimination, **1977** 384, 392
sentencing
and double jeopardy, **1980** 978, 986-988
excessive prison terms, **1983** 659
sex bias
in education, **1984** 202-203, 213-214
by Jaycees, **1984** 467-475
in pension plans, **1983** 691, 694-701
snail darter protection from dam project, **1978** 433
Social Security benefits
sex bias in, **1977** 169, 171-174
for widowers, **1975** 178-184
sodomy and privacy right, **1986** 601, 608
student aid and draft registration, **1984** 496
students' rights
and corporal punishment, **1977** 293, 303
and free speech, **1986** 731, 739
and newspaper censorship, **1988** 38, 45-46
in searches, **1985** 15, 24-26
tax increase to promote desegregation, **1990** 227-228, 229-232
televised trials, **1981** 170
tenure review disclosure, **1990** 23-34
treatment of severely handicapped infants, **1986** 543, 554
treaty termination, **1979** 918, 933, 938
tuition tax credit, **1983** 676, 684-688
uncompensated takings, **1987** 533, 549-553
unitary taxation, **1983** 645, 647-657
utilities regulation, **1982** 448
water rights, **1982** 689
wiretapping authorization by attorney general, **1974** 393, 403
worker health protection, **1981** 492-501
zoning
for adult theaters, **1986** 132, 133, 140-144
barring low-income and minority housing, **1977** 36, 43
Bresnahan, Timothy, Microsoft antitrust case ruling, **2002** 800-801
Bretton Woods Committee, Brady plan presented to, **1989** 137, 143
Bretton Woods Conference (1944), **1984** 356, 795-796; **1985** 624; **1986** 438; **1989** 138-139
Bretton Woods monetary system
collapse of, **1978** 743, 749-750
creation of, **1972** 815-816; **1978** 660
replacement of, **1974** 497-505; **1976** 3-12
Brewer v. Williams, **1977** 219-235
Brewster v. Gage, **1992** 462
Breyer, Charles, medical use of marijuana, **2001** 326
Breyer, Stephen G.
abortion
antiabortion demonstrations, **2000** 433
partial birth, **2000** 431-432, 434-440
affirmative action, **2003** 362, 363
federal government plans, **1995** 309, 323-326
campaign finance reform, **2003** 1160
congressional term limits, **1995** 260
death penalty
and International Court of Justice jurisdiction, **2005** 182
for juvenile offenders, **2002** 358; **2004** 797; **2005** 179
for the mentally retarded, **2002** 356
detentions in terrorism cases, **2004** 377, 378, 381-388
disabilities in the workplace, **2002** 6
disability, definition of, **1999** 319, 320, 325-332
drug testing of students, **1995** 339-346
eminent domain, **2005** 363, 364
endangered species on private lands, **1995** 359-368
free speech
ballot initiatives, **1999** 6
Internet and, **1997** 445
Internet pornography filters in public libraries, **2003** 388, 389, 397
gay rights discrimination, **1996** 286
grandparents' rights, **2000** 289, 290-295
gun-free school zone, **1995** 184, 190-191, 196-200
HIV as a disability, **1998** 379, 388-389
line-item veto, **1997** 612; **1998** 421, 431-433, 433-437
medical use of marijuana, recusal, **2001** 327, 330
Microsoft Corp. antitrust case, **2000** 309
Miranda warnings, **2000** 389
parochial school aid, **1997** 363, 375-380, 380-381
physician-assisted suicide, **1997** 461, 472-473, 478-479
presidential elections recount, **2000** 1000, 1002, 1003, 1019-1024
presidential immunity, **1997** 292
race-based redistricting, **1995** 371, 380-384; **1996** 370, 381-383, 383-387
religious clubs in public schools, **2001** 422
religious freedom, **1997** 408, 417-420
religious publications, **1995** 386, 393-395
religious symbols, **1995** 387, 396-404
school prayer, **2000** 367
school vouchers, **2002** 409
sentencing laws, **2003** 982; **2004** 359, 360, 366-374
sex offenders, right to confine, **1997** 383-384, 392-394
sexual harassment, **1999** 215
sodomy laws, **2003** 403
states' rights, **1999** 333, 345-349
student drug testing, **2002** 425, 426
Supreme Court appointment, **1993** 393, 396
Ten Commandments displays, **2005** 377-378, 383-384
unreasonable searches, **2001** 409, 410
Brezhnev, Leonid I.
ABM treaty, **2001** 928
on Alekseyeva emigration, **1981** 748-750
on Camp David accords, **1978** 607
career and death of, **1980** 139; **1982** 871-877
corruption and conservatism under, **1987** 79-80
Czechoslovakia invasion (1968),**1975** 240
dissidents
Carter support for, **1977** 190
crackdown on, **1986** 1092
Egyptian-Soviet relations, **1976** 170, 172-173
on European Communist parties, **1976** 434-450
European leaders, meetings with, **1980** 503-504
Gorbachev criticism of, **1986** 145

Brezhnev, Leonid I. *Continued*
intervention in Afghanistan, **1979** 966; **1980** 5, 9-15
Iran's revolution, noninterference in, **1978** 710, 713
on Middle East cease-fire proposals, **1973** 882, 885, 892
missile parity, U.S.-Soviet, **1981** 824
Moscow summit agreements, **1974** 535-569
nuclear freeze, **1982** 225-231
nuclear testing
ban, **1977** 737-738
for peaceful purposes, signing of treaty on, **1976** 369-374
party congress speeches, **1976** 143-155; **1981** 225-239
personality of, Nixon on, **1977** 341-342
Reagan's zero-option proposal to, **1981** 823-828
SALT I agreements, **1972** 431-463
SALT II negotiations and signing, **1977** 245; **1979** 413-414
Soviet constitution, **1977** 747-758; **1993** 772
U.S. as unreliable, **1980** 10, 13-14
U.S. leaders, contacts with, **1985** 749-750
Nixon during Arab-Israeli war, **1973** 898-900, 905, 907-908
Nixon in U.S., **1973** 587-609
Reagan letter on Soviet repression, **1982** 880
U.S. televised speech, **1986** 5
U.S. trade agreement, **1973** 792
U.S. trade benefits as goal of, **1974** 901
U.S.-PRC relations, **1978** 782
Vladivostok accord, **1974** 955-958, 967-972
West German agreements, **1973** 557-562
Yugoslavia, Soviet intentions toward, **1976** 869-870
Brezhnev doctrine, Soviet rejection of, **1989** 399-402
Bribery
of government officials, by international business, **1980** 512
for private immigration bills in Congress, **1979** 468-478
of public officials, combating, **1997** 800-807
Brickman, Lester, **1995** 517
Bridge, Peter J., **1972** 509
Bridgeport (Conn.), mayor on city bankruptcy, **1991** 303-307
Bridger-Teton National Forest, oil and gas drilling, **2004** 670
Bridgeton (tanker), Iranian attack on in Persian Gulf, **1987** 794
Bridgewater, Bill, **1995** 464
Brier, James H., **1988** 796
Brill, Kenneth, Iran nuclear weapons inspections, **2003** 1030
Brilliant, Lawrence B., **1978** 653
Brimmer, Andrew F., **1996** 784
Brindel, Glenn R., Iraqi attack on USS *Stark,* **1987** 792, 809-815
Brinegar, Claude S., **1973** 589
Brinker, Nancy A., on breast cancer research, **1993** 907
Brinkley, David, **1972** 712
Briseno, Theodore J., King case indictment and acquittal, **1992** 409; **1993** 633-637, 639, 641-642, 647, 650
Bristol-Myers, manufacturer of breast implants, **1995** 516
Britain. *See* Great Britain
British Broadcasting Corp. *See* BBC (British Broadcasting Corporation)
British Commonwealth, Zimbabwe membership suspension, **2003** 1114-1118
British Meteorological Office, **1987** 745
British North American Act (1867), **1980** 402-403; **1981** 813-822
Britt, Harry, **1989** 306
Brittain, Leon, on GATT, **1993** 542
Brizola, Leonel, **1985** 4
Broadcasting
See also Television broadcasting
cable TV, FCC rules on, **1972** 137-142
commercial, and license fees, **1979** 119-120, 128
deregulation of, **1984** 450-451
equal time rule, **1987** 625
for presidential candidates, **1976** 695
fairness doctrine, **1984** 451, 454, 460; **1987** 625-636
home video recording, **1984** 53-80
license renewal regulations, proposed changes in, **1973** 55-62
ownership of newspaper and radio or TV station in same community, FCC on, **1978** 419-432
public broadcasting, **1979** 119-134; **1984** 449-463
editorials in, **1984** 449-463
Broccoli
calcium in, **1992** 399, 403
as cancer preventative, **1992** 277-281
George H. W. Bush's opinion of, **1992** 277
Broder, David S.
aid for Eastern Europe, **1989** 414
on Clinton State of the Union address, **1995** 24
presidential debates, **1988** 721, 723
Wallace on World War II, **1975** 155
Broderick, Edwin B., **1972** 783
Brokaw, Tom, in vice-presidential debate, **1988** 806-807, 813-814, 819-820, 826-827
Bromwich, Michael R., FBI crime laboratory report, **1997** 221-228
Bronchitis, chronic, from smoking and other workplace hazards, **1985** 817
Bronfman, Edgar, **1997** 262
Bronson, Bennett, **1989** 540
Bronstein, Alvin, **1984** 479-480
Brooke, Edward W. (R-Mass.)
as consultant on HUD matter, **1989** 334
Ford economic and energy proposals, **1975** 17
Laird letters to on nuclear first strike, **1975** 496, 502-504
Nixon pardon, **1974** 812
Nixon resignation, **1974** 289
Brookings Institution
Brady plan at conference of, **1989** 137
independent counsel report, **1999** 168
proposed firebombing of, **1974** 350, 444
on succession in Saudi Arabia, **1992** 227
Brooklyn Naval Station (New York), closing of, **1988** 952
Brooks, Harvey, **1973** 783

Brooks, Jack (D-Texas)
crime bill, **1994** 576
on Twenty-seventh Amendment, **1992** 440
Brooks, Karen B., Indonesia relations, **2002** 703
Brooks, Leo A., Philadelphia raid on MOVE group, **1986** 240-251
Brothers to the Rescue, **1996** 93-97
Browder v. Gayle, **2005** 357
Brown, Bertram S., **1972** 155
Brown, Charles, **1982** 19
Brown, Curtis, *Discovery* space shuttle mission, **1998** 778-786
Brown, David M., *Columbia* astronaut, **2003** 633
Brown, Edmund G.
California farm labor law **1975** 377-378
EPA hazardous waste investigation, **1983** 749, 753
gubernatorial election defeat, **2004** 317
presidential nomination, **1976** 597
Proposition 13 passage, **1978** 397-398, 400-402
Brown, Edmund G., Jr. ("Jerry"), **1992** 669, 686
Brown, Franklin C., corporate fraud conviction, **2003** 332-333
Brown, George, on Britain's military, **1976** 804-806
Brown, Gordon
African economic aid, **2005** 406
British Labor Party leader, **2005** 394
Brown, Harold
Independent Panel to Review DOD Detention Operations, **2004** 212
national security strategy, **1986** 781-790
Panama Canal treaties, **1977** 593
sales of warplanes to Saudi Arabia, **1978** 126
SALT II, **1979** 417
secretary of defense appointment, **1976** 878
U.S. defense posture, **1980** 123-157
U.S.-PRC defense cooperation, **1979** 967
Brown, J. Larry, **1985** 189
Brown, Jesse
on Gulf War syndrome, **1994** 266
radiation testing on citizens, **1993** 988
Brown, Jodie
abortion pill, **2000** 784
on embryonic research, **1998** 66
Brown, Lee P., drug-free schools, **1995** 341
Brown, Lester R.
on drought, **1988** 863
on Soviet farming and agricultural trade, **1982** 823
Brown, Mark Malloch
Arab world development, **2002** 484
Srebrenica massacre, **2005** 854
UN chief of staff appointment, **2005** 236
as UN Development Programme head, **2004** 893
Brown, Michael (Palomar Observatory astronomer), planetary studies, **2002** 215
Brown, Michael D.
FEMA director resignation, **2005** 566, 568
Hurricane Katrina disaster, **2005** 566, 568, 569
Brown, Ronald H.
Corporate Citizenship Award, **1996** 42
death of, **1996** 204-209
Democratic convention (1992),**1992** 669
on labor-management relations report, **1995** 15, 17
Brown, Sarah, on teenage pregnancy, **1999** 386
Brown, Tod D. (bishop), sexual abuse by priest, apology for, **2005** 866
Brown, William H., III
EEOC sex discrimination guidelines, **1972** 313-314
investigation of Philadelphia raid on MOVE group, **1986** 240-251
Brown, Willie L.
California term limits, **1997** 887
Census Bureau undercount, **1991** 444-445
Brown v. Board of Education of Topeka, **1972** 935-937; **1979** 535-537; **1990** 230, 237, 430, 434, 616; **1991** 23, 27, 29; **1992** 35, 41, 42, 577, 578, 579, 581, 585, 599; **1995** 456, 458; **2000** 771-772
Brown v. Thomson, **1983** 601
Brown & Williamson Tobacco Corp., tobacco claims settlement, **1997** 331; **1998** 842
Brownback, Sam (R-Kan.)
on needle-exchange programs, **2005** 53
stem cell research guidelines, **2000** 669
stem cell research opponent, **2005** 319
Browner, Carol M., on smoking in public places, **1993** 64-65
Browning, Edmond L., consecration of woman Episcopal bishop, **1989** 49-54
Browning-Ferris Industries of Vermont, Inc. v. Kelco Disposal, Inc., **1993** 433-434, 437, 440
Bruce, David K. E., **1973** 293
Bruce, Margaret K., **1975** 508
Brugiere, Jean-Louis, French antiterrorism judge, **2004** 119
Brumbaugh, R. Dan, **1990** 816
Brundtland, Gro Harlem
global dietary guidelines, **2003** 484
mental health, **2001** 578
tobacco control treaty, **2003** 261
Bruno, Hal, **1976** 774
Brush, Peter, human radiation tests, **1993** 987-995
Bryan, United States v., **1990** 28
Bryant, Anne, on sexual harassment in schools, **1993** 355
Bryant, Barbara Everitt, **1990** 171; **1991** 443
Bryant, Ed (R-Tenn.), House Judiciary Committee impeachment inquiry, **1998** 708
Bryant, Gyude
Liberia interim government, **2005** 801
Liberian guerrilla leader, **2003** 772
Bryant, John (D-Texas), television violence, **1993** 489
Bryant, Robert, antiabortion violence, **1998** 813-814
Bryant, William, on national security break-ins, **1981** 371-372
Brzezinski, Zbigniew, **1980** 476
Carter trips, **1977** 897; **1978** 169
Iranian contacts with, **1979** 869
Nixon's speech on Russia, **1992** 260
SALT II, **1978** 550
Soviet invasion in Afghanistan, **1979** 966, 977-983
use of B. Carter's Libyan contacts, **1980** 908-909, 913-917
U.S.-PRC normalization of relations, **1978** 783
on Vietnam POWs, **1993** 114
B'Tselem (Israeli human rights organization), **2004** 812; **2005** 30
Buchanan, Bruce, **1990** 295-299

Buchanan, James, **1984** 20
Buchanan, Patrick J.
in 1992 primaries, **1992** 56
attacks Clinton on draft issue, **1992** 158
on English as official language, **1995** 573
as presidential candidate, **1996** 496, 563-564; **2000** 896
at Republican Party convention, **1996** 478
on U.S. bishops' pastoral letter, **1986** 985
Buchen, Philip W., **1974** 811
Buckheit, Bruce, air pollution, EPA investigations, **2004** 666
Buckley, James L. (C-N.Y.)
Nixon resignation, **1974** 191, 199-200, 289
suit on federal election law, **1976** 71-111
world population growth, **1984** 522
Buckley, William F.
hostage, **1991** 753
on John Paul II's criticism of capitalism, **1988** 166
kidnapping and killing of, **1986** 1015; **1987** 217; **1989** 316
Buckley v. American Constitutional Law Foundation (ACLF), **1999** 5-14
Buckley v. Valeo, **1976** 71-111; **1998** 435; **1999** 11; **2003** 1157, 1159
Buddhism
ethnic conflict in Sri Lanka, **1987** 615-616
position of Dalai Lama, **1989** 573, 575
Budget, federal
See also Balanced budget; Balanced budget amendment
AIDS funding, **1983** 533, 540-541
bipartisan agreement on, **1989** 72, 83-84
blacks, effect of cuts on, **1983** 41-42, 44-55
Bush administration proposals, **2002** 42; **2004** 60-61; **2005** 82-83
CBO on Reagan's proposed, **1982** 191-201
CEA report on, **2003** 86-87
comptroller general report on, **2005** 121-136
and economic outlook, CBO report on, **2003** 683-690
full-employment balance in, Nixon on, **1972** 115-118; **1973** 170, 177-178, 185, 187-190
poor, effect of Reagan cuts on, CBO analysis, **1983** 765-772
projections from 2004 through 2013, **2003** 687
Reagan revisions of Carter, **1981** 325-335
reduction efforts under Reagan, **1982** 78-79, 121, 125, 143-144, 150, 155-158
restraint in Carter's, **1978** 8, 13; **1981** 57, 61-62
spending cuts, **2005** 78
and tax package in Reagan's economic plan, **1981** 213-224, 639-646
Budget, states'. *See* States' budget crisis
Budget and Accounting Act (1921),amendments to, **1974** 586-587
Budget deficit
See also Budget, federal
Bush administration, **2001** 665, 913; **2002** 36, 42, 691, 693, 880; **2003** 68, 69, 86-87
criticisms of, **2003** 681-683
manageable limits, **2003** 678
proposal to cut in half, **2005** 78-79, 143
causes of, **2005** 121-122
Reagan economic report on, **1985** 79, 84-85
CBO report on, **2003** 678-690
CEA report on, **1991** 87
Democratic Party platform on, **1984** 555, 559-560, 565-568; **1992** 691
during Bush administration, **1991** 67-69
during Republican administrations, **1997** 605
economic summits on, **1983** 508, 511-513; **1985** 348-349, 351
executive-legislative agreement on, **1989** 71-74, 83-84
executive-legislative summit on, **1987** 834-836, 838
and Gramm-Rudman-Hollings legislation, **1985** 803-808; **1986** 40, 43-44, 49-50, 53-54; **1987** 3-8; **1989** 43-44
Court on separation of powers, **1986** 705
Greenspan remarks on, **2004** 235-237
growth in
Carter revisions to Ford budget, **1977** 125, 127
Ford CEA on financing, **1975** 105-106
mounting concern for, **2005** 121-123
under Ford economic and energy plan, **1975** 30
impact on business investment, **1974** 85-86
impact on inflation, **1974** 421, 424; **1976** 30-31, 46
impact on international monetary system, **1985** 624, 627, 630
in industrialized countries, effect on developing nations, **1983** 802, 804, 809-810
legal limit on U.S. debt, **2003** 68
in Nixon budget, **1972** 84, 116; **1974** 95-96, 98, 101
and Omnibus Budget Reconciliation Act, **1993** 182
as presidential campaign issue, **1984** 846, 849-852; **1988** 726-728, 769-770, 801, 803, 818-819, 825-826
projections
for fiscal 2003, **2003** 680-681
for fiscal 2004, **2003** 680-681; **2004** 20; **2005** 137
for fiscal 2005, **2005** 137
for fiscal 2006, **2005** 79, 137
long-term outlook and an aging population, **2005** 123-124
short-term focus, **2005** 124-125
projections of
in Carter budget, **1981** 61, 111
in Ford budget, **1976** 37, 40
by Ford CEA, **1975** 83, 85-86, 88-89
in Reagan budget, **1982** 143-144, 152-158; **1983** 101-102, 107, 107-110; **1984** 81-82, 88; **1985** 71-72, 76
in Reagan economic plan, **1981** 640, 645
reduction of
Carter plans for, **1977** 67, 70, 73; **1978** 70, 95-96, 98, 688, 694; **1979** 31
CEA report on, **1997** 53, 60-61; **1998** 86
Clinton plan for, **1995** 72-73; **1996** 21, 24, 51, 52, 65-67; **1997** 50-51; **1998** 74, 77, 81-82; **2000** 22
current economic expansion and, **1999** 95-97
by cutting spending, Reagan on, **1989** 3, 9
executive-legislative agreement on, **1988** 137, 149-150, 153-157, 163
GAO report, **1996** 147-155
and investment, **1995** 80-81

new budget process, Muskie on effectiveness of, **1976** 31
Reagan CEA on, **1983** 122, 125, 130-131; **1984** 136-139; **1985** 93-95; **1987** 117, 121-122, 125-126, 133-134
Reagan on proposed legislation, **1984** 99, 119, 126-127
Reagan plans for, **1985** 106-108, 111; **1987** 106-107, 111-112
by reforming budget, Nixon on, **1973** 178-180
tax cuts, **2003** 681-682, 752
zero deficit, **1998** 42
Republican platform on, **1976** 621-622; **1988** 616-617, 630
State of the Union, democratic response, **1991** 48
trade deficit and, **1985** 624-625, 627; **1987** 428
underestimation of, CBO on, **1982** 191, 195-197, 200
worldwide, and admission to European Union, **1998** 273
Budget Enforcement Act (1990), **2005** 124
Budget messages
Bush, **1989** 71, 73-82; **1991** 67-71
Carter, **1978** 95-102; **1979** 9-17
Ford, **1975** 83-98; **1976** 37-43; **1977** 57-63
Nixon, **1972** 115-119; **1973** 169-183; **1974** 95-112
Reagan, **1982** 143-162; **1983** 101-118; **1984** 99-117; **1985** 71-78; **1986** 49-58; **1987** 3-15; **1988** 149-163
Budget process
change of fiscal year, **1974** 585
changes in to reflect future effects, **1975** 97
congressional reconciliation and Reagan appropriations veto, **1981** 640-641, 831-834
history of, **1974** 574-575
reform, **1987** 14-15
Bush on (2-year), **1989** 74
details of (set of deadlines; priority setting), **1976** 177-178
implementation of (first budget-fiscal 1977), **1976** 39-40
to improve congressional control, **1973** 8-19
Nixon on, **1972** 116-117; **1974** 112
Reagan recommendations, **1988** 58, 62-63, 161-162; **1989** 10
recent congressional changes in, Ford on, **1977** 57, 63
to reduce deficits, Nixon recommendations, **1973** 178-180
remedies for, Burns on, **1974** 424
timetable for, **1974** 582
two-year, Nixon on planning for, **1973** 170, 176-177
unified, in Nixon budget, **1974** 96
zero-based, Carter plan for, **1977** 109, 125, 129; **1978** 72, 98, 101
Budget surplus
Clinton plan for, **1998** 74-75, 98; **1999** 90
Clinton remarks on, **1999** 350-356
Congressional Budget Office on, **1998** 500-509
projections, **1999** 42; **2000** 17, 45; **2004** 236
Buerganthal, Thomas, **1993** 237
Buffett, Warren
California gubernatorial recall election, **2003** 1009
insurance industry investigations, **2004** 418
Bugayev, Boris P., **1973** 589
Buitenen, Paul van, EC corruption, **1999** 156
Bukharin, Nikolai, **1987** 857-858
Bulgaria
attack on Israeli plane (1955), **1983** 775
EU membership issue, **2003** 43; **2004** 199, 977
human rights, **1990** 137
NATO membership, **2004** 136
political liberalization in, **1989** 635
power sharing by communist government, **1989** 710
Warsaw Pact dissolution, **1991** 399-401
Bullock, Clint, affirmative action, **2003** 364
Bullock, Thomas, **1981** 337
Bulow, Jeremy, underfunded pensions, **2003** 710
Bumpers, Dale (D-Ark.), Clinton impeachment trial defense summation, **1999** 20, 29-40
Bundy, McGeorge
East-West scientific organization, **1972** 834
no-first-use defense policy, **1982** 305-315
Bunning, Jim (R-Ky.), steroid use in baseball, **2005** 215
Buonomo, Joe, **1983** 526
Burch v. Louisiana, **1979** 263-268
Burchfield, Bobby, campaign finance reform, **2003** 1160
Burdick, Quentin N. (D-N.D.), **1972** 396
Burdzhanadze, Nino
on Georgian political situation, **2003** 1047-1049
Georgian presidential elections, **2003** 1042-1044; **2004** 72
Bureau of Immigration and Customs Enforcement, Federal Air Marshall Service, **2004** 146
Bureau of Indian Affairs (BIA), apology for mistreatment of Indians, **2000** 723-728
Bureau of Justice Statistics (BJS)
capital punishment report, **2004** 794-805
prison statistics, **2002** 786-787; **2005** 679-680
on rape, **1993** 386, 389-390
on violent crime, **1993** 377
Bureau of Labor Statistics (BLS)
data on young families, **1992** 356
U.S. employment situation, **2003** 441-449
Bureau of Land Management (BLM), logging in Oregon, **1992** 490
Bureau of Reclamation, water programs of, **1978** 387, 389, 392
Burford, Anne M. Gorsuch
congressional investigation of EPA, **1982** 965-970; **1983** 749-750
Justice Department investigation of EPA, **1983** 749-753
Reagan administration environmental policies, **1984** 83
Burg, Avraham, **1999** 362
Burgenthal, Thomas, Israeli security wall, World Court ruling on, **2004** 310
Burger, Anna, Change to Win coalition labor organizer, **2005** 487, 488, 495-497
Burger, Warren E.
abortion
and privacy right, **1973** 102
public funding of, **1977** 424-425; **1980** 515

Burger, Warren E. *Continued*
right to, **1983** 544-545, 565-566, 569; **1986** 559-561, 569-571
state restrictions on, **1976** 483
advertising prescription drug prices, **1976** 352, 360
affirmative action
job program, **1979** 495, 501-502
medical school admissions, **1978** 468-471, 491
minority promotions, **1986** 677
age discrimination, **1983** 232, 239
alimony for men, **1979** 193, 200
antitrust immunity of cities, **1982** 35, 43
auto search and seizure, **1978** 753; **1982** 425
Balanced Budget Act and separation of powers, **1986** 706, 708-718
bankruptcy and labor contracts, **1984** 182
bankruptcy law, **1982** 597
broadcast of offensive material, **1978** 515
campaign financing, **1976** 104-107
Carter inaugural, **1977** 89
census data confidentiality, **1982** 171-178
child pornography, **1982** 676
church and state separation, church's objection to liquor license, **1982** 955-961
clean air regulations, **1984** 427
congressional immunity, **1979** 467-475, 479-491
Constitution bicentennial, **1987** 765-766, 771-775
corporate free speech in referendum campaigns, **1978** 307-309, 315-317
Court workload, **1972** 953; **1982** 707, 724-727
criminal justice system, **1981** 191-196
criticism of lawyers, **1986** 767-768
on deadly force, **1985** 304, 312
death penalty, **1990** 313
constitutionality of, **1972** 499-500, 503-504
constitutionality of state laws, **1976** 489-490
mandatory, for murder of police officer, **1977** 397, 400
mitigating factors, **1978** 495-507, 511-514; **1982** 51-53, 56, 60
mother's request for stay against defendant's wishes, **1976** 918, 920-921
for rape, **1977** 517-518, 525-528
state's misuse of, **1980** 455, 457, 466-467
education for alien children, **1982** 490, 501
exclusionary rule, **1976** 523, 531-532; **1984** 506
federal and state powers, **1985** 169, 182
historic preservation and property takings, **1978** 453, 462
home video taping, **1984** 53
immunity of municipalities, **1980** 299, 308
indigents' right to psychiatric aid, **1985** 209
intra-enterprise conspiracy doctrine, **1984** 414, 415-422
involuntary commitment, **1979** 335-344
job bias suit against member of Congress, **1979** 399, 401, 408-410
judicial immunity, **1978** 260
judiciary, state of, **1972** 639-643
jury trials, split verdicts in, **1972** 423
Kent State parents' right to sue, **1974** 265-270
labor union members' freedom to resign, **1985** 415
legal system's problems, **1983** 392
legislative veto, **1983** 619-634
libel
appellate review of award, **1984** 300, 309
of private and public persons, **1986** 355, 357, 364
mental patients, right to treatment, **1975** 470, 476-480
mentally retarded, rights of, **1982** 522, 529
military draft, sex discrimination in, **1981** 521
minimum wage laws, **1976** 378
minority set-asides in federal contracts, **1980** 539-552
Miranda warnings, and definition of interrogation, **1980** 431
NAACP boycott, **1982** 656
national court of appeals, proposed, **1975** 456, 463
Nixon papers and tapes, **1974** 622-637; **1977** 466-467, 493-510
obscenity standards, **1973** 612-618, 621-622
parental child custody rights, **1982** 260, 271
passport revocation, **1981** 541, 543-552
patenting of living organisms, **1980** 493-500
peremptory challenge, **1986** 409, 411-412, 425-433
political firings from public jobs, **1980** 259, 260
pregnancy coverage in company disability plans, **1976** 892
presidential immunity, **1982** 551
press
access to pretrial hearings, **1979** 511-512, 521-522
confidentiality of sources, **1972** 507
gag orders and right to fair trial, **1976** 464-473
libel of public figure, **1979** 285
newsroom searches, **1978** 355
prison crowding, **1981** 478
prisoners' rights, searches, **1984** 479-485, 488-491
public aid for private schools, **1973** 641-646; **1977** 432, 440; **1985** 433, 453-454
public broadcasting editorials, **1984** 450, 461
public display of Nativity scene, **1984** 217-226
on racial criteria in redistricting, **1977** 151-153, 164-167
Reagan inaugural, **1981** 137; **1985** 40
reapportionment and one-man, one-vote rule, **1973** 278
redistricting, **1983** 600, 612-615
and gerrymandering, **1986** 629
on release of Marshall's papers, **1993** 339-340
resignation of, **1986** 591, 594, 597, 599
right of reply by political candidate, **1974** 524-527
right to counsel, **1981** 431, 433-441
and police procedure, **1977** 219, 221, 229-234
school book banning, **1982** 568, 580
school desegregation, **1979** 536
busing restrictions, **1982** 620, 633
remedies for, **1974** 639-648; **1977** 448, 457-463
school prayer, **1985** 380-381, 392-395
schools, judicial intervention in operation of, **1975** 68, 75
search and arrest at home without warrant, **1980** 283, 291
secrecy of CIA sources, **1985** 333, 334-342
seniority protections, **1984** 366
sentencing

and double jeopardy, **1980** 977
excessive prison terms, **1983** 660-661, 670-674
sex bias
in education, **1984** 202, 210
in pension plans, **1978** 293-294, 301-303; **1983** 691
in Social Security survivors' benefits, **1975** 178, 184; **1977** 170, 177
snail darter protection from dam project, **1978** 433-446
sodomy and privacy right, **1986** 601, 603, 607
Statue of Liberty centennial, **1986** 698
statutory rape laws, sex discrimination in, **1981** 339
student aid and draft registration, **1984** 495-500
student searches, **1985** 14
students' free speech, **1986** 731, 732-739
students' rights, corporal punishment, **1977** 293
suspects' rights, and public safety, **1984** 388
swearing-in
of Ford, **1973** 969, 971; **1974** 684
of Rockefeller, **1974** 987
tax exemptions for discriminatory schools, **1983** 489, 490, 491-502
televised trials, **1981** 163-176
treatment of severely handicapped infants, **1986** 543, 554
treaty termination, **1979** 917, 933
tuition tax credit, **1983** 676, 684-688
unitary taxation, **1983** 645, 657-658
utilities regulation, **1982** 448, 460
voter residence requirements, **1972** 283
warrants for OSHA safety inspections, **1978** 340
water rights, **1982** 689
wiretapping authorization by attorney general, **1974** 392, 399
worker health protection, **1981** 492, 503
Burger King, jobs for welfare recipients, **1997** 34, 622
Burgess, Guy, in Soviet spy network, **1979** 905-906, 908-909, 911, 913
Burgess, John
as first black Episcopal bishop, **1989** 49
on U.S.-Japan relations, **1987** 428
Burke, Anne M., sexual abuse of priests, **2004** 86
Burkina Faso, drought and famine in, **1984** 974, 979, 982
Burlington Industries, Inc. v. Ellerth, **1998** 439-442, 453-465
Burma
See also Myanmar
human rights in, **1989** 58, 64-65, 607-609
opium growing in, **1972** 646, 648-649
religious persecution, **1997** 567-568
Burnet v. Colorado Oil & Gas Co., **1991** 389
Burnham, Christine, UN undersecretary appointment, **2005** 236
Burnham, Frederic B., **1992** 381
Burnham, Gracia, Philippine hostage, **2001** 105
Burnham, Martin, Philippine hostage, **2001** 105
Burnley, James H., IV, **1988** 268-269
Burns, Arnold, **1988** 497
Burns, Arthur F.
controlling inflation, **1972** 961-970; **1974** 419-425, 862; **1975** 635-642; **1977** 718
international monetary reform, **1972** 413-418
size of federal budget, **1977** 127
Burns, Nicholas
Haiti elections, **2005** 330
Iraq War alliance, **2003** 43
Burns, William F. (Arms Control and Disarmament Agency director), on chemical weapons, **1989** 28
Burns, William J. (State Department asst. secy.)
Jenin "massacre" investigations, **2002** 934
Lebanon-Syria relations, **2004** 561
Middle East peace process, **2001** 366
U.S. relations with Libya, **2004** 172, 175
Burns, William M. (Roche chief executive), avian flu vaccine production, **2005** 752
Burroughs Wellcome Co., FDA approval of AZT, **1987** 327-329
Burt, Martha, on homelessness report, **1994** 253
Burt, Richard R.
Shcharansky release, **1986** 93
Soviet chemical warfare, **1981** 682-683, 687-694
Burton, Dan (R-Ind.)
and Clinton impeachment, **2001** 89
on financial disclosure for members of Congress, **1995** 701
Waco incident, **1999** 482
Burton, Harold H., Supreme Court justice papers, **1993** 340
Burundi
African peacekeeping force, **2003** 924
assassination of president Cyprien Ntaryamira, **1994** 541; **1999** 863; **2000** 452
child soldiers, **2002** 918, 925
human rights in, **1989** 598-599, 601; **1990** 135
hunger in, **2003** 756
peace agreement, **2003** 922-932
political situation, **1999** 866-867
refugees in Tanzania, **1999** 435
Tutsi and Hutu ethnic group conflicts, **2000** 64-65; **2003** 922-924
UN humanitarian aid, **2003** 926
UN peacekeeping mission, **2003** 450
UN refugee camp, attack on, **2004** 507
Busbee, George, **1982** 74
Busey, James B., Pan Am bombing, **1990** 304
Bush, Barbara
at inauguration of George W. Bush, **2001** 95
Wellesley commencement address, **1990** 353-356
Bush, George H. W.
Cabinet appointments, **1988** 892, 895; **1989** 105, 107, 355, 358; **2000** 1027-1028
campaigns and elections
acceptance speeches, **1980** 651, 653-654; **1984** 727-730, 741-745; **1988** 589-590, 604-613; **1992** 781-794
Perot challenge, **1992** 717
postelection press conference, **1988** 892, 894-900
postelection statement, **1992** 1019, 1023-1024
presidential debates, **1988** 721-783; **1992** 907-977
presidential elections, **2000** 896
Reagan on at Republican convention, **1988** 590, 597-598
Reagan victory statement, **1980** 960-961
on Republican Party platform, **1992** 799

Bush, George H. W. *Continued*
selection of Quayle, **1988** 800, 801
victory statement, **1988** 891-894
Central America
bipartisan accord with Congress on contras, **1989** 161-168
contra aid fight, **1988** 243
Noriega relations with U.S., **1988** 82
Panama invasion, **1989** 701-707
CIA director appointment, **1975** 875
defense policy
arms control, **1990** 19, 57
arms reduction and European cooperation treaties, **1990** 734-745
chemical weapons ban, **1989** 25-27
Iraq war resolution, **1991** 3, 6
missile defense system, **2000** 678; **2001** 928; **2003** 817
START agreement, **1991** 475-490
START II agreement, **1994** 17-20, 20-23
troop reductions in Europe, **1990** 15
underground nuclear test ban, **1999** 601
domestic policy
abortion funding vetoes, **1989** 368
Brady bill, **1991** 286
broccoli, opinion of, **1992** 277
Clear Air Act revisions, **1990** 715-720
cutting programs, **1992** 66
enterprise zone legislation veto, **1993** 212-213, 216
health care reform, **1992** 65-66, 101, 107
HOPE housing proposal, **1990** 101-102; **1992** 65, 107, 449
Hurricane Andrew, **1992** 534, 843-848
Hurricane Iniki, **1992** 843-848
Job Rights Bill, **1991** 759-765
Job Training 2000 initiative, **1992** 101, 106, 107-108
Job Training Partnership Act, **1992** 449
Magic Johnson's resignation from AIDS Commission, **1992** 891-893
real estate, **1992** 101, 114
regulatory moratorium, **1992** 57, 62, 100, 106
regulatory reform, **1990** 86
reneges on no-tax pledge, **1990** 409-417
Social Security, **1992** 55
unemployment benefits, **1992** 63
welfare reform, **1988** 848; **1992** 67
economic policy
budget compromise, **1997** 602
budget deficit, **1990** 50, 55, 84, 410; **2003** 679
budget message, **1989** 71, 73-82; **1991** 67-71
capital gains tax, **1992** 56-57, 63, 101, 106, 107
cut on capital gains tax, **1990** 53-54, 82, 93
enterprise zones, **1992** 65, 101, 107, 449
fighting recession, **1995** 55, 56-57, 61-65
investment incentives, **1992** 101
monetary policy, **1992** 62, 115-117
research and development, **1990** 54; **1995** 65
research and development tax credit, **1992** 57
savings and loan institutions, bailout plan, **1989** 463-468
economic reports, **1990** 81-104, 83-87; **1991** 73-81; **1992** 97-134
economic summits
Houston, **1990** 467, 468-469, 478-483
London, **1991** 451-473
Munich, **1992** 637-648
Paris, **1989** 411, 414, 430-435
Tokyo, **1992** 12
education programs, **1989** 86-87, 561-565; **1990** 51, 54, 86, 153-163; **1991** 219-226; **1992** 45
New American Schools program, **1992** 64
environmental policy
climate change, **2002** 298-321; **2004** 841
forest fire guidelines, **2000** 714
Rio summit, **2002** 595
Europe
Baltic states' freedom statements, **1989** 471
Berlin Wall opening, **1989** 627-630
conventional forces cut, **1989** 297-304
on German reunification, **1989** 627
Hungary and Poland visits, **1989** 411-424, 430-437
Netherlands visit, **1989** 411, 435-437
Poland, U.S. lifting of trade sanctions against, **1987** 185
Walesa award, **1989** 524
on West Germany's postwar role, **1989** 489
executive orders
on Haitian refugee asylum, **1992** 453-468
union political activity, **1992** 345-351
federal government work furlough, **1981** 832
federal officials' salaries, **1989** 196
flag protection, **1989** 343-345
foreign policy
Baltic states, U.S. relations, **1991** 545-549
China-U.S. relations, **2001** 738-739
Chinese students in U.S., **1990** 50
drug summit at Cartagena, **1990** 115-126
drug war strategy, **1989** 499-508
Earth Summit (Rio), **1992** 499-506
El Salvadoran peace plan, **1992** 25
end of Cold War, **1992** 432
environmental issues, **1990** 480-481
food aid to Soviet Union, **1990** 807-814
Gorbachev resignation, **1991** 810-811
Gulf War coalition, **2003** 49
Haitian refugees, **1992** 453-458; **1993** 413; **1994** 436-437
Iraqi invasion of Kuwait, **1990** 533-543, 551-556, 767, 773-776
Irgan, U.S. downing of Iranian airliner, **1988** 704
Labor victory in Israeli elections, **1992** 655-665
Lithuanian independence, **1990** 185
London Declaration, **1990** 455, 456, 461-466
Mandela meeting, **1990** 68
Mexico, free trade agreement, **1993** 954
Middle East Peace Conference (Madrid), **1991** 719, 721-723
Persian Gulf war, **1990** 551-556, 767-782
Russia
summit with Yeltsin, **1992** 519-531
U.S. aid, **1992** 255-265, 519-521
Somalian aid, **1992** 1067-1072

Soviet Union
address on end of, **1991** 811-812
Washington summit with Gorbachev, **1990** 331-350
UN praised in address, **1990** 629, 646-651
Vietnam relations, **1995** 473
war powers debate, **1990** 663-679
funerals
eulogy for Ronald Reagan, **2004** 320
Hirohito funeral, **1989** 100, 102-103
Iran-contra affair
on North and Poindexter, **1986** 1050
pardon of Weinberger, **1992** 1073-1079
role in, **1989** 393-395; **1994** 8-9, 16
Marshall resignation, **1991** 377-379
National Rifle Association resignation, **1995** 208-211
Pakistan, earthquake relief efforts, **2005** 479
on peace dividend, **1989** 662
Pearl Harbor fiftieth anniversary, **1991** 775-784
Persian Gulf War, **1995** 55, 59-60
address to nation, **1991** 20-22
Geneva Talks, **1991** 16-17
letter to Hussein, **1991** 17-18
victory speech, **1991** 121-128
PRC repression of prodemocracy demonstrations, **1989** 275, 277-278, 281-286
presidential inaugurals
bicentennial celebration, **1989** 125, 133-135
inaugural address, **1989** 41-48
at inauguration of George W. Bush, **2001** 95
presidential pardons, **2001** 90
presidential transition period, **2000** 1027-1028
Reagan assassination attempt, **1981** 352, 358-359
Reagan presidential library dedication, **1991** 735-738
Reagan transfer of power, **1985** 491, 494, 495
regulatory reform, **1992** 469
regulatory relief task force, **1981** 492
Republican Party convention, **2000** 509
riots after Rodney King beating, **1992** 407-429
Rushdie death threat, **1989** 95-98
school prayer amendment, **1984** 241
Soviet relations
Akhromeyev meeting, **1989** 440
Chernenko meeting, **1984** 145, 149
Gorbachev meetings, **1985** 274; **1988** 927-929
Malta summit with Gorbachev, **1989** 643-645, 647-648, 650-660
Soviet changes, **1989** 175-176, 179-181
space exploration, on *Discovery* success, **1988** 796
State of the Union addresses, **1990** 49-62; **1991** 35-49; **1992** 55-68
Sununu resignation as Chief of Staff, **1991** 769-773
Supreme Court
appointments, **1990** 615-628; **1991** 551-615; **1992** 553
praise for Justice Brennan, **1990** 616
terrorism, **1984** 934
military response to, **1989** 317, 320
Munich killings of Israeli athletes, UN resolution, **1972** 751-754
U.S. hostages in Lebanon, **1989** 317, 319-320
trade policy
Enterprise for the Americas Initiative, **1992** 64
General Agreement on Tariffs and Trade, **1990** 87
Japanese trade talks, **1992** 12, 14-15, 17-18
NAFTA, **1992** 64; **1993** 954
Soviet Union, **1990** 331-332, 336-337
trade mission to Japan, **1992** 11-22
tsunami relief effort, **2005** 992
volunteerism summit, **1997** 40, 238-239, 240-241
on Watergate, **1973** 500
Bush, George W.
agricultural policy, farm bill and agricultural subsidies, **2002** 450
budget deficit, promises to cut in half, **2005** 78-79, 143
cabinet during second term, **2005** 44-45
cabinet nominations, **2001** 96-97; **2004** 778-779
campaign finance reform, **2002** 38
campaigns and elections
California voters, **2003** 1006
Hispanic voters, **2003** 350
midterm campaign speech, **2002** 818-829
presidential, **2000** 520, 609, 618
Florida recount, **2000** 999-1024
presidential debates, **2000** 797-810, 817-832
presidential victory speech, **2000** 1025, 1030-1033
See also below presidential elections
communications policy, **2004** 626-638
"compassionate conservatism," **2000** 508
defense policy
ABM treaty, **2001** 281-282, 516, 894
notice of withdrawal from, **2001** 927-934; **2002** 276
chemical and biological weapons, **2001** 516, 677
confronting an "axis of evil," **2002** 33-34, 40-41, 56, 612, 614, 635, 714, 732; **2003** 19, 875, 1025, 1219; **2004** 867; **2005** 579
Global Threat Reduction Initiative, **2004** 326-327
Iran nuclear weapons program, **2003** 1027
military restructuring, **2001** 181-182
missile defense system, **2000** 680-681; **2001** 281-289, 739-740; **2002** 1026-1031; **2003** 817-823; **2004** 176-185
NATO expansion, **2004** 135-141
North Korean relations, **2003** 592-598
Nuclear Nonproliferation Treaty, **2005** 931, 933-934
nuclear weapons, **2003** 904-905
Proliferation Security Initiative, **2004** 323, 324
and Russian nuclear facilities, **2001** 7, 21-22
Russian-U.S. nuclear arms control treaty, **2002** 275-286
September 11 terrorist attacks, **2001** 614-623, 624-630; **2003** 546
small arms trade, **2001** 516-518
UN address on terrorist threat, **2003** 19-20
UN peacekeeping missions, criticism of, **2001** 820-821
war on terrorism, **2001** 637-649; **2003** 29-32
weapons of mass destruction, **2002** 437-445; **2003** 19
domestic and social policy

Bush, George W *Continued*
abortion
abortion pill controversy, **2000** 781
counseling, funding ban for overseas programs, **2001** 127-131; **2005** 52
opposition to, **2000** 429; **2002** 223
partial-birth abortion ban, **2003** 1000-1001
affirmative action, **2002** 973; **2003** 359-360
death penalty
McVeigh execution, **2001** 433
support of, **2005** 179, 798
end-of-life care, Schiavo case intervention, **2005** 154
faith-based initiatives, **2001** 95, 132-140, 174, 178-179, 420-421; **2002** 37, 406-407, 823; **2003** 27-28; **2004** 29
gay marriage, **2003** 401-402, 405-406; **2004** 21; **2005** 79, 85
gun control and ballistic "fingerprinting," **2002** 961-962
hate crimes legislation, **2000** 161
immigration policy, **2001** 764-771; **2005** 79, 83
Prisoner Re-Entry Initiative, **2004** 29-30
proposals, **2002** 36-38
public opinion, **2002** 877
retirement security, **2002** 43
Social Security reform, **2001** 173-174, 177, 182-183, 913-926; **2005** 41, 84-85, 111-120
private retirement accounts, **2004** 236-237; **2005** 77, 85, 123, 198
privatization, **2002** 105; **2004** 27
social values issues, **2004** 20-21
social welfare initiatives, **2003** 27-28
tobacco industry regulation, **2000** 557
economic policy
budget deficit, **2004** 20, 236; **2005** 78-79, 143
corporate governance, **2002** 392, 400
economic stimulus package, **2001** 663, 666-667
jobless recovery, **2003** 441-442, 445-446
national debt, **2001** 179
public opinion, **2005** 138
tax code reforms, bipartisan panel on, **2005** 83, 143
tax cut plans, **2001** 54-55, 171, 172-173, 179-181; **2002** 36-37, 878-879; **2003** 22-23, 25-26, 70
tax relief, **2001** 400-406, 666; **2002** 43; **2003** 69, 74; **2004** 19-20, 26
economic reports, **2002** 51-66; **2003** 68-74; **2004** 56-71; **2005** 137-144
education policy
education reform, **2003** 25
federal programs, **2001** 173, 176-177; **2005** 83
intelligent design, **2005** 1011
"No Child Left Behind" program, **2002** 42-43; **2004** 20, 26; **2005** 83
school prayer, **2000** 367
school vouchers, **2002** 406
energy policy, **2001** 213
alternative fuels for automobiles, **2003** 22, 27
energy conservation, **2005** 779
energy "crisis" in California, **2001** 182, 331, 332-334
national energy policy, **2002** 309; **2003** 1120
national policy, Bush task force on, **2001** 331-336; **2003** 1017-1018
omnibus energy bill impasse, **2003** 1014, 1017
environmental policy, **2001** 212-213, 217-219
Arctic National Wildlife Refuge, oil drilling, **2002** 824; **2003** 182, 1017; **2004** 670
arsenic levels in water, **2001** 212-215, 219-221, 541
Bridger-Teton National Forest, oil and gas drilling, **2004** 670
brownfields cleanup, **2001** 178
Clear Skies Initiative, **2002** 299, 894, 898-899; **2003** 27, 179-180; **2004** 666-667; **2005** 79, 83, 95, 98-99
global warming, **2001** 109-115, 215, 516, 677; **2002** 298-321; **2003** 861-873
Healthy Forests Initiative, **2003** 27, 181
industrial pollution, **2002** 894-905
Johannesburg summit, **2002** 595
national parks, **2001** 178, 216-217
new source review rules, **2004** 664-665
ocean protection, **2004** 605
foreign policy
Afghanistan
postwar period, **2003** 1089-1090
war against Taliban regime, **2001** 686-697
Africa
economic development, **2001** 504
five-nation tour, **2003** 453-454, 473-474, 770
Argentine financial crisis, **2002** 83
Bosnia peacekeeping mission, **2000** 141
Brazil
relations with, **2003** 7-8; **2005** 765-776
state visit, **2005** 767-768
China
American spy plane incident, **2001** 247-253
meetings with Hu Jintao, **2002** 852; **2005** 613, 615
U.S. relations, **2001** 738-745; **2003** 1179-1180
U.S. trade relations, **2000** 215
visits to, **2005** 613-614
Colombia
aid program, **2000** 844; **2002** 574
Plan Colombia, **2002** 574
Congo peacekeeping mission, **2003** 294
Cuba
Commission for Assistance to a Free Cuba, **2004** 246-257
Haiti political situation, **2001** 396
India-Pakistan dispute over Kashmir, **2002** 325-331
International Criminal Court, opposition to, **2003** 99, 101-102
trade sanctions, **2000** 266, 268-269
U.S. policy, **2002** 234-235, 236
cultural diplomacy, **2005** 579-588
European-U.S. relations, **2005** 582
German-U.S. relations, **2005** 874, 878-879
India-U.S. relations, **2005** 462-471
Iraq
abuses of Iraqi prisoners, **2004** 207-234
capture of Saddam Hussein, **2003** 1192, 1198-1199, 1221

confronting, **2002** 612-623
economic sanctions, **2000** 581; **2001** 851
elections, **2005** 944, 948, 951-952
reconstruction, **2005** 717
"regime change," **1998** 938; **2002** 35, 56, 484, 612-614, 713
security threat to U.S., **2001** 849-854; **2003** 19
sovereignty, **2003** 1189; **2004** 23-24, 402, 407-411
Iraq War
Iraq-Niger uranium sales allegations, **2003** 20-21, 876; **2005** 248-249, 699-700
justifications for, **2004** 24-25, 236, 480-481, 677, 713, 714
prospect of war, **2003** 18-20, 135-151; **2004** 713
speech from aircraft carrier *Abraham Lincoln,* **2003** 144
Israel
air strikes against Syria, **2003** 1202
disengagement policy, **2005** 530-531
meetings at Texas ranch with Sharon, **2005** 531, 536
West bank settlement, **2004** 303-304; **2005** 535-536
Kosovo peacekeeping mission, **2000** 141
Latin America, **2002** 779
Lebanon, Syrian troop withdrawal, **2004** 557
Liberia, **2003** 769-771
Libya
economic sanctions lifting, **2004** 168-175
U.S. relations, **2003** 1219
Middle East
promoting democracy in Arab lands, **2004** 628-629; **2005** 42-43, 164, 269, 581
state visit to, **2003** 196
Middle East peace
Geneva Accord, **2003** 1205
international "roadmap" for peace, **2003** 191-205, 1205-1208; **2004** 303
Middle East-U.S. Partnership Initiative, **2002** 483-484, 487; **2003** 957-959; **2004** 628-629; **2005** 272
North Korea
nuclear programs, **2004** 24
six-party talks, **2003** 1178; **2004** 871-872, 937; **2005** 604-611
U.S. relations, **2001** 267-278; **2002** 634
Northern Ireland peace negotiations, **2005** 509, 510
Pakistan, Musharraf's military role, **2004** 1011
Pakistan relations, **2002** 165-166, 168; **2004** 1011
Palestinian Authority, economic aid, **2005** 34
Palestinians
new leadership, **2002** 369-381
relations with Arafat, **2004** 301
Russia
Bush-Putin talks, **2001** 893, 895; **2003** 250; **2005** 305-306
relations with Putin, **2004** 570
U.S. relations, **2001** 892-893; **2003** 250
Rwandan genocide, **2000** 450
South Korea state visit, **2002** 732
Syria, economic sanctions against, **2004** 557-560
U.S. relations, **2003** 1209
Uzbekistan, "Strategic Partnership" agreement, **2005** 429
Venezuela coup attempt, **2002** 203-204, 206
Zimbabwe economic sanctions, **2003** 1116
funeral services
comments on death of John Paul II, **2005** 291
eulogy at Ronald Reagan state funeral, **2004** 320-322
remarks on Chief Justice Rehnquist, **2005** 551-557
health care policy
abstinence-only sex education, **2001** 458; **2004** 21, 29
AIDS initiative, **2003** 21-22, 453-454, 780-783; **2004** 432, 433-441; **2005** 51-53
AIDS prevention programs, **2002** 469-470, 473-474
coverage, **2001** 177-178
flu pandemic, U.S. preparations for combating, **2005** 747, 750-751
flu vaccine shortage, **2004** 641
health care system, **2003** 26-27; **2005** 143
for health insurance, **2002** 669; **2004** 983
health savings accounts, **2005** 143
HealthierUS initiative, **2002** 624, 626
medical records privacy, **2000** 1066; **2001** 485
Medicare reform, **2003** 23, 26, 1119-1128
mental health care, **2002** 268
nursing home staffing levels, **2002** 121
prescription drug benefit for seniors, **2002** 949-950; **2003** 23, 1119-1120; **2004** 20, 27; **2005** 143
prescription drug benefit reform, **2000** 131, 134; **2001** 713
SARS outbreak, **2003** 127
stem cell research, **2000** 667-668
opposition to federal funding for, **2002** 513; **2005** 79, 86, 317-539-546
tobacco control treaty, **2004** 284
inaugural address, **2001** 94-101; **2005** 41-49, 305, 582
critiques of, **2005** 43-44
Iraq war, "Plan for Victory" speeches, **2005** 838-839, 842-850
media policy, **2005** 644-655
Middle East Free Trade Area, **2003** 958
national security
aviation security, **2003** 720
commission on terrorist attacks testimony, **2004** 454-455
domestic surveillance without court warrants, **2005** 80, 958-969
Homeland Security Department, **2002** 36, 42, 530-545
intelligence agency reform legislation, **2004** 970, 971-972
national security strategy, **2002** 633-665
preemption doctrine, **2002** 633-665; **2003** 809-810, 905; **2004** 889
Project BioShield Act, **2004** 442-449
Project BioShield proposal, **2003** 30; **2004** 445
State of the Union address on, **2002** 33-34
terrorists, bin Laden denunciation of, **2004** 536
USA Patriot Act and, **2003** 607-611; **2005** 80

Bush, George W. *Continued*
presidential approval ratings, **2003** 18-19; **2004** 479; **2005** 41, 138, 567
presidential election (2000)
dispute and Florida recount, **2001** 94, 522-523; **2005** 305, 553
results, **2004** 773
presidential election (2004)
bin Laden denunciation of Bush, **2004** 536
campaign, **2004** 478-484, 773-778; **2005** 487
campaign issues
bioterrorism protection, **2004** 641
environment, **2004** 664
"moral values," **2004** 776
Vietnam-era service, **2004** 482
debates, **2004** 483, 675-708
"mandate" from the voters, **2005** 41
nomination acceptance speech, **2004** 493-501
results, **2004** 17, 478, 777-778
victory speech, **2004** 782-783; **2005** 77
Republican Party
convention acceptance speech, **2000** 521-523, 527-535
platform, **2000** 508
presidential candidate, **2000** 519
space programs
future of, **2003** 631, 633; **2004** 3, 9-16
speech at NASA on, **2004** 13-16
State of the Union addresses, **2001** 171-187; **2002** 33-48; **2003** 18-39; **2004** 17-30, 711
terrorist interrogation policy
detainees, denouncing use of torture, **2004** 340
as "enemy combatants", and Geneva Conventions, **2003** 310; **2004** 212-213, 336-337, 377
State of the Union addresses, **2001** 171-187; **2002** 33-48; **2003** 18-39; **2004** 17-34, 537, 711; **2005** 77-94
Supreme Court nominations, **2005** 41, 77, 79, 558-565, 814-815
trade policy
Asia-Pacific Economic Cooperation forum, protests against, **2004** 938
free trade, **2003** 741
trade negotiations, **2003** 744
tsunami disaster, U.S. response, **2004** 993-995
Bush, Jeb (Florida governor)
death penalty, **2000** 989
election reform, **2001** 527
energy exploration in Florida coastal waters, **2001** 338
Florida election process investigations, **2000** 1000
gubernatorial election, **2002** 235, 819-820, 822
at inauguration of George W. Bush, **2001** 95
Lott resignation, **2002** 972
Schiavo case intervention, **2005** 155, 156, 159
tsunami disaster relief, **2004** 994; **2005** 992
Bush, Laura
HealthierUS initiative, **2002** 624, 626
at Republican Party convention, **2000** 511; **2004** 484
at State of the Union address, **2002** 44
state visits
China, **2005** 614
Egypt, **2005** 166
stem cell research, **2004** 160
youth gang prevention initiative, **2005** 86
Bush, Neil, Silverado savings and loan affair, **1990** 818
Bush v. Gore, **2005** 553
Bush v. Lucas, **1992** 189-190, 194
Bush v. Vera, **1996** 368-387
Bushnell, Prudence, U.S. embassy security concerns, **1998** 556, 557
Business
See also Corporations; Industry; Investment, business capital
costs of air pollution control regulations, **1972** 253-258; **1981** 276-277
education role of, **1983** 419, 424; **1986** 816; **1988** 298
ethics in, and defense contractors, **1982** 87-89, 90-93
fixed investment, **2005** 147
integration of women into, **1977** 861, 864
inventories, **2005** 147
investment in, outlook for, **1987** 120, 124-125, 130-131, 133
job creation by
Carter program, **1978** 8, 13, 20-21, 65, 69, 99-100
Ford on, **1976** 13-14, 19, 30
management responsibilities of
John Paul II on, **1981** 695, 707-709
U.S. bishops on, **1984** 965-966
on minimum and subminimum youth wage, **1983** 785-790
minority, Carter proposals on assistance to, **1980** 51
and national security export controls, **1987** 29-30, 34-38, 41-42
organized crime as, **1986** 179-180, 210-213
price freezes impact on, in economic stabilization program, **1973** 703-705, 710-711
safety inspections of, with warrants, **1978** 339-353
takeovers and mergers, **1986** 971-972, 978
tax cuts for
Carter CEA on, **1981** 106, 135
in Ford economic plan, **1975** 17, 20, 25, 88, 104
trade secrets, FOIA exemption for, **1981** 394, 398
use of by CIA as cover, **1976** 255-256
Business, small
job creation by, Joint Economic Committee on, **1981** 305
role in U.S. economic growth, Democratic platform on, **1984** 585-586
support for, Republican platform on, **1984** 671-672
Business Roundtable (BRT), economic growth, **2002** 53
Business Week, on Milken's junk bonds, **1990** 252
Busing
See also School desegregation
to achieve racial balance
Florida constitutional amendment banning, **1972** 201-206, 260
moratorium on proposed by Nixon, **1972** 259-260, 269
Bussereau, Dominique, agricultural subsidies, **2005** 411

Bustamente, Cruz M., California gubernatorial recall election, **2003** 350, 577, 1006-1009
Buthelezi, Mangosuthu Gatsha, **1976** 677-678; **1992** 285-286
AIDS, death of family member, **2004** 429
and Zulu-based Inkatha Freedom Party, **1994** 247; **1995** 102; **1998** 758
human rights, **1990** 140
Butler, Lord, British prewar intelligence gathering, **2004** 718-719
Butler, R. Paul, planet explorations and discovery, **1999** 174, 176-177
Butler, Richard, UN weapons inspections in Iraq, **1997** 768-769; **1998** 936, 937; **1999** 147-148
Butler, Robert, on aging U.S. population, **2002** 194
Butler, Shelby, **1986** 41, 48
Butler v. Michigan, **1997** 454
Butterfield, Alexander P., on White House taping system, **1973** 697-701, 948; **1974** 24
Buttiglione, Rocco, European Commission cabinet nomination challenged, **2004** 202
Butts, Calvin O., III, **1995** 337
Butz, Earl L., **1973** 338, 427
Buyer, Steve (R-Ind.), House Judiciary Committee impeachment inquiry, **1998** 707-708
Buyoya, Pierre
Burundi presidential elections, **2003** 923
resigns as president, **2003** 924
Buzhardt, J. Fred, Jr.
Agnew plea bargaining, **1973** 828-830
memo to Watergate committee, **1973** 660
on White House taping system, **1973** 698
Bybee, Jay S., terrorist interrogation guidelines memo, **2004** 338, 343-346
Byelorussia
See also Belarus
Alma-Ata Declaration, **1991** 804-806
Commonwealth Pact, **1991** 803-804
Nuclear Arms Pact, **1991** 806-808
nuclear weapons, **1991** 787
Soviet Union restructuring plan, **1991** 532-533
U.S. expulsion of UN mission personnel, **1986** 267, 271
Bynon, Joseph P., **1973** 643
Byock, Ira, end-of-life care, **1997** 325
Byrd, Harry F., **1990** 42
Byrd, James, hate crime victim, **2002** 239
Byrd, Robert C. (D-W.Va.)
antidrug program, **1989** 501
appointment of Iran-contra committee, **1986** 1052
AWACS sale to Saudis, **1981** 788-793
Bork nomination, **1987** 719-720
charges against Torrijos, **1978** 179
Clean Air Act revisions, **1990** 716
Clinton impeachment trial, **1999** 17
at congressional bicentennial, **1989** 126-127
draft evader pardon, **1977** 97
line-item veto, **1997** 612; **1998** 420-421
Nixon pardon, **1974** 812
North and Poindexter, **1986** 1051
nuclear test ban treaty, **1999** 602
Reagan appropriations bill veto, **1981** 831
responses to Reagan State of the Union, **1984** 84; **1987** 107; **1988** 59
Rockefeller nomination, **1974** 709
SALT II debate, **1979** 967
Senate historian, **1998** 153
START talks, **1988** 355
Thomas confirmation hearings, **1991** 600-602
on Twenty-seventh Amendment, **1992** 440
on unfunded mandates, **1995** 143
U.S. Capitol bicentennial, **1993** 897
Byrd amendment, on Rhodesian chrome imports, **1976** 288, 291
Byrd v. Raines, **1997** 612
Byrne, David, cigarette labeling, **2001** 226
Byrne, W. Matthew, Jr.
dismissal of Pentagon Papers case, **1973** 537-542
offer of FBI director job, **1973** 538, 744-745
White House meeting, **1974** 208
Byrnes, James
"speech of hope," **1996** 655, 658
on U.S. joining the UN, **1985** 709
Byron, Beverly F. (D-Md.), **1987** 672
Byron, William H., **1986** 758, 764

C

CAB. *See* Civil Aeronautics Board
Cabana, Robert, **1998** 932
Cabell, Enos, **1986** 170
Cabinet
Carter administration reorganization, **1979** 561-562, 570-579
executive privilege claimed for members of, **1973** 338, 340-342
president's changes in size of, **1988** 873
Cabinet Committee on International Narcotics Control, world opium survey, **1972** 645-650
Cable News Network, Inc. v. Noriega, **1990** 721-725
Caceres-Collazo, Carlos, death of UN relief worker, **2000** 702
Cady, John R. , food safety agency, opposition to, **1998** 523
Cafardi, Nicholas P. , sexual abuse by priests, **2004** 87
Cafaro, Vincent, pretrial detention of, **1987** 492-496, 502-503, 507
CAFTA. *See* Central America Free Trade Agreement
Cahill, Mary Beth, Kerry presidential campaign, **2004** 480
CAIR. *See* Clean Air Interstate Rule
Cairo (Egypt), UN population conference, **1994** 721-725
Calder, Iain, libel suit against, **1984** 248, 253-256
Calder v. Bull, **2005** 371
Calder v. Jones, **1984** 247-248, 253-256
Caldera, Louis, Korean War massacre, army secretary on, **1999** 552-558
Caldwell, Earl, confidentiality of news sources, **1972** 507-509, 512-514
Caldwell, United States v. , **1972** 507-509, 512-519
Calero, Adolfo, **1987** 639
Calero-Toledo v. Pearson Yacht Leasing Co., **1993** 432, 435
Calfa, Marian, **1989** 637

Califano, Joseph A., Jr.
abortion funding, **1977** 409-410
Cabinet appointment, **1976** 879
Cabinet reorganization, **1979** 561
cancer-causing substances in the workplace, **1978** 633-641
Carter's welfare plan, **1977** 553, 564
House members' sexual misconduct, **1982** 730-731, 735-740; **1983** 727
national health plan, **1978** 543, 545
student drug testing, **2002** 427
swine flu, **1978** 669-670, 672
on teenage substance abuse, **2002** 178
Califano v. Goldfarb, **1977** 169-181
California
See also Los Angeles; San Diego; San Francisco; University of California
affirmative action (Proposition 209), **1996** 759-763; **1997** 183-194
Agricultural Labor Relations Board, creation of, **1975** 378, 381-385
air quality in Ventura, **1981** 275
ballot initiatives, **1999** 4
bilingual education initiative (Proposition 227),**1998** 313-319
budget deficit and shortfalls, **2003** 72, 1007
drug use survey, **1999** 464
employee pension plans, **2005** 198
energy "crisis," **2001** 55, 182, 331, 332-334; **2003** 1007, 1015; **2004** 416
English-only law, **1986** 959-962
farm labor law, **1975** 377-399
greenhouse gas emissions reduction, **2004** 832
gubernatorial recall election, **2003** 72, 350, 577, 850, 1005-1013
hazardous waste disposal in Lathrop, **1979** 782, 785, 791, 793, 799
high school certificates of proficiency, **1975** 692
human cloning research ban, **2002** 515-516
immigration (Proposition 187), **1994** 388-389; **1995** 563
medical use of marijuana (Proposition 215), **1996** 755-758; **2001** 325-330
morning-after pill controversy, **2003** 999
Native American population, **2003** 577
prison abuse scandal, **2004** 764
same-sex couples, spousal benefits, **2004** 37
same-sex marriages
ban, **2000** 158, 161; **2004** 37, 39
legislation vetoed, **2005** 863, 868
science textbooks and creation-evolution controversy, **1972** 843-844
sexual abuse by priests settlement, **2004** 87
stem cell research (Proposition 171), **2004** 157, 161-162
taxation and spending limits (Proposition 13), **1978** 397-402; **1999** 4
term limits (Proposition 140), **1997** 886-891
"three-strikes" law upheld, **2003** 983-984
welfare reform, **1999** 260-261
California v. Ramos, **1983** 710
California Coastal Commission, land-use regulation and beach access, **1987** 531, 533, 547-563
California Federal Savings and Loan v. Guerra, **1987** 17-27
California Highway Patrol (CHP), **1992** 426-427
California Overseas Bank, indictment of with Marcoses, **1988** 867-872
California United Homecare Workers, **2005** 489
Callaghan, James, at economic summits, **1977** 367; **1978** 533; **1979** 3-6
Calley, William L., Jr. , reversal of conviction of, **1974** 857-860
Callins v. Collins, **1994** 161-171
Callister, Marion J. , on ERA deadline extension, **1981** 923-924; **1982** 612
Calvert, Jack, **1983** 200
Cambodia
See also Kampuchea (Cambodia)
Clinton's UN address, **1993** 806, 813
conflict in
after Paris peace accords, **1973** 447, 450
Soviet support for Vietnamese, **1985** 708, 715
debt relief program, **2005** 407
fall of, **1975** 251, 302, 353, 356, 496
human rights in, **1988** 103-104
human trafficking, **2002** 343-344
Khmer Rouge demise, State Department on, **1998** 971-975
land mine casualties, **1995** 47, 48
Mayaguez seizure, **1975** 311-318
political settlement, **1991** 691-711
political situation after coup, State Department on, **1997** 639-646
self-determination for, Vietnam peace negotiations on, **1972** 870, 872, 875; **1973** 124, 131-132, 142-143
Senate POW/MIA report, **1993** 120-122, 124-125
UN peace plan, **1990** 561-569
UN report on refugees, **1991** 672-673
UN role in, **1995** 355
U.S. aid policy, **1974** 278, 281-283; **1975** 224, 227-228, 230; **1997** 640, 645
U.S. bombing in, **1973** 516, 525
House Judiciary Committee on, **1974** 728-730, 736-740, 742-744, 747-748
leaks to press on (1969),**1976** 159-165
Nixon on, **1973** 731-735
proposed article of impeachment on, **1974** 655, 660
Senate testimony on, **1973** 729-730
U.S. invasion of, Nixon on, **1977** 323, 342-343, 346-347
U.S. MIAs in
commission on, **1977** 214-215, 217
House report on, **1976** 925-936
U.S. military aid to, **1972** 59
Vietnamese invasion of, **1979** 184-186, 190
Camdessus, Michel
Asian financial crisis, **1997** 832-843; **1998** 722
plunge of U.S. dollar, **1985** 624
Russian economic crisis, **1998** 604
Camejo, Peter, **1976** 695
Cameroon
AIDS epidemic, **2002** 470
carbon dioxide eruption in, **1987** 61-77

John Paul II's visit to, **1985** 500, 504-509
Caminiti, Ken, steroid use in baseball, **2005** 213
Camp, Carter, **1973** 532
Camp David, Carter retreat for crisis of confidence speech, **1979** 559-560, 563-564
Camp David accords, **1978** 605-632
as betrayal of Arab cause, Castro on, **1979** 685
Democratic platform on, **1980** 762, 768
failure of, Fahd on, **1981** 634-635
framework for Egyptian-Israeli peace treaty, **1978** 605-606, 611, 614-615, 623-624; **1979** 223-224
framework for peace in Middle East, **1978** 605-606, 608-613, 616, 619-620, 622-623; **1980** 778, 790
negotiations' progress following, **1981** 631-632
Shamir on, **1983** 832
on Sinai return to Egypt, **1982** 337-344
and U.S. vote in UN on Israeli settlements, **1980** 236, 241-242
Campaign contributions. *See* Campaign financing
Campaign finance reform, **1996** 551, 553-554; **1997** 31, 33, 826-827; **1998** 50; **1999** 42, 56; **2002** 38
Campaign financing
attorney general investigations, **1997** 822-831; **1998** 890-902; **2000** 763
Chinese government and, **1998** 976
congressional hearings, **1997** 825-826
dairy industry, to Nixon's campaign, **1973** 948-949, 960, 963-964; **1974** 3-4, 6, 11-14
Democratic Party platform on, **2000** 615-616
disclosure of, **1975** 681-687; **1976** 71-74, 87-92, 104-108
federal candidates' use of personal wealth in, **1976** 72-73, 75, 85, 109-110
federal laws on, **1973** 549, 551; **1976** 71-111
foreign sources of, Watergate committee on, **1974** 604, 615
illegal
from corporations, Watergate prosecutor on, **1975** 654, 659, 662-663, 668-669, 684-687
in presidential campaigns (1972),**1974** 603-605, 613-614
issue ads restrictions, **2003** 1155, 1157, 1158, 1159
legislation, Supreme Court on, **2003** 1155-1172
limits on
Nixon proposals for, **1974** 215-218
Senate Watergate committee on, **1974** 614
linked to ITT antitrust settlement, **1972** 395-406
misuse of funds, censure of Wilson by House, **1980** 485-491
from PACs, **1988** 808-809
presidential elections, **1997** 21; **2004** 776-777
public, **1974** 215-219, 606, 615; **1976** 71-74, 92-98, 106-107, 110-111
for congressional elections, Carter proposal for, **1977** 199-201, 203-204
Rebozo's handling of, **1973** 898, 906, 975-977
secret funds
for break-in defendants, **1973** 501
of Republican finance committee, **1973** 413-414
"soft money" contributions ban, **2003** 1155-1156, 1159, 1160-1161
solicitation of, rules on, **1974** 612
spending limits, **1974** 614; **1976** 71-87, 105-110
Vesco investigation by SEC, **1973** 564
Campaign for Tobacco-Free Kids, **2000** 536; **2003** 263; **2004** 282
Campaign for Working Families, **2004** 40
Campaign practices
abuses of incumbent's power, **1974** 601-603, 610-613
espionage and sabotage, **1973** 549, 551; **1975** 653, 687-688
misuse of bank funds and plane for, Lance investigation, **1977** 626, 654, 658-660
Campaign reform
Democratic platform on, **1972** 587
Nixon on, **1973** 962-963; **1974** 215-220
Campbell, Alastair, British prewar intelligence on Iraq, **2003** 884
Campbell, Ben Nighthorse (R-Colo.)
BIA apology to Indians, **2000** 725
on Native American skeletal remains, **1989** 539-543
party switch, **2001** 377
Campbell, Carroll A., Jr. (R-S.C.)
education goals, **1990** 54, 154-163
education summit, **1989** 561-562
national standards for educational testing, **1992** 46-47, 48-49
South Carolina abortion bill, **1990** 217
Campbell, John, **1989** 215
Campbell, Keith, cloning research, **1997** 213, 214-215
Campbell, Kim, at economic summit (Tokyo), **1993** 541-557
Campbell, William, nicotine levels in cigarettes, **1994** 214-217
Campeau, Robert, **1990** 253
Campolo, Tony, churches and volunteers, **1994** 49; **1997** 243
Campos, Roel C. , accounting board nominations, **2002** 1034
Canada
acid rain report, causes and remedies, **1983** 197-210
antismoking laws, **1988** 311-312
Caribbean economic aid from, **1982** 180, 186
chemical warfare study, **1982** 237, 257
constitutional reform in, **1981** 813-822; **1982** 317-323; **1984** 408, 411-412
defense missile system, **2004** 181
economic summits, **1976** 425; **1978** 533, 536, 538; **1981** 591; **1982** 469; **1983** 507-514
Houston, **1990** 467-482
Munich, **1992** 637-648
emigration from to U.S., **1981** 606, 615
gay marriage legislation, **2004** 42; **2005** 869
inter-American dialogue, **1983** 375
John Paul II's visit, **1984** 777-787
land route for Alaska pipeline, **1972** 272, 280-282
liberalism in, **1984** 409-412
nuclear materials sale to India, **1975** 361
as oil supplier, increased world interest in, **1981** 800
ozone depletion, **1992** 79-80
poverty summit, **1981** 770
Quebec independence, **1998** 592-598

Canada *Continued*
Quebec separatism, **1976** 855-862; **1980** 401-410; **1990** 367-372
SARS (severe acute respiratory syndrome) outbreak, **2003** 123, 124, 132
smoking report, **1992** 267-275
student test scores, **1992** 90
U.S. boundary dispute, **1985** 638
U.S. invasion of Grenada, **1983** 850
U.S. relations, **1984** 408-409, 411-412
U.S. trade agreement, **1988** 392, 396, 571-578
Canady, Charles T. (R-Fla.)
affirmative action programs, **1995** 485; **1998** 856-857
gay rights legislation, **1996** 286
House Judiciary Committee impeachment inquiry, **1998** 706
same-sex marriages, **1996** 688
school prayer amendment, **1995** 548
Canary Capital Partners, mutual funds scandal, **2003** 694, 700-706
Cancer
alcohol consumption and, **1982** 508, 516
among minorities, **1985** 685-687, 689, 696-697
deaths, **2001** 867
declining, NCI report on, **1996** 790-793
diet
broccoli study and, **1992** 277-281
carcinogens in, **1996** 71-79
for reduced risk of, **1982** 507-520; **1992** 277-281
as a disease of interactions, **1978** 634, 642, 649-650
health care for patients, presidential panel on, **2001** 867-879
interferon as treatment for, **1986** 481-485
physical fitness and, **1989** 613-617
smoking linked to, surgeon general's report, **2004** 288-290
women and smoking, **2001** 232-233
workplace exposure to substances causing, **1978** 633-651
Cancer, breast
hormone replacement therapy and risk of, **2002** 506
mammograms for diagnosis of, **1997** 142-149; **2001** 869-870; **2002** 265, 510
mortality rates, **1996** 791-793; **1997** 142
report, **1993** 905-922
rescue of South Pole doctor, **1999** 611-613
support groups for women, **2001** 869
treatment with drug tamoxifen, **1998** 194-202
Cancer, lung
mortality rates, **1996** 791-793
radon exposure and, **1988** 3-4, 6-8
and smoking, **1985** 809, 811-813, 816; **1986** 1081; **1988** 311-312
of cigarettes, **1972** 50-51; **1982** 163-169
damage suits, **1992** 563-573
health care costs, **1985** 616-617
from involuntary smoking, **1986** 1082, 1084-1085
of low-tar cigarettes, **1981** 3-4, 6-8; **1982** 164, 168
marijuana smoking, **1982** 204-205, 207-208
secondhand smoke, EPA report on, **1993** 63-69
and women, **1980** 17, 20-22; **2001** 232
urban air pollution and, **1972** 775-781
Cancer, prostate, screening and treatment, **2001** 870; **2002** 265
Cancer, skin, as effect of ozone layer reduction, **1973** 235-244; **1975** 438-439, 442; **1992** 82
Cancer, thyroid, from nuclear testing fallout, **1997** 591-601
Cannon, Christopher B. (R-Utah) , House Judiciary Committee impeachment inquiry, **1998** 712
Cannon, Lou, **1988** 392
Cannon v. University of Chicago, **1992** 189, 190, 191-192, 194-195, 198
Canseco, Jose, steroid use in baseball, congressional testimony on, **2005** 213-214, 218-219
Cantwell v. Connecticut, **1992** 546
Cape Krusenstern National Monument, **1978** 736-737
Capellas, Michael D. , WorldCom collapse, **2002** 395; **2003** 333, 334
Capital gains taxes
Bush advocates, **1991** 75; **1992** 56-57, 63
in McGovern's economic program, **1972** 737-740
reducing rate for, Bush on, **1989** 72, 75
Capital punishment/Death penalty
Amnesty International on, **1988** 883; **1989** 597; **1990** 131, 138
Blackmun opposition to, **1994** 161-171
Brennan opposition to, **1985** 664-666
Bureau of Justice Statistics report on, **2004** 794-805
Catholic teaching on, **1995** 146-147, 152-153; **1999** 830
in China, **1993** 560
constitutionality of, **1972** 499-505; **1977** 518
death row prisoners appeals, **1983** 707-723; **1993** 141-152
as deterrent, Republican platform on, **1980** 568, 594
discrimination against minorities, **2000** 990
in drug cases, **1986** 842
enemy combatant cases and, **2003** 113
EU membership and, **2002** 910
fairness of, Supreme Court on, **2001** 387-394; **2005** 555
humane and uniform standards for imposing, **1982** 51-63
indigents' right to psychiatric aid, **1985** 207-219
jurors opposed to, **1986** 445-456
Justice Department report on, **1999** 828-835; **2000** 988-998
for juveniles, **2002** 357-358; **2004** 797
Supreme Court on, **2005** 177-196, 555
mandatory, and mitigating factors, **1978** 495-514
for mentally retarded prohibited, **2001** 388, 391-394; **2002** 353-368; **2005** 177, 555
Moral Majority on, **1983** 818
moratorium, **2002** 353-355
in Nigeria, hanging of dissidents, **1995** 696-699
number of executions, **2004** 804-805; **2005** 178
declining, **2004** 794-795
one thousandth in U.S., **2005** 178
as political campaign issue, **1988** 723, 736-737, 754
public opinion on, **1983** 711
racial bias or discrimination in, **1987** 463-476; **2001** 387-394; **2002** 358-359

Rehnquist position on, **1990** 311-317; **2005** 552
restoration of, Nixon on, **1973** 305-306, 325-326
in South Africa
constitutional ban, **1996** 251
court ruling on, **1995** 283-287
state legislation, **1972** 500; **1976** 917-919; **2004** 800-801
constitutionality, **1977** 518
mandatory or discretionary, **1976** 489-507
for rape, **1977** 517-528
for terrorist acts, **1974** 43, 60
for Timothy McVeigh, for Oklahoma City bombing, **1997** 626; **2001** 387, 390, 433-437
unconstitutional, **2002** 355-356
in U.S., UN report on, **1998** 183-193
U.S. military tribunals, **2001** 629
World Court and, **2005** 181-182
Capitalism
criticism of by John Paul II, **1981** 696, 706-709; **1988** 165-166, 168-169, 174
PRC constitution on, **1978** 159
shortcomings of, Brezhnev on, **1976** 143, 152; **1977** 747-748, 754; **1981** 232-233
triumph of, Reagan on, **1989** 6, 16, 20
Capitol (U.S.)
bicentennial, **1993** 893-904
service for slain Capitol policemen, **1998** 510-517
Capitol Square Review v. Pinette, **1995** 385, 387, 396-404
Caplan, Arthur, medical errors, **2003** 851
Capps, Thomas E. , national energy policy, **2001** 337
Capps, Walter (D-Calif.) , death of, **1998** 41
CAPPS II system. *See* Computer Assisted Passenger Prescreening System (CAPPS II) program
Caramanlis, Constantine, **1975** 354
Carbohydrates, dietary guidelines on, **2005** 12
Carbon dioxide
gas eruption in Cameroon, **1987** 61-77
increased levels of, and climate change, **1988** 861-864
Card, Andrew H., Jr.
Bush reelection campaign and, **2004** 775
FDA drug safety review system, **2004** 854
and Hurricane Andrew, **1992** 534, 844
as White House chief of staff, **2005** 45
Card, David, minimum wage, **1996** 564
Cardenas Ramirez, Blandina, **1983** 915
Cardin, Benjamin (D-Md.)
Democratic Party agenda, **2005** 81
and Gingrich ethics violations case, **1997** 17-19
Cardiopulmonary resuscitation, physicians' informing patients about, **1984** 276, 281-285
Cardiovascular disease
See also Heart disease
and involuntary smoking, **1986** 1086
and smoking, **1985** 616-617; **1986** 1082
Cardoso, Fernando Henrique
Brazil economic situation, **2002** 775; **2003** 3
IMF loan, **2003** 6
Careerism, vs. liberal arts in undergraduate colleges, **1986** 940, 943-944, 949
Carey, Hugh L. (D-N.Y.)
IRA prison hunger strike, **1981** 402, 404
New York City blackout, **1977** 546-547
New York City fiscal crisis, **1975** 862, 866-867, 869; **1977** 568
regulation of oil exploration, **1975** 168
Carey, Mary, California gubernatorial recall election, **2003** 1008
Carey, Ron
statement on UPS strike, **1997** 631-634
Teamsters union president ousted, **1997** 628, 630-631
Carey v. Piphus, **1992** 193
Carey v. Population Services International, **1992** 594
Carhart, LeRoy, abortion rights, **2000** 431; **2003** 998
Carhart et al. v. Ashcroft, **2003** 1002
Caribbean
Cuban-Soviet presence in, **1982** 83, 180, 187-188
Democratic platform on, **1984** 640
Hurricane Hugo's impact on, **1989** 667-668, 670
Republican platform on, **1984** 709
smoking in the America's, **1992** 267-275
U.S. military presence in, **1979** 763-764, 768
Caribbean Basin Initiative, **1982** 83, 179-190; **1983** 78; **1984** 40-41
Carifa, John D. , mutual funds scandal, **2003** 696
Carjackings, **1999** 616
Carlin, George, broadcast of offensive material, **1978** 515-531; **1986** 732
Carlson, Arne, **1993** 486
Carlsson, Ingvar, **1988** 348; **1999** 861
Carlucci, Frank C.
military base closings, **1988** 951-952
NSC appointment, **1986** 1049; **1987** 208
SDI strategy, **1988** 325
U.S. downing of Iranian airliner, **1988** 705-717
Carmona, Pedro, Venezuela transitional government, **2002** 203
Carmona, Richard H.
obesity, countering, **2003** 480-491
prescription drug importation, **2004** 985
smoking, health consequences of, **2004** 280-298
Carnahan, Jean (D-Mo.)
midterm election defeat, **2002** 36, 821
senatorial election, **2000** 907; **2001** 97
Carnahan, Mel (Missouri governor)
death of, **2001** 97; **2002** 821
Midwest floods, **1993** 486
Carnal Knowledge, as obscene material, **1974** 515-519
Carneal, Michael, **1998** 736-737
Carnegie Commission on the Future of Public Broadcasting, report of, **1979** 119-134
Carnegie Corporation, Forum on Education and the Economy, on teaching profession, **1986** 457-478
Carnegie Endowment for International Peace
Democracy and Rule of Law Project, **2005** 44
South African sanctions, **1990** 67
Carnegie Foundation for the Advancement of Teaching
on education reform, **1983** 415
on higher education, **1985** 583-602
international math and science test, **1992** 85-96
on undergraduate colleges, **1986** 939-958
on urban school crisis, **1988** 195-219

Carothers, Robert L., on college drinking, **2002** 176
Carothers, Thomas, on war on terrorism, **2005** 44
Carpenter, David, in insider trading case, **1987** 882, 884, 886
Carpenter v. United States, **1987** 881-889
Carr, Michael H.
  Galileo imaging team, **1997** 204
  water on Mars, reaction to possibility of, **2000** 380-382
Carrasco, Gilbert Paul, **1987** 255
Carrie, Elliott, on crime rates, **1999** 615
Carrillo, Santiago, on Communist Party in Spain, **1976** 434, 450-455
Carrington, Lord
  Falklands war, **1982** 285; **1983** 4-22
  Zimbabwe independence, **1979** 939, 941; **1980** 335
Carroll, John, **1989** 619-623
Carroll, Ted, Hartford school privatization, **1994** 410
Carroll v. President and Commissioners of Princess Anne, **1994** 316, 317
Carroll v. United States, **1982** 425-526
Cars. *See* Automobile industry; Automobile safety; Automobiles
Carswell, G. Harrold, **1987** 717, 726; **1994** 164
Cartagena group, **1984** 795
Carter, Ashton B., **1984** 258
Carter, Billy
  Libyan contacts of, Justice Department investigation, **1980** 907-917
  peanut warehouse investigation, **1979** 801-803, 805-807
Carter, H. E., **1973** 781
Carter, Hodding, III, on Iran situation, **1978** 714-716
Carter, Jimmy
  administration
    accomplishments of
      Carter on, **1981** 57-104
      Mondale on, **1980** 772-773, 787-791
    advisers, government experience of, **1976** 805-806
    civil service reform, **1978** 137-138, 137-148, 140-148
    crisis of confidence speech, **1979** 559-560, 562-569, 574, 576
    fireside chats
      on energy and the economy, **1977** 103-112
      on Panama Canal treaties, **1978** 178, 181-187
    Ginsburg appointment to Appeals Court, **1993** 392
    judicial appointments, **1987** 52
    Lance resignation, **1977** 625, 627-628, 675-685
    political dismissal of U.S. attorney, **1978** 51-53, 61-64
    public broadcasting, **1979** 119, 122
    public broadcasting editorials, **1984** 449, 454
    radio call-in program, **1977** 183-188
    Vance resignation, **1980** 475-476
    White House staff appointments process, **1976** 854
    Young's resignation, **1979** 648-649, 652, 654, 656
  assets of on taking office, **1977** 28, 33-34
  budget
    defense of at Democratic conference, **1978** 765-766, 769-771
    revisions, **1977** 125-129
  budget messages, **1978** 95-102; **1979** 9-17; **1980** 109-121
  Cabinet
    appointments, **1976** 846, 850-851, 877-880, 883-885
    reorganization, **1979** 561-562, 570-579
  campaigns and elections
    1980 campaign, **1984** 648
    1980 party platform, **1984** 550
    acceptance speeches, **1976** 595-604; **1980** 771-783
    activities curtailed by hostage crisis, **1979** 879
    campaign funds investigated, **1979** 801-802, 806, 809-812
    concession statement, **1980** 959-960, 962-963
    debates
      with Ford, **1976** 693-719, 733-757, 797-821
      with Reagan, **1980** 919-951
    Democratic Party platform, **1976** 543
    Democratic Party's midterm conference, **1978** 765-775
    federal election system reform, **2001** 526
    nomination battle with Kennedy, **1980** 701-702, 709, 711-712, 771-772, 774
    Reagan-Anderson debate, **1980** 847-849
    reform proposals, **1977** 199-205
    Republican convention view of, **1984** 663-725, 727-729, 743
    town meetings of, **1977** 185
    victory statement, **1976** 841-843
  at Clinton's inaugural, **1993** 131
  death penalty for juveniles opponent, **2005** 179
  defense policy, **1980** 29, 39, 44, 86-96
    arms control, UN speech on, **1977** 737-745
    arms sales, **1978** 105-109
    B-1 bomber cancellation, **1977** 529-533
    draft evader pardon by, **1977** 95-99
    draft registration, **1981** 522-523
    intelligence agencies restricted under, **1981** 83, 861
    MIAs, **1977** 207-209
    NATO, U.S. support for, **1978** 373-376
    NSC under, **1987** 212, 215
    SALT II
      deferring action, **1979** 418, 967
      negotiations, **1977** 243-245, 250-256; **1978** 549
      ratification urged, **1979** 415, 454-461, 463, 465-466, 764-765, 769-770
      signing, **1979** 413-415
    SALT II, efforts to rally support for, **1978** 550-567
    warplanes sales in Middle East, **1978** 125-127, 129-131
  Democratic Party convention speech, **2004** 483
  domestic policy
    abortion, federal funds for, **1977** 409-410
    legal and medical professions, **1978** 327-338
    National '80s Agenda, **1981** 39-40
    national health plan, **1978** 543-547
    proposals, **1980** 28, 36-38, 41-86

social program proposals, **1980** 42-43, 57-71
Social Security reform proposals, **1977** 377-381
urban policy proposals, **1978** 241-258
welfare reform plan, **1977** 551-565; **1979** 389-395
welfare reform plan, women's opposition to, **1977** 866-867
economic policy, **1980** 37, 39, 45-52
anti-inflation program, **1978** 533-537, 683-684, 686-693, 686-697; **1980** 243-257
CEA reports, **1978** 65-93; **1979** 81-117; **1980** 159-171; **1981** 105-115
Chrysler loan guarantee, **1979** 693-695
dollar value, program to strengthen, **1978** 683, 697
dollar-strengthening moves, **1978** 683-686, 697-698
economic growth projected by, Joint Economic Report on, **1977** 717, 726-727
Federal Reserve Board action to restrain credit and fight inflation, **1979** 771-774, 776-780
IMF-World Bank meeting, **1978** 659-663
IMF-World Bank speech, **1977** 687-691
inflation and, **1998** 501
multilateral trade negotiations, completion of, **1979** 637-644
"October Surprise" report, **1993** 3-16
economic summits, **1977** 367; **1979** 3-4, 6-7; **1980** 503-504
Education Department, creation of, **1979** 157-161
energy policy
coal miners' strike settlement, **1978** 111-124
oil price decontrol and windfall profits tax, **1979** 319-320, 323-324
OPEC oil price increase, **1979** 253, 258-259
program, **1977** 277-292; **1978** 533-537
Three Mile Island nuclear accident, **1979** 824, 826, 861-863
environment, rejection of bubble concept, **1984** 427
environmental policy
Alaskan lands, preservation of, **1978** 731-734
population and environment study, **1980** 665, 667
water policy, **1978** 385-395
ethics standards, **1977** 27-34, 625, 676, 681-683
farewell address, **1981** 31-37
Federal Emergency Management Agency, **1992** 533
foreign policy
Amin's message to, **1977** 143-148
Australia, apology to for Skylab, **1979** 553, 558
Belgium visit, **1977** 897, 900
Bosnia cease-fire negotiations, **1995** 719
Bosnia mission, **1994** 552
Brazil, on human rights and nuclear proliferation, **1978** 269-270, 272-280
China relations, **1997** 95
China-Taiwan relations, **2003** 1180
Cuban refugees in Mariel boatlift, policy on, **1980** 337-350
Cuba-U.S. relations, **2002** 232-238
developing countries, cooperation of industrialized countries with, **1978** 269-270
El Salvador, control of aid for, **1981** 242
France visit, **1977** 897, 900
Geneva Accord (for Middle East peace), **2003** 1204
Haiti, **1994** 437-438
human rights emphasis in, **1977** 4; **1980** 35-36, 39, 44-45, 99-100, 194-195, 479; **1981** 179; **1986** 97; **1990** 728
human rights issues, **2002** 637
Iran
revolution in, and support for shah, **1978** 699-716
Rushdie death threat, **1989** 98
visit to, **1977** 897-900, 913-918
Iran, American hostages in
agreement on, and frozen assets of Iran, **1981** 559, 561-568
attempted rescue of, **1980** 351-354
effect on election outcome, **1981** 145
farewell address on, **1981** 36-37
negotiations for release of, **1980** 999-1000, 1007-1009
nullification of claims against Iran, **1981** 559-573
release of, **1981** 138, 145-147, 156-158
taking of, **1979** 867-884
Latin American policy of, Vance on, **1979** 713-721
in Liberia, **1978** 271
Libya, brother's contacts with, **1980** 907-917
Mexico meetings with López Portillo, **1979** 169-181
Middle East, U.S. sales of warplanes in, **1978** 125-134
in Nigeria, on conflicts in Africa, **1978** 269-271, 281-287
North Korea, **1994** 603, 608
Panama Canal, **1992** 650
transfer ceremony, **1999** 850-855
treaties, benefits of, **1977** 592-593
treaty ratification, **1978** 177-178, 180-190
treaty signing, **1977** 591-594
Poland
Soviet intervention in, **1980** 795, 802; **1987** 184
visit, **1977** 897-913
PRC relations, **1984** 24
aviation, textiles, and shipping agreements, **1980** 829-833
invasion of Vietnam, **1979** 185
normalization of, **1978** 781-785
scientific and cultural agreements, **1979** 135-143, 149-151, 153-154
U.S. goals in, **1979** 669-678
Saudi Arabia
restraint on oil prices, **1976** 938
visit, **1977** 897, 900
South Korea, Park assassination, **1979** 896-897
Soviet diplomatic personnel, U.S. limits on, **1986** 268
Soviet relations, **1984** 811
after SALT II signing, **1979** 454-461
combat troops in Cuba, **1979** 763-770
invasion of Afghanistan, **1979** 966-967, 970-972, 976-977; **1980** 27-33, 40, 84, 86-87
Sakharov exile, **1980** 105
and Soviet buildup, **1978** 223-240

Carter, Jimmy *Continued*
Taiwan treaty, termination of, **1979** 917-938
Venezuela
coup attempt negotiations, **2002** 201, 205, 983
referendum on the presidency, **2004** 549, 550
visit to Cuba, **2002** 232-238, 983
Guantanamo Bay prison, **2005** 450
Holocaust Museum, **1993** 308
on Hubert Humphrey, **1978** 3-4, 18-19
John Paul II meeting, **1979** 729
at Kennedy presidential library dedication, **1979** 813-819
Middle East peace
and Begin as prime minister, **1983** 834
Camp David accords, **1978** 605-607, 615-617, 619-624; **1979** 223-225
Egypt visit, **1977** 897-899, 902
Israeli-Egyptian peace treaty, **1980** 34, 39, 40, 94
Israeli-Palestinian Peace Accord, **1993** 748, 749, 761-762
negotiations, **1993** 748, 749
Sadat-Begin initiatives, **1977** 830, 849
UN vote on Israeli settlements, **1980** 235-242
minority status, commission on, **1988** 187
New York City blackout, **1977** 545, 547
New York City debt, **1976** 864
Nobel Peace Prize recipient, **2002** 232, 981-989
Playboy interview, **1976** 774, 787, 797, 800-801
presidential election (1980), **2004** 316, 317
presidential inaugural address, **1977** 89-93
press conferences, **1976** 845-854; **1988** 843
at Reagan presidential library dedication, **1991** 735-736, 744-746
State of the Union addresses, **1978** 7-19, 19-50; **1979** 19-28, 28-79; **1980** 27-102; **1981** 57-104
Sun Belt migration, **1981** 40
Thatcher election, **1979** 381
volunteerism summit, **1997** 238, 239, 240-241
Carter Center, referendum on Venezuelan president, **2003** 281-282; **2004** 550-551
Cartolini, Nestor Cerpa, Peruvian hostage leader, **1997** 235
Carver, Lord, representing UN in Rhodesia, **1977** 585
Carville, James, on Paula Corbin, **1997** 290
CASA. *See* National Center on Addiction and Substance Abuse
Casey, George W.
insurgency in Iraq, **2004** 877
U.S. forces in Iraq commander, **2004** 214
Casey, Mike, labor union organizer, **2005** 488
Casey, Robert P. (Pennsylvania governor), abortion rights, **1992** 590; **2003** 1001
Casey, William J.
business dealings, Senate investigation of, **1981** 855-859
CIA manual, **1984** 904-906
CIA terrorism report, **1981** 462
fatal illness of, **1994** 20
Iran-contra affair, **1986** 1016, 1018; **1987** 226, 232-233, 892; **1991** 652; **1994** 17
congressional oversight requirements, **1987** 896
covert operations, use of NSC for, **1987** 903, 906, 918
diversion of funds to contras, **1986** 1051; **1987** 894; **1989** 392, 394
North conviction, **1990** 493
secrecy within executive branch, **1987** 898, 923
mining of Nicaraguan ports, **1984** 340
"October Surprise" report, **1993** 4-5, 7, 10-11
Cash, Herman Frank, church bombing suspect, death of, **2002** 241
Casper, Gerhard, separation of powers, **1998** 911
Cassase, Antonio
Sudan war crimes, **2004** 594
UN International Commission of Inquiry on Darfur chair, **2005** 515
Cassell, Christine, end-of-life care, **1997** 325
Cassidy, Cardinal Edward Idris, Holocaust repentance report, **1998** 121-130
Cassini orbiter to Saturn, **2004** 6-7; **2005** 502
Casswell, Paul G. , Miranda warning, **2000** 386
Castaldi, David, sexual abuse by priests scandal, **2005** 867
Castano, Carlos
drug trafficking in Colombia, **2000** 841; **2002** 573
human rights violations in Colombia, **2003** 428
Castille, Ronald D., **1986** 241
Castle, Michael N. (R-Del.), **1998** 953
Castle Coalition, **2005** 364
Castor, Betty, **1992** 144
Castro, Fidel
CIA actions in Chile and, **1974** 806; **1975** 884-885, 892
CIA plot to assassinate, **1975** 401; **1984** 904
Senate investigation of, **1975** 710, 715-716, 725-756, 769-774, 778-780, 789-792
encounter with Clinton at Millennium Summit, **2000** 702
health of, **2004** 246
human rights in Cuba, **1984** 158
Lula da Silva's relations with, **2003** 7
Mariel boatlift of Cuban refugees, **1980** 337-350
Morales visit to Cuba, **2005** 770
at nonaligned nations' conference, **1979** 681-688
Pope John Paul II, death of, **2005** 291
Pope John Paul II, state visit to Cuba, **1998** 30-31
Soviet troops in Cuba, **1979** 764-765
support for Nicaragua, **1989** 163, 165-168
support for Salvadoran rebels, **1987** 640
tape-recorded congressional testimony, **1978** 912
U.S. agreement with on Cuban detainees, **1987** 929-930, 932-934
Venezuelan relations, **2002** 202
visit of Jimmy Carter, **2002** 232-238, 983
Cataracts, UV radiation and, **1992** 77, 81-82
Catastrophic illness. *See* Health insurance, catastrophic coverage
Caterpillar Tractor Co. , on Soviet pipeline sanctions, **1982** 881
Catholic Bishops' Conference (Ireland), **1992** 250
Catholic Church
See also Benedict XVI (pope); John Paul II (pope); Liberation theology; Vatican
in Africa, **1985** 499-514

and Argentine presidency, **1981** 184
in Canada, **1984** 777, 778
canon law code revised, **1983** 93-100
changes in practices of and clergy dissent, **1978** 596; **1988** 489-494
child sexual abuse by priests scandal, **1993** 407-411; **2002** 867-876; **2003** 523-543; **2004** 82-93; **2005** 8, 294, 865-867
on contraception, **1980** 871-873, 876-878, 880
Diplomatic Accord with Israel, **1993** 1033-1040
dissent in
Dutch, **1985** 363-367, 372-374
U.S. bishops on (1968),**1986** 759, 763-764
domestic partners' rights and, **1989** 307
economic questions, Pope's encyclical on, **1993** 229-241
evangelization, **1985** 773
in Far East, **1984** 327-338
Holocaust, or "Shoah", repentance, **1998** 121-130
homosexual rights laws, **1992** 723-730
homosexuals, pastoral care of, **1986** 909-911
in India, **1986** 23-25, 29-30
Jewish relations, **2005** 293
in Latin America, **1979** 726, 733; **1986** 639-649
lay participation, revised canon law on, **1983** 94-97
life-sustaining measures, **1975** 805-806, 814-815; **1976** 206-208
moral theology, Pope's encyclical on, **1993** 843-850
nuclear freeze, U.S. bishops on, **1982** 396, 885-901; **1983** 270
papal succession, **1978** 595-603
parochial schools and public aid, **1973** 643
in Poland, political role of, **1979** 725-728; **1981** 885; **1985** 119-121; **1987** 185-187; **1989** 524-528, 533
Pope John Paul II
"Day of Pardon" mass and visit to the Holy Land, **2000** 77-87
Denver visit, **1993** 659-669
funeral mass for, **2005** 290-298
twenty-fifth anniversary of reign of, **2003** 524
visit to U.S., **1987** 699-716
on reproductive technologies, **1987** 267-287
shortage of priests, **2005** 294
Spanish democratic constitution and, **1978** 810, 815
stem cell research, opposition to, **2005** 317
in Switzerland, **1984** 399-406
U.S.
as affected by Vatican II, **1985** 571-581
dissent in, John Paul II on, **1987** 699-701, 708-710
history of, **1989** 619-623
visit of John Paul II, **1987** 699-716
Vatican synod of bishops, on Vatican II, **1985** 765-780
in Western Europe, liberalism in, **1986** 909
women in, **1983** 95; **1985** 766, 777; **1986** 985; **1987** 701, 712-713, 715; **1988** 785-792
Catholic clergy
celibacy for, John Paul II on, **1979** 725, 729, 754-755
collegiality among, **1985** 766, 775-776
disciplining of, **1986** 757-765
dissent among U.S., **1986** 985-986
duties and mission of, **1984** 400, 402-406
female priests ban, **1994** 276-280
political activism of, **1979** 725, 727-728, 734, 736
John Paul II on, **1980** 967-970; **1986** 640, 647-648
in U.S., **1986** 318, 910-911
Vatican views on, **1980** 411-413, 416; **1984** 759-775; **1986** 317-319, 333, 335-338
sexual abuse by priests, **1992** 507-518; **1993** 407-411
U.S. bishops on economic policies, **1984** 957-972; **1986** 983-1011
Catholic Conference (U.S.) , on political asylum decision, **1987** 255
Catholic University of America, Vatican disciplining of Father Curran, **1986** 757-765
Caulfield, John J., **1974** 601
Causey, Richard A. , Enron Corp. fraud case, **2004** 416
Cavallo, Domingo, Argentine monetary policy, **2002** 81, 83
Cavazos, Lauro F.
education goals, **1990** 154, 155
education secretary, lack of leadership, **1991** 219
education secretary appointment, **1988** 892
Cavic, Dragan, Bosnia-Herzegovina constitutional reform, **2005** 858-859
Cavoli, Richard, **1986** 41, 47
CBO. *See* Congressional Budget Office
CBS. *See* Columbia Broadcasting System
CCSSO. *See* Council of Chief State School Officers
CDC. *See* Centers for Disease Control and Prevention
CDF. *See* Children's Defense Fund
CEA. *See* Council of Economic Advisers
Ceausescu, Nicolae
on Communist Party in Romania, **1976** 435, 452-455
execution of, **1989** 635, 709, 711-712
on population expansion in developing countries, **1974** 778
Cedras, Raoul, **1993** 454
CEECs. *See* Central and Eastern European countries
CELAM. *See* Latin American Bishops Council
Celebrex, drug safety, **2004** 640, 852-853, 855
Celeste, Richard F., **1990** 289-291
Cell line, defined, **1987** 354, 356-357
Cendant, WorldCom accounting fraud case settlement, **2004** 418
Censorship
daytime broadcast of offensive material, **1978** 515-531
decency standards in the arts, **1998** 405-418
Internet censorship in China, **2005** 619-620
Rushdie death threats, **1989** 95-98; **1998** 687-691
school book banning, **1982** 567-585
student newspaper censorship, **1988** 37-46
Census Bureau (U.S.)
access to federal tax returns, **1975** 849-850, 853-854
aging of U.S. population, **1996** 296-301
birth expectation decline, **1972** 301
census proclamation, **1990** 169-174
data confidentiality, Court on, **1982** 171-178
foreign-born population, **1995** 563-569

Census Bureau (U.S.) *Continued*
health insurance coverage, **1994** 463-471; **1999** 561-567; **2000** 787-794; **2001** 710-711; **2002** 666-675; **2003** 846-857
Hispanic population report, **2001** 314-324; **2003** 349-357
illegal immigrants in the U.S., **2001** 765
immigration report, **1997** 175-182
income inequality, **1996** 396-400
Internet use in the U.S., **2002** 67-79
measures of well-being report, **1999** 390-400
portrait of the nation's social, economic status, **1992** 475-478
retirement data, **2002** 104
undercount dispute, **1990** 170-171; **1991** 443-449
voter participation by young first-time voters in 1972 election, **1973** 35-38
working women, **2001** 548
young families data, **1992** 356
Centennial Olympic Park (Atlanta), bombing incident, **1996** 233, 445-449
Center for Auto Safety, on Firestone tire recall, **1978** 720-721
Center for Biosecurity, University of Pittsburgh Medical Center, **2004** 444, 445
Center for Democracy and Technology, medical records privacy,**1997** 582
Center for International Security and Cooperation (Stanford University), Chinese technology transfer, **1999** 239-240
Center for National Security Studies, detainees rights, **2004** 376
Center for Patient Safety, proposed, **1999** 780, 782
Center for Responsive Politics, campaign financing, **2004** 776-777
Center for Science in the Public Interest (CSPI), Chinese food and nutrition report, **1993** 689-694
Center for Strategic and International Studies
Haig address on first-strike defense, **1982** 305-315
Iraq reconstruction report, **2004** 406
Center for Study of the States, state aid for the poor report, **1991** 827-842
Center for the Study of Social Policy, **1983** 766
Center on Addiction and Substance Abuse, **2002** 427
Center on Alcohol Marketing and Youth, **2002** 178
Center on Budget and Policy Priorities, **1989** 334
income inequality, **1999** 391
poverty in aftermath of Hurricane Katrina, **2005** 141
state aid for poor report, **1991** 827-842
Center to Improve Care of the Dying, **1997** 329
Centers for Disease Control and Prevention (CDC)
AIDS, **1986** 887-888, 891-892, 905
adolescents with, **1992** 339-343
cases and deaths, **1993** 447; **1997** 81
HIV infection cases and, **1998** 380
HIV transmission risk during dental treatment, **1998** 380
rate of infection, **1983** 534
testing of pregnant women, **1995** 441-452
in the workplace, **1985** 733-747
AIDS/HIV programs
AIDS incidence in minorities in U.S., **2004** 433
antiretroviral drug therapy, **2005** 50-63
incidence in U.S., **2005** 55
biological and chemical threats, **2001** 73
bird flu in Texas, **2004** 924
cigarette smoking, **1993** 64, 65; **1999** 539-540
diabetes and obesity, **2000** 242-243
drug testing labs, accuracy of, **1986** 841
drug-resistant bacteria and overuse of antibiotics, **1999** 185, 186-187, 190, 192-193, 195
flu pandemic, preparations for, **2005** 750
flu vaccine, recommendations and shortages, **2004** 639-640
food contamination recalls, **2002** 582
food poisoning, **2000** 884
FoodNet program (foodborne illnesses), **1998** 529-530
gun-related deaths, **2001** 723
hazardous chemicals in Love Canal, **1983** 479-498
laboratory security guidelines, **2002** 744-745
obesity and overeating, **1997** 159-160
obesity-related deaths and diseases, **2002** 625; **2005** 5-6
SARS outbreak, **2003** 122, 127
sendentary lifestyle, **1993** 625-628
smoking among teenagers, **1998** 845
smoking-related illnesses, treatment costs, **2000** 558
steroid use by high school students, **2005** 218
swine flu program, **1978** 670, 673-674, 676-677
teenage smoking statistics, **2004** 281
tuberculosis control program, **1993** 853, 859-865
"VERB. It's What You Do" ad campaign, **2002** 626-627
youth violence prevention, **2001** 74
Centers for Medicare and Medicaid Services (CMS), nursing home abuse, **2002** 119-120
Central African Republic, John Paul II's visit to, **1985** 500-501
Central America
See also El Salvador; Nicaragua
conflicts in
and security issues, **1984** 44-51
and UN ineffectiveness, **1982** 769
democracy, development of, **1984** 38, 48-49
economic development in, **1983** 375-390; **1984** 31-33, 34-37, 39-40
human development in, **1984** 42-43, 51-52
human rights in, **1983** 181-195; **1984** 155-156, 159-162, 164-165; **1985** 146, 150-153
and Reagan policy, **1983** 440-442, 445-446
Kissinger commission report on, **1984** 31-52
military and economic aid for, debate on, **1983** 439-454
Nicaragua's activities in, **1985** 637, 639
peace in, conditions for, **1984** 38, 44, 48-50
peace plan, **1987** 637-638
in presidential debates, **1984** 877-880
refugees from, and political asylum in U.S., **1987** 254-255
Soviet activities in
Malta meeting on, **1989** 644, 650, 657-658, 666

Republican platform on, **1980** 641
trade growth in, conditions for, **1984** 40-41
U.S. policy, **1984** 289; **1985** 260-261
Democratic platform on, **1984** 637-640
Kissinger commission recommendations, **1984** 31-52
Republican platform on, **1984** 662, 707-709
use of U.S. military, **1984** 1005-1006, 1014
Central America Free Trade Agreement (CAFTA), **2005** 412-413
Central American Bank for Economic Integration, **1984** 37
Central American Common Market Fund, **1984** 37
Central American peace plan
Burger on, **1987** 774-775
Nicaraguan compliance with, **1989** 61-62
progress of compliance, **1987** 1007-1011
provisions, **1987** 637-648
Central and Eastern European countries (CEECs), Munich economic summit on, **1992** 644-645
Central Intelligence, Director of (DCI)
informing Congress of covert actions,**1976** 117, 119
role and authority of, **1976** 117, 120-121
in Ford reorganization, **1976** 127, 134-135
Rockefeller commission on, **1975** 414-416
Senate committee on, **1976** 238, 244-246
Senate investigation of Casey, **1981** 855-859
Central Intelligence Agency (CIA), **2005** 706
See also Central Intelligence, Director of (DCI)
abuses of, **1976** 235-236, 251
activities and procedures
House draft report on, **1976** 683-686
House investigation of, **1976** 115-124
Afghanistan war involvement, **2001** 689
in Africa, Amin on, **1977** 143, 145-147
Ames espionage case, **1994** 475-497
Bali bombing incident, **2002** 704
bin Laden, Osama, assassination attempts, **2001** 806-807
bombing of, by White Panther Party, **1972** 486
budgetary authority over, **1976** 237, 252
Center for the Study of Intelligence, **1992** 3
chemical weapons warnings during Gulf War, **1997** 742
Chile, campaigns against Allende in, **1974** 805-810; **1975** 873-875, 882-899, 899-910; **1977** 323, 351-352
China AIDS projections, **2002** 470-471
Chinese nuclear-espionage matter, **1999** 238
congressional oversight of, **1975** 412-413
creation of, **1997** 811
and Daniloff arrest, **1986** 820, 824-825
detention facilities at Guantanamo Bay, **2004** 380
disclosure of covert intelligence operatives, **2003** 20, 21; **2005** 699-716, 907
dissident groups, investigation of, **1975** 401-403, 409, 419-424, 429-430
domestic intelligence activities, **1975** 401-436, 523-528, 709; **1976** 238, 267-269
investigative techniques, **1975** 417-427
prohibition on, **1974** 609
drug experimentation by, **1975** 402, 432
and drug traders, **1972** 646
Ellsberg break-in support, **1973** 537-538, 540, 542-544, 548
employee of spying for Ghana, **1985** 604
executive branch oversight of, **1975** 412-414
FOIA, and ability to restrict information, **1981** 394
Gates nomination hearings, **1991** 651-669
government secrets, **1994** 525-526
intelligence gathering failures, **2002** 531-532, 992, 994, 995; **2004** 965-966
on Iran and position of shah, **1978** 699, 701
Iran-contra affair, **1986** 1015-1018, 1024; **1987** 896, 903, 906-912, 924
estimates of diverted funds, **1986** 1052
North conviction, **1990** 493
role of officials, **1992** 1073-1079; **1994** 17
Tower commission on, **1987** 218-219, 223-228, 232-233, 240-241
Iraq political situation, **1996** 680-686; **2004** 400
Iraq weapons of mass destruction reports, **2002** 35; **2004** 711, 712
Iraq-Niger uranium sales allegations, **2003** 20-21, 876; **2005** 248-249, 699-700
in Kennedy assassination investigation, **1978** 910-911, 915; **1979** 594, 606-607, 613-615
leak of agent's identity, investigations into, **2005** 77-78, 80, 246, 249, 562, 567, 631, 699-726, 767-768, 907
Middle East peace talks, **2001** 365
on Middle East terrorism, **1985** 466, 470
Mineta, Norman H., appointment as director, **2001** 97
mining of Nicaraguan ports, **1984** 340-341; **1985** 256-257, 637
misuse of in Watergate activities, **1974** 605, 675-683
Nicaraguan contras, support for, **1987** 639; **1989** 241
Nicholson espionage case, **1996** 794-800
Noriega of Panama and, **1990** 273; **1992** 651
North Korea, **1994** 602-603
North Korea political situation, **2001** 267-278
Office of Public Affairs, **1992** 3
passport revocation of former agent, **1981** 541-555
plausible denial doctrine, Senate committee on, **1975** 720, 793-795
political assassination plots, **1975** 401-403
Senate investigation of, **1975** 709-799
psychological operations manual, **1984** 847, 878-879, 903-916
recruitment restrictions for counterterrorism, **2000** 278-279
reform of, **1992** 3-10
research contracts of, Ford rules on, **1976** 126, 136
restrictions on
and possible dismantling of, Ford on, **1975** 224, 237
relaxation of, **1981** 861-868
role and authority of, **1975** 409-412; **1976** 235, 237, 246-252
specified by Ford, **1976** 126, 134-136
Roswell incident, **1997** 397
Russian nuclear testing, **1999** 604
secrecy of intelligence sources, **1985** 333-344

Central Intelligence Agency (CIA) *Continued*
secret detentions of "ghost detainees," **2002** 833-835; **2004** 213, 339; **2005** 905, 906-909
September 11 terrorists, **2003** 155, 219, 545-546
on Soviet forced labor, **1982** 857-859
Soviet propaganda about, **1981** 760
on terrorism, international, **1981** 461-475
terrorist interrogations
allegations of abuse and "secret prisons," **2005** 582
guidelines, **2004** 337-338
terrorist threat assessments, **2002** 740, 741-742
terrorist watch lists, **2003** 158, 566-567
TIPOFF system (terrorist watchlist), **2003** 157, 169; **2004** 469
TWA flight 800 crash, **1997** 780
U.S. bombing of Chinese embassy, **1999** 306, 309
Vietnam war, enemy troop counts in, **1985** 160
Watergate misuse of, **1974** 158, 162-164, 655, 657
Webster's testimony on Persian Gulf war, **1990** 776-779
world trends report, **2000** 1047-1062
Central Intelligence Agency (CIA) v. Sims and Wolfe, **1985** 333-344
CEQ. *See* Council on Environmental Quality, President's
Cerezo Arévalo, Vinicio
election of, **1987** 639
human rights in Guatemala, **1987** 195-196
signing of Tela accord, **1989** 161, 172
Cernan, Eugene, manned space missions, **2004** 10, 14
Cerulli Associates, retirement accounts, **2002** 103
César Aguirre, Alfredo
backed by Costa Rica, **1987** 638
Nicaraguan cease-fire, **1988** 242
Ceylon. *See under its later name* Sri Lanka
CFE. *See* Conventional forces in Europe
CFTC. *See* Commodity Futures Trading Commission
CHA. *See* Chicago Housing Authority
Chabad-Lubavitch v. Burlington, **1995** 397
Chabad-Lubavitch v. Miller, **1995** 397
Chabot, Steve (R-Ohio) , House Judiciary Committee impeachment inquiry, **1998** 709
Chad
human rights in, **1990** 136; **1993** 559-560
refugees from Darfur region, **2005** 515, 518
Chadha, Immigration and Naturalization Service v., **1983** 617-644
Chafee, John H. (R-R.I.)
Clinton impeachment trial, **1999** 20
and Republican Party, **2001** 378
takeover legislation, **1988** 923
war hero, **1999** 39
Chafee, Lincoln D. (R-R.I.) , Clear Skies plan, **2005** 99
Chafetz, Morris E., **1972** 193-194
Chai Zemin, **1980** 842
Chakrabarty, Ananda M. , patent of bacterium,**1980** 493-495
Chalabi, Ahmad
Iraq humanitarian aid, **2001** 853
Iraqi exile returns to Iraq, **2003** 936, 948; **2005** 942
Iraq's biological weapons, **2005** 250
and United Iraqi Alliance, **2004** 404
Challenger space shuttle
accident/disaster, **1986** 39, 41-42, 47; **2003** 632, 636
and future of program, **1987** 649-650, 653, 664, 669
investigation of, **1986** 515-539
tribute to crew, **1988** 795-798
Chamber of Commerce (U.S.)
lifting of wage and price controls, **1973** 46
minimum and youth wage, **1983** 785-790
parental leave, **1987** 19
in Taiwan, on U.S.-PRC relations, **1979** 672
U.S.-China trade relations, **2000** 215
Chambers, Julius L. , on blacks during Reagan administration, **1987** 44, 51-52
Chambers, Ray, volunteerism summit, **1997** 243
Chamblain, Jodel (Haiti rebel leader), Haiti political situation, **2004** 95, 98
Chambliss, Robert E. , church bombing trial (Birmingham, 1963) conviction, **2002** 241
Chambliss, Saxby (R-Ga.), **2002** 821
Chamorro, Edgar, and CIA manual, **1984** 905
Chamorro, Pedro Joaquín
murder of, **1979** 585
opposition to Somoza, **1987** 641
Chamorro, Violeta Barrios de
inaugural address, **1990** 259-266
in Nicaraguan transitional government, **1979** 582
Chand, Prem, **1977** 585
Chandler, Michael, al Qaeda terrorist network, monitoring support for, **2002** 1017; **2004** 540
Chandler v. Florida, **1981** 163-176
Chanet, Christine, Cuban dissidents, treatment of, **2004** 250
Chaney, James, civil rights worker murder (1964), **2002** 239; **2005** 353-361
Change to Win coalition (labor federation), **2005** 485, 487-489, 495-497
Channel Two Television Co. v. National Citizens Committee for Broadcasting, **1978** 419-432
Channell, Carl R. , Iran-contra affair, conviction and role in, **1991** 619; **1994** 12, 15
Chanos, James, on Enron business practices, **2001** 859
Chao, Elaine L.
confirmation as labor secretary, **2001** 97
reinstatement of Davis-Bacon Act, **2005** 489
United Way president, **1992** 306
Chaote, Pat, Reform Party vice-presidential nomination, **1996** 552
Chapel v. Center Moriches Union Free School, **2001** 421, 425-432
Chapin, Dwight, Watergate involvement, **1974** 321, 323, 333
Chaplinsky v. New Hampshire, **1990** 361; **1992** 546
Chapman, Clark, *Galileo* imaging team, **1997** 204
Chapman, Mark David, **1991** 814
Chapman v. California, **1991** 175-176, 179-180, 183, 382
Charaa, Farouk, Hariri assassination, UN investigation, **2005** 691
Charest, Jean, **1998** 594
Charles (prince of Wales)
on death of Diana, **1997** 647

at Hong Kong transfer ceremony statement, **1997** 502, 504-505
royal family affairs, **1992** 1059-1063; **1997** 648
wedding of, **1981** 601-603
at Zimbabwe independence ceremony, **1980** 317, 332, 333-334
Charles, Robert B. , Colombian drug control program, **2003** 431
Charles Schwab, mutual funds scandal, **2003** 696
Charter, Richard, offshore drilling, **2004** 604
Charter Crude Oil Co. , Billy Carter's Libyan contacts on behalf of, **1980** 908-911
Charter of Paris for a New Europe, **1990** 727, 734-745
Chase, Robert, school vouchers, **2002** 409
Chase Manhattan Bank, and New York City's fiscal crisis, **1977** 568-569, 577
Chasis, Sarah, Bush ocean protection policy, **2004** 605
Chaskalson, Arthur, South African court ruling on death penalty, **1995** 284, 285-287
Chaves, Aureliano, **1985** 4
Chavez, Cesar, organizing of farm workers by, **1975** 377-378
Chavez, Hugo
home-heating oil program, **2005** 780
Lula da Silva's relations with, **2003** 7
mass protest against, **2004** 549
military coup attempt, **2004** 125, 548-549, 552
national referendum on the presidency, **2003** 279-287; **2004** 548-554
negotiations with Jimmy Carter, **2002** 201, 983
U.S. relations, **2005** 765-767, 770-771
Venezuela political situation, **2002** 201-211
Venezuelan presidential promises, **2002** 775
Chavez, Linda
civil rights commission, **1983** 915
labor secretary nomination resignation, **2001** 97
women in combat, **1993** 335
Chavez, United States v. , **1974** 392-393, 400-405
Chavez-Thompson, Linda, **1995** 681, 683
AFL-CIO union leader, **1995** 681, 683
race relations panel, **1997** 316, 322
Chavis, Benjamin, Jr.
address of NAACP director, **1993** 579-584
at March on Washington thirtieth anniversary, **1973** 679-681; **1993** 678
resignation from NAACP, **1995** 453
Chawla, Kalpana, *Columbia* astronaut, **2003** 633
Chazov, Yevgeny I. , Nobel Peace Prize, **1985** 781-784
Chechen rebels
Beslan hostage crisis, **2004** 535, 564-576; **2005** 299, 300, 303
bombings, Russian airliners, **2004** 566
hostage taking in Moscow theater, **2002** 763-773
Russia negotiations, Putin on, **2004** 567
Russia relations, **2004** 569-570
suicide bombings of Russian planes, **2004** 144, 566
terrorist attacks, **2003** 245, 249-250, 1052; **2004** 565-566; **2005** 304-305
Chechnya, elections, **2003** 248-249; **2004** 565-566
Chechnya war, **1995** 93-94, 99-100; **1996** 432; **1999** 909-916; **2000** 175-176; **2001** 257, 894; **2005** 304-305
casualties of, **2002** 768
Chemical Bank, and New York City's fiscal crisis, **1977** 568, 577
Chemical control
hazardous waste disposal by, **1979** 785, 787, 792, 795, 799
regimes for illicit drugs, **1992** 210, 211
Chemical industry, tax for hazardous waste cleanup, **1982** 965-970
Chemical Manufacturers Association, studies of ozone layer, **1987** 745
Chemical weapons
See also Biological weapons; Bioterrorism; Terrorism; Weapons of mass destruction (WMD)
banning of
Brezhnev on, **1976** 144, 151
Bush on, **1989** 80
discussed at Malta summit, **1989** 645, 648, 652
proposed, **1985** 751, 754, 758
Clinton administration policy, **1998** 49-50
destruction of, Gorbachev on, **1986** 11, 17-19
Gulf War syndrome and, **1994** 264-275; **1997** 740-745; **2001** 908
in Iran-Iraq war, **1984** 749, 754; **1987** 610, 612; **1988** 531
Iraq
facilities inspections, **1991** 192
mobile biological weapons laboratories, **2003** 880-881
threat from, **2003** 877, 882; **2004** 716, 727-730
UN weapons inspection, **1997** 768; **1998** 934-944
use of in internal conflicts, **1989** 58, 68-69
Libyan mustard gas stores, **2003** 1221; **2004** 170
nonproliferation of, discussed at Iceland summit, **1986** 876
Paris declaration condemning use of, **1989** 25-30
reduction of, Bush UN speech on, **1990** 648-649
Soviet use of, **1981** 681-694, 724; **1982** 235-257
U.S. destruction of, beginning of, **1972** 323
U.S.-Soviet agreements on, Moscow summit, **1988** 356, 371
U.S.-Soviet negotiation on, **1987** 998
U.S.-Soviet reduction agreements, **1990** 332-333, 337-338, 349-350
verification issue, **1999** 603
worldwide proliferation of, **1996** 210-230
Chemical Weapons Convention (CWC)
Clinton support for, **1995** 358; **1997** 42
secretary of state on, **1997** 195-201
Senate ratification fails, **1996** 210-211
Senate ratification of, **1998** 50
UN secretary general on, **1996** 740-743
Chemical Weapons Treaty, **1993** 71-79
Chen Shui-bian
assassination attempt (2004), **2004** 258, 260
China relations, **2005** 622-623
first term as president, **2004** 259
pro-independence movement, **2004** 943
Taiwan independence referendum, **2003** 1180-1181; **2004** 259, 261
Taiwanese presidential elections, **2003** 1180; **2004** 258-259, 943
Taiwanese presidential inaugurations, **2000** 190-200; **2004** 258-267

Cheney, Daniel, TWA flight 800 crash, **1997** 782
Cheney, Lynne V.
humanities education, **1987** 681-696
marketing violent entertainment to children, **2000** 731
state of humanities, **1988** 517-518
Cheney, Richard B. "Dick"
Afghanistan, Karzai inauguration ceremony, **2004** 917
China, state visit, **2004** 939
CIA leak case, **2005** 702, 703, 704-705
Clarke testimony on terrorist attacks, **2004** 453
as defense secretary
chemical weapons treaty, **1996** 741
military base closings, **1988** 951
Navy's sexual harassment problems, **1992** 1004-1005
nuclear test ban treaty, **1999** 601, 608
Patriot Missile Performance report, **1992** 865-874
Somalian relief, **1992** 1068
war powers debate, **1990** 665-666
women in combat report, **1992** 1030
defense secretary appointment, **1989** 107
energy policy task force, **2005** 648, 779, 781-782
Enron Corp. meetings with energy policy task force, **2001** 863
global warming, **2001** 112
Halliburton Co.
former vice president, **2003** 947; **2005** 722
investigations, **2004** 893
at inauguration of George W. Bush, **2001** 95
Iran nuclear weapons program, **2005** 595
Iran-contra committee, **1986** 1052; **1987** 893
Iraq
chemical weapons, **2004** 716
nuclear weapons program, **2004** 714-715
weapons inspections program, **2002** 615, 616; **2003** 881
Iraq War
CIA intelligence and, **2004** 713
insurgency in its "last throes," **2005** 659, 660
response of Iraqi people, **2003** 141
McCain amendment on treatment of detainees, **2005** 909-910
national commission on terrorist attacks testimony, **2004** 454-455
national energy policy task force, **2001** 331, 334-335, 338-346; **2003** 1017-1018; **2004** 189
omnibus energy bill impasse, **2003** 1017
presidential executive authority, **2005** 961
Republican Party convention, acceptance speech, **2000** 521-522, 523-527
Republican Party convention speech, **2004** 484
September 11 terrorist attacks, **2001** 617
Social Security reform plan, **2005** 113
tax cut proposals, **2001** 402; **2005** 124
vice presidency
campaign, **2004** 480, 481
debates, **2000** 797, 800, 810-817; **2004** 678
nomination, **2000** 520-521
role in, **2001** 171-172
tie-breaker on House votes, **2000** 906-907; **2001** 378
Vietnam War military draft deferments, **2005** 837
Cheney v. United States District Court, **2004** 189
Cherkasky, Michael G. , Marsh & McLennan CEO appointment, **2004** 418
Chernenko, Konstantin U.
on antisatellite weapons ban, **1984** 259
death of, **1985** 271-275, 749
interview with U.S. reporter, **1984** 813-814
rise to power, **1984** 145-148, 150-154
on U.S.-Soviet relations, **1984** 917-923
Chernobyl nuclear accident
cleanup after, **1986** 386, 401-405
and emergency plans requirement, **1990** 196
industrialized nations on, **1986** 437, 439
Soviet report on, **1986** 383-407
Chernomyrdin, Viktor S. , Russian economic reform, **1995** 94-95; **1998** 602-605
Cherrey, John, U.S. war hero in Kosovo,**2000** 30
Cherry, Bobby Frank, church bombing trial (Birmingham, 1963), **2002** 239-246; **2005** 353
Chertoff, Michael
Homeland Security Department secretary appointment, **2005** 895-896
Hurricane Katrina disaster, DHS response, **2005** 567-569
Cheshin, Mishael, Demjanjuk war crime acquittal, **1993** 622-623
Chessie System, in railroad reorganization, **1975** 529, 534-535
Chestnut, Jacob J., Capitol policeman slain, **1998** 510-517
Chestnut, Wei Ling (Mrs. Jacob J.), **1999** 44
Chevron
merger with Unocal, **2005** 615-616
oil company profits, congressional hearings on, **2005** 781-782
Chevron v. Natural Resources Defense Council, **1984** 427-437; **1991** 258, 261
ChevronTexaco, affirmative action, **2003** 362
Chevron U.S.A. Inc. v. Echazabal, **2002** 5-6
Cheysson, Claude, **1982** 880
Chiang Ching-kuo
on Japan-Taiwan diplomatic relations, **1972** 827
Taiwan presidential elections, **2004** 258
on U.S. withdrawal of recognition of Taiwan, **1978** 782-783, 786-787
Chiang Kai-shek, ruler of Taiwan, **2004** 258
Chicago, B.& Q. R. Co. v. Chicago, **1994** 302
Chicago Board of Trade, in stock market crash, **1987** 835, 837, 841
Chicago Housing Authority (CHA), **1995** 294-301
discrimination charged in siting of public housing, **1976** 223-233
Chicago Mercantile Exchange
in stock market crash, **1987** 835, 837, 841
trading reform, **1988** 12
Chicago Tribune, on Nixon tape transcripts, **1974** 289, 301-302
Child abuse
See also Child labor; Child soldiers
atrocities against in Afghan conflict, **1986** 927, 933-934, 935
child pornography case, **1992** 313-327

HHS report, **1996** 778
ILO report, **1996** 776-783
rape study, **1992** 386
in refugee camps, **2002** 919-920
sexual abuse by priests, **1992** 507-518; **1993** 407-411; **2002** 867-876; **2003** 523-543; **2004** 82-93; **2005** 294
sexual exploitation of UNICEF director on, **2001** 955-962
violent crimes against, **1999** 617
Child Abuse Prevention and Treatment Act, and handicapped infants, **1983** 283
Child care
Democratic platform on, **1980** 734
federal funds for, women's conference support for, **1977** 861, 863-864
private, Reagan on, **1983** 86
quality, GAO testimony, **1994** 116-122
Republican platform on, **1980** 580-581; **1988** 615, 634-635
and Social Security benefits for surviving spouse, **1975** 177-185
tax credits, **2000** 25
for teen parents, **1986** 1062
for welfare mothers, **1988** 847-852
White House Conference on, **1998** 47
women and the workplace, **1985** 800-801
for world's women, right to, **1975** 512-513, 518-519
Child development, Perot Reform Party nomination speech on, **1996** 560-561
Child health,
AIDS, children with, **1988** 421-422, 436-437
AIDS epidemic impact on, **1998** 886-887; **1999** 386-387
alcoholism effects on, **1983** 342-344
antidepressants and suicide, **2004** 640, 746-752
cloning-to-produce children, ethics of, **2002** 521-523
cow's milk for infants, **1992** 398-399, 401
in Eastern Europe, **1994** 415-430
federal funding, **1998** 88
federal legislation, **2001** 134
HIV prevention and drug therapy, **2005** 61
HIV/AIDS epidemic, **2001** 449-450, 957-958
indicators of, **1999** 388-389
infant formula vs. breast-feeding, in developing countries, **1981** 447-458, 917
insurance coverage, **1999** 566-567; **2000** 24
malnutrition of children, **1985** 190-193, 196-203; **2002** 222
mental health, **2001** 577
obesity in children and, **2005** 6-7
obesity prevention, Institute of Medicine report, **2004** 652-663
overweight, **2001** 936-937; **2002** 625; **2003** 481-482
physical fitness and, **1993** 626-628
secondhand smoke exposure and, **1980** 23; **1986** 1082, 1084-1085, 1088
smoking by children, **1989** 31-32, 35, 38-39
smoking prevention programs, **1999** 49
smoking report and, **1994** 172-184
surveys on well-being of children, **1997** 424-425
vaccinations for children, **1999** 387
Child labor
ILO report on, **2002** 222
report, **1996** 776-783
Wal-Mart store agreement, **2005** 738-739, 740-744
workplace protections, **1997** 207
Child nutrition
diets of children, **1999** 385
malnutrition of children, **1985** 190-193, 196-203; **2002** 222
Child nutrition programs
Carter restoration of to budget, **1977** 127
consolidation of, in Ford budget, **1977** 58, 62
in schools, **1988** 196, 207, 218
Child Online Protection Act (COPA), **2002** 287, 290; **2003** 387
Child pornography
criminal penalties for possession, **1990** 239-249
entrapment of suspects, **1992** 313-327
using, **1982** 675-688
Child Pornography Prevention Act, **2002** 287-288; **2003** 387
Child Protection Act (1984), **1992** 314, 316
Child Rights Caucus, **2002** 223
Child slavery
trafficking in humans, State Department report on, **2002** 332-352; **2004** 125, 126
UN protocol on, **2002** 224-225
Child soldiers
Lord's Resistance Army (LRA), in Uganda, **2003** 470-479
UN protocol on, **2002** 224-225
UN secretary general report on, **2002** 916-926
Child support
case enforcement, **1997** 38, 618; **2000** 26
Democratic Party platform, **1996** 638
enforcement
Reagan on, **1983** 85
in welfare reform legislation, **1988** 849, 851
federal program spending cuts, **2005** 78
Child welfare
Convention on the Rights of the Child, **2002** 224-225
progress and problems, **2002** 222-223, 916
reform, **1996** 457-458
well-being of children report, **1997** 425; **1999** 384-400
world fit for, UN special session on, **2002** 221-231, 916
World Summit for (1990),**2002** 222
Children
See also Child welfare; School violence
adult attitudes toward, **1997** 422-443; **1999** 386
of aliens, right of to education, **1982** 489-506
atrocities against in Afghan conflict, **1986** 927, 933-934, 935
behavior and social indicators, **1999** 389
black Americans in poverty, **1989** 450, 457
Catholic Church's World Youth Day, **1993** 659-669
custody rights
of frozen embryo, **1989** 551-559
of lesbian parents, **1977** 861, 863, 866
of parents, **1982** 259-280
and surrogate mothers, **1987** 373-387; **1988** 71-79

Children *Continued*
dangers and threats to, **1999** 385
deaths of, UNICEF remedies for, **1981** 911-921
DeBoer adoption case, **1993** 515-529
discarded, programs for, **1989** 671-686
economic security indicators, **1999** 388
Eisenhower Foundation inner cities report, **1993** 211-233
food program budget cuts and, **1983** 49, 765-766, 770, 772
foster, in Jonestown mass suicide, **1979** 375-376
and grandparents' rights, Supreme Court on, **2000** 287-298
handicapped, Reagan on rights of, **1983** 269, 273, 282-283
HIV/AIDS epidemic, **1999** 387
homeless report, **1994** 257
marketing violent entertainment to, **2000** 729-739
National Commission on Children report, **1991** 349-365
nuclear testing fallout, effect on, **1997** 592-593
population and family characteristics, **1999** 387-388
in poverty, **1999** 384-385; **2002** 55
lack of health care and insurance, **1987** 149-152, 161-164
in U.S., **1988** 877-880
U.S. Catholic bishops on, **1986** 984, 988, 999
right to biological parents, Vatican on, **1987** 268, 278-279, 281, 284-285
and TV violence, effect on social behavior, **1972** 61-66; **1982** 365-383
UN Population Conference, **1994** 355, 356-357
Waco cult, **1993** 294
Children's Defense Fund (CDF), **1992** 353-360
on infant mortality and health care, **1987** 147-164
on student suspensions, **1975** 67
Children's Health Act, **2001** 134
Children's Health Insurance Program (CHIP), **2000** 24, 49, 788; **2001** 59, 130, 711-712
Children's Internet Protection Act (CIPA), **2002** 288-289, 293-297; **2003** 388, 393, 394
Chile
Alwyn's presidential address, **1990** 187-193
Beagle Channel Islands, dispute with Argentina, **1983** 8
Catholic clergy in, **1986** 318
China trade relations, **2004** 938
CIA covert action in, **1974** 805-810; **1975** 402-403, 899-910
Nixon on, **1977** 323, 351-352
democracy in, **1975** 883-884
human rights in, **1980** 191; **1983** 187-188; **1985** 149-150; **1986** 102-103; **1987** 193-194; **1988** 100-101; **1989** 58-59; **1990** 189
military coup in, CIA support for, **1975** 710, 715, 763-770, 776, 874-875, 895-910
military in, CIA contacts with, **1975** 907-910
nationalization of copper companies, U.S. economic retaliation for, **1972** 67, 329, 332-335
political situation, **2005** 771
revolution in, Brezhnev on, **1976** 152
sex trade and trafficking, **2004** 126
smoking report, **1992** 267-275
U.S. policy on, history of, **1975** 883-884, 891-893
Chilean Commission on Human Rights, **1990** 189
Chiles, Lawton (D-Fla.), **1987** 4
on Cuban immigrants, **1995** 204
domestic violence case, **1993** 288
Hurricane Andrew, **1992** 534, 844
Chiluba, Joseph, Zambian elections, **2001** 504
China, People's Republic of (PRC)
AIDS drug distribution, **2003** 780, 784
AIDS epidemic, **2001** 438, 440; **2002** 331, 470-471, 855; **2003** 1175; **2004** 429, 430; **2005** 55
Albania, relations with, **1985** 325, 326, 327
banking system reforms, **2003** 1177
Bush-Jiang meeting, **2001** 741-742
capture of U.S. fliers (1952),Nixon on, **1973** 194, 205-206
Catholic Church relations with, **1981** 204
Chinese students in U.S., **1990** 50
claims against U.S. for frozen assets, as issue in normalization of relations, **1973** 292, 296, 298-300
Clinton-Jiang news conference, **1998** 466-478
Communist Party congress, **1973** 767-778
constitution of, **1975** 43-53
citizens' rights and duties under, **1978** 158, 172-175
Cultural Revolution (1966-1976), **1980** 955-958; **1984** 165; **1997** 95, 97-98
death penalty, **1989** 597, 600; **1993** 560
early human remains discovered, **1992** 136-137
economic and political reform, **1989** 275, 278, 282
economic growth, **2002** 692, 853-854; **2003** 69, 765; **2004** 940; **2005** 413, 617-618
economic situation, **2000** 1049, 1059-1060
foreign direct investment, **2003** 754
environment and health, **2002** 855
environmental issues, **2005** 620-621, 919
expansion and economic growth of, **2005** 15
family planning in, **1984** 525, 540-541
Gang of Four, **1980** 955-958; **1997** 97-98
as a great power, **2005** 14, 28-29, 81, 612
HIV testing program, **2004** 429
Hong Kong
return of, **1984** 1045-1050
transfer ceremony, **1997** 501-506
Hong Kong pro-democracy demonstrations, **2004** 942
human rights in, **1980** 190, 197-198; **1984** 165-166; **1986** 98; **1988** 884, 887, 888; **1989** 59; **1990** 129, 135, 142-143; **1993** 559-560, 564-567; **1994** 74-84; **1996** 133-138; **1997** 735-738
IMF and World Bank membership for, **1980** 884, 891-892
intellectual property rights, WTO compliance, **2004** 939, 945
Internet censorship, **2005** 619-620
Iran nuclear materials, **2003** 1030
Japan
diplomatic relations with, **1972** 827-830
dispute with, **2005** 621-622
peace treaty with, **1978** 585-588
rapprochement with, **1972** 745-746
relations with, **1998** 540-541
Khmer Rouge, **1990** 562

leadership transition, **2002** 850-866; **2004** 941
Lin Piao's coup plot, **1974** 271-275
manned space missions, **2005** 503
military buildup, U.S. concerns about, **2005** 613, 614-615
missile threat to U.S., **1998** 487-488
Nixon on, **1992** 263
Nixon state visit, **1972** 183-192; **2002** 855
Shanghai communiqué, **1972** 187-190
North Korea
relations with, **1972** 523; **1999** 577; **2003** 1178
six-party talks, **2003** 1178; **2004** 871-872, 937
North Vietnam aid in violation of peace accords, **1975** 252, 259-260, 275-276
nuclear nonproliferation treaty, **1975** 363
nuclear secrets theft, U.S. accusations of, **1999** 235-256, 304
nuclear weapons development, **1994** 373; **1996** 217
Palestinian terrorist acts, defense of, **1972** 752
People's Liberation Army, modernization of, **2003** 1175
political protests, repression of, **2005** 618-620
political reforms, **2003** 1173-1188; **2004** 942
population control, **1999** 586-587
population of, **1974** 779; **1984** 522-523, 529; **1987** 455, 457
poverty summit, **1981** 770
prodemocracy movement
Dalai Lama on, **1989** 577, 581-582
demonstrations, **1989** 275-288
intellectuals in, **1989** 278-281
Tiananmen Square repression, **1989** 275-277
property rights and privatization, **2003** 1177
Reagan trip, **1984** 287-298
religious persecution, **1997** 562, 563, 568-570
Russian relations, **2001** 740
SARS outbreak
cover-up, **2003** 124-126, 784, 1174
and economic growth, **2003** 754
government response, **2003** 1174-1175
Soviet relations
normalization of, **1989** 276
and PRC alliances, Brezhnev on, **1981** 225, 228-229
propaganda about, **1981** 763
and struggle against Maoism, Brezhnev on, **1976** 144, 146
under Andropov, **1984** 146
space exploration, **2003** 301, 304-305; **2005** 621
strategic balance, impact on, **1972** 179-182
student test scores, **1992** 90, 93, 94
Taiwan relations, **2000** 190-200; **2002** 856; **2003** 1173, 1180-1181; **2004** 942-943; **2005** 17, 622-623
and U.S.-PRC relations, **1984** 23-24
Taiwan reunification policy, **2003** 1181
technology transfer, **1998** 976-982; **2003** 1030
Tiananmen Square protest, **1997** 94, 95, 728-729, 736-737; **1998** 467-468; **2001** 739; **2003** 1174
crackdown on 15th anniversary of, **2004** 941
Zhao Ziyang refusal to use force against protesters, **2005** 620
Tibet occupation by, **1989** 573-581
trade
arms embargo, **2005** 615
as a "market economy," **2004** 938
trade deficit with U.S., **2004** 237
trade practices, U.S. trade representative on, **2004** 937-948
trade relations with U.S., **2000** 19, 50, 213-221
UN admission of (1971), **1972** 183
UN peacekeeping mission, first-ever, **2004** 939
U.S. accord on economic, scientific, and cultural cooperation, **1984** 287-298
U.S. agreements on aviation, textiles, and shipping, **1980** 829-846
U.S. bombing of embassy in Yugoslavia, **1999** 236, 304-316, 726; **2001** 247
U.S. consular agreement, **1980** 829-830, 832, 834, 842-843
U.S. policy on, Republican platform on, **1980** 644-645; **1984** 713
U.S. recognition of, **1978** 585; **2004** 258
U.S. relations, **1999** 304-316; **2000** 29-30; **2001** 738-745; **2004** 939-940; **2005** 612-630
after Tiananmen Square, **1989** 277-278, 281-288
American spy plane incident, **2001** 247-253, 738; **2002** 855; **2003** 1179
defense cooperation, **1979** 967, 977
Democratic platform on, **1984** 643
most-favored nations status, **1994** 73-74; **1997** 731
normalization of, **1975** 235; **1976** 733, 744-745; **1978** 781-787; **1979** 3-4, 6-8, 73, 669-678; **1980** 790
opening of liaison offices, **1973** 291-300
reestablishment of contact, **1972** 7-9, 74, 78; **1973** 515, 521-523, 525; **1977** 337, 359-360
Republican platform on, **1972** 651, 653, 655, 657, 661
state visits, **2005** 612
and termination of Taiwan treaty, **1979** 918-919, 921-922
trade agreement, **2004** 939
trade relations, **2003** 754
and U.S. claims against, **1973** 292, 296, 298-300
U.S. scientific and cultural agreements, **1979** 135-154
U.S. summit meeting, **1997** 728-739
U.S. trade agreements, **1979** 670-671, 675-676; **1980** 44, 92-93; **1984** 23-30
U.S.-China bilateral trade agreement, **1999** 724-734, 797
Vietnam cease-fire agreement, support for, **1973** 332-333
Vietnam invasion, **1979** 137, 183-190
Vietnam peace talks, role in, **1972** 121, 132
WTO compliance, **2004** 943-948
WTO membership, **2001** 738; **2002** 851-852; **2003** 1179-1180
China, Republic of. *See* Taiwan (Republic of China)
China National Offshore Oil Corporation (CNOOC), **2005** 615-616
Chirac, Jacques
agricultural subsidies, **2002** 450
apology for French complicity with Nazis, **1995** 478-482

Chirac, Jacques *Continued*
on capture of Saddam Hussein, **2003** 1194
EU British rebate controversy, **2005** 343-344
EU constitution referendum, **2005** 339-341, 344-346
European defense force, **1999** 819
funeral for Hariri, **2005** 687
inaugural address of French president, **1995** 228-232
Iraq, UN resolution on disarmament of, **2003** 41-43, 51-52
Ivory Coast, UN peacekeeping, **2004** 821
Ivory Coast peace agreement, **2003** 239
meeting with Qaddafi, **2004** 168
Middle East peace, **2003** 1204
NATO charter with Russia, **1997** 515
NATO participation of France, **1997** 516
nuclear test ban treaty, **1999** 603
security measures against terrorist bombings, **1986** 829-838
social welfare system, **1997** 341
at Tokyo economic summit, **1986** 438
worldwide poverty, **2000** 477
Chirau, Jeremiah
Rhodesian internal agreement, **1978** 149-155
in Rhodesian talks, **1977** 584
Chiron Corporation
bird flu vaccine production, **2005** 751
bird flu vaccine research, **2004** 925-926
flu vaccine (Fluvirin) shortage, **2004** 639-651, 747
Chisholm, Shirley (D-N.Y.)
at Democratic convention, **1972** 590, 592
on Haitian refugees, **1980** 339
Chisholm v. Georgia, **1999** 338, 345
Chissano, Joaquin, Zimbabwe political situation, **2003** 1115
Chlorofluorocarbons (CFCs)
Bush and CEA on, **1990** 103-104
CFC reductions, **1988** 223
cutting production and use of, **1987** 747-756; **1988** 221-223
London Declaration, **1990** 469, 476
and ozone depletion, **1987** 746-748, 756, 758, 763; **1992** 75-83
Chmielewski, Waldemar, Polish priest's killing, **1985** 120-123, 125
Choice in Dying (New York City), **1997** 330
Cholesterol
dangers of too-low cholesterol, **1992** 398
debate about dangers of, **1987** 780-781
and heart disease, **1984** 1039-1043
identifying and treating levels of, **1987** 779-790
NIH guidelines, **2001** 475-476, 478
Cholestyramine, **1984** 1039-1040
Chopko, Mark, school voucher plans, **1997** 364
Chou En-lai
death of, **1976** 687
diplomatic relations with Japan, **1972** 827-830
Nixon visit, **1972** 184-185
party congress report by, **1973** 767-770, 773-778; **1975** 44
U.S. two-China policy, **1973** 292
Chow, Jack C. , AIDS in Asia, **2005** 54
CHP. *See* California Highway Patrol
Chrétien, Jean
Africa reform, **2003** 452
aid to Africa, **2002** 449-450
at economic summit (Denver), **1997** 342
land mines ban treaty, **1997** 844
Quebec independence, **1998** 594-595
U.S.-Canada Power System Outage Task Force investigation, **2003** 1015
worldwide poverty, **2000** 477
Christensen, Philip R. , Mars space exploration, **2003** 304
Christianity
compared with Judaism, **1986** 339-346
incompatibility with Marxism, **1984** 766-774
public display of Nativity scene, **1984** 217-239
relations with Jews, **1987** 700, 702-705; **1988** 405-414
shared values with Islam, **1985** 499-501, 509-514
Christie, Thomas P. , missile defense system, **2004** 177
Christopher, Warren M.
chemical weapons treaty, **1996** 742
Iranian support of terrorism, **2001** 796
on land mines, **1995** 46
on Los Angeles riots, **1992** 409
NATO expansion plans, **1996** 655-661; **1997** 515
negotiations on release of U.S. hostages in Iran, **1980** 999; **1981** 153-156
on Panama after Noriega, **1992** 649
terrorist threats, task force on, **2002** 743
Vietnam relations, **1995** 472
Christopher Reeve Paralysis Foundation, **2004** 161
Christy, Jack, **1986** 489
Chromosome damage, from toxic chemicals at Love Canal, **1980** 445-446, 452-454
Chronicle of Higher Education
faculty tenure review case, **1990** 25
interpreting another culture, **1990** 279
Chrostowski, Waldemar, **1985** 121-122
Chrysler Corp., bankruptcy and loan guarantee, **1979** 693-712
Chun Doo Hwan
on democratic reforms in South Korea, **1987** 583-585, 590-594
and human rights in South Korea, **1987** 199
ouster of, **1988** 854
persecution of Kim Dae Jung, **1997** 893, 894
on Reagan visit to U.S. troops, **1983** 895
sentencing of Kim Dae Jung, **1980** 825-828
Chung, Johnny, **1997** 825, 829
Chung Seung Hwa, assassination of Park, **1979** 895-897, 899-904
Church, Albert T. , Abu Ghraib prison abuse investigations, **2005** 911
Church, Frank (D-Idaho), **1973** 117
CIA involvement in Chile, **1974** 806
congressional vs. presidential powers, **1973** 5
on Nixon budget, **1974** 98
release of documents on CIA and NSA, **1975** 709-711, 799-803
report on intelligence agencies, **1976** 236
SALT II, **1979** 417-418

U.S. intelligence gathering, **2002** 991
Church and state separation
charitable choice, **2001** 132-140
deaf parochial student, **1993** 399-406
Democratic Party platform on, **1984** 606
John Paul II on, **1984** 778, 780-783
"one nation, under God" pledge of allegiance phrase, **2002** 382-390
parochial school aid, **1997** 361-381
public aid to private schools, **1973** 641-658; **1977** 431-445
public display of Nativity scene, **1984** 217-239
religious groups with political agenda, **1983** 817, 819-823
school prayer, **1992** 553-562
school vouchers, Supreme Court on, **2002** 406-423
in Spanish democratic constitution, **1978** 810, 815
use of school facilities by religious groups, **1993** 363-370
U.S.-Vatican diplomatic relations, **1984** 19-21
Church Arson Prevention Act (1966), **1997** 301, 306, 307, 308
Church of Jesus Christ of Latter-Day Saints. *See* Mormon Church
Church of Lukumi Babalu Aye, Inc. v. Hialeah, **1997** 421
Churchill, Winston, **1986** 792; **1992** 431, 433, 438
CIA. *See* Central Intelligence Agency
Ciampi, Carlo Azeglio, at Tokyo economic summit, **1993** 542
Cicerone, Ralph, global warming, **2001** 112
Cicippio, Joseph James
captivity of, **1989** 315-317, 320
hostage, **1991** 751, 753
Cigarette Advertising and Labeling Act (1970), **1973** 64
Cigarette Labeling and Advertising Act (1965), **1972** 46
Cigarettes
See also Pregnancy, smoking during; Smoking
additives in, health risks of, **1981** 3-5, 10-11
advertising
legislation, **1972** 46; **1973** 64
and promotion, **1988** 310-312, 314-315
radio and TV ban on, **1972** 46; **1989** 33
dangers of smoking, **1992** 267-275, 563-573
low-tar and low-nicotine, **1980** 17, 19, 25-26; **1981** 3-12
and lung cancer, **1972** 50-51, 775-776, 779, 781; **1981** 3-4, 6-8; **1982** 163-169
nicotine addiction, **1988** 309-317, 319-322
restrictions on sale of, **1989** 31-32, 39
taxes on, **1985** 615-616
warning labels on, **1972** 46; **1982** 164-165; **1988** 310-312, 314; **1989** 33
Cigars and pipes, health effects of smoking, **1973** 63-65, 71-77
Cin-Made Co., **1996** 43
CIPA. *See* Children's Internet Protection Act; Classified Information Procedures Act
Ciparick, Carmen Beauchamp, ruling on America's Cup, **1989** 184-188
Cipollone, Rose, **1988** 311
Cipollone v. Liggett Group, **1992** 563-573
Cirincione, Joseph, on intelligence community, **2005** 251
Cisneros, Henry G.
on homelessness, **1994** 252
on housing shortages for low-income people, **1996** 167
Los Angeles earthquake and, **1994** 5, 6
presidential pardon, **2001** 89
and President's Service Summit, **1997** 40
public housing takeover in Washington (D.C.), **1995** 499
Citgo Petroleum Corporation, air pollution requirements, **2004** 668
Citibank, and New York City's fiscal crisis, **1977** 567, 569, 577
Cities
See also City finances; *names of individual cities*
air pollution in linked to lung cancer, **1972** 775-781
crisis of
Democratic platform on, **1972** 550-554; **1976** 566-569; **1984** 576-577
and Vietnam war's distortion of national priorities, **1972** 481-483
decay of, in Carter-Reagan debate, **1980** 929-930
infant mortality in, **1987** 149, 155-156
inner cities, Eisenhower Foundation report on, **1993** 211-233
national parks in or near, **1972** 796, 800-801, 803-804
problems of studied in Kerner commission update, **1988** 185-194
programs for, in Reagan-Anderson debate, **1980** 848-849, 858-861
schools in, Carnegie plan for, **1988** 195-219
state of, HUD report on, **1998** 364-377
Citigroup, WorldCom fraud case settlement, **2004** 418
Citizen Service Act, **2003** 27
Citizen's Commission on Hunger in New England, **1985** 190
Citizens for Fairness in Education, **1982** 4
Citizenship education
in colleges, **1985** 584-587, 593-596, 598-600
Reagan on, **1989** 17, 21-22
recruitment to government service and, **1989** 201-202
City Council of Los Angeles v. Taxpayers for Vincent, **1993** 368; **1994** 293
City finances
Bridgeport (Conn.), bankruptcy of, **1991** 303-307
New York City, fiscal crisis, **1975** 861-869; **1976** 863-867; **1977** 567-579
City of Boerne v. Flores, Archbishop of San Antonio, **1997** 406-421
City of Cleburne v. Cleburne Living Ctr. , **1997** 191
City of Ladue v. Gilleo, **1994** 289-297
City of Richmond v. J.A. Croson Co. , **1995** 308, 315-316, 322, 323; **1997** 191, 193; **1998** 862, 867
Civil Aeronautics Board (CAB) , approval of Hughes airline purchase, **1973** 976
Civil disorder
See also Dissident groups; Kerner commission
intelligence community's response to, **1975** 419-424

Civil disorder *Continued*
Kent State antiwar demonstrations, parents' right to sue, **1974** 265-270
Los Angeles riots, **1992** 407-429
Civil law
damage awards, ABA on tort reform, **1987** 165-169, 172-178
on reproductive technologies, Vatican call for, **1987** 267, 269, 284-285
Civil rights
See also Civil rights movement; USA Patriot Act
Chavis NAACP address, **1993** 579-584
Clinton political discourse and citizenship speech, **1995** 426-660
D.C. voting representation in Congress, **1978** 589-590
Democratic Party platform on, **1972** 541-544; **1980** 739-741; **1984** 598-613; **1992** 694-695; **1996** 650-652
detainees
detentions in terrorism cases, Supreme Court on, **2004** 375-398
"enemy combatant" cases, **2002** 835-837; **2003** 106, 111-112, 310
Guantanamo Bay detentions, British Court on, **2002** 830-841; **2004** 375
secret domestic detentions, **2002** 833-835
enforcement
by Carter administration, **1979** 54-55; **1980** 78; **1981** 83
by Nixon administration, **1973** 227-234
by Reagan administration, **1983** 41-55, 913-917; **1987** 43-48, 51, 58-59; **1989** 17
Evers-Williams NAACP address, **1993** 453-462
executive power and, **2005** 901
FBI domestic security guidelines, **1983** 257-261
federal role in, National '80s Agenda on, **1981** 40, 53
in Hong Kong after British, **1984** 1046, 1048
Humphrey's commitment to, **1978** 3-5
intelligence agencies' domestic activities, **1975** 401-407; **1976** 237, 264-265, 284, 322-323
Johnson's contribution to legislation on, **1972** 938-940
of mentally retarded, **1982** 521-530
national identity card, **2002** 535
Pentagon "data mining" system and, **2002** 559-568
Polish government on reform, **1989** 526-528
in PRC constitution, **1975** 44, 48, 52; **1978** 158, 172-175
property tax increase for school desegregation, **1990** 227-238
Republican platform on, **1984** 663, 697-702; **1988** 642-643
rights of accused vs. citizen protection, Burger on, **1981** 191-196
security vs., **2001** 640-642
separation of military from domestic law enforcement, **2002** 534-535
sex discrimination in language of laws on, Justice Department on, **1983** 756
in Soviet constitution, **1977** 748, 754-755, 761-763
in Spanish constitution, **1978** 809-810, 814-818
student drug testing, Supreme Court on, **2002** 424-436
under Polish martial law, **1981** 881-882, 892
warrantless domestic surveillance, by NSA, **2005** 80, 958-959
Warren Court rulings on, **1972** 935-938
Civil Rights Act (1866)
discrimination in private school admissions, **1976** 391-404
reverse discrimination in firing employees, **1976** 405-407, 409-410
Civil Rights Act (1871), **1974** 266
Civil Rights Act (1957), **1972** 938-939; **1983** 913
Civil Rights Act (1964), **2003** 361
discrimination in federally assisted programs, **1976** 224-225, 229-231
provisions of, Warren on, **1972** 939
school desegregation plan's continued balance, **1976** 413-423
Title IX, **1992** 191
Title VI, **1992** 189-190, 191
reverse discrimination, **1978** 469-473, 478-487, 490-492
Title VII, **1993** 423-430, 939-945
affirmative action, **1986** 652-678
EEOC enforcement powers, **1972** 313-315
job discrimination, **1979** 400-401, 406-407; **1987** 17-27; **1989** 321-332
promotion opportunities for women, **1987** 331-349
reverse discrimination, **1976** 405-409; **1979** 493-507
seniority and discrimination, **1977** 383-393, 871-881; **1984** 366-370, 373-376, 383-385
sex discrimination in employer plans, **1976** 891-905; **1978** 293-306
Civil Rights Act (1968), **1972** 939
Civil Rights Act (1991), **1991** 759; **1992** 190
Civil Rights Commission
employment of minorities and women, **1982** 919-944
Florida presidential election findings, **2001** 523-524
in Nixon administration, **1973** 227-234
in Reagan administration, **1983** 78, 85, 913-917
Civil rights movement
Beckwith trial for murder of Medgar Evers, **2002** 239; **2005** 353
church bombing trial (Birmingham, 1963), **2002** 239-246; **2005** 353
civil rights workers slayings trial (Mississippi, 1964), **2005** 353-361
death of Rosa Parks, **2005** 353-354
FBI surveillance of, **1975** 874, 877-878
King's role in, **1983** 883, 885-888
lynchings, Senate apology for, **2005** 356-357
March on Washington, **1993** 583-584
thirtieth anniversary, **1993** 677-685
NAACP economic boycott during, **1982** 655-674
Civil Rights Remedies Equalization Amendment (1986), **1992** 195, 199
Civil Rights Restoration Act (1987), **1992** 195
Civil Service Commission
conflicting responsibilities of, **1978** 138, 140-141, 143-146

Fitzgerald whistleblowing case, **1973** 194-195, 202-204
Civil service reform, in Carter administration, **1978** 8, 15, 31, 137-148; **1979** 29, 36-39; **1981** 57, 81
Civil Service Reform Act (1978)
and drug testing of employees, **1986** 841
provisions, **1978** 137-148
Civil service retirement
Grace commission proposal on, **1984** 170, 174-175
in Reagan budget, **1983** 83, 115; **1984** 112
Social Security reform, **1983** 57, 65
Civiletti, Benjamin R., **1979** 562
B. Carter's Libyan contacts, **1980** 908, 911-912, 915-917
Carter warehouse investigation, **1979** 802
political dismissal, investigation of, **1978** 52, 54-56, 63
Claiborne, Harry E., **1993** 81
impeachment of, **1986** 849-857; **1989** 583
Clark, Barney, artificial heart implant patient, **2001** 476
Clark, Bob, Brzezinski interview, **1979** 977-979, 982
Clark, Kenneth B. , on riot commission reports, **1993** 214
Clark, Laura Blair Salton, *Columbia* astronaut, **2003** 633
Clark, Marcia, Simpson prosecutor's rebuttal, **1995** 613, 619-621
Clark, Ramsey, on drug dealers' punishment, **1973** 29
Clark, Russell G., **1990** 228
Clark, Vernon, USS *Cole* bombing, **2001** 4-5
Clark, Wesley K.
Kosovo crisis, NATO campaign, **1999** 137-138
Milosevic war crimes trial testimony, **2003** 464
presidential candidate, **2003** 464; **2004** 479, 480
Clark, William P., **1981** 848; **1982** 562; **1983** 827, 829
human rights in foreign policy, **1981** 779, 781-785
U.S. defense strategy, **1982** 395-403, 886, 896-901
Clark v. Arizona, **2005** 182
Clark Air Force Base (Philippines), U.S. POWs' return to, **1973** 245
Clarke, Richard, computer infrastructure security, **1998** 677
Clarke, Richard A. , commission on terrorist attacks testimony, **2004** 453
Clarridge, Duane R. , Iran-contra conviction, **1994** 12
Classified information
court handling of in Iran-contra trials and investigations, **1989** 393-395
leaks of by congressional committees, **1976** 115-117, 130
leaks of by executive branch officials, Ford proposed rules on, **1976** 125-129, 141
leaks of from congressional committees, House investigation of Schorr source, **1976** 683-686
procedures for classifying and declassifying, **1972** 235-245; **1976** 117, 123
scientific projects for military, **1972** 381-383
secrecy and disclosure of, proposed legislation on, **1976** 237, 263
use of secrecy classifications by Nixon administration, **1972** 23-24
Classified Information Procedures Act (CIPA), **1990** 494-495, 503, 505-506
Clausen, A. W.
departure from World Bank, **1985** 645
protectionism among industrialized nations, **1984** 796, 800-801
rain forests and World Bank projects, **1986** 860-861
World Bank role in world economies, **1984** 797, 800-802
Clausen, Cara, adoption case, **1993** 515-529
Clawson, Ken W., **1973** 630
Clay, Henry, as Speaker of the House, **1995** 6-7
Claybrook, Joan, **1978** 720
Clayton, Paul, medical records security, **1997** 581
Clayton Antitrust Act (1914)
conglomerate mergers and ITT settlement, **1972** 395
intra-enterprise conspiracy doctrine, **1984** 414, 422
CLC. *See* Cost of Living Council
Clean Air Act
See also Clear Skies Initiative
amendments (1977)
definitions of stationary pollution source, **1984** 427-437
NCAQ on effectiveness of, **1981** 275-295
amendments (1990), Bush on, **1990** 715-720
California initiative, **2004** 832
carbon dioxide emissions, **2003** 865
coal development and, **1973** 474-475; **1979** 666
environmental protection and, **1998** 92-93
industrial pollution law suits, **2002** 896
"new source review" dispute, **2002** 895-897, 902-905; **2003** 173-190; **2004** 664-666; **2005** 100
requirements postponed, Nixon on, **1974** 42, 54
requirements revisions, **2005** 101
Clean Air Interstate Rule (CAIR), **2004** 667; **2005** 95, 99-100
Clean Water Act
Clinton proposals, **1994** 39
and planning for oil spill, **1989** 226
storms and sewage drainage, **2004** 670
wetlands preservation and, **2004** 670
Clean Water Initiative, **1998** 51
Clear Skies Initiative, **2002** 299, 894, 898-899; **2003** 27, 179-180; **2004** 666-667; **2005** 79, 83, 95, 98-99
Cleland, Max
commission on terrorist attacks, resignation, **2003** 547
election defeat, **2002** 36, 533, 821
Cleland, Max (D-Ga.), **1977** 184
Clemency Board, Presidential, creation of, **1974** 820-821, 825-826
Clemens, Luis, economic development in developing countries, **2002** 449
Clements, Diane, on death penalty for juveniles, **2005** 180-181
Clergy
See also Catholic clergy
child sexual abuse by priests, **2002** 867-876; **2003** 523-543; **2004** 82-93; **2005** 294, 865-867
gay clergy controversy, **2004** 42-44
gay seminarians prohibition, **2005** 863-872
Cleveland, Grover, **1986** 699

Clifford, Clark M.
attorney for Bert Lance, **1977** 628
BCCI banking scandal, **1991** 621-636
Climate change
See also Greenhouse effect; Kyoto Protocol on Climate Change (UN treaty)
adverse effects of, **2002** 303, 312, 318-320
Arctic Climate Impact Assessment, **2004** 827-840
from burning coal, **1980** 418, 423, 427-430
Bush administration policy, **2004** 831-832
caused by ozone-depleting chemicals, **1975** 438-439, 442; **1980** 669, 691
Clinton comments on, **2000** 33
Conference of the Parties (or COP-10), **2004** 829
Council of Economic Advisers' Report, **1990** 102-104
economic summit statement on, **1988** 397
effects of, **1988** 863-866
effects of SST, **1973** 236
EPA report on, **2002** 298-321
Global Climate Change Initiative, **2002** 299
from greenhouse effect, **1988** 861-866
greenhouse gas emissions, **2001** 109; **2005** 919, 920, 925-927
Houston economic summit, **1990** 468-469, 476
hurricanes and, **2005** 926-927
impact of, **2000** 337-358
in nuclear winter, **1983** 857-878
record high temperatures and, **1998** 945-950
scientific research studies, **2004** 830-831; **2005** 920-921, 925-926
state initiatives, **2002** 305; **2005** 924-925
study of, U.S.-Soviet agreement on, **1972** 806, 811
UN Framework Convention on Climate Change (UNFCC, Rio treaty), **2000** 337; **2002** 300, 305-321, 593-594; **2004** 829
UN scientific panel report, **2001** 109-126
UN treaty, **1998** 945, 947; **2000** 337; **2001** 109-115, 109-126, 516, 541, 677
UN treaty conference (Kyoto), **1997** 481, 859-876
U.S. policy on global warming, GAO report on, **2003** 861-873
WMO report on global temperatures, **2004** 833; **2005** 926
worldwide heat waves and temperature increases, **2003** 866
Climate Change Technology Advisory Committee, **2005** 922
Climate Orbiter mission to Mars, **2003** 302; **2004** 4
investigation, **1999** 711-717; **2000** 89, 90, 95-102
Clines, Thomas G., **1991** 619
Clinger, William F. (R-Pa.) , on unfunded mandates legislation, **1995** 141-142
Clinton, Bill (William Jefferson)
See also Clinton Foundation; Lewinsky, Monica
affirmative action endorsement, **1998** 856
campaigns and elections
acceptance speech, **1992** 675-684; **1996** 602-603, 609-622
challenge from Perot, **1992** 717
Chinese government contributions, **1999** 237
finance practices, **1997** 822-825, 827-831
finance reform, **1997** 30-31, 33
nomination, **1992** 667-670
postelection statements, **1992** 1019-1021, 1024-1027; **1996** 747-749, 749-753
presidential campaign, **1997** 21
presidential debates, **1992** 907-977; **1996** 707-709, 709-718, 724-731
commerce secretary
Mickey Kantor appointment, **1996** 204
Ronald Brown, statement on death of, **1996** 204-209
communications policy, **2004** 627
congressional election results, **1994** 513, 515-519
on Contract with America, **1995** 427-428, 430
defense policy
chemical and biological weapons, **1998** 49-50
computer security, **1996** 312; **1998** 677
defense budget, **1999** 53-54
land mines ban treaty, **1997** 844, 846
military homosexual ban, **1993** 153, 156-162, 328-329; **1997** 761
missile defense system, **2000** 677-687; **2001** 928; **2003** 817; **2004** 176
national security issues, **1997** 40-43
national security needs, **1997** 811, 814
No Gun Ri (Korea) incident regrets, **2001** 33, 38
nuclear nonproliferation treaty, **1995** 233-238
nuclear test ban treaty, **1999** 600-607
security abroad, **1995** 38-40
spending cuts, **1994** 39, 45
U.S. role, **1994** 45-46; **1996** 31-32
U.S.-Russian arms control, **2000** 205-206
weapons development and nonproliferation policy, **1996** 227-228
defense secretary nomination, **1994** 22-25
Democratic Party convention
speech, **2004** 483
valedictory speech, **2000** 596-608
disbarment proceedings, **2000** 766
domestic and social policy
on advertising of distilled spirits, **1996** 770-771, 774-775
affirmative action endorsement, **1995** 483-496, 574-575
antiterrorism bill, **1996** 231-236
apparel workplace investigations, **1997** 206-211
aviation security, **1996** 662-664
child care programs, **1998** 47-48
child welfare, Convention on the Rights of the Child, **2002** 224
church arson prevention, **1997** 303, 306, 310, 311
consumer product liability, **1996** 275-276
crime bill, **1994** 35, 47-48; **1995** 33-34; **1996** 29; **1997** 39
drug control policy, Dole challenge to, **1996** 572
farm bill, **1996** 199
gay marriage, **2003** 405
health care reform, **1993** 781-804; **1994** 34-35, 42-45, 50-51, 127-128; **1995** 74-75; **1998** 46-47
Human Genome Project, **2000** 397-409
juvenile curfews, **1996** 325
medical records privacy, **2001** 486-487
Miranda warnings, **2000** 386

National Performance Review, remarks on, **1993** 733-735
partial birth abortion ban veto, **2003** 995
patients' bill of rights, **1999** 562-563
proposals, **1998** 39-40
same-sex marriages, **1996** 687-690; **1997** 761
Social Security reform, **2005** 84
tobacco claims settlement, **1997** 331-332, 335
unemployment system reform, **1994** 40
unfunded mandates legislation, **1995** 141-145
on violent crime, **1992** 376
volunteerism summit, **1997** 40, 238-244
welfare reform, **1994** 35, 40-42; **1995** 25, 74-75; **1996** 450-461; **1997** 33-34, 617-622; **1998** 46, 356-357
economic policy
balanced budget, **1995** 24-25, 32-33; **1996** 53; **1997** 30, 33, 602-605; **1998** 40, 77
balanced budget amendment, signing ceremony, **1997** 605-608
budget deficit reduction, **1998** 77
budget impasse, **1995** 737-745
budget surplus, **1998** 502; **1999** 350-356
on Bush's proposals, **1992** 58
corporate responsibility, **1996** 41-42
Democratic convention speech, **1996** 610-612
economic plan, **1994** 39
expanding the middle class, **1995** 34-38
five-year plan, **1993** 181-196
globalization ("Washington consensus"), **2000** 476; **2001** 87
middle class bill of rights, **1994** 610-614
minimum wage advocate, **1996** 563-569
tax increases, **1994** 38-39
Tokyo economic summit, **1993** 541-557
economic reports, **1994** 123-129; **1995** 69-76; **1996** 50-54; **1997** 52-54; **1998** 73-79; **1999** 85-92; **2000** 43-62; **2001** 52-60
economic summits, Denver, **1997** 341-342
education goals, **1990** 54, 154-163
education policy
Democratic convention speech on, **1996** 612-613
education and training programs, **1999** 53
inaugural address on, **1997** 24-25
national education standards, **1997** 29, 30, 34-35
State of the Union address on, **1997** 34-37; **1998** 43-44; **1999** 46-48; **2000** 22-24
uniforms in public schools, **1996** 84
education summit, **1989** 561-562
environmental policy, **1994** 39-40; **1996** 30-31; **1997** 39; **2001** 212-213
clean air and water initiatives, **1998** 51-52
climate change, **2005** 923
Everglades restoration project, **1996** 80-83; **1997** 39
industrial pollution law suits, **2002** 895-896; **2004** 665
lead levels for drinking water, **2003** 174
logging decision, **1993** 495-499
mercury emissions rules, **2005** 96
pesticide regulation reform, **1996** 467-470
Utah's Red Rocks region preservation, **1997** 39
executive orders
declassifying government secrets, **1994** 524-527
security clearances, **1995** 532-545
striking workers, **1995** 129-133
farewell speech, **2001** 86-93
FBI director appointment
Freeh nomination, **1993** 612-615
Sessions dismissal, **1993** 611-612
foreign policy
abortions overseas, federal funding for, **2005** 52
activist policy, **1999** 699-710
Africa, U.S. support for, **2000** 63-73
African state visit, **1998** 159-168, 221; **1999** 54, 428; **2000** 64-65
Angola, recognition of Dos Santos government, **2002** 153
Bosnia
humanitarian air lift, **1994** 45
NATO peacekeeping mission, **1995** 717-726; **1996** 818-819; **1998** 49
Burundi peace accord, **2003** 923
Chechnya war, **1999** 913
chemical weapons treaty, **1997** 195, 196-197
China
apology for U.S. bombing of Chinese embassy, **1999** 304
and human rights, **1994** 73-74
news conference, **1998** 466-478
summit meeting, **1997** 728-739
U.S. relations, **2001** 739
Colombia
Haiti, political situation, **2001** 396; **2004** 95
Plan Colombia, **2000** 842-844; **2002** 570, 573
state visit, **2000** 844
CSCE European security summit, **1994** 583-591
Cuba, boat people agreement, **1995** 203-207
Cuban airline attack response, **1996** 95-97
Democratic convention acceptance speech, **1996** 621-622
East Timor, UN peacekeeping forces, **1999** 513
Haiti
political situation, **2000** 959-960
U.S. forces in, **1994** 433-434
Haitian refugee interdiction, **1993** 413-421
Indonesia, political situation, **1999** 718-723
Iraq
air strikes against, **1998** 934-944; **2001** 850; **2003** 875, 1190
troop buildup on Kuwait border, **1994** 431-435
U.S. humanitarian aid, **2001** 853
weapons inspections, **2003** 875
Israel, eulogy for Yitzhak Rabin, **1995** 692
Israel-Syria peace negotiations, **1999** 894-895, 897
Kosovo, air war against Serbian forces, **1999** 134-143
Middle East
Declaration of Principles, **1993** 747-748, 761-763, 768
Israel-Jordan peace agreement, **1994** 331-333
West bank agreement, **1995** 622, 625-626
Middle East peace negotiations, **2001** 361; **2002** 370, 927

Clinton, Bill (William Jefferson) *Continued*
Camp David summit, **2000** 494-507; **2001** 360, 361; **2003** 1204
Geneva Accord, **2003** 1204
Israel and Palestinian concessions, **2004** 304
Millennium summit talks, **2000** 702
Wye River agreement, **1998** 747-749, 750; **1999** 52-53, 700
Nobel Peace Prize statement, **1993** 880, 881-882
North Korea
state visit proposed, **2000** 868-869
U.S. relations, **2002** 634
Northern Ireland, peace efforts, **1995** 727-733; **1998** 204
peacekeeping missions, **1999** 52-53
pre-election speech, **1992** 257
on religious freedom, **1998** 19, 22-23
Russia, economic crisis, **1998** 601-613
Rwanda genocidal war, apology for failure to act, **2004** 116
Rwanda genocidal war, U.S. apology for inaction, **1999** 860-861
Somalia, peace-keeping mission, **1994** 45
Somalian relief, **1992** 1068
Sudan, sanctions against, **2003** 840-841
Turkey, visit after earthquake, **1999** 467
UN address, **1993** 805-817
UN secretary general, statement on, **1996** 824-825, 826-827
United Nations, U.S. dues payment, **2001** 129, 901
U.S. embassy bombings, **1998** 558, 561-563
Vietnam
diplomatic relations, **1995** 472-477
state visit, **2000** 913-922
trade embargo, lifting of, **1994** 95-99
Yugoslavia, diplomatic relations with, **2000** 837-838
Foster, Henry, Jr., nomination for surgeon general, **1995** 67-68
Foster, Vincent, Jr. (White House counsel), suicide investigations, **1993** 531-539
gay rights, speech to Human Rights Campaign, **1997** 760-766
gay rights march on Washington, **1993** 327-331
Ginsburg Supreme Court appointment, **1993** 393-398
government reform, reinventing government, **1995** 30-31
health care policy
AIDS epidemic initiatives, **2000** 413-414
AIDS research, **1995** 428, 433, 434-435
consumers bill of rights, **1997** 787
medical records privacy, **2000** 1063-1071
stem cell research guidelines, **2000** 667
human radiation experiments, apology for, **1995** 633-638
impeachment trial, **1999** 15-40, 351; **2001** 88-89; **2002** 382; **2003** 1159; **2005** 553
inaugural addresses, **1993** 129-134; **1997** 20-26
International Criminal Court (ICC), **2002** 607
Iran-contra pardons, **1992** 1075
Justice Department nominations, **1993** 135-139
Korean War veterans memorial dedication, **1995** 506, 509-511
letter on draft, **1992** 155-161
on Los Angeles riots, **1992** 407
medical research, **1997** 37-38
natural disasters
floods in Midwest, **1993** 483-486
Los Angeles earthquake, **1994** 3-7
Nazi Germany, investigations into neutral aid to, **1997** 257-272
Nixon funeral remarks, **1994** 243-244
on Oklahoma City bombing, **1995** 176-177
passport search report, **1992** 1045-1052
political discourse and citizenship speech, **1995** 426-440
presidency
approval ratings, **1999** 42; **2005** 41
censuring the president, **1998** 633, 699
first year, **1994** 36
line-item veto, **1997** 611-616
public opinion on job performance, **1993** 585
presidential pardons, **2001** 86, 89-91
reprieve for Garza, **2001** 390
on Quayle's "Murphy Brown" speech, **1992** 444-445
on race-based redistricting, **1995** 371
racism
in America, **2000** 771-780
commencement speech on, **1997** 314-324
and inaugural address, **1997** 22
pleas to end in America, **1995** 646-654; **1997** 22, 29, 315
race initiative, State of the Union address on, **1999** 56-57
statement for March on Washington thirtieth anniversary, **1993** 684-685
Schultz, Charles (cartoonist) death, statement on, **1999** 859
security
clearances for government employees, **1995** 532-545
Pennsylvania Avenue closing, **1995** 254-258
shooting of Capitol policemen, **1998** 515-516
sexual harassment suit, **1997** 21, 290-298; **1998** 39, 565, 633-634, 638-639, 962; **1999** 16, 21-22
space program
support for, **1996** 471
talk with woman astronaut Shannon Lucid, **1996** 691-694
State of the Union addresses, **1994** 34-53; **1995** 24-42; **1996** 21-35; **1997** 29-44; **1998** 38-54; **1999** 41-57; **2000** 16-40
terrorism
U.S. air strikes against terrorists, **1998** 586-591
USS *Cole* bombing, **2000** 861-865
trade policy
China trade agreement, **2000** 213-221
"fast-track" negotiations, **1997** 612; **1998** 75
free trade in the Americas, **2002** 779
GATT, remarks on, **1994** 555-559
GATT renewal, **1993** 997-1002
and labor practices, **1998** 45
market expansion, **1997** 53-54
NAFTA, remarks on, **1993** 953-958; **1997** 541-549

Uruguay Round trade talks, **1993** 542
WTO meeting in Seattle, **1999** 799
tsunami relief work, UN special envoy, **2005** 991
UN fiftieth anniversary remarks, **1995** 350-358
U.S. Capitol bicentennial, **1993** 903-904
Vietnam War memorial, Memorial Day ceremony remarks, **1993** 347-349
visit with John Paul II, **1993** 660
Waco compound incident, **1995** 293-301
on welfare reform, **1988** 850, 852
White House Travel Office probe, **1993** 531-539; **1997** 21; **2000** 765
Whitewater investigation and scandal, **1994** 36; **1997** 21; **1998** 633; **2000** 762-770
World War II fiftieth anniversary commemoration, **1995** 216-221
Clinton, Hillary Rodham (First Lady; D-N.Y.)
book advance payments, **2000** 910
breast cancer report, **1993** 905
child care and family reform issues, **2000** 26
Clinton's inaugural address, **1993** 129, 131
Crawford FDA commissioner nomination, **2005** 816
Democratic Party conventions, **1992** 669; **1996** 602; **2000** 612; **2004** 483
economic summit (Tokyo), **1993** 549, 552
as First Lady, **2000** 907
Flowers (Gennifer) allegations, **1992** 156
Foster (White House counsel) suicide investigations, **1993** 531, 533, 539
gays in the military, **1999** 900
Ginsburg appointment, **1993** 398
health care reform plan, **1993** 781-804
Leavitt EPA administrator nomination, **2003** 174
presidential wife's role, **1992** 1021
Republican Convention, **1992** 781
Senate election, **2001** 86-87
and victory speech, **2000** 906-912
Starr investigation, **1998** 566
at UN Conference on Women, **1995** 581-587
Whitewater investigation, **1994** 36; **1996** 22, 839; **1997** 21; **1998** 393-394; **1999** 22; **2000** 762-770, 907
Clinton v. City of New York, **1998** 419-437
Clinton v. Jones, **1997** 290-298
Clinton, Roger, presidential pardon, **2001** 89
Clinton Foundation
AIDS generic drug treatment negotiations, **2003** 780, 784; **2004** 431-432
childhood obesity prevention programs, **2005** 6
Clohessy, David, sexual abuse by priests, **2002** 870; **2005** 866
Clonaid, human cloning research, **2002** 516-517
Cloning research, **1997** 212-220; **2000** 669
cloning defined, **2002** 519
ethics of, president's council on, **2002** 512-529; **2004** 157-167
human cloning
banning of, **1997** 213-214, 341, 351
defined, **2002** 519
UN resolution on, **2005** 323
of human embryos, **2001** 541; **2004** 158-159
state legislation, **2002** 515-516
stem cells from human embryos, South Korea research scandal, **2005** 317, 320-322
Club for Growth, **2005** 112
Club of Rome
Gorbachev on, **1992** 437
on limits to world growth, **1972** 215-220
Coal
burning of
and cancer-causing polluted air, **1972** 775, 777
emissions as cause of acid rain, **1983** 197-198
environmental effects, **1975** 193; **1980** 418, 423, 427-430
conversion to
in Carter energy plan, **1976** 708-709; **1977** 279, 281-284, 286, 290-291
Democratic platform on, **1976** 545, 575
in energy crisis, Nixon on, **1973** 914, 916; **1974** 105
FEA on, **1974** 912-913, 915
in Ford energy program, **1975** 17, 22-24, 29, 38
development of
Carter on, **1977** 103, 106
economic summit on, **1977** 373; **1978** 537-758; **1980** 503-504, 509
environmental allowances for, **1973** 467-468, 474-475; **1975** 91-92
in Ford energy program, **1976** 20
Nixon on, **1974** 105
Schlesinger on, **1979** 659-660, 665-666
expanded use of, Ford CEA on, **1975** 103; **1977** 85
research on extraction and use, U.S.-Polish agreement on, **1974** 884-885
surface mining of, standards for in energy crisis, **1973** 914, 920
as transition resource, Republican platform on, **1980** 615
world resources of, **1973** 467; **1980** 417-422, 425-427
Coal industry
market limitations and production, **1981** 40, 48, 65
strike in, negotiations and settlement, **1978** 111-124
Coal miners, respiratory disease in, and smoking, **1985** 818-819
Coalition Against Unsolicited Commercial E-Mail, **2002** 70
Coalition of Catholics and Survivors, **2002** 871
Coalition of Essential Schools, **1992** 47
Coalition Provisional Authority (CPA), **2003** 138-139, 142-144, 935; **2004** 208, 399, 879; **2005** 941
Coard, Bernard, **1983** 849
Coast Guard
Haitian refugees returned, **1992** 453-460, 467-468; **1993** 413-421
and homeland security, **2002** 51, 530, 532
Mariel boatlift of Cuban refugees, **1980** 339-340, 343, 345-346
responsibility in Alaska oil spill cleanup, **1989** 226, 228-229, 230, 232-234
Coastal Zone Management Act, **2004** 602
Coats, Dan (R-Ind.) , timing of U.S. air strikes, **1998** 587-588
COBE. *See* Cosmic background explorer

Coble, Howard (R-N.C.), House Judiciary Committee impeachment inquiry, **1998** 704
Coburn, Tom (R-Okla.)
  physician-assisted suicide, **1999** 442
  professional services ban, congressional ethics ruling, **2005** 636
  transportation spending debate, **2005** 125
Coca Cola, affirmative action, **2003** 362
Cocaine
  See also Drug use
  chemicals in production of, **1989** 513-514
  crack cocaine, **1986** 181; **1997** 682; **1999** 460
  demand for, **1986** 839-840
  emergence of crack, **1986** 181
  sentencing for sales of, **1997** 245-254
  use in U.S., **1996** 575-576, 579; **1999** 460, 463
Cochran, John, Bush presidential campaign, **2004** 479
Cochran, Johnnie L. , Simpson defense attorney's closing arguments, **1995** 613, 615-618
CODESA (Convention for a Democratic South Africa), **1992** 284-285, 288
Coelho, Tony (D-Calif.)
  Donovan indictment, **1984** 805
  Reagan-Gorbachev summit, **1987** 993
  resignation, **1989** 240
Cohen, Eliot, "smart" weapons performance, **1996** 403
Cohen, Jonathan, on condom use and AIDS prevention, **2004** 432
Cohen, William S. (R-Maine; Defense Department secretary)
  affirmative action, **2003** 362
  antiharassment training for military personnel, **1999** 900
  appointment, **1996** 673
  burial at sea of John F. Kennedy Jr., **1999** 424
  cost-cutting measures, **1997** 812
  defense spending, **1999** 819
  Gulf War syndrome investigations, **1997** 741
  Iraq, air strikes against, **1998** 936-937
  Kosovo, NATO air strikes, **1999** 127
  limits on gifts to members of Congress, **1995** 701
  Middle East diplomatic role, **2000** 862
  and national security, **2000** 32
  NATO expansion, **1997** 516
  No Gun Ri (Korea) incident, **2001** 34
  North Korean missile threat, **1999** 820
  Panama Canal, U.S. Policy, **1999** 852
  retirement from Congress, **1995** 558-559
  Russian submarine *Kursk* disaster, **2000** 635-641
  sexual harassment and discrimination in the military, **1997** 656
  on terrorist threat, **2004** 452
  Tomb of the Unknowns, disinterment remarks, **1998** 281-283
  U.S. embassy bombings, **1998** 558, 559-560
  USS *Cole* bombing, **2001** 6
  women in the military, **1987** 672; **1998** 335-336
Cohen v. Cowles Media Co., **1991** 317-318, 326-330
Cohen v. Jenkintown Cab Co., **1998** 398, 402, 404
Cohn, Samuel M., **1974** 573-574
Coifman, Jon, greenhouse gas emissions, **2002** 300
Coker v. Georgia, **1977** 517-528
Colak, Barisa, Bosnia-Herzegovina constitutional reform, **2005** 858-859
Colby, William E.
  ban on CIA assassinations, **1975** 796-797
  CIA actions in Chile, **1974** 805-810; **1975** 403
  CIA domestic intelligence, **1975** 523-528
  replaced as CIA director, **1975** 875
  secrecy of Senate report, **1975** 710
Cold War, **2004** 630-632
  See also Berlin Wall
  end of, Gorbachev speech on, **1992** 431-438
  end of, CIA on, **1992** 4, 6-7
Cole (USS, navy destroyer), bombing of, **2000** 277, 861-865; **2001** 3-16, 805; **2003** 30
Cole, David G. , civil rights of September 11 detainees, **2003** 314
Cole, James M.
  special counsel appointment, **1995** 749
  special counsel report on Gingrich ethics violations, **1997** 3-19
Cole, Norman, **1993** 369
Cole, Philip, cancer death rates, **1996** 790
Coleman, J. Marshall
  gubernatorial election, **1990** 42-43
  senatorial election campaign, **1994** 10
Coleman, James S. , on school desegregation, **1975** 613-633
Coleman, Mary Sue
  affirmative action, **2003** 363
  health insurance coverage, **2002** 669; **2004** 983
Coleman, Norm (R-Minn.)
  on call for Annan's resignation, **2004** 892; **2005** 236
  senatorial election, **2002** 822
  UN oil-for-food program scandal, **2004** 892
Coleman, Russell, death penalty case, **1998** 185-186
Coleman v. Thompson, **1991** 382-383
Coles, Matthew
  and Americans with Disabilities Act, **1998** 380
  domestic partnerships, **1989** 307
Collective bargaining
  agreements, and bankruptcy of companies, **1984** 181-199
  for farm workers in California, **1975** 377-399
  Pittston coal strike settled, **1990** 19-22
  steel industry labor-management agreement, **1973** 437-444
College Entrance Examination Board
  on gender-biased tests, **1992** 143
  on student test scores, **1975** 691
College Savings Bank v. Florida Prepaid Postsecondary Ed. Expense Bd., **1999** 334, 340
Colleges and universities
  accreditation reform, **1998** 5, 17
  active learning in, **1985** 589, 600-602
  affirmative action
    admissions programs, **1978** 467-492
    in California, **1996** 759-763; **1997** 186
    Supreme Court on, **2003** 358-386
  all-male policy, **1991** 309-316
  athletes steroid use policy, **2005** 218
  Barbara Bush's speech at Wellesley commencement, **1990** 353-356
  black athletes, **1989** 213-223

Catholic, academic freedom at, **1986** 758-760
CIA contacts in, **1976** 247, 253-254
CIA outreach to, **1992** 9
citizenship, teaching, **1985** 584-587, 594-596, 598-600
collaboration with urban public schools, **1988** 215-216, 218-219
college drinking, national task force report on, **2002** 175-192
computer-related field graduates, **1997** 670
costs of higher education, **1998** 3-18, 43-44
curriculum recommendations, **1985** 127-144
curriculum reform, **1986** 940-944, 949-951
degree, declining value of, **1985** 127-133
foreign student tracking, **2002** 843-845
goals for reform of, **1986** 939-958
HOPE scholarship program, **1998** 43, 78, 87; **1999** 46; **2000** 24, 47; **2001** 58
Knight report on college athletics, **1991** 129-142
liberal arts role, **1986** 939-958
math and science degrees granted, **1992** 628-629
minority enrollment, **1997** 186
nurturing creativity in, **1985** 596-597
Pell Grant scholarships, **1998** 43, 87, 150, 154; **2000** 24; **2001** 59; **2005** 144
police corps opportunities, **1997** 244
quality of life in, **1986** 941, 944-945, 954-956
research, role of, **1985** 589, 591-592
science and engineering programs and personnel, **1973** 787-789
segregation
Mississippi colleges, **1992** 575-587
Southern Education Foundation report on, **1995** 239-253
sex discrimination and federal aid, **1974** 507-513; **1984** 201-214
speeches marking 1970 Kent State deaths, **1990** 289-294
student aid programs, **1996** 115-117; **1998** 18; **2000** 48
and draft registration, **1984** 493-503
restructuring, **1993** 171-179
teaching vs. research, **1985** 127-129, 132-137; **1986** 939, 941, 944, 951-952; **1988** 517, 520-522
tenure decision for faculty, Supreme Court, **1990** 23-34
transition from high school, **1986** 941, 943, 947-948
tuition tax credit proposal, **1997** 30, 36; **1998** 87
undergraduate programs
for basic skills, **1986** 940-941, 943, 950; **1988** 380
exchanges with Soviet Union, **1990** 341
governing, **1986** 941, 945, 956-957
humanities in, **1984** 997-1003
western civilization curriculum, **1984** 997-1003
vocational orientation of students, **1988** 519
work/study programs, **1985** 585, 590
Collette, Alec, hostage, **1991** 751-752
Collins, Addie Mae, church bombing victim, **2002** 240, 244
Collins, Christopher, on disabilities in the workplace, **2002** 4-5
Collins, Eileen M. , *Discovery* space shuttle mission, **2005** 499-501
Collins, Francis, Human Genome Project, **2000** 399-400, 405-407
Collins, Sally, Forest Service rules, **2002** 900
Collins, Sarah, church bombing victim, **2002** 240, 244
Collins, Susan (R-Maine)
Clinton State of the Union address, Republican response, **2000** 19-20, 36-38
Hurricane Katrina disaster, **2005** 566
prescription drug advertising, **2002** 948
and Republican Party, **2001** 378
September 11 panel recommendations, **2004** 967, 969
Collor de Mello, Fernando, **1992** 502
Collyer, Rosemary M. , collective bargaining rights, **2005** 489
Colombia
Caribbean economic aid from, **1982** 180, 186
Contadora Group, **1987** 638
democratic security and defense policy, **2003** 425-438
drug control program, **2003** 431-432
drug summit, **1990** 115-126; **1992** 201-221
drug traffickers of, **1986** 185-189
drug trafficking, **2000** 31; **2002** 569-570
drug war in, **1989** 499-501, 511-515
human rights in, **1989** 603; **1990** 144-145
John Paul II's visit, **1986** 639-649
kidnappings, **2002** 570-571; **2003** 426-427
National Liberation Army (ELN), **2002** 570; **2003** 427
nuclear weapons material, **2004** 327
Plan Colombia, **2000** 842-851; **2002** 570, 573, 574; **2003** 429
political situation, **2005** 771
Revolutionary Armed Forces of Colombia (FARC), **2000** 841-842; **2002** 570-571; **2003** 426-427; **2005** 771
smoking in the Americas, **1992** 269
United Self-Defense Forces of Colombia (AUC), **2000** 841; **2002** 570, 573; **2003** 427-428
Uribe presidential inauguration, **2002** 569-578
U.S. aid program, **2002** 569
GAO report on, **2000** 840-851
U.S. involvement, **2002** 573-574; **2003** 429-431
U.S. military aid, **1989** 500-501, 504-505; **2002** 574
Colonialism, condemnation of by women's conference, **1975** 509, 521
Colorado
ballot initiatives legislation, **1999** 3-14
gay rights legislation, **1996** 284-295, 689
Colorado for Family Values, gay rights legislation, **1996** 285
Colosio, Luis Donaldo, assassination of, **1994** 563-564
Colson, Charles W.
Ellsberg break-in involvement, **1973** 545-547; **1974** 157, 205-210, 411-417, 443-447, 662
memo on ITT settlement, **1974** 408
on Supreme Court appointments, **2005** 379
Watergate indictment and sentencing, **1974** 157, 161, 163-165, 167; **1975** 143
Watergate involvement, **1974** 321-322, 334-343, 353, 364-366, 375

Columbia Broadcasting System (CBS)
Cronkite interview with Rebozo, **1973** 975-981
libel suit and protection of editorial process, **1979** 285-311
Rather interview with Nixon, **1972** 3-13
Westmoreland libel suit, **1983** 401-412; **1985** 159-165
Columbia space shuttle
disaster
background, **2003** 631-638
causes of, **2003** 635-636, 640-643, 676-677
Debris Assessment Team, **2003** 653-654
future program needs, **2003** 677
Investigation Board Report, **2003** 638-677; **2004** 9; **2005** 498
investigations, reaction to report, **2003** 637-638
NASA decision making leading up to accident, **2003** 648-653
organizational causes, **2003** 657-668
program management, **2003** 654-656
rescue or repair options, **2003** 657
history of missions, **1981** 417-426
Columbine High School (Littleton, Colo.), shooting incident, **1999** 179-184, 615; **2000** 729, 873, 875-876; **2001** 347-359
Columbus, Christopher, Amnesty International Indigenous Americans Abuses Report, **1992** 897-905
Columbus Board of Education v. Penick, **1979** 535-546
Colwell, Rita, on South Pole emergency rescue operation, **1999** 611-613
Colyandro, John, money laundering indictment, **2005** 633, 634, 637, 639-643
Combest, Larry (R-Texas)
government secrecy, **1997** 103
intelligence community, **1996** 796
Comey, James B. , torture in terrorism interrogations denounced, **2004** 343, 346-347
Commager, Henry Steele, **1983** 270
Commerce clause. *See under* Constitution (U.S.), Article I
Commerce Department
auto manufacturers, **1992** 20
in Carter's urban proposal, **1978** 243, 247, 251-253
consolidation of trade functions in, **1979** 638
digital economy report, **2000** 299-307
national security export controls, **1987** 30, 40, 41
pollution controls, study on costs of, **1972** 253
secretary Mickey Kantor appointment, **1996** 204-209
secretary Ronald Brown, death of, **1996** 204-209
technology worker shortage, **1997** 669-678
Y2K preparations, **1999** 760-768
Commercial Sexual Exploitation of Children, Second World Congress Against, **2001** 955-962
Commission for Assistance to a Free Cuba, **2004** 246-257
Commission for Reception, Truth, and Reconciliation (East Timor), **2002** 261; **2004** 756
Commission on America's Urban Families, **1992** 67
Commission on Intelligence Capabilities of the U.S. Regarding Weapons of Mass Destruction, **2005** 246-266
Commission on Protecting and Reducing Government Secrecy, report, **1997** 103-112
Commission on Safety and Abuse in America's Prisons, **2005** 679
Commission on the Future of Worker-Management Relations, report of, **1995** 15-23
Commission on the Media and the Electorate, report on voter participation, **1990** 295-299
Commission to Assess the Ballistic Missile Threat to the United States (Rumsfeld Commission), **1998** 481-499
Committee for Public Education and Religious Liberty v. Nyquist, **1973** 641-643, 646-656; **1983** 676-688
Committee for the Re-election of the President (CRP), as White House group, Watergate committee on, **1974** 600, 602, 616
Committee for the Study of the American Electorate, **2002** 820
Committee on Foreign Intelligence, establishment of, **1976** 127, 132-133
Committee on the Consequences of Uninsurance, **2002** 669
Committee on the Present Danger, on SALT II, **1978** 551
Committee to Prevent Wrongful Executions, **2001** 390
Commodities
See also Raw materials
price stabilization for exports of developing countries, **1975** 588-589, 592-593, 604; **1983** 380
Kissinger to UNCTAD on, **1976** 299-300, 304-309, 315-319
nonaligned nations on, **1983** 263-265
poverty summit on, **1981** 769, 777-778
UNCTAD resolution on, **1976** 427, 431
UNCTAD's integrated fund for, OPEC contribution to, **1976** 939
Commodity Credit Corporation, **1990** 808, 811
Commodity Future Modernization Act, **2001** 862
Commodity Futures Trading Commission (CFTC)
power company exemptions, **2001** 862
stock market crash (1987),**1987** 835; **1988** 9
regulatory role after, **1988** 11-12, 15, 30-31, 34
Common Cause
disclosure of Nixon campaign contributions, **1974** 604
on Wright investigation, **1989** 240
Common Fund for Commodities, **1984** 360
Common Market. *See* European Community (EC)
Commonwealth Club of California, **1992** 443
Commonwealth of Independent States, founding of, **1991** 786-787, 803-806
Commonwealth of Nations
accord on South Africa, **1986** 581-590
sanctions against South Africa, **1986** 372
Communication Workers of America v. Beck, **1992** 345-347
Communications Act (1934)
broadcast restrictions of, **1978** 515-531
license renewals, proposed changes on, **1973** 56, 58-62
telecommunications policy, revision of, **1982** 18

Communications Decency Act (CDA, 1996), **1996** 353; **1997** 444-458; **2003** 387
Communications industry
deregulation of, **1981** 59
minority broadcasters, **1990** 419-435
Communism
collapse of in Eastern Europe, **1989** 625-626, 635-639
as dehumanizing, John Paul II on, **1981** 696, 706-709
power sharing in Eastern Europe, **1989** 710
power sharing in Poland, **1989** 400, 489, 523-525, 537, 635, 710
Reagan administration policy, **2004** 318-319
Reagan on evils of, in British Parliament address, **1982** 478, 483
threat of
and CIA action in Chile, **1975** 884-885, 899-900
effect on CIA attitudes, **1975** 771-773
Communist Party
democracy within Czech, Dubcek on, **1975** 239-249
in Eastern Europe, evolution of, **1976** 434-435, 453-455, 459-461
in Italy, role in government, **1976** 341, 345-346, 426, 447-448, 456-457
PRC constitution and, **1975** 44-46, 49
in Western Europe
evolution of from Soviet dominance, **1976** 433-434, 456-457
special situation of, **1976** 433-434, 437, 441, 447-448, 450-452, 458
Communist Party of the Soviet Union (CPSU)
25th congress, Brezhnev speech, **1976** 143-155
26th congress, Brezhnev speech, **1981** 225-239
27th congress, Gorbachev speech, **1986** 145-168
28th congress, **1991** 528
agriculture report to, from Gorbachev, **1989** 145-152
congress's purpose and leadership, **1981** 225-226
and economic development, **1984** 151
in elections, **1989** 173-179
electoral system reforms, **1987** 79-81, 89-94
Gorbachev's resignation from, **1991** 527-530
leadership of, **1984** 145, 148-150
management reforms, **1987** 79, 90-91, 93-103
reforms under *perestroika,* **1988** 447-451, 458-464
role in new Soviet constitution, **1977** 747-748, 751, 755, 759
Community and Migrant Health Centers, funding of, **1987** 152
Community Communications Company, Inc. v. City of Boulder, Colorado, **1982** 35-49
Community Decency Act, **2002** 287
Community development
block grants for
Reagan on, **1983** 117
Urban League on targeting, **1983** 52, 54
loans and grants for, in Carter's urban plan, **1978** 242, 246-249, 252-256
neighborhood organizations, in Carter's urban plan, **1978** 241-245, 247, 255-257
Nixon proposals for, **1972** 101-103; **1973** 303-305, 314-321, 805-806
private sector initiatives in, Reagan plan for, **1982** 82
revenue sharing for, **1972** 101-102
Nixon on, **1973** 304-305, 314-317
Republican platform on, **1972** 651, 685-686, 694; **1980** 568, 591-592
urban enterprise zones
Reagan on, **1983** 54, 78
Republican platform on, **1980** 568, 591-592
Community Development Department, proposed, **1972** 101-102; **1973** 305, 316-317
Community Empowerment Act, **1997** 71
Community Mental Health Centers (CMHC) Act, **1990** 576, 585-587
Community Renewal Tax Relief Act (2000), **2001** 134
Community service
teaching commitment to, **1985** 584-585, 589-590, 598
as welfare requirement, **1988** 849, 851-852
Community Services Block Grant Program, **2001** 134
Compassion in Dying, **1997** 462
Competitiveness, U.S.
agricultural, **1986** 287, 290, 302, 306
corporate takeovers, Reagan CEA on, **1985** 101-104
Democratic platform on, **1984** 557, 584-589
education changes required, **1986** 457-458, 460-462; **1989** 86-87, 90
foreign, unfair
multilateral trade agreement on, **1979** 639-640
Republican platform on, **1980** 568, 598, 648-649
Japan's trading practices and, **1987** 428-429, 436
in military technology, and export controls, **1987** 38
Reagan and CEA on, **1987** 106, 112, 117, 123, 126, 137; **1989** 8, 13
regulations as hindrance to, Ford on, **1976** 50
strengthening, Nixon on, **1972** 85; **1973** 379-382, 385-386, 389-390
technological
Bush program for, **1989** 75-76
and export controls, **1987** 29-30, 34-38, 41-42
work ethic and, **1972** 390-391
world currency realignment and, **1972** 389
Comprehensive Alcohol Abuse and Alcoholism Prevention, Treatment, and Rehabilitation Act (1970), **1972** 193
Comprehensive Crime Control Act (1984),and sentencing reform, **1987** 407, 409-411
Comprehensive Drug Abuse Prevention and Control Act (1970), **1972** 291, 298
Comprehensive Employment and Training Act (CETA, 1973)
Carter budget cuts in], **1979** 11, 15
Carter support for, **1978** 20-21; **1979** 34-35, 390
contributing to employment growth, **1978** 85
job assistance to New York City, **1977** 547
passage of, **1974** 57
Reagan budget cuts in, **1981** 641
state and local choice in, Nixon on, **1974** 107
tax credits to employers, in Carter urban program, **1978** 242, 244, 246, 250
Comprehensive Environmental Response, Compensation, and Liability Act of 1980, **1995** 113

Comprehensive Health Manpower Training Act (1971), on hospital construction costs, **1972** 921
Comprehensive Nuclear Test Ban Treaty (CNTBT), **1995** 234-235, 234-237, 236, 237, 553-557; **1998** 49
postponed by India and Pakistan nuclear testing, **1998** 326, 329
ratification defeated by Congress, **1999** 43, 53, 600-610, 699, 819
ratification efforts, **2000** 31
Republican Party platform opposition to, **1996** 542
Compton, Ann, in presidential debates, **1988** 723, 756-757, 764-765, 772-773, 780-781
Comptroller General
budget review by, **1974** 587-590
employee pension plans, **2002** 101-113
federal budget issues, **2005** 121-136
role in Gramm-Rudman-Hollings, **1986** 705-730
role in impoundment control, **1974** 593-594
Comptroller of the Currency, Lance investigation by, **1977** 627-640
Computer Assisted Passenger Prescreening System (CAPPS II), **2003** 722, 726-727, 731; **2004** 144-145, 148-149
Computer Associates International, corporate scandal, **2004** 423
Computer security
cyberterrorism, **2002** 746
GAO report on, **1998** 676-686; **2002** 746
issues, **1997** 711-720
medical records security, **1997** 580-587
Computers
See also Internet
change in labor markets, **1992** 124
chess victory of IBM computer, **1997** 273-276
"digital divide" issue of access to, **1999** 368-383; **2002** 68-69
digital economy, **2000** 299-307
E-rate program, **1999** 371; **2000** 48
Microsoft Corp. antitrust case, **1999** 654-689; **2000** 105-130, 308-324; **2001** 775-792, 797-817
Netscape Navigator vs. Internet Explorer, **2000** 107-108
Pentagon "data mining" system, **2002** 559-568
privacy issues, **2002** 70-71
procurement agreement with Japan, **1992** 15
spam e-mail messages, **2002** 70-71
technology, and stock market crash (1987),**1988** 13, 15, 34
technology workers, shortage of, **1997** 669-678
threats to Pentagon systems, **1996** 312-324
year 2000 (Y2K) conversion, **1997** 534-540; **1998** 543-554; **1999** 51, 760-768; **2000** 3-15
Conable, Barber B. (R-N.Y.)
on Nixon impeachment, **1974** 674
World Bank appointment, **1986** 861
Conahan, Frank C., USS *Iowa* explosion investigation, **1990** 321
Conboy, Kenneth, **1997** 631
Concentration camps. *See* Nazi concentration camps
Concorde, opposition to overflights of U.S., **1976** 331, 342-343
Condition of Education report, **1992** 623-636
Condoms, and teenage pregnancy, **1986** 1060
Condon, Charles, unreasonable searches, **2001** 410
Condon, Dennis, **1993** 369
Cone v. West Virginia Pulp & Paper Co., **1990** 231
Confalonieri, Carlo, **1978** 596
Conference of Latin American Bishops (CELAM), and activist clergy, **1980** 412-413
Conference of the Parties (or COP-10), **2004** 829
Conference on Security and Cooperation in Europe (CSCE)
See also Helsinki Conference on Security and Cooperation in Europe (1975)
Charter of Paris for a New Europe, **1990** 727, 734-745
Clinton remarks, **1994** 585-588
conventional armed forces treaty, **1990** 727-732
Joint Declaration of Twenty-Two States, **1990** 727, 732-734
London Declaration of Peaceful Intent, **1990** 455-466
market economies, **1990** 473
structures and institutions, **1990** 743-745
Yeltsin remarks, **1994** 583-584, 588-591
Conference on Urgent Actions for Nuclear Non-Proliferation and Disarmament, **1998** 541
Conflict resolution
peaceful, Helsinki Final Act on, **1975** 563
peaceful, John Paul II on, **1985** 365, 369-371
restructuring of UN to promote negotiating groups, **1975** 325, 327, 332, 345
UN effectiveness in, **1973** 753-760; **1982** 769-779
Confucius, Chinese party attack on, **1974** 174, 271-272
Congo, Republic of
See also under its earlier name Zaire
casualties of war, **2005** 1032
child soldiers, **2002** 918, 925
conflict in, **1999** 428, 430, 431, 435-436, 645-653; **2000** 71-72; **2005** 1030-1031
Ituri region, **2004** 508, 588
Kinshasa, **2004** 505-506
North and South Kivu/Bukavu Crisis, **2004** 506-507, 508-509, 510-513
Congolese Rally for Democracy (DRC), **2002** 500, 548, 549; **2003** 290
Congo-Rwanda peace agreement, **2002** 546-555
Disarmament, Demobilization, Repatriation, Resettlement, and Reintegration (DDRRR), **2004** 509
disarmament of militias, **2005** 1030-1031
elections, **2005** 1027-1029
humanitarian situation, **1999** 649-650; **2002** 552-553
hunger in, **2003** 756
Ituri region conflict and violence, **2003** 290-292
Kabila leadership, **1998** 161
Lusaka cease-fire agreement, **1999** 434, 436, 646-647, 647-649; **2000** 979-980
Movement for the Liberation of Congo, **2002** 548; **2003** 290
natural resources exploitation, **2002** 551-552; **2003** 294-295
nuclear weapons material, **2004** 327
peace agreements, **2002** 447
political situation, **1997** 877-885; **1998** 220
UN secretary general on, **2004** 505-516

progress towards democracy, UN secretary general on, **2005** 1027-1035
Rwanda troop withdrawal, **2002** 547, 550; **2003** 290-292; **2004** 506-507
Uganda troop withdrawal, **2002** 547, 550; **2003** 290-292
UN peacekeeping mission, **1997** 151, 154, 155, 156; **2000** 450, 643; **2001** 161; **2002** 547; **2003** 288-297, 450, 453; **2004** 505-516; **2005** 1028, 1029-1030
sexual abuse scandal, **2004** 894; **2005** 237-238, 1030
war crimes tribunal, **2003** 99, 101
war in, UN secretary general report, **2000** 978-987; **2001** 159-170
Zimbabwe troop withdrawal, **2002** 550
Congregation for Catholic Education, homosexuality, Catholic Church policy, **2005** 863-864
Congress
See also House of Representatives; Joint Economic Committee; Senate; Supreme Court appointments
armed forces responsibility
base closing decision, **1988** 951-954
exclusion of women from draft, **1981** 521-530
bicentennial of, **1989** 123-133
budget reform passage, **1974** 573-597
Bush address to joint session of, **2001** 171-187
climate change proposals, **2005** 921-922
close of 104th Congress, congressional leaders on, **1996** 695-703
commerce power, and contest with local government, **1985** 167-187
Cuba Working Group, **2002** 235
Czechoslovakian president addresses, **1990** 4, 5-11
defense planning oversight, **1985** 670-671, 680-682
Democratic control of, **1972** 893; **1976** 841; **1986** 1027-1028; **1987** 105, 107; **1988** 891-892, 900; **1989** 41
Carter on working with, **1976** 845, 848-849
Carter-Ford debate on, **1976** 694-695, 714-715
Republican platform on, **1976** 617, 621, 623, 639, 645-646
election results
Clinton response, **1994** 513, 515-519
Gingrich response, **1994** 513-514, 519-523
Elizabeth II's address, **1991** 247-251
end-of-life care, Schiavo case intervention, **2005** 154, 156-157, 161-163
energy legislation, **2005** 782-783
ethics investigations, **2005** 632-634
executive privilege in testimony before
Burford contempt citation in EPA inquiry, **1982** 965-970
Nixon claim of, **1973** 337-342, 413-414
FDA drug regulation of "unsafe" drugs hearings, **2004** 853-854
flag protection legislation, **1989** 343-346
flu vaccine
for members and employees, **2004** 641-642
shortage hearings, **2004** 640, 642, 747
foreign policy
conflict with president on aid to Southeast Asia, **1975** 251, 256-261, 280-281, 290, 293-294
intervention by, Ford and Kissinger on, **1975** 4-5, 10-13, 223, 226, 228, 232, 235, 238
foreign policy powers
abdication of, **1973** 13, 15
circumvention of in Iran-contra affair, **1987** 893, 905, 915, 925
GATT approval, **1994** 555-559
Grace commission proposals, analysis of, **1984** 169-179
Gramm-Rudman-Hollings, and delegation to comptroller general, **1986** 705-730
impeachment powers, **1993** 81-91
intelligence agencies legislation, **2004** 968-970
intelligence gathering failures, Senate report on, **2004** 712-713, 965-966
intelligence oversight, **1976** 237, 240, 244; **1984** 340; **2004** 476
and Iran-contra affair, **1987** 207-210, 218-219, 227-229, 239, 241, 893, 898-905, 908-912, 914
Iran-contra affair, investigations by, **1986** 1018; **1987** 891-928
Iraq War resolution, **2002** 714-715, 719-723; **2003** 19
Iraqi prison abuse scandal, investigations and hearings, **2004** 211
members
FBI files on, **1975** 879-880
pay raises for, **1989** 196-197, 200-201, 203-204
right to choose staff, **1979** 401, 408-411
mercury emission regulations, **2005** 98
Nicaraguan contras
aid ban, **1987** 217-218, 221, 225, 227, 230
and diversion of funds, **1986** 1013-1014, 1016-1018, 1021, 1049-1053
aid request, **1985** 255-257; **1987** 1008-1009
bipartisan accord with Bush on, **1989** 161-168
oil company profits hearings, **2005** 780-782
pension funding legislation, **2005** 200-201
Persian Gulf crisis, reflagging of vessels, **1987** 793-794
Persian Gulf War resolution, **1991** 3-13
power of purse
and Iran-contra affair, **1987** 901-904, 925-926
pork barrel projects, **1977** 62-63
presidential impoundment of appropriated funds, **1973** 3-19, 88-90, 92-93, 171, 193, 204-205; **1975** 135-140
powers of vs. presidential power
appointment of FEC commissioners, **1976** 71-75, 98-104
McGovern on, **1973** 87-95
Nixon on, **1973** 801-802, 808
omission of OEO from Nixon budget, **1973** 453-464
PRC repression of prodemocracy demonstrations, resolutions on, **1989** 275, 277, 285
public broadcasting editorials, ban on, **1984** 449-463
race-based redistricting, **1993** 459-481
"racial gerrymandering," **1993** 459-481
religion and congressional powers, **1997** 406-421
Republican control of
first one hundred days, House Leaders on, **1995** 165-175

Congress *Continued*
opening remarks, **1995** 3-14
resignations, Packwood speech, **1995** 592-599
retirements, **1995** 558-559
ricin poison discovery, Senate Office Building, **2004** 268, 442-443
rules and procedures reform, **1973** 19
Democratic platform on, **1972** 584-586
Republican platform on, **1976** 628-629
Schwarzkopf's address, **1991** 243-246
sentencing guidelines, commission on, **2004** 359
September 11 terrorist attacks
congressional panel on, **2003** 544-575; **2004** 451
response to, **2004** 470
stem cell research, **2005** 318-320, 322-323
steroids in baseball, congressional hearing on, **2005** 212-227
tax returns, committees' access to, **1975** 857-858
term limits, **1992** 792-793, 796, 940-941; **1995** 259-275
trade relations with Japan, **1985** 319-322; **1987** 427-429
treaty termination, powers of, **1978** 782; **1979** 917-938
UN Zionism resolution, resolutions on, **1975** 825-826
unfunded mandates legislation, **1995** 141-145
U.S. Vietnam policy, **1995** 474-475
use of the filibuster compromise, **2005** 79, 559-560
Walesa's speech to, **1989** 523-525, 534-538
war powers
and ending Vietnam war, **1973** 3-19
McGovern on asserting, **1973** 88-89, 92
presidential consultation with, **1975** 311-314
resolution on, **1973** 923-930
women in combat, **1993** 333-334
Yeltsin's speech, **1992** 519-520, 526-531
Congress of National Black Churches, **1997** 304, 306
Congressional Advisory Panel to Assess Domestic Response Capabilities for Terrorism Involving Weapons of Mass Destruction, **2000** 281
Congressional Black Caucus
Carter defense budget, **1978** 97
censure of Trent Lott, **2002** 971, 973
cocaine penalties, sentencing for, **1997** 247
House inquiry on King assassination, **1978** 911
response to Reagan State of the Union, **1984** 84
Congressional Budget and Impoundment Control Act (1974)
amendment to, **1985** 804
budget reconciliation process, **1981** 640
changes in budget procedures, **1975** 97; **1976** 39-40, 177-178
effect on Carter budget, **1978** 96
Congressional Budget Office (CBO)
budget cut effects on poor, **1983** 765-772
budget deficit under Bush, **1990** 410
budget surplus, **1998** 500-509
consumer spending, **2004** 58
defense budget analysis, **1976** 184-185; **1982** 192, 195-196, 200
drug benefit plans, **2003** 1122
establishment of, **1974** 578-582; **1975** 97; **1976** 39-40, 177
estimates during Bush administration, **1990** 82
federal budget deficit, **1987** 4; **2003** 678-690
first annual report of, **1976** 177-189
first critique of president's budget, **1976** 45
Grace commission report, **1984** 169-179
Gramm-Rudman-Hollings role, **1986** 705-706
health insurance coverage, **2003** 848
King holiday costs, **1983** 884
missile defense system spending, **2002** 1027-1028; **2004** 179
multilateral trade agreement, **1979** 638-639
Reagan budget, **1982** 191-201
retirement and baby boomers, **2003** 711
structural budget deficit, **2000** 56-57
unemployment estimates during Ford administration, **1976** 39-40, 177
unfunded federal mandates, cost of, **1995** 141, 142, 144
Congressional elections
midterm elections, **2005** 113, 124-126
Bush campaign speech, **2002** 818-829
results, **2002** 36, 533
Congressional employees
duty of to report improper conduct, **1978** 847, 907-908
pages, improving system of, **1982** 729-735
right to sue for discrimination, **1979** 399-411
Congressional ethics
Abscam bribery investigation, **1980** 899-906
bribery of member for private immigration bill, **1979** 467-478
censure
of Crane and Studds, **1983** 725-734
of Diggs, **1979** 623-631
of Wilson, **1980** 485-491
DeLay, Tom
allegations of financial bribery, **2004** 577, 580-581
money laundering in Texas indictment, **2005** 78
denunciation of Talmadge, **1979** 623, 625, 631-636
expulsion
of Myers, **1980** 899-906
of Williams, **1981** 673-679
financial misconduct by member, **1979** 623, 625, 631-636
Gingrich House ethics violations, **1995** 746-751; **1996** 838-849; **1997** 3-19, 603; **1998** 800-801
Hays's employment of nontypist Ray, **1976** 365-368
House drug use and sexual misconduct inquiry, **1982** 729-740
"Keating Five" Investigation, **1991** 107-118
Korean influence-buying scheme, **1977** 769-819; **1978** 845-908; **1979** 897-898
limits on gifts to members, **1995** 700-709
misuse of clerk-hire funds by member, **1979** 623-631
punishments for members, **1979** 623-625
Rostenkowski indictment, **1994** 281-286
Sununu as Chief of Staff, **1992** 293-299
Tom DeLay's indictments, **2004** 577, 580-581; **2005** 631-643

trips paid for by foreign government, **1978** 900-902, 904-905
Wright investigation, **1989** 239-257
Congressional immunity
from job bias suits, **1979** 399-411
for legislative acts, **1979** 467-478
from libel suits, **1979** 479-491
Congressional Medal of Honor, investigation of claim for, **1989** 697-700
Congressional Research Service (CRS)
and CIA manual, **1984** 903, 906
gun laws, and terrorists, **2003** 159
Iraq War, U.S. escalating costs, **2005** 835
North conviction, **1990** 493
small arms trade, **2001** 519
Social Security price indexing, **2005** 116
Conkling, James B., **1981** 754
Connally, Greg, teenage smoking campaigns, **2004** 282
Connally, John B.
Burns's influence on, **1972** 962
campaign support for Nixon, **1972** 385
Kennedy assassination anniversary, **1993** 959, 962
on nationalization and U.S. development aid, **1972** 67
Thieu meeting with, **1973** 448
Watergate acquittal, **1975** 143
Connally, Nellie, Kennedy assassination anniversary, **1993** 959-960, 962-963
Connaughton, James
air quality at ground zero, **2003** 548
Kyoto Protocol, **2004** 829
Connecticut
abortion restrictions on, **1977** 407-409, 419-427
civil unions of same-sex couples, **2005** 863, 868
Connecticut National Bank v. Germain, **1992** 461
Connelly, James Patrick, Jr. , mutual funds scandal conviction, **2003** 696
Connelly, Paula, **1987** 19
Conner, Dennis, **1989** 184
Connerly, Ward, affirmative action, **1996** 761; **1997** 186, 317
Connolly, Marie-Therese, on nursing home abuse and neglect, **2002** 117
ConocoPhillips, oil company profits, congressional hearings, **2005** 781
Conrad, Clifton, **1991** 310
Conrad, David, **1993** 485
ConRail. *See* Consolidated Rail Corp.
Conroy, Dan, Waco investigation, **1993** 820, 828
Conroy, Glenn C. , discovery of first North Americans, **1992** 136
Conroy, Thomas F., **1993** 249-258
Conroy v. Aniskoff, **1993** 249-258
Conservation. *See* Environmental protection
Conservation Foundation, on national park system, **1972** 795-804
Conservative Political Action Conference, Reagan speech to on election victory, **1981** 325
Conservatives
Kennedy speech to Moral Majority, **1983** 817-825
Nixon on, **1972** 886-887, 891-892
Reagan speech to evangelicals, **1983** 269-277
and Republican platform, **1988** 615-616
Consolidated Edison Co. v. NLRB, **1995** 198
Consolidated Edison Co. of New York, New York City blackout, **1977** 545-550
Consolidated Rail Corp. (ConRail)
creation of in railroad reorganization, **1975** 529-542
sale of, **1988** 230-231, 238
Consolidated Rail Corp. v Darrone, **1992** 194, 197
Constantine, Thomas A. , warning letter to doctors on prescribing drugs for suicide, **1997** 462
Constellation, racial unrest aboard, **1972** 901
Constitution (Afghanistan), **2003** 1097-1098
Constitution (Canada) , constitutional reform, **1980** 402-403; **1981** 813-822; **1982** 317-323
Constitution (Iraq), **2005** 945-947
Constitution (PRC), **1975** 43-53; **1978** 157-175
Constitution (South Africa)
changes in, **1983** 889-892; **1984** 1027; **1993** 1003-1032
text of new constitution, **1996** 249-264
Constitution (Spanish) , approval of, **1978** 809-843
Constitution (U.S.)
Article I
bill of attainder
custody of Nixon papers and tapes, **1977** 465-467, 482-486, 492-493, 507-510
student aid and draft registration, **1984** 493-501
commerce clause
federal regulation of utilities, **1982** 447-467
gun-free school zone, **1995** 183-200; **1999** 335
minimum wage laws applied to state and local governments, **1976** 377-389; **1985** 167-187
state water rights, **1982** 689-701
patents and copyrights, **1980** 495, 501; **1984** 60-61, 70, 74
speech or debate clause, congressional immunity, **1979** 399-402, 407-411, 467-478, 479-491
Article II
appointment clause, **1976** 71-75, 98-104; **1988** 467-478
disability clause, **1985** 491-492
impeachment trial clause, **1993** 81-91
presidential impeachment grounds, **1974** 137-143
presidential succession, **1981** 352
subpoena of presidential materials for criminal trial, **1974** 623, 633
Article III
case or controversy requirement, **1979** 194-198, 200-205
judicial powers and independence, **1982** 597-610
Article VI, supremacy clause, damage suits for tobacco-related ills, **1992** 563-573
bicentennial of, **1987** 107-108, 113-115, 765-775, 771-775
Bill of Rights
applied to states, **1985** 480, 484-488, 654-668
Washington call for, **1989** 124-125
interpretation of, Meese-Court dispute on, **1985** 479-490, 653-655, 657-660, 666-668
president as commander-in-chief, war powers debate, **1990** 663-679
Constitutional amendments (proposed)
abolishing electoral college, **1977** 199-200, 204-205

Constitutional amendments (proposed) *Continued*
banning abortion, **1976** 545, 562, 811-812; **1985** 53-56; **1988** 65
D.C. voting representation in Congress, **1978** 589-591
flag burning prohibition, **1990** 359
flag protection, **1989** 343-346
on marriage, **2004** 21, 40; **2005** 79, 85
process, **1989** 346
on school prayer, **1976** 812; **1983** 85, 269, 272; **1984** 83, 91, 241-245; **1985** 381
Constitutional amendments (U.S.)
First Amendment
applied to states, **1985** 653-655, 660-664, 666-668
establishment clause
deaf parochial student, **1993** 399-406
parochial school aid, **1997** 361-381
pledge of allegiance, **2002** 382-390
religion in schools, **1995** 546-547
religious clubs in school, **2001** 420-432
religious publications, **1995** 386, 388-395
religious symbols, **1995** 387, 396-404
school prayer, **2000** 365-378
school vouchers, **2002** 406-423
Ten Commandments displays, **2005** 376-389
establishment of religion
churches' voice in government, **1982** 955-963
creation science in schools, **1982** 5-8, 16; **1987** 565-576
justices on, **1985** 654-655, 666
Meese on, **1985** 479-480, 486-488
political causes of religious groups, **1983** 817, 819-823
public aid to private schools, **1973** 641-658; **1977** 431-445; **1985** 433-461
public display of Nativity scene, **1984** 217-239
public funding of abortions, **1980** 516-522
religion in curriculum, **1987** 597-598, 600-601, 603-605
religious organizations' use of campus building, **1981** 869, 879
school prayer, **1985** 379-395
tuition tax credit for private school parents, **1983** 675-677
use of school facilities by religious groups, **1993** 363-370
free press
access to pretrial hearing, **1979** 511-513, 520-527
candidates' right to reply, **1974** 523-528
confidential sources, **1972** 507-519; **1976** 684-686
coverage of Grenada invasion, **1983** 850
gag orders on criminal trials, **1976** 463-479
libel of public figure, **1979** 285-311
libel suits against news media, **1984** 247-254, 299-312; **1985** 47-52; **1986** 355-368
media ownership, **1978** 419-432
newsroom searches, **1978** 355-372
press attitudes toward Court, **1979** 311-318
prior restraint, Noriega phone calls broadcasted, **1990** 721-725
privacy for editorial process, **1983** 401
public broadcasting editorials, **1984** 449-462
student newspaper censorship, **1988** 37-46
free speech
advertising prescription drug prices, **1976** 351-363
antiabortion demonstrations, **2000** 432-433
antiabortion protesters and RICO law, **1994** 26-33
ballot initiative petitions, **1999** 5
broadcast of offensive material, **1978** 515-531
campaign contribution and spending limits, **1976** 72-87; **1985** 277-294
campaign finance reform, **2003** 1159, 1160
child pornography, **1982** 675-688; **1990** 239-249
CIA exposé, **1981** 541, 544
in civil rights movement, **1982** 655-674
compensation law, **1991** 813-825
for corporations in referendum campaigns, **1978** 307-324
decency in the arts, **1998** 405-418
fairness doctrine, **1987** 625-636
family-planning clinic advice, **1991** 257-273
flag burning, **1989** 343-354; **1990** 357-365
gay rights to march, **1995** 327-335
hate crimes, **1992** 175-185
on the Internet, **1997** 444-458
Internet pornography ban, **1996** 353-361
Internet pornography filters, **2003** 387-400
lawyer advertising, **1982** 65-71
libel from misquotation, **1991** 317-329
local prohibition of "for sale" signs, **1977** 313-320
obscenity standards, **1973** 611-628; **1974** 516, 520-522; **1987** 480-490
pornography destroyed, **1993** 431, 432, 438-446
racially motivated assault, **1993** 385-389
religious organizations' use of campus buildings, **1981** 869-879
religious publication, **1995** 385-395
religious symbols, **1995** 385, 387, 396-404
residential signs, **1994** 289-297
in satire, **1988** 175-182
school book banning, **1982** 567-585
school prayer, **1992** 553-562
student's offensive language, **1986** 731-742
tenure review disclosure, **1990** 23-34
zoning for adult theaters, **1986** 131-144
freedom of association
campaign contribution limits, **1976** 72, 74-81
custody of Nixon papers and tapes, **1977** 465, 468, 480-482
discriminatory admission to private school, **1976** 392, 395-396
domestic surveillance of citizens, **1976** 237, 264-265
open political primaries, **1986** 1066-1073
political dismissals from public jobs, **1980** 259-271
sex discrimination by private clubs, **1984** 465-478; **1988** 399-403
religious freedom, **1997** 406-421

Second Amendment, right to bear arms, **2001** 722-737; **2002** 959-968
Fourth Amendment
search and seizure
automobile exception, **1982** 425-446
automobile passengers' rights, **1978** 753-764
covert entry for electronic surveillance, **1979** 269-271, 274-280
custody of Nixon papers and tapes, **1977** 465-466, 492
drug searches, **1995** 339-349
drug testing of employees, **1986** 841
Ellsberg break-in, **1974** 206, 411-417, 664
exclusionary rule, **1976** 521-536; **1981** 648, 661-663; **1984** 507-519; **1985** 224-253
newsroom protection, **1978** 355-372
OSHA safety inspections, **1978** 339-353
prisoners' rights, **1984** 479-488
sodomy and privacy right, **1986** 601-603, 611-612
students' rights, **1985** 13-26
unreasonable, **2001** 407-419
use of deadly force, **1985** 303-315
warrantless arrests at home, **1980** 281-297
warrantless FBI break-ins, **1981** 371-373
warrantless wiretaps by federal law enforcement, **1972** 485-489
student drug testing, **2002** 424-436
Fifth Amendment
double jeopardy clause
in impeachment of federal judge, **1989** 584, 586-587
in sentencing, **1980** 977-988
sex offenders, right to confine, **1997** 382-394
due process
abortion rights, **1990** 387-407; **1992** 589-613
family-planning clinic advice, **1991** 257-273
minority set-asides, **1980** 539-566
preventive detention, **1987** 491-493, 496-500, 503-506
public funding of abortions, **1980** 516-530
right to privacy, **1986** 605-606
sex bias in Social Security survivors' benefits, **1977** 169-181
sex bias suit against member of Congress, **1979** 399-408
property takings
coastal land, **1992** 615-620
developers and public land, **1994** 298-310
eminent domain, **2005** 362-375
frozen Iranian assets, **1981** 559, 561-568, 572
historic landmarks, **1978** 453-465
land use regulation, **1987** 531-553
self-incrimination
draft and student aid, **1984** 495-503
interrogation and psychiatric interview, **1981** 432-445
Justice Department access to tax returns, **1975** 829, 855
Miranda warning, **1984** 388-397; **1985** 223-253; **1990** 785-793; **2000** 385-395
right to counsel pre-Miranda, **1974** 473-485
travel rights, passport revocation, **1981** 541, 544
Sixth Amendment
right to counsel
offense punishable in prison, **1979** 207-214
in proceedings, **1977** 219-235
self-incrimination, **1981** 432-445
right to fair trial
closed pretrial hearing, **1979** 511-533
jury composition, **1975** 55-66; **1986** 410-413, 425-426, 445-456
jury size, **1979** 263-268
press coverage, **1976** 463-479
right to trial by jury, sentencing guidelines, **2004** 358, 362-374
Eighth Amendment
cruel and unusual punishment
appeals from death row prisoners, **1993** 141-152
beating of prison inmates, **1992** 175-185
corporal punishment in schools, **1977** 293-309
death penalty
constitutionality, **1972** 499-505
for juveniles, **2005** 177-196
mandatory, **1977** 397-405
for mentally retarded, **2001** 387-394; **2002** 353-368; **2005** 177
mitigating factors and, **1978** 495-514; **1982** 53-63
and race, **1987** 464, 472, 475
for rape, **1977** 517-528
state laws, **1976** 489-507
excessive prison sentences, **1983** 659-674
prison crowding, **1981** 477-490
rights of mentally retarded, **1982** 53-63, 521-530
excessive bail, **1987** 492, 496, 500-507
excessive fines, for drug-trafficking, **1993** 431-438
immunity of states, **1992** 195
murder case sentencing, **1991** 381-395
sentencing guidelines, Supreme Court on, **2004** 358-374
sentencing laws, three strikes-law upheld, **2003** 983-984
Tenth Amendment
reserved powers, **1982** 36-45, 447-467; **1983** 231-239; **1985** 168, 184-187
congressional term limits, **1995** 259-275
Eleventh Amendment
executive immunity, **1974** 265-270
states' rights, immunity from suits, **1999** 333-356
Fourteenth Amendment
consolidation of districts to desegregate, **1972** 15-21
due process
abortion, **1990** 387-407
women's right to choose, **1992** 589-613
child custody rights, **1982** 259, 261-280
damages for consumer product liability, **1996** 274-283
grandparents' rights, **2000** 287-298
involuntary commitment, **1979** 335-344
jury composition, **1986** 445-456
murder case sentencing, **1991** 381-395

Constitutional amendments (U.S.) *Continued*
physician-assisted suicide, **1996** 125-126; **1997** 459-479
prisoner appeals, **1991** 205-218; **1993** 141-152
for prisoners, **1984** 479, 482, 485, 491
religious freedom, **1997** 406-421
right to die, **1990** 373-386
right to privacy, **1986** 604-610
rights of mentally retarded, **1982** 521-530
same-sex marriage laws, **2004** 38
sex offenders, right to confine, **1997** 382-394
sodomy laws, **2003** 402-404, 406-413
students' rights, **1975** 67-80; **1977** 293-309
equal protection clause
abortion clinic blockades, **1993** 93-112; **1994** 311-326
affirmative action, **1995** 307-326; **1997** 183-194; **1998** 855-868; **2003** 358-386
alimony for men, **1979** 193-194, 196-201
death penalty and racial bias, **1987** 464, 467-469; **2002** 358-359
draft, sex discrimination in, **1981** 522-523
education for aliens, **1982** 492-498, 502-504
gay rights, **1996** 284-295
jury selection, **1986** 409-433; **1994** 223-236
minority set-asides, **1980** 539-566
physician-assisted suicide, **1996** 123-124; **1997** 329
private club discrimination, **1988** 399-403
redistricting, **1973** 277-289; **1986** 616-632
redistricting, race-based, **1993** 459-481; **1995** 369-384; **1996** 368-387
religious freedom, **1997** 406-421
reverse discrimination, **1978** 467-492
same-sex marriage laws, **2004** 38
school desegregation, **1979** 536-539, 543, 547-548, 550; **1982** 619-652; **1991** 23-33
school financing, **1972** 221; **1973** 361-377
segregated colleges, **1992** 575-587
sodomy laws, **2003** 402-404, 406-413
statutory rape laws, sex discrimination in, **1981** 339-349
unreasonable searches and seizures, under USA Patriot Act, **2003** 609-612
voter residence requirements, **1972** 283-290
zoning regulations barring low-income housing, **1977** 35-44
privacy right, and abortion, **1973** 102-107, 110-114
unlawful state conduct, tax increase to desegregate schools, **1990** 227-238
Fifteenth Amendment, right to vote, **1993** 459-481
Twenty-third Amendment, D.C. presidential vote, **1978** 590-591
Twenty-fifth Amendment
transfer of presidential power, **1985** 491-495
vice-presidential vacancy, **1973** 827, 969-971; **1974** 710, 987-991
Twenty-sixth Amendment, vote for 18-year-olds, **1973** 35
Twenty-seventh Amendment, congressional pay raises, **1992** 439-442
Constitutional Convention (1787), **1987** 765-769, 771-772
Construction industry
New York, corruption in, **1986** 180, 205
stabilization of hospital construction costs, **1972** 922, 927
wages and price controls on, in Nixon's anti-inflation program, **1973** 43, 45, 48, 51-52
Consumer Federation of America, food safety, **2002** 581
Consumer nations
cooperation on energy and raw material supplies, **1974** 123-127, 530, 835; **1975** 5-7, 9, 236, 588, 591-592, 600
and EC proposal to Arab states, **1974** 185-188
meeting with energy producers, **1974** 982-984; **1975** 326-327
Consumer price index (CPI), **1997** 59; **1998** 73, 74, 79; **1999** 86; **2001** 62; **2005** 139, 150
projections for 1996 to 1998, **1996** 69
Consumer product liability
Firestone tire recall, **1978** 719-727; **2000** 688-699
Supreme Court on, **1996** 274-283
Consumer protection
Carter on agency for, **1977** 187
Democratic platform on, **1972** 547-548; **1976** 558-559; **1984** 583-584
health care bill of rights, **1997** 787-799
hospital patient's bill of rights, **1974** 39-42
information on prescription drug prices, **1976** 351-363
Consumer Reports, manufacturer's libel suit against, **1984** 299-312
Consumer spending, **2002** 53, 58-59; **2004** 56-57; **2005** 137, 138, 146
Contadora Group
mediation by, **1985** 257, 261, 264-268
objectives for Central America, **1984** 49-50; **1987** 638, 642-643
Container Corp. of America
sex discrimination charges against, **1972** 314
state's right to tax multinational earnings, **1983** 645-658
Container Corp. of America v. Franchise Tax Board, **1983** 645-658
Conte, Victor, "designer drugs" conviction, **2005** 213
Continental shelf
See also Outer continental shelf
definition of, and Law of the Sea Treaty, **1982** 354
Contraception
See also Birth control; Family planning
Catholic teaching on, **1979** 725, 729, 757; **1983** 93, 242; **1988** 786; **1995** 145-146, 149-151
noncompliance with, **1980** 871-873, 876-878, 880
improved methods to reduce world population projections, **1981** 14, 18
information about, in developing countries, **1987** 457, 459
methods, research on, **1987** 441, 450, 458
for teenagers, **1972** 301, 311; **1986** 1058-1062, 1064
parental notification, **1983** 269, 272
Contract with America
CEA challenges to, **1995** 70

Clinton comments on, **1995** 427-428, 430
during first one hundred days of Congress, **1995** 165-167
Gingrich comments on, **1995** 4, 8-9, 168, 170
Gingrich strategic plan, **1998** 696, 800
House Republican election pledges, text of, **1994** 374-378
and line-item veto, **1998** 419
unfunded mandates legislation, **1995** 141-142
Contracts
government, striking workers and, **1995** 129-133
for government services, **1988** 230, 234, 237
private, discrimination in private school admission, **1976** 391-404
with surrogate mothers, legality of, **1987** 373-387; **1988** 71-79
Contras. *See* Iran-contra affair
Controlled Substances Act, **1997** 459, 462; **1999** 442; **2001** 293, 329
Convention of the High Seas (1958), **1992** 457
Convention on Conventional Weapons (CCW), **1995** 52-53, 54; **1997** 845
Convention on Prohibition and Destruction of Biological Weapons (1972), Soviet violations of, **1981** 682, 685-686
Convention on the Prevention and Punishment of the Crime of Genocide. *See* Genocide Convention
Convention on the Prohibition of the Development, Production, Stockpiling and Use of Chemical Weapons and on Their Destruction, **1993** 71-79
Convention on the Safety of United Nations and Associated Personnel, **1998** 541
Conventional Armed Forces in Europe Treaty, **1990** 728-732
Conventional forces in Europe (CFE)
readiness of, Clark on, **1982** 396, 400
reduction of, **1985** 751, 754, 757-758
Bush proposal, **1989** 297-304
Gorbachev on, **1986** 18; **1988** 927, 937-940; **1989** 400, 405
Reagan proposal, **1982** 478-480
U.S.-Soviet talks on, **1989** 645, 665
strengthening of, **1975** 497-498, 502-505; **1978** 373-378
treaty, **1990** 727-732
U.S. requirements, **1980** 129-134
Conyers, John, Jr. (D-Mich.)
church arson prevention, **1997** 306
on Clinton impeachment, **1998** 697; **2001** 89
on government staff reductions, **1993** 720
House Judiciary Committee impeachment inquiry, **1998** 701-702
on judicial impeachment, **1989** 584
Lott's racial remarks, **2002** 971
nomination of Dellums, **1976** 596
Patriot missile critic, **1992** 865
Reno resignation encouraged, **1993** 295
on Rockefeller nomination, **1974** 988
Rosa Parks as staff member for, **2005** 357
screening immigrants, **2002** 845
Starr report public release, **1998** 636
Cook, Frederick A. , North Pole discovery claim, **1988** 832-833; **1989** 687-688, 690
Cook, Joe, student drug testing, **2002** 424
Cook, Richard, space mission failures, **1999** 714
Cook, Robin, Rushdie death threat lifted, **1998** 690-691
Cook, Suzan Johnson, race relations panel, **1997** 317, 322; **1998** 668
Cooke, Francis, **1973** 102
Cooke, Lawrence H., **1976** 863
Coomaraswamy, Radhika, human rights in Afghanistan, **1999** 527
Cooper, Charles, **1986** 888-889
Cooper, Kenneth, stem cell research, **2001** 542
Cooper, Matthew, CIA leak case, **2005** 701
Cooper Clinic, on physical fitness and health, **1989** 613-617
Cooper Institute for Aerobics Research, physical activity report, **1996** 419-420
Cooperative Institutional Research Program, University of California at Los Angeles, on student goals, **1986** 940
Cooperative Threat Reduction (CTR) program, **1994** 369-370; **1996** 143, 228-230
Coordinating Committee on Multilateral Export Controls (CoCom), **1987** 29-32, 34-35, 37-40, 42
COPA. *See* Child Online Protection Act
COPAZ (National Commission for the Consolidation of Peace), **1992** 29-30
Copper companies, Chile's nationalization of, **1972** 67, 329, 332-335
Copperweld Corp. v. Independence Trade Corp., **1984** 413-426
Copyright
agreement with Vietnam, **1997** 490
and home video taping, **1984** 53-80
Copyright Act (1976),and home video taping, **1984** 53, 56-57, 67, 69-74
Corallo, Mark
sentencing laws, **2003** 982
USA Patriot Act, **2003** 611
Corday, Eliot, **1987** 780
Corddry, Charles, in Reagan-Anderson debate, **1980** 847, 855-857
Corder, Frank Eugene, **1995** 255
Cordesman, Anthony, on Iraq link to terrorist groups, **2003** 882
Cordia, Louis J., **1983** 751
Cordovez, Diego, **1988** 257
Corell, Robert W. , Arctic Climate Impact Assessment study, **2004** 827, 828
Corey, Elias J. , Nobel in chemistry, **1990** 796
Cornéa, Aurel, **1986** 833
Cornelius v. NAACP Legal Defense and Education Fund, Inc. , **1993** 367, 368
Cornell, Robert J. (D-Wis.), **1980** 413
Cornyn, John (R-Texas) , midterm elections, **2002** 820, 825
Corporate accountability
employee pension plans, **2002** 101-113
and Enron collapse, **2002** 37-38, 54
mutual funds scandals, **2003** 693-706
reform backlash, **2004** 421-422
responsibility, **1996** 633

Corporate accountability *Continued*
responsibility for economic growth, Democratic platform on, **1984** 581-588
scandals and bankruptcies, **2002** 54-55, 878; **2004** 415-428
and SEC failures, GAO report on, **2002** 1032-1043
underfunded pension plans, **2005** 197-211
WorldCom fraud case, **2002** 391-405; **2003** 332-348
Corporate management, and U.S. competitiveness, **1986** 971-973, 978-980
Corporate mergers
AOL (America Online)-Time Warner, **2000** 1034-1046
communications mergers, **2000** 1037
Dynegy Inc.-Enron merger, **2001** 860-861
FTC Chairman on, **1998** 338-353
major mergers, **2000** 1037-1038
Reagan CEA on, **1985** 81, 102-104
Corporate Responsibility, Conference on, **1996** 41-49
Corporate takeovers
analysis of, **1988** 921-925
Democratic platform on, **1984** 581
junk bonds, Milken's guilty plea, **1990** 251-257
U.S. and Reagan administration values, Urban League on, **1987** 46
Corporation for Public Broadcasting (CPB)
editorials and federal funding, **1984** 449-463
structural flaws in, **1979** 119-122, 130, 133-134
system leadership and programming conflicts, **1979** 121, 124-127, 130
Corporations
See also Corporate accountability
campaign contributions from
and free speech, **1978** 307-324
in Watergate scandal, **1974** 603-604; **1975** 654, 659, 662-663, 668-669, 684-687
clean air enforcement and use of bubble concept, **1984** 427-437
collaboration with urban public schools, **1988** 216-217
opposition to ERA, **1982** 612
sponsorship of national parks, **1996** 582
and subsidiaries, intra-enterprise conspiracy doctrine, **1984** 413-426
tax cuts for, Ford economic plan, **1975** 17, 20, 25, 88, 104
Corporations, multinational
activity in Chilean election, **1975** 875, 888, 897
development role and conduct of, Kissinger on, **1975** 595-597
exploitation of developing countries, **1972** 332-336; **1974** 255, 258-260
nationalization of by developing countries, U.S. economic retaliation for, **1972** 67-71
reinvestment in host countries, **1975** 326
unitary taxation of, **1983** 646, 647
Corps of Engineers, Midwest floods, **1993** 484
Corr, William V. , tobacco company lawsuit, **2003** 263
Corrigan, Dara, Medicare cost estimates, and intimidation of HHS employee, **2004** 579
Corson, Dale R. , on technology transfer, **1982** 814
Cosmic background explorer (COBE), **1992** 379-383
Cossiga, Francesco, at economic summit, Venice, **1980** 504
Cost of Living Council (CLC)
administration of price freeze, **1973** 704, 711, 713
management of voluntary restraints on wages and prices, **1973** 44-45, 47-54
Costa Mendez, Nicanor, on Falklands (Malvinas) war, **1982** 289-291
Costa Rica
Central American peace plan, **1987** 637-638, 642-648, 1007-1011
Central American presidents' accord, **1989** 163
as demilitarized country, Dalai Lama on, **1989** 581
economic pressures on, **1987** 638
John Paul II's visit to, **1983** 241-244
Nicaraguan activity in, **1985** 264
smoking in the Americas, **1992** 269
U.S. economic aid to, **1984** 32
Costantino, Joseph, tamoxifen trials, **1998** 198-200
Costle, Douglas M. , on hazardous waste regulations, **1980** 446-452
Cot, Jean-Pierre, **1983** 969
Cotter, William, **1993** 172
Cotting, James C., **1988** 11
Cotton dust exposure, and smoking, **1985** 820-821
Couch, John, II, school prayer, **2000** 367
Coudaris, Marcel, **1986** 833
Coughlin, Paula, Tailhook scandal and, **1994** 109
Coulson, Danny O. , Waco incident, **1999** 481
Council for Mutual Economic Assistance (Comecon)
dismantling of, **1991** 400
Gorbachev on EC cooperation with, **1989** 401, 405-407
Council for Science and Technology, on fluorocarbons, **1975** 438
Council of Chief State School Officers (CCSSO), **1992** 144
Council of Economic Advisers (CEA)
annual reports (Bush, George H. W.), **1990** 87-104; **1991** 73-74, 81-96; **1992** 97-134
annual reports (Bush, George W.), **2002** 51-66; **2003** 75-95; **2004** 61-71; **2005** 145-153
annual reports (Carter), **1978** 66-67, 77-93; **1979** 81-83, 94-117; **1980** 159-160, 171-186, 210, 212, 215; **1981** 105-107, 115-143, 214
annual reports (Clinton), **1994** 123-124, 129-146; **1995** 69-71, 76-91; **1996** 50-51, 55-70; **1997** 50-52, 54-73; **1998** 73-76, 79-97; **1999** 85-88, 92-102; **2000** 43-46, 50-62; **2001** 53, 60-72
annual reports (Ford), **1975** 99-100; **1976** 45-47, 52-70; **1977** 66-67, 75-88
annual reports (Nixon), **1973** 185-191; **1974** 69-94
annual reports (Reagan), **1982** 121-122, 128-141; **1983** 121-141; **1984** 119-121, 128-144; **1985** 79-81, 88-104; **1986** 59-69; **1987** 117-119, 125-144; **1988** 117-118, 126-148; **1989** 3-5, 12-14
creation of, **1979** 216
midyear update on inflation (Nixon), **1974** 419
new members, **1990** 82; **1992** 99
Council of Europe
CIA secret detentions investigations, **2005** 906, 908
Election Observation Mission (CEEOM), Kosovo elections, **2001** 819-825

Gorbachev speech to, **1989** 399-409
Council of State Governments, position on ballot initiatives, **1999** 5
Council on Competitiveness, **1992** 469
Council on Environmental Quality, President's (CEQ)
creation of, **1972** 90; **1973** 215
fluorocarbons, task force on, **1975** 438
pollution controls, costs of, **1972** 253
population and the environment, **1980** 665-697
remedies for global problems, **1981** 13-14, 22-27
water policy review, **1978** 387, 389
Council on Food Safety, establishment of, **1998** 523
Council on Foreign Relations
AIDS epidemic report, **2005** 54
al Qaeda assets in Saudi Arabia, **2002** 1018
terrorist threat task force report, **2002** 740-763
Council on International Economic Policy
annual reports, **1973** 379-391; **1974** 113-122; **1975** 187-199
economic retaliation for nationalization, **1972** 70-71
Council on Wage and Price Stability
on coal strike settlement, **1978** 114
role in fighting inflation, **1974** 863, 865-866, 873, 878; **1978** 697; **1979** 34, 83
Counsel, right to. *See* Criminal law, right to counsel
Counterintelligence
executive branch oversight of, **1976** 244, 248-249
FBI role in, **1976** 283-284, 321-322
Counterterrorism
British antiterrorism legislation, **2005** 398-399
Bush State of the Union address on, **2005** 87
color-coded alerts system, **2004** 268-269
computer system failures, **2005** 897-898
counterfeit document identification, **2003** 219-220, 223-226
Defense Department Antiterrorism/Force Protection (AT/FP) plan, **2001** 4-5, 8-16
disrupting plots, **2003** 1056-1057
drivers license information, **2002** 535
Emergency Alert System, **2002** 744
"no-fly" terrorist watch lists, **2003** 157; **2004** 145; **2005** 898
Pentagon "data mining" system, **2002** 559-568
Terrorism Information and Prevention System (TIPS), **2002** 564; **2003** 613
terrorism threat levels, **2005** 896-897
UN recommendation for international treaty to combat terrorism, **2005** 230
UN resolution supporting, **2001** 625, 631-632
UN role, **2004** 902-903
Country Reports on Human Rights Practices, **1977** 3-25; **1980** 189-198; **1981** 179-190; **1982** 107-119; **1983** 181-195; **1984** 155-168; **1985** 145-157; **1986** 97-113; **1987** 189-204; **1988** 93-115; **1989** 57-70
as policy instrument, **1981** 780-781, 784-785
Courtney, Michael (archbishop), killed by gunmen in Burundi, **2003** 926
Courts, British, detentions at Guantanamo Bay, **2002** 830-841; **2004** 375
Courts, federal and state
See also Federal courts
gay marriage, Massachusetts Supreme Court on, **2003** 401-402, 404-405; **2004** 37-55
intelligent design, **2005** 1010-1026
Internet pornography in libraries, **2002** 287-297
Killen trial for civil rights workers slayings, **2005** 353-361
mutual funds, New York State Court on, **2003** 693-706
partial birth abortion case, **2003** 1002
Schiavo end-of-life care case, **2005** 154-163
Ten Commandments displays, **2005** 376-377
Courts, federal appeals
affirmative action ban panel, **1997** 183-194
California term limits, **1997** 886-891
detention of terrorism suspects, **2003** 105-120
Elian Gonzalez political asylum case, **2000** 265-276
Hamdan detainee case, **2005** 446-447, 453-461
impeachment of judges, **1999** 18
Internet pornography ban, **1996** 353-361
judicial vacancies, **1998** 48
Microsoft antitrust case, **1999** 654-689; **2000** 105-130; **2001** 775-792; **2002** 797-817
breakup ruling, **2000** 308-324
physician-assisted suicide, **1996** 121-132
pledge of allegiance, **2002** 382-390; **2005** 376
Republican Party platform reforms, **1996** 515-516
right to bear arms, **2001** 722-737
Courts, foreign, Demjanjuk acquittal by Israeli court, **1993** 617-623
Courts, international. *See* International Court of Justice; International Criminal Court
Courts, military, Tailhook court-martial decisions, **1994** 107-115
Courts, U.S. *See* Supreme Court cases; Supreme Court opinions
Covert action
by CIA
in Chile, **1974** 805-810; **1975** 882-883, 887-891, 911-914
as foreign policy tool, **1975** 717-720
CIA and NSC role in, in Ford reorganization, **1976** 126-127, 133
executive branch review of, **1976** 237, 241-244, 251-252
informing Congress of, House recommendation on, **1976** 117, 119
by NSC in Iran-contra affair, **1987** 216-219, 222, 224, 226-230, 240
restrictions on, proposed legislation, **1987** 908-912
as routine in intelligence bureaucracy, **1976** 240, 250-251
violations of law in Iran-contra affair, **1987** 892, 896, 902-903
Covertino, Richard G. , September 11 attacks trials, federal prosecutor, **2004** 273
Covey, Harvey O., **1988** 798
Covey, Richard O., *Discovery* space shuttle mission, **2005** 499
Cowall, Charles, **1989** 689
Cowper, Steve, **1989** 227
Cox, Archibald
access to Watergate tapes, and erasure, **1974** 23-24
access to White House tapes, **1973** 698, 737, 742; **1974** 622
federal court rulings on, **1973** 839-857

Cox, Archibald *Continued*
firing of, **1973** 698, 839, 859-880; **1974** 622
and Bork confirmation report, **1987** 718, 720, 725, 739-740
Nixon explanation of, **1973** 897-898, 902-904
special prosecutor fired, **1998** 906
and Watergate prosecution report, **1975** 654-661
Cox, Christopher (R-Calif.)
Chinese technology transfer, **1998** 977, 979-982
color-coded threat alert system, **2004** 269
House committee on national security and theft of nuclear secrets chair, **1999** 236
Cox, Patrick
EU membership celebration, remarks on, **2004** 204
on European Commission, **1999** 157
Cox, William, **1977** 410-411; **1993** 168
Cox committee. *See* House Select Committee on U.S. National Security and Military/Commercial Concerns with the People's Republic of China
Coyle, Philip, missile defense system testing, **2003** 819
CPB. *See* Corporation for Public Broadcasting
CPI. *See* Consumer price index
CPSU. *See* Communist Party of the Soviet Union
Crack cocaine
See also Cocaine
emergence of, **1986** 181
epidemic ebbing, **1997** 682
users, **1999** 460
Cragin, Charles, No Gun Ri (Korea) incident investigation, **2001** 34
Craig, Gregory B., Clinton impeachment trial, **1999** 19
Craig, Larry (R-Idaho)
climate change proposals, **2005** 921
nuclear testing fallout, **1997** 591
Cramer, Robert J. , counterfeit documents/identification, **2003** 218-219, 223-226
Crane, Daniel B. (R-Ill.) , House censure of, **1983** 725-734
Cranston, Alan (D-Calif.)
Glaspie-Hussein pre-war meeting, **1991** 158-159, 160-161
on Israeli raid on Iraq, **1981** 508
"Keating Five," investigations, **1990** 817; **1991** 107-118; **1992** 756
on limits of government, **1978** 9
and Lincoln Savings, **1989** 465
on Nixon budget, **1974** 98
on Reagan's new federalism, **1982** 74
Cravero, Kathleen, AIDS prevention for women, **2004** 431
Crawford, Lester M.
antidepressants and risk of suicide in children, **2004** 749-750
FDA commissioner nomination, **2005** 816
FDA flu vaccine inspections, **2004** 642-643
FDA rulings on controversial issues, **2005** 816
FDA suppression of research results, response to, **2004** 854
Crawford v. Los Angeles Board of Education, **1982** 619-652
Craxi, Bettino, **1986** 438
Jaruzelski meeting, **1987** 185
Reagan meeting, **1985** 709
Creation science
in California textbooks, National Academy of Sciences on, **1972** 843-844
teaching in schools, **1987** 599, 604-605
Credit Suisse First Boston, corporate scandal, **2004** 422-423
Creppy, Michael J. , secret domestic detentions, **2002** 834
Crespo-Velasco, Jorge, **1990** 117
Cresson, Edith, European Commission corruption, **1999** 156-157
Crestor, drug safety of, **2004** 853
Creusot-Loire, U.S. trade sanctions against, **1982** 880
Creutzfeld-Jacob disease (CJD), **2000** 880, 881, 882, 891-892; **2003** 1234
Crick, Frances, DNA discovery, **2000** 398
Crile, George, Westmoreland libel suit against CBS, **1983** 401; **1985** 159, 161-162, 164
Crime and law enforcement
See also Hate crimes; Law enforcement; Organized crime; Police conduct; Violence
against property, **1993** 376, 378
alcoholism and involvement in, **1983** 335
Boston, Stuart murder hoax, **1990** 35-40
bribery of public officials, combating, **1997** 800-807
broadcast of Noriega taped phone calls, **1990** 721-725
burglary statistics as justification for deadly force, **1985** 304
Clinton administration record on Crime and law enforcement prevention, **2000** 26-27
Clinton proposals, **1994** 35, 47; **1995** 33-34; **1996** 29-30; **1997** 39
congressional legislation, **1994** 575-576
counterfeiting of U.S. currency, **1996** 98-105
death penalty, **1990** 311-317
death penalty effect on, **1983** 711
Democratic Party platform, **1984** 619-621; **1996** 634-636; **2000** 614
Dole convention speech on, **1996** 492-493
domestic violence prevention, **1983** 357-364
federal, sentencing reform, **1987** 407-426
fight against with help of judicial appointees, Nixon on, **1972** 720-721
and human nature, Reagan on, **1981** 648, 667-670
identity theft, **2002** 785-786
judicial system's failure to control, Burger on, **1981** 191-196
mentally ill in prisons and jails, **1990** 579-581
Miranda rule upheld, **1990** 785-793
rape report, **1992** 385-395
rate in U.S., **2002** 784-785; **2003** 980-981, 986-987; **2004** 761; **2005** 677
Republican Party platform, **1984** 693-695; **1988** 655-656; **1996** 521-524
use of DNA "fingerprints" as evidence, **1992** 361-366
victims of, compensation law, **1991** 813-825
violent
Attorney General's task force on, **1981** 647-667
FBI report on, **1994** 574-582; **1995** 710-716

Justice Department reports on, **1992** 375-378
Crime in the United States (FBI report), **1995** 710-716; **1996** 732-739; **1997** 681-689; **1998** 869-877; **1999** 614-622; **2000** 852-860; **2001** 746-757; **2002** 784-793; **2004** 761-770; **2005** 677-685
Crime statistics
FBI report on, **1995** 710-716; **1996** 732-739; **1997** 681-689; **1998** 869-877; **1999** 614-622; **2000** 852-860; **2001** 746-757; **2002** 784-793; **2003** 979-992; **2004** 761-770; **2005** 677-685
school crime and safety reports, **2000** 873-879; **2001** 350-351
trends for children, **1999** 384
Crime Victims Research and Treatment Center, rape study, **1992** 385-395
Criminal justice system
coerced confessions, **1991** 175-184
excessive prison sentences, **1983** 659-674
fair administration of, and access to Nixon tapes, **1974** 621-638
fair trial, TV's effect on, **1981** 163-176
FBI domestic security guidelines, **1983** 257-261
federalism in, attorney general's violent crime task force on, **1981** 663-667
increased spending on, Ford proposals, **1976** 15, 22-23
inequity in, Democratic platform on, **1972** 566-570
insanity defense, **1982** 531-537
minorities and, **2000** 772-774
murder case sentencing, **1991** 381-395
plea bargain, eliminating for drug dealers, **1973** 27, 30-31
reform of
Carter on, **1978** 327-328, 330-332, 334
Nixon on, **1973** 305, 323-324
Reagan on, **1983** 86, 114
sentencing for cocaine penalties, **1997** 245-254
Simpson trial, **1994** 63-64; **1995** 611-621
Criminal law
assassination of high federal official, **1978** 911, 917-918
deadly force to stop burglary suspect, **1985** 303-315
exclusionary rule, **1984** 505-519
Attorney General's violent crime report on, **1981** 648, 661-663
and *habeas corpus* claims, **1976** 521-536
fair trial, and gag order on press coverage, **1976** 463-479
indigents' right to psychiatric aid, **1985** 207-219
insanity defense, **1983** 25-40; **1985** 207-219
jury selection
in death penalty cases, **1986** 445-456
racially motivated, **1986** 409-433
service for women, **1975** 55-66
size and unanimous verdict, **1979** 263-268
Meese criticism of Court decisions, **1985** 480-481, 485-486
Miranda warnings
before second confession, **1985** 223-253
and interrogation definition, **1980** 431-444
and suspects' rights, **1984** 365-385
parole, and sentencing reform, **1987** 407, 411, 413
plea bargain, and sentencing reform, **1987** 418, 425-426
preventive detention of felony suspects, **1987** 491-508
procedure, phone company ordered to assist in electronic surveillance, **1977** 883-896
right to counsel
for offense punishable in prison, **1979** 207-214
pre-Miranda, **1974** 473-485
and self-incrimination, **1977** 219-235; **1981** 431-445
sentencing reform proposals, **1987** 407-426
Criminal liability, for terminating life-support systems, **1976** 198, 217-218
Criminal offense, as impeachment requirement, **1974** 137-143, 145-146, 149-150, 194-195, 199
Crippen, Robert L., **1981** 417, 420
Crisp, Mary Dent
abortion rights, **1992** 800
Republican National Committee resignation, **1980** 568
Cristiani, Alfredo
El Salvador peace treaty, **1992** 23, 24
signing of Tela accord, **1989** 161, 163, 172
violence in El Salvador, UN Truth Commission report on, **1993** 237, 239
Critical Infrastructure Protection, President's Commission on, **1997** 711-720
Critical Mass, on Three Mile Island report, **1979** 825
Critical thinking, and colleges' failures, **1985** 128, 137-138
Croatia
civil war, **1998** 827
elections, **2003** 465
EU membership issue, **2004** 976-977; **2005** 342-343, 857-858
history of, **2003** 56
independence declaration, **1991** 367-376
NATO membership candidacy, **2004** 136; **2005** 857
political situation, **2000** 152-153
UN peacekeeping efforts, **2003** 811
Ustasha regime wartime treasury, **1998** 293, 310-312
Crocetti, Annemarie F., on NCAQ clean air report, **1981** 277, 288-292
Crocker, Charles, Angolan Peace Accord, **1991** 288
Crocker, Chester
accord on Angola and Namibia, **1988** 948
Namibian independence, **1990** 200
Cronkite, Walter
Carter's call-in radio program, **1977** 183, 185
Rebozo interview, **1973** 975-981
Sadat interview, **1977** 828
Crook, Shirley, murder victim, **2005** 179-180
CrossCountry Energy Corp., **2003** 336; **2004** 417
Crouch, William W., USS *Cole* bombing, **2001** 5-6
Crowe, William J.
affirmative action, **2003** 362
embassy security, **1999** 690, 691
on nuclear test ban treaty, **1998** 49
terrorist threats, task force on, **2002** 743
U.S. downing of Iranian airliner, **1988** 704-717

CRP. *See* Committee for the Re-election of the President
CRS. *See* Congressional Research Service
Cruel and unusual punishment
death penalty for juveniles, Supreme Court on, **2005** 177-196
sentencing guidelines, Supreme Court on, **2004** 358-374
sentencing laws, three-strikes law upheld, **2003** 983-984
Cruz Neto, Armando da, Angola peace agreement, **2002** 154
Cruzan, Nancy, **1990** 373-386
Cruzan v. Director, Missouri Dept. of Health, **1990** 373-386; **1996** 122, 127, 130; **1997** 465, 471
Cryogenics, and frozen embryo rights, **1989** 551-559
CSCE. *See* Conference on Security and Cooperation in Europe
CSPI. *See* Center for Science in the Public Interest
Cuba
See also Guantanamo Bay detainees; Havana (Cuba)
aid to Nicaragua, **1985** 256, 261-262, 264-265, 639-641
arms shipments to El Salvador, State Department on, **1981** 241-242, 244-250
biological weapons, **2002** 233
boat people agreement, **1995** 203-207
Bush administration policy toward, **2004** 246-257
Central America instability and, Kissinger commission on, **1984** 32, 45-46, 51
Central American threat, Reagan on, **1983** 439-440, 443, 445
CIA assassination plots in, Senate investigation of, **1975** 710, 715, 725-756, 769-772, 778-780, 789-792
CIA documents about Bay of Pigs and missile crisis, **1992** 10
civilian airplanes attack, **1996** 93-97; **1998** 33
colonialism in Latin America, Reagan on, **1982** 83, 180, 187-188
communism in, and U.S. action in Chile, **1975** 884-885, 892
as defense threat for U.S., **1980** 127-128, 130
dissidents, crackdown on (2003),**2004** 249-250
Elian Gonzalez political asylum case, **2000** 265-276
end to support for Nicaragua urged by U.S., **1989** 163, 165-166, 167-168
Grenada coup and, **1983** 847-853
human rights in, **1977** 189; **1980** 191; **1984** 158-159
human trafficking, **2004** 125
Hurricane Georges damage, **1998** 790
inter-American dialogue on role of, **1983** 376-377, 386-390
Kennedy assassination, investigation of link to, **1978** 910, 914; **1979** 606-609
Mariel boatlift of refugees from, **1980** 337-350; **1981** 605; **2002** 232-233
U.S.-Cuba agreements on, **1987** 929-934
military buildup in, **1983** 307, 311-312
religious freedom, **1997** 564, 571-572
religious freedom, papal address on, **1998** 30-37
smoking in the Americas, **1992** 269
Soviet combat troops in, **1979** 417-418, 713-714, 720, 763-770; **1983** 443
Soviet propaganda about, Project Truth on, **1981** 763
Soviet relationship with, Castro on, **1979** 682-684
support for Argentina in Falklands war, **1982** 287
terrorism supported by, **1981** 463, 469; **1985** 464, 466, 471-472, 476
travel restrictions, **1995** 205; **2002** 235-236
U.S. economic blockade against, **1979** 686-687
U.S. economic sanctions, **1995** 204; **1996** 95-97; **1998** 30, 32-33; **2000** 266, 268; **2002** 233; **2004** 246
U.S. policy, **2002** 232-238; **2004** 246-257
U.S. relations with
antihijacking agreement, **1973** 265-268
Carter on, **1977** 184, 186
Varela Project (anti-Castro democratic movement), **2002** 234; **2004** 249
withdrawal from Angola, **1988** 356, 947-950
Cuba, Commission for Assistance to a Free, **2004** 246-257
Cuban American National Foundation, **2004** 248
Cuban Americans
and Elian Gonzalez political asylum case, **2000** 265-269
and relatives in Cuba, **2002** 235-236
U.S. restrictions on, **2004** 247-248
visits to Cuba, **2004** 247
Cullen, Robert, on Shevardnadze resignation, **1990** 826
Cults
Branch Davidian sect, **1995** 177, 209; **1996** 362; **1997** 123; **1999** 480-488
Heaven's Gate mass suicide, **1997** 122-126
Jonestown (Guyana) suicide, **1997** 123
Cultural agreements
Soviet-European, Gorbachev on, **1989** 401, 405-406
U.S.-PRC, **1984** 288, 296-298
U.S.-Soviet
Geneva summit, **1985** 749-750, 755, 759
Moscow summit, **1988** 356, 371
Washington summit, **1987** 1000-1001, 1005
Cultural diplomacy
for improved U.S. foreign relations, **2005** 579-588
national commission on September 11 recommendations, **2005** 903-904
Cultural freedom, and voluntary exile of Rostropovich and Vishnevskaya, **1975** 161-165
Cultural heritage, destruction of in Afghan conflict, **1986** 927, 935
Culver, John C., **1990** 295-299
Cummings, Sam R. , right to bear arms, **2001** 725
Cummins, Anthony, **1997** 407
Cunningham, Randy "Duke," bribery and tax invasion indictment, **2005** 631, 636
Cuomo, Andrew M.
affordable housing, **1999** 392
on homelessness, **1994** 253
Cuomo, Mario M., **1992** 669; **1993** 393
at Democratic Party convention, **1996** 601-602
speech at Democratic convention, **1984** 648-649
on surrogate motherhood, **1988** 72-73
Cupit, James Hopkinson, Jr., **1989** 50

Curran, Charles E.
on birth control, **2005** 293
Vatican censure of, **1993** 845
Vatican disciplining of, **1986** 318, 757-765, 985
Curran, James W.
on spread of AIDS, **1985** 734; **1986** 888
voluntary AIDS testing for pregnant women, **1995** 442
Curran, Paul J. , Carter warehouse investigation by, **1979** 801-812
Currency
See also Dollar
Chinese yuan
devaluation of currency, **2003** 1180; **2004** 940; **2005** 616-617
floating of, **2004** 238-239
linked to the dollar, **2005** 412
counterfeiting of U.S., **1996** 98-105
euro
coins and bills, **1998** 271-280
and the eurozone, **2003** 752, 753; **2004** 197, 199, 238, 239
U.S. dollar
devaluation of, **2003** 752, 753, 758; **2004** 56, 235, 238-239; **2005** 412
strengthening, U.S. Treasury intervention, **1978** 683, 685, 698
Currency exchange rates
change in, Group of Five Communiqué, **1985** 623-630
flexible
economic summit (Puerto Rico) agreement on, **1976** 425-430
economic summit (Rambouillet) agreement on, **1976** 425-426, 428-429, 431
IMF (Jamaica) agreement on system reform, **1976** 3-12
IMF interim measures for management of, **1974** 497-505
impact on inflation, **1975** 639-640
Joint Economic Committee on, **1980** 229-230
Reagan CEA commitment to, **1989** 13
international monetary crisis, 14-nation Paris accord on, **1973** 343-345, 350-352
realignment of
Nixon administration on, **1972** 82-85; **1973** 386-388
U.S. proposals at IMF (Washington), **1972** 815-826
stability in, economic summit (Bonn) on, **1978** 535-536, 540-541
and U.S. competitiveness, Reagan on, **1986** 41, 45; **1987** 123, 137
Curriculum
upgrading of in U.S. education, **1989** 86, 92
Western civilization as component of, **1988** 518, 522-523
Currie, Betty, Lewinsky scandal, **1998** 574-576, 583, 635, 644-645, 650-651
Currie, Nancy J., **1998** 931
Curry-Lindahl, Kai, on national parks, **1972** 796
Curseen, Joseph P. , anthrax mailings victim, **2001** 674
Curtis, Carl T. (R-Neb.), **1974** 675
Curtiss-Wright Export Corp., United States v., **1998** 429
Cushman, Robert E., Jr., **1972** 901
Custodio, Luther, in B. Aquino assassination conspiracy, **1984** 927, 929-931
Customs Service (U.S.), **1992** 318-319
and gun shipments to Jonestown, **1979** 349, 367-368, 373
Cutler, Lloyd, **1981** 560
federal election system reform, **2001** 526
Russian nuclear weapons panel, **2001** 17, 19
Cyprus
Democratic Party platform on, **1992** 706
EU membership, **2004** 198, 974
EU membership for Turkey, **2004** 976
Greek-Turkish conflict over, U.S. arms used in, **1975** 224, 232-233
peace negotiations, **2004** 977
political situation, **1997** 360
Republican Party platform on, **1996** 541
Cywinski, Bogdan, **1983** 925
Czech Republic
EU membership, **2004** 198
Iraq War, support for, **2003** 42, 49-51
NATO membership, **1997** 514, 516; **1999** 119, 120, 122-124; **2004** 136, 198
Czechoslovakia
Civic Forum, formation of, **1989** 636-639
Havel statements, **1990** 3-18
human rights in, **1988** 884, 888
Dubcek on, **1975** 239-242, 246-247, 249
political liberalization in, and communist concessions, **1989** 635-639, 710
Prague Spring, **1975** 239-240, 242-245; **1989** 636-637
Public Against Violence, formation of, **1989** 637-639
Soviet invasion of (1968),**1989** 399-400
and aftermath, Dubcek on, **1975** 239-249
Warsaw Pact condemnation of, **1989** 646
Warsaw Pact dissolution, **1991** 399

D

Dacca University (Bangladesh), Kennedy speech at, **1972** 163-165
Dae Jung, Kim, No Gun Ri (Korean War) incident, **2001** 38
Dahmer, Vernon, murdered civil rights advocate, **2005** 355
Daily, Edward, No Gun Ri (Korean War) incident, **1999** 552-553; **2001** 36
Daimler-Chrysler
health benefits for domestic partners, **2000** 162
Internet-based parts exchange, **2000** 302
Dairy industry
cow's milk and children, **1992** 398-399, 401
osteoporosis and dairy products, **1992** 402
political campaign contributions to Nixon, **1974** 3-4, 6, 11-14, 604-605, 616
Dalai Lama
meeting with John Paul II, **1986** 24
Nobel Prize acceptance, **1989** 573-581

D'Alema, Massimo, **1999** 913
D'Alessandro, David, Olympics bribery scandal, **1999** 107
Daley, Richard J., **1972** 590
Daley, William M.
computer access initiative, **1999** 371
on electronic business, **2000** 299
Panama Canal transfer ceremony, **1999** 853
Dalia v. United States, **1979** 269-284
Dallagher, John R., resignation from Air Force Academy, **2003** 793
Dallaire, Romeo
Rwanda genocidal war, **2003** 1075; **2004** 116, 117
UN peacekeeping mission in Rwanda, **1999** 862; **2000** 451
Daly, Brendan, gun control legislation and the NRA, **2001** 723
Dam, Kenneth W., **1992** 305, 306, 308
Damages
compensatory, **1987** 178
punitive, for pain and suffering, **1987** 166-169, 174-178
D'Amato, Alfonse M. (R-N.Y.)
on Freeh, FBI director nomination, **1993** 611
Gulf War syndrome investigations, **1994** 264
neutral aid to Nazi Germany, **1997** 262
presidential commission on aviation security and terrorism, **1990** 301-310
Whitewater investigations, **1996** 839
Dames & Moore v. Regan, **1981** 559-573
Dan, Wang, **1996** 134
Danforth, John C. (R-Mo.)
civil rights legislation, **1991** 715
desegregation plan and tax increases, **1990** 228
Iraq war resolution, **1991** 5
Japan's open-market plan, **1985** 319
Lebanon, Syrian troop withdrawal, **2004** 560
school prayer amendment, **1984** 243-244
Sudan, sanctions on *janjaweed* militia, **2004** 592
Sudanese peace negotiations, **2003** 837
Thomas, relationship with, **1992** 35, 37
Thomas confirmation hearings, **1991** 604-605, 609-612
UN ambassador resignation, **2004** 891
Waco investigation, **1999** 165, 480, 482-488
Daniels, Mitchell E., Jr., budget deficit, **2001** 665
Daniloff, Nicholas S., arrest of in Moscow, **1986** 269, 819-827
Dannemeyer, William E. (R-Calif.), **1983** 884
Daoud, Muhammed, ouster of, **1979** 968-969
Darby, Joseph M., Abu Ghraib abuse scandal, **2004** 208
Darby, United States v., **1995** 188
D'Arcy, John (bishop of Indiana), gay seminarians prohibition, **2005** 864
Darden, Christopher, Simpson prosecutor's rebuttal, **1995** 612, 618-619
Darden, Edwin, student drug testing, **2002** 427
Darfur region. *See under* Sudan
Darman, Richard G.
in budget negotiation, **1989** 72
budget warnings, **1990** 50, 410
national education goals, **1990** 154-163
OMB economic forecasts, **1991** 68
on presidential press conferences, **1988** 836
on tax reform and corporate management, **1986** 971-981
White House adviser, **1991** 769
Darwin, Charles, **1982** 4
Daschle, Tom (D-S.D.)
104th Congress
first one hundred days, Democratic response, **1995** 165, 174-175
remarks on closing of, **1996** 698-699
anthrax mailings, **2001** 674
Bush State of the Union address, **2001** 174-175, 183-187; **2004** 21, 30-32
faith-based initiatives, **2001** 136
on Hillary Clinton in the Senate, **2000** 909-910
and Jeffords party switch, **2001** 379
missile defense system, **2001** 284
national energy policy, **2001** 338
nuclear test ban treaty, **1999** 602
pledge of allegiance unconstitutional, **2002** 382
Senate election defeat, **2004** 773; **2005** 81
Senate majority leader appointment, **2001** 380-381
Starr report, **1998** 633
tax cut initiatives, **2001** 666; **2004** 20
terrorist threat from "axis of evil," **2002** 34
war on terrorism, **2001** 638-639
warrantless domestic surveillance, **2005** 961
DASH (Dietary Approaches to Stop Hypertension) Eating Plan, **2005** 8-9
Dash, Samuel
Democratic counsel resignation, **1998** 699
on independent counsel legislation, **1999** 168
D'Aubuisson, Roberto, **1984** 34; **1993** 239
Davenport, Charles, IRS study by, **1975** 830-859
David and Lucile Packard Foundation, **2001** 548
Davidoff, Constantino, in Falklands war, **1983** 4, 18
Davidovic, Slobodan, war crimes convictions, **2004** 854
Davidson, Daniel I., on Vietnam peace negotiations, **1972** 351-352
Davidson, Michael, **1993** 83
Davies, David, tobacco company conspiracy, **2000** 539
Davies, John G., sentencing of LAPD officers, **1993** 631-651
Davies, Thomas D., on Peary's North Pole claim, **1988** 833; **1989** 688
Davis, Gray (California governor)
energy "crisis," **2001** 332-333; **2003** 1015
Enron and energy market manipulation, **2001** 859
health insurance coverage, **2003** 850
pledge of allegiance unconstitutional, **2002** 382
recall election, **2003** 72, 350, 850, 1005-1009, 1015
stem cell research supporter, **2002** 515-516
Davis, Jacquelyn K., on discrimination against women in military, **1987** 671-679
Davis, Javal C., Abu Ghraib prison abuse conviction, **2004** 215, 220, 221
Davis, LaShonda, **1999** 216
Davis, Lynn, Russian nuclear weapons panel, **2001** 19
Davis, Sara, on China's AIDS/HIV prevention programs, **2005** 55

Davis, Shirley, job bias suit against member of Congress, **1979** 399-411
Davis, Thomas M., III (R-Va.)
congressional midterm elections, **2002** 818
steroid use in baseball, congressional hearings on, **2005** 214, 215
Davis v. Bandemer, **1986** 615-635; **1993** 463, 465, 470
Davis v. King, **1989** 551-559
Davis v. Monroe County Board of Education, **1999** 216-234
Davis v. Monsanto Chemical Co., **1993** 945
Davis v. Passman, **1979** 399-411; **1992** 189, 192, 193-194
Davis-Bacon Act
Grace commission proposal on, **1984** 170, 178-179
for Hurricanes Katrina and Rita, **2005** 489
Dawson v. Delaware, **1993** 388
Dayan, Moshe
Egyptian-Israeli Sinai disengagement, **1974** 31
Syrian-Israeli disengagement, **1974** 436
U.S. assurances to Israel, **1979** 225
Days of Remembrance, Holocaust commemoration, **1981** 381-389
Dayton Bd. of Education v. Brinkman, **1977** 447-457; **1979** 535-536, 546-552
Dayton peace agreement (Bosnia), **2002** 717; **2003** 461, 463; **2004** 953
tenth anniversary, **2005** 851-853, 859-862
DDC (dideoxycytidine), in treatment of AIDS, **1987** 328
De Chastelain, John, IRA weapons decommissioning, **2001** 759-760; **2005** 510-511
De Diego, Felipe, Ellsberg break-in, **1974** 205-206, 208-210, 411-417
De Gaulle, Charles, **1976** 331
De Klerk, Frederick W.
bombing cover-up charges, **1998** 757
death penalty and, **1995** 283-284
in inaugural address, **1989** 545-550
Mandela's release, **1990** 72; **1994** 247
Namibian independence, **1990** 199-201, 203
National Party withdrawal from South African coalition government, **1996** 251
Nobel Peace Prize
acceptance speech, **1993** 877-884
winner, **1994** 247
repeal of apartheid laws, **1991** 53-65
South African constitution, **1992** 283-292; **1993** 1003, 1005
and South African elections, **1994** 247-248
South African government leader, **1999** 297-298
South African human rights issues, **1998** 756
South African speeches, **1990** 65-72
De La Beckwith, Byron, retrial for Evers' assassination, **1994** 100-106
De la Garza, E. "Kika" (D-Texas), wife's testimony in Korean influence buying inquiry, **1977** 789-794
De la Rua, Fernando
Argentine financial crisis, **2002** 82-83
Argentine presidential election, **2002** 82
De Larosiere, Jacques, on world inflation, **1979** 771, 774-776
De Mello, Sergio Vieira
East Timor independence, **1999** 511; **2001** 594-595
Guantanamo Bay detainees, **2003** 109
Iraq, detainee abuse scandal, **2004** 208
UN mission in Iraq, killed in bombing, **2003** 109, 808-809, 810, 939, 940, 944; **2004** 208
UN Transitional Administration in East Timor (UNTAET), **2002** 258
De Mita, Ciriaco, **1988** 392
Dead Sea scrolls, access granted to, **1991** 637-639
Deal, Duane, *Columbia* space shuttle disaster report, **2003** 638
Dean, Howard, former governor, presidential campaign, **2004** 17, 479-480
Dean, John W., III
executive privilege claimed for, **1973** 337-338
on Ford's involvement in Watergate, **1976** 760-762, 764
guilty plea, **1975** 659
release from prison, **1975** 143
resignation, **1973** 499, 502, 504, 509, 564
taped conversations with Nixon, **1974** 160, 173-175, 189-191, 193, 195, 200, 294-296, 303-384
Watergate break-in planning, **1973** 501
Watergate committee testimony, **1973** 550, 659-679; **1975** 658
Watergate investigation by, **1973** 414
White House suspicions about, **1973** 660-662, 673-677; **1974** 991-992, 994-1001
Dean, Richard, **1996** 33-34
Death and dying
See also End-of-life care; Physician-assisted suicide
end-of-life care report, **1997** 325-330
euthanasia, John Paul II on, **1987** 701, 712
right to die
definition of death, and terminating life-support systems, **1983** 279, 281-282, 290-291
Quinlan case, **1975** 717, 805-806, 811-813; **1976** 197-198, 200-201, 204-205, 212; **1983** 281
and terminating life-support systems, commission on, **1983** 279-282, 285-289, 291-299
Death penalty. *See* Capital punishment/Death penalty
Death Penalty Information Center
abolition of capital punishment, **2005** 177-178
death penalty for juvenile offenders, **2002** 358
declining numbers of death sentences, **2004** 794
number of executions, **2001** 387; **2002** 354
Death rates. *See* Mortality rates
Deaver, Michael K., conviction under independent counsel law, **1988** 465-466
DeBoer, Jessica, adoption case decision, **1993** 515-529
Debt, national
See also Budget deficit
cost of interest on, **1975** 33; **1982** 144, 153
inflationary strains on, **1975** 167
need to reduce spending, Reagan on, **1981** 215-216, 218, 330
in Nixon budget, **1974** 95-96, 102
raising of ceiling on, **1985** 806, 808
Debt crisis, of developing countries
Baker plan for relief of, **1989** 137-138, 140
Brady plan for relief of, **1989** 137-144
Democratic platform on, **1984** 644-645

Debt crisis *Continued*
economic summits, **1988** 391-393, 396-397; **1990** 475
Gorbachev on, **1988** 933-934
IMF
on status of, **1977** 696-697
and World Bank role, **1977** 708; **1983** 801-802, 806-812; **1989** 4
inter-American dialogue on, **1983** 376-381
Kissinger proposal for, **1976** 300-301, 305, 313-314
nonaligned nations summit (India) on, **1983** 264-266
OECD survey of, **1982** 971-978
Reagan CEA on, **1983** 137-139; **1986** 78-83
Republican platform on, **1988** 617, 632-633
U.S. economic policy, U.S. bishops on, **1986** 984, 1006-1010
in U.S. presidential debates, **1988** 751-752
and world trading system, Allende on, **1972** 334
Declaration of Atlantic Relations, signing of, **1974** 529-533
Declaration of Cartagena, **1990** 117-126; **1992** 201, 213, 215
Declaration of Independence, bicentennial celebrations of, **1976** 15-16, 26, 509-516, 537-542
Declaration of San Antonio (1992), **1992** 206-221
DeConcini, Dennis (D-Ariz.)
Ames espionage case, **1994** 477
declassifying government records, **1994** 525
"Keating Five," investigations, **1990** 817; **1991** 107-118
and Lincoln Savings, **1989** 465
Panama Canal treaty, reservations about, **1978** 179-180, 220
on school prayer amendment, **1984** 244
Souter confirmation hearings, **1990** 627-628
Thomas confirmation hearings, **1991** 552, 566-570, 599
Deep Space missions investigations, **2000** 89-92, 95-102
Defectors. *See* Asylum, political
DeFend, Alan, nursing home abuse, **2002** 119
Defenders of Wildlife, **1995** 360
Defense Advanced Research Projects Agency (DARPA), Information Awareness Office, **2002** 560, 564-568
Defense Advisory Committee on Women in the Services (DACOWITS), on sexual harassment in military, **1987** 671-679
Defense Base Closure and Realignment Act (1990), **1995** 410
Defense Base Closure and Realignment Commission, military base closings, **1993** 501-513; **1995** 407-418
Defense budget
See also Defense spending
CBO analysis
of Ford's, **1976** 184-185
of Reagan's, **1982** 192, 195-196, 200
and Gramm-Rudman-Hollings restrictions, **1986** 39-40, 44
increases in
Carter, **1978** 16, 49-50, 97, 100; **1979** 9-11, 13-14, 25, 27, 70-71; **1980** 110, 112-113, 123-125, 136-137; **1981** 57, 59-60, 89
Ford, **1975** 84, 86, 90-94; **1976** 13, 15, 25, 37-39, 42; **1977** 58, 61
Nixon, **1972** 115-116; **1974** 43, 50, 62, 96, 98-99, 103
Reagan, **1981** 214, 219-220, 326; **1982** 87-88, 96-97, 143-145, 158-161; **1983** 101-102, 307-310, 755; **1984** 99-100, 104, 109, 126; **1988** 149-150, 156
reduced increases in, Reagan, **1986** 49-51, 53, 55; **1987** 4-6, 9-10, 14
reductions in
Bush (George H. W.), **1989** 71, 79-80
as Gramm-Rudman-Hollings requirement, **1985** 803-805, 807
in McGovern's economic program, **1972** 738-739
Reagan vs. Congress on, **1983** 307-309
reorganization of process, Packard commission on, **1986** 679-680, 682-684, 693-695
savings in
Carter revisions, **1977** 126, 128; **1980** 248-249
Reagan on, **1983** 78, 103, 109
of UN members, Gromyko on devoting to development aid, **1973** 810, 820-821
Defense buildup
Carter plans for, **1979** 462-466; **1980** 773, 777, 788
Democratic platform on, **1980** 756-758
as presidential campaign issue, **1980** 920-925, 936-937
Reagan's, **1982** 478, 487-488; **1983** 88, 106; **1985** 105-107, 114-115; **1989** 15-16, 19
Rickover on, **1982** 88, 96-97
and Soviet threat, **1982** 903-904, 910-911; **1985** 39-40, 44-45
and U.S.-Soviet relations, **1984** 812, 826-827
Republican platform on, **1976** 652-653; **1988** 615-617, 688-702
and Soviet threat, Republican platform on, **1984** 662-664, 718-726
Defense contractors
corporate mergers, **1998** 341
enforcement of laws governing, **1986** 679-681, 690-693
Rickover on, **1982** 87-89, 90-93
Tower's relationship with, **1989** 106, 110, 112-115, 117
Defense conversion, Democratic Party platform on, **1992** 691
Defense Department
See also Cheney, Richard B. "Dick"; Cohen, William S.
Antiterrorism/Force Protection (AT/FP) plan, **2001** 4-5, 8-16
arms sales, and U.S. influence, **1978** 107
arms sales, to Iran, role in, **1986** 1016, 1018, 1024, 1051
ban on scientific presentations affecting security, **1982** 813-819
base closings, **1988** 951-954; **1993** 501-513; **1995** 407-418
budgeting challenges, **2005** 131-132
chemical agents exposure, **2001** 908
chemical weapons, rules for dismantling, **1989** 26
computer security, **1996** 312-324

computer systems
"data mining" system, **2002** 559-568
inventory, **1999** 762
security matters, **1998** 676-677
Cooperative Threat Reduction (CTR) program, **1996** 143, 228-230
cost-cutting measures, **1997** 811-812
deserter clemency program, **1974** 820; **1977** 97, 184
discrimination in Medal of Honor award, **1989** 699-700
draft evaders, amnesty for, **1974** 820
in drug war, **1989** 500, 504-505
Grenada invasion, **1983** 847, 849
helicopters for Mexico, **1992** 202
hostages in Iran, attempted rescue of, **1980** 351-385
Hurricane Andrew, **1992** 534
intelligence agencies in, proposed restructuring of, **1976** 258-259
in Iran-contra affair, circumvention of, **1987** 899, 902, 913, 922, 924
management and efficiency of, Rickover on, **1982** 87-89, 96-102
MIAs in Southeast Asia, **1976** 925-927, 930, 933-934
military construction bills, **1997** 613
military homosexual ban, **1993** 153-164
military readiness, letters questioning, **1994** 528-534
national security needs, **1993** 695-715
nuclear weapons proliferation report, **1996** 210-230
Panama invasion, costs of, **1989** 703
Pentagon Papers, **1973** 539; **1974** 33-37, 205-206
POW repatriation, information to aid, **1973** 246, 248-262
procurement reform, Democratic platform on, **1976** 546, 585-586
reorganization of, **1985** 669-683; **1986** 679-695
satellite and aerial reconnaissance, **1992** 5
on SDI, changing focus of, **1988** 323-331
secretary of
nomination, **1994** 22-25
proposed strengthening of authority, **1985** 670, 681
standards of conduct, **1989** 108-115, 117, 120
sexual harassment and discrimination against women, **1987** 671-679
on Soviet acquisition of military technology, **1985** 603-614
on Soviet military strength, **1981** 717-730
Tailhook scandal, court-martial decisions, **1994** 107-115
technology export controls, **1987** 30, 40-42
on terrorist attack on Marines in Beirut, **1983** 933-966
terrorist bombing in Saudi Arabia, **1996** 672-679
Tomb of the Unknowns disinterment remarks, **1998** 281-283
Total Information Awareness (TIA) project, **2003** 613
on U.S. defense posture, **1980** 123-157
on U.S. downing of Iranian airliner, **1988** 703-717
USS *Cole* bombing, **2001** 3-16
women in combat debate, **1992** 1029-1044
Y2K conversion, **1999** 762; **2000** 4, 11
Defense Department Authorization Act (1983), **1984** 493-503
Defense Information, Center for
nuclear arms race, **1975** 496
Persian Gulf attacks, **1988** 705
Defense Information Systems Agency (DISA), computer security, **1996** 313, 315-316, 322, 323
Defense Intelligence Agency (DIA), **1976** 122, 258-259
Abu Ghraib prison scandal, **2004** 214
intelligence gathering investigations, **2002** 994
Defense of Marriage Act, **2003** 405; **2004** 29
Defense policy
See also Military force; Nuclear deterrence
European defense force, **1999** 817-827
Republican Party platform on, **1996** 541-543
Defense posture
See also Military strength
Soviet, Akhromeyev congressional testimony on, **1989** 439-444
strategy, former national security officials on, **1986** 781-790
U.S.
Moorer on, **1972** 179-182
Soviets on naval force of, **1989** 440-441
Defense Science Board, U.S. Strategic Communication Task Force, **2004** 626-638
Defense spending
See also Defense budget
and budget deficit, **2004** 236
Bush administration, **1991** 68
Bush defense budget proposals, **2002** 35-36, 42
of capitalist countries, Brezhnev on, **1981** 233-234
CEA report on, **1992** 105
Clinton proposal to increase, **1999** 53-54
comptroller general report on, **2005** 131-132
cost-cutting measures, **1997** 811-812
decline in military spending, **2005** 139
Democratic platform on, **1972** 527, 576-577; **1976** 546, 585-586; **1984** 566; **1988** 558, 560, 566
Dole support for, **1995** 576
and economic priorities, U.S. Catholic bishops on, **1986** 984, 989, 997
maintaining after Vietnam war, Nixon on, **1973** 428, 432-433
negotiating from strength, Nixon on, **1972** 74, 78-80, 723
as presidential campaign issue, **1988** 741-745, 761-764, 778-779
Reagan defense buildup, **2002** 35
Republican platform on, **1972** 651, 661-664; **1980** 569, 624-632
and SALT agreement, Carter on, **1979** 461-466
and Soviet threat, Reagan on, **1981** 646
and Soviet threat, Reagan on MX missile, **1982** 903-913, 917-918
Tower's support for, **1989** 105-106
for Vietnam War, congressional vs. executive control over, **1973** 3-4, 7, 12-13, 15, 17
Deficit, budget. *See* Budget deficit
Deficit Reduction Act, **2000** 22
Deforestation
impact on natural resources and environment, **1980** 666, 669-670, 681-682, 685, 689-690, 695

Deforestation *Continued*
population pressure in developing countries, **1987** 440-441, 446-448
World Bank projects, **1986** 859-873
DeGeneres, Ellen, **1997** 761
DeHaven, Ron, mad cow disease, testing for, **2003** 1238
Dehr, Donald, **1999** 109
Del Ponte, Carla
UN war crimes tribunal for Kosovo war, **2001** 830, 831; **2003** 1072; **2004** 952; **2005** 854
UN war crimes tribunal for Rwanda, **2003** 99-101, 1072-1073
Delahanty, Thomas K., **1981** 351-352; **1991** 185
Delahunt, William D. (D-Mass.)
Cuban Working Group, **2002** 235
House Judiciary Committee impeachment inquiry, **1998** 709
Delahunty, Robert J., Afghanistan detainees, prisoner-of-war status and Geneva Conventions, **2004** 336
Delainey, David W., Enron Corp. collapse, **2003** 337
Delaney, James J. (D-N.Y.), and carcinogens in food, **1996** 73, 467
Delaney clause, **1990** 176, 180
DeLauer, Richard D., **1983** 307
DeLaughter, Bobby, De La Beckwith's retrial for Evers assassination, **1994** 100-106
Delaware, smoking prevention program, **2004** 282
DeLay, Paul, AIDS epidemic, **2000** 411
DeLay, Tom (R-Texas)
on "activist" judges, **2005** 364
assault weapons ban, **2004** 764
bribery and money laundering investigations, **2004** 577, 580-581; **2005** 78
Clinton campaign contributions, **1999** 237
Clinton resignation campaign, **1998** 954
eminent domain, **2005** 364
and Gingrich ethics violations, **1997** 4, 5
House majority leader, **2005** 632
House majority leader resignation, **2005** 78
indictments, **2005** 631-643
midterm elections, **2002** 820
NASA moon-Mars missions supporter, **2004** 11
prescription drug benefits for seniors ad campaign, **2004** 577
Republican senior leader, **1998** 952
Schiavo end-of-life care case, **2005** 157, 158, 364-365
stem cell research opponent, **2005** 319
Ten Commandments displays, **2005** 379
U.S.-China trade relations, **2000** 215-216
Delbanco, Thomas, **1984** 276, 281-285
Deleuze, Olivier, Kyoto Protocol on Climate Change, **2001** 115
Delfico, Joseph F., child care quality testimony, **1994** 116-122
Dellinger, Walter E., III
on affirmative action, **1997** 185
on physician-assisted suicide, **1996** 124
Dellums, Ronald V. (D-Calif.)
on Kissinger Vietnam Study, **1972** 361
praise from Gingrich, **1995** 4, 8
in vice-presidential balloting, **1976** 596
Deloitte & Touche, federal oversight, **2004** 423
Delors, Jacques
at economic summits, **1984** 356; **1986** 438; **1988** 392
Soviet aid package, **1990** 467
Delphi (auto parts supplier), bankruptcy, **2005** 200, 486
Delta State University, **1992** 576, 578-587
Delvalle, Eric Arturo, **1988** 81
Dembo, Antonio, death of, **2002** 153
Demining Assistance Program, **1995** 47-48
Demirchian, Karen, shooting of, **1999** 639
Demirel, Suleyman
on conflict with Greece over Cyprus, **1975** 354
Middle East peace negotiations, **2001** 361
military takeover in Turkey, **1980** 807-808
Demjanjuk, Ivan, war crimes acquittal, **1993** 617-623
Democracy
assailed in UN, Moynihan on, **1975** 648-650
in Central America, and Reagan policy, **1983** 440-441, 443-449
Chinese movement in favor of, **1989** 275-282, 284
conflict with secrecy required by intelligence agencies, **1976** 236, 240
development of
in friendly countries, Reagan administration on, **1983** 182, 895, 912
Reagan before British Parliament, **1982** 478, 480-481, 484-485
and human rights, Reagan administration on, **1987** 189, 191
inter-American dialogue on, **1983** 376, 378, 381-383
movements toward, Dalai Lama on, **1989** 574, 577
Polish movement toward, **1989** 523-538
Soviet constitution and movement toward, Brezhnev on, **1977** 753, 756
U.S. support for in world, **1983** 87-89, 114; **1984** 717-718; **1985** 115-116; **1988** 617, 632
values of, economic summit on, **1984** 357-358
world movement toward
Bush on, **1988** 608; **1989** 80-81
Gorbachev on, **1988** 930-933
Reagan on, **1988** 58, 60, 66, 67; **1989** 16, 20-21
Democracy and Rule of Law Project, **2005** 44
Democratic Forces for the Liberation of Rwanda (FDLR), **2004** 506
Democratic Front for the Liberation of Palestine, **1988** 907
Democratic Leadership Council (DLC), **1992** 668, 685
Democratic National Committee (DNC)
civil suit by, White House strategy on, **1973** 663
primary rules, **1986** 1067
registration of young voters, **1973** 36
Watergate break-in at headquarters of, **1973** 413-415, 423-425; **1974** 23, 157-184, 657, 659; **1975** 142, 653, 655
Democratic Party
See also Congress, Democratic control of
campaign finances
attorney general investigations, **1998** 890-902
Chinese contributions to, **1997** 825
convention, Boston (2004)

Kerry nomination acceptance speech, **2004** 483-484, 485-493
speeches, **2004** 483-484
Gephardt comments on role of, **1995** 6
Iraq stabilization plan, **2005** 81, 93
Kennedy decision against running, **1974** 854
midterm conference, **1978** 765-780
open primaries, **1986** 1067
policies of, Republican convention on, **1988** 590-591, 594-596
presidential debates, **1984** 858-861
primary campaign, **2004** 479-480
on Reagan State of the Union, **1983** 78-79; **1988** 59
response to State of the Union address, **1990** 51, 59-62
State of the Union address
Daschle's response, **2004** 32-34
Gephardt's response, **2001** 174-175, 183-187; **2002** 38, 46-48
Locke's response, **2003** 23-24, 36-39
Pelosi's response, **2004** 21-22, 30-32
state redistricting plan, **1986** 615-635
traditional values of, Kennedy on, **1980** 701-709
unity of, **1984** 647-648
vision/agenda for the future lacking, **2005** 81
wars during administrations of, Dole on, **1976** 773-774, 792-793
Democratic Party and Democratic National Committee v. NCPAC, **1985** 277-294
Democratic Party conventions
AIDS speech, **1992** 709-713
Atlanta, **1988** 533-559
Chicago, **1996** 600-622
first-ballot rule, **1980** 701, 711, 771-772
Los Angeles
Clinton speech to, **2000** 596-608
speeches, **2000** 617-634
Miami Beach, **1972** 527-528, 589-597, 599-600
Eagleton nomination and acceptance, **1972** 597-600
openness of through reforms, **1972** 527, 589-592
New York City, **1976** 595-607; **1980** 711-713, 771-791; **1992** 667
Kennedy speech, **1980** 701-709
unity of, **1976** 543-544, 595-596, 604
rule changes for, **1978** 765, 767, 778-780
San Francisco, **1984** 549-551, 647-649, 647-658
Democratic Party platform, **1972** 527-588; **1976** 543-594; **1980** 701-704, 711-770; **1984** 549-646; **1988** 557-569; **1992** 685-707; **1996** 623-652; **2000** 609-616
Democratic reforms
Bonner lecture on Soviet reforms, **1990** 207-213
Gorbachev address to Soviet 28th Party Congress, **1990** 439-453
Havel address to Czechoslovakian nation, **1990** 3-11
Havel address to U.S. Congress, **1990** 4, 11-18
Democratic Republic of the Congo. *See* Congo, Republic of
Democratization
Bush promoting democracy in Arab lands, **2004** 628-629; **2005** 42-43, 164, 582
"third wave" of, **2005** 22
UN promoting democracy in Arab lands, **2005** 269-289
Demographic trends, and financial condition of Social Security system, **1975** 115-121, 125-126
Dempsey, Mary, Internet pornography filters, **2003** 390
Denali National Monument, **1978** 731, 736
Deng, Francis M., Chechnya war, **1999** 914-916
Deng Xiaoping
China-Taiwan relations, **2000** 199
Chinese leadership, **2002** 851; **2003** 1174
dominance in new government, **1978** 157
economic reforms, **2000** 214
and GATT, **1999** 725
Hua on criticism of, **1976** 691
and human rights, **1984** 165; **1986** 98
Jiang Qing's attacks on, **1980** 955-956
peace treaty with Japan, **1978** 585
on PRC's invasion of Vietnam, **1979** 185
president Jiang Zemin on death of, **1997** 94-100, 728
repression of Chinese prodemocracy demonstrations, **1989** 275, 277-278, 282-283, 287-288
U.S. visit, **1978** 781, 785-786; **1984** 23
U.S.-PRC normalization of relations, **1979** 669
U.S.-PRC scientific and cultural agreements, **1979** 135-142, 149-151, 153-154
Denmark
Arab oil embargo against, **1974** 221-222
support for Iraq, **2003** 42, 49-51
Dennis, Edward S. G., Jr., Waco incident, **1993** 819-820
Dennis, Michael J., **2002** 224
Dennis, W. Glenn, Roswell incident, **1997** 396
Denny, Reginald, **1992** 409, 414, 422
Dental care, oral health in America, surgeon general's report on, **2000** 222-239
Dental diseases, smoking linked to, surgeon general's report on, **2004** 293
Denton, Jeremiah (R-Ala.)
FBI domestic security guidelines, **1983** 258
freedom of religious speech, **1983** 272
return as POW from Vietnam, **1973** 245
Denver (Colorado)
air quality of, **1981** 275, 289
John Paul II's visit, **1993** 659-669
Deoxyribonucleic acid. *See* DNA
Department of Energy (DOE), GAO report on nuclear cleanup priorities, **1995** 113-119
DePasquale, Daniel A., on closed pretrial hearings, **1979** 511, 516-517, 526-527, 533
Deportation
of Cuban detainees, **1987** 929-937
and political asylum, **1987** 253-265
Depression
antidepressant drugs and suicide in children, **2004** 746-752
prevalence in U.S. adult population, **1984** 833-840
screening for, federal task force on, **2002** 265-274
"The Deputy" (Hochhuth), **1998** 123
Deregulation
See also Airline industry; Trucking industry

Deregulation *Continued*
expanded, Reagan economic report on, **1986** 59-60, 63, 67-68, 85-87
increased, National '80s Agenda on, **1981** 40, 46-47
as privatization, **1986** 68; **1988** 237
progress in, Carter on, **1981** 59, 81-82, 109, 115
Republican Party platform on, **1992** 821
in transportation industry, Carter on, **1978** 22, 29; **1979** 24, 30, 36-37, 39-40, 84, 88
Deri, Aryeh, Israeli Shas Party leader, **1999** 360, 361
Derrick, Butler, Russian nuclear weapons panel, **2001** 19
Dervis, Kemal, Turkish economics minister resignation, **2002** 907
Desai, Morarji R., election of, **1977** 237-241
Desai, Nitin, on aging world population, **2002** 193
D'Escoto, Miguel, **1980** 412
Desert One Operation, **1980** 357, 360-361, 370-373, 378-385
Desertification
and carrying capacity in world, **1980** 669-670, 686-687
and population pressure in developing countries, **1987** 441, 447-448
DeSeve, G. Edward, computer security issues, **1998** 678
DeShaney v. Winnebago County Dept. of Social Services, **1991** 265
DeSutter, Paula A., Libya nuclear weapons program dismantled, **2004** 171
Detainees' Parents Support Committee, on South African torture, **1982** 797-811
Détente
accomplishments of, Gromyko on at UN, **1974** 833, 835, 843-844
and human rights in Soviet Union, **1973** 791-800; **1975** 560
Nixon on, **1974** 114, 117
Sakharov on, **1975** 917, 922-923
NATO cooperation on, **1974** 530-531, 533; **1975** 357-358; **1982** 479
Nixon-Brezhnev relations at Moscow summit, **1974** 536
nonaligned nations' role in, **1974** 834, 838-839
opportunities of, Waldheim on, **1972** 631-634; **1973** 758-759
in practice, Carter on, **1978** 225, 234, 236, 239-240
progress in
Gromyko on, **1973** 816-818
Kissinger on, **1973** 811-812
Republican platform on, **1976** 618, 651
and risk of military confrontation, **1973** 881-896, 937
Solzhenitsyn's expulsion, effect of on, **1974** 129, 146, 152
and Soviet invasion of Afghanistan, **1979** 966, 981-982
and trade expansion, economic summit on, **1976** 427, 430
Deterrence. *See* Nuclear deterrence
Detroit (Michigan)
impact of Chrysler on economy of, **1979** 695, 710
school desegregation remedies for, **1974** 639-654
Detroit Bank v. United States, **1995** 313
Deukmejian, George, **1984** 729
Deutch, John
CIA counterterrorism recruitment restrictions, **2000** 278
computer security, **1996** 312; **1997** 711-712
government secrecy, **1997** 103
Gulf War syndrome investigations, **1994** 265, 270
Iraq situation report, **1996** 680-686
national security, **1993** 695; **1999** 502-503
Nicholson espionage case, **1996** 794-800
presidential pardon, **2001** 89
Developing countries
agricultural subsidies, opposition to, **2003** 8, 14, 743
aid to
Democratic platform on, **1972** 583
economic summits on, **1981** 591, 597-598; **1982** 470, 475; **1985** 353
for food and agriculture, food conference on, **1974** 939-953
for privatization, **1988** 235-236
Republican platform on, **1988** 617, 632-633
from UN members' military budgets, Gromyko on, **1973** 810, 820-821
in world recession, Ford on, **1975** 189
arms sales to, **1977** 251, 265, 267
balance of payments deficits, and IMF assistance, **1976** 4, 6, 8
basic needs and development of, Carter on, **1977** 190, 194-195
Catholic Church in, **1985** 766, 768
children and disease in, UNICEF on, **1981** 912, 917-918
chlorofluorocarbon reduction by, **1987** 747-748, 753-756; **1988** 223
debt of, **1985** 626, 627
Baker plan on, **1985** 643-652
economic summits on, **1984** 355-356, 359-361; **1986** 438, 441-442; **1988** 391, 392-393, 396-397; **1989** 425-427; **1991** 466-468
inter-American dialogue on, **1983** 376, 378-381
John Paul II on, **1986** 639-646; **1988** 165-166, 168
McNamara on, **1977** 707-709
OECD survey of, **1982** 971-978
and protectionism among industrialized countries, **1983** 381; **1984** 795-802
Reagan economic report on, **1986** 78-83
debt reduction, Brady plan for, **1989** 138-139, 141-144
demographic change in, **1984** 529-534, 544-545
economic aid, **1997** 481-482
economic cooperation with industrialized countries, **1973** 810, 813-815; **1975** 587-611; **1976** 427-428, 431
economic development
and human dignity, **1988** 165-174
and industrial accidents, **1984** 1024-1025
and population growth in, **1975** 919
progress of, McNamara on, **1977** 698-704
role of education, **1980** 889-890
sustainable, **1981** 15-17, 27-28, 774
economic situation, **1999** 392-394

employment and services in, McNamara on, **1972** 859-865
energy supplies and costs of, IMF aid to, **1977** 368, 374
export commodities of
and industrialized countries' responsibilities, **1977** 688-689, 704-707
price stabilization for, **1976** 427, 431; **1983** 263-265, 380-381
UNCTAD integrated program for, **1976** 299-300, 305, 308, 315-319
food shortages and price increases for, impact of world recession on, **1975** 196-197
foreign investment in, mutual codes of conduct for, **1975** 595-596
hazardous waste imports, **1989** 154-156
health care in, restructuring, **1980** 890-891
improving conditions in, and world growth limits, **1972** 218-219
income and population, impact on resources, **1980** 666, 674-679, 681-690
independence and economic growth in, U.S. support for, **1980** 476-477, 482-483
and industrialized countries' deficits, **1983** 802, 804, 809-810
infant formula marketing in, WHO code on, **1981** 447
Latin American, economic participation of, **1979** 713-716, 718, 721
liberation theology in, **1984** 759-775
life expectancy in, **1984** 531-532
meeting basic human needs in, McNamara on, **1977** 700-704, 710-715
and multilateral trade agreement, **1979** 639, 641
nationalization of U.S. firms, U.S. economic retaliation for, **1972** 67-71, 329, 332-335
natural disasters in, **1984** 973-995
and new international economic order, **1975** 325-331, 349, 587-591, 603
nonaligned nations summit on, **1983** 263-268
nondemocratic, demands of in UN, Moynihan on, **1975** 645-651
nuclear technology for, **1975** 361-362, 368
oil price increases, impact on, **1974** 222, 255-256; **1979** 251, 254-257; **1980** 504-505, 507, 510-511, 884-886, 891, 895; **1981** 179, 181
OPEC assistance to, **1976** 939
population control in, **1987** 439-453, 458-461
family planning, **1984** 521-523, 534, 536-543, 545-546
population growth in, **1984** 522, 524-528, 534-537
support for, **1974** 777-779
poverty of children in, **1988** 878-879
at poverty summit, **1981** 769
public services in, McNamara on, **1977** 710-715
as raw materials producers, power of, **1975** 4, 325-327
resettlement programs, **1987** 444-445, 447
resources of
control of, **1974** 255-264
and Law of the Sea Treaty, **1982** 345-346
resources of exploited by industrialized world, **1972** 329-336; **1974** 255, 258-260
self-determination for and exploitation of, **1974** 833-839
"Singapore issues" trade negotiations, **2003** 743-744
smoking trends in, **1989** 33, 37, 40
social and economic inequities in, **1985** 58-61
social unrest in due to austerity measures, **1989** 137, 140
Soviet propaganda about, Project Truth on, **1981** 761
tariff preferences for, U.S. pledge on, **1972** 471, 474
tobacco control efforts, **2000** 547-548
in UN, challenge to industrialized countries, **1975** 325-327, 330-331
as UN bloc, Scali on, **1975** 645
UN Zionism resolution, **1975** 825-826
U.S. aid to
Nixon on, **1974** 278, 283-285
Reagan on, **1981** 773
and U.S. economic policy, U.S. bishops on, **1986** 984, 988-989, 993, 1004-1010
U.S. relations with in Carter administration, **1978** 269-290; **1979** 647, 650-651
and U.S. withdrawal from UNESCO, **1983** 967-968
women in, needs and rights of, **1975** 507-522
women's roles in, **1985** 556-561, 564-567
World Bank projects in, **1986** 859-873
WTO Doha Development Agenda, **2003** 742, 746, 766
Y2K-related problems, **2000** 12-14
DeWaal, Caroline Smith
food safety agency, **1998** 523
salmonella testing, **2001** 701
DeWine, Mike (R-Ohio), intelligence gathering failures, **2002** 995
DeWitt, John L., **1988** 289
Dhaliwal, Herb, massive power blackout investigation, **2003** 1015
DHS. *See* Homeland Security Department
Di Rita, Larry, strategic communications report, **2004** 627-628
Diabetes
among minorities, **1985** 685-687, 690, 702-704
and job accommodations, **1998** 380-381
and obesity, **2000** 242-243
research and treatment, **1997** 217-218
in women who smoke, **2001** 234-235
Diamond v. Chakrabarty, **1980** 493-502; **1987** 352, 358
Diamond smuggling, "conflict diamonds," **2002** 252
Diana (princess of Wales)
death of, **1997** 647-653; **1999** 422
land mines ban, **1997** 845
royal family problems, **1992** 1059-1063
Diarra, Seydou, Ivory Coast prime minister appointment, **2003** 239; **2004** 820
Diaz Herrera, Roberto, **1989** 704
Dickerson, Vivian, morning-after pill controversy, **2003** 999
Dickerson v. United States, **2000** 385-395
Dickey, Jay (R-Ark.), embryonic research funding, **1998** 66; **2000** 669
Dickey, Nancy, medical safety, **1999** 781

Dicks, Norman (D-Wash.), Chinese technology transfer, **1998** 977, 979-982; **1999** 236
Diem, Ngo Dinh, as target of CIA activity, investigation of, **1975** 401, 710, 715, 763, 770, 776
Diet
See also Child nutrition; Nutrition; Obesity
carbohydrate recommendations, **2005** 12
carcinogens and, **1996** 71-79
cholesterol levels, **1987** 780, 782-783, 785-788
dietary trans fatty acids, **1992** 399, 403-404
federal dietary guidelines, **1996** 3-16; **2000** 240-261; **2001** 936; **2005** 3-13
global dietary guidelines, **2003** 481, 484-485
and health, **1997** 160-161
heart disease risk and, **1984** 1039-1043
nutrition revisionism, **1992** 397-403
obesity
FTC report on weight loss advertising, **2002** 624-632
surgeon general's report on, **1997** 167; **2001** 935-954; **2003** 480-491
obesity and overeating, **1997** 159-160
reducing risk of cancer, **1982** 507-520
sodium and potassium recommendations, **2005** 12
vegetarian diets, **1996** 5, 8
weight management, **2005** 10
Dietary Guidelines Advisory Committee (DGAC), **2005** 8
Dietary Guidelines for Americans (HHS report), **2005** 7-13
Dieter, Richard
on abolition of capital punishment, **2005** 177-178
death penalty for juvenile offenders, **2002** 358
Dietz, Park E., **1982** 533
Diez, Francisco, referendum on Venezuelan president, **2003** 281
DiFrancesco, United States v., **1980** 977-988
DiGenova, Joseph E., **1989** 394; **1992** 1047
Diggs, Charles C., Jr. (D-Mich.), House censure of, **1979** 623-631; **1980** 485
DiIulio, John J., Jr., faith-based initiatives, **2001** 132, 133
Dillingham, Gerald D.
aviation security, **2001** 652
FAA and airline safety inspections, **1996** 239, 240-246
on FAA procedures, **1997** 114
Dillingham, Steven D.
on rape study, **1993** 386
on violent crime, **1993** 377
Dillon, John T., on economic recovery, **2002** 53
DiMaggio, Joe, baseball record, **1995** 588-589
Dimpfer, Michael, Yushchenko dioxin poisoning, **2004** 1006
ad-Din, Fu'ad Muhyi, on Sadat assassination, **1981** 735, 738-739
Dine, Thomas A., on Baker speech, **1989** 290
Dingell, John D., Jr. (D-Mich.)
on Brady commission, **1988** 11
Clean Air Act revisions, **1990** 716-717
on corporate takeovers, **1988** 923
on fairness doctrine, **1987** 627
patients' bill of rights, **1999** 562
Dingell, John D., Sr. (D-Mich.), national health insurance, **1993** 782
Dinh, Viet
domestic detentions, **2002** 833
USA Patriot Act author, **2003** 609
Dinitz, Simcha, and Israeli protest of Scranton's remarks, **1976** 192
Dinkins, Carol, and special prosecutor law, **1988** 467
Dinkins, David N.
Census Bureau undercount, **1991** 444
election of, **1989** 368; **1990** 42
gay/lesbian march on Washington, **1993** 327
DiNois, Augustine, on Catholic moral theology, **1993** 845
Diouf, Jacques, worldwide famine reduction, **2002** 690
Diplomacy
ABM treaty negotiation process, **1987** 290-291, 312-315
Angola-Namibia peace accord, **1988** 947-950
confidentiality in, **1975** 258-259, 574
continuity in, Kissinger on, **1975** 274
Nixon achievements in, Republican platform on, **1972** 655-657
PRC-Japan, establishment of relations, **1972** 827-830
regional, and Contadora Group, **1984** 49-50
Syria, break in relations with U.S., Britain, and Canada, **1986** 832
U.S.-British extradition treaty, **1986** 751-756
U.S.-Egyptian normalization of relations, **1973** 931
U.S.-Iran diplomatic relations, and hostage taking by Iran, **1979** 867-872, 878-879, 885-888
U.S.-Libyan relations, **1986** 347-354
U.S.-PRC consular agreement, **1979** 136, 139, 151-153; **1980** 829-830, 832, 834, 842-843
U.S.-PRC opening of liaison offices, **1973** 291-300
U.S.-Soviet, and arrests of Daniloff and Zakharov, **1986** 819-827
U.S.-Syrian relations, resumption of, **1974** 451, 462-464
U.S.-Vatican relations, **1984** 19-22
Diplomatic immunity, U.S. entering of Nicaraguan embassy in Panama, **1989** 703
Diplomats
expulsions of Nicaraguan and U.S., **1988** 243
expulsions of Soviet and U.S., **1986** 267-272
hostage taking and attacks on, economic summit on, **1980** 506
size of UN missions, convention on (1946), **1986** 268
Soviet in U.S., number of and espionage by, **1985** 606
Dirceu, Jose
Brazil political corruption scandal, **2005** 768
Brazilian Workers Party leader, **2002** 776
Director of National Intelligence (DNI). *See* National Intelligence Director (NID)
Dirksen, Everett McKinley (R-Ill.), **1984** 242
Disabled persons
children, life-sustaining measures for, **1983** 269, 273, 282-283
consolidation of welfare payments, **1979** 391, 394

definition of, Supreme Court on, **1999** 317-332; **2002** 3-4
disability programs, Reagan budget cuts in, **1983** 766-767, 769-772
disability rights vs. seniority rights, **2002** 3, 6
EEOC employer guidelines on mental disabilities, **1997** 127-141
expulsion of disruptive students from schools, **1988** 47-56
federal programs for, **2005** 132-133
HIV-positive people, Supreme Court on, **1998** 378-392
persons with contagious diseases as, **1987** 245-246, 248-252
Republican Party platform on, **1988** 644-645
right to work, John Paul II on, **1981** 715
rights of, John Paul II on, **1984** 778-780
in the workplace, Supreme Court on, **2002** 3-14
Disappeared persons, Brazilian government action on, **1984** 157-158
Disarmament
See also Nuclear nonproliferation
destruction of biological and toxin weapons, convention on, **1972** 323-328
nonaligned nations summit on, **1983** 263-264, 266-268
Sakharov plan for, **1975** 918, 923-924
women's conference support of, **1975** 522
Disarmament, Demobilization, Repatriation, Resettlement, and Reintegration (DDRRR), in the Congo, **2004** 509
Disaster relief
See also Federal Emergency Management Agency; Hurricane Katrina disaster; Hurricane Rita disaster
effectiveness of, **1984** 973-976, 985-995
floods of Red River (North Dakota and Minnesota), **1997** 229-233
Homeland Security Department response, **2005** 893
Hurricane Mitch relief effort, UN report on, **1998** 789-798
Disasters
See also Earthquakes; Floods; Hurricane disasters; Natural disasters
carbon dioxide gas eruption in Cameroon, **1987** 61-77
Chernobyl nuclear accident, **1986** 383-407; **1990** 196
human behavior in, **1984** 986-989
Three Mile Island nuclear accident, **1979** 823-863; **1990** 196
worldwide, **1999** 468-469
Discovery space shuttle mission, **1998** 53-54, 776-786, 930
NASA reports on, **2005** 498-506
tribute by, to *Challenger* victims, **1988** 795-798
Discrimination
against AIDS victims, **1988** 439-441
against aliens, **1982** 489-506; **1986** 964-965, 966-967
against homosexuals, as result of AIDS, **1983** 534-535
in education, and school financing based on property tax, **1973** 361-377
minorities and the death penalty, **2001** 387-394
and voting rights, **2001** 523-524
Discrimination, age
mandatory retirement, **1985** 397-407
by state and local governments, **1983** 231-240
Discrimination, job
affirmative action promotion of women, **1987** 331-349
against African Americans, **1993** 423-430
against women, proposed laws on, **1977** 864
among minorities and women, **1982** 919-944
charitable choice and, **2001** 134-135, 136
contagious diseases and, **1987** 245-252
definition of disabled, Supreme Court on, **1999** 317-332; **2002** 3-4
Democratic platform on, **1988** 560-561
disabilities in the workplace, Supreme Court on, **2002** 3-14
and education, Democratic platform on, **1984** 551, 571, 599-608
EEOC employer guidelines on mental disabilities, **1997** 127-141
fetal protection policies, **1991** 143-153
by members of Congress, **1979** 399-411
proof of, **1989** 321-322, 324-329
seniority rights after maternity leave, **1977** 871-881
seniority systems
and affirmative action, **1984** 365-385
predating Civil Rights Act, **1977** 383-393
sex discrimination law suits, **2001** 549-550
and sexual harassment, **1998** 438
Discrimination, race
See also Blacks; Minorities; Minority business; School desegregation
and black college athletes, **1989** 214, 220
and blacks' economic status, **1989** 445, 447-449, 451-453, 459
in death penalty, **1987** 463-476
Democratic platform on, **1984** 598-601, 605-608, 612
in military, **1972** 901-906
NAACP boycott to combat, **1982** 655-656
by private clubs, **1988** 399-403
in private school admission policies, **1976** 391-404
remedies for past, minority set-asides, **1980** 539-566; **1989** 323-324
in zoning regulations, **1977** 35-44
Discrimination, religious
in India, **1986** 25, 27
and Medal of Honor award, **1989** 697-700
and student speech, **1983** 272
Discrimination, reverse
in firing employees, **1976** 405-411
in medical school admissions, **1978** 467-492
in work training program, **1979** 493-507
Discrimination, sex
See also Sexual assault and harassment
in alimony, **1979** 193-206
college all-male policies, **1991** 309-316
Democratic platform on, **1984** 598-601
in education, *Grove City* decision, **1984** 201-214
in employment, **1982** 919-944; **1985** 789-801

Discrimination, sex *Continued*
company disability plans, **1976** 891-905
EEOC guidelines on, **1972** 313-319
parental leave and job reinstatement, **1987** 17-27
payments in pension plans, **1978** 293-306; **1983** 691-705
segregation in workplace, **1985** 789-801
in employment training, **1985** 790, 794, 798-800
ERA on, **1982** 611-615
fetal protection job policies, **1991** 143-153
juries, exclusion from, **1975** 55-66
in language of laws, **1983** 756-763
lawsuits, **2001** 549-550
by members of Congress, **1979** 399-411
in military, **1987** 671-679; **1989** 115-116
in military draft, **1981** 521-540
O'Connor on, **1981** 577
and poverty, **1986** 984, 988, 992, 997, 999, 1001
by private clubs, **1984** 465-478; **1988** 399-403
in school admissions and programs, HEW rules on, **1974** 507-513
in Social Security survivor benefits, **1975** 56, 177-185; **1977** 169-181
in statutory rape laws, **1981** 339-349
in textbooks, **1974** 507
Thomas confirmation hearings, **1991** 562-563
women's conferences on, **1975** 507-522; **1977** 861-867
women's right to work, John Paul II on, **1981** 696-697
in workplace, **1993** 939-945
Diseases
See also Alzheimer's disease; Heart disease; Respiratory disease
avian influenza (bird flu) outbreaks, **2004** 923, 924-925; **2005** 747-749
Creutzfeld-Jacob disease (CJD), **2000** 880, 881, 882, 891-892
drug-resistant infections and, **1999** 185-199
flu pandemic, WHO preparations for, **2004** 923-928
flu vaccine shortage, GAO report, **2004** 639-651
global warming and, **2002** 304
gonorrhea, **1999** 193
Gulf War syndrome, **1997** 740-745
Gulf War veterans with Lou Gehrig's disease, **2001** 907-912
infectious disease preparedness, GAO report, **2004** 645-651
infectious diseases, **1996** 302-311; **1997** 348-349
mad cow disease, **2000** 880-892; **2002** 583; **2003** 1234-1244
obesity-related, **2001** 935-954; **2003** 480-491
SARS (severe acute respiratory syndrome) outbreak, **2003** 68-69, 121-134, 754, 757; **2004** 924
smoking-related, **2004** 280-298
Spanish flu pandemic (1918), **2004** 924
turberculosis control program, **1993** 853, 859-865
veneral disease, **1972** 343-350
Disney, corporate scandal, **2004** 423
Dissident groups (U.S.)
CIA investigation of, **1975** 401-403, 409, 419-424, 429-430, 523-528
and domestic security intelligence plan, Nixon on, **1973** 567-569
FBI surveillance of, **1975** 874; **1976** 322-327
NSA monitoring of cable traffic of, **1975** 711, 802
warrantless wiretapping of by Justice Department, **1972** 485-489
Distilled Spirits Council of the United States (DISCUS), on liquor advertising on television, **1996** 770-775
District of Columbia
bicentennial fanfare, **1993** 893-904
drinking water crisis, **1993** 261-263
federal support for, **1998** 51
financial crisis, **1995** 497-505
financial crisis in schools, **1996** 784-789
Gay/Lesbian march, **1993** 327-331
Holocaust Museum dedication, **1993** 307-313
home rule, **1978** 590; **1995** 497, 500
home rule charter, **1995** 497
infant mortality in, **1987** 149, 154, 156
Korean War veterans memorial, **1995** 506-511
March on Washington thirtieth anniversary, **1993** 677-685
Persian Gulf War victory parade, **1991** 243-244
privatization of schools, **1994** 411
voting representation in Congress, **1978** 589-591; **1984** 610-611
District of Columbia Financial Responsibility and Management Assistance Authority, school crisis report, **1996** 784-789
Ditlow, Clarence, **1978** 720
Dittemore, Ron
Columbia space shuttle disaster investigation, **2003** 633-634
NASA resignation, **2003** 634
Ditton, Paula, mental illness of prisoners, **1999** 839
Divorce
Catholic teaching on, **1979** 725, 729, 757; **1980** 871, 873, 876, 880
condemned by John Paul II, **1982** 837
dispute between Vatican and Dutch Catholics, **1985** 363-364, 372
in revised Catholic canon law, **1983** 93
student newspaper discussion of, **1988** 37-40, 44-46
Dixon, Alan J. (D-Ill.)
judicial impeachment, **1986** 850, 856-857
military base closings, **1995** 408
school prayer amendment, **1984** 244
Dixon, Julian C. (D-Calif.), **1989** 240; **1995** 499
Dixon, Sharon Pratt, election, **1990** 709
Djerejian, Edward P., U.S. diplomacy in Arab world, **2003** 959-960
Djindjic, Zoran
assassination of, **2003** 57-60; **2004** 955
on extradition of Slobodan Milosevic, **2001** 828; **2003** 58
Yugoslavian political leader, **2001** 828, 831
Yugoslavian presidential candidate, **2000** 835
Djoudi, Hocine, **2000** 450
DLC. *See* Democratic Leadership Council
DNA (deoxyribonucleic acid)
as evidence in capital crime cases, **2000** 990
fingerprints in criminal cases, **1992** 361-366

testing
as evidence in capital crime cases, **2004** 799
exonerations and overturned convictions and, **2002** 354; **2004** 794
DNC. *See* Democratic National Committee
Doar, John M.
impeachment inquiry report, **1974** 138
Watergate grand jury report, **1974** 225, 227
Dobbert v. Florida, **1977** 519
Dobbin's Distillery v. United States, **1993** 435
Dobriansky, Paula
global climate change, U.S. policy, **2004** 828
partnerships with developing countries, **2002** 595-596
Dobrynin, Anatoly F.
Arab-Israeli peace negotiations, **1973** 932
arms control talks, **1984** 260
denied promotion to Politburo, **1987** 81
Soviet troops in Cuba, **1979** 764
U.S.-PRC relations, **1979** 137
Dobson, James, Ten Commandments displays, **2005** 379
Doctors without Borders (Médecins sans Frontières), **1999** 288, 491; **2002** 472; **2004** 914
Darfur region rape reports, **2005** 518
Haiti, violence-related injuries, **2005** 331
DOD (Department of Defense). *See* Defense Department
Dodd, Christopher J. (D-Conn.)
on Genocide Convention, **1986** 117
on Reagan policy on Central America, **1983** 441
and Tower nomination, **1989** 105
Dodd, Thomas J. (D-Conn.)
Clinton presidential nomination speech, **1996** 602
Senate censure of, **1979** 623
violence on television hearings, **1993** 488
Doder, Dusko, Chernenko interview, **1984** 917-923
Dodge, David, hostage, **1991** 751
Dodic, Milorad, Bosnia-Herzegovina constitutional reform, **2005** 858-859
DOE (Department of Energy). *See* Energy Department
Doe, Samuel K.
coup in Liberia, **1980** 275-280
death of, **2003** 768
military coup and elections in Liberia, **2003** 768
Doe v. Bolton, **1973** 101-102, 111-114
Doha Development Agenda, **2003** 742, 746, 766; **2005** 410, 411
Doherty, Joseph Patrick Thomas, **1986** 752
Dohrn, Beatrice, same-sex marriages, **1999** 899
Dolan, Michael P.
apology to taxpayers, **1998** 131
IRS disputes with taxpayers, **1997** 662
Dolan v. City of Tigard, **1994** 298-310
Dole, Elizabeth Hanford
Pittston coal strike settled, **1990** 19-22
Republican Party convention speech, **1996** 479; **2000** 511-512
secretary of transportation appointment, **1982** 563
Dole, Robert (R-Kan.)
affirmative action, **1995** 483-484, 574-575; **1996** 759
affirmative action, opposition to, **1995** 483-484, 574-575
Bork nomination, **1987** 719
budget compromise, **1990** 412-413
budget negotiations, **1985** 71; **1986** 41
Clinton State of the Union
Republican response to, **1996** 21-23, 35-38
response to, **1994** 35, 50-53
Congress
bicentennial, **1989** 131-132
limits on gifts to members of, **1995** 701, 702
resignation from Senate, **1996** 270-273
term limits, **1995** 259
defense policy
chemical weapons treaty, **1996** 211, 742
draft evader pardon, **1977** 96
START talks, **1988** 355
domestic and social policy
abortion issue, **1996** 496; **2000** 509-510
consumer product liability, **1996** 275-276
drug legislation, **1986** 842
drug prevention programs, **1996** 570, 572
social issues speech, **1995** 573-580
Social Security reform, **1983** 62
on striking workers, **1995** 130
tobacco sales to children, **1996** 592
welfare reform, **1988** 849, 852; **1996** 451
economic policy, minimum wage, **1996** 565
economic policy, on Clinton five-year plan, **1993** 181
on Farrakhan and Million Man March, **1995** 647, 657
flag burning amendment, **1990** 359
foreign policy
Bosnia peacekeeping mission, **1998** 49
chemical weapons treaty, **1997** 196, 197
Iran-contra affair, **1986** 1051, 1052; **1987** 207; **1991** 618; **1992** 1075
Iraq war resolution, **1991** 4, 5, 11
Israeli kidnapping of Obeid, **1989** 316
Nicaraguan contras, bipartisan accord on, **1989** 164
U.S.-Vietnam relations, **1995** 472
Foster nomination, **1995** 63
Gingrich supporter, **1997** 5
independent counsel legislation, **1999** 168
Inman nomination, **1994** 23, 24
Nixon funeral remarks, **1994** 241-242
Nixon impeachment, **1974** 674-675
presidential campaign, **1997** 21; **2000** 509, 896
debates, **1996** 707-709, 709-718, 724-731
postelection statement, **1996** 747-749, 753-754
Republican convention acceptance speech, **1996** 478-480, 486-495
Reagan State of the Union, **1983** 79
Republican Party convention speech, **2000** 511
on striking workers, **1995** 130
Thomas confirmation hearings, **1991** 613-615
Tower nomination, **1989** 107
U.S. Capitol bicentennial, **1993** 896-897
vice presidential candidacy, **1976** 665-667, 673-676, 773-796
Volcker reappointment, **1983** 595-597

Dole, Robert (R-Kan.) *Continued*
war hero, **1999** 39
war powers debate, **1990** 665, 666-667
Watergate exoneration, **1974** 600
Watt resignation, **1983** 828
World War II service record, **1996** 31
Dollar
appreciation of (1980-1985), and U.S. competitiveness, **1987** 117-118, 123, 126, 135, 137
in Bretton Woods system, role of, **1972** 816; **1985** 624
convertibility of, in international monetary reform, **1972** 417
decline in value of
and Carter anti-inflation program, **1978** 659, 661-662, 683-686, 697-698; **1979** 93-94, 97, 106-107, 574-575, 578-579
as reason for OPEC price increase, **1978** 790-792
and stock market crash, **1987** 833, 835-836, 840
declining value of, **2003** 752, 753, 758; **2004** 56; **2005** 412
devaluation of, **1972** 413; **1973** 343-350; **1985** 623-630
effect on OPEC oil prices, **1979** 253, 257-258
and European Monetary System, **1978** 741-743, 749-750, 752
floating of, **1976** 4
overvaluation of, economic summit on, **1976** 426, 429
stability of
in Carter's economic report, **1980** 160-161, 170-171
de Larosière on, **1980** 885
Fed policy, **1987** 512
impact of inflation, Carter on, **1979** 82-84
strength of
and budget deficit, **1985** 348
impact of inflation and U.S. oil imports, **1978** 533
and trade deficit, **1984** 119-120, 124, 130, 140-141; **1985** 320, 322
Dombeck, Mike, national forest road construction moratorium, **1999** 592, 594-595
Domenici, Pete V. (R-N.M.)
climate change proposals, **2005** 921
energy prices and oil company profits, congressional hearings on, **2005** 780, 781, 785-786
immigration policy, **1996** 636-637
Kissinger commission report, **1984** 33
legislative veto, **1983** 619
mental health legislation, **2002** 267-268
mental health treatment, **1996** 389-390
Nixon budget, **1987** 5
recovery of John Paul II, **1981** 428
Russian nuclear weapons programs, **2001** 21
Volcker reappointment, **1983** 595-597
war hero, **1999** 39
Domestic partnerships, California and New York recognition of, **1989** 305-311
Domestic security. *See* Security, domestic; Surveillance, domestic
Domestic surveillance
background on, **2005** 959
congressional response, **2005** 960-961
FBI investigations of groups, **2002** 562-563; **2003** 611
New York Times report, **2005** 960, 963
NSA surveillance program, **2005** 959-960
NSA warrantless surveillance, **2005** 80, 958-969
Domestic violence
against women, **1994** 62-72
crime statistics on, **2000** 854
study on, **1993** 287-291
and women's rights, **2000** 327-328
Dominican Republic
Christopher Columbus Memorial Lighthouse, **1992** 899-900
CIA involvement in, Senate investigation of, **1975** 710, 715, 759-763, 770-772, 777, 785-789
elections in, **1979** 716
hurricane damage and relief efforts, **1998** 789, 790
Iraq troop withdrawal, **2004** 882
John Paul II's visit to, **1979** 726
smoking in the Americas, **1992** 269
Dominion Virginia Power Company, "new source" review, **2003** 177
Dominique, Jean, murder of, **2001** 397
Donahue, Thomas R., **1995** 681, 683
Donaldson, Denis, Sinn Féin leader revealed to be British informer, **2005** 511
Donaldson, Sam, interview of Sakharov, **1986** 1093-1094
Donaldson, William H.
mutual funds scandal, **2003** 695, 698, 699
SEC chairman nomination, **2002** 1034; **2003** 338
SEC mutual funds rulings, **2003** 697; **2004** 420, 421
Donors, human, rights of, **1987** 351-372
Donovan, Raymond J.
indictment of, **1984** 803-809
investigations of, **1982** 587-596
Dooling, John F., **1977** 408
Dorgan, Byron (D-N.D.)
campaign contributions, **2005** 635
nuclear test ban treaty, **1999** 601-602
prescription drug importation, **2004** 985
Dornan, Robert K. (R-Calif.), **1989** 395
Dos Santos, José Eduardo
Angolan conflict, **2002** 152-154
Angolan peace accord, **1991** 288
Doss, Alan, Liberia elections, **2005** 803
Dostum, Abdul Rashid
Afghanistan presidential candidate, **2004** 916, 917
Afghanistan warlord, **2001** 882; **2003** 1096
Dothard v. Rawlinson, **1991** 149
Double jeopardy clause. *See under* Constitutional amendments (U.S.), Fifth Amendment
Douglas, Jim (Vermont governor), prescription drug imports lawsuit, **2004** 984
Douglas, Paul W., Pittston strike settlement, **1990** 19-22
Douglas, William O.
abortion and privacy right, **1973** 102
class action suits, **1974** 428, 432-433
death penalty as discriminatory, **1972** 499-501
jury trials, split verdicts in, **1972** 423, 428-429
legislative apportionment and one-man, one-vote rule, **1973** 278-279, 284

national court of appeals, **1975** 455-456
obscenity, **1973** 612, 619-621; **1974** 516, 520, 521
papers of, **1993** 340
pre-Miranda right to counsel, **1974** 474, 484-485
press sources, confidentiality of, **1972** 508, 517-518
school desegregation remedies, **1974** 639-640, 649, 651
school financing based on property tax, **1973** 362, 372
vagrancy laws, **1972** 207-211
wiretapping authorization by attorney general, **1974** 393, 403-405
Douglas-Home, Alec, **1972** 467
Doumar, Robert G., "enemy combatant" case, **2002** 836; **2003** 111
Dove, Rita, U.S. Capitol bicentennial, **1993** 893, 899-900
Dow Chemical
breast implants lawsuits, **1995** 517
regulation of chemical discharge from, **1977** 131-141
workplace cancer, **1978** 645
Dow Corning, manufacturer of breast implants, bankruptcy of, **1995** 515, 516, 517
Dowd, Edward, Waco incident, **1999** 483
Dowd, John M.
investigation of political dismissal, **1978** 57-58, 64
Rose investigation, **1989** 478-481
Dowling, Robert, artificial heart implants, **2001** 479, 481-484
Downey, John T., release of by China, **1973** 194, 205-206, 292, 296
Downey, Thomas J. (D-N.Y.)
on military draft, **1992** 157
welfare reform, **1988** 848, 852
Downing, Thomas N. (D-Va.), **1978** 911
Downing, Wayne, Saudi Arabia bombing investigation, **1996** 673-674, 675-679
Doyle v. Ohio, **2000** 393
DPRK (Democratic People's Republic of Korea). *See* North Korea
Draft registration. *See* Military draft, registration
Dragonovic, Father, **1983** 739
Draper, Morris, **1983** 472
Drath, Connie, **1980** 19
Draude, Thomas V., **1992** 1030
Drauthammer, Charles, Lott resignation, **2002** 970
Drayden v. Needville Independent School District, **1992** 191
Drea, Edward J., **1989** 699
Dred Scott v. Sandford, **1992** 613
Dresser (France) S. A., **1982** 880
Drew, Elizabeth, at Carter-Ford debate, **1976** 693, 699-700, 705-706, 711-712, 717
Drexel Burnham Lambert, Milken's guilty plea, **1990** 251-257
Dreyfuss, Richard, Geneva Accord for Middle East peace, **2003** 1204
Driggs, John Douglas, **1984** 4
Drinan, Robert F. (D-Mass.)
on Rockefeller nomination, **1974** 988
Vatican order to leave Congress, **1980** 411-416, 968; **1981** 696; **1984** 761
Drinking water. *See* Water quality
Drori, Amir, **1983** 166, 178
Drought
and global warming, **1988** 861, 863, 865
in sub-Saharan Africa, and relief efforts, **1984** 973-985
Drug abuse. *See* Drug use
Drug Abuse, National Advisory Council on, **2004** 843
Drug Control Policy, Office of National, creation of, **1989** 499-500
Drug enforcement
See also Drug trafficking
Attorney General's violent crime task force on, **1981** 647, 649-650
budget for, **1991** 70
bureaucratic duplication in, **1989** 510-511
Bush program for, **1989** 71, 76-77, 499-511
Clinton administration proposals, **1997** 39
Democratic Party platform on, **1988** 562; **1996** 635-636
drug summit (Cartagena), **1990** 115-126
drug summit (San Antonio), **1992** 201-221
economic summit, Houston, **1990** 477-478
Ford proposals for, **1976** 15, 23
international cooperation in, **1972** 104; **1985** 349; **1988** 393-395; **1989** 414, 429-431, 513-515
Nixon programs, **1972** 104; **1973** 306, 326-328
and organized crime, **1984** 111
progress in, Republican platform on, **1972** 682-683
in Reagan budget, **1988** 150, 155
Republican Party platform on, **1988** 656-657, 679-680; **1996** 524-525
strengthened in drug legislation, **1986** 842
U.S. strategies, **1986** 189-200
Drug Enforcement Administration (DEA), **1992** 203
drug testing of employees of, **1986** 840
support for Bolivian enforcement, **1986** 181-182
warnings to doctors on prescription drugs for suicide, **1997** 459, 462-463; **1999** 441, 442
Drug Free America Foundation, **2002** 427
Drug policy, national, **1973** 393-412; **1986** 189-190, 197-201
Drug Policy Alliance, **2002** 427
Drug Price Compensation and Patent Term Restoration Act (1984), **1993** 198
Drug safety
See also Celebrex; Vioxx; *and under names of individual drugs*
antidepressant drugs and suicide in children, **2004** 640, 746-752
drug safety office proposal, **2004** 854
FDA black box warning, **2004** 749-750
protecting patients from unsafe drugs, FDA officials on, **2004** 850-866
Drug testing
accuracy and constitutionality of, **1986** 841
compulsory, organized crime commission on, **1986** 179-181, 199-200
by employers, **1986** 171
of federal employees, **1986** 254-255, 839-846
for pregnant women, **2001** 409-410
random, **1995** 339-349
of students

Drug testing *Continued*
Bush State of the Union address on, **2004** 21, 28
Supreme Court on, **2002** 424-436
Drug trafficking
See also Drug enforcement
Afghanistan opium trade, **2003** 1101; **2004** 919
asset forfeiture case, **1993** 431-438
in Colombia, U.S. aid program, **2000** 840-851; **2003** 430-431
Colombian war against, **1989** 499-501, 511-515
death penalty for, **1988** 610
international efforts, **1991** 470-471
mandatory life sentences for, **1973** 27-33
mandatory sentences for, **1973** 306, 327-328, 394
Noriega involvement in, **1988** 81-92; **1989** 704-705
Noriega sentenced for, **1992** 649-653
and organized crime, **1986** 182-200
prevention programs, **1997** 350
sentencing for cocaine penalties, **1997** 245-254
on U.S.-Mexican border, **1979** 169, 181
war against drugs, **1992** 203
world, U.S. report on, **1972** 645-650
Drug use
addiction
prevalence of, **1973** 27-28
smoking as, **1988** 309-322
and AIDS, **1988** 416, 421, 431, 435-436
public health measures to combat, **1986** 889-891, 894-895
among jail inmates, **2000** 855
antidepressant drugs and suicide in children, **2004** 640, 746-752
in Arizona, **1999** 464
Barry sentencing for, **1990** 707-711
in California, **1999** 464
and child neglect, **1989** 672, 674-675, 679-680, 684-685
children and women "caught in the net" of drug abuse, **2005** 679
by congressional employees, **1983** 727, 728
declining, **1998** 48
"designer steroids" and, **2005** 213
education about risks of, **1973** 393, 405
Exxon Valdez crew and, **1989** 225-237; **1990** 523-524; **1991** 641-648
federal surveys, **1996** 570-579; **1999** 459-464
health consequences of, **1986** 183-185
by House members, inquiry into, **1982** 729, 731, 738
and human behavior, **1973** 403-410
illicit drug use, **1999** 461-462
injection-drug users and HIV infection prevention, **2005** 62-63
and insanity defense, **1983** 30-31, 38
in major-league baseball, penalties for, **1986** 169-175
marijuana, effects on health, **1982** 203-211
National Center for Education Statistics Report, **1992** 624
needle-exchange programs for addicts, **1997** 81, 82, 87-88
prevention programs, **1996** 30
PRIDE Report, **1992** 1013-1016
in public schools, Senate report on, **1975** 213, 219
rehabilitation for drug addicts, **1992** 220
research on, **1989** 511
steroid use in sports, **2004** 29; **2005** 212-227
treatment
Bush on funds for, **1989** 76
in Bush's war on drugs, **1989** 505-506, 510
Carter program for, **1979** 45
Democratic platform on, **1988** 562
Eisenhower Foundation report, **1993** 223-234
for federal employees, **1986** 840-846
Nixon on, **1972** 104-105; **1973** 326-328
Republican platform on, **1972** 681-683
treatment for addictions, Bush statement on, **2003** 28
trends in new use, **1999** 463-464
use of term drug abuse, in drug policy, **1973** 393, 397-398
Drug-Free Schools Coalition, **2002** 424
Drugs
See also Prescription drugs
abortion pill controversy, **2000** 429
in alcoholism treatment, **1983** 347-349
alternative development programs, **1990** 118-119
antibiotics and drug-resistant bacteria, **1999** 185-199
antituberculosis, **1992** 1007-1011
Bolivia-U.S. chemicals agreement, **1990** 126
Democratic Party platform on, **1992** 699-700
experimentation with by intelligence agencies, **1975** 402, 432; **1976** 139
generic AIDS drugs, **1999** 491-492
HIV transmission and, **1992** 339-340
minors' access to, and paraphernalia sales, **1982** 215-223
prescription
advertising of prices, **1976** 351-363
national policy on, **1973** 394, 396-397, 399-400
for treatment of high cholesterol, **1987** 780, 788-789
prescription drugs, prices, **1993** 197-209; **1994** 87-94; **2000** 131-140
searches
in autos, **1982** 425-428
of students, **1985** 13-26
war on
as presidential campaign issue, **1988** 724-725, 814-815
Reagan support for, **1986** 181; **1987** 107, 112
Drumtra, Jeff, child abuse in refugee camps, **2002** 919
D'Souza, Dinesh, **1991** 331
Du Daobin, political dissident arrested, **2004** 941
Duarte, José Napoleón
El Salvador elections and U.S. aid, **1984** 34
election of, and insurgency, **1987** 640
and human rights in El Salvador, **1985** 146, 150-151; **1986** 103-104
request for U.S. economic aid, **1981** 242
and talks with guerrillas, **1987** 194-195
Dubcek, Alexander
protest letter to Czech assembly, **1975** 239-249
reappearance of, **1989** 636-637

Duberstein, Kenneth, International Olympics Committee investigations, **1999** 108, 109
Dubinin, Yuri, **1989** 525
DuBois, Arthur B., **1972** 775
Dubs, Adolph, **1979** 968
Duckworth v. Franzen, **1992** 181
Due process clause. *See under* Constitutional amendments (U.S.), Fourteenth Amendment
Duelfer, Charles A., weapons of mass destruction in Iraq, **2004** 676-677, 711-733
Duffus, James, III, testimony on National Park Service, **1995** 120-128
Duffy, Trent, tobacco control treaty, **2004** 284
Duhalde, Eduardo
  Argentine economic policy, **2002** 84-85
  Argentine presidential elections, **2002** 82, 83-84, 85; **2003** 824
Duisenberg, Willem F.
  European Central Bank president appointment, **1998** 273
  on euro currency, **1999** 75-84
Dukakis, Michael S., **1988** 848; **1989** 49
  acceptance speech, Democratic convention, **1988** 533-534, 536-542
  competence as theme of campaign, **1988** 534, 537-538
  and Democratic platforms, **1976** 544; **1988** 535, 557-559
  health insurance coverage, **2000** 787
  postelection press conference, **1988** 892, 900-904
  presidential debates, **1988** 721-783
  presidential nomination, **2000** 619
  refuses to submit plans for Seabrook nuclear plant, **1990** 196
  response to Reagan State of the Union, **1984** 84
  tone of presidential campaign, **1989** 41, 43
  U.S. relations with Noriega, **1988** 82
  warmth as campaign issue, **1988** 721-723, 731-733, 758-759
Duke, David, **1991** 715, 760
Duke, Doris, **1988** 868
Dulles, Allen, and CIA Castro plot, **1975** 734-735, 737-741, 778-779, 782-783
Dumas, Reginald, Haiti economic situation, **2004** 94
Dumont, Rene, **1974** 777
Duncan, Charles W., Jr., appointments of, **1976** 878; **1979** 562, 572-573
Duncan, David, Enron Corp. collapse, **2002** 397
Duncan v. Louisiana, **1992** 327
Dundee, Angelo, **1984** 1020
Dunham, Richard L., **1977** 545
Dunlap, Albert J., **1996** 44
Dunlop, John T.
  appointment to CLC, **1973** 44, 47
  Social Security's financial condition, **1975** 117
Dunlop Commission. *See* Commission on the Future of Worker-Management Relations
Dunn, Jennifer (R-Wash.), Clinton State of the Union address, Republican response, **1999** 43, 58-60
DuPont de Nemours & Co., E. I., on chlorofluorocarbon reductions, **1988** 223
DuPont et al. v. Train, **1977** 131-141
DuPont-Columbia University Survey of Broadcast Journalism, **1973** 57
Duran, Francisco Martin, **1995** 256
Durbin, Richard "Dick" (D-Ill.)
  animal feed regulations, **2003** 1239
  on Democratic Party platform, **2000** 611
  drivers license information standards, **2002** 535
  food safety system, **2001** 700
  on independent counsel, **1999** 167
  terrorist threat alerts, **2004** 270
  tobacco company lawsuit, **2001** 225-226
Durenberger, Dave (R-Minn.)
  budget deficits, **1985** 107-108
  infant formula code, **1981** 448
  North and Poindexter's silence, **1986** 1050
Durmus, Osman, on earthquake in Turkey, **1999** 466
DuVal, Merlin K., **1973** 64-65
Duvalier, François, **1986** 98
Duvalier, Jean-Claude
  Haitian dictator, **2005** 329
  human rights in Haiti, **1977** 8-9
  ouster of, **1986** 98-99, 106-107; **1987** 191, 196
DVA. *See* Veterans Affairs Department
Dwyer, Jim, death penalty, **2000** 990
Dwyer, William L., spotted owl decision, **1991** 275-285
Dybul, Mark, on AIDS policy, **2005** 53
Dynegy Inc., Enron Corp. lawsuit, **2001** 860-861, 864-865
Dziwsz, Stanislaw (Archbishop and pope's personal secretary), on death of John Paul II, **2005** 291

E

Eagle Forum
  on "Baby M" case, **1987** 376
  on Bork nomination, **1987** 719
Eagleburger, Lawrence S.
  chemical weapons treaty, **1993** 72; **1997** 195-196
  Clinton's Passport Search, **1992** 1046
  Cuban foreign policy, **1998** 33
  Glaspie-Hussein pre-war meeting, **1991** 256
  Haiti, trade embargo against, **1993** 454
  on Middle East weapons, **1993** 72
  North Korea, **1993** 547
  START II treaty, **1994** 18-20, 23-29, 39-40
Eagleton, Thomas F. (D-Mo.)
  on executive encroachment on congressional power, **1973** 3
  vice presidential nomination, **1972** 589, 591, 597-605
EAI. *See* Education Alternatives, Inc.
Earle, Ronnie, Delay indictment, **2005** 633, 634
Earls, Lindsay, student drug testing case, **2002** 425
Earned Income Tax Credit (EITC), **1995** 78; **1996** 28, 54, 59; **2000** 18, 25, 47, 50; **2001** 58
Earth, studies of, NASA goals for, **1987** 649, 651, 653, 655-658, 667
Earth Summit (Rio de Janeiro), **1992** 499-506, 641-642; **1999** 403; **2002** 593
Earthquakes
  See also Tsunami disaster in Indian Ocean Region
  California
    Los Angeles (1994), **1994** 3-7

Earthquakes *Continued*
San Fernando Valley (1971), **1994** 4
San Francisco area (1989), **1989** 667-670; **1994** 4
Colombia, Red Cross relief, **1999** 468
Indian Ocean region, **2004** 991, 992
Iran, **2003** 1033
Pakistan-held Kashmir, **2005** 468, 472, 477-479
prediction of, U.S.-Soviet cooperation in, **1972** 805-806, 811-812
Turkey, U.S. aid, **1999** 465-471
Earthscan, on disaster relief, **1984** 973-995
East, John P. (R-N.C.), **1982** 165
East Anglia University, study of climate change, **1988** 861
East Asia. *See* Asia
East Germany. *See* German Democratic Republic
East Timor
elections, **2001** 597; **2002** 257-258
human rights violations, **2002** 261; **2004** 756
independence
statements on, **2002** 256-264
UN human rights commissioner on, **1999** 511-523
UN secretary general on, **2001** 593-599
Indonesian army involvement, **2002** 707
National Liberation Front (Fretilin), **2001** 595
Revolutionary Front for an Independent East Timor (Fretilin), **2002** 257
"truth and friendship" commission, **2002** 261; **2004** 756
UN peacekeeping forces, **1999** 513-514, 718-719
UN Transitional Administration (UNTAET), **1999** 514; **2002** 258-259
war crimes prosecutions, **2004** 756-757
Easterbrook, Gregg, **1991** 244
Easterling, Barbara, **1995** 681, 683
Eastern Airlines, labor-management discord, **1988** 268-269
Eastern Europe
boundaries and Soviet domination of, and Helsinki Final Act, **1975** 481, 483, 488, 559-560, 562-563
Chernobyl nuclear accident, effects of, **1986** 384-385
economic summit, London, **1991** 464-465
health problems in, **1994** 415-430
Houston economic summit, **1990** 473-474
human rights in, **1980** 191
Polish liberalization as threat to, **1980** 794-795
political reform in, **1989** 399-400, 411-424, 430-435, 523-524, 535-538, 625-639, 660-661, 709-712
in presidential debates, **1984** 882-883
self-determination for, Bush on, **1989** 180
Soviet domination of, Ford on, **1976** 733-734, 741-742, 760, 766-768, 786-787
Soviet military buildup in, **1980** 124, 126, 129-131, 141, 153-155
Soviet missiles in, Andropov plan for reduced, **1982** 983-988
Soviet nonintervention in, **1989** 644-645, 652, 656-657, 663
Soviet position in, Kennan on, **1989** 210-211
Soviet troop cuts in, **1989** 299, 303
and Soviet Union's democratic reforms, **1987** 81
U.S. policy toward
Democratic platform on, **1984** 636
Republican platform on, **1984** 711
Warsaw Pact dissolution, **1991** 399-401
Western trade with, **1982** 469-470
Eastern Slavonia, UN peacekeeping mission, **1997** 151, 154, 156
Eastman Kodak v. Image Technical Services Inc., **2000** 109, 121-126
Eastman Kodak Company, nuclear testing warnings, **1997** 593
Eaton, Paul D., Iraqi security force training, **2004** 881
Ebadi, Shirin
Nobel Peace Prize recipient, **2003** 1033, 1129-1137; **2004** 929
U.S. sanctions on publications from Iran, **2004** 932
Ebbers, Bernard J., WorldCom collapse fraud case, **2002** 393-395; **2003** 333-335, 342-348; **2004** 417-418
Ebert v. Poston, **1993** 252-253, 255-256, 257
EC. *See* European Community
Ecevit, Bulent, **1980** 807-808
as Turkish prime minister, **2002** 907
Echaveste, Maria, apparel industry sweatshops, **1997** 209
Echeverria Alvarez, Luis, on U.S. cooperation with developing countries, **1972** 471-474
Echo-Hawk, Walter, on Native American skeletal remains, **1989** 539, 542
Eckhardt, Bob (D-Texas), **1979** 781-782
Eckstein, Otto
on Carter anti-inflation program, **1980** 246
supply-side economic model of, **1980** 210
Economic boycotts. *See* Boycotts
Economic cooperation
of developing and industrialized countries, U.S. proposals on, **1975** 587-603
or economic nationalism, Kissinger on, **1974** 848-850
in food and oil crises, Nixon call for, **1974** 103, 113-122
international, Kissinger on, **1975** 4, 13-14
in NATO, **1974** 530, 533
to promote development, UN resolution on, **1975** 587-589, 603-611
UN restructuring for, **1975** 325-351
Economic development
in Africa, **2001** 504-515
aid to developing countries, **1997** 481-482
and Bhopal accident, **1984** 1024-1025
community empowerment zones, **1997** 39, 71
empowerment zones and enterprise communities, **1998** 90-91; **1999** 91; **2001** 59
environmental consequences of, **1986** 859-873
financing of, UN resolution on, **1975** 605-608
global slowdown, **2001** 56-57
globalization, **2000** 481-482, 701, 1047-1048, 1054
as goal of Soviet democratic reforms, **1987** 79-81, 83-89, 98-104
integration of women in, **1975** 511-514, 518, 520-521; **1985** 556-561, 564-567
jobs and services to alleviate poverty of children, UNICEF on, **1981** 912, 920-921
New Markets agenda, Clinton administration proposals, **2000** 28, 49-50

New Markets and Renewal Communities Initiative, **2001** 59
nonresidential investment in U.S., **2003** 78-79
pessimism about, John Paul II on, **1988** 165-174
and population control, **1984** 521-522; **1987** 440-443, 449, 452-453, 459-460
set-aside programs abolished, **1998** 856
small and medium-sized enterprises, **1997** 344-345
in the U.S., **1999** 50
U.S. aid for, Nixon request from Congress, **1974** 277-278, 283-285
world poverty eradication
G-8 summit on, **2000** 475-487
UN Millennium Summit Declaration, **2000** 706-708
Economic growth
Bush and OMB projections, **1991** 68-69, 75-79
Clean Air Act's effect on, **1981** 276, 278-279
forecasts
by CBO and Reagan administration, **1982** 192, 198
by Joint Economic Committee, **1981** 310-312
and inflation, OECD on effects of, **1973** 683-685, 689-690
Joint Economic Committee proposals for, **1981** 293-295, 299-309, 312-324
Nixon economic report on, **1973** 185, 187-189
Reagan first-term achievements, **1984** 742-743; **1985** 43-44, 88-91, 105, 108-109
Reagan on administration's successes, **1989** 3, 5-12
Republican platform proposals for, **1980** 567-568, 570-571, 596-597
restoring, National '80s Agenda on, **1981** 39-47
targets
Carter to IMF-World Bank, **1977** 687-691
for economic summit countries, **1977** 367-369
world slowdown in, consequences for trade, **1977** 687-688, 691-698
Economic Growth and Taxpayer Relief Reconciliation Act (EGTRRA, 2001), **2003** 75, 85-86, 687; **2004** 68-69
Economic justice
and black America, **1987** 49, 51, 59
Democratic commitment to, Kennedy on, **1980** 701-709, 711-712
Democratic platform on, **1972** 527, 534-535
John Paul II on, **1979** 735-736, 752; **1985** 58, 60-61; **1986** 639-646; **1988** 165-171
in McGovern's proposed tax reforms, **1972** 737-742
in U.S. economic policies, Catholic bishops on, **1984** 957-972; **1986** 983-1011
Vatican on liberation theology, **1984** 759-775; **1986** 317-338
and world resources, **1980** 666, 668, 674-679
Economic order, new international
developing countries' call for, **1974** 777-778, 789
and UN restructuring, **1975** 325-331, 349
U.S. response to, **1975** 587-591, 650-651
nonaligned nations on, **1979** 687-688, 690
women's conferences on, **1975** 507, 513-514, 519-521; **1985** 556-557, 560-561
Economic performance
See also Economic reports
aftermath of September 11, **2001** 663-671
assumptions in Reagan budget, **1984** 101-105; **1985** 72, 73-75; **1986** 51-53; **1987** 3, 5
and blacks' economic status in U.S., **1989** 449-451, 453-454
budget surplus, CBO report on, **1998** 500-509
Bush State of the Union address, **2003** 23-24; **2004** 25-27; **2005** 82-83
Daschle's response, **2004** 33
CEA projections
Bush administration, **2002** 62-66; **2003** 75-95; **2004** 61-71; **2005** 145-153
Clinton administration, **1994** 123-124, 129-146; **1995** 71, 76-77, 79-80; **1996** 68-70; **1997** 51-52, 63-69; **1998** 84-85, 7981; **1999** 88; **2000** 50-62
Reagan administration, **1984** 128-131, 133-135, 144; **1985** 79-104; **1986** 59-65, 70-72, 74-75; **1987** 117, 119-120, 124-125, 127-132, 136-137, 144; **1988** 117-120, 126-128, 135-142
comptroller general report, **2005** 121-136
deflation, **2002** 51
Democratic Party platform, **1996** 626-629
European growth projections, **2001** 667; **2002** 691-692
global economy, U.S. role in, **2002** 691
Greenspan on "faltered" business recovery, **1991** 851-856
and human development, UN report on, **1996** 438-444
labor productivity, CEA report on, **2004** 69-71
"misery index," **1996** 52; **1997** 59; **1999** 95
"New Economy" in U.S., CEA report on, **2001** 60-64
October stock market crash, **1987** 834-838
peacetime expansion, **1999** 42
productivity growth, CEA report on, **2001** 64-68; **2004** 69-71
Reagan recovery plan, **1981** 213-224, 325-335, 639-644; **1982** 75-78, 121-128, 131-132; **1983** 77-78, 81-84, 87-88, 101-118, 121-141
slowdown, **2000** 45-46; **2001** 55-57
stagnation causes and remedies, Nixon's CEA on, **1974** 69-83
standard of living, **2000** 51
stock market volatility, **1997** 721-727
UN global economic outlook, **2002** 689-701
uncertainty as factor in, **2004** 65-66
U.S. economy, **2003** 752; **2004** 236
Greenspan on state of, **2002** 877-884
worldwide
CEA report on, **2003** 90-93
imbalances in, **2005** 413-414
IMF report on, **2003** 751-766
predictions, **2004** 56
Economic Policy Board, creation of, **1974** 877-878
Economic Policy Institute (EPI)
economic outlook, **1994** 124
health care costs and family finances, **1993** 271-285
work and leisure report, **1992** 163-173
Economic recession. *See* Recession
Economic Recovery Tax Act (ERTA, 1981), **1984** 125, 134; **1985** 89
and business investment, **1985** 80, 86, 90
provisions, **1981** 639-643

Economic reports
Bush (George H. W.) and CEA, **1990** 81-104; **1991** 97-134; **1992** 73-96
Bush (George W.) and CEA, **2002** 51-66; **2003** 68-95; **2004** 56-71; **2005** 137-153
Carter and CEA, **1978** 65-67, 77-93; **1979** 81-117; **1980** 159-161, 171-186; **1981** 105-135
Clinton and CEA, **1994** 123-146; **1995** 69-91; **1996** 50-70; **1997** 50-73; **1998** 73-97; **1999** 85-102; **2000** 43-62; **2001** 52-72
Ford and CEA, **1975** 99-113; **1976** 45-70; **1977** 65-88
Nixon and CEA, **1973** 185-191; **1974** 69-94
Reagan and CEA, **1982** 121-141; **1983** 121-141; **1984** 119-144; **1985** 79-87; **1986** 59-92; **1987** 117-144; **1988** 117-148; **1989** 3-14
Economic reports, international
Ford, **1975** 187-199
Nixon, **1973** 379-391; **1974** 113-122
Economic Rights and Duties of States, Charter of (1974), **1973** 810, 815; **1975** 325, 328
Economic sanctions
al Qaeda terrorist network, UN panel on, **2002** 1014-1025
countries denying religious freedom, **1998** 19, 21
UN role, **2004** 903-904
Economic sanctions (by country)
Afghanistan, **1999** 524, 525-526
Arab oil embargo,**1974** 221, 223; **1975** 3-4
Cuba, **1998** 30, 32-33
India
lifting of, **2001** 627
for nuclear testing, **1998** 327, 328-329
Iran, **2001** 794, 795; **2005** 595
U.S. oil embargo, **1979** 869, 873, 875
Iraq, international embargo against, **1990** 545-550, 768
Libya, **1986** 347, 349; **2001** 795; **2003** 1223-1224
lifting of, **2004** 168-175
Nicaragua, U.S. embargo against, **1990** 260-261
North Korea, **2005** 606
Pakistan
lifting of, **2001** 627
for nuclear testing, **1998** 327, 328-329
Panama, **1988** 81-82; **1989** 702-703, 705-706
Poland, **1981** 884-885, 895-896; **1982** 563, 879, 949; **1987** 183-188
PRC after Tiananmen Square, **1989** 275, 277, 282-285
Rhodesia, UN sanctions, **1976** 288, 290-292; **1979** 940-942
South Africa, **1985** 531-540; **1986** 99; **1987** 190; **1989** 547, 549-550
lifting of, **1991** 53-65
UN arms embargo, **1977** 823-825
Soviet Union
grain embargo, **1979** 967; **1982** 824
pipeline suppliers, **1981** 884; **1982** 879-884
for Polish martial law, **1981** 884-885, 896
Sudan, **2004** 125
U.S., by European Union, **2003** 446
Vietnam, lifting of embargo, **1994** 95-99
Economic Stabilization Act (1971), **1973** 43, 47, 49, 54
Economic stabilization program
Phase III, **1973** 43-54, 220, 223-224, 577-585
Phase IV, **1973** 703-713
Economic summits
Bonn, **1978** 533-542; **1985** 347-355, 626, 628
Denver, **1997** 340-360
Houston, **1990** 124, 467-482
London, **1977** 367-375; **1984** 355-364; **1991** 451-473
Munich, **1992** 637-648
Ottawa, **1981** 591-599, 774
Paris, **1989** 414, 424-434; **1992** 124
Puerto Rico, **1976** 425-431
Tokyo, **1979** 253; **1986** 437-444; **1992** 21-22; **1993** 541-557
Toronto, **1988** 391-397
Venice, **1980** 503-513; **1987** 511-512, 525-530
Versailles, **1982** 469-476
Williamsburg, **1983** 507-514
Economics
demand-side, Joint Economic Committee on, **1981** 293-294, 298
supply-side, **1999** 94-95
Carter and advisers on, **1981** 105-106, 133-134
Joint Economic Committee on, **1980** 209-231; **1981** 293-294, 298-299, 319
in Reagan economic plan, **1981** 214, 327, 639-642
Ecosystems
aquatic, acid rain effects on, **1983** 198-207, 210
ecosystem forest management approach, **1992** 489-492
nuclear war effects on, **1983** 859, 879-881
Ecstasy (drug), use among teenagers, **1999** 460-461
Ecuador
drug summit, **1992** 201-221
human trafficking, **2004** 125
John Paul II's visit, **1985** 57, 58
nationalizations in, **1972** 67
and OPEC oil price, **1981** 799
political situation, **2005** 770-771
smoking in the Americas, **1992** 269
U.S. trade preferences denied to, **1975** 224, 233
Ecumenicism
Catholic and Orthodox church relations, **1979** 730, 760-761
dispute between Vatican and Dutch Catholics on, **1985** 363-364
in Ireland, John Paul II on, **1979** 728-729, 742-748
in U.S. Catholic Church, **1985** 572-573, 576, 579
and women as Episcopal bishops, **1989** 51-53
Eddings v. Oklahoma, **1982** 51-63; **1983** 709
Edelin, Kenneth, **1975** 544
Edelman, Marian Wright
on economic plight of young families, **1992** 353
infant mortality in U.S., **1987** 147
MIA commission, **1977** 208
Edgett, Kenneth S., war on Mars, **2000** 380-381
Edison Electric Institute
coal strike settlement, **1978** 114
global warming, **2002** 299
"new source" review, **2003** 178
Three Mile Island report, **1979** 825
Edmonson, Drew, WorldCom fraud case, **2003** 335; **2004** 418

Education
See also Bilingual education; Colleges and universities; Head Start program; Literacy; School desegregation; Schools; Sex education; Students' rights; Teachers
accountability, **1999** 47-48, 90-91
after-school activities and drug testing, **2002** 424-436
basic skills, **1975** 692; **1988** 196, 207-209, 218
of blacks, **1983** 42-43, 47-53; **1985** 29, 34, 36, 37; **1987** 43-45, 51, 58-59
book banning in, **1982** 567-585
California bilingual education initiative, **1998** 313-319
CEA on human capital investment, **1997** 53, 64-66
character counts program, **1997** 36
for congressional pages, **1982** 730, 734
deaf parochial student, **1993** 399-406
Democratic Party platform on, **1980** 732-734; **1984** 555, 571-573; **1988** 558, 561-562; **1992** 693, 697; **1996** 629-631; **2000** 614
on drug dangers, **1989** 506, 510
elementary
community's role in, **1986** 804, 808-809
curriculum for, **1986** 804-807, 809-813
equal opportunity in, **1972** 201-206, 222-224, 259-269, 675-676, 703-704
federal funding
Bennett on, **1986** 804-805
Bush budget, **1989** 71, 75-76
in Carter administration, **1979** 158, 160-162
compensatory grants for poor schools, **1972** 267
Democratic platform on, **1980** 732-734
for more teachers and training, **1999** 66-67
public aid to parochial schools, **1977** 431-445; **1985** 433-461, 480, 486-487
Reagan administration block grant funding, **1981** 641, 644-645
Reagan budget, **1981** 217; **1983** 766-767, 769, 771; **1984** 100, 107
voucher systems, **1985** 435; **1986** 40, 45; **1988** 233, 237
federal role in
Bush State of the Union address, **2004** 20, 26; **2005** 83
Daschle's Democratic response, **2004** 33
Clinton administration and, **1995** 82; **1996** 27, 53, 62; **1997** 24-25, 29, 34-37, 64-65; **1999** 46-48, 90-91; **2000** 22-24, 48; **2001** 58, 59
Clinton Democratic nomination speech, **1996** 612-613
flexibility in, **1989** 562, 564-568
Nation at Risk report on, **1983** 414-415, 424
national education policy for inner cities, **1993** 221
Reagan goals, **1983** 77-79, 85-86; **1987** 107, 112
Reagan on, **1983** 110-111, 415
Republican platform on, **1980** 583-585, 603
State of the Union address, **1990** 51, 54
financing of, based on property tax, **1973** 361-377
Four-Point Plan for Educational Excellence, **2000** 20, 37-38
G-8 Summit commitment to, **2000** 486
G.I. Bill for America's Workers, **1997** 37
international comparisons, **1992** 624
in Arab countries, **2002** 485-486, 495-497
Japanese studies, Japan's funding of in U.S., **1973** 718, 721
job skills training, **1998** 82
knowledge, students' application of, **1989** 85-86, 88-94
for knowledge-based economy, **1986** 457-458, 460-462
legal, **1983** 391-393, 398-400
linguistic rights in, **1981** 813-814, 818-819
local control of, Reagan on, **1983** 414-415
multicultural
national standards, **1992** 48
textbooks, **1991** 331-347
national education goals, **1990** 153-163
national education standards, **1997** 30, 34-35; **1998** 44, 88
national education strategy (America 2000 plan), **1991** 219-226
national goals for instruction, reshaping of, **1989** 86, 93-94
national goals of, **1986** 816-817
national standards report, **1992** 45-54
of Native Americans, **2003** 582
"No Child Left Behind" program, **2002** 42-43; **2004** 20, 26; **2005** 83
parental role in, **1986** 219-223; **1989** 562, 565, 569
Perot Reform Party nomination speech on, **1996** 559-561
in prisons, **1981** 192, 194-196, 663-664, 667
public opinion on, **1983** 424-425; **1989** 16-17
religion, teaching about, **1987** 597-608
remedial, **1977** 447-448, 457-464; **1983** 419; **1985** 130
Republican Party platform on, **1984** 663, 689-693; **1988** 615, 649-653; **1996** 527-529; **2000** 512-513
research on teaching and learning, **1986** 217-238
right to
for alien children, **1982** 489-506
in PRC constitution, **1975** 52
and student suspension, **1975** 67-80
for women of world, **1975** 517-519
science curriculum
creation science, **1982** 3-16; **1983** 818
intelligent design, federal court on, **2005** 1010-1026
math and science, **1983** 414-416, 429-430; **1988** 377-390; **1992** 85-96, 627, 628
sexual harrasment of students, **1992** 146, 187-189; **1993** 353-361
skills vs. process training, **1987** 683-687
on smoking dangers, **1982** 164; **1988** 310, 315
state regulations for, flexibility in, **1989** 563, 565, 567
state responsibility in, **1972** 221-225, 232-233; **1983** 414-415
student aid
draft registration and, **1984** 494
loan programs, **2005** 78
Pell grant scholarships, **2001** 59; **2005** 144

Education *Continued*
student financial aid, Nixon on, **1972** 105; **1974** 48-49, 59
tax exemptions for discriminatory schools, **1983** 489-505
teaching profession, upgrading, **1986** 457-478
technology issues, **2002** 69
television's effect on, **1982** 366, 371-372, 381-382
testing
biases, **1975** 692
scores of U.S. students, **1983** 418-419; **1988** 297, 302-303
tuition tax credits for, **1973** 304, 310; **1983** 53, 111, 675-687; **1984** 83, 91
U.S. competitiveness, **1983** 413-414, 416-417, 422; **1986** 972, 979-980
veterans' benefits extension, **1988** 277-285
vocational, **1972** 227-228, 677; **1992** 624
of women and girls
Afghanistan girls, **2003** 1099-1100
in developing countries, **1980** 889-890
on infant health, **1981** 447, 449-450, 452
relation to birth rates, **1984** 527, 534, 536
schools shortchange girls, **1992** 141-154
worldwide, UNICEF report on, **1998** 920-928
Education, higher. *See* Colleges and universities
Education Accountability Act, **1999** 47-48
Education Alternatives, Inc. (EAI), privatization of schools, **1994** 409-414
Education Amendments (1972)
gender discrimination ban, **1999** 216
Title IX, **1984** 203; **1992** 188
discrimination prohibited, **1992** 142, 150
HEW rules on sex discrimination, **1974** 507-513
money damages under, **1992** 187-189
sex discrimination and federal aid, **1984** 201-214
Education and Consolidation and Improvement Act (1981), **1985** 434-435
Education Commission of the States, **1992** 48
Education Department
abolition proposal, **2000** 510
civil rights enforcement, **1983** 914
creation of, **1978** 8, 15, 27; **1979** 16, 19, 36, 51, 157-168
startup budget, **1979** 161, 163, 165
elementary education, **1986** 803-817
international math and science testing, **1992** 85-96
math and science assessment, **1988** 377
National Center for Education Statistics report, **1992** 623-636
National Education Goals panel report, **1992** 46
Office of Educational Research and Improvement (OERI), **1992** 153
progress in U.S. education, **1989** 85-94
reorganization, **1979** 157
research on teaching and learning, **1986** 217-238
on sex-equity programs, **1992** 143
State of American Education address, **1996** 106-117
student aid and draft registration, **1984** 494
undergraduate education, **1984** 998
uniforms in public schools, **1996** 84-92
Women's Educational Equity Act Program (WEEAP), **1992** 151
Education for All Handicapped Children Act (1975), and expulsion of disruptive students, **1988** 47-56
Education for Economic Growth, National Task Force on, **1986** 459
Education reform, **1986** 939-940
CEA report on, **1991** 90
and humanities, **1987** 681-696
Nation at Risk on, **1983** 413-437
neglect of urban schools, **1988** 195-200
progress of, **1988** 297-306; **1989** 85-94
reshaping instructional goals, **1989** 86, 93-94
summit of governors and president, **1989** 561-570
Education summit, **1990** 51; **1992** 45, 50
Educational achievement
by gender, **1992** 627, 634-636
goals, **1991** 356-357
race and ethnicity, **1992** 147-148
socioeconomic status and, **1992** 147-148
sports participation and, **1997** 168
Educational attainment
computer and Internet use and, **2002** 74-75
of foreign-born, **1997** 180
for Hispanic Americans, **2003** 356
minority employment and, **1982** 919-920, 929-930, 932, 936-943
Educational Excellence Act (1989), **1989** 564
Educational Testing Service (ETS)
on gender-biased tests, **1992** 143
international math and science test, **1992** 85-96
math and science assessment, **1988** 377
state of U.S. education, **1989** 85-94
student reading ability, **1990** 155
Edwards, Don (D-Calif.)
FBI domestic security guidelines, **1983** 258
judges' pay, **1989** 197
judicial impeachment, **1989** 585, 590-595
Rockefeller nomination, **1974** 988
Session investigation, **1993** 610
Edwards, Edwin W. (D-La.), in Korean influence-buying scheme, **1978** 846, 859-860, 869-870, 872
Edwards, Harry T., Microsoft antitrust case, **2001** 776
Edwards, Jack (R-Ala.), **1988** 952
Edwards, James B., **1982** 563
Edwards, John (D-N.C.)
jobs and job growth, **2003** 442
medical malpractice, **2004** 20
vice presidential campaign, **2004** 20, 479, 480-481, 775
vice presidential debates, **2004** 678
Edwards, Mickey (R-Okla.)
bipartisan accord on contras, **1989** 164
Contra aid, **1988** 243
Edwards v. Aguillard, **1987** 565-576; **2005** 1011
Edwards v. Arizona, **1981** 431-433, 441-445; **1990** 786-793
Edwards v. South Carolina, **1995** 331
Edwards Air Force Base (Calif.), *Columbia* space shuttle landings, **1981** 417, 419-420, 424
EEOC. *See* Equal Employment Opportunity Commission
EEOC v. Arabian American Oil Co., **1992** 462
EEOC v. Franklin and Marshall College, **1990** 27
EEOC v. Shell Oil Co., **1990** 29-31

EEOC v. University of Notre Dame du Lac, **1990** 27
Efaw, Fritz, **1976** 596
Efrat, Yona, **1982** 783; **1983** 163
EFZ Properties v. Rodriguez, **1992** 615
Egan, Cardinal Edward M., sexual abuse by priests, **2004** 86
Egan, Michael J., investigation of political dismissal, **1978** 56-57, 59, 61-64
Egeberg, Robert, **1972** 343
Egeland, Jan
North Korea humanitarian aid, **2005** 610
Sudan conflict, humanitarian aid, **2004** 590
tsunami disaster, UN relief effort, **2004** 991, 993, 994; **2005** 992
Uganda conflict, **2003** 472
Eglin, Colin, **1986** 371
Eglin Air Force Base (Florida), Cuban refugees at, **1980** 338, 340, 342
EGTRRA. *See* Economic Growth and Taxpayer Relief Reconciliation Act
Egypt
See also Muslim Brotherhood
Arab relations
acceptance into Arab League, **1989** 292
diplomatic ties, **1987** 869-871, 874
and Egyptian peace initiatives, **1977** 829
and peace treaty with Israel, **1980** 4
suspension from Arab League, **1979** 224, 226
control of Gaza Strip (1949), **1988** 581
election reforms, **2005** 164-174, 399, 581
elections, Muslim Brotherhood participation in, **2005** 270, 273
Gaza Strip border area (Philadelphia route), **2004** 304, 314
Israeli relations
accord on partial return of Sinai, **1975** 473-586
cease-fire agreement, **1973** 931-935
cease-fire negotiations, **1973** 881-896
disengagement agreement, **1974** 29-32
framework for peace treaty, in Camp David accords, **1978** 605-606, 614-616, 620, 623
normalization of, **1979** 224-225, 243-245
peace negotiations, **1980** 236-237, 241-242, 504; **1989** 291, 292
peace treaty, **1979** 223-250; **1980** 34, 39, 40, 94
Sadat peace initiative, **1977** 827-855
Sinai return, **1982** 337-344
Israeli-Lebanese security agreement, **1983** 472
Mubarak meets with Rabin, **1992** 657
parliamentary elections, **2005** 168-170
PLO forces relocated in, **1982** 744
political opposition groups (Al Ghad-"Tomorrow"-political party), **2005** 165-168
political reform, **2003** 961
Sadat assassination, **1981** 733-746
Sharon disengagement policy, **2004** 303
Soviet relations
abrogation of friendship treaty, **1976** 169-175
Brezhnev on, **1976** 147
end of Soviet aid, **1978** 126-128, 130
Soviet aid in war, **1973** 883-884, 890
trade agreement, **1976** 171
state visit of Condoleezza Rice, **2005** 165, 167-168
state visit of Laura Bush, **2005** 166
Sudanese refugees assaulted, **2005** 169-170
Suez Canal and Bab-el Mandeb strait opening, in disengagement agreement, **1974** 30
terrorist bombings at Red Sea resorts, **2004** 535, 812; **2005** 165, 168, 399
U.S. relations, **2003** 958
arms sales, **1976** 169-172
Carter visit, **1977** 897-899
Nixon visit, **1974** 449-455
sale of warplanes, **1978** 106, 125-131
U.S. aid, **1974** 277, 279-282, 449-451, 457-458; **1975** 574, 585
Egyptair, hijacking at Cairo, **1985** 463, 467-468
Egyptian Movement for Change (*kifayah*, "enough"), **2005** 165, 273
Ehrlich, Robert L., Jr. (Maryland governor)
death penalty moratorium, **2002** 355
health insurance benefits legislation, **2005** 737
Ehrlichman, John D.
Ellsberg break-in, **1973** 538, 546-547; **1974** 35-39, 205-214, 411-417, 661-665, 668-669; **1975** 667
ITT case, order to Kleindienst concerning, **1974** 407-410
Nixon's confidence in, **1973** 738, 748-749, 948, 955
political intelligence gathering by, **1974** 601
preparation of Republican platform, **1972** 652
resignation of, **1973** 499, 502-504, 508, 510-511, 564
Watergate committee testimony, **1973** 550, 660-661
Watergate cover-up, **1974** 227-228, 306, 337, 360, 369, 991-992; **1975** 141-144, 146-151
indictment, **1974** 157-159, 161-167, 176-180
subpoena of Nixon in trial, **1974** 991
in White House taped conversations, **1974** 999-1002
and wiretaps in Nixon White House, **1976** 160
Eichman, United States v., **1990** 357-365
Eide, Kai, Kosovo political situation, **2004** 951, 957-964; **2005** 855-856
Eiffel, Alexandre Gustave, **1986** 699
Eigen, Peter, on bribery of public officials, **1997** 801
Eilberg, Joshua (D-Pa.)
conflict of interest indictment, **1978** 51-64
on Rockefeller nomination, **1974** 988
Einaudi, Luigi, Haiti political situation, **2001** 396
Eisen, Phyllis, on immigrant legislation, **1995** 565
Eisen v. Carlisle & Jacquelin, **1974** 427-433
Eisenach, Jeffrey, and GOPAC activities, **1997** 8, 13
Eisenhower (Milton S.) Foundation, inner cities report, **1993** 211-233
Eisenhower, Dwight David
Cabinet rejection, **1989** 107
and Castro, plots against, **1975** 725-729, 734-735, 737-738, 778-779, 789
and Lumumba assassination, **1975** 710, 720-723, 770, 789
NSC under, **1987** 212, 214
nuclear test ban, **1999** 601
pledge of allegiance amendment, **2002** 384
political uses of FBI, **1975** 873, 877
presidential approval ratings, **1989** 16; **2005** 41

Eisenhower, Dwight David *Continued*
press conferences of, **1988** 841
transfer of power, **1985** 492
Vietnam involvement, **1984** 349
Eisenhower, Milton, **1988** 289
Eisenhower, Susan, Russian nuclear weapons panel, **2001** 19
Eisenman, Robert H., Dead Sea scrolls, **1991** 638
Eisenstadt v. Baird, **1992** 594
Eisner, Michael, Disney chairman resignation, **2004** 423
Eisold, John F., flu vaccine for Congress and congressional staff, **2004** 641-642
Eitan, Rafael
Israeli invasion of Lebanon, **1983** 833
Palestinian refugee camp massacre, **1983** 166, 178
Eizenstat, Stuart E., **1979** 559
neutral nations aid to Nazi Germany, **1997** 257-258; **1998** 291-312
Ejercito, Luisa, Philippine senator, **2001** 104
El Al Israeli Airlines
attempted bombing of plane in Britain, **1986** 832
Rome and Vienna airport bombings, **1985** 468
El Mercurio, CIA influence on content of, **1975** 875, 894-895, 901-902
El Niño-La Niña
El Niño-Southern Oscillation (ENSO) phenomenon, **2001** 118, 124
impact from, **1998** 726, 947-948
El Salvador
activist Catholic clergy in, **1984** 761
American missionaries killed in, **1981** 242
arms buildup in, State Department on, **1981** 241-261
Central American peace plan, **1987** 637, 640, 642-648, 1007, 1008
civil war in, **1984** 44-45, 48-49; **1987** 640
Cuban-Soviet colonialism in, Reagan on, **1982** 180, 187-188
death squads in, **1987** 191, 194; **1989** 598, 604-605
Duarte's political position in, **1981** 243
elections in, **1984** 34, 49
forest conservation, **2001** 114
human rights in, **1981** 180, 185-186; **1982** 109-113; **1983** 189-191, 442; **1984** 156, 159-162; **1985** 146, 150-151; **1986** 103-104; **1987** 191, 194-195; **1989** 59; **1990** 145-147
and U.S. aid, **1984** 32-34, 46-48
hurricane and flood damage, **1998** 791
Jesuit priests' massacre, **1993** 238, 243
John Paul II visit, **1983** 242, 246-250
Nicaraguan support of guerrillas, **1984** 340-341, 345; **1985** 256, 263, 266, 269; **1989** 650, 657-658, 666
pledge to discontinue, **1989** 163-164, 167, 171-172
peace accord, on reintegration of Nicaraguan contras, **1989** 165
peace treaty, **1992** 23-32
Reagan policy on, **1984** 816
Kissinger commission recommendations, **1984** 31-34
Republican platform on, **1984** 662
refugees from, U.S. asylum for, **1987** 254-255
Romero assassination, **1980** 412
smoking in the Americas, **1992** 269
Soviet policy on, **1984** 827
Soviet propaganda about, Project Truth on, **1981** 763
UN report on refugees, **1991** 672
U.S. aid to, **1981** 242, 253, 261; **1982** 181, 188-189; **1983** 439-449, 452-454; **1984** 32-34, 46-48
violence in, UN Truth Commission report on, **1993** 237-248
Elazer, David, **1974** 30
ElBaradei, Mohammed
India, U.S. nuclear-energy supplies sales to, **2005** 466-467
Iran nuclear weapons inspections, **2003** 1025-1036; **2004** 868, 870; **2005** 594
Iraq weapons inspections, **2002** 718; **2003** 46, 878-879; **2005** 467
Iraq-Niger uranium sales fraud, **2003** 20; **2005** 700
Libyan nuclear weapons dismantled, **2004** 171
Libyan nuclear weapons inspections, **2003** 1222
Nobel Peace Prize recipient, **2004** 929; **2005** 931-940
North Korean nuclear weapons program, **2002** 734; **2004** 870
nuclear weapons proliferation controls, **2003** 906; **2004** 326, 329-335; **2005** 931-934
Elde, Espen Barth, on Nobel Peace Prize controversy, **2004** 931
Elder, Nan, **1977** 778-781
Elderly. *See* Senior citizens
Elders, Jocelyn, surgeon general resignation, **1994** 592-594; **1995** 61
Eldridge, Joseph, **1993** 455
Elections
See also Campaign finance reform; Campaign financing; Campaign practices; Presidential elections; Voter participation; Voter registration; *and* under names of individual countries
congressional midterm elections, 2002 36, 533; **2005** 113, 124-126
Bush campaign speech on, **2002** 818-829
state
corporate free speech and spending in, **1978** 307-324
run-off primaries, Democratic platform on, **1984** 551, 609-610
system reform, bipartisan commission on, **2001** 522-535
voter participation, report on, **1990** 295-299
Electoral college, constitutional amendment to abolish, **1977** 199-200, 204-205
Electric power industry. *See* Energy industry; Power plants
Electronic commerce (e-commerce), **2000** 301-302
Electronic Frontier Foundation, **2002** 561
Electronic Privacy Information Center (EPIC), Secure Flight proposal, **2004** 145
Elementary and Secondary Education Act (1965), Title I, and parochial school aid, **1985** 434, 450-452, 455-460
El-Hage, Wadih, embassy bombing conviction, **2001** 803
Elizabeth (New Jersey), hazardous waste disposal at, **1979** 785, 792-793, 795

Elizabeth I (queen of the United Kingdom), **1984** 316
Elizabeth II (queen of the United Kingdom)
on American bicentennial, **1976** 537-542
on bombings of London, **2005** 395
Canadian constitutional reform, **1982** 317-318, 320-323
death of Diana, statements on, **1997** 647-648, 650-651
knowledge of Blunt's work as Soviet spy, **1979** 906, 908, 912-913
meeting with John Paul II, **1982** 409-410
meeting with Reagan, **1982** 478
royal family problems, **1992** 1059-1063
Schwartzkopf knighthood bestowed by, **1991** 244, 248
speech for new prime minister, **1997** 277-283
on Thatcher government, **1979** 379, 381-384
visit to U.S., **1991** 247-251
Elliott, Emerson J., **1992** 87
Elliott, J. Robert, reversal of Calley's conviction, **1974** 857-860
Ellis, Harry, in Carter-Reagan debate, **1980** 920, 925-928, 939-940
Ellis, Jim, money laundering indictment, **2005** 633, 634, 637, 639-643
Ellis Island (New York City)
deteriorating condition of, **1995** 124, 125
Statue of Liberty centennial, **1986** 697-699
Ellsberg, Daniel
dismissal of Pentagon Papers trial, **1973** 537-548; **1974** 205-206
leak of Pentagon Papers, **1973** 537, 539; **1974** 33-38
psychiatrist's office break-in, **1973** 745-746; **1974** 33-40, 205-214, 661-664; **1975** 142, 656-657, 663, 667
CIA support for, **1975** 403, 428
national security grounds for, **1974** 411-417
Sorensen affidavit for, **1976** 880
White House efforts to defame, **1974** 38, 40, 443-447; **1975** 143
and White House wiretaps, **1976** 159-160
Ellwanger, Paul, **1982** 4-5
Ellwood, Robert, on cults, **1997** 124
El-Maati, Amer, terrorist suspect, **2004** 276
Elmardoudi, Abdel-Ilah, terrorist-related conviction, **2004** 273
Elrod v. Burns, **1980** 259-267
Elson, Edward, **1979** 120
Ely-Raphel, Nancy, trafficking in persons, **2002** 334
Embargo. *See under* Economic sanctions (by country)
Embassies
bombings in Kenya and Tanzania, **1998** 555-563; **1999** 53, 524, 690; **2000** 277, 278; **2001** 3, 617, 688; **2002** 1014-1015; **2003** 453, 841; **2004** 520
convictions, **2001** 803-804
consolidation proposal, **1999** 691
diplomatic posts evaluation, State Department on, **1999** 690-698
employment of host country workers, **1986** 269-270
human rights and religious freedom issues, **1998** 25-26
inviolability of, and Iran hostage taking, **1979** 870-871, 878-880, 890-891
security against terrorist attack, **1981** 463
security lapses, **1998** 557; **1999** 690-692
U.S. bombing of Chinese embassy in Yugoslavia, **1999** 304-316, 726; **2001** 247
Embryos
See also Stem cell research
frozen, custody and rights of, **1989** 551-559
research on human, Vatican teaching on, **1987** 267-268, 273-277
Emergency preparedness
Emergency Alert System, **2002** 744
exercises for terrorist attacks, **2003** 903-904
first responders, **2002** 745
communications technology, **2005** 894
response to September 11 terrorist attacks, **2004** 470
Emergency Wartime Supplemental Appropriations Act (2003), **2003** 684
Emerson, Timothy Joe, **2001** 725
Emerson, United States v., **2001** 726-737; **2002** 963
Emigration
of Jews to Palestine, British action on (1939), **1983** 144
of Soviet Jews, under Brezhnev, **1982** 871-872
of Soviets
increase of, **1989** 66-67
slowdown of, **1975** 561
Emigration, right of
See also Travel, freedom of
discussed at Washington summit, **1987** 991, 993, 1003
East Germany's lifting of restrictions, **1989** 625-629
Sakharov and Bonner hunger strike for, **1981** 747-752
Sakharov on, **1975** 915, 918, 925-926
Soviet policy on, **1988** 355-356, 359
Republican platform on, **1980** 637-638
and U.S. trade agreement, **1972** 846; **1973** 380, 792-793, 797-798, 800; **1976** 143, 149
and U.S. trade privileges, **1973** 587-588; **1974** 42, 55, 114, 117, 901-906; **1975** 224-225, 235
Western pressure on, **1973** 810, 822-823
in Soviet Union, and U.S. trade agreement, **1989** 645
Eminent domain
public use defined, **2005** 362-364
state legislation, **2005** 363
Supreme Court on, **2005** 362-375
Emmert, Mark A., affirmative action, **2003** 363
Emmervall, Madelaine, **1988** 347
Empey, Reg, Ulster Unionist Party leader, **2005** 510
Employee Benefit Research Institute
pension plans, **2004** 737
retirement plan survey, **2002** 104
Employee benefits
Clinton administration policy, **1996** 27-39
corporate responsibility for, **1996** 41-49
for partners of homosexual employees, **1996** 689
Employee Retirement Income Security Act (ERISA, 1974), **2002** 108-113; **2004** 734; **2005** 198
Employment
See also Discrimination, job; Discrimination, sex

Employment *Continued*
Democratic platform on, **1984** 564-565, 576-577; **1988** 559-560, 563
drug testing in, **1986** 840-841
economic advisers' report, **1990** 98-101
economic justice in, U.S. bishops on, **1986** 983-984, 987-988, 992, 996-998
as economic summit concern, **1983** 508, 512-514
equal opportunity in, Democratic platform on, **1972** 531-532
during Carter administration, **1979** 83, 85, 94-95, 104-105; **1981** 58-59, 62-63, 107
during Ford administration, **1976** 667, 670, 672
during Nixon administration, **1973** 220-221
during Reagan administration, **1988** 118-121, 126, 137-142
expected from U.S.-Soviet trade agreement, **1972** 846
impact on inflation, **1976** 709-710; **1977** 67-68, 81, 87-88
growth in, Joint Economic Committee plan for, **1981** 295-297, 304-306
guaranteed, McGovern on, **1972** 594-595
hiring practices, EEOC guidelines on, **1972** 314-318
of illegal aliens, **1981** 46, 265, 268, 270-272, 605, 613; **1986** 963-969
inflation controls' impact on, **1980** 701-706, 711-713, 715-717, 769-770
mandatory retirement, **1985** 397-407
minimum and youth wage effect on, **1983** 785-790
of minorities and women, **1982** 919-944
outlook, Reagan and advisers on, **1987** 120-121, 125-128, 130-133, 144
overtime pay vs. workers compensatory/"comp" time, **2003** 445
Republican platform on, **1980** 567, 570, 595-599
right to refuse dangerous work, **1980** 199-207
stimulation of, Reagan administration plan for, **1981** 214, 216, 218, 223-224, 325
Sun Belt migration in search of, **1981** 39-40, 49-54, 327
underground economic activity, **2003** 444
in U.S., CEA report on, **2005** 149
U.S. situation, Bureau of Labor Statistics report, **2003** 441-449
for veterans and minorities, Nixon on, **1972** 95-98, 107-109
youth assistance, **1983** 77, 84, 115, 116
Employment, public service
Burns on, **1974** 425; **1975** 635-636, 641-642
Carter plan for, **1977** 108, 551, 554, 556-557, 559-560
CETA cuts by Reagan, **1981** 641
Democratic platform on, **1972** 532
domestic economic summit on, **1974** 861-863, 865, 870, 873, 879
Ford proposals, **1975** 88; **1976** 709-710
for hard-core unemployed, **1977** 67, 73, 87
for job losses in energy crisis, **1974** 768
Muskie on, **1976** 14, 29
phasing out in Ford budget, **1976** 38
Joint Economic Committee on, **1975** 35
Reagan budget cuts in, **1981** 641
Republican platform on, **1976** 619, 622
Employment cost index (ECI), **2005** 150
Employment Division v. Smith, **1997** 406-407, 410, 411, 416, 418-420, 421
Employment Nondiscrimination Act, **1997** 762, 764; **1999** 56; **2000** 35
Employment programs
See also Job training
in Carter budget, **1977** 126-128; **1979** 10-11, 15
in Carter welfare reform proposal, **1979** 389-390, 392-394
incentives to hire the hard-core unemployed, Carter's urban proposals, **1978** 242, 244, 246, 249-250, 252
Reagan budget cuts to, CBO on, **1983** 766-767, 769, 771
Republican platform on, **1972** 667-668
Employment Service (U.S.), staff reductions in, **1981** 326
Endangered species
coral communities, **2004** 621
as effect of climate change, **1988** 865
impact on environment, **1980** 666, 680, 692-693
marine mammals, **2004** 620-621
monitoring and protection of, Nixon on, **1972** 151
preservation of, U.S.-Soviet agreement on, **1972** 806, 809-810
Endangered Species Act, **2001** 218-219
and EPA pesticides regulation, **2004** 670-671
recovery of spotted owl, **1992** 490
ruling on protection of spotted owl, **1991** 275-285
salmon in fisheries considered "wild," **2004** 670
snail darter protection, **1978** 433-452
Supreme Court on, **1995** 359-368
Endara, Guillermo
election of, **1989** 702-703, 705-706
and money-laundering operations, **1992** 649-650
presidential election, **1992** 651
suit against Noriega, **1990** 723
Enders, Thomas O., on aid for El Salvador, **1981** 242, 257-261
End-of-life care
See also Death and dying; Right to die
"culture of life"
politics of, **2005** 157-159
John Paul II statements on, **2005** 293
Schiavo case
autopsy results, **2005** 159
congressional intervention, **2005** 154, 156-157, 161-163
Florida Court rulings, **2005** 154-157, 160-161
Supreme Court ruling, **2005** 154-163
Energy conservation
after Iran's hostage taking, Carter on, **1979** 872
alternative energy sources, **2001** 336-337
alternative fuels for automobiles, **2003** 22, 27
Carter administration questionnaires on, **1977** 185
Carter anti-inflation program, **1980** 247, 251-252
Carter energy program, **1977** 103, 106, 111, 277-292; **1978** 11, 96, 99; **1979** 319-320, 323-324
Democratic Party platform on, **1976** 545-546, 575, 579; **1980** 713, 749-752; **1984** 594-595
domestic summit on, **1974** 863, 869, 877

Ford administration program, **1975** 16-18, 22-23, 28-29, 36-38, 83; **1976** 20, 709; **1977** 71
fuel allocation restrictions, **1973** 914-918
government role in, Nixon on, **1973** 480-481
home efficiency measures, tax credits for, **1974** 910, 915; **1975** 104
impact on oil supply, **1980** 996; **1982** 979
incentives for
in Carter program, **1979** 560, 568; **1980** 28, 36-37, 54-55, 169-170
in Ford program, **1975** 84, 86-87, 91, 103-104, 110-111
Nixon CEA on, **1974** 81-82
world cooperation in, **1981** 14, 20-22
industrialized countries' cooperation on, **1974** 982, 984; **1977** 368-369, 373-374, 690; **1980** 508-510; **1981** 778
by industry and utilities, during coal strike, **1978** 111-112, 115, 119
insulation standards revision, **1972** 149
Joint Economic Committee on, **1980** 211, 231
low-income assistance for, **1979** 320, 324; **1980** 731-732
mandatory measures, FEA on, **1974** 909-911, 914-918
in Nixon program, **1974** 42, 46-47, 54, 99, 104
Nixon's emergency plans, **1973** 913-919
progress in
Nixon on, **1974** 146-147
Reagan on, **1983** 113-114
Reagan-Anderson debate on, **1980** 848, 852-855
Republican Party platform on, **1976** 645
Energy costs
See also Oil prices
and Carter anti-inflation measures, **1980** 243, 245, 251-252, 255-256
Carter CEA on, **1980** 159-162, 165-166, 168, 172-173, 178-179
as cause of inflation, Burns on, **1974** 419-421
to developing countries, **1980** 666, 669, 683-685, 694
and IMF and World Bank aid, **1977** 368, 374
poverty summit on, **1981** 778
impact on world economy
de Larosière on, **1980** 894-895
Ford on, **1975** 187-194
prices at replacement value, in Carter energy plan, **1977** 283, 288-289, 291
Energy crisis
Carter administration's leadership, **1979** 559-560, 562-564, 567-569
construction in deepwater ports, **1973** 465, 479
impact on inflation, Nixon CEA on, **1974** 69-70, 72, 74-75
as moral equivalent of war, Carter on, **1977** 103, 106-107, 111
Nixon program for dealing with, **1973** 465-486
nonaligned nations on, **1979** 686-687, 690
as priority, Nixon on, **1974** 41-42, 45-47, 54, 56
reality of, Schlesinger on, **1979** 663-664
remedies for, National '80s Agenda on, **1981** 39-40, 47-48
Energy Department (DOE)
carbon dioxide emissions report, **2001** 215-216
closing of Hanford nuclear plant, **1986** 386
compliance with environmental laws, **1989** 355-362
creation of, **1976** 879; **1977** 106, 185, 283, 292; **1978** 32, 39; **1979** 16, 29, 51
decontrol of domestic oil prices, **1979** 324, 326
energy price predictions, **2005** 779-780
fuel reallocation during coal strike, **1978** 111-112, 115, 120-121, 123-124
GAO report on nuclear cleanup priorities, **1995** 113-119
Global Threat Reduction Initiative, **2004** 326-327
global warming studies, **2001** 113
greenhouse gas emissions, **2005** 926
human radiation experiments, **1993** 987-995; **1994** 54-61; **1995** 633-634
Iraq nuclear weapons development, **2004** 715
laboratory security, **2003** 902
national policy, Bush task force plans, **2001** 331-346; **2003** 1017-1018
[nuclear] material protection, control, and accounting (MPC&A) systems, **1996** 142-146
nuclear weapons plants cleanup, **1994** 339-348
Republican platform on, **1984** 662, 673
Russian nuclear weapons report, **2001** 17-32
Energy industry
See also Oil and gas industry; Oil industry
deregulation of, Republican platform on, **1980** 568, 613-618
Enron Corp. bankruptcy, **2001** 862; **2004** 416-417
incentives for, Bush on, **1988** 611
massive power blackout
causes of, **2003** 1014-1024
final report on, **2004** 190
new electric power plants, **2001** 335
New York City blackout, **2003** 1016
oil company profits, congressional hearings on, **2005** 781-782
power industry deregulation, **2003** 1015, 1016-1017
reserves and production of, information on, **1977** 291-292
Seabrook nuclear plant, **1990** 195-198
Energy policy
achievements in, Carter on, **1981** 57, 59, 64-67, 86, 99-100, 109, 113
congressional legislation, **2005** 782-783
Democratic Party platform on, **1988** 565; **1991** 47; **1992** 694
economic effects of, Carter CEA on, **1978** 66, 70-71, 93
energy "crisis" in California, **2001** 55, 182, 331, 332-334; **2003** 1007, 1015
Ford CEA on, **1975** 102-104, 109-112; **1977** 71-72, 85-86
Joint Economic Committee plan, **1981** 307-308
London economic summit on, **1991** 463-464
national
Bush task force on, **2001** 331-346; **2003** 1120; **2004** 189
Carter plan for, **1978** 11, 19-21, 38-39; **1979** 60-64
National Commission on Energy Policy, **2004** 189
omnibus energy bill impasse, **2003** 1014, 1017

Energy policy *Continued*
options and strategies, FEA report, **1974** 909-918
Republican Party platform on, **1984** 672-673; **1996** 536-537; **2000** 515
Schlesinger farewell observations, **1979** 659-667
world development, UN summit on, **2002** 599, 602-603
Energy Policy and Conservation Act (1975), **1976** 51, 574-575; **1979** 321, 324
Energy prices
See also Oil and gas prices
energy company executives on, **2005** 777-799
Federal Reserve Board chairman on, **2004** 186-194
high prices, **2005** 414
Energy research and development
Democratic platform on, **1972** 559-560
in developing countries, **1981** 769-770, 778
Ford program, **1976** 39, 42
international cooperation on, **1972** 834
of new technologies
Ford on, **1975** 17, 22-23
Nixon CEA on, **1974** 83-85
Nixon program, **1973** 465-469, 481-483, 914-915, 920-921; **1974** 96, 99, 105
Reagan program, **1984** 100, 109
Energy Research and Development Administration (ERDA), **1975** 17
atmospheric research by, **1975** 447
creation of, **1973** 466-467, 921; **1975** 92
nuclear fuel reprocessing and recycling evaluation, **1976** 824, 830, 836-837
Energy security
Carter proposals for, **1980** 28, 36-37, 41-42, 52-56, 112-114
trust fund, creation of, **1979** 258, 320-321, 324-325, 330-333
Energy Security Corp., **1979** 560, 567-568, 570
Energy self-sufficiency
Ford on progress in, **1977** 46, 52-53
Ford program, **1975** 15-17, 21-24, 28-29, 99-100, 102-104, 111-112; **1976** 15, 20, 51
Nixon program, **1973** 913-921; **1974** 98-99, 104-106
Republican Party platform on, **1980** 613-618, 649-650
Energy shortages. *See* Energy crisis; Energy supply
Energy sources development
alternative
in Carter budget, **1977** 128; **1978** 96, 99
Carter on during campaign, **1980** 772, 775, 779
Carter proposals for, **1979** 253, 258-259, 321-322, 324, 560, 567-568, 570
Carter-Reagan debate on, **1980** 939-942
Democratic Party platform on, **1976** 545-546, 573-576, 582; **1980** 712, 749-751
economic summit on, **1980** 503-505, 508-510
Ford plans for, **1974** 771
industrialized countries' cooperation on, **1974** 982, 984; **1978** 538; **1980** 509
Kissinger on, **1975** 6
Republican Party platform on, **1972** 691-692; **1976** 645
domestic
in Carter budget, **1979** 14, 61-63
in Ford budget, **1975** 84, 86, 92
Ford program, **1974** 771; **1975** 194-195
incentives for, Reagan on, **1980** 652, 657
Nixon program, **1973** 465-477, 481-486, 805; **1974** 120
economic summit on, **1981** 598-599
and environmental restrictions, **1980** 617-618; **1981** 276, 279
exploration and leasing
Ford proposal, **1975** 17, 22-23, 38
Republican Party platform on, **1976** 645-646
federal management of, Carter on, **1979** 61, 63-64
renewable
coal as transition to, **1980** 417-418, 421-423, 425-427
Democratic Party platform on, **1980** 712-713, 749-751; **1984** 592-594
Energy supply
allocation of in coal strike, **1978** 111-112, 115, 120-121, 123-124
domestic
assessment of, **1974** 912-913
environmental impact of accelerated production, **1974** 909-910, 913-914
oil as diminishing resource, world coal report on, **1980** 417-418, 420-421, 423-426
reliability of
Ford on, **1974** 877
international cooperation to ensure, **1973** 483; **1974** 955-956, 968; **1975** 589, 591-592
world, U.S. consumption of, **1973** 466-467, 913, 919
Energy technology
U.S.-Mexican collaboration on, **1979** 169-171, 179-180
U.S.-Soviet cooperation in, **1974** 535-536, 538-542, 567
Engen, Donald D.
on air traffic safety, **1986** 254-255
on aviation regulation, **1988** 269
Engineers, in research and development, **1973** 781-782, 786-788
England. *See* Great Britain
England, Gordon R.
DOD interrogations of detainees policy directive, **2005** 910
Guantanamo Bay detainees, **2005** 448
England, Lynndie R., Abu Ghraib prison abuse case, **2004** 215, 220; **2005** 911-912
England-Joseph, Judy A., testimony on Chicago Housing Authority, HUD takeover of, **1995** 294-301
Engle, Joe H., **1981** 419
Engle v. Vitale, **1985** 379, 389-390; **1992** 557, 559, 561-562; **1995** 547
Engler, John, and balanced budgets, **1995** 11
English, Diane, **1992** 444
English language
plain, regulations written in, **1977** 104, 109
slang dictionary for returning POWs, **1973** 246-253
teaching of to immigrants, **1983** 415; **1986** 960-961
as U.S. official language, **1986** 959-962; **1995** 573-574, 577-578; **1996** 521
Enhanced Border Security and Visa Entry Reform Act (2002), **2003** 166, 167

Enhanced radiation weapons (ERW). *See* Neutron weapons
Enmund v. Florida, **1991** 385
Enola Gay (B-29 bomber), Smithsonian Institution exhibit, **1995** 55-58
Enrile, Juan Ponce
coup attempt against Aquino, **1987** 844-846
criticism of Aquino, **1986** 1037-1039
ouster of Marcos, **1986** 308-309
Enron Corporation
bankruptcy and collapse, **2001** 333, 857-866; **2002** 37, 54, 101-113, 391, 395-396, 1032-1033, 1036-1037; **2005** 201-202
Bush presidential campaign donor, **2003** 1158
collapse and pension funds, **2003** 710
fraud investigation, **2003** 332, 333, 336-337
indictment of CEO Kenneth L. Lay, **2004** 415-417, 424-428
Ensign, Tod, **1977** 96
Enterprise for the Americas initiative, **1992** 208, 213
Enterprise zones
Chavis of NAACP remarks on, **1993** 583
for community development, **1983** 54, 78; **1985** 106, 110-111
Republican platform on, **1980** 568, 579, 591
and community empowerment zones, **1997** 39, 71; **1998** 90-91; **1999** 91; **2001** 59
failure of programs, **1993** 212-213, 214-216
Entertainment industry, marketing violence to children, **2000** 729-739; **2001** 73, 75-76
Entrapment
Barry (mayor of D.C.) on drug charges, **1995** 498
Barry sentencing, **1990** 707
in sting operations, **1992** 313-327
Environment
Alaska pipeline impacts on, **1972** 271, 277-280
Alaskan oil spill, **1990** 513-530
biotechnology in agriculture, impact of, **1986** 288, 295-296, 306
Bush and CEA on, **1990** 102-104
Charter of Paris, **1990** 741-742
Clear Air Act revisions, **1990** 715-720
dangers to from technological progress, **1975** 919-920, 922
degradation of as cause of natural disasters, **1984** 975-985
energy strategies, impact on, **1974** 909-910, 913-916
Global Environment Outlook, **2002** 594-595, 855
Houston economic summit, **1990** 468-469, 476-477
nuclear war, consequences of, **1983** 857-882; **1985** 541-554
population impact on, **1980** 665-667, 670, 685-693
Reagan administration policies, **1983** 828-830; **1984** 81-83, 90; **1989** 17
Republican platform on, **1984** 662-663, 685-686
Seabrook nuclear plant, **1990** 195-198
Shevardnadze statement, **1990** 644-645
urban environment study, U.S.-Soviet agreement on, **1972** 806, 808-809
World Bank projects, **1986** 859-873
Environmental Defense Fund, **1990** 719
genetically altered crops, **1999** 403
land use permit for Alaska pipeline, **1972** 271
offshore oil and gas leases, **2004** 604
rain forests in Indonesia, **1986** 859-873
Environmental protection
See also Acid rain; Air pollution and air quality; Climate change; Hazardous waste; Natural resources; Ocean pollution; Ozone layer; Toxic chemicals; Water pollution
arsenic levels in water, **2001** 212-221, 541
biotechnology in agriculture, **1999** 401-411
in Bush (George H. W.) budget, **1989** 71, 77
Carter goals for, **1978** 40-42; **1979** 64-66
Carter on challenges and accomplishments, **1981** 31-32, 35, 83-85
CEA report on, **1998** 92-93
clean water, **2003** 180-181
clear cutting timber, **1992** 489-492
Clear Skies Initiative, **2002** 299, 894, 898-899; **2003** 27; **2004** 666-667; **2005** 79, 83, 95, 98-99
Clinton administration, **1996** 30-31, 64-65; **1997** 39; **2000** 32-33
Clinton clean air fund proposal, **1999** 55-56
Clinton Democratic acceptance speech, **1996** 619-621
and coal, conversion to, **1977** 282-283, 290
Democratic Party platform on, **1972** 556-558; **1980** 751-752; **1984** 550, 556, 595-598; **1988** 564; **1992** 697-698, 706-707; **1996** 648-650
Democratic Party response, **2003** 38
drug cultivation affecting, **1992** 218-219
Earth Summit (Rio), **1992** 499-506
as economic consideration, nonaligned nations on, **1983** 266
economic growth, compatibility with, **1974** 105; **1976** 545-546, 578-579
electric automobile production, **1996** 17-20
and energy development, **1973** 468-469, 471-476, 479; **1977** 71; **1980** 939-942
Everglades restoration project, **1996** 80-83
farm legislation and, **1996** 200-201
Ford administration record in, **1976** 807-808
of forest lands, Clinton "roadless initiative," **2001** 216; **2002** 899; **2004** 668-669
forest lands, Clinton "roadless initiative," **1999** 592-599
global
and biological diversity, **1981** 23-24
conference on, **1972** 475-479
Democratic platform on, **1976** 584
economic summits on, **1985** 354-355; **1989** 414, 427-430
economics on, **1991** 468-470
as NATO concern, **1975** 354, 358
U.S. remedies for, **1981** 13-14, 22-27
global issues, **1997** 345-348
global warming, **2002** 298-321
Healthy Forests Initiative, **2002** 894, 899-900; **2003** 27, 181
industrial pollution, EPA regulations, **2002** 894-905
Lands Legacy Initiative, **1999** 56; **2000** 32
lead levels in drinking water, **2003** 174
Livability Agenda, **1999** 56
logging policy, **1993** 495-499

Environmental protection *Continued*
mercury pollution regulations, **2005** 95-110
mining permits, **2001** 217
Nixon program, **1972** 90-91, 147-153; **1973** 214-219
Superfund proposal, **1980** 44, 82
ocean protection, presidential commission on, **2004** 602-625
oil and gas development, **2003** 182
pesticide regulation reform, **1996** 467-470
as presidential campaign issue, **1988** 776-777, 805-806, 811-812, 817-818
regulation, **2001** 218
regulation enforcement, **2002** 901; **2003** 181-182
Republican Party platform on, **1972** 651, 688-690; **1976** 646-648; **1984** 685-686; **1988** 616, 668-671; **1992** 829, 830-832; **1996** 533-535
Tallgrass Prairie restoration, **1993** 885-891
UN earth summit conference
New York City, **1997** 480-488
Rio de Janeiro, **1997** 480, 860; **1999** 403; **2002** 593
UN global warming treaty, **1997** 859-876
U.S.-Soviet agreements on cooperation in, **1972** 805-813; **1985** 751, 755; **1987** 994, 1000
in water projects, **1978** 385-391, 394-395
water quality, **2001** 217-218
Environmental Protection Agency (EPA)
acid rain study, **1983** 200
air quality in New York City after September 11 attacks, **2003** 174, 547, 548
air quality regulations, **2004** 664-674
Alaskan oil spill, **1989** 231-232
atmospheric research, **1975** 447
Bush on, **1990** 55
chlorofluorocarbons ban, **1992** 76
chlorofluorocarbon reductions, **1987** 747; **1988** 222-223
chemical discharge into waterways, regulations on, **1977** 131-141
Clean Air Act
requirements, **1981** 280-284
revisions, **1990** 715-720
clean air enforcement, bubble concept, **1984** 427-437
climate change, **1988** 861-866
creation of, **1972** 90; **1973** 215
Earth Summit (Rio), **1992** 499
enforcement activities, **2002** 901
genetically engineered foods, **1992** 470
hazardous waste
cleanup, congressional investigation of, **1982** 965-970; **1988** 465, 467
disposal, **1972** 148; **1979** 781-784, 788-790
in Love Canal, **1983** 479-487
management, **1980** 446-452
shipment, **1989** 154
industrial pollution regulations, **2002** 894-905
Justice Department investigation of, **1983** 749-753
mercury pollution regulations, **2005** 95-110
merit awards for young people, **1972** 152-153
"new source review," **2002** 895-897, 902-905; **2003** 176-179; **2004** 664-674; **2005** 100
pesticides and pest management, **1972** 150
pesticides in food, **1996** 467-469
plant biotechnology, **1986** 288
pollution control costs, **1972** 253
radon testing, **1988** 3, 4
in Reagan budget, **1984** 82-83, 90, 100
safe drinking water report, **1993** 261-270
secondhand smoke, **1993** 63-69
urban air pollution, **1972** 775; **1978** 247, 252
water treatment funds, impoundment of, **1975** 135-140
Environmental Protection Agency v. Natural Resources Defense Council, **1984** 427-437
Environmental regulations
business investment and, **1974** 86
costs of to business, **1972** 253-258; **1975** 640-641
economic basis for, Reagan on, **1989** 7
flexibility of, National '80s Agenda on, **1981** 40
lifting to ease burden on business, **1974** 862-863
relaxing of, during energy crisis, **1973** 914, 918
Environmental tobacco smoke (ETS)
effects of, EPA report, **1993** 63-69
health dangers of, **1986** 1079-1080, 1083-1089
Environmental warfare
Brezhnev on, **1976** 151
U.S.-Soviet discussion of, **1974** 558-559
EPA. *See* Environmental Protection Agency
EPI. *See* Economic Policy Institute
Episcopal Church, consecration of woman bishop, **1989** 49-54
Episcopal Church in the United States, gay clergy controversy, **2004** 42-44
Epperson v. Arkansas, **2005** 1011
Equal Access Act, **2001** 421
Equal Employment Opportunity Act (1972), and affirmative action, **1986** 659-661
Equal Employment Opportunity Commission (EEOC)
Clarence Thomas chairs, **1992** 38, 39
disabilities in the workplace, **2002** 3, 5, 9, 11-13
discrimination claims, **1997** 322
employer guidelines on mental disabilities, **1997** 127-141
enforcement, **1985** 790, 796
faculty tenure review case, **1990** 23-34
health care benefits for retirees, **2005** 489
labor union's discriminatory practices, **1986** 651-667
mandatory retirement, **1985** 399, 403, 405
sex discrimination guidelines, **1972** 313-319; **1976** 891-892, 898-899, 903-905
sex discrimination law suit, **2001** 549
sexual harassment regulations, **1993** 943
Equal Employment Opportunity Commission v. Wyoming, **1983** 231-240
Equal opportunity
CEA report on, **1998** 97
Republican Party platform, **1996** 517-518
Equal protection clause. *See under* Constitutional amendments (U.S.), Fourteenth Amendment
Equal Rights Amendment (ERA)
Carter support for, **1977** 184; **1979** 55; **1980** 770; **1981** 59, 83
Carter-Reagan debate, **1980** 921, 947-949

Democratic Party platform on, **1972** 543; **1976** 545, 562; **1980** 712, 739-740; **1984** 603-604, 607
and draft registration, **1981** 523-524
expiration of deadline for, **1982** 611-617
Kennedy on, **1980** 708
Moral Majority on, **1983** 818
National '80s Agenda support for, **1981** 40
not ratified, **1992** 440
population commission support for, **1972** 307
progress of, **1975** 56, 509; **1980** 43, 77-78
ratifying procedures, federal court on, **1981** 923-938
Reagan on, **1980** 655; **1983** 755-757
Republican Party platform on, **1972** 699-700; **1976** 635-636; **1980** 568, 652; **1982** 612; **1984** 662; **1988** 617
school prayer measure attached to, **1984** 242
women's conference on, **1977** 861-864
Equal time rule, in broadcasting, **1976** 695; **1987** 625
Equatorial Guinea, human trafficking, **2004** 125
Erbakan, Necmittin, as Turkish prime minister, **2002** 908
ERBD. *See* European Bank for Reconstruction and Development
Ercan, Ahmet, on earthquakes in Turkey, **1999** 467
Erdman, Karen, care of the mentally ill report, **1990** 573-598
Erdogan, Recep Tayyip
Cyprus peace negotiations, **2004** 977
EU membership invitation, **2004** 973
EU membership status, **2004** 975-976
Turkish Islamic leader, **2002** 906-908
U.S.-Turkish relations, **2004** 978
Erectile dysfunction, smoking linked to, **2004** 293
Erekat, Saeb
Gaza Strip, Jewish settlers withdrawal from, **2004** 302
Israel-Palestine conflict, **2003** 1207
Ergonomics, OSHA standards, **1999** 769-778
Ericksen, Michael, on addictive power of cigarette smoking, **1999** 539
Erickson, William H., Columbine High School shooting incident, **2001** 348-349
Erie R. v. Tompkins, **1992** 569
Eritrea
border dispute with Ethiopia, **1999** 431; **2000** 753-761
UN report on refugees, **1991** 673
Eritrean Liberation Front, Libyan support for, **1986** 348
Ermacora, Felix, on human rights in Afghanistan, **1986** 919-936
Ernst & Young, federal oversight, **2004** 423
Eros (asteroid), landing on, **2001** 143-149
Ervin, Sam J., Jr. (D-N.C.)
busing moratorium, **1972** 259
impoundment of funds, **1973** 4, 171
Nixon pardon, **1974** 812
political uses of tax information, **1975** 830
testimony of White House aides, **1973** 338-339, 501
Watergate hearings, opening statement, **1973** 549-554
Watergate investigation, Nixon cooperation with, **1974** 42
Watergate report, **1974** 600, 605
White House tapes, **1973** 841, 860-861, 870
ESA. *See* European Space Agency
Eskander, Amin Soliman, on U.S.-Egyptian relations, **2005** 273
Espionage
American spy plane incident in China, **2001** 247-253, 738; **2002** 855; **2003** 1179
Ames case, **2001** 150-151, 155
Senate report on, **1994** 475-497; **1996** 794
charges of
arrests of Danilov and Zakharov, **1986** 819-827
Cambodia on *Mayaguez*'s mission, **1975** 312-318
Iran on U.S. hostages, **1979** 869-870, 873-876
U.S. and Soviet expulsion of diplomats, **1986** 267-272
Chinese theft of U.S. nuclear secrets, **1999** 235-256
combating, relaxation of intelligence restrictions on, **1981** 861-868
Nicholson case, CIA-FBI statement on, **1996** 794-800
Pitts case, **1996** 794, 795-796
Robert Hanssen case, **2001** 150-158, 893
Soviet acquisition of military technology, **1985** 603-614; **1987** 30-33, 37
U.S.-Soviet spy swap, **1986** 93-94
Walker spy ring, **1985** 603-604, 606
Wen Ho Lee spy case, **2000** 740-752
Esposito, Bill, FBI crime laboratory report, **1997** 224
Espy, Mike
agriculture secretary resignation, **1994** 403-408; **1998** 906
corruption charges, **1998** 906, 907-908
and NPR proposals, **1993** 720-721
Esquipulas, Guatemala, meeting of Central American presidents (1986), **1987** 639, 642-643
Esquipulas II agreement (1987), **1987** 637-648; **1989** 162-163, 165-168
Essner, Robert A., Wyeth class action suits, **2002** 507
Essy, Amara, African Union secretary general, **2001** 506
Establishment clause. *See under* Constitutional amendments (U.S.), First Amendment
Estabrook, Ronald, **1996** 72-73
Estelle v. Gamble, **1992** 178-183
Estelle v. Smith, **1981** 431-441
Estes, Bille Sol, **1981** 164
Estes, Richard, sexual exploitation of children, **2001** 956
Estes v. Texas, **1981** 164, 169-171
Estonia
economic situation, **2004** 199
EU membership, **2004** 198
freedom statement of, **1989** 469-473
NATO membership, **2004** 136, 198
Soviet restructuring plans, **1991** 532-533
U.S. diplomatic relations, **1991** 545-549
Estrada, Joseph, Philippine president ousted from office, **2001** 102-104
Ethics. *See* Bioethics; Congressional ethics; Government ethics

Ethics in government. *See* Government ethics
Ethics in Government Act (1978)
  Donovan investigation, **1982** 587
  on independent counsel, **1988** 465-478
  Meese investigation, **1988** 495
Ethiopia
  AIDS epidemic, **2002** 470
  border dispute with Eritrea, **1999** 431; **2000** 753-761
  conflict in, and Soviet advisers, **1985** 708, 715
  desertification, and population pressure, **1987** 441, 445, 459
  drought and famine in, **1984** 973-974, 978, 982, 990; **1985** 195
  executions in, **1989** 602
  human rights in, **1982** 113-114; **1985** 151-152; **1986** 99-101; **1987** 191-192; **1988** 884; **1989** 58; **1990** 132
  political obstacles to food delivery, **1985** 350, 353
  refugees in
    increase in, **1981** 179
    UN report, **1991** 671
Ethnic conflicts
  See also under names of individual countries
  Amnesty International on killings in, **1989** 598-602, 609
Ethnic groups
  and academic achievement, **1992** 147-148
  relations among in Soviet Union, **1987** 96-97
Etler, Dennis A., **1992** 137
ETS. *See* Educational Testing Service; Environmental tobacco smoke
Euclid v. Ambler Realty Co., **1994** 303
Eureka, European space project, **1985** 349, 355
Eureka College, Reagan speech on START, **1982** 385-393
Euro. *See under* Currency
Euro-Atlantic Partnership Council (EPAC), **1997** 518, 520-521
Europe
  See also Conventional forces in Europe; Eastern Europe; Western Europe
  Charter of Paris for a New Europe, **1990** 727, 734-745
  communist leaders in, focus on national needs, **1976** 144-145
  confidence-building measures in, Geneva summit, **1985** 751, 754, 758
  defense balance in, **1980** 124, 126, 129-132, 141, 153-157
  economic development forecasts, **2005** 15
  human rights cases in, **1981** 182
  Iran nuclear weapons development negotiations, **2004** 869-870
  population growth in, **1987** 443-444
  reconciliation of
    and East German reforms, **1989** 632-634
    and German postwar guilt, **1989** 487-497
    Walesa on, **1989** 535-536
  sex trade and human trafficking, **2004** 124, 126, 129
  Soviet cooperation with, **1989** 399-409, 433-435
  work and leisure compared with U.S., **1992** 171-172
European Bank for Reconstruction and Development (EBRD)
  aid to Eastern Europe, **1992** 644
  aid to Russia, **1992** 257
  established, **1990** 473
European Central Bank (ECB), monetary policy, **1999** 75-84
European Coal and Steel Community, **1998** 272; **2004** 197; **2005** 339
European Commission
  establishment of, **1999** 155-156
  EU executive body reorganization, **2004** 197
  leadership, **2004** 201-202
  reform report, **1999** 155-164
  role of the presidents, **2004** 200-201
European Communist and Workers' Parties, Conference of, **1976** 433-461
European Community (EC)
  agricultural subsidies, **1990** 480
  Argentine imports, ban on, **1982** 284, 298
  Britain's contribution and EC budget, **1984** 439-445
  Chernobyl nuclear accident, **1986** 384
  common agricultural policy (CAP), **1984** 441
  Eastern Europe, changes in, **1989** 633
  economic and technical cooperation proposed with Arab oil producers, **1974** 113, 123, 185-188, 530
  economic summits, **1981** 591; **1986** 441
    Houston, **1990** 467, 470-471, 480
    Munich, **1992** 638, 640
  European currency unit, **1991** 843-850
  European currency unit, president on, **1998** 271
  European Parliament, Reagan speech, **1985** 359
  floating of currencies of members, **1973** 345
  food aid to Soviet Union, **1990** 807
  formation of, **1978** 743, 749
  French antiterrorist measures, **1986** 829, 832, 834
  inflation, cooperation in fighting, **1974** 982-983
  Irish abortion case, **1992** 250
  on PLO participation in peace talks, **1980** 504
  and Rushdie death threat, **1989** 97
  on Saudi peace plan, **1981** 633
  South Africa, sanctions against, **1985** 532; **1986** 372
  Soviet cooperation with, **1989** 401, 405-407
  Thatcher government's commitment to, **1979** 379-381, 387
  trade embargo against Haiti, **1992** 454
  trade policies, **1973** 492; **1985** 348, 350, 352
  on U.S. air strike against Libya, **1986** 350-351
  Yugoslavia, economic sanctions, **1991** 367
European Council
  European defense force proposal, **1999** 817-827
  presidency, **2004** 200-201
European Currency Unit (ECU), creation of, **1978** 742-748
European Economic Community (EEC)
  See also European Community; *under its later name* European Union (EU)
  membership, **2004** 197
European Environment Agency, climate change research, **2004** 830
European Monetary Cooperative Fund, creation of, **1978** 742

European Monetary System (EMS), agreement on, **1978** 741-752
European Monetary Union, **2003** 752
European Security and Defence Identity (ESDI), **1997** 522
European Space Agency (ESA)
and International Space Station, **1998** 930
Mars Express probe launch, **2003** 301-309; **2004** 6; **2005** 502
European Union (EU)
See also European Commission
Africa economic development aid, **2005** 408
Bosnia peacekeeping mission, **2004** 135, 138, 197, 954
budget controversy, **2005** 343-344
Bush speech on Middle East conflict, **2005** 582
Chinese textile import quotas, **2005** 617
cigarette labeling, **2001** 222, 226
constitution, **2003** 41; **2004** 197, 200-201
French and Netherlands referendums, **2005** 339-342, 344-346
new constitution fails, **2005** 338-350
ratification process, **2005** 338-339
death penalty
ban for members, **2002** 910
opponent, **2005** 179
economic growth and, **2003** 753
euro currency, and monetary policy, **1999** 75-84
euro currency adopted, **1998** 271-280; **1999** 155
European defense force, **1999** 817-827; **2002** 889; **2003** 463
expansion
membership for Turkey, **1999** 158, 466-467
potential members, **1999** 158
genetically altered seeds moratorium, **1999** 403
HIV prevention policy, **2005** 53
human trafficking, combating, **2004** 132
International Criminal Court, opposition to U.S. exemptions, **2003** 101-102
Internet antispam regulations, **2003** 393
Iran nuclear nonproliferation, **2003** 1027
Israeli security wall controversy, **2003** 1209
Kosovo, international policy toward, **2004** 951
Kyoto Protocol on Climate Change (UN treaty), ratification of, **2002** 303-304
Liberia, Election Observation Mission, **2005** 800-813
Libya, relations with, **2004** 168, 171-173
mad cow disease rulings (beef export prohibitions), **2000** 880, 882-883
membership, **2002** 608-609, 887
for Bosnia, **2003** 460; **2005** 851, 852-853, 857-858
for Bulgaria, **2005** 338
for Croatia, **2005** 342-343
for Cyprus, **2004** 974
future members, **2005** 342-343
of new members threatened, **2003** 43; **2005** 338
for Poland, **2004** 198; **2005** 340
for Romania, **2005** 338
standards for membership (Copenhagen criteria), **2004** 974
ten new members, **2002** 679-688; **2003** 753; **2004** 135, 197-206; **2005** 338
for Turkey, **2002** 906, 909-910; **2004** 197, 973-980; **2005** 338, 340, 342-343
for Ukraine, **2004** 1002; **2005** 66, 338, 342
mercury emissions treaty, **2005** 97
Microsoft antitrust challenge, **2001** 775, 780; **2002** 798
North Korean humanitarian aid, **2002** 736
North-South Korea negotiations, **2001** 267, 268
Parliament, Blair speech to, **2005** 346-350
Russia political situation, **2004** 569
Rwandan presidential election, **2003** 1071
Stability Growth Pact (budget deficit limits), **2003** 753
Sudan conflict, **2004** 593
Thatcher's resistance, **1990** 747-748
U.S., economic sanctions against, **2003** 446
U.S. poultry and egg ban, **2004** 924-925
Uzbekistan, weapons sales ban, **2005** 433
Yugoslavia, economic aid, **2001** 829
Zimbabwe, diplomatic sanctions, **2003** 116
Euskadi Ta Askatasuna (ETA, Basque Homeland and Freedom), **2004** 105-108
Euthanasia
See also Physician-assisted suicide
Catholic teaching on, **1995** 146, 155-158
John Paul II on, **1987** 701, 712; **1988** 171
Supreme Court case, **1990** 373-386
Evangelicals, National Association of
Reagan speech on domestic and foreign policies, **1983** 269-277
Reagan speech on religious values, **1984** 242
Evangelization, in U.S. Catholic Church, **1985** 572, 575-576, 579
Evans, Daniel J. (R-Wash.), **1988** 292-293
Evans, David, student drug testing, **2002** 424
Evans, Donald I.
commerce secretary confirmation, **2001** 97
prescription drug importation, opposition to, **2004** 985
Evans, Jimmy, Hunt ethics law conviction, **1993** 303-305
Evans, Lane (D-Ill.), apparel industry sweatshops, **1997** 209
Evans, Richard, Medicare prescription drug benefits, **2003** 1122
Evans, Rowland, **1989** 440
Everett, Robert R., **1988** 324
Everglades (Florida), restoration of, **1996** 80-83
Evers, Charles, **1982** 656
Evers, Medgar
assassination of, **1995** 456
Beckwith trial for murder of, **2002** 239; **2005** 353
Beckwith's retrial, **1994** 100-106
NAACP activities, **1995** 455
Everson v. Board of Education of Ewing, **1992** 556; **1993** 405
Evers-Williams, Myrlie, address as new NAACP chairman, **1995** 453-462
Evert, Lawrence G., Vietnam War casualty victim, **2000** 916
Evidence
admissibility of

Evidence *Continued*
and congressional immunity for legislative acts, **1979** 467-478
given outside presence of counsel, **1977** 219-235
obtained in good faith, **1981** 647-648, 661-663; **1984** 505-519
from unreasonable search, **1976** 521-536
from warrantless search of auto, **1978** 753-764
Evolution
See also Creation science; Intelligent design
teaching theory of in public schools, **1982** 3-16
theories of universe's origins, **1992** 379-383
Evren, Kenan
human rights in Turkey, **1985** 156
military takeover in Turkey, **1980** 807-810
Evron, Ephraim
on AWACS sale to Saudis, **1981** 798
on Saudi peace plan, **1981** 632
Ewing v. California, **2003** 984
Ex post facto laws, conviction for, and death penalty, **1977** 519
Exchange rates. *See* Currency exchange rates
Exclusionary rule
claims of illegal search and *habeas corpus* proceedings, **1976** 521-536
good faith exception to, **1981** 647-648, 661-663; **1984** 505-519
Meese on Court rulings on, **1985** 480-481, 485-486
and Miranda warnings, **1974** 473-485; **1977** 224-235; **1985** 223-253
passengers' rights in auto search, **1978** 753-764
Reagan support for easing of, **1985** 107, 114
and student searches, **1985** 14-15
Executions, government, Amnesty International report on, **1989** 597-606
Executive branch
See also Cabinet; Executive privilege
access of to federal tax returns, **1975** 829-830, 849-857
appointment powers of, and independent counsel, **1988** 465-478
drug testing of employees, **1986** 839-846
foreign policy power, and Iran-contra affair, **1987** 893, 895-905, 908-915, 919-923, 926-927
intelligence oversight by, **1976** 237-239, 241-244
interpreting powers of, judicial restraint in, **1981** 809
power of
Bork's views according to Senate committee, **1987** 738-739
in international claims, **1981** 559, 567-571
Mansfield on, **1974** 41, 62-63
public confidence in, **1976** 667-671, 674, 714, 798, 801, 819
reorganization of
Nixon call for, **1972** 88-89, 881, 884-886; **1973** 181
and Nixon's extension of executive privilege, **1973** 3, 5-6, 13, 18
Republican platform on, **1972** 651, 694
responsiveness of, Democratic platform on, **1972** 586
and treaty ratification, role of Senate, **1987** 290, 292-304, 312-315
vs. legislative power, in worker health suit, **1981** 492, 504
Executive branch agencies
creation of new in Nixon administration, **1974** 111
political uses of
House Judiciary Committee on, **1974** 655, 658-659, 715-716, 719-721, 752-753
Watergate Committee on, **1974** 601-603, 609-613, 616-617
Executive branch officials
ethics guidelines for, **1977** 27-34, 104, 110
financial disclosure, **1977** 27-34
pay raise for, **1977** 183-184, 188; **1989** 196-197, 201-204
turnover in, **1989** 200
Executive Office of the President (EOP), Sununu ethics issue, **1992** 296
Executive orders
classifying and declassifying documents, **1972** 235-245
drug testing of federal employees, **1986** 181, 255, 839-846
economic sanctions against South Africa, **1985** 531-532, 536-540; **1986** 99
economic stabilization controls, **1973** 43-45, 48-54, 577-585, 703-713
intelligence agencies
increased authority for, **1981** 861-868
reorganization, **1976** 125-128, 131-142, 236
internment of Japanese-Americans, **1988** 288-289, 292
military draft
clemency board for draft evaders, **1974** 825-826
draft evader pardon, **1977** 95-99
reforms, **1972** 247
race initiative, **1998** 668
regulations, cost-benefit analysis of, **1981** 59, 492
security clearances, **1995** 532-545
striking workers, **1995** 129-133
union political activity, **1992** 345-351
Executive privilege
at civil service hearing, in whistleblowing case, **1973** 194-195, 202-204
claimed for Nixon Cabinet officials, **1973** 3, 5-6, 13, 18
claimed for Nixon White House aides, **1972** 404-405; **1973** 413-414; **1974** 321, 326, 332, 383
Democratic platform on, **1972** 585
Gorsuch claim of in EPA investigation, **1982** 965-967
intelligence documents, congressional subpoena of, **1976** 115-116
Nixon policy on, **1973** 566, 574, 664-669, 671-673, 960-961; **1974** 287, 291-293
Nixon tapes and documents
access of Watergate committee to, **1973** 698
access of Watergate prosecutor to, **1973** 698, 859-880; **1975** 653, 658-671; **1982** 967
Court rulings on, **1973** 839-857; **1974** 621-625, 627-629, 631-638; **1977** 465-466, 471-476, 491-492, 510-516

Nixon's waiver of, **1973** 500-501, 503, 909; **1974** 296
president's congressional testimony, Ford on pardon, **1974** 887-888
Exercise. *See* Physical exercise
Exon, Jim (D-Neb.)
ban on Internet pornography, **1996** 353-354
Thomas confirmation hearings, **1991** 605-606
Export Administration Act (1979), **1987** 30
Export Control Act (1949), **1987** 30
Export controls
on chemical weapons materials, **1989** 28
on equipment for Soviet pipeline, U.S. lifting of, **1982** 879-884
on food products, Nixon request for authority over, **1973** 577, 581
on hazardous wastes, **1989** 153-160
on military technology, **1985** 605-613; **1987** 29-42
on military useful equipment to Soviets, U.S.-European agreement on, **1982** 881, 883
Export-Import Bank
credits for Soviets, in trade agreement, **1972** 845, 858
loans to China, **1984** 24
Polish credit insurance suspended for martial law, **1981** 884, 895
Exports. *See* Agricultural exports; Commodities; Trade, exports and imports
Express Scripts, antidepressant drug use in children, **2004** 747
Expropriation. *See* Nationalization
Extradition
of Noriega, **1988** 81-82
political offense exception, and U.S.-British treaty, **1986** 751-756
of terrorists, U.S.-sponsored UN proposals on, **1972** 752, 756, 759-760
Extraterrestrial life
Galileo's inspection of Jupiter's moon, **1997** 202-205
life on Mars, **1996** 471-477; **1997** 510
Extremists, in U.S. Army, task force on, **1996** 178-185
Exxon Mobil
antitrust probe of and oil prices, **1983** 921
homosexual employees policy, **1999** 901
oil company profits, congressional hearings, **2005** 781-782
Exxon Valdez (oil tanker), Alaskan oil spill, **1989** 225-237; **1990** 513-530; **1991** 641-648
Eyadema, Gnassingbe, Togo elections, **2003** 451
Eye diseases, smoking linked to, surgeon general report on, **2004** 294
Eyster, Janet, **1978** 654

F

FAA. *See* Federal Aviation Administration
Fabius, Laurent
EU constitution debate, **2005** 340
Greenpeace affair, **1985** 631-634
Fabrikant, Jacob I., **1988** 4
Faden, Ruth, **1995** 633-634, 635-636
Fadl, Jamal Ahmed, **2001** 804
Fagan, Jeffrey, crime rate declining, **1997** 681
Fagnoni, Cynthia M., welfare reform, congressional testimony on, **1999** 258-259, 261-271
Fahd bin Abdul Aziz (king of Saudi Arabia)
death of, **2005** 272
on Iraqi activities, **1981** 636
on Lebanon peace, **1981** 636-637
Middle East peace plan of, **1981** 631-637
political reform, **2003** 234
stroke victim, **2003** 229
U.S. policy in Middle East, **1981** 634-635
U.S. troop arrival, **1990** 557-560
Fahim, Makhdoom Amin, Musharraf's military role in Pakistan, **2004** 1012
Fahim, Mohammed Qasim
Afghanistan elections, **2004** 915-916, 917; **2005** 973
Afghanistan military situation, **2002** 19; **2003** 1095, 1096
Fahmy, Ismail
Arab-Israeli peace negotiations, **1973** 932
meeting with Soviet official, **1976** 171
resignation, **1977** 829
Fahrenkopf, Frank
Democratic Party platform, **1988** 557-558
parties' primary rules, **1986** 1067
political gerrymandering, **1986** 618
Fahringer, Herald Price, **1982** 676
Fair Employment and Housing Act (FEHA), California, **1987** 18-27
Fair Housing Act (1968), and zoning regulations, **1977** 36-37, 42
Fair Labor Standards Act (FLSA), **1999** 336-337, 341, 344, 345, 347, 349
1974 amendments, **1976** 377-389; **1985** 167-187
Fairbank, John K., **1973** 293
Fairchild, Wiley, in impeachment case, **1989** 584-585, 590-596
Faircloth, Lauch (R-N.C.), church arson prevention, **1997** 306
Fairfax-Brewster School, racial discrimination in admission, **1976** 392-395
Fairness doctrine, **1984** 451, 454, 460
FCC abolition of, **1987** 625-636
proposed strengthening of, **1973** 56, 59-60
Faisal (king of Saudi Arabia)
assassination of, **2003** 228
on Nixon visit to Arabia, **1974** 451, 459-462
Faisal (prince of Saudi Arabia), as foreign minister, on detentions of terrorists, **2004** 522
Falkland Islands (Malvinas) war, **1982** 283-304, 769
and Argentine disappeared persons, **1984** 791
British report, **1983** 3-23
economic summit on, **1982** 473
Haig's peace efforts, **1982** 285, 299
John Paul II on, **1982** 410
military hardware used in, **1982** 287
peace efforts in, **1982** 285-286, 294, 299-301
U.S. support for British, **1982** 478, 484, 562
Fallaci, Oriana, on U.S. in European affairs, **1973** 488, 495-498
Falun Gong (religious organizations), Chinese suppression of, **2003** 1182; **2005** 614
Falwell, Jerry
on Kennedy speech to Moral Majority, **1983** 818

Falwell, Jerry *Continued*
magazine parody of, **1988** 175-182
political influence of, **1984** 846
Republican Party convention, **2000** 512
on school prayer, **1984** 242
Ten Commandments displays, **2005** 378
on U.S.-Vatican diplomatic relations, **1984** 21
Families
See also Domestic violence
adult attitudes toward children, **1997** 422-443
African-American described by Dan Quayle, **1992** 447-448
allowances for heads of households, John Paul II on, **1981** 697, 705
Alzheimer's disease, burden on caregivers, **1987** 392-393, 397, 399-401
black
economic status of, **1983** 42, 45; **1989** 447, 451, 456-457
with female heads, **1983** 43, 47; **1985** 28-29, 35-36
state of in U.S., **1985** 27-29, 33-36
breakup of
and discarded children, **1989** 671-686
U.S. bishops on, **1985** 573, 577
Catholic ministry to, **1980** 871-882
Contract with America, **1994** 374-378
Democratic Party platform on, **1992** 696; **1996** 646-647; **2000** 614-615
divorce and alcoholism, effect of on, **1983** 335
economic plight of young families, **1992** 353-360
government offenses against, **1980** 875-876, 880
immigrant, reunification of, **1975** 559, 568-569; **1977** 908; **1981** 266, 272-273
parental consent for abortion, **1983** 543-576
parental notification of children's use of contraception, **1983** 269, 271-273
parental rights in child custody, **1982** 259-280
preservation of
programs for, **1989** 671, 676-677
Republican Party platform on, **1980** 580-581, 583, 588-589
protection of by governments, world population conference on, **1974** 784
Republican Party platform on, **1992** 801, 804-807; **1996** 526-527; **2000** 512
rights of, proposed charter of, **1980** 875-877, 880
stability of, Carter's welfare reform plan, **1977** 551, 553, 555-557
strengthening American families, **1996** 25-26
support for
Republican Party platform on, **1988** 633-639
services for poor women, **1987** 147-149, 151-154, 162-164
and U.S. economic policies, **1986** 984, 986-987, 989, 994, 999, 1001-1002
TV viewing in, **1982** 370-371
two-earner, **1992** 130-131
UN Population conference, **1994** 351-359
unwed mothers, Quayle's "Murphy Brown" speech, **1992** 443-452
values of
Bush on, **1988** 609, 612; **1989** 74
John Paul II on, **1979** 727, 737; **1982** 837-839, 847; **1985** 500-501, 506; **1986** 35-37
Reagan on, **1980** 652, 659; **1989** 59, 65
Republican Party platform on, **1984** 702-703, 715
vice-presidential debate on, **1992** 995-998
violence in, **1983** 357-364
women's role in, John Paul II on, **1981** 697, 705; **1987** 561-564
work and young parents, **1992** 167
working women and, **1985** 794-795, 800-801
Families USA
health care bill of rights, **1997** 790
health care coverage report, **2003** 848
prescription drug pricing, **2002** 947
Family and Medical Leave Act, **1997** 38; **1998** 47, 78; **1999** 48
Family Assistance Plan, Nixon proposal, **1972** 738; **1977** 553
Family law
Elian Gonzalez political asylum case, **2000** 265-276
grandparents' rights, **2000** 287-298
Family planning
abortion as means of, **1972** 301, 309
aid for population control, **1981** 13-14, 18-19
in developing countries, **1984** 521-523; **1987** 439, 441, 445-446, 449-452, 455-461
in India, **1977** 238, 241
as partial solution to economic problems, **1974** 779
in PRC constitution, **1978** 158, 174
as a right, population conference on, **1974** 778, 782
and rights and needs of women, **1975** 512-513, 519
school-based clinics for, **1986** 1058, 1064
Family Planning Services and Population Research Act, Title X, **1986** 1060
Family Support Act (1988)
amendments to, **1994** 41
signing of, **1988** 847-852
Family Violence Prevention Fund, domestic violence study, **1993** 287-291
Famine
in Africa, John Paul II on, **1985** 507-508
after nuclear war, **1985** 541, 543, 553
economic class of victims, **1984** 982-983
in North Korea, **1999** 572; **2000** 360; **2001** 271-272
in South Africa, **2002** 156-157
in sub-Saharan Africa
and disaster relief, **1984** 973-983
economic summit on aid, **1985** 350, 353-354
in Zimbabwe, **2002** 156-157
Fanfan, Duncan, sentencing of, **2004** 361
Fanfani, Amintore, **1987** 525
Fannie Mae
financial management investigations, **2004** 420
regulatory oversight, **2004** 420
Fannin, Paul J. (R-Ariz.), **1973** 466
FAO. *See* Food and Agriculture Organization
Farabundo Marti National Liberation Front (FMLN), **1984** 160; **1987** 640
El Salvador human rights, **1993** 237-239
El Salvador peace treaty, **1992** 23-32; **1993** 237
Faragher v. City of Boca Raton, **1998** 439-442, 443-452

Farah, Douglas, Liberia, support for president Charles Taylor, **2003** 771
"Farewell" papers, on Soviet technology acquisition, **1987** 33
FARL. *See* Lebanese Armed Revolutionary Faction
Farland, William, on secondhand smoke, **1993** 64
Farley, Dean E., **1988** 334
Farley, Reynolds, **1975** 614-615
Farm Animal Reform Movement (FARM), on Sweden's animal-rights law, **1988** 348
Farm price supports, reform of, **1987** 10
Farm subsidies. *See* Agricultural subsidies
Farm workers
collective bargaining for, California law, **1975** 377-399
Democratic Party platform on, **1972** 539
dignity of, John Paul II on, **1981** 714
hazards faced by, **1975** 377
hiring of temporary residents, **1986** 964-965, 968-969
Farmer, John J., Jr., racial profiling, **2000** 773
Farmers Home Administration, Grace commission proposal for, **1984** 175-176, 179
Farms
See also Agriculture
animal rights on, Swedish law on, **1988** 347-351
family
Democratic Party platform on, **1972** 571-573
U.S. bishops on survival of, **1986** 984, 987, 1002-1005
size and structure of, effect of biotechnology on, **1986** 287-306
Farooqi, Amjad Hussain, death of, **2004** 1012
al-Farouq, Omar, al Qaeda terrorist arrested in Indonesia, **2002** 703-704
Farr, William T., **1972** 509
Farrakhan, Louis
and Million Man March, **1995** 453, 455, 646, 647-648, 655-669
and NAACP, **1993** 580
Farrell, Carolyn, **1980** 413
Fascell, Dante B. (D-Fla.), Iraq war resolution, **1991** 4
Fast, Barbara, Abu Ghraib prison abuse scandal, **2004** 215; **2005** 912
Fastow, Andrew, Enron Corp. collapse, **2001** 859; **2002** 396; **2003** 336-337; **2004** 416
Fastow, Lea, Enron Corp. conviction, **2004** 416
Fatah movement, **2002** 370, 372, 1040, 1045; **2004** 807
generational conflict within, **2005** 32-33
Hamas challenge to, **2005** 33-34
Fatah political party, Palestinian elections, **2005** 27
Fattal, Antoine, **1983** 471-472
Fattouh, Rawhi, Palestinian Authority president, **2004** 808
Fauci, Anthony, biomedical research laboratories, **2004** 446-447
Faulkner, Brian, on Northern Ireland power-sharing plan, **1973** 354
Fauntroy, Walter E. (D-D.C.), **1978** 912; **1979** 649
Faux, Jeff, economic outlook, **1994** 124
Fay, Calvina, student drug testing, **2002** 427
Fay, George R., detainees prison scandal, **2004** 213
Fay, Kevin, **1987** 748
Fay, Michael, America's Cup rulings, **1989** 183-184; **1990** 267-273
Fayed, Emad "Dodi," **1997** 647, 649
Fazio, Vic (D-Calif.), **1983** 729
FBI. *See* Federal Bureau of Investigation
FCC. *See* Federal Communications Commission
FCC v. League of Women Voters of Calif., **1984** 449-463; **1987** 626-627, 633-634, 636; **1991** 263-264
FCC v. National Citizens Committee for Broadcasting, **1978** 419-432
FCC v. Pacifica Foundation, **1978** 515-531; **1986** 732, 738, 742; **1991** 821; **1997** 447-448, 451
FDA. *See* Food and Drug Administration
FDIC. *See* Federal Deposit Insurance Corporation
FEC. *See* Federal Election Commission
Federal Air Marshall Service, **2004** 146
Federal Aviation Administration (FAA)
air traffic control security, **2003** 729, 732
on air traffic safety, **1986** 253-266
airline safety enforcement, **1998** 169-179
Alaska Airlines flight 261 crash, **2000** 490
aviation security requirements, **1996** 663-671
aviation security responsibilities, **2001** 654-659; **2003** 728-729
changes in air traffic control, **1978** 793-807
commuter airline safety, **1994** 535-540
Federal Air Marshall Service, **2004** 146
fuel tank requirements, **1997** 782
inspection procedures, **1979** 949-953, 957-959, 961-963
inspection program, **1997** 115, 116; **1999** 113-114
mandatory retirement regulations, **1985** 397, 400-401, 405
performance of, **1997** 113
reorganization of, **1988** 267-272, 275-276
report on aviation safety and terrorism, **1990** 301-310
striking air controllers banned from, **1981** 622-629
TWA flight 800 crash, **1997** 780
and White House Commission report, **1997** 113-121
Y2K conversion, impact of, **1999** 762; **2000** 8-9
Federal Aviation Reauthorization Act, **1998** 170
Federal Bar Association, Stevens speech on Court role, **1985** 653-655, 666-668
Federal budget. *See under* Budget deficit; Budget, federal; Budget surplus
Federal Bureau of Investigation (FBI)
Abscam investigation, **1980** 899-906; **1981** 673-679
Allen investigation, **1981** 847-854
anthrax attack investigations, **2004** 443
antiterrorism guidelines, **2000** 279
CIA coordination with, **1975** 401-403, 419-422, 425, 433-434, 524-526
civil rights workers slayings (1964) investigations, **2005** 354
computer system failures, **2005** 897-898
counterintelligence responsibilities, **1976** 136-137, 248
on crime increase, **1981** 647
crime laboratory credibility, **1997** 785-786
crime laboratory report, **1997** 221-228
Director nomination, **1993** 609-615

Federal Bureau of Investigation (FBI) *Continued*
DNA databanks, **1992** 362-363, 366
domestic intelligence guidelines, **1976** 124, 127, 321-323, 328-330; **1983** 257-261
domestic security responsibilities, **1976** 235-236, 266, 275-283
Donovan investigation, **1982** 588, 594-596
drug testing of employees, **1986** 840
electronic surveillance, phone company assistance, **1977** 883-896
Ellsberg break-in investigation, **1974** 205-207, 211-213
espionage
Aldrich Ames case, **2001** 150-151, 155
Ames case, **1994** 475-497
Nicholson case, **1996** 794-800
Robert Philip Hanssen case, **2001** 150-158
Wen Ho Lee case, **2000** 742-745
Zakharov case, **1986** 820
foreign intelligence activities, **1976** 136-137; **1981** 83, 861
"Freemen" surrender, **1996** 362-367
Fulminante trial, **1991** 176
Guantanamo Bay detainee interrogations, **2004** 380-381
gun purchasers, records of, **2001** 722, 725-726; **2002** 959; **2003** 156, 158-160
intelligence gathering failures, **2004** 455, 468
congressional panel investigations, **2002** 531-532, 992, 995, 1007-1009, 1013; **2003** 545-546
internal security review, **2001** 154
investigative subjects and techniques, **1976** 275-281
Iowa explosion, **1989** 518, 520
Kennedy assassination investigation, **1978** 910-911, 915; **1979** 593-595, 608, 613-614
King, Martin Luther, Jr., monitoring by, **2002** 562
King, surveillance of, **1977** 113-115, 120-121
King assassination investigation, **1977** 113-123; **1978** 910, 917; **1979** 620-621
Los Angeles riots, **1992** 409-410, 413-429
National Crime Information Center, **2003** 157
national security leaks, investigation of, **1974** 487-495
pardons for former officials, **1981** 371-373
political uses of, **1976** 321-328
Senate intelligence committee on, **1975** 873-882
political uses of in Watergate, **1974** 158-163, 167-169, 176, 179, 181
House Judiciary Committee on, **1974** 657-659
Senate committee on, **1974** 601-602, 609, 617
special prosecutor on, **1975** 677-680
White House tapes on, **1974** 316, 326-327, 339-340, 347
public image of, **1975** 874-875, 877-879
reorganization of, **1976** 321, 323, 328-330
September 11 commission supports, **2004** 967
September 11 detainees (PENTTBOM investigation), **2003** 312, 314, 317-331
Sessions removal as director, **1993** 609-615
Soviet diplomats, travel rules for, **1986** 268
surveillance/investigations of groups without restrictions, **2002** 562-563; **2003** 611
terrorist watch list consolidation, **2003** 157-158; **2005** 897-898
Till, Emmett, murder investigation, **2005** 353
Tower investigation, **1989** 105-106, 111
TWA flight 800 crash, **1997** 780-786
uniform crime report, **1992** 376-378; **1995** 710-716; **1996** 732-739; **1997** 681-689; **1998** 869-877; **1999** 614-622; **2000** 852-860; **2001** 746-757; **2002** 784-793; **2003** 979-992; **2004** 761-770; **2005** 677-685
rape reports, **1992** 389-390
United Way investigation, **1992** 305
USA Patriot Act
expansion of powers under, **2003** 607, 612-613
library search requests, **2003** 609
"sneak and peek" searches, **2003** 613
violent crime report, **1994** 574-582
Violent Gang and Terrorist Organization File, **2003** 159
Virtual Case File system, **2005** 897
Waco compound incident, role in, **1993** 293-301, 819-840
Waco incident, **1999** 480-488
Watergate investigation by, **1973** 337, 500, 511-512, 571-572, 665-666, 740-741; **1974** 674-683
White House mishandling of files, **2000** 765
White House Travel Office, **1993** 531-533, 535-536
wiretaps
on Ellsberg, **1973** 538-541, 544-545
in Nixon White House, **1976** 159-168
Federal Cigarette Labeling and Advertising Act, **1992** 566-568, 572
Federal Communications Commission (FCC)
cable TV rules, **1972** 137-142
campaign advertising, **1998** 50
competitors for AT&T, **1982** 18
equal time for candidates, **1976** 695
fairness doctrine, **1984** 451, 454, 460; **1987** 625-636
Internet pornography filters in public libraries, **2003** 390
license renewal rules, **1973** 56-62
liquor advertising, **1996** 772
minority broadcasters, **1990** 419-435
offensive language on radio, **1978** 515-531
ownership of different media in same community, **1978** 419-432
public broadcasting editorials, **1984** 449-454, 456-457, 461
telecommunications company mergers, **1998** 339, 340-341
television rating system, **1997** 527
and television violence, **1993** 489
v-chip requirement ruling, **1997** 527
Federal Contract Compliance Programs, Office of, and sex segregation in the workplace, **1985** 690, 796
Federal Corrupt Practices Act (1910), **2003** 1157
Federal Corrupt Practices Act (1925), **2003** 1157
Federal courts
See also Courts, federal and state; Federal judges; Supreme Court
AT&T deregulation and antitrust settlement, **1982** 17-33
congressional impact statement for new legislation, Burger proposal, **1972** 639, 641-642

creation science in public schools, **1982** 3-16
dismantling of OEO, **1973** 453-464
electronic surveillance by law enforcement, **1977** 883-896
ERA ratification procedures, **1981** 923-938
executive privilege for subpoenaed White House tapes, **1973** 839-857
habeas corpus
claim in, based on illegal search, **1976** 521-536
death penalty appeals guidelines, **1983** 707-723
Hinckley trial for attempted assassination of Reagan, **1982** 531-537
judicial activism in, Justice Department on, **1981** 803-809
libel awards, independent appellate review of, **1984** 299-300, 302, 305-307, 309-312
national court of appeals, proposed, **1972** 953-959; **1975** 455-467
political questions considered by, **1986** 616-623, 629-632
school desegregation
busing orders, **1972** 15-21, 259-260, 264-267, 269; **1977** 447-464; **1979** 535-552
order of continued balance in, **1976** 413-423
school operation, intervention in, **1975** 68-69, 75, 78-80
state and local challenges to constitutionality of federal laws, **1985** 167-187
three-judge panels, elimination of recommended, **1972** 639-640, 642, 958
on treaty termination power, **1979** 917, 919-932
urban segregation, public housing in suburbs as remedy, **1976** 223-233
workload of, Justices on remedies for, **1982** 706, 712-719
workload of, morale, and salaries in, **1989** 195-197, 202-204
Federal Death Penalty Act, **2002** 355
Federal Deposit Insurance Corporation (FDIC)
bank failures drain funds, **1990** 815-823
challenges to, **1986** 61, 90
insolvent banks, **1988** 914-915
savings and loan bailout, **1989** 464, 468
Federal Election Campaign Act (1971)
Amendments of 1974, **2003** 1157
Nixon campaign violations of, **1973** 502
PAC spending limits, **1985** 277-294
validity of, **1976** 71-111
Federal Election Commission (FEC)
appointment of commissioners, **1976** 71-75, 98-104
campaign contribution and spending limits, **2003** 1157
Carter election reform proposals, **1977** 202, 204
creation of recommended, **1974** 611, 613
equal time for candidates, **1976** 695
limits on campaign financing, **1976** 71-111
Federal Election Commission v. National Conservative Political Action Committee, **1985** 277-294
Federal Emergency Management Agency (FEMA)
arson prevention and training grants, **1997** 304, 309-310
Brown resignation, **2005** 566
House Appropriations Committee Report, **1992** 533-542
hurricane and earthquake disasters, **1989** 668-669
Hurricane Andrew, **1992** 843-848
Hurricane Iniki, **1992** 843-848
Hurricane Katrina response, **2005** 543, 544, 566, 567, 569-571
Los Angeles earthquake, **1994** 5-6
merger with Homeland Security Department, **2005** 569
midwest floods and, **1993** 485, 486
nuclear power accidents, **1979** 858, 862
Red River floods, **1997** 232
Y2K problems, **2000** 7
Federal employees
AIDS employment policy, **1988** 417
civil service reform, **1978** 137-148
cuts in hiring and cap on pay increases, **1978** 688-689; **1979** 88-89
discharge for political beliefs, **1980** 259, 268
drug testing of, **1986** 180-181, 254-255, 839-846
hiring freezes, **1980** 247-248, 254, 652, 658-659; **1981** 138, 335
incompetent, flexibility in firing, **1978** 137-139, 143
increase in number of, **1974** 97
merit pay for managers, **1978** 137-139, 143
pay adjustments of, CBO analysis of, **1976** 187-188
pay increases for, **1974** 97, 111; **1977** 183-184, 188; **1987** 13-14
political rights of, and Hatch Act revision, **1976** 543; **1977** 199, 201, 205
productivity cost of King holiday, **1983** 884
smoke-free environment for, **1986** 1080-1081, 1090
strikes by, **1981** 621-629, 805
work furlough for, **1981** 642, 831-834
Federal Energy Administration (FEA), options and strategies for decade (1975-1985), **1974** 909-918
Federal Energy Regulatory Commission (FERC), "standard market design" for public utilities, **2003** 1016-1017
Federal Express, labor union campaigns, **2005** 487
Federal Food, Drug and Cosmetic Act, Delaney Clause, **1996** 73, 467-468
Federal Home Loan Bank Board
charter for Rebozo associate, **1973** 976
cost of savings and loan crisis, **1988** 913
replacement of, **1989** 463-464
Federal Interagency Forum on Child and Family Statistics
well-being of children indicators, **1997** 425
well-being of children report, **1999** 384, 387-400
Federal judges
See also under names of Supreme Court justices
"activist" judges, **2005** 364
Carter appointments, **1987** 52
impeachment of, **1989** 583-596; **1999** 18
Nixon appointments, **1972** 881, 890
Reagan appointments, **1987** 43-45, 51-52
reconfirmation of, American Party platform on, **1972** 617
retention of, **1975** 456
salaries of, **1977** 183-184; **1989** 195-204
selection of on merit, **1978** 327, 333

Federal judges *Continued*
sentencing discretion of, **1987** 407-409, 413, 416-418
workload of, Burger on, **1972** 639-643
Federal Judicial Center, studies of federal courts, **1972** 953-954
Federal Labor Relations Authority
creation of, **1978** 139, 144, 147
PATCO decertification by, **1981** 622
Federal Legal Council, Smith speech on judicial activism, **1981** 805-809
Federal Mediation and Conciliation Service, **1997** 629
in coal miners' strike, **1978** 112, 115, 124
Pittston coal strike settled, **1990** 21
Federal Power Commission (FPC), on New York City blackout, **1977** 545-550
Federal Railroad Administration (FRA), railroad safety regulations, **1996** 189-198
Federal Reserve Board
Bush economic report, **1992** 98
chairman
Bernanke confirmation hearings, **2005** 142
Greenspan appointment, **1987** 511-516
Volcker reappointment, **1983** 595-597
changing role under Bush, **1990** 81-82
"destabilizing" policies of, Republican platform on, **1984** 661-662, 669-670
discount rate increase, **1978** 683-686, 698
economic recovery, **1975** 100, 102, 106
and gradual reduction in money growth, **1984** 130-131
Greenspan on, **1991** 850-856
and moderate growth policy, **1983** 121-122, 124, 129-130
and monetary restraint, **1977** 717-719, 725, 728-731; **1980** 159, 175-176, 178-179
and tight money growth, Reagan CEA, **1985** 87
energy prices, **2004** 186-194
independence of, **1976** 716-717; **1980** 568, 621-622; **1981** 213, 222
inflation control, **1972** 961-970; **1984** 101
with credit restraint, **1979** 771-774, 776-780; **1980** 244-246, 249-250, 255
and gradual reduction in money growth, **1982** 30, 121, 127
moderate growth of money supply and credit, **1974** 419, 423-424
with monetary restraint, **1974** 862; **1980** 110
and monetary targets, **1981** 107, 111-112, 125-129
and stable monetary policy, **1980** 219, 223-228
interest rates, **2002** 51, 52; **2005** 139
and monetarist view of Reagan CEA, **1986** 59-60, 72-74, 77; **1988** 117-118, 129-132
money growth targets, Joint Economic Committee on, **1981** 294-296, 299-301, 318-319
stock market crash (1987)
action in, **1987** 834, 837, 841-842; **1988** 10, 14, 27, 132-135
regulatory role after, **1988** 11-12, 15, 30-31, 118, 132-133
tight monetary policy, and debt crisis, **1982** 972
trade and budget deficits, **2004** 235-245
Federal Savings and Loan Insurance Corporation (FSLIC), depletion of fund, **1988** 913-918
Federal Trade Commission (FTC)
alcohol advertising and youth, **2002** 178
America OnLine-Time Warner merger, **2000** 1034-1046
cigarette advertising, **1992** 565-566; **1994** 173, 175
cigarette health warnings, **1972** 46; **1982** 164-165
claims of U.S. Jews against East Germany, **1974** 802
corporate mergers, **1998** 338-353
first black member of, **1992** 33
liquor advertising, **1996** 772-773
marketing violent entertainment to children, **2000** 729-739; **2001** 73
prescription drug price advertising, **1976** 352
spam e-mail messages, **2002** 70
tobacco advertising, **2003** 265
TV advertising of little cigars, **1973** 64
weight-loss advertising, **2002** 624-632
Federal Trade Commission Act (1914), intra-enterprise conspiracy doctrine, **1984** 414, 422
Federal Water Pollution Control Act Amendments (1972), EPA authority to regulate chemical discharge, **1977** 131-141
Federalism
Court on federal and state powers, **1985** 168-169
in criminal justice, violent crime task force on, **1981** 663-667
new, in Nixon budget, **1973** 169; **1974** 98-99, 106-108
new, Reagan proposal, **1982** 73-74, 80-81, 124, 161-162
new, scaled-back Reagan plan, **1983** 77, 86
and states' rights, Meese criticism of Court, **1985** 480, 484-485
Federation of American Health Systems, on for-profit hospitals, **1986** 489
Federation of American Scientists, **1990** 755
on White House science adviser reorganization, **1973** 782-783
Fedorov, Yevgeny, **1972** 805-806
Feeney, Tom (R-Fla.), on judicial reform and separation of powers, **2005** 181
Fehr, Donald, **1986** 171
steroid use in baseball, **2005** 214-216
Feig, Stephen, breast cancer study, **1993** 907
Fein, Bruce E.
on affirmative action decision, **1987** 334
on civil rights rulings, **1989** 324
Feinberg, Kenneth R., September 11 attacks victim's fund, **2003** 544-545
Feingold, Russell D. (D-Wis.)
campaign finance reform, **1997** 31, 33, 827; **1998** 50, 893; **1999** 56; **2003** 1155; **2004** 777
Clinton impeachment trial, **1999** 17
police powers legislation, **2001** 641
warrantless domestic surveillance, **2005** 962
Feinstein, Dianne (D-Calif.)
base closings in California, **1995** 409
California gubernatorial recall election, **2003** 1007
on California's English-only law, **1986** 960
Clinton censure resolution, **1999** 21
on domestic partners measure, **1989** 306

Feith, Douglas J., on NATO alliance, **2002** 885
Feldblum, Chai, disability, definition of, **1999** 319
Feldman, William, on moon ice findings, **1998** 116, 119
Feldstein, Martin S.
  economic report, **1983** 121; **1984** 119-121
  on Reagan budget, **1984** 102
  resignation, **1985** 80
  on Soviet pipeline sanctions, **1982** 881
Felici, Pericle, **1980** 872
Felipe (crown prince of Spain), demonstrations against terrorists, **2004** 107
Felis, Kenneth P., in insider trading case, **1987** 882, 884-885
Fellay, Bernard, excommunication of, **1988** 490, 492
Fellner, William J., **1974** 70
Fel-Pro, Inc., **1996** 42
Felt, W. Mark
  on FBI break-ins, **1976** 322
  Reagan pardon for, **1981** 371-373
FEMA. *See* Federal Emergency Management Agency
Feminist Majority Foundation, antiabortion demonstrations, **2000** 433
Feminists for Life, **2005** 561
Fenyvesi, Charles, **1989** 340
FERC. *See* Federal Energy Regulatory Commission
Fergany, Nader, Arab world development, **2002** 484
Ferguson, Sarah (Duchess of York), **1992** 1060
Ferguson v. City of Charleston, **2001** 407
Fernald, Ohio, nuclear plant, radiation leak from, **1989** 356
Fernandez, Carlos, general strike leader arrested, **2003** 280-281
Fernandez, Ferdinand F., pledge of allegiance, constitutionality of, **2002** 385, 390
Fernandez, Joseph F.
  Iran-contra activities of, **1989** 393
  Iran-contra trial, **1991** 430; **1994** 12, 17
Fernando, Enrique, **1984** 926
Fernstrom, Madelyn, on dietary guidelines, **2005** 4
Ferrarese, Laura, age of universe, **1994** 462
Ferraro, Geraldine A. (D-N.Y.)
  acceptance speech, **1984** 647, 649, 655-658
  Senate candidacy in 1992 and 1998, **2000** 906
  vice presidential candidacy, **1984** 550, 728; **2000** 906
Ferrell, Trevor, **1986** 41, 48
Ferrer, Jaime, **1987** 845
Ferro, Simon, Panama Canal transfer ceremony, **1999** 853
Fertilization, in vitro
  frozen embryo custody, **1989** 551-559
  Vatican on, **1987** 267-268, 276, 281-282
Feshbach, Murray, AIDS in Russia study, **2005** 54
Fessler, Pamela, **1992** 520
Fetal protection
  aborted, standard of care for, state laws on, **1976** 484, 488
  Supreme Court on, **1991** 143-153
Fetal research
  Catholic teaching on, **1995** 155
  ethics of, HEW regulations on, **1975** 543-556
Fhimah, Lamen Khalifa, Lockerbie case acquittal, **2003** 1223
Fichtenberg, Robert G., **1973** 57
Field v. Clark, **1998** 428
Field Foundation, task force on hunger, **1985** 190
Field Museum, on Native American skeletal remains, **1989** 540
Fielding, Fred T., **1985** 493
Fielding, Lewis J.
  office break-in, **1974** 33-40, 205-214, 443, 661-664; **1975** 656-657, 663, 667
    national security grounds for, **1974** 411-417
Fields, Cleo (D-La.), **1995** 370
Fields, Jack (R-Texas), "v-chip" for televisions, **1993** 489
Fiers, Alan D., Jr.
  Iran-contra affair, **1991** 429-436, 619, 651-652; **1992** 1073-1079
  Iran-contra conviction, **1991** 619; **1994** 12, 17, 18
Figueiredo, Joao Baptista, **1985** 4
Figueredo, Reinaldo, **1993** 237
Fillmore, Millard, **1992** 717
Finance Committee to Re-elect the President, secret funds of, **1973** 413-414; **1974** 604, 613-614
Financial Accounting Standards Board, **2004** 421
Financial disclosure
  Carter assets on taking office, **1977** 28, 33-34
  by executive branch officials, **1977** 27-34
Financial institutions
  See also Banks and banking; Savings and loan institutions
  mergers, **1998** 339-340
  reform, CEA report on, **1991** 93-96
Financial Institutions Reform, Recovery, and Enforcement Act (1989), **1990** 816-817
  signing of, **1989** 463-468
Financial markets
  See also Stock market
  reaction to Fed restraint, **1979** 771-772
  regulation of, **1984** 143-144
Financial policy. *See* Recession
Findings, presidential
  overriding embargo on arms sales to Iran, **1986** 1016, 1024
    inadequate consultation on, **1987** 222-223, 225, 229
  overriding U.S. embargo on arms to Iran, **1986** 1052-1053
  requirement for covert operations, **1987** 897, 904, 908-910, 912
Findley, Paul (R-Ill.), **1982** 181
Fine, Glenn A.
  INS visa investigations, **2002** 844
  treatment of September 11 detainees, **2003** 312-314, 315; **2004** 376
  Virtual Case File system, **2005** 897
Fineberg, Harvey V., on swine flu immunization, **1978** 670-681
Finland
  EU membership, **2004** 197
  euro currency, **1998** 271
  Gorbachev visit, **1989** 400
Finley, James K., **1990** 575

Finn, Chester E., Jr., education reports, **1986** 218; **1987** 682; **1988** 378
Fire Management Policy Review Team, report of, **1988** 941-946
Firefighters Local Union No. 1784 v. Stotts, **1984** 365-385
Firestone Tire & Rubber Co.
tire recall agreement, **1978** 719-727
tire recall and Ford sport utility vehicle accidents, **2000** 688-699
First, Neal, cloning research, **1997** 212, 215
First Accounts program, **2000** 50
First American Bankshares, Inc., BCCI banking scandal, **1991** 621-636
First English Evangelical Lutheran Church of Glendale v. Los Angeles County, **1987** 531-546
First National Bank of Boston v. Bellotti, **1978** 307-324
FirstEnergy Corporation, massive power blackout, **2003** 1014, 1015, 1021; **2004** 190
Firyubin, Nikolai P., **1972** 494-495
FISA. *See* Foreign Intelligence Surveillance Act
Fiscal policy
See also Government spending
CBO analysis of for 1977 budget, **1976** 177, 179, 183
in economic plan of Joint Economic Committee, **1981** 301-303, 320-322
encouraging economic growth, **1980** 219-221, 223
Nixon's CEA on, **1974** 69-71, 78-79
Fischer, Dean E.
Israeli annexation, **1981** 900
Shostakovich refugee status, **1981** 375-377
Fischer, Joschka
and ABM treaty, **2001** 284
German foreign minister, **2005** 873-874
Israeli-Palestinian conflict, **2004** 629
nuclear weapons proliferation, **1999** 603
Fischer, Markus, **1984** 400
Fischer, Stanley, Thailand economy, **1998** 725
Fish, Hamilton, Jr. (R-N.Y.), on Twenty-seventh Amendment, **1992** 440
Fish and Wildlife Service (FWS)
management of Alaskan lands, **1978** 732
spotted owl ruling, **1991** 275-285; **1993** 496
Fish industry and fisheries
Alaskan oil spill impact on, **1989** 225, 227-230
Chesapeake Bay crab and oyster fisheries, **2004** 603
climate change and, **1988** 865
conservation of, UN treaty on, **1995** 524-531
dead zone in Gulf of Mexico, **2004** 603
in exclusive economic zones, and Law of the Sea Treaty, **1982** 346, 352-355
fish farms, federal regulation, **2004** 603
as food resources, **1980** 680-681, 689
and Mount St. Helens eruption, **1980** 812-814, 820-822
ocean protection policy, **2004** 602-625
Polish rights in U.S. waters, suspension of, **1981** 884, 896
salmon and dams, **2004** 668-669
sustainable fisheries, **2004** 619-620
Fishback, Ian, McCain amendment on treatment of detainees, **2005** 909-910
Fisher, Louis, North Iran-contra conviction, **1990** 493
Fisher, Mary D.
appointment to AIDS commission, **1992** 892
Republican convention speaker, **1992** 709-710, 713-715, 783
Fisher v. United States, **1998** 402
Fisheries. *See* Fish industry and fisheries
Fiske, Robert B., Whitewater investigations, **2000** 763
Fissile Material Cut-Off Treaty, **2004** 327
Fitzgerald, A. Ernest
whistleblowing case
Nixon on, **1973** 194-195, 202-204
and presidential immunity, **1972** 540-559
Fitzgerald, Garret
British-Irish accord on Northern Ireland, **1985** 723-732
New Ireland Forum, **1984** 315
Fitzgerald, Patrick, illegal disclosure of covert CIA agent, special investigator, **2005** 249, 701-705
FitzGerald, Peter (Irish deputy police commissioner), Hariri assassination, UN investigation, **2005** 690-692
Fitzgerald, Peter G., charitable choice, **2001** 135
Fitzwater, Marlin
on apartheid vote, **1992** 285
on Beck executive order, **1992** 346
FBI files on, **2000** 765
funding antidrug program, **1989** 501
Japanese criticism of U.S. workers, **1992** 13
Los Angeles riots, **1992** 407
Marcos indictment, **1988** 869
Nicaraguan cease-fire, **1988** 242
Quayle's "Murphy Brown" speech, **1992** 444
Washington summit, **1987** 993
Flag, respect for, Dole view on, **1995** 579
Flag burning
court cases, **1990** 357-365
desecration as free speech, **1989** 343-354
Flag Protection Act, **1990** 357-365
Flake, Jeff (R-Ariz.), Davis-Bacon Act, reinstatement of, **2005** 489
Flavin, Daniel, alcoholism definition, **1992** 849
FleetBoston Financial Group, mutual funds scandal, **2004** 419
Fleischer, Ari
ABM treaty withdrawal, **2001** 930, 934
ballistic "fingerprinting," **2002** 962
Brazil-U.S. relations, **2002** 779
Bush administration abortion policy, **2001** 128
Bush presidential campaign and election, **2000** 1027; **2001** 525
campaign finance reform legislation, **2002** 38
Chechnya, international terrorists in, **2001** 894
Iraq-Niger uranium sales claim, **2005** 700
sex education and sexual health, **2001** 458
Social Security reform, presidential commission on, **2001** 915
U.S. military action against Iraq, **2001** 851
Venezuela coup attempt, **2002** 203-204, 206
Fleischer, David, Enron Corp. earnings, **2001** 860
Fleisher, Belton M., on minimum and youth wage, **1983** 785-790

Flemming, Arthur S., **1983** 915
Flerov, Inessa, **1986** 822
Flerov, Viktor, **1986** 822
Fletcher, James, future of NASA, **1987** 650-651, 653
Fletcher, Joseph, **1988** 833
Flight Safety Foundation, on air traffic control system, **1986** 253, 265
Flinn, Kelly, **1997** 656
Flint, Lara, terrorism watch lists, **2004** 145
Flood, Ann, on breast cancer research, **1993** 907
Flood, Daniel J. (D-Pa.), bribery indictment, **1978** 51-64
Floods
  See also Tsunami disaster in Indian Ocean Region
  Haiti floods and hurricanes, **2004** 99
  Midwest floods, Clinton remarks, **1993** 483-486
  Red River area (North Dakota and Minnesota), Clinton remarks, **1997** 229-233
  Venezuela, **1999** 469
Florida
  abortion restrictions, **1989** 367-368
  busing issue, **1972** 201-206
  death row executions, **1999** 829-830
  presidential elections vote recount, **2000** 999-1024; **2001** 522
  Schiavo end-of-life care case, **2005** 154-161
  tobacco industry class-action case, **2000** 557-558
Florida v. College Savings Bank, **1999** 334
Florio, James J. (D-N.J.), **1989** 368
Flowers, Gennifer, **1992** 155-156
Flowers, Robert B., **1997** 742
Flowers, Walter (D-Ala.), **1974** 714
Floyd, Henry F., Padilla detainee case, **2004** 451
Flu pandemic
  See also Avian influenza (bird flu)
  preparedness, congressional response, **2005** 753
  swine flu immunization (1976), **1978** 669-672, 674
  U.S. government plan for combating, **2005** 744-764
  vaccine production, **2005** 751-752
Flu vaccine shortage
  congressional hearings, **2004** 640, 642, 747
  FDA officials on, **2004** 640, 642, 747, 850
  GAO report, **2004** 639-651
  WHO on, **2004** 643, 925
Fluorocarbons 11 and 12, proposed banning of, **1975** 437-453
Flynn, Laurie M., care of the mentally ill report, **1990** 573-598
Flynn, Michael T., Guantanamo Bay detentions, **2002** 832
Flynn, Raymond L.
  Bosnia crisis, **1993** 660
  Census Bureau undercount, **1991** 444
  Stuart murder hoax, **1990** 35-40
  Vatican-Israel Diplomatic Accord, **1993** 1035
Flynn, Robert J., release of by China, **1973** 292, 296
Flynt, John J., Jr. (D-Ga.), Korean influence-buying investigation, **1977** 769, 771-774; **1978** 846-847
Flynt, Larry, free speech in satire of public figures, **1988** 176-182
FMC Corp., EPA regulation of chemical discharge, **1977** 131-141
FMLN. *See* Farabundo Marti National Liberation Front
FNLA. *See* National Front for the Liberation of Angola
Focus on the Family
  abortions, and ultrasound technology, **2005** 818
  Ten Commandments displays, **2005** 379
Fogarty, William M., on U.S. downing of Iranian airliner, **1988** 704, 707
Foley, James B.
  Aristide resignation, **2004** 96
  on international bribery, **1997** 801
Foley, Kathleen M., end-of-life care, **1997** 326
Foley, Laurence, U.S. diplomat killed by terrorists in Amman, **2002** 740; **2005** 400
Foley, Thomas S. (D-Wash.)
  bipartisan accord on Nicaraguan contras, **1989** 164
  Bush victory speech, **1991** 121-122
  Bush's leadership, **1990** 51
  Bush's no-taxes pledge, **1990** 409
  congressional bicentennial, **1989** 130-131
  Constitutional amendment (27th), **1992** 440
  election defeat, **1994** 514
  election to speaker, **1989** 240-241
  funding antidrug program, **1989** 501
  Iraq war resolution, **1991** 4, 5
  NAFTA, **1993** 956
  Somalian relief, **1992** 1068
  State of the Union address, Democratic response to, **1990** 59-62; **1992** 57, 68-72
  U.S. Capitol bicentennial, **1993** 895, 901-903
Foley Brothers, Inc. v. Filardo, **1992** 461-462
Folsom, Jim, Jr., appointment as governor, **1993** 303
Food aid
  for developing countries
    UN conference on, **1974** 939-941, 952-953
    UN resolution on, **1975** 610
  federal programs, and hunger in U.S., **1984** 3-17; **1985** 190-191, 193, 199-205
  and human behavior, **1984** 973, 976, 985-986, 992-994
  private programs in U.S., **1984** 6, 10-11, 16-17
  and production, U.S. Catholic bishops on, **1986** 1002-1005, 1009
  state and local programs in U.S., **1984** 6, 15
  as stopgap measure, poverty summit on, **1981** 769, 773-774, 777
  surplus commodities, efficient distribution of in U.S., **1984** 9-10
  suspension of to Poland, **1981** 883-884, 895
  U.S.
    to developing countries, **1974** 833-834, 841-843, 850
    increase in world, Carter proposal, **1981** 13-14, 19-20
Food and Agriculture Organization (FAO)
  African drought, **1984** 973, 978-979, 982, 992-993
  agricultural production in developing countries, **1972** 859-860, 865-866
  flu pandemic prevention, **2005** 750
  role in World Food Council, **1974** 940
  tobacco industry, support for, **2000** 54
  worldwide famine reduction, **2002** 690

Food and Agriculture Organization (FAO)
Continued
worldwide hunger, **2003** 756-757
Food and Drug Administration (FDA)
abortion pill controversy, **2000** 429
acupuncture treatments, **1997** 750
AIDS generic combination drug approvals, **2004** 432; **2005** 51
anthrax vaccine drug approval, **2004** 446
antidepressants and suicide in children, **2004** 640, 746-752
artificial heart implants, **2001** 476
AZT approval, **1987** 327-330
cigarette regulations
authority for, **1999** 538-539; **2000** 556-557; **2001** 223
proposed, **1995** 670-679; **1997** 331
Crawford commissioner nomination, **2005** 816
drug names, **1999** 780
drug safety review system, protecting patients from unsafe drugs, **2004** 850-866
flu vaccine inspections, **2004** 640, 642, 747, 850
food inspections, **1997** 692; **1998** 523-524
food labeling rules, **1990** 175-181
food safety system, **1994** 379-386; **1997** 690; **2001** 699-700; **2002** 583
genetically engineered foods, **1992** 469-473
HIV screening, **1992** 336
interferon approval, **1986** 481-485
lovastatin approval, **1987** 780
morning-after pill controversy, **2003** 998-999; **2005** 814-831
nicotine as a drug, **1997** 331, 333
nicotine levels in cigarettes, **1994** 205-217; **1997** 333, 334
nutrition labeling for trans fats, **2003** 483
Prempro labeling, **2002** 505
prescription drug advertising, **2002** 947-949
prescription drug importation rules, **2004** 984
silicone breast implants, **1992** 367-373; **1995** 515-523
smoking as "pediatric disease," **1997** 336
tobacco products regulation, **1999** 538-539; **2000** 555, 556-557; **2003** 261, 264-265; **2004** 282-283
tobacco sales to children, regulations against, **1996** 589-599
TPA approval, **1987** 875-879
trials of AIDS drugs, **1988** 429-430
Food and Drug Administration Modernization Act (FDAMA), **1998** 89; **2005** 9
Food and nutrition. *See* Nutrition
Food Assistance, Presidential Task Force on, **1984** 3-17
Food guide pyramid, **1992** 397, 400; **1996** 4-5
revised, **2005** 3-5
Spanish-language version, **2005** 5
Web site, **2005** 5
Food labeling
of fat content, **1984** 1040, 1043
FDA rules, **1990** 175-181
for trans fatty acids, **2003** 482-483
Food prices
as cause of inflation, **1974** 419-421
controls on in Nixon program, **1973** 43-44, 48, 52-53, 220, 222, 577-585, 703-710, 712-713
increases in
and meat price ceilings, **1973** 427-428, 430-431, 434-435
and poor harvests, **1974** 864
increases on, impact on world economy, **1975** 187-193, 195-197
Nixon CEA on, **1973** 186, 189-190; **1974** 70, 76, 78
Food production
in developing countries, trade policies promoting increase in, **1975** 609-610
genetically engineered foods, **1992** 469-473
impact of population, income, and resources on, **1980** 666, 668-670, 677-680
self-sufficiency, in Third World, **1984** 980-981, 984-985
Food pyramid. *See* Food guide pyramid
Food Quality Protection Act, **1996** 467-470
Food safety
agency established, **1998** 523
agency proposals, **1997** 693; **2001** 700
agriculture department initiative, **1997** 690-698
beef and poultry recalls, **2002** 581-582
bioterrorism and, **2004** 446
enforcement, **2001** 700-701
federal dietary guidelines on, **2005** 13
food labeling rules, **1990** 175-181
foodborne illness
contaminated salad bars in Oregon, **2001** 699
GAO report on, **1998** 521-531
genetically altered foods, **1992** 469-473; **1999** 401-411
ground beef contamination, **1994** 404
Hazard Analysis and Critical Control Points (HACCP), **1996** 415, 416-417; **1997** 690, 694-697; **1998** 521-522, 525, 527, 528; **2000** 883-884; **2001** 700-701; **2002** 58-581
inspection service, **1994** 379-386, 404
inspections, GAO report on, **2002** 579-589
mad cow disease and, **2000** 883-884; **2001** 698-699; **2002** 583; **2003** 1234-1244
meat inspection rules, **1996** 414-417
National Residue Program (NRP), **1994** 381, 382-383
pesticide regulation reform, **1996** 46-470
salmonella testing, **2001** 699, 700-701
threats to food supply, GAO report on, **2001** 698-709
unsafe chemicals in food, **1994** 379-386
Food Safety and Inspection Service (FSIS), **1998** 523-524, 523-528; **2001** 699-700; **2002** 579
Food Security Act (1985), **1986** 83-84; **1987** 10, 141
Food shortages
global
dealing with, Kissinger on, **1975** 10
NATO concern about, Ford on, **1975** 354, 358
recurrent, food conference on, **1974** 939-953
international cooperation to overcome, **1974** 113-115, 118, 955-956, 968
and population growth, **1974** 777-780, 790; **1987** 441, 448
Food stamp program
in Carter budget, **1977** 127

cutbacks, **1996** 453
guaranteed "minimum security" income to replace, **1981** 40
hunger task force recommendations for, **1984** 15-16
participation in, **1984** 7-9, 14; **1985** 190, 200-201
Reagan budget cuts in, **1982** 145; **1983** 41-42, 49, 109, 766-767; **1985** 190-191, 202, 203
reform of, Carter on, **1979** 390, 394; **1981** 68-69
revision of eligibility for
in Ford budget, **1977** 59
in Reagan budget, **1981** 218, 641
state responsibility for, Reagan proposal, **1982** 74, 81
strengthening, Physician Task Force on, **1985** 190-191, 203
use declining, **1999** 391
Y2K computer conversion, **1998** 553
Food supplies
building reserves in U.S., Humphrey on, **1974** 873
international reserves system, U.S. proposal, **1974** 842, 850
maintaining global, Kissinger on, **1973** 809, 814-815
stability of, international cooperation on, Kissinger proposal, **1975** 598-599
Foot, Michael, at Reagan address to British Parliament, **1982** 478
Footwear, U.S. restriction of imports, **1988** 339, 341, 344-346
Forbes, Malcolm S. "Steve," Jr., tax reform, **2001** 401
Forced labor. *See* Human trafficking; Slavery
Ford, Betty, **1977** 862; **1993** 906
Ford, Carl, Jr., on Bolton UN ambassador appointment, **2005** 237
Ford, Gerald R.
arms control
nuclear nonproliferation, **1976** 823-824, 826-829, 832-834
nuclear testing for peaceful purposes, treaty on, **1976** 369-374
assassinations, congressional testimony on, **1978** 912
bicentennial of Declaration of Independence, **1976** 509-516
budget, CBO analysis of, **1976** 178-179, 181-182
budget messages, **1975** 83-98; **1976** 37-43; **1977** 57-63
campaigns and elections
acceptance speech, **1976** 665-673
campaign financing, **1976** 759-771
concession statement, **1976** 841-843
debates with Carter, **1976** 693-719, 733-757, 797-821
potential vice presidential nominee, **1980** 651
presidential nomination, **1976** 665-666
at Republican convention, **1984** 728-729; **1988** 590
Republican Party platform, **1976** 617-618
Congress, first message to as president, **1974** 696-697, 699-705
economic policy
domestic summit on inflation and recession, **1974** 861, 876-880
economy and energy TV message, **1975** 16-17, 27-32
Giscard d'Estaing meeting, **1974** 981-985
on recession, **1974** 975-980
economic reports, **1975** 99-100; **1976** 45-52; **1977** 65-66, 68-74
international, **1975** 187-199
Egyptian abrogation of Soviet treaty, **1976** 170
Elizabeth II visit, **1976** 538-541
federal election system reform, **2001** 526
food and energy shortages, UN speech, **1974** 833-834, 841-843
foreign policy
military aid and arms sales, **1977** 4
presidential power in, **1975** 223, 226, 228, 232, 235, 238
speech to Congress, **1975** 223-238
healing of U.S. by, Carter on, **1977** 89-90
health insurance plan, **1978** 544
on Helsinki agreement, **1975** 560
intelligence, withholding documents from Congress, **1977** 116
intelligence agencies
CIA activities, **1976** 115
CIA activities in Chile, **1974** 805; **1975** 874
guidelines for, **1975** 403; **1976** 236
reorganization of, **1976** 125-142
Senate's CIA report, **1975** 710
Japan visit, **1974** 955-956, 958-965
Mayaguez incident, **1975** 311-314
minorities, commission on status of, **1988** 187
NATO, U.S. commitment to, **1975** 353-359
New York City fiscal crisis, **1975** 861-869; **1976** 863-864
Nixon pardon, **1974** 811-817; **1975** 143; **1977** 323, 355-356
agreement on presidential files, **1975** 667-668
congressional testimony on, **1974** 887-900
as option, **1974** 766-769, 774
Nixon's Middle East trip, **1974** 469-470
NSC under, **1987** 212
nuclear first-use in Korea, **1975** 496, 504
nuclear fuel and technology controls, **1976** 823-838
oil crisis
prices and economic breakdown, **1975** 4
Saudi's moderate price increase, **1976** 937
use of force in, **1975** 5
oil price shocks, **1998** 501
Panama Canal treaties, **1977** 593
Polish trade and technology agreements, **1974** 883-886
presidential election, **2004** 317
presidential materials legislation, **1977** 465, 468-469
presidential power to impound funds, **1975** 136
presidential swearing-in, **1974** 684, 686, 688-689, 695-699
presidential transfer of power, **1985** 492
press conferences, **1974** 765-775; **1976** 759-771; **1988** 843
Reagan presidential library dedication, **1991** 735, 743-744
Rockefeller vice presidential nomination, **1974** 707-711, 987

Ford, Gerald R. *Continued*
South Korea visit, **1974** 955-956, 965-967
Soviet relations
Solzhenitsyn in U.S., **1975** 481-482
Vladivostok agreement, **1974** 955-958, 967-972; **1977** 244, 250, 252; **1979** 413, 455; **1985** 750
State of the Union addresses, **1975** 15-16, 18-27; **1976** 13-26; **1977** 45-56
swine flu immunization program, **1978** 669-672, 674-676, 681
trade bill signing, **1974** 902
UN, U.S. relations with, **1975** 826
UN Zionism resolution, **1975** 825-826
vetoes, **1975** 18; **1976** 709-713, 780
vice presidency
appointment, **1974** 696
confirmation, **1973** 969-970
nomination, **1973** 827
swearing-in ceremony, **1973** 969-973
Vietnam war
accounting for MIAs, **1977** 207-208
draft evader clemency program, **1977** 95, 97-98; **1984** 349
U.S. domestic reconciliation, **1975** 251-253, 262-266
U.S. evacuation from Saigon, **1975** 266
volunteerism summit, **1997** 238, 239-240
Watergate
defense of Nixon, **1974** 674, 889, 891
investigation of involvement, **1976** 760-764, 802-803
lesson of, **1974** 236
Ford, Guillermo, election of, **1989** 702, 706
Ford, Harold P., Gates CIA confirmation hearings, **1991** 651, 661-664
Ford, Holland
on Advanced Camera for Surveys (ACS), **2002** 217
age of universe, **1994** 462
Ford, Leslie
breast cancer screening, **2002** 510
tamoxifen trials, **1998** 200-201
Ford, Tyrone, **1986** 41, 48
Ford, Wendell H. (D-Ky.), **1988** 270
Ford, William D. (D-Mich.), **1989** 195
Ford v. Wainwright, **1993** 149-150, 151
Ford Motor Co.
economic situation, **2005** 137, 140
Firestone tire recall, **2000** 688-699
health benefits for domestic partners, **2000** 162
Internet-based parts exchange, **2000** 302
"junk bond" credit rating, **2005** 200
SUV sales declining, **2005** 780
underfunded health liability, **2005** 200
underfunded pension plans, **2004** 738; **2005** 200
Ford Motor Co. v. EEOC, **1998** 450
Fordice, Kirk, desegregation in Mississippi colleges, **1992** 575-587
Fordice, United States v., **1992** 575-587; **1995** 239, 242, 245-247
Foreign Agents Registration Act, B. Carter's Libyan contacts, **1980** 907-917
Foreign aid
See also Arms sales; Military aid
congressional opposition to, **1999** 700-702
Democratic platform on, **1976** 583-584
food aid to Soviet Union, **1990** 807-814
former Russian republics, **1992** 520-521, 530
humanitarian, for Southeast Asia, Ford requests for, **1975** 223-225, 227-230
Israel, **1992** 655-657
Nixon request for, **1974** 277-286
Nixon speech on aid to Russia, **1992** 255-265
in Reagan budget, **1984** 111-112
Republican Party platform on, **1980** 646-647; **1984** 715-716
Sheik Jaber's UN address, **1990** 656, 659
tied to human rights, **1977** 3-4, 10, 12-13, 19-20; **1980** 189, 192, 194-195; **1982** 107, 109
Ukraine, **1994** 364
Foreign Assistance Act (1961), human rights report required by, **1985** 145
Foreign Assistance Act (1971), and countries protecting drug traffickers, **1972** 647
Foreign Corrupt Practices Act, **1997** 800-807
Foreign Espionage Act, **1999** 241
Foreign governments, donations from, in Iran-contra affair, **1987** 897-898, 901-902, 904, 920
Foreign Intelligence Advisory Board
CIA oversight by, **1975** 413-414
Reagan recommissioning of, **1981** 862-864
Foreign Intelligence Surveillance Act (FISA), **2002** 562; **2003** 613; **2005** 959
Foreign languages
competence of Americans, and Japan trade, **1985** 320, 322
early study of, **1983** 414, 428-431; **1986** 812
need for emphasis on, **1987** 683, 687-688, 695-696
in undergraduate education, **1984** 998-1003; **1985** 128, 143
Foreign Military Assistance Act (1976), and human rights in recipient countries, **1977** 4
Foreign policy
See also State Department
activist policy, Clinton on, **1999** 699-710
agricultural trade's role in, **1982** 823-835
arms sales as tool of U.S., **1978** 107
Carter priorities in, **1979** 69-78
Clinton Democratic Party convention, **1996** 621-622
confronting an "axis of evil," Bush on, **2002** 33-34, 40-41, 56, 612, 614, 635, 714, 732; **2003** 19, 875, 1025, 1219; **2004** 18; **2005** 579
congressional intervention in, Kissinger on, **1975** 4-5, 10-13
congressional powers in, McGovern on, **1973** 88-89, 92-93
congressional-executive conflicts
on aid to Central America, **1983** 439-454
on aid to Southeast Asia, **1975** 223-224, 227-231, 251, 256-258, 260-261
continuity in, Ford pledge of, **1974** 703-704
contradictions in, Iran-contra affair, **1987** 895-901
cultural diplomacy, **2005** 579-588
Democratic Party platform on, **1980** 713, 754-769; **1984** 621-622, 632-646; **1988** 558, 566-568
diplomatic posts evaluation, State Department on, **1999** 690-698

goals and strategies, Vance on, **1980** 476-483
human rights in
as Carter emphasis, **1977** 89, 91; **1978** 7, 16, 43; **1979** 77-78; **1980** 35-36, 39, 99-100, 194-195; **1981** 57, 59-60, 101-102
Carter UN speech on, **1977** 189-190, 195-197
Democratic Party platform on, **1976** 580-581, 588, 590, 592-594; **1980** 755, 759-761
and foreign aid, **1981** 183-184
Mondale on, **1979** 677; **1980** 789-791
as presidential campaign issue, **1976** 742-743, 750-752, 756-757; **1980** 778, 935
Reagan policy, **1981** 462, 779-781, 784-785; **1982** 108; **1983** 181; **1985** 145-148
and support for shah, **1978** 705-708, 711-712
Vance on, **1976** 887; **1980** 479
and world respect for U.S., **1978** 773, 775
morality and pragmatism in, Kissinger on, **1975** 257-259; **1976** 907-908, 913
morality in
Carter on, **1976** 735, 739, 742-743, 750-752; **1977** 105, 111; **1978** 43
Republican Party platform on, **1976** 651
national commission on September 11 recommendations, **2005** 902-903
Nixon survey of, **1973** 515-530
presidential power in
congressional restriction of war powers, **1973** 923-930
Ford assertion of, **1975** 223, 226, 228, 232, 235, 238
to make agreements, Iranian-U.S. settlement, **1981** 560
private individuals in implementation of, **1987** 217, 219, 224, 226, 241-242
Reagan legacy in, Bush on, **1984** 743-744
religious persecution, U.S. position on, **1998** 19-29
Republican Party platform, **1984** 663, 707-718; **1988** 616-617, 673-688; **1996** 538-546
secrecy in
Carter on, **1976** 735, 739-740, 746, 752
Democratic Party platform on, **1972** 574-575, 583-584
Republican Party platform on, **1976** 617-618
tracking foreign visitors, GAO report on, **2003** 218-226
U.S. relations, overseas view of, **2005** 579-588
U.S. role as world leader, **1995** 580
U.S. role in the world, Bush administration on, **2003** 40
use of military force in, National Academy of Sciences on, **1972** 381-382
weakened position of U.S., Reagan on, **1980** 652, 660-663
Foreign Policy Association, U.S. policy on Latin America, Vance speech, **1979** 713-721
Foreign Terrorist Tracking Task Force, **2001** 765-766, 768
Foreign-born population. *See* Immigrants and immigration
Foreman, Carol Tucker, food safety, **2001** 700, 701; **2002** 581
Forest Service (U.S.)
clear-cutting and spotted owl controversy, **1993** 496-497
ecosystem management approach, **1992** 489-492
fire-management policy of, **1988** 941-946
management of Alaskan lands, **1978** 732
multiple-use management, **1973** 21-26
national forests development, **2004** 669
spotted owl ruling and, **1991** 275
Forests
Clinton "roadless initiative," **1999** 592-599; **2001** 216-217; **2002** 899; **2004** 668-669
conservation and global warming, **2001** 113-114
ecosystem management approach, **1992** 489-492
effect of climate change on, **1988** 864-865
fire management policy for, **1988** 941-946
fire prevention guidelines, **2000** 712-722
"Healthy Forests" Initiative, **2002** 894, 899-900; **2003** 27, 181
Save America's Forests, **1999** 594
Forgione, Pascal D., Jr., teacher quality survey, **1999** 65
Formula, infant, marketing practices in developing countries, WHO on, **1981** 447-458
Forney, John M., Enron Corp. scandal, **2004** 416
Fornos, Werner, on world population control efforts, **1987** 439-461
Forrester, Douglas, senatorial election, **2002** 821
Forrester, Jay, **1972** 215
Fort Chaffee (Arkansas), riot of Cuban refugees at, **1980** 338
Fort Dix (New Jersey), closing of, **1988** 952
Fort Douglas (Utah), closing of, **1988** 952
Fort Meade (Maryland), closing of, **1988** 952
Fort Sheridan (Illinois), closing of, **1988** 952
Fort Wayne Books v. Indiana, **1993** 442
Fortas, Abe, **1987** 580
chief justice nomination, **2005** 559
Fortier, Lori, testimony in Oklahoma City bombing case, **1997** 624-625
Fortier, Michael J., and Oklahoma City bombing, **1995** 177; **1997** 624-625
Forty Committee, authorization of covert action in Chile, **1975** 886, 888-890, 892-893, 895-899, 901-903, 912
Forum for the Future, European-U.S.-Middle East foreign ministers meetings, **2004** 629; **2005** 273
Foster, Arnold, **1978** 470
Foster, Henry W., Jr.
surgeon general nomination, **1995** 61-68
surgeon general nomination, NAACP support for, **1995** 454
and White House travel office firings, **1998** 394
Foster, Jodie, and Hinckley case, **1981** 351; **1982** 532
Foster, Marcus, killing of, **1974** 247, 250-251
Foster, Richard S., Medicare chief actuary, intimidation of, **2004** 579-580
Foster, Vincent W., Jr.
meeting with attorney James Hamilton, **1998** 393
suicide, **1993** 531-539; **1998** 633
Foster homes, shortage of, **1989** 673, 677, 683
Foundation on Economic Trends, **1986** 288; **1992** 470
Fourie, Bernardus G., **1984** 1029

Fowler, Donald
abortion issue, **1996** 624
Democratic Party fund-raising violations, **1996** 839-840
Fowler, Tillie K.
Air Force Academy sexual misconduct investigation panel, **2003** 794, 795
Independent Panel to Review DOD Detention Operations, **2004** 212
Fox, James Alan (FBI official)
crime rate, **2003** 981
juvenile crime, **1995** 711; **1998** 871; **1999** 615
Marcos indictment, **1988** 869
youth and gang killings, **2004** 761
Fox, Michael F., therapeutic cloning research, **2002** 515; **2005** 318
Fox, Vicente
Mexican citizens and death penalty in U.S., **2004** 798
Mexico presidential election, **2000** 963-977
U.S. immigration policy, **2001** 764-765
Venezuela coup attempt, **2002** 204
Foxman, Abraham H., **1989** 700
Foys, Roger, sexual abuse by priests settlement, **2005** 867
FPC. *See* Federal Power Commission
Framework Conventions. *See* United Nations conventions
Frampton, George T., Jr., **1988** 942
France
Air France flight 4590 crash (Concorde plane) investigations, **2000** 488-493
arms sales to Iraq, **1984** 750, 752
Barbie case
extradition, **1983** 737-747
trial, **1987** 517-524
Berlin, four-power agreement on, **1972** 467-470
Carter visit, **1977** 897, 900
Chirac apology for complicity with Nazis, **1995** 478-482
Chirac inaugural address, **1995** 228-232
Communist Party in, **1976** 434, 457-458
compensation to U.S. for 1966 troop pullout, **1974** 982, 985
at economic summits, **1976** 425; **1978** 533, 536; **1979** 3-8; **1981** 591; **1982** 469-471; **1983** 507-514
economic summits
Houston, **1990** 467-482
Munich, **1992** 637-648
embassy attack in Liberian coup, **1980** 277
energy crisis, multilateral cooperation in, **1974** 123-124, 126-127, 185-189
EU constitution referendum, **2005** 339-342, 344-346
euro currency, **1998** 271
European Monetary System, participation in, **1978** 741
exchange rate instability, **1985** 623-630
Genocide Convention ratification, **1986** 115
Germany, division of, **1986** 792-793, 796, 798
heroin refining in, **1972** 646, 649
Iraq War, opposition to, **2003** 40-43, 48, 51-52
Ivory Coast peace agreement, **2003** 237-239
John Paul II to, **1980** 968-969
missiles of, Soviet position on, **1982** 983, 986-987; **1983** 792; **1986** 10, 13
Muslim immigrants, **2005** 340
NATO consultations, **1974** 529
NATO participation of, **1975** 354; **1976** 331, 336, 339-341
nonproliferation treaty abstention, **1975** 363
nuclear plant exports of, **1976** 332
and Palestine mandate, **1988** 581
PLO departure from Lebanon, role in, **1982** 741, 744
at poverty summit, **1981** 770
proposed Atlantic charter, **1973** 488
Rwanda, peacekeeping forces to, **1994** 542-543
sabotage of Greenpeace ship, **1985** 631-634
student test scores, **1992** 90
terrorist attack on Beirut barracks of, **1983** 933
terrorist bombings in, and security measures, **1986** 829-838
UN membership for two Germanys, four-power agreement on, **1972** 897, 900
UN sanctions against South Africa, **1977** 823-824; **1985** 533
on U.S. invasion of Grenada, **1983** 850
U.S. relations, improvement in, **1974** 981-985
U.S. sanctions against Soviet pipeline, **1982** 880
Franco, Francisco
followers of, and democratic constitution, **1978** 809
Spanish civil war, **1978** 812
Frank, Barney (D-Mass.)
at gay/lesbian march on Washington, **1993** 327
House Judiciary Committee impeachment inquiry, **1998** 702
HUD investigation, **1989** 336-337
immigration law, **1986** 964-965
Japanese-America reparations, **1988** 289
on military homosexual ban, **1993** 154
same-sex marriages, **1996** 688
U.S.-China trade relations, **2000** 216
Frank, Ellen, on depression studies, **1993** 654
Frankel, Jeffrey, U.S. economic growth, **1999** 88
Frankel, Max, **1976** 735
Franklin, Benjamin, on power of God, **1995** 14
Franklin, Christine, **1992** 187-199
Franklin, John Hope, presidential advisory panel on race relations, **1997** 314, 316, 322, 323; **1998** 665, 668
Franklin v. Gwinnett County Public Schools, **1992** 187-189
Franks, Gary A. (R-Conn.), **1995** 372
Franks, Lord, **1983** 3
Frascone, Salvatore, **1984** 804, 806
Fraser, Douglas A.
Carter budget, **1978** 766
worker concessions to Chrysler, **1979** 695
Fraser, Malcolm J.
Skylab's return in Australia, **1979** 553, 558
study group on South Africa, **1986** 582
at Zimbabwe independence, **1980** 318
Fraternity of St. Pius X, conflict with Vatican, **1988** 490-493
Frates, William S., **1974** 663-665

Frattini, Franco, European Commission cabinet appointment, **2004** 202
Frazier, Bernard W., **1978** 720
Frazier, Lynn, recall election, **2003** 1006
Frechette, Louise, UN oil-for-food program scandal, **2005** 234
Fred Alger Management, mutual funds scandal, **2003** 696
Freddie Mac, corporate scandal, **2003** 332, 339
Frederick, Ivan L., II, Iraqi detainee abuse conviction, **2004** 208, 215
Frederick, Pauline, **1976** 735
Free Access to Clinic Entrances, **1998** 810
Free Congress Foundation, **1987** 719
Free Iraqi Forces, **2003** 936
Free speech. *See under* Constitutional amendments (U.S.), First Amendment; Speech, freedom of
Free the Slaves, on temporary worker (T visas) program, **2004** 124-125
Free trade. *See* General Agreement on Tariffs and Trade (GATT)
Free Trade Agreement, U.S.-Canadian, **1988** 58, 65
Free Trade Area of the Americas (FTAA), **2002** 779; **2003** 8, 14; **2005** 766
Freed, James, **1993** 308
Freedman, Wendy L., age of universe controversy, **1996** 265-268
Freedom
  Bush inaugural address on, **2005** 46-49, 581
  economic, Reagan to Soviet dissidents and students, **1988** 359-363
  political freedom in the Arab world, **2002** 485
  public use of audiotaped court cases, **1993** 935-937
  Western, Solzhenitsyn warnings on, **1978** 409-410
Freedom Commission on Mental Health, **2002** 268
Freedom Forum First Amendment Center, **2002** 407
Freedom Initiative for Americans with Disabilities, **2001** 178
Freedom of Access to Clinic Entrances (FACE) Act, **1994** 313; **1998** 810, 814
Freedom of information, declassification of CIA documents, **1992** 3-10
Freedom of Information Act (FOIA), **2005** 649
  briefing of Ryan on Jonestown trip, **1979** 349-350, 369-370, 372, 377
  census data, **1982** 171-178
  Clinton's passport search report, **1992** 1045-1052
  revised guidelines, **1981** 393-400, 655-658
  secrecy of CIA sources, **1985** 333-344
Freedom of religion. *See under* Constitutional amendments (U.S.), First Amendment
Freedom of speech. *See under* Constitutional amendments (U.S.), First Amendment
Freedom Support Act (1992), **1992** 520, 521
Freeh, Louis J.
  FBI director nomination, **1993** 609-615
  "Freemen" surrender, **1996** 362-367
  Hanssen espionage case, **2001** 150-158
  investigations into campaign finance practices, **1997** 824, 830-831
  Nicholson espionage case, **1996** 794-800
  on Russian intelligence efforts, **1996** 794
  Waco incident investigation, **1999** 481
  Wen Ho Lee spy case, **2000** 742-744
Freeman, Douglas Southall, **1989** 124
Freeman, Harold P., cancer patient care, **2001** 868
Freemen (militia group), surrender of, FBI statement on, **1996** 362-367
Freidman, Milton, school vouchers, **2002** 407
Frelinghuysen, Peter H. B. (R-N.J.), **1974** 280
French language
  linguistic and educational rights in Canada, **1981** 813-814, 818-819
  as an official language of Canada, **1981** 817-818
  and Quebec separatist votes, **1976** 855-856, 861; **1980** 401-410
Frenzel, Bill (R-Minn.), **1983** 729
Fresno, Juan Francisco, **1986** 318
Freund, Paul A., **1972** 953
Frey, Robert, on corporate management and responsibility, **1996** 43
Friday, William C., **1991** 129
Fried, Charles
  on civil rights rulings, **1989** 324
  on *Roe v. Wade,* **1985** 54
Friedan, Betty, **1974** 779
Friedes, Josh, on same-sex marriages, **2004** 40
Friedman, Jerome I., Nobel in physics, **1990** 796
Friedman, Leon, Miranda warning, **2000** 386
Friedman, Louis, on Mars exploration, **2000** 93
Friedman, Michael
  food recalls, **1997** 691
  on tamoxifen trials, **1998** 197
Friedman, Rob, marketing violent entertainment to children, **2000** 731
Friedman, Stanton T., Roswell incident, **1997** 400
Friedman, Stephen, White House National Economic Council director, **2002** 880
Friedman, Thomas
  Guantanamo Bay prison, **2005** 450
  Nixon on Russian aid package, **1992** 256
  Saudi peace initiative, **2002** 370
Friendly, Fred, **1973** 58
Friends of the Earth
  land use permit for Alaska pipeline, **1972** 271
  Reagan record on environment, **1989** 17
Frink, Al, **2004** 59
Frisby v. Schultz, **1994** 320
Frist, Bill (R-Tenn.)
  AIDS initiative, **2003** 21-22
  CIA secret detentions, **2005** 907
  Clinton State of the Union address, Republican response, **2000** 19-20, 38-40
  during shooting of Capitol policemen, **1998** 511
  filibuster "nuclear option" threat, **2005** 559
  food safety system, **2001** 700
  health coverage for the uninsured, **2003** 847
  insider trading allegations, **2005** 631, 635-636
  patient safety hearings, **1999** 782
  poison ricin discovery, **2004** 268, 442-443
  prescription drug importation, **2004** 984
  Schiavo end-of-life care case, **2005** 157, 158
  Senate majority leader election, **2002** 819, 969-970, 973
  stem cell research, **2004** 160; **2005** 319-320

Frohn, Wolf-Georg, **1986** 93
Frohnmayer, David, on ballot initiatives, **1999** 5
From, Al, Democratic Party platform, **1992** 668
Frontiero v. Richardson, **1995** 313
Frost, David, Nixon interviews, **1977** 321-365
Frost, Gary L., **1995** 337
Frost, Martin (D-Texas), U.S.-China trade relations, **2000** 215
FSLIC. *See* Federal Savings and Loan Insurance Corporation
FSLN. *See* Sandinista National Liberation Front
FTAA. *See* Free Trade Area of the Americas
FTC. *See* Federal Trade Commission
Fuel Cycle Evaluation Conference, International, Carter speech on nuclear fuel repository, **1977** 273
Fuhrman, Mark, racist police detective in Simpson trial, **1995** 612-613, 617, 646; **1997** 74
Fujimori, Alberto
  capture of Shining Path leader, **1992** 859-864
  Drug Summit (San Antonio), **1992** 201, 202-203
  human rights report, **1993** 571-572, 574
  Peruvian hostage crisis, **1997** 234-236
  Peruvian president's accomplishments, **2000** 923-926
Fukuda, Takeo, **1977** 367
  PRC peace treaty, **1978** 585-586
  trade surplus reduction pledge, **1978** 533-534, 539
Fulbright, J. W. (D-Ark.), on noninterference in Soviet domestic affairs, **1973** 792, 799-800
Full Employment and Balanced Growth Act (1978), **1978** 21; **1979** 90-91; **1983** 140
  employment goals, **1978** 66-67
  reporting requirements, **1987** 131-132
Fullam, John P., libraries and pornography, **2002** 288
Fuller, Graham, Gates CIA confirmation hearings, **1991** 652, 657-661
Fullilove v. Klutznick, **1980** 539-566; **1990** 421, 425-426; **1995** 312, 314, 321, 323-324
Fulminante, Oreste C., **1991** 175-184
Fulz, Keith O., aviation security, testimony on, **1996** 665-671
Fund for a Conservative Majority, **1985** 277-278
Fund for Religious Liberty, **2002** 407
Fund for Rural America, **1996** 201
Funk, Sherman M., **1992** 1045-1052
Funk v. United States, **1998** 398, 402
Furman v. Georgia, **1972** 499-505; **1976** 490-502; **1978** 495-497, 503-510, 513-514; **1980** 455-466, 471; **1983** 708; **1990** 313
Futrell, Mary Hatwood
  education funding, **1988** 299
  merit pay for teachers, **1986** 459

G

G-7. *See* Group of Seven
Gabon
  human trafficking, **2002** 344
  and OPEC oil prices, **1981** 799
Gacumbitsi, Sylvestre, Rwanda war crimes conviction, **2004** 118
Gadahn, Adam, terrorist suspect, **2004** 276
Gaete, Marcelo, California gubernatorial election, **2003** 350
Gaffney, Frank J., Jr., **1996** 741
Gaidar, Yegor, **1994** 186
Gairy, Eric, **1983** 847
Galan, Luis Carlos
  assassination of, **1989** 500, 512; **1990** 116
Galarreta, Alfonso de, excommunication of, **1988** 490, 492
Galbraith, John Kenneth, **1987** 883
Gale, Robert, **1986** 384
Gale, William G., Bush economic team, **2002** 880-881
Galiber, Joseph L., indictment, **1984** 803, 805-809
Galileo mission to Jupiter, **2003** 305
Gallagher, Cornelius E. (D-N.J.), in Korean influence-buying scheme, **1978** 846, 857-860, 867-869
Gallagher, Maggie, government-funded propaganda, **2005** 645
Gallegly, Elton (R-Calif.), House Judiciary Committee impeachment inquiry, **1998** 705-706
Galluci, Robert L., on North Korean nuclear agreement, **1994** 602-610
Galman, Rolando, B. Aquino assassination, **1984** 926-931
Galson, Steven
  FDA suppression of research results, response to, **2004** 853
  morning-after pill over-the-counter sales, FDA ruling, **2005** 816
Galtieri, Leopóldo, Falklands (Malvinas) invasion, **1982** 285; **1983** 11-12
Galvin, Cristina, AIDS in Russia study, **2005** 54
Galvin, William F., mutual funds scandal, **2003** 695
el-Gamasy, Ghany, **1976** 171
el-Gamasy, Mohammed Abdel, **1974** 30
Gambari, Ibrahim, Angola peace agreement, **2002** 154
Gambling
  sentencing of Pete Rose, **1990** 483-487
  on sports events, **1989** 477-484
Gamboa, Anthony H., Scully's penalty for threatening HHS employee Foster, **2004** 579, 583-587
Gandhi, Indira
  address at nonaligned nations summit, **1983** 263-268
  assassination, **1984** 933, 945-949
  declaration of state of emergency, **1977** 237-239
  resignation, **1977** 237-239
  at Zimbabwe independence, **1980** 318
Gandhi, Mohandas K., John Paul II on, **1986** 24, 26-27
Gandhi, Rajiv (Indian prime minister)
  assassination of, **2002** 93, 94; **2004** 348
  on assassination of I. Gandhi, **1984** 945, 947-949
  Indo-Sri Lankan accord on ethnic conflict, **1987** 615-622
  warning to two superpowers, **1985** 710
Gandhi, Sanjay, **1977** 238
Gandhi, Sonia, Indian elections and controversial background, **2004** 348, 349; **2005** 467
Gandy, Kim, abortion protests, **1994** 28
Gangs
  legislation controlling, **1997** 39
  Williams of Crips gang death penalty execution, **2005** 178

youth gangs
Bush initiative for prevention of, **2005** 86
Justice Department report on, **2001** 73, 75
Gann, Paul, **1978** 397
Gannett Co., Inc. v. DePasquale, **1979** 317-318, 511-533
Gannon, James P., at Carter-Ford debate, **1976** 693, 697-698, 703-704, 709-710, 716
GAO. *See* General Accounting Office; Government Accountability Office
Gao Qiang, AIDS/HIV epidemic in China, **2003** 1175; **2005** 55
Garambe, François, Rwanda genocidal war, **2004** 116
Garamendi, John, California gubernatorial recall election, **2003** 1008
Garang, John
accidental death of, **2005** 514, 520-521
Sudanese peace talks, **2003** 838-840
Garcia, Alan, drug summit at Cartagena, **1990** 115-126
Garcia, Michael, terrorism threat alerts, **2004** 272
Garcia, Robert (D-N.Y.), **1988** 499
Garcia v. San Antonio Metropolitan Transit Authority, **1985** 167-187, 480, 484; **1999** 334, 347
Gardner, Booth (D-Wash.), education goals, **1990** 54, 154-165
Gardner, Neil, death of at Columbine School shooting, **2000** 875-876
Garfield, James A.
assassination of, **1978** 138
illness of, **1985** 492
Garland, Lillian, **1987** 18
Garment, Leonard
assurances to AIM at Wounded Knee, **1973** 531-532
Marc Rich presidential pardon, **2001** 90
presidential counsel appointment, **1973** 499, 509
Garn, Jake (R-Utah), on Volcker reappointment, **1983** 595-597
Garner, Jay M., postwar Iraq operations, **2003** 935; **2005** 941
Garofalo, Lucia, **1999** 499
Garrett, H. Lawrence, III
Tailhook incident, **1992** 190, 482-483, 879-880; **1993** 316
USS *Iowa* explosion report, **1990** 320
Garrett, Laurie, AIDS epidemic report, **2005** 54
Garriott, Owen Kay, **1973** 940
Garrison v. Louisiana, **1991** 321
Garrow, David, **1995** 657
Garten, Jeffrey E.
corporate scandals, **2002** 393
U.S. economy, **2001** 57
Gartner Group, on year 2000 computer conversion, **1997** 534, 536; **2000** 5
Garvey, Jane E., aviation fuel tank requirements, **1997** 782
Garvey, Steve, baseball record, **1995** 588
Garwin, Richard L., **1984** 527
Garwood, Robert R., court-martial and conviction of, **1981** 197-201
Garza, Cutberto, federal nutritional guidelines, **2000** 240
Garza, Juan Raul, death penalty sentencing of, **2000** 990; **2001** 387, 390; **2002** 356
Garzon, Lucho, elections in Colombia, **2003** 429
Gas, natural
See also Oil and gas prices
decontrol of prices
Ford and CEA on, **1976** 51, 56-57
Nixon on, **1973** 465-466, 470-471
increased production of, Nixon on, **1973** 914, 919
Siberian, U.S. importing of, **1972** 846
Gas emissions. *See* Greenhouse gas emissions
Gas pipeline, Soviet
forced labor on, **1982** 857-869
U.S. economic sanctions against companies involved in, **1982** 879-884
Gasch, Oliver H., **1979** 917, 919
Gasoline prices. *See* Oil and gas prices
Gasoline rationing
as emergency conservation measure, **1975** 18, 23, 36
standby plan for, **1974** 81; **1979** 560, 568, 579
Gasoline shortages, status of, Nixon on, **1974** 146-147, 149-150
Gasoline tax
See also Oil and gas prices
Anderson proposal, **1980** 848, 852, 854
standby plan for, **1974** 910; **1977** 278, 287; **1980** 109, 120
Gates, Bill
children, UN special session on, **2002** 221-222
HIV/AIDS prevention programs, **2002** 472
Microsoft antitrust case, **1999** 655; **2001** 776; **2002** 798, 799
Gates, Daryl F., **1991** 403, 405, 417, 425; **1992** 409, 414-415, 416, 417-429
Gates, Robert M.
Ames espionage case, **1994** 488
CIA reform, **1992** 3-10
Inman nomination, **1994** 24
nomination hearings, **1991** 429, 651-669
Vietnam War POW/MIAs, Senate report on, **1993** 127
Gates Foundation, HIV/AIDS prevention programs, **2002** 472
Gates of the Arctic National Monument, **1978** 731, 739
GATT. *See* General Agreement on Tariffs and Trade
Gavin Group (Boston), child sexual abuse by priests investigation, **2004** 83
Gaviria, Cesar
Haiti political situation, **2001** 396
Venezuelan political situation, **2002** 204-206, 209-211; **2003** 280-282; **2004** 551
Gaviria Trujillo, Cesar, at U.S.-Latin American drug summit, **1992** 201
Gay, Hobart R., Korean War massacre incident, **1999** 556
Gay marriage. *See under* Marriage, same-sex marriage
Gay rights
See also Homosexual rights; Marriage, same-sex marriage
and the clergy, **2004** 42-44

Gay rights *Continued*
seminarians, Vatican prohibition on, **2005** 863-872
Clinton speech to Human Rights Campaign, **1997** 760-766
discrimination against gays, Supreme Court on, **1996** 284-295
march on Washington, **1993** 327-331
parade marchers, **1995** 327-335
recognition of domestic partnerships, **1989** 305-311
same-sex civil unions
international legislation, **2004** 42
Vermont legislation, **2000** 158-167; **2004** 37
and security clearances, **1995** 532, 533; **1997** 761
sodomy laws, Supreme Court on, **2003** 401-424
Gayle, Helene, AIDS prevention, **2002** 472
Gaza Strip settlements
See also Israel, occupied territories; Palestinians
border area with Egypt (Philadelphia route), **2004** 304, 314
Israeli withdrawal from Jewish settlements in, **2003** 1200, 1204, 1206; **2004** 301-315; **2005** 27, 529-538
Operation Penitence, **2004** 811
Operation Rainbow, **2004** 811
peace plan for West Bank and Gaza Stirp, **1977** 855-857
postwithdrawal chaos, **2005** 31-32
terrorist bombing of U.S. diplomatic convoy, **2003** 1202-1203
Gbagbo, Laurent
Ivory Coast elections, **2002** 251-252; **2003** 238
Ivory Coast peace agreement, **2003** 238-240
peace negotiations, **2004** 818-825; **2005** 804-805
GCC. *See* Gulf Cooperation Council
Geagea, Samir, Lebanese political prisoner released, **2005** 690
Gearan, Mark, radiation tests on citizens, **1993** 990
Gearhart, John, on embryonic research, **1998** 66
Gebser v. Lago Vista Independent School District, **1998** 442; **1999** 222, 228, 229
Gehman, Harold L., Jr.
Columbia space shuttle disaster, **2003** 633
USS *Cole* bombing, **2001** 5-6
Gehrig, Lou, baseball record, **1995** 588-591
Gehring, Perry, **1978** 635
Geiger, Keith, **1991** 221
Geisel, Ernesto, **1978** 270
Gekas, George (R-Pa.), House Judiciary Committee impeachment inquiry, **1998** 703
Gelb, Leslie, **1986** 10
Geldof, Bob, antipoverty campaign, **2005** 406, 409
Gellar, Kenneth S., **1979** 920; **1993** 250
Gemayel, Amin
resignation of cabinet, **1984** 84
role in Israeli-Lebanese security agreement, **1983** 471-473
and terrorist attack on Beirut Marine barracks, **1983** 933
Gemayel, Bashir, assassination of, **1982** 781; **1983** 163-164, 170; **1985** 50-51
Gender discrimination. *See* Discrimination, sex
Gender Discriminatory Agency Review, **1983** 756-763
Geneen, Harold, ITT political contributions and antitrust settlement, **1972** 397, 404-406
Genentech, Inc., FDA approval of TPA, **1987** 875-876, 879
General Accounting Office (GAO)
See also under its later name Government Accountability Office (GAO)
air traffic safety, **1986** 253-266
Amtrak testimony, **1994** 197-204
aviation safety enforcement, **1998** 169-179
aviation safety report, **1997** 112-121
aviation security, **1996** 662-671; **2001** 650-659; **2003** 720-739
Balkans political situation, **2000** 141-157
biotechnology, **1986** 288
bioterrorism preparation, **2001** 672-685; **2004** 444
census undercount, **1990** 171; **1991** 444
child care quality testimony, **1994** 116-122
Colombia aid program, **2000** 840-851
computer security, **2002** 746
computers
security of systems, **1998** 676-686
Y2K (year 2000) conversion, **1997** 534-540; **1998** 543-554
counterfeiting of U.S. currency, **1996** 98-105
deficit reduction, **1996** 147-155
District of Columbia financial crisis, **1995** 497-505
drinking water, threat to safety of, **1993** 261-270
drug prices report, **1994** 87-94
drug-resistant bacteria, **1999** 185-199
energy policy task force, **2003** 1018
explosion on USS *Iowa* report, **1990** 319-330
FAA and airline safety inspections, **1996** 237-246
federal aviation security, **2004** 142-154
federal election system reform, **2001** 526-527
financial markets, **1988** 9
food safety
foodborne illness, **1998** 521-531
inspections, **2002** 579-589
threats to food supply, **2001** 698-709
Food Safety Agency proposal, **1997** 693
foreign visitors, tracking of, **2003** 218-226
global warming policy, **2003** 861-873
Grace commission report, **1984** 169-179
graduation by college athletes, **1989** 215-216
Gulf War, "smart" weapons performance, **1996** 403-413; **1997** 493-500
Gulf War syndrome, **1997** 741
hazing and other practices at military academies, **1992** 481-487
health insurance coverage, **1998** 139-150
hospital construction costs, **1972** 921-931
HUD programs, **1996** 169
identity theft, **2002** 785
intelligence agencies audit, **1976** 117, 121
missile defense systems, **2004** 176-185
monitoring of block grants, **1983** 54
National Park Service
conditions, **1996** 580-588
testimony, **1995** 120-128
on National Performance Review projections, **1993** 720
"new source" review, **2003** 178-179
nuclear material in the former Soviet Union, **1996** 139-146

nuclear wastes cleanup, **1994** 339-348; **1995** 113-119
nursing home abuse, **2002** 117-132
OEO legal services program, **1973** 454
Patriot Missile Performance report, **1992** 865-874
Pentagon computer systems, threats to, **1996** 312-324
prescription drug advertising, **2002** 945-958
railroad safety, **1996** 189-198
Republican committee violations of federal election law, **1973** 414, 502
role in Gramm-Rudman-Hollings, **1986** 706
Roswell incident, **1997** 397
Russian nuclear weapons reports, **2001** 19
school vouchers, **2002** 410
Securities and Exchange Commission failures, **2002** 1032-1043
Social Security system solvency, **1998** 98-109
Sununu ethics issue, **1992** 296
terrorism, **1997** 711
terrorist watch lists, **2003** 155-172
threat alert system, **2004** 269
UN Oil for Food program, **2004** 892
UN peacekeeping operations report, **1997** 150-157
UN reform, **2000** 179-189
unsafe chemicals in food testimony, **1994** 379-386
U.S. military aid to Pakistan, **1972** 163
U.S. missile defense system, **2003** 817-823
welfare reform, **1998** 354-363; **1999** 257-271
General Agreement on Tariffs and Trade (GATT)
See also under its later name World Trade Organization (WTO)
Bush on, **1990** 478-479; **1992** 19, 101, 506
CEA report on, **1998** 83
Clinton renewal, letter to Congress, **1993** 997-1002
Clinton support for, **1994** 46, 555-559
Democratic Party platform on, **1992** 704
industrialized nations on, **1986** 442
negotiations, U.S. trade reform to prepare for, **1973** 379-381, 388-389
progress on, economic summits on, **1978** 539; **1982** 470
proposed round, **1985** 348, 354
Republican Party platform on, **1992** 823, 828
Uruguay Round, **1993** 541-543; **1994** 142; **1995** 74, 85; **1997** 53, 61-62; **1998** 83, 92; **1999** 798; **2001** 59; **2003** 742
agricultural subsidies, **1990** 469, 471-473
and bilateral agreements, **1988** 574
Bush on, **1990** 87
Group of Seven on, **1992** 640
Reagan support for, **1987** 122
US-EC dispute over agricultural subsidies in Europe, **1992** 639
General Electric (GE)
Hudson River pollution and, **2001** 218
patent of bacterium, **1980** 493-494
Soviet pipeline sanctions, **1982** 881
General Electric Co. v. Gilbert, **1976** 891-905
General Mills (GM), affirmative action, **2003** 362
General Motors (GM)
affirmative action, **2003** 362
economic situation, **2005** 137, 140
health benefits for domestic partners, **2000** 162
Internet-based parts exchange, **2000** 302
"junk bond" credit rating, **2005** 200
Los Angeles riots and, **1992** 409
prescription drug benefit reform, **2000** 134
selling electric automobiles, **1996** 17-20
SUV sales declining, **2005** 780
truck safety, **1994** 443-448
UAW strike, **1998** 320-325
underfunded health liability, **2005** 200
underfunded pension plans, **2003** 709; **2004** 738; **2005** 200
General Services Administration (GSA), FEMA and, **1992** 538-539
Genetic engineering
controls and safeguards on, Asilomar conference on, **1975** 319-324
farm-animal rights, **1988** 350-351
FDA approval of TPA, **1987** 875-879
patent of bacterium, **1980** 493-502
Genetic Saving & Clone, **2002** 517
Genetics
biotechnology in agriculture, **1999** 401-411
cloning research, **1997** 212-220
genetic testing in the workplace, **1998** 63-72
Human Genome Project, **1997** 37-38; **2000** 34, 397-409
stem cell research, **2000** 667-673
Geneva Conventions
Afghanistan detainees and, **2004** 212-213, 337, 338
detainees of war on terror, **2005** 447
Iraqi prisoners, **2004** 213
on the Laws of War (1949)
Afghanistan conflict, **1986** 930-931
Israeli occupied territories, **1976** 195-196
Nicaraguan conflict, **1985** 258
Noriega sentencing, **1992** 649-651, 653
on Prohibition of Use in War of Asphyxiating and Poisonous Gases and Bacteriological Methods of Warfare (1925), **1972** 323-324, 841; **1981** 682, 685-686; **1989** 25, 28-29
Relative to the Protection of Civilian Persons in Time of War (1949), **1976** 195-196
Geneva summit
Reagan-Gorbachev, **1985** 749-761
effect on U.S.-Soviet relations, **1986** 3-8
and prisoner exchange, **1986** 93-94
Genocide
See also Burundi; Rwanda
Congo conflict, in Ituri region, **2004** 508, 588
defined, **2004** 593-594
Sudan conflict in Darfur region, secretary of state on, **2004** 588-601
Genocide Convention
on definition of genocide, **2004** 593-594
U.S. Senate ratification of, **1986** 115-130; **2002** 605
Genscher, Hans-Dietrich, **1985** 348
on Holocaust, **1990** 602
nonagression treaty with Soviet Union, **1990** 601, 608-614
Geoghan, John J.
murder in prison, **2003** 526; **2004** 87; **2005** 867

Geoghan, John J. *Continued*
  priest sexual offender case, **2002** 868; **2003** 524; **2005** 867
George, Francis (cardinal), sexual abuse of priests, **2004** 86-87
George, Clair E.
  Iran-contra affair, **1991** 652; **1992** 1073-1079
  Iran-contra conviction, **1994** 12
George v. Evans, **1992** 181
George Air Force Base (Calif.), closing of, **1988** 952
Georgetown University
  Brennan speech on role of Court, **1985** 653
  Haig speech on first-strike policy, **1982** 305-315
Georgia
  See also University of Georgia
  abortion restrictions, **1973** 101-102, 111-114
  death penalty law, constitutionality of, **1976** 489-503
  intelligent design case, **2005** 1013
Georgia (country)
  Adzharia province independence movement, **2004** 72, 74-75
  Burdzhanadze on political change in, **2003** 1039-1049
  economic reform, **2004** 79-80
  enriched uranium removed from, **2001** 19
  governance reform, **2004** 78-79
  interim government, **2003** 1043-1044
  political situation, **2005** 43, 64
  "Rose Revolution" (parliamentary elections), **2003** 1039-1043; **2005** 306
  Saakashvili anticorruption campaign, **2004** 73-74
  Saakashvili antiseparatist campaign, **2004** 75-76
  security reform, **2004** 79
  separatist/rebel regions of, **2003** 1045-1046; **2004** 75-76
  Shevardnadze removed from office, **2004** 1001
  Soviet Union restructuring plans, **1991** 532
  transition to democracy, **2004** 72-81
  U.S. involvement, **2003** 1044-1045; **2004** 73
Geothermal energy
  contribution to energy supply, **1974** 910, 913
  development of, **1975** 29, 84, 92
  leasing for development of, **1973** 469, 473
  research, **1974** 105
Gephardt, Richard A. (D-Mo.)
  104th Congress
    closing remarks, **1996** 699-701
    first one hundred days, Democratic response, **1995** 165, 172-174
    opening remarks, **1995** 3-6
  Bush State of the Union address, Democratic response, **2001** 174-175, 183-187; **2002** 38, 46-48
  campaign finance reform, **2002** 38
  election to majority leader, **1989** 240
  free trade agreements, **1997** 543; **1998** 75
  House impeachment vote, **1998** 961-962, 967
  House minority leader resignation, **2002** 818, 822
  House Speaker elections, **1997** 3; **1998** 803
  presidential candidate, **2003** 446; **2004** 479, 480
  Reagan State of the Union, **1986** 39
  Social Security reform, **2001** 915
  Starr report, **1998** 633, 636
  trade legislation, **1987** 429
  vice presidential candidate, **2004** 480
  war in Iraq, congressional resolution on, **2002** 714-715, 818
Geraghty, Timothy, **1983** 935
Gerard, Jean, **1983** 968
Gerasimov, Gennadi I.
  on Brezhnev doctrine, **1989** 400
  on London Declaration, **1990** 456
  Soviet Union, collapse of, **2004** 319
  on U.S. invasion of Panama, **1989** 703
Gerberding, Julie L.
  flu vaccine shortage, **2004** 640, 642
  on obesity-related deaths, **2005** 6
Geremek, Bronislav, at NATO membership ceremony for Poland, **1999** 121, 126-127
Gergen, David R.
  presidential press conferences, **1988** 836, 838
  Reagan assassination attempt, **1981** 353-354
Gerlack, Howard L., **1983** 935
Germain, Adrienne, sex education for children, **2002** 224
German Democratic Republic (East Germany)
  apology for Holocaust, **1990** 106
  Berlin four-power agreement, impact of, **1972** 467
  Berlin Wall, opening of, **1989** 625-630
  Berlin Wall construction (1961), **1986** 791-799
  human rights in, **1988** 884, 888
  Jewish reparations from, **1974** 801-802
  market economy, Kohl on shift to, **1989** 631-632
  political liberalization in, **1989** 635-636, 710
  U.S. diplomatic relations, **1974** 801-803
  Warsaw Pact withdrawal, **1991** 399
  West German relations, **1972** 897-900; **1986** 791-799
German reunification
  East and West German views of, **1972** 897-898
  and European security organization, **1975** 560
  final settlement treaty, **1990** 599-608
  Gorbachev response, **1990** 332, 599
  Kohl's legacy, **1998** 816
  Kohl's plan for, **1989** 627, 630-634
  Kohl's response to rabbi, **1990** 105-112
  Malta summit talks on, **1989** 658-659, 664
  NATO allies' concerns about, **1989** 626-627
  NATO membership, **1990** 332, 455
  Soviet fears of, **1990** 467
  Soviet-German treaty, **1990** 608-614
  U.S. conditions for, **1989** 627-629, 634
  Weizäcker unity day speech, **1990** 681-693
Germany
  See also Holocaust; Nazi Germany; War crimes
  economic situation, **2002** 689, 692; **2005** 873-876
  economic summits, Munich, **1992** 637-648
  euro currency, **1998** 271
  Gerhard Schroeder's legislative plans, **1998** 815-826
  history of, **1986** 794-798
  Iraq War, opposition to, **2003** 40-43, 48, 51-52
  Kristallnacht anniversary, **1975** 825
  Medium Extended Air Defense System (MEADS), **2004** 180-181
  nonagression treaty with Soviet Union, **1990** 601, 608-614

unemployment rate, **2005** 874
UNSC membership proposal, **2003** 812
U.S. relations, **2005** 874, 878-879
war guilt of, **1989** 487-497
war on terrorism, military support for, **2001** 627, 628
World War II causes, Wallace on, **1975** 155-156, 160
Germany, Federal Republic of (West Germany)
arms reductions in Europe, **1989** 297-298
Atlantic charter, proposed, **1973** 488
Berlin
crises, **1986** 791-799
four-power agreement on, **1972** 467-470
Berlin Wall, Reagan at, **1982** 477-479
Catholic clergy in, John Paul II address to, **1980** 968, 970-971
East German relations, **1972** 897-900; **1986** 791-799
EC action on VAT, **1984** 443
economic growth of, **1978** 533-534, 536
IMF on, **1977** 688, 692, 697
economic summits, **1976** 425-426; **1979** 3-8; **1981** 591; **1982** 469; **1983** 507-514; **1990** 467-482
European Monetary System, **1978** 741
exchange rate stabilization, **1985** 623-630
Genocide Convention ratification, **1986** 115
international economic organization, proposed, **1981** 769
Law of the Sea Treaty abstention, **1982** 345-361
Libyan chemical weapons plant, **1989** 28
Mengele extradition order, **1985** 410, 412
nuclear technology sale to Brazil, **1975** 363
peace movement in, **1981** 718; **1982** 479
poverty summit, **1981** 770
Reagan's Bitburg visit, **1985** 357-362
Soviet technical and cultural agreements with, **1973** 557-562
terrorism in, and Syrian relations, **1986** 833
U.S. invasion of Grenada, **1983** 850
U.S. missile deployment in, **1982** 983; **1983** 792-793
U.S. sanctions against Soviet pipeline, **1982** 880
war guilt of, Kohl on, **1989** 487-497
Gerow, Bert, **1989** 540
Gerrymanders, racial. *See* Minorities, race-based redistricting
Gerson, Allan, and Meese investigation, **1988** 498, 514
Gesell, Gerhard A., **1990** 491, 492, 493
on Cox firing, **1975** 662
Ellsberg break-in case, **1974** 445, 447, 661-669; **1975** 667
national security defense, **1974** 34, 39, 411-417
federal aid to hospitals treating seriously ill infants, **1983** 283
sentencing of North, **1989** 391, 393-397
Geyer, Georgie Anne, at presidential debates, **1984** 876-879, 889-892
Ghailani, Ahmed Khalfan, suspect in terrorist bombings captured, **2004** 537-538, 1012
al-Ghamdi, Ali Abd al-Rahman al-Faqasi, al Qaeda leader arrested, **2003** 229
Ghana
cancellation of Kissinger visit, **1976** 288
Clinton state visit, **1998** 159
Ghanem, Shokri, Libyan economy, **2003** 1226
Ghani, Ashraf, Afghanistan finance minister resignation, **2004** 917
Gherebi, Falen, Guantanamo Bay detainees, **2003** 111
Gherebi v. Bush; Rumsfeld, **2003** 118-120
Ghorbanifar, Manucher, and U.S. arms sales to Iran, **1986** 1052; **1987** 223-224, 226, 233
Ghotbzadeh, Sadegh, **1979** 870
Ghufron, Ali (*aka* Mukhlas), Indonesian Islamic extremist, **2002** 706
GI Bill
extension of benefits and alcoholism, **1988** 277-285
restoration of, **1985** 585, 590
Giaimo, Robert N. (D-Conn.), **1977** 59; **1978** 96
Giamatti, A. Bartlett
bans Pete Rose from baseball, **1990** 429, 491, 493
and Rose gambling case, **1989** 477-484
Vincent's resignation as baseball commissioner, **1992** 855-858
Giambi, Jason, steroid use in baseball, **2005** 213, 214
Giancana, Sam
and CIA Castro plot, **1975** 728-731, 742-744
links to Kennedy assassination, **1979** 595
Gianni, Matthew, on conservation of world fisheries, **1995** 524
Gibbons, John J., jury selection and racial bias, **2004** 796
Gibbons, Sam M. (D-Fla.), Gulf of Tonkin resolution, **1991** 5
Gibbons v. Ogden, **1995** 186-187
Gibson, Charles, presidential debates moderator, **2004** 676, 691-701
Gibson, Edward George, **1973** 940
Gibson, Everett K., **1996** 471, 474-476
Gibson, Ian, on *Mars Express* probe launch failure, **2004** 6
Gibson, John M., Capitol policeman slain, **1998** 510-517
Gibson, Lynn (Mrs. John M.), **1999** 44
Gibson, Robert "Hoot," **1995** 420-424
Gibson, William F.
on Chavis as NAACP director, **1993** 579
and NAACP scandal, **1995** 453-454
Gideon v. Wainwright, **1979** 207-208, 211-212; **1985** 208; **1993** 935
Gidzenko, Yuri, **1998** 932
Gierek, Edward
arrest of, **1981** 882
as host to Carter, **1977** 898, 908-911
ouster of, **1980** 793-795
U.S.-Polish trade and technology agreements, **1974** 883-886
Gierow, Karl Ragnar, **1972** 727
Gifford, Kathie Lee, apparel industry sweatshop investigations, **1997** 206-207, 209
Giglio v. United States, **1991** 208-209
Gildenberg, Bernard D., Roswell incident, **1997** 400
Gille, John, **1988** 222
Gilleo, Margaret P., **1994** 289-297
Gilley, Bruce, Chinese leadership, **2002** 853
Gilligan, Andrew, British prewar intelligence on Iraq, **2003** 883
Gilman, Benjamin A. (R-N.Y.), **1976** 926
Gilmartin, Raymond, Vioxx withdrawal, **2004** 851

Gilmore, Gary Mark, death penalty execution of, **1976** 917-923; **2005** 178
Gilmore, James S., III (Virginia governor), on terrorism, **1999** 502; **2000** 281; **2001** 673
Gilmore v. Utah, **1976** 917-923
Gilmore Commission. *See* Congressional Advisory Panel to Assess Domestic Response Capabilities for Terrorism Involving Weapons of Mass Destruction
Gimes, Mikos, **1989** 341
Gingrey, Phil (R-Ga.), eminent domain, **2005** 365
Gingrich, Newt (R-Ga.)
affirmative action, **1997** 316
antimissile defense policy, **1998** 483
balanced budget amendment, **1995** 738-740, 744-745
signing ceremony, **1997** 604, 608-610
budget controversy, **1996** 148; **1997** 3; **1998** 800
Clinton debate, **1995** 427; **1996** 21
Clinton visit to China, **1998** 469
Congress
election results, **1994** 513-514, 519-523
first one hundred days, **1995** 165, 167-172
House censure of Crane and Studds, **1983** 726-727
House ethics rules violations, **1995** 746-751; **1996** 838-849; **1997** 3-19, 603; **1998** 800-801
House Speaker reelection, **1997** 3-4
House Speaker resignation, **1998** 698, 799-808, 951; **2005** 632
limit on gifts to members of, **1995** 701
lobbyist registration bill, **1995** 702
opening remarks, **1995** 3-5, 6-14
shooting of Capitol policemen, **1998** 514-515
flag protection amendment, **1989** 345
Jiang Zemin state visit, **1997** 730
minimum wage, **1996** 565
national security commission member, **1999** 500
on NEA funding, **1998** 407
Renewing American Civilization course, **1997** 7-11, 14-15
at Republican Party convention, **1996** 478; **2000** 509
welfare reform bill, **1996** 461
Wright investigation, **1989** 240
Ginn, Rosemary, **1972** 599
Ginsberg v. New York, **1990** 394; **1997** 447, 451, 454-457
Ginsburg, Douglas H.
Meese action on AT&T, **1988** 497, 505-506
nomination to Court, **1987** 720
Ginsburg, Ruth Bader
abortion
antiabortion demonstrations, **2000** 433
partial birth, **2000** 432, 440-441, 441
abortion clinic protests, **1994** 312-320
affirmative action, **2003** 362, 363
affirmative action, federal government plans, **1995** 309, 320-326
campaign finance reform, **2003** 1160
child pornography and "community standards," **2002** 291
congressional term limits, **1995** 260
death penalty, **2004** 795
for juvenile offenders, **2002** 358; **2004** 797; **2005** 179
for the mentally retarded, **2002** 356
defense attorneys, ineffectiveness of, **2002** 353
detentions in terrorism cases, **2004** 377, 378, 388-391
disabilities in the workplace, **2002** 6
disability, definition of, **1999** 319-320, 325-332
drug testing of students, **1995** 339-346
eminent domain, **2005** 363
endangered species on private lands, **1995** 359-368
free speech
ballot initiatives, **1999** 5-12
decency and the arts, **1998** 408
and the Internet, **1997** 445
Internet pornography filters in public libraries, **2003** 388, 390, 399-400
gay rights discrimination, **1996** 286
grandparents' rights, **2000** 289, 290-295
gun-free school zone, **1995** 184
HIV as a disability, **1998** 379, 389
line-item veto, **1998** 421
medical use of marijuana, **2001** 327
Miranda warnings, **2000** 389
parochial school aid, **1997** 363, 374-375, 375-380, 380-381
physician-assisted suicide, **1997** 461, 472-473, 478
presidential elections recount, **2000** 1002, 1003-1004, 1019-1024
public lands and developers, **1994** 299, 306-309
punitive damages, for consumer product liability, **1996** 275, 282-283
race-based redistricting, **1995** 371, 380-384; **1996** 370, 381-383, 383-387
religious clubs in public schools, **2001** 422, 430-432
religious freedom, **1997** 408
religious publications, **1995** 386, 393-395
school prayer, **2000** 367
school vouchers, **2002** 409, 416-423
sentencing laws, **2003** 984; **2004** 360
sex offenders, right to confine, **1997** 384, 392-394
sexual harassment, **1998** 461; **1999** 215
in workplace, **1993** 939-945
sodomy laws, **2003** 403
states' rights, **1999** 333, 345-349
student drug testing, **2002** 426-427, 433-436
Supreme Court appointment, **1993** 391-398
Ten Commandments displays, **2005** 378
unreasonable searches, **2001** 409, 410
Gioiosa, Tommy, and Rose gambling case, **1989** 478-480
Giordano, United States v., **1974** 392-399
Girod, Christophe, Guantanamo Bay detainees, **2003** 109
Giscard d'Estaing, Valéry
at economic summits, **1977** 367; **1978** 533; **1979** 3-5; **1980** 503-504; **1984** 355
EU constitution draft document, **2004** 200
EU membership expansion, **2004** 974
European Monetary System, **1978** 741-744, 750
Ford meeting on economic cooperation, **1974** 981-985
Gorbachev initiatives, **1989** 298-299

international monetary reform, **1972** 817
NATO participation, **1976** 331, 336, 339-341
U.S. visit, **1976** 331-343
Giuliani, Rudolph W. (New York City mayor)
and Hillary Clinton's senatorial campaign, **2000** 908-909
on Marcos indictment, **1988** 869
parochial school aid, **1997** 363
Republican Party convention speech, **2004** 484
September 11 attacks, **2001** 648
Glacier Bay National Monument, **1978** 731, 735, 738
Glacier Bay National Park, **1995** 126
Glaciers, effects of global warming on, **2002** 304
Glantz, Stanton A., on secondhand smoke, **1995** 673
Glaser, Elizabeth, Democratic convention speaker, **1992** 669, 709-713, 783
Glasnost (openness)
Elena Bonner analyzes, **1990** 207, 209
Gorbachev on, **1987** 79-80, 89, 94-95, 858-859, 862; **2004** 319
and human rights, **1987** 190
in political debate, **1988** 447-450, 454-456, 459-460
Glaspie, April C., Hussein pre-war meeting, **1991** 155-163; **1992** 966-969
Glasser, Ira, **1989** 345
Glaudemans, Jennifer L., Gates CIA nomination hearings, **1991** 652, 664-665
Glavin, William F., **1986** 973
GlaxoSmithKline
flu vaccine suppliers, **2004** 645
Paxil, risk of suicide as side effects for children, **2004** 748
Glazer, Nathan, multicultural textbooks, **1991** 332, 343-344
Gleaton, Thomas, PRIDE drug abuse report, **1992** 1013-1016
Glemp, Jozef
martial law in Poland, **1982** 948
Polish priest's killing, **1985** 120-121
visit of John Paul II to Poland, **1987** 555
Glendening, Parris N. (Maryland governor), death penalty moratorium, **2002** 355
Glenn, John (D-Ohio)
campaign finances, **1998** 894
Discovery space shuttle mission, **1998** 53-54, 776-786, 930
election campaigns, **1998** 777
"Keating Five" investigation, **1990** 817; **1991** 107-118
and Lincoln Savings, **1989** 465
radiation testing on citizens, **1993** 989
Reagan budget, **1987** 5
SALT II verification, **1979** 418
SDI, **1984** 259
student treatment in the military academies, **1992** 482
VA status, **1988** 875
women in combat, **1991** 492, 499-506, 512
Glickman, Dan (D-Kan.; agriculture secretary)
biotechnology in agriculture, **1999** 401-411
declassifying government records, **1994** 525
on farm bill, **1996** 199-203
food recalls, **1997** 691-692
food safety system, **1997** 693-698; **1998** 523
forest and national fire plan, **2000** 712-722
meat inspection rules, **1996** 414-417
war powers debate, **1990** 664
Global 2000 Report, **1980** 665-697
Carter proposals resulting from, **1981** 13-30
Global AIDS Alliance, **2005** 52
Global Climate Coalition, **1997** 862
Global Crossing, bankruptcy and collapse of, **2002** 102, 391, 399
Global Environment Outlook, **2002** 594-595, 855
Global Fund to Fight AIDS, Tuberculosis, and Malaria. *See* United Nations Global Fund to Fight AIDS, Tuberculosis, and Malaria
Global HIV Prevention Working Group, **2002** 472
Global Protection Against Limited Strikes, **2000** 678
Global Surveyor (MGS) mission, **2000** 89, 95-102, 379-384
Global Threat Reduction Initiative, **2004** 326-327
Global warming. *See* Climate change
Globalization
See also Economic development
defined, **2004** 241
Greenspan remarks on, **2004** 239-245
impact of, National Intelligence Council report on, **2005** 16, 19-21
Glover, Calvin, beating death of Barry L. Winchell, **1999** 900
Glover v. Patten, **1998** 399
Gluck, Michael, on tuberculosis, **1993** 852
GM. *See* General Mills; General Motors
Godfrey v. Georgia, **1980** 455-472; **1983** 708-709
Goering, Curt, on human rights, **1993** 560
Goislard, Bettina, killed by gunmen, **2003** 1091
Gokhale, V. P., **1984** 1023-1026
Golan Heights
See also Israel, occupied territories
Israeli annexation of, **1981** 788, 899-900
Israeli-Syria negotiations, **1995** 623
Israeli-Syrian disengagement of forces in, **1974** 435-439
Gold
as basis of world currency values, **1972** 816, 823
IMF accord on changes in, **1976** 3-9, 11
as IMF reserve asset, **1972** 413, 416
replacement of, **1974** 499, 502, 504
market price as basis for valuation, French-U.S. agreement on, **1974** 982-983
rising price of, and international monetary crisis, **1973** 343-345, 347
U.S. abandonment of convertibility of dollars into (1971), **1972** 816; **1974** 498
U.S. sales of, to improve trade deficit, **1978** 685, 698
Gold, Steven D., **1991** 828
Goldberg, Arthur J.
American Jewish Commission on Holocaust, **1981** 382-383; **1983** 143, 145
papers of, **1993** 340
Rockefeller financing of biography of, **1974** 988
UN in U.S. foreign policy, **1972** 337-340
Goldberg, Milton, **1990** 155

Goldberg, Suzanne, sodomy laws, Supreme Court case, **2003** 404
Goldblat, Jozef, **1972** 323
Golden, Soma, in Reagan-Anderson debate, **1980** 847, 864-865
Goldfarb, Cecilia, **1986** 821
Goldfarb, David, **1986** 821, 826-827
Goldfinger, Nat, **1975** 635-636
Goldin, Daniel S.
  "faster, better, cheaper" philosophy, **2000** 88-92; **2003** 632, 636
  Glenn space shuttle mission, **1998** 777
  life on Mars, **1996** 471-477; **1997** 510
  Mars mission failures, **1999** 712, 714; **2000** 88, 90-92
Goldin, Harrison J., and New York City's fiscal crisis, **1977** 567, 573, 575-576
Goldman, Janlori, medical records privacy, **2001** 487
Goldman, Ronald L., murder of, **1995** 611-621; **1997** 74
Goldschmid, Harvey J., accounting board nominations, **2002** 1034
Goldschmidt, Neil E., FAA regulation study, **1979** 952
Goldsmith, Arthur, African elections, **2003** 451
Goldsmith, Judy, on sex discrimination, **1983** 693, 756
Goldsmith, Stephen, faith-based initiatives, **2001** 133
Goldsmith-Grant Co. v. United States, **1993** 435
Goldstein, Barry L., **1987** 334
Goldstein, Cynthia, **1989** 307
Goldwater, Barry (R-Ariz.), **1973** 87
  D.C. voting representation in Congress, **1978** 590
  Defense Department reorganization, **1985** 669, 671
  draft evader amnesty, **1974** 821; **1977** 96
  foreign aid requests, **1974** 280
  intelligence agencies, Senate committee report on, **1976** 236
  Mecham resignation, **1988** 250
  Nixon's White House tapes, **1973** 697; **1974** 288
  Reagan endorsement of, **2004** 317
  at Republican Party convention, **1984** 729
  school prayer amendment, **1985** 381
  termination of Taiwan treaty, **1979** 917-938
Goldwater v. Carter, **1979** 917-918, 920, 932-938
Gomaa, Noaman, leader of Egyptian Al-Wafd party, **2005** 168
Gomez, Ciro, Brazilian presidential candidate, **2002** 777
Gomillion v. Lightfoot, **1993** 465, 467-468, 469, 471, 477
Gomulka, Wladyslaw, **1980** 794
Goncalves, Vasco, **1975** 354
Gongadze, Georgiy, murder investigation of journalist, **2005** 66-67
Gonzales, Alberto
  affirmative action, **2002** 974
  Afghanistan detainees, and Geneva Conventions, **2004** 337, 338
  attorney general nomination, **2004** 342, 778
  death-row inmate case reviews, **2005** 181
  Justice Department memo on terrorist interrogation guidelines, **2004** 337, 343-346; **2005** 45, 910
  Padilla detainee case, **2005** 452
  sentencing guidelines, **2005** 681
  warrantless domestic surveillance, **2005** 962
Gonzalez, Arthur J.
  Enron Corp. bankruptcy, **2004** 417
  WorldCom collapse, **2003** 334
Gonzalez, Elian, political asylum case, **2000** 265-276
Gonzalez, Felipe, **1982** 837
Gonzalez, Henry B. (D-Texas)
  BCCI banking scandal, **1991** 623, 631
  House inquiry on assassinations, **1978** 911-912
  savings and loan crisis, **1989** 465
Gonzalez, Juan Miguel (father of Elian), **2000** 265-268
Gonzalez, Virgilio R., Watergate break-in, **1973** 415, 419-423; **1974** 159-161
Good, Harold, IRA weapons decommissioning, **2005** 511
Good News Club v. Milford Central School, **2001** 420-432
Goode, W. Wilson, and Philadelphia police raid on MOVE group, **1986** 239-251
Goodell, Charles E. (R-N.Y.), clemency program for draft evaders, **1974** 821; **1977** 97
Goodlatte, Robert W. (R-Va.), House Judiciary Committee impeachment inquiry, **1998** 707
Goodling, William F. (R-Pa.), **1989** 563
Goodman, Andrew, civil rights worker murder (1964), **2002** 239; **2005** 353-361
Goodman, DeWitt S., **1987** 780
Goodman, Julian, **1973** 56
Goodman, Mark, **1988** 39
Goodman, Melvin A., Gates CIA confirmation hearings testimony, **1991** 652, 653-657
Goodridge v. Department of Public Health, **2003** 404, 414-424; **2004** 38-39, 44-55
Goodwin, Alfred T., pledge of allegiance unconstitutional, **2002** 382-384, 386-390
Goodwin, Thomas G., **1986** 489
GOPAC (political action committee), and Gingrich ethics violations, **1995** 748-751; **1996** 840-848; **1997** 6-14
Gorbachev, Mikhail S.
  Afghanistan, withdrawal from, **1988** 257-258, 928-929, 935
  agriculture program, **1989** 145-152
  arms control proposals, **1986** 9-20; **1988** 927-928, 938-940
    Bush response to, **1989** 297, 300-301, 303-304
    and SDI, **1986** 782, 784
  Baltic states
    freedom statements, **1989** 470
    independence, **1990** 184-185
  Berlin Wall, **1990** 107
  Bolshevik revolution anniversary, **1987** 857, 859-861, 867-868
  Bonner lecture on, **1990** 207-213
  Brezhnev doctrine, rejection of, **1989** 399-402
  Bush-Gorbachev statement on invasion of Kuwait, **1990** 550-551
  Bush's NATO press conference, **1990** 465
  Central America, U.S. pressure to end support for leftist regimes in, **1989** 163, 165-168, 644, 650, 657-658, 666
  Chernobyl nuclear accident, **1986** 385, 388, 406

coup attempt, **1991** 400, 475, 515-525, 527, 531
Daniloff arrest, **1986** 820, 821
defense as military strategy, **1989** 439-444
democratic reforms, **1987** 79-104; **1989** 173-177
domestic problems, **1990** 333
Eastern Europe political liberalization, **1989** 339-341, 412, 422-423, 523, 535, 625-626, 630, 635
economic reforms of, **1987** 185
economic summits
London, **1991** 451-473; **1997** 340
desire to join, **1989** 431-434
end of Cold War speech, **1992** 431-438
European cooperation, **1989** 399-409, 433-435
food aid from U.S., **1990** 807-808
friendship with Shevardnadze, **2003** 1039
Geneva summit, **1985** 707-709, 713-714, 718, 749-756
German reunification treaty, **1990** 599
Iceland summit, **1986** 875-885
INF treaty signing, **1987** 945-950
Katyn massacre by Stalin, **1990** 223-224
Lithuanian declaration of independence, **1990** 184-185
Malta meeting with Bush, **1989** 643-645, 648-660
Middle East Peace Conference (Madrid), **1991** 719, 723-725
Moscow summit, **1988** 353-373
NATO membership for unified Germany, **1990** 455, 600
New Year's Day message to U.S., **1986** 3-6
Nobel peace prize, **1990** 796-797
party congress speech (27th), **1986** 145-168
perestroika (restructuring), **1987** 857-858, 862, 864-866; **1988** 447-464, 929-931, 936-937; **2004** 319
power of, **1988** 448; **1989** 175, 211-212, 302
PRC visit, **1989** 276-277
resignation as Soviet leader, **1991** 785, 808-811
resignation from Communist Party, **1991** 527-529; **1993** 771
restructuring the Soviet Union, **1991** 531-541
rise to leadership, **1985** 271-275
Russian leader, **1999** 917; **2000** 173
Sakharov release, **1986** 1091-1094
Shevardnadze's resignation speech, **1990** 825-832
Soviet Party Congress, **1990** 439-448, 449-453
START agreement, **1991** 475-490
test ban moratorium, **1986** 783
troop reductions in Europe, **1990** 15
Vaclav Havel on, **1990** 13
Washington summit, **1987** 991-1004; **1990** 331-350
as world leader, **1992** 261
Gorbachev, Raisa, Wellesley College commencement, **1990** 354
Gorbachev Foundation, **1992** 432
Gordiyevsky, Oleg, **1985** 604
Gordon, Edmund G., multicultural textbooks, **1991** 332
Gordon, Robert, productivity studies, **2000** 301
Gore, Al, Jr. (D-Tenn.; vice president)
aviation safety report, GAO on, **1997** 113-121; **1998** 171-172; **1999** 114; **2001** 652
Brady bill signing, **1993** 966
campaigns and elections
acceptance speech, **1992** 670-675; **1996** 602, 603-608
attorney general investigations of campaign finance, **1998** 898-902
finance practices, **1997** 823-824, 825, 827-831
nomination, **1992** 667, 668-669
postelection statements, **1992** 1020, 1026
presidential campaign, **1999** 800; **2000** 131, 161, 520, 609, 618-619; **2004** 479, 480
presidential debates, **2000** 797-810, 817-832
presidential elections
concession speech, **2000** 1025-1027, 1028-1030
Florida recount, **2000** 999-1024; **2001** 524-525
presidential nomination acceptance speech, **2000** 617, 620-621, 625-634
vice presidential debates, **1992** 907, 909, 977-1001; **1996** 707-709, 718-724
vice presidential nomination acceptance speech, **2000** 763
Capitol bicentennial, **1993** 895, 897-898
church arson prevention, **1997** 310
Clinton inaugural address, **1993** 129, 130
defense policy
gays in the military, **1999** 900-901
missile defense system, **2000** 680
Democratic Party convention speech, **2004** 483
draft issue, **1992** 158
economic policy, **2001** 58
entertainment industry regulations, **2000** 729, 731
environmental issues
Everglades restoration project, **1996** 80-83
global warming, **1997** 861
oil production in Arctic refuge, **2001** 336
support for environmental protection, **2001** 212
faith-based initiatives, **2001** 134
foreign policy
China-U.S. relations, **2001** 739
China-U.S. trade relations, **2000** 215
Elian Gonzalez political asylum case, **2000** 269
Rwandan genocide, **2000** 450
South Africa, U.S. trade sanctions, **1999** 491
gay rights, Ellen DeGeneres "coming out," **1997** 761
gun control issue and NRA lobby against, **2001** 724
hate crimes legislation, **2000** 161
Holocaust Museum Dedication, **1993** 310
House impeachment vote, **1998** 968-969
human genetic engineering commission proposal, **1983** 526
at inauguration of president Bush, **2001** 94-95
IRS and customer service, **1998** 131-138
job discrimination, and genetic testing, **1998** 64-65
midwest floods, **1993** 485
NAFTA, **1993** 955, 956
National Performance Review report, **1993** 695, 717-733
nuclear nonproliferation treaty, **1995** 234, 238
Omnibus Budget Reconciliation Act, **1993** 181
ozone depletion, **1992** 77
prescription drug benefit reform, **2000** 131, 134
presidential elections, California voters, **2003** 1006
school prayer, **2000** 367

Gore, Al, Jr. (D-Tenn.; vice president) *Continued*
school violence, Columbine High School commemoration speech, **1999** 179-184
shooting of Capitol policemen, **1998** 515
television rating system, **1997** 529-531
tobacco industry regulation, **2000** 557
and UN summit on poverty, **1995** 135
U.S. Capitol bicentennial, **1993** 897-898
volunteerism summit, **1997** 238
Gore, Rich, **1981** 418
Gore, Tipper
at Democratic Party national convention, **2000** 612
and education, **1997** 36
mental health initiative, **1999** 49, 837; **2000** 25
"trash lyrics" legislation, **1990** 509, 511
Gore, Bush v., **2000** 999-1024
Gorelick, Jamie S., national commission on terrorist attacks, **2004** 452
Gorsuch, Anne M. *See* Burford, Anne M. Gorsuch
Gorton, Slade (R-Wash.), **1995** 359
election and Indian voters, **2003** 577
Gosh, Salah Abdall, Darfur region conflict, **2005** 517
Goss, Porter J.
CIA director confirmation, **2004** 968, 970
congressional intelligence failures panel, **2002** 991; **2003** 885
McCain amendment on treatment of detainees, **2005** 909-910
September 11 panel recommendations, **2004** 968
on terrorist networks, CIA director's comments on, **2005** 402
Goss v. Lopez, **1975** 67-80; **1995** 348
Gotovina, Ante, war crimes, **2003** 465
Goulart, Joao, **1985** 5
Gould, George D., **1988** 10
Gover, Kevin, BIA apology to Indians, **2000** 723-728
Government
accountability of, and FOIA revisions, **1981** 395
decentralization of, Republican platform on, **1980** 568, 608-610
dependence on
as cause of inflation, **1974** 421
to control risk, **1987** 127, 141-143
economic justice in policies of, U.S. bishops on, **1986** 983-985, 994, 997-998, 1000-1011
limiting role of
Bush on, **1989** 74
Carter on, **1980** 948
Democratic Party platform on, **1984** 560-561
Mondale on, **1980** 784
Nixon on, **1972** 882, 891-892
with privatization, **1988** 229-239
Reagan on, **1980** 652, 656-659, 947; **1987** 117, 120-123, 127, 141-142; **1988** 59, 121-122; **1989** 3-9, 12
Republican Party platform on, **1980** 571-572, 583-584, 586, 601-603, 608-610
Thatcher government on, **1979** 379, 382, 385
lowered expectations of
Carter on, **1978** 7-11, 65, 69, 95, 98, 102
Ford on, **1976** 13, 16-17
Nixon on, **1973** 80-81, 83-84, 211-213
news media coverage of, **1973** 629-639
public confidence in
Carter on, **1976** 797-798, 800-801
Mondale and Carter on, **1976** 597-600, 603, 605-607
reducing size of, **1985** 39, 44
Joint Economic Committee support for, **1979** 215-216
public opinion on, **1989** 17
Reagan on, **1981** 137-140; **1985** 72, 74, 77
Republican Party platform on, **1984** 665-666, 705-706
responsiveness of, Democratic Party platform on, **1976** 555-558
running against, Ford on, **1976** 714
service in, recruitment and pay, **1989** 198-202
shutdown of with veto of appropriations bill, **1981** 831-834
Government Accountability Office (GAO)
See also under its earlier name General Accounting Office (GAO)
Education Department propaganda prohibition, **2005** 644-655
federal advisory panels appointments, **2004** 843-844
flu vaccine shortage, **2004** 639-651
Homeland Security Department audit, **2005** 896
Iraq reconstruction, **2005** 718
Medicare cost estimates withheld from Congress, **2004** 577-587
mercury pollution regulations, cost-benefit analysis, **2005** 95, 98
morning-after pill over-the-counter distribution, FDA ruling, **2005** 814-831
National Guard preparedness, **2004** 784-793
presidential election problems investigations, **2004** 778
spending and tax policies review, **2005** 124
Government assets
sale of as privatization technique, **1988** 230, 232, 234-237
sale of to raise revenue, **1987** 3-4, 11
Government ethics
See also Congressional ethics
Allen's financial disclosure, **1981** 847-854
Bush on public service, **1988** 611
Carter administration, guidelines for, **1977** 27-34, 104, 110; **1978** 332-333
Casey's business dealings, **1981** 856, 858-859
Democratic Party platform on, **1972** 596-597; **1980** 746-747; **1984** 602-603, 618-619
Donovan investigation, **1982** 587-596
ethics office reports, **1992** 293-299
Ford pledge to uphold, **1974** 697, 704-705
HUD scandal, **1989** 333-337
as issue in presidential debates, **1988** 781-782
patronage, and dismissal on political grounds, **1980** 261, 268-271
paying for propaganda, **2005** 644-655
and recruitment to public service, **1989** 198-202
Republican Party platform, **1988** 647-649; **1996** 512-513
Sununu White House chief of staff's travels, **1992** 293-299

Watergate scandal
abuse of power in, **1975** 670-672
effect on young people, **1974** 190-191, 197
moral issues of, **1973** 723-727
whistleblowing and presidential immunity, **1982** 539-559
Government management
See also Privatization
civil service reform, Carter on, **1979** 37; **1980** 72
competence in
Bush on, **1988** 606
Carter on, **1976** 597, 600-601
Democratic Party platform on, **1988** 559
decision making in swine flu immunization program, **1978** 670-677
efficiency in
Carter program for, **1977** 104, 109-110; **1979** 19, 35-39, 84; **1980** 71-72; **1981** 59, 80-82
Democratic platform on, **1972** 533; **1980** 744-748
Ford plans for, **1976** 32-33
Nixon on, **1973** 181; **1974** 98, 100, 110-112
paperwork reduction, **1978** 8, 15, 33; **1979** 16; **1980** 747-748; **1981** 82
"plain English" regulations, Carter on, **1977** 104, 109
Reagan program for, **1982** 157-158; **1983** 105, 110, 116-117; **1984** 112-117; **1985** 77, 112; **1986** 56-57; **1987** 6, 12-13; **1988** 160-161
under FOIA and revised guidelines, **1981** 394-395, 397-399
Grace commission proposals, **1984** 169-179
Government reorganization
See also Civil service reform
Carter on savings from, **1976** 700
Carter plan for, **1976** 703-704; **1977** 104, 109; **1978** 15, 19, 32-33, 101, 769; **1979** 12, 16-17
Clinton reinventing government plan, **1995** 75, 83-85; **1996** 32-34, 54, 63-64
Democratic Party platform, **1996** 639-640
Ford plan for, **1976** 672; **1977** 46, 53
Mondale on, **1976** 777
reduction in size of, **1997** 54
Republican Party platform, **1976** 626-627; **1996** 511-513
Government spending
ceiling on, **1972** 669-670; **1973** 178-180, 223-224; **1976** 31
congressional control of, **1973** 171; **1974** 573-575
freeze in
in Reagan budget, **1983** 101-105, 108-109; **1985** 74-77, 79, 81-86
Republican Party platform on, **1988** 616, 629-630
and inflation control
Burns on, **1972** 961-962, 965-967; **1974** 419, 421
Carter on, **1978** 684, 688, 692-694; **1979** 22-23, 84, 88, 102-104, 109-110; **1981** 58
congressional reaction to Nixon budget, **1974** 95-96, 98-101
domestic summit on, **1974** 862-877
Ford on, **1974** 765-766, 769-770; **1976** 18-19, 710
Nixon on, **1973** 172, 176, 221, 428, 431-433, 711-712, 804, 808
Republican Party platform on, **1976** 618-623, 649-650
moratorium on growth in, in Ford budget, **1975** 16, 20-21, 30-31, 83-84, 86, 89, 105
as presidential campaign issue, **1976** 675-676, 694-695, 698; **1980** 862-863, 920-921, 927-929, 951
reduction in
in Carter budget, **1980** 244, 246-249, 254-255
Ford on, **1976** 37-38, 41
Joint Economic Committee on, **1979** 216-217; **1981** 294-296, 303, 310, 313, 321-322
Reagan CEA on, **1988** 119, 121, 124
in Reagan economic plan, **1981** 213-224, 325-335, 639-640, 644-645
Reagan on, **1980** 652, 656-660, 663; **1984** 126, 132-134; **1985** 105-106, 111-113; **1989** 3, 8-11
Thatcher government on, **1979** 379-380, 385
restraint in
in Carter budget, **1978** 96, 98
Carter CEA on, **1978** 65-66, 70-72, 83, 89; **1979** 109-110
Ford CEA on, **1976** 55-56
Ford on, **1974** 701; **1976** 13, 18-19, 55-56, 669-670, 672; **1977** 57-58, 60
Joint Economic Committee on, **1979** 216-218
Nixon on, **1972** 115-119; **1973** 43, 46-47, 170-178, 210, 213, 219, 801
OECD on, **1973** 686, 693
Reagan CEA on, **1986** 66, 75-76; **1987** 117, 121-122, 125, 133-134
restraint on, Ford on, **1977** 66, 69-70, 73-74, 76-77
taxpayer revolt against, **1978** 397-402
Governmental Affairs Institute, on voting by young people, **1973** 35-36
Gow, Ian, **1985** 725
Grace, J. Peter, report on government efficiency, **1984** 169-177; **1988** 231
Grace commission
CBO/GAO analysis of report of, **1984** 169-179
enactment of proposals, **1986** 40, 44
on privatization, **1988** 231
recommendations of, **1984** 87, 105-106, 115-116, 126-127, 169-170
Grachev, Pavel S.
Chechnya War, **1995** 94
on Russian military readiness, **1994** 530
Gradison, Bill (D-Ohio), on health insurance premiums, **1998** 141-142
Graham, Billy, on shooting of John Paul II, **1981** 428-430
Graham, Bob (D-Fla.)
congressional intelligence failures panel, **2002** 991
presidential candidate, **2004** 479
START treaty, **2002** 280
Graham, David J., Vioxx study and FDA drug safety review, congressional testimony, **2004** 851, 853, 854, 855-861
Graham, Gary, death penalty execution, **1993** 142; **2000** 991
Graham, Jim, **1992** 709
Graham, John, peer reviews for regulatory science, **2004** 844-845

Graham, Lindsey (R-S.C.)
Andijon killings, Uzbekistan, investigation, **2005** 432
Clinton impeachment inquiry, **1998** 699
detainee rights, **2005** 451
House Judiciary Committee impeachment inquiry, **1998** 712-713
McCain amendment on treatment of detainees, **2005** 909-910
Social Security personal retirement accounts supporter, **2005** 113
Graham, Patricia A., **1986** 218
Graham, Thomas, Jr., nuclear nonproliferation treaty, extension of, **1995** 233-238
Grain reserves, international system of, **1975** 598-599, 610
Grain sales
U.S. to Poland, Carter on, **1977** 906
U.S. to PRC, **1980** 829-831, 845-846
U.S.-Soviet, **1990** 337
embargo on, **1979** 967; **1980** 115-116
suspension, **1981** 884
Grainer, Charles A., Jr., Abu Ghraib prison abuse conviction, **2004** 215; **2005** 911
Gramm, Phil (R-Texas)
abortion opponent, **1995** 62
budget reduction legislation, **1985** 803
commodities futures legislation, **2001** 862-863
on IMF funding, **1983** 803
Jeffords party switch, **2001** 380
party switching, **2001** 377
as presidential candidate, **1995** 573
Gramm, Wendy
CFTC chairman and Enron Corp., **2001** 862-863
on stock market crash, **1988** 10, 12
Gramm-Rudman-Hollings Act. *See* Balanced Budget and Emergency Deficit Control Act (1985)
Grams, Rod (R-Minn.), Cuban foreign policy, **1998** 33
Grand Central Terminal (New York City), landmark status of, **1978** 453-465
Grand Rapids School District v. Ball, **1985** 433-452, 457, 459, 480, 486-487; **1993** 403; **1997** 361, 368-371, 373, 375-379
Grand Staircase-Escalante National Monument (Utah), **2001** 217
Grand Teton National Park (Wyoming), snowmobile regulation, **2001** 218; **2002** 902
Granderson, Colin, UN peacekeeping reform panel, **2000** 643
Grandparents' rights, Supreme Court on, **2000** 287-298
Graner, Charles, Abu Ghraib prison abuse scandal, **2005** 913
Grass, Martin L., Rite Aid Corp. fraud conviction, **2003** 332; **2004** 422
Grassley, Charles E. (R-Iowa)
antidepressants and risk of suicide in children, **2004** 749
border security, **2003** 220
closing of PLO offices, **1988** 479
drug safety office proposal, **2004** 854
FDA suppression of research study results, **2004** 853, 854
Iraq war resolution, **1991** 5
Nursing Home Compare Web site, **2002** 120
oil company profits, **2005** 781
prescription drug importation, **2004** 984
Social Security reform, **2005** 114
Grasso, Richard
SEC board resignation, **2003** 698
stock market scandals, **2003** 332, 693, 697-698; **2004** 422
Gratz v. Bollinger, **2003** 362-363, 381-386
Gravel, Mike (D-Alaska)
on Alaska federal lands, **1978** 733
and Kissinger Vietnam study (1969), **1972** 361
Gray, C. Boyden
lobbyist, **2002** 896
Supreme Court nominees, **1990** 615
White House counsel, **1991** 760; **1992** 293, 295-299
Gray, L. Patrick, III
confirmation hearings, **1973** 337-338, 666-667; **1974** 328-329
FBI break-ins, **1976** 322; **1981** 372
FBI investigation of Watergate, **1973** 740-741; **1974** 675-682
political use of FBI by White House, **1975** 873, 876
withdrawal of FBI nomination, **1973** 500-501, 511-512
Gray, Laman, artificial heart implants, **2001** 479-483
Gray, Nellie J., antiabortion rally, **1985** 53-55
Gray, William H., III (D-Pa.)
Bush State of the Union address, **1990** 50
election to majority whip, **1989** 240
on Reagan budget, **1987** 5
Grayned v. City of Rockford, **1994** 319
Grealy, Mary R., medical records privacy, **2001** 488
Great Britain
Afghanistan war against Taliban regime, **2001** 686-697
antiterrorism legislation, **2005** 398-399
Berlin, four-power agreement on, **1972** 467-470
British-Irish peace efforts, **1993** 923-931
Canadian constitutional reform, **1980** 402-403; **1981** 813-814; **1982** 317-323
death of Princess Diana, **1997** 647-653
defense funds for development aid, **1973** 810
EC contribution, **1984** 439-442
economic summits, **1976** 425-426; **1978** 533, 536-537; **1979** 3-8; **1981** 591; **1982** 469, 471; **1983** 507-514
Munich, **1992** 637-648
election of prime minister Blair, **1997** 237-283
Elizabeth II's visit to U.S., **1991** 247-251
English law on impeachment, **1974** 138, 140-142
Eurocurrency, rejection of, **1997** 278
European Monetary System, **1978** 741, 751
exchange rate stabilization, **1985** 623-630
in Falkland Islands (Malvinas) war, **1982** 283-304; **1983** 3-23
free trade, nineteenth century movement toward, **1985** 81, 96-97
gay marriage legislation, **2005** 869
Genocide Convention ratification, **1986** 116
Germany, division of, **1986** 792-793, 796, 798
health care, prescription drug prices, **1994** 87-94

Holocaust, acquiescence or indifference to, **1983** 143-144, 148, 150
Hong Kong agreement, **1984** 1045-1050
Houston economic summit, **1990** 467-482
human rights, **1990** 134, 141-142
intelligence service, Soviet spies in, **1979** 905-914
Iran, diplomatic relations with, **1989** 95-97
Iraq War
letter of support, **2003** 49-51
support for, **2003** 811
Israel, role in formation of, Arafat on, **1974** 927-928, 933
John Paul II's visit to, **1982** 409-418
Law of the Sea Treaty, **1982** 345-361
London terrorist bombings, **2005** 393-404, 473-474
mad cow disease, **2000** 880-892; **2001** 698-699
missiles of, Soviet position on, **1982** 983, 986-987; **1983** 792; **1986** 10, 13
NATO membership for Spain, **1975** 354
nonproliferation treaty signing, **1975** 363
Northern Ireland
accord with Irish Republic on, **1985** 723-732
IRA prison hunger strike, **1981** 401-416
peace agreement, **1998** 203-219
peace negotiations, **2005** 507-513
presence in, New Ireland Forum on, **1984** 316-326
shared political power plan for, **1973** 353-359
troop withdrawal, **2005** 510
on Osama bin Laden, **2001** 802-818
ozone depletion research, **1992** 79
and Palestine mandate, **1988** 581
poverty summit, **1981** 770
privatization in, **1988** 230, 238
proposed Atlantic charter, **1973** 488
Reagan speech to Parliament, **1982** 477-488
Rhodesia
cease-fire proposal, **1979** 944-948
lifting of economic sanctions against, **1979** 940-942
pressure for black majority rule in, **1978** 149-150
settlement proposals, **1976** 288, 291, 721-725, 908-909; **1977** 583-590
royal family problems, **1992** 1059-1063
South Africa, economic sanctions against, **1977** 823-824; **1986** 583
Soviet pipeline sanctions defied by, **1982** 880
student test scores in England, **1992** 90, 92, 95
Syria, diplomatic break with, **1986** 832
Thatcher
election victory, **1979** 379-387
resignation of, **1990** 747-752, 761-766
UN membership for East and West Germany, four-power agreement on, **1972** 897, 900
U.S. air strike against Libya, **1986** 350-351
U.S. extradition treaty with, **1986** 751-756
U.S. invasion of Grenada, **1983** 850
U.S. missile deployment in, **1981** 717-718; **1983** 793
Vatican diplomatic relations with, **1984** 21
wedding of Charles and Diana, **1981** 601-603
Zimbabwe independence, role in, **1979** 939-948; **1980** 317-319, 332-336
Great Lakes, water quality report, **1994** 147-152
Grechko, Andrei A., **1976** 171
Greece
conflict with Turkey over Cyprus, **1975** 224, 232-233, 354
earthquake relief for Turkey, **1999** 466
human trafficking, **2002** 344
NATO participation, **1975** 354, 357; **1982** 420
relations with Albania, **1985** 327
wartime atrocities in, **1986** 743-745
Greeley, Andrew, **1993** 408
Greeley, Ronald, and *Galileo* imaging, **1997** 204
Green, Bill (R-N.Y.), in Holocaust commemoration, **1981** 388-389
Green, Joyce Hens, Guantanamo Bay detainees case, **2005** 448
Green, Pincus, **2001** 89
Green, Robert L., **1975** 614
Green, Stanley E., Abu Ghraib prison abuse scandal investigations, **2005** 912
Green v. County School Bd., **1998** 865
Green v. New Kent County School Board, **1991** 27, 29; **1992** 582
Green Belt Movement, in Kenya, **2004** 929-936
Green Party, Nader as presidential candidate, **2000** 611, 617, 895-905
Greenberg, Daniel, in presidential debate, **1980** 847, 853-854
Greenberg, Jack, **1972** 500
Greenberg, Jeffrey W., CEO of Marsh & McLennan resignation, **2004** 418
Greenberg, Maurice, SEC investigation of AIG, **2004** 418
Greenberger, Marcia D., gender discrimination, **1991** 310
Greene, Harold
on AT&T divestiture, **1982** 18-21, 28-33
and Persian Gulf War declaration, **1990** 666
Greene, Mike, **1990** 509
Greenhouse, Bunnatine H., Halliburton no-bid contracts, **2005** 723
Greenhouse, Linda
on congressional term limits, **1995** 259
on Rehnquist legacy, **2005** 552
Greenhouse effect
from burning coal, **1980** 418, 423, 427-430
and climate change, studies on, **1988** 861-866
Earth Summit (Rio), **1992** 499-506
Houston economic summit, **1990** 468
impact of SST, **1973** 236
and loss of ozone layer, **1987** 746; **1988** 222
Greenhouse gas emissions
See also Climate change; Kyoto Protocol on Climate Change (UN treaty)
earth summit (Rio de Janeiro), **1997** 860
and global warming, **1998** 945; **2000** 337, 346
Great Britain policy, **1997** 481
"greenhouse gas intensity," **2002** 299
inventory, **2002** 310-311, 313-315
reduction of, **1997** 861-862; **2000** 341
trends and projections, **2002** 312, 315-318
U.S. policy, **1997** 861-862
Greenpeace International
French sabotage of ship, **1985** 631-634

Greenpeace International *Continued*
hazardous waste exports, **1989** 154
world fisheries conservation, **1995** 524-525
Greenspan, Alan
budget strategies, **2005** 124
Bush tax cut plan, **2001** 402
corporate scandals, **2002** 393
and economic expansion, **1997** 51; **1998** 75-76, 502; **2002** 56
energy prices, **2004** 186-194; **2005** 779
Federal Reserve Board appointment, **1987** 511-516
Federal Reserve Board chairman, **2005** 141-142
Federal Reserve Board resignation, **2005** 141
"home equity extraction," **2005** 139
influence noted, **1990** 82
monetary policy, **1999** 86
on negative personal savings, **2005** 139
savings and loan bailout, **1990** 817
Social Security benefits, **2005** 115
Social Security reform, **1983** 59-60, 62
state of the economy, **2002** 877-884
stock market crash, **1988** 10, 12
stock market volatility, **1997** 721-727
trade and budget deficits, **2004** 234-245
Greenspan, Hank, **1973** 976
Greenstein, Robert, **1984** 5; **1991** 828
tax cuts for social service programs, **2005** 141
Greenstock, Jeremy, U.S. intervention in Liberia, **2003** 769
Greenwald, Gerald, **1986** 973
Greer, George W., Schiavo end-of-life care case, **2005** 155-157
Greer, Germaine, **1974** 779
Gregg, Judd (R-N.H.)
education reform, **2002** 42
Medicare prescription drug benefit, **2003** 1122
Gregg v. Georgia, **1976** 489-503; **1980** 455-465, 468, 472; **1983** 708; **1990** 313
Gregoire, Christine, Washington gubernatorial election, **2004** 778
Gregory, Gwendolyn
disruptive handicapped students, **1988** 48
public aid to parochial schools, **1985** 434
Gregory, Wilton D. (bishop), child sexual abuse by priests, **2002** 870, 871; **2003** 526; **2004** 83, 85, 87
Gregory v. Ashcroft, **1992** 463; **1995** 186
Gregory v. Chicago, **1995** 331
Grenada
military buildup in, **1983** 307, 312
U.S. invasion of, **1983** 847-853
Grey, Robert, nonproliferation treaty, **2000** 204
Griffey, Ken, Jr., and home run championship, **1998** 627
Griffin, Arlee, Jr., **1995** 337
Griffin, Michael D.
Discovery space shuttle mission, **2005** 499, 501
Hubble Space Telescope mission, **2005** 503
Griffin, Robert P. (R-Mich.), **1978** 179-180
Griffin v. Prince Edward County School Board, **1990** 231-232
Griffin v. Wisconsin, **1995** 342
Griffith, Winthrop, **1975** 377
Griggs v. Duke Power Co., **1989** 321-322, 325, 328
Grigson, James
psychiatric testimony of, **1981** 432-439
testimony in capital punishment cases, **2000** 991
Grimmett, Richard F., small arms trade, **2001** 519
Griswold, Erwin N.
Court workload, **1975** 459, 463-464, 466
flag protection amendment, **1989** 345
ITT antitrust suit, **1974** 5
Griswold v. Connecticut, **1990** 623; **1992** 594, 596
Grocholewski, Zenon (cardinal), gay seminarians prohibition, **2005** 864
Groer, Anne, in presidential debates, **1988** 723, 729-730, 736-737, 744-745, 750-751
Gromyko, Andrei A., **1973** 587
arms control negotiations, **1977** 243-244, 257-268; **1979** 414; **1984** 260, 917-919
Berlin, four-power agreement on, **1972** 467
change in role of, **1985** 272-273
defense budget percentages for development aid, proposal of, **1973** 810, 820-821
Munich terrorism, **1972** 752
resignation as president, **1988** 448
on Soviet troops in Cuba, **1979** 764
UN speech on U.S-Soviet relations, **1974** 833, 835, 843-844; **1984** 811-813, 821-829
U.S. trade concessions and Soviet emigration policy, **1974** 902, 905-906
Gross, H. R. (R-Iowa), **1974** 280
Gross domestic income (GDI), **2005** 152-153
Gross domestic product (GDP), **2001** 60; **2002** 52, 53; **2004** 61; **2005** 138-139, 145-146, 151-152
compared with other nations, **1992** 125
growth in, Clinton economic report on, **1996** 69; **1998** 73, 79; **1999** 95-96; **2000** 44
predicted, **1992** 109
Gross national product (GNP), **2000** 50, 62
Grossman, Marc, Iraq reconstruction efforts, **2004** 405
Grosvenor, Gilbert M., **1989** 688-689
Grosz, Paul, and John Paul II's visit to Austria, **1988** 406-407, 409-411
Group of 24 (G-24)
Houston economic summit, **1990** 473-474
Munich economic summit, **1992** 644
Group of 77, call for new world trade structure, **1976** 299
Group of Eight (G-8, *formerly* G-7)
African economic assistance, **2005** 405-427
AIDS initiative and, **2003** 782; **2005** 51
Bush-Putin talks, **2001** 893
climate change declaration, **2005** 920-921
final statement, **1997** 340-360
food safety, **1999** 405
Hu Jintao, first Chinese leader to meet with, **2003** 1179
Kosovo conflict, **1999** 286
Middle East Initiative, **2004** 628-629
NATO expansion, **1997** 340, 516
New Partnership for African Development (NEPAD), **2002** 446-466; **2003** 451-452, 1226
Palestinian economic aid, **2005** 34
Russian weapons arsenal security, **2003** 907

sanctions against India and Pakistan for nuclear testing, **1998** 328
summit meetings
Gleneagles, Scotland (2005), **2005** 395, 405-427
St. Petersburg (2006), **2005** 299
terrorist threats, **2004** 270
weapons of mass destruction, **2002** 437-445
world poverty, summit on, **2000** 475-487
Group of Friends (Salvadoran peace process), **1992** 24-25
Group of Seven (G-7)
African economic development, **2001** 504
aid to Russia, **1992** 257
economic aftermath of September 11, **2001** 664
economic summits
Houston, **1990** 467-482
London, **1991** 451-473
Munich, **1992** 637-648
environmental issues, **1992** 503, 505
world debt relief, **1999** 701-702; **2000** 69
Group of Twenty, **1999** 393-394
Grove City College v. Bell, **1984** 201-214; **1992** 196
Growe v. Emison, **1993** 471
Grupper, Pessah, **1983** 832
Grutman, Norman Roy, **1988** 176-177
Grutter v. Bollinger, **2003** 362, 364-381, 383
GSA. *See* General Services Administration
GSCP. *See* Salafist Group for Call and Combat (GSCP)
Guadeloupe summit, **1979** 3-8
Guam, abortion legislation, **1990** 217
Guantanamo Bay detainees
abuse allegations, **2004** 380-381; **2005** 449-450
Afghan detainees, **2005** 976-977
Ashcroft on, **2002** 830, 833; **2003** 108
British antiterrorism legislation influenced by, **2005** 399
British Courts on, **2002** 830-841; **2004** 375
Bush administration policy on "enemy combatants," **2003** 310; **2004** 212-213, 336-337
CIA detention facility, **2004** 380
closing proposals, **2004** 450
combatant status-review tribunals, **2004** 376, 379-380; **2005** 447-449
congressional hearings, **2005** 450-451
detentions in terrorism cases, Supreme Court on, **2004** 207, 375-398
due process rates of detainees, **2005** 448
foreign views of U.S. and, **2005** 580
Graham amendment, **2005** 450-451
interrogations of terrorist suspects, Justice Department on, **2004** 336, 338-339
treatment of
abuse allegations investigations, **2005** 449-450
International Red Cross monitoring of, **2003** 107, 109; **2004** 380
Justice Department on, **2003** 310-331
Koran incident, **2005** 449, 450
U.S. Court of appeals rulings, **2003** 106, 107-109; **2005** 446-461
Guantanamo Bay Naval Base (Cuba), Haitian refugees, **1992** 453-468; **1993** 371-383, 413-421
Guardians Assn. v. Civil Service Commission of New York City, **1992** 191, 194
Guatemala
Central American peace plan
compliance with, **1987** 637, 638-639, 642-648, 1007, 1008
signing of agreement in, **1987** 637-648, 1007; **1989** 162-163, 165-168
CIA documents about 1954 coup, **1992** 10
Cuban-Soviet colonialism in, Reagan on, **1982** 180, 187-188
human rights in, **1981** 180; **1985** 146, 152; **1986** 104-106; **1987** 191, 195-196, 638-639; **1990** 137, 147-148
hurricane and flood damage, **1998** 791
insurgency in, Cuban and Nicaraguan support for, **1985** 264
John Paul II's visit, **1983** 242, 251-253
peace agreement, **1996** 850-856
political killings in, **1989** 599, 605
smoking in the Americas, **1992** 269
U.S. military and economic aid to, **1984** 32
Guccione, Bob, **1973** 612-613
Gucht, Karel de, U.S. policy on torture, Rice statements on, **2005** 908
Guckert, James D., Internet blogger, **2005** 646
Guei, Robert, Ivory Coast coup leader, **2002** 251; **2003** 238
Guerrilla warfare
CIA manual on in Nicaragua, **1984** 903-916
John Paul II on in Peru, **1985** 58-59, 65-67
Guffey, Roger, **1987** 512-513
Guillain-Barre syndrome, and swine flu immunization, **1978** 669, 673, 676-677, 680
Guinea, on coup in Liberia, **1980** 277
Guinier, Lani, on minority rights, **1995** 611
Guinn v. United States, **1993** 467
Guisti, Carlos, death of Peruvian hostage, **1997** 235
Guiteau, Charles Julius, **1978** 138
Gul, Abdullah
legislative program, **2002** 911-915
Turkish prime minister election, **2002** 906-908
Gulag Archipelago, publication of in West, **1974** 129-130; **1975** 482
Gulf Cooperation Council (GCC), **2001** 626
attempted mediation of Iran-Iraq war, **1984** 750, 752-754
Gulf of Tonkin resolution, **1990** 663-664, 665
Gulf War. *See* Persian Gulf War
Gun control
American Party platform on, **1972** 615, 617-618
assault weapons ban, **2002** 960-961; **2004** 764
assault weapons in crime, **1995** 470-471
attorney general's violent crime task force on, **1981** 647-648, 651-655
automatic weapons, **1995** 468
background checks on gun purchasers, **2001** 722, 725-726; **2002** 959; **2003** 156, 158-160
ballistic "fingerprinting," **2002** 959, 961-962
Brady bill signing, **1993** 965-969
Bush position on, **1988** 559, 591, 610
Carter position on, **1976** 813
Clinton administration proposals, **1999** 42, 43, 54-55; **2000** 27
crime bill, **1994** 576

Gun control *Continued*
crime statistics, **1994** 580-581
Democratic Party platform on, **1972** 528, 568; **1976** 570-571; **1992** 700; **1996** 634-635
Eisenhower Foundation inner cities report, **1993** 227
firearm use, **1996** 733
Ford position on, **1976** 812-813, 816
gun safety laws, **2000** 27, 386
gun use in crimes, **1995** 463-471
gun violence report, **1992** 493-498
gun-free school zones, Supreme Court on, **1995** 183-200; **1998** 735-736; **2005** 552
guns in the home study, **1993** 871-876
Nixon position on, **1973** 201-202, 329
NRA on, **1981** 648
presidential debates on, **1992** 937-940
Reagan position on, **1981** 648; **1991** 185-188
Republican Party platform on, **1980** 568, 594; **1988** 616, 645; **1996** 519; **2000** 513
right to bear arms, federal appeals court on, **2001** 722-737; **2002** 959-968
small arms trade, **2001** 516-521
Urban League recommendation on, **1983** 55
Gunderson, Steve (R-Wis.), **1996** 688
Gun-Free School Zones Act (1990), **1995** 185-186
Gun-Free Schools Act (1994), **1998** 735-736
Gunn, David, abortion clinics, **1993** 95
Gunn, James, age of universe, **1994** 462
Gup, Ted, **1991** 276
Gurney, Edward J. (R-Fla.), **1974** 606
Gusinsky, Vladimir, Russian entrepreneur, or "oligarch," **2000** 174; **2001** 256
Gusmao, Jose Alexandre (Xanana)
East Timor independence, **1999** 515; **2002** 263-264
East Timor presidential elections, **2002** 257-258
Guterres, Eurico
East Timor human rights violations, **2002** 260
East Timor war crimes conviction, **2004** 756
Gutierrez, Carlos, as Commerce Department secretary, **2005** 45
Gutiérrez, Gustavo, and liberation theology, **1984** 759-760; **1986** 317
Gutierrez, Lucio, Ecuador president ousted, **2005** 771-772
Gutknecht, Gil (R-Minn.), prescription drug importation, **2004** 985
Guyana
human trafficking, **2004** 125
at poverty summit, **1981** 770
relationship with People's Temple, **1979** 349, 371-372, 374
Guyer, Tennyson (R-Ohio), **1976** 926
Guyot, Lawrence, on lynchings, **2005** 356
Guzman Reynoso, Abimael, capture, **1992** 202, 859-864
Gvishiana, Jermen M., **1972** 833
Gwynn, Tony, baseball season cancellation, **1994** 361

H

H. L. v. Matheson, **1990** 392, 398, 402, 403
Habash, George, **1988** 907
Habeas corpus
See also *Constitutional amendments (U.S.), Fourteenth Amendment, due process*
claims of in federal court, **1976** 521-536
Habib, Mamdouh, Australian detainee case, **2005** 448, 914
Habib, Philip C.
Philippine change of government, **1986** 308
PLO departure negotiations, **1982** 741, 743, 755
Habib v. Bush, **2003** 115
Habibie, B. J.
East Timor, UN peacekeeping forces, **1999** 513
East Timor independence, **1999** 512
elections in Indonesia, **1999** 514, 718, 719
president of Indonesia, **1998** 284-288; **1999** 719-720; **2001** 563
Habiger, Eugene E., nuclear weapons security, **1999** 240
Habitat for Humanity
low-income housing, **1999** 56
and rebuilding of burnt churches, **1997** 304, 306, 311
Habyarimana, Juvenal
assassination of, **1994** 541; **1998** 614; **1999** 863; **2000** 452, 455
Rwanda genocidal war, **1999** 861, 862
Hackworth, Donald E., General Motors UAW strike statement, **1998** 323, 324-325
Hadda, William F., **1977** 569
Hadley, Stephen J., secret detentions and torture allegations, **2005** 907
Haekkerup, Hans, UN peacekeeping mission in Kosovo, **2001** 820
Hagan, Carl I., on Nobel Peace Prize controversy, **2004** 931
Hagel, Charles "Chuck" (R-Neb.)
climate change proposals, **2005** 921-922
Cuban trade sanctions, **2000** 268
federal budget deficit, **2003** 682
food safety system, **1997** 692
global warming, **2001** 112
Iraq reconstruction efforts, **2004** 405
Iraq War troop withdrawal, calling for, **2005** 836
missile defense system, **2000** 681
Hagelin, John, **1996** 707
Haggerty, United States v., **1990** 357-365
Hague v. Committee for Industrial Organization, **1995** 334
al-Haidri, Ali, Iraq elections, **2005** 943
Haig, Alexander M., Jr.
after Reagan assassination attempt, **1981** 352, 354-355; **1985** 493
appointment to chief of staff, **1973** 499
at economic summit, **1982** 469
El Salvador, rebel arms buildup in, **1981** 241-243
Falklands war, **1982** 285, 299, 562
human rights and quiet diplomacy, **1981** 779
Israeli raid on Iraq, **1981** 508
NSC wiretaps, **1974** 488-489, 492
nuclear arms reduction, **1982** 386
nuclear first-strike defense, **1982** 305-315
Poland, martial law in, **1981** 883-884
Reagan administration, disputes within, **1982** 562

resignation from State Department, **1982** 561-566
on Soviet chemical warfare, **1981** 681-685; **1982** 235-252
on Soviet pipeline sanctions, **1982** 562
Soviet support of terrorism, **1981** 462
Watergate
Ford meetings with on Nixon's future, **1974** 889-891
negotiations on Nixon materials, **1975** 663, 665
Haig v. Agee, **1981** 541-555
Haile-Mariam, Mengistu
famine in Ethiopia, **1984** 974
human rights in Ethiopia, **1985** 151; **1987** 191-192
rule of, **1986** 99-100
Haines, Gerald K., Roswell incident, **1997** 397
Haiti
Aristide's return to, **1994** 436-444
casualties from violence in, **2005** 331
elections
disputes, **2001** 395-396
preparing for, **2005** 329-331
elections in
and cutoff of U.S. aid, **1987** 939-941
and UN, **1995** 355
human rights, and U.S. aid, **1977** 3, 8-11
human rights abuses, **1986** 97-99, 106-107; **1988** 94, 101-103, 884, 888; **2004** 98
hurricane damage and disasters, **1998** 789, 790; **2004** 99; **2005** 334
independence, two hundredth anniversary, **2004** 94
interim government, **2004** 96; **2005** 329
John Paul II's visit to, **1983** 241, 253-255
legislative elections, **2000** 953-955
natural disasters, **2004** 99
political prisoners, **2005** 333
political situation, **2000** 952-960; **2001** 395-399; **2004** 94-102
political violence and gang warfare, **2005** 331-333
population growth in, **1987** 440, 443
post-Aristide era, UN Security Council on, **2004** 94-102
presidential elections, **2000** 955-956
refugees from
agreement with U.S., **1982** 114
political asylum, **1993** 371-383
returned to, **1992** 453-468; **1993** 413-421
U.S. classification of, **1980** 338-339, 341, 344, 348-349
U.S. interdiction of, **1981** 606-607
Resistance Front, **2004** 95
security situation and gang violence, **2005** 331-333
smoking in the Americas, **1992** 269
Taiwan diplomatic relations, **2005** 332
UN economic assistance, **2005** 334
UN peacekeeping mission, **1997** 150, 151, 154, 155, 156
UN Stabilization Mission (peacekeeping force), **2004** 785, 949; **2005** 329-337
U.S. economic aid package, **2004** 98; **2005** 333-334
U.S. forces in, **1994** 433-434, 437-438, 529
U.S. led-ousting and forced exile of Aristide, **2004** 94-96
Haitian Refugee Center v. Baker, **1992** 460; **1993** 417
Haitian Refugee Center v. Gracey, **1992** 468; **1993** 417
al-Hakim, Abdul Aziz
Iraqi Governing Council leader, **2003** 946
United Iraqi Alliance and, **2004** 404
Hakim, Albert A.
Iran-contra conviction, **1991** 619; **1994** 12
role in Iran-contra affair, **1987** 892, 899, 901, 906, 919, 927
trial of, **1989** 392-393
al-Hakim, Ayatollah Mohammed Bakir, killed in bombing, **2003** 940; **2004** 404
Haldeman, H. R.
campaigns and elections
organization of CRP by, **1974** 600
secret funds, **1973** 414
Nixon's confidence in, **1973** 738, 748-749, 948, 955
resignation, **1973** 499, 502-504, 508-510, 564
Watergate
committee testimony, **1973** 550, 660-662
court proceedings in case of, **1974** 157-167, 171-176, 225-228, 991-992; **1975** 141-142, 144-146, 151
cover-up, White House tapes on, **1974** 306, 308-315, 321-322, 333-334, 363-381
defendants, payments to, **1974** 189-191, 193, 198, 201
Watergate tapes
conversations with Nixon, **1974** 673, 675-680, 991-992, 994-1002
erasure of, **1974** 23-27
instructions to destroy, **1977** 324, 358
wiretaps in Nixon White House, **1976** 160
Hale, Kate, Hurricane Andrew, **1992** 844
Hale, Mother, **1985** 117
Hale, Wayne, space shuttle program, **2005** 501
Halevy, David, and Sharon libel suit, **1985** 49-51
Halilovic, Safet, Bosnia-Herzegovina constitutional reform, **2005** 858-859
Hall, James E.
air bag safety, **1997** 775
air safety standards for foreign airlines, **1999** 113
on airline safety, **1994** 535
aviation safety, congressional testimony on, **1999** 116-118
and de-icing procedures, **1998** 171
on National Transportation Safety Board funding, **1999** 115
on railroad safety, **1996** 189
TWA flight 800 crash, **1997** 781, 783-786
Hall, Tony P. (D-Ohio), abortion issue, **1996** 624
Halliburton Company
Iraq reconstruction contracts, **2003** 947; **2005** 722-723
UN Oil for Food program, **2004** 893
Halons
cutting production and use of, **1988** 221-223
and ozone layer loss, **1987** 747-748, 756
Halper, United States v., **1993** 434, 436, 437
Halperin, Morton
FOIA suit by, **1975** 523

Halperin, Morton *Continued*
wiretap on, **1974** 488; **1976** 159-168
Ham, Linda, NASA resignation, **2003** 634
Hamadeh, Marwan (Lebanon minister of economy), assassination attempt, **2004** 561-562
Hamadi, Mohammed Ali, **1989** 316
Hamas (Islamic resistance movement)
cease-fire agreement, **2003** 196
Fatah party challenger, **2005** 33-34
Palestinian Authority elections, **2004** 809; **2005** 27, 34, 271, 273
Rantisi assassination, **2004** 301, 302
suicide bombings, **2001** 363-365, 367; **2002** 927, 929-931, 933; **2003** 191, 192, 195, 196, 841, 1053, 1211; **2005** 31
Syria as refuge for, **2003** 1202; **2004** 559
Yassin assassination, **2004** 301, 302
Hambali. *See* Isamuddin, Riduan
Hamdan, Mustapha, Hariri assassination plot, UN investigation, **2005** 691
Hamdan, Salim Ahmed, "enemy combatant" case, **2004** 379-380; **2005** 446-447
Hamdan v. Rumsfeld, **2005** 446-447, 453-461
Hamdi, Yaser Esam, "enemy combatant" case, **2002** 835-836; **2003** 106, 111-112; **2004** 376, 377; **2005** 555, 962
Hamdi v. Rumsfeld, **2004** 377, 381-392; **2005** 555, 962
Hamilton, Charles V., **1985** 27
Hamilton, James, meeting with Foster, posthumous confidentiality, **1998** 393
Hamilton, Joseph G., human radiation experiments, **1993** 989
Hamilton, Lee H. (D-Ind.)
congressional intelligence failures panel, **2002** 990, 997
Glaspie-Hussein pre-war meeting, **1991** 156
government secrecy, **1997** 103
Iran-contra committee, **1986** 1052; **1987** 893
Israeli kidnapping of Obeid, **1989** 316
national commission on terrorist attacks
recommendations, **2005** 893-904
vice chairman, **2003** 547; **2004** 450, 451, 457, 458, 967, 968, 970
national security commission member, **1999** 500
national security strategy, **2002** 637
North trial, documents in, **1989** 394-395
"October Surprise" report, **1994** 4
Reagan's knowledge of Iran-contra affair, **1986** 1051
Russian nuclear weapons panel, **2001** 19
U.S.-Taiwan relations, **2000** 192
Yeltsin's congressional speech, **1992** 519
Hamilton, Wendy, on teenage drinking, **2002** 178
Hamilton, William, **1972** 253
Hamling v. United States, **1974** 515-517, 520-522
Hammer, Armand, **1986** 821
presidential pardon, **2001** 90
Hammerschmidt, John Paul (R-Ark.), presidential commission on aviation security and terrorism, **1990** 301-310
Hammond, Jay S., **1978** 733
Hammonds, Tom, food safety, **2001** 699
Hamre, John, Y2K computer conversion, **1998** 545; **1999** 762
Han Sung-Joo, **1999** 861
Hancho Kim, in Korean influence-buying scheme, **1977** 770, 776, 786-789; **1978** 849-852, 881-887
Hancock, J. Steward, Jr., **1990** 269, 273
Hand, Brevard, on secular humanism in schools, **1987** 598-599
Handal, Shafik, weapons purchased for El Salvador by, **1981** 241, 243, 247-251, 254-255
Handel, William, **1987** 376
Handgun control. *See* Gun control
Handicapped persons. *See* Disabled persons
Handler, Philip
defense of Sakharov, **1973** 793-794
on East-West scientific organization, **1972** 833-834
Hanfling, Robert I., Russian nuclear weapons panel, **2001** 19
Hanford Nuclear Reservation (Washington), cleanup efforts, **1994** 340-341; **1995** 114-115, 117-118
Hanna, Mark, campaign finance, **2003** 1156-1157
Hanna, Richard T. (D-Calif.), in Korean influence-buying scheme, **1977** 770, 800, 803-804; **1978** 846, 850, 855-856, 862-866, 874
Hannaford, Peter D., in Allen investigation, **1981** 848, 850
Hannan, Ahmed, terrorist-related conviction, **2004** 273
Hanover, Donna, **2000** 908
Hans v. Louisiana, **1999** 339
Hansen, Charles M., Jr., on labor unions, **1999** 632
Hansen, James, **1988** 861
Hansen, Joseph, Wal-Mart illegal workers, **2005** 739
Hanssen, Robert Philip, espionage case, **2001** 150-158, 893
Haradinaj, Ramush
Alliance for the Future of Kosovo leader, **2004** 952
as Kosovo prime minister, **2004** 952
UN Kosovo war crimes tribunal, **2004** 952; **2005** 856
Harakat al-Muqawamah al-Islamiyya (Hamas). *See* Hamas (Islamic resistance movement)
Haram as-Sharif, violence at, **1976** 191, 194-195
al-Haramain Islamic Foundation (HIF), **2003** 231, 1058; **2004** 520-521, 522-537
al-Harazi, Mohammed Omar, **2000** 863; **2001** 6
Harbi, Khaled, Saudi Arabian militant, **2004** 519
Harding, Warren G., **1988** 840
Hare, Kenneth, **1983** 199
Hariri, Rafiq
assassination of, **2005** 80-81, 271, 272, 686-696
as prime minister of Lebanon, **2004** 557-558, 560, 561
resignation of Hariri and his cabinet, **2004** 562
al-Hariti, Abu Ali, CIA assassination of, **2002** 1016
Harjo, Susan Shown, **1989** 539
Harkin, Tom (D-Iowa)
apparel industry sweatshops, **1997** 209
disability legislation, **1999** 319
on disruptive students, **1988** 48
farm bill opponent, **1996** 200
FDA regulation of tobacco products, **2004** 283
flu pandemic preparedness, **2005** 753

food safety, **2002** 581
on Negroponte national intelligence director nomination, **2005** 253
nuclear testing fallout, **1997** 593
Vietnam war opponent, **1992** 156
war powers debate, **1990** 674
Harlow, Bill, CIA counterterrorism recruitment restrictions, **2000** 278-279
Harman, Jane (D-Calif.), congressional intelligence gathering investigations, **2003** 885
Harman, John, unsafe chemicals in food, **1994** 379-386
Harman, Sabrina, Abu Ghraib prison abuse suspect, **2004** 220, 221
Harmon, Melinda, Enron Corp. collapse, **2002** 397
Harpootlian, Dick, midterm elections, **2002** 820
Harriman, Averill, **1980** 318
Harrington, Emmet, **1973** 643
Harrington, Michael J. (D-Mass.), on CIA involvement in Chile, **1974** 805-810
Harris, Barbara Clementine, consecration of as bishop, **1989** 49-54
Harris, Eric, Columbine High School shooter, **1999** 179; **2000** 875-876; **2001** 347, 348, 352
Harris, Fred R. (D-Okla.)
Kerner Commission report update, **1988** 186
poverty and race, **1998** 667-668
Harris, James A., **1975** 208
Harris, Jean, **1991** 814
Harris, Katherine
2002 midterm elections, **2002** 822
Florida elections, **2000** 1000
Harris, Patricia Roberts
appointment to HEW, **1979** 561, 577-578
appointment to HUD, **1976** 878-879
Carter's urban policy proposals, **1978** 241
smoking by women, **1980** 18, 20
Harris, Teresa, **1993** 439-945
Harris v. Forklift Systems, Inc., **1993** 939-945; **1998** 462
Harris v. McRae, **1980** 515-535
Harris v. New York, **2000** 393
Harrison, Patricia de Stacy, cultural diplomacy programs, **2005** 581
Harrison, Selig S., **1972** 523
Harry Ptasynski, United States v., **1983** 517-523
Hart, Doug, **1993** 974
Hart, Gary (D-Colo.)
on air quality, **1981** 275-276
campaign for Democratic Party nomination, **1984** 647; **1992** 336
Democratic Party platform, **1984** 549-551
national security, **2001** 639
national security commission member, **1999** 500
Russian nuclear weapons panel, **2001** 19
terrorist threats, task force report, **2002** 740-763
Hart, George L., Jr., **1974** 409
Hart, Philip A. (D-Mich.), **1973** 81
Hartford Public Schools (Connecticut), privatization of, **1994** 409-414
Hartigan v. Zbaraz, **1990** 388
Hartman, Arthur A., negotiation of accord with East Germany, **1974** 802-803
Hartwig, Clayton M., USS *Iowa* explosion, **1989** 517-520; **1990** 319-321; **1991** 679-680
Hartzler, Joseph H., **1997** 623
Hartzog, George B., **1972** 796
Haruk-ul-Islam (Islamic extremist group), **2003** 214
Harvard Medical School, physicians on terminally ill, **1984** 275-281
Harvard Medicare Project, **1986** 273-285, 1026
Harvard School of Public Health
Medicare drug benefit for seniors, **2004** 578-579
survey on children, **1997** 424-425
weight-related deaths, **2005** 6
Harvard University
Bok report to on legal system, **1983** 391-400
commission on presidential press conference, **1988** 835-845
liberal arts program and 350th anniversary, **1986** 940
Solzhenitsyn speech on spiritual decline of West, **1978** 403-417
stem cell research, **2004** 161
Vance speech on foreign policy, **1980** 475-483
Harvey, Kenneth D., sexual harassment of women in military, **1987** 671-672, 674
Harvey, Rachel, Aceh province conflict, **2004** 993
Hasenfus, Eugene, American pilot shot down in Nicaragua, **1994** 13
al-Hashemi, Akila, assassination of, **2003** 813, 940
Hashimoto, Ryutaro
at economic summit (Denver), **1997** 342
on hostage crisis in Peru, **1997** 234-237
Japanese economic stimulus package, **1998** 532, 535
al-Hashiri, Abd al-Rahim, al Qaeda leader captured, **2002** 1016
al-Haski, Hasan, terrorist bombings in Madrid, **2004** 110
Hassan, Margaret, hostage killed in Iraq, **2004** 876
Hassan II (king of Morocco), **1985** 501
Hassan Morales, Moises, **1979** 582
al-Hassani, Hajim, Iraq assembly speaker, **2005** 945
Hassayampa, racial unrest aboard, **1972** 901
Hasson, Kevin J., school vouchers, **1995** 386; **2002** 407
Hastert, J. Dennis (R-Ill.)
candidate for House Speaker, **1998** 954
CAFTA, **2005** 413
CIA secret detentions, **2005** 907
"Clear Skies" Initiative, **2002** 899
energy legislation, **2005** 782
as House Speaker, **2005** 632
intelligence agency reform legislation, **2004** 970
Iraq War troop withdrawal, **2005** 837
national commission on terrorist attacks, **2004** 452, 458
national energy policy, **2001** 337
tax reform issues, **2000** 18
U.S.-China trade relations, **2000** 220
Hastings, Alcee L. (D-Fla.), impeachment of, **1989** 583-590; **1993** 82-83
Hatch, Orrin (R-Utah)
abortion, **1983** 546
affirmative action opponent, **1997** 185-186

Hatch, Orrin (R-Utah) *Continued*
baseball exemption from antitrust laws, **1994** 361-362
Bork nomination, **1987** 720
D.C. voting representation in Congress, **1978** 590
Donovan indictment, **1984** 805
FOIA revisions, **1981** 394
nursing home abuse, **2002** 120
physician-assisted suicide, **1997** 462
religious freedom, **1997** 408-409
school prayer amendment, **1984** 243
Sessions investigation, **1993** 610
Social Security reform, **2005** 116
stem cell research supporter, **2005** 319
Thomas confirmation hearings, **1991** 554, 600, 602-603
torture in terrorism investigations, **2004** 341
Hatch Act (1939)
Justice Department officials in political activities, **1974** 612-613
revision of
Carter proposal on, **1977** 199, 201, 205
Democratic Party debate on, **1976** 543
Hatcher, Mike, civil rights workers slayings trial, **2005** 355
Hate crimes
abuses against Muslims, **2005** 678
church arson cases, **1997** 301-313
church bombing trial (Birmingham, 1963), **2002** 239-246
Democratic Party platform on, **2000** 614
extremists in U.S. Army, task force on, **1996** 178-185
FBI crime report, **1998** 874; **1999** 616-617, 619; **2000** 857; **2001** 751-752; **2002** 789; **2003** 991; **2004** 770; **2005** 685
FBI report, **1997** 686
legislation, Supreme Court on, **1992** 543-551
racially motivated, **1993** 385
Hate Crimes Prevention Act, **1999** 56; **2000** 35
Hatfield, Mark O. (R-Ore.)
freedom of religious speech, **1983** 272
new federalism, **1982** 74
Reagan budget, **1987** 5
START and nuclear freeze, **1982** 386
Hatfill, Steven J., anthrax attacks suspect, **2004** 443
Hathaway, William D. (D-Maine), **1973** 454
Hatton, Melinda R., medical records privacy, **2000** 1065; **2001** 487, 488
Hauck, Frederick H., on *Challenger* victims, **1988** 795, 798
Haughey, Charles J., **1985** 725
Hauslohner, Peter, **1984** 148
Hauspurg, Arthur, **1977** 545
Havana (Cuba), nonaligned nations' conference in, **1979** 681-691
Havel, Vaclav
addresses to nation and U.S. congress, **1990** 3-18
Bush on, **1990** 52
as Czech leader, **1989** 637
German minority in Czechoslovakia, **1990** 130
NATO membership for Czech Republic, **1997** 516
Nobel Peace Prize nominee, **2003** 1131
on Warsaw Pact dissolution, **1991** 399
Haver, Richard L.
and CIA intelligence, **1992** 4
secretary of defense for military intelligence appointment, **2002** 994
Havlick, Mike, Gulf War veterans with ALS, **2001** 909
Hawaii
morning-after pill, without prescription for, **2003** 999
same-sex couples, spousal benefits, **2004** 37
same-sex marriages, **1996** 689; **1999** 4, 898-899
Hawaii Housing Authority v. Midkiff, **2005** 369-371, 373-374
Hawatmeh, Nayef, **1988** 907
Hawi, George, anti-Syrian protester killed in bombing, **2005** 690
Hawking, Stephen, **1992** 379
Hawkins, Augustus F. (D-Calif.)
on education, **1986** 961; **1989** 87, 563
on welfare reform, **1988** 850
Hawkins, David, **1981** 276
Hawkins, Gains, **1985** 161
Hawkins, Vernon, **1996** 784
Hawley, Willis D., **1992** 87-88
al-Hawsawi, Mustafa Ahmed
linked to September 11 terrorist attacks, **2001** 620; **2003** 1055
terrorist suspect captured in Pakistan, **2003** 1055-1056
Hayakawa, S. I. (R-Calif.), **1986** 959
Hayden, Michael V.
as Negroponte's chief deputy on national intelligence, **2005** 253
NSA intelligence gathering, **2002** 991-992
Hayden, Tom (D-Calif.), on Democratic Party platform, **2000** 611
Hayes, Robin (R-N.C.), CAFTA, **2005** 413
Haynes, Charles C., school vouchers, **2002** 407
Haynes, William J., II, detainee interrogations, torture prohibited by conventions, **2004** 340
Haynsworth, Clement F., **1987** 717
Hays, United States v., **1995** 370
Hays, Wayne L. (D-Ohio)
House ethics investigation of, **1976** 365-368
resignation from House, **1980** 902
Haz, Hamzah (Indonesian vice president)
election, **2002** 704
and Islamic extremist groups, **2002** 705
September 11 attacks on U.S., **2001** 566
Hazard Analysis and Critical Control Points (HACCP) system, **1998** 521-522, 525, 527, 528; **2000** 883-884; **2001** 700-701; **2002** 580-581
Hazardous Substances and Hazardous Waste Response Liability and Compensation Act (1980), **1980** 452; **1981** 84; **1982** 965-970; **1983** 479-480
Hazardous waste
See also Nuclear waste management; Toxic chemicals
cleanup
funding for in Reagan budget, **1984** 83, 90
politics in EPA, investigations of, **1982** 965-970; **1983** 749-753
progress in, **1981** 84

control of, Global 2000 proposals on, **1981** 26-27
disposal
regulations on, House inquiry on, **1979** 781-800
standards for, Nixon call for, **1973** 216-217
health of Love Canal residents, **1983** 479-487
industry, organized crime in, **1983** 750
international trade in, treaty on, **1989** 153-160
management, EPA regulations on, **1980** 446-452
radioactive, from nuclear plants, **1989** 355-362
Hazelton, Dennis Robert, testimony in Korean influence-buying inquiry, **1977** 812-819
Hazelwood, Joseph J., and Alaska oil spill, **1989** 225-226, 232-234, 238-240; **1990** 513-530; **1991** 642
Hazelwood School District v. Kuhlmeier, **1988** 37-46
al-Hazmi, Nawaf, September 11 attacks hijacker, **2002** 992; **2003** 546, 555-561, 566-567
Head Start program
Bush (George H. W.) supports, **1992** 57, 101, 106, 108
Bush (George W.) administration support for, **2002** 43
and creation of Education Department, **1979** 158, 164-165
federal support for program, **1993** 212, 217-218; **1997** 36, 73; **1998** 88; **2000** 23; **2001** 58
full funding recommended, **1992** 355, 360
increased funding for in urban schools, **1988** 196, 207, 218
National Commission on Children report, **1991** 350
Healey, Denis, **1982** 478
on world currency stability, **1978** 660-661
Health
See also Cancer; Child health; Mental health; Public health; Smoking; Women's health
air quality standards for protection of, **1981** 277, 281-282
benefits for girls in sports, **1997** 158-171
benefits of drinking, **1995** 3-4, 16
CEA report, **1998** 88-90
cholesterol, NIH recommendations on, **1984** 1039-1043; **2001** 475-476, 478
connective tissue disease and breast implants, **1995** 520-521
costs of rising, **2000** 789
depression screenings, **2002** 265-274
diet and nutrition effects on, **1982** 507-520
in Eastern Europe, **1994** 415-430
foods, cholesterol, milk, margarine, **1992** 397-403
HealthierUS initiative, **2002** 626
hormone replacement therapy, **2002** 503-511
mammogram screenings, **1997** 38, 142-149; **2001** 869-870; **2002** 265, 510
marijuana for medical uses, **1996** 755-758
of minorities, progress in U.S., **1985** 685-706
physical exercise, benefits of, **1996** 418-429
physical fitness and death rates, **1989** 613-617
prostate cancer screenings, **2001** 870; **2002** 265
radon exposure, **1988** 3-8
sedentary lifestyle, CDC report on, **1993** 625-628
TV's effects on, **1982** 366-367, 378-379
"Walk for Better Health" campaign, **2002** 627
Health, public. *See* Public health
Health and Human Services (HHS) Department
AIDS
and discrimination, **1986** 888
spending, **1986** 887
AZT approval, **1987** 327-330
catastrophic illness coverage, **1986** 273, 1025-1035
child abuse and neglect, **1996** 778
federal dietary guidelines, **1996** 3-16
flu pandemic, emergency plan, **2005** 747-764
flu vaccine price gouging, **2004** 641
food labeling rules, **1990** 175-181
funding cutbacks, **1981** 326
and civil rights enforcement, **1983** 914
and smoking education, **1982** 164
hospital oversight, inspector general on, **1999** 412-421
infant and maternity care, **1987** 149, 153, 158-161
interferon approval, **1986** 481-485
medical records privacy, **1997** 580-587; **2000** 1063-1071; **2001** 485-503
minority health, **1985** 685-706
nursing home staff shortages, **2002** 117
prescription drug benefit for seniors, ad campaign challenged, **2004** 577, 580
prescription drug importation, task force report on, **2004** 981-990
Social Security reform, **1983** 74
treatment of severely handicapped infants, **1986** 541-558
welfare reform studies, **1999** 269-270
Health care
See also Diet; Health care costs; Health care financing; Nutrition
access to
and for-profit hospitals, **1986** 490, 496-498, 503-507
and health insurance coverage, **2001** 716-717
medical ethics commission on, **1983** 317-334
Nixon plan for improving, **1972** 91-93
privately provided, Thatcher government on, **1979** 380, 384, 385
in recession, **1983** 318
acupuncture treatments, NIH panel on, **1997** 747-759
for AIDS victims, **1988** 420-424
alcoholism causes and treatment, **1983** 335-354
for Alzheimer's disease victims, **1987** 391-406
for black Americans, **1987** 59
effects of Reagan budget cuts, **1983** 42, 45, 49, 53
heart attack incidence and care, **1993** 671-675
and socioeconomic status, **1987** 59; **1989** 446, 449, 452, 455-456
for children, UNICEF on inadequacies of, **1981** 911-913
Democratic Party platform on, **1980** 725-728; **1984** 569-570, 613-614; **1988** 558, 563-564; **1996** 631-632; **2000** 615
in Eastern European nations, **1994** 415-430
end-of-life care, **1997** 325-330
in for-profit hospitals, **1986** 487-513
health care system reform, Bush on, **2003** 26-27
infant and maternity programs, **1986** 1061-1062; **1987** 147-164

Health care *Continued*
information and education for minorities, **1985** 687, 690-691
long-term care proposals, **1999** 46
mammograms and mastectomies, **1997** 38, 142-149
medical mistakes, Institute of Medicine on, **1999** 779-793; **2001** 191, 192, 193
medical records security, **1997** 580-587
Medicare reform proposals, **1986** 273-285
nursing shortages, **2001** 191-192, 194
oral health in America, **2000** 222-239
patients' bill of rights, **1973** 39-42; **1997** 787-799; **1998** 46-47, 89, 140; **1999** 48-49, 562-563
for the poor, effects of Reagan budget cuts, **1983** 766-767, 771-772
prescription drug coverage for seniors, **2001** 713; **2003** 18, 23, 38-39; **2004** 20, 27-28, 33-34; **2005** 143
preventive programs
in Carter budget, **1979** 14, 43-44
in developing countries, **1980** 890-891
government investment in, **1978** 633-634, 636-637
Republican Party platform on, **1972** 673-675; **1984** 683-685; **1988** 636-639; **1996** 529-530; **2000** 514
smoking dependence, treatment of, **1988** 310, 314, 321-322
state and local responsibility for, Reagan plan for, **1982** 74, 81
for women, **1993** 653-658; **1997** 38
Health care costs
for AIDS victims, **1988** 443-445
of alcoholism treatment, **1983** 337
containment of, Carter's insurance proposal, **1978** 543, 545-547
controls on, Nixon's anti-inflation program, **1973** 43, 45, 48, 52
deficit reduction and, **1996** 67
facilities construction costs, **1972** 922-926
family finances and, **1993** 271-285
in for-profit hospitals, **1986** 494-496
improvement in efficiency and effectiveness of, **1977** 73-74
long-term, education about, **1986** 1031
medical ethics commission on, **1983** 317-319, 324-326, 331-334
prescription drug prices, **1994** 87-94; **2000** 131-140
reducing, Reagan on, **1983** 86, 112
rising costs of, **2001** 712; **2004** 981-982; **2005** 122, 137
of smoking, **1985** 615-622
spending on health care, **1998** 142
Health care financing, **2005** 133-134
block grants to states for, in Reagan economic plan, **1981** 641, 644-645
health savings accounts, **2003** 847, 1125, 1127; **2005** 143
Health Care Financing Administration (HCFA), **1986** 1026
hospital quality oversight, **1999** 412-421
Health Care Leadership Council, **2001** 488
Health care quality
hospital care, **1999** 412-421
in U.S., IOM report, **2001** 191-211, 868-869
U.S. health care, IOM report on, **2001** 191-211, 868-869
Health care reform
CEA report on, **1991** 91-93
Clinton proposals, **1993** 781-804; **1994** 143-144; **1995** 74-75, 88-90; **1997** 38
Eisenhower Foundation report, **1993** 224
Health care workers
AIDS education for, **1987** 320, 323-326
AIDS management, **1987** 818, 822-826
and AIDS transmission, **1985** 736, 739-745
Catholic, and medical intervention in procreation, **1987** 268-269, 283
training of, **1972** 91-92, 673
Health, Education, and Welfare Department (HEW)
alcohol and health report, **1972** 193-200
ban on sex discrimination in schools, **1974** 507-513
cutting waste and fraud in welfare system, **1979** 390, 392, 394
enforcement of civil rights laws, **1992** 578-579
fetal research regulations, **1975** 543-556
funding of, **1972** 116; **1974** 863
hospital construction costs, **1972** 922, 925-926, 928-930
limits on tar and nicotine content in cigarettes, **1973** 46
marijuana and health, **1972** 155-162
occupational safety programs, **1978** 637-641
renaming of, **1979** 158
segregation of smokers working at, **1972** 47
smoking by women, **1980** 18-26
social insurance programs, **1977** 552
Social Security system's income, **1975** 116
swine flu immunization, **1978** 669, 673
Health insurance
benefits, for Wal-Mart employees, **2005** 737-738
benefits for retirees, **2005** 489
Bush administration proposals, Daschle's Democratic response, **2004** 34
catastrophic coverage
Carter plan for, **1978** 545-546
CBO analysis of, **1976** 186
employment-related illness, **1986** 1026-1027, 1033-1034
HHS recommendations, **1986** 1025-1035
legislation on, **1988** 334
in Medicare, **1976** 14, 21, 38, 42
Reagan on, **1987** 107, 112
Republican Party platform on, **1976** 633-634
Census Bureau report, **1994** 463-471
Clinton administration proposals, **1999** 49; **2000** 49
coverage
Census Bureau on, **1999** 561-567; **2000** 787-794; **2001** 710-711; **2002** 666-675; **2003** 846-857
for children, **1999** 566-567; **2000** 49
GAO report, **1998** 139-150
mental health parity, **2002** 267-268
myths and realities, **2001** 711-712, 714-716
for prescription drugs, **2001** 712; **2002** 949-950; **2003** 23, 38-39

retiree benefits, **2002** 667-668
universal/guaranteed health care, **2004** 982-983
Democratic Party platform on, **1992** 693-694
employer disability plans, maternity leave in, **1977** 871-872, 874-877, 880-881
employer disability plans, pregnancy coverage in, **1976** 891-905
extension of to domestic partners, **1989** 305-309
Hispanics, **2001** 712; **2003** 854
and length of hospital stay, **1988** 333-337
for mental health treatment, **1996** 388-390
numbers of, **2001** 711; **2002** 945; **2003** 846-848; **2004** 58
portability, **1999** 564
premiums
for a family of four, **2005** 485
rising costs of, **2004** 982
private
and for-profit hospitals, **1986** 487-488, 503
market changes, **1986** 1032-1033
Republican Party platform on, **1992** 809-810
tax credit for long-term care, **1986** 1031-1033
uninsured
Black/African American Americans, **2001** 712; **2003** 853
consequences of, **2002** 669
IOM report on, **2001** 710-721; **2004** 981, 982
numbers of, **1998** 142-143; **1999** 563-564
universal coverage, **1999** 564
Health insurance, national
Carter proposal for, **1976** 597, 601; **1978** 26, 543-547; **1979** 14, 23, 43-44; **1981** 58, 68
costs of, **1978** 328, 337-338
Clinton reform proposals, **1994** 34-35, 42-45, 50-51, 127-128, 463-465
Democratic Party platform on, **1972** 549; **1976** 545, 559-561
Kennedy on, **1978** 765-766, 776-777
Mondale support for, **1976** 782, 793
National '80s Agenda on, **1981** 40
Nixon on, **1973** 304, 308; **1974** 41, 47-48, 53, 58, 96, 99-100, 109
Regional Health Alliances, **1993** 783-784
Republican Party platform on, **1972** 652, 674; **1976** 634
Health Insurance Association of America (HIAA), ad campaign, **1994** 35
Health Insurance Portability and Accountability Act (HIPAA, 1996), **1997** 72; **1998** 78, 140-142, 143-150; **2000** 1063; **2001** 486
Health maintenance organizations (HMOs). *See* Managed care
Health Privacy Project, **2001** 488
Health Research and Education Trust, health insurance survey, **2004** 982
HealthSouth, corporate scandal, **2003** 332, 339-340
Healthy Forests Initiative, **2002** 894, 899-900; **2003** 27, 181
Healthy Lunch Pilot Program, **2004** 656
Healthy Start program, **1992** 108
Hearn, Ruby P., child health care, **1997** 425
Hearst, Patricia. *See* Shaw, Patricia Hearst
Hearst, Randolph A., food distribution program, **1974** 247-253
Heart disease
See also Cardiovascular disease
among minorities, **1985** 685-686, 689, 697-698
anticlotting drugs for heart attack prevention, **1987** 875-879
and cholesterol, **1984** 1039-1043; **1987** 780-784
and cholesterol levels, NIH guidelines, **2001** 475-476, 478
first artificial heart implant, **2001** 479-484
Heart and Estrogen/Progestin Replacement Study (HERS), **2002** 505
and physical fitness, **1989** 613-617
research, U.S.-Soviet cooperation on, **1974** 535-536, 538, 544-546, 549, 567
smoking and risk of, **1972** 48-49; **1981** 3-4, 6-8, 11-12
smoking linked to, surgeon general's report, **2004** 290
Heath, Clark, nuclear testing fallout, **1997** 591
Heath, Edward, **1985** 725
Heatwole, Nathaniel, aviation "security breaches" with baggage, **2003** 721
Heavily Indebted Poor Countries (HIPC) debt-relief initiative, **2003** 761
Hebert, Curt, California energy "crisis," **2001** 333
Hebert, F. Edward (D-La.)
Navy's racial problems, **1972** 902
U.S. bombing of Cambodia, **1973** 730
Hechinger, Fred M., **1982** 4-5
Hecker, JayEtta Z., impact of NAFTA, **1997** 543
Hecker, Michael H. L., **1974** 25
Heckler, Margaret M.
AIDS policy, **1983** 533-541; **1985** 733; **1986** 888
American diet, **1984** 1040
antiabortion rally, **1985** 53
minority health, **1985** 685-688
treatment for seriously ill infants, **1983** 283
Heddell, Gordon S., Wal-Mart child labor lawsuit, **2005** 738
Heffron v. International Soc. for Krishna Consciousness, Inc., **1995** 398
Hefley, Joel (R-Colo.), park service opponent, **1995** 121
Heflin, Howell (D-Ala.)
Senate impeachment powers, **1993** 83
Souter nomination, **1990** 616
Thomas confirmation hearings, **1991** 552, 579-580, 598-600
Tower secretary of defense nomination, **1989** 105
Hefner, Bill (D-N.C.), on radio talk shows, **1993** 586
Hefner, Hugh, Gore supporter, **2000** 613
Hegemony
contention for, U.S. and Soviet, PRC on, **1973** 768, 776-777
rejection of
in PRC-Japanese peace treaty, **1978** 586-587, 782
in U.S.-PRC agreement, **1978** 782, 784
Heimann, John G., on Lance investigation, **1977** 627-640
Heinbecker, Paul, impunity from war crimes, **2002** 608

Heineman, Ben W.
  Justice Powell's retirement, **1987** 579
  treatment of handicapped infants, **1986** 544
Heinrich, Janet
  bioterrorism preparation, **2001** 673, 677
  flu vaccine shortage, **2004** 640, 644, 645-651
Hekmatyar, Gulbuddin, Islamist *mujahideen* opposed to Karzai, **2003** 1091
Helgesen, Vidar, cease-fire in Sri Lanka, **2002** 94
Heller, H. Robert, **1987** 513
Heller, Mark, "roadmap" for Middle East peace, **2003** 197-198
Heller, Walter, **1973** 45
Helmly, James R., Army Reserve forces, preparedness, **2004** 788
Helms, Jesse (R-N.C.)
  affirmative action, **1991** 760
  AIDS research, opposition to, **1995** 428, 433, 459
  AIDS testing, **1987** 320
  chemical weapons treaty opponent, **1996** 741; **1997** 196
  Clinton unfit as Commander in Chief, **1994** 529-530
  D.C. voting representation in Congress, **1978** 590
  death penalty in U.S., **1998** 185
  food aid, **1984** 5
  GATT critic, **1994** 556
  Genocide Convention, **1986** 116
  government secrecy, **1997** 103
  King holiday, **1983** 883-884
  National Endowment for the Humanities, attack on, **1990** 511
  nuclear test ban treaty, **1999** 601, 608, 699
  reparations to Japanese-Americans, **1988** 289, 293
  school prayer amendment, **1984** 244; **1985** 381
  on tobacco industry, **1996** 592
  U.S. role in UN, **1995** 350-351; **1997** 153; **1999** 701; **2001** 901
  U.S.-British extradition treaty, **1986** 752-753
Helms, Richard C.
  CIA activity in Chile, **1975** 403
  CIA as White House cover in Watergate, **1974** 675-680, 682
  CIA ban on assassinations, **1975** 792, 796-797
  CIA plot against Castro, **1975** 730-734, 744, 747-756, 779-781, 784
Helsinki Accords, **1990** 14, 728
Helsinki Conference on Security and Cooperation in Europe (1975)
  Communist Party leaders on, **1976** 436-437, 442, 445, 453
  Final Act, **1975** 559-570
    Brezhnev on, **1976** 148, 151
    as context for German reunification, **1989** 627-630, 633-634, 659, 662
    and European cooperation, Gorbachev on, **1989** 654
    human rights provisions
      Carter on, **1977** 898, 904-905
      Ford on, **1975** 358
      Sakharov on, **1975** 915, 924-925
    implementation of, **1976** 347-348
    and Soviet emigration policy, **1981** 747-752; **1987** 190, 202
    and Soviet policies, economic summit on, **1987** 528
    Western eagerness to sign, Solzhenytsin on, **1975** 481-482, 487-488
  Madrid Concluding Document, **1984** 168
  and Soviet domination in Eastern Europe, Carter on, **1976** 734, 740-742
  and Soviets' right to travel, **1986** 1092
Helsinki II, Gorbachev proposal for, **1989** 645, 654
Helsinki Watch, **1983** 182; **1984** 156; **1985** 146
  Elena Bonner co-founds, **1990** 208
  formation of, **1981** 748
  Vaclav Havel visits, **1990** 5
Helstoski, Henry (D-N.J.), **1979** 467-478
Helstoski, United States v., **1979** 467-478
Henderson, Lenneal J., on effect of tax reform on blacks, **1987** 44, 52-55
Henderson, Wade J.
  affirmative action programs, **1998** 856
  civil rights rulings, **1989** 324
  political asylum ruling, **1987** 255
Hendricks, Leroy, sex offender confinement case, **1997** 382-394
Hendrickson, David C., on Bush's "freedom crusade," **2005** 44
Henix, Amos, **1972** 783
Henry, Ernst, **1979** 907
Henry, Greg, planet detection, **1999** 175
Henry J. Kaiser Family Foundation
  health insurance premiums, **2002** 667
  media role in obesity, **2004** 653
Hensley, Jack, hostage killed in Iraq, **2004** 876
Henson, Matthew, with Peary at North Pole, **1989** 687, 689, 693, 696
Hepatitis B, transmission of, **1985** 738-739
Hepps, Maurice S., libel suit of, **1986** 356, 358-359
Herbert, Anthony B., libel suit against CBS, **1979** 285-311, 315-318
Herbert, Victor, acupuncture, **1997** 750
Herbert v. Lando, **1979** 285-311, 315-318; **1998** 402
Hercules Inc., EPA regulation of chemical discharge of, **1977** 131-141
Hercus, Dame Ann, UN peacekeeping reform panel, **2000** 643
Herdman, Robert K., SEC chief accountant resignation, **2002** 1033-1034
Herdman, Roger C., on tuberculosis incidence, **1993** 851
Heritage Forests Campaign, **1999** 594
Heritage Foundation, **1987** 334
Herman, Alexis
  apparel industry sweatshops, **1997** 209
  consumer health care, **1997** 787, 791
  ergonomics standards, **1999** 769
  UPS strike, **1997** 630
  welfare system, **1997** 620
Hermaniuk, Maxim, on family rights charter, **1980** 873, 875-877
Hernandez, Keith, **1986** 170, 171
Hernu, Charles, **1985** 632
Heroin
  history of use in U.S., **1973** 399-401
  production, price, and market, **1972** 645-650

Herrera v. Collins, **1993** 141-152
Hersh, Seymour
  on CIA's domestic activities, **1975** 401, 709
  Iraq prison abuse scandal, **2004** 208
Hershaft, Alex, **1988** 347-348
Herter, Christian A., Jr., **1972** 476
Hertzstein, Robert, **1986** 744
Herzog, Chaim
  on UN debate on Israeli occupied territories, **1976** 192
  on UN Zionism resolution, **1975** 825
Herzog, Jesus Silva, **1983** 802
Hesburgh, Theodore M.
  college athletics reform, **1991** 129
  resignation from Civil Rights Commission, **1973** 228
  on U.S. immigration policy, **1981** 265
Heseltine, Michael, **1990** 748, 749
Hess, Dan, **1973** 194
Hess, Stephen, on Bush State of the Union address, **2004** 18
Hester, Jeff, on Hubble space telescope pictures, **1995** 291-293
Heston, Charlton, **1992** 346
HEW. *See* Health, Education, and Welfare Department
Heyman, I. Michael, *Enola Gay* exhibit announcement, **1995** 55-58
Heymann, Philip, sentencing guidelines, **2005** 681
Heymann, Philip B., Waco incident, **1993** 819
Hezbollah (Party of God, Shi'ite militant group)
  French hostages held by, **1986** 831-832
  gun purchases in U.S., **2003** 159
  hostage taking by, **1985** 465-466
  Iranian support for, **2001** 796-797; **2003** 942
  and Khobar towers bombing indictments, **2001** 807
  leader of kidnapped, **1989** 315-319
  Lebanon parliamentary elections, **2005** 271, 273
  Lebanon political demonstrations, **2005** 688
  Syrian support of, **2004** 558-559
  terrorism infrastructure, **2004** 811
  terrorist attack on U.S. Marines in Beirut, **1983** 934
HHS. *See* Health and Human Services (HHS) Department
Hickel, Walter J., **1991** 642
Hickey, James A.
  on Curran's suitability to teach theology, **1986** 758-760, 762-763
  on Vatican statement on bioethics, **1987** 269
Hickman v. Block, **2002** 964-968
Hicks, David, Australian detainee at Guantanamo Bay, **2003** 110; **2004** 378-379; **2005** 447
Hicks, Jerry, **1986** 965
Hicks, John J., FBI crime laboratory report, **1997** 223
Hicks, Katherine, **1997** 661
Hidalgo, Edward, **1990** 301-310
Hidoyatova, Nigora, Uzbekistan activist arrested, **2005** 432
Hier, Marvin (rabbi)
  German unity, **1990** 105-110
  on Jewish-Christian relations, **2000** 79
Higginbotham, A. Leon, Jr., letter to Clarence Thomas, **1992** 33-43
Higgins, John P., Jr., Education Department propaganda, **2005** 645
Higgins, William R.
  hostage, **1991** 751, 753
  killing of, **1989** 315-316, 319
High school
  California certificates of proficiency, **1975** 692
  dropout rate, **1988** 297, 299-300, 305
  integration at Little Rock Central High School, fortieth anniversary, **1997** 317
  reorganization of urban high schools, **1988** 196, 198-199, 208-212
  shooting incident at Columbine High School (Colorado), **1999** 179-184, 615; **2000** 729, 873, 875-876
  unsafe sex risks of students, **1992** 339-343
Higher education. *See* Colleges and universities
Higher Education Act (1965), Title IV, student aid and draft registration, **1984** 496-503
High-Level Panel on Threats, Challenges, and Change, report, **2004** 887-911
Highway Trust Fund, proposed funding of mass transit, **1973** 305, 319
Highways
  reduction in speed limit during energy crisis, **1973** 914-915, 917-918
  repair program consolidation, **1981** 73
Hijackers, punishment and extradition of, U.S.-sponsored UN proposals on, **1972** 752, 754-757, 762
Hijacking
  Achille Lauro, **1985** 463, 467
  Air France, and holding of Israeli hostages at Entebbe, **1976** 517-520
  death penalty for, **1977** 518
  Egyptair, **1985** 467-468
  international cooperation against, economic summits on, **1978** 533, 535, 541-542; **1988** 393, 394
  TWA, Beirut, **1985** 463-466, 469; **1986** 1015
  U.S.-Cuban agreement on, **1973** 265-268
Hill, Andrew, **1992** 188-191
Hill, Anita F.
  sexual harassment issue, **1991** 760; **1993** 354-355
  Thomas confirmation hearings, **1991** 553-554, 582-616; **1992** 33, 187-188; **1993** 354
Hill, Christopher
  Kosovo political situation, **1998** 830
  Six-Party Talks negotiations, **2005** 607-608
Hill, Clarence A. Mark, women in combat, **1993** 334-335
Hill, Eleanor, congressional intelligence failures panel, **2002** 991
Hill, Henry, **1991** 814
Hill, Julia, **1990** 228
Hill, M. Charles, Iran arms sales, **1994** 18
Hill, Paul, shooting death of abortion doctor, **2003** 999-1000
Hill, United States Term Limits, Inc. v., **1995** 263
Hill v. Colorado, **2000** 433
Hilliard, William, in Carter-Reagan debate, **1980** 920, 929-931, 943
Hills, Carla A.
  lobbying for DRG Funding Corp., **1989** 335

Hills, Carla A. *Continued*
NAFTA, **1992** 760-761
Hills, Lee, **1974** 524; **1991** 129
Hills v. Gautreaux, **1976** 223-233
Hilmers, David C., **1988** 797
Hilton, Claude, **1989** 393
Hinckley, John W., Jr.
attempted assassination of Reagan, **1981** 351, 362-363; **1985** 493; **1991** 185
insanity defense, **1982** 531, 533-534; **1983** 25, 31-32, 35
verdict, **1982** 531-537
Hinckley, John W., Jr., United States v., **1982** 531-537
Hindawi, Nezar, **1986** 832
al-Hindi, Abu Issa, terrorism suspect, **2004** 271
Hinduism
ethnic conflict in Sri Lanka, **1987** 615-616
practice of in India, **1986** 23
religious conflict in India, **1984** 945-949
Hinerfeld, Ruth J., in presidential debates, **1980** 847, 849, 921
Hinshaw, Andrew J., **1972** 615
Hinson, David R.
commuter airline safety, **1994** 536
FAA and airline safety, **1996** 237-238
Hinton, Henry L., Jr., Patriot Missile Performance report, **1992** 867-874
HIPC. *See* Heavily Indebted Poor Countries (HIPC) debt-relief initiative
Hirabayashi v. United States, **1995** 313; **1997** 190
Hirohito (Emperor of Japan)
Ford meeting with, **1974** 955-956, 962-963
funeral of, **1989** 99, 101-103
Hirsch, E. D., **1988** 518
Hirsch, Martin S., **1985** 735
Hispanic Americans
adult literacy report, **1993** 742-743
AIDS Commission report, **1993** 447, 451
alcoholism effects on, **1983** 345
California English-only law, **1986** 959-961
California voters, **2003** 1009
Census undercount, **1991** 443-449
college enrollment, **1997** 186
economic characteristics, **2003** 356-357
educational attainment, **2003** 356
educational opportunities, **1992** 629, 632-634
employment disparities among, **1982** 919-944
employment gains among, Carter on, **1981** 59
Hartford Schools privatization, **1994** 409-414
health insurance, **1994** 467-468, 470
health problems of, **1985** 685-687, 693, 695-700, 703-706
homeless report, **1994** 257-258, 261
immigration reform and, **1986** 964, 965
John Paul II's speech to in U.S., **1987** 699-700, 705-707
labor market, **1999** 101-102
Los Angeles riots, **1992** 407-408, 416-417
mental health, surgeon general's report on, **2001** 587-588
NCES report, **1992** 623-624, 632-634
population, U.S. Census report on, **2001** 314-324; **2003** 349-357
poverty data, **2003** 357
race-based redistricting, **1993** 459-481
research studies, **2003** 351-353
sexual harassment in public schools, **1993** 357-360
Spanish as predominant foreign tongue, **1992** 475
teenage birth rates, **1998** 261-262
Thomas confirmation hearings, **1991** 568-570
uninsured, **2001** 712
urban poverty and unemployment among, **1988** 185-194
violence against women report, **1994** 65-67
Hiss, Alger, **1994** 237-238
Historic preservation
of Grand Central Terminal, **1978** 453-465
and property takings, **1978** 453-461
right to develop or change landmarks, **1978** 453-465
Historically black colleges and universities (HBCUs), **1995** 241, 247, 249
segregated in Mississippi, **1992** 575-587
History
emphasis on in education, **1987** 681-685, 689, 695
teaching religion's influence on, **1987** 598-601, 603
Hitler, Adolf
German guilt for crimes of, **1989** 488, 490-492, 494, 496
nonaggression pact with Stalin (1939), **1989** 469-472
Waffen SS under, **1985** 357
HIV. *See* Human immunodeficiency virus (HIV) infection
Hizv-ut-Tahrir, Andijon killings, **2005** 429-431
Hoagland, Jim, on South African apartheid system, **1993** 880
Hobbs, Charles D., **1988** 850
Hochhuth, Rolf, **1998** 123
Hockey, season delay, **1994** 361
Hodel, Donald P., **1982** 563
Hodgkinson, Harold, **1986** 218
Hodgson v. Minnesota, **1990** 387-398; **2005** 194
Hoeveler, William
Noriega phone call broadcast, **1990** 721-722
Noriega sentencing, **1992** 649-653
Hoffa, James P. (son of Jimmy Hoffa), Teamsters election defeat, **1997** 628
Hoffa, James R., **1979** 610-611
Hoffman, Bruce
terrorism movement, **2004** 538
war on terrorism in Afghanistan, **2003** 1053
Hoffman, Mark William, **1981** 337
Hoffman, Walter E., charges against Agnew, **1973** 827-830
Hoffman Estates v. Flipside, **1982** 215-223
Hoffman-La Roche, production of alpha interferon, **1986** 482
Hoffmeister, John, oil company profits, congressional testimony on, **2005** 796-799
Hogan, Thomas F., CIA leak case, **2005** 701
Hoge, James, **1976** 774

Holbrooke, Richard C.
Bosnia
Dayton peace agreement, **1999** 737, 740; **2000** 142-143; **2002** 717; **2003** 463
Declaration of New York, **1999** 737
Congo, Lusaka agreement, **1999** 647
East Timor refugees, **1999** 515
Kosovo peace negotiations, **1998** 830; **1999** 136
United Nations, U.S. dues payment, **2000** 182; **2001** 901
Holder, Angela Roddey, **1973** 40
Holder, Barbara, Evers assassination retrial, **1994** 103-104
Holder, Eric H., Jr.
jury selection and racial bias, **2002** 359
on Rostenkowski indictment, **1994** 281, 283-286
Holdren, John, National Commission on Energy Policy, **2004** 189
Holkeri, Harri
resignation, **2004** 951
UN Mission in Kosovo administrator, **2003** 1139-1140, 1142-1143; **2004** 950-951
Holland, Al, **1986** 170
Holland, J. Russel, *Exxon Valdez* final agreement, **1991** 641-648
Holland v. Illinois, **1990** 427
Holley, David, sexually abusive priests, **1993** 407-411
Holliday, George, Rodney King beating, **1991** 403; **1993** 631-632, 637-638
Hollinger International, corporate scandal, **2004** 423-424
Hollings, Ernest F. (D-S.C.)
Alaska oil spill, **1989** 228-230, 233-235
budget reduction legislation, **1985** 803
decontrol of natural gas prices, **1973** 466
FAA responsibilities, **1988** 270
television violence, **1993** 489
war powers debate, **1990** 675-676
Holman, Carl, **1981** 40
Holmes, Cheryl, testimony in Korean influence-buying inquiry, **1977** 805-811
Holmes, Donald G., Alabama statute on school prayer, **1985** 380, 383, 386-387, 391
Holmes, Eugene, **1992** 155, 159-161
Holmes, Kim R.
on right of self-defense of nations, **2004** 890
UN Security Council expansion, **2003** 812
Holmes Group, on education reform, **1986** 458-459
Holmes Norton, Eleanor (D-D.C.), **1995** 499
Holmstead, Jeffrey R., "Clear Skies" Initiative, **2002** 898
Holocaust
and Austrian Jewish community, papal visit, **1988** 406-414
Catholic Church repentance for, **1998** 121-130
Demjanjuk war crimes acquittal, **1993** 617-623
French complicity with Nazis, apology for, **1995** 478-482
German guilt and remorse for, Kohl on, **1989** 488-491
German reunification, **1990** 105-112
Hans-Dietrich Genscher, **1990** 602
Jerusalem commemoration of, **1981** 382
and Jewish-Christian relations, **1987** 700, 703-704
Nazi war crimes, Barbie trial, **1987** 517-524
Nazi-confiscated art, return of, **1998** 294-295
neutral nations aid to Nazi Germany, **1998** 299-312
and Reagan's Bitburg visit, **1985** 358-360
survivors and liberators, conference of, **1981** 382
Swiss banks and, **1998** 293-294
tracing victims, **1993** 310
U.S. commemoration of, **1981** 381-389
U.S. Jews' role in, **1983** 143-161
victims of, restitution investigations, **1997** 257-272
and Waldheim's war service, **1986** 743-746, 749-750
Walesa apology for Poland's role, **1991** 253-256
Wiesel's descriptions of, **1986** 1075-1077
Holocaust Memorial Council, U.S., **1981** 381-382; **1986** 1076
Holocaust Museum, dedication of, **1993** 307-313
Holst, Johan Joergen
Middle East peace negotiations, **1993** 748
Nobel Prize statement, **1993** 880-881
Holsted, James L., **1982** 3-4
Holt, Cooper, **1977** 96
Holton, Gerald, **1983** 415
Holtz-Eakin, Douglas J.
number of uninsured, **2003** 848
on tax breaks for businesses, **2005** 122
Holtzman, Elizabeth (D-N.Y.)
on Nixon pardon, **1974** 888, 898-900
on Rockefeller nomination, **1974** 988
Holum, John D., **1992** 686
Homeland security. *See* National security
Homeland Security, Office of. *See* White House, Office of Homeland Security
Homeland Security Act (2002), **2003** 162, 166, 167-168, 726
Homeland Security Department (DHS)
See also Transportation Security Administration (TSA)
air marshal program, **2004** 145-146
biometric identification program, **2003** 221
bioterrorism assessment, **2004** 444
Bush proposal for department, **2002** 36, 42
Bush State of the Union address on, **2005** 86-87
collective bargaining rights, **2005** 489
congressional panel proposes new agency for intelligence gathering, **2002** 994
creation of, **2002** 530-545, 740, 818-819, 823; **2003** 25; **2005** 893
FEMA merger with, **2005** 569
foreign visitors, tracking of, **2003** 156, 221
Hurricane Katrina disaster response, **2005** 566
immigration law enforcement functions, **2003** 315
Kerick nomination withdrawal, **2004** 272
London bombings, response to, **2005** 395
registration of selected immigrants, **2003** 317
Scarlet Cloud (anthrax attack exercise), **2003** 904
secretary appointment, **2002** 531, 533
secretary Ridge resignation, **2004** 272
Secure Flight program, **2004** 144-145
staff changes, **2005** 895-896
terrorist attacks, emergency preparedness exercises, **2003** 903-904

Homeland Security Department (DHS) *Continued*
terrorist watch list consolidation, **2003** 155, 157, 158, 161, 170, 221
threat alert system, **2004** 268-269
TOPOFF (Top Officials Series), attack modeling exercise, **2003** 903, 911-921
Homelessness
blacks in America and Reagan social policies, **1987** 49, 59
Bush on, **1988** 607; **1989** 78
children, underfunded programs for, **1989** 672, 675, 679, 685
Democratic Party platform on, **1984** 617-618
economic report of the president, **1990** 101-102
homeless population, **1994** 253-254
characteristics of, **1994** 256-257
Interagency Council on the Homeless report, **1994** 252-263
as issue in presidential debates, **1988** 734-736
mentally ill, **1990** 576-579
national survey of, **1999** 392
Republican Party platform on, **1988** 640-642; **1992** 812
Homicide
among minorities, **1985** 685-687, 690, 704-705
FBI crime report statistics, **2001** 753-754; **2002** 790-791; **2003** 988; **2004** 767; **2005** 682
gun availability and risk of, **1993** 871
Homicide rate, **1994** 415; **1995** 710, 714; **1999** 620; **2001** 753-754
Homosexual rights
See also Gay rights
Catholic Church on, **1992** 723
charitable choice and discrimination, **2001** 135
child custody for, **1977** 861, 863, 866
contagious disease and job discrimination, **1987** 246-247
Democratic Party platform on, **1980** 712; **1984** 550, 612
exclusion from city human rights law, **1989** 306
gay seminarians, Vatican prohibition on, **2005** 863-872
gay/lesbian march on Washington, **1993** 327-331
gays in the military, **1999** 899-901; **2000** 160-161; **2004** 37-38, 42
military ban, **1993** 153-164; **1997** 761; **1999** 901
New York City legislation on, **1986** 910
recognition of in California and New York, **1989** 305-311
same-sex civil unions, **1999** 898-899; **2000** 158-167
same-sex marriages, **1996** 687-690
in France, **1999** 901
sodomy and right to privacy, **1986** 601-614
Vermont Supreme Court on, **1999** 898-908
Homosexuality
Catholic teaching on, **1979** 729, 758; **1985** 363-364, 373
gay gene, existence of, **1993** 599-608
Homosexuals
AIDS impact on, **1983** 534-535
Moral Majority on, **1983** 818
pastoral care of, Vatican on, **1986** 909-918; **1987** 701, 714
Honasan, Gregorio, coup attempt against Aquino, **1987** 845-846
Honberg, Ronald S., on EEOC guidelines on mental disabilities, **1997** 129
Honda, Raisuki, **1989** 101
Honduras
and Central American peace plan, **1987** 637-640, 642-648
hurricane damage, UN situation report, **1998** 789-791, 792-798
Iraq troop withdrawal, **2004** 882
John Paul II's visit to, **1983** 242
Nicaraguan contra activity in, **1985** 264; **1987** 638-639
population growth in, **1987** 440, 443
smoking in the Americas, **1992** 269
Tela accord on Nicaraguan contras, **1989** 161-162, 168-172
U.S. economic aid to, **1984** 32
Honecker, Erich
Berlin Wall anniversary, **1986** 791-792
ouster of, **1989** 626
Honegger, Barbara, **1983** 756-763
Hong Kong
British agreement to return to PRC, **1984** 1045-1050
China sovereignty, **2003** 1181-1182
elections, **2003** 1182
political situation, **1997** 358-359, 501, 503-504; **1998** 468
pro-democracy demonstrations, **2003** 1181-1182; **2004** 942; **2005** 623
protests in against PRC government, **1989** 278
SARS (severe acute respiratory syndrome) outbreak, **2003** 131, 754
stock market plunge, **1997** 722, 834
transfer to China ceremony, **1997** 501-506; **2000** 192
Hong Soon Young, Korean War massacre incident, **1999** 553
Honig v. Doe, **1988** 47-56
Hood, Jay W., Guantanamo Bay and mishandling of Koran, **2005** 449
Hood, John, civil rights workers slayings (1964) trial, **2005** 354-356
Hook, Sidney, **1991** 551-552
Hooker Chemical Corp.
dumping of hazardous chemicals by, **1979** 782, 785, 791, 800; **1980** 445-446
Love Canal evacuation, **1983** 479-487
Hooks, Benjamin L.
affirmative action rulings, **1978** 470; **1979** 495; **1984** 367
civil rights rulings, **1989** 324
on Los Angeles riots, **1992** 408
NAACP leader, **1993** 579
Sun Belt migration, **1981** 40
Hooks, Iain, victim of Israeli-Palestinian conflict, **2002** 919
Hoover, Herbert, **1988** 840
Hoover, J. Edgar
church bombing investigation (Birmingham, 1963) closed by, **2002** 240-241

FBI break-ins, **1976** 322, 325-326; **1981** 372
King, surveillance of, **1977** 115; **1983** 885
political uses of FBI by presidents, **1975** 876-879
and "Verona" project, **1997** 104
wiretaps in Nixon White House, **1974** 489; **1976** 159-168
Hoover Institution, on CFC production, **1992** 77-78
HOPE scholarship program, **1998** 43, 78, 87; **1999** 46; **2000** 24, 47; **2001** 58
Hopewell Furnace National Historic Site (Pennsylvania), **1995** 124, 125
Hopwood v. State of Texas, **1998** 862-863
Horinko, Marianne (EPA acting administrator), "new source" review, **2003** 177-178
Horn, Alan, marketing violent entertainment to children, **2000** 731
Horn, Steve (R-Calif.), Y2K computer conversion crisis, **1998** 545
Horn, Wade, Education Department propaganda, **2005** 645
Hornby, William, **1974** 524
Horner, Charles A., Independent Panel to Review DOD Detention Operations, **2004** 212
Horner, Garnett D., interview with Nixon, **1972** 881-892
Horowitz, Michael, religious persecution, **1997** 562-563
Horton, Frank (R-N.Y.), Patriot Missile Performance report, **1992** 867-874
Horton, John P., **1983** 751
Hosokawa, Morihiro, resignation of Japanese Prime Minister, **1994** 221-224
Hospital construction
cutbacks of in Nixon budget, **1974** 96
federal financing of, GAO study on, **1972** 921-931
Hospital costs
for catastrophic illness care, **1986** 1026-1028
containment of, Carter on, **1978** 22, 25-26, 76; **1979** 11, 15, 19-20, 23, 31, 84-85
Hospital insurance, financing costs of, **1975** 116-117, 130
Hospitals
business and social responsibilities of, **1986** 487-513
for-profit, evaluation of care provided by, **1986** 487-513
medical mistakes, Institute of Medicine report on, **1999** 779-793
occupancy rate trends, and length of stay, **1988** 333-335
patient's bill of rights, **1973** 39-42
payment of
limiting increases in, Carter on, **1977** 127-128
and Medicare reform, **1986** 281-282
public, abortion restrictions of, **1977** 407-409, 427-430
quality of, **1999** 412-421
treatment of seriously ill infants, **1983** 273, 282-283, 303
treatment of severely handicapped infants, **1986** 541-558
Hosseinian, Hadi Nejad, **2001** 796
Hostages
See also under Terrorism
in Attica prison uprising, **1972** 783-788
Moslem captors release, **1990** 277-278
terrorist victims in the world, CIA on, **1981** 471-474
Hostages, American
in Iran, **1995** 351
and B. Carter's Libyan contacts, **1980** 908-909, 913-917
Carter on, **1980** 28, 29-31; **1981** 31, 36-37, 85-87, 156-158
CIA on, **1981** 473
negotiations for release, **1980** 999-1009
Reagan on, **1980** 661
release of, **1981** 137-138, 145-162; **2003** 1033
rescue attempt, **1980** 351-385, 475-476
U.S.-Iran settlement on, **1981** 145-146, 559-573
world opinion on, **1979** 867, 869-871, 877, 881
in Lebanon, **1985** 465-466
Bush on, **1989** 47
as presidential campaign issue, **1988** 746-747, 820-821
and U.S. arms sales to Iran, **1986** 1013-1022, 1049, 1054; **1987** 206, 208, 216-221, 226-227, 230-231
and U.S. terrorism policy, **1980** 932-936
Hostages, French, held by Hezbollah, **1986** 831-833
Hostages, Israeli, rescued from Entebbe, **1976** 517-520
Hostages, Japanese, in Peru, **1997** 234-237
Hotz, Robert, **1988** 796
el-Houderi, Ali A., **1980** 908
Houphouet-Boigny, Felix, ousted in military coup, **2002** 251
House v. Bell, **2005** 182
House Administration Committee, power of over members, **1976** 365-367
House Appropriations Committee, report on FEMA, **1992** 533-542
House Armed Services Committee
Akhromeyev testimony, **1989** 439-444
military readiness, letters questioning, **1994** 528-534
Tailhook Incident, **1992** 880
on terrorist attack on Marines in Beirut, **1983** 933-938
House Armed Services Special Subcommittee on Intelligence
Colby testimony on CIA involvement in Chile, **1974** 805-810
Liddy's refusal to testify, **1974** 205
House Banking Committee, BCCI banking scandal hearings, **1991** 621-636
House Budget Committee, formation of, **1974** 574, 576-577; **1976** 177-179
House Commerce Subcommittee on Oversight and Investigations, on hazardous waste disposal, **1979** 781-800
House Committee on Standards of Official Conduct (Ethics committee)
censure of Diggs, **1979** 623-631
Gingrich violations, **1995** 746-751

House Committee on Standards of Official Conduct *Continued*
Hays investigation, **1976** 366
investigation of intelligence leaks, **1976** 117
Korean influence-buying investigation, **1977** 769-819; **1978** 845-908; **1979** 897-898
Wright investigation, **1989** 239-257
House Democratic Steering and Policy Committee, plan for economic and energy crises, **1975** 15-18, 32-41
House Foreign Affairs Committee
Iran-contra affair investigation, **1986** 1050-1052
Jonestown and Ryan murder investigation, **1979** 347-378
House Foreign Affairs Subcommittee on Human Rights and International Organizations
Korean influence-buying investigation, **1979** 898
testimony on UN, **1990** 630-635
House Government Operations Subcommittee
on Employment and Housing, HUD investigation, **1989** 333-337
on Government Information and Individual Rights, investigation of cable monitoring, **1975** 710-711
IRS misconduct inquiry, **1975** 830
House Intelligence Committee
CIA reforms, **1992** 4
establishment of recommended, **1976** 117-118
recommended merger with Senate committee, **1987** 207, 241
war powers debate, **1990** 664
House International Relations Committee, release of State Department human rights report by, **1977** 3
House International Relations Subcommittee on International Organizations, on Korean influence buying, **1977** 771
House Interstate and Foreign Commerce Subcommittee on Oversight and Investigations, on Firestone tire recall, **1978** 720
House Judiciary Committee
access to White House tapes, **1974** 189-192, 194, 196-197, 201-203
impeachment inquiry, **1974** 145-149; **1998** 695-721
access to White House tapes, **1974** 302-304, 622, 673-674, 680-682
articles of impeachment, **1974** 655-660
final report, **1974** 713-763
members' support for impeachment, **1974** 683
Nixon on, **1974** 41-42, 52
Nixon's income taxes, **1974** 236, 238-239
release of grand jury report on Nixon, **1974** 225-232
release to of edited transcripts of White House tapes, **1974** 287-299, 303-387
staff report, **1974** 137-142
Watergate special prosecutor cooperation with, **1975** 664-666
wiretaps in Nixon White House, **1974** 487-489
impeachment trial, **1999** 15-40
members' reactions to White House tapes, **1974** 673-674
Rockefeller confirmation as vice president, **1974** 707, 709, 987-989
House October Surprise Task Force, **1994** 3-16
House of Representatives
See also Joint Economic Committee
Agnew request for investigation by, **1973** 828, 832-834
budget reconciliation in, **1981** 640-641
Calley's access to testimony before, **1974** 857-860
censure of
Crane and Studds, **1983** 725-734
Diggs, **1979** 623-631
Wilson, **1980** 485-491
Chinese technology transfer, **1998** 976-982
Civil Rights Commission appointments, **1983** 913-914
EPA hazardous waste investigations, **1982** 965-970; **1983** 749-750
ERA, reintroduction of, **1982** 611-617
expulsion, of Myers, **1980** 899-906
Gorsuch contempt citation, **1982** 965-970
Holocaust commemoration, **1981** 382
impeachment charges against Judge Claiborne, **1986** 849, 851-853
impeachment vote, **1998** 958-970
IRA prison hunger strike, resolution on, **1981** 402, 413
passage of NAFTA, Clinton remarks on, **1993** 953-958
physician-assisted suicide legislation, **1999** 441-442
Rockefeller confirmation, **1974** 987-989
sexual misconduct and drug use by members and pages, **1982** 729-740
speaker of, and transfer of presidential power, **1985** 493
Speaker of the House
election, **1997** 3-4
Gingrich resignation, **1998** 698, 799-808, 951
Livingston resignation, **1998** 799, 951-957, 959, 962
Wright resignation, **1997** 5; **1998** 800
spending responsibilities, abdication of, **1973** 4, 8-10
transfer of power from Democratic to Republican Party, **1995** 3-14
WHO infant formula code, resolution on, **1981** 448, 457-458
Wright as Speaker of, **1989** 241, 258
House of Representatives v. Immigration and Naturalization Service, **1983** 617-644
House Post Office, Rostenkowski indictment and, **1994** 281-286
House Resources Committee, on endangered species, **1995** 360-361
House Select Committees
on Assassinations, **1992** 10
Kennedy and King assassination investigation, **1978** 909-921; **1979** 593-622
reviving of, **1977** 114
on Children, Youth, and Families, on discarded children, **1989** 671-686
on Intelligence
intelligence agencies investigation
leaks from, **1976** 115-117, 683-686
recommendations, **1976** 115-124
Iran-contra investigation, **1986** 1050; **1987** 891-928

on Missing Persons in Southeast Asia, **1976** 925-936; **1977** 208
on Narcotics Abuse and Control, drug trafficking, **1990** 117
on U.S. National Security and Military/Commercial Concerns with the People's Republic of China (Cox committee), **1999** 235-256
House Standards of Official Conduct Committee (Ethics committee), Gingrich violations, **1995** 746-751; **1996** 838-849; **1997** 3-19
House Subcommittees
Census and Population, **1990** 171
Crime and Criminal Justice, **1992** 203
Financial Institutions, **1990** 816
Health and the Environment, nicotine levels in cigarettes, **1994** 205-217
Regulation, Business Opportunities, and Technology, child care quality hearings, **1994** 116-122
Transportation and Hazardous Materials, Amtrak hearings, **1994** 197-204
House Ways and Means Committee, Greenspan on "faltered" business recovery, **1991** 843-850
Housing
adequate and affordable, Democratic Party platform on, **1984** 577, 579-580
affordable, lack of, **1994** 260-261; **1998** 253-259, 355, 364; **1999** 391-392
discrimination in
New York laws prohibiting, **1974** 708
Urban League on, **1987** 47
equity in, Democratic Party platform on, **1972** 554-556; **1984** 606
fair, enforcement of, **1981** 83; **1983** 78, 86; **1987** 45
home ownership
characteristics in 1990, **1992** 476, 478
Republican Party platform on, **1984** 681, 702-703; **1988** 628
Home ownership and Opportunity for People Everywhere program, **1992** 449
integrated, promotion of by prohibiting "for sale" signs, **1977** 313-320
low-income
barred by zoning regulations, **1977** 35-44
cutbacks in Reagan budget, **1982** 145
federal assistance for, Urban League on, **1983** 52
and lobbyist fees paid by developers of, **1989** 333-337
privatization of, **1988** 230, 232, 237
programs for, Carter on, **1981** 72-73
public
Chicago Housing Authority, HUD takeover of, **1995** 294-301
problems created by, Republican platform on, **1984** 681-682; **1988** 629
in suburbs, as remedy for racial segregation, **1976** 223-233
rental housing market crisis, **1996** 167-177
Republican Party platform, **1996** 509-510
rising cost of, Carter CEA on, **1980** 159-164, 175, 182
segregation in
and economic status of American blacks, **1989** 446, 451-452, 458
and schools' racial population, **1975** 614-615, 624-625, 630
Housing and Community Development Act (1974), authority of HUD and local governments under, **1976** 224, 231-232
Housing and Urban Development Department (HUD)
in Carter's urban proposal, **1978** 243, 247, 249, 251-253
Chicago Housing Authority takeover, **1995** 294-301
church arson rebuilding program, **1997** 302-303, 304, 308-309
cities, state of the, **1998** 364-377
on homeless families, **1989** 672, 679
housing the poor, **1998** 253-259, 355, 364
investigation of, **1989** 333-337
public housing in suburbs, **1976** 223-233
rental housing market, **1996** 167-177
Housing construction
response of to oil prices and credit supply, **1974** 77, 80, 92, 420, 422, 425; **1980** 161, 163-164, 177
U.S.-Soviet cooperation on materials and techniques, **1974** 535-536, 542-544, 549, 567
Housing industry
emergency aid to, Democratic plan for, **1975** 18, 35-36
reversal of decline in, Ford CEA on, **1975** 100-101, 108-109
tax incentives and credit relaxation called for by, **1974** 863
Housing market
and consumption, **2003** 77-78
and "home equity extraction," **2005** 139
median price in U.S., **2004** 57
mortgage refinancing, **2004** 67
prices
CEA report on, **2003** 76
inflation or housing bubble, **2005** 139, 414
residential investment, **2003** 79-80; **2005** 146
Housing segregation. *See under* Housing
Houston (Texas)
air quality of, **1981** 275, 289
national women's conference in, **1977** 861-867
Howard, A. E. Dick
Florida recount case, **2000** 1004
on Supreme Court Justice Powell's retirement, **1987** 579
Howard, J. Daniel, Tailhook Convention Report, **1992** 880, 884
Howard, J. Timothy, Fannie Mae investigations, **2004** 420
Howard, John
Iraq War coalition and, **2003** 138
Kyoto Protocol on Climate Change ratification, **2002** 303-304
on terrorist bombings in Bali, **2002** 703
Zimbabwe elections, **2002** 133
Zimbabwe membership in British Commonwealth, suspension of, **2003** 1114
Howard, Michael
Conservative Party leader, **2005** 394
on London bombing terrorist suspects, **2005** 396

Howarth, James, **1983** 727
Howe, Geoffrey, **1990** 748
Howe, Jonathan, **1988** 38
Hoxha, Enver, death of, **1985** 325-331
Hoyer, Steny (D-Md.), minority whip election defeat, **2001** 549
Hruska, Roman L. (R-Neb.), on proposed court of appeals, **1975** 455-457
Hrusovsky, Pavol, on fall of the Berlin Wall, **2004** 198
Hu Jintao
  China space exploration program, **2003** 305
  Chinese military buildup, **2005** 615
  Chinese political repression, **2005** 618-619
  Chinese social distress, **2004** 937
  Chinese yuan, **2004** 238-239
  Japan relations, **2005** 621-622
  Latin American trade relations, **2004** 938
  military commission chairman, **2004** 941
  new Chinese leader/president, **2002** 850, 852-853; **2003** 1173, 1174
  North Korea relations, **2005** 605
  on U.S. bombing of Chinese embassy, **1999** 305
  U.S. visit, **2005** 612
    postponed, **2005** 568, 613
  Uzbekistan, meeting with president Karimov, **2005** 433
Hu Na, **1984** 288
Hu Nim, on U.S. spying on Cambodia, **1975** 312-313
Hu Yoabang, **1989** 276
Hua Guofeng
  eulogy of Mao and elevation to new posts, **1976** 687-691
  invitation to Carter to visit PRC, **1979** 136, 154
  on normalization of relations with U.S., **1978** 783, 786
  reappointment, **1978** 157-158
  resignation, **1980** 956
Huang, John, campaign finance contributions, **1997** 825; **1998** 894
Huang Chen, **1973** 293
Huang Hua, **1979** 151
Huang Shu-tse, **1974** 779
Hubbard, Carroll, Jr. (D-Ky.), BCCI banking scandal, **1991** 632-633
Hubbard, R. Glenn, on economic recovery, **2002** 52
Hubbard, Scott
  Columbia space shuttle disaster investigation, **2003** 634
  on *Lunar Prospector* mission, **1998** 118
  NASA Mars mission programs director, **2000** 92-93
Hubbell, Webster L., Whitewater indictment, **1998** 633; **2000** 764
Hubble, Edwin, on expanding universe, **1992** 380
Hubble space telescope
  age of the universe, **1994** 458-462; **1996** 265-269
  birth of stars, **1995** 288-293
  flaws, **1990** 753-754, 755-757, 758
  future of program, **2003** 631; **2004** 11-13; **2005** 502-503
  galaxy images from new camera, **2002** 212-218; **2004** 7
  mission repairs, **1999** 712
  mission repairs and flaws in, **2003** 632; **2005** 502-503
  planet outside the solar system, **1998** 115
HUD. *See* Housing and Urban Development Department
Hudson, David L., on third party visitation rights, **2000** 288
Hudson, Keith, **1992** 175-185
Hudson v. McMillian et al., **1992** 175-185
Hudson v. Palmer, **1984** 480-488
Huerta, Michael P., on year 2000 computer conversion, **1997** 534-535
Huffington, Arianna, California gubernatorial recall election, **2003** 1008
Hufnagle, Vicki, on medical specialties, **1993** 655
Hufstedler, Shirley, **1975** 464
Hugel, Max, resignation from CIA, **1981** 856, 858-859
Hughes, Francis, **1981** 402
Hughes, Harold E. (D-Iowa), on Colson's conversion, **1974** 444-445
Hughes, Howard R., Nixon campaign contributions from, **1973** 975-977; **1974** 605, 616
Hughes, Karen P., cultural diplomacy programs, **2005** 581
Hughes Space and Communications Co., **1999** 237, 250
Human cloning. *See under* Cloning research
Human experimentation
  with chemicals, by intelligence agencies, **1976** 261-262, 269-270
  fetal research, public funding for, **1975** 543-544
  with hallucinogenic drugs, by CIA, **1975** 402, 432
  radiation experiments, **1993** 987-995; **1994** 54-61; **1995** 633-638
  in testing biological weapons, **1997** 768
Human Genome Project, **1997** 37-38; **2000** 34, 397-409, 668
Human immunodeficiency virus (HIV) infection
  See also AIDS (acquired immunodeficiency syndrome); United Nations Programme on HIV/AIDS
  in African nations, **1999** 489-498
  and child abuse in refugee camps, **2002** 919
  children infected with, **1999** 387; **2001** 957-958
  in China, **2003** 1175
  as a disability, Supreme Court on, **1998** 378-392; **1999** 317
  drug prevention, federal guidelines on, **2005** 50-63
  global HIV/AIDS epidemic, **1998** 878-889; **2002** 469-482; **2004** 429-441
  neviripine for pregnant women, **2002** 473
  in Russia increasing, **2001** 255
  transmission risks during dental treatment, **1998** 379-380
  in U.S., **1997** 84
  U.S. drug patents and treatment for, **2003** 742
  worldwide estimates, **1997** 83-84
  worldwide impact of, **1996** 306-307; **1997** 348-349
  worldwide incidence of, **2003** 781; **2005** 50
  young people and, **1998** 888-889
Human Life Amendment, National Committee for a, on federal funds for abortion, **1977** 410-411
Human needs
  meeting in developing countries
    Carter on, **1977** 691

McNamara on, **1977** 700-704, 710-715
Human reproduction, Vatican teachings on, **1987** 267-287
Human rights
See also under names of individual countries
Afghanistan, **1999** 531-534
Amnesty International reports, **1988** 883-889; **1989** 597-609; **1990** 129-142; **1993** 559-578
Burundi war atrocities, **2003** 924, 925
Chechnya war, **1999** 909-916; **2000** 175-176
China, People's Republic of, **1994** 73-84; **1996** 133-138; **1997** 729, 735-738; **1998** 467-468, 469-470
Congo, sexual exploitation by UN personnel, **2004** 509
Congo conflict, **2002** 553; **2003** 291
defined by State Department report, **1984** 156-157
and democracy, G-8 statement on, **1997** 355-356
Democratic Party platform on, **1984** 625-626, 645-646; **1988** 568; **1992** 705
East Timor independence and, **1999** 511-523; **2002** 260-261
education, **2001** 612-613
El Salvador, **1993** 237-248
Gorbachev on, **1992** 437
growth of institutions protecting, State Department on, **1981** 181-183
Haiti political situation, **2004** 98
Helsinki Final Act provisions on, **1975** 559-561, 564, 568-570
international consensus on, **1980** 192
Iraq, **1999** 144-152; **2000** 581-595
abuses of Iraqi prisoners, U.S. Army report on, **2004** 207-234
John Paul II UN speech on, **1995** 639-645
Kosovo conflict, **1998** 837-839; **1999** 802-816
Nigeria, **1995** 696-699
as peace requirement, Sakharov on, **1975** 915-918; **1985** 717
Republican Party platform on, **1984** 716-717
Sierra Leone civil war, **2002** 249-250
South African Truth and Reconciliation Commission report, **1998** 755-775
State Department reports on, **1977** 3-25; **1980** 189-198; **1981** 179-190; **1982** 107-119; **1983** 181-195; **1984** 155-168; **1985** 145-157; **1986** 97-113; **1987** 189-204; **1988** 93-115; **1989** 57-70; **1990** 129-131, 142-152; **1994** 73-84; **1996** 133-138
status of women, UN conference on, **1975** 507-522
strengthening of as function of UN, Waldheim on, **1973** 754, 760
Sudan, **2003** 839-840
trafficking in humans, State Department reports on, **2002** 332-352; **2004** 125, 126
Turkey, torture issue, **2002** 910
Uganda conflict, **2003** 470-479
UN Conference on Women, **1995** 581-587
UN Millennium Summit Declaration, **2000** 708-709
UN position on, **1995** 358
U.S. *See* Abu Ghraib prison abuse scandal; Guantanamo Bay detainees
U.S.-Soviet discussions of differences on
Geneva summit, **1985** 750, 759
Iceland summit, **1986** 875-876, 879, 881
Moscow summit, **1988** 354-360, 370
Reagan's New Year's message, **1986** 4, 8
SALT talks, **1977** 243-245, 247-248, 252-253, 266-267
at UN, **1985** 712-713
Washington summit, **1987** 991, 993, 999, 1002, 1005
Uzbekistan, killings in Andijon, **2005** 429-433, 436-445
violations, UN secretary general on, **2000** 701
world struggle for, Carter farewell address on, **1981** 31-32, 35-36
world violations of, Wiesel on, **1986** 1075-1078
Human Rights, Universal Declaration of
John Paul II on, **1979** 729, 740, 749-750
Reagan on, **1984** 815; **1985** 712
Human Rights Campaign
Clinton speech on gay rights, **1997** 760-766
domestic partner benefits, **2000** 162
gay rights political action committee, **1997** 760; **1999** 4
Human Rights Center, University of California at Berkeley, human trafficking study, **2004** 123
Human Rights Watch
Afghanistan
detainees, abuse of, **2004** 216-217
political situation, **2002** 16
warlords, **2002** 20; **2003** 1096
Bagram base detentions, **2002** 832
Burundi war atrocities, **2003** 924, 925
Chechnya war, **2002** 766
China, political repression, **2005** 619
China AIDS/HIV prevention programs, **2005** 55
Colombia guerillas, **2002** 572; **2003** 428
Congo conflict, **2002** 553
death penalty opponent, **2005** 179
Indonesia and East Timor independence, **2001** 596
Iraq
Abu Ghraib prison scandal, **2004** 214, 340, 341
civilian casualties, **2003** 145
legal system, **2003** 1196
repression of Kurds, **2003** 1195-1196
U.S. troops fire on demonstrators, **2003** 941
Jenin "massacre" investigations, **2002** 934-935
Kosovo, Albanian attacks on Serbs, **2004** 950
Kosovo conflict, **1999** 290
Palestinian suicide bombings, **2002** 931
racial divide in criminal justice system, **2000** 774
religious vs. political rights, **1997** 563
trafficking in humans, **2002** 324, 335
Uganda conflict, **2003** 470-479
U.S. civil liberties, **2002** 830
U.S. domestic detentions, **2002** 834
U.S. secret detentions, **2005** 906-907
Uzbekistan, in aftermath of Andijon killings, **2005** 431-432
Venezuela Supreme Court appointments, **2004** 552
Human settlement, earliest in North America, **1992** 135-139
Human trafficking
Congressional Research Service report on, **2004** 122-134
State Department reports, **2002** 332-352; **2004** 125

Human trafficking *Continued*
Sudan conflict and, **2002** 332-352
trafficking to U.S., **2004** 131
UN peacekeeping forces in Kosovo, **2004** 893
in Venezuela, **2004** 552-553
victims of, **2004** 128
Humanitarian Law Project (Los Angeles), **2003** 612
Humanities
in American public, **1988** 517, 519, 523-527
colleges' failures in, **1985** 128, 138-139, 143
in education, **1987** 681-696; **1988** 517-523
Humberto Meuia, Oscar, **1985** 152
Humberto Romero, Carlos, overthrow of, **1981** 243, 252
Hume, Brit, in vice presidential debate, **1988** 808-810, 815-816, 821, 823
Hume, John
at New Ireland Forum, **1984** 315-316
Northern Ireland peace negotiations, **1998** 203
Humphrey, Harold, **1978** 654
Humphrey, Hubert H. (D-Minn.)
campaign contributions to, **1974** 603
death of, **1978** 3-6, 18-19
in Florida Democratic primary, **1972** 201
labor union support for, **1992** 345
Nixon budget, **1973** 171; **1974** 96
nomination of Mondale, **1976** 596
unemployment and fighting inflation, **1974** 861, 870-873
withdrawal from presidential race, **1972** 590
Humphrey, Hubert H., III, on Jaycees decision, **1984** 467
Hun Sen
Cambodian coup, **1997** 639-641; **1998** 971, 972
Cambodian peace talks, **1991** 692
Hundler, Donald W., on electric vehicles, **1996** 19, 20
Hungary
abandonment of communism, **1989** 400
East German exodus to, **1989** 626
economic aid to, Bush on, **1989** 412-413, 418-419, 422-423, 432-433
economic situation, **2004** 199
EU membership, **2004** 198
Iraq War, support for, **2003** 42, 49
Nagy tribute, **1989** 339-342
NATO membership, **1997** 514, 516; **1999** 119, 120; **2004** 136, 198
political liberalization in, **1989** 339-341, 413, 416-424, 433-435, 635-636
power sharing by communist government, **1989** 710
student test scores, **1992** 87, 90
uprising in (1956), **1989** 340-342
Warsaw Pact dissolution, **1991** 399-401
Hungate, William L. (D-Mo.), on Nixon pardon, **1974** 888, 896
Hunger
See also Famine
bishops' letter on economic policies, **1984** 963
Carter administration war on hunger worldwide, **1981** 100-101
causes of, **1984** 3-6, 8
definitions of, **1984** 11-13, 17
Democratic Party platform on, **1984** 617-618
during Reagan administration, **1983** 765-766, 770, 772; **1984** 3-6, 11-14
FAO report on, **2003** 756-757
infant formula link to malnutrition, **1981** 447, 450, 917
in large cities, U.S. Conference of Mayors report on, **2003** 73
Physician Task Force report on, **1985** 189-205
Republican Party platform on, **1984** 677
worldwide, remedies proposed in Global 2000 report, **1981** 13-14, 19-20, 27-28
Hunger strikes
of IRA prisoners, **1981** 401-416
of Sakharov and Bonner, **1981** 747-752
Hunt, E. Howard, Jr.
Ellsberg break-in, **1973** 538, 542-548; **1974** 205-206, 208-210; **1975** 428-429
Watergate break-in, **1973** 415, 417-423; **1975** 142
memo on White House commitments to defendants, **1974** 992-994
White House payments to, **1974** 158-167, 306-308, 348-353, 359, 361, 364-370, 375, 377-378
Hunt, Guy, ethics law violation conviction, **1993** 303-305
Hunt, James B. "Jim" (North Carolina governor), teaching standards, **1997** 35; **1999** 47
Hunt, Jeneane Michelle, **1991** 176
Hunt, Rex, in Falklands war, **1982** 284, 292
Hunt v. Blackburn, **1998** 398
Hunt v. McNair, **1973** 643-644
Hunter, Duncan (R-Calif.)
Chinese ownership of U.S. oil firms, **2005** 615-616
intelligence agency reform legislation, **2004** 969-970
Hunter v. Erickson, **1997** 188, 192
Hunthausen, Raymond G., Vatican disciplining of, **1986** 757, 911, 985-986
Huntington Library (San Marino, Calif.), Dead Sea scrolls, **1991** 637-639
Huntress, Wesley, on moon ice findings, **1998** 114, 117
Huong, Tran Van, and collapse of South Vietnam, **1975** 269, 279, 291, 295
Hurd, Douglas, **1990** 749
Hurley, Jayne, Chinese food report, **1993** 689-694
Hurley v. Irish-American Gay, Lesbian and Bisexual Group of Boston, **1995** 327-335
Hurricane disasters
See also Hurricane Katrina disaster; Hurricane Rita disaster
Andrew, FEMA and, **1992** 533-542, 843-848
climate change and, **2005** 926-927
Haiti disaster, UN economic assistance, **2005** 334
Haiti floods and hurricanes, **2004** 99
Hugo, damage from, **1989** 667-668, 670
Iniki, **1992** 843-848
Mitch relief effort, UN report on, **1998** 789-798
UN report on damage, **1998** 789-798
Hurricane Katrina disaster, **2005** 539-548
Bush administration response, **2005** 77, 539, 566-578
chaos in New Orleans, **2005** 541-542
congressional response and appropriations, **2005** 101, 137-138, 140-141

demolition and reconstruction, **2005** 543-544
economic impact, **2005** 78, 546-547
emergency response, **2005** 540
investigations of inadequacy of, **2005** 569-571
evacuations and displacement, **2005** 542-543
FEMA response, **2005** 543, 566, 567, 569-571
"Gulf Opportunity Zones" (for economic development), **2005** 571
Homeland Security Department response, **2005** 893
National Weather Service warning, **2005** 548
oil and gas industry, **2005** 779
poverty and, **2005** 140-141
rebuilding the levees, **2005** 544-546
reconstruction contracts, fraud and mismanagement of, **2005** 570
Hurricane Rita disaster
congressional response, **2005** 101
Homeland Security Department response, **2005** 893
oil and gas industry, **2005** 779
Texas and Louisiana evacuation, **2005** 541
Husak, Gustav
regime of, Dubcek letter on, **1975** 239-244, 246-247
resignation, **1989** 637
Husam, Taher Husam, Hariri assassination plot, UN investigation, **2005** 692
Husband, Rick D., *Columbia* commander, **2003** 632, 633
Hushen, John W., **1974** 813
Huskey, Kristine, Guantanamo Bay detentions, **2003** 108
Hussain, Hasib Mir, London terrorist bombing suspect, **2005** 396-397
al-Hussein, Hanif Shah, Afghan parliamentary elections, **2005** 972
Hussein, Saddam. *See* Saddam Hussein
Hussein, Uday (Saddam Hussein's son), killed during gun battle, **2003** 938-939, 1191
Hussein ibn Talal (king of Jordan)
on Arab leaders' use of Palestinians, **1974** 920
and Arab solidarity, **1987** 870, 872
Carter meeting with, **1977** 899, 902
conditions for joining peace talks, **1978** 606
death of, **1999** 890-891
eulogy for Yitzhak Rabin, **1995** 691, 693-694
and Israeli peace agreement, **1994** 329-335
and Israeli peace proposal, **1985** 710-711
Middle East peace negotiations, **1999** 890-891
Nixon meeting with, **1974** 449, 451, 467-469
Persian Gulf peacemaking efforts, **1990** 558-559
PLO in peace talks, **1982** 754
renunciation of ties to West Bank, **1988** 579-585, 906
West Bank peace agreement, **1995** 622
Wye River peace agreement, **1998** 744, 753-754
Hustler magazine, libel suits against, **1984** 247-253; **1988** 175-182
Hustler Magazine and Larry C. Flynt v. Falwell, **1988** 175-182
Hutchings, Robert L., and world trends, **2005** 14
Hutchinson, Asa (R-Ark.)
House Judiciary Committee impeachment inquiry, **1998** 711
House Judiciary Committee impeachment trial, **1999** 18
medical use of marijuana, **2001** 327
Hutchinson, Billy, **2001** 761
Hutchinson, Edward (R-Mich.)
on impeachment inquiry report, **1974** 138
review of Nixon tapes, **1974** 288, 291, 298
Hutchinson, Ronald R., libel suit against Proxmire, **1979** 479-491
Hutchinson v. Proxmire, **1979** 479-491
Hutchison, Kay Bailey, Kennedy assassination anniversary, **1993** 960, 961
Hutchison Whampoa Ltd., **1999** 852
Hutton, Lord, British prewar Intelligence on Iraq inquiry, **2003** 884; **2004** 718-719
Hutu (ethnic group). *See* Burundi; Rwanda
al-Huweirini, Abdulaziz, assassination attempt, **2003** 230-231
Huygens robot mission, **2004** 6-7; **2005** 502
Hwang Woo Suk, South Korean stem cell research scandal, **2005** 320-322
Hybels, Bill, Clinton interview on Monica Lewinsky affair, **2000** 598-599
Hybridoma technology, defined, **1987** 354, 357
Hyde, Henry J. (R-Ill.)
abortion rights, **1992** 799-800
and public financing of, **1977** 408, 411; **1980** 516; **1983** 273
and antiterrorism bill, **1995** 179
church arson prevention, **1997** 306
death penalty, **2000** 989
extra-marital affair, **1998** 697
House impeachment inquiry, **1998** 696, 697, 700-701
House Judiciary Committee and impeachment trial, **1999** 16, 17-19, 22-29; **2001** 89
House vote on impeachment, **1998** 959
on human rights policy, **1981** 780
India-U.S. relations, **2005** 466
"October Surprise" Task Force chairman, **1994** 4
physician-assisted suicide legislation, **1997** 462; **1999** 441-442
on Reno conflict of interest, **1997** 824
Starr report public release, **1998** 636
Hyde amendment, on public financing of abortion, **1977** 407-408, 410-411; **1980** 515-535; **1983** 273
Hyland, William, **1992** 256
Hypertension
DASH (Dietary Approaches to Stop Hypertension) Eating Plan, **2005** 8
and obesity, **2004** 653

I

Iacocca, Lee A., **1979** 694; **1986** 699; **1992** 11
IAEA. *See* International Atomic Energy Agency
IBM Corporation
benefits for partners of homosexual employees, **1996** 689
chess victory of "Deep Blue" computer, **1997** 273-276
pension plan case, **2004** 737

IBM Corporation *Continued*
purchase by Lenovo Group Ltd., **2004** 939; **2005** 616
ICA. *See* International Communication Agency
Icahn, Carl, **1986** 972, 978
ICAO. *See* International Civil Aviation Organization
ICBMs. *See* Missile systems, intercontinental ballistic
ICC. *See* International Criminal Court
Iceland summit (1985), **1986** 784, 875-885
ICJ. *See* International Court of Justice
Idaho
abortion restricted by legislation, **1990** 215-219
reversal of ERA approval, **1981** 923-938; **1982** 612
Idaho v. Coeur d'Alene Tribe of Idaho, **1999** 348
Idaho v. Freeman, **1981** 923-938
Idaho National Engineering Laboratory, nuclear waste cleanup, **1995** 118
IDEA. *See* Individuals with Disabilities Education Act
Ieng Sary, **1975** 312
Ifill, Gwen, vice presidential debates moderator, **2004** 678
Ignagni, Karen, mental health legislation, **2002** 268
Ikard, Frank, **1975** 168
ILA. *See* International Longshoremen's Association
Ilchman, Alice S., **1985** 789
Iliescu, Ion, **1989** 711
Illarionov, Andrie N.
Kyoto Protocol, Russian opposition to, **2003** 865
Russian envoy to G-8 meetings, **2005** 301
Yukos oil seizure, criticism of, **2005** 301
Illing, Sigurd, Uganda conflict, **2003** 473
Illingworth, Garth, images of the universe, **2002** 217
Illinois, death penalty moratorium, **2002** 353, 354-355
Illinois v. Krull, **1995** 346
Illinois v. McArthur, **2001** 407
Illinois Broadcasting Co. v. National Citizens Committee for Broadcasting, **1978** 419-432
ILO. *See* International Labor Organization
Imag, David G., **1992** 144
IMClone Systems, insider trading scandal, **2002** 399-400; **2004** 420
Imesch, Joseph L., **1988** 786
IMF. *See* International Monetary Fund
Immigrants and immigration
See also Asylum, political
aid to immigrants, **1996** 452-453, 455-456; **1997** 34
alien legalization and amnesty, **1981** 265-273, 605-606, 611-612
bills, payment to members of Congress for, **1979** 468-478
California, Proposition 187, **1994** 388-389; **1995** 563
California drivers' licenses, **2003** 1009
California's English-only law, **1986** 959-961
Census Bureau reports, **1992** 475, 477; **1997** 175-182; **2001** 765
crises in, Reagan plan for, **1981** 606, 612-613, 616-618
Cuban and Haitian refugee boatlifts, U.S. policy on, **1980** 337-350; **1981** 76-77, 605-607; **1995** 203-207
Cuban detainees in U.S., agreement on, **1987** 929-930, 932-934
Democratic Party platform, **1996** 636-637
domestic detentions of immigrants, **2002** 833-835
Economic Advisers' Report, **1990** 82, 99-101
economic effects of, Reagan CEA on, **1986** 91-92
entry-and-exit tracking system, **2003** 220-221
foreign student tracking, **2002** 843-845
foreign-born population, in U.S., **1990** 170-171; **1995** 563-569; **1997** 175-182
Hispanics in U.S., John Paul II on, **1987** 699-700, 706-707
housing markets and, **2003** 80
illegal immigrants
citizenship for children of, **2000** 510
education for children of, **1982** 489-506
Mexico to U.S., **1979** 169-172, 175, 181
as presidential campaign issue, **1984** 889-890
Republican Party platform on, **1984** 703-704
U.S. enforcement and, **1981** 265-266, 270-273, 605-606, 608-610, 616-618
Immigration Enforcement Bureau, **2001** 767
Immigration Services Bureau, **2001** 767
in labor market, **1987** 144
language instruction for, federal funding of, **1983** 415
legal immigrants, number of, **1995** 564-656
legalization of, **1981** 265-266, 271-272, 605-606, 611-612; **1986** 964-965
National Security Entry-Exit Registration System (NSEERS), **2002** 845-849
prohibitions on, American Party platform on, **1972** 624
reform
Reagan's signing statement, **1986** 963-969
U.S. Commission report, **1994** 387-400
refugee policy
coordinated, Carter on, **1981** 76-77
Democratic Party platform on, **1984** 611-612
Reagan proposals on, **1981** 605-618
registration of selected immigrants, **2003** 316-317
Republican Party platform, **1996** 520-521
screening, attorney general on, **2002** 842-849
skilled workers proposed, **1990** 82, 100-101
student visa abuses, **2001** 765, 769
temporary guest workers program, **2005** 79, 83
temporary worker program/temporary visas (T visas), **2004** 20, 27, 124-125
U.S. and British policies on, and the Holocaust, **1983** 144, 149-150
U.S. policy, **2003** 957
executive order tightening, **2001** 764-771
U.S. strength in diversity, **1997** 43
Wal-Mart workers, **2005** 739-740
Immigration and Customs Enforcement Agency, terrorism threat alert, **2004** 272
Immigration and Nationality Act (1952), **1987** 256-265
Haitian refugees issue, **1992** 456, 459-468; **1993** 414, 415-418
Immigration and Naturalization Service (INS)
See also Homeland Security Department (DHS)
abolition proposal, **1997** 175
amnesty program for illegal aliens, **1986** 965

border inspections, **2003** 219
Chinese student visas, **1989** 277-278, 281-282
drug testing of employees, **1986** 840
Haitian refugees, **1992** 455
and homeland security department, **2002** 530, 842; **2003** 219
Mariel boatlift of Cuban refugees, **1980** 345-346, 348-350; **1987** 932-934, 936
political asylum
and deportation, **1987** 253-265
for Elian Gonzalez, **2000** 266, 269
from religious persecution, **1998** 26-28
for women, new rules on, **1995** 276-280
reorganization of, **2001** 764, 766-767; **2002** 842
screening immigrants, **2002** 842-843
September 11 detainees
"hold until cleared" policy, **2003** 312-313
"INS Custody List," **2003** 311
Student and Exchange Visitor Program, **2003** 222
Transit Without Visa program, **2003** 222
visa application and issuing process, **2003** 222-223
visas for terrorist hijackers, **2002** 842-843; **2003** 219
Immigration and Naturalization Service v. Cardoza-Fonseca, **1987** 253-265; **1992** 463, 465
Immigration and Naturalization Service v. Chadha, **1983** 617-644; **1998** 427
Immigration and Naturalization Service v. Lopez-Mendoza, **1984** 508
Immigration and Naturalization Service v. Phinpathya, **1992** 464
Immigration and Refugee Policy, Select Commission on, **1981** 77, 265-273, 605
Immigration Reform and Control Act (1986), signing of, **1986** 963-969
Immunity. *See* Congressional immunity; Diplomatic immunity; Judicial immunity; Presidential immunity
Immunization
federal program, funding of, **1987** 152
swine flu program, analysis of, **1978** 669-681
Impeachment, gubernatorial, **1988** 249-256
Impeachment, judicial, **1986** 849-857; **1989** 583-596
Impeachment, presidential
Clinton impeachment
articles of impeachment, **1998** 964-967; **1999** 20
censure resolution, **1999** 21
grounds for, in Starr report, **1998** 637-638
House Judiciary Committee inquiry, **1998** 695-721
House votes, **1998** 958-970
and plea-bargain agreement, **2001** 88-89
Starr independent counsel investigations, **1998** 38-39, 393, 395, 565-566, 905, 907, 960; **2001** 88
Starr investigation report, **1998** 632-664
and timing of air strikes against Iraq, **1998** 937
trial, statements from, **1999** 15-40
constitutional requirements for, **1974** 137-143, 145-149
criminal offense requirement for, **1974** 194-195, 199
House Judiciary Committee inquiry
access to presidential documents, **1974** 192, 196-197, 202-203
final report on Nixon, **1974** 713-763
Nixon income taxes, **1974** 236, 238-239
Nixon on cooperation with, **1974** 41-42, 52
release of Watergate grand jury report to, **1974** 225-232
Johnson impeachment, **1998** 697, 959; **1999** 15
Nixon impeachment
articles of impeachment, **1974** 655-660
House vote, **1998** 959
impact on country, Nixon on, **1974** 292-293
Senate impeachment powers, **1993** 81-91
Impoundment of funds by president
budget reform passage, **1974** 573-575, 591-597
and congressional power of purse, **1973** 3-19, 88-90, 92-93
Nixon on, **1973** 193, 204-205
OECD on, **1973** 686
Inaugural addresses
Bush, George H. W., **1989** 41-48
Bush, George W., **2001** 94-101; **2005** 41-49, 43-44, 305, 582
Carter, **1977** 89-93
Clinton, **1993** 129-134; **1997** 20-26
Ford, **1974** 695-705
Kennedy, **1973** 80; **2001** 95
Nixon, **1973** 79-85
Reagan, **1981** 137-143; **1985** 39-46
INC. *See* Iraqi National Congress
Income assistance
Democratic Party platform on, **1972** 527, 532-533, 545
guaranteed income, National '80s Agenda on, **1981** 40
Republican Party platform on, **1972** 651-652, 679
taxable grant of $1,000, McGovern proposal, **1972** 719, 738
Income disparities. *See* Economic justice
Income distribution
among young families, **1992** 353-360
basic needs report, **1999** 391, 394-400
CEA report on, **1992** 127-134
Census Bureau report, **1992** 475-478
human development, UN report on, **1996** 438-444
median income of foreign-born, **1997** 181
Income inequality
CEA on, **1997** 52; **2000** 52-53
CEA on causes of, **2000** 58-61
Census Bureau on, **1996** 396-400; **1999** 390-391
in developing countries, **1999** 392-393
Income insurance, in McGovern's economic program, **1972** 738, 741-742
Income policies. *See* Wage and price standards
Income redistribution, as priority in developing countries, **1972** 862-864
Inculturation, and Catholic clergy in India, **1986** 24-25, 28-30, 32-33
Independence Day
bicentennial celebrations, **1976** 331-343, 509-516, 537-542
Statue of Liberty restoration, **1986** 697-703
Independent counsel
See also Lewinsky, Monica; Special prosecutor; Watergate special prosecutor; Whitewater investigations

Independent counsel *Continued*
constitutionality of, **1988** 465-478; **1989** 393
dissatisfaction with, **1998** 634
future of, Starr congressional testimony on, **1999** 165-172
history of, **1988** 466
in Iran-contra affair, **1986** 1052, 1054-1055
role of the, **1998** 905-911
Independent Election Commission of Iraq, **2005** 947
Independent International Commission on Decommissioning (IICD), **2001** 759-760, 762; **2005** 510-511
Independent Panel to Review DOD Detention Operations, **2004** 212-213
Independent Petroleum Association, **1983** 518
Inderfuth, Karl F., India and Pakistan economic sanctions, **1998** 329
India
See also Kashmir
AIDS drug distribution and manufacture, **2003** 780, 784
AIDS epidemic, **2002** 471; **2004** 429, 430
assassination of I. Gandhi, **1984** 945-949
Bhopal gas poisoning, **1984** 1023-1026; **1985** 295-302
bombings in New Delhi, **2005** 468
Carter visit, **1977** 897, 900
cyclone in Bay of Bengal, **1999** 468-469
Dalai Lama's exile in, **1989** 573, 578
Dalit (*formerly* Untouchables), racism against, **2001** 605
Desai as head of government, **1977** 237-241
economic growth, **2003** 754, 765
economic situation, **2000** 1061; **2004** 351-352
elections, **2004** 348-350; **2005** 463
expansion and economic growth of, **2005** 15
family planning program, **1977** 238, 241
as a great power, **2005** 14, 18-19
human rights, **1990** 133-134, 138
John Paul II visit, **1986** 23-37
Lahore Declaration, **1999** 623-624
missile threat to U.S., **1998** 491-492
nonalignment policy of, **1977** 237, 241
nuclear reactors, **2005** 464-465
nuclear test explosion by, **1975** 361-363
nuclear weapons and population of, Wallace on, **1975** 156, 158-159
nuclear weapons testing, **1998** 483, 541; **1999** 623-624; **2000** 203
opium growing in, **1972** 646, 648-649
Pakistan relations, **2001** 963-970; **2002** 325-331; **2003** 209-217; **2004** 352-353
Pakistani conflict with
Nixon administration policy toward, **1972** 163, 580; **1977** 322, 339-341
secession of East Pakistan, **1977** 538
and U.S. economic aid, **1972** 23-39
U.S.-PRC Shanghai communiqué on, **1972** 188-189
Pakistani guerrilla attack on parliament, **2001** 963-970; **2002** 325, 326; **2003** 209
Pakistani terrorist bombings, **2002** 326-327; **2003** 210-211, 212
population of, **1984** 522, 525, 531
at poverty summit, **1981** 770
programs and priorities, prime minister on, **2004** 348-357
relations with Pakistan, **1999** 623-629
Rushdie death threat, impact in, **1989** 95
sex trade in children, **2001** 956; **2004** 126
Sri Lanka accord with on ethnic conflict, **1987** 615-622
state of emergency in, Moynihan on, **1975** 648
tsunami disaster, **2004** 348
tsunami relief effort, **2005** 1003-1004
UNSC membership proposal, **2003** 811
U.S. relations, **2004** 1011; **2005** 462-471
U.S.-India defense cooperation agreement, **2005** 463
weapons of mass destruction proliferation, **1996** 213, 222-223
Indian Mineral Lease Act, **2003** 579
Indian Ocean, military limitations in, **1977** 247, 251, 738-739, 744
Indian Schools Program, **1979** 158, 166
Indiana, welfare reform, **1999** 258
Indians. *See* Native Americans
Individual Development Accounts (IDAs), **2000** 26
Individual Retirement Accounts (IRAs), **1984** 119, 125, 235; **1992** 57, 63, 106
Individuals with Disabilities Education Act (IDEA), **1993** 399, 402-405; **1999** 318
Indochina. *See* Southeast Asia
Indonesia
See also East Timor; West Timor
Aceh province
cease-fire agreement, **2002** 707-708; **2004** 993
tsunami disaster, **2004** 753, 993, 995; **2005** 993-995
AIDS epidemic, **2002** 471; **2004** 430
economic situation, **1998** 722, 724; **1999** 720-721; **2002** 707
elections, **1999** 719-720
family planning in, **1987** 451
human rights in, **1977** 3, 11-13; **1990** 134
human trafficking, **2002** 344-345
IMF aid package, **1997** 836; **1999** 721
independence movements, **1999** 721-722
OPEC oil prices
cuts, **1981** 799
increase in, **1976** 938
political situation, **1998** 604; **1999** 718-723
population pressure and resettlement programs, **1987** 445, 447
Powell visit to, **2002** 703
presidential elections, **2004** 753-755
rain forests of, impact of World Bank projects, **1986** 859-873
SARS (severe acute respiratory syndrome) outbreak, **2003** 132
Suharto resignation, **1998** 284-288, 722; **2001** 562-563; **2004** 753
Sukarnoputri address on challenges in, **2001** 562-574
Sukarnoputri presidential election defeat, **2004** 753-755

terrorist bombings
in Bali, **2002** 702-712, 1014, 1016; **2003** 1052; **2004** 754-756; **2005** 399-400
in Jakarta, **2004** 754-755, 756
tsunami relief efforts, **2005** 1001-1002
unemployment, **1998** 726
U.S. relations, **2002** 703-704
Wahid resignation, **2001** 563-564
Wiranto presidential candidate, **2004** 753-754
Yudhoyono presidential inauguration, **2004** 753-760
Industrial pollution
Clean Air Interstate Rule, **2004** 666
New Source Review (NSR) program, **2002** 894-905; **2003** 173-190; **2004** 664-674; **2005** 100
Industrialized countries
See also Developing countries; Economic summits
aid to developing countries, **1972** 859-861, 864-865
balance-of-payments problems of, economic summit on, **1976** 426-427, 429-430
challenged by developing countries in UN, **1975** 325-327, 330-331
chlorofluorocarbon reduction by, **1988** 223
deficits in, impact on developing countries, **1983** 802, 804, 809-810
economic cooperation with developing countries, **1973** 810, 813-815; **1975** 587-611; **1976** 427-428, 431
economic growth in, and threat of protectionism, **1984** 795-796, 797-798, 800
exploitation of resources of developing countries, **1972** 329-336; **1974** 255, 258-260; **1984** 760, 763, 778; **1986** 317, 319, 323-324
food aid from, **1974** 939-942, 952-953
gap between developing countries and, John Paul II on, **1988** 165-171
infant mortality in, U.S. compared with, **1987** 147-149, 152-154
oil price rise and development aid, **1980** 884-887, 891
population control
responsibility for, **1972** 215, 218-219
support for, **1974** 777-779
teenage pregnancies in, **1986** 1057, 1059
urbanization and aimlessness in, Sakharov on, **1975** 919-920
use of world resources by, **1974** 778, 780
women in, needs and rights of, **1975** 507-512, 514-519
Industry
as acid rain source in U.S. and Canada, **1983** 197, 208
hazardous waste dumping by, **1979** 781-800
industrial output, compared with other nations, **1992** 103
pollution control by, economic costs to, **1972** 253-258; **1981** 276-277
U.S.-PRC agreements on trade and technology, **1984** 23-30
Indyk, Martin S.
on new Palestinian leader, **2002** 375
U.S.-Iran relations, **1998** 689
INF. *See* Intermediate-range Nuclear Force (INF) Treaty
Infant mortality
among minorities in U.S., **1985** 685, 687, 690, 705-706
causes of in U.S., **1987** 147-164
in developing countries, **1984** 527, 530-533; **1987** 440-441, 446, 449, 452, 458, 461
in Eastern European nations, **1994** 425
female infanticide, **2000** 327
and hunger in U.S., **1985** 190, 196-197, 199
link to smoking during pregnancy, **1973** 63-71
racial differences in the U.S., **1987** 147-151, 154, 156
worldwide, **1996** 306
Infants
formula for, WHO code on, **1981** 447-458
low-birthweight
effects of, **1987** 147-148, 150-153, 155, 157, 160-161, 164
link to smoking during pregnancy, **1972** 52; **1973** 63-71
seriously ill, medical treatment for, **1983** 282-283, 288-289, 299-303
severely handicapped, medical treatment for, **1986** 541-558
Infectious diseases
See also Diseases
and job discrimination, **1987** 245-252
WHO report on, **1996** 302-311
worldwide prevention, **1997** 348-349
Infertility
health effects of toxic substances, **1994** 149-152
Vatican teaching on remedies for, **1987** 269, 279, 284
Inflation
budget deficit's effect on, **1976** 30-31
Carter's anti-inflation program, **1978** 7, 12-14, 21-22, 67-70, 683-684, 686-697; **1979** 20, 22-24, 30-34, 84-90, 94-97, 105-109, 559, 567, 577
revised, **1980** 243-257; **1981** 106, 110-113, 131-133
causes and remedies, Burns on, **1972** 961, 963-965; **1974** 419-425
CEA report on, **2003** 83
consumer spending and saving, impact on, Ford CEA on, **1976** 57-58
control of
in Nixon budget, **1973** 169-172, 176
OECD on U.S., **1973** 683-695
credit availability as means of controlling, Joint Economic Committee, **1981** 300-301, 306-310
credit restraint as means of controlling, **1979** 771-774, 776-780
decline in
Ford CEA on, **1977** 65, 67-68
Ford on, **1976** 667, 669-670, 672
Reagan CEA on, **1984** 119-121, 123-124, 129-130; **1985** 79-80, 82-83, 88, 90-92
Reagan on, **1984** 101-102, 105, 117, 731-733
decline in world economy, economic summits on, **1986** 437, 440
Democratic Party platform on, **1976** 544, 548, 551-552; **1984** 568-569
in developing countries, **1981** 179, 181; **1982** 971-972, 975, 977

Inflation *Continued*
domestic economic summit, **1974** 699, 701-702, 861-880
economic growth without
economic summits on, **1976** 425-426, 428-429; **1978** 533-537; **1981** 591-592, 596; **1983** 507-508, 511, 513
Ford CEA on, **1975** 99-102, 107
Ford on, **1975** 16-17, 28; **1976** 14, 18
employment tradeoffs with control of
economic summit on, **1977** 367, 369, 371
Ford CEA on, **1976** 45-49; **1977** 81, 87-88
Joint Economic Committee on, **1977** 718, 720-722, 727-728
Kennedy-Carter debate on, **1980** 701-706, 711-713, 715, 717, 769-770
energy crisis contribution to
Ford on, **1975** 83, 87-88
Nixon CEA on, **1974** 69-83
Nixon on, **1974** 56
in energy prices, **1978** 790-792
Carter CEA on, **1980** 160, 162, 172-173, 175, 177-179
decline, Reagan and CEA on, **1987** 120, 124-125, 127
Ford on, **1976** 50
impact on industrialized countries, **1979** 251, 253, 258
and Ford recession-fighting plan, **1974** 975-976, 979-980
forecast, **2002** 63
government spending restraint as means of controlling
in Carter budget, **1978** 95-97; **1979** 9-10, 12-13
Carter CEA on, **1978** 65; **1979** 87-88, 109
Carter on, **1978** 766, 771
CBO on, **1976** 179, 183
in Ford budget, **1976** 37-38, 41
Nixon CEA on, **1973** 185-190
government spending to offset, in Nixon budget, **1974** 95-101
and hunger in U.S., **1985** 191, 201-202
in industrialized countries, effect on world economy, **1983** 802, 807-811
Joint Economic Committee on, **1979** 215-219, 221; **1980** 214, 221, 228-229
minimum wages, youth impact on, **1983** 786-790
money supply impact on, **1981** 294, 313-320; **1983** 595-597
Reagan CEA on, **1986** 70-71
Nixon's economic stabilization program, **1973** 43-54, 427-428, 430-431, 434-435, 577-585, 703-713
as persistent problem, Carter CEA on, **1978** 65, 67-70, 75-77, 80-81, 85-86, 93
as presidential campaign issue, **1972** 530-534; **1980** 848, 851, 920, 925-929
as priority problem, Ford and CEA on, **1976** 45-48, 50, 52-54
productivity slowdown's effect on, **1979** 81-82, 84, 86, 113-117
projections of
Carter CEA on, **1976** 697; **1980** 176-179, 181-183
CBO on, **1982** 192, 198
Joint Economic Committee on, **1977** 726-728; **1978** 723-725
Nixon CEA on, **1973** 185-190
Reagan CEA on, **1987** 119, 130; **1989** 4-5, 12-14
rate, **1998** 74, 75; **2000** 44, 52, 58; **2001** 62
Reagan economic program on control of, **1981** 213-215, 223-224, 294, 325, 327, 331, 642, 644; **1982** 121-124, 133-141, 144, 152-155; **1983** 121-122, 127-128, 139-140
Republican Party platform on, **1976** 617-619, 622, 641; **1980** 567-570, 620-622
Social Security benefits adjustment for, **1975** 115-116, 119-122, 124, 127; **1977** 378, 380
stagflation, Reagan on, **1981** 214, 293; **1982** 129, 134
tax increases as result of, **1977** 57, 61, 732
tax policy impact on, **1980** 861-864
U.S. pledge to reduce, Carter and IMF on, **1978** 660-666
Vietnam war as cause of, Nixon on, **1972** 82-84
wage and price controls
Ford opposition to, **1974** 765-766, 769-770, 772-773
in Nixon's program, **1973** 186, 188-190; **1974** 42-43, 55
in wages and prices, **1975** 635-642; **1976** 52-54; **1978** 85-88; **1979** 105-106
in world economy
Carter CEA on, **1980** 170-171
de Larosière on, **1979** 773-776; **1980** 894, 896
economic summit on, **1980** 507
Ford CIEP on, **1975** 187-188, 192-193; **1979** 190
IMF on, **1977** 688, 692
Inflation rate, **1996** 51, 69; **1997** 50, 53
Influenza
See also Flu vaccine shortage
nature of disease, **1978** 671, 678-680
swine flu immunization program, **1978** 669-681
Information
control of by Nixon administration, National Press Club on, **1973** 629-632, 635-639
freedom of, Sakharov on importance of, **1975** 915, 918, 922, 925-926
Information, government
See also Classified information; Freedom of Information Act (FOIA)
procedures for requests for, **1972** 236
Information technology (IT)
See also Science and technology
digital economy, Commerce Department report on, **2000** 299-307
and globalization, **2000** 481-482
and health care delivery, **2001** 207-208
and the "New Economy," **2001** 64, 68-72
productivity paradox, **2000** 300-301
revolution in, **2000** 54-55
Information Technology Agreement (ITA), **1998** 92
Information Technology Association of America (ITAA), technology worker shortage, **1997** 669, 670
Infrastructure
Democratic platform on, **1984** 576-580

protecting, **1997** 711-720
Ingle, Bob, Arthur Ashe as AIDS victim, **1992** 336
Inglis, Bob (R-S.C.), House Judiciary Committee impeachment inquiry, **1998** 706-707
Inglis, Oliver Michael, **1998** 616
Ingraham v. Wright, **1977** 293-309; **1992** 178; **1995** 348
Inhofe, James (R-Okla.), Clear Skies Initiative, **2004** 667
Inkatha Freedom Party, **1992** 285; **1995** 102
Inman, Bobby Ray
defense secretary nomination withdrawal, **1993** 695-696; **1994** 22-25
embassy security, **1999** 691
national security export controls, **1987** 30
Innocence Protection Act, **2002** 354
Inouye, Daniel K. (D-Hawaii)
Buzhardt memo, **1973** 660
as chair of intelligence committee, **1976** 237
energy prices and oil company profits, congressional hearings on, **2005** 786
Iran-contra committee, **1986** 1052; **1987** 892, 894
Iraq war resolution, **1991** 5
public financing of federal elections, **1974** 606
reparations to Japanese-Americans, **1988** 289-291
SDI, **1983** 308
television violence, **1993** 489
war hero, **1999** 39
INS. *See* Immigration and Naturalization Service
Insanity defense
in criminal trials, **1983** 25-40
in Hinckley trial, **1982** 531-537
Insider trading
allegations, **2005** 631, 635-636
Milken's guilty plea, **1990** 251-257
scandals (1986-1987), **1987** 881-883
SEC definition of, **1987** 883
and *Wall Street Journal* reporter, **1987** 881-882, 884-889
Institute for Aerobics Research, on physical fitness and health, **1989** 613-617
Institute for Historical Review, **1981** 381
Institute for International Sports, **1989** 215
Institute for Justice
eminent domain, **2005** 364
school vouchers, **2002** 409
Institute of Medicine (IOM)
See also National Academy of Sciences
bioterrorism, new vaccines against biological weapons, **2004** 444
childhood obesity prevention, **2004** 652-663
end-of-life care report, **1997** 325, 327-328
on health consequences of marijuana, **1982** 203-211
health insurance coverage, **2001** 710-721; **2003** 848-849
consequences of forgoing, **2002** 669
universal health care, **2004** 981
medical mistakes, **1999** 779-793; **2001** 191, 192, 193
quality of U.S. health care, **2001** 191-211, 868-869
thyroid cancer from radiation study, **1997** 592, 594, 598
Insurance industry
fraud investigations, **2004** 418
liability and malpractice, rising cost of, **1987** 165-169, 172-173
private
in Carter's health plan, **1978** 543-544, 546-547
incentives of, **1987** 127, 141-143
and sex bias in pension plans, **1983** 691-694
Insurance Information Institute, Hurricanes Andrew and Iniki, **1992** 844-845, 847-848
Insurgent groups, and weapons development, **1996** 224-225
Intel Corporation, and Microsoft Corp. antitrust case, **2000** 106
Intellectual freedom, for Soviet scientists, **1973** 793-796
Intellectual property rights, Chinese compliance with WTO rules, **2004** 939-940, 945
Intelligence, domestic
See also Surveillance, domestic
CIA involvement in, **1975** 401-436, 523-528
FBI revised guidelines for, **1976** 321-330
gathering, and secrecy of CIA sources, **1985** 333-344
in Nixon administration, **1973** 567-569; **1974** 327
restrictions on, **1976** 125-126, 137-138
restructuring and oversight of, Senate report on, **1976** 235-239, 264-285
review of policy on, Watergate prosecutor recommendation, **1975** 653, 679-680
use of by NSC staff, **1987** 209, 218-219, 223-224, 226-227, 231
Intelligence, foreign
British, Soviet spies in, **1979** 905-914
cable interception operation, **1975** 709, 711, 800-803
quality of U.S., and Soviet combat troops in Cuba, **1979** 763-766, 768
restructuring and oversight of, Senate report on, **1976** 238-264
surprised by Iranian revolution, **1979** 868, 878-879
U.S., failures of in Iran, **1978** 699, 701
Intelligence, military, covert action by, House recommendation to prohibit, **1976** 123
Intelligence, political, gathering of by White House aides, **1974** 600-601, 608-611, 657-658
Intelligence agencies
See also Central Intelligence Agency
budgets of, **1976** 235, 237, 240, 252, 260-261
congressional oversight of, **1974** 609; **1976** 117, 120-121
Democratic Party platform on, **1976** 546, 587
expanded authority for, by Reagan executive order, **1981** 861-868
national intelligence director, **2004** 474-475, 965, 968; **2005** 246
reorganization of and relations with Congress, House inquiry on, **1976** 115-124
restrictions on, Ford on, **1975** 224, 236-237
Senate investigations of CIA and FBI, **1975** 873-914
Silberman-Robb commission recommendations, **2005** 252-253

Intelligence agencies *Continued*
U.S. intelligence agencies, Bush on reform of, **2004** 965-972
Intelligence Capabilities of the United States Regarding Weapons of Mass Destruction, Commission on, **2005** 246-266
Intelligence community
abuses and wrongdoing by, **1976** 125
expanding powers of, **1996** 796-797
leak of House draft report on, **1976** 683-686
reform of, **1976** 14-15, 25, 27, 33-34
reorganization of, Ford plans for, **1976** 125-142
Republican Party platform on, **1996** 547-548
restoring confidence in, Republican Party platform on, **1976** 653
Intelligence gathering, domestic, **2005** 963-964
See also Domestic surveillance; Federal Bureau of Investigation (FBI)
FBI activities, **2002** 531, 532
national commission on September 11 recommendations, **2005** 900-901
Pentagon "data mining" system, **2002** 559-568
Intelligence gathering, international
See also Central Intelligence Agency (CIA)
CIA's pre-Iraq War intelligence gathering, **2004** 712-713
Commission on Intelligence Capabilities of the U.S. Regarding Weapons of Mass Destruction, **2005** 246-266
national commission on September 11 recommendations, **2005** 900-901
National Intelligence Estimate report, **2003** 874, 875; **2004** 714; **2005** 247
political use of intelligence, **2005** 250-252
Senate Intelligence Committee report, **2005** 712-713
U.S. intelligence failures, congressional joint panel reports on, **2002** 990-1013; **2003** 544-575
White House disclosure of CIA operative investigations, **2005** 78, 80, 246, 562
Intelligence Oversight Board, President's
creation of, **1976** 127-128, 139-141, 242-243
reestablishment of, **1981** 862-864
role in Iran-contra affair, **1987** 225-226
Intelligence Reform and Terrorism Prevention Act (2004), **2004** 970, 971-972; **2005** 256
Intelligent design, federal district court on, **2005** 1010-1026
Interagency Border Inspection System, **2003** 169
Interagency Council on the Homeless, report, **1994** 252-263
Interagency Task Force on Inadvertent Modification of the Stratosphere, **1975** 437-453
Interagency Task Force to Monitor and Combat Trafficking in Persons, **2002** 335
Inter-American Development Bank
U.S. aid requested for by Nixon, **1974** 285
U.S. contributions to, and nationalization of private U.S. firms, **1972** 69-71
Inter-American Dialogue Commission, **1983** 375-390
Inter-American Human Rights Commission, **1978** 279
Intercontinental ballistic missile (ICBM), **1992** 60, 520-521, 522
Interdependence, global economic
growing and inevitable, Nixon on, **1973** 381-384
Joint Economic Committee on, **1981** 322
and migration, **1981** 266-268
and oil price increase, **1975** 187-199; **1976** 913-914
poverty summit on, **1981** 769, 776
and raw materials of developing countries, **1976** 300, 302-303
and U.S. policy, Catholic bishops on, **1986** 984, 987-988, 1005-1010
Interest groups, single-, Carter on threat of, **1981** 31-34
Interest rates, **1997** 721; **1998** 76; **2002** 51, 52; **2005** 139, 152
control of, Reagan plan for, **1981** 642, 646; **1982** 144, 152-155
decline of, economic summit on, **1986** 437, 440
and developing countries' debt, **1982** 971-973; **1983** 802, 807-808, 811-812
financial institutions, impact on, **1985** 90
forecasts by CBO and Reagan administration, **1982** 192, 198
investment, impact on, **1981** 295, 300
targeting, Reagan CEA on shift from, **1983** 122, 126, 129-130
tax relief plan and, **2003** 88-90
U.S., economic summits on impact of, **1981** 592, 596; **1982** 470, 474; **1983** 508-509, 511-512
and U.S. trade deficit, **1983** 126; **1985** 320; **1987** 120, 128, 130, 135
Interferon, FDA approval of, **1986** 481-485
Intergovernmental Authority on Development (IGAD), **2003** 837
Interior Department (U.S.)
Alaska pipeline, environmental and economic impacts of, **1972** 271-280
Alaskan lands, preservation of, **1978** 731-740
coordination of water projects by, in Carter plan, **1978** 385, 387, 392, 394
on endangered species, **1995** 359
fire-management policy of, **1988** 941-946
Indian trust fund accounting lawsuit, **2003** 576, 578-579
national parks conference, **1972** 795
oil and gas deposits offshore, exploitation of, **1975** 168-169
recovery of spotted owl, **1992** 490
Watt resignation, **1983** 827-830
wildfire prevention guidelines, **2000** 712-722
Intermediate-range Nuclear Force (INF) Treaty, **1988** 57-58, 67
economic summit statement on, **1988** 394
exchange of instruments of ratification, **1988** 353, 358, 367, 369, 372
former U.S. officials on reductions in, **1986** 783, 790
negotiations, **1983** 507, 510, 791-800
progress toward at Geneva summit, **1985** 749, 751, 753, 758
ratification of, **1988** 353-354, 373
signing of, **1987** 945-989
Internal Revenue Service (IRS)
audit and settlement procedures, **1975** 829-836

children's tax credit, **1992** 359
citizen advocacy, **1998** 50-51
collection of delinquent taxes, procedures for, **1975** 829, 836-844
Customer Service Task Force report, **1998** 131-138
employees of, access to tax returns, **1975** 858-859
Grace commission proposal on, **1984** 177
impact of year 2000 computer conversion on, **1997** 535
mistakes and abuses, **1997** 661-668
Nixon income taxes, **1974** 235-241, 245
operations of, Administrative Conference study of, **1975** 829-859
People's Temple tax exemption, **1979** 350, 377
political uses of in Watergate, **1973** 662-664; **1974** 323, 601-602, 609, 617, 655, 658-659; **1975** 677-680
reform bill, **1997** 663; **1998** 51, 56
reforms and customer service, **1998** 131-138
and tax exempt organizations, **1997** 9-13, 15
United Way investigation, **1992** 305
use of for domestic spying, **1976** 235, 272-273, 278
wage and price monitoring by, **1973** 44, 704
withholding tax reduced, **1992** 57, 62, 67, 101, 107, 118-119
International Action Network on Small Arms, **2001** 518
International Advisory and Monitoring Board of Iraq, **2004** 893
International AIDS Society, **2004** 433
International Assessment of Educational Progress (IAEP), **1992** 88-96, 624
International Association for the Evaluation of Educational Achievement, **1992** 85
International Association of Chiefs of Police, **1985** 305
Reagan address to on crime, **1981** 648, 667-670
International Association of Firefighters v. Cleveland, **1986** 652-653, 667-678
International Association of Machinists, **1988** 269
International Atomic Energy Agency (IAEA)
Chernobyl accident report, **1986** 385-407
Democratic Party platform on strengthening of, **1992** 703
Iran nuclear weapons program, **2003** 1025-1036; **2004** 867-873
Iraq nuclear weapons development, **2002** 718; **2003** 33, 46, 878-879; **2004** 715
joint US-USSR statement of nonproliferation, **1990** 346-350
Libya, dismantling nuclear weapons program, **2004** 169
North Korean nuclear weapons program, **2002** 734, 736-737, 738-739
North Korean nuclear weapons sites inspections, **1994** 602, 606-609
nuclear nonproliferation, IAEA director on, **2004** 323-335
PRC's nuclear capability, **1984** 288
radioactive materials safety, **2002** 441-442
reforms at end of cold war, **1992** 437
upgrading of, Ford proposal, **1976** 824, 832-834, 836
U.S. support for, **2003** 31
verification of nuclear energy for peaceful purposes, **1975** 362-363, 365-367
International Bank for Reconstruction and Development. *See* World Bank
International Brotherhood of Teamsters, **2005** 487
International Brotherhood of Teamsters v. United States, **1977** 383-393
International Campaign to Ban Landmines, **1997** 845
International Civil Aviation Organization (ICAO), on downing of South Korean airliner by Soviets, **1983** 777, 781-782
International Commission of Jurists
on Amin regime in Uganda, **1975** 645
on human rights in Iran, **1977** 14-15
International Committee of the Red Cross
Baghdad terrorist bombing, relief assistance, **2004** 876
Beirut hijacking and, **1985** 465
Colombia earthquake disaster relief, **1999** 468
detention centers report, warnings of abuse, **2004** 208, 211, 213
Guantanamo Bay detainees, monitoring of, **2003** 107, 109; **2004** 380; **2005** 449
Haitian refugees, monitoring return of, **1981** 606-607
North Korea aid, **2005** 609
Philippines detention centers, inspection of, **1977** 22
secret detainees allegations, **2005** 906
Swedish, disasters relief, **1984** 973-995
International Communication Agency (ICA), **1981** 780
Soviet propaganda countermeasures by, **1981** 753-767
International Conference on AIDS and STIs in Africa (Kenya), **2003** 786-790
International Convention on Civil and Political Rights (ICCPR), and death penalty, **1998** 183, 184, 189, 190, 192, 466, 469
International Convention on Elimination of All Forms of Racial Discrimination, **2001** 605-606
International Council of Scientific Unions, environmental consequences of nuclear war, **1985** 541-554
International Court of Arbitration, on sovereignty of Beagle Channel Islands, **1983** 8
International Court of Justice (ICJ, World Court)
death penalty and, **2005** 181-182
execution of foreigners in U.S., **2004** 797-798
Genocide Convention and, **1986** 115-117, 121-123
Israeli security wall in the West Bank, **2004** 309-310
John Paul II's speech to, **1985** 365, 369-371
jurisdiction over Nicaragua, **1984** 341
PLO observer mission to UN, closing of, **1988** 480
U.S. and compulsory jurisdiction, **1984** 341; **1985** 637-641; **1986** 116, 117, 121-123
U.S. hostages in Iran, **1979** 870-871, 885-887, 890-892; **1985** 639
U.S. mining of Nicaraguan ports, **1984** 339-345; **1985** 256
U.S. relations, **2005** 181-182

International Court of Justice (ICJ) *Continued*
West Bank security wall ruling, **2005** 536
International Criminal Court (ICC)
Bush administration opposition to, **2003** 99, 101-102; **2005** 516-517
Congo war crimes trial, **2003** 289
Darfur human rights violations, **2005** 516-517
establishment of, **2003** 100-101
first session, UN secretary general on, **2003** 99-104
proposal, UN secretary general on, **2002** 605-611
U.S. objections to, **2002** 606-607; **2003** 99, 101-102
U.S. peacekeeping troops, exemptions from jurisdiction of, **2004** 891
use of child soldiers, as a war crime, **2002** 918
International Criminal Tribunal for Rwanda, **1998** 614-625; **1999** 866; **2003** 99-100, 1069-1088; **2004** 117-118
International Criminal Tribunal for the Former Yugoslavia, **2003** 99, 464, 1144
International Crisis Group
Afghanistan military situation, **2002** 19
Congolese disarmament, **2004** 509
Georgian political situation, **2003** 1041
Haiti political situation, **2004** 94, 97
Sudan conflict in Darfur, **2004** 589
Zimbabwe elections, **2002** 137
International Development Association, **1974** 284-285; **1986** 442
International Emergency Economic Powers Act, **1990** 536-537
International Energy Agency, **2005** 778
creation of, **1975** 236
development of alternative energy sources, **1975** 190, 195
raw materials prices, **1975** 588
world oil consumption rates, **1981** 800
International Fund for Agricultural Development, establishment of, **1974** 940-942, 949-950
International Indian Treaty Council, on skeletal remains, **1989** 541
International Institute for Strategic Studies
al Qaeda terrorist network, **2004** 537
on SALT strategic balance, **1972** 765-774
International Institute of Applied Systems Analysis, formation of, **1972** 833-835
International Islamic Relief Organization, **2003** 1058
International Joint Commission (IJC), Great Lakes water quality report, **1994** 147-152
International Labor Organization (ILO)
child labor, **2002** 222; **2004** 133
child labor report, **1996** 776-783
famine victims, **1984** 975, 982-983
labor standards, **1999** 52, 800
sex trade in children, **2001** 956
Soviet labor practices, **1982** 857, 860
U.S. contributions to, **1972** 339, 342
U.S. withdrawal from, **1975** 826; **1983** 969
women's rights, **1975** 508
International law
See also Diplomacy; International Court of Justice; United Nations
hostage taking by Iran, **1979** 867-893
limits on diplomatic missions, **1986** 268-272
ocean resources and seabed mining, law of sea treaty on, **1982** 345-361
International Longshoremen's Association (ILA)
corruption in, **1986** 180, 200
strike, **1972** 385, 389
International Monetary Fund (IMF)
Africa debt relief program, **2000** 450, 479; **2005** 406-407
aid to Russia, **1992** 257, 521
amendment to Articles of Agreement, **1976** 3-12
Argentine debt relief, **2003** 826-828; **2005** 768-769
Argentine economic crisis, **2002** 80, 82-91
Asian financial crisis, **1997** 832-843; **1998** 723-724
Belgrade meeting, **1979** 771, 773-776
Brazilian loan program, **2002** 775, 777; **2003** 6-7
Club of Ten, **1976** 4
critics of, **2002** 86
debt crisis
Baker plan for relief of, **1985** 643-652
Brady plan for relief of, **1989** 138, 141-143
economic summit on, **1984** 356, 359-360
monitoring of, **1986** 441, 442
debt reduction, **1999** 702
development loans, increased funding for, **1975** 589, 592-594, 601-603; **1977** 689; **1980** 883-885
energy costs, help for developing countries with, **1977** 368, 374
establishment of, **1985** 624
foreign exchange markets, stability of, **1978** 659-660, 663, 665-666
independence of, economic summit on, **1982** 470, 472
India and Pakistan loans suspended, **1998** 328
Indonesia economy, **1999** 721
Iraq economic situation, **2005** 720
Japanese economy, **1998** 534
Latin America economic growth, **2005** 765
Latin American debt, Reagan and Larosière on, **1983** 801-814
Liberia economic situation, **2005** 801
monetary system reform, **1972** 815-820; **1974** 497-505
Multilateral Debt Relief Initiative, **2005** 407-408
Munich Economic Summit on, **1992** 643
new funds to developing countries, **1982** 475, 973
Poland's membership in, **1987** 184
policy recommendations of, **1986** 79-80, 82
proposed economic organization of developing countries, **1981** 769, 773
Russian economic crisis, **1998** 601, 604
Russian loan suspension, **1999** 913-914
Sierra Leone debt relief, **2002** 249
Soviet economy report, **1990** 467-468, 474, 813
Soviet Union status, **1990** 808, 809-810
special drawing rights (SDRs)
change in value of, **1976** 3-4, 6-8, 11
as medium for monetary exchange, Shultz proposal, **1972** 816, 822-823
as principal reserve asset, **1974** 497-505
revisions in, Burns on, **1972** 416-417
U.S. sales of, **1978** 685, 698
U.S. employment and underground economic activity, **2003** 444

U.S. support for, **1998** 46
world economic situation
de Larosière on, **1984** 795-799
Witteveen speech on, **1977** 687-688, 691-698
worldwide economic outlook, **2003** 751-766
worldwide economic recovery, **2002** 689
worldwide economic slowdown, **2001** 667
Zimbabwe economy, **2003** 1111-1112
International Obesity Task Force, **2002** 628
International Olympics Committee (IOC), bribery scandal investigations, **1999** 105-112
International Partnership on Avian and Pandemic Influenza, **2005** 750
International penal tribunal, U.S. reservation to Genocide Convention, **1986** 119, 129-130
International Planned Parenthood Federation (IPPF), **1987** 454-458
on school-based clinics, **1986** 1058
International Red Cross. *See* International Committee of the Red Cross
International Rescue Committee, Congo conflict, mortality studies, **2002** 546; **2004** 509
International resources bank, Kissinger proposal for, **1976** 300-301, 306-309, 427
International Security Assistance Force (ISAF), NATO peacekeeping force in Afghanistan, **2003** 1093-1094; **2004** 138
International Society for Human Rights, **1982** 857
International Telephone and Telegraph Corp. (ITT)
antitrust settlement and political contributions, **1972** 395-406; **1974** 3-5, 16-21, 407-410; **1975** 143, 654-656, 666
involvement in Chilean election, **1975** 402-403
International Trade Commission (ITC), economic effects of Mount. St. Helens eruption, **1980** 811-824
International Union for Conservation of Nature and Natural Resources, **1972** 795
International Union of Bricklayers v. Meese, **1992** 468
International Women's Year, National Commission on the Observance of, **1977** 862
International Women's Year, world conference of
Declaration of Mexico opted at, **1975** 507, 518-522
plan of action, **1975** 507-518
Internet
access
digital divide initiative, **1999** 368-383; **2000** 48; **2002** 68-69
E-rate for classroom connections to, **1999** 371; **2000** 48
digital economy, **2000** 299-307
free speech, Supreme Court on, **1996** 353-361; **1997** 444-458
future generation, **1998** 53
Internet Explorer vs. Netscape Navigator, **1999** 654-689
into the classrooms, **1997** 37
into the hospitals, **1997** 37
Microsoft Corp. antitrust case, **1999** 654-689; **2000** 105-130, 308-324; **2001** 775-792
online investing, **1999** 20
pornography ban, **1996** 353-361
pornography filters in public libraries, Supreme Court on, **2003** 387-400
pornography in libraries, federal court on, **2002** 27-297
public release of Starr report on, **1998** 636-637
spam, **2003** 392-393
use in the U.S., Census survey on, **2002** 67-69
viruses and worms, **2003** 390-392
Interstate Commerce Commission (ICC)
on ConRail, **1975** 530-531
relaxation of regulations of, **1974** 863
Intifada
Israeli human rights abuses, **1989** 57-58, 69-70
Palestinian, **1988** 906, 909
transformation of into dialogue, Baker on, **1989** 289-290, 295
Intra-enterprise conspiracy doctrine, **1984** 413-426
Investigative Group, Inc. (IGI), **1992** 303, 307-308
Investigator magazine, libel action against, **1986** 357-358
Investment, business capital
budget deficit's impact on
Nixon CEA on, **1974** 85-86
Reagan CEA on, **1983** 121, 125
energy crisis impact on, Nixon CEA on, **1974** 91-92
growth in, forecast by Carter CEA, **1981** 106, 108
inflation's impact on
Burns on, **1974** 422
Carter and CEA on, **1978** 66, 68, 70, 75, 79
Ford and CEA on, **1976** 46, 49, 58-59, 67-70
outlook for, Reagan and advisers on, **1987** 120, 124-125, 130-131, 133
progress in economic recovery, Joint Economic Committee on, **1977** 720, 723, 732-733
reduction in projected by Ford CEA, **1975** 100, 107-108
strength of
Carter CEA on, **1979** 97, 100-101
Reagan CEA on, **1985** 80-82, 89-90
tax incentives for
Burns on, **1972** 961, 967; **1975** 640
Carter CEA on, **1980** 210, 219, 222
to fight inflation, **1972** 961, 967
Ford and CEA on, **1977** 65, 69, 75-76, 78-80, 83
Ford on, **1974** 862, 864-865, 978, 980; **1975** 16, 25, 29-30, 102-103, 107-108
Joint Economic Committee on, **1979** 215-217, 222; **1980** 210, 222; **1981** 293-296, 301-302, 304-306, 315-316
National '80s Agenda on, **1981** 40, 42
Nixon on, **1972** 389-390
in Reagan budget, **1981** 326-327, 639
world need to increase, **1977** 694-696
Investment, foreign
in developing countries
Kissinger proposal, **1975** 593-596; **1976** 301, 305-307, 427
Nixon on, **1973** 390
in U.S., controls on, and dollar devaluation, **1973** 349, 351
by U.S. firms
and nationalization, **1972** 67-71
Nixon's encouragement of, **1973** 380, 389-390

Investment firms, layoffs in after stock market crash (1987), **1987** 836
Investor Responsibility Research Center, **1990** 67
Investors, institutional, and stock market crash (1987), **1988** 11, 13, 34
Iowa (USS)
explosion and deaths on, **1989** 517-521
explosion investigation, **1991** 679-689
GAO report on explosion, **1990** 319-330
Statue of Liberty centennial, **1986** 698
IPPF. *See* International Planned Parenthood Federation
IRA. *See* Irish Republican Army
Iran
Afghan refugees in, and human rights, **1986** 920, 922-926
and "axis of evil," Bush State of the Union address, **2002** 33-34, 40-41, 612, 614, 635, 714; **2003** 19, 875, 1025, 1219; **2004** 18, 867; **2005** 579
Carter visit to, **1977** 897, 899-900, 913-918
chemical weapons stockpile, **1997** 198
chemical weapons treaty, **1993** 72
claims of U.S. firms nullified, **1981** 146, 149, 151-152, 559-573
counterfeiting of U.S. currency, **1996** 100
earthquake, **2003** 1033
Ebadi Nobel Peace Prize recipient, **2003** 1033, 1129-1137
ethnic conflict in, **1979** 871
executions in, **1984** 163; **1989** 58, 68, 597
Expediency Council, **2005** 590, 591, 594
foreign relations, **2005** 589-603
French contacts with on hostages in Lebanon, **1986** 832
frozen assets of
negotiations on, **1980** 999-1009
in U.S., **1981** 150-151, 559, 561-568
Great Britain diplomatic relations, **1998** 687-689
Guardian Council, **2003** 1032-1033; **2004** 871; **2005** 589-590
Hezbollah, support for, **2001** 796-797
human rights in
report, **1993** 560
under Khomeini, **1980** 190, 196; **1984** 155, 162-163; **1989** 58, 67-68
under shah, **1972** 3; **1977** 13-16; **1978** 705-707, 711-712
human trafficking, **2002** 345
Islamic fundamentalism in, **1989** 315, 317-318
Israeli-Palestinian Peace Accord, **1993** 750
Khatami presidential election, **1997** 284-289
Khatami UN address "Dialogue Among Civilizations," **2001** 793-801
Khomeini's death, **1989** 315-318
missile threat, **1998** 482, 489-490; **2003** 1031
national security needs review, **1993** 696, 702
nuclear weapons program, **1994** 364; **2005** 81, 591
Ahmadinejad UN speech on "nuclear issue," **2005** 593, 595, 600-603
ElBaradei remarks on, **2005** 594
European and U.S. opposition to, **2005** 592-596
IAEA inspections, **2005** 593.594
IAEA resolutions on, **2003** 1025-1036; **2004** 325, 867-873
potential costs to U.S., **2005** 17
Silberman-Robb commission on, **2005** 252
nuclear weapons proliferation, **1996** 212
OPEC oil prices, **1976** 938; **1981** 799
OPEC oil production quotas, **1982** 980
political situation, **2003** 1031-1033; **2004** 871; **2005** 81
population growth in, **1987** 440, 443
presidential elections, **2005** 589-592
reform movement, **2002** 742; **2004** 871
religious persecution of Baha'i sect, **1997** 564, 572-573
revolution in, **1979** 867-871
Brezhnev on, **1981** 230-231
effect on oil production and prices, **1978** 791-792; **1980** 995, 1000
and global oil supply, **1979** 3-4, 252, 662-663
U.S. support for shah, **1978** 699-716
Rushdie death threat
and diplomatic relations, **1989** 95-98
lifted, **1998** 687-691
Russian arms sales, **2001** 893
Saudi Arabia bombing, role in, **2000** 280
SAVAK police force, **1977** 14-15; **1978** 701
Soviet military presence in, Carter on, **1979** 971, 982-983
Soviet propaganda about, Project Truth on, **1981** 763
terrorism supported by, **1985** 464-465, 468, 470-471, 476
CIA on, **1981** 463, 465, 469
U.S. hostages in Lebanon, **1989** 315-320
U.S. arms sales to
in Carter administration, **1978** 106
Ford and Carter debate on, **1976** 743-745
in Reagan administration, **1986** 1013-1024, 1049-1055; **1987** 205-206, 208, 217-230, 527; **2004** 320
U.S. diplomatic relations, **1998** 689-690; **2001** 794-796
U.S. economic sanctions, **2001** 794, 795
U.S. hostages in
Algerian intermediary role, **1985** 464
attempted rescue of, **1980** 351-385, 475-476, 503-504, 506
Carter on, **1980** 28-31; **1981** 31, 36-37, 85-87, 156-158
communication with ICJ on, **1979** 888-890
ICJ rulings on, **1979** 870-871, 890-892; **1985** 638-639
negotiations for release, **1980** 999-1009
"October Surprise" theory, **1993** 3-16
release from Lebanon, **1991** 751-758
release of, **1981** 137-138, 145-162; **2003** 1033
taking of, **1979** 729, 867-893
UN efforts fail, **1995** 351
and U.S. defense posture, **1980** 123, 125, 127, 137
U.S. diplomatic efforts for, **1979** 970-971
U.S. relations with
during shah's regime, **1979** 867, 870, 876, 889

Islamic countries on, **1980** 4-5
weapons development, **1996** 212, 218, 219
Westernization of by the Pahlevis, **1978** 700-702, 708, 711
Iran Air Flight 655, U.S. downing of, **1988** 703-717
Iran U.S. arms sales to, legality of, **1987** 892, 894, 905, 921, 927-928
Iran-contra affair
basic facts of, **1994** 12-13
Bush's pardon of Weinberger, **1992** 1073-1079
convictions and disposition of cases, **1994** 12
and independent counsel law, **1988** 466, 468
Independent Counsel report on, **1994** 8-21
as issue in presidential debates, **1988** 741, 747, 749
legal outcomes of, **1989** 391-397; **1994** 12
Meese statement, **1986** 1014, 1023-1024
new pleas and charges, **1991** 429-441
North charges dismissed, **1991** 617-620
North conviction appeal, **1990** 491-507
North sentencing, **1989** 391-397
"October Surprise" theory connection to, **1993** 3-4
Poindexter conviction, **2002** 561
Reagan administration involvement, **2004** 320
Reagan statements on, **1986** 1013, 1017-1023, 1049, 1053-1055; **1987** 105-107, 109
and Reagan's strength abroad, **1987** 525-526
as reflection of administration values, Urban League on, **1987** 45-47
Senate and House investigating committees
on law violations, **1987** 891-892, 895, 903-905, 919, 926-928
minority report, **1987** 891, 894-895, 914-928
report, **1987** 891-928
Tower commission report on, **1987** 205-242
legal issues, **1987** 224-226, 227-230, 241
NSC, decision-making process, **1987** 222-226
Iranians in U.S., screening of for deportation or asylum, **1979** 869, 882
Iran-Iraq War
Arab League on threat of, **1987** 869-873
Brezhnev on, **1981** 225, 231
chemical weapons in, **1989** 27-28
economic summits on, **1982** 473; **1984** 357, 364; **1987** 525, 527, 530
military balance in, **1984** 747-755
nonaligned nations on, **1983** 268
OPEC appeal for resolution of, **1980** 995-997
origins of, **1984** 747-748; **1988** 529-530
Persian Gulf shipping, danger to, **1987** 793-794; **1988** 703-706
and release of U.S. hostages, **1980** 1000
truce, **1988** 529-532
UN ineffectiveness during, **1982** 769
UN Security Council resolution on, **1987** 609-613
U.S. arms sales to Iran, **1986** 1014-1015, 1018-1022; **1987** 206, 208, 219, 221, 224
Iran-Libya Sanctions Act (ILSA, 1996), **2004** 173-174
Iran-United States Claims Tribunal, **1981** 146, 149, 152-156, 559-573
Iraq
See also Iran-Iraq War; Iraq, postwar period; Iraq War; Persian Gulf War; Saddam Hussein
and "axis of evil," Bush State of the Union address, **2002** 33-34, 40-41, 612, 614, 635, 714; **2003** 19, 875, 1025, 1219; **2004** 18, 867
biological weapons, **2004** 715-716, 730-733; **2005** 249-250
chemical weapons, **2004** 716, 727-730
chemical weapons use, **1989** 27-28; **1991** 192-193; **1993** 72; **1994** 272; **1996** 212; **1997** 740-745; **1998** 49-50
in internal conflict, **1989** 27, 58, 68-69, 598-600
deadline pressure on Saddam Hussein, **1990** 767-782
disarmament, UN resolution, **2002** 713, 715-717, 724-728
economic sanctions, **1990** 545-550, 769; **1991** 4, 7-9, 166-167
Egyptian diplomatic relations with, breaking of, **1977** 829
executions in, **1989** 597
Governing Council, **2003** 936, 944, 946, 950-954, 1192, 1196; **2004** 24
human economic and social development, UN report on, **2005** 276
human rights in, **1989** 58, 60, 68-69; **1990** 148-150; **1993** 559, 567-571; **1999** 144-152; **2000** 581-595
interim/transitional government, **2004** 23-24, 399-411; **2005** 271, 941
International Advisory and Monitoring Board, **2004** 893
Israeli raid of nuclear plant in, **1981** 507-519, 636
Kuwaiti invasion. *See* Persian Gulf War
links to al Qaeda terrorist network, **2002** 617-618; **2003** 19, 46-47; **2005** 401-402
missile threat to U.S., **1998** 482, 490-491
nuclear arms buildup, **1981** 511-513
nuclear weapons program, **1991** 192-193; **1994** 364; **1996** 212; **2004** 714-715, 726-727; **2005** 248-249, 466-467
oil production and prices, break with OPEC on, **1976** 940-941
oil-for-food program, **1999** 146-147; **2004** 717, 887, 891-893; **2005** 228, 233-235
OPEC oil prices, **1978** 791; **1979** 252; **1981** 799
Operation Desert Fox, **1999** 53
Patriot Missile Performance report, **1992** 865-874
PLO forces relocated in, **1982** 744
political situation, CIA report on, **1996** 680-686
power struggles in, and reliability of oil supply, **1979** 663
presidential debate on, **1992** 968-970
religious persecution, **1997** 564, 573-574
Sadat assassination, reaction to, **1981** 734
security threat to U.S., Bush on, **2001** 849-854; **2003** 19
Shevardnadze statement, **1990** 637-638
sovereignty, **2003** 1189; **2004** 399-411
Stark (USS), attack on, **1987** 791-815; **1988** 703-704
terrorism by, CIA on, **1981** 463, 465, 468
troop buildup on Kuwait border, **1994** 431-435
UN peace terms, **1991** 191-203
UN postwar report, **1991** 165-174

Iraq *Continued*
UN resolution, response to, **2002** 717-719, 728-730
UN sanctions against, **1995** 355-356; **1997** 767, 769-770; **2000** 581, 583-585; **2001** 849-850; **2002** 614
UN weapons inspections, **1998** 934-944; **1999** 147-148; **2000** 585; **2001** 850; **2002** 609, 613, 718-719; **2003** 41, 878-880
U.S. antiterrorism attacks, support for, **2001** 687-688
U.S. confronting, **2002** 612-623
U.S. military readiness, **1994** 530-531
U.S. "regime change" policy, **1998** 938; **2001** 852-853; **2002** 35, 56, 484, 612-614, 713
weapons development, **1996** 212, 218, 219
weapons inspections, UN Special Commission, **1997** 767-773
weapons of mass destruction, **2002** 437, 713, 718, 742; **2003** 874-900; **2004** 711-733
Iraq, postwar period
antiwar movement, **2005** 835-836
Bush administration plans, **2003** 934-935, 948-950; **2005** 79-80
Bush defense of war in, **2004** 399-400
Bush democratization plans, **2005** 42
Bush "Plan for Victory" speeches, **2005** 838-839, 842-850
Bush State of the Union address on, **2005** 88-90
capture of Saddam Hussein, **2003** 135, 934, 1189-1199, 1221
reaction to, **2003** 1193-1194
casualties. *See under* Iraq War
Coalition Provisional Authority (CPA), **2003** 138-139, 142-144, 935; **2004** 208, 399, 879; **2005** 722-723, 941
constitution, **2005** 945-947
costs, U.S. escalating, **2005** 835
detainees
abuses of Iraqi prisoners
International Red Cross report on, **2004** 208, 211, 213
U.S. Army report on, **2004** 207-234
McCain proposal on ban on abuse of, **2005** 80
terrorist suspect interrogations, Justice Department on, **2004** 336-347, 375
Development Fund for Iraq (oil money), **2005** 721-723
economic situation, **2005** 720-721
elections, **2005** 270-271, 581
December elections, **2005** 947-949
Independent Electoral Commission of Iraq (IECI), **2005** 952-957
international observers on, **2005** 941-957
January elections, **2005** 942-944
Sunni boycott, **2005** 271, 942-943, 944
legality or legitimacy of, **2005** 273, 952-953
preparing for, **2004** 403-404
UN role, **2004** 890-891
Fallujah, battles for control of, **2004** 880-881
hostage takings/kidnappings of foreigners, **2004** 876; **2005** 666
insurgency and violence against U.S., **2003** 1194; **2004** 535, 539, 874-884; **2005** 660-661, 670-671
counterinsurgency efforts, **2005** 661
major violent attacks, **2004** 877; **2005** 666-669
number of fighters, **2005** 659
international coalition, Democratic Party support for, **2004** 31
Iraqi prison abuses, **2005** 662-663
Mahdi Army, **2004** 879; **2005** 664
militias, **2005** 72-673, 663-664
NATO training program, **2004** 138
oil industry, **2005** 720-721
Peshmerga (Kurdish army), **2005** 664, 673
reconstruction, **2004** 405-406
U.S. special inspector general, **2005** 717-733
sectarian violence (Sunnis, Shi'ites, and Kurds), **2005** 659
security challenges, **2003** 937-938; **2004** 874-884
stabilization and security, **2005** 659-676
Bush remarks to World Affairs Council, **2005** 673-676
Defense Department on, **2005** 669-673
Democratic Party plan, **2005** 81, 93
training Iraqi police and soldiers, **2005** 661-663
Supreme Council for the Islamic Revolution in Iraq (SCIRI), **2005** 663-664, 673, 942
terrorist bombings, **2003** 939-943, 1052; **2004** 876; **2005** 664-665
troop strength, **2005** 659, 832-833
troop withdrawals
coalition troops, **2004** 882-883; **2005** 833-834
Rep. Murtha call for, **2005** 80, 836-838, 837, 840-842
Spanish troops, **2004** 105, 108-109
UN headquarters bombing in Baghdad, **2003** 109, 614, 808-809, 939, 1091; **2004** 876
UN mission, **2003** 810
UN sanctions lifted, **2003** 934
UN Security Council on, **2003** 933-954
unemployment, **2005** 720
UN-U.S. cooperation, **2004** 890-891
Iraq Liberation Act, **2001** 852
Iraq Survey Group, **2003** 880-881; **2004** 712
Iraq War
African reform and, **2003** 452-453
antiwar movement, **2005** 836
Brazil opposition, **2003** 7-8
French opposition, **2002** 715-716; **2003** 40
German opposition, **2003** 40
MoveOn.org campaign, **2005** 836
Russian opposition, **2003** 40, 250
Sheehan personal crusade, **2005** 836
British intelligence failures, **2004** 718-719
Bush address to the nation (March 17, 2003), **2003** 146-149
Bush address to the nation (March 19, 2003), **2003** 150-151
Bush on prospect of, **2003** 135-151
Bush State of the Union address, justification for, **2003** 18-19; **2004** 18-19, 711
Bush Thanksgiving visit to the troops, **2003** 934
capture and release of missing U.S. army soldiers, **2003** 142
casualties
during postwar Iraq attacks, **2003** 941, 1090

iraqbodycount.net (British-based Web site), **2004** 879; **2005** 665
Iraqi civilians, **2003** 145; **2004** 878-879; **2005** 665
Iraqis, **2005** 659
pictures of flag-draped coffins, **2005** 648-649
U.S. troops, **2003** 144, 941; **2004** 875; **2005** 659, 665, 674, 834-835
child soldiers (Ashbal Saddam, Saddam's Lion Cubs), **2002** 917
China support for UN resolutions, **2003** 1179
Coalition Provisional Authority (CPA), **2003** 138-139, 142-144; **2004** 399
congressional resolution, **2002** 714-715, 719-723; **2003** 19
costs of, **2004** 236; **2005** 835
early days of the war, **2003** 139-142
European leaders on the prospect of, **2003** 40-52
Iraqi response to "liberation," **2003** 933
justifications for, **2004** 24-25, 236, 454-455, 713, 714, 889; **2005** 894
Mandela's comments on, **2003** 454
National Intelligence Estimate report, **2003** 874, 875; **2004** 714; **2005** 247
preemption doctrine of U.S., **2002** 633-665; **2003** 809-810, 905; **2004** 889
rescue of Private Jessica Lynch, **2003** 142; **2004** 713
"shock and awe" bombings, **2003** 140
Spain support for, **2004** 105, 108
Turkish response, **2002** 910-911
UN resolution authorizing fails, **2003** 47-49
U.S. economy and, **2003** 752
weapons of mass destruction, Powell's UNSC speech, **2003** 45, 47; **2004** 717-718
Iraq War, postwar period
Abu Ghraib prison abuse scandal, **2004** 207-234, 336-347, 375, 881; **2005** 663
al Qaqaa munitions dump, looting of, **2004** 717
Iraqi Commission on Public Integrity, **2005** 722
Iraqi Governing Council, **2003** 936, 944, 946, 950-954, 1192, 1196; **2004** 24; **2005** 941
interim constitution, **2004** 400, 401
Iraqi National Congress (INC), U.S. support for, **2001** 852-853; **2003** 936
IRAs. *See* Individual Retirement Accounts
Ireland, Northern
British plan for shared political power in, **1973** 353-359
British Prime Minister Major on, **1994** 449-457
British-Irish accord on, **1985** 723-732
British-Irish peace efforts, **1993** 923-931
cease-fire and end to violence, **2005** 507-513
Clinton on peace efforts in, **1995** 727-733
conflict in, **1973** 353-355; **1981** 401-402; **1984** 315-321; **1985** 723-724
John Paul II on, **1979** 725, 728-729, 741-748
Democratic Party platform on, **1992** 706
elections, **2005** 508
Good Friday agreement, **1999** 753-754, 756
home rule in, **1985** 724
human rights in, **1988** 112-113; **1990** 134, 140-141
IRA prison hunger strike in, **1981** 401-416, 471-472
IRA weapons decommissioning, **2001** 758-763; **2005** 508, 510-511
New Ireland Forum proposals, **1984** 315-326
peace agreement, **1998** 203-219
peace process, **1999** 753-759; **2001** 758-760
terrorism in
Thatcher government on, **1979** 380, 383, 387
U.S.-British extradition treaty, **1986** 751-753
U.S. economic aid to, **1986** 753
Ireland, Patricia
RICO and abortion protests, **1994** 27
same-sex marriages, **1996** 687
Ireland, Republic of
abortion case, **1992** 249-254
accord with British on Northern Ireland, **1985** 723-732
euro currency, **1998** 271
and European Monetary System, **1978** 741, 751
governing a united Ireland, **1984** 317, 321-326
history of British rule in, **1984** 316-317
John Paul II's visit, **1979** 725, 728-729, 741-748
New Ireland Forum proposals, **1984** 315-326
Republican Party platform, **1996** 541
student test scores, **1992** 90
unification of
British power-sharing plan on, **1973** 353, 359
New Ireland Forum on, **1984** 317, 321-326
U.S. economic aid to, **1986** 753
Irian Jaya (New Guinea), independence movement, **2001** 566-567
Irish Family Planning Association, **1992** 250
Irish Republican Army (IRA)
bank robbery allegations, **2005** 508
British-Irish peace efforts, **1993** 923-931
ceasefire agreement, **1994** 449-452; **1995** 727
ceasefire and end to violence, **2005** 507-513
exclusion from New Ireland Forum, **1984** 315
Libyan support for, **1986** 348
Major's statement on Northern Ireland, **1994** 449-457
in Northern Ireland conflict, **1985** 723-724
peace process and decommissioning of, **1999** 753-759
provisional wing of
and British power-sharing plan for Northern Ireland, **1973** 354
prison hunger strike, **1981** 401-416, 471-472
terrorism by, CIA on, **1981** 463, 471-472
Sinn Féin, **1984** 315; **1994** 449-451; **1995** 728-729
U.S. extradition of terrorists to Britain, **1986** 751-756
weapons destruction by, **2001** 758-763
Irish-American Gay, Lesbian and Bisexual Group of Boston (GLIB), **1995** 327-335
Irons, Peter, **1993** 935-937
IRS. *See* Internal Revenue Service
Isaacman, Alton F., **1988** 176
Isaacs, Alick, **1986** 482
Isamuddin, Riduan (*aka* Hambali)
Islamic extremist leader, **2002** 705, 706
terrorist linked to Bali bombings arrested, **2003** 1052; **2004** 23
Isbister, John, **1978** 654-655

Iselin, John Jay, **1984** 451
Iselin v. United States, **1992** 463
Islam
  See also Muslim countries
  conflicts between Muslim and Western societies explained, **1990** 277-287
  gulf between Western culture and, **1989** 95-98
  in Pakistan, **1977** 538, 541
  regime in Iran and human rights, **1984** 162-163
  revival of in Africa, **1985** 499-501, 509-514
  Saudi Arabian constitution, **1992** 225-248
  Sunni vs. Shi'ite in Iran-Iraq War, **1984** 747-748; **1988** 530-531
  UN Population Conference and Islamic fundamentalist views, **1994** 351-352
  violence at the Temple Mount, **1990** 697, 704
  al-Islam, Ansar, attacks and bombings in Iraq, **2003** 943
Islamic Amal, and terrorist attack on Marines in Beirut, **1983** 934
Islamic Conference, Organization of, on Soviets in Afghanistan, **1980** 3-15
Islamic Holy War, kidnapping by, **1989** 316
Islamic Jihad, **2001** 363-365; **2002** 930, 933; **2003** 196, 841, 1211
  founded in Egypt, **2003** 1054
  Palestinian elections, **2004** 809
  suicide bombings, **2005** 29, 31
  in Syria, **2003** 1202; **2004** 559
Islamic resistance movement. *See* Hamas (Islamic resistance movement)
Island Trees Union Free School District v. Pico, **1982** 567-585
Ismail, Mohammed F., **1973** 932
Ismail, Mustafa Osman
  Sudan conflict, **2004** 592
  Sudan peace negotiations, **2003** 841
Ismail, Razali, UN earth summit, **1997** 482
Ismailia (Egypt), Begin's visit to, **1977** 827, 829, 847-855
Isolationism, new
  Clinton challenges, **1995** 350, 357
  Nixon decries, **1992** 256, 258
Israel
  See also Gaza Strip settlements; Jerusalem; West Bank settlements
  African countries' severing ties with, **1974** 256
  on Arab (Fez) peace plan, **1982** 754
  Arab boycott of U.S. firms trading with, **1976** 734, 742, 755-756
  assassinations by Jewish underground, **1983** 832
  Barak on new government programs, **1999** 359-367
  Bulgarian downing of plane (1955), **1983** 775
  casualties of conflict, **2002** 928-929; **2004** 812-813; **2005** 31
  chemical weapons treaty, **1993** 72
  combating terrorism against, Shultz on, **1984** 941
  Dead Sea scrolls, **1991** 637-639
  Demjanjuk war crimes acquittal, **1993** 617-623
  economic situation, **2003** 1211-1212
  economy of, **1983** 831, 833, 837-839
  Egyptian relations
    Camp David accords, **1978** 605-606, 614-616, 620, 623
    cease-fire agreement, **1973** 931-937
    military disengagement agreement, **1974** 29-32, 221-224
    normalization of, **1979** 224-225, 243-245
    peace talks, economic summit on PLO participation in, **1980** 504
    peace treaty, **1979** 223-250; **1980** 4, 34, 39-40, 94
    return of Egyptian territory urged by EC, **1974** 186
    Sadat peace initiative, **1977** 827-859
    Sinai
      return of, **1982** 337-344
      withdrawal from, **1975** 473-586; **1978** 614-615
  elections, **2003** 192
  Entebbe raid and release of hostages, **1976** 517-520; **1977** 143, 145-146
  extinction of, Amin on, **1975** 645-646, 649
  formation of state of, **1988** 581
    Arafat on, **1974** 926-933
  Hebron withdrawal, **1996** 339-340
  human rights, **1990** 130, 136, 150-152
  human trafficking, **2002** 345
  intelligence exchanges with France, **1986** 832
  international "roadmap" for peace, **2003** 191-205, 1213-1216; **2004** 303
  Iran relations, Admadinejad anti-Israel rhetoric, **2005** 591-592
  Israeli-Palestinian Peace Accord, **1993** 747-768
  Jenin "massacre" investigations, **2002** 934-935
  Jordan peace agreement, **1994** 329-335
  kidnapping of Obeid, **1989** 315-319
  Labor Party victory in elections, **1992** 655-665
  land mine warfare, **1995** 51
  on law of sea treaty, **1982** 345
  Lebanon
    agreement on pullout from, **1983** 833, 840-842
    PLO departure from, **1982** 741-749
    security agreement with, **1983** 471-477
    Syrian role in conflict with, **1982** 742-744
  Libyan plane, attack on (1978), **1983** 775
  Middle East Peace Conference (Madrid), **1991** 719-731
  Middle East peace initiative, **1985** 710-711
    U.S. proposal, reactions of coalition government to, **1989** 290-293
  Netanyahu election as prime minister, **1996** 337-342
  Nixon visit, **1974** 449, 451, 464-467
  nuclear weapons capability of, **1989** 28
  nuclear-free zone proposed by, **1981** 514-515, 748
  "October Surprise" report, **1993** 14-15
  October war
    cease-fire negotiations, **1973** 881-896
    movement behind Egyptian lines, **1973** 882, 892, 894, 931-933
    U.S. airlift of equipment to, **1977** 338-339
  Oslo peace agreement (1993), **2004** 807; **2005** 33-34
  Palestinian conflict, **2001** 603-604; **2002** 927-941; **2003** 191-205, 1210-1211; **2004** 535

Bush European Union speech, **2005** 582
cease-fire negotiations, **2005** 29-32, 530
Disengagement Plan, **2003** 1200-1217; **2004** 301-317, 628; **2005** 27, 529-538
home demolitions, **2004** 310-311
suicide bombings, **2004** 811-812; **2005** 29
UN human development report on, **2005** 276
violence in Gaza Strip, **2004** 305
Palestinian deportation, **1992** 658
Palestinian refugee camp massacre, **1982** 781-795; **1983** 163-180
Sharon libel suit, **1985** 47-52
Persian Gulf War, **1991** 99-100
political situation, **1999** 359-367; **2002** 936-937; **2005** 529, 534-535
population projections, **2003** 1206
Rabin on labor election victory, **1992** 655-665
as racist and terrorist aggressor, Arafat on, **1974** 919-920, 922-924, 926-933, 936-937
raid on Iraqi nuclear plant, UN on, **1981** 507-519
religious persecution, **1997** 574-575
right to exist, PLO acceptance of, **1988** 905-908
Saudi Arabia and, **1992** 226
Saudi peace initiatives, **2002** 370-372
and Saudi peace plan, **1981** 631, 635
security for, John Paul II on, **1987** 700, 704
Shamir speech to Knesset as prime minister, **1983** 831-845
Soviet relations, establishment of, **1974** 835
student test scores, **1992** 90, 92, 94, 95
supporters of
Arab oil embargo against, **1975** 3-4
Arab oil production cutbacks to penalize, **1973** 932, 936; **1975** 4
Syria, disengagement agreement with, **1974** 435-439
Syria peace negotiations, **1999** 890-897, 893-894
Syria relations, **1999** 362; **2003** 1202-1203
terrorism against
attacks on El Al Israeli Airlines, **1985** 468; **1986** 832
retaliation for Munich attack on Olympic athletes, **1972** 751-753
TWA hijacking to Beirut, **1985** 463, 465
Turkey, earthquake rescue teams, **1999** 466-467
UN war crimes files, efforts to open, **1987** 519
UN Zionism resolution, **1975** 825-827
UNESCO, exclusion from meetings of, **1975** 326; **1983** 967-969
U.S. arms sales to
Ford and Carter on, **1976** 743-745
Ford on, **1976** 762
role in sales to Iran, **1986** 1013, 1015-1018, 1022-1023, 1050, 1053; **1987** 221
Tower commission on, **1987** 206, 217, 222-223, 228, 233-234
warplanes sales, **1978** 106
warplanes sales to Egypt and Saudi Arabia, **1978** 125-134
warplanes sales to Saudis, **1981** 787-789, 792, 796, 798
U.S. economic and military aid, **1974** 277, 279-282
Nixon offer of, **1974** 450-451, 465-466
in Sinai accord, **1975** 574, 582-585
and Syrian-Israeli disengagement, **1974** 436
U.S. policy, **2002** 369-381; **2004** 629
U.S. relations
Carter on, **1977** 738, 743-744
Democratic Party platform on, **1972** 527, 579
forces in southern Lebanon, Carter on, **1978** 273
Haig support of, **1982** 562
Kissinger on, **1973** 935-937
military agreement, suspension of, **1981** 900, 907-909
military and political cooperation, **1983** 834-835
Republican Party platform on, **1972** 659
strain over U.S.-Soviet declaration, **1977** 738
trade agreements, **1988** 573
and U.S. hostages in Lebanon, **1989** 315-317
Young meeting with PLO UN observer, **1979** 647-657
and U.S.-Egyptian resumption of relations, **1976** 170-172
Vatican Diplomatic Accord, **1993** 1033-1040
Vatican diplomatic relations with, support for in Austria, **1988** 411, 413
violence on the Temple Mount, **1990** 695-711
on Waldheim's war service, **1986** 744, 746
Washington Declaration, **1994** 329-335
West Bank security "wall," **2002** 936; **2003** 191, 1205, 1208-1210; **2004** 304, 309-310, 313; **2005** 530, 536
West Bank settlement policy, **2004** 302-304, 313, 628; **2005** 529-530, 535-537
women's conference, delegation to Nairobi, **1985** 556
Wye River agreement with Palestinians, **1998** 742-754; **1999** 52-53, 700, 891-893
Israel, John, Abu Ghraib prison scandal, **2004** 210
Israel, occupied territories
See also Gaza Strip settlements; West Bank settlements
Golan Heights annexation, U.S. on, **1981** 788, 899-900
human rights in, **1986** 112-113; **1989** 57-58, 69-70
human rights of Palestinians in, **1983** 268; **1988** 94, 113-115, 884, 889
and "land for peace" formula, **1989** 289, 295
Palestinian autonomy in, **1979** 224-226
Palestinian claims to, **1988** 581-582
Palestinian deaths in, **1989** 598
Palestinian declaration of independence, **1988** 905-911
peace negotiations with U.S. and Egypt, **1980** 236-237, 241-242
settlements in, **1978** 606, 616, 620, 621; **1979** 226
and Reagan peace plan, **1982** 753-767
UN vote on dismantling of, **1980** 235-242
U.S. opposition to, **1976** 191-196; **1979** 649; **1983** 832, 834
UN Zionism resolution on, **1975** 825-827
withdrawal from, Sadat and Begin on, **1977** 828-829, 836-837, 839, 846
Issa, Darrell (R-Calif.), California recall election, **2003** 1005, 1008

Issacs, Amy
on Democratic Party platform, **2000** 611
views on Ralph Nader, **2000** 897-898
Istook, Ernest J., Jr. (R-Okla.)
lobbyist legislation, **1995** 702-703
Ten Commandment displays, **2005** 379
Italy
Agca's trial jurisdiction, **1981** 427-428
CIA support for political party in, **1976** 167
Communist Party in government, **1975** 353; **1976** 341, 345-346, 426, 447-448, 455-457
economic summits, **1976** 425-426; **1978** 533, 536; **1981** 591; **1982** 469, 471; **1983** 507-514
Houston, **1990** 467-482
Ethiopian invasion by, use of incendiary weapons, **1972** 838
euro currency, **1998** 271
and European Monetary System, **1978** 741, 751
Iraq War supporter, **2003** 42, 49-51
Medium Extended Air Defense System (MEADS), **2004** 180-181
missiles of, Soviet position on, **1983** 792-793
Munich Economic Summit, **1992** 637-648
PLO departure from Lebanon protected by, **1982** 741, 744
Reagan visit, **1982** 477
Soviet pipeline sanctions defied by, **1982** 880

J

J. E. B. v. Alabama, **1994** 223-236
J. I. Case Co. v. Borak, **1992** 193, 195
J. W. Hampton, Jr. & Co. v. U.S., **1998** 436
Jaber, Sheik of Kuwait, UN address, **1990** 655-660
Jablonski, Henryk, **1978** 597
Jabr, Bayan, Iraqi prison abuses, **2005** 663
Jackson, Andrew, **1989** 107
campaign financing, **2003** 1156
Jackson, Henry M. (D-Wash.)
ABM treaty amendment, **1979** 413
ABM treaty ratification, **1987** 294-299
energy legislation, **1973** 466, 914, 918
Nixon's credibility, **1974** 24
nuclear reactor sales to Middle East, **1974** 451
placed in nomination at Democratic convention, **1972** 590, 592
SALT amendment on missile equality, **1972** 766
SALT II debate, **1979** 415-416
South Vietnam aid, **1975** 280-281
Soviet forces in Middle East, **1973** 882, 887
trade concessions linked to Soviet emigration policy, **1974** 538, 901-905
Jackson, Jesse L.
Clinton's affirmative action speech, **1995** 485
Democratic national conventions, **1972** 590; **1988** 534-535, 557-558; **1992** 669; **1996** 601-602; **2000** 612
Democratic Party platform, **1984** 549-551
individual retirement accounts, opposition to, **1998** 100
at March on Washington thirtieth anniversary, **1993** 679, 681-684
at Million Man March, **1995** 656
NAACP director, withdrawal for candidacy, **1993** 580-581
presidential candidacy of, **1984** 647; **1985** 27, 32
as "race-hustling poverty pimp," **1997** 31
on Schott suspension for racist remarks, **1993** 168
Sierra Leone peace negotiations, **2000** 1073, 1074
speeches at Democratic conventions, **1984** 648; **1988** 535, 546-556
on Texaco executives racial slurs, **1996** 765, 766
Thomas Supreme Court nomination, **1991** 552
Young's resignation from UN, **1979** 469
Jackson, Kenneth T., multicultural education, **1991** 332, 344-345
Jackson, Linda McGinty, artificial heart implants, **2001** 479
Jackson, Michael, NATO Kosovo Force commander, **1999** 288
Jackson, Thomas Penfield, **1990** 708-709
line-item veto, **1997** 612
Microsoft antitrust case, **1997** 654-689
Microsoft antitrust ruling, **2000** 105-130, 308-324; **2001** 775-777; **2002** 799-802
sentencing guidelines, **2004** 361
Jackson v. Georgia, **1972** 499-505
Jackson v. Virginia, **1993** 148
Jackson State University (Miss.), **1992** 576, 578-587
antiwar protesters' deaths remembered, **1990** 292
Jackson-Lee, Sheila (D-Texas)
House Judiciary Committee impeachment inquiry, **1998** 707
U.S.-Africa policy, **2000** 72
Jackson-Vanik Act (1974), **1990** 808, 809, 811-813
Jacob, John E.
on black America, **1985** 27-28; **1987** 43, 44-51
on racial progress in post-Reagan era, **1988** 186
Jacobsen, Carl, **1984** 148
Jacobsen, David P., release of, **1986** 1016, 1021
Jacobson, Keith, **1992** 313-327
Jacobson, Michael, **1993** 690; **1996** 5
Jacobson, Michael F., on dietary guidelines, **2005** 4
Jacobson v. Massachusetts, **1990** 377
Jacobson v. United States, **1992** 313-327
Jacoby, Charles, Jr., U.S. detention facilities inspections, **2004** 217
Jacoby, Lowell E., Abu Ghraib prison scandal, **2004** 214
Jacoby v. Arkansas Dept. of Ed., **1999** 336
Jaffee v. Redmond, **1996** 388-395
Jaffree, Ishmael, silent prayer in schools case, **1985** 379, 383
Jagielski, Mieczyslaw, **1980** 794
Jagland, Thorbjoern, Middle East peace negotiations, **2001** 361
Jai Hyon Lee, **1977** 781-786
Jaish-e-Muhammad (Kashmiri guerrillas), **2002** 166, 167, 326; **2003** 210, 212
Jakes, Milos, ouster of, **1989** 636
Jalai, Ali Ahmad, Afghan interior minister resignation, **2005** 974
Jalal, Masooda, Afghanistan presidential candidate, **2004** 916
Jallow, Hassan, Rwanda war crimes tribunal prosecutor, **2004** 118

JAMA. *See Journal of the American Medical Association*
al-Jamadi, Manadel, terrorist detainee, **2005** 913
Jamai, Khalid, on capture of Saddam Hussein, **2003** 1193
Jamaica, on Caribbean Basin Initiative, **1982** 181
Jamaica accord, IMF on reform of world monetary system, **1976** 3-12
Jamali, Zafarullah Khan
  Pakistan prime minister election, **2002** 169; **2003** 214
  relations with India, **2003** 211, 216-217
  resignation as prime minister, **2004** 1010-1011
James, Daniel, student drug testing case, **2002** 425
James Webb Telescope, plans for, **2004** 12
Jamieson, John, **1989** 50
Jamison v. Texas, **1994** 296
Janjalani, Auarak Abubakar, Abu Sayyaf leader, **2001** 106
Janszen, Paul, **1989** 479-480
Japan
  Allen investigation in, **1981** 847, 849
  in Atlantic community, Kissinger on, **1973** 487, 489-490, 492, 495
  bird flu outbreak, **2004** 924-925
  Bush's trade mission to, **1992** 11-22
  China relations, **1998** 540-541; **2003** 1178; **2005** 621-622
  defense policy, share of burden, Reagan on, **1983** 893-894, 898-899, 902-903
  economic growth and recovery, **2003** 69, 753-754; **2004** 937; **2005** 413
    IMF on, **1977** 688, 692, 697
  economic recession, **2002** 689, 691-692
  economic situation, **1997** 835; **1998** 532-542; **2000** 1049, 1060; **2001** 56, 667
  economic summits, **1981** 591; **1982** 469; **1983** 507-514
    Houston, **1990** 467-482
    Munich, **1992** 637-648
  emperor's divine status, **1989** 99-101
  environmental project funding, **1992** 500
  Ford visit, **1974** 955-956, 958-965
  Hosokawa resignation, **1994** 221-224
  hostage crisis in Peru, **1997** 234-237
  John Paul II visit, **1981** 203-204, 208-211
  Koizumi economic reform plans, **2001** 304-313
  Korean jetliner shot down by Soviets, **1983** 776
  Liberal Democratic Party (LDP), **1994** 221-223
  math and science skills of students, **1988** 379, 390
  missile defense system, **2004** 180
  monetary policy, **1987** 629-630
  national security export controls, **1987** 29
  North Korean relations, **1999** 576-577; **2003** 1178
  Pearl Harbor attack
    statement of remorse for, **1991** 776-777, 783
    and U.S. internment of Japanese-Americans, **1988** 287-289, 293
  population growth in, **1984** 530
  poverty summit, **1981** 770
  PRC relations
    establishment of diplomatic, **1972** 827-830
    peace treaty, **1978** 585-588
    reactions to Nixon's trip, **1972** 183
  Reagan visit, **1983** 893-908
  Russia relations, **1998** 540
  security alliance with U.S., **1992** 14
  South Africa, sanctions against, **1986** 372
  Soviet propaganda about, Project Truth on, **1981** 763
  space exploration program, **2003** 303-304
  Taiwan, peace treaty with (1952), **1972** 827-828
  Tokyo subway terrorist nerve gas incident (Arum Shinrikyo group), **1999** 502, 503; **2000** 278, 282
  UN Security Council, permanent seat for, **1973** 718, 722, 809, 814
  UN treaty conference (Kyoto), **1997** 481, 859-876
  UNSC membership campaign, **2003** 811-812; **2005** 465, 622
  U.S. foreign policy, **1998** 540-542
  U.S. investment in, measures to encourage, **1985** 321, 322-323
  U.S. relations
    Democratic Party platform on, **1984** 642-643
    Nixon on strengthening, **1973** 515, 518, 522, 525-526
    Tanaka meeting with Nixon, **1973** 717-722
    U.S. return of Okinawa, **1972** 41-42
  U.S. trade relations, **1972** 41-43; **1993** 541, 543
    consumer purchase of U.S. products urged, **1985** 319-320, 323
    lifting of U.S. economic sanctions, **1987** 526
    opening of markets, **1987** 428-431, 434, 436-437
    U.S. deficit, **1972** 745, 747-749; **1983** 122, 134-136; **1985** 319-323, 624-627, 629; **1986** 972, 975; **1987** 118, 136; **1989** 100
    U.S. sanctions against, **1987** 427-437
  war on terrorism, military support for, **2001** 627
  World War II
    apology for suffering, **1995** 302-306
    Wallace on causes of, **1975** 155-157, 160
Japan Society, Darman speech to, **1986** 971-981
Japanese American Citizens League, **1988** 290
Japanese Americans, internment, reparations for, **1983** 211-228; **1988** 287-295
Jardine, James S., **1978** 61
Jarmin, Gary, **1984** 244
al-Jarrallah, Ahmed, on capture of Saddam Hussein, **2003** 1194
Jarrell, Jerry, hurricane damage, **1998** 790
Jaruzelski, Wojciech
  human rights in Poland, **1985** 153
  John Paul II in Poland, **1983** 577, 579-580, 584-587; **1987** 555
  Katyn massacre, **1990** 223-224
  martial law
    imposition of, **1981** 881-882, 886-891
    lifting of, **1982** 947-953; **1987** 184-185
  on Nobel Prize for Walesa, **1983** 926
  power sharing by, **1989** 523-524, 527
  relations with Catholic Church, **1985** 119-120
Jarvis, Gregory B., *Challenger* accident, **1986** 515, 521; **1988** 795
Jarvis, Howard A., **1978** 397
Jatti, B. D., **1977** 237-239

Javits, Jacob K. (R-N.Y.)
monetary policy, **1977** 719
nuclear reactor sales to Middle East, **1974** 451
OEO phaseout, **1973** 454
Republican platform, **1980** 568
Soviet emigration policy, **1974** 538
vice presidential selection procedure, **1972** 599
Javorsky, Jaroslav, **1986** 93
Jaworski, Leon
access to White House tapes, **1974** 289-290, 302-303; **1975** 663
Colson plea bargain, **1974** 443-446
House investigation of Korean influence buying, **1977** 769-770, 774-778; **1978** 847, 849
Kleindienst plea bargain, **1974** 409
Nixon involvement and possible prosecution, **1975** 664, 667
Nixon pardon, **1974** 811
resignation as Watergate prosecutor, **1974** 814; **1975** 668
subpoena of Nixon tapes, Court ruling on, **1974** 621-622; **1975** 665
Watergate prosecutions, Ford on, **1974** 766, 769
Watergate prosecutor appointment, **1973** 859, 954; **1975** 661-662
White House tape erasure, **1974** 24
Jaycees, U.S., sex discrimination by, **1984** 465-478
Jayewardene, Junius, Indo-Sri Lankan accord, **1987** 615-622
Jaynes, Gerald D., **1989** 445-447
Jdey, Abderraouf, terrorist martyr, **2004** 275
Jean-Juste, Gerard, pro-Aristide priest arrested, **2004** 100
Jefferson, LaShawn R., trafficking in humans, **2002** 334
Jefferson Parish Hospital District No. 2 v. Hyde, **2000** 109, 121-126
Jeffords, James M. (R-Vt., I-Vt.)
on financing higher education, **1993** 173
health insurance for disabled persons, **1999** 49
health insurance premiums, **1998** 141
patient safety hearings, **1999** 782
Republican Party defection, **2001** 171, 377-384, 400, 403; **2002** 821, 970
Jehovah's Witness, religious freedom issues, **1997** 407, 564, 572
Jemaah Islamiyah (terrorist network), **2002** 705-706; **2003** 1052; **2004** 539, 754-755, 756; **2005** 400
Jenco, Lawrence, release of, **1986** 1016
Jenkins, Bill (R-Tenn.), House Judiciary Committee impeachment inquiry, **1998** 710
Jenkins, Roy, on European Monetary System, **1978** 742-743, 749-752
Jenkins v. Georgia, **1974** 515-522
Jenner, Albert E., Jr.
impeachment inquiry report, **1974** 138
on release of Watergate grand jury report, **1974** 225, 227
Jenness, Craig, Iraq elections, **2005** 949
Jenninger, Philipp, **1989** 488
Jennings, Jerry D., **1992** 534
Jenrette, John W., Jr. (D-S.C.), conviction and resignation from House, **1980** 900-901
Jepsen, Roger W. (R-Iowa), on Joint Economic Committee report, **1981** 293, 297-299
Jeremiah, David, Chinese nuclear espionage matter, **1999** 238
Jerome, John, **1984** 183
Jerusalem
East, status of, **1977** 854; **1979** 225-226
holy sites in, administration of, **1976** 191-192, 194-195
Palestinian militant suicide bombings, **2004** 302
Sadat visit to, **1977** 827-847
status of
Begin on, **1977** 847, 854
Sadat on, **1977** 837, 854
UN resolution on, **1980** 235-237, 239-240, 242
U.S. policy on, **1976** 195; **1995** 623
Temple Mount violence, **1976** 191, 194-195; **1990** 695-705
Jesse-Petersen, Soren, UN Mission in Kosovo administrator, **2004** 951, 952
Jesuit order. *See* Society of Jesus
Jet Propulsion Laboratory (Pasadena, Calif.)
Galileo's inspection of Jupiter's moon, **1997** 202-205
Mars *Climate Orbiter* mission, **2000** 89
Spirit rover mission, **2004** 7-8
Jett v. Dallas Independent School District, **1989** 323
Jewell, Richard, Olympic Park bombing suspect case, **1996** 445, 446-447
Jewish Community Relations Council, Shultz speech on terrorism, **1984** 933, 935
Jewish Material Claims Against Germany, Conference on, **1974** 802
Jews
See also Anti-Semitism; Holocaust
Admadinejad on the "myth" of the Holocaust, **2005** 592
American
Arafat meeting with, **1988** 907-908
claims against Nazi Germany, **1974** 801-802
Holocaust commemoration by, **1981** 381-389
human genetic engineering, **1983** 525
John Paul II, meeting with, **1987** 699-700, 702-705
nuclear arms, **1983** 270
Reagan's Bitburg visit, **1985** 358-362
role in Holocaust, **1981** 382-383; **1983** 143-161
and same-sex unions, **2000** 162
U.S. government role in Holocaust, **1983** 143-144, 149, 150-152
U.S. sale of planes in Middle East, **1978** 125-134; **1981** 787
U.S. vote in UN on Israeli settlements, **1980** 236, 238
Waldheim meeting with John Paul II, **1988** 406
and Young meeting with PLO, **1979** 647-649
Austria, John Paul II visit, **1988** 406-407, 409-414
British policies on genocide and emigration of, **1983** 144, 148-149
Christians, relations with, **1987** 702-705; **1988** 405-414
East German reparations to, **1974** 801-802

French apology for complicity with Nazis, **1995** 478-482
Nazi genocide of, **1983** 143-145, 147-150; **1989** 488, 490-491, 494, 496
Barbie trial, **1987** 517-524
Catholic Church response, **2005** 293
in Germany, **1990** 105-112
Holocaust Museum, **1993** 307-313
oppression of, John Paul II on, **1986** 339-344
Roman Catholic Church Holocaust repentance statement, **1998** 121-130
Soviet
emigration of, **1974** 901-905; **1986** 93-96, 98, 112; **1987** 190, 202-203
harassment of, **1988** 111-112
Shostakovich on anti-Semitism, **1981** 376, 378
Jia Qinglin, Chinese leadership, **2003** 1174
Jiang Qing
arrest of, **1976** 688
trial of, **1980** 955-958
Jiang Zemin
Bush meeting with, **2005** 613
China-Taiwan relations, **2000** 193, 199; **2002** 856
China-U.S. relations, **2001** 738-745
China-U.S. summit meeting, **1997** 728-739; **1999** 726
Chinese leadership transition, **2002** 850-866; **2003** 1174; **2004** 941
and Clinton news conference in China, **1998** 466-478
on death of Deng Xiaping, **1997** 94-100
on earthquake in Taiwan, **1999** 468
Hong Kong transfer ceremony statement, **1997** 502, 505-506
Japan state visit, **1998** 541
military commission chairman, **2002** 850; **2004** 941
UN peacekeeping mission reforms, **2000** 703
visit to U.S., **2002** 856
Jihad, Laskar, and al Qaeda terrorist network, **2001** 567
Jilani, Jalil Abbas (Pakistan ambassador), support for guerrillas, **2003** 211
Jin Linbo, North Korea negotiations, **2005** 606
Job creation
See also Employment, public service
Bush economic growth initiative, **2003** 87-88; **2004** 26-27
Democratic response, **2004** 33, 56
Bush six-point plan, **2004** 60
in Carter's welfare reform plan, **1977** 551, 553-554, 556-557, 559-560
CEA report on, **2004** 57-58
Democratic Party platform, **1996** 629, 632-633
in developing countries, **1972** 859-860, 863-864
economic stimulation for, **1972** 82-83
government spending for, Ford on Carter plan, **1977** 66-67, 73
and inflation, economic summits on, **1977** 367, 369, 371; **1982** 470-471, 473-474
Jobs for the 21st Century program, **2004** 26
outsourcing/offshoring impact on, **2004** 58-59, 237-238
presidential elections and, **2004** 58-59
private sector, **1978** 66-67, 69
Carter on, **1978** 8, 13, 20-21, 99-100
Ford on, **1976** 694, 697
Republican Party platform on, **1976** 619, 622
public sector
in Carter budget, **1979** 34-35
CBO analysis of, **1976** 185
congressional Democrats on, **1975** 18, 34-35
Republican Party platform, **1988** 621-622, 623; **1996** 506-507
tax incentives for, **1972** 83; **1975** 20, 30; **1976** 13-14, 19, 30
technology worker shortage, **1997** 669-678
Job Creation and Worker Assistance Act (JCWAA, 2002), **2003** 75; **2004** 68
Job discrimination. *See* Discrimination, job
Job Opportunities and Basic Skills (JOBS), state programs for welfare, **1988** 849
Job rights bill, **1991** 759-765
Job training
in Carter welfare reform proposal, **1979** 390, 392-394
Democratic Party platform on, **1972** 531, 546
for displaced farmers, **1986** 303-306
for long-term unemployed, in Carter budget, **1979** 31, 34-35
for minorities and women, **1982** 920, 939-941
in prisons, **1981** 192, 194-196, 663, 667
and programs, in Carter budget, **1979** 91
and relocation assistance, **1981** 54
Republican Party platform on, **1980** 598-599
sex segregation in, **1985** 794, 798-800
and transitional assistance, Democratic Party platform on, **1984** 574-575
Urban League proposals, **1985** 29, 34-35, 37
for veterans, Carter plan for, **1977** 108
for welfare mothers, **1988** 847-852
for youth
Carter on, **1981** 58, 62-63
in Reagan budget, **1981** 326
Job Training Partnership Act (JTPA, 1982)
and blacks, **1985** 29, 35
Quayle's sponsorship of, **1988** 591, 603, 800, 821, 824
Reagan's support for, **1983** 115-116, 124; **1984** 108; **1985** 106, 111
Jobless rate. *See* Unemployment rate
JOBS. *See* Job Opportunities and Basic Skills
Jobs and Growth Tax Relief Reconciliation Act (JGTRRA, 2003), **2003** 684, 686; **2004** 60, 68-69; **2005** 147
Jobs for the 21st Century program, **2004** 26
Joe DiMaggio Children's Hospital, **1999** 385
Johanns, Mike, as agriculture department secretary, **2005** 45
John, Sir Elton, gay marriage to David Furnish, **2005** 869
John Brown P.L.C., **1982** 880
John Jay College of Criminal Justice, child sexual abuse by priests, **2004** 83, 84
John Paul I (pope), installation as pope and death, **1978** 595-600

John Paul II (pope)
assassination attempt on, **1981** 427-430, 697; **2000** 77
book advance payment, **2000** 910
on canon law, revised, **1983** 93-100
Catholic-Jewish relations during the Holocaust, **1998** 121-122, 124; **2000** 79
on contraception, **1980** 872
"culture of life," statements on, **2005** 293
"Day of Pardon" mass, **1998** 77-87
death of, **2005** 290-291
economic questions, encyclical on, **1991** 229-241
on economic rights of mothers, **1981** 697, 705
on economic supremacy, **1984** 958, 962-963, 965-966, 970-971
excommunication of Lefebvre, **1988** 489-494
on Falklands war, **1982** 286, 410
on families, **1980** 873-875
female priests ban, **1994** 276-280
funeral mass
foreign dignitaries attending, **2005** 291
Ratzinger homily, **2005** 290-298
on Gospel of Life ("culture of death"), **1995** 145-161
on human rights
and dignity of human person, **1979** 734; **1981** 204-206; **1983** 242, 251-255
during economic development, **1988** 167, 170, 173-174
and government exploitation, **1985** 500-501, 505-506, 508
threats against, **1979** 749-753
UN speech, **1995** 639-645
of workers, **1981** 695, 709-715
Indigenous Americans abuses report, **1992** 900
land mines ban, **1997** 845
legacy of, **2005** 292-294
and liberation theology, **1984** 759-775; **1986** 317
moral theology, encyclical on, **1993** 843-850
Nobel Peace Prize nominee, **2003** 1131
on Nobel Prize for Walesa, **1983** 926
peace, joint statement with Reagan on, **1982** 477-488
on Poland
ban on Solidarity, **1982** 948
economic sanctions against, **1987** 184
martial law, **1981** 885
on political activism among Catholic clergy, **1980** 411-413, 416
reassertion of orthodoxy, **1986** 757
religious freedom in Cuba, **1998** 30-37
Rome synagogue visit, **1986** 339-346
selection and installation as pope, **1978** 595-597, 600-603
sexual abuse by priests, **1993** 407-411; **2002** 869; **2005** 294
social concerns, encyclical on, **1988** 165-174
social justice, encyclical on, **1980** 967-968, 971-976
state visits
Cuba, **1998** 30-31
to the Holy Land, **1998** 77, 79-81
twenty-fifth anniversary of his reign, **2003** 524
UN address, **1979** 729, 748-753
and U.S. Catholic Church, **1986** 909
U.S.-Vatican diplomatic relations, **1984** 19, 21
on Vatican II, **1985** 571, 765-767
Vatican-Israel Diplomatic Accord, **1993** 1033, 1035
visits to
Africa, **1985** 499-514
Argentina, **1982** 410
Austria, **1988** 405-414
Canada, **1984** 761, 777-787
Central America and Caribbean, **1983** 241-255
Colombia, **1986** 639-649
Dominican Republic, **1979** 726
Far East, **1981** 203-211; **1984** 327-338
Great Britain, **1982** 409-418
India, **1986** 23-27
Ireland, **1979** 725, 728-729, 741-748
Mexico, **1979** 726-728, 730-738
Netherlands and Belgium, **1985** 363-376
Poland, **1979** 725, 727-728, 738-741; **1983** 577-593; **1987** 555-564
South America, **1985** 57-67
Spain, **1982** 837-853
Switzerland, **1984** 399-406
Turkey, **1979** 725, 729-730, 760-761
U.S., **1979** 725, 728-729, 748-760; **1987** 699-716
with Clinton, **1993** 660
Denver, **1993** 659-669
on women, role of, **1988** 785-792
work, encyclical on, **1981** 695-715
John XXIII (pope)
honored by Jews at death, **1986** 342
Vatican II reforms, **1978** 596; **1983** 94; **1985** 571, 765-766
Johns Hopkins University
Applied Physics Laboratory, *NEAR (Near Earth Asteroid Rendezvous) Shoemaker* mission to Eros, **2001** 143-149
School of Medicine, cancer study, **1992** 277-281
Sexual Disorders Clinic (Baltimore), **1997** 385
Johnson, Andrew, impeachment of, **1975** 139; **1998** 697, 959; **1999** 15
Johnson, Ben, Olympic athlete disqualified for drug use, **2005** 212
Johnson, David R., Salt Lake Olympics committee, **1999** 106, 107
Johnson, Ervin "Magic"
person with AIDS, **1998** 880-881
resignation from AIDS commission, **1992** 710-711, 891-893
retirement from basketball and AIDS announcement, **1991** 747-749; **1992** 335, 340
Johnson, Gregory, in flag burning case, **1989** 343-344, 346-348
Johnson, Jerome, Tailhook convention report, **1992** 883
Johnson, Lady Bird, **1977** 862
Johnson, Lyndon Baines
appointment of Kerner commission, **1988** 185
budget deficits, **2003** 679
CIA plot against Castro, **1975** 754-756
civil rights legislation of, Warren on, **1972** 938-940
death of, **1973** 97-99
economic policy, **1998** 500-501

as Kennedy's running mate, **1988** 533
Medicare enactment (1965), **1986** 273
Medicare prescription drug benefits, **2003** 1121
political uses of FBI, **1975** 873, 878-882
press conferences of, **1988** 842
transfer of presidential power, **1985** 492
U.S. bombing of North Vietnam, **1972** 491-497
vice presidential papers donation, **1973** 947, 957
Vietnam war
on trial U.S. bombing halt, **1972** 493
and Westmoreland suit, **1985** 159, 161-162
on vision of the educated young, **1972** 789-793
Johnson, Magic. *See* Johnson, Ervin "Magic"
Johnson, Mickey, church bombing trial, **2002** 241
Johnson, Mitchell, **1998** 736
Johnson, Nancy L. (R-Conn.)
and ERA, **1988** 617
Gingrich ethics violations, **1995** 748
Johnson, Nicholas, **1973** 56-57
Johnson, Paul, **1987** 331-349
Johnson, Paul, Jr., contractor kidnapped and beheaded in Saudi Arabia, **2004** 519
Johnson, Richard, Social Security crisis, **2002** 105
Johnson, Stephen L., mercury emissions from power plants, EPA guidelines, **2005** 96, 99
Johnson, Sterling, Jr., **1992** 459-460
Johnson v. Eisentrager, **2003** 108, 115-117, 119-120; **2004** 378, 392-398
Johnson v. Glick, **1992** 178, 180, 181
Johnson v. Louisiana, **1972** 423-426, 428-429
Johnson v. Mississippi, **1993** 149
Johnson v. Transportation Agency, Santa Clara, California, **1987** 331-349
Johnson v. Zerbst, **1990** 792-793
Johnson and Johnson, affirmative action, **2003** 362
Johnson C. Smith University (North Carolina), **1992** 577
Johnson-Sirleaf, Ellen, **2000** 450
Liberian presidential elections, **2005** 802-803
visit to U.S., **2005** 803
Johnston, Henry S., **1988** 249
Johnston, J. Bennett (D-La.), **1995** 114-115
Johnston, Kelly, food safety, threats to food supply, **2001** 700
Johnston, Lloyd D., drug use among adolescents, **1996** 571
Joint Center for Political Studies, **1983** 766
Joint Chiefs of Staff
attempted rescue of U.S. hostages in Iran, **1980** 351-385
and Iran-contra affair, **1986** 1051
proposed dismantling of, **1985** 670-671, 674, 676-677, 681, 683
restructuring of, **1982** 325-336; **1986** 679, 681, 684-685
on Seabed Treaty, **1972** 167-168
Joint Commission on the Accreditation of Health Care Organizations (JCAHO), **1999** 413; **2001** 193
Joint Committee on Internal Revenue Taxation, on Nixon tax deductions, **1974** 235-245
Joint Economic Committee
Burns testimony on government spending, **1972** 962
creation of, **1979** 216
reports of, **1977** 717-733; **1979** 215-222; **1980** 209-231; **1981** 293-324
Rickover farewell testimony to, **1982** 87-104
Joint Study Committee on Budget Control, **1974** 575
Joint U.S.-Russian Commission on POW-MIAs, **1992** 521, 525
Jones, A. Elizabeth, Chechen-Russian conflict, **2004** 570
Jones, Ben, **1995** 748, 750; **1996** 840
Jones, Bob, III, **1983** 491
Jones, Christina, **2002** 42
Jones, David C.
on Joint Chiefs restructuring, **1982** 325-336
on nuclear test ban treaty, **1998** 49
on U.S. defense posture, **1980** 123
Jones, Hugh R., **1976** 892
Jones, James R. (D-Okla.), **1982** 145
Jones, Jim, People's Temple and mass suicide, **1979** 347-348, 357-366, 376
Jones, John E., III, intelligent design case, **2005** 1012, 1013, 1014-1026
Jones, Nathaniel R., **1992** 34
Jones, Paul L., GAO report on student treatment at military academies, **1992** 481-487
Jones, Paula Corbin, sexual harassment suit, **1997** 21, 290-298; **1998** 39, 565, 633-634, 638-639, 962; **1999** 16, 21-22, 166; **2000** 763
Jones, Robert E., physician-assisted suicide, **2001** 293
Jones, Roy C., **1985** 381
Jones, Shirley, libel suit against *National Enquirer,* **1984** 248, 253-256
Jones, Tommy Lee, Democratic national convention, **2000** 612
Jones, Walter (R-N.C.), Iraq War troop withdrawal, calling for, **2005** 836
Jones, William B., **1973** 453-464
Jones Institute for Reproductive Medicine (Norfolk, Virginia), **2001** 531
Jones v. Alfred H. Mayer Co. (1968), **1976** 392-403
Jonestown, Guyana, mass suicide of People's Temple members, **1979** 347-349
Jopel Contracting and Trucking Corp., indictment of, **1984** 803-809
Jordan
arms transfers to Pakistan, **1972** 34, 37-39
and Camp David accords, **1978** 605-607, 609-611, 622, 624
elections, **2003** 961
free-trade agreement, **2001** 627
Israel peace agreement, **1994** 329-335
legal and administrative links to West Bank, **1988** 579-585
Nixon visit, **1974** 449, 451, 467-469
PLO forces relocated in, **1982** 744
population growth in, **1987** 440, 443, 446
role in Israeli-Lebanese security agreement, **1983** 472
role in Reagan Middle East peace proposal, **1982** 753, 758-760, 763
student test scores, **1992** 91, 93, 95
territories captured from in 1967 war, **1983** 834, 932

Jordan *Continued*
terrorist bombings in Amman, **2005** 400-401
UN Oil for Food Program, **2004** 717
U.S. aid to, **1974** 277, 279, 282, 451, 468
U.S. arms sales to, **1978** 106
Jordan, Anthony, Baptist view on women and the family, **1998** 334
Jordan, Barbara (D-Texas), immigration reform, **1995** 565
Jordan, Hamilton
appointment to chief of staff, **1979** 561, 573
Perot Campaign, **1992** 718
Jordan, J. Phillip, **1978** 62
Jordan, James, civil rights workers slayings trial, **2005** 355
Jordan, Larry R., on extremists in the military, **1996** 179
Jordan, Robert W. (Saudi Arabia ambassador), security of Americans in Saudi Arabia, **2003** 229
Jordan, Steven L., Abu Ghraib prison abuse scandal, **2005** 912
Jordan, Vernon, Jr., Lewinsky scandal, role in, **1998** 577-580, 635, 649-650; **1999** 17
Jordan, Vernon E., **1978** 243
Joseph, Stephen C., **1981** 448
Jospin, Lionel, and French antiterrorist measures, **1986** 831
Joss, Sally, small arms trade, **2001** 518
Joste, Bruce, tobacco industry fraud suit, **1999** 538
Journal of the American Medical Association (JAMA)
alcoholism definition, **1992** 849-852
end-of-life care report, **1997** 325-330
gun violence report, **1992** 493-498
physical activity report, **1996** 420
physical fitness and health study, **1989** 613-617
Journalism. *See* Mass media; News media; Press
Jovanovi, Zvezdan, Serbia war crimes, **2003** 59
Jovic, Borisav, **1991** 368
Jovic, Ivo Miro, Dayton peace agreement, tenth anniversary, **2005** 861-862
Joyce, Diana, affirmative action case, **1987** 331-349
Joyce, Philip G., federal budget deficit, **2005** 123
Joyce, Terrance, glaciers, effect of global warming on, **2002** 304
JTPA. *See* Job Training Partnership Act
Juan Carlos I (king of Spain)
and Marc Rich presidential pardon, **2001** 90
Panama Canal transfer ceremony, **1999** 853
signing of democratic constitution, **1978** 809-812
Soviet-forged letter from Reagan to, **1981** 754
terrorist bombings of Madrid, **2004** 107, 111-112
Jubeir, Adel, terrorist bombings in Riyadh, Saudi Arabia, **2003** 230
Judaism
See also Jews
Christianity compared with, **1986** 339-346
Judges. *See* Federal judges
Judicial activism
boundaries of justiciability, **1981** 803-804, 806-807
O'Connor on, **1981** 576, 581-582, 585-590
Republican platform on, **1984** 704
use of remedial powers, **1981** 803-804, 808-809
Judicial appointments, and views on abortion, **1980** 569, 619, 865-866
Judicial Conference of the United States, **1990** 311-312
on judge's impeachment, **1989** 584
on judicial pay raise, **1989** 195-196, 202-204
justices on Court workload, **1982** 706, 718-719, 722-723
Schmults address to on FOIA, **1981** 394
Judicial immunity, from suits resulting from judicial acts, **1978** 259-268
Judicial powers, vs. legislative, on federal minimum wage laws applied to state governments, **1976** 378, 388-389
Judicial review, of executive branch, Court ruling on Nixon tapes, **1974** 621-637
Judicial system
See also Federal courts
Court workload remedies, justices on, **1982** 705-727
failure of to control crime, Burger on, **1981** 191-196
federal court appointments, **1998** 48
reform of
Burger's suggestions for, **1972** 639-643
Carter on, **1979** 41
Judicial Watch, national energy policy task force, **2003** 1018
Judiciary, Spanish, in democratic constitution, **1978** 811, 832-834
Juliana I (queen of the Netherlands), abdication of, **1980** 387-392
Jumblatt, Walid, Lebanese cabinet member resignation, **2004** 561
Jumper, John P., sexual misconduct at Air Force Academy investigations, **2003** 793, 794, 797
Juncker, Jean-Claude, EU British rebate controversy, **2005** 343
Junk bonds
Japanese view of, **1992** 21
and leveraged buyouts, **1988** 922, 924
Milken's guilty plea, **1990** 251-257
Jupiter
NASA explorations, **1999** 175-176; **2003** 305
Voyager I mission, **1980** 989
Jupiter Communications, online stock trading study, **1999** 203
Juppé, Alain, French government programs, **1995** 229-230
Jury selection
in death penalty cases, **1986** 445-456
exclusion of women, **1975** 55-66
gender-motivated peremptory challenges, **1994** 225-236
racially motivated peremptory challenges, **1986** 409-433
Jury trials
awards in personal injury or liability cases, **1987** 165-169, 174-178
instructions, error in, **1987** 479, 481, 483-487
split verdicts, constitutionality of, **1972** 423-429
unanimous verdicts and six-person juries, **1979** 263-268

Justice and Equality Movement, **2004** 589
Justice Department
activism of under Meese, **1985** 481, 655
affirmative action consent decree, **1984** 365-376, 381-385
Agnew investigation and charges, **1973** 827-836
Allen investigation, **1981** 847-854
Aramco antitrust investigation, **1983** 921-924
AT&T antitrust suits, **1982** 17-33
B. Carter's Libyan contacts, investigation of, **1980** 907-917
on Barbie affair, **1983** 737-747
Bureau of Justice Statistics, use of guns in crime report, **1995** 463-471
capital punishment report, **1999** 828-835; **2000** 988-998; **2001** 390
child pornography, definition of, **2002** 290
and CIA's authority to investigate own agents, **1975** 402, 413-414
civil rights enforcement by, **1983** 46, 51, 914, 916-917; **1987** 43-45, 48, 58
Clinton secretary nomination, **1993** 135-139
closing of PLO observer mission to UN, **1988** 479-485
Cuban detainee agreement, **1987** 929-932, 935-937
curfews for juveniles, **1996** 325-333
draft evader clemency program, **1977** 97
Enron CEO (Kenneth Lay) indictment, **2004** 415-417, 424-428
EPA investigation by, **1983** 749-753
in ERA ratification defense, **1981** 924
executive privilege, in Gorsuch lawsuit against House, **1982** 966
FBI crime laboratory, Office of the Inspector General (OIG) investigations, **1997** 221-228
FBI gun purchaser background checks, **2001** 725-726; **2003** 156, 158-160
flag burning, **1990** 357-365
FOIA suits, **1981** 394-396
Haitian refugee asylum, **1992** 453
House members' misconduct, investigations of, **1982** 730-731, 738
Hughes antitrust case, **1973** 976
human trafficking cases, **2004** 124
and insider trading, **1987** 881
Iran-contra affair, North conviction, **1990** 493
Iran-contra affair, on diverted funds, **1986** 1013-1014, 1017, 1022-1024, 1052
ITT antitrust settlement, **1972** 395-406; **1974** 3-5, 16-21, 407-410; **1975** 143, 654-656, 666
on judicial restraint, **1981** 803-809
Kennedy assassination investigation, performance in, **1978** 910, 915
King assassination investigation, performance in, **1977** 113-123; **1978** 910, 917
Korean influence-buying investigation, **1978** 846-848
on life-sustaining measures for infants, **1983** 283
Los Angeles riot investigation, **1992** 411
Love Canal enforcement action, **1980** 445, 447
Marcos indictment, **1988** 868-872
Merck investigations, **2004** 852
Microsoft antitrust settlement, **2002** 797, 798, 802
Milken's junk bonds, **1990** 252
National Crime Survey, rape victims reported, **1992** 386
Noriega indictments, **1988** 81-92
Office of Special Investigations (OSI), discovery of Mengele, **1985** 409-414
on Pentagon Papers publication, **1973** 539
political dismissal investigation, **1978** 51-64
political involvement of officials, Watergate committee recommendations on, **1974** 612-613
political uses of, in Watergate cover-up, **1974** 158-163, 167-169, 176, 179, 181, 657, 659
on press protections, **1972** 508-509
prison occupancy standards, **1981** 477
prosecution function, independence of, **1975** 654, 672-678
protective function privilege for Secret Service officers, **1998** 396, 566
race-based redistricting, **1995** 369-372, 378-379
rape victims and emergency contraception guidelines, **2005** 817
reports on violent crime, **1993** 375-378
sexual misconduct investigation of House members, **1983** 728
tax returns, access to, **1975** 829, 849-855
telephone industry, policies on and Meese investigation, **1988** 496-497, 505-506
terrorist detainees, treatment of, **2003** 310-331; **2005** 910
terrorist interrogations, use of torture in (torture memo), **2004** 207, 336-347, 375, 778; **2005** 906
terrorist watch list consolidation, **2003** 158
TIPS (Terrorism Information and Prevention System), **2002** 564; **2003** 613
tobacco company lawsuit, **2003** 261, 263-264; **2004** 284
tobacco industry health risks fraud allegations, **1999** 536-551
violence against women report, **1994** 62-72
Waco incident report, **1993** 819-821, 829-840
on Waldheim
barring of from U.S., **1988** 405
war service of, **1986** 745-746
war on terrorism and, **2001** 642
Watergate investigation by, **1973** 859, 862, 874, 877
wiretaps
authorization procedures, **1974** 391-405
in domestic security cases, **1972** 485-489
youth gang activity report, **2001** 73, 75
Justice for All, **2005** 180
Justice Policy Institute, sentencing reform, **2002** 786-787
Juvenile justice system
curfew ordinances, **1996** 325-333
death penalty, **1998** 187
Democratic Party platform, **1996** 635
and discarded children, **1989** 671, 673, 675-678, 681
juvenile crime bill, **1998** 48
juveniles in adult prisons, **2000** 855
Republican Party platform, **1996** 522-523
rise in juvenile crime, **1995** 711
violent crime, **1996** 733

K

Kabarebe, James, Congo resource exploitation, **2002** 551
Kabbah, Ahmad Tejan
  Sierra Leone elections, **2000** 1073; **2002** 249
  Sierra Leone peace negotiations, **1999** 430; **2002** 247-255
Kabila, Joseph (son of Laurent)
  Congolese leader, **2001** 160, 161
  coup attempts, **2004** 506
  peace agreement, **2002** 547-555; **2003** 288-290
  political infighting in Kinshasa, **2004** 505-506
  transitional government leader, **2005** 1027-1028
Kabila, Laurent
  assassination of, **2001** 159-161; **2002** 548; **2003** 289; **2005** 1027-1028
  Congo resources plundered, **2003** 294
  Congolese leader, **1998** 161; **1999** 430, 645-646
  war in the Congo, **2000** 643, 978, 979; **2002** 547-548
  Zaire coup and new Congo leader, **1997** 877, 879-885
Kabuga, Felicien, Rwanda war crimes suspect, **2004** 117
Kaczmarek, Jerzy, **1986** 93
Kaczynski, David, role in conviction of brother as Unabomber, **1998** 233-234
Kaczynski, Theodore J.
  Unabomber manifesto, **1995** 600-610
  Unabomber sentencing, **1998** 233-252
Kadar, Janos, **1989** 341
Kaddoumi, Farouk, al Fatah leader, **2004** 808
Kaden, Lewis B., **1999** 692
Kadish, Ronald T., U.S. missile defense system, **2003** 818; **2004** 177
Kadyrov, Akhmad
  assassination of, **2004** 565
  Chechen presidential election, **2003** 249
Kagame, Paul
  Congo peace agreement, **2002** 548-555
  plane crash with presidents of Rwanda and Burundi, involvement in, **2004** 119
  Rwanda genocidal war remembrance, **2004** 116
  Rwanda peacekeeping mission in the Sudan, **2004** 592
  Rwanda-Congo conflict, **2004** 507
  Rwandan Tutsi president, **2000** 454; **2003** 1069-1070
Kagan, Robert, U.S.-China relations, **2001** 250
Kahan, Yitzhak, investigation of Palestinian refugee camp massacre, **1982** 783; **1983** 163; **1985** 48, 50, 51
Kahn, Abdul Qadeer, nuclear weapons technology trafficking, **2004** 169, 323, 327-329, 1009, 1013; **2005** 934
Kahn, Ann P., **1988** 378
Kahn, Chip, privacy of medical records, **2000** 1065
Kahn, Ismail
  Afghanistan warlord, **2002** 20; **2004** 914
  son assassinated, **2004** 914
Kahn, Mohammed Naeem Noor, al Qaeda communications expert captured, **2004** 538
Kahn, Mohammed Sidique, London terrorist bombing suspect, **2005** 398
Kaifu, Toshiki, Soviet aid, **1990** 467
Kaiser, Karl, European defense force, **1999** 818
Kaiser Aluminum & Chemical Corp. v. Weber, **1979** 493-507
Kaiser Commission on Medicaid and the Uninsured, **2003** 846
Kaiser Family Foundation
  health insurance coverage, **2004** 982
  Medicare drug benefit for seniors, **2004** 578-579
Kaiser Permanente
  prescription drug benefit reform, **2000** 134
  Vioxx study, and risk of heart attacks or strokes, **2004** 851, 853
Kajelijeli, Juvenal, Rwanda war crimes conviction, **2003** 1075
Kalam, Abdul, India elections, **2004** 350
Kalb, Bernard, **1986** 352
Kalb, Marvin
  Chernenko interview, **1984** 918
  in presidential debates, **1984** 877, 880-881, 893-895
  on presidential press conferences, **1988** 835
Kalinic, Dragan, Bosnia war criminals, **2004** 953
Kalish, Steven, **1988** 83, 88-91
Kallstrom, James, TWA flight 800 crash, **1997** 781, 783-786
Kalmbach, Herbert W.
  payments by for political investigations, **1974** 338-339, 354, 601, 604, 610-611
  payments to Watergate break-in defendants, **1974** 307, 331, 338-339, 353-354
  release from prison, **1975** 143
  secret campaign funds, **1973** 501
  Watergate guilty plea of, **1974** 153
Kalugin, Oleg, **1993** 114
Kamal, Mohamed, on Egyptian political system, **2005** 166
Kambanda, Jean, Rwandan genocide trials, **1998** 614-625; **2000** 454-455
Kamel, Mohammed Ibrahim, **1978** 607
Kamenar, Paul D., **1979** 920
Kamenske, Bernard H., **1981** 754
Kamisar, Yale, **1987** 579
Kamorteiro, Abreu, Angola peace agreement, **2002** 154
Kampuchea (Cambodia)
  See also Cambodia
  chemical warfare in, **1981** 682; **1982** 235-236, 244-245, 256-257
  human rights in, **1980** 190, 197; **1981** 180, 187; **1982** 109, 115-116; **1983** 191-193
  self-determination for, economic summit on, **1981** 594
  UN ineffectiveness at resolving conflict in, **1982** 769, 773
Kamuhanda, Jean de Dieu, Rwanda war crimes conviction, **2004** 118
Kanaan, Ghazi, suicide death of, **2005** 691
Kanans, Peter, African debt relief program, **2005** 408
Kandarian, Steven A.
  PBGC investment policy, **2004** 737

underfunded pension plans, **2003** 708, 711-719; **2004** 735
Kang Sok Joo, North Korean nuclear weapons program, **2002** 733
Kang Sok Ju, Roh Tae Woo's UN address, **1988** 855
Kania, Stanislaw, **1980** 794-795
Kanka, Megan, sex offender victim, **1997** 384
Kansas
intelligent design case, **2005** 1013-1014
Sexually Violent Predator Act, **1997** 382-394
Kansas v. Hendricks, **1997** 382-394
Kansas v. Marsh, **2005** 182
Kansas City (Missouri) School District (KCMSD), **1990** 227-238
school uniform policy, **1996** 90
Kantor, Mickey, commerce secretary appointment, **1996** 204
Kapila, Mukesh, Sudan conflict, **2004** 590
Kaplan v. Burlington, **1995** 397
Kaposi's sarcoma, **1985** 734
Karadzic, Radovan
Bosnian war criminal, **2001** 826; **2003** 461, 463; **2004** 138, 953; **2005** 851, 853-854
Kosovo war criminal, **1995** 718; **1999** 738, 803; **2000** 837
Karami, Omar
as prime minister of Lebanon, **2004** 562; **2005** 687
resignation and reinstatement, **2005** 688
Karami, Rashid, death of, **2005** 690
Karcher v. Daggett, **1983** 599-616
Karimov, Islam
Andijon killings and trial, **2005** 429-433
Uzbekistan presidential election, **2005** 428-429
Karlan, Pamela, **1995** 372
Karmal, Babrak
replacement of, **1986** 919
Soviet installation of, **1979** 965, 969-970; **1980** 190, 195
Karon, John M., AIDS statistics, **1996** 158-159
Karpinski, Janis, Abu Ghraib prison abuse scandal, **2004** 209-210, 215, 233-234; **2005** 912
Karrazi, Kamal, Rushdie death threat lifted, **1998** 691
Karrubi, Mehdi, Iranian presidential candidate, **2005** 590
Kartman, Charles, U.S.-North Korea diplomatic relations, **1999** 570
Karzai, Ahmed Wali, Afghanistan reconstruction, **2003** 1100
Karzai, Hamid
Afghanistan constitution, **2003** 1097-1098
Afghanistan interim government prime minister, **2001** 691, 880-882; **2003** 1089, 1094, 1095-1096
Afghanistan parliament address, **2005** 970-989
Afghanistan president of transitional government, **2002** 15-19
assassination attempts (2003), **2004** 916
government of, **2005** 973-974
Nobel Peace Prize nominee, **2002** 983
parliamentary elections, **2005** 970-973
presidential inauguration, **2004** 912-922
U.S. relations, **2005** 974
visit to U.S., **2002** 39
Kashmir
crisis in, White House statement on, **2002** 325-331
earthquakes, **2005** 468, 472, 477-479
elections in, **2002** 329-330
India-Pakistan disputes, **1999** 624-625; **2001** 963-966; **2002** 166; **2003** 209-217; **2004** 352, 1010; **2005** 17, 468
India-Pakistan peace negotiations, **2005** 472, 476
Kasich, John (R-Ohio)
debt-relief program, **2000** 479
welfare reform, **1996** 461-462
Kasparov, Garry, chess victory of IBM computer, **1997** 273-276
Kass, Leon
human cloning research, ethics of, **2002** 513; **2004** 158
stem cell research, **2001** 541
Kassal, Bentley, ruling on America's Cup, **1989** 184, 193
Kassebaum, Nancy Landon (R-Kan.), **1995** 130
on criticism of South Africa, **1984** 1029
Glaspie-Hussein pre-war meeting, **1991** 159
Tower nomination, **1989** 105
women in combat debate, **1991** 511
Kassebaum-Baker, Nancy Landon (R-Kan.)
chemical weapons treaty, **1997** 201
integration of women for military training, **1997** 657
striking workers, **1995** 130
women in the military, **1998** 336
Kassir, Samir, journalist killed in Lebanon, **2005** 689
Kassirer, Jerome P., gun control laws advocate, **1993** 872
Kasten, Bob (R-Wis.)
investigation of Medal of Honor award, **1989** 699
World Bank projects in Indonesia, **1986** 860
Kastenmeier, Robert W. (D-Wis.)
judicial impeachment, **1989** 585
legislative intent, **1993** 250
Rockefeller nomination, **1974** 988-989
Kastigar v. United States, **1990** 492, 494, 495-497
Kasyanov, Mikhail (Russian prime minister)
appointment, **2000** 173
critic of Putin, **2005** 301
questions Yukos Oil seizure, **2003** 247; **2005** 301
Katmai National Monument, **1978** 731, 735-736
Katrina disaster. *See* Hurricane Katrina disaster
Katsav, Moshe
on Israel Gaza Strip withdrawal, **2005** 532
Israel-Syria diplomatic relations, **2004** 559
Katyn Massacre, **1990** 223-225
Katz, David L., on dietary guidelines, **2005** 4
Katz, Harvey, on UAW General Motors strike, **1998** 321-322
Katz, Julius, trade negotiations, **1999** 797
Katzenbach v. Morgan, **1997** 415
Kauffman, Bruce W., on Philadelphia MOVE raid, **1986** 240-241, 244, 248-251
Kauffmann, John R., and King assassination, **1979** 595, 618-619
Kaufman, Frank J., Roswell incident, **1997** 401
Kaufman, Irving R., **1986** 179
Kaunda, Kenneth, **1976** 288

Kavan, Jan, at NATO membership ceremony for Czech Republic, **1999** 121, 122-124
Kawamoto, Nobuhiko, **1992** 12
Kay, David, U.S. weapons search in Iraq, **2003** 880, 881-883, 886-900; **2004** 712
Kazakhstan
  Alma-Ata Declaration, **1991** 804-806
  Commonwealth Pact, **1991** 803-804
  human trafficking, **2002** 345-346
  national security needs review, **1993** 714
  Nuclear Arms Pact, **1991** 806-808
  nuclear weapons, **1991** 787; **1993** 554; **1994** 363-373; **1996** 219-221
    dismantling of, **2001** 18; **2004** 169
  Soviet Union restructuring plans, **1991** 532-533
  START I, **1993** 18, 21, 24, 30, 32, 36, 54; **1994** 585
  START II, **1993** 23, 29, 36, 59
Kazin, Alfred, on Holocaust Museum controversy, **1993** 307
Kazini, James, Congo resource exploitation, **2002** 551
Kbaki, Mwai, Kenya presidential inauguration speech, **2002** 1044-1051
Kealy, Edward R., national education strategy, **1991** 221
Kean, Michael H., **1992** 47
Kean, Thomas H. (New Jersey governor)
  congressional intelligence failures panel, **2002** 990, 997
  education summit, **1989** 562
  national commission on terrorist attacks chairman, **2003** 547; **2004** 450, 451, 454, 457, 967, 968, 970
  national commission recommendations, **2005** 893-904
  race relations panel, **1997** 316, 322; **1998** 668
  racial stereotyping, **1998** 666
  at Republican convention, **1988** 590
Keating, Charles H., Jr.
  "Keating Five" investigations, **1991** 107-118; **1992** 756
  Keating inquiry, **1990** 817
  savings and loan scandals, **1989** 465
Keating, Frank
  on Oklahoma City bombing, **1995** 176, 179-180
  sexual abuse by priests controversy, **2003** 523, 527-528
Keeler, William H.
  antiabortion issue, **1998** 812
  female priests ban, **1994** 276-277
  U.S. Catholic bicentennial mass, **1989** 620-623
  Vatican-Israel Diplomatic Accord, **1993** 1034-1035
Keeley, Robert, **1980** 318
Keenan, Nancy, Roberts Supreme Court nomination, **2005** 815
Keeton, Kathy, **1984** 247-248, 249
Keeton v. Hustler Magazine, **1984** 247-253
Kefauver, Estes (D-Tenn.), drug industry pricing hearings, **1993** 198; **1994** 88
Keith, Damon, secret domestic detentions, **2002** 835
Keizer, Col. Herman, Jr., Army's first Muslim chaplain, **1993** 973-975
Keker, John W., **1989** 394-395
Keldysh, Mstislav V., **1973** 794-796
Keller, Ric (R-Fla.), restaurant obesity lawsuits, **2003** 484
Kellerman, Arthur
  guns in the home study, **1993** 871-876
  uninsured, **2001** 711
Kelley, Clarence M.
  FBI's domestic intelligence guidelines, **1976** 321-330
  Hearst kidnapping, **1974** 249
Kelley, Paul X., on terrorist attack on Marines in Beirut, **1983** 935
Kelley, Virginia, **1992** 1046, 1052
Kelling, George, violent crime, **1997** 682
Kellner, Leon B., **1988** 83
Kelly, David, suicide, **2003** 884; **2004** 718
Kelly, J. Michael, **1978** 58
Kelly, James (UPS spokesman), UPS strike statement, **1997** 634-635
Kelly, James A. (State department asst. secy.), North and South Korean talks, **2002** 732-733
Kelly, Jean, **1975** 438
Kelly, John, Wen Ho Lee spy case, **2000** 741
Kelly, Richard (R-Fla.), conviction of, **1980** 900-901
Kelo, Susette, eminent domain case, **2005** 363
Kelo v. City of New London, **2005** 362-375
Kelso, Adm. Frank B., II
  Iowa (USS) explosion investigations, **1991** 679-689
  Tailhook scandal court-martials, **1994** 107-115
  women in combat, **1991** 507; **1993** 334
Kemble, Penn, **1973** 36
Kemeny, John G., Three Mile Island report, **1979** 823-825
Kemeny commission on Three Mile Island accident, **1979** 823-863
Kemp, Jack F. (R-N.Y.)
  comment on Lott's racial remarks, **2002** 971
  on HUD scandal, **1989** 334-335
  on Nixon budget, **1974** 98
  at Republican convention, **1984** 729
  tax relief plan, **1980** 567-568, 574
  vice presidential campaign, Republican Party acceptance speech, **1996** 478, 480, 481-486
  vice presidential debates, **1996** 707-709, 718-724
Kemp-Roth plan, **1980** 567-568, 574
  in Carter-Reagan debate, **1980** 920, 926, 928
  Democrats' attack on, **1980** 772, 781, 785-786
Kempthorne, Dirk (Idaho governor), national forests development, **2004** 669
Kemptner, Thomas, hostage, **1991** 751
Kenai Fjords National Monument, **1978** 731, 735, 737
Kendall, David E.
  grand jury investigations, **1998** 567
  on Whitewater investigations, **2000** 765
Kendall, Henry W., Nobel in physics, **1990** 796
Kendall v. United States, **1992** 192, 196
Kennan, George F.
  Carter response to Soviet invasion of Afghanistan, **1980** 29-30
  end of cold war, **1989** 207-212
  no-first-use defense policy, **1982** 305-315
Kennard, William E.
  ballot initiatives, **1999** 6
  telecommunications industry mergers, **1998** 341

Kennedy, Anthony M.
abortion
antiabortion demonstrations, **2000** 433
parental consent for teenage, **1990** 387-407
partial birth, **2000** 429, 432, 442-444
state restrictions on, **1989** 366-367
abortion clinics
blockades, **1993** 93, 101-102
protesters and RICO law, **1994** 33
protests, **1994** 312, 322-326
affirmative action, **2003** 362, 363, 376-381
federal government plans, **1995** 308, 310-319
asset forfeiture
drug trafficking, **1993** 432-438
pornography seized, **1993** 432, 440-446
campaign finance reform, **2003** 1160, 1165, 1171-1172
child pornography, **1990** 239-245
coastal property rights, **1992** 616
coerced confessions, **1991** 175, 182-184
compensation law, **1991** 814-815, 823-825
congressional term limits, **1995** 260-261, 270
damages for tobacco-related ills, **1992** 564
deaf parochial student, **1993** 399-403
death penalty
for juvenile offenders, **2002** 358; **2004** 797; **2005** 177, 179-180, 183-192
for the mentally retarded, **2002** 356
detentions in terrorism cases, **2004** 377, 378, 381-388, 395-396
disabilities in the workplace, **2002** 6
disability, definition of, **1999** 319, 320
discrimination by private clubs, **1988** 403
drug testing of students, **1995** 339-346
eminent domain, **2005** 363
endangered species on private lands, **1995** 359-368
entrapment in child pornography case, **1992** 322-327
faculty tenure review disclosure, **1990** 23-34
flag burning, **1989** 343-344, 350-351; **1990** 357-362
free speech, and the Internet, **1997** 445
freedom of residential signs, **1994** 290-297
gay rights discrimination, **1996** 284-286, 287-291
gay rights to march, **1995** 327-335
grandparents' rights, **2000** 289, 297-298
gun-free school zone, **1995** 184, 192-194, 260
Haitian refugee interdiction, **1992** 453, 459-468; **1993** 413-421
hate crimes, **1992** 543-551; **1993** 385-389
HIV as a disability, **1998** 379, 381-388
impeachment, Senate's authority to remove judge, **1992** 81-87
job discrimination
fetal protection, **1991** 144, 151-153
involving African Americans, **1993** 423-429
jury selection, gender discrimination, **1994** 233
legislative intent, **1993** 250-253
libel from misquotation, **1991** 318, 319-325
line-item veto, **1998** 421, 430-431
minority set-aside programs, **1989** 324; **1990** 421, 429-435
Miranda rule affirmed, **1990** 785-790
Miranda warnings, **2000** 389
nomination to Court, **1987** 720-721
Noriega phone calls dispute, **1990** 721-724
parochial school aid, **1997** 363
physician-assisted suicide, **1997** 461
pornography
child pornography and "community standards," **2002** 291
child pornography ban, **2002** 290
Internet filters in public libraries, **2003** 388, 389, 396-397
presidential elections recount, **2000** 1002-1003, 1005-1019
prison inmates, beaten by guards, **1992** 175-182
prisoner appeals, **1991** 205, 207-215
from death row, **1993** 141-148
public lands and developers, **1994** 299, 300-306
race discrimination, **1989** 321, 323
race-based redistricting, **1993** 459-474; **1995** 369, 371, 373-380; **1996** 369, 371-379, 381
religious clubs in public schools, **2001** 422
religious freedom, **1997** 407-417
religious publications, **1995** 385-395
religious symbols, **1995** 387, 396-400
right to die, **1990** 373-382
school desegregation, **1991** 24
school facilities, use by religious groups, **1993** 363-369
school prayer, **1992** 553-562; **2000** 367
school vouchers, **2002** 408
sentencing laws, **2003** 982, 984; **2004** 359, 360, 368-374
murder case sentencing, **1991** 389-391
sex offenders, right to confine, **1997** 383
sexual harassment, **1998** 439-441, 453-461; **1999** 215, 217, 227-234
at school, **1992** 188-197
in workplace, **1993** 939-944
sodomy laws, **2003** 403, 406-413
states' rights, immunity from suits, **1999** 333, 335, 336-344
student drug testing, **2002** 426
tax increase for school desegregation, **1990** 227, 228-229, 232-238
Ten Commandments displays, **2005** 377, 380-383
unreasonable searches, **2001** 409, 410, 416-419
women's right to choose abortion, **1992** 589-609
Kennedy, Carolyn Bessette, death of, **1999** 422
Kennedy, David, death of, **1999** 423
Kennedy, Donald, science and technology appointments, **2004** 843
Kennedy, Edward M. (D-Mass.)
AIDS legislation, **1987** 320
Bangladesh independence, **1972** 163-165
Carter budget, **1979** 10-11
Carter tribute to, **1980** 772, 774
Chappaquiddick incident, **1999** 422-423
church arson prevention, **1997** 306
CIA involvement in Chile, **1974** 806
civil rights Court rulings, **1989** 324
D.C. voting representation in Congress, **1978** 590
at Democratic midterm conference, **1978** 765-766, 775-777

Kennedy, Edward M. (D-Mass.) *Continued*
at Democratic national conventions, **1980** 701-712; **1984** 649; **2000** 612
Democratic Party platform, **1984** 550
draft evader pardon, **1977** 96
education reform, **2002** 42-43
Elizabeth II's visit to U.S., **1991** 248
eulogy for John F. Kennedy Jr., **1999** 422-427
food aid, **1984** 5
food safety system, **2001** 700
genetic engineering controls, **1975** 320
government-funded video news releases, **2005** 647
health insurance
catastrophic illness coverage, **1986** 1027
costs, **1998** 141
for disabled persons, **1999** 49
national health insurance, **1978** 544-545, 765-766, 776-777
IRA peace process, **2005** 509
IRA prison hunger strike, **1981** 402-404, 412-413
Iraq War, justifications for, **2003** 24; **2004** 714
Iraq War troop withdrawal, calling for, **2005** 836
JFK assassination thirtieth anniversary, **1993** 959
John Paul II, shooting of, **1981** 428
Kennedy Library dedication, **1979** 813-815, 819-821
Kennedy School of Government speech, **1991** 713-717
King holiday, **1983** 884
Kleindienst confirmation, **1972** 396, 404-406
Love Canal, **1980** 445
McGovern nomination, **1972** 590-591
Medicare reform legislation, **2003** 1119-1120; **2004** 580
on minimum wage, **1996** 564
Moral Majority speech, **1983** 817-825
nephew's date rape case, **1992** 388
"no fly" terrorist lists, **2004** 145
O'Connor confirmation hearings, **1981** 577
patient safety legislation, **1999** 782
as presidential candidate, **1979** 813-815; **1980** 771-772, 774; **1984** 648
Rehnquist appointment, **1986** 591-592
rejection of presidential race, **1974** 853-855
religious freedom, **1997** 409
same-sex marriages, **1996** 688
school choice proposal, **1991** 221
screening immigrants, **2002** 845-846
SDI, **1983** 306
Seabrook nuclear plant, opposition to, **1990** 197
Souter nomination, **1990** 617-618
START proposal, **1982** 386
Thomas confirmation hearings, **1991** 562-563
UN vote on Israeli settlements, **1980** 238
warrantless domestic surveillance, **2005** 960-961
women in combat, **1991** 497-499, 508-510
Kennedy, John F.
administration
access to federal tax returns, **1975** 856
CIA plots
against Castro, **1975** 725, 729-733, 736, 739-754, 774, 778-779, 789-792
against Trujillo, **1975** 777, 788-789
FBI, political uses of, **1975** 873, 879
assassination of, **1999** 422
acoustical analysis of, **1978** 909-911, 914, 921; **1979** 594, 601-603, 621-622
CIA involvement, **1997** 104
CIA link to, Rockefeller commission on, **1975** 409, 436
CIA materials declassified, **1992** 3, 10
conspiracy theory, **1979** 593, 595, 603-605; **1980** 596
House investigation of, **1978** 909-916; **1978** 921; **1979** 593-596; **1979** 600-615; **1980** 596
thirtieth anniversary, **1993** 959-963
Berlin Wall construction, **1986** 792-793
choice of running mate, **1988** 533
Clinton inaugural address, **1993** 130-131
inaugural address, **1973** 80; **2001** 95
on leadership, **1997** 49
Mansfield tribute to, **1973** 965-966
NSC under, **1987** 212, 214
Peace Corps, **1993** 189
presidential library dedication, **1979** 813-821
press conferences of, **1988** 842
Quayle compared to, **1988** 799, 820
tax cut proposal, **1999** 93
Thurgood Marshall's papers, **1993** 341
transfer of power, **1985** 492
White appointment to Supreme Court, **1993** 393
Kennedy, John F., Jr., eulogy for, **1999** 422-427
Kennedy, Joseph, Jr., death of, **1999** 422
Kennedy, Joseph P., III (D-Mass.)
boycott of Elizabeth II's visit, **1991** 248
on death of Robert F. Kennedy, **1979** 814
JFK assassination thirtieth anniversary, **1993** 959
liquor advertising, **1996** 772
Kennedy, Michael, death of, **1999** 423
Kennedy, Patrick F., embassy security, **1998** 557
Kennedy, Richard T., on human rights in foreign policy, **1981** 781-785
Kennedy, Robert F. (D-N.Y.)
animosity of organized crime toward, **1979** 595, 610-611, 615
assassination of, **1999** 422
CIA Castro plot, and organized crime figures, **1975** 742-744, 774-775
Kennedy Library exhibits on, **1979** 813
Kennedy, William, III, White House Travel Office, **1993** 531-532, 535-536
Kennedy Library, dedication of, **1979** 813-821
Kennedy v. Mendoza-Martinez, **1993** 434
Kennedy-Kassebaum bill. *See* Health Insurance Portability and Accountability Act
Kennesaw State College (KSC), Gingrich Renewing American Civilization course, **1997** 8, 14
Kenney, Stephen, Guantanamo Bay detainees, **2003** 110
Kennicutt, Robert, age of universe, **1994** 460, 462
Kent State University
speeches marking 1970 student deaths, **1990** 289-294
suits on deaths in demonstrations (1970), **1974** 265-270

Kenya
  drought in, **1984** 974, 984
  early human remains discovered, **1992** 136
  embassy bombings, **1998** 555-563; **1999** 53, 524, 690; **2001** 3, 617, 688; **2002** 1014-1015, 1046; **2003** 841; **2004** 520
  free elections, **2002** 447
  Green Belt Movement, **2004** 929-936
  John Paul II visit, **1985** 501
  Kbaki presidential inauguration speech, **2002** 1044-1051
  Kenya African National Union (KANU), **2002** 1044-1047
  Nairobi women's conference, **1985** 555-570
  National Rainbow Coalition (NARC), **2002** 1045
  parliamentary elections, **2004** 931
  population growth in, **1984** 530, 533; **1987** 440, 443
  Sudanese peace negotiations, **2003** 837
Kenyatta, Jomo, Kenyan leader, **2002** 1044
Kenyatta, Uhuru, Kenya presidential candidate, **2002** 1045-1047
Keohane, Nan, **1990** 353-354
Kerick, Bernard, Homeland Security Department secretary nomination, **2004** 272
Kern, Paul, detainees prison scandal, **2004** 213
Kerner, Otto, **1988** 185
Kerner Commission (1968)
  Eisenhower Foundation inner cities report, **1993** 211-233
  report, update on, **1988** 185-194; **1998** 667-668
Kerr, Andy, logging policy, **1993** 495
Kerr, Donald M., Jr., FBI crime laboratory director, **1997** 221
Kerr, Richard
  Ames espionage case, **1994** 488
  weapons of mass destruction, prewar intelligence, **2003** 874; **2004** 713
Kerrey, Bob (D-Neb.)
  Clinton and Vietnam, **1992** 156
  commission on terrorist attacks appointment, **2003** 547; **2004** 452
  homosexuals in the military, **1993** 160
  IRS reform, **1997** 663
  Social Security reform, **1998** 100
  on U.S.-Vietnam relations, **1995** 472
  war hero, **1999** 39; **2000** 918
Kerry, John (D-Mass.)
  Abu Ghraib prison scandal, **2004** 214
  campaign issues, Iraq stabilization and security, **2005** 665
  Clinton's passport search, **1992** 1047
  gay marriage issue, **2004** 40-41
  Glaspie-Hussein pre-war meeting, **1991** 162-163
  global warming, **1997** 862; **2001** 112
  health insurance coverage expansion, **2004** 983
  homosexuals in the military, **1993** 160
  Iraq War, position on, **2004** 482-483, 677
  medical malpractice, **2004** 20
  MIAs in Russia, **1992** 521
  national commission on terrorist attacks recommendations, **2004** 458
  outsourcing jobs overseas, **2004** 59
  presidential election
    campaign, **2004** 17, 478-484, 773-779
    campaign issues
      "backdoor draft," **2004** 787
      bioterrorism protection, **2004** 641
      environment, **2004** 664
      gay marriage, **2004** 40-41
      jobs and employment, **2004** 59
      stem cell research, **2004** 160, 842
    concession speech, **2004** 773-774, 779-781
    debates, **2004** 483, 675-708
    endorsements, by Nobel laureates and prominent scientists, **2004** 842-843
    nomination acceptance speech, **2004** 485-493
    results, **2004** 478; **2005** 41
    Vietnam service record, **2004** 480-481
  presidential elections, endorsements, union-backed, **2005** 487
  tax reform, **2004** 20
  terrorist threat alerts, **2004** 270
  U.S.-Vietnam relations, **1995** 472
  Vietnam trade embargo, **1994** 96-98
  Vietnam War record, **2004** 480-481
  Vietnam War veteran, **2000** 918
  war powers act, **1990** 665, 668-671
Kessler, David A.
  cigarette regulations, **1995** 670-679
  drug safety review, **2004** 854
  FDA regulations, testimony on, **1996** 598-599
  nicotine levels in cigarettes, **1994** 205, 208-213
  silicone breast implants, **1992** 367-373; **1995** 515-523
  smoking and health panel, **1997** 334
  smoking ban proposal, **1994** 205-206
  tobacco industry conspiracy, **2000** 538
  tobacco product regulation, **2000** 556
Kessler, Gladys
  Clinton executive order on striking workers, **1995** 131
  secret domestic detentions, **2002** 835; **2003** 316
Kevorkian, Jack (Dr. Death), physician-assisted suicide cases, **1994** 502-503; **1996** 122; **1997** 329; **1999** 442
Keyes, Alan L., **1985** 556
Keyishian v. Board of Regents, **1990** 31, 32-33; **1991** 265
Keynes, John Maynard, **1999** 93
Keyworth, George A., **1982** 813-814
KGB (Government Committee for State Security)
  Daniloff arrest, **1986** 820-821, 826-827
  technology espionage, **1985** 610-612
  travel rules for U.S. diplomats, **1986** 268
Khadzhimba, Raul, South Ossetia leader for independence from Georgia, **2003** 1046
Khalid v. Bush, **2005** 448
Khalifa, Muhammad Jamal, **2001** 106
Khalil, Hassan, Hariri assassination, UN investigation, **2005** 691
Khalil, Mustafa, **1979** 225
Khalizad, Zalmay
  Afghanistan, UN peacekeeping forces, **2002** 18-19
  U.S. ambassador to Iraq, **2005** 946

Khamenei, Ayatollah Ali (Iranian president)
  Ahmadinejad endorsement for president, **2005** 591
  denounces Guardian Council, **2003** 1032
  Iran elections, **2004** 871
  Iran nuclear weapons program, **2003** 1028
  Iranian Islamist cleric leader, **2005** 589
  Iran-Iraq truce, **1988** 531-532
  Rushdie death threat, **1998** 688, 689
  September 11 terrorist attacks, response to, **2001** 625, 793-796
Khan, Mohammad Sidique, London terrorist bombing suspect, **2005** 396
Khan, Muhammad Naeem Noor, al Qaeda operative captured, **2004** 271
Kharrzi, Kamal, Iranian foreign minister, **2001** 796; **2002** 34
Khashoggi, Adnan
  U.S. arms sales to Iran, **1986** 1052
  U.S. indictment with Marcoses, **1988** 867-872
Khashoggi, Jamal, *al-Watan* editor fired, **2003** 234
Khatami, Mohammad
  Iran nuclear weapons program, **2003** 1026; **2004** 869
  Iran political reforms, **2003** 1031-1032, 1130; **2005** 589-590
  Iran presidential election, **1997** 284-289; **1998** 687, 688; **2004** 871; **2005** 589-793-794
  Iran reform movement, **2002** 34, 742; **2004** 871
  UN address "Dialogue Among Civilizations," **2001** 793-801
  U.S.-Iran relations, **1998** 687; **2001** 793-794
  al-Khatanii, Mohamed, detainee abused by interrogators, **2004** 381
Kherchtou, L'Houssaine, **2001** 804
Khieu Samphan, **1998** 972-975
Khmer Rouge (Cambodian guerillas), **1990** 561-562; **1991** 691-693
  collapse of the, **1998** 971-975
Khodorkovsky, Mikhail
  Russian entrepreneur case, **2003** 247-248
  Yukos chairman arrested and jailed, **2004** 569; **2005** 302-303
Khomeini, Ayatollah Ruhollah
  acceptance of cease-fire with Iraq, **1988** 529-532
  anti-Israeli sentiments, **2005** 591
  death of, **1989** 97, 315-318; **1998** 688
  exile of, **1978** 701-702
  human rights in Iran, **1984** 162-163
  Iran-Iraq War, **1984** 748-749, 754
  Islamic leader of Iraq, **2003** 1190; **2005** 589
  regime of, **1980** 190, 196
  Rushdie death threat, **1989** 95-98; **1998** 687
  strengthened position of, **1979** 871
  support for terrorism, **1987** 609-610
  U.S. hostages
    conditions for release of, **1980** 999-1000; **1981** 145-146, 148-152
    crimes of, **1979** 867-870, 873-875
  U.S. relations with, **1986** 1014
Khouri, Rami
  Arab intellectual freedom, **2003** 957
  on Iraq and U.S. sovereignty, **2005** 273
Khrushchev, Nikita S.
  Berlin crisis, **1986** 793
  Gorbachev's praise for, **1987** 857-859, 863-864
  Hungarian uprising, **1989** 340-341
  ouster of (1964), **1987** 80, 857-858, 863
  personality of, Nixon on, **1977** 341
  relations with Hoxha, **1985** 327
  Sakharov appeal to on nuclear testing, **1981** 748
  on Solzhenitsyn's work, **1972** 728; **1974** 130
Kidan, Adam, fraud charges, **2005** 633, 635
Kidder, Peabody & Co., insider trading case, **1987** 882, 885
Kikhja, Mansur R., **1975** 646
Kilberg, William, on sexual harassment policy, **1998** 441
Kilburn, Peter, **1989** 316; **1991** 753
Killen, Edgar Ray, civil rights workers slayings conviction, **2005** 353-361
Kilpatrick, Dean, **1992** 386
Kilpatrick, James J., **1989** 345
Kim, Jim Yong, WHO HIV drug therapy program, **2005** 51
Kim Chong Il, **1987** 199
Kim Dae-jung
  death sentence for, **1980** 825-828
  and democratic reforms in Korea, **1987** 583-584, 586, 588, 591
  Japan relations, **1998** 541
  No Gun Ri (Korean War) incident, **2001** 38
  Nobel Peace Prize for "Sunshine Policy" with North Korea, **2000** 867; **2001** 268; **2002** 731
  North Korea relations, **1999** 576; **2000** 193
  North-South Korea talks, **2001** 270-271; **2002** 268; **2005** 606
  North-South Korea reunification efforts, **2000** 359-364, 679, 866, 867; **2001** 268-269; **2002** 731
  release from house arrest, **1986** 109
  South Korean economic crisis, **1997** 894
  South Korean elections, **1997** 835, 892-897
Kim Dong Jo, influence buying in Congress by, **1977** 769-771, 775-786, 790-793; **1978** 846-849, 860, 887-894
Kim Hyung Wook, testimony in Korean influence-buying inquiry, **1977** 794-802
Kim Il Chol, North Korean-U.S. relations, **2002** 736
Kim Il Sung
  death of, **1994** 603; **2000** 868; **2001** 267
  dialogue with South Korea, **1972** 523; **1988** 853-859
  human rights in North Korea, **1987** 198
  and Korean War, **1995** 507
Kim Jae Kyu, **1979** 895-904
Kim Jong Il
  North Korean nuclear weapons program, **2005** 604
  North Korean president, **1994** 603
  North-South Korea reunification efforts, **2000** 193, 359-364, 679
  North-South Korea talks, **1997** 895; **2001** 268, 270-271; **2005** 606
  regime collapse, **2005** 609
  Six-Party Talks, **2005** 606
  state visit of Madeleine Albright, **2000** 866-872
  U.S. relations, **2002** 736; **2003** 36

visit to China, **2001** 272
Kim Jong Pil, South Korean prime minister, **1997** 894
Kim San Keun, **1977** 786-789
Kim Sou Hwan, Stephen, **1986** 318; **1987** 585
Kim Un Yong, International Olympics Committee investigations, **1999** 106, 108
Kim Young Sam
and democratic reforms in Korea, **1987** 584, 586
Korean War veterans memorial dedication, **1995** 506, 508-509
release from house arrest, **1986** 109
South Korean president, **1997** 892, 893
Kimche, David
Israeli-Lebanese security agreement, **1983** 471-477
U.S. arms sales to Iran, **1986** 1015
Kincannon, Charles Louis, Hispanic largest minority group in U.S., **2003** 349
King, Angela, women's rights, **2000** 325
King, Carolyn Dineen, sentencing laws, **2003** 983
King, Coretta Scott, at March on Washington thirtieth anniversary, **1993** 677, 679
King, Jeffrey C., on maternal mortality, **1996** 344-345
King, Martin Luther, Jr.
assassination of
conspiracy theory, **1979** 616-619
FBI investigation of, **1977** 113-123
House investigation of, **1978** 909-912, 916-917, 921; **1979** 593, 595, 616-621
celebration of, on Inauguration Day, **1997** 22, 25
FBI campaign against, **1975** 874, 881
FBI surveillance of, **1977** 113-115, 120-121; **2002** 562
Justice Department campaign against, **1978** 910-911, 917
March on Washington, **1993** 583-584, 677, 679
March on Washington and "I Have a Dream" speech, **2002** 240
national holiday honoring, **1983** 883-888; **1988** 249
Nobel Peace prize and, **1983** 885
King, Peter (R-N.Y.), Davis-Bacon Act, reinstatement of, **2005** 489
King, Rodney
beating, **1991** 403; **1992** 407-429; **1993** 214
sentencing of LAPD officers, **1993** 631-651
King, Rufus, **1984** 20
King, Tom, **1985** 726
King, William Lyon MacKenzie, **1984** 407, 410
King, Willie, victim of medical mistake, **1999** 782
King v. St. Vincent's Hospital, **1993** 252
Kingsley Books v. Brown, **1993** 444
Kinkel, Kipland P. "Kip," **1998** 736
Kinkel, Klaus, NATO expansion, **1996** 657
Kinnock, Neil
European Commission commissioner, **1999** 156, 158
Thatcher resignation, **1990** 749, 750
Kirby, Robert G., **1988** 11
Kirchner, Nestor
Argentine debt relief, **2005** 768-769
Argentine presidential elections, **2003** 824-826
Summit of the Americas, **2005** 767
Kirghizia
Alma-Ata Declaration, **1991** 804-806
Commonwealth Pact, **1991** 803-804
Soviet Union restructuring plans, **1991** 532-533
Kirillin, Vladimir, **1980** 104
Kiriyenko, Sergei, Russian economy, **1998** 603, 604
Kirk, Paul G., Jr.
Democratic Party platform, **1988** 557
parties' primary rules, **1986** 1067
Kirkingburg v. Albertson's, **1999** 319
Kirkland, Lane, **1992** 346
bankruptcy and labor contracts, **1984** 183
Carter budget, **1980** 111
at March on Washington thirtieth anniversary, **1993** 679
Pittston coal strike settled, **1990** 19-22
retirement from AFL-CIO, **1995** 680-681
Kirkpatrick, Jeane J.
Haig disputes with, **1982** 562
on Israeli raid on Iraqi nuclear plant, **1981** 508, 515-518
nuclear test ban treaty, **1999** 608
at Republican conventions, **1984** 728-729; **1988** 590
UN appointment of, feminists on, **1983** 756
UN ineffectiveness, **1982** 770
Kirsch, Irwin, **1993** 738-739
Kirsch, Philippe, ICC (World Court) presiding judge, **2003** 100
Kiser, Jackson L., VMI all-male policy decision, **1991** 309-316
Kissinger, Henry A.
achievements of, Dole on, **1976** 784-785
Africa policies of U.S., **1976** 287-295
Arab-Israeli peace negotiations
Egyptian-Israeli cease-fire, **1973** 931-937
Egyptian-Israeli disengagement, **1974** 29-31; **1976** 170
impact of Arafat's UN speech on, **1974** 920
Israeli-Syrian disengagement, **1974** 435-436
in shuttle diplomacy, **1975** 575
U.S. and Soviet roles in, **1973** 881-896
Central America policy, commission recommendations, **1984** 31, 33
chairman national commission on terrorist attacks resignation, **2002** 990, 996-997; **2003** 547; **2004** 451
CIA activities in Chile, **1974** 805; **1975** 875
Cuban foreign policy, **1998** 33
developing countries
exports of, **1976** 299-301, 304-305, 307-310
investment in, **1976** 299-315, 427
Moynihan's attack on, **1975** 646
as Ford's secretary of state, **1974** 689, 696
foreign aid, Nixon requests for, **1974** 278-280
foreign policy
congressional intervention in, **1975** 4-5, 10-13
focuses for year, **1973** 515-516
France, U.S. relations with, **1974** 981
gold valuation, **1974** 982
Gorbachev foreign policy initiatives, **1989** 298-299
ILO, U.S. withdrawal from, **1983** 969
Indo-Pakistani conflict, U.S. position on, **1972** 23-39
intelligence documents, withholding from Congress, **1976** 115-116

Kissinger, Henry A. *Continued*
International Olympics Committee investigations, **1999** 109
Iran hostage crisis, **1979** 880-881
and Israeli protest of Scranton's UN remarks, **1976** 192
Kennan's analysis of cold war, **1989** 208
military coup in Chile, **2002** 606
Namibian independence, **1976** 613
national security wiretaps, **1974** 449-450, 487-495; **1976** 159-168
NATO
news conference, **1976** 907
proposed new charter for, **1973** 487-495
reinvigoration of relations within, **1974** 529-530
U.S. commitment to, **1976** 346
Nixon funeral remarks, **1994** 240-241
Nixon Middle East trip, **1974** 450
Nixon on, in Frost interviews, **1977** 322, 342-346, 354-355, 361-362
Nixon resignation, **1974** 684, 693
nomination to secretary of state, and retention at NSC, **1973** 737, 739
North Vietnam trip, implementation of peace accords, **1973** 193, 195-196
nuclear test ban treaty, **1999** 601
oil crisis
EC proposed cooperation with Arab states, **1974** 186
emergency fund for hard-hit consuming nations, **1974** 982
long-term supply, **1974** 124
military force in, **1975** 3-5, 8-9
Panama Canal treaties, **1977** 593
peace as U.S. goal, **1973** 809-816
PRC
normalization of relations with, **1973** 291-300
prodemocracy movement in, **1989** 278
producers associations, dangers of, **1974** 256
Rhodesia
peace plan for, **1977** 585
settlement negotiations, **1976** 613, 721-722
Rogers feud with, Nixon on, **1977** 344-345
SALT agreements, **1972** 460-463
strategic balance in, **1972** 766
SALT II ratification, **1979** 417
SALT negotiations, **1974** 536-537
and earlier promises on cruise missiles, **1977** 244, 250, 252, 254
on Solzhenitsyn
asylum for, **1974** 129
receiving at White House, **1975** 481
South Africa's apartheid policy, **1976** 678
Soviet relations
noninterference in internal affairs, **1973** 792, 796-799
trade concessions linked to emigration policy, **1974** 901-906
testimony on Ellsberg, **1974** 664
U.S. foreign commitments, credibility of after Vietnam, **1975** 252-262, 272
Vance as successor to, **1976** 878, 886, 888-889
Vietnam peace accords, **1973** 116-117, 120-133
Vietnam peace negotiations
deadlock in, **1972** 941-951
secret, **1972** 127-133
settlement provisions, **1972** 867-868, 871-878
Thieu on, **1975** 283-284, 286
Vietnam war
POWs and, **1993** 113-114, 117, 122
report on status of (1969), **1972** 361-379
and U.S. domestic reconciliation, **1975** 251, 254-261
use of French intermediaries with North Vietnam, **1972** 491, 495-496
Vladivostok accord, **1974** 957
world economic cooperation, **1974** 834-835, 845-851; **1975** 4, 13-14, 587-603
Kissinger Commission on Central America, **1984** 31-52, 93, 112
Kittinger, Joseph W., Jr., Roswell incident, **1997** 396, 401
Kitty Hawk, racial unrest aboard, **1972** 901
Kitzhaber, John, physician-assisted suicide, **1997** 463; **2001** 293
Kitzmiller v. Dover Area School District, **2005** 1014-1026
Klarsfeld, Serge, on Barbie trial, **1987** 518-519
Klaus, Patsy, **1993** 375
Klausner, Richard
cancer death rates, **1996** 790
mammogram advocate, **1997** 144, 145-149
on tamoxifen trials, **1998** 194, 197-198, 202
Klebold, Dylan, Columbine High School shooter, **1999** 179; **2000** 875-876; **2001** 347, 348, 352
Klein, Herbert G., **1973** 630, 635
Klein, Jacques
Liberia and U.S. intervention, **2003** 770
UN mission in Liberia, **2003** 772
Klein, Joel, Microsoft Corp. antitrust ruling, **1999** 658-659
Klein, Robert N., II, California stem cell research initiative, **2004** 161-162
Kleindienst, Richard G.
confirmation and reaffirmation as attorney general, **1972** 395-406
conviction, **1975** 653, 666
on disclosure of wiretap transcripts, **1972** 486
guilty plea, **1974** 407-410
ITT antitrust suit, **1974** 5
Liddy's appeal to for Watergate defendants, **1974** 158, 162, 348
resignation, **1973** 499, 502, 504, 509
sentencing, **1974** 409; **1975** 143
Kleindienst v. Mandel, **1992** 463
Kleinfield, Andrew J., **1997** 184
K-Mart, corporate scandal, **2003** 332, 340
Knauff v. Shaughnessy, United States ex rel., **1992** 467
Knight, Hal M., **1973** 729
Knight Foundation Commission on Intercollegiate Athletics, **1991** 129-142
Kobuk Valley National Monument, **1978** 731, 739
Koch, Edward I.
amnesty for Vietnam draft evaders, **1973** 194
mayoral election, **1977** 568

Statue of Liberty centennial, **1986** 697
Koch, Robert, and tuberculosis, **1993** 852
Kocharian, Robert, shootings in Armenian parliament, **1999** 639-642
Koecher, Hana, **1986** 93
Koecher, Karl, **1986** 93
Kogut, Alan, **1992** 381
Koh, Harold Hongju
race relations, **2000** 772
on violence in Kosovo, **1999** 805-806
Kohl, Helmut
aid for Soviets, **1990** 467-468
arms reductions in Europe, **1989** 298
Berlin Wall anniversary, **1986** 791-792, 794-799
Bush on working relationship, **1990** 482
campaign finance scandal, **2005** 874-875
Chazov's Nobel Prize, **1985** 782
economic summits, **1986** 438; **1987** 526; **1988** 392
Denver, **1997** 342
Munich, **1992** 638, 639
Tokyo, **1993** 542
euro currency plans, **1998** 272-273
German economic reforms, **1998** 816-817
German guilt and remorse for war, **1989** 487-497
German reunification, **1989** 627, 630-634; **1990** 599, 682; **2005** 873
German unification, **1998** 816
on Holocaust and German reunification, **1990** 105-106, 111-113
Libyan chemical weapons plant, **1989** 28
mentorship of Merkel, **2005** 874-875
Reagan's Bitburg visit, **1985** 358
Reagan's consultation with, **1985** 709
reelection defeat, **1998** 273, 815; **1999** 77
Kohl, Herbert (D-Wis.)
investigation of Medal of Honor award, **1989** 699
Thomas confirmation hearings, **1991** 571-575
war powers debate, **1990** 667-668
Kohlberg Kravis Roberts & Co., and RJR Nabisco buy-out, **1988** 922
Kohler, Foy D., **1972** 493-495
Köhler, Horst
aid to Argentina, **2002** 85
German elections, legality of, **2005** 875
German president, **2005** 874
WTO trade talks, **2003** 744
Kohut, Andrew
on public opinion of the economy, **2005** 137
Social Security indexing plan, **2005** 114
U.S. foreign relations, overseas views of, **2005** 579
Koivisto, Mauno, **1989** 400
Koizumi, Junichiro
aid on Africa, **2002** 450
China-Japan dispute, **2005** 621
economic reform plans, **2001** 304-313
election to prime minister, **2001** 304, 305-306
Japanese economic reform, **2002** 692
North Korean state visit, **2002** 732
Kokinda, United States v., **1991** 265
Kokum, Bajram, as Kosovo prime minister, **2005** 856
Kolb, Ben, death of, **1999** 782
Kolbe, Jim (R-Ariz.)
Republican Party convention speech, **2000** 512
Social Security reform, **1998** 101
Kolbe, Lloyd, **1992** 340
Kolesnikov, Dmitri, Russian submarine disaster, **2000** 637
Kollar-Kotelly, Colleen
Guantanamo Bay detentions, **2002** 832-833; **2003** 108
Microsoft antitrust case, **2001** 778, 780; **2002** 797-817
Koller, Arnold, **1997** 259
Kolvenbach, Peter-Hans, **1984** 761
Kondracke, Morton M., in presidential debate, **1984** 877, 883-885, 897-898
Konner, Joan, **1990** 295-299
Konopliv, Alex, gravity map of the moon, **1998** 117
Kony, Joseph, Lord's Resistance Army spiritual leader, **2003** 471, 474
Koo-do, Chung, No Gun Ri (Korean War) incident, **2001** 38
Kooijmans, Pieter, Israeli security wall, World Court ruling on, **2004** 310
Koon, Carl B., **1989** 669
Koon, Stacey C., King case indictment and sentencing, **1993** 409, 631-651
Koop, C. Everett
on AIDS education, **1986** 889; **1987** 320
antiabortion rally, **1985** 53
antismoking campaign, **1989** 31-40
gun violence report, **1992** 493-498; **1993** 872
involuntary smoking, **1986** 1079-1081
nicotine addiction, **1988** 309-322
partial-birth abortion ban, **2003** 1001
smoking and cancer, **1982** 164
smoking and health, **1997** 332, 334
smoking in the workplace, **1985** 809-811
Koop, James Charles, antiabortion protester, **1998** 811
Kopechne, Mary Jo, death of, **1999** 423
Koplan, Jeffrey, childhood obesity, **2004** 654
Kopp, James Charles, abortion shooting, **2001** 130
Koppel, Ted, Brzezinski interview, **1979** 978-981
Koran, **1990** 280
Korb, Lawrence, on homosexuals in the military, **1993** 154
Korea, Democratic Republic of (North Korea). *See* North Korea
Korea, Republic of (South Korea). *See* South Korea
Koreagate, House influence-buying investigation, **1977** 769-819; **1978** 845-908; **1979** 897-898; **1980** 485-487
Korean Central Intelligence Agency (KCIA), involvement in influence buying in Congress, **1977** 769-819; **1978** 846-847, 856, 860-868, 881-884, 888-896, 901
Korean demilitarized zone, Reagan speech to U.S. troops, **1983** 893, 895
Korean War (1950-1953), **1972** 523; **1988** 853, 855-856
background, **1995** 507-508
land mine warfare, **1995** 50
No Gun Ri incident, **1999** 552-558; **2001** 33-51
use of incendiary weapons, **1972** 838
veterans' memorial dedication, **1995** 506-511
Korean-Americans, Los Angeles riots and, **1992** 412, 417, 423

Korematsu v. United States, **1994** 326; **1995** 313
Koresh, David, Branch Davidian cult leader, **1993** 293-295, 819-840; **1997** 123; **1999** 480
Koroma, Ernest, Sierra Leone presidential candidate, **2002** 248
Koryagin, Anatoly, **1985** 782-783
Koskinen, John A., Y2K conversion, **1998** 543-544; **1999** 761, 764; **2000** 3-15
Kosor, Jadranka, Croatia presidential elections, **2005** 857
Kosovo
  Albanian Muslims/Kosovar Albanians, **2001** 554-555; **2005** 855
  Alliance for the Future of Kosovo, **2004** 952
  Democratic League, **2004** 952
  Democratic Party, **2004** 952
  economic situation, **2003** 1151-1152
  elections, **2001** 819-825
  human trafficking, **2002** 335
    NATO and UN peacekeeping forces engaged in, **2004** 893
  Kosovo Force (KFOR), NATO peacekeeping force, **2003** 1138, 1140, 1141; **2004** 138-139, 949-950
  political situation, **2003** 1138-1154; **2005** 851, 854-856
  political situation report, **2000** 141-157
  property rights, **2003** 1152
  Serb minority, **2003** 1140-1141
  UN Mission in Kosovo (UNMIK), **2003** 1138-1154; **2004** 785, 949-964; **2005** 855-856
  UN "standards before status," **2004** 950-951
  UN war crimes tribunal, **1998** 831; **2001** 826-848
Kosovo Liberation Army, **2001** 820; **2003** 1142, 1144; **2004** 952
Kosovo Protection Corps (KPC), **2003** 1142, 1153-1154
Kosovo war
  human rights violations, **1999** 802-816
  Milosevic's role in, **2000** 834
  NATO air strikes against Serbian forces, **1999** 119, 122; **2000** 143, 834; **2001** 819
    Clinton announcement, **1999** 134-143
    UNSC resolution on, **1999** 285-296
  Racak massacre, **1999** 135
  rape of women and children, **2001** 957
  Srebrenica massacre, **1999** 735-752, 860; **2001** 826-827, 899; **2005** 851, 853-854
  UN economic assistance, **1999** 429
  UN peacekeeping mission (United Nations Mission in Kosovo, *or* UNMIK), **2000** 141, 144-151; **2001** 554-555, 820-821
  UN situation report, **1998** 827-841
  U.S. involvement, **1999** 601; **2000** 599
Koss, Mary P., **1992** 386
Kostunica, Voislav
  on extradition of Milosevic, **2001** 829
  Kosovo independence, opposition to, **2004** 952; **2005** 856
  Serbian political situation, **2003** 60
  Serbian presidential candidate, **2003** 58; **2004** 955-956
  Serbian prime minister, **2004** 955; **2005** 856
  Srebrenica massacre
    tenth anniversary memorial, **2005** 854
    war criminals arrested, **2005** 854
  Yugoslavian presidential elections, **2000** 141; **2001** 827, 831; **2003** 56, 58
  Yugoslavian presidential inauguration, **2000** 833-839
Kosygin, Alexei N., **1972** 491
Kotze, Petrus, **1982** 797-798
Koubriti, Karim, terrorist-related conviction, **2004** 273
Kouchner, Bernard, UN peacekeeping mission in Kosovo, **1999** 287-288; **2000** 145-146; **2001** 820
Kouri, Alberto, Peruvian government corruption, **2000** 925
Kovalev, Anatoly G., collects Nobel for Gorbachev, **1990** 796-797
Kowloon Peninsula, return of to China, **1984** 1045, 1047-1048
Kozlowski, L. Dennis, Tyco International scandal, **2002** 398; **2004** 422
Kozyrev, Andrei V., **1992** 524
KPMG, federal oversight, **2004** 423
KPMG Peat Marwick, volunteer program, **1997** 240
Kraehenbuehl, Pierre, Iraqi prison abuse scandal, **2004** 211
Kraft Foods Inc., advertising of snack foods for children, **2005** 7
Kramer, Victor, **1989** 241
Krause, Allison, **1990** 289, 291
Krause v. Rhodes, **1974** 265-270
Krauthammer, Charles, on California stem cell research initiative, **2004** 162
Kravchenko, Yuri F.
  Gongadze case investigations, **2005** 66-67
  suicide death of, **2005** 67
Kravchuk, Leonid, START I ratification, **1993** 19
Kreisky, Bruno, **1974** 449
Krenz, Egon, **1989** 626, 646
Kreps, Juanita M., **1976** 878-879
  Commission on the Future of Worker-Management Relations member, **1995** 15
Krikalev, Sergei, **1998** 932
Krim, Mathilde
  on AIDS commission report, **1988** 417
  on AIDS contagion, **1986** 889
Kristallnacht, anniversary of, **1989** 488
Kristof, Nicholas D., anthrax attacks, reporting on, **2004** 443
Kristol, William
  Lott resignation, **2002** 970
  Miers nomination, **2005** 562
  Social Security reform, **2005** 112-113
  U.S.-China relations, **2001** 250
Krogh, Egil, Jr.
  Ellsberg break-in, **1974** 205-207, 209-210, 412
    as covert operation, **1974** 662, 664
  sentencing, **1974** 33-40
Kropp, Art, **1987** 719
Krstic, Radislav, Srebrenica massacre indictment, **2001** 826-827
Krueger, Alan B., minimum wage, **1996** 564
Krueger, Anne, Argentine debt relief, **2003** 827

Kruger, James, **1982** 798
Krugman, Paul, on California recall election, **2003** 1006
Kryuchkov, Vladimir A.
  anti-Western speeches, **1990** 808, 826
  Soviet coup attempt, **1991** 515, 517
Krzyzewski, Mike, **1989** 216
Ku Klux Klan
  church arson cases, **1997** 302
  church bombing trial (Birmingham, 1963), **2002** 239-246
  civil rights workers slayings, **2005** 354, 355
  religious symbols, **1995** 387, 396-404
Kubicina, Kathy, **1989** 518
Kuchma, Leonid
  nuclear weapons treaty, **1994** 364
  as Ukrainian president, **2004** 1001, 1002; **2005** 65
Kucinich, Dennis J. (D-Ohio)
  on Democratic Party platform, **2000** 611
  presidential candidate, **2004** 479
Kuhlik, Bruce, prescription drug advertising, **2002** 948
Kujawa, Artur, **1985** 121
Kulkov, Felix
  dissident freed by Kyrgyzstan protesters, **2005** 434
  as Kyrgyzstan security services acting head, **2005** 434-435
  parliamentary elections, **2005** 435
Kumar, Sanjay, securities fraud and obstruction of justice conviction, **2004** 423
Kumaratunga, Chadrika (Sri Lankan president)
  assassination attempt, **2002** 93, 95
  Sri Lanka peace process, **2002** 95
Küng, Hans, **1986** 757
Kunin, Madeleine M., on adult literacy, **1993** 738
Kunkel, Dale, television rating system, **1997** 528
Kupolati, Rufus M., **1999** 861
Kurban, Ira J., **1987** 255
Kurdish peoples
  human rights abuses, **1990** 136-137
  Iraq situation report, **1996** 680-686
  and Iraqi chemical weapons, **1996** 740
  Iraqi suppression of, **1991** 191-192
Kurdistan Workers Party, unlawful support for, **2003** 612
Kurylo, Michael, on ozone depletion, **1992** 77-80
Kusa, Musa, Libyan weapons and U.S. sanctions, **2003** 1221
Kushner, Gary, Espy resignation, **1994** 405
Kusnetsov, Vasily V., **1977** 749
Kutz, Gregory D., weapons materials security exercise, **2003** 902, 907-910
Kuwait
  Arab League support for in Persian Gulf crisis, **1987** 870, 873
  Bush liberation announcement, **1991** 104-105
  chemical weapons treaty, **1993** 72
  elections, **2003** 961; **2005** 272
  Iraq invasion of, **2003** 1190
  Iraq War, support for, **2003** 138, 140
  Iraqi invasion, **1990** 533-543; **1994** 431
  Iraqi troop buildup, **1994** 431-435
  missing in action in Iraq, **2000** 589-591
  national security needs review, **1993** 702, 710, 712
  OPEC oil price cut, **1981** 799
  OPEC oil price increase, **1976** 938
  Sheik Jaber's UN address, **1990** 655-660
  terrorist attack on American Embassy in, **1983** 934
  U.S. military readiness, **1994** 528, 531, 533
  U.S. protection of Persian Gulf vessels, **1987** 793-794; **1988** 705
  voting rights for women, **2005** 272
Kweder, Sandra L., FDA drug safety system, congressional testimony, **2004** 854, 861-866
Kyi, Aung San Suu, Nobel Peace Prize recipient, **2002** 982
Kyl, Jon (R-Ariz.)
  chemical weapons treaty, **1996** 741, 742
  computer security issues, **1998** 678
  homeland security plan, congressional review, **2002** 533
Kyllo v. United States, **2001** 407-419
Kyoto Protocol on Climate Change (UN treaty), **1998** 945, 947; **2000** 337, 341-342; **2001** 109-115
  Bonn agreement, **2001** 114-115
  Bush opposition to, **2001** 109, 112-113, 215, 516, 677; **2002** 298, 595, 597; **2003** 861-862; **2004** 827, 828; **2005** 920
  credits for greenhouse gas emissions, **2002** 302
  EU ratification, **2002** 303-304
  greenhouse gas emissions limits, **2002** 594
  international debate on, **2002** 302-304; **2003** 864-866
  Marrakech negotiations, **2001** 115
  ratification and implementation, **2004** 828-830
  Russia
    opposition to, **2003** 862
    ratification, **2004** 827, 829
  UN Climate Change Conference (Montreal), **2005** 922-924, 927-930
Kyrgyzstan
  parliamentary elections, **2005** 434-435
  political uprising in, **2005** 428, 433-436
  refugees from Uzbekistan, **2005** 431-432
  U.S. base, **2005** 433
Kyrgz Republic, human trafficking, **2002** 346

L

La Bella, Charles, campaign finance investigations, **1998** 891
La Force, J. Clayborn, Jr., **1984** 4
Laboa, José Sebastian, **1989** 701-702
Labor Department
  civil rights enforcement by, **1983** 914-915
  coal miners' strike, **1978** 113, 115-118, 121, 124
  Donovan investigations, **1982** 587-596
  employee rights in dangerous workplaces, **1980** 199-207
  federal rules applied to local public agencies, **1985** 167-187
  OSHA safety inspections, warrants for, **1978** 339-353
  productivity of workers, **1992** 14
  women's earnings report, **2001** 547-553

Labor Department *Continued*
worker health protection, costs of regulating, **1981** 491-505
Labor market, developments in, **1999** 97-102; **2003** 81-84
Labor unions
See also Work force; Workers; Workplace
AFL-CIO split by several unions, **2005** 485-497
air controllers' strike, **1981** 621-629
anti-Wal-Mart campaign, **2005** 487, 488, 735-737
coal miners' strike and settlement, **1978** 111-124
contracts with, and bankruptcy of companies, **1984** 181-199
corruption in, **1986** 179-180, 200-210
Democratic Party commitment to, **1984** 550
discriminatory practices of, **1986** 651-667
employer wage and benefit concessions, **2005** 486
for farm workers, California law on, **1975** 377-399
federal employees
right to join, **1978** 138-140, 144
strikes by, **1981** 621-629, 805
and foreign competition, **1973** 380
protection from, **1988** 339, 345
freedom of members to resign, **1985** 415-429
hospital construction costs, cooperation in stabilizing, **1972** 922, 927
John Paul II on role of, **1981** 695-696, 713-714; **1987** 556-560
labor movement advances, **1999** 630-638
longshoremen's strike, **1972** 385, 389
as measure of human rights, State Department report on, **1983** 182
for medical profession, **1999** 632-633
membership declining, **2005** 486, 487
on minimum and youth wage, **1983** 786
Pittston coal strike settled, **1990** 19-22
in Poland
formation of, **1980** 793-802
Solidarity activities, **1981** 882-883; **1983** 926-932; **1987** 183-187
power of, Thatcher government on, **1979** 379-380, 382, 385-386
protection from workplace hazards, **1985** 810; **1986** 1080
right-to-work laws, Republican Party platform on, **1988** 616, 645-646
seniority, and affirmative action, **1984** 365-385
sex discrimination in, EEOC guidelines on, **1972** 313
skilled labor needs, **1990** 82, 99-101
steel industry agreement with, **1973** 437-444
union political activity, **1992** 345-351
and U.S. economic policies, U.S. bishops on, **1984** 958, 965
wage increases obtained by, economic impact of, **1972** 964; **1975** 638-640
WTO and, **1999** 799-800
Laborers' International Union of North America, **2005** 487
Labor-Management Committee, White House, **1974** 878
Labor-management relations
and economic growth, Democratic Party platform on, **1984** 582-583
future of, **1995** 15-23
steel industry agreement, **1973** 437-444
Laboulaye, Edouard-Réne de, **1986** 699
Labrecque, Thomas G., **1977** 569
Lacovara, Philip A.
on release of Watergate grand jury report, **1974** 225, 227-228
resignation, **1974** 814
Lacy, Lee, **1986** 170
Lader, Phillip, on government as a conglomerate, **1993** 719
LaDuke, Winona, Green Party vice presidential candidate, **2000** 895
LaFalce, John J. (D-N.Y.), **1983** 481
Laffey, Alice L., **1988** 786
Lafontaine, Oskar
German elections, **2005** 875
German reunification, **1990** 682
Laghi, Pio, **1984** 22
Lagos Declaration for Action Against Apartheid, **1977** 824
Lagumdzija, Zlatko, Bosnia-Herzegovina constitutional reform, **2005** 858-859
LaHood, Ray (R-Ill.), House impeachment vote, **1998** 961
Lahoud, Emile
Lebanese presidential elections, **2004** 560, 561
presidential term extension, **2005** 686-687
Syria relations, **2004** 560
Laingen, R. Bruce
hostage taking in Iran, **1979** 868-869
hostages' release, **1981** 161-162
Laird, Melvin R.
Calley denied right to call as witness, **1974** 858-859
defense spending, **1972** 179
military draft, end of, **1972** 733
national security export controls, **1987** 30
national security strategy, **1986** 781
nuclear first-strike potential, **1975** 496, 502-504
privatization commission, **1988** 229
U.S. bombing of Cambodia, **1973** 729-730, 732
U.S. troop withdrawal from Vietnam, **1972** 55-59
Lake Clark National Monument, **1978** 731, 737-738
Lake Mead National Recreation Area (Nevada), **1995** 124, 126, 127
Lake Nyos, Cameroon, carbon dioxide gas eruption in, **1987** 61-77
Lakhani, Hemant, arms dealer arrested, **2003** 617
Lakwena, Alice, Uganda guerrilla spiritual leader, **2003** 471
Lalonde, Brice, **1989** 154
Lamb, Joan, **1984** 494
Lamberth, Royce, Interior Department Indian trust fund account lawsuit, **2003** 576, 578
Lamb's Chapel v. Center Moriches Union Free School District, **1995** 390-391, 393, 398, 399
Lamm, Richard D.
on physician's responsibility to terminally ill, **1984** 276
Reform Party candidate, **1996** 551
Lammert, Nobert, on Merkel as first woman German chancellor, **2005** 878

Lamy, Pascal
"Singapore issues" trade negotiations, **2003** 743-744
WTO negotiations, **2005** 411
Lance, Bert
appointment to OMB, **1976** 877-878, 881, 884-885, 889-890
and Carter bank loan investigation, **1979** 802
on Carter budget revisions, **1977** 125-126
confirmation investigation, **1977** 643-646
Senate testimony and resignation, **1977** 625-628, 640-685
Lancet, study of PBB-contaminated animal feed, **1978** 653-658
Land mines
global ban on antipersonnel land mines, **1997** 358, 844-858
Kosovo conflict, **1998** 837
military history of, **1995** 49-51
State Department report on, **1995** 46-54
treaty banning, **1997** 844-858; **1998** 541
Landau, Jack C.
editorial process, **1979** 287, 317
newsroom searches, **1978** 357
press access to pretrial hearings, **1979** 513
Lando, Barry, libel suit against CBS, **1979** 285-311, 315-318
Landrieu, Mary (D-La.)
Hurricane Katrina disaster response, **2005** 540
lynchings, Senate apology for, **2005** 356
therapeutic cloning, **2002** 515
Landrieu, Moon, **1979** 562
Landsbergis, Vytautas, **1990** 183, 185
Land-use regulation
public uses and developers, **1994** 298-310
and uncompensated takings, **1987** 531-553
Lane, Mark
on Kennedy assassination, **1978** 911
on King assassination, **1978** 912
Laney, James T., U.S.-North Korean relations, **2001** 269
Lange, David
Anzus pact, **1985** 633
French sabotage of Greenpeace ship, **1985** 632-633
Lange, Joep, on AIDS ARV treatment, **2004** 433
Langevin, Jim (D-R.I.), stem cell research supporter, **2005** 318
Languages
See also Bilingual education; English language; French language; Spanish language
in education, Canadian constitution on, **1981** 813-814, 818-819
French, and Quebec separatists, **1976** 855-856, 861; **1980** 401-410
official
Castillian in Spain, **1978** 811, 813
English in states of U.S., **1986** 959-962; **1995** 573-574, 577-578
French and English in Canada, **1981** 817-819
Russian, rejection of in Baltic states, **1989** 470
Lansbergis, Vytautis, **1991** 546
Lansky, Meyer, **1979** 595
Lantos, Tom (D-Calif.), HUD investigation by, **1989** 335-336
Lanza, Robert, cloning and stem cell research, **2002** 517; **2005** 322
Lao Tsu, on leadership, **1998** 154
Laos
chemical warfare in, **1981** 682, 684-694; **1982** 235-236, 243-244, 255-256
fighting in after Paris peace accords, **1973** 447, 450
human rights in, **1988** 884
missing Americans in, House report on, **1976** 925-936
opium growing in, **1972** 646-649
self-determination for
Vietnam peace accords on, **1973** 124, 131-132, 142-143
in Vietnam peace negotiations, **1972** 870, 872, 875
U.S. aid to, **1974** 278, 281-283; **1977** 214, 217
U.S. bombing of (1970-1972), **1973** 730
U.S. MIAs in, **1977** 209, 213-214
U.S. relations with, improvement in, **1977** 213-214
Lapidus, Lenora, drug abuse policy, **2005** 679
LaPierre, Wayne, and the National Rifle Association, **1995** 208-215
Lapointe, Archie E., **1989** 86; **1992** 86, 87
Lappe, Mark, **1993** 368
Lappin, Harley, Timothy McVeigh's execution, **2001** 433-437
Largent, Steve (R-Okla.), Clinton State of the Union address, Republican response, **1999** 58, 60-63
Larinjani, Mohammed Jiwad, **1987** 610
Larosière, Jacques de
inflation and energy crisis, **1980** 885, 894-896
Latin American debt crisis, **1983** 802, 807-814
PLO observer to IMF-World Bank meeting, **1980** 884
world economic situation, **1984** 795-799
Larre, René, **1972** 414
Larry, R. Heath, **1973** 437-438
Larsen, Terje Rod, Middle East violence, **2000** 934; **2001** 365
Larson, Richard, on tax exemptions for discriminatory schools, **1983** 491
Lashkar-e-Jhangvi (Kashmiri guerrillas), **2002** 167
Lashkar-e-Taiaba (Kashmiri guerrillas), **2002** 326; **2003** 210, 212; **2004** 539; **2005** 468
Lasser, Lawrence, Putnam Investments chairman resignation, **2003** 695
Lathrop (California), hazardous waste disposal at, **1979** 782, 785, 791, 793, 799
Latin America
See also Central America; *individual countries*
Carter trip to, **1978** 269-270, 272-280
Catholicism in, **1986** 639-649
Cuban-Soviet colonialism in, Reagan on, **1982** 180, 187-188
debtor nations of, **1984** 795-797, 799
Democratic Party platform, **1996** 645
Drug Summit Agreement (San Antonio), **1992** 201-221
economic situation, **2000** 1050; **2002** 689, 693; **2003** 754

Latin America *Continued*
fertility in, **1984** 533
free trade negotiations, **1994** 595-601
human rights in, **1985** 145-146
inter-American dialogue on, **1983** 376, 378, 383-384
U.S. promotion of, **1979** 714, 716-717, 719
Indigenous Americans Abuses Report, **1992** 897-905
inter-American dialogue on, **1983** 375-390
and liberation theology, **1984** 759-761, 764, 768, 778; **1986** 317-318
Republican Party platform, **1996** 545-546
sex trade and human trafficking, **2004** 123-124, 126, 130-131
smoking in the Americas, **1992** 267-275
terrorism in, CIA on, **1981** 465-466, 473-474
trade relations with China, **2004** 938
urbanization of, **1984** 530
U.S. and IMF aid to, **1983** 802
U.S. defense relations, **1993** 713
U.S. invasion of Panama, **1989** 703-706
U.S. policy toward
Carter on, **1981** 60, 97-99
Democratic Party platform on, **1972** 581; **1984** 637-641
Republican Party platform on, **1984** 707-709
Vance on, **1979** 713-721
U.S. relations, **2005** 765-776
during Falklands (Malvinas) war, **1982** 287
and Panama Canal treaties, **1977** 591-593; **1978** 178, 183, 185
Latin American Bishops Council (CELAM), John Paul II at, **1979** 726-727, 730-732
Latortue, Gerard
Haiti elections, **2005** 331
Haiti prime minister, **2004** 96, 97, 98; **2005** 329, 333
Latrobe, Benjamin Henry, Capitol building and, **1993** 894
Latty, Louise, **1985** 435
Latvia
Bush visit to Baltic states, **2005** 305-306
EU membership, **2004** 198
freedom statement of, **1989** 469-473
NATO membership, **2004** 136, 198; **2005** 306
Soviet restructuring plans, **1991** 532-533
U.S. diplomatic relations, **1991** 545-549
Lau v. Nichols, **1986** 961; **1998** 313
Laurel, Salvador, **1986** 308, 1038
Lautenberg, Frank J. (D-N.J.)
government-funded video news releases, **2005** 647
oil company hearings, **2005** 781
senatorial election, **2002** 821-822
terrorists and gun purchaser background checks, **2003** 159, 160
Lautenberg, Frank R. (D-N.J.), presidential commission on aviation security and terrorism, **1990** 301-310
Lavagna, Robert, Argentine economic situation, **2002** 85
Lavelle, Rita M., in congressional investigation of EPA, **1982** 966; **1983** 750-751
Law, Bernard (cardinal)
antiabortion issue, **1998** 812
posted to Vatican in Rome, **2005** 294
sexual abuse by priests, **2002** 865-866, 872; **2003** 523-525; **2004** 82, 86; **2005** 294, 865-867
resignation as archbishop of Boston, **2004** 87
Law, Sim, fraud and conspiracy charges against Lay (CEO Enron Corp.), **2004** 416
Law enforcement
See also Crime and law enforcement; Federal Bureau of Investigation (FBI); Police conduct
aggressive driving and, **1997** 554, 556-558
auto search and seizure, **1982** 425-428
"broken windows" theory, **1997** 682-683
community policing, **1997** 39; **2001** 59
in drug war, **1989** 499, 502, 504, 507, 509-510
employees in U.S., **1996** 739; **1997** 689; **1998** 877; **1999** 622; **2000** 860; **2001** 757; **2002** 793; **2004** 770; **2005** 685
federal, integrity of, **1975** 653-654, 677-679
immigration control, **1981** 265, 271-272, 605-606, 609-610, 613
intelligence agencies' assistance to, **1976** 123, 139; **1981** 867
Nixon State of the Union message on, **1973** 303, 305-306, 321-326
police corps, **1997** 244
police murder, mandatory death penalty for, **1977** 397-405
revenue sharing for, Nixon on, **1973** 305, 321-323
searches by, and exclusionary rule, **1976** 521-536
sting operations, **1992** 313-327
wiretaps
attorney general's approval of, **1974** 391-405
national security, **1972** 485-489
Law Enforcement Assistance Agency (LEAA), reorganization of, **1978** 332
Law of the Sea Treaty, **1982** 345-361
Law of the Sea Treaty, Convention on, **2004** 605-606
Lawrence, David M., health care, **1997** 791
Lawrence v. Texas, **2003** 403, 406-413; **2004** 41
Lawrence Livermore National Laboratory (California)
on Chernobyl accident, **1986** 386-387
nuclear freeze protest at, **1982** 886
Lawson, Nigel, **1985** 623
Lawyers
advertising by, **1982** 65-71; **1986** 768, 772
attorney-client privilege, Supreme Court on, **1998** 393-404
Carter's criticism of, **1978** 327-337
client privilege, abuses of, Senate Watergate Committee on, **1974** 618
economic pressures on, **1986** 768, 771-772, 774-775
ethics of, **1986** 767-778
and moral issues of Watergate, **1973** 723-727
personal injury cases and contingency fees, **1987** 166-167, 169-170
right to. *See* Criminal law, right to counsel
state regulation of profession, **1986** 771-773
Lawyers Committee for Human Rights, **1993** 455
Lawyers Committee for International Human Rights, **1983** 182; **1984** 156; **1985** 146

Lawyers for Louisiana, **1987** 566
Laxalt, Paul (R-Nev.)
D.C. voting representation in Congress, **1978** 590
nomination of Reagan, **1976** 666
at Republican convention, **1984** 729
Lay, Kenneth, Enron Corp. collapse, **2001** 857, 858, 859, 861, 863, 865; **2002** 396; **2003** 336
Lay Commission on Catholic Social Teaching, **1986** 984-985
Lazio, Rick A., senatorial campaign, **2000** 906-909
Le Duc Tho
Paris peace accords, negotiation and signing of, **1973** 115-118
in Paris peace negotiations, **1972** 122-124, 130, 941, 947, 949
Le Grange, Louis, **1986** 371
Le Kha Phieu
on U.S. imperialism, **2000** 916
U.S.-Vietnam trade agreement, **2000** 919
Le Van Bang, Vietnam ambassador, **1997** 489
LEAA. *See* Law Enforcement Assistance Agency
Leach, Jim (R-Iowa), on Gingrich as House Speaker, **1997** 3-4
Leach, Margaret, **1988** 891
Lead poisoning, protection of children from, **1972** 152
Leadership Conference on Civil Rights
Bork nomination, **1987** 719
civil rights Court rulings, **1989** 324
economic status of blacks, **1989** 447
Education Fund, "digital divide" issue, **2002** 69
Lott resignation, **2002** 973
Reagan civil rights record, **1989** 17
Voting Rights Act extension, **1983** 47
League of Nations
Palestine mandates, **1988** 581
South African mandate for South West Africa (Namibia), **1976** 611
League of Women Voters
sponsorship of debates
Carter-Reagan, **1980** 919-920, 951
Ford-Carter, **1976** 693-695
Reagan-Anderson, **1980** 847-848, 849, 867-868
Reagan-Mondale, **1984** 848, 876
vote ratings of, **1976** 789-790
League of Women Voters of California, ban on public broadcasting editorials, **1984** 449, 451
Leahy, Patrick (D-Vt.)
anthrax mailings, **2001** 674
Casey investigation, **1981** 855
farm legislation, **1996** 200-201
federal sentencing guidelines, **2004** 359
judicial impeachment, **1989** 585
land mines ban, **1997** 845, 846
medical records security, **1997** 582-583
Reagan presidency, **1989** 17
Rehnquist appointment, **1986** 592
Roberts Supreme Court nomination, **2005** 561 562
Thomas confirmation hearings, **1991** 570-571, 603
tobacco company lawsuit, **2001** 225
torture in terrorism interrogations investigations, **2004** 340, 341
tsunami relief effort, **2004** 994
USA Patriot Act, **2003** 611
war on terrorism, **2001** 642, 643
Leape, Lucian, medical mistakes, **1999** 781
Leavitt, Mike (Utah governor; EPA secretary)
abortion and premature babies, **2005** 819-820
clean air programs, **2003** 180; **2004** 666, 667
Crawford FDA commissioner nomination, **2005** 816
EPA pesticides regulation, **2004** 670
EPA secretary appointment, **2003** 174
flu pandemic preparedness, **2005** 753
health and human services secretary appointment, **2005** 45
Salt Lake Olympics corruption scandal, **1999** 106
Leavy, Edward, **1997** 184
Lebanese Armed Revolutionary Faction (FARL), **1986** 831
Lebanon
See also Beirut (Lebanon)
conflict in
economic summit on, **1982** 473
and UN ineffectiveness, **1982** 769
elections, **2005** 689-690
Hezbollah participation in, **2005** 271, 273
parliamentary elections, **2005** 270-273
Fahd on peace in, **1981** 636-637
French hostages in, **1986** 831-833
Hariri assassination, UN commission on, **2005** 686-696
human trafficking, **2002** 346
Israeli forces in, Carter on, **1978** 273
Israeli raids in, **1972** 751-752; **1982** 741-744
Israeli-Lebanese security agreement, **1983** 471-477, 833
mass protests against Syria, **2004** 562
Palestinian refugee camp massacre, **1982** 781-795; **1983** 163-180; **1985** 47-51
peacekeeping mission, **1985** 464
PLO departure from, **1982** 741-749
political protests, **2004** 561-562; **2005** 167, 272, 687-688
release of hostages, **1991** 751-758
Syrian role in, **1982** 742-744
Syrian troop withdrawal, **2004** 557-563; **2005** 80, 271, 686, 688-689
Taif peace accord, **2004** 557
terrorism in, **1983** 933-966; **1984** 935, 937, 940; **1985** 463-466, 469
terrorist bombings in, **1998** 555-556; **2001** 3; **2004** 319; **2005** 686-687
UN Oil for Food Program, **2004** 717
UN peacekeeping mission, **1997** 151, 154, 155, 156
U.S. hostages in, **1986** 1013-1022
and Iran-contra affair, **1987** 206, 208, 217, 219-221, 226-227, 230-231
and Israeli kidnapping of Obeid, **1989** 315-320
U.S. troops in, **1984** 83-84, 93, 1006, 1012
U.S.-led peacekeeping missions, **2004** 319-320
Lebedev, Platon, Yukos oil company partner convicted, **2005** 302
Lebow, Cynthia, on National Transportation Safety Board, **1999** 115
Lederberg, Joshua, **1975** 319-320

Lederberg, Joshua *Continued*
Gulf War syndrome investigations, **1994** 265, 270
Lederer, Raymond F. (D-Pa.), **1980** 900-901
Ledford, Andrew K., Abu Ghraib prison abuse scandal, **2005** 913
Lee, Barbara (D-Calif.), U.S.-Africa policy, **2000** 72
Lee, Barbara Combs, death with dignity, **1997** 462
Lee, Bill
nomination for Office of Civil Rights, **1997** 765
race relations, **2000** 772
Lee, James, **1986** 861
Lee, Martin, Hong Kong prodemocracy advocate, **1997** 502; **2005** 623
Lee, Pascal, water on Mars, reaction to possibility of, **2000** 381-382
Lee, Rex E.
on affirmative action and seniority, **1984** 367
Court's hearing of abortion cases, **1983** 546
restraint as solicitor general, **1985** 655
Lee, Robert E., **1972** 137-138
Lee, Wen Ho
espionage accusations, **1999** 235, 241
spy case, **2000** 740-752
Lee Jong Wook, WHO AIDS ARV treatment, **2004** 433
Lee Teng-hui, **2000** 190, 196
Taiwan presidential elections, **2004** 258
Lee v. Weisman, **1992** 553-562; **1993** 370; **1995** 547; **2005** 382
Leete-Guy, Laura, **1992** 163-173
Lefebvre, Marcel
excommunication of, **1988** 489-494
traditionalist movement in Catholic Church, **1984** 400
Lefever, Ernest W.
and infant formula controversy, **1981** 449, 780
nomination and withdrawal of, **1982** 108
Legal Defense and Education Fund, **1983** 711
Legal services, political goals of, Nixon administration on, **1973** 454
Legal Services Corporation
expansion of, **1978** 327, 334
funding for, **1981** 641; **1985** 29, 35
Legal system
See also Criminal justice system; Judicial system
Bok on problems of, **1983** 391-400
ensuring treatment for seriously ill infants, **1983** 289
illegal drugs as strain on, **1989** 499, 502, 504, 507, 509-510
standards of proof in, **1982** 260-280
Legalism, as scale of Western society, Solzhenitsyn on, **1978** 405, 408-409
Legislative intent, **1993** 249-258
Legislative reform, Clinton on unfunded mandates legislation, **1995** 141-145
Legislative Reorganization Act (1946), **1974** 574
Legislative Reorganization Act (1970), **1974** 587-589
Legislative veto, unconstitutionality of, **1983** 617-644
Lehman, Betsy, death of, **1999** 782
Lehman, John, national commission on terrorist attacks hearings, **2004** 453
Lehman, William (D-Fla.), **1981** 388
Lehn, Kenneth, **1988** 921-925
Lehrer, Jim
Mugabe interview, **1980** 322-328
in presidential and vice presidential debates, **1988** 723-726; **1992** 909-912, 918, 929, 955-977; **1996** 709-731
presidential debates moderator, **2004** 675, 679-690
Leibel, Rudolph, on obesity-related diseases, **2005** 6
Leigh-Pemberton, Robin, **1985** 623
Lemaitre, Georges, "Big Bang" theory, **1992** 379-380
Lemon v. Kurtzman, **1983** 677, 680-681; **1985** 380-381, 385-388, 394, 435, 439-449, 452-455; **1987** 567-569, 572, 575-576; **1992** 554, 556; **1993** 264, 369, 370; **1997** 372; **2005** 381
Lempert, Richard, affirmative action case, **2003** 367
Lenfant, Claude
cholesterol levels and heart disease, **2001** 478
heart disease in women and hormone replacement therapy, **2002** 506, 508
Leng May Ma v. Barber, **1993** 419
Lenhoff, Donna
Nursing Home Compare Web site, **2002** 120
nursing home staffing standards, **2002** 121
Lenin, V. I.
New Economic Policy of, Gorbachev on, **1986** 145-147, 153, 156, 158; **1987** 857-858, 860-861; **1989** 146-149
Soviet reforms traced to, **1988** 448-451, 455, 458-460, 464
Lenovo Group Ltd. (Chinese computer maker), purchase of IBM, **2004** 939; **2005** 616
Lenzner, Terry, **1992** 307
Leo XIII (pope), **1985** 369
Leon, Gloria, **1983** 337
Leon, Richard J., Guantanamo Bay detainees case, **2005** 448
Leon, United States v., **1984** 505-519; **1985** 480-481, 485
Leonard, Graham, **1989** 51
Leonard, Jeff, **1986** 170
Leonard, John, news conference on Y2K conversion, **2000** 6
Leonard, William A., **1979** 287, 316
Lerner, Kenneth, unreasonable searches, **2001** 408
Leshner, Alan, research on marijuana for medical purposes, **1996** 757
Lesotho, dependence on South Africa, **1986** 582, 585
Lessig, Lawrence, Microsoft antitrust case, **2001** 777-778
Leukemia, interferon as treatment for, **1986** 481-485
Leval, Pierre N., Westmoreland suit against CBS, **1983** 401-402; **1985** 162
Leventhal, Harold, **1973** 842
Leveraged buyouts (LBOs), growth of, **1988** 921-924
Lévesque, René
on Canadian constitution, **1982** 318
on Canadian educational language guarantees, **1981** 813-814, 818-819
election victory of, **1976** 855-862
Quebec separatism, **1980** 401-402, 407-410; **1990** 368, 369
Levi, Edward H., **1977** 113
Levi, Virgilio, **1983** 580

Levin, Carl M. (D-Mich.)
limits on gifts to members of Congress, **1995** 701, 702
missile defense system testing, **2001** 284-285; **2002** 1029
nuclear weapons policy, **2002** 278
separation of military from domestic law enforcement, **2002** 535
Levin, Sander (D-Mich.), U.S.-China trade relations, **2000** 216
Levin, Shlomo, Demjanjuk war crime acquittal, **1993** 620-621
Levine, Arnold J., AIDS research, **1996** 157
Levine, Irving R., bank failures, **1990** 818-823
Levitas, Elliott H. (D-Ga.), on EPA investigation, **1982** 966; **1983** 751
Levitt, Arthur, online investing, SEC chairman on, **1999** 203-214
Levitt v. Committee for Public Education and Religious Liberty, **1973** 641-642, 644-646
Levy, David, Israel foreign minister appointment, **1999** 362
Levy, Mark, union for interns and medical residents, **1999** 633
Lewinsky, Monica
alleged Clinton affair, **1998** 38-39; **1999** 601
Clinton apology to the nation, **1998** 568-569
Clinton denial to staff, **1998** 581-582
Clinton grand jury testimony, **1998** 564-585, 651-652, 655-656
Clinton plea-bargain agreement, **2001** 88-89
Clinton public denials, **1998** 566; **1999** 15
Clinton public discussion with evangelical ministers, **2000** 598-599, 610
Clinton refusal to testify, **1998** 661-662
Clinton-Lewinsky denial of affair, **1998** 38-39, 565
Clinton-Lewinsky meetings, **1998** 572-574, 656-657
dress stains and DNA sample, **1998** 639
Flynt of *Hustler* magazine muckraking campaign, **1998** 953
gifts, concealment of evidence, **1998** 583-584, 635, 643-645, 656-657, 658-659
House impeachment vote, **1998** 958-970
House Judiciary Committee impeachment inquiry, **1998** 695-721
impeachable offenses
abuse of constitutional authority, **1998** 635, 653-654, 662-663
grounds for, **1998** 637-638
obstruction of justice, **1998** 635
perjury, **1998** 634, 654-656
witness tampering, **1998** 635, 660-661
impeachment trial, **1999** 15-40
job search for, **1998** 582-584, 635, 647-649, 659-660
Jordan (Vernon) involvement, **1998** 577-580, 584, 635, 649-650, 660; **1999** 17
Livingston resignation speech calling for Clinton resignation, **1998** 955-957
Republican campaign for Clinton resignation, **1998** 954
secretary Betty Curie's role in, **1998** 574-576, 583, 650-651
sexual relationship, **1998** 570-572, 584-585, 640-641
Starr independent counsel investigations, **1998** 38-39, 565-566, 907, 960; **1999** 15-16, 22, 166-167; **2000** 763-764
Starr report, **1998** 632-664
testimony, **1998** 576-577
Tripp (Linda) tapes, **1998** 565-566
Lewis, Bernard
Islam and the West, **1990** 277-287
Rushdie death threat, **1989** 97
Lewis, Drew
and Republican Party platform, **1984** 661
resignation, **1982** 563
Lewis, Floyd W., **1979** 825
Lewis, John (D-Ga.), **1995** 372
affirmative action programs, **1998** 859
civil rights, **1995** 372
"no-fly" terrorist watch lists, **2004** 145
Lewis, Judith, on food shortages in South Africa, **2002** 157
Lewis, Pamela A., affirmative action, **1996** 761
Lewis, Samuel W., on Israeli annexation of Golan Heights, **1981** 900, 905-907
Lewis, Stephen
AIDS epidemic in Africa, **1999** 490
AIDS pandemic, **2003** 780-781, 786-790
Bush AIDS emergency relief plan, **2004** 432; **2005** 53
Rwandan genocidal war investigations, **2000** 450, 453
Lewis Mumford Center for Comparative and Urban Regional Research (SUNY, Albany), Hispanic studies survey results, **2003** 351-352
Lexington (USS), accident on, **1989** 519
Leyraud, Jerome, **1991** 753
Li Peng
Chinese leadership, **2002** 850; **2003** 1174
repression in China, **1989** 277
Li Ruihuan, Chinese leadership, **2002** 851
Li Zhaoxing, China-Japan dispute, **2005** 621
Liability
coverage for oil spill disasters, **1989** 227, 230-231
Firestone tire recall, **2000** 688-699
multinational enterprise, and Bhopal accident, **1985** 297
Supreme Court on punitive damages, **1996** 274-283
tort, ABA recommendations for reform of system, **1987** 165-181
al-Libbi, Abu Faraj, al Qaeda operative captured, **2005** 473
Libby, I. Lewis "Scooter"
indictment for disclosure of CIA agent, **2005** 78, 80, 246, 249, 631, 699-726, 767-768, 907
Marc Rich presidential pardon, **2001** 90
Libby, John W., military recruitment, **2004** 789
Libby, United States v., **2005** 705-716
Libel
awards, court review of, **1984** 299-311
from misquotation, Supreme Court on, **1991** 317-329
of private persons, burden of proof, **1986** 355-357, 358-368

Libel *Continued*
of public figures
burden of proof, **1986** 355-356, 357-358
and congressional immunity, **1979** 479-483, 490-491
and editorial process of news media, **1979** 285-311, 315-318
protections in federal law, **1974** 215-216, 220
suits against media, **1984** 247-256, 299-312
Sharon suit against *Time* magazine, **1985** 47-52
Westmoreland suit against CBS, **1985** 159-165
Libel Defense Resource Center, **1984** 300
Liberalism
need for rejuvenation of, McGovern on, **1973** 87-88, 91
as presidential campaign issue, **1988** 722, 733-734, 760-761, 778
Liberation theology, **2005** 293
and activist Catholic clergy, John Paul II on, **1979** 726-727, 730-731, 734-737; **1980** 412-413; **1985** 57-58, 63; **1986** 640, 647-648
and renewal of Vatican II, **1985** 766, 778-780
Vatican statements on, **1984** 759-775, 778; **1986** 317-338
Liberation Tigers of Tamil Eelam. *See* Tamil Tigers
Liberia
Carter visit, **1978** 271
child soldiers, **2002** 918, 925
civil war, **2002** 251; **2003** 767-773
coup led by Doe, **1980** 275-280
elections, **2005** 800-813
founding of, **1980** 275, 276
human rights in, **1993** 559
hunger in, **2003** 756
interim government, **2005** 801
natural resources exploitation, **2003** 769
political situation, **2005** 800-801
UN economic sanction and arms embargo, **2003** 768, 769
UN Mission in Liberia (UNMIL), peacekeeping force, **2003** 450, 767-779, 772; **2005** 801
UN report on refugees, **1991** 672, 673
U.S. aid to, **1980** 277
U.S. intervention, **2003** 453, 454, 769-771
Liberians United for Reconciliation and Democracy (LURD), **2002** 251; **2003** 768-769, 772
Liberty Baptist College, Kennedy speech to Moral Majority, **1983** 817-825
Liberty Council, Ten Commandments displays, **2005** 378
Liberty Lobby, **1981** 381
Libraries
FBI investigations of patron records, **2002** 563
Internet filters in public libraries, Supreme Court on, **2003** 387-400
Internet pornography in, federal court on, **2002** 287-297
Library Services and Technology Act (LSTA), **2003** 388, 394
Libya
on Arab cease-fire with Israel, **1973** 932-933
Arab League meeting, boycott of, **1987** 869
Arab oil embargo, lifting of against U.S., **1974** 221, 224
chemical weapons plant in, **1989** 28
contacts with B. Carter, **1980** 907-917
downing of jet by Israeli planes (1973), **1983** 775
on Egyptian peace initiative, **1977** 829
human rights in, **1987** 203-204
on Israeli-Lebanese security agreement, **1983** 473
Lockerbie bombing, involvement in, **2004** 171
nuclear weapons program
dismantling of, **2003** 901, 1025, 1031, 1218-1233; **2004** 169-171, 323
North Korea link, **2005** 605
oil price increases, **1979** 251, 252, 254
and OPEC oil prices, **1978** 791; **1980** 995-996; **1981** 799
and OPEC production quotas, **1982** 980
political situation, **2003** 1225-1227; **2004** 168-175
relations with EU, **2004** 168, 171-173
on Sadat after Camp David accords, **1978** 607
on Sadat assassination, **1981** 734
Syria, support for against Britain, **1986** 832-833
terrorism supported by, **1982** 83; **1985** 464, 466-473, 476; **1986** 439, 444
CIA on, **1981** 462-463, 465, 467-468
UN sanctions, **2003** 1223-1224
U.S. air strikes against, **1986** 347-354; **1998** 586
U.S. economic sanctions, **2001** 795; **2003** 1223-1224
Bush administration lifting of, **2004** 168-175
U.S. relations, **2003** 1218-1219; **2004** 171-173
U.S. relations with, breaking of, **1981** 462
weapons inspections, **2003** 1219-1222
weapons programs, **2005** 248
weapons proliferation, **1996** 212-213, 218; **1997** 198
Lichtenstein, Marshall, **1973** 36
Lichtenstein, Nelson, Wal-Mart store image problems, **2005** 740
Lichtman, Judith, **1991** 259
Liddy, G. Gordon
appeals on behalf of Watergate break-in defendants, **1974** 158-163
Ellsberg break-in, **1973** 538, 545-546, 548
indictment, **1974** 205-206, 208-210
national security grounds for, **1974** 411-417
trial and sentencing, **1974** 661-662, 665-666
Watergate break-in, **1973** 415, 418-419
White House tapes on involvement of, **1974** 330, 335-336, 341-346, 348, 353
Watergate conviction, for refusal to testify, **1975** 666-667
Lieberman, Joseph I. (D-Conn.)
affirmative action programs, **1995** 485
charitable choice and employment discrimination, **2001** 134-135, 136
Clinton censure resolution, **1999** 21
entertainment industry regulations, **2000** 729, 731; **2001** 76
global warming
and carbon dioxide emission controls, **2003** 866
greenhouse gas emissions, **2005** 922

Homeland Security Department proposal, **2002** 531, 533, 534
Hurricane Katrina disaster relief management, **2005** 570
presidential candidate, **2004** 479
September 11 panel (national commission on terrorist attacks) recommendations, **2004** 458, 967, 968, 969
vice presidential campaign, **2000** 520, 609
debates, **2000** 797, 800, 810-817
vice presidential nomination, **2000** 619-620
acceptance speech, **2000** 621-625
Whitman resignation, **2002** 897
Liebman, James, capital punishment cases study, **2000** 989-990
Lien Chan
China-Taiwan relations, **2005** 622-623
Taiwanese presidential candidate, **2004** 260
Taiwanese vice president, **2000** 191
Life expectancy
in African countries declining, **1998** 879, 886; **2000** 63, 70
in the U.S., **2000** 51, 70; **2005** 6
worldwide, **1996** 305; **1999** 588
Life-sustaining measures
See also Death and dying
medical ethics and law on terminating, **1976** 197-219; **1983** 279-303
patient's right to refuse, **1973** 39-41; **1983** 280
Quinlan case, **1975** 805-824; **1976** 197-219
for severely handicapped infants, **1986** 541-558
for terminally ill patients, **1984** 275-285
Lifflander, Matthew L., **1992** 718
Ligachev, Yegor K., **1989** 147; **1990** 441
Liggett Group Inc.
lung cancer death liability case, **1988** 311
smoking and addiction, **1988** 311; **1997** 333
Lillestrand, Robert, **1988** 832
Lilly, Frank, **1988** 415
Lima, Declaration of, on sovereignty over natural resources, **1972** 330, 334, 336
Liman, Arthur L., **1972** 783
Limbaugh, Rush, **1993** 585
Lin Piao
coup plot of, **1973** 767-774; **1974** 271-275; **1997** 97
death of, **1977** 360-361
Lincoln, Robert Todd, presidential nomination, **2000** 519
Lincoln Savings and Loan Association, failure of, **1989** 465
Lindemann, Jean, **1986** 482
Lindgren, Astrid, **1988** 348
Lindgren, Mark, universal health care coverage, **2002** 671
Lindh, John Walker, enemy combatant with Taliban regime, **2002** 835; **2003** 106
Lindor, Brignol, journalist killed in Haiti, **2001** 397
Lindsay, Germaine, London terrorist bombing suspect, **2005** 396-397
Lindsay, John V. (R-N.Y.) (1959-1965)
campaign contributions to, **1974** 603
on punishment for drug dealers, **1973** 28-29
Lindsey, Bruce R., presidential attorney-client privilege, **1998** 393
Lindsey, Lawrence B., resignation, **2002** 880
Link, Perry, **1989** 276
Linmark Associates, Inc. v. Willingboro, **1977** 313-320; **1994** 292-293, 295
Linnoila, Markku, **1983** 336
Linowes, David L., on privatization, **1988** 229-230
Linowitz, Sol, **1983** 375
Lippmann, Walter, **1989** 208
Lippold, Kirk S., *Cole* (USS) captain, **2000** 862; **2001** 4, 5, 6
Litan, Robert E., **1990** 816
Literacy
See also Education; Reading
adult Americans
functional literacy of, **1975** 691-705
literacy for women, **2000** 326
survey report, **1993** 737-746
in African countries, **2000** 69-70
America Reads Challenge, **1997** 35, 64-65; **1998** 77, 88
among youth, **1983** 414
colleges' failures, **1985** 128, 138-139
functional competence of adult Americans, **1975** 691-705
in U.S.
for adults, **1999** 50
workers and young adults, **1988** 298-299
Literature
book banning in schools, **1982** 567-585
need for emphasis on in education, **1987** 681-685, 689, 695
role in conveying life experience, Solzhenitsyn on, **1972** 727-731
teaching religion's influence on, **1987** 599-603
in undergraduate education, **1984** 997-1003
Lithuania
declaration of independence, **1990** 183-186
Elena Bonner on, **1990** 212
EU membership, **2004** 198
freedom statement of, **1989** 469-473
NATO membership, **2004** 136, 198
sex trade in children, **2001** 956
Soviet restructuring plans, **1991** 532-533
U.S. diplomatic relations, **1991** 545-549
U.S. policy, **1990** 185
Litigation, reduction of unnecessary, Carter on, **1978** 327, 335-336
Little, Greg, tobacco industry fraud suit, **1999** 538
Little, Rory K., on abolition of capital punishment, **2005** 177
Littlefield, Warren, **1993** 489
Liu Shao-chi, **1975** 44
Livingston, Robert L. (R-La.)
air strikes against Iraq, **1998** 937
on Clinton education agenda, **1997** 29
extra-marital affair, **1998** 953
House Speaker challenge, **1998** 802
House Speaker resignation, **1998** 799, 951-957, 959, 962
Livingston, Robert R. (chancellor of New York), at George Washington's inauguration, **1989** 124

Livni, Tzipi, Israel justice minister, **2005** 534
Liwei, Yang, Chinese astronaut, **2003** 301
Lloyd-Jones, David, **1979** 952
Lobbyists
See also Koreagate
registration and financial disclosure, **1995** 700, 702-703
Local governments
abortion restrictions of, **1977** 407-409, 427-430; **1983** 543-576
affirmative action for firefighters, **1986** 652-653, 667-678
age discrimination against employees of, **1983** 231-240
business regulation by, subject to antitrust laws, **1982** 35-49
census data, access to, **1982** 171-178
community development responsibility of, **1973** 304-305, 314-319; **1980** 858-859; **1987** 12
control of hazardous waste disposal, **1979** 786-787, 799-800
crisis management by, **1986** 239-251
development planning by, federal assistance in, **1972** 551-554
drug paraphernalia sales, restrictions on, **1982** 215-223
economic cooperation, intergovernmental, Democratic Party platform on, **1984** 581-582
emergency plans for nuclear accidents, **1979** 824, 827, 838-840
federal minimum wage laws applied to, **1976** 377-389; **1985** 167-187
federal tax returns, access to, **1975** 858
immunity of officials from damage suits, **1980** 299-316
law enforcement, federal assistance in, **1973** 305, 321-323
and minority set-asides in federal contracts, **1980** 539-566
participation in Carter's urban program, **1978** 244-245, 247, 249, 252, 254-257
privatization of services, **1988** 237-238
problem solving at level of, Republican Party platform on, **1976** 618, 620, 627, 641-642
Proposition 13, impact in California, **1978** 397-402
racial integration
ban on "for sale" signs, **1977** 313-320
public housing in suburbs, **1976** 223-233
revenue sharing
in block grants, Reagan plan, **1981** 217, 219, 334-335, 644-645
in Carter administration, **1977** 127, 129; **1981** 78
Ford on, **1976** 14, 23-24, 47, 62
in Nixon budget, **1973** 169, 174-175, 181-182; **1974** 98-99, 106-108
social service provision by
Nixon on, **1973** 304-309
Reagan on, **1986** 56
spending growth in, **1978** 83-84
zoning regulations
on adult theaters, **1986** 131-144
barring low-income housing, **1977** 35-44
Locke, Gary (Washington governor), **1997** 43
election, **2004** 778
State of the Union address, Democratic response, **2003** 23-24, 36-39
Lockett v. Ohio, **1978** 495-511; **1983** 708
Lockhart v. McCree, **1986** 445-456
Lockheed, loan guarantee for, **1979** 693
Lockheed Martin Astronautics, Mars *Climate Orbiter* mission, **2000** 89
Lockyer, Bill, medical use of marijuana, **2001** 327
Lockyer v. Andrade, **2003** 984
Lofgren, Zoe (D-Calif.), House Judiciary Committee impeachment inquiry, **1998** 707
Logdson, John M., space exploration cost reduction, **1999** 712
Logging, preservation of Alaskan lands from, **1978** 731-732
London, Ephraim, **1973** 612
London, Julius, **1975** 438
London Declaration of Peaceful Intent, **1990** 455-466
Long, Huey, **1993** 586
Long, Russell B. (D-La.), **1977** 97
Long Beach (California), school uniform policy, **1996** 89
Longshoremen's Association. *See* International Longshoremen's Association
Loomis, Carol, **1980** 847, 850-851
Lopez, Alfonso, Jr., **1995** 183
Lopez, United States v., **1995** 183-200, 260
Lopez Obrador, Andres Manuel, Mexico presidential candidate, **2005** 772
López Portillo, José
Carter meetings with, **1979** 169-181
at poverty summit, **1981** 770, 775-778
Loprest, Pamela, welfare reform report, **1999** 259
Loral Space and Communications Systems Ltd., **1999** 237, 250
Lord's Resistance Army (LRA), **2003** 470-479, 840
Lorillard Tobacco Co.
claims settlement, **1997** 331; **1998** 842
liability in lung cancer death, **1988** 311
Los Alamos National Laboratory (LANL)
nuclear secrets theft, **1999** 235, 241; **2000** 740-752
security threat, missing hard drives, **2000** 744-745
Los Angeles (California)
air quality in, **1981** 275, 289
earthquake, **1994** 3-7
police department
abuses, **1991** 403-428
sentencing of convicted officers, **1993** 631-651
riots (1992), **1993** 213, 214
riots after Rodney King beating, **1992** 407-429, 496
Los Angeles Bar Association, Carter address to, **1978** 327-337
Los Angeles County, land-use regulation, **1987** 531-546
Los Angeles Department of Water and Power v. Manhart, **1978** 293-306; **1983** 692, 695-704
Losonczy, Geza, **1989** 341
Lott, Trent (R-Miss.)
AIDS epidemic, **2000** 414
air strikes against Iraq, **1998** 937, 961
aviation security, **2001** 653
balanced budget agreement, **1997** 604

campaign finance reform, **1997** 31, 827; **1998** 893
chemical weapons treaty, **1996** 742; **1997** 196-197
Clinton State of the Union address, Republican response, **1998** 40-41, 54-59
Congress
closing remarks at 104th Congress, **1996** 701-703
limits on gifts to members of, **1995** 701
Senate "Leaders Lecture Series," **1998** 151
Senate majority leader election, **1996** 271
shooting of Capitol policemen, **1998** 513-514
Elian Gonzalez political asylum case, **2000** 269
health care reform, **1997** 791
on Hillary Clinton in the Senate, **2000** 910
Jeffords party switch, reaction to, **2001** 379
Jiang Zemin state visit, **1997** 730
limits on gifts to members of Congress, **1995** 701
liquor advertising, **1996** 772
nuclear test ban treaty, **1999** 600-603, 607-610
Panama Canal, U.S. policy, **1999** 852
Senate majority leader resignation, **2002** 240, 819, 969-980; **2003** 360
television rating system, **1997** 529
warrantless domestic surveillance, **2005** 961
Louisell, David W., **1975** 545
Louisiana
creationism legislation, **1987** 565-576
juries
six-person, **1979** 263-268
women serving on, **1975** 55-66
mandatory death penalty law, **1976** 489-490, 506-507; **1977** 397-405
Lounge, John M., **1988** 797
Lovastatin, FDA approval of, **1987** 780
Love, John A., **1973** 466
Love Canal, New York
hazardous waste disposal at, **1979** 782, 785-787, 791, 793, 796-798, 800; **1983** 479-487
health effects of, **1980** 445-447, 452-454
Lovell v. Griffin, **1994** 296
Loving v. United States, **1997** 296
Loving v. Virginia, **1995** 313
Lovitt, Robin, death sentence commuted to life in prison, **2005** 178
Low, George M., **1979** 952
Low Income Housing Information Service, on HUD scandal, **1989** 334
Lowe, Ira N., at Ehrlichman sentencing, **1975** 142, 144, 146-150
Lowery, Joseph E., at March on Washington thirtieth anniversary, **1993** 678-679
Lowey, Nita (D-N.Y.)
and investigation of Medal of Honor award, **1989** 699
U.S. aid to Colombia, **2002** 573
Lown, Bernard, Nobel Peace Prize recipient, **1985** 781-787
Lowry, Mike (D-Wash.), **1982** 908
Loy, Frank, on global warming, **2000** 342
Loy, James, aviation baggage screening, **2003** 723
LRA. *See* Lord's Resistance Army
LSTA. *See* Library Services and Technology Act
Lu, Annette, Taiwanese vice presidential candidate, **2004** 260
Lubbers, Ruud
sexual harassment complaints against, **2005** 238
UN High Commissioner for Refugees resignation, **2005** 238
Lucas, David H., land-taking compensation, **1992** 615-620
Lucas v. South Carolina Coastal Council, **1992** 615-620
Lucent Technologies, retirement fund losses, **2002** 102
Luciana, Albino. *See* John Paul I (pope)
Lucid, Shannon W., space flight, **1996** 691-694; **1999** 611
Luckasson, Ruth A., on mental retardation, **2002** 356-357
Ludwig, David, obesity-related diseases in children, **2005** 6
Ludwig, Frederick G., Jr., Tailhook convention, **1992** 882, 884
Lugar, Richard G. (R-Ind.)
Agriculture Department reorganization, **1994** 404
chemical weapons treaty, **1996** 741
Glaspie-Hussein pre-war meeting, **1991** 161
Guantanamo Bay detainees, **2005** 449
Law of the Sea Treaty, **2004** 606
NATO expansion, **1997** 517
nuclear materials in former Soviet states, **1996** 141
nuclear test ban treaty, **1999** 602, 608
Russian nuclear weapons, **2001** 18; **2002** 437-440
Ukraine elections monitor, **2004** 1003
U.S. policy on South Africa, **1984** 1029
U.S.-British extradition treaty, **1986** 752-753
war powers debate, **1990** 665, 666-667
Lujan, Manuel, Jr., spotted owl recovery plan, **1992** 490
Lukamba, Paulo, Angola peace agreement, **2002** 154
Luken, Thomas A. (D-Ohio), on urban priorities, **1972** 481-483
Lukovic, Milorad, Serbian gang leader, **2003** 59
Lukyanov, Anatoly I., **1989** 175; **1991** 517
Lula da Silva, Luiz Inacio
antipoverty programs, **2005** 768
Brazil presidential election, **2002** 774-783
Brazil presidential inauguration speech, **2003** 3-17
economic policy, **2003** 3
political corruption scandal, **2005** 768
trade mission to China, **2004** 938
U.S. relations, **2005** 765-776
visit to Washington, D.C., **2002** 779
Lumumba, Patrice, assassination of, **1975** 710, 715-716, 720-724, 769-772, 778, 780, 789; **1984** 904
Lundberg, Ferdinand, **1974** 709
Lundberg, George D., **1984** 1021
gun violence report, **1992** 493-498
gunshot wound treatment, **1993** 872
Lundgren, Ottilie, anthrax mailings victim, **2001** 675
Lundgren v. Superior Court (Ct. App. 1996), **1997** 189
Lung disease
See also Cancer, lung
and smoking, **1972** 49-50; **1986** 1082
and smoking in the workplace, **1985** 809, 811-813, 816-817

Lungren, Dan (R-Calif.), **1983** 213
Luns, Joseph M. A. H.
  Kissinger's contribution, **1976** 908
  SALT progress, **1976** 346
  Spain's entry into NATO, **1982** 410
LURD. *See* Liberians United for Reconciliation and Democracy
Lurie, Nicole, health care for women, **1993** 653-658
Lusaka accord, **1999** 434, 436, 646-647, 647-649; **2000** 979-980; **2002** 154-155, 163-164
Luthuli, Albert, Nobel Peace Prize recipient, **1984** 1027; **1993** 877-878, 880-881, 883
Luwum, Janani, **1977** 143-145
Luxembourg
  euro currency, **1998** 271
  John Paul II visit, **1985** 363
Luzhkov, Yuri, **1993** 772
Lynch, James
  crime rate and counterterrorism, **2004** 761
  crime rates, **2003** 981
Lynch, Jessica, rescue of, **2003** 142
Lynch v. Donnelly, **1984** 217-239; **1992** 556; **1995** 399; **2005** 381
Lynchings, Senate apology for, **2005** 356-357
Lynn, Barry W.
  intelligent design case, **2005** 1013
  school prayer amendment, **1984** 244
  Ten Commandments displays, **2005** 379
Lynn, James T., **1973** 338
Lynn, Joanne
  end-of-life care, **1997** 327, 328-330
  religious clubs in public schools, **2001** 423

M

Ma Ying-jeou, **2000** 191
Maathai, Wangari
  Kenya parliamentary elections, **2004** 931
  Nobel Peace Prize recipient, **2004** 929-936
Macapagal, Diosdado, Philippine president, **2001** 104-105
MacDonald, Donald Ian, **1988** 417
Macedo, Carlyle Guerra, **1992** 269, 271-272
Macedonia
  Albanian Muslim guerrilla rebellion, **2001** 554-555
  ethnic conflicts in, **2001** 554-555, 820
  independence, **1991** 368
  NATO membership candidacy, **2004** 136
  NATO peacekeeping mission, **2001** 554-558
  peace agreement, **2001** 554-561; **2004** 956-957
  political situation, **2003** 56
  recognized as Republic of Macedonia, **2004** 957
Machel, Graça
  NEPAD member, **2003** 452
  UN on HIV/AIDS in Africa, **2003** 787, 789
Mack, John P., **1989** 241-242
MacKinnon, George E.
  access to White House tapes, **1973** 842, 853-854
  treaty termination, **1979** 919, 931
Maclean, Donald, in Soviet spy network, **1979** 905-906, 908-909, 911, 913
MacMillan, Michael, **1983** 832
MacNeil, Robert
  government control of public television, **1973** 58
  Mugabe interview, **1980** 321-322, 324-326, 328-329
MacNeish, Richard S., **1992** 135-139
Macroeconomic policy, **1999** 93-94; **2002** 58-62; **2003** 75-77, 84-90
MAD. *See* Mutual Assured Destruction
Mad cow disease (bovine spongiform encephalopathy), **2000** 880-892
  and food safety, **2000** 883-884; **2001** 698-699; **2002** 583
  origin of, **2000** 880-881, 884-885; **2003** 1235
  protections against, **2003** 1237-1239
  secretary of agriculture on, **2003** 1234-1244
Maddox, Lester, **1976** 695
Madigan, Edward, Food Guide Pyramid withheld, **1992** 397
Madison, James
  on the constitution, **1997** 416
  on D.C. voting rights, **1978** 590
  at first presidential inaugural, **1989** 124
  twenty-seventh constitutional amendment, **1992** 439
Madrid (Spain), terrorist bombings, **2004** 105-114, 137, 268, 535, 540; **2005** 393
Madrid, Migule de la, free trade agreement, **1993** 954
Madrid Declaration on Euro-Atlantic Security and Cooperation, **1997** 514-526
Madsen v. Women's Health Center, **1994** 311-326
Mafart, Alain, **1985** 633
Magaziner, Ira, health care policy, **1993** 783
Magruder, Jeb Stuart
  offers of clemency and cash to, **1974** 158, 163
  release from prison, **1975** 143
  on Watergate break-in planning, **1973** 501
Mahan v. Howell, **1973** 277-289
Mahdi, Adel Abdul, Iraq interim government, **2005** 945
Mahdi Army (*aka* Jaysh al Mahdi), **2004** 879; **2005** 664, 673
Maher v. Roe, **1977** 407-409, 419-427
Maheu, Robert, **1973** 976
Mahon, George (D-Texas)
  Ford budget, **1976** 40
  national debt with Nixon budget, **1974** 95
Mahoney, James, global warming, U.S. policy on, **2003** 864; **2004** 831
Mahoney, Patrick J., Ten Commandments displays, **2005** 379
Mahoney, Roger M. (archbishop of Los Angeles), sexual abuse by priests, **2004** 86, 87
Mahoney, William P., **1981** 578
Mai Van Bo, **1972** 496-497
Mail
  See also Postal Service (U.S.)
  interception of by intelligence agencies, **1976** 126, 129-130, 138, 239, 273-274
    CIA, **1975** 401, 409, 418-419, 426, 524, 527-528
  use of for allegedly obscene brochure, **1974** 515-516, 520-522
  and wire fraud, in insider trading, **1987** 881-889

Maine
Canada-U.S. trade agreement and industry in, **1988** 573
smoking prevention program, **2004** 282
Maine et al., United States v., **1975** 167-175
Maisano, Frank, Clean Air Act, **2002** 897
Maizière, Lothar de
agreement to Soviet Union, **1990** 602, 607-608
first government after reunification, **1990** 107
Major, John
on apartheid vote, **1992** 285
British-Irish peace efforts, **1993** 923-927
on mad cow disease, **2000** 881-882
on Munich economic summit, **1992** 637
on Northern Ireland, **1994** 449-457
ousted by Tony Blair, **1998** 204
as prime minister, **1997** 277-278, 279
resignation of Prime Minister Thatcher, **1990** 747, 749
royal family problems, **1992** 1059, 1062-1063
at Tokyo economic summit, **1993** 542
Makuza, Bernard, Rwanda prime minister appointment, **2003** 1071
Malawi, HIV/AIDS victims, **2004** 429
Malaysia
economic crisis, **1998** 722
financial crisis, **1997** 833
human trafficking, **2002** 346-347
as oil supplier, **1981** 800
tsunami relief effort, **2005** 1005
Maldives, tsunami relief effort, **2005** 1002-1003
Malecela, John, **1986** 582
Malek, Frederic V., **1974** 97
Maleter, Pal, **1989** 340-341
Mali, drought and famine in, **1984** 974, 979-980
Malik, Yakov, **1973** 882
Malin, Michael C., water on Mars, possibility of, **2000** 380-382
Malinowski, Tom, Abu Ghraib prison scandal, **2004** 340
Mallerais, Bernard Tissier de, excommunication of, **1988** 490, 492
Mallick, George, in Wright ethics investigation, **1989** 240, 248-257, 262-264
Mallightco, Inc., in Wright ethics investigation, **1989** 240, 251-257, 259-263
Mallon, Seamus, Northern Ireland peace agreement, **1998** 205; **1999** 754, 756
Malloy v. Hogan, **2000** 390
Malnutrition
causes and effects of, **1985** 190-193, 195-199, 201
infant formula linked to, **1981** 447, 450, 917
Malone, James L., Law of the Sea Treaty, **1982** 346
Malone, James W.
dissent among U.S. clergy, **1986** 985
U.S. bishops' letter on economic policies, **1984** 959
U.S.-Vatican diplomatic relations, **1984** 21
Vatican II report, **1985** 571-572
Malta, EU membership, **2004** 198
Malta summit, Gorbachev-Bush, **1989** 643-660
Maltais, Vern, Roswell incident, **1997** 401
Maluf, Paul, in Brazil election, **1985** 3-5
Malvinas. *See* Falkland Islands (Malvinas)
Malvo, Lee Boyd, sniper shootings in Washington, D.C., **2005** 180
Mammograms, **1997** 38, 142-149; **2001** 869-870; **2002** 265, 510
Manafort, Paul, **1989** 335
Managed care
health insurance coverage, Census Bureau on, **1999** 561-567
and patients' rights, **1998** 46-47
Manatt, Charles, **1983** 79
Mancuso, Salvatore, human rights violations in Colombia, **2003** 428
Mandel, Marvin, felony conviction, **1993** 303
Mandela, Nelson
AIDS epidemic, **2000** 415; **2002** 473
Burundi conflict mediator, **1999** 867; **2000** 65; **2003** 923
children, UN special session on, **2002** 221
Clinton state visit, **1998** 161-167
on death penalty, **1995** 283
on executions in Nigeria, **1995** 697, 698
imprisonment, **1986** 582, 586-589; **1989** 546
inaugurations as president of South Africa, **1994** 247-251
Iraq War, views on, **2003** 454
land mines ban, **1997** 845
Lockerbie case agreement, **2003** 1223
Namibian independence, **1990** 199-200
Nobel Peace Prize
acceptance speech, **1993** 877-884
winner, **1994** 247
release, **1985** 516, 525, 533
remarks opening Parliament, **1995** 101-109
South African constitution, **1992** 284-285, 888; **1993** 1003, 1005; **1996** 249
South African leadership and legacy, **1999** 297-299
South African speech and U.S. visit, **1990** 65-68, 76-80
South African Truth and Reconciliation Commission report, **1998** 756
Mandela, Winnie, human rights abuses, **1998** 758, 771-772
Mandell, Shelley, sexual harassment, **1993** 941
Mandelson, Peter, WTO negotiations, **2005** 411
Mandil, Claude, oil prices, **2005** 778
Manezes, Jean Charles de, British police killed by mistake, **2005** 397
Mangieri, United States v., **1990** 494
Mankiewicz, Frank, **1979** 120
Mankiw, Gregory N., outsourcing and international trade, **2004** 59
Manley, Audrey F., physical activity report, **1996** 418
Manley, Dexter, **1989** 215
Mann, James R. (D-S.C.), **1974** 288
Mann, John, suicide in adolescents, **2004** 748
Mann, Thomas E., **1986** 1067
MANPADS. *See* Man-Portable Anti-aircraft Defense Systems
Man-Portable Anti-aircraft Defense Systems (MANPADS), **2004** 152
Mansfield, Mike (D-Mont.)
on civility in the Senate, **1998** 151-158
congressional vs. executive powers, **1973** 4-11

Mansfield, Mike (D-Mont.) *Continued*
Democratic proposals at inflation summit, **1974** 861-862, 867-870
Kennedy tribute by, **1973** 965-966
limited test ban agreement, **1974** 538
Mayaguez incident, **1975** 311
MIA commission, **1977** 207
Nixon defense spending, **1973** 802
response to Nixon State of the Union, **1974** 41-42, 62-65
Sinai accord, U.S. monitoring of, **1975** 574
support for Kissinger, **1974** 488-489
White House taping system, **1973** 697
Manufacturer's Hanover Trust Co., and New York City's fiscal crisis, **1977** 568, 577
Manywa, Azaria Ruberwa, vice president of Congo, **2003** 290
Mao Zedong
See also Jiang Qing
attempted assassination of, **1973** 767-774; **1974** 271-275; **1980** 955-958
Chinese leadership, **1997** 94, 95, 97, 98; **2002** 851
constitution's reliance on, **1978** 158-160, 163
death of, **1976** 687-691; **1997** 95
Hoxha, relations with, **1985** 327
leadership of, **1984** 165
Nixon meeting, **1972** 187; **1977** 337-338
as reinforcement of legitimacy of, **1972** 183
party congresses
absence from, **1975** 43-44
presiding over, **1973** 768-769, 773-775, 778
and Soviet communism, Nixon on, **1977** 361
Tanaka meeting, **1972** 828
Mapplethorpe, Robert, **1990** 510, 511; **1998** 406
Maran, Stephen, **1992** 379
Marburger, John H., III, Bush administration science and technology accomplishments, **2004** 842-843
Marbury v. Madison, **1997** 417; **1998** 909
Marcelino, Juan M., mutual funds scandal, **2003** 695
March v. Chambers, **2002** 385
Marchais, Georges, on Communist Party in France, **1976** 434, 457-458
Marchenko, Anatoly T., death of, **1986** 95, 1091, 1094; **1987** 190, 202
Marchenko, Ivan, holocaust, **1993** 618-619
Marcos, Ferdinand
B. Aquino assassination, **1984** 925-927
conflict with Catholic Church, **1981** 203-204
and coup attempt against C. Aquino, **1987** 843-844
human rights under, **1977** 20-24; **1984** 166; **1985** 154; **1986** 98, 110-111
indictment of in U.S., **1988** 867-872
John Paul II opposition to, **2005** 293
martial law ended by, **1981** 204
ouster of, **1986** 307-314, 1037-1038; **1987** 190, 201
Philippine president resignation, **2001** 102
wealth of, **1986** 309-310
Marcos, Imelda
B. Aquino assassination, **1984** 926
indictment of in U.S., **1988** 867-872
preparations for papal visit, **1981** 203
wealth of, **1986** 309-310
Marcovich, Herbert, as U.S. intermediary with North Vietnam, **1972** 491, 495-496
Marcus, Yoel, **1983** 833
Marcus v. Hess, United States ex rel., **1993** 434
Marcy, Geoffrey, planet explorations and discovery, **1999** 174-177; **2001** 146-147
Mardian, Robert C.
Watergate cover-up
conviction and sentencing, **1974** 991-992; **1975** 141, 144, 150-151
indictment, **1974** 157, 159, 161, 163-164
Marei, Sayed, accepting Sadat's Nobel Prize, **1978** 607, 624-625
Margolis, Jon, in vice presidential debate, **1988** 804-805, 810-812, 817-818, 823-825
Mariel boatlift, **1980** 337-350; **1981** 605; **1993** 413
agreement on Cuban detainees in U.S., **1987** 929-937
Marijuana
See also Drug use
decriminalization of, **1972** 155, 291, 295-299; **1996** 571
effects on health, **1972** 155-162; **1982** 203-211
history of use in U.S., **1973** 399-401
law enforcement recommendations on, **1972** 291, 295, 297-300
legalization for medical use, **1996** 755-758; **1997** 462; **2001** 293
prevalence of use in U.S., **1972** 156-157
social policy recommendations on, **1972** 291-297
Supreme Court on, **2001** 325-330; **2005** 552
therapeutic uses of, **1972** 162
use in U.S., **1996** 575, 579; **1999** 460, 463
Marine Corps (U.S.)
barracks bombing in Beirut, **1983** 933-966; **1985** 464
discrimination against women, **1987** 671-679
terrorist attack on in Lebanon, **1983** 933-966
Marine ecosystem
See also Ocean pollution
Alaskan oil spill impact on, **1989** 225, 227-230
protection of, Law of the Sea Treaty on, **1982** 347, 355-356
Mariotta, John, Wedtech conviction, **1988** 498, 500, 503
Maris, Albert B., on federal control of offshore oil, **1975** 168-173
Maris, Roger, home run record, **1998** 626
Maritime shipping, U.S.-PRC agreement on, **1980** 829, 832, 834-836
Market economy
East German shift to, Kohl on, **1989** 631-632
international, Soviet interest in cooperation in, **1989** 647, 651
Polish shift to, **1989** 524, 530-533
Marketing, of infant formula in developing countries, **1981** 447-448, 452, 455-456
Markey, Edward (D-Mass.)
on human radiation experiments, **1993** 989
Nuclear Nonproliferation Treaty, **2005** 466
and stock market crash, **1988** 12
television rating system, **1996** 833; **1997** 529
television violence, **1993** 489-490

Markle Commission on the Media and the Electorate, **1990** 295-299
Markovic, Mirjana, **2000** 834
Markowitz, Harry M., Nobel in economics, **1990** 796
Marks, Gerald M., **1987** 428
Marks v. United States, **1990** 243, 244
Marlowe, Howard, **1984** 183
Marovic, Svetozav, president of Serbia and Montenegro, **2003** 57
al-Marri, Ali Saleh Kahlah, enemy combatant case, **2003** 112
Marriage
  Catholic Church on
    annulments among Catholics, **1980** 871-872; **1983** 95
    canon law revised, **1983** 95, 98
    sanctity of, John Paul II on, **1980** 874; **1982** 837, 847
    unity of, **1980** 879, 881-882
  child marriage, **2001** 957
  constitutional amendment
    banning same-sex marriage, **2004** 21
    defining marriage, **2004** 21, 41
  domestic partners measure, Catholic Church on, **1989** 307
  entry or exit permits to allow, Helsinki Final Act on, **1975** 487, 559, 569
  forced, and women's rights, **1975** 507-508, 521-522
  polygamy in Mormon church, **1981** 337
  same-sex civil unions, **2000** 158-167
  same-sex marriage, **1996** 687-690; **1997** 761; **1999** 4
    Bush administration on, **2003** 401-402; **2004** 21; **2005** 79
    Canadian legislation, **2004** 42; **2005** 869
    constitutional amendment on marriage, **2004** 21, 40; **2005** 79, 85
    in Europe, **2000** 162
    international legislation, **2005** 869
    Massachusetts Supreme Court ruling on, **2003** 401-402, 404-405; **2004** 37-55; **2005** 863
    state legislation, **2004** 39-40; **2005** 863, 868-869
  as union of a man and a woman, **2004** 29, 37, 41
Mars (planet)
  Bush plan for missions to, **2004** 9-16
  Climate Orbiter (MCO) mission, **1999** 711-717; **2000** 89, 90, 95-102; **2003** 302; **2004** 4
  Express probe, **2003** 301-309; **2004** 6
  Global Surveyor (MGS) mission, **2000** 89, 95-102, 379-384; **2002** 213-215; **2003** 302, 304; **2004** 4
  life on, NASA statements on, **1996** 471-477; **2000** 379-384
  mission failures, NASA report on, **2000** 88-102; **2003** 632
  NASA explorations, **1999** 175-176
  Odyssey mission, **2000** 379
  Opportunity rover, **2003** 303; **2004** 3; **2005** 501-502
  Pathfinder mission, **1997** 509-513; **1999** 712; **2000** 89; **2003** 302; **2004** 3
  Polar Lander (MPL) mission, **1999** 711-717; **2000** 89, 95-102; **2003** 302; **2004** 4
  rovers mission, NASA on, **2004** 3-8
  Spirit rover mission, **2003** 303; **2004** 3-8, 9; **2005** 501-502
  U.S. manned mission to, **1987** 649, 651, 655-656, 662-664, 667-669
  Viking 1 and *Viking 2* missions, **2003** 302; **2004** 3
  water on, possibility of, **2000** 379-384; **2002** 214-215
Marsh, Robert T., infrastructure commission chairman, **1997** 712
Marsh v. Chambers, **1992** 561-562
Marsh & McLennan Companies, lawsuit, **2004** 418
Marsh Inc., lawsuit, **2004** 418
Marshall, Andrew, climate change report, **2004** 830
Marshall, Burke, **1972** 783
Marshall, Cecelia, **1993** 340
Marshall, F. Ray
  affirmative action ruling, **1979** 495
  aid for New York City after blackout, **1977** 547
  appointment to labor secretary, **1976** 878-879
  coal miners' strike, **1978** 113, 115-188
  Commission on the Future of Worker-Management Relations member, **1995** 15
  employee rights in dangerous workplaces, **1980** 199-207
Marshall, George C., **1984** 440
Marshall, Margaret H., gay marriage legislation, **2003** 404, 414-424
Marshall, Thurgood
  abortion
    family-planning clinic advice, **1991** 259, 266-272
    parental consent for, **1990** 387-407
    and privacy right, **1973** 102
    public funding of, **1977** 408, 414, 416-418, 425, 428; **1980** 515-516, 525, 528-533
    right to, **1986** 559
    state restrictions on, **1983** 544, 565-566, 569-572; **1989** 367, 379
  affirmative action
    admissions to medical school, **1978** 468-471, 478, 487-489
    discrimination by labor union, **1986** 654
    job program, **1979** 494
    promotion of women, **1987** 332
  alcoholism and veterans' benefits, **1988** 279, 284
  alimony for men, **1979** 193
  antitrust immunity of cities, **1982** 35
  auto search and seizure, **1978** 754, 761; **1982** 425, 427-428, 439
  Balanced Budget Act and separation of powers, **1986** 707, 718
  bankruptcy and labor contracts, **1984** 182, 193
  bankruptcy court system, **1982** 597-610
  broadcast of offensive material, **1978** 515, 517, 526, 531
  child pornography, **1982** 677; **1990** 240, 245-249
  church and state separation, **1982** 955-961
  class action suits, **1974** 428, 432
  coerced confessions, **1991** 175-176
  commercial speech, promoting integration by preventing, **1977** 313-320
  congressional immunity, **1979** 467
  Constitution bicentennial, **1987** 767-768

Marshall, Thurgood *Continued*
corporate speech in referendum campaigns, **1978** 307, 318
Court workload, **1982** 706, 722-723
creation science, **1987** 566
death penalty, **1993** 142-143
competency of willing defendant, **1976** 918, 921-923
as cruel and unusual punishment, **1972** 499, 502-503; **1978** 507-508, 514; **1980** 455, 457, 462-466
ex post facto, **1977** 519
jurors opposed to, **1986** 447, 454-456
mandatory for murder of police officer, **1977** 397
mitigating factors, **1982** 51
racial discrimination in, **1987** 463, 473
for rape, **1977** 517, 525
state laws on, **1976** 489-490
summary procedures for appeal, **1983** 709-710, 717-719
discrimination
compensation for, **1984** 366-367, 376
settlements, **1989** 322, 331
drug paraphernalia sales, **1982** 215-223
education for alien children, **1982** 490
electronic surveillance, **1974** 393, 403; **1977** 884, 891; **1979** 269, 279
employer pension plans, women's payments in, **1978** 293-294, 303-305
exclusionary rule, **1984** 506-508, 516
faculty tenure review disclosure, **1990** 23-34
federal minimum wage laws applied to states, **1976** 378, 385
flag burning, **1989** 343; **1990** 357-362
home video taping, **1984** 54, 69
indigents' right to psychiatric aid, **1985** 208-217
intra-enterprise conspiracy doctrine, **1984** 414, 422
job discrimination
age discrimination, **1983** 232
parental leave and, **1987** 17-25
proof of, **1989** 322, 328, 331
seniority systems and, **1977** 384, 392-393
suit against member of Congress, **1979** 399
judicial immunity, **1978** 260, 266
jury trials
racially motivated selection of jurors, **1986** 412, 421-425
size of jury, and unanimous verdict, **1979** 264, 268
split verdicts in, **1972** 423
labor union members, freedom to resign, **1985** 415, 424
legislative apportionment and one-man, one-vote rule, **1973** 278, 284
legislative veto, **1983** 610
libel from misquotation, **1991** 329-330
libel of private and public persons, **1986** 355, 357
Marcoses' petition to, **1988** 868
maternity leave, seniority rights after, **1977** 872, 877
media ownership, **1978** 419-432
medical treatment for severely handicapped infants, **1986** 543, 545
minority set-aside programs, **1980** 539-540, 558-560; **1990** 419-428
Miranda warnings, **1984** 388, 395-397; **1985** 225-226, 236
and definition of interrogation, **1980** 431, 433, 439-441
rule affirmed, **1990** 785-790
Noriega phone calls dispute, **1990** 721-725
obscenity
and harmless error, **1987** 479, 485
standards for, **1973** 612, 622; **1974** 516, 519, 522
OSHA safety inspections, **1978** 340
PAC spending limits, **1985** 279, 290
papers, complaints over release of, **1993** 339-345
parental rights in child custody, **1982** 260
passport revocation, **1981** 541, 552
patenting of living organisms, **1980** 494, 500
political asylum, **1987** 253
political campaigns
candidates' personal wealth in, **1976** 110
gerrymandering and, **1986** 618
open political primaries, **1986** 1065-1066, 1068-1071
political firings from public jobs, **1980** 259
pregnancy coverage in company disability plans, **1976** 892, 900
presidential immunity, **1982** 539, 552
press freedom
access to pretrial hearings, **1979** 511, 513, 525
confidentiality of sources, **1972** 508
gag orders and right to fair trial, **1976** 464, 473
libel of public figures, **1979** 285, 307-311
newsroom searches, **1978** 355, 367
prison crowding, **1981** 478-488
prisoner appeals, **1991** 205, 215-218
property takings
for historic preservation, **1978** 453
uncompensated, **1987** 549
public display of Nativity scene, **1984** 219, 231
racial segregation, public housing in suburbs, **1976** 233
resignation from Supreme Court, **1991** 377-379
reverse discrimination in firing employees, **1976** 406-411
right to counsel, **1974** 482; **1977** 220, 228; **1979** 207, 211
right to die, **1990** 375, 382-386
school book banning, **1982** 568-578
school desegregation, **1977** 463; **1991** 24, 29-33
continued balance, **1976** 414, 421-423
cross-district remedies for, **1974** 639-640, 649, 651-654
restrictions on busing, **1982** 620, 644
school financing
based on property tax, **1973** 362-363, 372-377
public aid to parochial schools, **1977** 431-432, 441-443; **1985** 433
searches
evidence from illegal, and *habeas corpus* claim, **1976** 523, 532
prisoners' rights in, **1984** 480-481, 485, 491
of students, **1985** 15, 24
secrecy of CIA sources, **1985** 333, 335, 342-344

sentencing
double jeopardy and, **1980** 978, 986
excessive prison sentences, **1983** 659
in murder cases, **1991** 381, 391-395
preventive detention, **1987** 491-493, 502-508
sex discrimination
in education, **1984** 202, 213
by Jaycees, **1984** 468
in military draft, **1981** 521, 532-540
in pension plans, **1983** 691-692, 694-701
in Social Security survivors' benefits, **1977** 169
in statutory rape cases, **1981** 346
snail darter protection from dam project, **1978** 433
sodomy and privacy right, **1986** 601, 608
student aid and draft registration, **1984** 496, 500-503
student newspaper censorship, **1988** 38, 45
students' free speech, **1986** 731, 733, 739-740
students' rights, corporal punishment and, **1977** 293, 303
succeeded by Clarence Thomas, **1994** 33, 34, 36, 38-39
tax increase for school desegregation, **1990** 227-228, 229-232
treaty termination, **1979** 917, 933
tuition tax credit, **1983** 676, 678, 684-688
unitary taxation, **1983** 645
utilities regulation, **1982** 448
voter residence requirements, **1972** 283-290
water rights, **1982** 689
worker health protection, **1981** 492
zoning
for adult theaters, **1986** 133, 140
barring low-income and minority housing, **1977** 36, 43
Marshall v. Barlow's, Inc., **1978** 339-353
Marshall Plan, as basis for EC, **1984** 440
Marston, David W., dismissal of, **1978** 51-64
Martin, Graham, former ambassador to Vietnam, **1997** 489
Martin, John S., sentencing laws, **2003** 982
Martin, Paul (Canadian prime minister)
defense missile system, **2004** 181
election defeat, **2005** 409
meeting with Qaddafi, **2004** 168
UN Climate Change Conference address, **2005** 922-923, 927-930
Martin v. Struthers, **1994** 296
Martin v. Wilks, **1989** 322, 324, 329-332
Martin Marietta Corp., **1990** 754
Martinez, Bob (R-Fla.), **1989** 367; **1990** 217
Martinez, Eugenio R.
Ellsberg break-in, **1974** 205-206, 208-210, 411-417, 661-662, 667-668
Watergate break-in, **1973** 415, 419-423
Martinez, Marty (D-Calif.), apparel industry sweatshops, **1997** 209
Martinez, Mel (R-Fla.)
Guantanamo Bay prison, **2005** 450
Schiavo end-of-life care case, **2005** 159
Martinez, Ricardo
aggressive driving, **1997** 550
air bag regulations, **1996** 801-806; **1997** 774-775
Martinez-Fuerte, United States v., **1995** 342
Martinique (French West Indies), Ford-Giscard d'Estaing meeting, **1974** 981
Martonyi, Janos, at NATO membership ceremony for Hungary, **1999** 121, 124-125
Marty, Dick, CIA secret detentions investigations, **2005** 908
Marulanda, Manuel "Sureshot," Colombia peace negotiations, **2000** 842; **2002** 570
Marxism
criticism of by John Paul II, **1988** 165-166, 168-169, 174
and liberation theology, **1984** 759-762, 766-773
John Paul II on, **1985** 57-58; **1986** 640, 648
Vatican on, **1986** 317, 319, 323
Marya S. Norman-Bloodsaw et al. v. Lawrence Berkeley Laboratory et al., **1998** 66-72
Maryland
death penalty moratorium, **2002** 353, 354-355
health insurance benefits legislation, **2005** 737
welfare reform, **1999** 258
Marzen, Thomas, **1986** 544
Masaryk, Jan, death, **1990** 4
Masaryk, Thomas Garrigue, **1990** 8-9, 12
Mashek, John, in presidential debates, **1988** 723, 726-728, 734-735, 741-742, 749-750
Masire, Ketumile
Botswanan leader, **2001** 161
Lusaka peace agreement, **2000** 979
Masire, Q. K. J., **2000** 450
Maskhadov, Aslan (Chechen rebel leader)
Chechnya war, **1999** 910
death of, **2005** 304
Moscow subway bombing, **2004** 565
al-Masri, Abu Hamza, London mosque fiery sermons, **2005** 396
el-Masri, Khaled, wrongful detention, **2005** 914
Mass Democratic Movement, **1989** 546
Mass media
See also News media
electronic, and fairness doctrine, **1987** 627, 629-630, 632-634, 636
sex and violence in, John Paul II on, **1987** 701, 710-711
voter participation report, **1990** 295-299
Mass transit
Carter programs for, **1979** 320, 324; **1981** 73-74
Nixon proposals for, **1972** 102-103; **1973** 305, 319; **1974** 41, 48, 60-61, 107
privatization in, **1988** 236
Massachusetts
child sexual abuse by priests, attorney general on, **2003** 523-543
gay marriage, Supreme Court ruling on, **2003** 401-402, 404-405; **2004** 37-55
political campaigning by banks and corporations, **1978** 307-324
same-sex marriage legislation, **2005** 868
Massachusetts v. Morash, **1993** 252
Massachusetts v. Oakes, **1990** 244
Massachusetts v. Sheppard, **1984** 508
Massachusetts Freedom to Marry Coalition, **2004** 40

Masselli, Nathan, in Donovan investigations, **1982** 588, 595-596
Masselli, William P.
  in Donovan investigations, **1982** 588, 595
  indictment, **1984** 803-809
Massey, Douglas S., **1989** 447
Massiah v. United States, **1991** 207, 209-211, 214-215
Masson, Jeffrey M., libel case, **1991** 317-326
Masson v. New Yorker Magazine, **1991** 317-326
Massoud, Ahmed Shah, Afghan Northern Alliance leader assassinated, **2004** 915
Massoud, Ahmed Zia, Afghanistan vice presidential candidate, **2004** 915
Matanza, in El Salvador (1932), **1987** 640
Maternal and Child Health Block Grant, **1987** 152
Maternal mortality, UNICEF report on, **1996** 343-352
Maternity policies. *See* Parental leave; Pregnancy
Mathematics education
  math and science gender gap, **1992** 142, 148
  reform of, **1983** 414-415, 419, 429-430, 433
  students' progress in, **1988** 377-382
  upgrading of, **1989** 86-91
Mather, John, **1992** 381
Mather Air Force Base (Calif.), closing of, **1988** 952
Mathews, David, and swine flu program, **1978** 670, 674, 681
Mathews v. Eldridge, **1990** 402
Mathews v. United States, **1992** 320
Mathias, Charles McC., Jr. (R-Md.), **1980** 568; **1990** 295-299
Matloff, Norm, **1997** 669
Matsch, Richard P., **1997** 624
Matsui, Robert (D-Calif.)
  reparations for Japanese-American internees, **1988** 289
  Social Security reform, **2001** 915-916
Matsunaga, Spark M. (D-Hawaii), on reparations to Japanese-Americans, **1988** 289, 290-291
Matthews, Gabriel Baccus, **1980** 276
Matthews, Gary, **1986** 171; **1993** 169
Mauer, Marc
  crime rates increasing, **2003** 982
  prison reform, **2002** 787
Mauritania
  drought and famine in, **1984** 974, 979-982
  human rights, **1990** 135
May, Richard, UN war crimes tribunal for Kosovo war, **2001** 830
May, William, dismissal from President's Council on Bioethics, **2004** 843
Mayardit, Salva Kiir, Sudan rebel leader, **2005** 521
Mayers, Daniel, Russian nuclear weapons panel, **2001** 19
Mayfield, Brandon, wrongful arrest for Madrid bombings, **2004** 110
Mazuz, Menachem, Sharon corruption charge case dropped, **2004** 306
Mbeki, Thabo
  African aid, impact of Iraq War, **2003** 453
  African conflict resolution, **2002** 447
  African Union summit meeting, **2003** 454
  AIDS, questioning causes of, **2000** 410, 414-415; **2003** 784
  AIDS prevention and treatment, **2002** 473; **2003** 784
  amnesty, **1998** 759
  ANC human rights violations, **1998** 756
  Burundi peace agreement, **2003** 924-925
  Ivory Coast peace negotiations, **2005** 804-822
  New African Initiative, **2001** 507; **2002** 447
  New Partnership for African Development (NEPAD), **2002** 447-448, 450-4511
  South Africa presidential inauguration speech, **1999** 297-303
  U.S. trade sanctions, **1999** 491
  World Summit on Sustainable Development speech, **2002** 596
  Zimbabwe elections, **2002** 133
  Zimbabwe-South Africa relations, **2003** 1114-1116
M'Bow, Amadou-Mahtar, **1983** 969
McAdams, Francis H., **1979** 950-951
McAfee, Robert, **1987** 817
McAleese, May, **1999** 756
McAndrew, James, Roswell incident, **1997** 396-405
McAuliffe, Christa, *Challenger* accident, **1986** 515, 520-521; **1988** 796
McBride, Bill, Florida gubernatorial campaign, **2002** 822
McBride, Richard P.
  on academic freedom at Catholic universities, **1986** 760
  on papal order on Drinan, **1980** 411
McCaffrey, Barry R.
  cocaine penalties, sentencing for, **1997** 246
  Colombia drug emergency, **2000** 843
  drug control programs, **1996** 617
  drug czar appointment, **1996** 30
  drug use among teenagers, **1996** 571-572
  drug use survey, **1999** 459, 461
  marijuana law enforcement, **1996** 756; **1997** 462
  national commission on terrorist attacks recommendations, **2004** 458
McCain, John (R-Ariz.)
  campaign finance investigations, **1996** 840
  campaign finance reform, **1997** 31, 33, 826-827; **1998** 50, 893; **1999** 56; **2000** 619; **2004** 777
  and carbon dioxide emission controls, **2003** 866
  detainees treatment amendment, **2005** 80, 909-910
  entertainment industry, marketing violence to children, **2000** 731
  Georgia (country), free parliamentary elections, **2003** 1040
  greehnouse gas emissions, **2005** 922
  Inman nomination, **1994** 24
  International Olympics Committee investigations, **1999** 108
  Jeffords party switch, reaction to, **2001** 379-380
  "Keating Five" investigation, **1989** 465; **1990** 817; **1991** 107-118
  line-item veto, **1997** 611; **1998** 422
  Medicare prescription drug pricing, **2003** 1123
  movie industry rating system, **2000** 732
  prescription drug importation, **2004** 985
  presidential campaign, **2000** 520

on presidential credibility abroad, **1995** 720
Republican Party and, **2001** 378
at Republican Party convention, **2000** 511
Republican Party convention nomination speech, **1996** 479
Senate debate on women in combat, **1991** 492, 506-508, 510-512
space program, future of manned space flight, **2003** 637
steroid use in baseball, **2005** 216-217
tax cut proposal, **2001** 401
television rating system, **1997** 529
tobacco claims settlement, **1998** 841
UN sanctions against Iraq, **2004** 714
U.S. intelligence gathering commission, **2005** 247
on U.S.-Vietnam relations, **1995** 472-473
vice presidential candidate, **2004** 480
Vietnam trade embargo, **1994** 97-98
war hero, **1999** 39; **2000** 918
women in combat, **1981** 511-512; **1991** 506-508, 510
McCain-Feingold law. *See* Bipartisan Campaign Reform Act
McCann, Mark, U.S. detention facilities inspections, **2004** 217
McCarthy, Colman, **1985** 783
on moral theology, **1993** 845
McCarthy, Eugene J. (D-Minn.)
campaign financing limits, **1976** 71-111
equal time demands of, **1976** 695
support for in presidential election, **1976** 841
McCarthy, James J., global warming, **2001** 111
McCarthy, John, **1991** 753
McCarthy, Timothy J., **1981** 351-352; **1991** 185, 188
McCartney, Robert, death of, **2005** 508-509
McCarver, Ernest P., death penalty, **2001** 388
McChesney, Kathleen, child sexual abuse by priests, **2004** 83
McChristian, Joseph, **1985** 161
McChrystal, Stanley (Maj. Gen.), Iraq War, **2003** 143
McClain, Charles W., Jr., Patriot missile performance report, **1992** 866
McClellan, Mark
Medicare premium increase, **2004** 582
morning-after pill, without prescription for, **2003** 998
prescription drug advertising, FDA warning letters, **2002** 948
prescription drug benefit for seniors enrollment, **2004** 578
prescription drug importation, **2004** 985
McClellan, Scott
Bagram base prisoner treatment, **2002** 832
death penalty, **2005** 179
global warming policy, **2002** 300
government-funded video news releases (VNRs), **2005** 647
Iraq War troop withdrawal, **2005** 837
Middle East roadmap to peace, **2003** 1207
stem cell research ethics, **2004** 160
Uzbekistan Andijon killings, **2005** 432
McCleskey v. Kemp, **1987** 463-476; **1990** 314
McCleskey v. Zant, **1991** 205-218
McClintock, Tom, California gubernatorial recall election, **2003** 1008, 1009
McClory, Robert (R-Ill.)
impeachment inquiry report, **1974** 138
Nixon resignation, **1974** 674
Rockefeller's qualifications, **1974** 988
McCloskey, Paul N., Jr. (R-Calif.), **1972** 711-712
McClure, Herbert R., **1986** 255
McClure, James A. (R-Idaho; attorney), **1978** 590
Russian nuclear weapons panel, **2001** 19
McCollum, Bill (R-Fla.)
BCCI banking scandal, **1991** 634
House Judiciary Committee impeachment inquiry, **1998** 702-703
McCollum v. Board of Education, **1993** 406
McCone, John, and CIA plot against Castro, **1975** 734-736, 744, 749, 751, 779-785, 792
McConnell, Mitchell (R-Ky.)
campaign finance reform law opponent, **2003** 1156, 1158
husband of Elaine Chao, **2001** 97
limits on gifts to members of Congress, **1995** 701
Senate majority leader candidate, **2002** 973
McConnell v. Federal Election Commission, **2003** 1155-1172
McCool, William C., *Columbia* astronaut, **2003** 633
McCord, James W., Jr.
grand jury testimony, **1973** 500
letter to Sirica, **1973** 415-417; **1975** 655
offers of clemency and cash to, **1974** 158-163
Watergate committee testimony, **1973** 550
McCormack, Ellen, **1976** 597
McCormack, Sean, Israel security wall controversy, **2003** 1209
McCormick, Richard, **1987** 269
McCorvey, Norma, abortion rights, **2003** 999
McCoy, Alfred W., **1972** 646
McCreary County v. ACLU of Kentucky, **2005** 376-380, 384-389
McCulloch v. Maryland, **1992** 567; **1999** 347
McCullough, David, U.S. Capitol bicentennial, **1989** 132-133; **1993** 893, 895, 899
McCurdy, Dave (D-Okla.)
on anti-Clinton sentiments, **1994** 610
CIA reforms, **1992** 5, 10
McCurry, Michael D.
on outreach events, **1997** 761
security clearance reform, **1995** 532
McDermott, Jim (D-Wash.), single-payer health insurance, **1993** 784
McDonald, Brian, **1994** 241
McDonald, Henry, space shuttle program safety, **2000** 93-94
McDonald, Larry P. (D-Ga.), **1983** 775
McDonald and Laird v. Santa Fe Trail Transportation Co., **1976** 405-411
McDonald's
obesity lawsuit, **2003** 483-484
smoking ban, **1994** 206
McDonnell Douglas Corp., DC-10 crash investigation, **1979** 949-963
McDonnell Douglas Corp. v. Green, **1993** 424-427, 429-430

McDonough, William J., SEC accounting board, **2003** 338
McDougal, James B. and Susan, Whitewater investigation, **2000** 763, 764
McDougal, Susan, presidential pardon, **2001** 89
McDowell, Barbara, gun control laws, **1995** 185
McElroy, William G., Jr., **1972** 419-422
McEntee, George, W., **1995** 681
McFall, John J. (D-Calif.)
House reprimand, **1978** 845-846, 879-880
in Korean influence-buying scheme, **1978** 874
McFarland v. Scott, **1994** 162
McFarlane, Robert C.
arms control talks, **1984** 259
Iran
U.S. arms sales, **1986** 1051, 1053
U.S. contacts with, **1986** 1015-1017, 1021
Iran-contra affair, **1991** 618; **1992** 1073-1079
conviction, **1994** 12
role in, **1987** 216, 225, 228, 232, 892, 897, 899, 906, 924; **1994** 11, 13, 14, 16
sentencing, **1989** 392-394
and Oliver North Iran-contra conviction, **1990** 493
NSC appointment, **1983** 829
"October Surprise" report, **1993** 11
South Africa, lack of change in, **1985** 533
Soviet pipeline, and investigation of Meese, **1988** 498, 512-515
McGarr, Frank, death penalty panel, **2000** 989
McGhan Medical Corp., **1993** 369
McGhee, James D.
black families, single-parent, **1985** 27-28
effects of recession on blacks, **1983** 42
McGill, William J.
National '80s Agenda, **1981** 39
public broadcasting report, **1979** 120, 122
McGinn, Ricky, death penalty execution, **2000** 991
McGinty, Kate, logging policy, **1993** 498
McGovern, George S. (D-S.D.)
acceptance speech, **1972** 589, 591-596
antiwar support for candidacy of, **1972** 407
campaign contributions to, **1974** 603
congressional vs. presidential power, **1973** 87-95
and Democratic Party platform, **1972** 527; **1992** 686
draft evader pardon, **1977** 96
economic program of, **1972** 737-742
election concession, **1972** 893-896
Kent State protesters commemorated, **1990** 290, 291-294
minority views of, Nixon on, **1972** 886
presidential campaign, **1994** 239
SALT II, effect on arms race, **1979** 416
size of military force, **1972** 733
vice presidential choices, **1972** 597-608
young voter support for, **1973** 36-37
McGowan, Carl
access to White House tapes, **1973** 842
treaty termination, **1979** 919
McGowan, Daniel, health care, **1997** 791
McGrath, Mary, **1993** 369
McGraw, Steven C., Foreign Terrorist Tracking Task Force, **2001** 766
McGuinness, Jeffrey C., **1995** 130
McGuinness, Martin, **1994** 449; **1999** 756; **2001** 759
McGwire, Mark
home run record, **1998** 626-631
steroid use in baseball, congressional hearings on, **2005** 213-215, 220-221
use of steroids, **1999** 461
McHenry, Donald F.
UN appointment, **1979** 651
UN vote on Israeli settlements, **1980** 235-238
McHugh, James T., **1995** 145-146
McIntyre, James T., Jr.
appointment to OMB, **1977** 628
Carter budget, **1980** 110
creation of Education Department, **1979** 162-168
privatization commission, **1988** 229
McKay, David S., **1996** 472, 474-476
McKay, James C., Meese investigation, **1988** 466, 495-516; **1998** 906
McKay, Robert B., commission on Attica Prison uprising, **1972** 783-788
McKay, Ronald, stem cell research, **2005** 320
McKee, Alice, **1992** 141, 142
McKelvey v. Turnage, **1988** 277-285
McKennon, Keith, **1993** 368-369
McKiernan, David D., Iraqi detainee abuse investigations, **2004** 208
McKinley, Brunson, on presidential elections in Haiti, **1987** 939-941
McKinley, William, presidential campaign, **2003** 1157
McKinney, Cynthia A. (D-Ga.), **1995** 370
McKinney, Gene C., military sexual harassment case, **1997** 656-657; **1998** 336
McKinnon, Don, British Commonwealth membership, Zimbabwe suspension, **2003** 1115
McKusick, Victor A., **1992** 362, 364
McLaren, Richard W., on ITT antitrust settlement, **1972** 396, 398-400, 403
McLarty, Thomas F., III, **1992** 1021
McLaughlin, Ann, **1990** 301-310
McLaughlin, John, on Nixon's morality, **1974** 302
McLaughlin, John E.
CIA deputy director forced out of agency, **2004** 968
North Korea political situation, **2001** 267-268
McLaughlin v. Florida, **1995** 313
McLaurin v. Oklahoma, **1992** 41
McLaury, Bruce K., **1996** 785
McLean, Bethany, on Enron Corp., **2001** 859
McLean v. Arkansas Bd. of Education, **1982** 3-16
McLucas, William, WorldCom collapse fraud case, **2003** 335
McMahon, John Alexander, **1973** 39
McManus, Michael, government-funded propaganda, **2005** 645
McMillan, John L. (D-S.C.), and D.C. home rule charter, **1995** 497
McMillen, Tom (D-Md.), Knight report on college athletics, **1991** 130
McMullen, Peter, **1986** 752
McNair, Denise, church bombing victim, **2002** 240, 244
McNair, Ronald E., *Challenger* accident, **1986** 515, 520; **1988** 795

McNamara, Robert S.
CIA's Mongoose operation, **1975** 752-753
developing countries' needs, **1977** 687-689, 698-716
no-first-use defense policy, **1982** 305-315
order of Pentagon Papers study, **1972** 491, 493
population and environment study, **1980** 667
population growth, **1984** 523
testimony in Westmoreland libel suit, **1985** 160
World Bank farewell speech, **1980** 883-893
McNealy, Scott, on Microsoft Corp. antitrust ruling, **2000** 110
McNeill, John J., on Catholic Church's view of homosexuals, **1986** 909-911
McNerney, Walter J., **1986** 488
McNichols v. Baldrige, **1982** 171-178
McPeak, Merrill A. (Gen.), women in combat, **1993** 333-334
McPherson, M. Peter, **1981** 449
McQuillian, Thomas R., **1992** 534
McVeigh, Timothy
death penalty and execution of, **2002** 356
and Oklahoma City bombing, **1995** 177; **1996** 178; **1997** 623-627; **1999** 480; **2001** 387, 390, 433-437
McWherter, Ned, **1992** 685
McWilliams, David, interrogation of terrorist suspects, **2004** 380
Mead, Kenneth, and airport security, **1999** 114
Mead, Margaret, **1974** 779
Meadows, Dennis L., on limits to world growth, **1972** 215-217
Meadows, William H., oil exploration in Arctic National Wildlife Refuge, **2001** 336
MEADS. *See* Medium Extended Air Defense System
Means, Russell
Christopher Columbus Legacy, **1992** 899
Wounded Knee occupation by AIM, **1973** 532-533
Meany, George
affirmative action ruling, **1979** 495
Carter cabinet appointments, **1976** 879
détente, **1975** 482
lifting of wage and price controls, **1973** 45
support for Carter and Mondale, **1976** 773, 788-790
Thieu meeting, **1973** 448
Mears, Walter, **1976** 774
Mease, Darrell, death sentence commuted, **1999** 830
Meat imports, authority to suspend tariffs and quotas, Nixon on, **1973** 428, 434
Meat prices
ceilings imposed on, **1973** 427-428, 430-431, 434-435
freeze on, lifting of, **1973** 703-704, 709, 712-713
Mecham, Evan, impeachment and conviction of, **1988** 249-256
Medact, Iraq medical system, **2004** 406
Médecins sans Frontières. *See* Doctors without Borders
Medeiros, Humberto, on attempted assassination of John Paul II, **1981** 428-429
Medellin, Jose Ernesto, on Texas death row, **2004** 798
Medellin v. Dretke, **2004** 798
Medellin drug cartel, Noriega's assistance to, **1988** 83-87
Medicaid
abortion funding, **1977** 407-427; **1980** 516-518, 522-535
alcoholism causes and treatments, **1983** 335-336, 339-343, 346-350
Alzheimer's care, **1987** 393-395, 397, 399, 402-404
catastrophic illness expense, **1986** 1026-1027, 1035
consolidation of into block grant, in Ford budget, **1976** 38, 43
contraceptives for teenagers, **1986** 1060
eligibility, **1998** 88; **1999** 564
equitable access to health care, **1983** 317-320, 326, 329-331, 333
hospital stay, length of, **1988** 333, 335-337
hospitals, for-profit, **1986** 487-488, 491-492, 496, 498, 506
infant and maternity programs, cuts in, **1987** 149, 152, 162-163
for persons with disabilities, **1999** 320
Reagan budget cuts in, **1982** 145, 156; **1983** 755; **1984** 100; **1986** 50
CBO on, **1983** 772
effect on blacks, **1983** 42, 45, 49, 53
in Reagan's new federalism proposal, **1982** 74, 79, 81
reform, **1996** 451, 557
shortcomings of, **1985** 200, 203
smoking, costs of, **1985** 615, 618-619
spending, **2002** 54-55; **2005** 78
spending growth, **1997** 52, 63-64
Medical care. *See* Health care; Health insurance; Physicians
Medical devices
artificial heart implants, **2001** 475-484
heart pumps (ventricular assist devices, VADs), **2001** 477
Medical errors. *See* Medical mistakes
Medical ethics. *See* Bioethics; Physician-assisted suicide
Medical Expenditure Panel Survey (MEPS), **2000** 139
Medical liability reform, **2005** 144
Medical malpractice, cap on awards for damages, **2003** 850-851; **2004** 20
Medical mistakes
Bush State of the Union address on, **2004** 28
IOM report on, **1999** 779-793; **2001** 191, 192, 193
and malpractice damage awards, **2003** 851
Medical records
parents and minors rights, **2001** 498-500
privacy issue, **1997** 580-587, 795; **2000** 400-401
privacy regulations, **2000** 1063-1071; **2001** 485-503
Medical research
See also Biomedical research
and animal rights, **1988** 348
commercialization of, **1987** 351-372
ethics of cloning, president's council on, **2002** 512-529; **2004** 157-167
on fetuses, HEW regulations on, **1975** 543-556
Medicare
alcoholism care and costs, **1983** 335-336, 343, 352-353
Alzheimer's care, **1987** 393-395, 397, 399, 402-404
benefits changes, in Ford budget, **1977** 58

Medicare *Continued*
budget surplus and, **1999** 42, 43, 45-46, 90, 354-356
catastrophic coverage in Ford budget, **1976** 14, 21, 38, 42
coverage for mammograms, **1997** 38
Democratic Party platform on, **2000** 615
enactment of (1965), **1986** 273-274
equitable access to health care, **1983** 318-320, 329-331, 333
financial crisis, **2004** 582-583
for-profit hospitals, **1986** 487-491, 495-496, 506-508, 510
growth in outlays for, Reagan CEA on, **1984** 132
payment system changes, in Reagan budget, **1984** 100, 109; **1986** 50
premium increase, **2004** 582
prescription drug benefit
cost estimates controversy, **2004** 577-587
reform, **2003** 18, 23, 38-39; **2004** 20, 27-28
prescription drug benefit reform, **2000** 18, 24-25, 131-140
Reagan budget cuts in, **1982** 145, 156; **1987** 4, 10
CBO on, **1983** 772
in Reagan's new federalism proposal, **1982** 81
reform, **1996** 557, 712-713; **1998** 89, 93-94
Harvard proposals, **1986** 273-285
legislation, **2003** 18, 26, 847, 1119-1128
restructuring of, **1986** 1025-1026, 1027, 1029-1030
smoking, costs of, **1985** 615, 618-622
spending cuts, **2005** 78
spending growth, **1997** 52, 63-64
tax credits for uninsured, **2000** 24
trust fund, **2001** 58
vouchers as means to privatize, **1988** 235
Medicare Modernization Act, **2004** 577
Medicare Prescription Drug Act (2003), Bush remarks on, **2003** 1119-1128
"Medigap" insurance industry, **1986** 1027-1028, 1030
Medimmune, flu vaccine supplier of FluMist, **2004** 640
Medium Extended Air Defense System (MEADS), **2004** 180-181
Medrano, Juan Ramon, **1992** 26
Medvedev, Roy A.
election of, **1989** 175
Gorbachev speech on revolution anniversary, **1987** 858
Soviet reforms, **1975** 482
Meech Lake Accord, **1990** 367-372
Meehan, Martin T. (D-Mass.)
campaign finance reform, **1997** 33; **1998** 893; **1999** 56; **2003** 1155
House Judiciary Committee impeachment inquiry, **1998** 708-709
Meek v. Pittenger, **1993** 403, 406; **1997** 366, 377
Meese, Edwin, III, **1988** 495, 497
agreement with Cuban detainees, **1987** 931
confirmation of, **1985** 481
criticism of Court, **1985** 479-490, 653-655, 666-668
diversion of funds to contras, **1986** 1013-1014, 1017, 1022-1024, 1050
ethics investigation of, **1988** 466, 495-516
hunger in U.S., **1983** 765; **1984** 4; **1985** 189-190
independent counsel law, **1988** 466-467
investigation of, **1998** 906
Iran-contra inquiry by, **1987** 894, 897, 906, 919, 924; **1989** 392; **1994** 16-17
school prayer amendment, **1985** 381
sentencing guidelines, **2005** 681
transfer of presidential power, **1985** 493
Meester, Douglas, Air Force Academy cadet court-martialed for sexual misconduct, **2003** 793
Megawati Sukarnoputri, **1999** 718-720
Mehlis, Detlev, Hariri assassination, UN investigation, **2005** 690-692
Mehmood, Anser, terrorist suspect detained, mistreatment of, **2003** 624-625
Meinhold, Keith, homosexual discharged from military, **1993** 155
Meir, Golda
Israeli-Egyptian disengagement, **1974** 30
Israeli-Syrian disengagement, **1974** 435-436
Nixon meeting, **1974** 467
peace negotiations, **1973** 932
Meirelles, Henrique, Brazil economic situation, **2002** 778
Meisinger, Susan R.
on EEOC guidelines on mental disabilities, **1997** 129
on sexual harassment policy and practice, **1998** 441
Meislin, Richard J., **1984** 522
Meissner, Doris M., Elian Gonzalez political asylum case, **2000** 266
Mellman, Kenneth, Social Security privatization plan, **2005** 112
Mellon, Margaret, **1992** 470
Melnikov, Vladmir I., on Soviet elections, **1989** 174, 178
Memoirs v. Massachusetts, **1973** 611, 614-617, 626; **1990** 244
Memphis (Tennessee)
affirmative action in fire department, **1984** 365-385
school uniform policy, **1996** 91
Men
and affirmative action promotion of women, **1987** 331-349
mental health services used by, **1984** 833-834, 840-841, 843
military draft, sex discrimination in, **1981** 521-540
Social Security survivors' benefits for, **1975** 56, 177-185
statutory rape laws, sex discrimination in, **1981** 339-349
Menchu, Rigoberta, human rights issues, **2001** 613
Mendel, Gregor, genetics research, **2000** 398
Mendoza, Enrique, Venezuelan opposition leader, **2004** 552
Menem, Carlos
Argentine economic policy, **2002** 81-82
Argentine presidential elections, **2002** 81, 82; **2003** 825
IMF-World Bank joint meeting address, **2002** 82

Menéndez, Mario Benjamin, surrender in Falklands war, **1982** 284, 302, 304
Menendez, Robert (D-N.J.), Cuban Americans, restrictions on, **2004** 248
Mengele, Josef, discovery of body, **1985** 409-414
Mental health
of black Americans, environmental influences on, **1983** 42-43, 49
care of mentally ill report, **1990** 573-598
depression screening, federal task force on, **2002** 265-274
EEOC mental disabilities guidelines, **1997** 127-141
federal legislation, **2002** 267-268
and insanity defense, **1982** 531-537; **1983** 30, 34-39
and marijuana use, **1972** 161; **1982** 204, 206-207
mentally retarded, rights of, **1982** 521-530
minority mental health, surgeon general's report on, **2001** 575-592
prevalence of disorders in U.S. adult population, **1984** 833-843
psychiatric testimony in trials, **1983** 707, 710, 715, 720-722
services, use of and need for, **1984** 833-834, 841-843
services for discarded children, **1989** 671, 673, 675, 678, 680, 682
surgeon general's report on, **1999** 836-849; **2001** 575, 868
therapist-patient privilege, Supreme Court on, **1996** 388-395
TV violence, effect on, **1982** 365-383
uncertainties of treatment of illness, **1975** 470, 476
White House Conference on, **1999** 49; **2000** 25
Mental patients
involuntary commitment of, standard of proof for, **1979** 335-344
rights of to liberty and to treatment, **1975** 469-480
Mentally retarded
death penalty, **1998** 187-188
death penalty prohibition, **2001** 387-394; **2002** 353-368; **2005** 177
Mentor Corp., **1993** 369
Mercer, Thomas, **1992** 1054
Merck
drug safety, **2004** 850-866
SEC investigations, **2004** 852
Vioxx withdrawal, **2004** 850-852
MERCOSUR, **1998** 95
Mercury Bay Boating Club, **1989** 183-184
Mercury emissions regulations, **2004** 667, 842; **2005** 95-110
MACT (maximum achievable control technology) vs. cap-and-trade approach, **2005** 102, 104, 106-110
state lawsuits against, **2005** 98
Meredith Corp., and FCC complaints, **1987** 626, 628, 635-636
Mergers. *See* Corporate mergers
Merhige, Robert R., Jr., on Richmond school desegregation plan, **1972** 15-21
Meridia, drug safety of, **2004** 853
Merisotis, Jamie, **1993** 173
Merit Systems Protection Board, creation of, **1978** 138, 141-142, 144, 146-147
Meritor Savings Bank v. Vinson, **1992** 197; **1993** 942-945; **1998** 438, 445-446, 449, 455-457, 460, 463
Merkel, Angela
coalition building among political parties, **2005** 876-878
election campaign, **2005** 875-876
EU budget controversy, **2005** 344
EU membership for Turkey, **2005** 342-343
first woman as German chancellor, **2005** 878
German chancellor agenda for change speech, **2005** 879-890
political career and Kohl mentorship, **2005** 874-875
U.S.-German bilateral meeting with Rice, **2005** 908
Merlo, Thomas J., **1992** 303, 308
Merola, Mario, on Donovan indictment, **1984** 804-807
Merriam, William R., Beard memo to on ITT settlement and political contributions, **1972** 395-398
Merrill, William H., Ellsberg break-in prosecution, **1974** 663-664
Merrill Lynch, stock market scandals, **2003** 696
Merrill Lynch, Pierce, Fenner and Smith, Inc., New York City's fiscal crisis and, **1977** 567, 577
Merrill Lynch, Pierce, Fenner and Smith, Inc. v. Curran, **1992** 195
Merriman, Walker, **1982** 165
Merz, Friedrich, German parliamentary elections, **2005** 875
Mesa, Carlos, Bolivian president forced from office, **2005** 769
Meselson, Matthew, **1982** 237
Mesic, Stjepan, Croatian presidential elections, **2000** 141
Messemer, Robert, Wen Ho Lee spy case, **2000** 742
Messing, David, Air France flight 4590 crash, **2000** 489
Metcalf, Joseph, III, **1983** 849
Metcalf, Lee (D-Mont.), **1978** 18
Metro Broadcasting, Inc. v. FCC, **1995** 308, 312, 315-316, 322-323
Metromedia, Inc. v. San Diego, **1994** 292, 293
Metropolitan Edison Co., expertise on nuclear accidents, **1979** 824-827
Metzenbaum, Howard M. (D-Ohio)
food labeling proposal, **1990** 176
on General Motors truck safety settlement, **1994** 445
Rehnquist appointment, **1986** 592
Souter nomination, **1990** 625-626
on television violence, **1993** 488
Thomas confirmation hearings, **1991** 563-565
Metzler, Cynthia, apparel industry sweatshops, **1997** 209
Mexican-Americans. *See* Hispanic Americans
Mexico
assassination investigations, **1994** 563-564
Caribbean economic aid from, **1982** 180, 186
Chiapas rebellion, causes of, **2004** 931
and Contadora Group, **1987** 638
debt relief for under Brady plan, **1989** 138-139
drug summit, **1992** 201-221
elections, **2005** 772

Mexico *Continued*
financial crisis, **2002** 82
human rights, **1990** 131, 139-140
immigration to U.S., **1997** 176-177
ceiling raised, **1981** 606, 615
Institutional Revolutionary Party (PRI), **1994** 563-564
John Paul II's visit to, **1979** 726-728, 730-738
NAFTA, **1992** 759-763; **1993** 953-958
Octavio Paz wins literature Nobel, **1990** 795-806
as oil supplier, **1981** 800
peso devaluation and debt crisis in, **1982** 971-972
political situation, **2005** 772
poverty summit in, **1981** 769-778
religious persecution, **1997** 564
smoking in the Americas, **1992** 269
temporary worker program in U.S., **1981** 605, 611
trade agreements with U.S., **1988** 573
U.S. relations, **1979** 169-181; **2001** 764-765
attention to developing countries, **1972** 471-474
improvement in, **1979** 713, 719
Vicente Fox presidential inauguration, **2000** 963-977
Zedillo inaugural address, **1994** 563-573
Mexico City, International Women's Year conference, **1975** 507-522
Meyer, Edward C., **1982** 327
Meyer v. Grant, **1999** 5
Meyer v. Nebraska, **2000** 292
Meyerhoff, Al, **1996** 72
Meyerhoff, Harvey M. "Bud," **1993** 308
Mezvinski, Edward (D-Iowa), **1974** 988
Mfume, Kweisi (D-Md.)
Congressional Black Caucus activities, **1993** 581
Lott's racist statements, **2002** 971, 973
at Million Man March, **1995** 656
president and CEO of NAACP, **1995** 453, 454-455
Schott suspension for racist remarks, **1993** 168
Texaco executives racial slurs, **1996** 765, 766
Miami Herald Publishing Co. v. Tornillo, **1974** 523-528
Michael H. v. Gerald D., **1990** 380
Michael M. v. Superior Court of Sonoma County, **1981** 339-349
Michel, Robert H. (R-Ill.)
appointment of Iran-contra committee, **1986** 1052
bipartisan accord on Nicaraguan contras, **1989** 164
federal election system reform, **2001** 526
House censure of Crane and Studds, **1983** 726
Iraq war resolution, **1991** 5
Reagan budget, **1982** 145
retirement as House Republican leader, **1998** 800
Soviet propaganda, **1981** 753
U.S. Capitol bicentennial, **1993** 900-901
Michelman, Kate, on Nader presidential campaign, **2000** 898
Michigan
See also University of Michigan
Jessica DeBoer adoption case, **1993** 515-529
PBB-contaminated animal feed in, **1978** 653-658
Michigan v. Tucker, **1974** 473-485; **2000** 392
Michigan Dept. of State Police v. Stitz, **1995** 342
Microsoft Corporation
affirmative action, **2003** 362
antitrust case, **1999** 654-689; **2000** 105-130, 302-303
breakup ruling, District Court on, **2000** 308-324
settlement, **2001** 775-792; **2002** 797-817
homosexuals, discrimination in the workplace, **2005** 869
Internet viruses and worms, **2003** 391-392
Microsoft Corporation, United States v., **2001** 780-792
Middle East
See also Arab states; Arab-Israeli conflict; Arab-Israeli war; Palestinians; *individual countries*
Bush on "new" democratic Iraq, **2003** 137-138
Bush plans for democratization of, **2005** 42-43, 164
Bush State of the Union address on, **2005** 80-81, 88
conflicts, Soviet views of, **1981** 763; **1984** 827-828
Democratic Party platform on, **1984** 636-637; **1996** 645; **2000** 616
economic situation, **2000** 1050-1051, 1059
economic summit (London), **1991** 466
Forum for the Future meetings, **2004** 629; **2005** 273
human rights, **1990** 130-131
nuclear-free zone proposed for, **1981** 514-515, 748
peace process
Barak comments on, **1999** 364-366
Brezhnev proposals for, **1981** 225, 231-232, 234-235
Bush plan, **1991** 122, 124-126
Camp David accords, **1979** 223-250
Egyptian-Israeli treaty, **1979** 227-250
framework for, **1978** 605-606, 608-613
Shamir on, **1983** 832, 842-843
Camp David summit, **2000** 475, 494-507
Declaration of Principles, **1993** 747-768; **1995** 622; **1998** 742
Democratic Party platform on, **1980** 713, 762, 768
Geneva conference on
as groundwork for further negotiations, **1973** 932, 935; **1975** 573-576, 586
Palestinian participation in, **1974** 835, 845
Israeli proposal, **1985** 710-711
Madrid Conference, **1991** 719-731
Millennium Summit talks, **2000** 702
negotiations
Carter on work toward, **1978** 9, 17, 47
U.S. offers to Israel and Egypt, **1975** 363
opportunities for, and U.S. foreign aid, **1974** 277-286
and Palestinian self-determination, **1974** 833-834, 837-838
Paris peace talks, **2000** 932
PLO observer, Young's meeting with, **1979** 647-657
progress in, Carter on, **1981** 60, 86, 94-95
prospects for, Kissinger on, **1976** 907-908, 910
Reagan initiative, **1982** 753-767; **1984** 816-817
requirements for

Baker on, **1989** 289-296
Brezhnev on, **1976** 147
Carter on, **1977** 738, 743-744
Gromyko on, **1974** 833, 835, 844
Sadat initiative, **1977** 827-855
Saudi plan for, **1981** 631-637
Sharm el-Sheikh (Egypt) peace talks, **2000** 933
Sinai
partial withdrawal from, **1975** 573-586
return of to Egypt, **1982** 337-344
statement of G-8, **1997** 359
terrorist opposition to, **1995** 39
U.S. role in, **1995** 623-624
Carter on, **1977** 899, 902, 906-907
Ford on, **1975** 233-234
Kissinger on, **1975** 12
and Saudi oil price, **1976** 937-938
West Bank agreement, **1995** 622-630
Wye River peace agreement, **1998** 742-754; **1999** 52-53, 700
Republican Party platform on, **1984** 711-712; **1988** 617, 683-684; **1992** 834-836; **1996** 544-545; **2000** 515
sex trade and human trafficking, **2004** 130
state visit of John Paul II, **1998** 77, 79-81
superpower balance in, Schlesinger on, **1979** 659, 661-662
terrorism in, **1983** 933-966
CIA on, **1981** 465-466, 473
economic summit on, **1981** 593
escalation of, **1985** 463-470
Reagan on, **1985** 463-464, 466, 468-475
Shultz on, **1984** 940-941
U.S. planes and weapons sales in, **1978** 105-107, 109, 125-134; **1981** 631, 637, 787-798
violence in, UN Human Rights Commissioner report, **2000** 930-951
violence on the Temple Mount, **1990** 695-711
weapons development, **1996** 217-218
Middle East Partnership Initiative, **2002** 483-484, 487; **2003** 957-959; **2004** 628-629; **2005** 272
Middle East peace
Geneva Accord, **2003** 1203-1205
Mitchell Commission report on, **2001** 360-376
post-Arafat diplomacy, **2004** 809-810
roadmap to peace/"Quartet" sponsors (U.S., EU, Russia, and the UN), **2002** 375-377; **2003** 191-205, 1200, 1203, 1207, 1213-1216
Sharm el-Sheikh (Egypt) peace talks, **2001** 361-362
and UN conference against racism, **2001** 613
Middle East Watch, **1990** 131
Middle-Class Bill of Rights, **1994** 610-616; **1995** 73-74, 86-87
Midwest Independent System Operator (MISO), power blackout investigations, **2003** 1015-1016, 1021-1022
Miers, Harriet, Supreme Court nomination, **2005** 79, 551, 558, 562-563, 767
Migration
See also Immigrants and immigration
economic and political, inter-American dialogue on, **1983** 377, 384-385
internal
proposed guidelines for in developing countries, **1974** 785-786
to Sun Belt and jobs, **1981** 39-40, 49-54, 327
to urban areas, **1992** 476
World Bank projects in Indonesia, **1986** 859-873
international
facilitating, **1974** 786-788
and global interdependence, **1981** 266-268
and population pressure in developing countries, **1984** 530-531, 546-547
preventing discrimination against workers, **1974** 787
as response to drought and famine, **1984** 974, 983-984
Migratory birds, and climate change, **1988** 866
al-Mihdhar, Khalid, September 11 attacks hijacker, **2002** 992; **2003** 545-546, 555-561, 566-567
Mikati, Najib, Lebanon elections, **2005** 689
Mikerevic, Dragan, Bosnian Serb prime minister resignation, **2004** 953
Mikolashek, Paul T., Iraqi prison abuse scandal, **2004** 211
Mikulin, Ivan, **1990** 456
Mikva, Abner J. (D-Ill.), **1978** 97
Milanovic, Branko, income inequality, **2002** 690
Milbank Memorial Fund, end-of-life care guidelines, **1997** 329
Miles, Richard
Georgian elections negotiations, **2003** 1044-1045; **2004** 72
ousting of Milosevic in Yugoslavia and, **2003** 1045
Military Academy (U.S.), hazing and other practices, **1992** 481-487
Military aid
See also Arms sales; Foreign aid; Human rights; *individual countries and regions*
Nixon requests for, **1974** 278-280, 285
reform of programs, Nixon on, **1972** 80-81
U.S. aid linked to human rights, State Department rationale, **1977** 3, 10, 12-13, 19-20, 23-25
U.S. and inter-American dialogue on, **1983** 375-377, 385-390
U.S. economic policies, U.S. bishops on, **1984** 961, 971
Military aircraft, administrators' use of, **1992** 293-299
Military base closings, commission report, **1988** 951-954; **1993** 501-513; **1995** 407-418
Military command, coordination of, **1985** 670, 677, 683
Military deserters
exclusion from Carter's pardon, **1977** 95, 184, 186
Ford amnesty program for, **1974** 813, 819-831
Military draft
amnesty for evaders of
Democratic Party platform on, **1972** 528, 576
Ford on, **1974** 768, 813, 819-831; **1976** 701-703
Nixon on, **1972** 12-13, 722; **1973** 193-194, 197-198
Clinton letter on, **1992** 155-161
ending
Democratic Party platform on, **1972** 577, 733
Nixon on, **1972** 733-736

Military draft *Continued*
Republican Party platform on, **1972** 663-664
history of, **1972** 734
opposition to, in Reagan-Anderson debate, **1980** 848, 855-858
pardon of evaders, Carter on, **1977** 95-99
procedural changes, **1972** 247-251
reduction in calls, Nixon on, **1972** 79, 98-99
registration
and federal student aid, **1984** 493-503
reinstituted under Carter, **1981** 523
of women, **1981** 522-525
reinstatement of, **1980** 28, 35
sex discrimination in, **1981** 521-540
system in Vietnam era, **1984** 349
Military force, use of
Carter-Reagan debate on, **1980** 920, 922-925, 946
conditions for, Weinberger on, **1984** 1005-1015
Ford-Carter debate on, **1976** 798, 803-804
in oil crisis, Kissinger and Ford on, **1975** 3-4, 8-9
president's consultation with Congress on, **1975** 311-314
to rescue U.S. hostages in Iran, **1980** 351-385, 475-476, 1009
or threat of, Helsinki Final Act on, **1975** 562
Military personnel
See also Air Force Academy (U.S.); Marine Corps (U.S.); Naval Academy (U.S.)
black soldiers, **1983** 43, 50, 52
casualties
bombing in Saudi Arabia, **1996** 672-679
Iraq War, **2003** 144, 941; **2004** 875; **2005** 659, 665, 674, 834-835
Vietnam War, **1984** 347-352
delayed-entry pool, **2004** 786
drug testing of, **1986** 840
in drug war, **1986** 181, 194-195, 842
expanding the Army, **2004** 786
extending tours of duty, **2004** 786, 875
hazing and other practices at military academies, **1992** 481-487
homosexual ban, **1993** 153-164, 328-329; **1997** 761
gays in the military and, **1999** 899-901; **2000** 510; **2004** 37-38, 42
lifted in Britain, **1999** 901
in Korean DMZ, Reagan speech to U.S., **1983** 893, 895
MIAs in Vietnam, **1984** 348, 350-351
National Guard and reserve units in Iraq and Afghanistan, **2004** 784-793, 875
pay increase for, **1972** 733, 735-736; **1979** 464; **1980** 848, 856-857
and upgraded training, **1981** 91; **1983** 88
racial and disciplinary problems, **1972** 901-906
recruitment and retention, **1980** 135-136, 661; **2004** 788-789
redeployments, **2004** 787
reenlistment bonuses, **2004** 787, 875
remedial education for, cost of, **1983** 419
sexual harassment
Army report on, **1997** 654-660; **1998** 335-336
prevention initiatives, **1992** 1003-1005
shortages, **2004** 785-786
stop-loss orders/backdoor draft, **2004** 785-786, 787, 875
stresses on soldiers and their families, **2004** 787-788
Tailhook incident, **1992** 879-890
volunteer force, Nixon on, **1972** 733-736
women
assignment and promotion of, **1972** 627-629; **1987** 671-673, 675-676, 679
in combat debate, **1987** 671, 673, 675-676; **1989** 704; **1991** 491-512; **1992** 1029-1044; **1993** 333-336
housing and working conditions for, **1987** 672, 676-677, 679
Military procurement
procurement reform, Democratic Party platform on, **1976** 546, 585-586
streamlining of, **1986** 679-681, 685-690
Military Selective Service Act (1967)
modifications of, **1972** 247
student aid and draft registration, **1984** 495-497
Military services
See also Army (U.S.); Marine Corps (U.S.); Navy (U.S.)
bureaucratic power of, **1985** 669-671, 675-677, 679
coordination of, **1985** 669-670, 673-674, 683
Democratic Party platform on, **1992** 701-703, 702-703
guard Bush at Cartagena drug summit, **1990** 116
Haitian refugees and Coast Guard, **1992** 453-455, 457-459
Hurricanes Andrew and Iniki, **1992** 844-846
Los Angeles riots, **1992** 408, 410, 426
Republican Party platform on, **1992** 840-841
rivalry among, **1982** 325-336; **1986** 681
Military spending. *See* Defense spending
Military strength
Democratic Party platform, **1996** 642-644; **2000** 616
as foreign policy, Wallace on, **1975** 157-158
maintaining
Carter on, **1976** 733, 736; **1981** 87-92
Ford on, **1976** 733, 736
and national security needs, **1993** 695-715
as negotiating tool
Nixon on, **1973** 802, 807
Republican Party platform on, **1972** 651, 661-663, 666
nuclear strength after cold war, **1992** 56
for peace
Nixon on, **1973** 515-516, 522-523
Reagan on, **1983** 87-88
readiness
for future wars, **1997** 813
improvement in, **1980** 123-124, 130, 132-135
questioning of, **1994** 528-534
Republican Party platform on, **2000** 515
Military support, for drug enforcement, **1986** 181-182, 192, 194-195
Military technology
export controls on, **1987** 29-42
Soviet acquisition of, **1982** 813-819; **1985** 603-614
Toshiba sales to Soviets, **1987** 427, 429

Military trials, Garwood court-martial and conviction, **1981** 197-201
Military tribunals, **2002** 836-837; **2003** 113
Milk price supports, increase in, **1974** 3-4, 6-15
and Nixon campaign contributions, **1973** 948-949, 960, 963-964; **1974** 604-605, 616
Milken, Michael R., **1990** 251-257
Millennium Challenge Account (AIDS program), **2003** 453-454, 766
Millennium Development Goals (UN). *See under* United Nations Millennium Summit
Millennium Round (WTO, Seattle), **1999** 797-801; **2000** 476; **2003** 742; **2005** 409
Millennium Summit. *See* United Nations Millennium Summit
Miller, Arnold, and coal strike, **1978** 111-112
Miller, Candice S. (R-Mich.), Medicare reform bill, **2004** 581
Miller, Edward S., Reagan pardon for, **1981** 371-373
Miller, Emilie F., **1991** 310
Miller, G. William
appointment to Federal Reserve, **1977** 718
appointment to Treasury, **1979** 562, 575
Chrysler loan guarantee, **1979** 693, 695
OPEC price increase, **1978** 790
strengthening the dollar, **1978** 685, 698
Miller, Geoffrey D.
Abu Ghraib prison scandal, **2004** 210; **2005** 450
detainee interrogations, **2004** 212
Guantanamo Bay detainees, **2004** 210, 212; **2005** 450
Miller, George (D-Calif.)
apparel industry sweatshops, **1997** 209
child labor laws, **2005** 738
discarded children report, **1989** 672
education reform, **2002** 42
and Gingrich ethics violation complaint, **1995** 748, 751
Miller, James C., III, **1985** 73; **1987** 4
Miller, Judith, CIA leak case, journalist jailed for protecting source, **2005** 699, 702
Miller, Merton H., Nobel in economics, **1990** 796
Miller, Richard R.
Iran-contra affair, conviction, **1991** 619; **1994** 12
Iran-contra affair, role in, **1994** 15
Miller, Thomas R., United States v., **1994** 109-115
Miller, United States v., **2001** 728-730; **2002** 964-968
Miller, Walter B., youth gang activity report, **2001** 75
Miller, William, advisory council appointment, **2004** 843
Miller, Zell (D-Ga.)
Clinton letter on the draft, **1992** 158
Jeffords party switch, **2001** 380
Republican Party convention speech, **2004** 484
Miller v. California, **1973** 611-621; **1974** 515-521; **1987** 480-487; **1990** 243, 244; **1997** 449-450
Miller v. Johnson, **1995** 369-384; **1996** 369
Miller-El, Thomas, jury selection and racial bias, **2002** 358-359; **2004** 796; **2005** 182
Miller-El v. Cockrell, **2002** 359; **2004** 796; **2005** 182
Milligan, Richard L., *Iowa* (USS) explosion investigation, **1989** 518; **1990** 319; **1991** 679-680
Milliken, William G., **1976** 666
Milliken v. Bradley, **1974** 639-654; **1976** 223-233; **1977** 447-448, 457-464; **1990** 230, 231, 235
Million Man March
Clinton remarks on, **1995** 646, 655
Farrakhan's remarks at, **1995** 655-669
Mills, Cheryl D., Clinton impeachment trial, **1999** 19
Mills, Wilbur D. (D-Ark.)
campaign contributions to, **1974** 603
as McGovern's proposed treasury secretary, **1972** 738
Nixon taxes, **1974** 235-236, 239
Soviet trade agreement, **1973** 791
trade reform bill, **1973** 381
Milosevic, Slobodan, **1991** 368; **1995** 717, 719
Bosnia conflict, **1995** 717, 719
Kosovo conflict, **1998** 828-831; **1999** 134-136, 139, 285-286; **2000** 30; **2003** 1138
ousted from presidency, **2000** 141; **2003** 56, 1040; **2004** 955; **2005** 64
as president of Yugoslavia, **2001** 821
presidential election concession, **2000** 833-837
war crimes, **1999** 738, 802-803; **2000** 837
war crimes trial, **2001** 826-848; **2002** 984; **2003** 99, 463-464, 1072-1073, 1144, 1195; **2004** 956; **2005** 851, 950
Yugoslavia's UN membership, **1992** 876-877
Milutinovic, Milan, war criminal, **1999** 803
Milwaukee (Wisconsin), drinking water crisis, **1993** 261-263
Milwaukee v. Illinois, **1992** 195
Mimeiri, Muhammed, U.S.-Sudan relations, **2003** 840
Mincberg, Elliot, **1992** 34
Miner, Roger J., **1996** 123-124
Mineta, Norman Y. (D-Calif.; secretary of transportation)
FAA responsibilities, **1988** 270
reparations to Japanese-Americans, **1988** 289
Tower commission report, **1987** 207
transportation secretary confirmation, **2000** 1027; **2001** 97; **2005** 45
Minh, Duong Van, and fall of South Vietnam, **1975** 269, 275, 279
Minimum wage, **1995** 70
Brazilian national minimum wage, **2003** 5
Clinton proposals for raising, **1995** 70; **1996** 59; **1999** 42, 43, 88
Clinton's remarks on, **1996** 563-569
Democrat vs. Republican position on, **1996** 697
elimination of, Reagan on, **1980** 920, 928, 932
federal laws on applied to local governments, **1976** 377-389; **1985** 167-187
increase
Carter on, **1981** 59
effect on welfare rolls, **1999** 257
Supreme Court ruling, **2005** 552
U.S., **2005** 485, 490
Wal-Mart public relations campaign and, **2005** 734, 736
and youth wage, **1975** 641; **1980** 932; **1983** 116, 785-790; **1984** 108, 123
Mining industry
coal, surface mining standards, **1973** 914, 920

Mining industry *Continued*
on Law of the Sea Treaty, **1982** 346
mining waste disposal, **2002** 901-902
mountain top mining and water quality, **2004** 670
and preservation of Alaskan lands, **1978** 731-732, 734
of seabed resources, **1982** 346-348, 351-352, 354-361
strip mining, and environment protection, **1976** 545, 575
Minish, Joseph G. (D-N.J.), **1983** 729
Minneapolis Star & Tribune Co. v. Minnesota Comm'r of Revenue, **1991** 820, 822
Minnick v. Mississippi, **1990** 785-793
Minorities
See also Blacks; Hispanic Americans; School desegregation; Women
abortion, effects of restrictions on, **1977** 417-418
affirmative action
charges of reverse discrimination, **1976** 405-411; **1978** 467-492; **1979** 493-507
and seniority system, **1984** 365-385
AIDS among, **1988** 423, 435
boxing as opportunity and danger, **1984** 1020-1021
breast cancer research and, **1993** 921-922
child welfare system, overrepresentation in, **1989** 681
civil rights enforcement
by Nixon administration, **1973** 227-234
by Reagan administration, **1983** 913-917
condition of education report, **1992** 629-634
Democratic Party platform on, **1980** 712, 723-724, 740, 743; **1984** 598-613; **1988** 562-563
discrimination
and the death penalty, **2000** 990; **2001** 387-394
by private clubs, **1988** 399-403
and economic recovery, Reagan on, **1980** 652, 660
education
college, access to, **1985** 584-585, 588, 590-591
high school dropout rate among, **1988** 297, 299-300, 305
of non-English-speaking, **1986** 817
opportunity in, Nixon on, **1972** 95-96, 108-109, 165, 261
progress in U.S. schools, **1989** 85, 87-90
reform movement's impact for, **1983** 415, 418, 428
employment disparities of, **1982** 919-944
on federal bench, **1987** 51-52
hazing and other practices at military academies, **1992** 481-487
health care, heart attack incidence and care, **1993** 671-675
health problems of, **1985** 685-706
job discrimination
Court rulings on, **1989** 321-332
and poverty, **1986** 984, 992, 996-997, 999, 1001
math and science skills among, **1988** 378, 380-381, 384-385
mental health, surgeon general's report on, **2001** 575-592
Navy programs for, **1972** 901-906
presidential advisory board on race relations report, **1998** 665-675
race-based redistricting, **1993** 459-481; **1995** 369-384; **1996** 368-387
Republican Party platform on, **1980** 568, 578-580, 582; **1984** 696-697, 701-702
seniority systems, discrimination in, **1977** 383-393
set-aside programs for broadcasting, **1990** 419-435
smoking trends among, **1989** 32, 36-37
standardized test biases, **1975** 692
in teaching profession, **1986** 475-476
tuberculosis rates, **1993** 856-867
TV watched by, **1982** 366
undercount, **1991** 443, 445
unemployment among, Carter on, **1978** 67-68, 74, 84, 92; **1981** 58-59, 62
and urban school crisis, **1988** 195-219
urban underclass, Kerner Commission update on, **1988** 185-194
voting rights, **2001** 523-524
women as, institutionalized bias against, **1977** 865
Minority business assistance
Democratic Party platform on, **1980** 722-723; **1984** 585-586
Reagan on, **1983** 115
Urban League on, **1983** 50, 54
Minority business set-asides
Carter program for, **1978** 36
in city construction projects, **1989** 323-324
and Donovan indictment, **1984** 803-809
in federal contracts, **1980** 539-566
Minority Participation in Education and American Life, Commission on, **1988** 185-187
Minors' Consent to Health Services Act, **1990** 390-391
Minshall, William E. (R-Ohio), in Korean influence-buying scheme, **1978** 846, 856, 874, 877-879
Miosz, Czeslaw, on Sakharov and Bonner, **1990** 208
Mir (space station)
Lucid flight experience, **1996** 691-694; **1999** 611
news conference from space, **1995** 419-425
service and decommissioning of, **1998** 929-930
Miranda v. Arizona
Court's determination of "interrogation," **1980** 431-444
interrogation after right to counsel invoked, **1981** 431, 433, 441-445
pre-Miranda right to counsel, **1974** 473-485
ruling upheld, Supreme Court on, **2000** 385-395
self-incrimination in psychiatric interview, **1981** 431-441
and voluntary confessions, **1985** 223-253
Miranda warning
Meese on Court rulings on, **1985** 481, 486
and public safety, **1984** 387-397
and right to counsel, **1974** 473-485; **1977** 219-235; **1981** 431-432, 433, 441-445
ruling upheld, **1990** 785-793; **2000** 385-395
and second confession, **1985** 223-253
Supreme Court ruling on upheld, **2000** 385-395
wording of, **2000** 385-386
Misauri, Nur, Philippine activist, **2001** 105-106
MISO. *See* Midwest Independent System Operator
Missile systems
See also MX missile

air-to-surface ballistic, SALT II provisions on, **1979** 421-448
antiballistic
agreement on number of sites, **1974** 535-537, 553-554
Soviet, U.S. response to, **1980** 147; **1986** 782, 785, 789
Anti-Ballistic Missile (ABM) treaty, **2000** 203, 205-206, 677-678, 680; **2001** 281-282, 516, 893-894, 927-934; **2002** 276
antimissile defense system, **1998** 483-484
antisatellite (ASAT), and Reagan budget, **1986** 51
Bush administration, **2001** 281-289, 739-740; **2002** 1026-1031; **2004** 842
GAO report on, **2003** 817-823; **2004** 176-185
Chinese missile sales to Iran and Pakistan, **2000** 218-219
Clinton administration, **2000** 677-687; **2001** 283-284
cruise
launched from B-52 bombers, **1977** 529-533; **1981** 90
SALT II negotiations on, **1978** 550, 556, 571-573
SALT II provisions on, **1978** 566-567; **1979** 414-415, 427-428, 439-440
Soviet, U.S. report on, **1981** 721, 725
status of under Vladivostok accord, **1977** 243-246, 248-250, 252-254, 257, 261-262
and U.S. defense posture, **1980** 124, 129, 133, 137, 156
U.S. deployment in Europe, **1982** 225, 232-233
defensive, presidential debates on, **1984** 847, 893-895
in Falklands war, **1982** 287
intercontinental ballistic
advanced, Ford support for, **1977** 46, 55
balance of in SALT negotiations, **1978** 568-570
MX (Peacekeeper), **2004** 318
SALT II provisions on, **1979** 413-447
Soviet, **1978** 555; **1980** 147, 152; **1981** 718-720, 722-723, 726-728
START II limitations on, **1993** 17-61
under Vladivostok accord, **1974** 957, 968
U.S., **1978** 550-551, 554; **1980** 126, 128-129, 151, 152; **1982** 903-905, 917
intermediate-range
freeze on, Brezhnev proposal, **1982** 225-231
reduction of, Gorbachev on, **1986** 10, 16-17
U.S. deployment in Europe, **1984** 289, 811-813, 822-823, 827
Iran medium-range missiles, **2003** 1031
Iraq missile program, **2004** 716
Medium Extended Air Defense System (MEADS), **2004** 180-181
Midgetman, U.S. strategy for, **1986** 782-786, 789-790
Minuteman missiles, **1992** 60
in nuclear balance, **1980** 124, 128, 152
in Reagan budget, **1987** 4
and SALT negotiations analysis, **1978** 565, 569, 572
North Korean missile program, **2001** 268-270
Patriot missile performance report, **1992** 865-874
Pershing II
in nuclear balance, **1980** 129, 133, 137, 156-157
U.S. deployment in Europe, **1982** 225-226, 232-233
reduction of
destruction of under INF treaty, **1987** 945-946, 951-953, 955-956
Reagan START proposal, **1982** 385-386, 391-392
Russian response to U.S. program, **2002** 1029
"Safeguard" system, **2000** 677
SALT II limitations on, **1979** 413-417, 419-449, 457-458
scud-based missile infrastructures, **1998** 488-492
sea-based missile defense, **2001** 283
short-range, future of, NATO allies' concern about, **1989** 297-298, 300-302
Soviet SS series
freeze announced by Brezhnev, **1982** 225-226, 230, 232-233
reductions in, Andropov proposal, **1982** 983-988
submarine-launched ballistic
SALT II negotiations on, **1978** 570-571
SALT II provisions on, **1979** 421-446
Soviet, **1978** 555; **1981** 720, 726
under Vladivostok accord, **1974** 957, 968
U.S., **1980** 124, 126, 151
surface-to-air, Soviet, **1980** 149; **1981** 720, 722
test failures, **2000** 679; **2004** 177-178
test firings, limits on, **1977** 247, 251
threats to U.S., Rumsfeld Commission on, **1998** 481-499
Titan, and U.S. defense posture, **1980** 124, 128, 152
Trident
Ford support for, **1977** 46, 54-55
and U.S. defense posture, **1980** 136, 152
U.S. and Soviet, numbers at time of SALT II signing, **1979** 449-451
U.S. deployment in Europe, **1981** 717-718, 823-830; **1982** 225-226, 232-233, 305-310; **1983** 792-793
Gorbachev on, **1986** 10, 17
U.S. sales to Saudis, **1981** 787
U.S.-China talks, **2000** 218-219
U.S.-Soviet balance in
Brezhnev on, **1981** 824
with SALT I agreements, **1972** 766-773
vehicle delivery (MIRVs), **1983** 366, 368
limited agreement on, **1974** 536-537
SALT II provisions on, **1979** 413-447
under Vladivostok accord, **1974** 957, 968
Missing in action (MIAs)
accounting for in Southeast Asia, **1995** 472-473, 475; **1999** 476
commission investigating, **1977** 207-218
declassificaiton of U.S. records, **1993** 349
House report on, **1976** 925-936
Republican platform on, **1972** 658
Senate report on, **1993** 113-127
U.S. trade embargo and, **1993** 115; **1994** 96-99
Vietnam, negotiations with, **1997** 491
Vietnam peace agreement on, **1973** 115, 120-121, 157-158

Missing in action (MIAs) *Continued*
Yeltsin on, **1992** 519-520, 521, 525
Mississippi
civil rights workers slayings (1964) trial, **2005** 353-361
smoking prevention program, **2004** 282
Mississippi Burning (movie), **2005** 354
Mississippi River, water quality report, **1994** 147-148, 152-160
Mississippi State University, **1992** 576, 578-587
Mississippi University for Women, **1992** 576, 578-587
Mississippi University for Women v. Hogan, **1991** 309
Mississippi Valley State, **1992** 576, 578-587
Missouri
abortion restrictions of, **1976** 483-488; **1989** 365-389
death row executions, **1999** 830
Missouri v. Jenkins, **1990** 227-238
Missouri ex rel. Gaines v. Canada, **1992** 41
Misty Fjords National Monument, **1978** 732
Mitchell, Andrea, in presidential debates, **1988** 723, 761-762, 769-771, 777-778
Mitchell, George J. (D-Maine)
bipartisan accord on Nicaraguan contras, **1989** 164
Bosnia, Dayton peace agreement, **1999** 736
budget compromise with Bush, **1990** 410
Bush inauguration, **1989** 42
on Bush leadership, **1990** 51
Bush State of the Union, response to, **1991** 36, 45-49
Clean Air Act revisions, **1990** 716
Clinton's economic stimulus package, **1993** 184
congressional bicentennial, **1989** 129-130
Disney board chairman, **2004** 423
independent counsel legislation, **1999** 168
Iran-contra pardons, **1992** 1075
Iraq war resolution, **1991** 4, 9-11
Irish Good Friday peace agreement, **2005** 508
Middle East peace process, Mitchell Commission report on, **2001** 360-376
military homosexual ban, **1993** 153
national commission on terrorist attacks resignation, **2002** 990, 996-997; **2003** 547
Northern Ireland peace negotiations, **1998** 204-205; **1999** 753, 754-755
Olympic bribery scandal investigations, **1999** 107-108, 109
Reagan State of the Union, response to, **1986** 41
Thomas confirmation hearings, **1991** 606-608, 612
tobacco industry lobbyist, **1997** 335
U.S. Capitol bicentennial, **1993** 893, 895-896
war powers debate, **1990** 664, 666
Mitchell, John N.
conviction, **1974** 991-992; **1975** 653-654
as CRP's moving force, **1974** 600
Dean's connection to, **1973** 660
indictment, **1973** 564; **1974** 157-159, 161-171
ITT antitrust settlement, **1972** 396-398, 400, 404, 406; **1974** 5
secret campaign funds, **1973** 414
sentencing, **1975** 141-145, 150
Watergate break-in
approval for, **1973** 501; **1974** 601
informing Nixon about, **1973** 738, 744
Watergate committee testimony, **1973** 550
Watergate involvement, White House tapes on, **1974** 335-336, 342-343, 345-347, 377, 382-387
wife of, Nixon on, **1977** 362-365
wiretaps
authorization procedures, **1974** 384, 391-405
in domestic security cases, **1972** 485
in Nixon White House, **1976** 159-168
Mitchell, Mark L., on takeovers and buyouts, **1988** 921-925
Mitchell, Martha
Mitchell on at sentencing, **1975** 142
and Watergate, Nixon on, **1977** 362-365
Mitchell, Parren J. (D-Md.)
on Carter defense budget, **1978** 97
on Joint Economic Committee report, **1979** 215
Mitchell, Todd, **1993** 385-389
Mitterrand, François
antipoverty proposal, **1995** 135
Cambodia settlement, **1991** 691
Charter of Paris, **1990** 728
chemical weapons ban, **1993** 72
chemical weapons use, **1989** 27
and deportation of Jews, **1995** 479
EC budget controversy, **1984** 439, 441
at economic summits, **1981** 591; **1982** 470; **1983** 509; **1985** 348-349, 352; **1986** 438; **1987** 526; **1988** 392
Munich, **1992** 638
Tokyo, **1993** 542
on German reunification, **1989** 626
and Greenpeace affair, **1985** 631
Soviet aid, **1990** 467
Statue of Liberty centennial, **1986** 697-698, 702-703
Mitzna, Amram, **2002** 937; **2003** 192
Miyazawa, Kiichi
Bush and, **1992** 12, 14-17, 21-22
Japanese monetary policy, **1998** 533
Japan-U.S. trade agreement, **1993** 541, 555-557
at Munich economic summit, **1992** 638
on U.S., **1992** 13, 165
Mjos, Ole Danbolt, Nobel Peace Prize controversy, **2004** 931-932
MKULTRA, CIA project, **1985** 334, 336-338, 341-342
Mladic, Ratko
Kosovo war criminal, **1999** 738, 739, 803; **2001** 826; **2003** 463; **2004** 138, 956; **2005** 851, 853-854
war criminal, **1995** 718
Mnangagwa, Emmerson, Congo resource exploitation, **1974** 551
Moakley, Joseph "Joe" (D-Mass.)
Jesuit murders in El Salvador, **1992** 25
leukemia victim, **2001** 172, 178
al-Moayad, Mohammed al Hasan, arrested for financing al Qaeda, **2003** 1056
Mobil Oil Corp., antitrust investigation of, **1983** 921
Mobutu Sese Seko
corrupt dictator, **2000** 978
ousted from Zaire, **1997** 877-879; **1998** 161, 220, 615; **1999** 428, 645, 863; **2001** 159; **2002** 547; **2005** 1027-1028

Rwandan genocidal war, **2000** 450
Modjeski, Leland William, **1995** 256
Moeller, Per Stig, International Criminal Court, **2002** 609
Mofaz, Shaul, defense minister, **2005** 534
Moffett, William A., access to Dead Sea scrolls, **1991** 639
Mofford, Rose, **1988** 250-251
Mohamad, Mahathir, Malaysian prime minister on currency trading, **1997** 833
Mohamed, Khalfan Khams, embassy bombing conviction, **2001** 803
Mohammad, Atta, Afghanistan warlord, **2003** 1096
Mohammadi, Mawlawi Mohammed Islam, Afghan parliamentary elections, **2005** 972
Mohammed, Khalid Sheikh (*aka* Muktar Balucci)
arrested in Pakistan, **2003** 1055-1056; **2004** 23, 537; **2005** 906
ghost detainee in secret detention, **2005** 906
interrogation techniques used on, **2004** 339
terrorist suspect linked to al Qaeda, **2002** 100, 993; **2003** 106, 563-564
Mohammed, Ramzi, London terrorist bombing suspect, **2005** 397
Mohammed, Shanaz, September 11 detainee, **2003** 314
Mohammed, Sheik Omar Bakri, departure from London, **2005** 398
Mohammed VI (king of Morocco), political reforms, **2005** 273
Mohaqeq, Mohammad, Afghanistan presidential candidate, **2004** 916, 917
Moi, Daniel Arap
Green Belt Movement, response to, **2004** 930-931
Kenyan presidential leadership, **2002** 447, 1044-1046, 1047
Moin, Mustafa, Iranian presidential candidate, **2005** 590
Mojadeddi, Sebaghatullah, Afghan parliamentary elections, **2005** 973
Moldavia
Alma-Ata Declaration, **1991** 804-806
Commonwealth Pact, **1991** 803-804
Molina, Mario J., **1975** 437-438
Molinari, Susan (R-N.Y.)
Republican Party convention keynote speech, **1996** 479
welfare reform, **1996** 462
Molitoris, Jolene, on railroad safety regulations, **1996** 190
Molyneaux, James, **1985** 725
Molz, Frederick, Microsoft antitrust case ruling, **2002** 798
Monaghan, Henry P., on commerce clause, **1995** 185
Moncini, United States v., **1992** 326
Mondale, Walter F. (D-Minn.)
acceptance speeches, **1976** 595-597, 604-607; **1980** 772-773, 783-791; **1984** 647-655, 661-662
Beijing University speech on U.S.-PRC relations, **1979** 669-678
budget reform, **1974** 573
Chrysler loan guarantee, **1979** 695
CIA manual, **1984** 905
Democratic Party platform, **1984** 549-551
Donovan charges, **1984** 805
Education Department creation, **1979** 161-168
election concessions, **1980** 959, 962-963; **1984** 953-956
election debates, **1976** 773-796; **1984** 845-902
eulogy for Humphrey, **1978** 3-6
Ford budget deficit, **1975** 85
Gromyko meeting, **1984** 812
intelligence agencies, oversight of, **1976** 236
Israel, U.S. commitment to, **1978** 127-128, 131-134
Mariel boatlift of Cuban refugees, **1980** 339-340
Nixon inaugural, **1973** 81
OEO, attempted dismantling of, **1973** 454
PAC contributions to, **1985** 278
presidential election (1984), **2004** 316
SDI, **1984** 259
senatorial election, **2002** 821
terrorism, **1984** 934
U.S.-Soviet relations, **1984** 919
vice presidential role, **1976** 846-847, 851
voter registration change, **1977** 199-200
Mones, Paul, child killers, **2001** 348
Monetary policy
Argentine peso, **2002** 81
CEA report on, **2003** 84-85; **2004** 66-67
credit restraint
domestic summit on relaxing, **1974** 862, 868, 870-872, 874, 877
to fight inflation, **1979** 771-774, 776-780
credit supply increase, congressional Democrats on, **1975** 34
dollar, strengthening of, **1978** 683-686, 697-698
economic growth, promotion of, **1972** 968-969; **1980** 216-219, 223-228
Ford CEA on, **1975** 100, 102, 106
Nixon CEA on, **1974** 69-71, 79-80
euro currency, **1998** 271-280; **1999** 75-84
European Community common currency unit, **1991** 843-850
European corporate bond market, **1999** 77-78
Mexican peso collapses, **2002** 82
moderate restraint in, Joint Economic Committee Democrats on, **1981** 295-297, 299-301
monetarism vs. Federal Reserve tight money policy, **1988** 117-118, 121-122, 128-129
money supply growth
Carter CEA on, **1978** 90-91
Ford CEA on, **1976** 55, 65-67
and inflation, Joint Economic Committee Republicans on, **1981** 294, 317-320
Nixon CEA projection, **1974** 79-80
OECD on U.S. moderation of, **1973** 686-688, 693
money supply restraint
effect on economic recovery, Joint Economic Committee on, **1977** 717-719, 725, 730-731
Fed action on, **1979** 772-774, 777-780
money supply restraint to fight inflation
Burns on, **1974** 419, 423-424
Carter CEA on, **1981** 111-112, 125-129
Joint Economic Committee on, **1980** 224-228
in Nixon stabilization program, **1973** 711
Reagan CEA on, **1982** 122, 127, 134-138

Monetary policy *Continued*
Reagan CEA on, **1984** 130-131; **1986** 59-60, 72-73, 76-78
restraint in, Joint Economic Committee on relaxing, **1979** 216-218
restraint in to fight inflation, Carter CEA on, **1980** 159, 163, 175-176, 178-179
restrictive
in Carter's anti-inflation program, **1979** 82-83, 87, 93, 96-97, 110-112
in Reagan economic plan, **1981** 213, 222, 325
Volcker impact on, **1983** 595-597
world economic outlook, IMF report, **2003** 751-766
Monetary system, international
See also Bretton Woods monetary system
effect of on debt crisis, **1982** 971-978
exchange rate stability, **1986** 437-438, 440-441
Paris accord on, **1973** 343
inter-American dialogue on, **1983** 376, 378-381
nonaligned nations on, **1983** 264-265
reform of
developing countries' role in, **1972** 329, 331, 333; **1975** 326, 328, 349-350; **1981** 778
economic summit on, **1984** 356, 360-361
elements needed in, Burns on, **1972** 413-418
IMF efforts in, **1974** 497-505; **1976** 3-12
Nixon on, **1972** 82-85
U.S. proposals, **1972** 815-826
stability in, **1973** 384-387; **1981** 100; **1985** 624
economic summit on, **1982** 470, 476
and U.S. interest rates, economic summit on, **1983** 507-508, 511-513
Money laundering
asset forfeiture case, **1993** 431-438
Cartagena drug summit, **1992** 124
drug summit at San Antonio, **1992** 211-212
in drug war, international cooperation against, **1989** 514
Noriega sentenced for, **1992** 649-653
Noriega indictment for, **1988** 83, 88-90; **1989** 704-705
Mongoose, covert action against Cuba, **1975** 744-754, 790, 792
Monk, Richard, UN peacekeeping panel, **2000** 643
Monopolies
See also Antitrust
intra-enterprise conspiracy doctrine, **1984** 414
Microsoft Corp. antitrust case, **1999** 654-689; **2000** 105-130, 302-303
Microsoft Corp. breakup ruling, **2000** 308-324
Postal Service (U.S.), proposed end to monopoly of, **1988** 230, 233-234
WTO antimonopoly powers, **1999** 393
Monsanto
EPA regulation of chemical discharge from, **1977** 131-141
jobs for welfare recipients, **1997** 34, 622
Montague, Michigan, hazardous waste disposal at, **1979** 785, 787, 791, 793, 795
Montazeri, Ayatollah Hussein Ali, **1989** 98
Montenegro
See also Serbia and Montenegro
political situation, **2003** 56
Monteneros of Argentina, terrorist acts of, **1984** 790-793
Montgomery (USS), and U.S. downing of Iranian airliner, **1988** 704-705
Montgomery, G. V. "Sonny" (D-Miss.), **1977** 208
Monticello (Charlottesville, Virginia), Declaration of Independence bicentennial celebration, **1976** 509-510
Montoya, Joseph M. (D-N.M.), **1974** 606
Montreal Protocol on Substances That Deplete the Ozone Layer, **1987** 745-756; **1988** 221-223, 397; **1990** 469, 476; **1992** 76; **2003** 182
Montt, Efrain Rios, **1996** 851
Montuoro, Mario, in Donovan investigations, **1982** 587, 589, 591-592
MONUC. *See* United Nations Organization Mission in the Democratic Republic of Congo
Moody, Tom, **1982** 37
Moody's Investors Service, Inc., **1977** 568
Moon, NASA missions to and outpost on, **1987** 649, 655-656, 660-662, 668-669
Moore, Charles B., Roswell incident, **1997** 400
Moore, Charles W., Jr., *Cole* (USS) bombing, **2001** 4-5, 6
Moore, Henson, forest preservation, **1999** 595
Moore, Roy S., removal from Alabama Supreme Court, **2005** 376
Moore, Thomas Gale
on ozone layer depletion, **1992** 77-78
on Reagan CEA, **1986** 60; **1988** 117; **1989** 4
Moorer, Thomas
Panama Canal transfer, **1999** 852
on U.S. defense posture, **1972** 179-182
Moorhead, William S. (D-Pa.), **1973** 338
Moosally, Fred P., *Iowa* (USS) explosion investigation, **1989** 519; **1990** 321
Moose, George E., UN death penalty report, **1998** 185
Moose, Richard M., **1979** 650
Moral Majority
Kennedy speech to, **1983** 817-825
on silent prayer decision, **1985** 381
Morales, Evo
Bolivian presidential elections, **2005** 765, 769-770
visit to Cuba, **2005** 770
Moran, Marcy C., bankruptcy of Bridgeport (Conn.), **1991** 303-307
Moreland, Pat, **1990** 509
Morgan, Thomas E. (D-Pa.)
on foreign aid requests, **1974** 279
Harrington letter to on CIA, **1974** 805-810
Morgan v. Nucci, **1998** 864
Morgan Guaranty Trust Co., and New York City's fiscal crisis, **1977** 567-568, 577
Morgan Stanley, mutual funds scandal, **2003** 696
Morganthau, Robert M., Enron Corp. collapse, **2003** 337
Mori, Yoshiro, Japanese prime minister, **2001** 305
Mormon Church
ERA opposition by, **1981** 924
leader succession, document on, **1981** 337-338
polygamy and, **1981** 337
Moro National Liberation Front (MNLF), **2001** 105
Moroccan Islamic Combat Group, **2004** 110

Morocco
  Casablanca bombings, **2003** 1052
  John Paul II visit, **1985** 501, 509-514
Morozov, Mark, death of, **1987** 190, 202
Morris, Dick
  Clinton campaign strategist resignation, **1996** 601
  Mexican president Fox campaign consultant, **2000** 965
Morris, James T.
  African aid programs, impact of Iraq War, **2003** 453
  Sudan conflict in Darfur, **2004** 591
  worldwide hunger, **2003** 757
  Zimbabwe food aid program, **2003** 1111
Morris, Stephen J., **1993** 114
Morris, Thomas L., Jr., anthrax mailings victim, **2001** 674
Morrison, Alan B.
  on independent counsel law, **1988** 468
  on sentencing reform, **1987** 409-410
Morrison, Alexia, and independent counsel law, **1988** 465-478
Morrison, Toni, Nobel Prize for Literature, **1993** 977-985
Morrison, United States v., **2000** 328
Morrison v. Olson, **1988** 465-478
Morse, Robert, Alcoholism definition, **1992** 850
Mortality rates
  See also Infant mortality
  cancer deaths, **1996** 790-793
  for children, **1999** 384
  in Eastern European nations, **1994** 425
  U.S. women, from cigarette smoking, **2001** 231-232
  world, programs to reduce, **1974** 780-781
  worldwide, **1996** 305-306
Morton, David, North Korea, UN humanitarian aid, **1999** 572
Morton, Rogers C. B. (R-Md.)
  on Alaska pipeline, **1972** 271-272
  at Stockholm environment conference, **1972** 476
Mosbacher, Robert A.
  Census Bureau undercount, **1991** 443-449
  Commerce secretary appointment, **1991** 770
Moscoso, Mireya
  first woman president of Panama, **1999** 851
  Panama Canal transfer ceremony, **1999** 853
Moscow summits
  Nixon-Brezhnev, **1972** 431-463; **1974** 535-569
  Reagan-Gorbachev, **1988** 353-373
Moseley-Braun, Carol, presidential candidate, **2004** 479
Moser, Susanne, global warming, **2002** 301
Mosholder, Andrew, antidepressants and risk of suicide in children, **2004** 749
Moskal v. United States, **1992** 464
Moslems. *See* Muslims
Moss, Frank (D-Utah), **1972** 46
Mossadegh, Mohammed, **1978** 700-701
Mosser, Thomas, victim of Unabomber, **1998** 234, 235, 237-238
Motesinos, Vladimiro, Peruvian intelligence officer, **2000** 923-927
Mother Teresa, John Paul II on, **1986** 25, 33-34
Mothers. *See* Families; Pregnancy; Women
Mothers of the Plaza de Mayo, **1984** 790
Motion Picture Association of America, on home video taping, **1984** 55
Motley, Constance Baker, **1988** 499
Mott, John, **1989** 698
Moulton, Brian, consumer spending, **2004** 57
Mount Pinatubo, **1992** 78-79
Mount Saint Helens, volcanic eruption of, economic effects, **1980** 811-824
Moussaoui, Zacarias
  detained, **2003** 311, 562
  London mosque and, **2005** 396
  September 11 terrorist attacks, involvement in, **2001** 619-620, 641; **2002** 834, 993, 999-1000
Moutardier, Hermis, **2002** 42
MOVE group, Philadelphia police raid on, **1986** 239-251
Movement for Democracy (Liberian guerrillas), **2003** 768
Movement for Democratic Change, **2002** 134, 136, 138-147
Movement for the Popular Liberation of Angola (MPLA), **1991** 287-300
Movement for the Student Vote, **1973** 36
MoveOn.org
  Iraq antiwar movement, **2005** 836
  voter turnout for presidential elections, **2004** 777
Movesian, Musheg, **1999** 639
Mowhoush, Abed Hamed, death at Abu Ghraib prison, **2004** 216; **2005** 913
Moyer, Bruce, on government personnel cuts, **1993** 720
Moyers, Bill
  interview with Carter, **1978** 708-710
  in Reagan-Anderson debate, **1980** 847, 849-850
Moyne, Lord, **1983** 832
Moynihan, Daniel Patrick (D-N.Y.), **1980** 111; **1990** 50
  criticism of developing countries in UN, **1975** 645-651
  Ginsburg nomination, **1991** 396-397
  government secrecy, **1997** 103-104
  health care costs, **1993** 783
  health insurance for disabled persons, **1999** 49
  intelligence agencies' authority, **1981** 862
  international economic cooperation, UN proposal of U.S., **1975** 589
  IRA prison hunger strike, **1981** 402, 404
  King holiday, **1983** 884
  new federalism, **1982** 74
  Social Security reform, **1983** 62; **1998** 100; **2001** 915, 917; **2005** 84
  vacating Senate office, **2000** 906
  welfare reform, **1988** 848-850, 852; **1996** 452
Mozambique
  drought and famine in, **1984** 974, 978-979
  economic sanctions against Rhodesia, lifting of, **1979** 941
  proposed U.S. aid to, **1976** 288, 291
  rejection of Rhodesian internal agreement by, **1978** 150
  on Rhodesian settlement plan, **1976** 721-722, 728-729

Mozambique *Continued*
student test scores, **1992** 91
UN role in, **1995** 355
MPLA. *See* People's Movement for the Liberation of Angola
Mrazek, Robert J. (D-N.Y.), **1988** 340
Mrdja, Darko, Serb war criminal, **2003** 464
Mubarak, Gamal (son of Hosni Mubarak), as potential future leader of Egypt, **2005** 165
Mubarak, Hosni
Arab states-Egyptian relations, **1981** 745-746; **1987** 871
on attacking Hussein in Iraq, **2001** 852
Bush Middle East Initiative, response to, **2004** 628
as Egyptian leader, **2005** 164-165
election of, **1981** 735, 740-746
election reforms, **2005** 164-174, 271, 581
eulogy for Yitzhak Rabin, **1995** 691, 694-695
Group of Eight (G-8) meeting, declined attending, **2004** 629
on hatred of Americans, **2004** 628-629
hijackers, reaction to U.S. interception of, **1985** 467
Hussein pre-war talks, **1991** 158
Israeli return of Sinai, **1982** 337-344
Middle East peace (Geneva Accord), **2003** 1204
peace negotiations proposal, **1989** 291
Persian Gulf war, **1990** 558-559
political reform, **2003** 961
Rabin's election in Israel, **1992** 657
Sadat assassination, **1981** 735-737
Sharon disengagement policy, **2004** 303
Sudanese extremists plot to kill, **2003** 840
West Bank peace agreement, **1995** 622
Much, Christian Walter, human cloning ban, **2002** 516
Mudge, Dirk, **1976** 612
Mueller, Robert S., III
on capture of Hawsawi, **2003** 1055
detainees treatment, **2003** 315
FBI internal security review, **2001** 154, 157
intelligence gathering, congressional panel investigations, **2002** 992, 995
library searches, **2003** 609
terrorism threat, news conference on, **2004** 268-279
Virtual Case File system, **2005** 897
Mueller v. Allen, **1983** 675-687; **1993** 401-403, 406
Mugabe, Robert
agreement on cease-fire, **1979** 941
AIDS, death of family member, **2004** 429
Congo peace negotiations, **2002** 548
demands of in Rhodesian conflict, **1977** 584
election of, and Zimbabwe independence, **1980** 317-333, 335-336
at funeral mass for John Paul II, **2005** 291
"land reform" program (white farm takeovers), **2001** 508; **2003** 1111
presidential elections in Zimbabwe, **2002** 133-137, 447-448; **2003** 1110, 1112-1113
rejection of Rhodesian internal agreement, **1978** 150
Zimbabwe political situation, **2003** 1110-1116, 1227
al-Mughassil, Ahmed, Khobar Towers bombing, **2001** 807
Muhammad, Abdul-Rasheed, first Army Muslim chaplain, **1993** 973-975
Mujaheddin-e Khalq (Iran guerrilla force), **2003** 1026
Mukai, Chiaki, Japanese astronaut, **1998** 776
Mukasey, Michael, Guantanamo Bay detainees, **2003** 112
Mukherjee, Pranab, India-U.S. defense cooperation agreement, **2005** 463
Mulfor, David C., **1989** 138
Mulligan, Deirdre K., medical records privacy, **1997** 582
Mullins, Janet, **1992** 1046
Mulroney, Brian
Canadian cabinet members, **1998** 594
economic summits, **1986** 438; **1988** 392
Munich, **1992** 638
election of, **1984** 407-409
Meech Lake separatism agreement, **1990** 367-372
on "Murphy Brown" controversy, **1992** 451-452
NAFTA, **1992** 761
Reagan pre-summit consultation with, **1985** 709
Soviet aid, **1990** 467
trade agreement with U.S., **1988** 58, 571-574, 577
Multiculturalism, Republican Party platform on, **2000** 513-514
Multilateral Debt Relief Initiative, **2005** 407
Multiple Use-Sustained Yield Act (1960), **1973** 22
Multiponics, Inc., in Casey investigation, **1981** 856
Multistate Tax Commission, on unitary taxation, **1983** 646
Muluzi, Makili, Zimbabwe political situation, **2003** 1115
Mulva, James, oil company profits, congressional testimony on, **2005** 791-794
Mumcu, Erkan, on earthquake in Turkey, **1999** 466
Mundy, Carl E., Jr.
chemical weapons, **1997** 201
on women in combat, **1993** 334
Mundy, R. Kenneth, **1990** 708
Munford, Sarah W., **1993** 610
Munoz, Heraldo, Analytical Support and Sanctions Monitoring Team, **2004** 540
Munoz-Flores, United States v., **1993** 91
Muntefering, Franz, German vice chancellor, **2005** 877
Munzel, Erica, affirmative action case, **2003** 367
al-Muqrin, Abdelaziz, death of al Qaeda leader, **2004** 519
Murad, Abdul Hakim, "bomb plot" using aircraft as weapons, **2003** 554
Murai, Tomohide, Chinese economic situation, **2004** 938
Murano, Elsa, *E. coli* contamination, **2002** 582
Murayama, Tomichi, apology for World War II suffering, **1995** 302-306
Murder. *See* Homicide
Murdoch, Rupert, **1995** 749-759
Muris, Timothy J., on spam e-mail messages, **2002** 70
Murkowski, Frank H. (R-Alaska), **1995** 114-115
global warming, **1997** 862
Hanford cleanup, **1995** 114-115
Murphy, Austin J. (D-Pa.)
on newborn infant care, **1983** 283
Puerto Rican statehood, **1993** 949

Murphy, John M. (D-N.Y.), conviction of, **1980** 900-902
Murphy v. United Parcel Service, **1999** 319
Murray, Alan, **1990** 818-823
Murray, Bruce C., **1990** 755
Murray, Craig, on torture of terrorism detainess, **2005** 429
Murray, Gilbert P., victim of Unabomber, **1998** 234, 237
Murray, James E. (D-Mont.), national health insurance, **1993** 782
Murray, John, on *Mars Express* probe, **2005** 502
Murray, Joseph E., Nobel in medicine, **1990** 796
Murray, Patty (D-Wash.), Crawford FDA commissioner nomination, **2005** 816
Murray v. Pearson, **1992** 41
Murroroa Atoll, and Greenpeace affair, **1985** 632
Murtha, John P. (D-Pa.), Iraq troop withdrawal, calling for, **2005** 80, 836-838, 837, 840-842
Museveni, Yoweri
  on condom use for HIV prevention, **2005** 53
  Uganda troop withdrawal from Congo, **2002** 550
  Ugandan leadership, **1998** 161; **1999** 646; **2003** 471, 474
Musharraf, Pervez (Pakistan president)
  assassination attempts, **2003** 213-214, 1053; **2004** 1009
  crackdown on guerrilla/terrorist attacks, **2002** 326-327; **2003** 209-211, 212
  India relations, **2003** 212; **2004** 352-353
  India-Pakistan peace negotations, **2005** 476
  Kahn weapons-smuggling network controversy, **2004** 328
  Kashmir dispute, **2001** 964-965; **2002** 166, 325-331; **2003** 209
  on London terrorist bombing suspects, **2005** 396, 473-474
  military and political role, **2004** 1009-1017
  military coup, **1999** 623-629; **2002** 325
  Pakistan election referendum, **2002** 165-174
  vote of confidence, **2003** 214
  war on terrorism, support of U.S., **2001** 626, 627, 632-636; **2002** 40, 165, 326, 327; **2003** 210, 213
Music, "trash lyrics" legislation, **1990** 509-511
Muskie, Edmund S. (D-Maine), **1977** 59; **1978** 96
  appointment as secretary of state, **1980** 476
  Global 2000 proposals, **1980** 667; **1981** 14
  hostages in Iran, negotiations on release of, **1980** 1000, 1007-1009
  Korean sentencing of Kim Dae Jung, **1980** 825, 828
  NATO communiqué on Poland, **1980** 795
  NSC operations, review of, **1986** 1018; **1987** 205
  PRC-U.S. consular agreement, **1980** 842-843
  presidential candidacy of, **1972** 202, 590; **1974** 602
  response to Ford State of the Union, **1976** 13-15, 26-35
  Vietnam war, ending of, **1972** 143
Muslim Brotherhood
  in Egyptian elections, **2005** 164, 166-169, 271, 273
  in Syria, political activities, **2004** 558
Muslim countries
  new "Caliphate" dominating, **2005** 14, 16-17
  public opinion surveys, on anti-American sentiments, **2004** 627
  U.S. policy toward, **2004** 626-628
  world trends in political islam, National Intelligence Council report on, **2005** 16-17, 21-22
Muslim religion. *See* Islam
Muslims
  Army's first Muslim chaplain, **1993** 973-975
  Bernard Lewis lecture, **1990** 277-287
  hate crimes, **2005** 678
Mussa, Michael
  Argentine debt crisis, **2002** 82, 86
  Asian monetary policy, **1998** 725
  monetarist theory supporter, **1988** 117
  resignation from CEA, **1989** 4
Mustafa, Abu Ali, assassination of, **2001** 364
Mustafa, Rustem, war crimes conviction, **2003** 1144
Mustafa, Xhemail, assassination of, **2000** 146
Muto, Kabun, **1992** 21, 22
Muttahida Majlis-e-Amal (United Action Forum), Pakistan religious coalition, **2003** 213; **2004** 1010, 1012; **2005** 473
Mutual Assured Destruction (MAD)
  Republican platform on, **1984** 726
  and SDI, **1984** 267
Mutual Balanced Force Reductions (MBFR) (in Europe), progress of talks in Vienna, NATO on, **1976** 346, 348-349
Mutual Defense Treaty (1954), U.S.-Taiwan, termination of, **1978** 781-783, 785, 787; **1979** 917-938
Mutual funds industry
  board chairmen controversy, SEC proposal, **2004** 419-420
  scandal, **2003** 693-706; **2004** 419-420
Muzorewa, Abel
  signing of internal agreement on constitution, **1978** 149-155
  in talks on Rhodesian government, **1977** 584
  in transitional Rhodesian government, **1979** 941-942
  and Zimbabwe independence, **1980** 318, 323
Mwanke, Katumba, Congo resource exploitation, **2002** 551
MX missile
  basing plans for, **1982** 399-400, 906-908, 912, 916
  building of, allowed by START proposal, **1982** 386
  commission recommendations on, **1983** 365-374
  congressional approval of, **1983** 369
  development of, **1983** 365-374
    urged by SALT II opponents, **1978** 550
  as essential, Carter on, **1981** 90
  program, in Reagan budget, **1987** 4
  Reagan and Anderson positions on, **1980** 848, 858
  in Reagan budget, **1983** 102, 369
  in Reagan defense strategy, **1982** 399-400, 903-908, 916
  role in restoring nuclear balance, **1980** 124, 129, 133, 136, 152
  and SALT II debate, **1979** 415, 417, 457-458, 463
  U.S. strategy for, **1986** 782-783, 784-786, 789-790
My Lai massacre, **1984** 349
Myanmar
  See also Burma
  human rights, **1990** 134
  human trafficking, **2002** 343; **2004** 125

Myanmar *Continued*
tsunami relief effort, **2005** 1005
Myers, Donald F., WorldCom collapse fraud case, **2002** 395; **2003** 335
Myers, Hardy, physician-assisted suicide, **2001** 293
Myers, Lewis, Jr., **1993** 580
Myers, Matthew
FDA tobacco regulation, **2003** 264
state smoking prevention programs, **2004** 282
worldwide tobacco regulation treaty, **2000** 536; **2003** 262
Myers, Michael J. "Ozzie" (D-Pa.), House expulsion of, **1980** 486, 899-906; **1981** 673; **1983** 727
Myers, Richard B.
Abu Ghraib prison scandal, **2004** 208, 209
Liberia, U.S. intervention, **2003** 770
al Qaeda terrorist network regrouping, **2002** 1017
Uzbekistan, U.S. relations, **2005** 429
Myers, Woodrow A., Jr., **1988** 416

N

NAACP. *See* National Association for the Advancement of Colored People
Naar, Alan, **1988** 311
Nachman Corp. v. Pension Benefit Guaranty Corp., **1992** 463
Nada, Youssef, funding terrorism, **2003** 1058
Nadel, Norbert A., **1989** 479
Nader, Ralph
Cipollone case, **1988** 311
on corporate mergers, **1998** 341-342
foreign aid, **1989** 17
milk price supports decision by Nixon, **1974** 3-4
NAFTA, **1993** 955
national forests, **1973** 21-26
presidential candidate, **2000** 611, 617, 895-905; **2004** 775
Nadler, Jerrold (D-N.Y.)
House impeachment vote, **1998** 961, 963
House Judiciary Committee impeachment inquiry, **1998** 705
NAEP. *See* National Assessment of Educational Progress
NAFTA. *See* North American Free Trade Agreement
Nagin, C. Ray (New Orleans mayor), Hurricane Katrina disaster response, **2005** 540, 542, 544-545, 567-568, 571
Nagorno-Karabakh conflict, **1999** 640-641
Nagy, Imre, Hungary's tribute to, **1989** 339-342, 413, 417
Nahimana, Ferdinand, Rwanda genocide war crimes conviction, **2003** 1073, 1075-1088
Naimi, Ali, oil prices, **2005** 778
Nairobi (Kenya)
UNCTAD meeting, **1976** 299-319, 427, 431
World Conference on Women, **1985** 555-570
Najibullah, rule of in Afghanistan, **1986** 919-920, 923-924, 926
Nakajima, Hiroshi, on infectious diseases, **1996** 302
Nakasone, Yasuhiro
at economic summits, **1983** 508; **1984** 356; **1986** 438; **1987** 525
on Gorbachev initiatives, **1989** 298-299
Reagan pre-summit consultation with, **1985** 709
Reagan visit, **1983** 894, 896-898
trade imbalance with U.S., **1985** 319-323
U.S. trade sanctions against Japan, **1987** 427, 433-436
Nakhla, Adel, Abu Ghraib prison abuse suspect, **2004** 220, 222
Namibia
Angola peace accord, **1988** 947-949
early human remains discovered, **1992** 136
independence, **2002** 152
independence from South Africa, **1988** 947-950; **1990** 199-206; **1991** 288
interim government in, proposal for, **1976** 611-615
majority rule in, Carter on progress toward, **1977** 738, 743; **1978** 270-272, 274, 282-283
Nujoma inaugural address, **1990** 204-206
settlement of conflict in, Kissinger on, **1976** 287, 292-293, 294
South African occupation of, **1986** 581
and human rights, **1981** 180
UN role in, **1995** 355
U.S. aid to, **1976** 294
Namphy, Henri
elections in Haiti, **1987** 939-941
government of, and human rights, **1987** 196
Nandan, Satya, **1995** 524, 526-527
Nanjing, Treaty of (1842), **1984** 1045
Napalm, effects of in war, UN report on, **1972** 837-841
NARAL Pro-Choice America, **2005** 561, 815, 819
Narcotics. *See* Drug trafficking; Drug use
NAS. *See* National Academy of Sciences
NASA. *See* National Aeronautics and Space Administration
Nashville Gas Co. v. Satty, **1977** 871-881
Nasreddin, Idris, funding terrorism, **2003** 1058
Nassau County, Florida, School Board v. Arline, **1987** 245-252, 828-829
Nasser, Gamal Abdel, leadership of (Egypt), **1976** 169-170; **1981** 733; **2005** 164
Nasser, Jac, **2000** 692, 697-699
Nastaste, Adrian, Romanian elections, **2004** 199
Natan-Zada, Eden, terrorist protest of Gaza Strip withdrawal, **2005** 531-532
Nathan, Andrew J., Chinese leadership, **2002** 853
Nathan, Irv, independent counsel statute, **1998** 908
Nathan, Judith, **2000** 908
Nation at Risk, education problems and proposed reforms, **1983** 413-437; **1989** 561-562, 564
Nation of Islam, **1993** 580, 974; **1995** 453, 455, 646, 657
National Abortion Federation, **2003** 998
National Abortion Federation v. John Ashcroft, **2003** 1003-1004
National Abortion Rights Action League, **1992** 591
National Academy of Engineering
on environmental effects of SST, **1973** 235-244
technology education, **2002** 69
National Academy of Public Administration
"new source review" dispute, **2003** 175-176, 183-188
on VA status, **1988** 875

National Academy of Sciences (NAS), **1992** 87, 361-366
AIDS, public health aspects of, **1986** 887-908
"big bang" theory evidence, **1992** 379-383
cosmic background explorer, **1992** 379-383
creation science in schools, **1972** 843-844; **1982** 4; **1987** 566
defense of Sakharov and threatened scientific exchanges, **1973** 791-796
diet for reduced cancer risk, **1982** 507-520
environmental effects of SST, **1973** 235-244
federal advisory panel appointments, **2004** 844
food supply, threats to, **2002** 579
genetic engineering research, safeguards on, **1975** 319-324
global warming panel, **2003** 864; **2005** 920-921
greenhouse effect, **1988** 862
hospitals, for-profit, **1986** 487-513
Hubble space telescope, **1990** 747-751; **1994** 458-462
Hubble space telescope report, **2004** 12
human cloning panel, **2002** 514
human embryonic stem cell research guidelines, **2005** 322
human radiation experiments, **1993** 988
mercury emissions study, **2005** 103
military force in foreign policy, **1972** 381-382
ozone depletion report, **1992** 75-81
reports on terrorist threats, **2002** 745
revision of charter of, **1972** 381-383
secret military research projects, **1972** 381-383
space program in U.S., future of, **1990** 747-749, 751-760
as sponsor of East-West scientific organization, **1972** 833-834
stratosphere, man-made impacts on, **1975** 438, 445, 453
technology transfer to Soviets
export controls, **1987** 29-42
through leaks, **1982** 813-819
urban air pollution and lung cancer, **1972** 775
Vietnam veterans, **2001** 908
water quality report, **2001** 218
National Academy of Television Arts and Sciences, Whitehead speech on license renewals, **1973** 55, 57-62
National Adult Literacy Survey, **1993** 737-746
National Advisory Commission on Civil Disorders. *See* Kerner Commission
National Advisory Council on Drug Abuse, **2004** 843
National Aeronautics and Space Administration (NASA)
administration of
"faster, better, cheaper" philosophy, **2000** 88-92; **2003** 632, 636
organizational flaws, **2003** 635-637
redirecting goals, **1990** 753, 754-755, 757-766
age of the universe estimates, **1996** 265-269
Challenger accident, **1986** 515-539
climate change study, **1988** 861
Climate Orbiter mission to Mars investigation, **1999** 711-717; **2000** 89, 90; **2003** 302; **2004** 4
Columbia space shuttle disaster, **2003** 631-677; **2004** 9
cosmic background explorer, **1992** 379-383
Discovery space shuttle mission, **1998** 776-786; **2005** 498-506
Galileo mission to Jupiter's moons, **1997** 202-205; **2003** 305
Global Surveyor mission to Mars, **2000** 89, 95-102, 379-384; **2003** 302, 304; **2004** 4
global warming studies, **2001** 113; **2002** 304
Hubble space telescope, **1990** 753-754, 755-757, 758; **2002** 212-218; **2003** 304, 306; **2004** 7
birth of stars, **1995** 288-293
Human Space Flight Center, **2003** 644-646
image and programs after *Challenger,* **1988** 795-798
International Space Station, **1998** 929-933
life and water on Mars, possibility of, **1996** 471-477; **2000** 379-384
Lunar Prospector findings of moon ice, **1998** 113-120
manned space missions, Bush speech on, **2004** 13-16
manned space station, **1984** 82, 90
Mars mission failures, **2000** 88-102; **2003** 302
Mars rovers mission, **2004** 3-8
multiplanet solar system discovery, **1999** 173-178
NEAR (Near Earth Asteroid Rendezvous) Shoemaker mission to Eros, **2001** 143-149
Office of Space Science and Applications, Astrophysics Division, **1992** 383
Opportunity mission to Mars, **2003** 303; **2004** 3; **2005** 501-502
ozone layer studies, **1975** 438, 446-447; **1987** 745-746, 756-764; **1988** 221-228; **1992** 75-81
Pathfinder mission to Mars, **1997** 509-513; **1999** 712; **2000** 89; **2003** 302; **2004** 3
radiation exposure experiments, **1993** 988
Return to Flight Task Group, **2005** 499
Skylab program, **1973** 939-946; **1979** 554-557
space program planning, Ride report, **1987** 649-669
space shuttle program, **1981** 417-426; **2000** 93-94; **2004** 10
Spirit mission to Mars, **2003** 303; **2004** 3-8, 9; **2005** 501-502
Spitzer Space Telescope, **2005** 503
Stardust spacecraft mission, **2004** 7
upper atmosphere satellite research, **1992** 78-79
Voyager mission, Saturn data, **1980** 989-993; **1981** 835-844
National Agenda for the 80s, commission report, **1981** 39-56
National Air and Space Museum, *Enola Gay* exhibit, **1995** 55-58
National Alliance for the Mentally Ill, care of mentally ill report, **1990** 573-598
National Archives
CIA records at, **1992** 9
Holocaust victims, **1993** 310
and Peary's North Pole notes, **1988** 831-833
student performance reports, **1990** 155
Supreme Court audiotapes, public use of, **1993** 935-937
Twenty-seventh Amendment, **1992** 439-442
National Assessment of Educational Progress (NAEP), **1992** 88, 624, 627

National Assessment of Educational Progress (NAEP) *Continued*
literacy trends, **1988** 298
math and science education, **1988** 377-390
minority students, **1985** 585
state of education in U.S., **1989** 85-94
student reading ability, **1990** 155
National Association for the Advancement of Colored People (NAACP)
affirmative action rulings, **1978** 470; **1979** 495; **1984** 367; **1987** 334
African American families, **1985** 28, 33
boycotts of, damages from, **1982** 655-674
Chavis address, **1993** 579-584
church arson prevention, **1997** 311
Coleman report on desegregation, **1975** 614
eminent domain, **2005** 364
Evers assassination retrial, **1994** 100-106
Evers-Williams address, **1995** 453-462
Haitian refugees, **1981** 606, 616-618
on hate crimes, **1992** 545
Legal Defense Fund
on Gilmore death penalty, **1976** 917-918
and racially motivated jury selection, **1986** 412
on Los Angeles riots, **1992** 408
on Lott resignation, **2002** 973
lynchings, opposition to, **2005** 356
migration to Sun Belt, **1981** 40
Perot appearance before, **1992** 719
on race-based redistricting, **1995** 372
Social Security reform, **2005** 113
Thomas Supreme Court nomination, **1991** 552
National Association for the Advancement of Colored People v. Claiborne Hardware Co., **1982** 655-674; **1994** 316, 317
National Association of Addiction Treatment Providers, **1988** 279
National Association of Black-Owned Broadcasters, **1990** 419
National Association of Broadcasters
on licensing fees, **1979** 120
Whitehead speech to on news media, **1973** 57
National Association of Broadcasters v. FCC, **1978** 419-432
National Association of Children's Hospitals, on seriously ill infants, **1983** 282-283
National Association of Evangelicals, **1997** 311
National Association of Home Builders, radon testing by, **1988** 4
National Association of Manufacturers
chlorofluorocarbon reductions, **1988** 223
and e-commerce, **2000** 301
global warming, **2002** 299
mercury emissions guidelines, **2005** 99
Soviet trade status, **1973** 588
National Association of Realtors, housing markets, **2005** 139
National Association of Recording Arts and Sciences, **1990** 509
National Association of Retail Merchandisers, **1990** 509
National Association of School Resource Officers, school crime statistics, **2001** 351
National Association of Secondary School Principals
on education summit, **1989** 563
sexual harassment in schools, **1999** 218
National Association of Securities Dealers (NASD)
regulation of, **1999** 204-205
suitability rule, **1999** 205
National Association of State Budget Officers, states' budget crisis, **2002** 54
National Association of State Mental Health Directors, **1990** 575
National Audubon Society, on coastal property rights, **1992** 616
National Automated Immigration Lookout System, **2003** 169
National Bank of Georgia, and Carter warehouse investigation, **1979** 801-812
National Basketball Association (NBA), drug use in, **1986** 170
National Bioethics Advisory Commission, cloning of humans moratorium, **1997** 213-214
National Bipartisan Commission on Central America. *See* Kissinger Commission on Central America
National Board for Professional Teaching Standards, **1997** 35
proposed, **1986** 458-459, 468-472
National Broadcasting Company (NBC), on license renewal proposals, **1973** 56
National Bureau of Economic Research (NBER)
economic recessions in U.S., **2001** 665
poverty rate, **2005** 111
recession defined, **2004** 62
U.S. business cycles, **2004** 62
National Campaign to Prevent Teen Pregnancy, **1998** 263; **1999** 386
National Cancer Act (1971), **2001** 867-868
National Cancer Institute (NCI)
breast cancer drug tamoxifen, **1998** 194-202
breast cancer report, **1993** 905-922
breast cancer screening, **2002** 510
cancer deaths, **2001** 867
cancer deaths declining, **1996** 790-793
on cancer-causing substances in workplace, **1978** 633-634, 640-641
Celebrex and heart problems, **2004** 852
decrease in lung cancer, **1985** 809
funding, **1998** 53
gay gene, existence of, **1993** 599-608
health effects of radon exposure, **1988** 4
mammogram controversy, **1997** 142-149
nuclear testing fallout, **1997** 591-601
weight-related deaths, **2005** 6
National Catholic Bioethics Center (Philadelphia), **2005** 322
National Center for Atmospheric Research, on ozone depletion, **1988** 222
National Center for Children in Poverty, child care quality, **1994** 117-118
National Center for Complementary and Alternative Medicine, **2002** 507
National Center for Education Statistics (NCES)
adult literacy report, **1993** 737-746
report, **1992** 87, 623-636
teacher quality survey, **1999** 64-71

National Center for Health Statistics (NCHS)
infant mortality rates, **1987** 150
low-birthweight infants, **1987** 148
murders with guns, **1992** 493-494
teenage pregnancy report, **1998** 260-267; **1999** 385
National Center for Missing and Exploited Children, sex offenders, **1997** 384
National Center for Tobacco-Free Kids, **1997** 335
National Center on Addiction and Substance Abuse (CASA), on teenage drinking, **2002** 175-176, 177-178
National Center on Child Abuse and Neglect (NCCAN), **1992** 509
National Cholesterol Education Program, **1987** 779-790; **1992** 398
National Church Arson Task Force (NCATF), report, **1997** 301-313
National Citizens' Coalition for Nursing Home Reform, **2002** 120, 121
National Clean Air Coalition, on proposed Clean Air Act revisions, **1981** 276
National Climate Change Technology Initiative, **2001** 113
National Coalition Against Pornography, **1990** 511
National Coalition Against Sexual Assault, **1993** 386
National Coalition of Girls Schools, **1992** 143
National Coalition of Health Care, **2004** 983
National Collegiate Athletic Association (NCAA)
on African American college athletes, **1989** 213-223
Knight report on collegiate athletics, **1991** 129-142
National Commission on AIDS
final report, **1993** 447-457
HIV-infected women, **1992** 710
National Commission on Air Quality (NCAQ), on Clean Air Act's impact, **1981** 275-295
National Commission on Children, **1991** 349-365
National Commission on Energy Policy, **2004** 189
National Commission on Excellence in Education, *Nation at Risk* report, **1983** 413-437; **1989** 561-562, 564
National Commission on Federal Election Reform, report, **2001** 522-535
National Commission on Marijuana and Drug Abuse, **1972** 291-300; **1973** 393-412
National Commission on Separation of Powers report, **1998** 905-911
National Commission on Social Security Reform, **1983** 57-75, 108
National Commission on Terrorism, **2000** 277-286; **2001** 765
National Commission on Terrorist Attacks Upon the United States
activities of, **2003** 544, 547
final report of commission, **2004** 450-477
hearings, **2004** 452-455
reaction to final report, **2004** 457-458
recommendations of commission, **2004** 456-457, 471-477, 966-967
terrorist financing in Saudi Arabia, **2004** 517-533
National Commission on the Causes and Prevention of Violence, **1999** 615
National Commission on the Cost of Higher Education, report on college costs, **1998** 3-18
National Commission on the Public Service, recommendations of, **1989** 196-202
National Commission Responsibilities for Financing Postsecondary Education, restructuring college aid, **1993** 171-179
National Committee for an Effective Congress, on congressional vs. presidential powers, **1973** 5, 12-19
National Committee on U.S.-China Relations, **2005** 613
National Conference of Catholic Bishops
See also United States Conference of Catholic Bishops (USCCB)
antiabortion crusade, **1998** 811-812
bicentennial of first Catholic diocese, **1989** 620
economic justice, **1986** 983-1011; **1987** 51
nuclear freeze, **1983** 270
nuclear war and deterrence, Reagan strategy, **1982** 885-896
physician-assisted suicide, opposition to, **1996** 124
report on Vatican II, **1985** 571-581
sexual abuse by priests, zero tolerance policy, **2005** 863
sexually abusive priests, **1993** 407-409
U.S. economic policies, **1984** 957-972
U.S.-Vatican diplomatic relations, **1984** 21
women, dignity and vocation of, **1988** 785-786
National Conference of Commissioners on Uniform State Laws, brain-death statutes, **1983** 282, 290-291
National Conference of Roman Catholic Bishops. *See* National Conference of Catholic Bishops
National Conference of State Legislatures
pledge of allegiance, constitutionality of, **2002** 383
on political redistricting, **1983** 600
state budget shortfalls, **2003** 72
National Coordinator for Security, Infrastructure Protection, and Counter-Terrorism, **1998** 677
National Corn Growers Association, Reagan to on farm exports to Soviets, **1982** 824
National Cotton Council v. Donovan, **1981** 491
National Council for Universal and Unconditional Amnesty, on draft evader pardon, **1977** 96
National Council of Chain Restaurants, smoking ban, **1994** 206
National Council of Churches
church arson prevention, **1997** 304, 306, 311
religious freedom, **1997** 408
on U.S.-Vatican diplomatic relations, **1984** 21
National Council of Churches of Christ, cease-fire proposal at Wounded Knee, **1973** 532
National Council of Community Health Centers, **1990** 575
National Council of Resistance of Iran, **2003** 1026
National Council of Senior Citizens, on for-profit hospitals, **1986** 489
National Council of Teachers of Mathematics (NCTM), **1992** 52
National Council on Disability, **2002** 269
National Council on Education Standards and Testing, **1992** 45-54, 85
National Council on the Arts, decency standards, **1998** 406
National Counsel for Economic and Social Development (Brazil), **2003** 4, 12

National Counterterrorism Center, **2004** 474, 966, 968, 970
National Crime Victimization Survey (NCVS), **1998** 869-870; **2001** 747-748
  analysis of results, **1994** 64-72
  rape reports, **1992** 389-390
  use of guns in crime, **1995** 463-471
  violent crimes, **1992** 375-380
National Declassification Center, **1997** 105, 108-109
National Defense Panel, national security needs, **1997** 811-821
National Development Bank, Carter urban proposal, **1978** 242-244, 251
National Earthquake Information Center (U.S.), **1999** 465
National Economic Council (NEC), **1997** 62
National Education Association (NEA)
  Education Department, creation of, **1979** 157, 159
  education funding, **1988** 299
  merit pay for teachers, **1986** 459
  school violence, **1975** 208
  school vouchers, **2002** 409
  student drug testing, **2002** 427
  students' rights and responsibilities, **1975** 221
  tuition tax credit, **1983** 678
National Education Goals Panel, **1991** 220; **1992** 46, 50, 107; **1996** 106
  Bush and governors' statements on, **1990** 153-163
  gender-equity issue and, **1992** 144
  international math and science test, **1992** 85
National Education Summit on Girls, **1992** 143-144
National Endowment for Democracy, **2003** 958; **2004** 552; **2005** 43
National Endowment for the Arts (NEA)
  decency in the arts, **1998** 405-418
  funding, **1998** 406, 407-408
  future of nonprofit arts, **1997** 699-710
  on humanities education, **1987** 681-696
National Endowment for the Arts v. Finley, **1998** 405-418; **2003** 395
National Endowment for the Humanities (NEH)
  humanities education, **1987** 681-696
  state of humanities, **1988** 517-527
  undergraduate education, **1984** 997-1003
National Energy Strategy, **1992** 101, 106
National Enquirer, libel suit against, **1984** 247, 248, 253-256
National Environmental Policy Act (NEPA), **2002** 901
  accomplishments of, **1973** 215
  Energy Department compliance with, **1989** 357, 359
  environmental impact statement requirement, **1972** 271
National Federation of Republican Women, Agnew speech on leaks of charges against him, **1973** 829
National Fish and Wildlife Foundation, **2005** 736
National Fisheries Institute, **2004** 604
National Food Policy Conference, **1990** 175
National Football League (NFL), drug use in, **1986** 170-171
National Foreign Affairs Training Center (NFATC), religious persecution training, **1998** 27
National Forest Management Act (NFMA), **1991** 277-285
National Front for the Liberation of Angola (FNLA), **2002** 152
National Gay Rights Advocates, on domestic partners measures, **1989** 307
National Geographic Society, and Peary's North Pole claim, **1988** 832; **1989** 687-689
National Governors Association (NGA), **1990** 153, 155-163
  education task force, **1989** 561-562, 566
  states' budget crisis, **2002** 54
National Guard
  Kent State University students killed by, **1990** 289-294
  Los Angeles riots and, **1992** 426, 427
  preparedness, GAO report, **2004** 784-793
  units in Iraq and Afghanistan, **2004** 784-793, 875
National Gulf War Resource Center, **2001** 909
National Heart, Lung, and Blood Institute (NHLBI)
  cholesterol and heart disease, **1984** 1039-1043
  cholesterol education, **1987** 779-790
  cholesterol guidelines, **2001** 475-476, 478
  cholesterol levels, **1992** 398
  hormone replacement therapy study, **2002** 503-511
National Highway Traffic Safety Administration (NHTSA)
  aggressive driving, **1997** 550-561
  automobile air bag regulations, **1996** 801-806; **1997** 774-779
  Firestone tire recall, **1978** 719-727; **2000** 688-699
  General Motors truck safety, **1994** 443-448
National Household Survey on Drug Abuse (NHSDA), **1996** 570-579; **1999** 459-464
National Hurricane Center, on Hugo, **1989** 667
National Institute for Health Care Management, **2002** 946
National Institute for Occupational Safety and Health (NIOSH), on cancer-causing substances in the workplace, **1978** 633-634, 640-641
National Institute of Allergy and Infectious Diseases, **2004** 447
National Institute of Child Health and Human Development, **1997** 425
National Institute of Environmental Health Sciences, on cancer-causing substances in workplace, **1978** 633-634, 640-641
National Institute of Justice (NIJ)
  DNA "fingerprints" study, **1992** 366
  on prison crowding, **1981** 478
National Institute of Mental Health (NIMH), **1990** 583, 590
  HEW report on marijuana and health, **1972** 155-162
  mental disorders in U.S. adult population, **1984** 833-843
  TV's effect on behavior, **1982** 365-383
National Institute of Standards and Technology, on DNA tests, **1992** 363
National Institute on Aging, study on physical fitness and health, **1989** 613-617
National Institute on Alcohol Abuse and Alcoholism, **2002** 176
  alcohol and health, **1972** 193-200
  alcoholism research, **1983** 336, 350, 353

National Institute on Drug Abuse, rape study, **1992** 385-395
National Institutes of Health (NIH)
acupuncture, panel on, **1997** 749-759
AIDS research, **1996** 156-166; **1997** 38, 83
alcoholism research, **1983** 336, 339
cholesterol, **1984** 1039-1043; **1987** 779
cholesterol guidelines, **2001** 475-476, 478
end-of-life care research, **1997** 327, 330
fetal research, **1975** 544
funding for, **1998** 53; **2001** 58
genetic engineering guidelines, **1975** 321
hormone replacement therapy, **2002** 503-511
marijuana study funding, **1982** 203
National Center for Human Genome Research, **1992** 366
plant biotechnology, **1986** 288
stem cell research grants, **2004** 159
stem cell research guidelines, **2000** 667-673; **2001** 540
youth violence prevention, **2001** 74
National Intelligence Authority, **2004** 970
National Intelligence Council
CIA reform and, **1992** 5
NIE report, **2003** 874, 875; **2004** 714; **2005** 247, 258-259
world trends, **2000** 1047-1062; **2005** 14-26
National Intelligence Director (NID), **2004** 474-475, 965, 968; **2005** 256
full budgetary authority, **2004** 969
Negroponte as first director, **2005** 246
National Intelligence Estimate (NIE), **2003** 874, 875; **2004** 714; **2005** 247, 258-259
National Intelligence Service, proposal, **2004** 969
National Labor Relations Act (Taft-Hartley Act, 1947), unfair labor practices, **1985** 415-429
National Labor Relations Board (NLRB)
and freedom of union members to resign, **1985** 415-429
and labor contracts of bankrupt companies, **1984** 181-182, 184-188, 190-197
labor organizing procedures, **2005** 488
on labor unions for hospital interns and medical residents, **1999** 633
and union political activity, **1992** 345-347
National Labor Relations Board v. Bildisco & Bildisco, **1984** 181-199
National Labor Relations Board v. Jones & Laughlin Steel Corp., **1995** 188, 191-192
National Labor Relations Board v. Mackay Radio and Telegraph, **1995** 129
National League of Cities (NLC)
antitrust immunity of cities, **1982** 37
budget cutbacks affecting cities, **1973** 454
child welfare, **1999** 385
residential signs, **1994** 290
National League of Cities v. Usery, **1976** 377-389; **1983** 231-232
National Legal Center for the Medically Dependent and Disabled, on treatment of handicapped infants, **1986** 544
National Longitudinal Study of Adolescent Health, **1997** 424
National Marine Fisheries Service, salmon as an endangered species, **2004** 669-670
National Mining Association, global warming, **2002** 299
National monuments
See also under names of individual monuments
boundary proposals, Norton on, **2001** 217
Bush administration, **2001** 217
Clinton administration designations, **2001** 217
creation of in Alaska, **1978** 731-740
National Museum of Natural History, on Native American skeletal remains, **1989** 540
National Museum of the American Indian, creation of, **1989** 540, 542
National Nuclear Security Administration, **1999** 240-241
National Ocean Council, proposal for, **2004** 604, 605
National Oceanic and Atmospheric Administration (NOAA)
creation of, **1972** 90; **1973** 215; **2004** 602
fish farm regulation, **2004** 603
global warming and record high temperatures, **1998** 946; **2000** 340
operations and mandate for, **2004** 604
ozone depletion studies, **1975** 447; **1987** 745-746; **1988** 223, 228
seafood inspection, **1990** 179-180
National Optical Astronomy Observatories, **1990** 754
National Organ Transplant Act (1984), **1987** 353-354
National Organization for Women (NOW)
abortion protesters and RICO law, **1994** 26-33
discriminatory language in federal laws, **1983** 756
ERA defeat, **1981** 924; **1982** 612
parental leave, **1987** 19
sex bias in pension plans, **1983** 693
Social Security reform, **2005** 113
National Organization for Women v. Joseph Scheidler et al., **1994** 26-33
National Parent-Teacher Associations, "trash lyrics" legislation, **1990** 510, 511
National Park Service (NPS)
criticism of, **1992** 489
fire-management policy, **1988** 941-946
GAO report on deteriorating conditions, **1996** 580-588
GAO testimony on management of, **1995** 120-128
new parks, **1996** 581
preservation as primary mission, **1972** 795-802
Vail Agenda, **1992** 329-334
vulnerability to terrorist groups, **2000** 282
working conditions, **1992** 329-330
National parks
Alaskan lands, preservation and protection of, **1978** 731-740; **1999** 593-594; **2001** 216-217
cities in or near, **1972** 796, 800-801, 803-804
corporate sponsorship of, **1996** 582
deteriorating condition of, GAO report on, **1996** 580-588
fire management policy, **1988** 942
forest preservation and roadless initiative, **1999** 592-599; **2001** 216-217; **2004** 668-669
historical and cultural mission of, **1972** 798-799, 802

National parks *Continued*
limiting commercial facilities in, **1972** 795-796, 798-801
preservation as primary mission, **1972** 795-802
recreation as mission of, **1972** 795-798, 800-804
snowmobiles in, **2001** 218; **2002** 902
"Vail Agenda" report on, **1992** 329-334
National Parks, World Conference on, **1972** 795-797
National Parks and Conservation Association, on fire-management policy, **1988** 942
National Parks Centennial Commission, **1972** 795
National Performance Review (NPR), report, **1993** 695, 717-735; **1995** 75, 83-85
National Press Club
news media relations with federal government, **1973** 629-639
Reagan speech on U.S. missile deployment in Europe, **1981** 823-830
Schlesinger on energy policy in farewell speech, **1979** 659-667
National Public Radio (NPR), recommendations for, **1979** 119, 128, 131-133
National Registry for Voluntary Emissions Reductions, **2002** 299
National Republican Committee for Choice, abortion rights, **1992** 800
National Research Act (1974), on research ethics, **1975** 543-544, 552, 556
National Research Council (NRC)
African Americans' economic status, **1989** 445-459
arsenic levels in water, **2001** 214-215
bioterrorism, new vaccines against biological weapons, **2004** 444
carcinogens in the diet, **1996** 71-79
DNA evidence in criminal cases, **1992** 361-366
food supply safety, **2002** 582-583
global warming, **2002** 308-309, 312, 320-321
math education, **1989** 87
medical records security, **1997** 581
radon exposure, **1988** 3-8
reorganization of, **1972** 381-383
sex segregation in workplace, **1985** 789-801
technology education, **2002** 69
teenage pregnancy, **1986** 1057-1064
National Review Board for the Protection of Children and Young People, **2004** 82-93
National Rifle Association (NRA)
Ashcroft member of, **2003** 158
assault weapon ban repeal efforts, **1995** 464-465
ballistic "fingerprinting," **2002** 959, 960
Brady bill signing, **1993** 965-969
Bush (George H. W.) resignation from, **1995** 208-215; **2001** 723
campaign finance reform law, **2003** 1158
crime bill, opposition to, **1994** 576
gun control, **2004** 764
Bush (George W.) administration support for, **2001** 722-724
gun control opponent, **1981** 648; **1992** 494, 498
guns in the home study, **1993** 872-873
National Right to Life Committee, **1990** 215, 376; **1992** 591
abortion, parental consent, **2005** 817
human cloning ban, **2002** 515
partial-birth abortion ban, **2000** 430; **2003** 997
National School Boards Association, **1992** 47; **1995** 341
child welfare, **1999** 385
disruptive handicapped students, **1988** 48
drug-testing for athletes, **1995** 341
public aid to parochial schools, **1985** 434
sexual harassment of students, **1999** 215
student drug testing, **2002** 427
of student newspaper censorship, **1988** 38
National Science Advisory Board for Biosecurity, **2004** 443
National Science Board, on education reform, **1983** 415-416, 420
National Science Foundation (NSF)
atmospheric research, **1975** 447
DNA "fingerprints" study, **1992** 366
emergency rescue of South Pole doctor, **1999** 611-613
funding for, **1998** 53; **2001** 59
international math and science test, **1992** 85-96
ozone layer studies, **1987** 745
science education, **1988** 379
science in U.S., **1973** 781-789
U.S. students compared with those in other countries, **1989** 87
National security
arms control in Nixon policy on, **1973** 519, 521, 525, 527-528
border security
arrests of potential terrorists, **2003** 38
biometric identifiers, **2003** 220-221
counterfeit documents, **2003** 219-220, 223-226
national commission on September 11 recommendations, **2005** 900
and terrorist watch lists, **2003** 163-164
tracking foreign visitors, **2003** 218-226
visa application process, **2003** 222-223
borders and immigration controls, **2004** 468
civil rights and, **2001** 640-642
clearances of government employees, **1995** 532-545
computer security, GAO report on, **1998** 676-686
computer security threats, **1996** 312-324; **1997** 111-112
declassifying government secrets, **1997** 105, 108-109
Defense Department force protection plan, **2001** 4-5
Democratic Party platform, **1996** 641-644
Dole Republican convention speech on, **1996** 493
domestic surveillance, warrantless wiretaps, **1972** 485-489
executive invoking of, Mansfield on, **1974** 63
in federal buildings, **1995** 178-179
and formation of White House intelligence unit, **1973** 563-573
as freedom of information exemption, **1981** 393
government secrecy report, **1997** 103-112
as grounds for Ellsberg break-in, **1973** 538-539, 546; **1974** 33-40, 205-214
Gesell rejection of, **1974** 411-417
Nixon on, **1973** 953-954, 956-957

Homeland Security Department
created, **2002** 530-545
proposal, **2002** 36
and Hunt blackmail threat, Nixon on, **1974** 295-296
infrastructure protection, **1997** 711-720
leaking of information, **1997** 106
missile threat, Rumsfeld Commission on, **1998** 481-499
National Defense Panel needs report, **1997** 811-821
National Security Strategy report, **2002** 534, 633-665; **2004** 889
nuclear weapons secrets theft by China, U.S. accusations of, **1999** 235-256, 304
and passport revocation, **1981** 541-555
Pennsylvania Avenue closing, **1995** 254-258
Pentagon needs review, **1993** 695-715
Pentagon Papers case, **1997** 104, 105-106
preemption doctrine, **2002** 633-665; **2003** 809-810, 905; **2004** 889
role of president and NSC, **1987** 209-217, 234-242
and secrecy of Senate's CIA investigation report, **1975** 710-711
secret classification of documents, **2005** 648
State of the Union address, Democratic response, **2004** 30-32
and technology transfer, **1982** 813-814; **1987** 29-42
terrorist watch list consolidation, **2003** 155-172
threats in the next century, **1999** 499-510
U.S. nuclear strategy, **1997** 811, 814
"Verona" project, **1997** 104
warrantless FBI break-ins, **1981** 372
White House wiretaps, **1974** 449-450, 487-495
wiretaps in previous administrations, Nixon on, **1973** 738, 748, 750
National Security Act (1947)
CIA sources, secrecy of, **1985** 334-344
CIA's role and authority, **1975** 409-412
creation of, **1997** 811
creation of Joint Chiefs, **1982** 325
and disclosure of intelligence information to congressional committees, **1976** 117, 122
and operation of NSC, **1987** 209, 211-212, 228-230, 234, 238-239
reorganization of intelligence agencies, **1976** 126, 129, 131-132
reorganization of oversight of intelligence agencies, **1976** 237, 241, 244, 246
National security adviser, Tower Commission on role of, **1987** 207, 212-216, 235-237, 239
National Security Agency (NSA)
cable traffic interception by, **1975** 709, 711, 799-803
domestic surveillance without court warrants, **2005** 80, 958-969
and Hanssen's espionage activities, **2001** 153
as independent agency, House recommendation, **1976** 120
intelligence gathering, congressional panel investigations, **2002** 991-992, 993, 994
proposed restructuring of, **1976** 258-259
National Security Council (NSC)
arms sales reduction policy, **1978** 107
background paper for presidential finding, **1986** 1053
Boland amendment application to, **1987** 892, 898, 919, 926-927
Committee on Foreign Intelligence, **1976** 242-243
covert operations
and intelligence gathering roles, **1976** 126-127, 132-133, 241-244
in Iran-contra affair, **1987** 892, 896, 902-904, 908-909, 911, 914, 918
creation of, **1997** 811
Foreign Operations Subcommittee, recommended, **1976** 117, 122
Forty Committee, **1976** 127, 241-242
involvement in operations, Tower Commission on, **1987** 238
Operations Advisory Group, establishment of, **1976** 127, 133, 242-243
staff of, **1987** 206-208, 214, 217-218, 224-226, 237-238
strategic communications policy, **2004** 627
wiretaps in, **1974** 449-450, 487-495; **1976** 159-168
workings of
in Iran-contra affair, **1989** 391-393
Tower Commission review of, **1986** 1017-1018, 1023; **1987** 205-242
National Security Entry-Exit Registration System (NSEERS), **2002** 845-849; **2003** 221
National Socialism, in Germany, **1998** 127
National Socialist Party of America v. Skokie, **1995** 331
National Space Council, **1990** 754
National Student Association, CIA funding for, **1975** 402
National Survey of America's Families, **1999** 259
National Telecommunications and Information Administration, report, **1999** 368-383
National Transportation Safety Board (NTSB)
Alaskan oil spill, **1990** 513-530
American Airlines crash investigation, **1979** 949-963
aviation safety, **1999** 115
commuter airline safety recommendations, **1994** 535-540
railroad safety recommendations, **1996** 189, 191
TWA flight 800 crash, **1997** 780-786; **2000** 491
ValuJet crash, **1996** 238
National Union for the Total Independence of Angola (UNITA), **1991** 287-300; **1999** 431; **2002** 151-164
accord on Angolan civil war, **1988** 947
National Urban Coalition, on migration to Sun Belt, **1981** 40
National Urban League
Carter's urban policy, **1978** 243
computer access programs, **1999** 371
economic disparities in U.S., **1989** 447
racial progress in post-Reagan era, **1988** 185-186
state of black America, **1983** 41-55; **1985** 27-37; **1987** 43-60
National Victim Center, rape study, **1992** 385-395
National Weather Service, Hurricane Katrina warning, **2005** 548
National Wildlife Federation, **1992** 470
National Women's Conference, Houston, **1977** 861-867

National Women's Law Center, **1992** 187
Nationalism, economic, dangers of to world economy, **1975** 187-188
Nationalization
of foreign interests in developing countries, **1974** 255-256, 260-261
investors' insurance against, Kissinger proposal, **1976** 301, 306
of property in Vietnam by PRG, **1975** 301, 306
of U.S. copper companies in Chile, **1974** 806
U.S. economic retaliation for, **1972** 329, 332-335
of U.S. firms by developing countries, Nixon policy on, **1972** 67-71
Native American Rights Fund, agreement with museums on skeletal remains, **1989** 539
Native Americans
AIM occupation of Wounded Knee, **1973** 531-535
alcoholism among, **1983** 345
Amnesty International Report on Abuses of, **1992** 897-905
BIA apology for maltreatment of Indians, **2000** 723-728
Catholic, and John Paul II visit, **1987** 699, 701
education, **2003** 582
federal governments failures, Civil Rights Commission report on, **2003** 576-591
health care, **2003** 580
health problems of, **1985** 686-687, 693-697, 700-701, 703-706, 786
housing, **2003** 580-581
land rights of
Democratic Party platform on, **1972** 527, 544
Republican Party platform on, **1972** 652, 705-706
law enforcement, **2003** 581
mental health, surgeon general's report on, **2001** 585-586
in North Carolina, **1993** 462
population, Census Bureau report, **2003** 576-577
religious freedom, **1997** 406-407, 410
skeletal remains, museum agreements to return, **1989** 539-543
suicide rate, **2001** 576
teenage birth rates, **1998** 261
Nativity scene, public display of, **1984** 217-239
NATO. *See* North Atlantic Treaty Organization
NATO-Russia Council, **2002** 886; **2004** 137
Natsios, Andrew, Iraq reconstruction efforts, **2004** 405
Natter, Robert J., *Cole* (USS) bombing, **2001** 4
Natural disasters
See also Disaster relief; Earthquakes; Floods; Hurricane disasters
tsunami in Indian Ocean region, **2004** 348, 753, 887, 891, 991-1000
Natural resources
acid rain effects on, **1983** 198, 200-210
global, U.S. remedies for problems in, **1981** 13-30
managing, Democratic Party platform on, **1984** 592
national forests
Clinton "roadless initiative," **1999** 592-599; **2001** 216-217; **2002** 899; **2004** 668-669
Healthy Forests Initiative, **2002** 894, 899-900; **2003** 27, 181
National Park Service, GAO testimony on, **1995** 120-128
in ocean, Law of the Sea Treaty on use of, **1982** 345-361
population pressure on, **1980** 665-666, 669-670, 677-685; **1987** 439-441, 446-448
protection of, Carter on, **1980** 44, 80-86; **1981** 83-85
report on National Park Service, **1992** 329-334
water regulation and conservation, **1982** 689-701
Natural Resources Defense Council (NRDC)
clean air regulations, **1984** 427-432
Clear Skies Initiative, **2002** 898
on environmental statement from Energy Department, **1989** 357
greenhouse gas emissions, **2002** 299
industrial pollution, **2002** 895
mercury emissions lawsuit, **2004** 667; **2005** 96, 97
Mississippi River water quality report, **1994** 147-148, 152-160
new source review, **2003** 178
wetlands preservation, **2004** 670
world fisheries conservation, **1995** 524
Natural Resources Department
Nixon proposal for, **1972** 148; **1973** 466, 484-485
proposal for, **2004** 604
Nature Conservancy
global warming and land use, **2001** 113
Tallgrass Prairie Reserve and, **1993** 885-891
Nature magazine, fluorocarbons' effect on ozone layer, **1975** 437-438
Naumann, Klaus, UN peacekeeping reform panel, **2000** 643
Navajo Nation
Interior Department Indian trust fund account lawsuit, **2003** 576, 578-579
population, **2003** 577
Naval Academy (U.S.)
Carter speech on Soviet policy, **1978** 223-225, 233-240
hazing and other practices, **1992** 481-487
Naval Petroleum Reserves
development of
FEA on, **1974** 910, 914
Nixon on, **1973** 918
sale of, **1988** 150, 156, 158, 235
Navarro Valls, Joaquin
on John Paul II's trip to Africa, **1985** 499
on UN Conference on Women, Vatican views, **1995** 583-584
Navigation Foundation, on Peary's North Pole claim, **1988** 833; **1989** 688-696
Navy (U.S.)
Cole (USS) bombing, **2000** 277, 861-865; **2001** 3-16, 805; **2003** 30
frigates, survivability and upgrading of, **1987** 791, 794-805
Gulf of Sidra, maneuvers in, **1986** 349
Iowa (USS), explosion on, **1989** 517-521; **1990** 319-330; **1991** 679-689
and Mariel boatlift of Cuban refugees, **1980** 339-341
nuclear-powered ships

Reagan proposals for, **1982** 145, 160
Rickover on, **1982** 89, 101
race relations, and shipboard incidents, **1972** 901-906
sexual harassment prevention initiatives, **1992** 1003-1005
Stark (USS), Iraqi attack on, **1987** 791-815
Tailhook scandal, **1993** 353-354; **2003** 791
court-martial decisions, **1994** 107-115
Defense Department report, **1993** 315-325
Pentagon report on, **1992** 879-890
women
assignment to warships, **1972** 627-629
in combat debate, **1992** 1029-1044
discrimination against, **1987** 671-679
Nayef bin Abdul Aziz (prince of Saudi Arabia)
terrorist bombings
linked to Zionists, **2004** 518
as threat to royal family, **2003** 230
Nazarbayev, Nursultan A., **1991** 532
Nazi concentration camps
Auschwitz-Birkenau, Mengele's activities at, **1985** 409-410, 412
Bergen-Belsen, Reagan's visit, **1985** 358, 360, 362
Birkenau (Auschwitz II), John Paul II at, **1979** 728, 738-741
French apology for complicity with Nazis, **1995** 478-482
French complicity with Nazis, **1995** 478
gold from victims of, **1997** 269
Mauthausen, John Paul II at, **1988** 406-409
refugees from to Switzerland, **1997** 265
Treblinka (Poland), war crimes at, **1993** 617-623
Wiesel's descriptions of, **1986** 1075-1077
Nazi Germany
anti-Semitism and the Shoah, **1998** 127-129
confiscated art, return of, **1998** 294-295
neutral nations aid to, **1997** 257-272; **1998** 291-312
war criminals
Barbie, **1983** 737-747; **1985** 409, 414; **1987** 517-524
in Bitburg cemetery, **1985** 357-362
Demjajuk acquittal, **1993** 617-625
Mengele, **1985** 409-414
Nazism
German guilt and remorse about, **1989** 487-497
and role of Austria in war, **1988** 405-408
Vatican response to, **1987** 700, 703
Nazi-Soviet nonaggression pact (1939), **1989** 469-473, 491
NBA. *See* National Basketball Association
NBC. *See* National Association of Broadcasters
NCAA. *See* National Collegiate Athletic Association
NCES. *See* National Center for Education Statistics
NCHS. *See* National Center for Health Statistics
NCI. *See* National Cancer Institute
NCVS. *See* National Crime Victimization Survey
Ndadaye, Melchoir, Burundi president assassination, **2003** 923
Ndayizeye, Domitien, Burundi president, **2003** 923, 924
Ndiaye, Bacre Waly, death penalty in U.S., **1998** 183-193
Ndombasi, Abdulaye Yerodia, vice president of Congo, **2003** 290
NEA. *See* National Education Association; National Endowment for the Arts
NEAR (Near Earth Asteroid Rendezvous) Shoemaker, **2001** 143-149
Near v. Minnesota ex rel. Olson, **1993** 439, 444-445
Neas, Ralph G.
on abortion issue, **2005** 560
civil rights Court rulings, **1989** 324
economic status of African Americans, **1989** 447
Reagan administration civil rights record, **1989** 17
Nebraska, partial-birth abortion ban, **2000** 430-431; **2003** 995-996, 998
Nebraska Press Association v. Stuart, **1976** 463-479; **1990** 725
Nedzi, Lucien N. (D-Mich.)
ouster from committee investigating CIA, **1975** 523-524
secret intelligence briefings for, **1976** 116
Needle exchange programs, for drug users, **1997** 81, 82, 87-88
Neglia, Peter, **1988** 498
Negligence, determining, in tort reform, **1987** 167-169, 179-181
Negroponte, John
"classified" vs. "sensitive information" policy, **2005** 649
International Criminal Court (ICC), U.S. opposition to, **2002** 608
as national intelligence director, **2005** 246, 252-253, 893, 895
U.S. ambassador to Iraq, **2004** 402, 891
war in Afghanistan, **2001** 628
war in Iraq, **2002** 716
NEH. *See* National Endowment for the Humanities
Nehru, Jawaharlal, **1984** 947
Neier, Aryeh
on draft evader pardon, **1977** 96
on government wiretaps, **1972** 486
Nelson, Bill (D-Fla.), on Poindexter's lying to Congress, **2002** 561
Nelson, Charles, uninsured Americans, **2000** 788
Nelson, Gaylord (D-Wis.)
on multilateral trade agreement, **1979** 638
on phaseout of OEO, **1973** 454
Nelson, George D., **1988** 798
Nemeth, Miklos, **1989** 339
NEPAD. *See* New Partnership for Africa's Development
Nepal, as zone of peace, **1989** 580
Neptune (planet), *Voyager*'s scheduled data collection on, **1981** 836
Neptune, Yvon, former Haitian prime minister imprisoned, **2005** 333
NERC. *See* North American Electric Reliability Council
Nero, Anthony V., Jr., **1988** 4
Nessen, Ron, **1974** 976
Nestlé Co.
infant formula marketing by, **1981** 448-449
Lefever's connection with, **1981** 449, 780
Netanyahu, Benjamin
Gaza Strip disengagement policy
opposition to, **2005** 531

Netanyahu, Benjamin *Continued*
voter referendum, **2004** 305, 307, 308
Israeli cabinet resignation, **2005** 532
Israel human rights, **1989** 58
as Israeli interim foreign minister, **2002** 937
Israeli prime minister election, **1996** 337-342
Israeli prime minister election defeat, **1999** 359-360, 890
Likud Party politics, **2005** 534
presidential challenge, **2000** 935
Wye River peace agreement, **1998** 742-747, 749-750; **1999** 891
Netherlands
Arab oil embargo against, **1974** 221-222; **1975** 3
Bush visit, **1989** 411, 435-437
coronation of Beatrix, **1980** 387-397
EU constitution referendum, **2005** 339-342
euro currency, **1998** 271
gay marriage legislation, **2005** 869
housing shortage in, **1980** 387, 389
immigration policy, **2005** 340
John Paul II visit, **1985** 363-374
Theo van Gogh murder, **2005** 340
troops in Iraq, **2004** 882-883
Netscape Communications Corp., and Microsoft Corp. antitrust case, **2000** 106-107, 110-130
Nettles, Bonnie Lu Trousdale, Heaven's Gate cult leader, **1997** 122-124
Nettleton, Joyce A., **1996** 72
Neuborne, Bert, **1995** 327
Neufeld, Peter, death penalty, **2000** 990
Neuharth, Allen H., **1979** 513
Neukom, William, Microsoft antitrust case, **2001** 777
Neustadt, Richard E., on swine flu immunization program, **1978** 670-681
Neutron weapons
and arms control, Carter on, **1977** 907-908
Soviet propaganda about, **1981** 764-767
Neves, Tancredo, election of, **1985** 3-12
Nevins, Allan, **1974** 709
New American Schools program, **1992** 57, 64
New England Journal of Medicine
on anemia in African American women, **1987** 148
on cow's milk, **1992** 399, 401
guns in the home study, **1993** 871-876
health care for women, **1993** 653-658
heart attacks and race, **1993** 671-675
reports on terminally ill, **1984** 275-285
New Ireland Forum, proposals of, **1984** 315-326
New Jersey
courts
Baby M case on surrogate mother contracts, **1987** 373-387; **1988** 71-79
Quinlan case on terminating life-support systems, **1976** 197-219
Megan's Law, for sex offenders, **1997** 382, 384
same-sex couples, spousal benefits, **2004** 37
stem cell research, **2004** 161
New Jersey v. T.L.O., **1985** 13-26; **1995** 342, 347, 348
New London Development Corporation (NLDC), eminent domain case, **2005** 362-375
New Markets and Renewal Communities Initiative, **2001** 59
New Markets Venture Capital Firms program, **2000** 49
New Mexico
early human remains, **1992** 135, 137-139
morning-after pill, without prescription for, **2003** 999
"prescribed fire" results in wildfires, **2000** 713
Wen Ho Lee spy case, **2000** 740-752
New Partnership for Africa's Development (NEPAD), **2003** 451-452, 766; **2005** 405-446-466
New Source Review (NSR) program, **2002** 895-897, 902-905; **2003** 173-190; **2004** 664-674; **2005** 100
New Territories (Hong Kong), return of to China, **1984** 1045, 1048
New World Foundation, task force on hunger, **1985** 190
New York (state)
Attica prison uprising, **1972** 783-788
compensation law, **1991** 813-825
drug dealers in, punishment for, **1973** 27-33
hazardous chemicals at Love Canal, **1983** 479-487
legislature's actions in New York City fiscal crisis, **1975** 861-864, 866-869
redistricting, racial criteria in, **1977** 151-167
Rockefeller governorship, **1974** 707-709
same-sex marriages in New Paltz, **2004** 39
state courts on America's Cup, **1989** 183-193
New York v. EPA, **2005** 100
New York v. Ferber, **1982** 675-688; **1990** 241-242, 243, 246, 247, 248-249; **1992** 319, 546-547
New York v. Quarles, **1984** 387-397; **2000** 392, 393
New York City
See also September 11 (9/11) terrorist attacks
air quality of, **1981** 275, 289
blackout, investigation of, **1977** 545-550
Declaration of Independence bicentennial celebrations, **1976** 509-510
discrimination by private clubs, **1988** 399-403
fiscal crisis
accounting and budgeting practices, **1977** 567-568, 571-573, 575-577
and debt moratorium, **1976** 863-867
federal financing for, **1975** 861-869
SEC on, **1977** 567-579
gay rights legislation, Catholic Church's view of, **1986** 910
landmark preservation law, and property takings, **1978** 453-465
public employee pension benefits, **2005** 197-198
New York City Transit Authority, Donovan indictment, **1984** 804, 806-809
New York Civil Liberties Union, on rights of mental patients, **1975** 470
New York Commissioner of Education, multicultural textbook report, **1991** 331-347
New York Daily News, on Quayle-Murphy Brown controversy, **1992** 443
New York Society of Economic Analysts, McGovern speech on economic program, **1972** 737-742
New York State Club Association v. City of New York, **1988** 399-403
New York State Power Commission, and New York City blackout, **1977** 546

New York Stock Exchange
conflict of interest of board member, **2003** 332, 693, 697-698
Grasso pay package, **2004** 422
market crash, **1987** 833, 835, 837, 839-840
market reform, **1988** 12
New York Telephone, United States v., **1977** 883-896
New York Times
aid to Russia, **1992** 256
Arthur Ashe story, **1992** 336
on CIA's domestic activities, **1975** 401, 523-528, 709
on DNA "fingerprints," **1992** 362
Dubcek letter in, **1975** 239-249
gun control, **1992** 494
Iowa (USS) explosion investigation, **1990** 320
on new nutrition studies, **1992** 397
Pentagon Papers in, **1972** 491-497; **1973** 537-539, 545; **1974** 206
on Yeltsin, **1992** 520
New York Times v. Sullivan, **1979** 286, 289-310, 315-317; **1986** 355-356, 359-368; **1988** 176-182; **1991** 321, 325-326
New York Times v. United States, **1990** 725
New Yorker
on Persian Gulf War, **1990** 546
on Shevardnadze resignation, **1990** 826
New Zealand
America's Cup rulings in New York courts, **1989** 183-193
French sabotage of Greenpeace ship, **1985** 631-633
nuclear-free zone, **1985** 633
Newberry, Truman H. (R-Mich.), **1981** 674
Newdow, Michael A., pledge of allegiance, constitutionality of, **2002** 382-390; **2005** 376
Newhouse, John, **1990** 546
Newman, Edwin, at presidential debates, **1976** 693; **1984** 877-902
Newman, Frank
on higher education, **1985** 583-602
on multicultural education, **1992** 47-48
Newman, Jim, **1998** 932
Newman, Troy, abortion pill, **2000** 784
Newport News Shipbuilding & Dry Dock Co. v. EEOC, **1991** 149
News media
See also Mass media; Press
Agnew case, leaks on, **1973** 828-830
broadcast programming, self-criticism of, **1973** 57
Chilean, CIA efforts in, **1975** 874-875, 894-897, 901-902
disinformation campaign of Reagan administration, **1986** 351-352
editorial processes, disclosure of, **1979** 286-311
fairness doctrine regulation, **1987** 625-632
FBI investigations of members of, **1975** 873, 878, 880
FOIA revisions, **1981** 395
government coverage by, **1973** 632-639
libel suits
awards to public figures, **1984** 299-300
on private persons, **1986** 355-357, 358-368
on public persons, **1986** 355-356, 357-358
Sharon against *Time* magazine, **1985** 47-52
vulnerability to, **1984** 247-256
Westmoreland against CBS, **1983** 401-412; **1985** 159-165
national security information, leaks of, **1973** 567-569; **1974** 449-450, 487-495
Nixon administration's relations with, **1973** 14, 55-58, 567-569, 629-639
Watergate coverage, **1973** 897-899, 903-905, 907-909
ownership in same community, FCC on, **1978** 419-432
presidential press conferences, **1988** 835-845
press freedoms, Court rulings on, **1979** 311-318
Reagan, assassination attempt on, coverage of, **1981** 352
restrictions on
during Grenada invasion, **1983** 850
during Polish martial law, **1981** 881-882
in South Africa, **1982** 799; **1986** 371-372
in South Korea, **1981** 190
travel and communication, Helsinki Final Act on, **1975** 559, 561, 569-570
UNESCO proposal for, **1983** 968-969
right to reply for political candidates, **1974** 523-528
sources and work product of, House subpoena of, **1976** 683-686
Three Mile Island accident, reporting on, **1979** 825, 828-829, 841-842, 860
trial coverage
access to pretrial hearings, **1979** 513
gag orders, **1976** 463-479
pretrial publicity and conviction reversal, **1974** 857-859
televised, **1981** 163-176
U.S. bureaus in PRC, **1979** 136, 150
White House press corps, **1988** 836, 839, 845
Newspapers
circulation fraud settlements, **2004** 423
ownership of, and of radio or TV station in same community, FCC on, **1978** 419-432
Newsweek magazine, on Kissinger Vietnam study (1969), **1972** 361
Ney, Bob (R-Ohio), fraud and conspiracy investigations, **2005** 635
NFL. *See* National Football League
NFMA. *See* National Forest Management Act
NGA. *See* National Governors' Association
Ngeze, Hassan, Rwanda genocide war crimes conviction, **2003** 1073, 1075-1088
Ngoma, Arthur Z'Ahidi, vice president of Congo, **2003** 290
Nguyen, Jean, **1985** 116-117
Nguyen, Kathy T., anthrax mailings victim, **2001** 675
NHTSA. *See* National Highway Traffic Safety Administration
Niasse, Moustapha, Congo peace negotiations, **2002** 548
Nicaragua
activist Catholic clergy in, **1980** 412; **1984** 761; **1986** 318
agricultural communes in, **1979** 584
cease-fire agreement with contras, **1988** 241-245

Nicaragua *Continued*
and Central American peace plan, **1987** 637-638, 640-648, 1007-1009
Chamorro inaugural address, **1990** 259-266
church-government relations in, **1986** 641
CIA mining of harbors, **1985** 256-257, 637
Contra support by Reagan, **1992** 651
Cuban support for, **1982** 180, 187-188; **1984** 45; **1985** 639
Cuban-Soviet colonialism in, Reagan on, **1982** 180, 187-188
democratic reforms in, **1988** 58, 66; **1989** 161-165, 167, 169
earthquake in, and exposure of government corruption, **1979** 585
elections in and compliance with peace plan, **1989** 161-162, 164-165, 167
embassy in Panama, U.S. forces in, **1989** 703
government overthrow by guerrilla warfare, CIA manual on, **1984** 847, 877-880, 903-916
human rights in
Americas Watch on, **1985** 146, 255, 258-260
Amnesty International on, **1989** 605-606
Reagan on, **1983** 445-446
State Department reports on, **1980** 191, 197; **1981** 180, 186-187; **1984** 164-165; **1985** 146, 153; **1986** 107-108; **1987** 191, 197-198; **1989** 58, 61-62
hurricane damage, **1998** 789, 791
ICJ ruling on U.S. mining of ports, **1984** 339-345; **1985** 637-641
Iraq, troop withdrawal from, **2004** 882
John Paul II visit, **1983** 241, 245-246
military, size of under Sandinistas, **1985** 263
military buildup in, **1983** 307, 312
peace in, conditions for, Kissinger commission on, **1984** 48-50
refugees from, and political asylum in U.S., **1987** 254-257
Republican Party platform on, **1988** 616, 675-676
revolution and guerrilla war in, Kissinger commission on, **1984** 44-45
revolution and ouster of Somoza regime, **1979** 581-591
U.S. reaction to, **1979** 575, 581-583, 585-588, 714, 716, 719-720
Salvadoran rebels, military support for, **1981** 249-251; **1989** 650, 657-658, 666
pledge to discontinue, **1989** 163-164, 167, 171-172
smoking in the Americas, **1992** 269
Soviet support for, **1984** 45, 827; **1985** 639, 708, 716
Soviet Union arms shipments, **1992** 24
support for Central American revolts, **1985** 637, 639
terrorism supported by, **1985** 464, 466, 472, 476
U.S. policy toward
Kissinger commission recommendations, **1984** 31-32
Reagan on goals in Central America, **1983** 439-454
U.S. trade embargo against, **1985** 257, 347-348
Nicaraguan contras
bipartisan U.S. accord on future of, **1989** 161-168
cease-fire agreement with Sandinistas, **1988** 241-245
church-government relations, **1986** 641
CIA training of, **1984** 903-916
demobilization and repatriation of, Tela declaration on, **1989** 161-162, 168-172
human rights abuses by, **1985** 146, 255, 258-260
Reagan commitment to, **1987** 106, 110
reintegration of into Nicaragua, **1987** 642
rise of, **1987** 638-640
U.S. aid to, **1985** 255-257, 260-269; **1988** 58, 66
congressional rejection of, **1985** 347
cutoff of, **1988** 241-243
Kissinger commission on, **1984** 31, 50
and Nicaraguan compliance with peace plan, **1987** 1007-1009
prohibition on, **1983** 441-442
U.S. bipartisan accord on, **1989** 161-168
U.S. diversion of funds to, **1986** 1013-1014, 1017, 1022-1024, 1049-1052, 1054
legality of, **1987** 891-892, 903-904, 919, 926
Reagan's knowledge of, **1987** 891, 894-895, 907, 916-917, 922-923
Tower Commission on, **1987** 205-208, 217-218, 221, 225-226, 230
Nichols, Terry L., and Oklahoma City bombing, **1995** 177; **1996** 178; **1997** 223, 623-627
Nicholson, Harold James, espionage case, **1996** 794-800
Nicholson, Jim, as veterans affairs secretary, **2005** 45
Nickles, Don (R-Okla.)
on Clinton legislative program, **1999** 42
Lott resignation, **2002** 972-973
tax cut initiatives, **2001** 666
Nicolaider, Cristino, **1982** 287
Nicolaides, Philip, **1981** 754
Nicotine addiction
See also Cigarettes
surgeon general on, **1988** 309-322
tobacco companies and, **1994** 205-217; **1995** 670-679; **1997** 333; **1999** 546-548
Niehaus, Bernd, small arms trade, **2001** 518
Nields, John W., Jr.
FBI break-in trial, **1981** 373
House investigation of Korean influence buying, **1978** 847, 849
Nielsen, Jerri, South Pole doctor, **1999** 611-613
Niezabotowska, Malgorzata, Katyn massacre by Stalin, **1990** 224
Niezvestny, Ernst, **1975** 162
Niger, drought and famine in, **1984** 974, 979-980, 983
Nigeria
AIDS epidemic, **2002** 470
Carter visit, **1978** 269-271, 281-287
Clinton state visit, **2000** 64
conflict in, **2002** 447
elections, **1999** 428
executions in, **1989** 597
human rights in, **1995** 696-699
inauguration of president Obasanjo, **1999** 272-282
Iraq uranium sales investigations, **2003** 20-21, 876; **2005** 248-249, 699-700

Liberian president Taylor exile to, **2003** 770, 771
OPEC oil prices, **1979** 251, 254; **1980** 995; **1981** 799
OPEC oil production quotas, **1982** 980
political conditions, **1998** 220
population control in, **1987** 441, 448
at poverty summit, **1981** 770
religious persecution, **1997** 575-576
U.S. policy, **1999** 275-276
U.S. response to hanging of dissidents, **1995** 696-699
U.S. technical training exchanged for oil, **1979** 650
NIH. *See* National Institutes of Health
NIJ. *See* National Institute of Justice
Nikolic, Tomislav, Serbian presidential candidate, **2003** 60; **2004** 956
NIMH. *See* National Institute of Mental Health
Nimitz (USS), attempted rescue of U.S. hostages, **1980** 352, 359-362, 369, 373, 379, 381, 383
NIOSH. *See* National Institute for Occupational Safety and Health
Nir, Amiram, **1986** 1016
Nirenberg, William A., **1983** 199
Niskanen, William A., **1984** 119; **1985** 80
Nistroy, Dietrich, **1986** 93
Nitze, Paul H.
critique of SALT II, **1978** 550-551, 567-582; **1979** 417
at Iceland summit, **1986** 876
in INF negotiations, **1983** 793
testimony in Westmoreland libel suit, **1985** 160
Nix v. Williams, **1984** 505-506
Nixon, F. Donald, wiretap on, **1973** 949, 959
Nixon, Richard M.
ABM treaty, **2001** 928
abortion and teenage contraceptive services, **1972** 301
administration
ABM treaty negotiation, **1987** 294-299, 301, 304, 306-310
Chilean coup, support for, **1975** 764-769, 787-788
CIA domestic surveillance during, **1975** 401-403, 409, 422, 425, 428-429, 523-528, 709
enemies list, **1973** 662-664, 677-679; **1974** 313-314
FBI, political uses of, **1975** 873, 880, 882
Indo-Pakistani conflict, position in, **1972** 23-40, 163
IRS, political uses of, **1975** 829-830, 849, 851, 856-857
Justice Department's domestic wiretaps, warrantless, **1972** 485-486
national security leaks and plumbers unit, **1974** 33-40
news media relations, **1973** 14, 55-58, 629-639, 898-899
papers and tapes from, custody of, **1977** 465-516
plumbers unit
Ellsberg break-in case, **1974** 33-37, 205-214, 661-669
Kissinger on, **1974** 488, 492-493
and Pentagon Papers trial dismissal, **1973** 537-548
planned raid on Greenspan, **1973** 976
responsibilities of, **1973** 563-573
public broadcasting, control of, **1979** 121-122
Rebozo's influence in, **1973** 975-976
record of, Nixon on, **1974** 41-42, 44-45
Soviet relations, noninterference in internal affairs, **1973** 792, 796-799
Vietnam peace agreement, on MIA search and aid for North Vietnam, **1977** 208, 212
Vietnam peace talks, secret, **1972** 121-134
Watergate-related illegal activities of, special prosecutor on, **1975** 653-664
White House aides
Colson plea bargain, **1974** 443-447
domestic intelligence gathering by, **1974** 600-601, 608-611
executive privilege for, **1973** 337-341, 413-414, 500-501, 503
and ITT antitrust settlement, **1972** 396-397, 401, 404-405
resignations in Watergate scandal, **1973** 499-504, 508-511
Watergate cover-up convictions, **1974** 991-1002
Agnew, charges against, **1973** 828-829, 831
Agnew resignation, **1973** 837-838
Arab-Israeli war
Egyptian-Israeli disengagement, **1974** 31
peace negotiations, **1973** 932
U.S.-Soviet avoidance of confrontation, **1973** 897-901, 905, 907-908
U.S.-Soviet role in cease-fire, **1973** 881-889
and black America, **1985** 27, 30-31
budget messages, **1972** 115-119; **1973** 169-183; **1974** 95-112
budget reform, signing of, **1974** 573
campaign reform proposals, **1974** 215-220
campaigns and elections
contributions handled by Rebozo, **1973** 975-977
corporate contributions to, **1974** 603-604
nomination acceptance speech, **1972** 711, 716-725
support by young voters, **1973** 36-37
victory speech, **1972** 893-895
Civil Rights Commission, Hesburgh resignation, **1983** 915
death penalty, **1972** 500
declassification of documents, **1972** 235-245
doctrine, **1972** 656-657, 663; **1973** 515-516, 523-524, 526
EC proposed cooperation with Arab states, **1974** 186
economic policy
CEA reports, **1973** 185-191; **1974** 69-94, 419
international report, **1973** 379, 381-382; **1974** 113-122
economic stabilization program, **1973** 43-54, 427, 430-431, 577-585, 703-713
Ellsberg break-in
authorization of, **1974** 411-416
question of involvement in, **1974** 33-37, 206
sworn statement on, **1974** 664
energy program, **1973** 465-486

Nixon, Richard M. *Continued*
executive privilege claims, **1973** 3, 5-6, 13, 18, 337-342, 698
FBI break-ins, warrantless, **1981** 372
finances, personal, **1973** 947, 956-959, 975-976
income taxes, **1973** 947, 956-959; **1974** 235-245, 656, 660, 730-735, 748-751
property improvements, **1974** 731
real estate capital gains, **1974** 235, 237-240, 244-245
Ford as vice president, **1973** 970
foreign aid
and drug trafficking, **1972** 647
requests, **1974** 277-286
Frost TV interviews with, **1977** 321-365
funeral of, **1994** 237-244
Geneva protocol, submission to Senate, **1972** 323-324
health policy
national insurance plan, **1978** 544
on venereal disease, **1972** 343
immunity in whistleblowing suit, **1982** 539-559
impeachment
articles of, **1974** 655-660
calls for, **1973** 860, 863, 903-904; **1974** 301-302, 673-675
impeachment inquiry
authorization by House, **1974** 137
final committee report, **1974** 713-763
impoundment of appropriated funds, **1973** 3-19; **1975** 135-140
inaugural address, **1973** 79-85
ITT antitrust settlement, **1974** 407-410
and political contributions, **1974** 3-5, 16-21
Japan relations
Sato meeting, **1972** 41-43
Tanaka meeting, **1972** 745-749; **1973** 717-722
Kissinger, working with, **1977** 322, 342-346, 354-355, 361-362
library and birthplace (Yorba Linda, Calif.), **1992** 256
Mexico relations, Echeverria meeting, **1972** 471
Middle East trip, **1974** 449-471
military draft, **1972** 247, 733-736; **1984** 349
milk price supports decision and dairy industry contributions, **1974** 3-4, 6-15
monetary policy
abandonment of gold standard, **1974** 498; **1985** 624
and Bretton Woods system, **1978** 743
reform proposals, **1972** 815-820
national security wiretaps, **1976** 159-168
nationalization of U.S. firms, **1972** 67-71
NATO relations, **1973** 488, 490; **1974** 529
NSC under, **1987** 212, 214-215
OEO
consolidation of, **1973** 312, 454
funding, **1973** 453-464
oil embargo, emergency steps, **1973** 913-921
oil pricing, **1998** 501
papers and tapes of, custody of, **1977** 465-516
pardon of, **1974** 811-817; **1975** 143, 145-146; **1977** 355-356
and agreement on presidential papers, **1975** 667-668
Dole and Mondale on, **1976** 773-774, 792
Ford explanation of, **1974** 887-900; **1976** 702
as option for Ford, **1974** 766-769, 774
peace
as legacy of, **1974** 41-46, 50-53, 687-688
through military strength, **1973** 269-270, 274-275
PRC relations, **1984** 24
PRC trip, **1972** 183-192; **1984** 287, 290
consequences of, **1978** 782, 784
presidential immunity, **1997** 291
press conferences, **1974** 145-154, 189-203; **1988** 843-844
public opinion on job performance, **1989** 16
Reagan presidential library dedication, **1991** 735, 742-743
resignation, **1975** 653, 666; **1977** 321, 323-324, 335-336, 354-355
announcement and farewell speech, **1974** 683-693
calls for, **1974** 301-302, 673-674
denial of plans for, **1973** 737, 747-748, 903-904, 913, 922; **1974** 42, 52, 145, 153, 189-191, 197-200
school finance commission appointment, **1972** 221
science advisers and science funding, **1973** 782-783
second-term plans, **1972** 881-892
Soviet relations
ABM treaty, **1972** 431-460
ABM treaty signing, **1972** 431-436, 452-453, 456-460; **1979** 413, 455
environment agreements, **1972** 806
Moscow summit agreements, **1974** 535-569
SALT agreements, **1972** 431-460, 766; **1974** 535-537
trade agreements, **1972** 845
trade benefits as goal of, **1974** 901
TV speeches to Soviet people, **1972** 439-442; **1974** 548-552; **1986** 5
space shuttle program, **1981** 417
speech on aid to Russia, **1992** 255-265
State of the Union address, **1972** 73-74; **1974** 41-53
State of the Union messages, **1972** 73-113; **1973** 209-225, 303-329, 801-808; **1974** 42-43, 53-62
state of world message, **1973** 515-530
tapes
Court ruling on, **1974** 637-638
edited transcripts of, **1974** 287-299
erasure on, **1974** 23-27
federal court rulings on, **1973** 839-857
release of, **1974** 673-682
tapes and files, Watergate prosecutor's access to, **1974** 621-638; **1975** 653-654, 658-666, 668-670
terrorism, deterrence of, **1972** 751
tobacco advertising law, **1973** 64
transfer of power, agreement with Eisenhower, **1985** 492
vice presidential papers, tax deduction for donation of, **1974** 146, 152, 154, 235-236, 239-240
Vietnam war
aid assurances to South Vietnam, **1975** 279-281, 285-299

amnesty for draft evaders, **1972** 12-13; **1973** 193-194, 197-198
antiwar demonstrations, **1973** 427-430, 433
bombing of North Vietnam, **1972** 385-388, 611; **1973** 3-4, 6-7, 9-13, 15, 17, 116; **1975** 273
Cambodia bombing, **1973** 751
ending of, **1984** 350
Paris peace accords, **1973** 115-120, 269-276
peace talks
on release of POWs, **1973** 331
secret, **1972** 121-126
return of POWs, **1973** 246
status report on (1969), **1972** 361-379
Thieu meeting, **1973** 447-451
troop withdrawal, **1972** 3-6, 55-56
war powers resolution, veto of, **1973** 923-924
Watergate
firing of special prosecutor, **1973** 859-880; **1987** 718, 740; **1988** 466
to managing editors, **1973** 947-964
and national security operations, **1973** 563-574
payments to break-in defendants, **1974** 306-308, 348-353, 356, 369-373, 375
responsibility accepted by, **1973** 499-501, 505
Watergate cover-up
Frost interviews on, **1977** 321-322, 324-335, 357-359, 362-365
involvement of White House staff, **1973** 414-415; **1974** 1002; **1975** 141-151
suspicion of Dean, **1974** 991-992, 994-1001
Watergate cover-up involvement of, **1974** 160, 173-175, 599, 606
Dean testimony on, **1973** 659, 662-672
and grand jury documents, **1974** 158, 225-232
House Judiciary Committee transcripts, **1974** 302-387
White House transcripts on, **1974** 287-299
welfare proposal, **1977** 553
White House enemies list, **1974** 602
Nixon, United States v., **1998** 401, 402
Nixon, Walter L., Jr., impeachment of, **1989** 583-585, 590-596; **1993** 81-91
Nixon v. Administrator of General Services, **1977** 465-516
Nixon v. Fitzgerald, **1982** 539-559; **1997** 294, 295
Nixon v. United States, **1974** 621-638; **1993** 81-91
Niyitegeka, Eliezer, Rwanda war crimes conviction, **2003** 1074
Nizamuddin, Mohammad, on aging population in the developing world, **2002** 194
Nkala, Enos, **1980** 318
Nkomo, Joshua
agreement to cease-fire, **1979** 941
demands of in Rhodesian conflict, **1977** 584-585
rejection of internal agreement, **1978** 150
Zimbabwe independence, **1980** 317-318, 320, 323, 329
Nkrumah, Kwame, African economic development proposals, **2001** 506
Nkurunziza, Pierre, Burundi peace negotiations, **2003** 924-925
NLC. *See* National League of Cities
NLRB. *See* National Labor Relations Board
No Child Left Behind Act, **2002** 42-43; **2004** 20, 26, 779; **2005** 83
No Child Left Behind program, video news services, as government propaganda, **2005** 647, 650-653
NOAA. *See* National Oceanic and Atmospheric Administration
Noatak National Monument, **1978** 731, 737
Nobel Peace Prize
Annan, Kofi, UN peace efforts, **2001** 517, 819, 899-906
Arias Sánchez of Costa Rica, **1987** 1007-1011
Begin, Menachem, Camp David accord, **2002** 981; **2003** 1131
Begin and Sadat, **1978** 607, 624-632; **1983** 834
Carter, Jimmy, lifetime work on human rights, **2002** 232, 981-989
Dalai Lama, policy of nonviolence, **1989** 573-581
Ebadi, Shirin, Iran human rights and political reform, **2003** 1033, 1129-1137
ElBaradei, Mohammed, for nuclear nonproliferation efforts, **2005** 594, 931-940
Kim Dae-jung, for Korean reunification efforts, **2000** 867; **2001** 268; **2002** 731
King, Martin Luther, Jr., **1983** 885
Kyi, Aung San Suu, Myanmar opposition leader, **2002** 982
Luthuli, Albert, nonviolent protest against racist laws, **1984** 1027; **1993** 877-878, 880-881, 883
Maathai, Wangari, sustainable development, **2004** 929-936
Mandela, Nelson, and Frederik W. De Klerk acceptance speeches, work to end racial segregation **1993** 877-884
Menchu, Rigoberta, Guatemala political activist, **2001** 613
Physicians for Prevention of Nuclear War (Chazov and Lown), **1985** 781-787
Rabin, Peres, and Arafat acceptance speeches, **1995** 691
Roosevelt, Theodore, Japan-Russia peace agreement, **2002** 981
Rotblat, Joseph, and nuclear disarmament, **1995** 553
al-Sadat, Anwar, Camp David accord, **2002** 981
Sakharov, Andrei D., Soviet human rights, **1975** 915-928; **1981** 748, 751-752
Trimble, David, Northern Ireland peace process, **2005** 508
Tutu, Desmond, speeches against apartheid, **1984** 1027-1037; **2002** 982
Walesa, Lech, trade union movement, **1983** 925-932
Wiesel, Elie, human rights, **1986** 1075-1078
Williams, Jody, land mines ban campaign, **1997** 846
Wilson, Woodrow, League of Nations, **2002** 981
Nobel Prize for Literature
Octavio Paz, **1990** 795-806
Solzhenitsyn, **1972** 727-731; **1974** 130-131
Toni Morrison, **1993** 977-985
Nofziger, Franklyn C. (Lyn)
ethics investigation of, **1988** 495, 499-501
and independent counsel, **1988** 466
al-Nogaidan, Mansour, political reform in Saudi Arabia, **2003** 234

Noguchi, Soichi, *Discovery* space shuttle mission, **2005** 500
Nol, Lon, **1991** 692
Nolan, Beth, Marc Rich presidential pardon, **2001** 91
Noles, Dickie, **1986** 171
Nollan v. California Coastal Commission, **1987** 531, 533, 547-553; **1994** 300, 302, 303, 306-307, 309-310
Nolte, Ernst, **1989** 488
Nominating conventions
  See also Democratic Party conventions; Republican Party conventions
  public financing of, **1976** 71, 74, 93, 97
Nonaligned nations
  access to nuclear technology for peaceful purposes, **1975** 361-363
  conferences
    Algiers, **1974** 255-256
    Havana, **1979** 681-691; **1983** 263
    New Delhi, **1983** 263-368
  cooperation on self-determination and use of resources, **1974** 255-257
  reform of international economic and trading system, **1983** 263-268
  resistance to bloc politics, **1979** 681-682, 688-691
  role in promoting détente, **1974** 838-839
Nonsmokers, health dangers from exposure to smoke, **1986** 1079-1090
NORAD. *See* North American Aerospace Defense Command
Norfolk & Western Railroad, in railroad reorganization, **1975** 534-535
Noriega, Manuel Antonio
  broadcast of taped phone calls, **1990** 721-725
  Bush on, **1992** 504
  as intelligence source for U.S., **1988** 82-83
  as issue in election debates, **1988** 722, 724-726, 741-742, 749, 801, 815
  rise of, **1989** 704-705
  sentenced for drug trafficking, **1992** 649-653
  surrender to U.S., **1989** 702-705
  U.S. indictments of, **1988** 81-92, 869
Norkfolk (Virginia), school uniform policy, **1996** 91-92
Norquist, Grover
  antitax activist, **2005** 632
  aviation security and CAPPS II program, **2003** 722
  CIA leak case, Rove involvement in, **2005** 703
Nortel Networks, retirement fund losses, **2002** 102
North, Oliver L.
  arms sales to Iran, **1986** 1015-1016, 1050
  Casey's Iran-contra role, **1987** 906
  congressional testimony, **1987** 892-893, 900, 917
  conviction and appeal, **1994** 12; **1998** 906
  destruction of documents, **1987** 916, 919
  diversion of funds, idea for, **1987** 917, 923
  failure to disclose activities to Congress, **1987** 900, 904-905
  firing of, **1986** 1017, 1023
  Iran arms sales, **1994** 9
  Iran-contra charges dismissed, **1991** 429, 617-620; **1992** 1075
  Iran-contra conviction appealed, **1990** 491-507
  Iran-contra role
    congressional investigation of, **1987** 892, 894, 896, 898-899, 906, 924
    Tower Commission on, **1987** 217-218, 224-227
  on presidential knowledge, **1987** 907, 917
  refusal to talk, **1986** 1050-1051
  secret attempts to release hostages, **1986** 1052
  senatorial election campaign, **1994** 9-10
  sentencing, **1989** 391-397
North America
  inter-American dialogue on critical issues of, **1983** 375-390
  population growth in, **1987** 443-444
North American accord, Reagan plan for, **1982** 183-184
North American Aerospace Defense Command (NORAD), **2003** 547
North American Electric Reliability Council (NERC), **2003** 1016, 1021
North American Free Trade Agreement (NAFTA)
  Bush on, **1992** 19, 101
  CEA report on, **1994** 142; **1995** 85; **1997** 53, 61-62, 68; **1998** 83, 95
  Clinton economic report, **1995** 74
  Clinton on impact of, **1997** 541-549; **2000** 47; **2001** 59
  Clinton remarks on House passage of, **1993** 953-958
  Republican Party support for, **1996** 510
North Atlantic Treaty Organization (NATO)
  Bosnia peacekeeping mission, **1995** 717-726; **1997** 342; **1998** 49; **1999** 286; **2001** 823; **2003** 463; **2004** 138
  charter, Kissinger on, **1973** 487-495
  charter with Russia, **1997** 514, 515
  conventional forces
    limitation of, Reagan proposal, **1982** 478-479
    reductions, Bush proposal, **1989** 176, 197-304
    strengthening, Carter on, **1981** 59-60, 90-93
    strengthening, Mondale on, **1984** 551
  danger of, Gromyko on, **1984** 822, 825-826
  Declaration on Atlantic Relations, **1974** 529-533
  defense program
    elimination of military interests of, Gorbachev on, **1989** 400, 403-405
    long-term, **1978** 373-381
  defense spending increase, Carter on, **1978** 97; **1979** 11, 13, 70-71
  defense strategy
    Akhromeyev on, **1989** 440-441, 443
    flexible response, **1973** 493-494
    maintaining defenses in time of détente, **1976** 907, 914-915
    nuclear deterrence, **1975** 503, 505
    technological superiority, **1987** 29-31
  European and world security, conference communiqué, **1976** 345-350
  European defense force and, **1999** 817-827; **2002** 889
  European nations and, **1995** 93, 100
  expansion
    Clinton support for, **1997** 40, 341; **1998** 48-49, 613; **1999** 54

cost issues, **1997** 517
G-8 discussions, **1997** 340, 516
Russian opposition to, **1998** 612-613
secretary of state report on, **1996** 655-661
statements marking, **1999** 119-133
summit meeting and, **1997** 514-526
fiftieth anniversary, Washington summit, **1998** 912; **1999** 119, 121-122
French participation in, **1976** 331, 336, 339-341; **1997** 516
future of
Clinton administration on, **1999** 120
secretary of state on, **1998** 912-919
Germany
Berlin and, **1986** 791, 796, 798
East German diplomatic relations, **1974** 801-802
German reunification and, **1989** 626-627, 634; **1990** 108, 332, 600
headquarters in Brussels, **2004** 135
historical background, **1981** 824-826; **1982** 419-420; **1999** 119-120
INF negotiations, **1983** 507-508
INF treaty, **1987** 946-947
Iraq training program, **2004** 138
Kosovo crisis
air strikes, **1999** 119, 122; **2001** 554-555, 819
Clinton announcement, **1999** 134-143
threat of, **1998** 829-831
UNSC resolution on, **1999** 285-296
Kosovo Force (KFOR) peacekeeping mission, **2003** 1138, 1140, 1141; **2004** 138-139, 949-950
London Declaration of Peaceful Intent, **1990** 455-466
Macedonia peacekeeping mission, **2001** 554-558
membership
for Bosnia, **2005** 851, 857
for Croatia, **2005** 857
partial memberships in, **1975** 354-355, 357
for Romania, **2002** 608
for Slovenia, **2001** 893
for Spain, **1982** 419-421
membership expansion, **2001** 895; **2002** 608-609, 885-893; **2003** 460; **2004** 135-141, 198
NATO Response Force (NRF), **2002** 889, 891
Partnership for Peace, **2003** 460
Poland
relations with, **1987** 184-185
Soviet intervention in, **1980** 795, 802-803
Republican Party platform, **1996** 539
role in changing Europe, **1989** 646, 654-655, 661-665
role today of, **2002** 888-889
Russia, new relationship with, **2001** 892-898; **2002** 276, 885, 886; **2004** 137
sharing of burdens in, **1973** 494
Nixon on, **1973** 253, 516, 519, 525
Soviet military buildup and, **1978** 223-224, 230-231, 238; **1981** 717-718, 722-724
Soviet propaganda about, Project Truth on, **1981** 763-764
Sudan, African Union peacekeeping mission supported by, **2005** 519
summit meeting (Madrid), **1997** 514-526
terrorism condemned by, **1981** 474
terrorist attacks on U.S., reaction to, **2001** 625
Thatcher commitment to, **1979** 380, 381, 386-387
theater nuclear force modernization (TNF), **1980** 91-92
U.S. buildup in and Soviet threat, **1980** 124, 130-131, 153-157
U.S. commitment to
after Vietnam, **1975** 353-356
Carter on, **1979** 462-463, 466
Democratic Party platform on, **1984** 633-634
Kissinger on, **1976** 907-908, 910-911
Reagan on, **1981** 823-827; **1984** 815
U.S. defense needs in, **1980** 124
U.S. involvement, **1993** 711-712
U.S. missile deployment in Europe, **1981** 823, 826-827; **1982** 225-226, 232-233, 305-310
U.S. troop pullout from France (1966), French compensation for, **1974** 982, 985
war on terrorism, reaction to, **2001** 630
North Carolina
death penalty executions, **2005** 178
mandatory death penalty law, **1976** 489-490, 503-507
race-based redistricting, **1993** 459-481
North Carolina State Bd. of Education v. Swann, **1990** 232
North Korea
See also Korean War
chemical weapons stockpiles, **1993** 72
economic and humanitarian aid, **2005** 609-610
famine and economic situation, **1999** 572; **2000** 360; **2001** 271-272; **2002** 731-732; **2003** 757
Grenada, secret treaties with, **1983** 849
human rights, UN resolution on, **2005** 608-609
human rights in, **1980** 190, 196; **1987** 198-199; **1988** 884
human trafficking, **2004** 125
humanitarian aid, **2001** 271-272
missile program, **2001** 268-270
missile threat to Europe, **1999** 820
missile threat to Japan (1998), **2004** 180
missile threat to U.S., **1998** 481-482, 489; **2000** 678; **2001** 739, 930; **2002** 1026; **2003** 818; **2004** 180
nonaggression pact with South Korea, **1972** 523-525
nuclear agreement, **1994** 602-609
nuclear weapons program
Agreed Framework (1994), **2002** 731, 735-736, 983
Bush statement on, **2003** 32; **2004** 24
Chinese response, **2002** 856; **2003** 1178
ElBaradei statement on plutonium processing, **2004** 872
IAEA monitoring of, **2002** 736
international oversight of, **2000** 204
Korean announcement of, **2002** 56, 733-734
Libya link, **2005** 605
materials suppliers, **2003** 1218
potential costs to U.S., **2005** 17
Silberman-Robb Commission on, **2005** 252
Six Party Talks, **2003** 1178; **2004** 871-872, 937; **2005** 604-611

North Korea *Continued*
violations of nonproliferation, **2004** 325
nuclear weapons proliferation, **1996** 211-212, 215-217
political situation, CIA report on, **2001** 267-278
religious persecution, **1997** 564
reunification of Korea, **2000** 359-364; **2002** 731
and Seoul Olympic Games, **1988** 854-855
Six-Party Talks, **2003** 1178; **2004** 871-872, 937; **2005** 604-611
South Korean overtures to, **1974** 956, 966; **1988** 853-859
South Korean relations, **1997** 895-896; **2001** 267-278; **2005** 606
state visit of Madeleine Albright, **1999** 571-572; **2000** 359, 679, 866-872; **2001** 268
terrorism supported by, **1985** 464, 466, 471-473, 476
terrorist attacks on U.S. condemned, **2001** 625
as threat to U.S., **1980** 128, 130-133
U.S. policy, **1999** 568-583; **2002** 634, 734-737
"axis of evil," Bush State of the Union address, **2002** 33-34, 40-41, 612, 614, 635, 714, 731, 732; **2003** 19, 875, 1025, 1219; **2004** 18, 867; **2005** 579
"dictatorship," State Department speech, **2003** 592-603
U.S.-PRC Shanghai communiqué on, **1972** 188-189
weapons exchange with Pakistan, **2002** 734
North Pole, discovery of, **1988** 831-833; **1989** 687-696
North Yemen, willingness to accept PLO, **1982** 744
Northeast States for Coordinated Air Use Management, **2004** 832
Northern Ireland. *See* Ireland, Northern
Northern Pipeline Construction Co. v. Marathon Pipe Line Co., **1982** 597-617
Norton, Gail A. (interior secretary)
confirmation, **2001** 97-98, 348; **2005** 45
national monument boundary proposals, **2001** 217
Norton Air Force Base (California), closing of, **1988** 952
Norway
Iraq troop withdrawal, **2004** 882
Sri Lanka cease-fire negotiations, **2002** 92-100
Norwegian Refugee Council, **2003** 1099
Norwood, Byron, American solider killed in Fallujah, **2005** 89-90
Norwood, Charlie (R-Ga.), patients' bill of rights, **1999** 562
Norwood, Janet L., **1988** 921
Norwood v. Harrison, **1973** 643
Notre Dame University, valedictory address on pursuit of honor, **1972** 419-422
Nott, John
Falklands War, **1983** 4, 10-14, 22
Soviet military buildup, **1981** 718
Nour, Ayman, Egyptian dissident jailed and released, **2005** 165-168
Novak, Robert, **1989** 440
Iraq-Niger uranium sales investigation, **2003** 11, 20; **2005** 249, 700-702
Novelli, Bill, smoking and health, **1997** 335
Novello, Antonia C., **1992** 267-271
NOW. *See* National Organization for Women
NPR. *See* National Performance Review; National Public Radio
NPS. *See* National Park Service
NPT. *See* Nuclear Nonproliferation Treaty
NRA. *See* National Rifle Association
NRC. *See* National Research Council; Nuclear Regulatory Commission
NRDC. *See* Natural Resources Defense Council
NSA. *See* National Security Act; National Security Agency
NSC. *See* National Security Council
NSF. *See* National Science Foundation
Ntakirutimana, Elizabeth and Gerard, Rwanda war crimes convictions, **2003** 1074
Ntaryamira, Cyprien, assassination of, **1994** 541; **1999** 863; **2000** 452
NTSB. *See* National Transportation Safety Board
Nuclear, chemical, and biological (NBC) weapons, proliferation of, **1996** 210-230
Nuclear defense
B-1 bomber, cancellation of, **1977** 529-533
first-use policy, Haig on, **1982** 305-315
no-first-use, Carter on, **1977** 738, 744-745
strategy, Reagan administration on, **1982** 395-407, 886-888, 896-901
Nuclear deterrence
effectiveness of, Kennan on, **1989** 209, 211
MX missile as component of, **1982** 903-918; **1983** 365-374
and no-first-use doctrine, **1975** 496, 504-505
SDI goals, **1984** 266-267, 270-271
strategic balance in U.S.-Soviet SALT agreements, **1972** 765-774
as U.S. defense policy, **1980** 143-146
Catholic bishops on, **1982** 396, 887, 893-895
Reagan administration on, **1982** 305-315, 397, 399-401, 403-407, 887, 897-901
and SALT II, **1978** 553-554, 580-581
Nuclear energy
See also Radiation
as alternative to oil, economic summit on, **1980** 503, 504, 509
breeder reactor development, Carter on commercial use for, **1977** 271-272, 274
capabilities and limitations of, Carter on, **1976** 707-708
Carter policy on, **1977** 271-276
contribution to energy supply, **1974** 910, 912-913, 916
development of
Carter on, **1977** 103, 106
economic summits on, **1977** 368-369, 374; **1978** 538
Ford on, **1975** 84, 92; **1976** 20
research on, **1977** 127-128
Schlesinger on, **1979** 659-660, 665-666
expanded use of, **1975** 103; **1980** 615-616
in former Soviet Union, **1996** 139-146, 228-229
future of in U.S., **1979** 861-863
Gorbachev on, **1992** 437
impact of Chernobyl accident, **1986** 383-386

peaceful uses of
Ford policy on controls, **1976** 823-838
U.S.-Soviet agreement to cooperate in, **1973** 588-589, 608
U.S.-Soviet treaty on underground testing for, **1976** 369-374
verification of by IAEA, **1975** 362-363, 365-367
safety standards for, Democratic Party platform on, **1976** 545, 576
setbacks for, National 80s Agenda on, **1981** 48
U.S.-PRC agreement on, **1984** 25
Nuclear Explosions for Peaceful Purposes, Treaty on Underground (PNE Treaty), signing, **1976** 369-374
Nuclear exports
for peaceful purposes, review of nonproliferation treaty, **1975** 361-370
responsibility of suppliers to world security, **1977** 741-742
U.S., controls on, **1976** 825-827, 829-832, 834-835; **1977** 271-276
U.S. proposed sale of reactors to Egypt and Israel, **1974** 449-451, 457-458; **1975** 466
U.S. sale of reactors to Iran, **1977** 899
U.S. sale of technology to PRC, **1984** 288-289, 294-295
Nuclear freeze
African Nuclear Weapon Free Zone Treaty, **1995** 236, 237
Gorbachev advocates, **1992** 436
Kennedy on, **1983** 823-824
on medium-range missile deployment, Soviet, **1982** 225-234
Moral Majority on, **1983** 818
movement
activities and protests of, **1982** 386, 396, 885-888, 904
and Nobel Peace Prize, **1985** 782-783, 787
Reagan administration opposition to, **1982** 226, 311, 886-888, 898-899
U.S. Catholic bishops on, **1982** 885-886, 895
Nuclear fuel
adequate supplies of, **1976** 51
cycle, evaluation of alternatives to, Carter on, **1977** 272-274, 741-742
Nuclear material, theft or diversion of, **1974** 848
Nuclear nonproliferation
Brazil's purchase of reprocessing plant, **1978** 270, 272, 274-276
commitment to
Carter on, **1977** 737, 740; **1978** 774; **1981** 66-67, 103
Gierek on, **1977** 909-910
control of weapons
Carter proposal, **1977** 737, 741-742; **1978** 17, 40, 44
Ford proposal, **1976** 823-824, 826-829, 832-834
Cooperative Threat Reduction Program, **2001** 18
Economic Summit (London) declarations, **1991** 453-456
ElBaradei's proposals, **2004** 326; **2005** 931-932
German agreement, **1990** 604
IAEA director on, **2004** 323-335
Iran-Europe agreement, **2004** 869-870
joint U.S.-Soviet statement, **1990** 346-350
policies and agreements, **1994** 366-368
Russian nuclear weapons programs, **2001** 17-32
safeguards
Carter policy on, **1977** 271-276
in transfer of technology, **1975** 361-370, 372-373
U.S. proposal on, **1974** 847-848
Shevardnadze statement, **1990** 641
statement of G-8, **1997** 356-358
treaty, extension of, **1995** 233-238, 554
United Nations conference on, **2000** 201-212
U.S. policy, **2003** 905-906
Nuclear Non-Proliferation Treaty (NPT, 1968)
Additional Protocol, **2003** 1026-1031; **2004** 171, 323, 324-325, 867-868
Iran ratification negotiations, **2004** 869
Admadinejad UN speech on "nuclear issue," **2005** 593, 600-603
background on, **2000** 201-202; **2004** 325-326
extension of, **1995** 233-238, 554; **1996** 228-229; **1997** 199
IAEA monitors compliance, **2004** 169
Iran nuclear weapons program, **2003** 1025-1036; **2004** 867-869
Libyan ratification, **2003** 1222
nonmember countries and, **2005** 462
North Korean withdrawal, **1994** 602; **2005** 604
review of, **1975** 361-373
UN Disarmament Committee session debates, **2004** 325-326
UN role with, **1995** 358
U.S. nuclear energy supplies sales to India, **2005** 462-467
U.S.-Soviet commitment to, **1985** 751, 753, 757
Nuclear power industry
attitudes and practices in, **1979** 830-833, 847-848, 853-854
expertise and training in, **1979** 824-825, 832-834, 845-846, 855, 862-863
monitoring equipment of, **1979** 855-857
safety responsibility of, **1979** 823, 832, 853-854, 857-858, 862-863
on Three Mile Island report, **1979** 825
waste from, environmental and safety problems in, **1989** 355-362
Nuclear power plants
construction of, **1975** 23-24, 29, 38
development and approval of, Nixon on, **1974** 105
emergency plans of, **1979** 824, 858-859
environmental and safety concerns about, **1989** 355-362
equipment orientation of, **1979** 823-826, 831-833
information access on accident, **1979** 827, 841-842, 859-861
Iraqi, Israeli raid on, **1981** 507
licensing of in energy crisis, **1973** 914, 917; **1977** 290-291
location of, **1979** 824, 839-840
safety of, **1976** 709; **1977** 283, 290
and design standardization, **1973** 467, 469, 475-477
Rickover on, **1982** 89, 102-103
safety of in former Soviet Union, **1992** 647-648

Nuclear power plants *Continued*
Seabrook nuclear plant, **1990** 195-198
Three Mile Island accident, **1979** 823-863
worker health in, **1979** 857-858
Nuclear Regulatory Commission (NRC)
attitudes of, **1979** 830, 842-845, 847-848
drug testing of employees, **1986** 841
establishment of, **1975** 92
and export controls, **1977** 272, 276
inspection and enforcement, **1979** 827, 842-843, 852-853, 862
licensing, **1979** 827, 842-843, 846-847, 852-853, 863
on radon exposure, **1988** 3
regulations of, **1979** 832, 842-844
reorganization of, **1979** 824-825, 830, 844-845, 848-849, 862; **1980** 28, 41, 43, 56
safety responsibility, **1979** 849-852, 861
Seabrook nuclear plant operations, **1990** 195-198
Y2K conversion problems, **2000** 8
Nuclear safety, **1997** 349
Nuclear technology
sales to China, **1997** 729
theft of, by China, **1999** 235-256, 304
Nuclear testing
ban on
Brezhnev on, **1976** 144, 151
Carter proposal, **1977** 737-738, 740-741
Comprehensive Test Ban Treaty, **1995** 553-557
former defense officials on, **1986** 781, 783, 790
treaty negotiations, **1995** 234-235
comprehensive ban on, **1995** 234-237, 553-557; **1998** 49; **1999** 600-610, 699, 819
discontinuance of, nonproliferation treaty on, **1975** 370-371
fallout, NCI report on, **1997** 591-601
by France, **1985** 631, 633
in India and Pakistan, **1999** 623-624
UN on, **1998** 326-332
monitoring of, U.S.-Soviet agreement on, **1987** 994, 997-998
reductions in, U.S.-Soviet discussion of, **1986** 875-876, 884
Soviet, Sakharov protest of, **1981** 748
Soviet moratorium on, **1986** 9, 11, 14-16, 385
treaty compliance verification, **1990** 338-339
underground
limitation of, U.S.-Soviet treaty on, **1974** 536-538, 555-558
on-site inspection of, **1972** 805; **1976** 369-370, 372
U.S.-Soviet treaty on, **1976** 369-374
U.S. policy, **2003** 905
verification of limits on, U.S.-Soviet discussion of, **1988** 357, 370
Nuclear war
biological consequences of, **1983** 857-882
defense strategy for
Reagan administration on, **1982** 395-407, 904-905
U.S. Catholic bishops on, **1982** 891-893
environmental consequences of, **1985** 541-554
horrors of, John Paul II on, **1981** 208, 210
increasing danger of, Carter on, **1981** 32, 34
limited, Reagan on outcome of, **1981** 824
medical risks of, **1985** 781, 783-784, 786
in presidential debates, **1984** 893
prevention of risk of, U.S.-Soviet agreement on, **1973** 589, 591-593, 595, 603
threat of, nonaligned nations on, **1983** 264, 267-268
as unwinnable, Reagan on, **1983** 791, 795
Nuclear waste management
cleanup priorities, GAO report on, **1995** 113-119
cleanup technologies, GAO report on, **1994** 339-348
Ford proposal on, **1976** 836-837
Nuclear weapons
See also Comprehensive Nuclear Test Ban Treaty (CNTBT); Nuclear nonproliferation; Strategic Arms Reduction Treaty (START II); Strategic Defense Initiative (SDI); Strategic weapons; Weapons of mass destruction (WMD)
arsenals available, **1985** 544-545
counterforce capability of U.S., Schlesinger on, **1975** 495-497, 502
dangers of
John Paul II on, **1979** 729, 740, 750-751
Rickover on, **1982** 89, 104
U.S. Catholic bishops on, **1982** 888-891
elimination of
Carter on, **1978** 16-17, 49
Gorbachev's proposal, **1986** 9-10, 12-14
U.S.-Soviet INF treaty, **1987** 945-989
environmental cleanup, GAO report on, **1994** 339-348
first-use option of U.S. and NATO, **1975** 495-505
fissile material production, **2004** 324
in former Soviet Union, **1996** 139-146
Gorbachev advocates freeze, **1992** 436
India, nuclear weapons program, **2005** 462
inspections of facilities under INF treaty, **1987** 946-947, 972-989
inventory of, U.S.-Soviet discussion of, **1977** 251, 255-256
Iran nuclear weapons program. *See under* Iran
Iraq nuclear weapons program, **2003** 876; **2004** 714-715, 726-727
buildup of, **1981** 511-513
hidden weapons, **1991** 192-193
Kahn nuclear weapons technology trafficking, **2005** 934
Libya dismantling, **2003** 1025, 1031, 1218-1233
Middle East nuclear-free zone, Israeli proposal for, **1981** 514-515, 748
missile threats, Rumsfeld Commission on, **1998** 481-499
modernizing to meet Soviet buildup, Carter on, **1978** 223-224, 230-231, 237-238
no-first-use debate, **1982** 305-315; **1984** 550-551
nonproliferation environment, **1998** 492-495
North Korea
nuclear agreement, **1994** 602-609; **1997** 41
Silberman-Robb Commission on, **2005** 252
Pakistan
nuclear weapons program, **2003** 1025
nuclear weapons testing, **1998** 326-332, 467, 541; **1999** 623-624; **2000** 203; **2005** 462

prohibition of on ocean floor, **1972** 167-171
proliferation of
OTA report, **1994** 363-373
worldwide, Defense Department report on, **1996** 210-230
reduction of
Bush support for, **1989** 80
in Europe, Andropov proposal, **1982** 983-987
Reagan START proposal, **1982** 385-393
U.S.-Soviet talks on, **1975** 361-362, 370-371; **1977** 243-268; **1986** 875-876, 880, 884
Republican Party platform on, **1992** 836-837
Russian missiles, **1997** 515
Russian nuclear weapons, Energy Department report on, **2001** 17-32
Soviet strength in, Defense Department on, **1981** 718-723, 725-730
strategic offensive, Vladivostok limitation on, **1974** 955-958, 967-968
Strategic Offensive Reductions Treaty, **2002** 280-282
terrorist threat preparedness, **2005** 894
UN conventions for nuclear terrorism prevention, **2005** 934-935
U.S. arsenal and strategy, Reagan on MX role in, **1982** 904-905
U.S. development of new weapons, **2003** 904-905
U.S. missile deployment in Europe, Reagan on, **1981** 823-830
U.S. policy, Nuclear Posture Review, **2002** 276-278
U.S.-Russian nuclear arms control treaty, **2002** 275-286; **2003** 907
U.S.-Soviet parity in, **1980** 124-129, 132, 142-148, 153-157
verification issue, **1999** 603-604
weapons smuggling, Kahn network, **2004** 169, 323, 327-329, 1009, 1013
world assumptions about never using, Kissinger on, **1974** 845-847
zero option reduction, Reagan on, **1983** 792, 796
Nuclear weapons testing. *See* Nuclear testing
Nuclear winter, biological consequences of, **1983** 857-882
Nujoma, Sam, **1976** 613; **1990** 199, 200-201, 204-206
Nunn, Louis B.
and HUD scandal, **1989** 334-335
ITT political contributions, **1972** 396-397
Nunn, Sam (D-Ga.)
ABM treaty interpretation, **1987** 289-317
Bush arms control proposal, **1989** 298
chemical weapons treaty, **1996** 741; **1997** 201
CIA manual, **1984** 904
Defense Department reorganization, **1985** 669
Gates confirmation hearings, **1991** 652
Iowa (USS) explosion investigation, **1990** 319-320
Iraq War resolution, **1991** 4, 5, 6-9
military base closings, **1995** 409
military homosexual ban, **1993** 153
naval explosions, **1989** 519
nuclear materials in former Soviet states, **1996** 141
Panama Canal treaties, **1978** 179
rejection of Tower nomination, **1989** 105-107
retirement from Congress, **1995** 558-559
Russian nuclear weapons, **2001** 18, 19; **2002** 438-440
SALT II, **1979** 417
SDI, **1988** 325
troop buildup in Middle East, **1990** 768-769
war powers debate, **1990** 674-675
women in combat, **1991** 492, 495, 510-511, 512
Nuon Chea, **1998** 972-975
Nursing homes
abuse and neglect, GAO report on, **2002** 117-132
care for Alzheimer's disease victims, **1987** 393, 403
Nursing Home Compare Web site, **2002** 118, 120
staff shortage, **2002** 120-122
Nussbaum, Bernard
on Foster suicide, **1993** 533
Whitewater investigations, **2000** 765
Nusseibeh, Sari, Middle East peace plan ("People's Voice"), **2003** 1203
Nutrition
See also Diet; Hunger; Malnutrition
breast cancer report, **1993** 911-912
calorie needs, **2005** 9-10
cancer risk and, **1982** 507-520
carbohydrate recommendations, **2005** 12
Chinese food report, **1993** 689-694
federal dietary guidelines, **2000** 240-261; **2001** 936; **2005** 3-13
food conference on, **1974** 944-946
food group recommendations, **2005** 11-12
food guide pyramid, **1992** 397, 400; **1996** 4-5; **2005** 3-5
global dietary guidelines, **2003** 481, 484-485
Healthy Lunch Pilot Program, **2004** 656
infant formula marketing, **1981** 447, 449-451, 917
school meals for children, **2004** 655-656, 662
surveillance system, national, **1985** 195-196, 204
trans fatty acids
consumption guidelines, **2005** 4, 12
labeling for, **2003** 482-483
TV's effect on, **1982** 366, 378-379
vegetarian diets and, **1996** 5, 8
Nyerere, Julius
Burundi peace negotiations, **2003** 923
death of, **1999** 867
and Rhodesian settlement plan, **1976** 721-722
Nyos, Lake, Cameroon, carbon dioxide gas eruption in, **1987** 61-77

O

Oak Ridge National Laboratory, Molten Salt Reactor Experiment, **1994** 340
Oakar, Rosemary (D-Ohio), BCCI banking scandal hearings, **1991** 634-635
Oakdale (Louisiana), riot of Cuban detainees, **1987** 929-932, 935-936
Oakland Cannabis Buyers' Cooperative; United States v., **2001** 325-330
Oakley, Phyllis E., refugee camps in Central Africa, **1996** 811-815
OAS. *See* Organization of American States
OASDI. *See* Old Age, Survivors, and Disability Insurance
OAU. *See* Organization of African Unity

Obaijayt, Hussein, terrorist killing of, **2000** 933
Obama, Barack (D-Ill.)
Democratic party convention speech, **2004** 483
Senatorial candidate, **2004** 483
Obando y Bravo, Miguel
church-government relations in Nicaragua, **1983** 241; **1986** 641
in Nicaragua-contra negotiations, **1987** 1008-1009
and Nicaraguan cease-fire, **1988** 242-243, 245
as political force, **1987** 641-642
Obasanjo, Olusegun
African economic development plan, **2002** 450, 451; **2005** 409
AIDS in Nigeria, **2001** 438
Carter meeting, **1978** 271, 287-290
Group-8 summit, **2005** 409
Liberian president Taylor exile to Nigeria, **2003** 770, 771
Nigerian internal conflicts, **2001** 505
Nigerian presidential inauguration speech, **1999** 272-282
study group on South Africa, **1986** 582
U.S. support for, **2000** 64
Zimbabwe elections, **2002** 133
Zimbabwe-Nigeria relations, **2003** 1114, 1115
Obeid, Abdul Karim, Israeli kidnapping of, **1989** 315-319
Obeid, Jean, Lebanon-Syria relations, **2004** 560
Oberdorfer, Don, **1992** 638
Obering, Henry A., defense missile system, **2004** 178
Oberstar, James L. (D-Minn.), presidential commission on aviation security and terrorism, **1990** 301-310
Obesity
See also Diet
adults in U.S., **2005** 3
body mass index (BMI), **2001** 936; **2004** 652
childhood obesity
causes of, **2004** 653-654
prevention, Institute of Medicine report, **2004** 652-663
in U.S., **2005** 3
deceptive weight loss advertising, **2002** 624-632
impact on health, **2005** 5-6
and incidence of diabetes, **2000** 242-243
and overeating, **2001** 935-954
surgeon general's report on, **2001** 935-954; **2003** 480-491
weight-related deaths, **2005** 3, 5-6
Obey, David R. (D-Wis.)
bipartisan accord on contras, **1989** 164
Iran-contra documents in North trial, **1989** 394
Obote, Milton, ousted from Uganda, **2003** 470
Obrenovic, Dragan, Serb war criminal, **2003** 464
O'Brien, Charles P., on marijuana's health effects, **1982** 204, 206-207
O'Brien, Jon, **1992** 250
O'Brien, Lawrence F.
Kleindienst letter to on ITT settlement, **1972** 396, 401
Watergate committee exoneration of, **1974** 600
O'Brien, Thomas J. (bishop)
hit-and-run accident, **2003** 527
resignation, **2003** 527
sexual abuse by priests, **2003** 526-527; **2004** 86
O'Brien, United States v., **1990** 360
Obscenity
See also Pornography
asset forfeiture and, **1993** 432, 438-446
Carnal Knowledge and, **1974** 515-519
community standards for, **1974** 515-522
definitions of, **1973** 611-628; **1982** 675
legal tests for, **1987** 479-490
"trash lyrics" legislation, **1990** 509-511
Obuchi, Keizo, on Japanese economic crisis, **1998** 532-542
Ocampo, Luis Moreno
Darfur region human rights crimes investigations, **2005** 517
International Criminal Court first prosecutor, **2003** 100-101
Occidental Petroleum Inc., hazardous waste disposal by, **1979** 782-783, 791, 793
Occupational safety and health
EEOC employer guidelines on mental disabilities, **1997** 127-141
ergonomics standards, **1999** 769-778
at nuclear plants, **1989** 356, 361
regulations on, **1978** 634-635, 636-637
Occupational Safety and Health Act (1970)
and employee rights, **1980** 199-207
worker health standards in, **1981** 491
Occupational Safety and Health Administration (OSHA)
and dangerous workplaces, **1980** 199-207
ergonomics standards, **1999** 769-778
smoking ban, **1994** 205-206
warrants for safety inspections, **1978** 339-353
Occupied territories. *See* Israel, occupied territories
Ocean commerce, U.S. sanctions against Soviets for Polish martial law, **1981** 884
Ocean dumping
international agreement on, **1972** 907-919
in northeast Atlantic, treaty on, **1972** 173-177
of waste material, international agreement on, **1972** 907-919; **1973** 215, 217
Ocean Policy Trust Fund, **2004** 604, 605, 623-624, 625
Ocean pollution
See also Ocean dumping
Global 2000 proposals for countering, **1981** 24-25
marine debris, **2004** 619
oil-spill agreements, **1972** 148, 152
study of, U.S.-Soviet agreement on, **1972** 806, 810
vessel pollution, **2004** 618
Ocean resources
Law of the Sea Treaty governing use of, **1982** 345-361
protection policy, presidential commission report on, **2004** 602-625
Oceanic Navigation Co. v. Stranahan, **1992** 468
Oceanography, U.S. Soviet agreement on cooperation in, **1973** 588, 609
O'Connor, Erin, anthrax mailings victim, **2001** 674
O'Connor, John, **1986** 910
O'Connor, Sandra Day
abortion, **1993** 339; **2005** 554

anti-abortion demonstrations, **2000** 433
clinic protests, **1994** 312-320
in confirmation hearings, **1981** 578, 582-585
family-planning clinic advice, **1991** 259, 266-272, 272-273
partial-birth, **2000** 432, 441
right to, **1986** 559-560, 562, 579-580
spousal notification, **2005** 563
trimester test in state regulations, **1983** 544-545, 557-564, 572; **1989** 366-367, 376-378
affirmative action, **1986** 676; **1987** 332-333, 346; **2003** 358-359, 362, 364-376; **2005** 554
federal government plans, **1995** 307-308, 309-319
and seniority, **1984** 366
age discrimination
against state and local employees, **1983** 232, 239
mandatory retirement, **1985** 397
alien children, education for, **1982** 490, 501
antitrust immunity of cities, **1982** 35, 43
appointment of, **1981** 575-590; **1983** 756
asset forfeiture
drug trafficking, **1993** 432-438
pornography seized, **1993** 432, 438-440
attorney-client privilege, **1998** 395, 401-404
auto search and seizure, **1982** 425
on bankruptcy and labor contracts, **1984** 182
bankruptcy law, **1982** 597
campaign finance reform, **2003** 1159, 1161-1169
child custody rights, **1982** 260, 271
child pornography, **1982** 676; **1990** 239-245
church and state separation
church objection to liquor license, **1982** 956
public display of Nativity scene, **1984** 218, 228-231
coastal property rights, **1992** 616-620
coerced confessions, **1991** 175, 182-184
compensation law, **1991** 813-814, 815-823
congressional term limits, **1995** 260, 271-275
creation science in schools, **1987** 566, 572
damages for tobacco-related ills, **1992** 564-573
deaf parochial student, **1993** 400, 403-406
death penalty
fairness of, **2001** 389, 391-394; **2004** 796
and International Court of Justice jurisdiction, **2005** 182
for juvenile offenders, **2002** 358; **2004** 797; **2005** 180, 192, 555
for the mentally retarded, **2002** 356; **2005** 555
mitigating factors, **1982** 51, 53, 59-60
racial discrimination in, **1987** 463
defense attorneys, ineffectiveness of, **2002** 353
detentions in terrorism cases, **2004** 377, 378, 381-388
disabilities in the workplace, **2002** 4, 7-14
disability, definition of, **1999** 318, 320, 321-325, 325-332
discrimination
by private clubs, **1988** 403
state and local government liability for, **1989** 323
disruptive handicapped students case, **1988** 48, 56
drug testing of students, **1995** 339, 340, 346-349
eminent domain, **2005** 362, 363, 371-375
endangered species on private lands, **1995** 359-368
entrapment in child pornography case, **1992** 322-327
exclusionary rule, **1984** 508
faculty tenure review disclosure, **1990** 23-34
federal and state powers, **1985** 169, 182
first woman on the Supreme Court, **2005** 555
flag burning, **1989** 343, 351; **1990** 358, 363-365
free speech
ballot initiatives, **1999** 6
decency in the arts, **1998** 405, 407, 408-415
and the Internet, **1997** 445-446, 454-458
Internet pornography filters in public libraries, **2003** 388
freedom of residential signs, **1992** 290-297
gay rights discrimination, **1996** 286
gay rights to march, **1995** 327-335
grandparents' rights, **2000** 287, 289, 290-295
gun-free school zone, **1995** 184, 192-194
Haitian refugee interdiction, **1992** 453, 459-468; **1993** 413-421
hate crimes, **1992** 544-551; **1993** 385-389
HIV as a disability, **1998** 380, 389-392
home video taping, **1984** 53
impeachment, Senate's authority to remove judge, **1993** 81-87
infants, treatment of severely handicapped, **1986** 543, 554, 558
intra-enterprise conspiracy doctrine, **1984** 414
job discrimination
fetal protection, **1991** 144
involving African Americans, **1993** 423-429
judicial restraint, **1981** 576, 581-582, 586-590
jury selection, gender discrimination, **1994** 226-227, 231-233
labor unions, freedom of members to resign, **1985** 415
legacy of Supreme Court rulings, **2005** 553-555
legislative intent, **1993** 250-253
legislative veto, **1983** 619
libel
award, appellate review of, **1984** 300-301, 310
from misquotation, **1991** 329-330
of private and public persons, **1986** 355-364
line-item veto, **1998** 421, 431-433, 433-437
minority set-aside programs, **1989** 324; **1990** 421, 429-434
minority status on court, **1992** 35
Miranda warnings, **1984** 388, 393-395; **1985** 223-224, 226-236; **2000** 389
rule upheld, **1990** 785-790
murder case sentencing, **1991** 389-390
NAACP boycott, **1982** 656
Noriega phone calls dispute, **1990** 721-725
obscenity, tests for, **1987** 479
parental consent for abortions, **1990** 387-407
parental leave and employment discrimination, **1987** 17
parochial school aid, **1997** 362-363, 364-375
physician-assisted suicide, **1997** 461, 472-473, 478-479
police use of deadly force, **1985** 304-305, 312-315
political asylum, **1987** 253

Continued
political gerrymandering, **1986** 617-618, 629-632
political primaries, open, **1986** 1065, 1072
presidential elections recount, **2000** 1002-1003, 1005-1019
presidential immunity, **1982** 539
preventive detention, **1987** 491
prison inmates, beaten by guards, **1992** 175-182
prisoner appeals, **1991** 206
from death row, **1993** 141-148
property takings, uncompensated, **1987** 541
public aid to parochial schools, **1985** 433, 435, 448-449, 455-461
public land and developers, **1994** 299, 300-306
race-based redistricting, **1993** 459-474; **1995** 369, 371, 373-380; **1996** 369-370, 371-379, 379-380
religious clubs in public schools, **2001** 422
religious freedom, **1997** 408, 410, 417-420
religious publications, **1995** 385-395
retirement/resignation from Supreme Court, **2005** 41, 79, 376, 379, 555, 560, 814
right to die, **1990** 373-382
school book banning, **1982** 568, 580
school desegregation, **1991** 24
restrictions on busing, **1982** 620, 633
school prayer, **1985** 380-381, 387-392; **1992** 553-562; **2000** 367
school vouchers, **2002** 408
searches, prisoners' rights in, **1984** 480
sentences, excessive prison, **1983** 660, 670-674
sentencing guidelines, **2004** 358, 360, 365, 366, 368-374
sex bias in education, **1984** 202, 210
sex bias in pension plans, **1983** 691-702, 704-705
sex discrimination by Jaycees, **1984** 468, 475-478
sex offenders, right to confine, **1997** 383
sexual harassment, **1998** 442; **1999** 215-217, 218-227
at school, **1992** 188-197
in workplace, **1993** 939-944
sodomy and privacy right, **1986** 601
sodomy laws, **2003** 403
states' rights, **1999** 333
student drug testing, **2002** 426-427, 433-436
student searches, **1985** 14
students' free speech, **1986** 731
Supreme Court appointment, **1993** 391
swing vote in *Webster,* **1990** 217
tax increase for school desegregation, **1990** 227, 228-229, 232-238
Ten Commandments displays, **2005** 378-379, 555
tobacco products regulation, **2000** 556
tuition tax credit, **1983** 676, 684-688
unitary taxation, **1983** 645, 657-658
unreasonable searches, **2001** 408, 409, 410, 416-419
use of school facilities by religious groups, **1993** 363-369
utilities regulation, **1982** 448, 460
water rights, **1982** 689, 699
women's right to choose, **1992** 589-609
O'Connor v. Donaldson, **1975** 469-480
"October Surprise" theory, **1991** 618; **1994** 3-16
Al Odah, et al. v. United States, **2003** 114-117
Odeen, Philip A., **1997** 812
Odeh, Mohammad Sadeek, embassy bombings, **1998** 558; **2001** 803
Oder-Neisse Line, recognition of, **1989** 627
Odierno, Raymond
on insurgents in Iraq, **2003** 1194
manhunt for Saddam Hussein, **2003** 1192
Odinga, Oginga, Kenyan opposition leader, **2002** 1045
Odinga, Raila, Kenyan opposition leader, **2002** 1045, 1047
Odom, William, **1989** 440
Odyssey mission to Mars, **2000** 379; **2002** 214-215; **2003** 302, 303, 304; **2004** 8
OECD. *See* Organization for Economic Cooperation and Development
OEO. *See* Office of Economic Opportunity
Office of AIDS Research (OAR), **1996** 156-166
Office of Civil Rights, Bill Lee nomination, **1997** 765
Office of Economic Opportunity (OEO)
antipoverty programs of, **1973** 304, 312; **1974** 96
attempts to dismantle, **1973** 453-464
phaseout of, **1974** 767, 773
Office of Federal Housing Enterprise Oversight, **2004** 420
Office of Government Ethics (OGE), report on Sununu, **1992** 293-299
Office of Management and Budget (OMB)
budget warnings, **1990** 50
dispute with FDA over food health claims issue, **1990** 176
federal budget deficit projections, **2003** 680
federal government furlough, **1981** 832
and Forest Service resources, **1973** 22, 26
Lance resignation, **1977** 625-685
peer reviews for regulatory science, **2004** 844-845
role in budget information controls, **1974** 589-590
role in Gramm-Rudman-Hollings, **1986** 705-706
year 2000 computer conversion cost estimates, **1997** 535-540
Office of Personnel Management (OPM)
creation of, **1978** 138, 141-143, 145-146
drug testing implementation, **1986** 839, 841-842, 846
Office of Professional Responsibility (OPR), Sessions FBI director investigation, **1993** 609-611
Office of Science and Technology, reorganization of, **1973** 782-783
Office of Technology Assessment (OTA) studies
Alzheimer's disease, care and services, **1987** 391-406
biotechnology and agriculture, **1986** 287-306
hazardous chemicals at Love Canal, **1983** 479-487
human tissues and cells, ownership of, **1987** 351-372
nuclear proliferation, **1994** 363-373
prescription drug prices, **1993** 197-209
smoking costs, **1985** 615-622
space-based missile defense, **1984** 257-258, 260, 267-272
tuberculosis, **1993** 851-869
U.S.-Russian space cooperation, **1995** 222-227
O'Flaherty, Edward, on Drinan's political career, **1980** 411, 415-416

Ogata, Sadako
Africa, UN economic assistance, **1999** 428-438
Congo, economic conditions, **1999** 646
UN refugee resettlement, **1991** 671-678
West Timor, attack on UN relief workers, **2000** 702
Oh, Angela E., race relations panel, **1997** 317, 322; **1998** 668
O'Hara, Jim, alcohol advertising and youth, **2002** 178
O'Hara, Joseph, **1984** 21
Ohio
death penalty law, **1978** 495-514
intelligent design case, **2005** 1013
public aid to parochial schools, **1977** 431-445
school desegregation orders, **1979** 535-552
Ohio v. Akron Center for Reproductive Health, **1990** 387, 395, 398-407
Ohira, Masayoshi, **1980** 504
Ohlone-Costanoan tribe, return of skeletal remains to, **1989** 540-541
Oil and gas industry
See also Oil industry
Chinese ownership of foreign companies, **2005** 615-616
company profits, **2005** 780-782
Hurricane Katrina disaster impact on, **2005** 546
Iraq oil industry, **2005** 720-721
Russian dismantling of private oil company Yukos, **2004** 569; **2005** 301, 302-303
Saudi Arabia oil industry, terrorist attacks on, **2004** 518
U.S. oil refineries, air pollution requirements, **2004** 667-668
Oil and gas prices
See also Oil taxes
ceilings on, in Nixon's stabilization program, **1973** 704
decontrol of, **1977** 278; **1980** 168-169
Democratic Party platform on, **1976** 545, 574
domestic summit on, **1974** 863
in Ford budget, **1975** 86
Ford CEA on, **1975** 103-104, 111; **1977** 71-72, 85-86
in Ford economic plan, **1975** 23; **1977** 52
Republican Party platform on, **1976** 645-646; **1988** 616, 665-666
under Carter administration, **1981** 50, 58, 64-65, 109
energy company executives on, **2005** 777-799
energy prices rising, **2004** 186-194
fluctuations in prices, **2004** 187-188, 190-194; **2005** 139
gasoline prices, **2005** 137, 139
federal control of new production and, **1977** 279, 289-290
Iraq gas price subsidies, **2005** 721
in U.S., **2005** 777
oil prices
Saudi Arabia price increases, **2004** 518
stabilizing, **2005** 414
world oil prices, **2005** 777
trade deficit and, **2004** 237
Oil and gas reserves
See also Strategic energy reserves
Arctic National Wildlife Refuge, **2001** 331, 335-336; **2003** 182, 1017; **2004** 670; **2005** 79
Iraqi oil reserves, **2005** 721
leasing expansion, in Ford energy program, **1975** 17, 23-24
leasing policies, Democratic Party platform on, **1976** 545, 575-576
Libyan reserves, **2004** 173
offshore oil and gas leases, **2004** 604
offshore resources, **2004** 622
worldwide supply and demand, **2004** 186-187
Oil consumers. *See* Consumer nations
Oil depletion allowance
elimination of, in McGovern's economic program, **1972** 737, 739
retention of, Nixon on, **1972** 385, 390
Oil embargo
Arab
against supporters of Israel, **1973** 932, 936
against U.S., Nixon's energy emergency plans, **1973** 913-921
against U.S. and Netherlands, **1975** 3-4
condition for ending, **1974** 187
as economic declaration of war, Carter on, **1976** 734, 742-744
extension of to Rhodesia, Portugal, and South Africa, **1974** 256
impact on developing countries' economies, **1975** 588
impact on U.S. economy, **1974** 73-76, 114, 119-121
impact on world economy, **1974** 114, 119-122
lifting of against U.S., **1974** 46, 124, 221-224
as model for raw materials producers, **1974** 255, 258
oil consumers, cooperation among, **1974** 123-124
use of military force against, **1975** 3-4, 8-9
U.S., on Iranian imports, **1979** 869, 872-873, 875
Oil exploration
in developing countries, **1980** 211
development of new domestic, Carter on, **1978** 39; **1979** 258
incentives for, Nixon on, **1973** 466, 472-473, 477
incentives in Carter energy plan, **1977** 279, 289-291
offshore
federal control of, **1975** 167-175
Nixon on stimulating, **1973** 465, 469-472
Oil for Food Program, UN, corruption scandals, **2004** 717, 887, 891-893; **2005** 228, 233-235
Oil imports
cost to U.S. of OPEC price increase, **1978** 789-790
decline in, **1979** 101-103
Carter on, **1981** 57-58, 64-66, 113
dependence on
and Carter budget, **1979** 14
Carter CEA on, **1978** 70, 79, 93
Carter on, **1976** 708; **1978** 8, 11, 20; **1979** 560-561, 567, 570
and Carter's energy program, **1977** 278, 280, 283-285, 292
Democratic Party platform on, **1980** 713, 717, 748-749, 763

Oil imports *Continued*
by developed and developing countries, **1977** 368, 370-372, 374
effect on U.S.-Libya relations, **1981** 463
Ford on, **1976** 20, 51; **1977** 52
Mansfield on, **1974** 867-869
and Middle East stability, **1981** 85-86, 95, 99-100, 107, 113, 116
Nixon energy program, **1973** 391; **1974** 83-84
Republican Party platform on, **1976** 645
Schlesinger on, **1979** 659-666
fees on
Carter anti-inflation measure, **1980** 243, 245, 251-252, 255
increase in, in Ford energy program, **1975** 17, 22-23, 29, 87, 103, 110
Iraqi oil export ban, **1991** 167
from Mexico, **1979** 169-172, 175, 179-180
quotas on
in Carter program, **1979** 560, 567
ending, **1973** 465, 477-479
reducing
Carter plan for, **1977** 690; **1979** 319-333
Carter pledge at IMF-World Bank meeting, **1978** 660-662
Ford plan for, **1977** 66, 71-72, 86
by industrialized countries, **1978** 533-535, 537; **1979** 253
Oil industry
See also Oil and gas industry
air pollution from, and lung cancer, **1972** 777
antitrust probe of Aramco and oil prices, **1983** 921-924
corporate mergers, **1998** 338-339
development incentives for, in Carter energy plan, **1977** 279, 289-291
OPEC on profits of, **1979** 255-256
shock after Iraq's invasion of Kuwait, **1992** 98-99, 102-103, 111, 113
taxed for hazardous waste cleanup, **1982** 965-970
Oil pollution. *See* Oil spills
Oil prices
See also Oil and gas prices
and arms purchases by oil producers, **1978** 107
assessment and projection (1975-1985) by FEA, **1974** 909-911
decline of
economic summit on, **1986** 437, 440, 443
impact on Nigeria, **1987** 441, 448
by OPEC, **1981** 799-801
Reagan CEA on, **1987** 117-119, 125, 127-129, 136
decontrol of, **1979** 319-321, 324-326
and energy conservation in U.S., **1974** 81
increases in
and alternative energy sources, **1980** 503-507, 509-510, 513
Carter CEA on, **1980** 159-163, 168, 170-173, 177-179, 182
Carter-Reagan debate on, **1980** 925-927, 939-940
and developing countries' debt, **1982** 971-972, 975
domestic, Ford CEA on, **1976** 51, 56
impact on developing countries, **1980** 884-886, 891; **1981** 179, 181
impact on U.S. economy, **1974** 70-76; **1978** 68; **1980** 245, 251-252, 255-256; **1981** 119
Ford on, **1975** 16, 21
Joint Economic Committee on, **1980** 210-212, 214, 220, 230
impact on world economy, **1974** 113-115, 118, 121-122; **1975** 187-196; **1976** 913; **1978** 68; **1981** 800
Nixon programs to counteract, **1974** 70-71, 76-84
OPEC's two-tiered, **1976** 937-942
and raw materials cartels among developing countries, **1975** 325-327
and strength of dollar, **1981** 592, 596
under Nixon economic controls program, **1974** 81
as threat to oil producers' markets, **1974** 849-850
Oil producers. *See* Producer nations
Oil shale, development of, **1973** 473; **1974** 910, 912
Oil spills
bacterium used in cleanup of, **1980** 493-495
Exxon Valdez
congressional hearings on, **1989** 225-237
report, **1990** 513-530; **1991** 641-648
national fund for cleanup and damage compensation, **1989** 227
Oil supply
allocation system, Nixon CEA on, **1974** 81-82
EC move toward cooperation with Arab states, **1974** 530
emergency sharing of, U.S.-Japan discussions of, **1973** 718, 720-721
and Iranian revolution, **1978** 701, 704, 712, 714; **1979** 3-4
and Iran-Iraq War, **1984** 747, 749-751, 754-755
Mexican exports to U.S., **1979** 169-172, 175, 179-180
reliable, international cooperation on, **1974** 71, 82-83, 113-115, 118-120
shocks to U.S. economy
Carter CEA on, **1981** 121-123
Joint Economic Committee on, **1981** 307-308, 319
U.S., and Soviet threat, **1980** 124, 127, 138
world, economic summit on, **1984** 357, 361, 364
world consumption of, **1980** 417-418, 420-421, 423-424, 426
decrease in, **1981** 65, 800
and world food production, **1980** 668-670, 679, 683-684, 688
Oil taxes
equalization tax on domestic, in Carter energy plan, **1977** 278-279, 287, 289-291
excise tax on domestic, in Ford program, **1975** 16, 18, 23-25, 29, 36-37, 87, 103-104
windfall profits tax on, **1979** 319-329, 332-333; **1983** 517-523
Carter support for, **1979** 568, 570-571, 577
Ford CEA on, **1975** 103, 111
in Nixon budget, **1974** 96, 101, 104
Ojdanic, Dragoljub, war criminal, **1999** 803

O'Keefe, Sean
  Columbia space shuttle disaster, **2003** 631-634
  Hubble space telescope mission controversy, **2004** 11-13
  NASA chief resignation, **2004** 12
  Navy's sexual harassment problems, **1992** 1004-1005
  space shuttle program, **2005** 498-499
  Spirit rover mission, **2004** 8
  Tailhook incident, **1992** 880
O'Keefe, Vincent, **1983** 94
O'Keefe, William K., **1997** 862
Okinawa, U.S. return of to Japan and removal of nuclear weapons, **1972** 41-42
Oklahoma
  bank failures in, **1988** 914
  welfare reform, **1999** 258
Oklahoma City bombing incident
  antiterrorism bill and, **1996** 231-232
  as evidence of terrorist threat, **1999** 502
  FBI crime laboratory reports, **1997** 221, 223
  gun control laws and, **1995** 183, 465
  McVeigh and Nichols trial and sentencing, **1997** 623-627; **1999** 480; **2001** 387, 390, 433-437
  militia group involvement, **1996** 178
  prayer service for victims, **1995** 176-182
Okun, Herbert S., limits on Soviet diplomatic personnel, **1986** 268, 270-272
Olalia, Rolando, **1986** 1038
Olasky, Marvin, faith-based initiatives, **2001** 135
Old Age, Survivors, and Disability Insurance (OASDI)
  See also Social Security
  addition to trust funds, **1977** 377-380
  benefits for widowers, **1975** 177-185; **1977** 169-172
  financial condition of system, **1975** 115-134
Older persons. *See* Senior citizens
O'Leary, Dennis O.
  hospital care oversight, **1999** 414
  medical mistakes, **2001** 193
  on Reagan's condition after shooting, **1981** 355-358
O'Leary, Hazel R.
  campaign finance practices, **1997** 824, 825, 828, 829
  human radiation experiments, **1993** 987-995; **1994** 54-61; **1995** 633-634
Oliart, Albert, **1982** 420
Olin Corp., EPA regulation of chemical discharge from, **1977** 131-141
Oliner, Stephen D., productivity paradox, **2000** 300
Oliver, Rene, **1983** 678
Olmert, Ehud
  Israeli acting prime minister, **2005** 529
  Israeli disengagement policy, **2004** 302
  Sharon cabinet appointment, **2005** 534
  withdrawal from Gaza Strip, **2003** 1206
Olmstead v. L.C., **1999** 319, 320, 325-332
Olshin, Lewis, **1981** 200-201
Olson, Pamela F., IRS disputes with taxpayers, **1997** 661
Olson, Theodore "Ted"
  affirmative action, **2002** 974
  campaign finance reform law, **2003** 1159
  Guantanamo Bay detainees, **2003** 110
  and independent counsel law, **1988** 465-478
  right to bear arms, **2002** 960
  secret domestic detentions, **2002** 835
Olympic Games
  Los Angeles (1984), Soviet boycott of, **1984** 260
  Moscow (1980)
    Islamic countries' boycott of, **1980** 4, 7
    U.S. boycott of, **1980** 28, 33, 713, 758, 777, 791
  Munich (1972), murder of Israeli athletes, **1972** 751-755
  Seoul (1988), **1988** 854-855
    and unrest in Korea, **1987** 584-585, 590, 593
  steroid use policy, **2005** 212-213
  summer games (London, 2012), **2005** 395
Olympics Committee. *See* International Olympics Committee (IOC)
O'Malley, Sean P., sexual abuse by priests settlement, **2003** 525-526
Omar, Mullah Mohammad, Taliban leader, **2001** 686, 691; **2002** 1015; **2003** 1054
Omar, Yassin Hassan, London terrorist bombing suspect, **2005** 397
OMB. *See* Office of Management and Budget
Omestad, Thomas, **1989** 636
Omnibus Budget Reconciliation Act (1990), **1992** 106
Omnibus Budget Reconciliation Act (1993)
  deficit reduction plan, **1996** 55-56
  earned income tax credit expansion, **1995** 78
  provisions of, **1993** 181-183
Omnibus Crime Control and Safe Streets Act (1968)
  covert entry by law enforcement, **1979** 269-271, 273-276, 279-284
  electronic surveillance by law enforcement, **1972** 485, 486; **1974** 391-405
  wiretap, phone company assistance ordered, **1977** 884, 886-896
Omnibus Trade and Competitiveness Act (1988), **1988** 339-344, 345
Oncale v. Sundowner Offshore Services, Inc., **1998** 441-442
One 1958 Plymouth Sedan v. Pennsylvania, **1993** 436
One America, President's Council for, **1998** 667, 673; **2000** 35
One Assortment of 89 Firearms, United States v., **1993** 436
One Lot Emerald Cut Stones v. United States, **1993** 436
Oneida tribe, return of skeletal remains to, **1989** 541
O'Neill, John, death of, **2001** 618-619
O'Neill, Paul H.
  Brazilian loan, **2002** 777
  New American Schools Development Corporation, **1991** 220-221
  resignation, **2002** 880
  tax cut plan, **2001** 54
  visit to Argentina, **2002** 84-85
O'Neill, Robert M., report on voter participation, **1990** 295-299
O'Neill, Thomas P. "Tip," Jr. (D-Mass.)
  acceptance of final impeachment report, **1974** 713
  budget cuts in social programs, **1983** 765-772
  Carter budget, **1979** 11

O'Neill, Thomas P. "Tip," Jr. (D-Mass.) *Continued*
Carter State of the Union, **1978** 9
congressional page system, **1982** 730
contra aid prohibition, **1983** 441-442
House censures of members, **1980** 485; **1983** 726, 728
as House Speaker, **1994** 37
IMF, U.S. funds for, **1983** 803
Korean influence-buying inquiry, **1977** 770
Nixon impeachment probability, **1974** 674
Nixon inaugural, **1973** 81
Northern Ireland
British-Irish accord, **1985** 726
economic aid to, **1986** 753
IRA prison hunger strike, **1981** 402, 404
Reagan budget, **1982** 145
Reagan State of the Union, **1983** 79-80; **1985** 105
Social Security reform, **1983** 59-60
as speaker, **1986** 39-40, 42
transfer of presidential power, **1985** 493
Onizuka, Ellison S., *Challenger* accident, **1986** 515, 520; **1988** 795
Ono, Masatoshi, Firestone tire recall, **2000** 692, 696-697
Onu, Peter, **1984** 974
OPEC. *See* Organization of Petroleum Exporting Countries
Opel, John R., **1988** 11
Open Society Institute, **1997** 329
Operation Candor
Nixon's defense of ITT antitrust settlement, **1974** 3-5, 16-21
Nixon's defense of milk price supports, **1974** 3-4, 6-15
Operation Desert Shield, **1990** 664-665
Operation Desert Storm
American deployment and coalition, **1991** 15
Patriot missile performance report, **1992** 865-874
"smart" weapons effectiveness, GAO report, **1997** 493-500
"smart" weapons performance report, **1996** 403-413
women in combat, **1993** 333
Operation Leprechaun, **1975** 830
Operation Rescue, **1994** 311, 313
Schiavo end-of-life care case, **2005** 158
OPIC. *See* Overseas Private Investment Corporation
Opinion polls. *See* Public opinion
Opium growing, economics of, **1972** 645-648
OPM. *See* Office of Personnel Management
Opp, Jeffrey, **1982** 729-730
Opportunity mission to Mars, **2003** 303; **2004** 3; **2005** 501-502
Oregon
Health Care Initiative, **2002** 670-671
health plan, **1992** 741-745
physician-assisted suicide legislation, **1994** 501-512; **1997** 461-463; **1999** 441-442; **2001** 290-293
Oregon v. Elstad, **1985** 223-253, 481, 486
Oregon v. Guzek, **2005** 182
Oregon v. Mitchell, **1997** 413-414, 415
Oregon Death with Dignity Act, **1994** 501-512
O'Reilly, David, oil company profits, congressional testimony on, **2005** 789-791
Organization for a Better Austin v. Keefe, **1990** 725
Organization for Economic Cooperation and Development (OECD), **1984** 359-361
business operations in conflict zones guidelines, **2002** 551
China economic growth, **2002** 692; **2005** 617
combating bribery of public officials, **1997** 800-807
curbing inflation, **1976** 426
developing countries' debt, **1982** 971-978
economic growth, U.S.-OECD comparison, **2005** 148-149
European economic growth projections, **2001** 667
hazardous waste shipments, **1989** 153-154
Kosovo conflict, **1998** 830-831
OPEC price increases, **1979** 254
survey of U.S. economy, **1973** 683-695
technological disasters, **1984** 1025
trade barriers, **1976** 430
world economic recovery, **2002** 689
Organization for Security and Cooperation in Europe (OSCE)
Georgian acting president Burdzhanadze speech, **2003** 1046-1048
Georgian elections, **2003** 1041
human trafficking prevention, **2004** 132-133
Kosovo human rights violations, **1999** 802-806, 814-816
Ukraine elections observer, **2004** 1003
Organization for the Prevention of Chemical Weapons, **2004** 169
Organization of African Unity (OAU)
See also African Union
on apartheid vote, **1992** 285
assessment of, **2001** 505-506
Congo, Lusaka cease-fire agreement, **1999** 650
coup in Liberia, **1980** 277
dissolution of, **2001** 504, 506
on drought, **1984** 974
Eritrea-Ethiopia border dispute, **1999** 431
Eritrea-Ethiopia war, peace negotiations, **2000** 754
on human rights charter, **1980** 193
Inter-Congolese dialogue, **2000** 979
Moynihan's attack on, **1975** 646, 649
replaced by African Union, **2003** 451
Rwandan genocide report, **2000** 449-474
summit (Algiers), **1999** 438
Zimbabwe independence, **1980** 319
Organization of American States (OAS)
antidrug efforts, **1992** 208
drug trafficking, **1992** 125
Haiti political situation, **2001** 395-399; **2004** 95
Haitian refugee interdiction, **1992** 454, 455, 458
human rights standards, **1980** 191, 193; **1981** 182-183
Malvinas (Falklands), sovereignty of, **1982** 287
Nicaraguan change of government, **1979** 581-584, 589
Panama Canal treaties, **1977** 591
Peru election monitoring, **2000** 924-925
Reagan's Caribbean proposal, **1982** 179-190
role in Central American peace, **1989** 163, 168-169
strengthening of, **1979** 717

U.S. invasion of Grenada, **1983** 850
U.S. invasion of Panama, **1989** 703
Venezuela political situation, **2002** 201, 204-205, 207-208; **2003** 279-287
Venezuela recall vote, **2004** 548-554
Organization of Arab Petroleum Exporting Countries (OAPEC), production cut, **1973** 932, 936
Organization of Eastern Caribbean States (OECS), request for U.S. aid in Grenada, **1983** 847-848, 851, 853
Organization of Petroleum Exporting Countries (OPEC)
accumulation of unused capital, effect on world economy, **1975** 4, 113
aid to developing countries, Kissinger on, **1975** 593
first economic summit and, **1985** 347
members of, Carter visit to, **1978** 269-270, 285
oil embargo
against U.S. and Netherlands, **1975** 3-4
lifting of against U.S., **1974** 221-224
as model for producers' associations, **1974** 255, 258
and U.S. denial of trade preferences, **1975** 224, 233
oil money in U.S. investments, **1975** 14
price cuts, **1981** 799-801
world oil price drop, **1987** 118
price fluctuations, Greenspan on, **2004** 190-194
price increases, **1978** 789-792; **1979** 251-258
Carter CEA on, **1980** 161-163, 167-168, 172, 174, 178, 182
combating future, **1979** 320, 325
crude oil production cuts and, **2003** 755; **2004** 287-288; **2005** 139
economic summit on, **1980** 507
Joint Economic Committee on, **1980** 210-212, 214, 220, 230
production quotas and, **2005** 777-778
quadrupling of prices, and other raw materials cartels, **1975** 325-327
quadrupling of prices, impact on world economy, **1974** 118-119, 121-122; **1975** 187-196
two-tiered, **1976** 937-942
prices
effect on developing countries' debt, **1982** 971
meetings on, **1980** 995-997
pricing and production policies of, **1980** 417-419, 424
production limits, **1982** 979-981
unreliability of, Schlesinger on, **1979** 659, 662-664
U.S. probe of Aramco, **1983** 921-922
Organization of the Islamic Conference, and Iran-Iraq War, **1984** 750
Organization of the Oppressed on Earth, killing by, **1989** 316
Organized crime
CIA use of in Castro assassination plots, **1975** 726-731, 734, 739, 742-744, 771, 774-775, 782-785
Donovan alleged link to, **1982** 587
efforts to combat, **1997** 349-350
Genovese family members under pretrial detention, **1987** 492-493, 495, 502-503, 507
in labor unions, **1986** 200-210
links to Kennedy assassination, House investigation of, **1978** 914; **1979** 594-595, 609-613, 615
and NBC weapons, **1996** 225
networking with terrorist groups, **2000** 1051
surveillance of, attorney general's authorization of, **1974** 391
in toxic waste industry, **1983** 750
UN role in combating, **2004** 903
Orlando, Michael, **1984** 804
Orlov, Irina Valitova, **1986** 821
Orlov, Yuri F.
emigration of, **1986** 821
in Soviet labor camp, **1981** 748
Ornstein, Norman, **1983** 618
Orr v. Orr; **1979** 193-206
Ortega, Carlos, general strike leader arrested, **2003** 281
Ortega, Katherine D., **1984** 728
Ortega Saavedra, Daniel
cease-fire with contras, **1988** 241-245
Central American peace plan, **1987** 641-642, 1008-1009; **1988** 242-243
church-government relations, **1986** 641
in Nicaraguan transitional government, **1979** 582
pledge to hold elections, **1989** 162
presidential election defeat, **1990** 259, 262
rise of, **1985** 257
signing of Tela accord on Nicaraguan contras, **1989** 161, 172
on U.S. military maneuvers, **1985** 708
Ortega Saavedra, Humberto, **1990** 260, 264
cease-fire with contras, **1988** 242, 245
compliance with peace plan, **1987** 1009
Orthodox church, relations with Catholic Church, John Paul II on, **1979** 730, 760-761
Ortiz, Carlos, medical records privacy, **2001** 487
Osborn, June E., **1992** 710
Osborn, Torie, at gay/lesbian march on Washington, **1993** 330-331
Osborn, United States v., **1998** 399
Osborne, Shane, American spy plane pilot, **2001** 248
Osborne v. Ohio, **1990** 239-249; **1992** 319
Oscamp, Paul J., **1988** 518
O'Scannlain, Diarmuid F., affirmative action court opinion, **1997** 184, 186-194
OSCE. *See* Organization for Security and Cooperation in Europe
Osgood, James, **1997** 626
OSHA. *See* Occupational Safety and Health Administration
Osheroff, Douglass, NASA reorganization, **2003** 638
Oslo (Norway), NATO conference in, **1976** 345-350
Osteoporosis, dairy products and, **1992** 402
OSTP. *See* White House, Office of Science and Technology Policy
Oswald, Lee Harvey
House investigation of, **1978** 909-910, 913-914; **1979** 593-595, 601, 603-613
Kennedy assassination anniversary, **1993** 960
Oswald, Russell G., and Attica prison uprising, **1972** 783-787
OTA. *See* Office of Technology Assessment
al-Otaiba, Mani Said, on OPEC price increases, **1978** 790; **1979** 253-256

Ottawa Declaration, **1990** 600, 603
Ottinger, Richard L. (D-N.Y.), **1975** 495
Otunnu, Olara A., child soldiers, **2002** 916, 918
Ouattara, Alassane, Ivory Coast elections, **2002** 251; **2003** 238; **2004** 822; **2005** 805
Outer continental shelf
  development of, **1974** 910, 914
  federal control of resources of, **1975** 167-175
  oil leasing on, **1973** 465, 469-472; **1975** 17, 23
Outer Continental Shelf Lands Act (1953), **1975** 169, 174-175
Outsourcing/offshoring
  as presidential campaign issue, **2004** 58-59
  and trade deficit, **2004** 237-238
Overseas Facilities Authority (OFA), **1999** 693, 695-696
Overseas Presence Advisory Panel, diplomatic posts evaluation report, **1999** 690-698
Overseas Private Investment Corporation (OPIC), **1974** 278; **1998** 165; **1999** 50
  dispute settlement procedures, **1972** 71
  and U.S. investment in PRC, **1979** 671, 676
Overton, William Ray, on creation science, **1982** 3-16
Ovitz, Michael S., Disney corporate scandal, **2004** 423
al-Owali, Mohamed Rashed Daoud, embassy bombings, **1998** 558; **2001** 803, 813-815
Owen, David, and Rhodesian settlement plan, **1977** 583-585
Owen, Priscilla R., Senate confirmation rejected, **2002** 823, 825-826
Owen, Roberts B., **1979** 887
Owen v. City of Independence, Mo., **1980** 299-316
Owens, Bill (Colorado governor)
  antidiscrimination bill, **2005** 868-869
  Columbine High School shooting incident, governor's commission on, **2001** 347-359
Owens, Wayne (D-Utah), **1974** 988
Own, Ahmed, Lockerbie case agreement, **2003** 1223
Oxfam America, and disaster relief, **1984** 974
Oxford University (England), McGovern speech on U.S. politics, **1973** 87-95
Oxley, Michael G. (R-Ohio)
  child pornography on the Internet, **2002** 291
  corporate reform act, **2002** 1033, 1035
Ozal, Turgut
  human rights in Turkey, **1985** 156
  military takeover in Turkey, **1980** 808
Ozone depletion
  aerosol propellants and, **1975** 437-453; **1980** 691
  biological and health effects of, **1975** 437-439, 442-443; **1987** 746
  CEA on, **1990** 103-104
  Democratic Party platform on, **1992** 706
  effects on climate, **1980** 669; **1988** 861-866
  Gorbachev on, **1992** 436
  NASA reports on, **1988** 221-228; **1992** 75-83
  skin cancer as effect of, **1973** 235-244; **1975** 438-439, 442; **1992** 82
  UN on, **1992** 75, 77-78, 81-83
  U.S.-Soviet agreement on, **1987** 747
Ozone layer
  Antarctic investigations of, NASA-coordinated, **1987** 745-746, 756-764
  effect of nuclear war on, **1985** 542, 548
  effect of SST on, **1973** 235-244
  pesticides, **2003** 182
  reduction
    ground-level, **1990** 716
    U.S. signs agreement, **1990** 468-469
  treaty exemptions, **2003** 182
  treaty to protect, **1987** 745-746, 747-756

P

Pachachi, Adnan, Iraq president of Iraqi Government Council, **2004** 24
Pacific Gas & Electric Co. v. Public Utilities Commission of California, **1995** 333
Pacific Southwest Airlines (PSA), San Diego collision and crash, **1978** 793-795
Pacifica Foundation
  ban on public broadcasting editorials, **1984** 449-451, 454
  Carlin broadcast on offensive language, **1978** 515-531
  right to be free of offensive materials, **1992** 323
Packard, David, defense management study, **1986** 679-680
Packard commission on defense management, recommendations of, **1986** 679-695
Packwood, Bob (R-Ore.)
  abortion
    as constitutional right, **1983** 546
    Republican stance on, **1989** 368
  Nixon pardon, **1974** 813
  resignation from Senate, **1995** 592-599
  sex discrimination, **1984** 203
  U.S.-Japan trade imbalance, **1985** 320
  welfare reform, **1988** 850, 852
PACs. *See* Political action committees
Padget, Ellie, computer security issues, **1998** 676
Padilla, Jose (*aka* Abdullah al-Muhajir)
  detainee case, **2003** 106, 112, 222; **2004** 376; **2005** 451-452
  "enemy combatant" case, **2002** 836; **2003** 106, 111-112; **2004** 376, 378
Padilla v. Rumsfeld, **2004** 378
Padre Island National Seashore (Texas), **1995** 123
Paek Nam Sun, North Korean-U.S. relations, **2002** 732
Page, Trevor, famine relief, **1984** 974
Pahlavi, Mohammed Reza (Shah)
  Iran on crimes of, **1979** 867-870, 873-874, 876, 884
  Iran under, **1988** 530
  overthrow of, **1986** 1014
  property and death of, **1980** 999-1000, 1004-1006
  rise and downfall of, **1978** 699-716
  secular goals of, **1989** 318
  U.S. admitting of, **1979** 868, 870, 874, 880-881
  on U.S.-Iranian relations, **1977** 913-915
  wealth of returned to Iran in hostage agreement, **1981** 145-146
Paige, Roderick R.
  Education Department propaganda, **2005** 645
  education secretary
    confirmation, **2001** 97

resignation, **2004** 778
Republican Party convention, **2004** 484
school vouchers, **2002** 406
Paisley, Ian
and British-Irish accord, **1985** 725
IRA weapons decommissioning, skepticism about, **2005** 510-511
Northern Ireland elections, **2005** 508-509
on Northern Ireland power-sharing plan, **1973** 355
Pakistan
See also Kashmir
Afghanistan
agreements with on peace and refugees, **1988** 257-264
Islamabad conference of on, **1980** 3-8
refugees in, **1980** 8; **1986** 919-920, 922-926, 936
election referendum, **2002** 165-174, 326
family planning in, **1987** 456-457
human rights in, **1980** 8; **1982** 109; **1986** 919-920, 922-926, 936
human trafficking, **2002** 347
hunt for al Qaeda leaders, **2004** 537; **2005** 472-473
impact of Rushdie death threat in, **1989** 95
Indian conflict
and secession of East Pakistan, **1977** 538
and U.S. aid, **1972** 23-39
U.S. policy on, **1977** 322, 339-341
U.S.-PRC Shanghai communiqué on, **1972** 188-189
Jaish-e-Muhammed (Kashmiri guerrillas), **2002** 166, 167, 326; **2003** 210, 212
Jamaat-e Islami (Islamic political party), **2003** 1056
John Paul II visit, **1981** 203
Lahore Declaration, **1999** 623-624
Lashkar-e-Taiba (Kashmiri guerrillas), **2002** 326; **2003** 210, 212; **2004** 539; **2005** 468
local elelctions, **2005** 475-476
military coup in, **1977** 537; **1999** 623-629
missile threat to U.S., **1998** 492
Musharraf as military and political leader, **2004** 1009-1017
Musharraf on Islamist extremism, **2005** 472-484
Muttahida Majlis-e-Amal (United Action Forum), **2004** 1010, 1012; **2005** 473
nuclear materials exports, **2003** 1030, 1031
nuclear weapons program, **2003** 1025
nuclear weapons smuggling, Kahn network, **2004** 169, 323, 327-329, 1009, 1013
nuclear weapons testing, **1998** 326-332, 467, 541; **1999** 623-624; **2000** 203
opium growing in, **1972** 646, 648-649
political situation, **2005** 475-476
relations with India, **1999** 623-629; **2001** 963-970; **2002** 325-331; **2003** 209-217; **2004** 352-353
religious persecution, **1997** 564, 576-577
sectarian (Shi'ite/Sunni) violence, **2005** 475
terrorist groups in, **2000** 279; **2002** 326-327
U.S. aid to, **1980** 28, 34, 44
U.S. security agreement with (1959), **1979** 966, 978-979, 982
and U.S.-PRC nuclear accords, **1984** 288-289
war on terrorism, support for U.S., **2001** 615, 626, 627, 632-636; **2002** 40; **2005** 472
weapons exchange with North Korea, **2002** 734
weapons of mass destruction proliferation, **1996** 213, 222-223
Pakistan Muslim League-Quaid (PML-Q), **2002** 168-169
Palacio, Alfredo, as president of Ecuador, **2005** 772
Palestine
Jewish emigration to, British policy on (1939), **1983** 144, 149
Labor Party victory in Israel, **1992** 655-665
partition of, Arafat on, **1974** 928
violence on the Temple Mount, **1990** 695-711
Palestine Liberation Organization (PLO)
on Camp David accords, **1979** 224
conditions of for peace negotiations, **1989** 290-291
and Egyptian-Israeli talks, **1980** 504
founding of, **2004** 806; **2005** 27
Israeli Peace Accord, **1993** 747-768
on Israeli raid on Iraq, **1981** 507
Israeli unwillingness to negotiate with, **1977** 829-830, 850
on Israeli-Egyptian disengagement, **1974** 31
Lebanon, departure from, **1982** 741-749; **1983** 471-473
Libyan support for, **1986** 348
Middle East Peace Conference (Madrid), **1991** 719-731
participation in Geneva peace conference, **1981** 225, 231-232
participation in peace talks on West Bank and Gaza, **1978** 605-606
as representative of Palestinians, **1988** 579-580, 582-583
Republican Party platform on, **1980** 640
on Sadat, **1977** 829; **1978** 607; **1981** 734
on Saudi peace plan, **1981** 633
terrorist acts of, **1981** 462-463, 470; **1985** 466-468
UN observer status for, extension of, **1975** 326
UN recognition of, and Arafat speech, **1974** 919-920, 934-937
U.S. attempt to close New York offices, **1988** 479-485
U.S. conditions for talks with, **1976** 192-193; **1981** 647-650, 653-657; **1988** 905-908
Young's meeting, **1979** 647-657
U.S. policy toward, **1975** 574, 586; **1981** 635; **1984** 289
West Bank agreement, **1995** 622-630
as World Bank-IMF conference observer, **1980** 884
Wye River peace agreement, **1998** 742-754; **1999** 53-54, 700, 891-893; **2001** 363
Palestine National Council
on access to Geneva peace talks, **1974** 437
declaration of independence, **1988** 905-911
on existence of Palestinian state, **1989** 291
Palestinian Authority, **2002** 927, 932-933; **2004** 807
See also Hamas (Islamic resistance movement)
Abbas on his presidential election, **2005** 27-40
elections, **2004** 807; **2005** 270-271, 273, 581
international economic aid, **2005** 34-35
Palestinian Liberation Organization (PLO), in Lebanon, **2004** 557
Palestinian National Charter (Cairo, 1968), **1988** 906

Palestinian state, **2002** 937; **2005** 27
Republican Party platform on, **1988** 617, 683
Saudi plan for, **1981** 631-632, 635
Palestinians
al-Aqsa Martyrs Brigade, **2002** 930-931; **2003** 196; **2005** 33
casualties of conflict, **2002** 928-929; **2003** 1210-1211; **2004** 812-813; **2005** 30-31
cause of
Castro on, **1979** 685
and peace discussions, **1985** 710-711
terrorist acts on behalf of, **1974** 435-436; **1985** 463-468
terrorists holding Israeli hostages at Entebbe, **1976** 517-520
cease-fire negotiations, **2003** 1201; **2005** 29-31
in drug trade, **1972** 647
economic situation, **2002** 935-936; **2003** 1211-1212
Geneva peace conference, participation in, **1974** 835, 845
guerrillas' attack on Israelis at Munich Olympic Games, **1972** 751-755
history and rights of, Arafat on at UN, **1974** 919-937
homeland for, John Paul II on, **1982** 342-343; **1987** 700, 704; **1988** 413-414
human rights situation, **2000** 937
international "roadmap" for peace, **2003** 191-205, 1200
Islamic Jihad, **2001** 363-365; **2002** 930, 933; **2003** 1202, 1211; **2005** 29
Israeli conflict, **2003** 191-205, 1210-1211; **2005** 582
Israeli home demolitions, **2004** 310-311
Israeli occupation, UN human development report on, **2005** 276
Israeli treatment of, **2001** 603-604
Israeli violence in West Bank, **2002** 927-941
Jenin refugee camp "massacre," **2002** 933-935
leadership of, **2002** 369-381; **2003** 192-193, 1200-1201
Lebanon, departure from, **1983** 471-473
Middle East violence, **2000** 930-951
national rights of, PLO on, **1974** 437
nationalism of, and Jordan's links to West Bank, **1988** 579-585
in occupied territories
autonomy for, **1977** 828-830, 848, 851, 855-857; **1978** 605-606, 609-610, 616, 621; **1979** 224-226, 649-650
human rights for, **1988** 93, 113-115, 884, 889; **1989** 57-58, 69-70
nonaligned nations' support for, **1983** 264, 268
political rights for, **1989** 289, 294-295
uprising of, **1988** 579-581, 583-585
Popular Resistance Committees, **2003** 1203
post-Arafat diplomacy, **2004** 809; **2005** 27-40
prime minister Mahmound Abbas appointment, **2003** 1200-1201
Red Crescent Society, **2004** 812, 813
refugee camp massacre in Lebanon, **1982** 781-795; **1983** 163-180; **1985** 47-51
right of return to Israel, **2004** 304
rights of, Carter on, **1977** 738, 744
self-determination for, **1974** 833-834, 837-838
suicide bombings, **2001** 363-365, 367; **2002** 927, 929-931; **2004** 535; **2005** 29
UN humanitarian aid, **2002** 919
Vatican policy, **2000** 79-80
West Bank homeland for, Sadat on, **1977** 828-830, 833, 837-839, 848, 852
West Bank Settlement policy, **2004** 303-304
Palila v. Hawaii Dept. of Land and Natural Resources, **1995** 366
Palme, Lisbet, **2000** 450
Palmeiro, Rafael
baseball suspension, **2005** 216
steroid use in baseball, congressional testimony on, **2005** 213-216, 221-222
Palmer, John L., Medicare financial situation, **2004** 582
Palmer, Russell Thomas, Jr., on prisoners' rights, **1984** 480, 482-483
Palmieri, Edmund, on closing of PLO observer mission to UN, **1988** 480-485
Palocci, Antonio
Brazilian economic policy, **2003** 6
Brazilian finance minister, **2002** 778
Pan Africanist Congress
ban on, **1989** 546; **1990** 69
on new South African constitution, **1992** 285
Pan Am (Lockerbie) bombing, **1990** 301-310; **1996** 662
Pan American Health Organization (PAHO), smoking in the Americas, **1992** 267-275
Panama
and Contadora Group, **1987** 638
elections in, **1989** 702-703, 706
human rights in, **1984** 155
John Paul II visit, **1983** 242
Noriega
indictments, **1988** 81-92
sentenced for drug trafficking, **1992** 649-653
ratification of canal treaties, **1977** 591; **1978** 177-222
smoking in the Americas, **1992** 269
stability of, and canal treaties, **1977** 593-594, 622; **1978** 177, 186
U.S. economic aid to, **1984** 32
U.S. economic sanctions against, **1988** 81-82; **1989** 702-703
U.S. invasion of, **1989** 701-707; **1990** 49, 52, 56; **1992** 649, 650
Bush on, **1992** 504
Panama Canal
control over, **1992** 650
employees, status of under treaties, **1977** 592, 603-606; **1978** 198-201
modernization of, Chinese funding for, **2004** 938
ownership of, **1978** 178-179, 184-185
protecting security of, **1989** 701, 705-707
sea-level canal in, **1977** 608; **1978** 203-204
treaties
as Carter accomplishment, **1980** 790; **1981** 60
negotiations on, **1977** 193
opponents of, **1977** 591-593; **1978** 178-179
ratification of
Carter call for, **1978** 9, 18-19, 47

controversy, **1977** 591-594; **1978** 177-186
by Senate, **1978** 177-222
Republican Party platform on, **1980** 642
Senate reservations to, **1978** 177, 179-180, 213-215, 220-222
signing of, **1977** 591-592, 594-617
support for in Ford-Carter debate, **1976** 733, 753-754
text of, **1978** 190-212
transfer ceremony, Carter speech, **1999** 850-855
and U.S.-Latin American relations, **1977** 591-593; **1979** 713, 718
U.S. sovereignty over, **1977** 184, 188
Panama Canal Neutrality Treaty, **1978** 177, 179-180, 215-220
signing of, **1977** 591-592, 618-622
Statement of Understanding, **1977** 593-594, 622-623
Panama Refining Co. v. Ryan, **1998** 436
Panamanian Defense Forces, in U.S. invasion, **1989** 701-705
Pandraud, Robert, **1986** 830
Panetta, Leon E. (D-Calif.)
budget critics, **1991** 68
California gubernatorial recall election, **2003** 1007
Clinton economic team, **1992** 1021
on disaster relief, **1994** 4
federal budget deficit, **2005** 123
ocean protection policy, **2004** 602
on Reagan budget, **1983** 103
Paniagua, Valentin, Peru presidential inauguration, **2000** 923-929
Panic, Milan, Yugoslavia's UN membership, **1992** 876
Panos Institute, **1986** 888
Panyarachun, Anand, UN reform panel, **2003** 809; **2004** 887
Paperwork reduction. *See* Government management, efficiency in
Pappas, In the matter of, **1972** 507-509, 511-512, 514-519
Pappas, Paul, confidentiality of news sources, **1972** 507-509, 511-512
Pappas, Thomas M., Abu Ghraib prison abuse scandal, **2004** 215; **2005** 912
Papua New Guinea, John Paul II visit, **1984** 328, 332-334
Paracha, Uzir, al Qaeda supporter convicted, **2003** 617
Paradise, United States v., **1990** 430
Paraguay
flexibility in drought, **1984** 984-985
smoking in the Americas, **1992** 269
Paramilitary organizations
Freemen surrender to FBI, **1996** 362-367
Waco and Ruby Ridge incidents, **1995** 178
Parden v. Terminal R. Co. of Ala. Docks Dept., **1999** 340
Pardew, James, Macedonia peace negotiations, **2001** 556
Pardo, Alvin, **1972** 167
Parens patriae, and Baby M case, **1987** 375, 377, 382, 387
Parental leave
and employment discrimination, **1987** 17-27
policies on in industrialized countries, **1987** 148-149, 154
seniority rights after, **1977** 871-881
U.S. compared with other industrialized nations, **1987** 147-148, 152-154
Parenting education, for teenagers, **1986** 1062
Parents
abortion consent for teenagers, **1976** 483, 486-487; **1990** 387-407
rights of
child custody and proof of neglect, **1982** 259-280
in medical treatment of child, **1973** 40
and private schools' discriminatory admissions, **1976** 392, 396
role in children's education, **1986** 804, 807-808; **1989** 86, 92
single, lambasted in "Murphy Brown" speech, **1992** 443-452
Parents' Music Resource Center (PMRC), **1990** 509-510, 511
Parents' rights, and grandparents' rights, Supreme Court on, **2000** 287-298
Parham v. J. R., **1990** 377, 380
Paris Adult Theatre I v. Slaton, **1973** 611-613, 621-628; **1992** 321
Paris Charter (1990), **1992** 437
Paris Club
Honduran and Nicaraguan disaster relief efforts, **1998** 792
international debt strategy, **1992** 643-644
Iraq debt reduction, **2004** 406
Russian participation, **1997** 341, 342-343
Paris peace accords (1973). *See* Vietnam War, Paris peace accords
Paris Reparations Conference (1946), **1997** 269-270
Parisi, Anthony J., on chemical wastes, **1980** 446
Park, Tongsun
influence buying in Congress, **1977** 770-771, 776-778, 795-819; **1978** 845-846, 849-881, 896-900; **1980** 485-487
Koreagate indictment of, **1979** 898
Park Chung Hee
assassination of, **1979** 895-904; **1980** 190-191, 825-826
on Communist victory in Vietnam, **1975** 252
Ford meeting with, **1974** 955-956, 965-967
and Korean influence-buying scheme, **1978** 858-859, 863, 865
military coup and, **1997** 894
possible talks with North Korea, **1972** 523
Parker, Barrington D., **1982** 533
Parker, Dave, **1986** 170
Parker, James A., Wen Ho Lee spy case, **2000** 741, 743-744, 746-752
Parker, Paul Michael "Mike" (D-Miss.)
Gingrich resignation, **1998** 803
on vote for Speaker of the House, **1995** 3
Parker, Robert, Taiwan-China relations, **1979** 672
Parker, Robert M., right to bear arms, **2001** 725
Parkinson, Kenneth W.
Watergate acquittal, **1974** 991-992; **1975** 141
Watergate indictment, **1974** 157, 159, 161, 165, 167

Parks, Rosa
  death of, **2005** 353-354
  at Million Man March, **1995** 656
  profile of, **2005** 357
Parmalat, corporate scandal, **2003** 332, 341
Parrish, Stephen, tobacco industry regulation, **2000** 557
Parry, Emyr Jones, stem cell research in Great Britain, **2005** 323
Parsons, Richard D., Social Security reform, **2001** 915, 917
Parsons, William
  Columbia space shuttle disaster, **2003** 634
  Discovery space shuttle mission, **2005** 500
Partial Birth Abortion Ban Act (2003), **2003** 995-1004
Partnership for Peace, **1994** 46; **1997** 521
Partnership for Progress and a Common Future with the Region of the Broader Middle East and North Africa, **2004** 629
Partnership for Public Warning, **2002** 744
Partnership for Supply Chain Management, **2005** 52
Pasadena City Board of Education v. Spangler, **1976** 413-423
Pashtoon, Yusuf, Afghanistan political situation, **2003** 1092-1093
Pasqua, Charles, **1986** 831
Passaro, David A., prison abuse case, **2005** 914
Passman, Otto E. (D-La.)
  job bias suit against, **1979** 399-411
  in Korean influence-buying scheme, **1978** 846, 857-858, 870-877
Passport Act (1926), **1981** 542, 545-547
Pasternak, Boris, **1972** 728
Pastora, Edén, **1987** 638, 641
Pastore, John O. (D-R.I.), on TV violence, **1972** 61-62
Pastrana, Andres
  Colombia presidential elections, **2000** 842
  peace negotiations, **1999** 468; **2000** 842; **2002** 569; **2003** 425
  Plan Colombia, **2000** 842-851; **2002** 570, 573, 574; **2003** 429
  U.S. aid to Colombia, **2000** 840
Patagonia, **1996** 43
Pataki, George (New York governor)
  greenhouse gas emissions, **2005** 924
  Medicaid-related veto, **1997** 613
  on Republican Party, **2000** 522
  September 11 attacks, **2001** 648
Patasse, Ange-Felix, Central African Republic president overthrown, **2003** 1226-1227
Pate, Russell R., on exercise, **1993** 626
Patent and Trademark Amendment Act (1980), **1987** 358-359
Patent law
  application to new life forms, **1987** 358-359, 364
  and genetically engineered bacterium, **1980** 493-502
  legal forum shopping in, **1975** 466-467
  and ownership of biological material, **1987** 358-359
Pathfinder mission to Mars, **1997** 509-513; **1999** 712; **2000** 89
Patients' Bill of Rights, **1997** 787-799; **1998** 46-47, 89, 140; **1999** 48-49, 562-563; **2000** 20, 38-40
Patman, Wright (D-Texas), **1973** 45
Patolichev, Nikolai S., **1973** 587-589
Patrawala, Marazan, **1985** 297
Patrick, Dennis R., **1987** 627
Patriot Act. *See* USA Patriot Act
Patten, Chris
  European Commission presidential candidate, **2004** 201
  on Hong Kong political situation, **1997** 501
  at Hong Kong transfer ceremony, **1997** 502
  North Korean missile program, **2001** 269
Patten, Edward J. (D-N.J.), in Korean influence-buying scheme, **1978** 846, 879-880
Pattern Makers' League v. National Labor Relations Board, **1985** 415-429
Patterson, Eugene, **1990** 295-299
Patterson, Russell H., Jr., **1984** 1020
Patterson v. McLean Credit Union, **1989** 322-324
Paul, Henri, **1997** 647
Paul, William, AIDS research, **1996** 157
Paul VI (pope)
  on activist clergy, **1980** 412
  on Catholic annulments, **1980** 872
  changes in church practice, **1978** 596; **1983** 94; **1988** 489-490
  on contraception, **1980** 872
  death of, **1978** 595-596
  on food aid, **1974** 941
  suspension of Lefebvre (1975), **1988** 490
Pauley, William H., III, investment banks settlement, **2003** 699
Paulison, David, FEMA acting director appointment, **2005** 568
Pavelic, Ante, **1998** 293
Pavkovic, Nebojsa, Kostunica military supporter, **2000** 836
Pavlov, Valentin S., **1991** 515
Pawtucket, Rhode Island, display of Nativity scene, **1984** 217-239
Paxon, Bill (R-N.Y.), and Gingrich ethics violations, **1997** 5
Paycheck Fairness Act, **2000** 25
Payne, Billy, on Centennial Olympic Park bombing, **1996** 448
Payne, Donald (D-N.J.), U.S.-Africa policy, **2000** 72
Payne v. Tennessee, **1991** 381-395; **1993** 142-143
Payton v. New York, **1980** 281-297
Paz, Octavio, **1990** 795-806
Paz, Robert, killing of in Panama, **1989** 704-705
Paz Zamora, Jaime
  drug summit (Cartagena), **1990** 115-126; **1992** 204
  U.S.-Latin America drug summit (San Antonio), **1992** 201, 204
PBGC. *See* Pension Benefit Guaranty Corporation
Peace
  See also Middle East peace; Nobel Peace Prize; Nuclear freeze, movement
  building in world, Nixon on, **1972** 721, 724-725; **1973** 82-83; **1974** 449-450, 452, 461, 469-471
  comprehensive and institutionalized, Kissinger on, **1973** 809-816
  dividend, **1992** 56
  issues, role of women in, **1985** 556, 567-570

Peace Corps, **2002** 37, 44
as alternative service for draft evaders, **1973** 193-194, 198
U.S. support for, **1981** 14
Peacebuilding Commission, UN proposal, **2004** 908
Peacekeeping
See also Middle East peace
African Union mission in Sudan, **2005** 518-519
multinational force in Israeli-Lebanese conflict, **1982** 741, 744-748
UN forces
negotiations on deployment and composition of in October war, **1973** 881-882, 886, 889-891, 898-900
U.S. support for, **1983** 798-800
UN ineffectiveness, remedies for, **1982** 769-779
UN Mission in Sudan (UNMIS), **2005** 520-521
UN missions, **1999** 860-889
in Congo, **2000** 450, 643
in East Timor, **1999** 513-514, 718-719
in Ethiopia-Eritrea, **2000** 755
in Haiti, **2000** 956
in Kosovo, **2000** 141, 144-151
Rwandan failure, **1999** 860-889; **2000** 643
in Sierra Leone, **1974** 250; **1999** 431; **2000** 450, 642, 1072-1077; **2002** 247-248, 547; **2005** 804
in Somalia, **1998** 222; **2000** 643
UN missions reform, **2000** 642-646, 702-703
UN missions sexual abuse scandals, **2004** 893-894
UN Stabilization Mission in Haiti (MINUSTAH), **2005** 329-337
UN use of force guidelines, **2004** 889-890, 904-905
UNEF, in Sinai accord between Egypt and Israel, **1975** 577-579, 581, 585
U.S. forces in Grenada, **1983** 849
Peacock, Susan C., CIA counterterrorism recruitment, **2000** 279
Pearl, Daniel, kidnapping and murder of journalist, **2002** 166, 740; **2005** 474
Pearl, Karen, morning-after pill, FDA ruling, **2005** 816
Pearl Harbor attack, fiftieth anniversary, **1991** 775-784
Peary, Robert E., North Pole discovery claim, **1988** 831-833; **1989** 687-696
Pease, Ed (R-Ind.), House Judiciary Committee impeachment inquiry, **1998** 711
Pechanek, Terry, antismoking campaigns, **2004** 282
Peck, Fred, on military homosexual ban, **1993** 154
Pei, I. M., **1979** 813
Pekala, Leszek, Polish priest's killing, **1985** 120-123, 125
Peking, Convention of (1860), **1984** 1045
Peking University. *See* Beijing University
Pell, Claiborne (D-R.I.)
dismantling of OEO, **1973** 454
Glaspie-Hussein pre-war meeting, **1991** 156, 160
Kennan congressional appearance, **1989** 207
UN charter, **1995** 354
Pell, Terence J., PRIDE drug abuse report, **1992** 1013-1016
Pell grant scholarships, **1985** 585, 590; **1993** 172, 176; **2001** 59; **2005** 144
and sex bias in education, **1984** 201, 204-206, 208-213
Pelletreau, Robert H., Jr., **1988** 908
Pelosi, Nancy (D-Calif.)
Bush State of the Union address, Democratic response, **2004** 21-22, 30-32; **2005** 81, 92-94
DeLay indictment, **2005** 634
first woman minority whip, **2001** 549
Gay/Lesbian March on Washington, **1993** 328
and Gingrich ethics violations case, **1997** 4
Iraq stabilization plan, **2005** 81, 93
warrantless domestic surveillance, **2005** 961
Peña, Federico
FAA and airline safety, **1996** 238
General Motors truck safety, **1994** 443-448
Los Angeles earthquake and, **1994** 5
and railroad safety regulations, **1996** 191
Pence, Mike (R-Ind.), stem cell research opponent, **2005** 318-319
Pendleton, Clarence M., Jr.
education cuts in Reagan budget, **1983** 914
employment disparities among minorities and women, **1982** 919-944
Pendleton Civil Service Act (1883), **1978** 138, 140
Peng Meng-chi, **1972** 827
Penn Central Transportation Co., bankruptcy of, **1975** 529-530
Penn Central Transportation Co. v. City of New York, **1978** 453-465
Penner, Rudolph G., **1981** 327
federal budget spending, **2003** 682
Pennhurst State School and Hospital v. Halderman, **1992** 196
Pennsylvania
See also Philadelphia
abortion restrictions of, **1977** 407-409, 411-419; **1989** 368; **1990** 217
intelligent design case, **2005** 1012, 1014-1026
Pennsylvania Avenue (Washington, D.C.), closing of, **1995** 178, 254-258
Pennsylvania Coal Co. v. Mahon, **1992** 617
Penny, Timothy, Social Security reform, **2005** 84
Penry v. Johnson, Texas Dept. of Criminal Justice, **2001** 387-394; **2004** 796
Penry v. Lynaugh, **2005** 187, 188
Pension Benefit Guaranty Corporation (PBGC)
financial condition, **2003** 713-714; **2004** 734-745; **2005** 132
investment policies, **2004** 737-738
role of the, **2005** 205-206
Social Security, underfunded pensions, **2003** 707-719
underfunded corporate pension plans, **2005** 197-211, 486
Pension plans. *See* Retirement plans; Social Security
Pentagon
See also Defense Department; September 11 (9/11) terrorist attacks
bombing in Saudi Arabia, **1996** 672
computer systems, threats to, **1996** 312-324
on satellite and aerial reconnaissance, **1992** 5
Pentagon Papers
case, **1997** 104, 105-106

Pentagon Papers *Continued*
dismissal of, **1973** 537-548, 745-746; **1974** 205-206, 661, 665
White House efforts to defame Ellsberg, **1974** 443-447
CIA participation in, **1975** 403
White House meeting with judge, **1974** 208
and wiretaps in Nixon White House, **1976** 160
final installment of, **1972** 491-497
leak of to press, and White House plumbers, **1973** 569-570; **1974** 33-37
Penthouse magazine, libel suit against *Hustler,* **1984** 247
Penzias, Arno, **1992** 380, 381
People for the American Way
Bork Supreme Court nomination, **1987** 719
hate crimes, **1992** 545
Roberts Supreme Court nomination, **2005** 560
school prayer and, **1984** 243
Thomas Supreme Court appointment, **1992** 34
People's Movement for the Liberation of Angola (MPLA), **2002** 152
People's Republic of China. *See* China, People's Republic of (PRC)
People's Temple, investigation of mass suicide at Jonestown, **1979** 347-378
PEPFAR. *See* President's Emergency Plan for AIDS Relief
Pepper, Claude (D-Fla.), **1988** 334
Percy, Charles H. (R-Ill.)
and Lance inquiry, **1977** 626, 628, 642, 647-648
on Republican Party platform, **1980** 568
Perelli, Carina, UN electoral assistance division staffer fired, **2005** 236
Peremptory challenge, racially motivated, **1986** 409-433
Peres, Shimon
Aqaba pipeline, and investigation of Meese, **1988** 498, 512-513
defeat by Netanyahu, **1996** 337
eulogy for Yitzhak Rabin, **1995** 692-693
French cooperation on terrorism, **1986** 832
as Israeli foreign minister, **2002** 937
Israeli-Palestinian peace accord, **1993** 747, 763-764
Israel's role in U.S. arms sales to Iran, **1986** 1050, 1053
Jenin "massacre" investigations, **2002** 934
Labor Party coalition with Sharon, **2005** 534
Nobel Peace Prize recipient, **2003** 1130
Palestinian peace negotiations, **2003** 1207
peace proposal, **1985** 710-711
Sharon disengagement policy, **2004** 306
on weapons control, **1993** 72
West Bank peace agreement, **1995** 622, 624, 689-690
Perestroika (restructuring)
Bush's NATO presss conference, **1990** 464
Elena Bonner analyzes, **1990** 207, 209-210
Gorbachev and Shevardnadze share task, **1990** 826
Gorbachev explanation of, **1987** 857, 858, 862, 864-866
Gorbachev on, **2004** 319
Gorbachev report to party congress, **1990** 442-448
Vaclav Havel on, **1990** 13
Peretz, Amir, Israeli elections, **2005** 534
Perez, Carlos Andres, **1992** 201
Pérez de Cuéllar, Javier
Angolan Peace Accord, **1991** 288
background and career of, **1982** 770
denial of U.S. visa to Arafat, **1988** 907
El Salvador
peace process, **1992** 24-25
violence report, **1993** 240
Falklands peace efforts, **1982** 285
Iran, hostage negotiations, **1991** 753
Iran-Iraq cease-fire, **1988** 531-532
Iran-Iraq War negotiations, **1987** 610-613
Iraq
peace mission to Baghdad, **1991** 16
postwar report, **1991** 165
pre-war appeal, **1991** 19-20
Nambian independence ceremony speech, **1990** 199-203
Peruvian presidential election, **2000** 923
recommendations to Israel, **1990** 696, 697
Soviet withdrawal from Afghanistan, **1988** 259
UN fortieth anniversary, **1985** 710
UN ineffectiveness, remedies for, **1982** 769-779
UN peace terms for Iraq, **1991** 192
U.S. withdrawal from UNESCO, **1983** 969
Perez del Castillo, Carlos, World Trade Organization (WTO) meeting (Cancún), **2003** 745-750
Perez v. United States, **1995** 198
Perkin-Elmer Corporation, **1990** 754
Perle, Richard
Hollinger International scandal, **2004** 424
Iraq-U.S. relations, **2001** 851
military technology espionage, **1985** 605
national security export controls, **1987** 30
Peron, Juan Domingo, Argentine economic policy, **2002** 80-81
Perot, H. Ross
Iran-contra affair, **1986** 1052
passport search, **1992** 1052
postelection statement, **1992** 1019-1020, 1021-1023
presidential debates, **1992** 907-977; **1996** 550
presidential election (1992), **1993** 130; **2000** 896
presidential election (1996), nomination, **1996** 550-562
statements on ending and reviving his campaign, **1992** 717-722
upstages Democratic Party convention, **1992** 667
Perry, Bruce D., psychiatric interviews with Waco cult members, **1993** 293
Perry, Daniel, stem cell research guidelines, **2000** 669-670
Perry, James M., on presidential debates, **1988** 721-722
Perry, Rick (Texas governor)
death penalty, **2001** 389; **2004** 798
Hurricane Katrina disaster response, **2005** 542-543
Perry, Robert M., **1983** 751
Perry, William J.
affirmative action, **2003** 362
air safety after Brown mission crash, **1996** 205-206

extremists in U.S. Army, task force on, **1996** 178
Gulf War syndrome investigations, **1994** 270
Kelso court-martial, **1994** 109
military base closings, **1995** 407, 408
military readiness, letters questioning, **1994** 528-529, 532-534
North Korea, U.S. policy, **1999** 568-583; **2000** 867
nuclear weapons proliferation, **1996** 210
secretary of defense nomination, **1993** 695; **1994** 23-24
terrorist bombing in Saudi Arabia, **1996** 672, 674
Perry v. Sindermann, **1991** 263; **1994** 309
Perry Education Assn. v. Perry Local Educators' Assn., **1993** 367; **1994** 313, 322
Persian Gulf
attacks on shipping in
Arab League on, **1987** 870, 873
during Iran-Iraq War, **1988** 530-532
Carter doctrine on, **1980** 27, 33, 90, 93-94
danger to merchant shipping in, Iran-Iraq War, **1987** 610, 611, 613
freedom of navigation in, **1987** 525, 527, 530
political situation in
during Iran-Iraq War, **1984** 747-755
Schlesinger on, **1979** 659, 661-663
U.S. presence in
downing of Iranian airliner, **1988** 703-717
expansion of, **1980** 124, 127, 133
Iraqi attack on *Stark* (USS), **1987** 792-794
and stock market crash, **1987** 833
Persian Gulf War
See also Operation Desert Shield; Operation Desert Storm
background, **2003** 135
Baker's congressional testimony, **1990** 779-782
Baker's UN remarks, **1990** 768, 769-771
birth defects of children of war veterans, **2001** 909-910
British veterans with illness, **2001** 910
budget deficit, **1990** 410
Bush, George H. W.
address to Congress, **1990** 551-556
on Geneva Talks failure, **1991** 551-556
ground war announcement, **1991** 101-102
on Kuwait liberation, **1991** 104-105
news conference, **1990** 773-776
ultimatum, **1991** 100-101
victory speech to Congress, **1991** 121-128
Bush-Gorbachev statement, **1990** 550-551
coalition, **2002** 717
congressional war resolution, **1991** 3-13
Dole on, **1991** 11
Mitchell on, **1991** 9-11
Nunn on, **1991** 6-9
Fahd on Iraqi threat, **1990** 557-560
Glaspie-Hussein pre-war meeting, **1991** 155-163
Gulf War veterans with ALS, **2001** 907-912
Iraqi invasion of Kuwait, **2003** 1190
Kuwaiti emir's address, **1990** 655-660
Patriot missile performance report, **1992** 865
Pérez de Cuéllar letter to Hussein, **1991** 19-20
prelude and onset of, **1991** 15-22
Saddam Hussein
deadline pressure to avoid war, **1990** 767-782
withdrawal speech, **1991** 102-104
Saudi Arabia and, **1992** 225, 226
Schwarzkopf's address to Congress, **1991** 243-246
Senate debate on women in combat, **1991** 491-512
Shevardnadze statements, **1990** 642-643, 828-829
"smart" weapons performance reports, **1996** 403-413; **1997** 493-500
State of the United Nations, State of the Union address, **1991** 35, 37-39, 43-46
United Nations
backing for, **1995** 351
peace terms, **1991** 191-203
report on postwar Iraq, **1991** 165-174
report on refugee resettlement, **1991** 671-673
resolutions, **1990** 545-550, 771-773
war powers debate, **1990** 663-679
Webster's congressional testimony, **1990** 776-779
women in combat, **1991** 491-512; **1992** 1029-1044
Persian Gulf War syndrome, **1994** 264-275; **1997** 740-745
Personal Responsibility and Work Opportunity Reconciliation Act (PRWORA, 1996), **1998** 357; **1999** 261
Persson, Goran, North Korean missile program, **2001** 269
Pertini, Alessandro, **1982** 477
Peru
and Contadora Group, **1987** 638
drug control measures, **1992** 217-218
Drug Summit, **1992** 201-221
drug war, U.S. military aid in, **1989** 500-501, 505
embassy in Havana, and political refugees, **1980** 337-338, 343, 345
essential drug chemicals agreement, **1990** 126-128
executions in, **1989** 598, 606
Falklands peace efforts of, **1982** 285
hostage crisis, **1997** 234-237
human rights in, **1984** 155; **1989** 62-64; **1993** 559-560, 571-575
and U.S. military aid, **1977** 3, 17-20
John Paul II visit, **1985** 57-59, 62-67
nationalization of private property by, **1972** 67
Paniagua presidential inauguration, **2000** 923-929
presidential elections, **2000** 924-925
Shining Path leader captured, **1992** 859-864
smoking in the Americas, **1992** 269
on U.S. invasion of Panama, **1989** 703
Peshmerga (Kurdish army), **2005** 664, 673
Pesticides
control of, Nixon environmental program, **1972** 147, 150
as environmental threat, Global 2000 report on, **1980** 666, 688-689, 695
methyl bromide ban, exemption for American farmers, **2004** 670-671
and the ozone layer, **2003** 182
regulation reform, **1996** 467-470
Pétain, Henri Philippe, complicity with Nazis, **1995** 478
Porter Novelli (public relations firm), food pyramid design, **2005** 5
Peters, Ron, **1989** 478-479

Petersen, Henry E.
  Agnew attacks on, **1973** 829
  taped conversation with Nixon, **1974** 303
  Watergate investigation by, **1973** 862; **1974** 347, 359, 374, 380-381
    Nixon instructions on, **1974** 297-298
Petersen, Jan, cease-fire in Sri Lanka, **2002** 94
Peterson, Douglas "Pete," U.S. ambassador to united Vietnam, **1997** 489; **1999** 476; **2000** 913, 918
Peterson, Peter G.
  development aid and nationalization, **1972** 67-68
  energy crisis, **1973** 465
  U.S.-Soviet trade agreement, **1972** 846, 852
Pethia, Richard D., Internet viruses and worms, **2003** 391
Petraeus, David, Iraqi security force (ISF) training, **2004** 881; **2005** 662
Petritsch, Wolfgang, Bosnian elections, **2003** 462
Petroleum Industry Response Organization, **1989** 227
Pettigrew, Thomas F., **1975** 614
Pew Center on Global Climate Change, **2002** 305; **2004** 832
Pew Charitable Trusts, ocean protection policy, **2004** 602
Pew Hispanic Center, research studies, **2003** 349, 352-353
Pew Internet and American Life Project
  Internet use in the U.S., **2002** 68
  spam and computer use, **2003** 392
Pew Research Center for People and the Press
  constitutional amendment barring gay marriage, **2004** 40
  foreign relations, overseas views of U.S., **2005** 579
  Social Security reform, **2005** 114, 116
  U.S. economy, public opinion on, **2005** 137
Pfeffer, Jeffrey, Enron Corp. bankruptcy, **2001** 862
Pfeiffer v. Marion Center Area School Dist., **1992** 191
Pfizer
  affirmative action, **2003** 362
  Celebrex and Bextra, drug safety studies, **2004** 852-853
  drug importation from Canada, **2004** 983-984
  eminent domain case, **2005** 362
PFLP. *See* Popular Front for the Liberation of Palestine
Phalangist Christians (Lebanon), and Palestinian refugee camp massacre, **1982** 781-795; **1983** 163-169, 172-173; **1985** 47-50
Pham Van Dong
  U.S.-Vietnam relations, **1977** 207, 209-210
  Vietnam peace negotiations, **1972** 495-496
Pharmaceutical industry
  drug pricing, **1993** 197-209
  Medicare reform legislation, **2003** 1123
  and prescription drug benefits, **2000** 134; **2003** 1123
Pharmaceutical Manufacturers Association, **1993** 198, 204
Phelan, John J., Jr., **1988** 12
Phelan, Richard J., **1989** 239
Philadelphia (Pennsylvania)
  air quality of, **1981** 275
  Declaration of Independence bicentennial celebrations, **1976** 509-510, 513-516
  police raid on MOVE group, **1986** 239-251
Philadelphia Daily News, on Quayle-Murphy Brown controversy, **1992** 443
Philadelphia Inquirer, libel suit against, **1986** 356, 358-359
Philadelphia Newspapers Inc. v. Hepps, **1986** 355-368
Philbin, Phil (D-Mass.), **1980** 413
Philby, H. A. R. "Kim," in Soviet spy network, **1979** 906, 908, 911, 913
Philip Morris, **1992** 564
  claims settlement, **1997** 331; **1998** 842
  FDA regulations on tobacco sales, **1996** 598-599
  liability in lung cancer death, **1988** 311
Philippe, Guy (Haiti rebel leader)
  and Haiti political situation, **2001** 397; **2004** 95, 96
  as Haiti presidential candidate, **2005** 331
Philippine Islands
  Arroyo presidential inauguration, **2001** 102-108
  B. Aquino assassination reports, **1984** 925-932
  Catholic clergy in, **1986** 318
  cease-fire agreement, **1986** 1037-1046
  constitution
    approval of, **1987** 844-845, 848
    provisional, **1986** 307-314
  coup attempt against C. Aquino, **1987** 843-850
  election of C. Aquino and ouster of Marcos, **1986** 307-314
  hostage in Iraq, **2004** 882
  human rights in, **1981** 187-188; **1984** 166-167; **1985** 154-155; **1986** 97-98, 110-111; **1987** 189-191, 201-202; **1988** 106-108; **1989** 58
    and U.S. aid, **1977** 3-4, 20-25
  Iraq troop withdrawal, **2004** 882
  as issue in U.S. presidential campaign, **1984** 897-899
  John Paul II visit, **1981** 203, 205-208
  labor strikes in, **1987** 843, 845-846, 850-851
  Marcoses' looting of funds from, **1988** 867-872
  political situation, **2001** 102-106
  at poverty summit, **1981** 770
  Reagan visit, cancellation of, **1983** 893
  SARS (severe acute respiratory syndrome) outbreak, **2003** 132
  terrorist link to al Qaeda network, **2001** 687
  terrorist sinking of a ferry, **2004** 536
  U.S. bases in, and U.S. aid, **1977** 4, 24-25
  U.S. policy toward, **1986** 307-310
  withdrawal of U.S. troops from, **1992** 1053-1058
Phillabaum, Jerry L., Abu Ghraib prison scandal, **2004** 209, 233
Phillips, Howard J., and dismantling of OEO, **1973** 453-464
Philosophy, in undergraduate education, **1984** 997-1003
Philpot, Charles, **1988** 942
Phoenix (Arizona), school uniform policy, **1996** 92
Photography, forensic, and Peary's North Pole claim, **1989** 688, 694-695
PHS. *See* Public Health Service
Physical exercise
  benefits of, **1993** 626

benefits of, surgeon general on, **1996** 418-429
recommendations, **2005** 10-11
Physical Fitness and Sports, President's Council on, **1997** 158-171
Physician Task Force on hunger in U.S., **1985** 189-205
Physician-assisted suicide
end-of-life care and, **1997** 326
federal appeals court on, **1996** 121-132
House bar on, **1999** 441-442
legalization of, **1997** 329
Oregon ballot measure approved, **1994** 501-512; **1997** 461-463
Oregon legislation, **2001** 290-293
Supreme Court on, **1997** 459-479
Physicians
Carter criticism of profession, **1978** 327-328, 337-338
choice of, in Carter's health insurance proposal, **1978** 543, 547
commercial interests in human tissues and cells, **1987** 351, 371-372
as entrepreneurs in for-profit hospitals, **1986** 489, 508-510
malpractice insurance, **1987** 166-167, 172, 175
minority admissions to medical school, **1978** 467-492
payment of, and Medicare reform, **1986** 280-281
responsibility toward terminally ill, **1984** 275-285
role in AIDS education and counseling, **1987** 822-824, 827
Physicians Committee for Responsible Medicine, **1992** 398-399
Physicians for Responsible Negotiations, **1999** 633, 812
Physicians for the Prevention of Nuclear War, International, Nobel Peace Prize, **1985** 781-787
Piccigallo, Philip R., **1992** 898
Picco, Giandomenico, hostage negotiations, **1991** 753
Pickens, T. Boone, Jr., as folk hero, **1986** 972, 978
Pickering, Charles W., Sr., Senate confirmation rejected, **2002** 823
Pickering, Thomas R.
U.S. air strikes against terrorists, **1998** 587
U.S. bombing of Chinese embassy, **1999** 306-316
violence on the Temple Mount, **1990** 696
Pien, Howard, flu vaccine shortage, **2004** 640
Pierce, Samuel R., Jr., HUD abuses under, **1989** 333-337
Pierce v. Society of Sisters, **2000** 292
Pietrasinski, Leszek, **1985** 120
Pietruszka, Adam, and Polish priest's killing, **1985** 120-123, 125
Pike, John E.
NASA's future goals, **1990** 755
space mission failures, **1999** 715
Pike, Otis G. (D-N.Y.), leaks from House committee, **1976** 116-117
Piks, Richard, NATO membership for Latvia, **2004** 136
Pilarcyzk, Daniel E., **1986** 986
Pilcher, Carl, on *Lunar Prospector* mission, **1998** 118
Pileggi, Nicholas, **1991** 814
Pilgrim, Gary, mutual funds scandal, **2003** 696
Pilgrim Baxter and Associates, mutual funds scandal, **2003** 696
Pillari, Ross, oil company profits, congressional testimony on, **2005** 794-796
Pillay, Navanethem, Rwanda war crimes tribunal, **2003** 1073
Pilling, Stephen, antidepressant therapy for children, **2004** 750
Pillinger, Colin, Mars *Express* launch leader, **2003** 303
Pinchot, Gifford, **1999** 593, 596
Pinchot, Peter, **1999** 593
Pincus, Harold, on depression, **2002** 267
Pine Ridge Indian Reservation, and AIM occupation of Wounded Knee, **1973** 531-535
Pinochet, Augusto
at Alwyn's presidential inaugural, **1990** 187-189
coup led by, **1975** 910-911
dictator of Chile, **2005** 771
free elections in Chile, **2005** 293
and human rights in Chile, **1985** 150; **1987** 193-194
war crimes, **2002** 606
Pioneer II, fly-by of Saturn, **1980** 990
Piot, Peter
AIDS epidemic in Africa, **1999** 489
AIDS treatment and prevention, **2003** 785; **2004** 431
global AIDS epidemic, UN reports on, **2000** 411-412; **2002** 469; **2004** 429-430; **2005** 50
HIV/AIDS epidemic, **1998** 878
Piotrowski, Grzegorz, Polish priest's killing, **1985** 120-123, 125
Pirkle, James, on secondhand smoke, **1993** 64
Pistole, John, FBI intimidation of suspects, **2003** 611
Pitney, Jack, midterm election results, **2002** 822
Pitofsky, Robert
entertainment industry regulations, **2000** 732
FTC chairman on corporate mergers, **1998** 338-353
on unionization of doctors, **1999** 633
Pitt, Harvey L.
accounting board controversy, **2002** 1032-1035
as SEC chairman, **2002** 1035-1036
SEC chairman resignation, **2002** 392, 880, 1032; **2003** 338
Pitts, Earl Edwin, espionage case, **1996** 794, 795-796
Pitts, Joy L., medical records privacy, **2001** 488
Pittsburg and Midway Coal Co., UMW contract with, **1978** 113
Pittston Company (Pittston Coal Group), **1990** 19-22
Pius VI (pope), creation of first U.S. Catholic diocese (1789), **1989** 619, 621
Pius XII (pope), and Jews during the Holocaust, **1998** 122, 123; **2000** 79
PJM Interconnection, power blackout investigation, **2003** 1015
Plaisted, Ralph, **1988** 833
Plakett, Thomas, Pan Am bombing, **1990** 304
Plame, Valerie, CIA leak case, **2003** 20, 21; **2005** 249, 699-716
Planned Parenthood Assn. of Kansas City, Mo., Inc. v. Ashcroft, **1983** 545, 565-571; **1990** 400, 401, 402

Planned Parenthood Federation of America
abortion, informed consent legislation, **2005** 819
morning-after pill, **2005** 816
partial-birth abortion, **2003** 998
Planned Parenthood of Central Missouri v. Danforth, **1976** 483-488; **1990** 391, 395, 400, 401, 402
Planned Parenthood of Southeastern Pa. v. Casey, **1992** 589-613; **1996** 125-127; **1997** 373, 465-466; **2000** 429-446
Plant Patent Act (1930), **1980** 493-494, 497-498, 501
Plant Variety Protection Act (1970), **1980** 443-494, 497-498, 501-502
Plavsic, Biljana, Kosovo war crimes, **2001** 826
Plaza, Galo, **1983** 375
Pledge of Allegiance
Bush on, **1988** 559, 591, 609, 613
federal court of appeals on, **2002** 382-390; **2005** 376
in presidential campaign, **1988** 722, 734; **1989** 344-345
Rehnquist views on, **2005** 552
Republican Party platform on, **1988** 651
Plessy v. Ferguson, **1990** 434-435; **1991** 31; **1992** 37-38, 42; **1995** 456
Pliusch, Ivan, **1991** 533
PLO. *See* Palestine Liberation Organization
Plowden, Warren, on sexual harassment in schools, **1999** 218
Pluto, as large object and not planet, **2002** 215-216
Plutonium
commercial reprocessing of, Carter on halt to, **1977** 271-272, 274
controls on use of, Ford policy, **1976** 823-825, 827-828, 830, 832, 836
Plyler v. Doe, **1982** 489-506
Podesta, John, Marc Rich presidential pardon, **2001** 91
Podgorny, Nikolai V.
ouster from Politburo, **1977** 748
signing of Soviet-Egyptian treaty, **1976** 169
U.S.-Soviet environment agreement, **1972** 806
Poe v. Ullman, **1997** 189, 476
Poelker v. Doe, **1977** 407-409, 427-430
Pohl, Karl Otto, **1985** 624
Poindexter, John M.
circumvention of Congress, **1987** 905
disinformation campaign against Libya, **1986** 351
indictment, **1989** 392-394; **1994** 9, 12
indictment and appeal, **1998** 906
Iran-contra affair
charges dismissed, **1992** 1075
conviction, **1990** 492, 493; **2002** 561
conviction overturned, **1991** 618-619
role in, **1986** 1016-1017, 1023, 1049-1051, 1053
congressional committee on, **1987** 892-893, 895, 897-899, 920
Tower Commission on, **1987** 208, 216, 218, 222, 225-226, 232
limited immunity for, **1987** 892
Pentagon "data mining" system, **2002** 559-568
shielding president, **1987** 897-898, 902, 907, 917, 919, 922-923, 925
Pokrovsky, Vadim, AIDS/HIV infection in Russia, **2002** 471
Pol Pot, death of, **1998** 972
Poland
anarchy in, Brezhnev on, **1981** 225, 228
border with East Germany, **1989** 627
Carter visit, **1977** 897-913
Catholic Church in, **1979** 727-728
debt rescheduling by, **1981** 885
economy and production, instability of, **1981** 883
elections in, **1989** 400, 523-538
EU membership, **2004** 198; **2005** 340
food supply and prices in, **1980** 793-794, 799-800
German designs alleged, **1990** 106, 108
German land claims, **1990** 600, 601
health problems, **1994** 415-430
human rights in, **1977** 898, 903-905; **1982** 107, 116-117; **1985** 153-154; **1988** 94
Iraq War, support for, **2003** 42, 49-51, 138
John Paul II visits, **1979** 725, 727-728, 738-741; **1983** 577-593; **1987** 555-564
Katyn massacre, **1990** 223-225
market reforms, **1992** 644
martial law, **1985** 119; **1987** 184-187
declaration of, **1981** 881-897
suspension of, **1982** 947-953
U.S. economic retaliation against Soviets, **1982** 563, 879-880, 882, 949
NATO membership, **1994** 583; **1997** 514, 516; **1999** 119, 120, 126-127; **2004** 136, 198
Nazi invasion of, anniversary of, **1989** 487-490, 492-494
Nobel Peace Prize for Walesa, government reaction to, **1983** 926
political liberalization in, **1989** 635-636
power sharing by communist government, **1989** 412-416, 420-421, 430-431, 434, 710
priest's killing, **1985** 119-126
Soviet domination over, **1989** 523, 525, 536-538
Soviet propaganda about, Project Truth on, **1981** 762
trade union activity in, **1980** 793-802; **1987** 183-186, 556-564
troops in Iraq, **2004** 882-883
U.S. economic aid for
Bush on, **1989** 412-414, 416, 420
Walesa plea for, **1989** 536-538
U.S. economic sanctions against, **1981** 884, 895-896
U.S. support for people of, **1981** 89; **1982** 83
U.S. trade agreements with, **1972** 846; **1974** 883-886
U.S. trade sanctions against, lifting of, **1987** 183-188
Walesa's apology to Israel for anti-Semitism, **1991** 253-256
Warsaw Pact
dissolution, **1991** 399, 399-401
military maneuvers in, **1981** 881, 894
Western economic aid for, **1989** 432-433
World War II struggles of, Walesa on, **1989** 524-525, 536
Poland, Greg, flu vaccine shortage, **2004** 642
Polar Lander mission investigation, **1999** 711-717; **2000** 89, 95-102; **2003** 302; **2004** 4

Poli, Robert E., **1981** 622
Police, murder of, mandatory death penalty for, **1977** 397-405
Police conduct
for access to medical records, **1997** 583
and exclusionary rule, **1984** 506-519
LAPD abuses, **1991** 403-428
and Miranda warning, **1985** 223-253; **1990** 785-793
Philadelphia raid on MOVE group, **1986** 239-251
racial profiling, **2000** 773; **2001** 179
riots after Rodney King beating, **1992** 407-429
Rodney King case, sentencing of officers, **1993** 631-651
rules for warrantless entry and home arrest, **1980** 283, 291, 295-296
use of deadly force, **1985** 303-315
Police Foundation, on domestic violence, **1983** 357-364
Polin, Colin, State Department appointment, **2000** 1027
Poling, Harold A., **1983** 12, 14, 19-20; **1992** 11
Polish Communist Party, trade unions' independence from, **1980** 793-797
Political action committees (PACs)
campaign contribution and spending limits, **1976** 72-73, 75-85
GOPAC and Gingrich ethics violations, **1995** 748-751
spending limits, constitutionality of, **1985** 277-294
Political affiliation, and discharge from public employment, **1980** 259-271
Political asylum. *See* Asylum, political
Political candidates, right to reply and media access, **1974** 523-528
Political participation
by American blacks, **1989** 446, 453
for blacks in South Africa, **1989** 545, 547, 550
and campaign financing limits, **1976** 71-87, 104-111
effect of Watergate scandal on, **1973** 550, 555; **1976** 14, 26-27
and open primaries, **1986** 1065-1073
Political parties
See also American Independent Party; Democratic Party; Republican Party
exhaustion of U.S., McGovern on, **1973** 87, 90
minor, financing of campaigns of, **1976** 89-90, 93-96, 106-107, 110-111
right of to hold open primaries, **1986** 1065-1073
strengthening, National '80s Agenda on, **1981** 39, 55-56
Political prisoners, Amnesty International report on, **1989** 597-609
Politkovskaya, Ana
hostage release in Russia, **2002** 764
on terrorist attacks in Russia, **2005** 304
Polk, James K., **1984** 20
Pollack, J. B., on effects of nuclear war, **1983** 857, 860-882; **1985** 542
Pollack, Ron
uninsured Americans (health), **2002** 666
uninsured and welfare reform, **2000** 788
Pollard, Jonathan J., **1998** 743-744
Pollock, Richard, **1979** 825
Pollution control
See also Air pollution and air quality; Hazardous waste; Ocean pollution; Water pollution
costs of
for industry, **1972** 253-258
Nixon on meeting in marketplace, **1973** 216
global cooperation in, **1973** 519, 523; **1981** 26-27
Polybrominated biphenyls (PBB), contamination of animal feed by, **1978** 653-658
Pombo, Richard W. (R-Calif.), Chinese ownership of U.S. oil firms, **2005** 615-616
Ponce, Ren Emilio, resignation of, **1993** 238
Ponte, Carla del, Kosovo war crimes investigations, **1999** 804
Pontifical Commission for Religious Relations with the Jews, **1998** 121, 124
Poole, William, CEA report, **1984** 119; **1985** 80
Pope (Catholic). *See under names of individuals*
Pope, Barbara Spyridon, **1992** 482
Pope v. Blue, **1993** 463
Pope v. Illinois, **1987** 479-490
Popieluszko, Jerzy, killing of, **1985** 119-126, 154; **1987** 557
Poppleton, Richard, Evers assassination retrial, **1994** 104
Popular Front for the Liberation of Palestine (PFLP)
Mustafa assassination, **2001** 364
PLO acceptance of UN resolution 242, **1988** 907
terrorism by, CIA on, **1981** 463-468
Population
aging in U.S., **1996** 296-301
Bucharest UN conference on, **1974** 777-797
Catholic Church views, **1994** 277, 351-352
environmental impacts of, **1980** 665-666, 670, 673-676, 696-697
Hispanic, U.S. Census report on, **2001** 314-324; **2003** 349-357
Native Americans, Census Bureau report, **2003** 576-577
UN Population Conference, **1994** 351-359
U.S.
Census 1990, **1992** 475-478
proclamation, **1990** 169-174
undercount, **1991** 443-449
ecologically sound level of, **1972** 301-312
U.S. population, U.S. census report on, **2001** 314-315
worldwide, **1996** 305; **1999** 584-591; **2001** 314, 318-319
Population control
See also Family planning
in China, **1999** 586-587
in developing countries, **1987** 439, 441, 448-453, 456-459
policy in, **1984** 528-529, 534-537
and food supply, UN conference on, **1974** 940-941, 948-949
Population growth
in developing countries
to bolster development, **1974** 777-779
impacts of, **1987** 439-453, 458-461
Sakharov on, **1975** 919
in world, **1974** 778, 780; **1984** 521-547

Population growth *Continued*
and maximum development of the earth, **1972** 215-220
NATO concern about, **1975** 354, 358
presidential debates on, **1984** 891-902
strategies to counteract, **1981** 13, 18-19
UNICEF on, **1981** 915-916
Population Growth and the American Future, Commission on, **1972** 301-312
Population Institute, on population growth in developing countries, **1987** 439-461
Population policy, of developing countries, **1984** 528-529, 534-547
Population Research Center, on racial segregation, **1989** 447
Pornography
See also Obscenity
advertising brochure for illustrated version of report on, **1974** 515-522
child, **1982** 675-688; **1990** 239-249; **1992** 313-327
decency in the arts, Supreme Court on, **1998** 405-418
definition of, **2002** 290
definitions of obscenity, **1973** 611-628
and the Internet, **1997** 444-458
Internet ban, **1996** 353-361
Internet pornography filters in public libraries, Supreme Court on, **2003** 387-400
Internet pornography in libraries, federal court on, **2002** 287-297
sale of in adult bookstores, and community standards, **1987** 479-490
virtual pornography, **2002** 289-290
zoning for adult theaters, **1986** 131-144
Poroshenko, Petro, Ukrainian cabinet resignation, **2005** 68
Porter, Anthony, victim of death row, **1999** 829
Porter, James R., **1993** 407, 507-508
Porter, John (Rev.), on hate crimes, **2002** 242
Porter, John Edward (R-Ill.), federal advisory panels, NAS study, **2004** 844
Porter, Roger B.
at education summit, **1989** 562
national education goals, **1990** 153-163
on parents' role in education, **1989** 86
Portland General Electric, **2004** 417
Portman, Rob (R-Ohio)
IRS reform, **1997** 663
WTO negotiations, **2005** 411
Ports, deepwater, construction of in energy crisis, **1973** 465, 479
Portugal
aid to Nazi Germany, **1997** 259, 262, 263; **1998** 291, 292
allied relations and negotiations with, **1998** 298-301
Angola's independence from, **1988** 947
Arab oil embargo against, **1974** 221, 256
Communist Party in, **1975** 276, 353-354
euro currency, **1998** 271
German assets, **1997** 267
Iraq War, support for, **2003** 42, 49-51
socialism in, **1976** 441
student test scores, **1992** 91, 94
Posey, Billy Wayne, civil rights workers slayings trial, **2005** 355
Posey, Robert Owen, church bombing trial, prosecution statement, **2002** 241, 242-246
Posner, Paul L., on deficit reduction, **1996** 147-148
Posner, Richard, Microsoft Corp. antitrust case, **1999** 654-689; **2000** 106
Posse Comitatus Act (1878), **2002** 534-535
Post Co. v. National Citizens Committee for Broadcasting, **1978** 419-432
Postal Service (U.S.)
See also Mail
child pornography sting, **1992** 314-318
private competition for, **1986** 59, 61, 88-89
proposed end to monopoly of, **1988** 230, 233-234
use of for domestic spying, **1976** 273-274
Postol, Theodore A., missile defense system, **2000** 679; **2002** 1029
Poston, Keith, on literacy and jobs, **1993** 739
Post-traumatic stress disorder (PTSD), among rape victims, **1992** 393-394
Potok, Mark, hate crimes, **2005** 678
Potomac International Corp., and Allen investigation, **1981** 848
Potsdam Conference, and division of Germany, **1986** 792
Potsdam Treaty, **1990** 599-600
Potter, John, anthrax mailings, **2001** 675
Potts, Stephen D., **1992** 295-299
Pound, Richard W., International Olympics Committee investigations, **1999** 106
Poussaint, Alvin F., on mental health of African Americans, **1983** 42-43, 49
Poverty
See also Social service programs; Welfare reform
and abortion, public funding for, **1977** 408-430
among blacks in America, **1983** 41-55, 766; **1987** 43-45, 48-50, 59
among children and the elderly in U.S., **1988** 877-880
among urban minorities, Kerner Commission update on, **1988** 185-194
among young families, **1992** 353-360
Annan report ("We the Peoples"), **2000** 700-701
Capability Poverty Measure, **1996** 439
Catholic Church's preference for the poor, **1984** 760, 762-764, 766, 770-772; **1985** 57-58, 60-61; **1986** 317-338
census figures show, **1992** 475-478
children in, **1999** 384-385
childrens' deaths and, UNICEF on, **1981** 911-912
combating with sustainable economic development, **1981** 15-16, 27-28
commitment to poor, Democratic platform on, **1984** 550, 598-600, 602, 616-618
in developing countries
John Paul II on, **1988** 167-168, 174
meeting basic human needs, **1977** 700-704, 710-715
dignity and human rights in, John Paul II on, **1981** 204, 206
economic aftermath of September 11, **2001** 670-671

economic growth's effect on, **1981** 42-43, 53; **1984** 868-871
and effects of tax reform and balanced budget legislation, **1987** 51-54
eradicating
as moral responsibility of industrialized countries, **1980** 887-893
as role for activist Catholic clergy, **1979** 725-727, 731
role of church in, John Paul II on, **1986** 25, 27-28, 30-34
and U.S. foreign aid policy, **1982** 107
extreme poverty defined, **2002** 689
Heavily Indebted Poor Countries (HIPC) debt-relief initiative, **2000** 483, 484; **2003** 761
Hurricane Katrina disaster aftermath and, **2005** 140-141
impact of Reagan budget cuts, **1981** 214, 216-217, 327, 640; **1983** 765-772
international summit (Cancún) on, **1981** 769-778
in Latin America, **1983** 375, 382, 452
minimum and youth wage effect on, **1983** 785, 788-789
minimum wage and, **2005** 490
opportunities for poor, Republican platform on, **1984** 696-697
Quayle on, **1992** 447-448
rates in America, **1997** 53, 60, 69; **1998** 74, 85, 365; **2002** 55; **2003** 73; **2004** 58; **2005** 111
among African Americans, **1999** 390; **2000** 53; **2002** 55
among children, **2002** 55
among the elderly, **1998** 99, 104; **2005** 111
among foreign-born, **1997** 181
among Hispanics, **1999** 390; **2000** 53
and sports opportunities for girls, **1997** 158-159, 168-169
UN summit on, **1995** 134-140
and urban school crisis, **1988** 195-199, 206-207, 218
in U.S.
declining state aid, **1991** 827-842
and health care access, **1983** 330, 333
and hunger and malnutrition, **1985** 190-193, 195-199, 201-202
and minority health, **1985** 687, 693
and U.S. economic policies, Catholic bishops on, **1984** 957-972; **1986** 984-985, 987-990, 992-994, 998-1002
in U.S. households headed by minority women, **1982** 931-932
world poverty reduction
G-8 summit leader on, **2000** 475-487
UN Millennium Summit Declaration, **2000** 706-708
Powell, Colin L.
affirmative action, **2003** 360, 368-370, 373, 383-386
Afghanistan detainees, and Geneva Conventions, **2004** 337
African economic development plan, **2002** 451
American spy plane incident in China, **2001** 249
Angolan humanitarian aid, **2002** 156
chemical weapons, **1997** 201, 742
Colombia, visit to, **2002** 574
Cuba, Commission for Assistance to a Free Cuba, **2004** 246-248, 250-257
on Farrakhan and Million Man March, **1995** 657
Georgia (country)
election negotiations, **2003** 1045
at presidential inauguration, **2004** 73
Guantanamo Bay detainees, **2003** 109
Haiti
on Aristide resignation and exile, **2004** 96
violence during visit, **2004** 100
India-Pakistan relations, **2001** 965
Indonesia, visit to, **2002** 703
Iran-contra affair and, **1994** 19
Iraq
disarmament, UN resolution on, **2002** 715-716
Niger uranium sales, **2005** 700
replacing Saddam Hussein, **2002** 614
UNSC speech, **2003** 45, 47; **2004** 717-718; **2005** 700
Liberia, U.S. intervention, **2003** 770
Libya
meeting at United Nations, **2004** 172
U.S. sanctions, **2003** 1223-1224
Lott's racial remarks, **2002** 972
McCain amendment on detainees treatment, **2005** 909-910
Middle East
cease-fire negotiations, **2002** 932
Geneva Accord, **2003** 1204, 1205
international "roadmap" for peace, **2003** 196
Israeli-Palestinian conflict, **2004** 629
Middle East Initiative, **2004** 628
peace process, **2001** 365-367; **2002** 372-373, 377
state visits, **2003** 198; **2004** 810
military homosexual ban, **1993** 153
missile defense system, **2000** 681
national security needs, **1993** 695
national security strategy, **2002** 634
NATO expansion, **2004** 136
North Korean relations, **2001** 268; **2002** 732
nuclear test ban treaty, **1998** 49
President's Volunteerism Summit, **1997** 40, 238-244
Republican Party convention speech, **1996** 478-479; **2000** 511
Russia
diplomatic relations, **2004** 569-570
nuclear weapons reduction, **2001** 21
role in NATO, **2001** 896
Saudi Arabia, state visit, **2003** 229; **2004** 522
secretary of state
nomination, **2001** 96
resignation, **2004** 629-630, 718, 778; **2005** 44-45
September 11 attacks, responsibility for, **2001** 804-805
Sudan
genocidal war, **2004** 115, 588-601; **2005** 515
peace negotiations, **2003** 841
Syria, U.S. sanctions against, **2004** 55
trafficking in humans report, **2002** 324
tsunami relief effort, **2004** 993-995; **2005** 992
Ukraine, at presidential inauguration, **2005** 65
UN conference against racism, **2001** 603-604

Powell, Colin L. *Continued*
UN multinational force authorization, **2003** 945
UN sanctions and weapons inspections, **2001** 850; **2003** 41, 879
UNSC speech on weapons of mass destruction, **2003** 45, 47; **2004** 717-718; **2005** 700
U.S. foreign policy adviser, **2003** 453
U.S.-Middle East Partnership, **2002** 487
U.S.-Russian nuclear arms treaty, **2002** 279-280
U.S.-Russian relations, **2001** 153
weapons of mass destruction, **2003** 877, 879
World Summit on Sustainable Development, **2002** 596
Zimbabwe
elections, **2002** 135
political situation, **2003** 1116
Powell, Donald, Hurricane Katrina disaster reconstruction (New Orleans), **2005** 545, 568
Powell, Jody
Carter warehouse investigation, **1979** 803
Carter's appointment of Jordan, **1979** 561
ethics guidelines, **1977** 28
presidential press conferences, **1988** 836
Powell, Laurence M., King case indictment and sentencing, **1992** 409; **1993** 631-651
Powell, Lewis, affirmative action, **2003** 362
Powell, Lewis F.
abortion
and privacy right, **1973** 102
public funding of, **1977** 408, 411-424; **1980** 515
right to, **1987** 579
state and local restrictions on, **1983** 543-557, 565-569, 573-576; **1986** 559
affirmative action
admissions to medical school, **1978** 468-469, 471-478
promotion of women, **1987** 332-333, 578
and seniority protections, **1984** 366
age discrimination, **1983** 232, 239
aliens, education for children of, **1982** 490
antitrust immunity of cities, **1982** 35
auto searches, **1978** 753; **1982** 425
bankruptcy and labor contracts, **1984** 182
bankruptcy law, **1982** 597
broadcast of offensive material, **1978** 515, 517, 525-526
child pornography, **1982** 675
church and state separation
church objection to liquor license, **1982** 956-961
public display of Nativity scene, **1984** 218
religious organizations' use of campus buildings, **1981** 869-875
civil rights cases, **1989** 321
class action suits, **1974** 427-432
clean air regulations, **1984** 427
corporate free speech in referendum campaigns, **1978** 307-308, 310-315
counsel, right to
and interrogation, **1981** 433
and police procedure, **1977** 220, 228-229
Court division, **1981** 576
Court workload, **1975** 462; **1982** 705-706, 712-715
creation science, **1987** 566, 572-574
death penalty, **1987** 578
constitutionality of state laws on, **1972** 499, 504; **1976** 489-491, 503, 506
mandatory for murder of police officer, **1977** 397
mitigating factors, **1982** 51-56
racial discrimination in, **1987** 463-473
for rape, **1977** 517, 528
standing of mother to request stay, **1976** 918, 920
state's misuse of, **1980** 455, 457
electronic surveillance
covert entry for, **1979** 269-278
by law enforcement without warrant, **1972** 485-489
federal and state powers, **1976** 378; **1985** 168-169, 182-187
handicapped infants, treatment of, **1986** 543, 545
home video taping, **1984** 54-55, 69
immunity of municipalities, **1980** 299-300, 308-316
intra-enterprise conspiracy doctrine, **1984** 414
job discrimination, suit against member of Congress, **1979** 399, 401, 408, 410-411
judicial deference to policy makers, **1987** 578
judicial immunity, **1978** 260-261, 266, 268
jury selection, racially motivated, **1986** 410-421
jury trials, split verdicts in, **1972** 423
labor unions, freedom of members to resign, **1985** 415-424
lawyer advertising, **1982** 65-71
legislative veto, **1983** 610, 634
libel of private and public persons, **1986** 355
mentally retarded, rights of, **1982** 521-529
minority set-asides in federal contracts, **1980** 539, 541, 552-558
Miranda warnings, and definition of interrogation, **1980** 431
NAACP boycott damages, **1982** 656
Nixon papers and tapes, custody of, **1977** 488-492
oath of office for Gov. Wilder, administered by, **1990** 41
obscenity, legal tests for, **1987** 479
open primaries, **1986** 1065
OSHA safety inspections, warrants for, **1978** 340
parental leave
and job discrimination, **1987** 17, 25
and seniority rights, **1977** 872, 877-880
parental rights in child custody, **1982** 260
patenting of living organisms, **1980** 494, 500
political asylum, **1987** 253-256, 262-265
political firings from public jobs, **1980** 259-260, 266-271
pregnancy coverage in company disability plans, **1976** 892
on presidential immunity, **1982** 539-550
press freedoms
access to pretrial hearings, **1979** 511-512, 522-524
confidentiality of sources, **1972** 507
gag orders and right to fair trial, **1976** 464, 478-479
libel of public figure, **1979** 285, 287, 297-298
newsroom searches, **1978** 355, 367
preventive detention, **1987** 491

prison crowding, **1981** 477-484
property takings, and historic preservation, **1978** 453
public aid to nonpublic schools, **1973** 642-643, 646-658; **1977** 432, 443-444; **1985** 433
racial discrimination, in private school admission, **1976** 392, 398-400
redistricting
gerrymandering in, **1986** 617-618, 632-635
one-man, one-vote rule, **1973** 279; **1983** 600, 612-616
racial criteria in, **1977** 152, 163
retirement of, **1987** 577-581, 717-718
school book banning, **1982** 567, 580
school desegregation
compensatory remedies for, **1977** 463-464
cross-district remedies for, **1974** 639
restrictions on busing, **1982** 619, 633
school financing based on property tax, **1973** 361-372
school prayer, **1985** 380-381; **1987** 578
schools, judicial intervention in operation of, **1975** 68-69, 75-80; **1979** 536-537, 542, 551
searches
evidence from illegal, **1976** 521-531
prisoners' rights, **1984** 480
sentences, excessive prison, **1983** 659-674
sentencing, and double jeopardy, **1980** 977
sex discrimination
in alimony payments, **1979** 193, 194, 205-206
in education, **1984** 202-203, 210-212
in employer pension plans, **1978** 293
by Jaycees, **1984** 468
in military draft, **1981** 521
in pension plans, **1983** 691-693, 701-704
in Social Security benefits, **1975** 178, 184-185; **1977** 169
in statutory rape laws, **1981** 339
snail darter protection from dam project, **1978** 434-435, 446-451
sodomy and privacy right, **1986** 601, 603, 607-608
state and federal powers, **1987** 579
students' rights
and corporal punishment, **1977** 293-303
free speech, **1986** 731
in searches, **1985** 14
suspects' rights and public safety, **1984** 388
tax exemptions for discriminatory schools, **1983** 490-491, 502-503
treaty termination, **1979** 917-918, 933-935
tuition tax credit, **1983** 676-677, 684-688
unitary taxation, **1983** 645, 657-658
utilities regulation, **1982** 448
water rights, **1982** 689
windfall profits tax on oil, **1983** 518-523
wiretapping authorization procedures of attorney general, **1974** 392, 399
zoning regulations
for adult theaters, **1986** 132-133
barring low-income and minority housing, **1977** 35-43
Powell v. McCormack, **1995** 262, 264, 267
Powell committee, **1990** 311, 316-317
Power plants
See also Energy industry; Nuclear power plants
air quality regulations, **2001** 215-216, 218
hydroelectric power, U.S. aid to China for, **1979** 670, 676
industry deregulation, **2003** 1015, 1016-1017
mercury emissions, EPA regulations on, **2005** 95-110
new electric power plants, **2001** 335
Poyakov, Vladimir P., **1976** 171
Prabhakaran, Velupillai (Tamil Tigers leader)
Indo-Sri Lankan accord, **1987** 617
Sri Lanka peace process, **2002** 94, 95-96
Prague Spring, **1975** 239-240, 242-245; **1989** 399-400, 636-637
Pratt Kelly, Sharon, mayor of D.C., **1995** 498
Pravda, on Soviet election, **1989** 176-177
Precourt, Charles, **1995** 423
Pregnancy
See also Parental leave; Teenagers, pregnancy
aids testing for pregnant women, **1995** 441-452
in employer disability plans, **1976** 891-905
employer policies on, EEOC guidelines on sex discrimination, **1972** 313, 319
and ethics of fetal research, **1975** 543-556
health care during, **1987** 147-164
and hunger in U.S., **1985** 193, 196-197, 199
maternal deaths, **1996** 343-352
of military women, **1987** 672, 677-678
prenatal diagnosis, Vatican teaching on, **1987** 268, 273-274
public funding for childbirth services, **1980** 515-516, 518-519, 524, 526-528, 530, 533
smoking and, surgeon general's report on, **2004** 292-293
smoking during, **1980** 17-18, 21, 23, 26
health dangers of, **1986** 1082
and low birth weight and infant mortality, **1972** 52; **1973** 63-71
stages of, and state restrictions on abortion, **1973** 101-114
unintended pregnancies, **2003** 999
Pregnancy Discrimination Act (1978), **1987** 18-27; **1991** 143-153
Premadasa, Ranasinghe, **1987** 617
Prescription drugs
abortion pill (RU-486/mifepristone) controversy, **2001** 128; **2003** 997
advertising, **2002** 945-958
directly to consumer, **2004** 852
GAO report on, **2002** 945-958
affordable drugs from Canada, **2004** 34
Bextra, safety problems, **2004** 852
Celebrex, safety problems, **2004** 640, 852-853, 855
cholesterol lowering, **2001** 475-476
coverage for senior citizens, **2002** 949-950; **2003** 18, 23, 38-39, 1119, 1120
discount plans, Bush support for, **2001** 713
discounted for AIDS treatment, **2001** 441-443
Effexor, and risk of suicide in children, **2004** 48
FDA black box warning, **2004** 749-750
generic AIDS drugs, **2002** 472-473
hormone replacement therapy, **2002** 503-511

Prescription drugs *Continued*
importation, task force report on, **2004** 981-990
importation from Canada, **2004** 983-984
Lipitor (cholesterol-lowering drug), **2004** 983
Medicare cost estimates withheld from Congress, **2004** 577-587
and Medicare reform, **2000** 18, 24-25, 131-140; **2001** 713; **2003** 18, 23, 1119-1128; **2004** 20, 27-28, 577
Paxil, and risk of suicide in children, **2004** 748
pharmacy requirements for filling, **2005** 817
prices and pricing, **2002** 820; **2003** 783-784; **2004** 34
Prozac, side effects, **2004** 747, 748
rising costs of, **2000** 789; **2002** 946-947
Vioxx, safety problems, **2004** 640, 747, 850-866

President, U.S.
appointment power
FEC commissioners, **1976** 71-75, 98-104
independent counsel, **1988** 465-478
nominee pledge to Congress, **1973** 5, 13, 18
Tower rejection, **1989** 105, 107, 116, 120
censuring president Clinton, **1998** 633, 699
confidentiality of conversations
Court ruling on Nixon tapes and documents, **1974** 621-625, 627-629, 631-638
executive privilege for Nixon aides, **1973** 337-342
federal court rulings on Nixon tapes and documents, **1973** 841, 850-851, 853-854
Nixon on, **1973** 742, 902-903; **1974** 189-192, 196-197, 202-203, 287, 291-293
and congressional power of purse
budget reform passage, **1974** 573-575, 591-597
impoundment of appropriated funds, **1973** 3-19, 171; **1975** 135-140
congressional testimony by, Ford and historical precedent, **1974** 887-888, 898
foreign policy powers
conflict with Congress on aid to South Vietnam, **1975** 251, 256-258, 260-261, 280-281, 290, 293-294
and congressional role, Ford on, **1977** 4, 50-51
negotiation of trade agreements, **1973** 379-381, 389
recognition of foreign governments, **1979** 918, 938
treaty termination, **1979** 917-938
illness in office, **1985** 491-492
immunity of
from civil damages for official action, **1982** 539-559
from subpoena, **1973** 839-857
impeachment of, constitutional requirements on criminality, **1974** 137-143, 145-146, 149, 194-195, 199
liability of to criminal prosecution, Watergate special prosecutor on, **1975** 653, 664, 667, 678-679
national security responsibility
and Ellsberg break-in, **1974** 411-416
Nixon on, **1973** 738, 748, 750-751
Tower Commission on, **1987** 209-211, 230-231, 234-235, 237
pardon power, **1974** 811, 815, 817, 893; **1977** 96
pardons by
See also Nixon, Richard M., pardon of
Carter of Vietnam draft evaders, **1981** 371
Reagan of Felt and Miller for FBI break-ins, **1981** 371-373
power of
abuse of by Nixon, House Judiciary Committee on, **1974** 658-659, 720-724
abuse of in use of intelligence agencies, **1972** 485-489; **1975** 873, 876-882; **1976** 27, 265
blocking of legal claims against Iran, **1981** 559-573
and congressional objectives for OEO, **1973** 453-464
impairment of, Nixon on, **1973** 801-802, 808; **1974** 41, 52, 145, 147, 153
in Reagan's terms, **1989** 16-17
standby authority to vary tax rates, **1973** 684, 693-694
usurping from Congress, McGovern on, **1973** 87-95
White House aides' view of, Watergate Committee report on, **1974** 600, 605
press conferences of, **1988** 835-845
rebuilding confidence in, Ford on, **1977** 45, 48
sons of former presidents, **2001** 94
transfer of power, **1985** 491-495
war powers
bombing of North Vietnam, **1973** 3-4, 6-7, 9-13, 15, 17
congressional restriction of, **1973** 923-930
Nixon on, **1977** 323, 349-350

Presidential Advisory Commission on Consumer Protection and Quality in the Health Care Industry, **1997** 787-799; **1998** 89, 140

Presidential approval ratings
for Bush, **2003** 18-19; **2004** 479; **2005** 41
for past presidents, **2005** 41

Presidential campaigns
See also Democratic Party platform; Nominating conventions; Republican Party platform
attorney general's separation from, **1975** 672-673, 678
busing issue in Florida Democratic primary, **1972** 201-206
funds, investigation of Carter's, **1979** 801-802, 806, 809-812
Iran hostage release delay, investigation of Reagan's, **1994** 3-16
of Kennedy, **1980** 701-709
nastiness of, **1988** 760, 765-766, 777-778, 783, 892, 899, 902-903; **1989** 43
negative tone of, **1976** 778-779, 797-798, 800-801
PAC spending limits, **1985** 277-294
public financing of, Carter proposal for, **1977** 199-200, 204
shortening of, Nixon on, **1972** 887-888; **1974** 215, 219
and timing of foreign policy initiatives, **1972** 7-10; **1984** 812

Presidential candidates, sons of former presidents, **2000** 519

Presidential Clemency Board, **1977** 97-98
Presidential commissions
Americans missing in Southeast Asia, **1977** 207-218
Assignment of Women in the Armed Forces, **1993** 334
Report on Women in Combat, **1992** 1029-1044
on Aviation Security and Terrorism, **1990** 301-310
coal industry, **1978** 119, 124
on Consumer Protection and Quality in the Health Care Industry, **1997** 787-799; **1998** 89, 140
on Critical Infrastructure Protection, **1997** 711-720; **1998** 677
ethics in biomedical and behavioral research, **1983** 279-303
food assistance in U.S., **1984** 3-17
government efficiency. *See* Grace Commission
HIV epidemic, **1988** 415-446
Holocaust, **1981** 382
on Implementation of U.S. Space Exploration Policy, **2004** 11
on Intelligence Capabilities of the U.S. Regarding Weapons of Mass Destruction, **2005** 246-266
National Agenda for the 80s, **1981** 39-56
on Ocean Policy, **2004** 602-625
organized crime
combating crime, **1986** 179, 210-216
drugs, **1986** 179-200
labor union corruption, **1986** 179-180, 200-210
privatization, **1988** 229-239
school financing, **1972** 221-233
stock market crash, **1988** 9-25
on Strengthening Social Security, **2001** 913-926
Three Mile Island accident, **1979** 823-863
on U.S. Intelligence Failures, **2005** 246-266
worker-management relations, future of, **1995** 15-23
Presidential debates
Bush (George H. W.)-Dukakis
U.C.L.A., **1988** 721-723, 754-783
Wake Forest University, **1988** 721-722, 724-753
Bush(George W.)-Gore debates, **2000** 797-800
first debate, **2000** 800-810
second debate, **2000** 817-824
third debate, **2000** 824-832
Bush(George W.)-Kerry debates, **2004** 675-708
first debate: focus on Iraq, **2004** 675-676, 679-690
second debate: town hall meeting, **2004** 676-677, 691-701
third debate: domestic issues, **2004** 677-678, 701-708
Carter-Reagan, Cleveland, **1980** 919-951
Clinton-Dole debates, **1996** 707-709, 709-718, 724-731
Ford-Carter
Philadelphia, **1976** 693-719
San Francisco, **1976** 733-757
Williamsburg, **1976** 797-821
Nader barred from attending, **2000** 798-799, 897
Perot Reform Party exclusion from, **1996** 50, 552, 707
Reagan-Anderson, Baltimore, **1980** 847-869
Reagan-Mondale
Kansas City, **1984** 846-847, 876-902
Louisville, **1984** 845-876
Presidential Debates, Commission on, as sponsor, **1988** 723
Presidential elections
Bush vs. Gore (2000), **2000** 520, 999-1024; **2001** 94, 522-525
Bush vs. Kerry (2004), **2004** 17, 40-41, 58-59, 259-262
direct popular vote, **1977** 199-200, 204-205
effect of Iran hostage taking, **1979** 879
Hispanic voters, **2003** 350
interference with, **1974** 608, 610-611
results, **1972** 893-896; **1973** 87-88, 90-91, 94; **1976** 841-843, 847-849, 851-853; **1980** 959-963; **1984** 953-956; **1988** 723, 891-904; **2004** 478
Presidential findings. *See* Findings, presidential
Presidential immunity, Supreme Court on, **1997** 290-298
Presidential impeachment. *See* Impeachment, presidential
Presidential inaugurations
See also Inaugural addresses
bicentennial of, **1989** 123-125, 133-135
Presidential papers
custody of Nixon's papers, Court on, **1977** 465-516
declassification of, **1972** 244
edited transcripts of White House tapes, release of, **1974** 287-299
executive privilege for, **1973** 742, 839-857, 859-880, 960-961
House Judiciary Committee's access to, **1974** 192, 196-197, 202-203, 302-304, 655, 659, 724-728, 751-752
Kennedy library dedication, **1979** 813-821
Nixon library, **1992** 256
Nixon on protection of, **1974** 189-192, 196-197, 202-203
ownership of, Nixon-Ford agreement on, **1974** 898-900
Reagan library dedication, **1991** 735-746
Watergate prosecutor's access to, **1973** 901-904; **1974** 23-25, 621-638
Presidential privilege. *See* Executive privilege
Presidential Proclamation No. 4771 (1981), on draft registration, **1984** 497, 499-500
Presidential Recordings and Materials Preservation Act (1974), Nixon challenge of, **1975** 670; **1977** 465-516
Presidential Task Force on Global Resources and Environment, **1980** 667; **1981** 13-30
President's Advisory Committee on Human Radiation Experiments, **1995** 633-638
President's Council for One America, **1998** 667, 673; **2000** 35
President's Council on Bioethics, human cloning, **2002** 512-529; **2004** 157-167
President's Council on Integrity and Efficiency, **1987** 6
President's Council on Physical Fitness and Sports, benefits for girls report, **1997** 158-171
President's Council on Year 2000 Conversion, **1998** 543-544; **2000** 3-15
President's Emergency Plan for AIDS Relief (PEPFAR), **2005** 51-53

President's Private Sector Survey on Cost Control. *See* Grace commission
President's Summit for America's Future (Philadelphia), **1997** 40, 238-244, 323
President's Task Force on Market Mechanisms. *See* Brady commission
Presidio (San Francisco)
  closing of, **1988** 952
  national park status, **1996** 581
Press
  See also Mass media; News media
  access to pretrial hearings, **1979** 511-533
  censorship
    by Chilean junta, **1975** 910
    laws in India, **1977** 237-241
    by PRG in Vietnam, **1975** 301-302, 306
  confidentiality of sources
    and grand jury subpoena, **1972** 507-519
    Supreme Court on, **1991** 317-329
  editorial process
    disclosure of in libel suit, **1979** 286-318
    and political candidate's right to reply, **1974** 523-528
  exhaustion of, and presidential power, McGovern on, **1973** 87, 90-91, 94
  free speech
    and libel awards, **1984** 299-312
    in satire of public figures, **1988** 175-182
  freedom and superficiality of, Solzhenitsyn on, **1978** 405, 410-411
  gag orders on coverage of criminal trials, **1976** 463-479
  and government corruption, Fallaci on, **1973** 488, 495-498
  newsroom searches, **1978** 355-372
  press conferences, presidential study of, **1988** 835-845
  public's right to know, and publication of Pentagon Papers, **1973** 537, 539
  role in society, Brennan on, **1979** 313-318
  Waco investigations, **1993** 820, 825-827
Press, Frank, **1982** 5
Presser, Jackie, ties to Reagan administration, **1986** 180, 206-207
Preval, Renee
  Haiti presidential candidate, **2005** 330
  Haitian president, **2000** 953
Preyer, Richardson (D-N.C.), **1978** 911-912
Price, Harold, **1978** 654
Price, Melvin (D-Ill.), **1974** 451
Prices. *See* Wage and price controls; Wage and price standards
PricewaterhouseCoopers, federal oversight, **2004** 423
Prieur, Dominique, **1985** 633
Primakov, Yevgeny
  confirmation as prime minister, **1998** 605-606
  NATO expansion, **1996** 656
  Russian economic plan, **1998** 606
  UN weapons inspections in Iraq, **1997** 769
Prince William Sound (Alaska), oil spill in, **1989** 225-237
Princeton Survey Research Associates, on children, **1997** 425
Principi, Anthony J., Gulf War veterans with ALS, **2001** 907-909
Prior, James, on IRA prison hunger strike, **1981** 414-416
Prisma Energy International Inc., **2003** 336; **2004** 417
Prison Fellowship Ministries, **2005** 379
Prison furloughs
  Bush on, **1988** 559, 591, 610
  as issue in presidential debates, **1988** 737
  Republican Party platform on, **1988** 616, 655
Prisoner Re-Entry Initiative, **2004** 29-30
Prisoners
  beaten by guards, **1992** 175-185
  job training and placement services, **2004** 29-30
  nonjudicial body to investigate complaints of, **1972** 958-959
  rights of in searches and visits, **1984** 479-491
Prisoners, political
  in Afghanistan, **1980** 195; **1981** 189-190
  in Bolivia, **1981** 185
  in Cuba, **1984** 158
  in Ethiopia, **1982** 113
  in Haiti, **1977** 8-9
  in Indonesia, **1977** 11
  in Iran, **1977** 14; **1980** 190
  in Nicaragua, **1980** 197; **1981** 186
  in North Korea, **1980** 196
  in Philippines, **1977** 21-23; **1986** 111
    release of, **1987** 191, 201
  in Poland, **1982** 117; **1985** 154
    release of, **1987** 183, 185-186
  in PRC, **1980** 190, 198
  Sakharov's plea for amnesty for in world, **1975** 915, 926-928
  in South Africa, **1988** 94-97
  in South Korea, **1986** 109; **1987** 200
  in Soviet Union, **1980** 191; **1984** 168; **1987** 190, 202-203; **1988** 111
    in psychiatric hospitals, **1980** 198; **1982** 119; **1984** 156; **1986** 111
  in Vietnam, **1981** 180, 188
Prisoners of war (POWs)
  See also Abu Ghraib prison abuse scandal; Guantanamo Bay detainees
  Americans in Southeast Asia, House investigation of, **1976** 925-936
  Bush administration policy on "enemy combatants," **2003** 310; **2004** 212-213, 336-337, 377
  Garwood court-martial for collaboration with captors, **1981** 197-201
  Geneva Convention on, and Iran-Iraq War, **1984** 751
  Iraqi prison abuses, U.S. Army report on, **2004** 207-234
  McCain ban on abuse of enemy detainees proposal, **2005** 80
  release of U.S.
    objective in bombing North, **1972** 611-612, 614
    Paris peace proposals on, **1972** 126, 133, 868, 874; **1973** 331
    tied to withdrawal of troops from Vietnam, **1972** 3, 5-7
  return of from Vietnam, **1973** 245-264

family adjustments, **1973** 246, 253-264
Nixon on, **1973** 196-197, 205, 427-430, 433
Paris peace agreement on, **1973** 115, 118-122, 125-126, 135-136, 155-157, 159-160
Vietnam
Ambassador Peterson, **1997** 489-490
declassification of U.S. records, **1993** 349
Senate report on, **1993** 113-127
U.S. trade embargo and, **1993** 115; **1994** 96-99
Prisons
See also Abu Ghraib prison abuse scandal
Attica uprising, McKay Commission report on handling of, **1972** 783-788
California prison system, abuse of inmates, **2004** 764
construction of, attorney general's violent crime task force on, **1981** 647-648, 664-666
crime statistics, **2005** 679-680
crowding in
double celling as cruel and unusual punishment, **1981** 477-490
link to crowded courts, **1981** 192, 664
drug use among jail inmates, **2000** 855
HIV infection prevention for inmates, **2005** 62
incarceration rates rising, **1998** 871-872; **1999** 616; **2000** 854; **2001** 748; **2003** 981-982; **2004** 763-764
juveniles in adult prisons, **2000** 855
likelihood of going to, **2000** 854-855
mental illness of prison population, **1999** 839-840
overrepresentation of African Americans in, **1983** 43
population growth slowing, **2002** 786-787
private sector management of, **1981** 666-667; **1988** 159, 234
riots of Cuban detainees, **1987** 929-937
vocational and educational programs in, **1981** 192, 194-196, 663-664
Pritchard, Paul C., **1988** 942
Privacy
attorney-client privilege, and posthumous confidentiality, **1998** 393-404
computer privacy and spam e-mail messages, **2002** 70-71
FOIA exemption for personal records, **1981** 394
genetic testing in the workplace, **1998** 63-72
invasions of
by arrests in suspects' homes, **1980** 281-297
by executive branch, Mansfield on, **1974** 63
by FBI, **1976** 237, 264-265, 280, 283-284, 324
of medical records, **1997** 580-587; **2000** 400-401, 1063-1071; **2001** 485-503
presidential right of, and custody of Nixon papers and tapes, **1975** 465-466; **1977** 476-480, 492, 502-507
right to
and abortion, **1973** 102, 104, 106-107, 110-112, 114; **1977** 408
and homosexual conduct, **1986** 601-614
and life-sustaining measures, **1975** 821-822; **1976** 198, 210-212
for prison inmates, **1984** 479-480, 482-487
private schools' discriminatory admissions, **1976** 392, 397
safeguards for, Nixon on, **1974** 43, 49, 60
TIPS (Terrorism Information and Prevention System) proposal, **2002** 564; **2003** 613
Privacy Act, and briefing of Ryan on Jonestown trip, **1979** 349-351, 369-370, 372, 377
Private charity, Bush on contribution of, **1989** 44, 46
Private clubs, discrimination against women and minorities by, **1988** 399-403
Private individuals, employment in U.S. covert operations, **1987** 894, 899, 901, 911, 923, 927-928
Private sector
in Carter's urban proposals, **1978** 241-244, 246, 249-252
contributions to solving U.S. economic and social problems, **1986** 984-985, 997-998, 1001
prison management by, **1981** 666-667
responsibilities for economic growth, **1984** 581-582
role in solving global problems, **1981** 13, 17-18, 29-30, 770
Private Sector Initiatives Program, Carter's, **1979** 34
Private Sector Initiatives Task Force, Reagan's, **1982** 82
Privatization
Grace Commission proposals on, **1984** 170, 178; **1988** 231
in Great Britain, **1988** 230, 238-239
in industrialized countries, **1988** 238-239
Reagan CEA on, **1986** 59, 61, 68, 88-89
Reagan support for, **1987** 11-12, 123-124; **1988** 122-123; **1989** 11
Republican Party platform on, **1984** 705; **1988** 627
sale of federal assets, **1988** 150, 152, 156, 158-159
sale of government loans, **1988** 230, 232
techniques and uses of, **1988** 229-239
Privert, Jocelerme, former Haitian interior minister imprisoned, **2005** 333
Prodi, Romano
at economic summit (Denver), **1997** 342
EU membership celebration, remarks on, **2004** 204-206
EU membership for Turkey, **2004** 975
European Commission
address to, **1999** 158-164
presidential appointment, **1999** 157-158
as European Commission president, **2004** 201
meeting with Qaddafi, **2004** 168
trade policy, **1999** 799
Producer associations, for control of raw materials, **1974** 255-256, 258-259, 261; **1975** 588-590, 598
Producer nations
arms purchases by, impact on oil prices, **1978** 107
contributions to agricultural development fund, **1974** 940-941
cooperation of on energy and raw materials, **1975** 588, 591-592, 600
investment of revenues of, **1974** 849
meeting with consumers of energy, **1974** 982-984
meeting with oil consumers at UN, **1974** 124
negotiating strength of, Castro on, **1979** 686-687
use of oil as political and economic weapon, **1974** 833-834, 841-843
world economic cooperation with, **1974** 834-835, 849-850

Production capacity, underutilization of in economic recovery period, **1977** 723-724, 732
Productivity
compared with other nations, **1992** 103
decline in, reasons for, **1986** 971-973, 975, 978-980
downward trend in, Ford CEA on, **1975** 99-102, 107
factors, **1992** 124-127
growth in, **1992** 99, 105-106
Carter CEA on, **1980** 160, 163, 174, 183-186
Joint Economic Committee proposals for, **1979** 215-219, 221-222; **1980** 209, 214, 216, 231
growth in U.S., CEA report on, **2005** 149
productivity paradox, **2000** 300-301
seen by Japanese, **1992** 13-14
slowdown in
Carter CEA on, **1979** 81-82, 84, 86, 96, 113-117
Ford CEA on, **1977** 66, 72, 75, 86-87
Professional Air Traffic Controllers Organization (PATCO)
effects of 1981 strike, **1986** 253-260; **1988** 268, 274
strike of, **1981** 621-629
Progress and Freedom Foundation (PFF), **1997** 8-9, 14
Progressive, **1990** 722
Progressive Policy Institute, **1992** 668
Project BioShield, Bush proposal for, **2003** 30; **2004** 445
Project BioShield Act (2004), **2004** 442-449
Project Independence, **1973** 914-915, 921; **1974** 47, 53, 84, 99, 104-105
continuation of under Ford, **1974** 767, 771
energy strategies for decade, **1974** 909-918
Project on Death in America, **1997** 326, 329
Project Truth, Soviet propaganda countermeasures by, **1981** 753-767
Pronk, Jan, Sudan conflict, **2004** 592, 595
Propaganda
armed, CIA manual, **1984** 903-916
CIA campaigns in Chile, **1975** 887, 890-896, 899, 902, 910-911
government funded video news releases (VNRs), **2005** 644-655
Soviet, Project Truth countermeasures to, **1981** 753-767
Property rights
activists and endangered species, **1995** 360-361
coastal land, **1992** 615-620
developers and public land, **1994** 298-310
Proposition(s). *See under* California
Prosper, Pierre-Richard, war crimes issues, **2002** 607
Protection of Human Subjects of Biomedical and Behavioral Research, National Commission on the, **1975** 543-556
Protectionism
American Party platform on, **1972** 623
among industrialized countries, impact on debt crisis, **1984** 795-796, 800-801
economic summit on, **1980** 512
Group of Five Communiqué on, **1985** 624, 626, 629-630
as hindrance for U.S. markets, Reagan CEA on, **1988** 118-119, 123, 125, 139, 142-144
and historical achievements of free trade, Reagan CEA on, **1985** 81, 95-100
IMF on, **1977** 688, 691, 693-694
pressures of trade deficit, Reagan CEA on, **1987** 118, 122, 126, 129, 139-140; **1988** 118-119, 123, 125, 139, 142-144
Reagan opposition to, **1983** 121-122, 137, 894, 897-900, 903-904; **1987** 106, 111
U.S. footwear and textile industries, **1988** 339-341, 344-346
U.S.-Japan trade dispute, **1985** 319-322; **1987** 434, 436
Protestant Unionists, and New Ireland Forum, **1984** 315-317
Protestantism. *See* Southern Baptist Convention
Providian Financial corporation, retirement fund losses, **2002** 102
Provost, Ronald D., child sexual abuse by priests, **1992** 508
Proxmire, William (D-Wis.)
bishops' letter on economic policies, **1984** 959
congressional immunity from libel suits, **1979** 479-491
Genocide Convention, **1986** 116
lifting of wage and price controls, **1973** 45
monetary policy, **1977** 718
multilateral trade agreement, **1979** 638
New York City's fiscal crisis, **1977** 568-569
Rickover testimony to, **1982** 88
stock market crash report, **1988** 12
on Tailhook incident, **1992** 881
unemployment projections, **1975** 85
women in military, **1987** 672
Prueher, Joseph W., **2001** 248, 249, 253
Hughes and Loral technology transfer to Chinese, **1998** 978
Pruitt, William, sexual abuse of missionary children, **2005** 867
Pryor, David (D-Ark.)
Claiborne impeachment, **1986** 850
on prescription drug prices, **1993** 197-199
Psychiatrists
criminal indigents' right to, **1985** 207-219
on insanity defense, **1982** 531, 534; **1983** 25-40
Ptasnyski, United States v., **1983** 517-523
Public Agenda, adult attitudes toward children survey, **1997** 422-443
Public assistance. *See* Social service programs; Welfare policy; Welfare reform
Public attorney, Senate Watergate Committee recommendation, **1974** 606-608
Public broadcasting
congressional ban on editorials, **1984** 449-463
future of, **1979** 119-134
Public Broadcasting Act (1967), **1984** 449-463
Public Broadcasting Service (PBS), responsibilities of, **1979** 131
Public Citizen, Crestor linked to kidney failure, **2004** 855
Public Citizen Health Research Group, **1993** 369
care of mentally ill report, **1990** 573-598
and secrecy of CIA sources, **1985** 333-344
Public Citizen Litigation Group, **1992** 564

on independent counsel law, **1988** 468
on prescription drug price advertising, **1976** 352
and secrecy of CIA sources, **1985** 333-344
on sentencing reform, **1987** 409-410
Public Company Accounting Oversight Board, **2002** 1033; **2004** 423
Public Discourse Project, **2004** 458
Public employees
dismissal of for political beliefs, **1980** 259-271
drug testing of, **1986** 839-846
reaction to Proposition 13 passage, **1978** 398-399
revolving door, between government and private employment, **1977** 27-30, 33, 104, 110
unions, on privatization, **1988** 230-231
Public health
See also Child health
AIDS and other sexually transmitted diseases, management of, **1987** 819-821, 826-829
AIDS epidemic, **1986** 887-908
alcoholism, new definition of, **1992** 849-852
alcoholism as problem of, **1972** 193-200
anthrax vaccine, **2004** 446
biological weapons, vaccines against, **2004** 444
contagious disease and job discrimination, **1987** 245-252
drug-resistant bacteria as threat to, **1999** 185-199
effects of toxic substances, **1994** 149-152
flu vaccine shortage, GAO report, **2004** 639-651
G-8 Summit commitment to, **2000** 485-486
Gulf War syndrome, **1994** 264-275; **1997** 740-745
hazardous waste disposal as danger to, **1979** 786, 796-799
hazards from Three Mile Island nuclear accident, **1979** 824, 835-836, 857-858
human radiation experiments, **1994** 54-61
infectious diseases, **1996** 302-311; **1997** 348-349
nuclear testing fallout, **1997** 591-601
population pressure's effect on in developing countries, **1987** 440, 445-446
programs for the poor, **1991** 832
silicone breast implants, **1992** 367-373; **1995** 515-523
suicide prevention, **1999** 439-455
swine flu immunization program, **1978** 669-681
tuberculosis, **1992** 1007-1011; **1993** 851-869
Public Health Cigarette Smoking Act (1969), **1992** 566-568, 572-573
Public Health Cigarette Smoking Act (1970), **1972** 46
Public Health Service (PHS)
on AIDS
education, **1987** 319-326
as epidemic, **1987** 327
testing, **1986** 889
on length of hospital stay, **1988** 333-337
physical fitness and health, **1989** 613-617
on smoking
antismoking campaign, **1989** 33-34
cigars and pipes, **1973** 64-65, 71-73, 76-77
during pregnancy, **1972** 52; **1973** 63-71
history of reports, **1972** 45-46
little cigars, **1973** 63-65, 73-76
nicotine addiction, **1988** 309-322
report, **1992** 267-275
tobacco and allergy, **1972** 46, 53
Public Health Service Act (1970), Title X, **1991** 257-273
Public officials
combatting bribery of, OECD treaty, **1997** 800-807
patronage, and dismissal on political grounds, **1980** 261, 268-271
Public opinion
on presidential elections, **1984** 845, 852, 858
radio talk show survey, **1993** 585-598
Public Service Co. of New Hampshire, **1990** 196-198
Public Telecommunications Financing Act (1978), **1979** 122, 124
Public utilities. *See* Utilities
Public Utility Regulatory Policies Act (1978), **1982** 447-448
Public Works Employment Act (1977), **1980** 539-566
Puckett, James, **1989** 154
Puerto Rico
Democratic Party platform on, **1992** 695
economic summit in, **1976** 425-431
Hurricane Hugo in, **1989** 668
self-determination for, Democratic platform on, **1984** 611
smoking in the Americas, **1992** 269
statehood for, Republican Party platform on, **1980** 568, 582
trade status with U.S., **1982** 180, 186
vote on future status, **1993** 947-952
Pugo, Boris K., **1991** 515
Puller, Lewis, Jr., Clinton's Vietnam memorial remarks, **1993** 347
Pulley v. Harris, **1990** 314
Putin, Vladimir
and ABM treaty, **2000** 680; **2001** 282, 927-934
as acting prime minister of Russia, **1999** 917, 921
Bush-Putin talks, **2001** 893, 895; **2005** 305-306
Chechen rebels
Beslan school hostage crisis, **2004** 535, 564-576; **2005** 299, 300, 303
hostage rescue from Moscow theater, **2002** 763-773
negotiations, **2004** 567
Chechnya war, **1999** 909, 911; **2001** 894
China relations, **2001** 740
India-Pakistan relations, **2002** 328, 329
Iraq, UN resolution on disarmament of, **2002** 716-717; **2003** 42-43, 51-52
Kyoto Protocol on Climate Change (UN treaty), **2002** 303; **2003** 862, 865; **2004** 827, 829
missile defense system, **2004** 181
on politics and morality, **2005** 313
presidential elections, **2000** 172-173
Russian presidential inauguration speech, **2000** 171-178
Russian State of the Nation address, **2001** 254-266; **2003** 245-259
Russian submarine disaster, **2000** 635, 637-638
Saakashvili visit to Moscow, **2004** 73
Ukraine
criticism from prime minister Tymoshenko, **2005** 66
Yanukovich for president supporter, **2004** 1003

Putin, Vladimir *Continued*
UN Security Council membership, **2004** 888-889
U.S. relations, **2001** 892; **2004** 137
U.S.-Russian arms control, **2000** 206; **2002** 275-286
Uzbekistan relations, **2005** 433
war on terrorism
support for U.S., **2001** 615, 626-627, 894
U.S. actions, **2001** 852
Putnam Investments, mutual funds scandal, **2003** 695; **2004** 419

Q

Qaddafi, Muammar
African economic development proposals, **2001** 506
boycott of Arab League meeting, **1987** 869
and human rights in Libya, **1987** 203-204
Libyan nuclear weapons program, dismantling of, **2003** 1218-1233; **2004** 18, 24, 323
rise of, **1986** 347-348
as sponsor of terrorism, **1985** 464, 466, 468-471; **1986** 1014
support of conversion to Islam, **1985** 499
terrorism by, CIA on, **1981** 462, 467-468
U.S. air strike against Libya, **1986** 347-354
U.S. relations, **2004** 168-175
Qadeer, Hashim, Pearl murder suspect, **2005** 474
Qadir, Haji Abdul, Afghan vice president assassination, **2002** 18
al Qaeda terrorist network
See also Bin Laden, Osama; Terrorist organizations
activities of, **2002** 740-741
African embassy bombings and, **2001** 617
attacks on, **2003** 1055-1056
Bali resort bombing linked to, **2002** 702, 1014, 1016
border arrests of potential terrorists, **2003** 38
British report on, **2001** 802-818
Bush State of the Union address, **2004** 537; **2005** 87
changing nature of, **2004** 538-540
Cole (USS) bombing, **2001** 3, 805; **2003** 30
congressional intelligence gathering joint panel report on, **2003** 544-575
financing, **2003** 1057-1058
Guantanamo Bay detentions, **2002** 830-841, 1016
as an ideology, **2003** 1051
international coalition against, **2001** 624, 641
Iraq links to, **2002** 617-618; **2003** 19, 46-47, 886, 901
links with guerilla leader Laskar Jihad, **2001** 566-567
Madrid terrorist bombings, **2004** 105-114, 137, 268, 535, 540; **2005** 393
manhunt for members of, **2004** 23, 537-538, 1012
in Mesopotamia, **2005** 401
as a movement rather than an organization, **2004** 538
nuclear weapons acquisitions, **2001** 17, 22, 282
recruitment of new members, **2003** 1051; **2004** 537, 538
refuge in Pakistan, **2002** 170; **2003** 210, 1050
sanctions against, UN panel on, **2002** 1014-1025
Saudi Arabia links to, **2003** 228-232; **2004** 517-533
September 11 attacks on U.S. linked to, **2001** 626; **2002** 33, 612; **2003** 546; **2004** 268, 517-533, 713
as source for terrorist attacks, **2005** 401-402
status of, Bush administration on, **2003** 1050-1051
superseded by other Islamic extremist groups, **2005** 24
support for, congressional joint panel on, **2003** 547
terrorist bombings in London, links to, **2005** 397-398
terrorist groups with links to, **2004** 539
testimony of defectors, **2001** 804
threat to U.S., **2004** 269-270, 457
National Intelligence Center forecasts, **2005** 15-16
UN sanctions against, **2003** 1050-1068
U.S. campaign against, **2002** 20; **2003** 1090-1091
U.S. intelligence failures, **2002** 990-1013
U.S. war against Taliban regime in Afghanistan, **2001** 686-697; **2002** 33
war on terrorism and, **2003** 29-30
weapons of mass destruction, **2002** 438
al-Qahtani, Mohammed, interrogations of detainee, **2005** 450
Qalibaf, Mohammed Baqur, Iranian presidential candidate, **2005** 590
Qanooni, Yonus
Afghan education minister resignation, **2004** 917-918
Afghan Northern Alliance leader, **2001** 881
Afghan parliamentary elections, **2005** 971
Afghan presidential candidate, **2004** 915-916
Qatar
human trafficking, **2002** 348
oil production increase, **1980** 996
OPEC meeting in, **1976** 937-942
OPEC oil prices, **1979** 252, 254; **1981** 799
political reform, **2003** 961
U.S. air base, **2003** 1054
al-Qattan, Ziyad, Iraq reconstruction investigations, **2005** 722
Quadrennial Advisory Council on Social Security, **1975** 115-117, 121-122
Quadrennial Commission, on federal judges' and officials' pay, **1987** 13; **1989** 197, 204
Quadripartite Agreement (1971). *See* Berlin, West, four-power agreement on (1971)
Quality of Health Care in America, Committee on, **2001** 191, 195
Quandt, William, **1992** 227
Quaoar (subplanet) discovery, **2004** 7
Quarles, Randall K., on pension plan funding, **2005** 201
Quattrone, Frank P., investment banker prosecuted for securities fraud, **2003** 699; **2004** 421-422
Quayle, Dan (R-Ind.; vice president)
acceptance speech, **1988** 589-591, 601-604; **1992** 783, 794-798
Bush on election results, **1988** 891, 893, 896
Council for Competitiveness, **1992** 469
draft issue, **1992** 158
inauguration, **1989** 41-42

as issue in presidential debates, **1988** 722, 749-750, 755-756, 766
mission to Latin America after Panama invasion, **1989** 703
"Murphy Brown" speech, **1992** 443-452
National Space Council, **1990** 754, 755
qualifications of, **1988** 799-823
on Tower rejection, **1989** 107
vice presidential debates, **1988** 799-829; **1992** 907, 909, 977-1001
Quebec
and Canadian constitution modifications, **1981** 813-814; **1982** 318
independence, Canadian Supreme Court on, **1998** 592-598
separatist vote in, **1976** 855-862; **1980** 401-410
Queen, Richard, **1981** 145
Quereia, Ahmed (*aka* Abu Ala), Palestinian leader appointed prime minister, **2003** 193, 1201; **2004** 807
Quincentennial of discovery of America, Amnesty International report, **1992** 897-905
Quindel, Barbara Zack, **1997** 630
Quinlan, Joseph, guardianship of daughter on life-support systems, **1975** 805, 807, 816-821, 824; **1976** 197-198, 200, 206-208, 218-219
Quinlan, Karen Ann
life-support systems for, **1975** 805-824; **1976** 197-219
right-to-die case, **1990** 375; **1996** 122
Quinn, Jack, Rich fraud case, Clinton pardon, **2001** 90
Quinn, Jane Bryant, in Reagan-Anderson debate, **1980** 847, 861-862
Quinn, John R., dialogue on contraception among Catholics, **1980** 871-872, 877-878
Quinn, Joseph, on retirement, **2005** 202
Quinn, William Joseph, **1986** 752
Quiroga, Jorge, Bolivia presidential elections, **2005** 769
Qureia, Ahmed (Palestinian prime minister)
on Jewish settlements on Palestinian land, **2004** 304
resignation retraction, **2004** 306
Qusay Hussein (Saddam's son), killed during gun battle, **2003** 938-939, 1191
Qwest Communications, retirement fund losses, **2002** 102

R

R. A. V. v. City of St. Paul, **1992** 543-551; **1993** 385, 387, 389
R. J. Reynolds Tobacco Co.
Joe Camel advertising campaign, **1997** 332, 334
tobacco settlement, **1998** 842
R. M. J., In re, **1982** 65-71
Rabbini, Burhanuddin
Afghan parliamentary elections, **2005** 972
former president of Afghanistan, **2001** 881, 882
Rabbo, Abed, Israel-Palestine peace agreement (Geneva Accord), **2003** 1204-1205
Rabe, Barry G., state's role in global warming, **2002** 305
Rabe, David, **1998** 407
Rabe v. Washington, **1990** 243, 244
Rabin, Yitzhak
assassination of, **1995** 622, 689-695; **1996** 337; **1998** 742; **1999** 890; **2004** 307, 309; **2005** 531
world leaders on, **1995** 689-695
Baker speech on Middle East peace, **1989** 290
Entebbe raid and dealing with terrorists, **1976** 517-520
Israeli-Palestinian peace accord, **1993** 747, 749, 767-768
and Jordanian peace agreement, **1994** 329-335
on labor election victory, **1992** 655-665
Nixon visit to Israel, **1974** 464-467
Nobel Peace Prize recipient, **2003** 1130
Oslo peace agreement (1993) and, **2005** 33-34
political life of, **1995** 690-691
Scranton's remarks on PLO, **1976** 192
signing of Sinai accord with Egypt, **1975** 575
West Bank agreement, **1995** 622, 623, 628-630
Raborn, William F., **1972** 492-493
Race relations
See also Blacks; Discrimination, race; Minorities
and Attica prison uprising, **1972** 783-784
Boston murder hoax, **1990** 35-40
busing and equal educational opportunity, Askew on, **1972** 201-206
Carter-Reagan debate on, **1980** 930-932
Clinton administration race initiative, **1998** 74, 665; **1999** 56-57
Clinton commencement speech on, **1997** 313-324
and Clinton inauguration, **1997** 22
computer and Internet use, **2002** 75-76
Eisenhower Foundation inner cities report, **1993** 211-233
Los Angeles Police Department, sentencing of officers in King case, **1993** 631-651
March on Washington thirtieth anniversary, **1993** 583-584, 677-685
in navy, and shipboard unrest, **1972** 627-629
presidential advisory board report, **1998** 665-675; **2000** 772
presidential advisory panel, **1997** 316-317
racial reconciliation, things you can do, **1998** 674-675
Virginia's first African American governor, **1990** 41-47
Racial Discrimination, Convention on the Elimination of, report to UN, **2000** 771-780
Racial segregation
See also School desegregation
apartheid ends in South Africa, **1992** 283-292
in housing and schools, in U.S. cities, **1988** 185-186, 190-191, 193
and public housing in suburbs, **1976** 223-233
race-based redistricting, **1993** 459-481; **1995** 369-384
tax increases in Missouri to combat, **1990** 227-238
Racial stereotyping, **1998** 672
Racicot, Marc
forest fire prevention policies, **2000** 714
lobbyist, **2002** 896
Racism
See also Civil rights, enforcement
in America, Clinton administration on, **2000** 771-780

Racism *Continued*
apology to African Americans for, **1995** 336-338
church arson cases, **1997** 301-313
church bombing trial (Birmingham, 1963), **2002** 239-246
Clinton plea to end in America, **1995** 646-654; **1997** 22, 29, 315
death penalty and racial bias, **2002** 358-359
and diversity in America, **1997** 43
institutional, and African American unemployment and poverty, **1983** 43, 49-50
Lott and his racial beliefs, **2002** 969-980
racial profiling of police, **2000** 773; **2001** 179
Schott suspension for racist remarks, **1993** 167-170
segregation on buses, **2005** 357
Texaco executives racial slurs, **1996** 764-769
UN Conference Against Racism, Racial Discrimination, Xenophobia, and Related Intolerance, **2001** 603-613
U.S. record on, **2001** 605-606
Zionism as, UN resolution on, **1975** 825-827
Racketeer Influenced and Corrupt Organizations Act (RICO)
antiabortion protesters and, **1994** 26-33
asset forfeiture and, **1993** 439-446
impact on organized crime, **1986** 211, 215-216
and pretrial detention, **1987** 492, 495
Racketeering
asset forfeiture, **1993** 431, 432, 438-446
Noriega sentenced for, **1992** 649-653
Radiation
and health of nuclear workers, **1978** 639, 646
human radiation experiments, **1993** 987-995; **1994** 54-61; **1995** 633-638
ionizing, smoking and lung cancer, **1985** 821
levels of after nuclear war, **1983** 858, 873-877
and nuclear plant safety, **1989** 355-357
Radio
ban on tobacco advertising on, **1972** 46; **1973** 64
Carter's call-in program, **1977** 183-188
daytime broadcast of offensive material, **1978** 515-531
public, proposed reorganization of, **1979** 119-121, 124-132
talk show survey, **1993** 585-598
Radio and Television News Directors Association, **1981** 395
Radio Católica, closing of by Nicaraguan government, **1986** 641
Radio Marti, and U.S.-Cuban agreement on Cuban detainees in U.S., **1987** 930
Radioactive waste. *See* Nuclear waste management
Radon, health effects of exposure to, **1988** 3-8
Raffarin, Jean Pierre (French prime minister), demonstration against terrorists in Spain, **2004** 107
Rafsanjani, Akbar Hashemi, Iranian presidential elections, **2005** 590, 594
Rafsanjani, Ali Akbar Hashemi, **1991** 753
on U.S. official visits to Iran, **1986** 1017
on Western hostages in Lebanon, **1989** 317-320
Rafshoon Advertising Agency, Gerald A., and Carter campaign funds investigation, **1979** 801, 805, 807, 809-812
Ragsdale, James, Roswell incident, **1997** 401
Rahkimov, Murtaza, as governor of Bashkortostan, **2005** 300
Rahkonen, Ossi J., **1981** 197
Rahman, Fazlur, Pakistan election referendum, **2002** 169
Rahman, Sheik Omar Abdul, World Trade Center bombing, **2001** 804
Raiffa, Howard, on East-West scientific organization, **1972** 833-835
Railroad industry
Amtrak
financial condition of, **1994** 197-204
GAO testimony on, **1994** 197-204
train accidents, **1995** 178; **1996** 189-190
deregulation of, **1978** 690; **1979** 24, 36, 40; **1980** 948; **1981** 59, 74
government reorganization of Northeast and Midwest, **1974** 87-89; **1975** 529-542
heavy regulation of, **1975** 529-532
impact on of technological progress in transportation, **1975** 529-532
rigidity of, **1974** 87-89
safety, GAO report on, **1996** 189-198
Raimondo, Anthony, asst. secy. of manufacturing nomination withdrawn, **2004** 59
Rain forests, tropical
global depletion of, U.S. aid in reversing, **1981** 13-14, 21-24
World Bank projects in Indonesia, **1986** 859-873
Rainbow Warrior, sabotage of, **1985** 631-634
Raines, Franklin D.
balanced budget agreement, **1997** 604
Fannie Mae investigations, **2004** 420
Raines, Tim, **1986** 171
Raines v. Byrd, **1998** 423
Rait, Ken, forest preservation, **1999** 594
Rajaie-Khorassani, Said, **1987** 610
Rajan, Raghuram, on worldwide economic imbalances, **2005** 414
Rajoy, Mariano, Spanish presidential election defeat, **2004** 105, 108
Rakas v. Illinois, **1978** 753-764
Rakoff, Jed S., death penalty unconstitutional, **2002** 355
Ralston, Joseph W.
Joint Chiefs of Staff nomination, **1997** 656
NATO peacekeeping forces in Bosnia, **2001** 823
Ram, Jagjivan, in Indian election, **1977** 238-239
Ramadan, Taha Yassin, U.S.-Iranian policy, **2002** 35
Ramazanadeh, Abdullah, **2001** 794
Rambouillet (France), economic summit, **1976** 425-426, 428-429, 431
Ramdass, Bobby Lee, death sentencing of, **2000** 992
Ramirez, Macario, **1986** 965
Ramirez Mercado, Sergio, **1979** 582
Ramo, Roberta Cooper, **1999** 109
Ramon, Ilan, *Columbia* astronaut, **2003** 633
Ramos, Fidel V.
and Aquino government, **1986** 1037, 1039; **1987** 844, 845
in ouster of Marcos, **1986** 308-309
Philippine presidential election, **2001** 103

withdrawal of U.S. troops from Philippines, **1992** 1053-1058
Ramos, William, abortion pill, **2000** 784
Ramsey, David J., acupuncture, **1997** 749
Ranariddh, Norodom (prince of Cambodia), **1997** 639; **1998** 971
Rand, Kirsten, gun control lobbying efforts, **2001** 724
RAND Corp.
international math and science tests, **1992** 87
leak of Pentagon Papers from, **1973** 537
Randall, Doug, climate change, **2004** 830-831
Randolph, A. Raymond
Guantanamo Bay detentions, **2003** 108
Hamdan detainee case, **2005** 447, 453-460
Randolph, Jennings (D-W.Va.), **1972** 922
Rangel, Charles B. (D-N.Y.)
Cartagena drug summit, **1990** 117
on Clinton State of the Union address, **1995** 26
drug treatment spending, **1986** 840
military draft legislation, **2004** 784
Nixon's resignation, **1974** 714
U.S.-China trade relations, **2000** 220
Rangel, José Vicente, referendum on Venezuelan president, **2003** 281; **2004** 550
Rantisi, Abdel Aziz, Hamas leader, **2002** 933
assassination, **2004** 301, 302, 810
Rao, P. V. Narasimha, India political situation, **2004** 351
Rape
Air Force Academy sexual misconduct investigations, **2003** 791-807
Congolese conflict, UN investigations, **2004** 508-509
date rape, **1992** 388, 394-395
death penalty for, state laws on, **1977** 517-528
during Kosovo conflict, **1999** 811
emergency contraception, Justice Department guidelines, **2005** 817
FBI crime report, **1998** 875; **1999** 620; **2000** 856-857; **2001** 754; **2002** 791; **2003** 989; **2004** 767-768; **2005** 682
FBI report, **1996** 737; **1997** 687-688
graduated penalties for, **1977** 865
Justice Department reports on violent crime, **1993** 375, 378
National Women's Study of, **1992** 385-395
statutory, sex discrimination in laws on, **1981** 339-349
violence against women report, **1994** 64-72
Ras Sudar oil fields, return of to Egypt, **1975** 583
Rasell, Edith, **1993** 271
Rasul, Safiq, British detainee at Guantanamo Bay case, **2004** 378-379
Rasul v. Bush, **2003** 114-115; **2004** 378-379, 392-398; **2005** 448, 451
Rather, Dan, Nixon interview, **1972** 3-13
Ratner, Michael, **1992** 456
Ratushinskaya, Irina, emigration from Soviet Union, **1986** 822
Ratzinger, Joseph (cardinal)
See also Benedict XVI (pope)
disciplining of Father Curran, **1986** 758-765
liberation theology, **1986** 317-338
on moral theology, **1993** 843
pastoral care of homosexuals, **1986** 909-918
reproductive technologies, **1987** 268
Rau, Johannes, European Union expansion, **2004** 198
Raudenbush, Stephen, affirmative action case, **2003** 368
Rauf, Tariq, nuclear nonproliferation, **2000** 204-205
Ravitch, Diane S.
on educational achievement, **1992** 625
on humanities education, **1987** 682
on math and science test scores, **1992** 86, 88
on sex-equity programs, **1992** 143
on teaching about religion, **1987** 599
Ravix, Remissainthe, Haitian gang leader killed, **2005** 333
Raw materials
See also Commodities
control of by developing countries, **1974** 255-264; **1975** 4
producer associations for, among developing countries, **1975** 187-188, 197-199, 325-327
reliable supply of for industrialized countries, **1975** 354, 358, 587-592
shortages of, relation to population growth, **1974** 777-778
world supply
economic cooperation on, **1974** 113-115, 118-119
proposed study of, **1975** 10
Rawl, L. W., on Exxon oil spill in Alaska, **1989** 225, 233-237
Rawlins, Dennis, on Peary's North Pole claim, **1988** 831-833; **1989** 688-689, 696
Ray, Charles, consul general in Vietnam, **1999** 476
Ray, Elizabeth, as congressional employee, **1976** 365-368
Ray, James Earl
as assassin of King, House inquiry on, **1977** 113-114, 116-118; **1978** 909-910, 916-917; **1979** 593, 595, 616-620
escape from prison, **1977** 116
Ray, Robert W., Whitewater investigations, closing of, **2000** 762-770; **2001** 88
Raymond, Harry, **1988** 832
Raymond, Lee, oil company profits, congressional testimony on, **2005** 781, 787-789
Raynor, Bruce, labor union dissident, **2005** 487
Razmara, Ali, **1978** 700
Raznatovic, Zeljko, death in Kosovo bombings, **2000** 834
RCRA. *See* Resource Conservation and Recovery Act
Reading
See also Literacy
America Reads Challenge, **1997** 35, 64-65; **1998** 77, 88
habits of U.S. public, **1988** 517, 524-526
teaching of, **1986** 219-220, 223-224; **1989** 89
Reagan, Maureen, **1985** 556
Reagan, Nancy
and Alzheimer's disease, **2001** 541
at British royal wedding, **1981** 602
honorarium for, and Allen investigation, **1981** 847, 849

Reagan, Nancy *Continued*
at Republican convention, **1988** 589-590, 592
at Statue of Liberty centennial, **1986** 698
stem cell research, federal funding for, **2004** 160; **2005** 318
therapeutic cloning, **2002** 515
volunteerism summit, **1997** 238, 240-241
war on drugs, **1986** 181, 840; **1988** 59, 64
Reagan, Ron (son of Ronald Reagan), Democratic Party speech supporting stem cell research, **2004** 483
Reagan, Ronald
on abortion, **1983** 546; **1985** 53-56
administration
accomplishments of
Reagan summing up, **1989** 15-23
Republican Party platform on, **1988** 619-620
acid rain studies, **1983** 197-210
affirmative action
enforcement, **1985** 789-790, 795-797
and reverse discrimination, **1987** 332
and seniority, **1984** 367
and African Americans, status of, **1983** 41-55; **1985** 29, 31-32; **1987** 51-55, 58-60
AIDS policy, **1987** 817-819, 822
education, government role in, **1987** 319-320
antitrust policy, **1984** 413-414
arms control
Democratic Party platform on, **1984** 624, 628
START proposal, differences on, **1982** 386
strategy, former security officials on, **1986** 781-784
verification of agreements, **1986** 11
catastrophic illness coverage, **1986** 273-274, 1025-1028
civil rights enforcement, **1983** 913-915
Democratic Party platform on, **1984** 600-605
debt crisis, international, **1983** 137-139; **1985** 643-652
defense policy
Democratic Party platform on, **1984** 622-624
Joint Chiefs reform, **1982** 325-336
limited nuclear war strategy, **1982** 395-407
nuclear first-strike, **1982** 305-315
nuclear freeze, **1982** 226, 232-234, 886-887
SDI and ABM treaty reinterpretation, **1987** 289-317
ecology and World Bank projects, **1986** 860
economic policy
bishops' criticism of, **1984** 957-972
Democratic Party platform on, **1984** 550, 552, 554-566
recovery program, **1984** 100-105
education
reform of, **1983** 413-437
sex discrimination in, **1984** 201
tax exemptions for discriminatory schools, **1983** 490-491
environment
development of natural resources, **1983** 828-829
investigation of EPA hazardous waste cleanup, **1982** 965-970; **1983** 749-753
exclusionary rule, **1984** 505-506
Falkland Islands policy, **1983** 8
family planning in developing countries, **1984** 521-522
foreign policy
Democratic Party platform on, **1984** 624-626, 630
human rights in, **1981** 179, 462, 779-785; **1985** 145-148; **1986** 97-113; **1987** 189-190
terrorism emphasis of, **1981** 170, 462
and gender gap, **1983** 755-763
HUD abuses during, **1989** 333-337
ICJ jurisdiction, **1985** 637-641
Iran-contra affair, **1986** 1013-1024
circumvention of policy processes, **1986** 1050-1053
conduct of, **1987** 891-928
legal outcomes of, **1989** 391-397
Japan, trade sanctions against, **1987** 427
Libya
disinformation campaign against, **1986** 351-352
expulsion of diplomats from U.S., **1981** 462
Middle East
Iran-Iraq War, and trade embargo, **1987** 609, 611
Saudi peace plan, **1981** 631
Sinai return to Egypt, **1982** 338-339
monetary policy, devaluation of dollar, **1985** 623-630
national security export controls, **1987** 30
Nicaragua policy, **1985** 255-257, 260-269
Panama, relations with Noriega and, **1988** 81-83
public broadcasting editorials, **1984** 449-450, 454
religion, and federal courts, **1984** 217; **1985** 479-480, 486-488
social program cutbacks, **1983** 765-772
food aid, **1983** 765-767, 770, 772; **1984** 3-17; **1985** 189-191, 193, 198-202
Soviet forced labor, **1982** 857-869
Soviet grain embargo, lifting of, **1982** 824, 831-835
Soviet pipeline sanctions, **1982** 879-884
Soviet propaganda, neutralizing, **1981** 753
student searches, **1985** 13
Supreme Court, differences with, **1985** 479-490, 653-655
trade, U.S. business protection against imports, **1982** 180
treatment of severely handicapped infants, **1986** 541-558
UNESCO withdrawal, **1983** 967-971
unitary taxation, **1983** 647
AIDS
commission report, **1988** 415, 417
education, **1987** 320
Allen resignation, **1981** 848
Alzheimer's disease announcement, **1994** 498-500
Alzheimer's disease victim, **2004** 160, 316; **2005** 318
arms control
chemical weapons, UN speech on, **1989** 27
INF proposal, UN speech on, **1983** 791-800
INF treaty signing, **1987** 945-949

and SDI, **1984** 259-260; **1986** 782, 784
Soviet nuclear freeze proposal, **1982** 225-226, 232
START proposal, **1982** 385-393
zero-option proposal, **1981** 823-825; **1983** 792, 796
assassination attempt, **1981** 351-367; **1982** 531-537; **1985** 493-494; **2004** 317
Berlin Wall anniversary, **1986** 791-792
biographical profile of, **2004** 316-320
biotechnology regulation, **1986** 289
Bitburg (West Germany) visit, **1985** 357-362; **1986** 1076; **1989** 488
British Parliament speech, **1982** 477-488
on British-Irish accord, **1985** 726
budget messages, **1982** 143-162; **1983** 101-118; **1984** 99-117; **1985** 71-78; **1986** 49-58; **1987** 3-15; **1988** 149-163
campaigns and elections
acceptance speeches, **1980** 651-664; **1984** 727-741
debate with Anderson, **1980** 847-869
debate with Carter, **1980** 919-951
debates with Mondale, **1984** 845-902
and Democratic Party unity, **1984** 647-649
election victory, **1980** 919, 959-962; **1984** 953-955
Kennedy (Edward M.) on policies of, **1980** 702, 704-705, 707-708
last convention speech, **1988** 589-590, 592-601
PAC contributions to, **1985** 277-278
presidential nomination, **1976** 665-666
Republican Party platform, **1976** 617-618; **1980** 567-568; **1984** 661-726
role of Moral Majority, **1983** 818
Canada-U.S. agreement, **1988** 571, 573-578
Caribbean Basin Initiative, **1982** 179-190
Central American policy, **1983** 439-454; **1984** 31-33; **1993** 238
Challenger commission, **1986** 516, 518
Civil Rights Commission, **1983** 913-916
Clark appointment to Interior, **1983** 829
communism, failure of, **1982** 477-478, 480, 482-486
Constitution bicentennial, **1987** 765-771
crime, speech to police chiefs on, **1981** 648, 667-670
death and funeral services for, **2004** 160, 320-322, 483; **2005** 318
defense policy, **1997** 814
bombing of Libyan targets, **2003** 1219
chemical weapons disposal, **1997** 198
military buildup, **1982** 478, 487-488; **1983** 88, 106; **1985** 39-40, 44-45, 105-107; **1989** 15-16, 19
missile defense system, **2000** 678; **2001** 928; **2003** 817
missile deployment in Europe, **1981** 823-830
MX missile, **1982** 903-918
nuclear war, threat of, **1983** 791, 795
nuclear weapons ban, **1999** 604
delivers Bush's first State of the Union address, **1990** 50
on *Discovery* success, **1988** 796
Donovan indictment, **1984** 805
drug war, **1986** 840, 842
economic organization, international, creation of, **1981** 770, 772-773
economic policy
budget deficit, **2003** 679
deficit spending, **1998** 501
economic plan, **1981** 213-224
recovery, **1982** 75-78
revisions of Carter budget, **1981** 325-328
supply-side economics, **1999** 94
tax reduction package, **1981** 639-646
economic reports, **1982** 121-141; **1983** 121-127; **1984** 119-120; **1985** 79-87; **1986** 59, 70-92; **1987** 117-124; **1988** 117-125; **1989** 3-112
economic summits
Bonn, **1985** 347-349, 351, 355
Geneva, **1985** 749-761
with Gorbachev, **1990** 333
Iceland, **1986** 875-885
London, **1984** 355-357, 362
Moscow, **1988** 353-373
Ottawa, **1981** 591
Tokyo, **1986** 438
Toronto, **1988** 391-393
Venice, **1987** 525-527
Versailles, **1982** 469-470
Washington, **1987** 991-1002, 1004-1006
Williamsburg, **1983** 508-509
education
school prayer, **1984** 241-242, 244; **1987** 597-598, 602
teaching and learning report, **1986** 217-218
teaching of values, **1986** 805
education policy, tuition tax credits, **2002** 407
on entitlements, **1982** 74, 79-80
EPA investigation, instruction to Gorsuch, **1982** 965-970
on ERA, **1982** 612, 615-616; **1983** 755-757
eulogy, by George W. Bush, **2004** 320-322
evangelicals speech, **1983** 269-277
executive orders
drug testing of federal employees, **1986** 839-846
intelligence agencies' authority, **1981** 861-868
regulations, cost-benefit analysis for, **1981** 492
South Africa sanctions, **1985** 518, 531-540; **1986** 99
Falklands War, **1982** 294, 478
"fantasy America" of, Democrats on, **1980** 772, 775-777, 779, 781, 785-786
Far East trip, **1983** 893-912
farewell address, **1989** 15-23
federal employees
air controllers strike, **1981** 621, 623-629
drug testing, **1986** 181, 839-846
pay increase for judges and officials, **1989** 197, 203
work furlough, **1981** 831-834
Federal Reserve Board appointments, **1983** 595-597; **1987** 511-516
food aid in U.S., **1984** 3-17
foreign policy
Angola-U.S. relations, **2002** 152

Reagan, Ronald *Continued*
goals, **1984** 814-815
and human rights, **1984** 156-157
Kim Dae-jung arrest intervention, **1997** 893
Middle East peace process, **2001** 362
UNESCO membership withdrawal, **2003** 810
Genocide Convention, **1986** 116
as governor of California, **2003** 1005
Grace Commission, **1984** 169, 170
Gramm-Rudman-Hollings signing, **1985** 803-804, 806-808
Grenada invasion by U.S., **1983** 847-853
gun control, **1991** 185-188
Haig resignation, **1982** 561-566
health, catastrophic illness coverage, **1986** 1025-1028
health of, **1987** 105-106
at Holocaust commemoration, **1981** 381-382, 386-387
hosts Gorbachev in California, **1992** 433
IMF funding, **1983** 801-807
immigration
reform, signing of, **1986** 963-969
refugees, interdiction of (esp. Haitian), **1981** 606, 613, 616-618
inaugural addresses, **1981** 137-143; **1985** 39-46
on independent counsel law, **1988** 465
IRA prison hunger strike, letter to from members of Congress, **1981** 402
Iran hostages
"October Surprise" theory, **1994** 3-16
welcomed home by, **1980** 1000; **1981** 146, 159-161, 461
Iran-contra affair
explanations of, **1986** 1013, 1017-1023
knowledge of contra diversion, **1986** 1050-1051, 1053
management of NSC, **1987** 205-208, 215-216, 222-225, 230-231
North conviction, **1990** 493, 502, 506-507
pardons, **1992** 1075
responsibility for, **1987** 891, 894-895, 907, 916-917, 922-925
role in, **1989** 392-394; **1992** 651; **1994** 8, 15-17
on Tower Commission report, **1987** 207-208
Italy trip, **1982** 477-488
Japan
trade imbalance with, **1985** 319
trade sanctions against, **1987** 427, 429-436
trip to, **1983** 893-908
Japanese-American reparations, **1988** 287-288
judicial appointments, **1987** 44-45, 51-52
on King holiday, **1983** 883-888
on Law of the Sea Treaty, **1982** 346, 360-361
Libya, air strike against, **1986** 347-354
Meese, relationship with, **1988** 495-496
Middle East
attack on U.S. Marines in Beirut, **1983** 933-934
AWACS sale to Saudis, **1981** 787-788, 793-798
on Begin, **1983** 834
Iran-Iraq War, **1987** 609, 611
Iraqi attack on USS *Stark*, **1987** 792
Israeli invasion of Beirut, **1982** 743-744
Israeli military and trade agreements, **1983** 834-835
Israeli raid on Iraq, **1981** 508
Palestinian refugee camp massacre, **1982** 784
peace plan, **1982** 753-760; **1988** 582
Saudi peace plan, **1981** 632
Soviet involvement in, **1983** 835
talks with PLO, **1988** 905-906, 908
U.S. downing of Iranian airliner, **1988** 704, 706
minimum wage and youth employment, **1983** 786
minority broadcasting, **1990** 420
NATO
Bonn meeting, **1982** 478-479
Spain's entry into, **1982** 420
new federalism, **1982** 73-74, 80-81; **1983** 53-54, 77, 86, 123, 415
Nicaragua
U.S. policy toward, **1984** 339-341, 904-905
U.S. trade embargo against, **1985** 257
Nicaraguan contras, support for, **1985** 256-257; **1987** 638-639, 641-642, 1008
on Nixon inaugural, **1973** 81
North American accord proposal, **1982** 183-184
organized crime commission, **1986** 179-180
overturns ban on health claims from food industry, **1990** 176
Panama Canal treaties, **1977** 593; **1978** 178
pardons for FBI break-ins, **1981** 371-373
Philippines
asylum for Marcos, **1988** 869
change of government, **1986** 308-309
Poland
letter to Brezhnev on repression in, **1982** 880
lifting of sanctions against, **1987** 183-188
martial law, and sanctions against, **1981** 884, 895-896
Nobel Peace Prize for Walesa, **1983** 925
at poverty summit, **1981** 769-775
PRC
trade and technology agreements with, **1984** 23-26
trip to, **1984** 287-298
presidential approval ratings, **2005** 41
presidential elections, **2004** 316, 317
presidential library dedication, **1991** 735-746
press conferences, **1988** 843-844
public opinion on job performance of, **1989** 16-17
regional conflicts, UN speech on, **1985** 707-719
regulatory burden on industry, **1984** 427-428
SDI, **1984** 257-258, 260, 267; **1988** 323-324, 326
announcement of, **1983** 305-316
and Gorbachev arms control proposal, **1986** 9
Social Security reform, **1983** 57-60
South Africa
constitutional changes, **1983** 890
economic sanctions against, **1985** 518, 531-540; **1986** 99, 372
meeting with Tutu, **1984** 1029
South Korea
sentencing of Kim Dae-jung, **1980** 825
trip to, **1983** 893-895, 908-912
Soviet relations
agricultural trade, **1982** 823-824, 831-835

Chernenko contact, **1984** 918-919
Daniloff arrest, **1986** 820
death of Andropov, **1984** 145-146, 148-150
emigration policies, **1981** 748-749
Gorbachev meeting at UN, **1988** 927-929
New Year's Day message to Soviets, **1986** 3-5, 7-8
pipeline sanctions, **1982** 879-884
and Polish martial law, **1981** 881-885, 894-897; **1982** 880, 882, 949
Soviet downing of Korean plane, **1983** 775, 777, 779-783
Soviet-forged letter to Juan Carlos, **1981** 754
summit meetings
Geneva, **1985** 749-761
Iceland, **1986** 875-885
Moscow, **1988** 353-373
Washington, **1987** 991-1002, 1004-1006
UN address on, **1984** 811-821
Western trade with Soviets, **1982** 469-470
and world terrorism, **1981** 461-462
State of the Union addresses, **1982** 73-85; **1983** 77-91; **1984** 81-95; **1985** 105-117; **1986** 39-48; **1987** 105-115; **1988** 57-68
Statue of Liberty centennial, **1986** 697-698, 700-702
stock market crash, **1987** 834-841
Supreme Court appointments, **1981** 575, 578; **1986** 591-599; **1987** 577-580; **1989** 321; **1990** 615-616
Bork nomination, **1987** 717-721
Taiwan, support for, **1984** 23-24
on terrorism, **1981** 461-462; **1984** 934; **1985** 463-477
transfer of power, **1985** 491-495; **1989** 42-43
UN, PLO observer mission to, **1988** 480
unemployment, reducing (State of the Union and CEA on recovery), **1983** 77-78, 84-85, 115-116, 121, 123-124, 131-133
urban enterprise zones, **1982** 81-82
U.S. promotion of democracy, **2005** 43
on U.S.-British extradition treaty, **1986** 752
Vatican
and assassination attempt on John Paul II, **1981** 427-429
diplomatic relations with, **1984** 19
John Paul II meetings, **1984** 327; **1987** 699
Veterans Affairs Department, **1988** 873, 875-876
vetoes
continuing appropriations bill, **1981** 642, 831-834
of fairness doctrine bill, **1987** 627
trade bills, **1988** 339-346
Vietnam unknown serviceman, **1984** 347-348, 350-352
welfare reform signing, **1988** 847, 850-852
women's rights, **1983** 755-763
Real estate, advertising sales of, and white flight, **1977** 313-320
Rebozo, Charles G. "Bebe," handling of Nixon campaign contributions, **1973** 898, 906, 975-977; **1974** 605, 616; **1975** 654, 660
Recall election, for Arizona governor, **1988** 250-251
Recession
See also Asia, financial crisis
1974-1975, with high inflation and unemployment, Burns on, **1975** 635-640
1981-1982
Fed policy during, **1987** 511-512
and savings and loan crisis, **1989** 463-464
Carter anti-inflation measures and, **1980** 243
deficit, Reagan on effect on, **1982** 143-144, 153-154
defined, **2004** 62
during Bush administration, **1991** 68-69, 74; **1992** 108-118; **1995** 55, 56-57, 61-65
emphasis on, in Ford economic program, **1975** 15-16, 19, 28
employment of minorities, effect of on, **1982** 919, 934
European, and monetary union, **1978** 742
fighting, Ford on before business leaders in D.C., **1974** 975-980
Greenspan on "faltered" business recovery, **1991** 851-856
health care, effect of on, **1983** 318
impact on Chrysler, **1979** 694, 700
in industrialized countries, effect of on world economy, **1983** 802, 804, 807-810, 812
Japanese economic crisis, **1998** 532-542, 722; **2001** 667; **2002** 689, 691-692
oil price increase effect on, **1981** 800
predictions
by Carter CEA, **1980** 159, 162-163, 165, 171-172, 174, 177-178
of continued, by Ford CEA, **1975** 99-101
dealing with, Joint Economic Committee on, **1980** 210, 220
Nixon's CEA on, **1974** 69, 73, 76
preventing
fiscal flexibility in Nixon budget, **1974** 95-98, 100-102
Nixon on, **1974** 41-43, 45, 53, 55
recovery from
balanced policy for, proper government role in, Carter on, **1981** 113-115
Carter on progress in, **1981** 57, 60-64, 105-108, 123
Ford and advisers on, **1976** 45-47, 52-54
Ford and CEA on progress toward, **1976** 45-47, 52-54; **1977** 45-46, 51
forecasts by Reagan CEA, **1982** 122, 139-141
Joint Economic Committee on, **1977** 717-722, 727, 731-732
progress in, Carter on, **1978** 67-68
under Carter, **1981** 105, 116
under Reagan, **1981** 642, 644; **1983** 101, 121, 127-128, 131-132, 139
reversing, Republican Party platform on, **1980** 567-568, 596-597
risk of U.S., and need for corrective action, OECD on, **1973** 682-695
in the United States, **1998** 532; **2001** 665; **2002** 52
and Ford budget, **1975** 83, 87-88
Volcker effect on, **1983** 595-597
worldwide
in aftermath of September 11, **2001** 667-668
economic summit on working out of, **1983** 508, 511-512
Ford CIEP on, **1975** 187-188, 190-192

Recession *Continued*
impact on developing countries, **1983** 263-266, 512, 802, 804, 807-810
oil surplus as result of, **1982** 979
recovery from
and global interdependence, **1976** 50-51
Joint Economic Report, **1977** 725-726
role of U.S. economy, Ford on, **1975** 25-26
Recombinant DNA research
ownership of biological material, **1987** 355, 357-358
potential hazards of, **1975** 319-324
Record, James F., Saudi Arabia bombing investigation, **1996** 673-674
Recording Industry of America, **1990** 509, 510
Recreation
as mission of national parks, **1972** 795-798, 800-804
and multiple-use management of national forests, **1973** 21-26
Recyling, construction of facilities for, **1972** 149
Red Cross. *See* American Red Cross; International Committee of the Red Cross
Red Lion Broadcasting Co. v. FCC, **1987** 629-630, 632-635; **1990** 426
Redistricting, political
equality of, **1983** 599-616
judicial review of, **1972** 935-938
use of racial criteria in, **1977** 151-167
Redman, Charles, **1986** 352
Reed, Bruce
on welfare rolls' decline, **1999** 257
welfare system, **1997** 619
Reed, Jack (D-R.I.), missile defense system, **2002** 1029; **2003** 818
Reed, John S., SEC board interim chairman, **2003** 698
Reed, Wornie L., **1989** 447
Reed v. Reed, **1995** 313
Reeker, Philip
on democracy in Pakistan, **2002** 168
Venezuela coup attempt, **2002** 206-207
Reese, Donald J., Abu Ghraib prison abuse scandal, **2004** 215
Rees-Jones, Trevor, **1997** 647, 649
Reeve, Christopher
death of, **2005** 318
at Democratic Party convention, **1996** 601
therapeutic cloning and stem cell research supporter, **2002** 515; **2004** 160; **2005** 318
Reeves, Keith, racism in U.S. survey, **2001** 606
Reflections of a Public Man, and Wright ethics investigation, **1989** 240, 244-247, 265-267
Reform Party
convention, Perot presidential nomination, **1996** 550-562
platform, **2000** 896
Refugee Act (1980), **1993** 414, 419-420, 421
applied to Shostakovich and son, **1981** 377
and political asylum, **1987** 253-265
refugee ceilings and emergency plans, **1981** 265
Refugees
See also Asylum, political
from Afghan conflict, **1986** 919-920, 922-927, 930-931, 936
Afghanistan, postwar, **2002** 20-22
Afghan-Pakistani agreement on, **1988** 258, 260-263
in Africa, John Paul II on, **1985** 508
Africa, UNCHR Ogata's address on, **1999** 432-438
Angolan conflict, **2002** 155-156
Bangladesh, in India, Kennedy on, **1972** 163-164
Central African refugee crisis, **1996** 809-815
Central American escaping hurricane and flood damage, **1998** 791
child abuse in, **2002** 919-920
Cuban boat people, U.S. policy on, **1980** 337-350; **1995** 203-207
economic summit's concern for, **1981** 594
Haitian
District Court on, **1993** 371-383
U.S. interdiction of, **1981** 606, 613, 616-618; **1992** 453-468; **1993** 413-421
Jews to Switzerland, **1997** 264-265
Kurdish refugees in Turkey, **2002** 911
Pakistani, return of from India, U.S. aid for, **1972** 32-36
Palestinian refugee camp in Jenin "massacre," **2002** 933-935
policy reform, Carter on, **1980** 44, 64; **1981** 76-77, 102
political, and U.S.-Cuban antihijacking agreement, **1973** 265-266, 268
population increases of in world, **1981** 179, 181, 188-190
Reagan administration policy on, **1981** 265, 605-607, 615-616
of religious persecution, U.S. policy, **1998** 26-28
Rwandan camps, UN security measures, **1994** 541-549
Shostakovich and son as, **1981** 375, 377
in Thailand, John Paul II visit to, **1984** 329, 336-338
UN on resettlement, **1991** 671-678
Vietnamese
evacuation of Da Nang, **1975** 201-204
evacuation of Saigon, **1975** 252-253, 267, 270-271, 274
resettlement in U.S., **1975** 224-225, 228-230; **1980** 100
Refugees International
sexual exploitation by peacekeepers report, **2005** 237
Zimbabwe AIDS epidemic, **2002** 137
Zimbabwe food shortages, **2002** 136
Refuseniks
See also Soviet Union, emigration rules
and release of Shcharansky, **1986** 94-95
Regal Tube Co., intra-enterprise conspiracy doctrine, **1984** 414-417, 421, 423, 425
Regan, Donald T.
on developing countries' concerns, **1984** 795
Feldstein resignation, **1985** 80
Iran-contra affair, **1986** 1053; **1987** 207, 222, 231-232
Japan's open-market plan, **1985** 319
transfer of presidential power, **1985** 493
as Treasury secretary, **1982** 469-470; **1984** 82, 119, 121
Regan v. Taxation with Representation of Wash., **1991** 262, 264

Regan v. Time, Inc., **1991** 820
Regents of the University of California v. Bakke, **1978** 467-492; **1993** 935; **1995** 313-314
Regional conflicts
  See also Afghanistan; Arab-Israeli War; Central America; Falkland Islands (Malvinas) War; Ireland, Northern; Middle East
  arms control agreements tied to, Gorbachev on, **1986** 20
  freedom fighters in, Reagan on, **1986** 40, 47
  resolution of
    Bush on Soviet cooperation in, **1989** 180
    Carter on, **1977** 738-739, 743-744; **1979** 74-76
    Reagan on, **1984** 816-817; **1986** 4, 8; **1989** 19-21
    UN ineffectiveness, **1982** 769-779
  Soviet exploitation of, NATO on, **1978** 374
  Soviet involvement in
    Carter on, **1978** 223-225, 229, 234-236, 239
    Reagan on, **1982** 180, 187-188; **1983** 307, 312, 439-454
  U.S. interference in, Gromyko on, **1984** 827-828
  U.S.-Soviet discussions of
    at Geneva summit, **1985** 750, 758-760
    at Iceland summit, **1986** 876, 879, 881
    at Malta summit, **1989** 644, 647, 650, 657-658, 666
    at Moscow summit, **1988** 356-357, 367
    at Washington summit, **1987** 991, 999, 1002, 1005
  world toleration of, Kissinger on, **1974** 845-846
Regional Greenhouse Gas Initiative, **2005** 924
Regional Rail Reorganization Act (1973), **1975** 529-530, 533
Regulation
  See also Deregulation; Transportation, deregulation of
  of auto standards, impact on Chrysler, **1979** 694, 697-698, 703, 711
  of broadcasting through fairness doctrine, **1987** 625-636
  budget for, to improve program efficiency, **1980** 211
  burden of to business, **1976** 676; **1980** 567, 602-603, 609-613
  cost to economic growth
    Ford CEA on, **1977** 66-67, 72-73, 79
    Reagan CEA on, **1985** 79, 82, 84, 86-87; **1988** 122-123, 138-139, 158
  cost to productivity
    Ford on, **1976** 19; **1977** 72-73
    Reagan reduction of, **1983** 103, 105, 118
  cost-benefit analysis of, **1978** 688-690, 694; **1981** 59, 491-505
    Joint Economic Committee on, **1981** 294, 295, 308-309, 313, 316-317, 322-324
    Reagan and advisers on, **1987** 117, 123-125
    Republican Party platform on, **1976** 624, 626-627
  criminal violation of, sentencing for, **1987** 419-420
  deregulation, in Carter-Reagan debate, **1980** 948
  economic
    reduction of
      Reagan on, **1983** 103-105, 118, 126
      Reagan on progress in, **1985** 105, 112-113
  environmental
    as burden on business and industry, **1975** 640-641; **1984** 427-430
    of hazardous waste disposal, **1979** 781-784, 788-790, 799
    impact on business investment, Nixon CEA on, **1974** 86
    impact on inflation, **1978** 76
    relaxation of to encourage competition, **1974** 862-863
  executive branch review of, **1982** 121, 126-127; **1984** 113; **1985** 77-78
  impact on inflation, **1978** 13; **1979** 218-220
  improving clarity and purpose of, Carter, **1977** 109; **1978** 33, 335-336
  interference with competition, **1976** 49-50
  of nuclear power industry, **1979** 832, 842-844
  reduction of
    Carter on, **1977** 104, 109
    Reagan on, **1989** 3, 5, 9, 11
    Reagan on progress in, **1984** 104, 113-114, 119, 124; **1987** 6-7, 12
  reversing growth of, in Reagan economic plan, **1981** 213, 219, 222, 325, 329; **1983** 123
  safety
    cost of, **1975** 640-641; **1978** 633-634, 636-637
    and government assumption of risk, **1987** 127, 141-142
  social
    costs of, Joint Economic Committee on, **1979** 217, 219-220
    effect on productivity, **1979** 82, 115-116
  state, of water export, **1982** 689-701
  of state utilities, **1982** 447-467
  unified calendar and sunset reviews of, **1978** 689, 694
Regulatory reform
  Carter proposals for, **1980** 43, 72-76, 169, 185, 779-780
  CEA economic report on, **1997** 61
  Democratic Party platform on, **1976** 544, 558; **1980** 716, 719, 744-745
  of financial markets, **1984** 143-144
  and government interference, Carter on, **1978** 15, 32-33
  Reagan task force on, **1981** 222, 492; **1984** 114
  Republican Party platform on, **1984** 670-671, 677, 687-688; **1988** 616, 626-627, 671-673; **1996** 514
Rehabilitation Act (1973), **1992** 189-190, 194, 195
  Section 504
    discrimination against alcoholics, **1988** 278-285
    job discrimination and contagious disease, **1987** 245-252
    treatment of severely handicapped infants, **1986** 541-558
Rehnquist, William H.
  abortion
    anti-abortion demonstrations, **2000** 433
    clinic protests, **1994** 312-320
    family-planning clinic advice, **1991** 260-266
    parental consent for, **1990** 387-407
    partial-birth, **2000** 432, 441, 444-446
    and privacy right, **1973** 102, 110-111, 114
    protesters and RICO law, **1994** 29-33
    public funding of, **1980** 515
    right to, **1986** 559-562, 571, 579

Rehnquist, William H. *Continued*
state restrictions on, **1983** 544-545, 557-564, 572; **1989** 365-367, 369-375
techniques, state restrictions on, **1976** 483
women's right to choose, **1992** 589, 611-613
advertising prescription drug prices, **1976** 352, 361-362
affirmative action, **1986** 677-678; **1987** 332-333, 346; **2003** 362, 363, 374, 376-386
federal government plans, **1995** 308
job program, **1979** 495, 502-507
and seniority protections, **1984** 366
age discrimination, **1983** 231-232, 239
alimony payments to men, **1979** 193-194, 200-205
antitrust immunity of cities, **1982** 35, 43
appointment to Chief Justice, **1986** 591-599
asset forfeiture
drug trafficking, **1993** 432-438
pornography seized, **1993** 432, 438-440
attorney-client privilege, **1998** 395, 397-401
auto searches, **1978** 753-761; **1982** 425
bankruptcy and labor contracts, **1984** 182, 184-193
bankruptcy law, **1982** 597
broadcast of offensive material, **1978** 515
campaign finance reform, **2003** 1160
child custody rights, **1982** 260-261, 271
child pornography, **1982** 675; **1990** 239-245
church-state separation
church's objection to liquor license, **1982** 956, 961
public display of Nativity scene, **1984** 218
Clean Air Act, **1990** 716
Clinton impeachment trial, **1999** 10, 16, 21; **2005** 553
coastal property rights, **1992** 616-620
coerced confessions, **1991** 175, 182-184
congressional immunity, **1979** 467
in job discrimination suit, **1979** 399, 401, 408-410
congressional term limits, **1995** 260, 271-275
counsel, right to, **1977** 219, 234; **1979** 207-210
Court division, **1981** 576
Court workload, **1982** 706-707, 723-724
damages for tobacco-related ills, **1992** 564-573
deaf parochial student, **1993** 399-403
death of, **2005** 41, 379, 447, 551-557, 558, 814
death penalty, **2005** 552-553
constitutionality of, **1972** 499, 505
constitutionality of state laws on, **1976** 489-490
ex post facto, **1977** 519
fairness of, **2001** 389
for juvenile offenders, **2002** 358; **2004** 797; **2005** 180, 192-196
mandatory for murder of police officer, **1977** 397-398, 400-405
for the mentally retarded, **2002** 356, 365-368
mitigating factors, **1978** 496-498, 510-511, 514; **1982** 51, 60
racial discrimination in, **1987** 463
for rape, **1977** 517-518, 525
remarks on, **1990** 311-317
standing of mother to request stay, **1976** 921
state's misuse of, **1980** 455, 457, 467
declassification of documents, **1972** 235
detentions in terrorism cases, **2004** 377, 381-388, 397-398
disabilities in the workplace, **2002** 6
disability, definition of, **1999** 318, 320
drug testing of students, **1995** 339-346
education
for children of illegal aliens, **1982** 501
creation science teaching, **1987** 567, 574
election campaigns
financing, **1976** 110-111
open political primaries, **1986** 1065, 1072
PAC spending limits, **1985** 278-290
eminent domain, **2005** 363, 371-375
endangered species on private lands, **1995** 360, 366-368
entrapment in child pornography case, **1992** 322-327
faculty tenure review disclosure, **1990** 23-34
flag burning, **1989** 343-344, 351-354; **1990** 358, 363-365
free speech
ballot initiatives, **1999** 6, 12-14
corporate, in referendum campaigns, **1978** 307, 309, 322-324
and the Internet, **1997** 445, 454-458
Internet pornography filters, **2003** 388-389, 393-396
in satire of public figures, **1988** 175, 177-182
freedom of residential signs, **1994** 290-297
funeral services, **2005** 551-557
gay rights discrimination, **1996** 286, 291-295
gay rights to march, **1995** 327-335
grandparents' rights, **2000** 289, 290-295
Guantanamo Bay detainees, **2003** 109-110
gun-free school zones, **1995** 184, 185-192
Haitian refugee interdiction, **1992** 453, 459-468; **1993** 413-421
hate crimes, **1992** 543-551; **1993** 385-389
HIV as a disability, **1998** 379-380, 389-392
home video taping, **1984** 54, 59
immunity of municipalities, **1980** 299, 308
impeachment, Senate's authority to remove judge, **1993** 81-87
at inauguration of president Bush, **2001** 94; **2005** 41
independent counsel law, **1988** 465, 467-477
intra-enterprise conspiracy doctrine, **1984** 414
job discrimination
and contagious disease, **1987** 246, 250-252
fetal protection, **1991** 151-153
hiring goals for minorities, **1989** 322, 329-331
involving African Americans, **1993** 423-429
judicial immunity, **1978** 260
judicial pay raise, **1989** 195-196, 202-204
jury selection
gender discrimination, **1994** 233-234
opposition to death penalty, **1986** 446-454
service by women, **1975** 55, 63-66
jury size and unanimous verdicts, **1979** 263-268
jury trials, split verdicts in, **1972** 423
labor unions, freedom of members to resign, **1985** 415

legacy of Supreme Court rulings, **2005** 551-553
legislative intent, **1993** 250-253
legislative veto, **1983** 619
libel
of private and public persons, **1986** 355, 357-358, 364
suits against news media, **1984** 247-256
libel award, appellate review of, **1984** 300-301, 310-312
line-item veto, **1998** 421
Marshall papers, letter over access to, **1993** 341-342
military draft, sex discrimination in, **1981** 521-522, 524-532
minimum wage laws applied to state governments, **1976** 377-385; **1985** 169, 182
minority set-aside programs, **1980** 539-540, 560; **1989** 324; **1990** 421, 429-434
Miranda warnings, **2000** 385-386, 388-389, 389-394
interrogation after right to counsel invoked, **1981** 433
interrogation definition, **1980** 431
pre-Miranda right to counsel, **1974** 474-482
rule upheld, **1990** 785, 786, 791-793
NAACP boycott damages, **1982** 656
Nixon papers and tapes, custody of, **1977** 466-467, 510-516
obscenity
community standards, **1974** 516-521
legal tests for, **1987** 479
OSHA safety inspections, warrants for, **1978** 340-341, 346
on Packwood investigation, **1995** 593
parental leave
and job discrimination, **1987** 17, 25
senority rights after, **1977** 871-877
parochial school aid, **1997** 363
patenting of living organisms, **1980** 493
peremptory challenge, **1986** 411, 425
physician-assisted suicide, **1997** 460-461, 463-472
political asylum, **1987** 254, 262
political dismissals from public jobs, **1980** 259-261, 266
Powell's retirement, **1987** 577
pregnancy coverage in company disability plans, **1976** 891-899
presidential elections recount, **2000** 1002, 1003
presidential immunity, **1982** 539
press
access to pretrial hearings, **1979** 511-512, 524-525
confidentiality of sources, **1972** 507-508
gag orders and right to fair trial, **1976** 464
libel of public figure, **1979** 285
newsroom searches, **1978** 355
right of reply by political candidate, **1974** 524, 527
preventive detention, **1987** 491, 493-502
prison crowding, **1981** 478
prison inmates, beaten by guards, **1992** 175-182
prisoner appeals, **1991** 205-206
from death row, **1993** 141-147
prisoners' rights in searches, **1984** 480
property takings
and historic preservation, **1978** 453-455, 462-465
uncompensated, **1987** 532, 534-541
proposed national court of appeals, **1975** 459, 462-463
psychiatric aid, indigents' right to, **1985** 209, 217-219
public aid to nonpublic schools, **1973** 642; **1977** 432, 440; **1985** 433, 435, 449, 455
public broadcasting editorials, **1984** 450-451, 461-463
public land and developers, **1994** 299, 300-306
punitive damages, for consumer product liability, **1996** 275, 282-283
racial discrimination in private school admission, **1976** 392, 401
redistricting, **1983** 600, 612-615; **1986** 629
one-man, one-vote rule, **1973** 277-284
race-based, **1993** 459-474; **1995** 369, 371, 373-380; **1996** 368-369, 371-379
racial criteria in, **1977** 152
religious clubs in public schools, **2001** 422
religious freedom, **1997** 408
religious publications, **1995** 385-395
religious symbols, **1995** 387, 396-400
reverse discrimination
in firing employees, **1976** 406
medical school admissions, **1978** 468-469, 471, 491
right to die, **1990** 373-382
school book banning, **1982** 568, 580
school desegregation, **1979** 536, 542-546, 551-552; **1991** 23-29
cross-district remedies for, **1974** 639
plan's continued balance, **1976** 413-421
restrictions on busing, **1982** 620-633
system-wide remedies for, **1977** 447, 449-455
school prayer, **1985** 380-381; **1992** 555; **2000** 367, 376-378
school vouchers, **2002** 408, 411-416
schools, judicial intervention in operation of, **1975** 68, 75
searches, home arrest without warrant, **1980** 283, 291, 297
sentencing
and double jeopardy, **1980** 977
excessive prison, **1983** 660, 670-674
murder case, **1991** 381, 383-389
sentencing laws, **2003** 980, 982, 983, 984; **2004** 360
sex discrimination
by Jaycees, **1984** 468
in pension plans, **1978** 293, 301; **1983** 691-692, 701-704
in Social Security survivors' benefits, **1975** 178, 185; **1977** 170, 177-181
sex offenders, right to confine, **1997** 383
sexual harassment
at school, **1992** 188-199; **1999** 215, 227-234
in workplace, **1993** 939-944
snail darter protection from dam project, **1978** 434-435, 451-452
sodomy and privacy right, **1986** 601
states' rights, **1999** 333

Rehnquist, William H. *Continued*
statutory rape laws, sex discrimination in, **1981** 339-344
student drug testing, **2002** 426
students' rights
and corporal punishment, **1977** 293
free speech, **1986** 731
searches, **1985** 14
suspects' rights and public safety, **1984** 388-392
tax exemptions for discriminatory schools, **1983** 490, 503-505
tax increase to fund school desegregation, **1990** 227, 228-229, 232-238
Ten Commandments displays, **2005** 377, 380-383, 552
terminal illness, **2005** 376
treaty termination, **1979** 917, 933, 935-937
tuition tax credit, **1983** 676-677, 679-684
unitary taxation, **1983** 645
unreasonable searches, **2001** 409, 410, 416-419
use of deadly force, **1985** 304, 312
use of school facilities by religious groups, **1993** 363-369
utilities regulation, **1982** 448, 460
virtual pornography, **2002** 290
water rights, **1982** 689-690, 699
wiretaps
authorization by attorney general, **1974** 392, 399
government case on warrantless, **1972** 485
worker health protection, **1981** 492, 503
zoning for adult theaters, **1986** 132, 134-140
Reich, Robert B.
apparel industry investigations, **1997** 209
on Clinton draft issue, **1992** 158
on corporate responsibility, **1996** 41-49
on illegal immigrants and the labor force, **1995** 565
on income inequality, **1996** 396
on labor-management relations report, **1995** 15, 17
Reid, Alex, IRA weapons decommissioning, **2005** 511
Reid, Harry (D-Nev.)
Bush State of the Union address, Democratic response, **2005** 81, 90-92
and Jeffords party switch, **2001** 379, 380
Senate majority leader election, **2005** 81
Social Security reform, **2005** 113
stem cell research, **2005** 310
warrantless domestic surveillance, **2005** 961
Reid, Richard C. ("shoe bomber"), terrorist hijacking attempt, **2001** 650; **2002** 836; **2005** 396
Reidl, Brian, federal budget deficit, **2003** 682
Reilly, Thomas F.
gay marriage legislation, **2003** 404; **2004** 38
Microsoft antitrust case, **2002** 798
sexual abuse by priests case, **2003** 523-543
Reilly, William K.
on Alaskan oil spill, **1989** 231-232
Bush appointment, **1990** 716
Earth Summit (Rio), **1992** 499-500, 505
on ozone layer, **1992** 76
Rein, Martin, **1988** 877
Reinecke, Ed (R-Calif.)
and ITT political contributions, **1972** 396-397, 404, 406
Watergate conviction of, **1975** 666
Reinhardt, Stephen
Guantanamo Bay detainees, **2003** 110-111
physician-assisted suicide, **1996** 123
pledge of allegiance, constitutionality of, **2002** 383, 384
right to bear arms, **2002** 961-968
Reinhardt College, and Gingrich Renewing American Civilization course, **1997** 8-9
Reinhold, Robert, **1981** 4
Reinventing Government Report. *See* National Performance Review
Reischauer, Robert D.
balanced budget agreement, **1997** 602
federal budget deficit, **2003** 682
Reisman, David, **1991** 310
Reiss, Albert J., on domestic violence, **1983** 358, 360
Reiss, David, on AIDS policy, **1997** 82
Relief organizations, international, effectiveness of, **1984** 973-976, 985-995
Religion
See also Catholic Church; Jews
Anglican-Catholic relations, John Paul II on, **1982** 409-410
Army's first Muslim chaplain, **1993** 973-975
Buddhism, John Paul II on, **1984** 327-330, 334
burial sites of Native Americans, museums' return of skeletal remains, **1989** 539-543
Bush administration faith-based initiative, **2001** 95, 132-140, 174, 178-179, 420-421; **2002** 37, 406-407, 823; **2003** 27-28; **2004** 29
church-state separation
Edward M. Kennedy on, **1983** 817, 819-823
public display of Nativity scene, **1984** 217-239
silent prayer in schools, **1985** 379-395
veto over liquor licenses, **1982** 955-963
Confucianism, John Paul II's visit to Far East, **1984** 327, 329
creation science in public schools, **1972** 843-844; **1982** 3-16; **1987** 565-576
cults, mass suicide of People's Temple members, **1979** 347-349, 356
and decision to terminate life-support systems, **1976** 209
ecumenicism, John Paul II on, **1984** 399-402; **1986** 24, 28-30, 32-33
freedom of, in Soviet Union, **1988** 355, 358-359
gay clergy controversy, **2004** 42-44
human genetic engineering, religious leaders on, **1983** 525
and Iran-Iraq War, **1984** 747-748
Judaism and Christianity compared, John Paul II visit to synagogue, **1986** 339-346
and moral status of human biological materials, **1987** 366-367
and Northern Ireland conflict, **1984** 315-322; **1985** 723-724
persecution and Holocaust, Reagan on, **1981** 381-382, 386-387
and politics, in presidential debates, **1980** 849, 864-866; **1984** 846, 855-858
public aid to parochial schools, **1973** 641-658
in public schools, **1995** 546-552
Rehnquist Supreme Court rulings on, **2005** 552

religious organizations' use of campus buildings, **1981** 869-879; **1983** 272; **1984** 245
sexual abuse by priests, **2002** 867-876; **2003** 523-543
state, Spanish democratic constitution on, **1978** 810, 815
teaching about, neglect of, **1987** 597-608
Ten Commandments displays, Supreme Court on, **2005** 376-389, 552, 555
tuition tax credit, effect of on parochial schools, **1983** 675-676, 677-678
and U.S. presidency, Carter on, **1977** 903
U.S.-Vatican diplomatic relations, **1984** 19-22
Religious freedom
in Cuba, **1997** 564, 571
in Cuba, papal address on, **1998** 30-37
"one nation, under God" phrase, **2002** 382-390
Supreme court case, **1997** 406-421
U.S. foreign policy, **1998** 19-29
Religious Freedom Day, **1998** 23
Religious Freedom Restoration Act (RFRA), Supreme Court on, **1997** 406-421; **1999** 335
Religious fundamentalists
Kennedy speech to Moral Majority, **1983** 817-825
Reagan speech to evangelicals, **1983** 269-277
Republican national convention, **1992** 781-798
on tax exemptions for discriminatory schools, **1983** 489, 491
Religious persecution
church arson cases, **1997** 301-313
State Department report, **1997** 562-579
U.S. policy, **1998** 26-28
Relman, Arnold S., on marijuana's health effects, **1982** 203-204, 210-211
Relyea, Harold, **1974** 887
Reno, Janet
anti-abortion violence, **1998** 809-813
attorney general nomination, **1993** 135-139
Brady Bill signing, **1993** 966
campaign finance investigations, **1997** 822-831; **1998** 890-902; **2000** 617, 763
capital punishment and minorities, **2000** 990
church arson cases, **1997** 301-303, 310
DEA and FBI reorganization proposal, **1993** 720
domestic violence prosecutions, **1993** 288
Elian Gonzalez political asylum case, **2000** 266, 267
FBI crime laboratory investigations, **1997** 221-222
FBI director, Sessions, resignation, **1993** 609-611
Foster suicide, **1993** 533, 539
Gore's "Reinventing Government" report, **1993** 720
Lewinsky affair investigations, **1998** 565-566
March on Washington thirtieth anniversary, **1993** 678
marijuana law enforcement, **1996** 756
Microsoft Corp. antitrust ruling, **1999** 658; **2000** 109
Nicholson espionage case, **1996** 797-798
physician-assisted suicide, **1997** 463; **1999** 441-442; **2001** 293
racial gerrymandering, Supreme Court case, **1993** 459-481
school safety, **1998** 738-739; **2000** 874-875
sentencing for cocaine penalties, **1997** 246
special counsel regulations, **1999** 165, 168-169
television violence, **1993** 490
tobacco industry fraud, **1999** 537
and violent crime, **1995** 710; **1998** 869
Waco compound incident, role in, **1993** 293, 295, 297-301, 821
Waco investigations, **1999** 480-488
Wen Ho Lee spy case, **2000** 742
Reno v. American Civil Liberties Union, **1997** 444-458
Renton v. Playtime Theatres, Inc., **1986** 131-144; **1997** 447-448
Repelita project (Indonesia), environmental consequences of, **1986** 859-873
Reporters Committee for Freedom of the Press
access to pretrial hearings, **1979** 513
Court ruling in libel suit, **1979** 287, 317
FOIA guidelines, **1981** 395
gag orders, **1976** 464
insider trading case, **1987** 882
newsroom searches ruling, **1978** 357
Reproductive freedom
See also Abortion; Contraception; Family planning
women's conference support for, **1977** 865-866
Reproductive technologies
artificial insemination, Vatican on, **1987** 267-269, 277-283
Catholic teaching on, **1987** 267-285
John Paul II on, **1987** 701, 711-712
Republic of China. *See* Taiwan (Republic of China)
Republic of Korea. *See* South Korea
Republican National Alliance (ARENA, El Salvador), **1993** 237, 239
Republican National Coalition for Life, **1992** 800
Republican National Committee (RNC)
campaign finance reform law, **2003** 1158, 1160
and Mary Dent Crisp resignation, **1980** 568
on parties' primary rules, **1986** 1067
on political gerrymandering, **1986** 618
Republican Party
See also Contract with America
congressional elections and, **1974** 696
on Democratic Party platform, **1988** 559
election losses, **1998** 801-802
Four-Point Plan for Educational Excellence, **2000** 20, 37-38
fund-raising efforts, **1998** 894
Indiana redistricting plan, **1986** 615-635
open primaries, **1986** 1065-1071
opening remarks of 104th Congress, **1995** 3-14
registration effort for 1972 election, **1973** 36
State of the Union address
Collins's response, **2000** 19-20, 36-38
Dole's response, **1996** 21-23, 35-38
Frist's response, **2000** 19-20, 38-40
Lott's response, **1998** 40-41, 54-59
Watts's response, **1997** 31, 44-49
Whitman's response, **1995** 25, 43-45
Watergate affair impact on, **1973** 499-500
welfare reform bill, **1996** 450-463
Republican Party conventions
Dallas, **1984** 661-664, 727-745
Detroit, **1980** 567-569, 651-664

Republican Party conventions *Continued*
Houston, **1992** 781-798, 799-839
ITT offer of contributions to, **1972** 395-406; **1974** 3-5, 16, 20-21
and antitrust case, **1974** 407-410
Kansas City, **1976** 665-676
Miami Beach, **1972** 651-652, 711-725
New Orleans, **1988** 589-613, 589-617
New York, **2004** 484, 493-501
Philadelphia, **2000** 519-535
San Diego, **1996** 478-496
Republican Party platform, **1972** 651-709; **1976** 617-664; **1980** 567-650; **1984** 661-726; **1988** 615-702; **1992** 799-839; **1996** 496-549; **2000** 508-515
Research and development (R&D)
CEA report on, **1997** 66-67; **1998** 82-83
tax credits proposed, **1992** 57, 65
Residential signs, **1994** 289-297
Resnick, Judith A., *Challenger* accident, **1986** 515, 520; **1988** 795
Resolution on Racial Reconciliation, **1995** 336-338
Resolution Trust Corporation (RTC), Seidman in charge, **1990** 817
Resource Conservation and Recovery Act (RCRA, 1976), **1995** 113
See also Superfund
regulations under, **1979** 781-782, 784, 788-790, 799
Respiratory disease
in coal miners, and smoking, **1985** 818-819
from involuntary smoking, **1986** 1082, 1085-1086
from smoking, health care costs of, **1985** 616-617
smoking linked to, surgeon general on, **2004** 291-292
Ressam, Ahmed, arrest for terrorist activities, **1999** 499; **2000** 861; **2001** 804; **2003** 553
Reston, James
acupuncture, **1997** 749-750
on Nixon's attacks on news media, **1973** 898
on Vance speech, **1980** 476
Retirement plans
See also Civil service retirement; Social Security
401(k) programs, **2005** 201-202, 485
baby boomers impact on, **2003** 711; **2005** 114-115
benefits and retirement age, **2005** 202
defined benefit system
status of the, **2005** 204-205
structural flaws in, **2005** 207-211
Democratic Party platform, **1996** 632
employee pension plans, comptroller general report on, **2002** 101-113
"moral hazard," **2005** 209-210
Reagan budget cuts to, **1982** 145, 150; **1983** 766-767, 769, 771-772
retiree demographic trends, **2003** 716
retirement security, **2002** 43
sex bias in, **1983** 691-705
Social Security, compared with payments, **1975** 115-134
underfunded corporate pensions, PBGC on, **2003** 707-719; **2005** 197-211
Universal Savings Accounts (USAs), **1999** 46, 90
Retrovir. *See* AZT (azidothymidine)
Reuss, Henry S. (D-Wis.)
federal aid to New York City, **1975** 863
Joint Economic Report, **1981** 293-297
monetary policy, **1977** 718
Rickover testimony to, **1982** 88
Reuther, Alan, on pension plan reform, **2005** 201
Revelle, Roger, **1988** 862
Revenue sharing
benefits of, Nixon on to South Carolina legislature, **1973** 270, 275
block grants
defined, **1976** 627-628
for social programs, **1976** 38, 43
to state and local governments, **1976** 14, 17, 23-24, 29-30
for community development, **1972** 101-102, 651, 685-686; **1973** 304-305, 314-317
cuts in for states, Joint Economic Committee on, **1979** 217
for education, **1972** 105-106, 230
in Ford budget, CBO analysis of, **1976** 186-187
general, extension of by Ford, **1975** 96; **1976** 47, 62
for human resources programs, **1973** 304, 307-310
for local law enforcement, **1973** 305, 321-323
shifting social programs to states, in Reagan budget, **1982** 74, 80-81
special and general compared, **1972** 694
for state and local governments, **1980** 28, 41-43, 65-67; **1981** 78
in Nixon budget, **1973** 169, 174-175, 181-182; **1974** 48, 53, 97-100, 106-108
support for, Democratic Party platform on, **1976** 566-567
for transportation, Republican Party platform on, **1972** 687-688
Revolutionary Justice Organization, **1989** 316-317
Revolutionary United Front (RUF), **2002** 247, 248, 249
Rexhepi, Bajram, Kosovo prime minister, **2003** 1139, 1143, 1144; **2004** 951
Rey, Juan Carlos, on Spain's entry into NATO, **1982** 420-421
Reynolds, Albert
British-Irish peace efforts, **1993** 923-927
Irish abortion case, **1992** 250
on Northern Ireland, **1994** 450
Reynolds, Frank, at Carter-Ford debate, **1976** 693, 695-697, 701-702, 707-708, 713-714
Reynolds, Robert E., and student newspaper censorship, **1988** 38-41, 44-46
Reynolds, William Bradford
appointment of, **1985** 481
Marc Rich presidential pardon, **2001** 90
sex discrimination language in laws, **1983** 756
treatment of severely handicapped infants, **1986** 544
Reynolds v. Sims, **1993** 465, 468
Rhode Island v. Innis, **1980** 431-444
Rhodes, Frank H. T., **1988** 187
Rhodes, James, **1974** 265
Rhodes, John J. (R-Ariz.)
Carter budget, **1978** 97; **1979** 11
Carter State of the Union, **1978** 9
Nixon impeachment, **1974** 674, 683
Nixon pardon, **1974** 812-813

Nixon resignation, **1974** 289, 302, 684
Rockefeller's qualifications, **1974** 988
Rhodes v. Chapman, **1981** 477-490; **1992** 179-180, 184
Rhodesia
See also Zimbabwe
Arab oil embargo against, **1974** 221, 256
cease-fire in, and plans for independence, **1979** 939-948
Democratic Party platform on, **1972** 580
elections in, Thatcher government on, **1979** 382, 386
internal agreement on constitution, **1978** 149-155
majority rule in, British plan for, **1976** 721-729
settlement in
British-U.S. plan for, **1977** 583-590
Kissinger on, **1976** 287-288, 290-292, 294, 613, 908-909, 912
UN sanctions against regime in, **1977** 193
white control of, **1978** 150
Riansofa, Laurence, Rwanda presidential elections, **2003** 1071
Ribicoff, Abraham (D-Conn.)
Lance inquiry, **1977** 628-629, 642-645, 663, 673-675
military base closings, **1988** 952
Soviet emigration policy, **1974** 538
Riccardo, John J., **1979** 694
Rice, Condoleezza
affirmative action, **2003** 360
Afghanistan, state visit, **2005** 971
Bolton UN ambassador nomination, **2005** 236
Dayton peace accords, tenth anniversary, **2005** 859-861
Egyptian state visit, **2005** 165, 167-168
European relations and visits to Europe, **2005** 582, 592, 907
global warming, **2001** 112
Haiti, visit to urge elections, **2005** 330
India-U.S. relations, **2005** 465
Iran nuclear weapons program, **2004** 868; **2005** 592
Iraq nuclear weapons program, **2004** 715
Iraq-Niger uranium sales, **2005** 700
Israel, state visit, **2005** 88
Khobar Towers bombing, **2001** 797
Lebanon, state visit, **2005** 690
Middle East
elections, **2005** 273
peace process, **2003** 196; **2005** 88
West Bank settlement policy, **2005** 535
national commission on terrorist attacks, congressional testimony, **2004** 453-454
national security adviser appointment, **2001** 96
national security strategy, **2002** 634
North Korea relations, **2005** 44, 605
North Korean nuclear weapons program, **2002** 735
"outposts of tyranny" list, **2005** 44, 605
secretary of state appointment, **2004** 629-630, 778; **2005** 44-45
Syria
troop withdrawal from Lebanon, **2005** 688
U.S. ambassador withdrawn from, **2005** 687
U.S. foreign policy adviser, **2003** 453
U.S. torture policy statements, **2005** 905-918
Rice, Norman B., election, **1990** 42
Rice v. Santa Fe Elevator Corp., **1992** 567
Rich, Denise, **2001** 90
Rich, Marc, presidential pardon, **2001** 89-91
Richard, Ivor
on Moynihan's attack on Zionism resolution, **1975** 646
peace plan for Rhodesia, **1977** 585
Richards, Ann, Texas gubernatorial elections, **2000** 520
Richards, Stephen, securities fraud conviction, **2004** 423
Richards, Thomas C., **1990** 301-310
Richardson, Bill (D-N.M.; energy department secretary)
GAO report on national parks, **1996** 581
nuclear weapons security, **1999** 240-241
on political compromise, **1996** 468
Russian nuclear weapons programs, **2001** 19
Wen Ho Lee spy case, **2000** 741
Richardson, Elliot L.
Agnew investigation by Justice Department, **1973** 828-829, 831-832
attorney general appointment, **1973** 499-500, 504, 506, 508
attorney general resignation, **1973** 839, 859-863, 874-876, 878-880, 897, 902-904; **1975** 660; **1987** 718, 725; **1998** 906
Nixon's cooperation in Watergate investigation by, **1973** 564, 574
at Republican convention, **1976** 665
on Watergate prosecutor's role, **1975** 655-656
White House tapes negotiations, **1973** 860-865, 870, 873-874, 878-879
Richardson, James T., on Star of Bethlehem, **1997** 125
Richardson, Michael Ray, **1986** 170
Richardson, Richard C., Jr., **1991** 310
Richardson, Warren, **1981** 381
Richardson, William, on medical mistakes, **1999** 780
Richer, Harvey B., age of the universe, **2002** 213
Richmond (Virginia)
minority set-asides in city contracts, **1989** 323-324
school desegregation plan, court-ordered, **1972** 15-21
school uniform policy, **1996** 90
Richmond, Fred (D-N.Y.), **1982** 88
Richmond, Julius B.
health consequences of smoking, **1981** 3-4
Medicare reform, **1986** 274
smoking by women, **1980** 17
Richmond, William C., and Philadelphia raid on MOVE group, **1986** 240-251
Richmond v. J. A. Croson Co., **1989** 323-324; **1993** 467; **1995** 308, 315-316, 322, 323
Richness, Michael, nicotine addiction, **1998** 845
Ricin poison discovery, Senate Office Building, **2004** 268, 442-443
Rickover, Hyman G., on Defense Department bureaucracy, **1982** 87-104
RICO. *See* Racketeer Influenced and Corrupt Organizations Act

Riddick v. New York, **1980** 281-297
Riddick v. School Bd. of City of Norfolk, **1991** 27
Ride, Sally K.
Challenger commission, **1986** 517
Columbia space shuttle disaster, **2003** 664
space program planning, **1987** 649-669
Ridge, Tom
anthrax threat response, **2001** 673-674, 676
food supply contamination, **2002** 583
Homeland Security Department secretary
appointment, **2002** 531, 533; **2005** 895-896
resignation, **2004** 272
homeland security strategy report, **2002** 534
terrorist threat alerts, **2004** 268
for chemical weapons, **2004** 272
for financial centers, **2004** 268, 270-271, 538
Terrorist Threat Integration Center, **2003** 158
terrorist watch list consolidation, **2003** 155
White House Office of Homeland Security, **2001** 637, 639-640; **2002** 36
Riding, Alan, **1985** 4
Ridings, Dorothy S., presidential debates, **1984** 848, 876
Riegle, Donald W., Jr. (D-Mich.)
Gulf War syndrome report, **1994** 264, 267, 270-271
"Keating Five" investigations, **1990** 817; **1991** 107-118
NAFTA, **1992** 761
savings and loans institutions, **1989** 465
Rifkin, Jeremy
genetically engineered foods, **1992** 470
human genetic engineering, **1983** 525
plant biotechnology, **1986** 288
Rifkind, Robert S., on Catholic Jewish relations, **1998** 123
Rigas, John J., fraud charge conviction, **2004** 415, 420
Rigas family, Adelphia Communications Corp. scandal, **2002** 399; **2004** 415, 422
Riggs, Frank (R-Calif.)
affirmative action programs, **1998** 858
bilingual education funding, **1998** 315
Right to die. *See* Death and dying; End-of-life care; Physician-assisted suicide
Right to life. *See* Abortion; End-of-life care
Right to Life Committee, National, **1986** 1058
Rights of the Child
Convention on the, **2002** 918
U.S. position on, **2002** 224-225
Riles, Wilson, **1975** 692
Riley, Joseph P., Jr., **1989** 668
Riley, Richard W.
on adult literacy, **1993** 739
national education standards, **1997** 35
parochial school aid, **1997** 363
restructuring college aid, **1993** 173
school safety, **1998** 738
State of American Education address, **1996** 106-117
Supreme Court appointment, consideration of, **1993** 393
teacher shortage, **1999** 65
Rimer, Barbara, mammogram advocate, **1997** 144, 145-149
Rindskopf, Elizabeth, on declassifying documents, **1994** 526
Ring v. Arizona, **2002** 353, 357; **2004** 360, 797
Rio Pact, and U.S. protection for Honduras, **1987** 640
Rio treaty. *See* United Nations conventions, Climate Change (UNFCCC)
Riordan, Richard, **1994** 4, 5, 7
California gubernatorial election, **2003** 1006, 1008
Ripken, Cal, Jr., on breaking consecutive baseball game record, **1995** 588-591; **1998** 628-629
al-Rishawi, Sajida Mubarak, terrorist bombing in Jordan, **2005** 401
Risner, Robinson, on return of POWs, **1973** 245-246
Rite Aid Corporation
corporate scandal, **2004** 422
retirement fund losses, **2002** 102
Ritter, Jorge, Panama Canal transfer ceremony, **1999** 853
Ritter, William Scott, Jr., UN weapons inspection in Iraq, **1998** 935-936
Rivera, Frederick P., gunshot wounds, **1993** 872
Rivera, Severina, on Marcos indictment, **1988** 868-869
Rivlin, Alice, **1976** 45; **1990** 709
Riza, Iqbal, UN chief of staff fired, **2005** 236
Rizal, Jose, Philippine resistance fighter, **2001** 107
RJR Nabisco
leveraged buyout of, **1988** 921-923
tobacco claims settlement, **1997** 331
RNC. *See* Republican National Committee
Roa Garcia, Raul, **1973** 265
Roadman, Charles H., nursing home staffing, **2002** 121-122
Robb, Charles S. "Chuck" (D-Va.)
Iraq war resolution, **1991** 4
senatorial election campaign, **1994** 10
supports Wilder, **1990** 43
U.S. intelligence gathering investigations, **2004** 712; **2005** 247
Vietnam War veteran, **2000** 918
Robelo Callejas, Alfonso
as contra, **1987** 638
in transitional government, **1979** 582
Robert Wood Johnson Foundation
child health care survey, **1997** 425
end-of-life care research, **1997** 326, 329, 330
Roberts, Francis, **1991** 33
Roberts, Jane Sullivan, antiabortion activist, **2005** 561
Roberts, John, **1983** 199
Roberts, John G., Jr.
abortion
parent notification, **2005** 818
views on, **2005** 815
Supreme Court confirmation as chief justice, **2005** 79, 447, 551, 558-565, 815
Roberts, Pat (R-Kan.)
CIA torture of detainees allegations, **2005** 906
farm bill, **1996** 200
National Intelligence Service, proposal, **2004** 969
U.S. intelligence gathering investigations, **2004** 713
Roberts v. Louisiana, **1976** 489-490, 505-507; **1977** 397-405
Roberts v. United States Jaycees, **1984** 465-478

Robertson, Carole, church bombing victim, **2002** 240, 243-244
Robertson, Dale F., **1992** 489-492
Robertson, George, Lord
Iraq, military force against, **2001** 852
Macedonia peace negotiations, **2001** 557
NATO, new role of, **2002** 888-889
NATO secretary general, **2004** 135
Russian role in NATO, **2001** 896
Robertson, Pat
capital punishment, **2000** 989
charitable choice, **2001** 135
Chavez assassination, comments suggesting, **2005** 770
on Clinton impeachment, **1999** 42
Liberian president Taylor, support for, **2003** 771
pharmacists' right to refuse filling prescriptions for moral or religious reasons, **2005** 817
at Republican convention, **1988** 590
on school prayer amendment, **1984** 244
stem cell research, **2001** 541
Robinson, Aubrey E., Jr., and injunction during coal strike, **1978** 113-114
Robinson, James M., Dead Sea scrolls, **1991** 638
Robinson, Mary
Chechnya war human rights violations, **1999** 913
child soldiers, **2002** 918
East Timor independence, **1999** 511-523
Middle East violence, **2000** 930-951
Robinson, Paul H., on sentencing guidelines, **1987** 409-410, 422-426
Robinson, Randall, **1989** 547
Robinson, Robert A., food safety, **1997** 693; **2001** 698-701
Robinson, Spottswood W., III
on treaty termination, **1979** 919
on White House tapes, **1973** 842
Robinson, Stephen (astronaut), *Discovery* space shuttle mission, **2005** 500
Robinson, Stephen L., Gulf War veterans with ALS, **2001** 909
Robinson, V. Gene, gay priest, Anglican ordination of, **2005** 865
Robles, Joseu, Jr., military base closings, **1995** 409
Robold, Warren, money laundering indictment, **2005** 633, 637
Rocca, Christina, visit to India, **2002** 327
Roche (firm), avian flu vaccine production, **2005** 752
Roche, Jacques, kidnapping and murder of, in Haiti, **2005** 331
Roche, James G., sexual misconduct at Air Force Academy, investigations, **2003** 792-795, 797
Rochin v. California, **1993** 149
Rockefeller, David, **1977** 569
Rockefeller, John D., III
on family planning, **1974** 779
on national population commission, **1972** 302
Rockefeller, John D., IV "Jay" (D-W.Va.)
children in America, **1991** 349
U.S. intelligence gathering, **2004** 713; **2005** 251
warrantless domestic surveillance, **2005** 961
Rockefeller, Laurance S., **1972** 476
Rockefeller, Nelson A.
commission on CIA's domestic activities, **1975** 401
inaction during Attica Prison uprising, **1972** 783-787
nomination of Nixon, **1972** 712-713
on punishment for drug dealers, **1973** 27-33
swearing-in as vice president, **1974** 987-990
and transfer of power, **1985** 492
vice presidential nomination and confirmation, **1974** 707-711, 988-989
vice presidential role of, **1974** 766-767, 770
Rockefeller commission on CIA's domestic activities, **1975** 401-436, 523-524; **1976** 115
Rocky Flats (Colorado), nuclear weapons facility, **1989** 356-359, 362; **1995** 114, 117
Rodgers, Kathy, sexual harassment rulings, **1998** 439-440
Rodino, Peter W., Jr. (D-N.J.)
bankruptcy legislation, **1984** 183
impeachment inquiry report, **1974** 138, 713
nomination of Carter, **1976** 597
reviewing Nixon tapes, **1974** 288, 291, 298
and White House review of Watergate grand jury report, **1974** 226
Rodionov, Igor, NATO expansion, **1996** 657
Rodrigo Franco Democratic Command, activity of in Peru, **1989** 64
Rodriguez de Quijas v. Shearson/American Express, Inc., **1997** 374
Rodu, Brad, cancer death rates, **1996** 790
Roe, Ralph R., Jr., NASA space shuttle program resignation, **2003** 634
Roe v. Wade, **1973** 101-111; **1977** 408-429; **1980** 515-534; **1981** 576; **1986** 559-580; **1989** 365-389; **1990** 215, 216, 387, 616, 624-625; **1991** 257, 272; **1992** 589-613; **1993** 339, 935; **1994** 317; **2000** 429-430, 434; **2001** 128; **2003** 995-1000; **2005** 554, 561, 563, 815, 819
anti-abortion rally, **1985** 53-55
Bork on, **1987** 718
Roed-Larsen, Terje
Jenin "massacre" investigations, **2002** 934
Lebanon, Syrian troop withdrawal, **2004** 560
Middle East peace initiatives, **2003** 1205
on Palestinian Authority, **2004** 807
Palestinian question, **2004** 806, 813-817
Syrian troop withdrawal from Lebanon, **2005** 688-689
Roemer, Buddy (D-La.)
abortion bill veto, **1990** 216-217
vetoes "trash lyrics" bill, **1990** 509-511
Rogan, James E. (R-Calif.), House Judiciary Committee impeachment inquiry, **1998** 712
Rogers, David E., Magic Johnson's resignation from AIDS commission, **1992** 891-893
Rogers, Don, **1986** 181
Rogers, Melissa, religious freedom, **1997** 408
Rogers, Richard M., Waco incident, **1999** 481
Rogers, Will, III, and U.S. downing of Iranian airliner, **1988** 703-717
Rogers, William D., Cuban foreign policy, **1998** 33
Rogers, William J.
on draft evader pardon, **1977** 96
on Panama Canal treaties, **1977** 593

Rogers, William P.
at Brezhnev-Nixon summit in U.S., **1973** 587
Challenger commission, **1986** 516
drug traffic report, **1972** 645
four-power Berlin agreement, **1972** 468
Kissinger feud with, Nixon on, **1977** 344-345
on minority status, **1988** 187
Paris peace accords signing, **1973** 117
on prevention of terrorism, **1972** 754-758
resignation, **1973** 737, 739
on return of POWs, **1973** 246
U.S. bombing of Cambodia, **1973** 516
U.S.-Cuban antihijacking agreement, **1973** 265-266
U.S.-PRC claims, negotiations, **1973** 292
U.S.-Soviet trade agreement, **1972** 846
Vietnam peace, international conference on, **1973** 331-332
Vietnam peace proposal, **1972** 143
Rogers v. EEOC, **1998** 462
Rogers v. Lodge, **1993** 466
Rogoff, Kenneth
global economy, **2003** 751
WTO trade talks, **2003** 755
Roh Moo-hyun
North Korea nuclear weapons, U.S.-South Korea statement on, **2005** 608
South Korean presidential elections, **2002** 731
South Korean stem cell research scandal, **2005** 321
Roh Sung-il, South Korean stem cell research scandal, **2005** 321
Roh Tae Woo, **1997** 894
democratic reforms in Korea, **1987** 583-590; **1989** 65
overtures to North Korea, **1988** 853-859
Rohani, Hassan, Iran nuclear weapons program, **2003** 1028; **2004** 868, 870
Rohrabacher, Dana (R-Calif.)
Innocence Protection Act, **2002** 354
stem cell research, **2004** 160
U.S.-China trade relations, **2000** 216
Rojas, Don, **1993** 580
Rollins, Edward J., **1992** 717-719
Rollins, Robert, **1981** 198
Roman, Agustin, **1987** 931
Roman, Peter, **1991** 400
Roman Catholic Church. *See* Catholic Church
Romania
Communist Party in, **1976** 435, 453-455
EU membership issue, **2003** 43; **2004** 199, 977
execution of Ceausescu, **1989** 709, 711-712
human trafficking, **2002** 348
NATO membership, **2004** 136
NATO membership candidacy, **1997** 516; **1999** 122
overthrow of government, **1989** 709-712
political liberalization in, **1989** 635
political situation, **2004** 199
UN population conference in Bucharest, **1974** 777-797
Warsaw Pact dissolution, **1991** 399-401
Romano, Sergio, U.S. foreign policy, **2003** 42
Romanov, Girgory V., **1985** 274
Rome (Italy)
airport attack, **1985** 463, 468
Treaties of, establishment of EC, **1984** 440, 444-445
World Food Conference, resolutions adopted by, **1974** 939-953
Romer, Roy (D-Colo.)
education goals, **1990** 154
educational testing standards, **1992** 46, 48-49
Romer v. Evans, **1996** 284-295
Romero, Anthony, terrorist suspects and civil liberties, **2003** 158, 611
Romero, Oscar A., assassination of, in El Salvador, **1980** 412-413; **1992** 24; **1993** 239, 242-243
Romney, George, volunteerism summit, **1997** 238
Romney, Mitt (Massachusetts governor)
death penalty, **2004** 798
gay marriage legislation, **2003** 404; **2004** 38-39
greenhouse gas emissions, **2005** 924
Rompilla v. Beard, **2005** 182
Ronald McDonald House Charities, **1997** 424, 426; **1999** 386
Roosevelt, Eleanor
as First Lady, **2000** 907
government position, **2000** 906
Roosevelt, Franklin Delano
on the American dream, **2005** 90
budget deficits during administration of, **2003** 679
democracy and, **2005** 43
and division of Germany, **1986** 792
fireside chats, **1977** 103
Gingrich comments on presidency of, **1995** 4
Japanese-American internment, **1988** 288-289, 293
midterm elections, **2002** 819
national forest preservation efforts, **1999** 596
New Deal measures and commerce clause, **1995** 184
political uses of FBI, **1975** 873, 876
press conferences, **1988** 840-841
Roper v. Simmons, **2004** 797; **2005** 177-196, 179
and Social Security system, **1978** 544
and Vatican-U.S. relations, **1984** 20
Roosevelt, Theodore R., press conferences, **1988** 839-840
Rose, Charlie (D-N.C.), U.S. Capitol bicentennial, **1993** 901
Rose, Eric A., artificial heart implants, **2001** 477
Rose, Noel, **1993** 369
Rose, Pete
banning of from baseball, **1989** 477-484
sentencing for filing false tax returns, **1990** 483-487
Roselli, John, and CIA Castro plot, **1975** 726-731, 735, 742-744
Rosen, Hilary, marketing violent entertainment to children, **2001** 76
Rosenbaum, Mark, and affirmative action, **1997** 284-285
Rosenberg, Mark, on domestic violence, **1993** 288
Rosenberger v. Rector and Visitors of the University of Virginia, **1995** 385-395; **1997** 368, 376
Ros-Lehtinen, Ileana (R-Fla.), Cuban-Americans, restrictions on, **2004** 248
Roslin Institute (Edinburgh), cloning research, **1997** 212-220; **2004** 161

Ross, Carl, forest preservation, **1999** 594
Ross, Jane L., Social Security shortfall, **1998** 99-100
Ross, Jerry, **1998** 932
Ross, United States v., **1982** 425-446
Rosselló, Pedro, **1993** 947, 950-951
Rossi, Dino, Washington gubernatorial election, **2004** 778
Rossi, Peter H., **1983** 358
Rossouw, Jacques, hormone replacement therapy, **2002** 503, 506, 509-510
Rostenkowski, Dan (D-Ill.)
health care reform, **1993** 783
indictment of, **1994** 281-286
on leveraged buyouts, **1988** 923
on welfare reform, **1988** 850, 852
Rostker v. Goldberg, **1981** 521-540
Rostow, Walt W.
on Berlin Wall anniversary, **1986** 792
Westmoreland libel suit against CBS, **1985** 160
Rostropovich, Mstislav, voluntary exile of, **1975** 161-165; **1981** 376
Roswell (New Mexico), UFO citings, Air Force report, **1997** 395-405
Rota, Robert V., House postmaster embezzlement, **1994** 282, 285
Rotberg, Iris C., **1992** 87
Rotblat, Joseph, Nobel Peace prize winner, **1995** 553
ROTC (Reserve Officers Training Corps), **1992** 155, 156-157, 159, 161
Roth, Kenneth
equal justice, **2000** 774
torture in terrorism interrogations investigations, **2004** 341
Roth, Loren, **1983** 25
Roth, Stanley O., Cambodian political situation, **1997** 641-646
Roth, William V., Jr. (R-Del.)
financing postsecondary education, **1993** 178
health insurance for disabled persons, **1999** 49
IRS hearings, **1997** 661
Senate Finance Committee chairman, **1995** 592
tax relief plan of, **1980** 567-568, 574
on Washington politics, **1993** 719
women in combat, **1991** 493-495, 496-497, 510-511
Roth v. United States, **1973** 611, 614-618, 622-623, 626-627; **1992** 546
Rothenberg, Joseph H., space shuttle program, **2000** 94
Rother, John, Social Security reform, **2001** 916
Rothman, Steven R. (D-N.J.), House Judiciary Committee impeachment inquiry, **1998** 711
Rothschild, Edwin, **1983** 922
Rothstein, Barbara J., **1996** 123
Roure, Amadou Toumani, **2000** 450
Rourke, Francis E., **1989** 43
Rove, Karl
Bush campaign strategy, **2004** 774, 776
as Bush political adviser, **2005** 45
CIA leak investigation, **2005** 78, 562, 631, 699-704
midterm elections, **2002** 819
Social Security privatization plan, **2005** 112
steel tariffs, **2003** 446
Rowan, Carl, **1984** 1019; **1993** 340
Rowe, James H., **1993** 490
Rowe, John W., National Commission on Energy Policy, **2004** 189
Rowen, Hobart
on Stockman on Reagan economics, **1985** 73
on trade deficit, **1985** 625
Rowland, Diane, on Medicaid, **1998** 143
Rowland, F. Sherwood, on chlorofluorocarbons' effect on ozone layer, **1975** 437-438; **1988** 222
Rowny, Edward L., **1979** 417
Roy, Joe, on extremists in the military, **1996** 178-179
Royal Dutch/Shell, oil and gas reserve fraud, **2004** 423
Royal Perth Yacht Club, America's Cup rulings, **1989** 183-184
Roybal, Edward R. (D-Calif.), House reprimand for Korean influence buying, **1978** 845-847, 879-880
Royce, Ed (R-Calif.), **2000** 72
Rozell, Pete, **1986** 171
Rubin, Asher, **1988** 48
Rubin, Carl, **1989** 479
Rubin, Howard A., on year 2000 computer conversion, **1997** 534
Rubin, Israel, **1989** 184
Rubin, James P.
Afghanistan, U.S. humanitarian aid, **1999** 527
Kosovo, NATO air strikes in, **1998** 829
Pakistan military coup, **1999** 625
on sub-Saharan African conflict, **1998** 220
Rubin, Robert E.
Asian financial crisis, **1997** 832; **1998** 725
on closing Pennsylvania Avenue, **1995** 255
IRS and customer service, **1998** 132-138
IRS reform, **1997** 663
and National Church Arson Task Force, **1997** 302, 310
Vietnam economic relations, **1997** 490
Rubin, Tony, **1988** 48
Rubin v. United States, **1992** 461
Rubino, Frank, **1990** 721
Rubitsky, David S., congressional Medal of Honor claim by, **1989** 697-700
Ruby, Jack, link to organized crime, **1979** 595, 609-613
Ruby Ridge incident, **1995** 178
Ruckelshaus, William D.
on acid rain, **1983** 200
appointment to FBI, **1973** 501
as EPA administrator, **1982** 967; **1983** 750
on FBI wiretaps of Ellsberg, **1973** 544-545
resignation as deputy attorney general, **1973** 839, 859-860, 862, 876, 897, 902-903; **1987** 718, 725; **1998** 906
at Stockholm environment conference, **1972** 476
Ruckelshaus v. Monsanto, Co., **2005** 369
Ruder, David C., on stock market crash, **1988** 10-12
Rudman, Warren B. (R-N.H.)
budget reduction legislation, **1985** 803
Chinese technology transfer study, **1999** 239
Gulf War syndrome investigations, **1997** 740
Iran-contra committee, **1986** 1052; **1987** 893-894
Middle East peace negotiations, **2001** 361
national security, **2001** 639

Rudman, Warren B. *Continued*
national security commission member, **1999** 500, 501-502
Oliver North Iran-contra conviction, **1990** 493
Souter nomination, **1990** 617
terrorist threats, task force on, **2002** 740-763
Rudolph, Eric, bombings at Olympics and of abortion clinics, **1998** 810; **2005** 820
Ruff, Charles F.
Clinton impeachment trial, **1999** 19
investigation of Ford campaign financing, **1976** 759-760
Ruffolo, Giorgio, **1989** 154
Rufo v. Inmates of Suffolk County Jail, **1997** 366
Rugova, Ibrahim
Democratic League of Kosovo leader, **2004** 952
Kosovo conflict, **1999** 288; **2000** 145
Kosovo independence, **2003** 1144
Kosovo presidential elections, **2001** 821; **2003** 1139
Ruiz Massieu, Jose Francisco, assassination of, **1994** 564
Rummel v. Estelle (1980), **1983** 660
Rumsfeld, Donald H.
ABM treaty, **2001** 894
Afghanistan
Karzai inauguration ceremony, **2004** 917
meeting with Karzai, **2005** 974
presidential elections, **2003** 1093
war reports, **2001** 692; **2003** 1090
Air Force Academy sexual misconduct investigation panel, **2003** 794
as cabinet member, **2005** 45
Chinese military buildup, **2005** 614-615
defense policy, **2002** 635
European relations, "Old Europe" and "New Europe" divide, **2005** 582
foreign policy, disdain for diplomacy, **2004** 630
Georgia (country), state visit, **2003** 1045
Guantanamo Bay detentions, **2003** 107, 109, 113; **2004** 376; **2005** 449
Guantanamo Bay interrogations, **2004** 338-339
Hanssen espionage case, **2001** 152
India-Pakistan relations, **2002** 328-329
India-U.S. defense cooperation agreement, **2005** 463
Iraq
Abu Ghraib prison abuse scandal, **2004** 207, 208, 210-211, 212
distortion of intelligence information allegations, **2005** 251
military preparedness, **2004** 779, 784
prewar intelligence, **2003** 881, 885; **2004** 453
Saddam loyalists, **2003** 942
security forces, **2003** 942
UN role, **2003** 949
U.S. military commitment, **2004** 874-875
U.S. military weapons shortages, **2004** 875
U.S. relations, **2001** 851
U.S. troop strength, **2005** 833
weapons inspections program, **2002** 615; **2003** 42
military intelligence, secretary of defense for, **2002** 994
missile defense system, **2001** 282-283; **2002** 1027-1028; **2004** 178
missile threat to U.S., **1998** 481-499; **2000** 678
national security strategy, **2002** 634
NATO Response Force, **2002** 889
North Korean nuclear weapons program, **2002** 733-734, 736
"old Europe" vs. "new Europe" statement, **2003** 42
replacement of at Cost of Living Council, **1973** 44, 47
Russia
NATO council, **2001** 896
nuclear weapons programs, **2001** 21
U.S. relations, **2001** 893, 894
Saudi Arabia, U.S. troop withdrawal, **2003** 233, 1054
Senate confirmation, **2001** 96
September 11 panel recommendations, response to, **2004** 968
terrorist attacks on the Pentagon, **2001** 617
tribunals and U.S. servicemen, **2002** 607
U.S.-China military relations, **2001** 251
Uzbekistan, U.S. relations, **2005** 429
war on terrorism, **2001** 627, 629-630, 643
Runcie, Robert
meetings with John Paul II, **1982** 410; **1986** 24
wedding of Charles and Diana, **1981** 602-603
women as Anglican bishops, **1989** 51
Runyon v. McCrary, **1976** 391-404; **1989** 323
Rural communities
effects of biotechnology and changing farm structure, **1986** 296-298, 305-306
rail service to, **1975** 530, 541-542
Rural Environmental Assistance Program (REAP), Nixon impoundment of funds for, **1973** 171
Rushdie, Salman
death threat against, **1989** 95-98
death threat lifted, **1998** 687-691
Rushford, Michael, sentencing reform, **2002** 787
Rusk, Dean
on Panama Canal treaties, **1977** 593
on U.S. bombing of North Vietnam (1965), **1972** 493-495
Russell, United States v., **1992** 319
Russello v. United States, **1993** 442
Russert, Tim, Hillary Clinton interview on Lewinsky affair, **2000** 908
Russia
See also Soviet Union; Yeltsin, Boris N.
ABM treaty, U.S. withdrawal from, **2001** 927-934; **2002** 276
AIDS/HIV infection epidemic, **2001** 255, 439; **2002** 471; **2004** 429, 430; **2005** 54
Alma-Ata Declaration, **1991** 804-806
arms control
START II agreement, **1993** 17-61
U.S. aid, **2002** 437-440
Bush summit with Yeltsin, **1992** 519-531
Chechen rebels
Beslan school hostage crisis, **2004** 535, 564-576; **2005** 299, 300, 303
hostages in Moscow theater, **2002** 763-773
terrorist attacks, **2005** 304-305
Chechen war, **1999** 909-916; **2000** 175-176; **2001** 257, 894; **2005** 304-305

China relations, **2001** 740
Commonwealth Pact, **1991** 787-791, 803-804
economic conditions, **1998** 75-76, 601-603, 722; **1999** 87; **2000** 1048-1049, 1060; **2001** 255
economic development forecasts, **2005** 15
economic recovery, **2002** 692-693
economic summit aid package, **1993** 541, 543
elections, **1995** 94; **1996** 139, 430-437; **1997** 515; **2000** 171, 172-173; **2003** 248
entrepreneurs arrested, for fraud and tax evasion, **2003** 246-248
foreign aid, **1992** 639
foreign policy, **1995** 100
homicide rate, **1994** 415
human trafficking, **2002** 348-349
Iran arms sales, **2001** 893
Iraq War, opposition to, **2003** 40, 42-43, 48, 51-52
Japan relations, **1998** 540
Kyoto Protocol on Climate Change, **2002** 303; **2003** 864, 865; **2004** 827
media, **1995** 98
media suppression by Putin government, **2003** 246, 247
military readiness, **1994** 530
missile threat, **1998** 487
NATO charter and cooperation, **1996** 656; **1997** 514, 515, 518, 521-522
NATO "new relationship," **2001** 892-898; **2002** 885, 886
NATO-Russia Council, **2002** 886
Nixon speech on aid, **1992** 255-265
North Korean diplomatic relations, **2003** 1178
Nuclear Arms Pact, **1991** 806-808
nuclear arms treaty, U.S.-Russian, **2002** 275-286; **2003** 907
nuclear materials, **2003** 1030
nuclear proliferation, **1994** 363-373; **1996** 219-221
nuclear testing, **1999** 604
nuclear weapons, **1991** 787
oil company takeovers, **2004** 187
Paris Club membership, **1997** 341, 342-343
privatization of, **1995** 96-97
Putin, Vladimir
  ABM treaty, U.S. withdrawal, **2001** 927-934
  presidential inauguration speech, **2000** 171-178
  State of the Nation address, **2001** 254-266; **2003** 245-259; **2005** 299-314
  U.S. relations, **2001** 892
  war on terrorism, support for U.S., **2001** 615, 626-627, 894
Putin-Bush talks, **2001** 893, 895; **2003** 250; **2005** 305-306
religious freedom, **1997** 564, 577-578
Republican Party platform, **1996** 540
social policy, **2005** 299-300
Soviet Union restructuring plans, **1991** 532-533
submarine *Kursk* disaster, **2000** 171-172, 635-641
U.S. missile defense system, **2002** 1029
U.S. policy, **2000** 29-30
U.S. relations, **2001** 892
and U.S. space station, **1995** 222-227, 419-425; **1998** 929-930
weapons of mass destruction, **2002** 437-438
weapons storage and security, **2003** 906-907; **2004** 323
Yeltsin, Boris
  address to parliament, **1994** 185-194; **1996** 430-437
  on crises in Russia, **1993** 769-779
  economic crisis, **1998** 601-613
  at economic summit (Denver), **1997** 340-342
  election victory, **1996** 139, 430-437; **1997** 515
  European security summit, remarks at, **1994** 583-584, 588-591
  postcoup dominance, **1991** 786
  Putin supporter, **2000** 171
  START II statement, **1993** 60-61
  state of the nation address, **1995** 92-101
  at Tokyo economic summit, **1993** 541, 543, 552-555
Yugoslavia's UN membership, **1992** 875-878
Yukos oil company seizure, **2004** 569; **2005** 301, 302-303
Russian language, rejection of in Baltic states, **1989** 470
Russian Orthodox church, millennium of, **1988** 355, 358, 459
Russo, Anthony J., Jr.
  dismissal of Pentagon Papers charges, **1974** 205-206
  leak of Pentagon Papers by, **1973** 537, 539
  Sorensen affidavit for, **1976** 880
Rust v. Sullivan, **1991** 257-273
Rutaganda, George, Rwanda war crimes conviction, **2003** 1075
Rutgers University, Brennan speech on the press and the Court, **1979** 285-311
Ruth, Henry S., Jr.
  and independent counsel legislation, **1999** 168
  on mandatory sentences for drug dealers, **1973** 28
  as Watergate special prosecutor, **1974** 814; **1975** 654, 668
Rutskoi, Aleksandr V., **1991** 517, 533; **1993** 769-779
Rwanda
  Clinton state visit, **1998** 159
  Congo-Rwanda peace agreement, **2002** 546-555
  Democratic Forces for the Liberation of Rwanda (FDLR), **2004** 506
  French forces in, **1994** 542-543
  genocidal war
    10th anniversary, **2004** 591
    Clinton apology for U.S. inaction, **1998** 160; **1999** 861
    Hutu and Tutsi ethnic conflict, **2003** 923
    number of victims, **2004** 115, 506
    OAU report on, **2000** 449-474
    remembrance of, UN secretary general on, **2004** 115-121
    Tutsi war casualties, **2000** 980-981; **2003** 923, 1069
    UN criminal tribunal, **2003** 1069-1088
    UN report, **1999** 860-889
    UN response, **1998** 222; **1999** 735; **2003** 811
    UN tribunal on, **1998** 614-625
  government of, **2000** 457-461
  Habyarimana assassination, **1994** 541

Rwanda *Continued*
Hutu and Tutsi, ban on distinctions between, **2004** 117
Ibuka ("remember" genocide survival group), **2003** 1072
post-genocide government of, **2004** 117
presidential and parliamentary elections, **2003** 1070-1071
refugee camps, State Department report, **1996** 809-815
refugee camps, UN security measures, **1994** 541-549
refugee relief, **1999** 434-435
troop withdrawal from Congo, **2003** 290
Tutsi-led intervention in the Congo, **2004** 506
UN Assistance Mission in Rwanda (UNAMIR), **1999** 862, 863-865, 869-884
UN humanitarian aid programs, **1999** 429
UN peacekeeping mission, **2003** 450
failure of, **1997** 151, 154, 155, 156; **1999** 860-889; **2000** 643
UN report on refugees, **1991** 672
UN war crimes tribunal, **2003** 99-100, 1069-1088; **2004** 117-118
U.S. military readiness, **1994** 528, 533
Rwandan Patriotic Front, **2004** 117, 119
Ryan, Allen A., on U.S. involvement with Barbie, **1983** 738, 739-747
Ryan, George (Illinois governor)
death penalty mass clemencies, **2004** 798
death penalty moratorium, **2000** 988; **2002** 354-355
Ryan, John D., **1973** 730
Ryan, Leo J. (D-Calif.), fatal trip to Jonestown, Guyana, **1979** 347-357, 363, 366-370, 372
Ryan, May Thomas, prescription drug importation, **2004** 984
Ryan, Mike, flu pandemic preparations, **2005** 750
Ryan, William, **1985** 571
Ryan White Act, reauthorization of, **2005** 86

S

Saah, Alfred, Magic Johnson's resumption of basketball, **1992** 892
Saakashvili, Mikhail
Georgian parliamentary elections demonstrations, **2003** 1041-1042
Georgian presidential elections, **2003** 1039; **2005** 306
Georgian transition to democracy, **2004** 72-81; **2005** 64
Russia, visit with Putin, **2004** 73
U.S. relations, visit with Bush, **2004** 73, 76
SAARC. *See* South Asian Association for Regional Cooperation
Sábato, Ernesto, **1984** 789
Sable Communications of Cal., Inc. v. FCC, **1997** 450
Sabo, Tim, Schott suspension, **1993** 167
Sabra, Palestinian refugee camp massacre, **1985** 47-51
Sabri, Naji, UN resolution on disarmament in Iraq, **2002** 717, 728-730
Sabri, Sheik Ikrima, state visit of John Paul II, **2000** 80
Sabshin, Melvin, **1990** 575
Sachar, Abram, interview of Warren, **1972** 936-938
Sacket, Ross, **1973** 612
al-Sadat, Anwar
Arab states' changed attitude toward, **1974** 436-437
assassination of, **1981** 632, 733-746; **2005** 164
background and career of, **1981** 733-734
Camp David accords, **1978** 605-608, 617-618; **1979** 223-224, 226
Carter meeting, **1977** 899, 902
cease-fire negotiations with Israel, **1973** 931-932
disengagement agreement with Israel, **1974** 30-31
Israeli-Palestinian Peace Accord, **1993** 749, 762
Jerusalem visit, **1977** 827-841; **1978** 607-608, 619, 621, 626-627, 630
as leader of Egypt, **2005** 164
Middle East peace, **1994** 331
Nixon visit, **1974** 450, 452-459
Nobel Peace prize recipient, **1978** 607, 625-628; **1983** 834; **2002** 981; **2003** 1130
Sinai accord with Israel, **1975** 575
Soviet friendship treaty, abrogation of, **1976** 169-175
U.S. relations, resumption of, **1973** 931-932
U.S. sale of warplanes to Egypt, **1978** 127-128, 130
Saddam Hussein
audiotapes while in hiding, **2003** 1191
Bush comments on, **2003** 18
Bush letter to, **1991** 17-18
Bush State of the Union address, **1991** 37, 44-45
Bush ultimatum to, **1991** 100-101
captured in Iraq by U.S. troops, **2003** 135, 934, 1189-1199, 1221; **2004** 18, 19, 404-405
cease-fire with Iran, **1988** 529-531
chemical weapons policy, **1997** 198; **1998** 49-50
child soldiers (Ashbal Saddam, Saddam's Lion Cubs), **2002** 917
deadline to avoid war, **1990** 767-782
final warning of U.S.-led invasion, **2003** 135-136
Glaspie pre-war meeting, **1991** 155-163
human rights in Iraq, **1999** 144-145; **2000** 581
human rights report, **1993** 568, 570
insurgency in postwar Iraq, role in, **2003** 1194
Iran-Iraq War, **1984** 748-750
Iraq invasion of Kuwait, **1990** 533-534, 542-543
Iraqi attack on USS *Stark,* **1987** 792
Iraqi relations in Arab world, **1987** 869-870
Iraqi troop buildup, **1994** 431-435
Kuwait withdrawal speech, **1991** 102-104
manhunt for, **2003** 1191-1192
ousted by U.S.-led military, **2003** 18, 135, 193, 194, 955, 1089, 1191; **2004** 399
political situation report, **1996** 680-686
post-Persian Gulf War period, **1991** 123
presidential debate on, **1992** 966-970
as ruler of Iraq, **2003** 1190-1191
terrorist attacks on U.S. linked to, **2001** 625; **2003** 877-878, 901
UN air strikes against Iraq, **1998** 934-944; **1999** 53; **2001** 850

UN resolution on Iran-Iraq War, **1987** 610
UN sanctions against Iraq, **2004** 714
UN weapons inspections, **1997** 767
U.S. policy toward, **2001** 629, 688, 849-854
U.S. "regime change" policy, **1998** 938; **2001** 852-853; **2002** 35, 56, 484, 612, 612-614, 713
war crimes trial, **2003** 1195-1196; **2005** 941, 949-951
weapons of mass destruction and, **2002** 34; **2003** 32-34; **2004** 714
al-Sadr, Ayatollah Mohammed Sadeq, assassination of, **1999** 145
al-Sadr, Moqtada
demonstrations against U.S., **2003** 940; **2004** 879-880
Mahdi Army (personal militia), **2004** 879; **2005** 664, 673
militant cleric and United Iraqi Alliance, **2004** 404
Saeed Sheikh, Ahmed Omar, Pearl trial conviction, **2002** 166; **2005** 474
Saenz v. Roe, **1999** 261
Safe and Drug-Free School Act, **1999** 55
Safe Drinking Water Safety Act (1974), **1993** 262-264, 267-268
Clinton proposals, **1994** 39
Safe Return Amnesty Committee, **1977** 96
Safire, William, Inman nomination, **1994** 23
Safran, Nadav, on Jordan and the Palestinians, **1988** 580-581
Sagan, Carl
on nuclear winter, **1983** 857, 860-870; **1985** 542
and Sagan Memorial Station, **1997** 509
on science education, **1988** 379
Sager, Alan, on prescription drug pricing, **2000** 135
Saguy, Yehoshua, role in Palestinian camp massacre, **1983** 166, 179
Saha, Abhjit, age of universe, **1994** 459, 462
Sahib, Shmed Abdul, Iraq reconstruction, **2005** 720
Said, Ibrahim Muktar, London terrorist bombing suspect, **2005** 397
Saidullayev, Abdul Khalim, as Chechen resistance leader, **2005** 304
Saigh, Fred, **1993** 168
Saigon (South Vietnam)
capture of by PRG, domestic policy statements, **1975** 301-307
U.S. evacuation from, **1975** 251-253, 266-277
Sainovic, Nikola, war criminal, **1999** 803
Saitoti, George, as Kenyan vice president, **2002** 1045
Sajudis movement, **1990** 183
Sakharov, Andrei D.
on Afghanistan invasion, **1981** 748
background and career, **1981** 180, 182, 747-748
Carter correspondence with, **1977** 189-190
defense of by American scientists, **1973** 791-796
election to Soviet congress, **1989** 176, 179
exile of, **1980** 103-108; **1986** 111-112
hunger strike by, **1981** 747-752
on internal Soviet reforms, **1975** 482
Nobel Peace Prize (1975), **1981** 748, 751-752
acceptance, **1975** 915-928
denial of visa to travel to ceremony, **1975** 561
release of, **1986** 95, 822, 1091-1095; **1987** 190, 202
Soviet campaign against, **1985** 782-783
and state of Soviet dissent, **1980** 191
Sakurauchi, Yoshio, **1992** 13, 20-21, 165
Salaam, Haji Mullah Abdul, Afghan parliamentary elections, **2005** 972
Salafist Group for Call and Combat (GSCP), **2004** 539
Sale v. Haitian Centers Council, **1993** 413-421
Saleh, Abdul Rahman, Indonesian attorney general appointment, **2004** 755
Saleh, Ali Abdullah (Yemini president), USS *Cole* bombing, **2001** 7
Salehi, Ali Akbar, Iran nuclear weapons inspections, **2003** 1029
Salerno, Anthony, pretrial detention of, **1987** 492-493, 495-496, 502-503
Salerno, United States v., **1987** 491-508; **1991** 20.260
Sales, Kirkpatrick, Indigenous People in Americas Report, **1992** 898
Salev, Hemi, Palestinian state, **2002** 375
Salid, Patricia, glass ceiling agreement, **1992** 748
Salim, Salim Ahmed, OAU secretary general, **2001** 506
Salinas de Gortari, Carlos
assassination of, **1994** 563-564
Brady plan for debt relief, **1989** 139
North American Free Trade Agreement, **1992** 760; **1993** 954
U.S.-Latin American Drug Summit, **1992** 201
Salisbury, Dallas L., pension plans, **2004** 737
SALT. *See* Strategic Arms Limitation Talks/Treaty
Saltik, Haydar, military takeover in Turkey, **1980** 808-809
Saltzman, Murray, **1983** 915
Salvation Army, and charitable choice, **2001** 135
Samar, Sima, Afghanistan Minister of Women's Affairs, **2002** 39
Samaranch, Juan Antonio, International Olympics Committee investigations, **1999** 106, 108, 109
al-Samaree, Ahmad, on Iraqi prison abuse scandal, **2004** 209
Sambor, Gregore J., and Philadelphia raid on MOVE group, **1986** 240-251
Same-sex marriage
See also under Marriage
Bush administration on, **2003** 401-402; **2004** 21, 37, 40
Samper, Ernesto, **2000** 842
Samples, United States v., **1994** 109-115
Sampson, Neil, **1992** 489
Samudra, Iman, Bali terrorist bombing, **2002** 706
Samuelson, Paul, **1973** 45
Samuelson, Robert J., **1992** 164
San Antonio Independent School District v. Rodriguez, **1973** 361-377; **1990** 230, 236
San Diego (California), air quality of, **1981** 275, 289
San Diego Yacht Club, America's Cup rulings in New York courts, **1989** 183-193
San Francisco (California)
earthquake (1906), intensity of, **1989** 669
earthquake (1989), damage from, **1989** 667-670
recognition of domestic partnerships by, **1989** 305-311

San Francisco (California) *Continued*
rise of People's Temple in, **1979** 350-352, 358, 364-366
Sanadar, Ivo, Croatia political situation, **2003** 465
Sanchez, Alex, baseball suspension for steroid use, **2005** 215
Sanchez, Loretta, Gore supporter, **2000** 613
Sanchez, Ricardo
Abu Ghraib abuse investigations, **2004** 208, 209, 213, 214-215; **2005** 912
on postwar Iraq, **2003** 1194
Sanchez de Lozada, Gonzalo, Bolivia presidential elections, **2005** 769
Sanctuary (USS), assigning navy women to, **1972** 627-628
Sanctuary movement, for Central American refugees, **1987** 254-255
Sandage, Allan R., age of universe controversy, **1996** 265-266, 268
Sandalow, David B., Nobel Peace Prize controversy, **2004** 931
Sanders, Barefoot, Kennedy assassination anniversary, **1993** 961-962
Sanders, Bernard "Bernie" (I-Vt.)
apparel industry sweatshops, **1997** 209
and Democratic Party, **2001** 378
Sanders, Dave (teacher shot at Columbine High School), **2001** 349, 352
Sanders v. United States, **1991** 215-217
Sanderson, James W., **1983** 751
Sanderson, Robert "Sandy," antiabortion protester victim, **1998** 810
Sandia National Laboratories, explosion on USS *Iowa* report, **1990** 319, 320, 323-324
Sandinista National Liberation Front (FSLN)
defeat by Chamorro, **1990** 259-265
and human rights in Nicaragua, **1984** 164-165
ouster of Somoza by, **1979** 581-585, 590-591
rise of, **1985** 257, 261-265; **1987** 641
use of Costa Rica, **1987** 638
Sandino, Augusto César, **1979** 584; **1987** 639-640
Sands, Robert, **1981** 401
Sanford, Bruce W., **1984** 299
Sanford, Terry (D-N.C.)
at Democratic convention, **1972** 590, 592
on smoking as addiction, **1988** 311
Sanger, David E., trade tariffs, **2003** 446
Sankoh, Foday
Sierra Leone guerrilla leader, **2000** 1073, 1075
Sierra Leone peace negotiations, **1999** 430-431
Sierra Leone RUF leader captured, **2002** 247
Sanofi-Aventis, avian flu vaccine production, **2005** 751
Santa Fe Independent School District v. Doe, **2000** 365-378; **2001** 423
Santer, Jacques
on euro currency, **1998** 274, 275-280
European Commission commissioner, **1999** 156-157
Santorum, Rick (R-Pa.)
Cuban foreign policy, **1998** 33
Senate majority leader candidate, **2002** 973
Santosky v. Kramer, **1982** 259-280; **1990** 379
Sarbanes, Paul S. (D-Md.)
corporate reform act, **2002** 1033, 1035
on HUD scandal, **1989** 334
on Rockefeller nomination, **1974** 988
Sarbanes-Oxley Act (2002), **2002** 1033, 1035-1036; **2003** 338; **2004** 421
Sarivola, Anthony, FBI informant, **1991** 176-181
Sarkisian, Aram, Armenian prime minister appointment, **1999** 639-640
Sarkisian, Vazgen
Armenian prime minister, **1999** 641
assassination of, **1999** 639
Sarmiento, Manny, **1986** 171
Sarney, José, **1985** 3-4
Sarnoff Corporation, bioterrorism assessment, **2004** 445
Sarobi, Habiba, first Afghan provincial governor, **2005** 974
Saro-Wiwa, Ken, execution of, **1995** 696-699
SARS (severe acute respiratory syndrome) outbreak
and Asian economic recovery, **2003** 69, 754, 757; **2005** 749
in China, **2003** 124-126, 784, 1174-1175
World Health Organization reports on, **2003** 121-134
Sasser, James "Jim" (D-Tenn.)
budget critic, **1991** 68
U.S. bombing of Chinese embassy, **1999** 305-306
SAT. *See* Scholastic Aptitude Test
Satanic Verses (Rushdie), death threat against author, **1989** 95-98
Satcher, David (surgeon general)
anthrax mailings, **2001** 676
on drug AZT therapy for pregnant women, **1995** 441
mental health, **1999** 836-849; **2001** 575
mental health of minorities, **2001** 575-592
obesity and health risks, **2001** 935-954; **2002** 626; **2003** 482; **2004** 652; **2005** 5
oral health in America, **2000** 222-239
on physical activity, **1996** 419
school violence study, **1999** 181
sexual health and responsible sexual behavior, **2001** 456-471
suicide prevention, **1999** 439-455, 836; **2001** 290-303; **2002** 268
teenage smoking, **1998** 845
tobacco use reduction report, **2000** 555-580
women and smoking, **2001** 222-244
youth violence, **2001** 73-85
Satellite communications, NASA launch of for PRC, **1979** 136, 139
Sato, Eisaku
meeting with Nixon, **1972** 41-43
trade relations with U.S., **1972** 746
Saturday night massacre, **1973** 839, 859-880; **1974** 622; **1975** 660-662; **1988** 466
Saturn, *Voyager* missions, **1980** 989-993; **1981** 835-844
Saudi Arabia
Arab League meeting and, **1987** 869-870, 873
Aramco antitrust probe and, **1983** 921-924
Camp David accords, **1978** 607; **1979** 226-227

Carter visit, **1977** 897, 900
economic situation, **2003** 227-228
elections, **2004** 517, 521-522, 626, 629; **2005** 270-272
Fahd on Iraqi invasion of Kuwait, **1990** 557-560
human trafficking, **2002** 349
Iraq War, support for, **2003** 138
Israeli-Lebanese security agreement, **1983** 473
Israeli-Palestinian peace initiatives, **2002** 370-372
links to al Qaeda terrorist network, **2003** 228-232
Mecca Grand Mosque seizure (1979), Soviet propaganda about, **1981** 753-754
Middle East peace plan of, **1981** 631-637
Nixon visit and U.S. aid, **1974** 449-451, 459-462
oil production after oil embargo, **1974** 222
OPEC oil prices, **1976** 937-942; **1979** 251-254; **1980** 995-996; **1981** 799
OPEC production quotas, **1980** 995-996; **1982** 980
political reform, **2003** 233-234; **2004** 521-522
poverty summit, **1981** 770
religious persecution, **1997** 564, 578-579
Saudization program, **2004** 522
social change in, and dependability of oil supply, **1979** 663
terrorist attacks, **2004** 518-520
terrorist bombings
of Khobar Towers apartment complex, **2000** 280, 861; **2001** 3, 796-797, 807
Pentagon report on, **1996** 672-679
in Riyadh, **2003** 227-244, 1052; **2004** 517-518, 535-536
text of first constitution, **1992** 225-248
U.S. forces withdrawal, **2003** 232-233, 1053-1054
U.S. sale of AWACS planes to, **1981** 631, 637, 787-798
U.S. sale of warplanes to, **1978** 106, 125-126, 128-131
war on terrorism, **2001** 627
Sauer, Beverly, bioterrorism attack response, **2001** 676
Sauter, Van Gordon, CBS documentary on Westmoreland, **1983** 402-403; **1985** 159
Sauvagnargues, Jean, **1974** 529
Savage, Gus (D-Ill.)
Elizabeth II's visit to U.S., **1991** 248
on white racism, **1995** 656-657
Savannah River (South Carolina), nuclear plant, safety of, **1989** 356
Save America's Forests, **1999** 594
Savimbi, Jonas
Angolan conflict, **2002** 151-153
Angola-Namibia peace accord, **1988** 947; **1991** 288
death of UNITA leader, **2002** 151, 153
U.S. support for, **2002** 152
Savings, personal
budget deficit and, **2005** 129
fell to negative savings, **2005** 139-140
impact of inflation on, **1976** 57-58; **1977** 732-733
incentives for, Joint Economic Committee support for, **1979** 215-216
for long-term medical care, **1986** 1031-1033
rate of, **1990** 82, 90-98
Savings and loan institutions
bailout of, **1989** 463-468
compared with problems in banking, **1990** 815, 816-818
crisis
Bush on plan for, **1989** 78-79
causes and remedies, **1988** 913-918
deregulation of, **1980** 948; **1988** 914
economic adviser's report, **1991** 93-96; **1992** 104, 114-115
"Keating Five" investigations, **1991** 107-118; **1992** 756
Milken's junk bonds, **1990** 252-253
problems of, Reagan CEA on, **1986** 60-61, 89-91
Savings Association Insurance Fund (SAIF), **1990** 816
creation of, **1989** 465, 467
Sawhill, Isabel, on teenage pregnancy, **1998** 263
Sawhill, John C.
bison release onto Tallgrass Prairie Reserve, **1993** 887-888
on energy conservation, **1974** 909
on energy supply, **1974** 910
Sawyer, Diane, in presidential debates, **1984** 848, 852-854, 861-864, 871-873
Saxbe, William B.
appointment to attorney general, **1975** 661-662, 665
on Nixon's tax returns, **1974** 239
Sayeed, Hafiz, founder of Lashkar-e-Taiaba in Pakistan, **2003** 210
al-Sayeed, Jamil, Hariri assassination, UN investigation, **2005** 691
al-Sayegh, Abdallah, **1975** 825
Saylor, John P. (R-Pa.), **1972** 797
Sayyaf, Abdul Rab Rassoul, Afghan parliamentary elections, **2005** 972
SBA. *See* Small Business Administration
Scali, John
on developing countries' coalition in UN, **1975** 645
U.S. position on UN actions, **1975** 326
Scalia, Antonin
abortion
anti-abortion demonstrations, **2000** 433
parental consent for, **1990** 387-407
partial-birth, **2000** 432, 441-442, 444-446
state restrictions on, **1989** 366-367, 378-379
abortion clinics
blockades, **1993** 93, 95-101
protests, **1994** 312, 316-317, 322-326
affirmative action, **1987** 332-334, 346-349; **2003** 362, 363, 376-381
federal government plans, **1995** 308, 319-320
appointment to Court, **1986** 560, 591, 593-597
asset forfeiture
drug trafficking, **1993** 432-438
pornography seized, **1993** 432, 438-440
attorney-client privilege, **1998** 395, 401-404
ballot initiatives, **1999** 6
campaign finance reform, **2003** 1160, 1169-1171
child pornography, **1990** 239-245
coastal property rights, **1992** 616-620
coerced confessions, **1991** 175-176, 182-184
congressional term limits, **1995** 260, 271-275
creation science, **1987** 567, 574-576

Scalia, Antonin *Continued*
deaf parochial student, **1993** 399-403
death penalty
fairness of, **2001** 389; **2004** 796
for juvenile offenders, **2002** 358; **2004** 797; **2005** 180, 192-196
for the mentally retarded, **2002** 356, 365-368
death penalty, racial discrimination in, **1987** 463
death row, appeals from death row prisoners, **1993** 141-147
detentions in terrorism cases, **2004** 377, 378, 390-392, 397-398
disabilities in the workplace, **2002** 6
disability, definition of, **1999** 318
discrimination by private clubs, **1988** 399-400, 403
disruptive handicapped students case, **1988** 48, 56
drug testing of students, **1995** 339-346
eminent domain, **2005** 363, 371-375
endangered species on private lands, **1995** 360, 366-368
entrapment in child pornography case, **1992** 322-327
faculty tenure review disclosure, **1990** 23-34
flag burning, **1989** 343; **1990** 357-362
free speech
decency in the arts, **1998** 405, 407, 415-417
and the Internet, **1997** 445
Internet pornography filters in public libraries, **2003** 388
freedom of residential signs, **1994** 290-297
gay rights discrimination, **1996** 284, 286, 291-295
gay rights to march, **1995** 327-335
grandparents' rights, **2000** 289, 297
gun-free school zone, **1995** 184
Haitian refugee interdiction, **1992** 453, 459-468; **1993** 413-421
hate crimes, **1992** 543-551; **1993** 385-389
HIV as a disability, **1998** 380, 389-392
impeachment, Senate's authority to remove judge, **1992** 81-87
independent counsel law, **1988** 468, 477-478
job discrimination
and contagious disease, **1987** 246, 250
fetal protection, **1991** 144, 153
involving African Americans, **1993** 423-429
jury selection, gender discrimination, **1994** 226, 234-236
legislative intent, **1993** 249-258
libel from misquotation, **1991** 325-326
line-item veto, **1998** 421, 431-433, 433-437
minority set-asides, **1989** 324; **1990** 421, 429-435
Miranda rule, **1990** 785, 786, 791-793
Miranda warnings, **2000** 389, 394-396
murder case sentencing, **1991** 389-390
Noriega phone calls dispute, **1990** 721-724
obscenity, tests for, **1987** 479-481, 484-485
parental leave and employment discrimination, **1987** 17
parochial school aid, **1997** 363
party primaries, open, **1986** 1065, 1072-1073
physician-assisted suicide, **1997** 461
political asylum, **1987** 253
presidential elections recount, **2000** 1002, 1003
preventive detention, **1987** 491
prison inmates, beaten by guards, **1992** 176, 182-185
prisoner appeals, **1991** 206
property takings, uncompensated, **1987** 533, 547-549
public lands and developers, **1994** 299, 300-306
punitive damages, for consumer product liability, **1996** 275
race-based redistricting, **1993** 459-474; **1995** 369, 371, 373-380; **1996** 369, 381
religious clubs in public schools, **2001** 422
religious freedom, **1997** 406-408, 409-417
religious publications, **1995** 385-395
religious symbols, **1995** 387, 396-400
right to die, **1990** 373-382
school desegregation, **1991** 24
school facilities, use by religious groups, **1993** 363-370
school prayer, **1992** 553-562; **2000** 367, 376-378
school vouchers, **2002** 408
segregated colleges, **1992** 576
sentencing laws, **2003** 984; **2004** 358, 360, 362-367
sex offenders, right to confine, **1997** 383
sexual harassment, **1998** 441, 442, 452, 461-465; **1999** 215, 227-234
at school, **1992** 188-199
in workplace, **1993** 939-945
sodomy laws, **2003** 403
states' rights, **1999** 333
student drug testing, **2002** 425, 426
tax increase to fund school desegregation, **1990** 227, 228-229, 232-238
Ten Commandments displays, **2005** 377, 378, 380-383
unreasonable searches, **2001** 408, 410, 411-416
virtual pornography, **2002** 290
women's right to choose, **1992** 589, 611-613
Scammon, Richard, on voting by young people, **1973** 35-36
Scanlon, William J.
bribery and fraud indictment, **2005** 633, 635
health insurance coverage report, **1998** 143-150
on insurance premium rates, **1998** 141
Schad v. Mount Ephraim, **1994** 296
Scharfenoth, Detlef, **1986** 93
Scharping, Rudolf, European defense force, **1999** 818
Schatten, Gerald P., South Korean stem cell research scandal, **2005** 321
Schechter Poultry Corp. v. United States, **1998** 436
Scheck, Barry, death penalty, **2000** 990
Scheffer, Jaap de Hoop
NATO membership and expansion, **2004** 136
NATO secretary general appointment, **2004** 135
U.S. policy on torture, Rice statements on, **2005** 908
Scheinberg, Phyllis F., GAO testimony on railroad safety, **1996** 189-198
Schell, Orville, **1989** 276
Schell, Walter, on EC proposal to Arab states, **1974** 185-186
Scheppach, Raymond C., Medicaid budget cuts, **2002** 55
Schering Corp., production of alpha interferon, **1986** 482

Scheuer, Michael, on al Qaeda terrorist network, **2004** 537
Scheuer v. Rhodes, **1974** 265-270
Schexnider, Alvin J., on blacks in the military, **1983** 43, 50
Schiavo, Michael, end-of-life care case, **2005** 155, 159
Schiavo, Terri, end-of-life care case, **2005** 154-163, 364-365, 376
Schiavone Construction Co.
  and Donovan investigations, **1982** 587
  indictment of, **1984** 803-809
Schieber, Sylvester J., retiree benefits, **2002** 668
Schieffer, Bob (presidential debates moderator), **2004** 677, 701-708
Schiff, Adam (D-Calif.), on separation of powers, **2005** 181
Schiff, Karena Gore, Democratic national convention, **2000** 612
Schiff, Steven, Roswell incident, **1997** 397
Schiffman, Lawrence H., Dead Sea scrolls, **1991** 638
Schifter, Richard, **1986** 97
Schilling, Curt, steroid use in baseball, congressional testimony on, **2005** 214, 222-223
Schindler, Bob and Mary, Schiavo end-of-life care case, **2005** 155-156, 159
Schiraldi, Vincent, sentencing reform, **2002** 787
Schiro v. Summerlin, **2004** 360, 797
Schlafly, Phyllis
  Baby M case, **1987** 376
  Bork nomination, **1987** 719
  ERA, **1977** 862-863; **1981** 925; **1982** 612, 616-617
  Law of the Sea Treaty, **2004** 606
  Republican Party platform, **1992** 800
Schlesinger, Arthur, Jr.
  Gorbachev reforms, **1989** 176
  multicultural education, **1991** 332, 345-347
  pledge of allegiance amendment, **2002** 383
Schlesinger, James R., **1992** 256, 258
  CIA domestic intelligence, **1975** 523, 526
  CIA involvement in Ellsberg break-in, **1973** 538
  energy policy, **1976** 879; **1977** 185; **1979** 659-667
  government career of, **1979** 660
  Independent Panel to Review DOD Detention Operations, **2004** 212, 342
  Mexico's price for natural gas, **1979** 169-170
  military aid, **1974** 279-280
  national security commission member, **1999** 500
  national security strategy, **1986** 781
  nuclear first-use option, **1975** 495-505
  nuclear test ban treaty, **1999** 601, 608
  resignation from Energy Department, **1979** 561, 572
  U.S. bombing of Cambodia, **1973** 729
  U.S. reaction to another oil embargo, **1975** 5
Schlesinger, Michael E., global warming, **2001** 113
Schlickeisen, Rodger, **1995** 360
Schmalensee, Richard L., **1992** 99
Schmemann, Serge, **1986** 146
Schmidt, Daniel, DeBoer adoption case, **1993** 515-529
Schmidt, Helmut
  economic summits, **1977** 367; **1978** 533-534; **1979** 3-4, 7-8; **1980** 504; **1981** 591
  and European Monetary System, **1978** 741-744, 750
  on global economic problems, **1975** 354
  on Soviet pipeline sanctions, **1982** 880
Schmidt, Randall M., Guantanamo Bay detainee abuse allegations investigations, **2005** 449-450
Schmidt, Stephen, Chinese food report, **1993** 689-694
Schmitz, John G. (R-Calif.), **1972** 615
Schmults, Edward D.
  on consequences of FOIA, **1981** 394
  and special prosecutor law, **1988** 467
Schneider, Carol, **1988** 518
Schneider, Rene, CIA support for groups opposed to, **1975** 710, 715, 763-770, 776, 787-789
Schneider, William C., **1973** 940
Schneider v. State, **1994** 296
Schneiders, Sandra, **1988** 786
Schnibbe, Harry, **1990** 575
Schnur, Dan, midterm elections, **2002** 818
Scholastic Aptitude Test (SAT)
  decline in scores on, **1975** 691-692
  and educational testing standards, **1992** 47
  emphasis on curriculum, **1987** 686, 688
  gender bias in, **1992** 142, 148
School desegregation
  busing moratorium, Republican Party platform on, **1972** 675-676
  colleges and universities, **1995** 239-253
  continued balance in, **1976** 413-423
  court-ordered busing
    across political lines, **1972** 15-21
    citywide, **1977** 447-464
    cross-district, **1974** 639-654
    and intention to discriminate, **1979** 535-552
    Nixon's alternatives to, **1972** 259-269, 715
    as presidential primary issue, **1972** 201-206
  impact of *Brown* ruling, **1972** 935-937
  methods of
    Democratic Party platform on, **1972** 563; **1976** 545, 563-564
    Republican Party platform on, **1976** 632-633
  in Mississippi colleges, **1992** 575-587
  Missouri tax increases to combat, **1990** 227-238
  and record of Reagan administration, Urban League on, **1987** 43-45, 58
  state restrictions on busing, **1982** 619-652
  Supreme Court on, **1991** 23-33
  trends in since 1966, **1975** 613-633
School integration
  colleges and universities, **1995** 239-253
  Little Rock Central High School fortieth anniversary, **1997** 317
School prayer
  Alabama statute requiring silent, Court ruling on, **1985** 379-395; **1987** 597, 604-605
  American Party platform on, **1972** 620
  constitutional amendment allowing
    Anderson position on, **1980** 866
    Ford support for, **1976** 812
    Reagan on, **1983** 85, 269, 272; **1984** 83, 91; **1985** 107, 113-114; **1987** 107, 112-113; **1988** 58, 65
    Senate rejection of, **1984** 241-245; **1985** 381
  Meese criticism of Court, **1985** 480, 487-488

School prayer *Continued*
Moral Majority on, **1983** 818
at public school graduation, Court ruling on, **1992** 553-562
in public schools, Supreme Court on, **2000** 365-378
Reagan support for, **1986** 40, 45
Republican Party platform on, **1972** 695; **1984** 662; **1988** 615-616, 642
voluntary
Bush on, **1988** 591, 610
Republican Party platform on, **1980** 568, 584
School violence
Columbine High School shootings, **1999** 179-184; **2000** 729, 873, 875-876; **2001** 73, 347-359; **2005** 678
crime in schools, FBI report on, **2005** 678
federal response, **1999** 181-182
and gun control, **2001** 723-724
gun-free school zones, Supreme Court ruling on, **2005** 552
legislative efforts to control, **1999** 55
school crime and safety reports, **2000** 873-879; **2001** 350-351
school safety report, **1998** 735-741
school shooter profiling, **2000** 874-875
school shooting incidents, **1999** 180-181; **2001** 347-348
youth violence, surgeon general's report on, **2001** 73-85
Schools
See also Education; High school; School desegregation; Teachers
accountability and evaluation of urban, **1988** 196-197, 201-206
affirmative action ban, **1998** 855-868
athletes steroid use policy, **2005** 218
charter schools, **1998** 88; **1999** 48
class time, efficient use of, **1988** 304-305
clusters within large urban, **1988** 196, 208-209
crime report, **1994** 575
curriculum, need for challenging, **1988** 303-305
D.C. schools, financial crisis, **1996** 784-789
discipline in, **1975** 67-80, 208-209, 219-221; **1985** 13-26; **1988** 299, 305-306
dropout rates among urban minorities, **1988** 196-197, 199, 210-212
education for handicapped in, **1988** 47-56
effectiveness of, **1986** 232-238
elementary, training of principal, **1986** 804-806, 814-815
enrollment
of children, **1999** 389
in Eastern European countries, **1994** 429
family planning clinics in, **1986** 1058, 1064
federal impact aid to, in Carter revision of Ford budget, **1977** 127
financing of
based on property tax, **1972** 74, 106-107, 676
Nixon's commission on, **1972** 221-233
Healthy Lunch Pilot Project, **2004** 656
high school certificates of proficiency in Calif., **1975** 692
magnet schools, **2002** 413
maintenance of buildings, **1988** 196, 198, 202, 212-214, 218, 306
Perot Reform Party nomination speech on, **1996** 559-561
prayer in schools, Supreme Court ruling on, **2005** 552
privatization of, **1994** 409-414
religion in public schools, **1995** 546-552
religious clubs in public schools, **2001** 420-432
school meals for children in, **2004** 655-656, 662
school safety, federal report on, **1998** 735-741
science equipment in, **1988** 385, 387-390
segregation in, and economic status of African Americans, **1989** 446, 448, 452, 454-455
sex discrimination in, HEW rules prohibiting, **1974** 507-513
sexual harassment, **1993** 353-361
uniforms policy in public schools, **1996** 84-92
urban
crisis in, Carnegie plan for, **1988** 195-219
high schools, reorganization of, **1988** 196, 198-199, 208-212
and segregation, Kerner Commission update, **1988** 190-191, 193
use of facilities by religious groups, **1993** 363-370
violence and vandalism in, Senate report on, **1975** 207-222
voucher plans, **1997** 363-364
GAO report on effectiveness of, **2002** 410
state legislation, **2002** 407-408
Supreme Court on, **2002** 406-423; **2005** 552
Schools, private
deaf parochial student, **1993** 399-406
parochial school aid, **1997** 361-381
public aid to
Court rulings on, **1973** 641-658; **1977** 431-445
Republican Party platform on, **1972** 677-678
studies by presidential commission, **1972** 221, 223, 226-227, 232
racial discrimination in admissions, **1976** 391-404
School-to-Work Opportunities Act, **1995** 73
Schopf, William, **1996** 472
Schor, Juliet B., **1992** 163-173
Schorr, Daniel
FBI investigation of, **1974** 602
and leak of CIA draft report, **1976** 683-686
Schott, Marge, suspension for racist remarks, **1993** 167-170
Schrire, Robert, on apartheid, **1993** 880
Schroeder, Gerhard
Afghanistan interim government, **2001** 881
bail-out of bankrupt company, **1999** 77
elections, **2005** 409, 874, 875-878
EU budget disputes, **2005** 344
and European Commission reforms, **1999** 157
European defense force, **1999** 819
German chancellor inaugural speech, **1998** 815-826
German economic situation, **2005** 873-874
and interest rates, **1998** 274
Iraq
on attacking Saddam Hussein, **2001** 852

capture of Saddam Hussein, **2003** 1194
UN resolution on disarmament, **2003** 41-43, 51-52
meeting with Qaddafi, **2004** 168
political profile, **1998** 817-819
tax cut plan, **2003** 753
U.S. relations, **2005** 874
war on terrorism, support of U.S., **2001** 628
Schroeder, Patricia (D-Colo.)
drug testing of federal employees, **1986** 842
at Gay/Lesbian March on Washington, **1993** 327
Grove City opinion, **1984** 203
House investigation of members' misconduct, **1982** 729-730
maternal mortality rate, **1996** 344
parental leave and job reinstatement, **1987** 19
response to Reagan State of the Union, **1984** 84
Tailhook incident, **1992** 880
Schuboroff, Berta, Argentine war crime trials, **2003** 828
Schuck, Peter, affirmative action in colleges and universities, **2003** 359
Schuker, Jill A., **1978** 703-707
Schuller, Robert, **1997** 43
Schultz, Marjorie, affirmative action proponent, **1997** 186
Schultze, Charles L.
Carter budget, **1979** 10
CEA report, **1981** 106
moves to strengthen dollar, **1978** 685
productivity slowdown, **1979** 82
Schulz, Charles M., retirement and death of, **1999** 856-859
Schulz, William F., on death penalty for juveniles, **2005** 180
Schumer, Charles E. (D-N.Y.)
Alito Supreme Court nomination, **2005** 815
BCCI banking scandal hearings, **1991** 635-636
Chinese import tariff, **2005** 617
drug trafficking, **1992** 203
FBI crime report, **2002** 785
House Judiciary Committee impeachment inquiry, **1998** 703
on monetary system reform, **1982** 973-974
religious freedom, **1997** 409
terrorist bombings in Saudi Arabia, **2003** 231
Schuster, Sharon, sexual harassment in public schools, **1993** 355
Schwalier, Terryl, **1996** 672-674
Schwartlander, Bernhard, AIDS prevention and treatment, **2002** 472
Schwartz, Bernard L., **1998** 978
Schwartz, Michael, Kent State protesters commemorated, **1990** 290, 293
Schwartz, Peter, climate change, **2004** 830-831
Schwarzchild, Henry, **1983** 711
Schwarzenegger, Arnold (California governor)
California budget plan, **2003** 1010
California employee pension plans, **2005** 198
California gubernatorial election, **2003** 72, 350, 577, 1005-1013, 1015
California prison system, abuse of inmates, **2004** 764
clemency for Williams denied, **2005** 178
greenhouse gas emissions, **2005** 924
inaugural address, **2003** 1005-1013
Indian voters, **2003** 577
Republican Party convention speech, **2004** 484
same-sex marriage legislation vetoed by, **2005** 863, 868
stem cell research supporter, **2004** 161
steroid drug use for bodybuilding, **2005** 213
Schwarzkopf, H. Norman
address to Congress, **1991** 243-246
affirmative action, **2003** 362
chemical weapons, **1997** 201
honorary knighthood from Queen Elizabeth II, **1991** 244, 248
Patriot missile performance report, **1992** 865-874
Persian Gulf War, **1991** 98-99, 101, 123; **1994** 434
at Republican Party convention, **2000** 511
Tallgrass Prairie Reserve, **1993** 886, 889-891
Schwarz-Schilling, Christian, UN administrator in Bosnia, **2005** 852
Schwebel, Stephen M., ICJ rulings on U.S.-Nicaragua dispute, **1984** 341, 344-345; **1985** 638
Schweiker, Richard S. (R-Pa.)
Nixon resignation, **1974** 289
as Reagan running mate, **1976** 618, 666
sex bias in pension plans, **1983** 693-694
Schweitzer, LeRoy, Freeman leader, **1996** 363, 365
Schwerner, Michael, civil rights worker murder (1964), **2002** 239; **2005** 353-361
Schwoebel, Richard L., **1990** 320
Science and technology
See also Military technology; Technology transfer
21st Century Research Fund, **2000** 34
advice to government on, **1972** 381-382
appointments to federal advisory panels, government panel on, **2004** 841-849
Assistant to the President for Science and Technology (APST), **2004** 845-847
Clinton administration initiatives, **2000** 33-34
and colleges' failures, **1985** 128, 139-141
and economic development, nonaligned nations on, **1983** 266
education about technology, **2002** 69
federal support for, **1995** 82-83
information technology revolution, **2000** 54-55
peaceful use of, John Paul II on, **1982** 838, 842-846
progress in, inseparability from open society, **1975** 915-916, 918-922
Republican Party platform, **1996** 508-509
social implications of
John Paul II on, **1981** 204-205, 210; **1984** 778-779, 783-785; **1985** 60-61
Vatican teaching on, **1987** 269-271, 277
for Soviet pipeline, U.S. ban on exports, **1981** 884; **1982** 879-884
U.S. position in, **1973** 781-782, 784-785
U.S.-European cooperation in, **1985** 355
U.S.-PRC agreements on, **1984** 23-30, 294-295
U.S.-Soviet agreements on, **1987** 994, 1000-1001, 1005
linked to treatment of Sakharov, **1973** 791-796
world trends, **2000** 1053-1054, 1057-1058

Science education
  creationism vs. evolution, **1972** 843-844; **1987** 565-576
  reform of, **1983** 414-415, 419, 429-430, 433
  upgrading of in U.S., **1989** 86-87, 89-92
  U.S. students' progress in, **1988** 378-379, 383-390
Scientific Committee on Problems of the Environment (SCOPE), on environmental consequences of nuclear war, **1985** 541-554
Scientific research
  basic vs. applied, government support of, **1973** 782-783, 785-786
  in Carter budget, **1978** 97, 100-101; **1979** 15-16, 51-52; **1980** 110, 114
  and development
    funding for, **1972** 109-111; **1973** 781-786, 789
    and U.S. technical preeminence, **1980** 160, 165, 169-170, 185-186
  East-West cooperation in, **1972** 833-835
  in Ford budget, **1977** 61-62
  genetic engineering, controls and safeguards on, **1975** 319-324; **1983** 525-532
  on human subjects, public funding for, **1975** 543-544
  in Reagan budget, **1983** 111; **1984** 108
  secret military projects, National Academy of Sciences on, **1972** 381-383
  and technology transfer to Soviets, **1982** 813, 815, 817-819
  universe's big bang origins, **1992** 379-383
Scientists
  in research and development, numbers of, **1973** 781-782, 786-788
  on SDI, **1984** 257-258, 260-266; **1988** 324
  U.S., defense of Sakharov by, **1973** 791-796
Scobee, Francis R. "Dick," *Challenger* accident, **1986** 515, 520; **1988** 795
Scobey, Margaret, U.S. ambassador to Syria withdrawn, **2005** 687
Sconiers, Daryl, **1986** 171
Scoon, Paul, **1983** 851
Scopes, John, and teaching of evolution, **1982** 4; **1987** 566
Scotland
  John Paul II visit, **1982** 409
  student test scores, **1992** 91, 92, 95
Scott, Edward W., **1986** 582
Scott, H. Lee, Jr., Wal-Mart public relations campaign, **2005** 736
Scott, Hugh (R-Pa.)
  Nixon inaugural, **1973** 81
  Nixon tape transcripts, **1974** 288, 301-302
  Paris peace accords, **1973** 117
  support for Kissinger, **1974** 489
Scott, Robert C. (D-Va.), House Judiciary Committee impeachment inquiry, **1998** 706
Scott, William L. (R-Va.), **1978** 590
Scott v. Illinois, **1979** 207-214
Scowcroft, Brent, **1992** 524
  chemical weapons, **1997** 201
  FBI files on, **2000** 765
  Iran-U.S. relations, **2001** 795
  MX missiles, **1983** 365, 368
  national security strategy, **1986** 781
  review of NSC operations, **1986** 1018; **1987** 205
  UN reform panel, **2003** 810; **2004** 887
Scranage, Sharon, **1985** 604
Scranton, William W. (R-Pa.)
  criticism of Israel at UN, **1976** 191-196
  veto of UN membership for Vietnam, **1977** 208
Scripps Institute of Oceanography, on greenhouse effect, **1988** 862
Scrutton, Hugh Campbell, victim of Unabomber, **1998** 234, 238-239
Scully, Thomas A.
  Medicare cost estimates, withholding from Congress, **2004** 579
  Nursing Home Compare Web site, **2002** 120
  penalty for threatening HHS employee Richard Foster, **2004** 577, 579-580
  resignation, **2004** 579
Scurry, Rod, **1986** 171
SDI. *See* Strategic Defense Initiative
SDRs. *See under* International Monetary Fund, special drawing rights
Sea Isle City, Iranian attack on in Persian Gulf, **1987** 794
Sea level, rise in, as effect of global warming, **1988** 866
Seabed Arms Control Treaty (1972), Senate consent to ratification of, **1972** 167-171
Seabed resources
  federal control of offshore, **1975** 167-175
  mining of under Law of the Sea Treaty, **1982** 346-348, 351-352, 354-361
Seabrook nuclear plant, **1990** 195-198
Seaga, Edward P. G., **1982** 181
Seamans, Robert C., Jr., claim of executive privilege by, **1973** 194-195, 202-204
Searches
  auto, and passengers' rights, **1978** 753-764
  drug testing of employees, **1986** 841
  electronic surveillance
    court-ordered phone company assistance, **1977** 883-896
    covert entry for, **1979** 269-284
    for foreign intelligence, with judicial warrant, **1976** 125-126, 129, 137
  exclusionary rule
    good-faith exception to, **1984** 505-519; **1985** 480-481, 485-486
    and *habeas corpus* claims, **1976** 521-536
  national security grounds for in Ellsberg break-in, **1974** 411-417; **1975** 654, 660, 680-681
  of newsrooms with warrants, **1978** 355-372
  prison inmates' rights, **1984** 479-491
  student, privacy vs. discipline, **1985** 13-26
  unreasonable, at home without warrant, **1980** 281-297
Sears, John P., **1976** 666
Seattle (Washington), school uniform policy, **1996** 89-90
Sebe, Lennox, **1985** 518
SEC. *See* Securities and Exchange Commission
Secord, Richard V.
  Iran-contra conviction, **1991** 619; **1994** 12

role in Iran-contra affair, **1986** 1015; **1987** 217, 224, 892, 899, 901, 906, 919, 927
trial of, **1989** 392-393
Secret Service
and homeland security, **2002** 532
Kennedy (John F.) assassination, and performance of, **1978** 910, 915; **1979** 613-614
political uses of
in impeachment articles, **1974** 658
Watergate Committee report on, **1974** 601
protective function privilege, **1998** 395-396, 566
Reagan assassination attempt, and performance of, **1981** 353
White House taping system, **1973** 698-701
Secularism, opposed to Islam, **1990** 277-287
Securities, investors in New York City, and city's fiscal crisis, **1977** 567-579
Securities and Exchange Commission (SEC)
access to federal tax returns, **1975** 854
accounting board nominations controversy, **2002** 1032-1035
Enron Corp. investigations, **2001** 860; **2003** 337-339
failures, GAO report on, **2002** 1032-1043
and insider trading, **1987** 881-883
Milken's junk bonds, **1990** 252
mutual funds scandal, **2003** 693-698
on New York City's fiscal crisis, **1977** 567-579
online investing, **1999** 203-214
pension fund accounting practices, **2004** 738
Pitt resignation, **2002** 880, 1032
and stock market crash, **1987** 835, 837, 840-841; **1988** 9, 11-12
regulatory role after, **1988** 11-12, 15, 30-31, 34
on takeovers and buyouts, **1988** 921-925
Vesco campaign contributions and mutual fund investigation by, **1973** 564
WorldCom fraud case, **2002** 391-405
Security, domestic
See also Homeland Security Department; National security; Surveillance, domestic
clearances of government employees, **1995** 532-545
declassifying government secrets, **1994** 524-527
FBI guidelines on, **1983** 257-261
in federal buildings, **1995** 178-179
intelligence restrictions on, relaxation of, **1981** 353, 359-364, 861-868
Japanese-American and Aleut native internment, **1983** 211-228
Pennsylvania Avenue closing, **1995** 254-258
Sedna (planetoid) discovery, **2004** 7
Seeber, Ronald, on unions, **1995** 682
Seevers, Gary L., **1974** 70
Segal, Eli J., welfare reform, **1997** 622; **1998** 357
Segregation. *See* Racial segregation; School desegregation
Segretti, Donald H.
political dirty tricks of, **1974** 602, 611
Watergate involvement, **1974** 318-319, 323, 335, 339
Seib, Philip M., **1973** 36
Seidman, L. William
bank failures' toll on deposit insurance funds, **1990** 815-823
on savings and loan crisis, **1988** 914-918
Seiple, Robert, religious freedom, **1998** 21
Sekule, William, Rwanda war crimes tribunal, **2003** 1075
Selassie, Haile, Ethiopian leader, **2000** 753-754
Selective Service Act (1948)
enactment of, **1972** 734
extension of military draft, **1993** 256
sex discrimination in draft, **1981** 523
violations of, Carter pardon for, **1977** 98-99
Selective Service System
draft evader pardon, **1977** 95-99
draft registration and student aid, **1984** 493-497, 500-501, 503
Selective Service System v. Minnesota Public Interest Research Group, **1984** 493-503
Selective Training and Service Act (1940), **1993** 257
Selig, Allan H. "Bud"
baseball commissioner on antisteroid use policy, **2005** 213-217
cancellation of baseball season, **1994** 360-362
steroid use in baseball, congressional testimony on, **2005** 224-227
suspension of Schott for racist remarks, **1993** 167-170
Semanza, Laurent, Rwanda war crimes conviction, **2003** 1074
Semiconductors, Japanese agreement with U.S. on, **1987** 427-429, 430-433
Seminole Tribe of Fla. v. Florida, **1999** 334, 336, 340, 345-346
Semyonov, Aleksei, emigration of, **1981** 747-749
Semyonov, V. S., SALT negotiations, **1972** 431, 454-459
Senate, U.S.
campaign finance hearings, **1998** 893-894
Democratic control of
impact on black America, **1987** 44-45, 50
impact on Reagan presidency, **1987** 4, 105, 108
denouncing of Talmadge, **1979** 623, 625, 631-636
ERA reintroduction in, **1982** 611-617
impeachment powers, **1993** 81-91
Japanese-American internees, debate on reparations for, **1988** 287-295
judicial impeachments
of Claiborne, **1986** 849-851, 853-857
of Hastings and Nixon, **1989** 583-596
King holiday, debate on, **1983** 884
Mansfield on civility in the, **1998** 151-158
president pro tempore, and transfer of power, **1985** 493
presidential appointees, confirmation of, **1973** 5, 13, 18
ratification of treaties, constitutional role in, **1987** 290, 292-304
resolutions
assassination attempt on John Paul II, **1981** 428
IRA prison hunger strike, **1981** 402, 413
Sakharov hunger strike, **1981** 749, 751-752
on Watergate pardons, **1974** 813
Rockefeller confirmation, **1974** 987
school prayer amendment, rejection of, **1984** 241-245

Senate, U.S. *Continued*
Seabed Arms Control Treaty, consent to ratification of, **1972** 167-171
spending responsibilities, abdication of, **1973** 4-10
WHO infant formula code, support for, **1981** 448
women in combat debate, **1991** 491-512
Senate v. Immigration and Naturalization Service, **1983** 617-644
Senate Armed Services Committee
criticism of Defense Department and Joint Chiefs, **1986** 681
Defense Department reorganization, **1985** 669-683
explosion on USS *Iowa,* report, **1990** 319-330
rejection of Tower nomination, **1989** 105-120
Subcommittee on Manpower and Personnel, hazing and other practices at military academies, **1992** 481-487
testimony on U.S. bombing of Cambodia, **1973** 729-730
war powers debate, **1990** 665-666
Senate Banking, Housing and Urban Affairs Committee, Gulf War syndrome report, **1994** 264-275
Senate Budget Committee, formation of, **1974** 573-574, 577-578; **1976** 177-179
Senate Children, Families, Drugs and Alcoholism Committee, **1992** 495
Senate Committee on Commerce, Science, and Transportation
on Exxon oil spill in Alaska, **1989** 225-237
hearings on AT&T divestiture, **1982** 19
Senate Environment Committee, Lavelle testimony to, **1982** 966
Senate Environmental Protection Subcommittee, Clean Air Act revisions, **1990** 717
Senate Ethics Committee, "Keating Five" investigation, **1990** 817; **1991** 107-108
Senate Finance Committee
budget compromise with Bush, **1990** 411
on Social Security system, **1975** 115-121
Senate Foreign Relations Committee
Arms Control Subcommittee, chemical warfare, Burt testimony on, **1981** 682-683, 687-694
cold war, Kennan on end of, **1989** 207-212
Iran-Iraq War and Persian Gulf, report on, **1984** 747, 750-755
Iraq's use of chemical weapons, **1989** 27
Kissinger confirmation hearings, and national security wiretaps, **1974** 487-494
Panama Canal treaties, concerns about, **1978** 177-178
SALT II hearings in, **1979** 415-418
Senate Governmental Affairs Committee, Lance testimony before, **1977** 628, 640-675
Senate Intelligence Committee
CIA reforms, **1992** 4
Gates CIA Director nomination hearings, **1991** 651-669
Senate Judiciary Committee
Bork nomination to Court, report of, **1987** 717-744
Constitution Subcommittee, FOIA revisions, proposed, **1981** 394
death penalty, **1990** 312
Gray confirmation hearings for FBI director, **1973** 337-338
Investigate Juvenile Delinquency Subcommittee, on violence and vandalism in schools, **1975** 207-222
Keating inquiry, **1990** 817
Kleindienst confirmation hearings for attorney general, **1972** 395-397, 400-406; **1974** 407-410
O'Connor confirmation hearings, **1981** 577, 579-590
Souter confirmation hearings, **1990** 615-628
special subcommittee investigation of B. Carter's Libyan contacts, **1980** 907-917
Thomas Supreme Court nomination hearings, **1991** 551-615
Senate Rules Committee, on Rockefeller confirmation, **1974** 707, 709, 987
Senate Select Committee on Ethics
denunciation of Talmadge, **1979** 623, 625, 631-636
Williams's expulsion recommended by, **1981** 673-679
Senate Select Committee on Intelligence
Casey investigation by, **1981** 855-859
CIA assassination plots, **1975** 709-799
CIA covert action in Chile, **1975** 873-875, 882-914
establishment of, **1976** 117, 237
FBI political abuses, **1975** 873-882; **1976** 321-322
Iran-contra affair investigation, **1986** 1050, 1053
report, **1987** 891-928
merger with House committee, Tower recommendation, **1987** 207, 241
Senate Select Committee on Presidential Campaign Activities (Watergate committee)
access to White House tapes, **1973** 737, 741-742, 841-842; **1974** 302
Butterfield testimony, **1973** 697-701
Dean testimony, **1973** 659-679
Ehrlichman testimony, **1973** 660-661
final recommendations, **1974** 599-619
Haldeman testimony, **1973** 660-662
hearings, **1973** 550
White House strategy for, **1973** 664-666, 672-673; **1974** 303, 330-332, 382-387
indictments for lying to, **1974** 157, 159-160, 170-176
interaction with special prosecutor, **1975** 655-658
investigations, **1973** 549-556; **1974** 41, 52
testimony of White House aides, **1973** 500-501, 503
Senate Select Committee to Study Governmental Operations with Respect to Intelligence Activities, inquiry on intelligence community, **1976** 115, 235-285
Sencer, David J., and swine flu program, **1978** 670-671, 675-676, 681
Sendero Luminoso (Shining Path), **1992** 202
Senegal
AIDS infection rate dropping, **2000** 412
Clinton state visit, **1998** 159
Senior citizens
See also Alzheimer's disease; Medicaid; Medicare
abuse of older persons, UN report on, **2002** 194
catastrophic illness expense
HHS recommendations, **1986** 1025-1033
Reagan on, **1983** 86; **1986** 41, 46
Contract with America, **1994** 374-378

Democratic Party platform on, **1972** 545-546; **1984** 614-616
economic status of, **1985** 99-101
health care
costs, **1993** 271-285
for-profit hospitals and, **1986** 487-513
health problems in Eastern Europe, **1994** 415-430
hunger in U.S. and, **1985** 193, 196, 198, 204
income floor for, Nixon on, **1972** 94-95
mental health disorders, **2001** 577
nursing home abuse and neglect, GAO report on, **2002** 117-132
opportunities and challenges of, **1997** 343-344
population in U.S., **1996** 296-301
in poverty in U.S., **1988** 877-880
prescription drug benefit plan, **2001** 712, 713; **2002** 945, 949-950; **2003** 18, 23, 38-39; **2004** 20, 27-28
Republican Party platform on, **1972** 700-702; **1984** 696; **1988** 639-640; **1996** 532-533
"safety net" for in Reagan economic plan, **1981** 214, 217; **1982** 156
suicide prevention, **1999** 454
UN World Assembly on Aging, **2002** 193-200
Senior Corps programs, **2002** 37, 44
Senior Executive Service (SES), creation of, **1978** 138-139, 142-143
Seniority systems
and affirmative action, **1984** 365-375, 379-381, 384
and racial discrimination, **1977** 383-393
rights after maternity leave, **1977** 871-881
Sens, Andrew D., on hazardous waste treaty, **1989** 153-154
Sensenbrenner, F. James, Jr. (R-Wis.)
on Clinton impeachment, **1999** 18
immigration law provisions of intelligence reform act, **2004** 969-970
INS reorganization, **2001** 767
Patriot Act II, **2003** 612
Schiavo end-of-life care case, **2005** 156
screening immigrants, **2002** 846
sentencing laws, **2003** 983
Sentelle, David B., **1990** 492
September 11 detainees' names secret, **2003** 315
Sentencing
appealing, and double jeopardy, **1980** 977-988
California "three-strikes" law upheld, **2003** 983-984
controversy, **2003** 982-983; **2004** 359
death penalty and mitigating factors, **1978** 495-514; **1982** 51-63
of federal criminals, reform of, **1987** 407-426
guidelines, Supreme Court on, **2004** 358-374; **2005** 680-681
mandatory, for drug trafficking, **1973** 27-33, 306, 327-328
racial discrimination in, **1987** 463-476
standards for, Carter support for, **1978** 327, 332
tougher guidelines, and higher incarceration rates, **2004** 763
Sentencing Commission (U.S.), **2003** 982; **2004** 359
proposed changes in procedures, **1987** 407-426
Sentencing Project, **2002** 786-787
Sentencing Reform Act (1984), **1997** 250-251, 253
Separation of church and state. *See* Church and state separation
Separation of powers
administrative powers for Congress, Court on Gramm-Rudman-Hollings, **1986** 706-730
appointment of FEC commissioners, **1976** 71-75, 98-104
appointment of independent counsel, **1988** 465-478
breaches of, **2000** 386
congressional investigations of executive branch
Iran-contra affair, **1986** 1018
Watergate committee hearings, **1973** 551-553
congressional resolution on judicial reliance on foreign sources, **2005** 181
congressional right to choose staff, **1979** 401, 408-411
and custody of Nixon papers and tapes, **1977** 465-467, 470-472, 487-491, 494-499, 502
executive privilege in congressional testimony, Nixon policy on, **1973** 337-342
judicial activism as intrusion on legislative domain, **1981** 581-582, 803-809
judicial review of executive branch, Court ruling on Nixon tapes, **1974** 621-623, 631-633
and line-item veto, **1998** 419-437
National Commission on Separation of Powers report, **1998** 905-911
presidential immunity from court processes, federal courts on Nixon tapes, **1973** 840-842, 845, 848, 854-857
Separatism, Quebec issue, **1990** 367-372
September 11 (9/11) Family Steering Committee, **2004** 450, 452
September 11 (9/11) terrorist attacks
See also Terrorist organizations
Arab world response, **2002** 483
aviation security, post-attack, **2001** 650; **2003** 218-219
bin Laden involvement in, **2001** 3, 614, 802-818
British government report on, **2001** 802-818
Bush statements on, **2001** 614-623; **2003** 19
Chinese response, **2001** 740-741
commission recommendations, **2005** 893-904
commission report, **2003** 544, 547; **2004** 339, 450-477, 517-533, 966-967, 1012-1013
congressional joint panel reports on, **2002** 990-1013; **2003** 544-575
detainees treatment, Justice Department on, **2003** 310-331
Indonesian reaction to, **2001** 565-567
intelligence gathering, congressional joint panel reports on, **2002** 990-1013; **2003** 544-575
international reaction to, **2001** 624-636
Iranian response, **2001** 795-796
Libyan response, **2003** 1224-1225
National Day of Prayer and Remembrance (National Cathedral), Bush statement, **2001** 621-623
offenders data, **2002** 793
postattack
economic aftermath, **2001** 52, 663-671
events following, **2001** 651-652, 894-895
NYC air quality, EPA report on, **2003** 174, 547, 548

September 11 (9/11) terrorist attacks *Continued*
U.S. military tribunals controversy, **2001** 629
victims data, **2002** 793; **2003** 544
victims fund administration, **2003** 544-545
war on terrorism, Bush plans for, **2001** 637-649
Serbia
Albanian Muslim guerrillas, **2001** 554-555
independence, **1991** 368
Lukovic gang trial, **2003** 59
ousting of Slobodan Milosevic, **2004** 1001
parliamentary elections, **2003** 1144
political situation, **2000** 153-155; **2003** 56; **2005** 856-857
presidential elections, **2003** 58, 60
Yugoslavia's UN membership, **1992** 875-878
Serbia and Montenegro
constitution adopted, **2003** 55-67
political situation, **2004** 955-956
union of states replaces Yugoslavia, **2003** 57
Serevent, drug safety of, **2004** 853
Sergeyev, Igor D., Russian submarine disaster, **2000** 635
Serpa, Horacio, Colombia presidential candidate, **2002** 571-572
Serra, Jose, Brazilian presidential candidate, **2002** 776-777
Serrano, Andres, **1998** 406
Serrano, Jose E., on Schott suspension for racist remarks, **1993** 168
Serushago, Omar, genocide trials, **1998** 616
Service Employees International Union (SEIU)
breakaway from AFL-CIO, **2005** 485-489, 735
home care workers union, **1999** 630, 631-632
hospital quality oversight, **1999** 414
SES. *See* Senior Executive Service
Seselj, Voijslav, Serbian war crimes trial, **2003** 59, 60; **2004** 956
Sessions, Alice, **1993** 610
Sessions, William
death penalty rulings, **2002** 355-356; **2004** 796
jury selection and racial bias, **2002** 359
removal as FBI director, **1993** 609
Sessler, Andrew, **1990** 208
Seuss, Hans, **1988** 862
Sevan, Benon V., UN oil-for-food program scandal, **2004** 892; **2005** 234-235
Sevareid, Eric
on Ford's swearing-in as vice president, **1973** 970
on Johnson's death, **1973** 98-99
Severe acute respiratory syndrome. *See* SARS (severe acute respiratory syndrome) outbreak
Sewall, Gilbert, Christopher Columbus Legacy, **1992** 897-898
Sex, extramarital
Catholic teaching on, **1979** 729, 757-758
dissent from, **1985** 363-364, 373
Sex discrimination. *See* Discrimination, sex
Sex education
about AIDS, **1986** 89, 893-894
in schools, **1987** 319-320, 323-325
abstinence-only programs, **1997** 83, 89; **2001** 128; **2002** 474; **2004** 21, 29
on contraceptives, **1986** 1060
Elders resignation as surgeon general, **1994** 592-594; **1995** 61
Moral Majority on, **1983** 818
reproductive health services for children, **2002** 223-224
safe sex for teenagers, **1997** 81, 82-83
sexual health and responsible sexual behavior, **2001** 456-471
Sex offenders
confining, Supreme Court on, **1997** 382-394
Megan's Law in New Jersey, **1997** 382, 384
Sex selection, ethics of embryonic research, **1998** 66
Sex tourism, **2001** 957; **2004** 131
Sexes, equality of, John Paul II on, **1988** 786-788
Sexual abuse and harassment
See also Rape
of children
abuse of missionary children, **2005** 867
National Review Board report, **2004** 82-93
by priests, **2002** 867-876; **2003** 523-543; **2005** 865-867
settlements, **2005** 867
"zero tolerance" rule, **2005** 863, 866
HIV prevention for victims of sexual assault, **2005** 61-62
Sudan violence, UN report, **2005** 514-525
Tailhook scandal, **2003** 791
UN peacekeepers abuse of women and children, **2004** 509, 893-894; **2005** 237-238
UN staff, **2005** 238
U.S. Air Force Academy, sexual abuse of women cadets, **2003** 791-807
Sexual assault and harassment
of children by priests, **1993** 407-411
Clinton-Jones law suit, **1997** 21, 290-298; **1998** 39, 565, 633-634, 638-639, 962; **1999** 16, 21-22; **2000** 763
of girls in athletic settings, **1997** 170
in the military, army report on, **1997** 654-660
in military academies, **1992** 481, 482-483, 485-486
Navy's Prevention Initiative, **1992** 1003-1005
in public schools, **1993** 353-361
of the same sex, **1998** 441-442
of students, **1992** 146, 187-199
by a classmate, **1999** 215-234
by a teacher, **1998** 442
Tailhook incident, Pentagon Report on, **1992** 879-890
in workplace, **1993** 939-945
Supreme Court opinion on, **1998** 438-465
Sexual Assault Project (Seattle), **1992** 386
Sexual behavior, among high school students, **1992** 339-343
Sexual ethics
Father Curran's dissent from Catholic teaching, **1986** 757-765
U.S. Catholic clergy on, **1986** 909-911
Sexual rights
honor killings of women, **2000** 327; **2001** 957
sexual exploitation of children, **2001** 955-962
trafficking in persons, **2000** 328; **2002** 335-352
of women, **2000** 326-327
Seychelles, tsunami relief effort, **2005** 1005

Seymour, Steven, **1977** 898
Shaath, Nabil, on Palestinian provisional state, **2002** 375
Shabazz, Betty, at Million Man March, **1995** 656
Shabdan, Kajikhumar, **1993** 565
Shadley, Robert D., sexual abuses on base, **1997** 655
Shafarevich, Igor, on voluntary exile of Soviet artists and intellectuals, **1975** 161-165
Shafer, Raymond P.
on drug problem, **1973** 393-394
social policy on marijuana, **1972** 291
Shafi, Haidar Abdul, Middle East Peace Conference (Madrid), **1991** 727-731
Shafir, Herzl, **1974** 436
Shah, Mohammad Zahir (Afghanistan king)
Afghan elections, **2005** 973
ousted in 1973, **2001** 881; **2004** 917
Shaheen, Jeanne, death penalty, **2000** 989
Shaheen, Michael, investigation of political dismissal, **1978** 52-61
Shaiken, Harley, on labor movement, **1999** 632
Shakhashiri, Bassam Z., **1988** 379
Shakhnovsky, Vasily, Russian entrepreneur case, **2003** 248
Shalala, Donna
consumer health care, **1997** 787, 791
dietary guidelines, **1996** 3
drug use among children, **1996** 570-572
drug use survey, **1999** 459, 461
girls in sports, **1997** 158-159
marijuana use, **1996** 756-757
medical records privacy, **1997** 580-587; **2000** 1063-1071
oral health in America, **2000** 223
physical activity, **1996** 4, 418
teenage pregnancy, **1998** 260
welfare system, **1997** 620
Shalikashvili, John M.
affirmative action, **2003** 362
antipersonnel land mines, **1997** 847
Georgian parliamentary elections, **2003** 1040
McCain amendment on detainees treatment, **2005** 909-910
on test ban treaty, **1998** 49
Shalom, Silvan
Israeli disengagement policy, **2004** 302, 303, 305
Israeli policy toward Arafat, **2003** 1201
Shalqam, Abdel-Rahman (Libyan foreign minister), meeting with Colin Powell, **2004** 172
Shamir, Yitzhak
background and career of, **1983** 832
election defeat, **1992** 655
election to prime minister, **1983** 831-845
Middle East Peace Conference (Madrid), **1991** 720, 725-727
Mubarak peace plan, **1989** 291
Palestinian elections on West Bank, **1989** 290, 294-295
Palestinian refugee camp massacre, **1983** 165, 176-177
Palestinian uprising, and human rights, **1989** 58
Reagan peace plan, **1982** 754, 760-766
relations with U.S., **1990** 695-696
Washington visit, **1983** 834-835
Shamrock, NSA operation of cable interception, **1975** 709, 711, 799-803
Shanab, Abu (Hamas leader), killed by Israelis, **2003** 197
Shanghai communiqué, U.S.-PRC, **1972** 187-190; **1978** 785-786
Shanker, Albert
affirmative action and seniority, **1984** 367
education summit, **1989** 563
education's problems, **1988** 299
school violence, **1975** 208, 213
science education, **1988** 379
teaching and learning research, **1986** 218
Shanley, Paul R., priest sexual offender case, **2004** 87; **2005** 867
Shannon, John, **1978** 398
Shannon, Thomas A., **1992** 47
Shannon, William, on Nixon administration and the press, **1973** 630, 637-639
Shapira, Avraham, Gaza withdrawal opponent, **2004** 307-308
Shapiro, Isaac, **1991** 828
Shapiro, Robert J., impact of Y2K computer failures, **1999** 762
Shapiro, Stephen
drug testing of students, **1995** 341
school voucher plans, **1997** 364
student rights, **1995** 341
Shapiro, Steven R., unreasonable searches, **2001** 409
al-Shara, Farouk, Israel-Syria peace negotiations, **1999** 896-897; **2000** 495
Sharansky, Natan, Gaza Strip withdrawal opponent, **2005** 531
Sharif, Nawaz
India-Pakistan Lahore Declaration, **1999** 623-624
Kashmir controversy, **2001** 964
ousted from Pakistan, **1999** 623, 625-626; **2001** 964; **2004** 1010
Pakistan election referendum, **2002** 167-169
Pakistani nuclear testing, **1998** 327
Sharm el-Sheik (Egypt), terrorist bombings of resorts, **2004** 535, 812; **2005** 165, 168, 399
Sharm el-Sheikh Fact-Finding Committee (Mitchell Commission), report, **2001** 360-376
Sharon, Ariel
Barak's election challenger, **2000** 931, 935
corruption scandal, **2004** 306
Gaza Strip withdrawal, **2003** 27; **2004** 301-315, 806-807, 810-811; **2005** 27, 529-538
invasion of Lebanon, **1983** 833
Israeli elections, **2003** 192
as Israeli prime minister, **2002** 937
Jenin "massacre" investigations, **2002** 934
Kadima Party (new centrist party), **2005** 529, 534-535
libel suit against *Time* magazine, **1985** 47-52
Middle East peace process
meetings with Rice and Abbas, **2005** 88
opposition to, **2001** 361, 364, 365, 366
Quartet "roadmap" for peace, **2002** 376; **2003** 194-198, 1200, 1207, 1213-1216; **2004** 303
settlement freeze, **2001** 363

Sharon, Ariel *Continued*
Palestinian conflict, **2003** 191
disengagement policy. *See above* Gaza strip withdrawal
on Palestinian leadership, **2002** 369-372
policy toward Arafat, **2004** 301
response to terrorist attacks, **2002** 930-931
uprising after visit to Temple Mount, **2001** 362
visit to U.S., **2002** 370; **2004** 628
and Palestinian refugee camp massacre, **1982** 782-793; **1983** 165, 175-176, 178
Palestinian uprising after visit to Temple Mount, **2000** 931
peace talks with Abbas, **2005** 28-30, 88, 530
return of Sinai to Egypt, **1982** 338
strokes and withdrawal from office, **2005** 529, 535
Sharp, Philip R. (D-Ind.), **1985** 806
Sharp, Ulysses S. Grant, **1985** 161
Sharpe, William F., Nobel in economics, **1990** 796
Sharpton, Al, **1991** 248
presidential candidate, **2004** 479
Shatila, Palestinian refugee camp massacre at, **1985** 47-51
Shatt-al-Arab waterway, Iran-Iraq dispute over, **1984** 748; **1988** 530, 532
Shattuck, John, religious freedom and human rights, **1998** 20
Shaw, Bernard, in presidential debates, **1988** 723, 754-755
Shaw, E. Clay (R-Fla.)
Social Security reform, **2005** 116
welfare reform, **1996** 463
Shaw, Patricia Hearst
kidnapping of, by SLA, **1974** 247-253
presidential pardon, **2001** 89
Shaw, Russell, sexual abuse by priests, **2002** 872
Shaw v. Hunt, **1996** 368; **1998** 866-867
Shaw v. Reno, **1993** 459-481; **1995** 370, 373-376, 378, 380, 380-382, 381-382, 384; **1996** 368, 370; **1997** 190, 193
Shawkat, Assef, Hariri assassination, UN investigation, **2005** 691
Shays, Christopher (R-Conn.)
campaign finance reform, **1997** 33; **1998** 893; **1999** 56; **2003** 1155
Gulf War illness, **2001** 909
Watt's "influence peddling," **1989** 334
Shcharansky, Anatoly B.
release of, **1986** 93-96
in Soviet labor camp, **1981** 748
Shcharansky, Avital, fight for husband's release, **1986** 94
Shea, Jamie, on U.S. bombing of Chinese embassy, **1999** 305
Shearer, Gail, comprehensive drug coverage, **2003** 1123
Shearson Lehman Hutton, and RJR Nabisco buyout, **1988** 922
Shedd, Dennis W., Senate confirmation, **2002** 823
Sheehan, Cindy, Iraq antiwar crusade, **2005** 836
Sheehan, John J., on clean air report, **1981** 277, 288-292
Sheehan, Michael, counterterrorism cooperation, **2000** 279
Sheehan, Neil, **1972** 492
Sheet Metal Workers' Local 28 v. Equal Employment Opportunity Commission, **1986** 651-667
Sheft, Mark, **1991** 828
Shehadeh, Sheik Salah, assassination of, **2002** 930, 933
al-Shehhi, Marwan, hijacker's visa status, **2002** 843-844
Shelby, Richard C. (R-Ala.)
on Clinton's performance, **1999** 42
intelligence failures, **2001** 154; **2002** 995; **2003** 546
party switch, **2001** 377
Sheldon, Louis P.
constitutional amendment banning gay marriage, **2004** 21
domestic partnerships, **1989** 306
Shell Oil USA, oil company profits, congressional hearings, **2005** 781
Shelton, Henry H.
Joint Chiefs of Staff nomination, **1997** 656
USS *Cole* bombing, **2001** 6
Shelton, Hugh, affirmative action, **2003** 362
Shen, James C. H., **1975** 43
Shenandoah National Park (Virginia), **1995** 123-124
Shenker, Albert, **1991** 221
Shepherd, Bill, **1998** 932
Sher, Neal, discovery of Mengele, **1985** 409-414
Sheraton Hotel Corp., funding of Republican convention, **1974** 3-5, 16, 20-21
Sherbert v. Verne, **1997** 410, 411
Sherlock, Stephen, Indonesian relations, **2002** 707
Sherman, Lawrence W., **1983** 358
Sherman v. United States, **1992** 316, 319, 320, 322, 324, 325
Sherman Antitrust Act (1890)
immunity of cities in regulating business, **1982** 35-49
intra-enterprise conspiracy doctrine, **1984** 414-415, 417-426
Sherrill, Kenneth, Clinton and gay rights, **1997** 760
Sherzai, Gul Agha, Afghanistan warlord, **2003** 1096
Shevardnadze, Eduard A.
Afghanistan, on violation of law in, **1989** 400
Afghanistan agreements, **1988** 258
Angola Peace Accord, **1991** 288
arrest of Daniloff and, **1986** 821
background, **1990** 827
on chemical weapons, **1989** 26, 28
food aid from U.S., **1990** 807-808, 809-814
foreign minister appointment, **1985** 273; **1991** 533
Georgian president ousted and resignation of, **2003** 1039-1044; **2004** 72; **2005** 64, 306
German reunification treaty, **1990** 600
Germany, nonaggression treaty with, **1990** 601, 608-614
London Declaration of Peaceful Intent, **1990** 456
meeting with Baker on START, **1989** 645
on regional conflicts, **1985** 708
resignation speech, **1990** 825-832
summit meetings
Iceland, **1986** 879
Washington, **1987** 993
UN address, **1990** 629, 635-646

Shevchenko, Arkady, **1986** 268
Shevtsova, Lilia, Russian political situation, **2001** 256
Shields, Dennis, affirmative action case, **2003** 366-367
Shifman, Pamela, Sudan human rights violations, **2004** 94
Shi'ite Amal militia, terrorist acts by, **1985** 465-466
Shi'ite Moslems
hostages held by, **1986** 831-833
influence in Iran, **1978** 700-701
Iran-Iraq War, history of, **1984** 748
Iraqi suppression of, **1991** 191-192
Lebanese
leader kidnapped by Israelis, **1989** 315-319
and TWA highjacking, **1986** 1015
role in terrorist attack on U.S. Marines in Beirut, **1983** 934, 943-944
Shimura, Hisako, UN peacekeeping reform panel, **2000** 643
Shin Yong Moon, human cloning, **2004** 158
Shining Path movement
activity of in Peru, **1989** 63, 606
capture of leader in Peru, **1992** 859-864
Fujimori defeat of, **2000** 923
John Paul II on, **1985** 58-59
Shintoism, Japanese belief in divine emperor, **1989** 100-101
Ships
antihijacking agreement, U.S.-Cuban, **1973** 265-268
Exxon Valdez (oil tanker), oil spill, **1989** 225-237; **1990** 513-530; **1991** 641-648
nuclear-powered, in U.S. Navy, **1982** 89, 101, 145, 160
ocean dumping from
international agreement on, **1972** 907-919
northeast Atlantic treaty on, **1972** 173-177
USS *Cole* (navy destroyer) bombing, **2000** 277, 861-865; **2001** 3-16, 805; **2003** 30
Al Shiraa, on Iran-contra link, **1986** 1017
Shiro, Michael, **1990** 106
Shoemaker, Eugene, **1998** 114; **2001** 143
Sholokhov, Mikhail A., **1972** 728
Shook, Karen H., **1996** 785
Shope, Robert E., tuberculosis report, **1992** 1007-1011
Short, Roger, killed in bombings in Turkey, **2003** 1052
Shostakovich, Maxim and Dmitri, defection of to U.S., **1981** 375-379
Shribman, David, on presidential debates, **1988** 721-722
Shriver, Maria, Schwarzenegger gubernatorial campaign, **2003** 1009
Shriver, R. Sargent, as McGovern's running mate, **1972** 598, 605-608
Shukrijumah, Adnan, terrorist suspect, **2004** 276
Shultz, George P.
Afghanistan agreements, **1988** 258-259
arms control talks, **1984** 260
California gubernatorial recall election, **2003** 1009
capital gains tax in McGovern plan, **1972** 738
chemical warfare by Soviets, **1982** 236, 252-257
Cuban foreign policy, **1998** 33
Daniloff arrest, **1986** 820-821
economic policy, recession, **1974** 97
economic summit, **1983** 507
Gromyko meeting, **1984** 813, 818, 918
Haiti aid, **1987** 939-941
Iceland summit, **1986** 875, 877, 879-880, 885
ICJ jurisdiction, **1985** 639-641
inflation control, **1972** 962; **1973** 578
price ceilings and import restrictions, **1973** 428, 434-435
price freeze administration, **1973** 704-705
Iran-contra affair, **1987** 232
arms sales to Iran, **1986** 1015-1016, 1051-1052
congressional report on, **1987** 893, 895, 899, 902-903, 922
Iran-Iraq War, UN resolution on, **1987** 609-610
Israeli-Lebanese security agreement, **1983** 472
Jordan's role in Palestinian-Israeli talks, **1988** 582
Libya, U.S. action against, **1986** 350, 352
monetary policy
dollar devaluation and international monetary crisis, **1973** 344-350
reform proposals, **1972** 815-816, 820-826
national security memo to, **1986** 781, 783
Nicaraguan cease-fire, **1988** 242-243
on Noriega negotiations, **1988** 81
PLO
denial of U.S. visa to Arafat, **1988** 907
departure from Lebanon, **1982** 743
observer mission to UN, **1988** 480
U.S. talks with, **1988** 908
Polish trade sanctions, lifting of, **1987** 185
secretary of state appointment, **1982** 561-563, 566
Seoul Olympic Games, **1988** 855
South Africa, sanctions against, **1985** 533
Soviet downing of Korean jetliner, **1983** 778
Soviet relations, **1984** 145
U.S. economic sanctions against, **1982** 563
terrorism, using force against, **1984** 933-944, 1006-1007
terrorist threats, task force on, **2002** 743
Washington summit
Nixon-Brezhnev, **1973** 589
Reagan-Gorbachev, **1987** 993
Shultz, Richard D., **1989** 216
Shumway, DeVan, **1973** 630
Shurberg Broadcasting of Hartford, Inc. v. FCC, **1990** 425
Shustov, Vladimir, UN peacekeeping reform panel, **2000** 643
Sibanda, Philip, UN peacekeeping reform panel, **2000** 643
Sichel, Daniel E., productivity paradox, **2000** 300
Sick, Gary, Iran hostage Six Party TalksOctober SurpriseSix Party Talks theory, **1993** 3-4
Sickle cell anemia, **1984** 614
Siddiqui, Aafia, terrorist suspect, **2004** 276
Sidgmore, John, WorldCom collapse, **2002** 394
Siegel, Michael, on secondhand smoke, **1993** 64
Siegfried, Richard S., sexual harassment in the military, **1997** 654
Sierra Club
anti-Wal-Mart campaign, **2005** 735, 736
national energy policy task force, **2003** 1018

Sierra Leone
  child soldiers, **2002** 917-918
  and coup in Liberia, **1980** 277
  elections, **2002** 248-249
  human rights, **2002** 249-250
  human trafficking, **2004** 125
  hunger in, **2003** 756-757
  kidnapping of children, **2001** 956
  Lomé peace accord, **1999** 433-434, 436; **2000** 1074, 1075
  peace negotiations, **1999** 428, 430, 433-434, 436; **2002** 247-255, 447
  Revolutionary United Front (RUF), **2002** 247, 248, 249
  UN peacekeepers captured, **2000** 1074-1075; **2002** 247
  UN peacekeeping forces (ECOWAS), **1999** 431; **2000** 450, 642, 1072-1077; **2002** 248, 547; **2003** 450, 772; **2005** 804
  UN war crimes tribunal, **2005** 803-804
  war atrocities, **1999** 430
Siewert, Jake
  Gore presidential acceptance speech and press leaks, **2000** 763
  Whitewater investigations, **2000** 765
Sigler, Andrew C., **1986** 973
Sigma Delta Chi, Whitehead speech on network news, **1973** 55-57
Signs on residential property, **1994** 289-297
Sihanouk, Norodom (prince of Cambodia), **1991** 692-693, 700
  and U.S. bombing of Cambodia, **1973** 731, 733
Sikhism, religious conflict in India, **1984** 945-949
Silberman, Laurence H., **1990** 492, 493, 505-507
  U.S. intelligence gathering investigations, **2004** 712; **2005** 247
Silberman-Robb commission. *See* Commission on Intelligence Capabilities of the U.S. Regarding Weapons of Mass Destruction
Silica exposure, and smoking, **1985** 819
Silicone breast implants, **1992** 367-373
Silva, Anibal Cavaco, **1991** 288
Silveria v. Lockyer, **2002** 962-968
Silverman, Leon, Donovan investigation, **1982** 587; **1984** 804
Simes, Dmitri K., **1984** 148
Simeus, Dumarsais, Haiti presidential candidate, **2005** 330-331
Simic, Aleksandar, on dissolution of Yugoslavia, **2003** 57
Simmons, Christopher, juvenile death penalty case, **2005** 179, 183-196
Simmons, Lt. Darlene, Tailhook scandal and, **1994** 109
Simon, Bill, California gubernatorial election, **2003** 1006, 1008
Simon, Don, campaign finance reform, **2003** 1156
Simon, Paul (D-Ill.)
  death penalty panel, **2000** 989
  on Puerto Rican statehood, **1993** 949-950
  Rehnquist appointment, **1986** 592
  Thomas confirmation hearings, **1991** 580-582
  violence on television, **1993** 488
Simon, Stanley, **1988** 498
Simon, Steven, bin Laden and al Qaeda network expansion, **2003** 1055
Simon, William E.
  Catholic bishops on economic policy, **1984** 95; **1986** 984-985
  Christopher Columbus defense, **1992** 898-899
  IMF amendments, **1976** 5
  IMF interim measures, **1974** 499
  inflation rate, **1974** 419
  on Nixon on impeachable offense, **1974** 674
  payments imbalances, **1976** 427
  Social Security system's financial condition, **1975** 117
Simon and Schuster, Inc. v. Members of N.Y. State Crime Victims Board, **1991** 813-825; **1992** 546, 548
Simon Weisenthal Center for Holocaust Studies, **1990** 105
Simopoulos v. Virginia, **1983** 545, 573-576
Simpson, Alan K. (R-Wyo.)
  fire-management policy, **1988** 942
  immigration laws, **1981** 607; **1986** 964; **1995** 563
  Japanese-American internment, **1988** 288-289, 294-295
  Russian nuclear weapons panel, **2001** 19
  Thomas confirmation hearings, **1992** 565-566
Simpson, Carole, presidential debate, **1992** 908, 931-954
Simpson, Nicole Brown, **1994** 63-64; **1995** 611-621; **1997** 74
Simpson, O. J. (Orenthal James)
  closing arguments in trial, **1995** 611-621
  final verdict, **1997** 29-30
  jurors' remarks, **1997** 74-80
  murder trial, **1994** 63-64
  and racism, **1995** 646
Sims, Charles, **1984** 367
Sims and Wolfe v. CIA, **1985** 333-338, 342-344
Sin, Jaime (cardinal)
  call for demonstrations against Estrada, **2001** 103-104
  conflict with Marcos, **1981** 203; **1986** 318
  on Marcos's election tactics, **1986** 308
Sinai Peninsula
  Camp David accords, Israeli withdrawal from, **1979** 225, 228, 231-242
  Egyptian-Israeli accords on
    disengagement in, **1974** 29-32
    return to Egypt, **1978** 606, 614-616, 623
    use of military force in, **1975** 573-586
  return of final portion to Egypt, **1982** 337-344
Singapore
  Iraq troop withdrawal, **2004** 882
  SARS (severe acute respiratory syndrome) outbreak, **2003** 132, 754
Singer, Israel, **1997** 262
Singer, Jana B., **1989** 553
Singer, Melanie, **1993** 636-637
Singer, S. Fred, global warming, **2001** 111
Singh, Giani Zail, on assassination of I. Gandhi, **1984** 948-949
Singh, Manmohan (Indian prime minister)
  India's programs and priorities, **2004** 348-357

India-U.S. relations, **2005** 462-471
as prime minister, **2005** 467-468
Singh, Natwar, **1989** 28
India-U.S. relations, **2005** 465
Singh, Sardar Swaran, **1986** 582
Single-sex education, Virginia Military Institute all-male policy, **1991** 309-316
Sinha, Yashwant, Pakistan referendum, **2003** 213
Sinhalese
cease-fire in Sri Lanka, **2002** 92-100
in Sri Lanka conflict with Tamils, **1987** 615-616
Siniora, Fuad, Lebanon prime minister, **2005** 690
Sinn Féin. *See* Irish Republican Army (IRA)
Sioux, negotiations on Wounded Knee occupation, **1973** 531-535
Sirica, John J.
grand jury report on Nixon's Watergate involvement, **1974** 158, 225-232
Hunt, immunity for, **1974** 205
Liddy sentencing, **1973** 418-419, 500
McCord letter to, **1973** 415-417
Nixon tapes
compromise plans for release of, **1973** 859-863
crucial 1972 conversation released to, **1974** 673, 680-681
release order, **1973** 698, 839-848
report of experts to, **1974** 23-27
Watergate prosecutor's access to, **1974** 289, 621-622, 638; **1975** 658-659, 664-665, 667
Watergate break-in defendants
convictions, **1975** 655
sentencing, **1973** 417-423
Watergate cover-up trial, **1974** 991-992; **1975** 141-151
Sisco, Joseph, **1973** 931
al-Sistani, Ayatollah Ali
Iraqi elections, **2003** 936; **2004** 400
Iraqi Governing Council "fundamental law", **2003** 946
meeting with De Mello of UN, **2003** 944
al-Sadr militia-U.S. agreement, **2004** 879-880
SCIRI militia, **2005** 663-664, 942
United Iraqi Alliance, **2004** 404
Sisulu, Walter, de Klerk's release of, **1989** 546; **1990** 65
Sithole, Ndabaningi
and internal agreement on constitution for Rhodesia, **1978** 149-155
in Rhodesian talks, **1977** 584
"Sixty Minutes," libel suit and freedom of press, **1979** 285-311
Sivits, Jeremy, Abu Ghraib prison abuse conviction, **2004** 215, 220
Sizer, Theodore R., **1992** 47
Skaggs, David, Russian nuclear weapons panel, **2001** 19
Skeete, Charles A. T., **1982** 181
Skilling, Jeffrey, Enron Corp. collapse, **2001** 859, 862; **2002** 396; **2003** 336; **2004** 416
Skin cancer, as effect of ozone layer reduction, **1973** 235-244; **1975** 438-439, 442; **1992** 82
Skinner, Richard L., Hurricane Katrina disaster relief contracts, **2005** 570
Skinner, Samuel B., Pan Am bombing, **1990** 304
Skinner, Samuel K.
on Alaskan oil spill, **1989** 230-233
travel practices, **1992** 294-295
White House chief of staff appointment, **1991** 769, 770
Skinner v. Railway Labor Executives' Association, **1995** 342, 343, 344, 345
Sklar, Morton, racism treaty, **2000** 772
Skylab space station, **1987** 650, 652
breakup and fall of, **1979** 553-558
launches and purposes of, **1973** 939-946
Skylstad, William (bishop of Spokane)
gay priests, **2005** 84
sexual abuse of priests, **2004** 87-88
SLA. *See* Symbionese Liberation Army
Slany, William Z., **1997** 257, 261
Slavery
See also Human trafficking
and reparations for, **2001** 604-605, 611-612
Sudan conflict and, **2003** 839-840
trafficking in humans, **2002** 332-352
in the U.S., **2004** 122-123
Slayton, Donald, **1981** 417
Sleeper, Jim, on racism, **1998** 667
Slepian, Barnett, antiabortion shooting victim, **1998** 809-811; **2001** 130
Sloan, Hugh W., Jr., **1973** 502
Sloan v. Lemon, **1973** 641-643, 656-658
Slovakia
EU membership, **2004** 198
NATO membership, **1999** 122; **2004** 136, 198
Slovenia
See also Bosnia
EU membership, **2004** 198
history of, **2003** 56
human rights report, **1993** 294-295
independence declaration, **1991** 367-376
international math and science test, **1992** 90, 91
NATO membership, **2001** 893; **2004** 136, 198
NATO membership candidacy, **1997** 516
Senate Yugoslav "Ethnic Cleansing" report, **1992** 772-779
Small Arms Survey, Haiti casualties of political violence, **2005** 331
Small Business Administration (SBA)
Grace Commission proposal on, **1984** 175-176, 179
Los Angeles earthquake, **1994** 5-6
Los Angeles riots and, **1992** 409
Small Business Job Protection Act (1996), **1996** 563-569
Smaltz, Donald C., Espy investigation, **1994** 405; **1998** 906, 907-908
Smeal, Eleanor
on ERA, **1981** 925; **1982** 612-615
on parental leave decision, **1987** 19
Smeeding, Timothy, **1988** 877
Smith, Bradford A., **1980** 989
Smith, Christopher (R-N.J.), human trafficking, **2002** 334
Smith, Emma, **1981** 338
Smith, Franklin L.
privatization of schools, **1994** 411

Smith, Franklin L. *Continued*
removed from D.C. schools, **1996** 784-785
Smith, Frederick W., on economic recovery, **2002** 53
Smith, Gerard C.
no-first-use defense policy, **1982** 305
SALT negotiations, **1972** 431, 454-459; **1987** 309
SDI, **1983** 306
Smith, Gordon H. (R-Ore.)
missile defense system, **2000** 681
physician-assisted suicide, **2001** 293
Smith, Henry P., III (R-N.Y.), **1974** 988
Smith, Herbert A., **1989** 698
Smith, Howard K., in Carter-Reagan debate, **1980** 920-922, 951
Smith, Ian D.
British plan for majority rule, **1976** 721-728
internal agreement on constitution, **1978** 149-155
leadership of, **1979** 939, 941-942; **1980** 317-318, 323
U.S. policy toward Rhodesia, **1976** 288
U.S.-British settlement plan, **1977** 583-585, 588
Smith, Jack, General Motors truck safety, **1994** 447
Smith, John F., Jr., GM electric vehicle development, **1996** 19-20
Smith, John Lewis, Jr.
on Gorsuch contempt case, **1982** 966
on sealed documents about King, **1983** 884
wiretaps in Nixon White House, **1976** 160
Smith, Joseph, Jr., on Mormon Church leader succession, **1981** 337-338
Smith, Judy, Magic Johnson's resignation from AIDS Commission, **1992** 891
Smith, Lamar (R-Texas)
and Gingrich ethics case, **1997** 4
House Judiciary Committee impeachment inquiry, **1998** 705
illegal immigrants, **1995** 565
Smith, Lonnie, **1986** 170
Smith, Marshall S., on national standards for educational testing, **1992** 47
Smith, Michael J., *Challenger* accident, **1986** 515, 520; **1988** 795
Smith, Neal (D-Iowa), on Twenty-seventh Amendment, **1992** 440
Smith, Nick (R-Mich.), allegations of Tom Delay's financial bribery, **2004** 577, 580-581
Smith, Philip E., release of by China, **1973** 292, 296
Smith, Richard G., **1979** 554
Smith, Robert, presidential candidate, **2001** 377-378
Smith, Sidney C., Jr., on cigarette regulations, **1995** 670
Smith, Thomas W., **1993** 408
Smith, Wallace B., **1981** 338
Smith, William A., **1985** 49
Smith, William French
Allen investigation, **1981** 848
as attorney general, **1985** 655
exclusionary rule, **1984** 505
FBI domestic security guidelines, **1983** 257
FOIA guidelines, **1981** 393-396
Hinckley verdict and insanity defense, **1982** 534
immigration policy, **1981** 605-616
judicial activism, **1981** 803-809
religion and federal courts, **1984** 217
terrorism and Soviet espionage, **1981** 862
Smith, William Kennedy
date rape, **1992** 394-395
rape case, **1992** 336
Smith v. Allwright, **1991** 389
Smith v. Cody, **1990** 626
Smith v. County of Albemarle, **1995** 397
Smith v. Daily Mail Publishing Co., **1991** 328
Smith v. Reeves, **1999** 339
Smith v. Texas, **2004** 797
Smithson, Amy E., on weapons of mass destruction, **2000** 281
Smithsonian Agreement (1971), on currency exchange realignment, **1972** 413-414; **1973** 344, 348, 387
Smithsonian Institution
agreement on returning Native American remains, **1989** 539-543
CIA declassified articles for, **1992** 8
Enola Gay exhibit, **1995** 55-58
Smoking
antismoking activists, **1992** 564
children and tobacco sales, FDA regulations, **1996** 589-599
cigarette advertising bans, **1997** 38, 332
cigarette labeling, European Union and, **2001** 226
cigarette regulations
FDA authority, **1999** 538-539
FDA proposals, **1995** 670-679
cigars and pipes, health effects of, **1973** 63-65, 71-77
damage suits for related ills, **1992** 563-573
decline in, **1999** 460
surgeon general on, **1981** 3
effects of quitting, **1989** 31-32, 34, 39
fraud of tobacco industry, allegations of, **1999** 536-661
Gore's vice presidential acceptance speech, **1996** 607-608
health consequences of
diseases and deaths caused by, **1989** 32-35, 37-38
surgeon general on, **1981** 3-12; **1982** 163-169; **1994** 172-184
surgeon general's report, **2004** 280-298
health costs of, **1985** 615-622
history of research in, **1988** 317-319
intervention programs in the workplace, **1985** 811, 815, 821-822
involuntary, health dangers of, **1972** 45-47, 53-54; **1982** 164, 167-168; **1986** 1079-1090
lung cancer, and air pollution, **1972** 775-776, 779, 781
in pregnancy, **1989** 32, 38
links to low birth weight and infant mortality, **1972** 52; **1973** 63-71
public attitudes toward (1964-1989), **1989** 31-40
in public places, restrictions on, **1972** 45-46; **1986** 1079-1081, 1087, 1090; **1989** 32, 37, 39
"quit smoking" help line, **2004** 281
and radon exposure, **1988** 3-4, 8
reduction, **1999** 539-540

secondhand smoke, **2004** 284-285
secondhand smoke, effects of, **1993** 63-69; **1995** 673
teenage smoking, **2004** 281-282
throughout the Americas, **1992** 267-275
tobacco companies
accountability, **1999** 49-50
lawsuit, **2003** 262, 263-264
liability in lung cancer death, **1988** 311
tobacco-related deaths, **2005** 5
trends, and declining death rates from, **1996** 791
trends in U.S., **1988** 309-311, 321-322
by women, and health risks, **1980** 17-26
women and health issues, **2001** 222-244
in workplace, **1986** 1079-1081, 1087, 1090
ban proposed, **1994** 205-206
and other hazardous substances, **1978** 635, 642, 645; **1985** 809-822
segregated areas, **1972** 46-47
young adults and, **1994** 172-184; **1997** 332, 335, 336; **1998** 47, 89; **1999** 49, 384
increasing, **1999** 460
Smoking or Health, Coalition on, **1988** 310
Smoot, George, **1992** 379-382
Smrkovsky, Josef, **1975** 240
SNAP. *See* Survivors Network of Those Abused by Priests
Snider, L. Britt, congressional intelligence failures panel resignation, **2002** 991
Snider, Stacy, marketing violent entertainment to children, **2000** 731
Snow, John W.
Chinese monetary policy, **2003** 1180
on economic growth and tax revenues, **2005** 122
employment projections, **2003** 442-443
on the eurozone, **2004** 239
Social Security reform plan, **2005** 113
Treasury secretary appointment, **2002** 880; **2005** 45
Snowe, Olympia (R-Maine)
integration of women for military training, **1997** 657
Medicare cost estimates withheld from Congress, **2004** 579
and Republican Party, **2001** 378, 380
sexual harassment in the army, **1997** 656
trade pact with Canada, **1988** 573
Soames, Lord Christopher
interim government in Zimbabwe-Rhodesia, **1979** 940, 942-944
role in Zimbabwe independence, **1980** 317-318, 332-333
Soares, Abillo, East Timor war crime conviction, **2004** 756
Soares, Joäo Clemente Baena, **1988** 242
Sobero, Guillermo, Philippine hostage, **2001** 105
Social inequities
John Paul II on, **1984** 778-779, 785-787; **1985** 365, 367-368, 372, 374-376
and liberation theology, **1984** 759-760, 763-764, 768; **1985** 57-58, 63
Vatican synod of bishops on, **1985** 766, 778-780
Social Security
See also Retirement plans
benefits
elimination of retroactive, **1977** 59
expansion of, **1975** 639
explained, **1985** 100-101
for widowers, **1975** 56, 177-185; **1977** 169-181
benefits for those who work, **1999** 320
budget surplus and, **1998** 40, 98; **1999** 42, 43, 45-46, 90, 354-356
cost-of-living adjustments (COLAs), **1985** 71-73
costs of
CBO on, **1982** 192, 200
Ford on methods of bearing, **1977** 73-74
and costs of smoking, **1985** 620-621
Democratic Party platform on, **1980** 728-730; **2000** 613-614
disability program cutbacks, **1983** 318, 333-334
eligibility requirements for dependents, **1977** 378
inflation's effect on, **1983** 108
as issue in presidential debates, **1980** 943-945; **1988** 771, 773-774
as issue in vice presidential debate, **1988** 804-805
long-term solvency, **2005** 132-133
optional participation in, American Party platform on, **1972** 615, 618
payroll tax base, adjustment to, **1975** 115-119, 121-122; **1976** 13, 21, 38, 43, 55, 188; **1978** 96-97
private retirement accounts, **2004** 236; **2005** 77, 85, 111-112, 123, 198
privatization, **2001** 914; **2002** 105; **2004** 27; **2005** 78, 112
public confidence in, **1983** 58, 60-61
in Reagan budget, **1981** 214, 217
reductions in outlays
Carter program for, **1979** 10-11, 15, 48-49
under Reagan, **1983** 53, 767, 771-772
reform
alternative proposals, **2005** 116
Bush presidential commission on, **2001** 913-926
Bush proposals, **2001** 173-174; **2004** 27, 236-237; **2005** 41, 78, 84-85, 111-120
Carter proposals, **1977** 377-381; **1981** 59, 71
CEA report on, **1998** 93-94
commission on, **1983** 57-75
Daschle on Democratic response to, **2004** 34
under Reagan, **1983** 57, 80-81, 108
reorganization of as independent agency, **1983** 73-74
Republican Party platform on, **1976** 640; **2000** 514
retirement benefits, and baby boomers impact on, **2003** 711; **2005** 114-115
solvency, GAO report, **1998** 98-109
spending growth, **1997** 52, 63-64
stability of, **1975** 115-134
strengthening the system, **1998** 43, 75
under Gramm-Rudman-Hollings, **1985** 804-805
women recipients of, **1983** 755
Y2K conversion compliance, **1998** 545, 550
Social Security, Presidential Commission on Strengthening, **2001** 913-926
Social Security, Quadrennial Advisory Council on
benefits for widowers, **1975** 177, 182
financial condition of system, **1975** 115-117, 121-122
Social Security Act, Title XIX, abortion restrictions on Medicaid funds, **1977** 407-427

Social Security Administration
dependency proof from widowers, **1977** 170
investigation of People's Temple, **1979** 374-375
Social Security Disability Insurance, **1999** 320
Social service programs
See also Welfare policy; Welfare reform
block grants to states for, Reagan proposal, **1981** 334-335, 641, 644-645; **1982** 74, 79-81
Bush budget, **1989** 71, 74-75, 78
Carter budget, **1978** 96-97, 99; **1979** 9-12, 14, 31, 43-51; **1980** 114-115
cuts in, **1978** 766, 771-772, 775-776; **1980** 110-111
revision of Ford budget, **1977** 122-129
Carter on meeting human needs, **1979** 90-92; **1980** 42-43, 57-71; **1981** 58, 67, 71-73
Carter urban proposal and, **1978** 255-256
consolidation of in Carter's welfare plan, **1977** 555, 557, 560-561, 563
costs of and self-deception about, Ford on, **1977** 66-67, 73
Democratic Party platform on, **1976** 545, 559-566; **1980** 712, 719-720, 725-739; **1984** 550, 555-556, 569-571, 602, 616-618
effectiveness of, Nixon on, **1972** 89-90; **1973** 80, 83-84, 303-304, 306-314
entitlements
in Nixon budget, **1974** 96-97, 100, 102, 108-109
in Reagan budget, **1982** 74, 79-80, 149-152; **1983** 101-103, 105, 107, 109, 117; **1988** 154, 157
faith-based and community initiatives, **2001** 132-140; **2004** 29
federal role in, National '80s Agenda on, **1981** 40, 49-50
Ford budget cuts in, **1975** 84-85, 89-90, 94-96, 98; **1976** 37-38, 40, 42-43; **1977** 58-59, 62
of Great Society, **1973** 97-98
as issue in vice presidential debates, **1976** 773, 781-783; **1988** 806-807
Nixon budget, **1974** 95-98, 100, 102, 108-110
cuts in, **1973** 169, 171, 173, 177
as prolonging poverty, Reagan on, **1989** 7
Reagan budget cuts in, **1982** 122, 143, 145, 149-150, 156-157; **1983** 83, 103-109, 125, 765-772; **1984** 100, 106; **1986** 49-51, 55; **1987** 4-5, 11
in economic plan, **1981** 214, 216-218, 326-328, 334-335, 639, 642, 644
effect on African Americans, **1983** 41-42, 44-55; **1987** 43-45, 48-50, 59-60
and hunger, **1985** 189-191, 193, 198-202
and infant and maternity health, **1987** 147-149, 151-152, 161-164
and poverty, **1983** 765-772; **1988** 186-190
women on, **1983** 755
Reagan policies on, Dukakis on, **1988** 722-723, 738-741
Republican Party platform on, **1984** 680-683
safety net
aid to states for, **1981** 644-645
and economic power, **1985** 105-106, 110-111
in Reagan economic plan, **1981** 214, 216, 326-327, 334
tax cuts' effect on, **1981** 640
Teen Challenge, **2001** 133, 135
Victory Fellowship, **2001** 133
Social values. *See* Ethics; Values
Socialism
mature, Soviet constitution as onset of, **1977** 747, 756-757
reaffirmation of PRC constitution, **1975** 44-45
Socialist countries
exploitation of people in, and military power, **1975** 920
national focus of, dangers of, **1976** 144-145
Socialist Workers Party, FBI burglarizing of, **1976** 322
Society of Jesus (Jesuits)
and liberation theology, **1984** 761
and papal order on Drinan, **1980** 411-416
Society of Professional Journalists, **1981** 395
Sodomy, and right to privacy, **1986** 601-614
Sofaer, Abraham D.
ABM treaty reinterpretation, **1987** 289, 295, 297-307, 310-315
ICJ jurisdiction, **1985** 639
Marcos indictment, **1988** 869
Sharon libel suit, **1985** 49
U.S.-British extradition treaty, **1986** 752-753
Soil conservation
and food production estimates, **1980** 679-680, 686, 695
Republican Party platform on, **1984** 677-678
Soil Conservation Service, watershed programs of, **1978** 387, 389, 391, 394
Sojourner mission to Mars, **1999** 712; **2000** 89; **2003** 302; **2004** 3
Solana, Javier
European defense force, **1999** 818
Iran nuclear weapons program, **2003** 1027
Kosovo air attacks, **1999** 136, 139
Macedonia peace negotiations, **2001** 556
Middle East peace negotiations, **2001** 361
Middle East visits, **2004** 810
North Korean missile program, **2001** 269
Solar energy
as alternative to oil, economic summit on development of, **1980** 503, 509
contribution to energy supply, **1974** 910, 913
development of, **1975** 29, 84, 92; **1976** 20; **1977** 103, 106; **1979** 61-62, 321
research on, **1974** 105
tax credit for in homes, **1977** 279, 281, 284, 286, 291
Solar system, exploration of
age of universe findings, **1994** 458-462
multiplanet solar system discovery, **1999** 173-178
NASA goals for, **1987** 653, 656, 658-660, 666-667
Soldiers' and Sailors' Civil Relief Act (1940), **1993** 249-258
Solem v. Helm, **1983** 659-674
Soler, Esta, on domestic violence, **1993** 287-288
Solidarity
achievements of, **1987** 183-187; **1989** 523-525, 534-535, 538
establishment of, **1980** 793-802

and John Paul II visits to Poland, **1983** 577-580; **1987** 556-557, 559-560
martial law restrictions on, **1981** 881, 888-889
power in Polish government, **1989** 412, 415-416, 523-524, 528
struggles of, John Paul II on, **1981** 696, 703
survival during martial law, **1982** 947-949, 952
Walesa's leadership of, **1983** 925-932
Solomon, David, **1990** 255-256
Solomon, Gerald B. H. (R-N.Y.), air strikes against Iraq, **1998** 937, 961
Solomon Islands, John Paul II visit, **1984** 328
Solovyev, Yuri, defeat of in Soviet election, **1989** 174, 177-178
Solow, Robert M., on minimum wage, **1996** 564
Solzhenitsyn, Alexander I.
denied travel to Nobel ceremony (1970), **1975** 916
détente and concessions by West, **1975** 481-491
expulsion from Soviet Union, **1974** 129-135, 146, 152; **1981** 376
Ford position on, **1976** 786-787
Nobel lecture on role of literature, **1972** 727-731
on West's spiritual decline, **1978** 403-417
Somalia
child soldiers, **2002** 918, 926
executions in, **1989** 602
human rights, **1990** 132
military aid from the U.S., **1992** 1067-1072
peace negotiations, **2002** 477
refugees from, **1981** 179
tsunami relief effort, **2005** 1005
UN peacekeeping mission, **1997** 151, 154, 155, 156; **1998** 222; **2000** 643; **2003** 450
Somerfield, William, **1989** 124
Somers, Anne R., **1972** 922
Somoza Debayle, Anastasio
ouster of, **1979** 581-585, 589-591; **1987** 638, 640-641
successors to, **1985** 153, 256, 262
Somoza Garcia, Anastasio, **1979** 584
Sons of the Gestapo, **1995** 178
Sontag, Camille, **1986** 833
Sony Corp. of America v. Universal City Studios, **1984** 53-80
Soong, James, **2000** 191
Taiwan presidential elections (2000), **2004** 258-259
Taiwan vice presidential candidate, **2004** 260
Sorensen, Theodore C., appointment to CIA, **1976** 879-880
Sorenson, Lary, **1986** 170
Sorkow, Harvey R., on surrogate motherhood contract, **1987** 373-387; **1988** 72
Soro, Guillaume, Ivory Coast civil war, **2004** 819
Soros, George
end-of-life care, **1997** 326
physician-assisted suicide, **1997** 462
Russian economy, **1998** 603
Sorrells v. United States, **1992** 319, 320, 322, 324, 325, 326-327
Sosa, Sammy
baseball home run record, **1998** 626-628
relief efforts in Dominican Republic, **1999** 54
steroid use in baseball, congressional hearings on, **2005** 213-214, 219-220
Souter, David H.
abortion
anti-abortion demonstrations, **2000** 433
clinic protesters and RICO law, **1994** 33
clinic protests, **1994** 312-321
family-planning clinic advice, **1991** 257, 259
partial birth, **2000** 432
affirmative action, **2003** 362, 363
affirmative action, federal government plans, **1995** 309, 323-324
asset forfeiture, drug trafficking, **1993** 432-438
campaign finance reform, **2003** 1160
child pornography, and Six Party Talkscommunity standards, Six Party Talks **2002** 291
coastal property rights, **1992** 616
coerced confessions, **1981** 182-184; **1991** 175
congressional term limits, **1995** 260
damages for tobacco-related ills, **1992** 546-573
deaf parochial student, **1993** 400, 403-406
death penalty
and ICJ jurisdiction, **2005** 182
for juvenile offenders, **2002** 358; **2004** 797; **2005** 179
for the mentally retarded, **2002** 356
detentions in terrorism cases, **2004** 377, 378, 388-391
disabilities in the workplace, **2002** 5, 6
disability, definition of, **1999** 319, 323, 325-332
drug testing of students, **1995** 339, 340, 346-349
eminent domain, **2005** 363, 364
endangered species on private lands, **1995** 359-368
entrapment in child pornography case, **1992** 313-322
free speech
ballot initiatives, **1999** 6
decency in the arts, **1998** 407, 417-418
and the Internet, **1997** 445
Internet pornography filters in public libraries, **2003** 388, 390, 399-400
freedom of residential signs, **1994** 290-297
gay rights discrimination, **1996** 286
gay rights to march, **1995** 327-335
grandparents' rights, **2000** 289, 295
gun-free school zone, **1995** 184, 195-196, 196-200
Haitian refugee interdiction, **1992** 453, 459-468; **1993** 413-421
hate crimes, **1992** 543-551; **1993** 385-389
HIV as a disability, **1998** 379
impeachment, Senate's authority to remove judge, **1993** 82-91
job discrimination, fetal protection, **1991** 144
job discrimination involving African Americans, **1993** 424, 424-430
jury selection and racial bias, **2005** 182
legislative intent, **1993** 250-253
libel from misquotation, **1991** 319, 329-330
line-item veto, **1998** 421
medical use of marijuana, **2001** 327
Miranda warnings, **2000** 389
murder case sentencing, **1991** 390
nomination, **1990** 217

Souter, David H. *Continued*
Noriega phone calls dispute, **1990** 721-724
parochial school aid, **1997** 363, 375-380, 380-381
physician-assisted suicide, **1997** 461, 476-478
presidential elections recount, **2000** 1002, 1003, 1019-1024
prison inmates, beaten by guards, **1992** 175-182
prisoner appeals, **1991** 206
from death row, **1993** 142, 149-152
public lands and developers, **1994** 299, 306-310
race-based redistricting, **1993** 461, 481; **1995** 371, 380-384; **1996** 370, 383-387
religious clubs in public schools, **2001** 422, 430-432
religious freedom, **1997** 408, 421
religious publications, **1995** 386, 393-395
religious symbols, **1995** 387, 396-404
school desegregation, **1991** 24
school prayer, **1992** 553-562; **2000** 367
school vouchers, **2002** 409, 415-423
Senate confirmation hearings, **1990** 615-628
sentencing laws, **2003** 984; **2004** 360
sex offenders, right to confine, **1997** 384, 392-394
sexual harassment, **1998** 439-441, 443-452; **1999** 215
at school, **1992** 188-197
in workplace, **1993** 939-944
sodomy laws, **2003** 403
states' rights, **1999** 333, 335-336, 345-349
student drug testing, **2002** 426-427
Ten Commandments displays, **2005** 378, 384-389
unreasonable searches, **2001** 408, 409, 410
use of school facilities by religious groups, **1993** 363-369
South, John, libel suit against, **1984** 248, 253-256
South Africa
See also African National Congress (ANC)
AIDS drug distribution and manufacture, **2003** 780, 784
AIDS prevention, **2002** 473; **2003** 784
apartheid laws repealed, **1991** 53-65
apartheid policies, **1987** 190, 193
Botha's reaffirmation of, **1985** 515-527
effects of, **1984** 1027-1037
Kissinger on, **1976** 287-289, 293-294
apartheid protests in U.S., **1985** 28-29, 33, 36
Arab oil embargo against, **1974** 221, 256
arms embargo against, UN resolution on, **1977** 823-825
Blacks (Urban Areas) Consolidation Act (1945), **1986** 369
Burundi peace negotiations, **2003** 924
Clinton state visit, **1998** 159
Commonwealth of Nations on problems of, **1986** 581-590
constitution of, **1983** 889-892; **1984** 1027; **1993** 1003-1032; **1996** 250
and corporate divestment, **1984** 1028; **1985** 146
De Klerk and Mandela on South African changes, **1990** 65-80
De Klerk on new constitution, **1992** 283-292
De Klerk reform plans, **1989** 545-550
death penalty, Supreme Court ruling, **1995** 283-287
Democratic Party platform on, **1972** 580; **1984** 641-642
elections, **1994** 247-248; **1999** 428
exclusion from UN session, **1975** 326
executions in, **1988** 883; **1989** 597
famine, **2002** 156-157
gay marriage legislation, **2005** 869
Group Areas Act (1950), **1986** 369, 586
homelands policy, **1976** 677-678, 680; **1984** 1029, 1031-1032; **1985** 516-517; **1986** 584-587
human rights in, **1981** 180; **1984** 167-168; **1985** 146-147, 155-156; **1986** 99, 101-102; **1987** 189-190, 192-193; **1989** 59-61; **1990** 131, 136, 140-141
Inkatha Freedom Party (IPC), **1995** 102; **1998** 758, 766-767, 773-774
majority rule in, Carter on, **1978** 271, 283-284
Mandela and De Klerk Nobel Peace Prize acceptance speeches, **1993** 877-884
Mandela's remarks opening Parliament, **1995** 101-109
Mbeki presidential inauguration, **1999** 297-303
military buildup and aggression against neighbors, **1977** 823-824
Mixed Marriages Act, repeal of, **1986** 586
Namibia
independence from, **1988** 947-950; **1990** 199-201, 203
interim government proposal, **1976** 611-615
occupation of, **1986** 581
nuclear capability of, **1975** 363
nuclear weapons, dismantling of, **2004** 169, 325
as outlaw, nonaligned nations on, **1983** 264, 268
Pan Africanist Congress (PAC), **1998** 772-773
pass laws, abolition of, **1986** 369-381, 584; **1987** 193
police use of force, **1988** 95-97
political prisoners in, **1984** 1028; **1988** 94-97
Amnesty International on, **1988** 883-884, 888
Population Registration Act, **1986** 586
presidential election, **1989** 545-548
presidential inauguration of Mandela, **1994** 247-251
press freedom in, **1987** 193
racial violence in, black leaders on, **1976** 677-680
Republican Party platform on, **1984** 715
Rhodesian settlement negotiations, **1976** 721-723
Satanic Verses banned in, **1989** 95
Soviet propaganda about, Project Truth on, **1981** 763
Squatting Act (1951), **1986** 371
state of emergency, **1985** 515-516, 524, 533; **1986** 370-372; **1987** 190, 193; **1988** 94-97
movement toward lifting, **1989** 547, 550
renewal of, **1989** 603
termination of urged by study group, **1986** 582, 584, 589
torture reported in, **1982** 797-811; **1988** 96-97
Truth and Reconciliation Commission
establishment of, **1995** 103, 107
report, **1998** 755-775
UN report on refugees, **1991** 672
UN role in, **1995** 355
UNSC membership proposal, **2003** 812
U.S. economic sanctions, **1978** 271, 287-288; **1984** 1029; **1985** 518, 531-540; **1986** 372, 583; **1987** 190; **1990** 67; **1992** 68

lifting of, **1991** 53-65
U.S. policy on, **1984** 816, 1028
Urban League on, **1987** 43, 45, 50
U.S. trade sanctions, **1999** 491
world economic sanctions against, **1986** 581, 583, 590
Zimbabwe independence, **1980** 319, 326-328
South African Communist Party, ban lifted, **1990** 69, 73
South African Council of Churches, **1984** 1027-1028, 1030, 1035
South Asian Association for Regional Cooperation (SAARC), **1998** 329
summit meetings, **2003** 211-212, 215
South Carolina
Hurricane Hugo in, **1989** 667-668
welfare reform, **1999** 258
South Carolina v. Gathers, **1991** 382-396
South Carolina v. Katzenbach, **1997** 412, 413
South Dakota, ballot initiatives, **1999** 3-4
South Korea
See also Korean War
assassination of Park, **1979** 895-904
Bush state visit, **2002** 732
Catholic clergy in, **1986** 318
Chun visit to Washington, **1981** 179
cloning of human embryonic stem cells research scandal, **2005** 317, 320-322
death sentence for Kim Dae-jung, **1980** 825-828
democratic reforms in, **1987** 583-594
economic development of, **1979** 897
economic situation, **1997** 896-897; **1998** 722, 723
elections, **1997** 835, 892-897; **2002** 731
financial crisis, **1997** 834-835, 892, 894
Ford visit, **1974** 955-956, 965-967
human cloning research, **2004** 158
human rights in, **1977** 189; **1979** 896-897; **1981** 179, 190; **1989** 60, 65-66
human trafficking, **2002** 348
IMF aid package, **1997** 836, 892
IMF-World Bank meeting, **1985** 643-652
influence buying in Congress, **1977** 769-819; **1978** 845-908; **1979** 897-898; **1980** 485-487
John Paul II visit, **1984** 217-332
martial law in, **1979** 895-897, 903
nonaggression pact with North Korea, **1972** 523-525
North-South Korea talks, **2001** 270-271; **2002** 268; **2005** 606
opposition to government, **1980** 825-827
ouster of Chun Doo Hwan, **1988** 854
overtures to North Korea, **1974** 956, 966
political situation, **1997** 896
Reagan visit, **1983** 893-895, 908-912
reconciliation with North Korea, Roh on, **1988** 853-859
relations with North Korea, **1997** 896-897; **1999** 576; **2001** 267-278; **2002** 731; **2003** 1178
reunification of Korea, **2000** 359-364; **2002** 731
security, **1997** 897
Soviet downing of airliner (1978), **1983** 775
Soviet downing of airliner (1983), **1983** 775-783; **1984** 146, 289; **1988** 704
student math and science test scores, **1992** 86-87, 91, 92, 94, 95
troops in Iraq, **2004** 882
unemployment, **1998** 726
U.S. arms sales to, **1978** 106
U.S. troops in, **1974** 956, 966-967
South Ossetia, civil war in rebel region of Georgia, **2003** 1046; **2004** 75-76
South West Africa. *See* Namibia
South West African People's Organization (SWAPO), **1988** 948; **1990** 199, 201, 204
compromise in Namibia, **1978** 274, 283
exclusion from interim government proposal, **1976** 611-613
exclusion from South African constitutional conference, **1976** 289
human rights practices of, **1981** 180
Nigerian support of, **1978** 288
South Yemen. *See* Yemen, South
Southeast Asia
collapse of non-Communist Vietnam and Cambodia, **1975** 251-253, 266-277
infant deaths in, UNICEF on, **1981** 911
missing Americans in
commission investigation of, **1977** 207-218
House report on, **1976** 925-936
refugee populations from, **1981** 179, 188-189
Soviet chemical warfare in, **1981** 681-694
threats to, Republican Party platform on, **1984** 712-714
U.S. aid requested for, **1974** 277-279, 281-283; **1975** 223-225, 227-231
U.S.-Soviet communiqué on, **1972** 450
withdrawal of foreign forces from, peace proposals on, **1972** 127, 133-134
Southeastern Promotions, Ltd. v. Conrad, **1993** 443
Southern Baptist Convention, **1995** 336-338
abortions, and ultrasound technology, **2005** 818
Dan Quayle on cultural elites, **1992** 445
on women and the family, **1998** 333-336
Southern Christian Leadership Conference, **1997** 311; **2002** 240, 242
eminent domain, **2005** 364
Southern Education Foundation, segregation report, **1995** 239-253
Southern Independent School Association, racial discrimination in admissions, **1976** 392-393
Southern Methodist University, violation of NCAA rules, **1989** 216
Southwest Airlines, Six Party Talkssecurity breaches-Six Party Talks with baggage, **2003** 721
Southwood, David, European Space Agency mission to Mars, **2003** 303, 307
Soviet Academy of Sciences, on U.S. scientists' defense of Sakharov, **1973** 791-796
Soviet Nuclear Threat Reduction Act (1991) (Nunn-Lugar initiative), **2001** 25
Soviet Union
See also Russia; *names of individual republics*
ABM treaty
interpretation of, **1987** 299-301, 304-306, 311-312

Soviet Union *Continued*
signing, **1972** 431-436, 452-458
violation of, **1987** 293-294
Afghanistan
agreement on withdrawal, **1988** 257-266
call for cease-fire, **1988** 928-929, 935
casualties in, **1986** 920, 934
Afghanistan invasion, **1979** 965-983; **1999** 524
Brezhnev on, **1980** 5, 9-12
and Carter budget, **1980** 110, 113, 115
Carter on, **1980** 27-33, 40, 84, 86-87
effect on U.S. hostage negotiations, **1979** 871
and human rights, **1980** 189-190, 195; **1982** 108-111, 118; **1986** 919-936
Islamic conference on, **1980** 3-15
and SALT II, **1979** 418
and U.S. defense posture, **1980** 123, 125, 127
agricultural policy
collective farmers' work styles, **1989** 145-147, 150-152
Gorbachev on, **1986** 146, 156-157; **1989** 145-152
agricultural trade, and U.S. foreign policy, **1982** 823-835
Albanian relations, **1985** 325-327
alcoholism in, **1987** 79, 101
Andropov's death, **1984** 145-154
Angola
civil war involvement, **1976** 287, 345-346; **1988** 947-948
support for Dos Santos government, **2002** 152
arms control
agreements, Republican Party platform on, **1972** 651, 660, 665-666
conventional forces cuts, Bush proposal, **1989** 297-304
goals, Gorbachev to Council of Europe, **1989** 400, 403-405
missile reduction proposal of Andropov, **1982** 983-988
nuclear freeze proposal of Brezhnev, **1982** 225-231
nuclear nonproliferation treaty, review of, **1975** 361-362, 370-371
nuclear testing for peaceful purposes, treaty signing, **1976** 369-374
proposals (since 1946), Gromyko on, **1977** 263-264
reaction to Reagan proposals, **1982** 385-393; **1983** 793-794
SALT I agreements
interim, **1972** 436-439, 446, 453-454
strategic balance in, **1972** 765-774
SALT II agreements, signing, **1979** 413-453
strategic balance in SALT II negotiations, **1978** 549-556
troop reductions by, **1988** 927-928, 937-939
underground test ban agreement, **1974** 535-569
Vladivostok accords, **1974** 955-958, 967-968; **1977** 243-268
and world political position, **1988** 449, 456-458
arms sales by, **1978** 107
Baltic states
annexation, **1989** 469-473
freedom statements, **1989** 470, 473-475
independence, **1990** 728
Berlin, four-power agreement on, **1972** 467-470
Brezhnev
death of, **1982** 871-877
speech to 26th party congress, **1981** 225-239
Bush-Gorbachev statement on Iraqi invasion of Kuwait, **1990** 550-551
Bush-Gorbachev Washington summit, **1990** 331-350
Central America
arms shipments to, **1989** 650, 657-658
destabilizing role in, **1983** 439-440, 443, 451; **1984** 32, 45-46, 51
chemical weapons, **1981** 681-694, 724; **1982** 235-257; **1989** 28
chemical weapons ban, **1989** 26, 28
Chernobyl nuclear accident report, **1986** 383-407
CIA materials declassified, **1992** 3, 10
cold war, **2004** 630-632
collapse of, **1991** 785-812; **1999** 120; **2003** 1039; **2004** 319; **2005** 307
constitution, adoption of, **1977** 747-767
consumer goods shortages in, **1988** 448, 451-453
cooperation with U.S. against Iraq, **1990** 545-551
coup attempt failure, **1991** 515-525
Cuban relations
Castro on, **1979** 682-684
military support for, **1979** 763-770
cultural exchanges, **1990** 340
cultural freedom, and voluntary exile of artists and intellectuals, **1975** 161-165
Czech invasion by (1968), Dubcek on, **1975** 239-244, 248
Czech president's addresses, **1990** 3-18
Democratic Party platform, **1996** 644
democratic reforms
Bush attitude toward, **1989** 179-181, 298, 302
and corruption, **1987** 79-80, 84-86, 101
and economic revitalization, **1987** 79-81, 83-89, 98-104; **1988** 448, 458
economic summit countries on, **1987** 525-528
Gorbachev on, **1988** 460-463, 932-933, 936-937
mass media in, **1989** 174, 178-179
proposed, **1987** 79-104
dissent in, **1974** 129-135; **1986** 94, 1091-1093
campaign against Sakharov, **1973** 791-795; **1980** 103, 105; **1986** 1091-1095
Solzhenitsyn imprisonment, **1972** 727-728; **1978** 404
treatment of dissidents, **1977** 189-190; **1980** 103-108; **1981** 180, 182, 375-379, 747-752
dissidents Sakharov and Bonner, **1990** 207-213
Eastern Europe
domination of legitimized by Helsinki Final Act, **1975** 481, 488, 559-560, 562-563
nonintervention policy in, **1989** 399-402, 644-645, 652, 656-657
economic development, aid, proposed instead of military spending, **1973** 810, 820-821; **1974** 797
economic policy
development reappraisal by Chernenko, **1984** 151-153

profit and accountability as goals, **1987** 80-81
economic reforms
Gorbachev on, **1986** 145-146, 152-160
plans for restructuring, **1991** 531-541
price reform, Gorbachev on, **1989** 147, 152
progress of, **1987** 858, 860-868
U.S. support for, **1989** 644-645, 647-648, 651
economic summits
Houston, **1990** 467, 474, 479-480, 481
London, **1991** 465
Munich, **1992** 645-648
Egyptian relations
abrogation of friendship treaty, **1976** 169-175
Brezhnev on, **1976** 147
closing of consulates in Egypt, **1977** 829
trade agreement, **1976** 171
El Salvador rebels, military support for, **1981** 241-242, 244-249
elections, **1987** 79-80, 90-93
Baltic representatives to new parliament, **1989** 471
for Congress of People's Deputies, **1989** 173-179
emigration of Jews, **1990** 332
emigration rules, **1983** 843-844; **1986** 1076, 1078; **1987** 190, 202-203; **1992** 808, 812-813
easing of, **1986** 821-822, 876, 879; **1988** 93, 110-111
environment, agreements with U.S. on, **1972** 805-813; **1987** 747
espionage
for military technology, **1985** 603-614
network in Britain, **1979** 905-911
by trade officials, **1985** 605, 612
in U.S., increase in, **1981** 862
in U.S. nuclear freeze movement, **1982** 887-888
in U.S. scientific and technological information, **1982** 813-819
ethnic relations, **1987** 96-97
European Communist parties' independence from, **1976** 433-435, 449-452, 454-458, 460-461
evils of communism, Reagan on, **1982** 477, 482-483; **1983** 270, 274
expansionism of
and SALT II, **1979** 416-418
and SDI, **1987** 106, 109-110
U.S. containment policy, **1989** 207-208
Falklands War, position on, **1982** 287
Five-Year Plan, twelfth (1985-1989), **1986** 145-168
food supply in, **1989** 145, 148, 151
foreign aid, **1990** 467, 479-480, 481, 807-814
foreign policy
Chernenko on, **1984** 153-154
constitution on, **1977** 760
Gorbachev on, **1986** 163-167
purposes of, **1980** 142-143
French détente with, **1976** 331-332, 335-336
gas pipeline, U.S. economic sanctions against, **1982** 471, 879-884
Genocide Convention, **1986** 115-116
Germany, division of, **1986** 792-793, 796, 798
Germany, East, **1990** 107
Germany, East and West, UN membership for, four-power agreement on, **1972** 897, 900
glasnost
Gorbachev on, **1987** 79-80, 89, 94-95, 858-859, 862
and human rights, **1987** 190
in political debate, **1988** 447-450, 454-456, 459-460
Gorbachev's end of cold war speech, **1992** 431-438
Grenada, coup and U.S. invasion, **1983** 847-849, 851, 853
historical revision by, **1987** 857-858, 861-862
and Holocaust, **1983** 143, 148-149, 152
housing shortages in, **1988** 448, 452-453
human rights in, **1980** 191, 198; **1982** 107-108, 118-119; **1984** 155, 168; **1986** 94-95, 98, 111-112; **1987** 190, 202-203; **1988** 93-94, 110-112, 449, 454, 459-460, 884; **1989** 57-59, 66-67; **1990** 130, 134-135
and communist system, **1978** 224-225, 234, 236-237; **1981** 779, 783
European-Soviet cooperation on legal framework for, **1989** 407-408
forced labor on gas pipeline, **1982** 857-869
and *perestroika,* **1988** 449, 454, 459-460
Reagan on at Moscow summit, **1988** 354-357, 358-360, 370
respect for, Bush on, **1989** 180-181
Sakharov on, **1975** 915-918, 920, 924-926
Shostakovich on, **1981** 376, 378
Solzhenitsyn on, **1974** 129-135; **1975** 481-491
trend toward openness, **1986** 1091-1095
under Brezhnev, **1982** 871-872
Western pressure to change, **1973** 791-800
and ICJ jurisdiction, **1985** 638, 640
industrial production
accountability in, **1988** 448, 453-454
disappointments of, **1976** 144, 154-155
internal affairs, Western interference in, **1973** 810, 822-823
Iranian revolution, **1978** 710-711, 713-714
Israeli relations, establishment of, **1974** 835
Japanese peace treaty with, **1972** 745
Japan-PRC treaty on third-power dominance, **1978** 586-587
Jewish emigrants in Israel, **1992** 655, 656
Katyn massacre, **1990** 223-225
Kennedy assassination link investigated, **1978** 910, 914; **1979** 605-606
Korean planes, attacks on, **1983** 775-783
Latin America, influence in, **1979** 713-714, 720; **1982** 180, 187-188; **1983** 375-377, 386-390
Law of the Sea Treaty, **1982** 345
leadership changes, **1984** 145-150, 153-154; **1985** 271-275
Lithuanian independence, **1990** 183-186, 332
Middle East
on Camp David accords, **1979** 227
on Egyptian-Israeli Sinai accord, **1975** 575
Iran-Iraq War, role in, **1984** 750-752
peace negotiations, cooperation in, **1973** 881-896, 897-901, 905, 907-908, 932, 934-937; **1974** 30
peace process involvement, Baker call for, **1989** 295-296
Syria, support for, **1983** 835

Soviet Union *Continued*
U.S. concern about presence in, **1979** 659, 661-662, 965-966, 982-983
military buildup
Carter on, **1978** 223-224, 228-229, 236
Defense Department on, **1980** 123-124, 126, 129, 131, 140-142, 154-155
and economic problems, **1980** 139-140
economic summit on, **1981** 593
Ford on, **1977** 52
MX missile as response to, **1982** 903-918; **1983** 365-374
NATO concern about, **1976** 345-346
Reagan on, **1981** 826-828
and SALT II debate, **1979** 416-417, 457, 462
SDI as response to, **1983** 305-307, 310-313
and U.S. defense policy, **1982** 84, 310, 406-407, 478, 903, 910-911
military spending for research and development, **1972** 180-182
military strategy, as defensive, **1989** 439-440
military strength
Defense Department on, **1981** 717-730
Kennan's assessment of, **1989** 209-212
Republican Party platform on, **1980** 569, 623-629, 632
military technology, acquisition of Western, **1987** 29-38, 42
Mir space station, **1998** 929-930
missile defense system, **2000** 677
NATO declaration of peaceful intent, **1990** 455-466
Nicaragua, support for, **1985** 257, 260-263, 265, 268, 639, 641; **1987** 641; **1989** 163, 165-166, 167-168
nonaggression treaty with Germany, **1990** 601, 608-614
North Korea, occupation of, **1972** 523
nuclear material in, **1996** 139-146
nuclear strategy, **1980** 150-151; **1984** 257-258
nuclear weapons, **2001** 18; **2003** 906-907
nuclear weapons reduction, **1991** 475-490
perestroika
and Baltic states' separation, **1989** 470-471, 473-475
and democratization in Eastern Europe, **1989** 339-341
progress of, **1988** 447-464, 929-932, 936-937
religious freedom under, **1988** 459-460
science and technology under, **1988** 454-456
Persian Gulf War peace initiative, **1991** 99
Poland
domination of, **1977** 903-907; **1983** 577-580, 927; **1989** 523, 525, 536-538
martial law in, **1981** 881-885, 894-896; **1982** 108, 116-119; **1987** 183-185
workers' demands, **1980** 793-795, 802-803
power of, and U.S. policy toward, Kennan on, **1989** 207-212
PRC criticism of desire for hegemony, **1973** 768, 776-777
PRC relations, **1978** 782-783
normalization of, **1989** 276
and Soviet struggle against Maoism, **1976** 144, 146
PRC relations with West
Reagan trip to PRC, **1984** 287, 289
reassurances to Soviets on, **1979** 3-4, 6-8
U.S.-PRC agreements, **1979** 137, 153
U.S.-PRC normalization, **1979** 414, 669-672, 674, 677
propaganda, **1981** 753-767
U.S., **1986** 146, 149
Western, Brezhnev on, **1977** 747-748, 753-756
regional conflicts, Reagan on support of, **1985** 707-708, 715-717
scientists at conference on nuclear war, **1983** 857-882
sex trade and trafficking, **2004** 126, 129
Shevardnadze's resignation speech, **1990** 825-832
social policies, Gorbachev on, **1986** 160-162
Soviet Party Congress, 28th congress, Gorbachev address, **1990** 439-453
Soviet-German treaty, **1990** 608-614
space program
emphasis of, **1987** 649-652, 655
manned missions, **1988** 797
student test scores, **1992** 87, 91, 92, 95
and Syrian support for terrorism, **1986** 832-833
terrorism by, CIA on, **1981** 462, 467
trade agreement, **1990** 331-332
United Nations
agencies under influence of, **1983** 968-969
Shevardnadze address, **1990** 629, 635-646
U.S.-Soviet statement, **1990** 652-654
U.S. defense against
classified plan for, **1982** 395-407
future of SDI, **1988** 323-325
MX missile, **1982** 903-918
response to SDI, **1984** 258-259, 261-263, 266, 271-272
U.S. relations, **1991** 472-473
and Afghanistan invasion, **1979** 966-967, 969-974, 976-982; **1981** 86-88
agreement on basic principles, **1972** 442-446
Bush on review of, **1989** 47-48, 80
Carter on, **1978** 223-240
Chernenko interview, **1984** 917-923
Daniloff arrest, **1986** 819-827
Democratic Party platform on, **1976** 546, 587-589; **1980** 758-759; **1984** 621-622, 628, 634-636, 643
détente in
Brezhnev on, **1976** 143-144, 147-151
concrete agreements, **1972** 74, 78; **1973** 515, 521, 525, 527, 529
Ford on, **1975** 224-225, 234-235, 357-358
NATO on, **1974** 530-531, 533
Solzhenitsyn on, **1975** 481-491
economic summit on, **1988** 391-394
expulsion of UN personnel, **1986** 820
expulsion of U.S. embassy personnel, **1986** 267-272
Geneva summit, Reagan-Gorbachev, **1985** 749-761
Gorbachev on, **1987** 858-859, 866-867

Gromyko on at UN, **1984** 811-813, 821-829
Iceland summit, Reagan-Gorbachev, **1986** 875-885
as issue in presidential debates, **1984** 847, 880-882; **1988** 742, 744-745
lend-lease settlement, **1972** 845, 855-858
Malta summit, Bush-Gorbachev, **1989** 643-660
Moscow summits
Nixon-Brezhnev, **1972** 445-452; **1974** 559-569
Reagan-Gorbachev, **1988** 353-373
mutual restraint, Kissinger on, **1976** 907, 914-915
New Year's Day messages, **1986** 3-8
Reagan on, **1983** 78, 89; **1984** 82, 93-94, 811-821; **1985** 40, 45, 707-708, 712-717
Republican Party platform on, **1976** 659-661; **1984** 663, 709-710; **1988** 616, 677-679
Vance on strategy and negotiation, **1980** 476-483
Washington summits
Nixon-Brezhnev, **1973** 587-609
Reagan-Gorbachev, **1987** 991-1006
U.S. trade agreement, **1972** 845-855
linked to emigration policy, **1972** 846; **1973** 380
rejection of Trade Act conditions, **1975** 5, 12-13
U.S. trade with
embargo on grain sales, **1979** 967; **1980** 13-14, 28, 32, 84-85, 213, 830
privileges linked to emigration policy, **1973** 587-588; **1974** 42, 55, 114, 117, 538, 901-906; **1975** 224-225, 235
Solzhenitsyn on, **1975** 481-482
U.S. economic sanctions, **1982** 563, 879-880, 882, 949
U.S. embargo on high-technology goods, **1980** 28, 32-33, 87
Vietnam, support for, **1979** 183-184, 186
Vietnam War
role as intermediary, **1972** 491, 494-495
support for cease-fire agreement, **1973** 332-333
support for North Vietnam, **1972** 407-408, 411, 493
in violation of Paris accords, **1975** 252, 259-260, 275-276
Warsaw Pact dissolution, **1991** 399-401
weapons development, **1996** 219-221
West, relations with, economic summit on, **1982** 469-470, 474, 476; **1984** 357, 362-363
Western economic policies, criticism of, **1986** 145, 148-152
worker productivity in, Gorbachev criticism of, **1987** 84-86, 88
Yugloslavian independence from, **1975** 869-873
Space exploration
See also Space program
Apollo space craft, **2003** 632
Beagle 2 surface-rover to Mars fails, **2003** 302-303; **2004** 3, 4
Cassini orbiter to Saturn, **2004** 6-7; **2005** 502
Challenger space shuttle accident, **2003** 632, 636
Chinese astronaut, Yang Lwei, **2003** 1178
Chinese manned space missions, **2005** 503, 621
Climate Orbiter mission to Mars investigation, **1999** 711-717; **2000** 89, 90; **2003** 302; **2004** 4
Clinton support for, **1997** 37
Columbia space shuttle disaster, **2003** 631-677; **2004** 9; **2005** 498
Deep Impact probe, **2005** 502
Discovery flight of John Glenn, **1998** 776-786
Discovery space shuttle mission, **2005** 498-506
Endeavor shuttle mission, **1998** 929-933
Express probe launch, **2003** 301-309; **2004** 6
Galileo
mission to Jupiter, **2003** 305
inspection of Jupiter's moons, **1997** 202-205
Hubble space telescope mission, **2002** 212-218; **2004** 7, 11-13; **2005** 502-503
Huygens robot mission, **2004** 6-7; **2005** 502
International Space Station, **1998** 929-933
James Webb Telescope plans, **2004** 12
Lunar Prospector findings of moon ice, **1998** 113-120
manned space missions, Bush on future of, **2004** 13-16, 18
Mars, life on, **1996** 471-477; **1997** 510
Mars *Global Surveyor* (MGS) mission, **2002** 213-215; **2003** 302, 304; **2004** 4
Mars mission failures, **2000** 88-102
Mars rovers missions, **2004** 3-8
Mir space station, **1995** 419-425; **1996** 691-694; **1998** 929-930; **1999** 611
NEAR (Near Earth Asteroid Rendezvous) Shoemaker, **2001** 143-149
New Horizons mission (exploration of Pluto), **2002** 216
Odyssey mission to Mars, **2002** 214-215; **2003** 302, 304, 393; **2004** 8
Opportunity mission to Mars, **2003** 303; **2004** 3; **2005** 501-502
Pathfinder mission to Mars, **1997** 509-513; **1999** 712; **2000** 89; **2003** 302; **2004** 3
Polar Lander mission investigation, **1999** 711-717; **2000** 89, 95-102; **2003** 302; **2004** 4
Republican Party platform on, **1996** 548
Salyut Soviet space station, **1998** 929
Sojourner mission to Mars, **1999** 712; **2000** 89; **2003** 302; **2004** 3
Spirit mission to Mars, **2003** 303; **2004** 3-8, 9
Unity space station, **1998** 931-933
Viking 1 and *Viking 2* missions to Mars, **2003** 302; **2004** 3
woman astronaut Shannon Lucid, **1996** 691-694; **1999** 611
Zarya Russian control module, **1998** 931-933
Space Exploration Policy, President's Commission on Implementation of U.S., **2004** 11
Space program
See also Solar system; Space exploration; Strategic Defense Initiative (SDI)
antisatellite weapons in
and ABM treaty interpretation, **1987** 289-317
Soviet position on, **1984** 812-813, 824
Bush on funding for, **1989** 75
domestic applications of
Nixon on exploiting, **1972** 74, 110-111
Republican Party platform on, **1972** 693
military projects in, spending for under Reagan, **1983** 305-316

Space program *Continued*
research, **1990** 753-766
Skylab launches and purposes, **1973** 939-946
Soviet development in, Defense Department on, **1981** 718, 728-729
Soviet leadership and goals in, **1987** 649-652, 655
strategic planning for, **1987** 649-669
U.S. leadership of, **1987** 649-656
Voyager mission, collection of data on Saturn, **1981** 835-844
Space shuttle program
budget cuts to, **1981** 418
budget patterns, **2003** 646
Challenger disaster, **2003** 632, 636
Challenger disaster, impact on, **1986** 517-518, 535-539
Columbia disaster, **2003** 631-677; **2004** 9; **2005** 498
Columbia voyage, **1981** 417-426
Discovery mission, **1988** 795-797; **2005** 498-506
Discovery's tribute to *Challenger,* **1988** 795-798
evolution of, **2003** 638-640
future of human space flight, **2003** 668-673; **2005** 498-501
NASA goals for, **1987** 649-650, 653-654, 662, 664, 669
post-*Challenger* disaster, **2003** 643-644, 646-648
retiring shuttle fleet, Bush plans for, **2004** 10
Soviet *Buran,* **1988** 797
Space station
Clinton support for, **1997** 37
international agreement, **1997** 351
manned, in Reagan budget, **1984** 82, 90, 108; **1988** 155
NASA goals for, **1987** 650-651, 653-654, 660-662, 665, 668-669
orbiting, studies of, **1984** 258
Sagan Memorial Station, **1997** 509
Soviet *Mir,* **1988** 797
space shuttle program safety, **2000** 93-94
unmanned, Skylab's return, **1979** 553-558
U.S. multination agreement on, **1988** 796
U.S.-Russian
cooperative effort, **1995** 222-227, 419-425
news conference from space, **1995** 419-425
Space Telescope Science Institute, **1996** 269
Spadolini, Giovanni
at economic summit, **1981** 591
Reagan meeting, **1982** 477
Spain
aid to Nazi Germany, **1997** 259, 262, 263; **1998** 291
allied relations and negotiations with, **1998** 301-304
civil war in, use of incendiary weapons, **1972** 838
Communist Party in, **1976** 434, 450-452
democratic constitution, **1978** 809-843
euro currency, **1998** 271
gay marriage legislation, **2005** 869
German assets, **1997** 267
Iraq War
support for, **2003** 42, 48, 49-51, 811; **2004** 108
troop withdrawal, **2004** 105, 108, 882
John Paul II visit, **1982** 837-853
legislature, in constitution, **1978** 810, 823-828
Madrid talks between Guatemala and insurgents, **1987** 639
mass demonstrations against terrorism, **2004** 107
NATO membership, **1975** 354, 358; **1982** 419-421
self-governing communities in, constitution on, **1978** 811, 836-840
Socialists in, government and policies of, **1982** 420, 837-853
Soviet-forged letter from Reagan to Juan Carlos, **1981** 754
student test scores, **1992** 91, 94
terrorist bombings in Madrid, **2004** 105-114, 137, 535, 540
war on terrorism, support for U.S., **2001** 627
Spangler v. Pasadena City Board of Education, **1991** 27
Spanish language
See also Bilingual education
Castillian as official language in Spain, **1978** 811, 813
as predominant foreign tongue, **1992** 475, 477
Spann, Johnny Michael, CIA officer killed in Afghanistan war, **2001** 691
Spann, William B., Jr., **1978** 328
Spasowski, Romuald, asylum granted to, **1981** 884, 891-893, 896-897
Speakes, Larry
press conferences, **1988** 835, 838-839
Syria's ties to terrorist acts, **1986** 832
U.S.-PRC nuclear accord, **1984** 288-289
U.S.-Vatican diplomatic relations, **1984** 21
Spears, Tony, Mars mission failures investigations, **2000** 90-91
Special counsel, Waco investigations, **1999** 165, 480-488
Special drawing rights (SDRs). *See under* International Monetary Fund
Special prosecutor
See also Independent counsel; Watergate special prosecutor
permanent, Watergate prosecutor on, **1975** 674-675
Species extinction. *See* Endangered species
Specter, Arlen (R-Pa.)
abortion rights ad, **2005** 561
Alito nomination, **2005** 563
Clinton impeachment trial, **1999** 20-21
Guantanamo Bay prison, **2005** 451
intelligence community, **1996** 796
on judicial impeachment, **1989** 586-589
national security, **1999** 503
and Republican Party, **2001** 378, 380
Saudi Arabia terrorist bombing, **1996** 674-675
State of the Union, Republican response, **1994** 50
therapeutic cloning and stem cell research supporter, **2002** 515; **2005** 320
Thomas confirmation hearings, **1991** 554, 576-579, 595-598
Waco cult attack, **1993** 299-301
warrantless domestic surveillance, **2005** 958, 961-962
Specter, Michael, tuberculosis report, **1992** 1008
Speech, freedom of
See also Constitutional amendments (U.S.), First Amendment

domestic surveillance and citizens' rights, **1976** 237, 264-265
in PRC constitution, **1975** 48, 52
Speer, Lisa, on world fisheries conservation, **1995** 524
Spellings, Margaret, education secretary nomination, **2004** 778-779; **2005** 45
Spence, David, **1985** 129
Spence, Floyd D. (R-S.C.), **1983** 726
military readiness, **1994** 528-534
terrorist bombing in Saudi Arabia, **1996** 675
Spencer, Earl, eulogy for Diana (princess of Wales), **1997** 648, 651-653
Spencer, Susan, economic summit (Tokyo), **1993** 548
Sperber, Murray, on college athletics, **1991** 130
Sperling, Gene
apparel industry code of conduct, **1997** 207, 209
on economic projections and the presidential campaign, **2000** 46
U.S.-China trade agreements, **1999** 726, 730
Speth, Gus
Global 2000 Report, **1980** 665, 667
proposed solutions to global problems, **1981** 13-14
Speth, James Gustave, human economic development report, **1996** 438-444
Spiegel, S. Arthur, **1990** 485, 486-487
Spies. *See* Espionage
Spirit mission to Mars, **2003** 303; **2004** 3-8, 9; **2005** 501-502
Spitzer, Arthur B., **1985** 209
Spitzer, Eliot L.
insurance industry fraud cases, **2004** 418
mutual funds investigations, **2003** 693-706; **2004** 415, 419
"new source" review dispute, **2003** 177
Wall Street analysts, **2002** 392, 397, 1036
Spock, Benjamin, on children consuming milk, **1992** 398-399
Sporhase v. Nebraska, **1982** 689-701
Sporkin, Stanley, **1993** 83
Sports
See also Athletics; Baseball; Basketball; Yachting
Arthur Ashe AIDS announcement, **1992** 335-338
boxing, AMA call for ban on, **1984** 1019-1021
chess victory of IBM computer, **1997** 273-276
health benefits for girls, **1997** 158-171
steroid use, **2004** 29; **2005** 212-227
Sports in Society, Center for the Study of, **1989** 215
Spotted owl, northern
Bush on, **1992** 506
ecosystem management approach, **1992** 489-492
Endangered Species Act and, **1995** 359-368
ruling on protection of, **1991** 275-285
Spragg, Howard E., on *Roe v. Wade,* **1973** 102-103
Sprague, Richard, and House inquiry on assassinations, **1978** 911-912
Spratt, John M., Jr. (D-S.C.), Chinese technology transfer, **1996** 98; **1999** 236, 237
Sprinkel, Beryl W.
CEA appointment, **1985** 80
CEA reports, **1986** 60-62; **1987** 119; **1989** 4
as monetarist, **1988** 117
proposed Medicare expansion, **1986** 1027
steps down from CEA, **1990** 82
Sprint, jobs for welfare recipients, **1997** 34, 622
Spudis, Paul, **1996** 473
Squadron, Howard, **1980** 238
Squibb, manufacturer of breast implants, **1995** 516
Squyres, Steve, on Mars rovers mission, **2004** 5
Srebrenica massacre, **2001** 826-827; **2005** 853-854
Serb assembly apology for, **2004** 953
tenth anniversary memorial ceremony, **2005** 854
UN report, **1999** 735-752, 860; **2001** 899
video on Belgrade television stations, **2005** 853-854
war crimes tribunal, **2005** 851
Wesley Clark testimony on, **2003** 464
Sri Lanka
accord with India on ethnic conflict, **1987** 615-622
cease-fire agreement, **2002** 92-100; **2004** 993
human rights, **1990** 133
human rights in, **1993** 559, 575-578
life expectancy and fertility decline in, **1984** 532
tsunami disaster, UN relief efforts, **2004** 993, 995
tsunami relief efforts, **2005** 995-996, 999-1001
St. Amant v. Thompson, **1991** 321
St. Clair, James D.
Colson testimony in impeachment inquiry, **1974** 445
constitutional standard for impeachment, **1974** 137, 139, 142-143
and June 23, 1972, Nixon-Haldeman conversation, **1974** 673, 680-681
Nixon tapes, **1975** 663, 665
compliance with Court on, **1974** 637-638
erasure on, **1974** 24
as executive branch dispute, **1974** 622-623
negotiations with House Judiciary Committee on, **1974** 190, 192
Nixon tapes and documents, release of, **1974** 302
Watergate grand jury report, release of, **1974** 225-227
St. George's University School of Medicine, and U.S. invasion of Grenada, **1983** 848-849, 852
St. Germain, Fernand J. (D-R.I.), **1983** 803
St. Mary's Honor Center v. Hicks, **1993** 423-430
St. Patrick's Day Parade, **1995** 327-335
Stafford, Robert, retirement, **2001** 378
Stagflation. *See under* Inflation
Stakic, Milomir, Serb war criminal, **2003** 464
Stalin, Joseph, **1992** 431-432, 434
agriculture policies, **1989** 146-147, 149-150
atrocities under, Polish officers massacred, **1990** 223-225
and division of Germany, **1986** 792-793, 796
Gorbachev criticism of, **1987** 857-859, 861-863
Khrushchev denunciation of, **1989** 340
nonaggression pact with Hitler (1939), **1989** 469-472, 491
Stals, Chris, NEPAD member, **2003** 452
Standard and Poor's Corp., and New York City's fiscal crisis, **1977** 568
Standard Oil, antitrust probe of Aramco, **1983** 921
Stanford, Kevin Nigel, death penalty case, **2002** 358
Stanford v. Kentucky, **2005** 179, 186-187, 188, 193-194
Stanford Daily, police search of newsroom, **1978** 355-372

Stanford University, collection of Native American skeletal remains, **1989** 540-541
Staniecki, Ted, parochial school aid, **1997** 363
Stanley, Justin, **1986** 768
Stanley v. Georgia, **1990** 239, 240, 241, 242, 244, 245, 248-249; **1992** 321
Stanley Commission on legal professionalism, report of, **1986** 767-778
Stans, Maurice H.
acquittal, **1975** 143
environmental controls, **1972** 253-254
as head of campaign finance committee, **1974** 604
indictment, **1973** 564
secret campaign funds, **1973** 414
Watergate committee testimony, **1973** 550
Star Wars. *See* Strategic Defense Initiative
Starbucks Coffee, **1996** 43
Stardust spacecraft mission, **2004** 7
Stark (USS), Iraqi attack on, **1987** 791-815; **1988** 703-704
Stark, Fortney H. "Pete" (D-Calif.)
catastrophic illness coverage, **1986** 1027
health costs of smoking, **1985** 615
Starovoitova, Galina, murder of, **1998** 606
Starr, Kenneth W.
abortion funding, **1991** 259
abortions for minors, **1990** 387
attorney-client privilege, **1998** 393, 395
campaign finance reform, **2003** 1159
Clinton rebuttal to Starr report, **1998** 654-664
euthanasia, **1990** 375-376
flag burning, **1990** 358
grand jury investigations, **1998** 567
independent counsel
Clinton investigations, **1998** 38-39, 565-566, 907, 960; **1999** 15-16, 22, 166-167
future of, **1999** 165-172
Whitewater investigations, **2000** 763; **2001** 88
minority broadcasting, **1990** 420
report to Congress, **1998** 632-653
on school prayer, **1992** 555
school prayer advocate, **2000** 366
on sting operations, **1992** 315
START. *See* Strategic Arms Reduction Treaty
State Children's Health Insurance Program (CHIP), **2000** 24, 49, 788; **2001** 59, 130
State courts
America's Cup, **1989** 183-193
DeBoer adoption case, **1993** 515-529
New York City debt moratorium, **1976** 863-867
pregnancy disability benefits, **1976** 892-893
surrogate motherhood contract, **1987** 374-375; **1988** 71-79
termination of life-support systems, **1976** 197-219
State Department
See also under names of secretaries of state
ABM treaty withdrawal, **2001** 932-933
Cambodia, Khmer Rouge demise, **1998** 971-975
Cambodian coup, **1997** 639-646
Central African refugee crisis, **1996** 809-815
chemical warfare
in Iran-Iraq War, **1984** 749
by Soviets, **1981** 681-694; **1982** 235-237, 240, 246-247, 250-253
China-U.S. relations, **2005** 612-630
Clinton's passport search report, **1992** 1045-1052
Cuban detainees agreement, **1987** 929-930, 932-934
cultural diplomacy, **2005** 579-588
diplomatic posts evaluation, **1999** 690-698
El Salvador, rebel arms buildup in, **1981** 241-261
employment of host country workers, **1986** 269-270
foreign arms sales, and U.S. influence, **1978** 107
Foreign Relations of the United States series, **1992** 10
Foreign Service, intelligence responsibility of, **1976** 259-260
global climate change policy, **2005** 920, 923
global human rights reports, **1990** 129-131, 142-152
global problems, U.S. strategies for, **1981** 13-30
Haitian refugees, **1993** 455
hazardous waste treaty, **1989** 153-154
human rights in China reports, **1996** 133-138
human rights policy, Reagan, **1981** 779-785
human rights reports, **1977** 3-25; **1980** 189-198; **1981** 179-190; **1982** 107-119; **1983** 181-195; **1984** 155-168; **1985** 145-157; **1986** 97-113; **1987** 189-204; **1988** 93-115; **1989** 57-70
in China, **1994** 73-84
ICJ, relations with, **2005** 181
Iran-contra affair
circumvention of, **1987** 892, 896-897, 899, 902, 922, 924
estimates of diverted funds, **1986** 1052
Oliver North conviction, **1990** 493
role of officials, **1994** 18-19
Iranian revolution
advisories to Americans, **1978** 702, 705-707
and position of shah, **1978** 00, 702-708, 710-711, 714-716
Kosovo human rights violations, **1999** 803, 806-814
land mine crisis, **1995** 46-54
MIAs in Southeast Asia, **1976** 925-930, 934-935
Namibian interim government proposal, **1976** 612-613
national security export controls, **1987** 30, 40
nationalizations, and economic aid cutoffs, **1972** 67
NATO expansion, **1996** 655-661
Nicaraguan ports, U.S. mining of, **1984** 339, 341
Noriega negotiations, **1988** 81-82
North Korean relations, **2003** 592-603
Office to Monitor and Combat Trafficking in Persons, **2002** 334
passport regulation authority, **1981** 541-555
PLO policy, **1976** 192
closing of observer mission to UN, **1988** 480-482
conditions for talks, **1988** 907-908
denial of visa to Arafat, **1988** 907
and Young's meeting with PLO observer, **1979** 647-657
Poland, martial law in, **1982** 950
population and the environment, **1980** 665-697
Powell, Colin, secretary of state nomination, **2001** 96
religious freedom abroad, **1998** 19-29

religious persecution report, **1997** 562-579
Rice, Condoleezza, secretary of state appointment, **2004** 629-630, 778; **2005** 44-45
Ryan's Jonestown trip, handling of, **1979** 347-351, 369-373, 376-378
SALT II negotiations, **1978** 551-567
Saudi Middle East peace plan, **1981** 632
security against terrorist attack, **1983** 934
Shostakovich defection, **1981** 375-379
South African constitutional changes, **1983** 890
Soviet arms control proposals, **1982** 226, 983
Soviet disinformation, **1981** 753-754
Soviet downing of Korean plane, **1983** 777-778
Soviet forced labor, **1982** 857-869
Stockholm environment conference, **1972** 476
terrorist watch list consolidation, **2003** 157, 158
trafficking in humans, **2002** 332-352; **2004** 125, 126
Turkish military takeover, **1980** 810
Uganda, safety of Americans in, **1977** 143-144
U.S. bombing of Chinese embassy, **1999** 304-316
Vatican, diplomatic relations with, **1984** 22
Venezuela political situation, **2002** 207
Vietnam, U.S. consulate in, **1997** 489-492
visa application process, **2003** 222; **2005** 580
State governments
abortion regulations, **1973** 101-114; **1976** 483-488; **1977** 407-427; **1983** 543-576; **1989** 365-389
access to federal tax returns, **1975** 858
as accountable service provider, **1976** 618, 620, 627
age discrimination by, **1983** 231-240
aid for the poor, **1991** 827-842
antitrust immunity of, for home-rule municipalities, **1982** 36-39
block grants for, **1991** 69
in Ford spending reduction plan, **1976** 38, 43
in Reagan budget revisions, **1981** 217, 219, 334-335, 641, 644-645
in Carter welfare reform plan, **1977** 551, 553-558, 561-562; **1979** 391, 394
in Carter's urban program, **1978** 242, 244, 248-249
child abuse, standard of proof for in custody cases, **1982** 259-280
community development responsibility of, **1973** 305, 314-317
countercyclical revenue-sharing grants to, Carter revision of Ford budget, **1977** 127, 129
drug paraphernalia sales restrictions, **1982** 215-216
education
for children of illegal aliens, **1982** 489-506
parochial school aid, **1977** 431-445
responsibility for, **1972** 221-225, 232-233; **1989** 561-570
role in reform, **1983** 414-415
role in urban public schools, **1988** 217
spending for, **1988** 299, 301-302
training for welfare mothers, **1988** 847-849, 852
emergency plans for nuclear accidents, **1979** 824, 840-841, 860-861
and employment-related catastrophic illness insurance, **1986** 1027, 1033-1035
federal laws applied to, **1985** 167-187
federal minimum wage laws applied to, **1976** 377-389
grants-in-aid to under Carter, **1981** 78
hazardous waste disposal, control of, **1979** 786-787, 799-800
immunity of officials, **1974** 265-270
judicial activism and reduced power of, **1981** 803
law enforcement, federal assistance for, **1973** 305, 321-323
legislative redistricting, **1986** 615-635
judicial review of, **1972** 935-938
one-man, one-vote principle, **1973** 277-289
mental institutions, and rights of retarded, **1982** 521-530
offshore oil resources, claim to, **1975** 167-175
parties' open primaries, **1986** 1065-1073
privatization of services, **1988** 237-238
and property tax cutting measures, **1978** 397-402
returning federal services to, **1986** 56; **1987** 12
revenue sharing for
Ford on, **1976** 14, 23-24, 47, 62
in Nixon budget, **1973** 169, 174-175, 181-182; **1974** 98-99, 106-108
role in U.S. economic growth, **1984** 581-582
school busing restrictions, **1982** 619-652
social service provision, Nixon on, **1973** 304-309
spending growth in, **1978** 83-84
televising trials, authority for, **1981** 164-176
utilities, federal regulation of, **1982** 447-467
water export regulation by, **1982** 689-701
water projects, federal cooperation with, **1978** 386-388, 390, 393-394
State Justice Institute, DNA "fingerprint" study, **1992** 366
State laws
constitutionality of, reviewed by courts, **1972** 639-640, 642
death penalty, constitutionality of, **1976** 489-507; **1977** 517-528
on jury service, exclusion of women, **1975** 55-66
State of New York v. Canary Capital Partners, **2003** 700-706
State of New York v. Microsoft Corp., **2002** 803-817
State of the Union addresses
Bush (George H. W.), **1990** 49-62; **1991** 35-49; **1992** 55-68
Bush (George W.), **2001** 171-187; **2002** 33-48; **2003** 18-39; **2004** 17-34, 537, 711; **2005** 77-94
Democratic response, **2001** 174-175, 183-187; **2002** 38, 46-48; **2003** 36-39; **2004** 21-22, 30-34; **2005** 81, 90-94
Carter, **1978** 7-19; **1979** 19-28; **1981** 57-104
accompanying messages, **1978** 19-50; **1979** 28-79
Clinton, **1994** 34-53; **1995** 24-45; **1996** 21-35; **1997** 29-49; **1998** 38-54; **1999** 41-63; **2000** 16-40
Republican responses to, **1996** 21-23, 35-38; **1997** 31, 44-49; **1998** 40-41, 54-59; **1999** 43, 58-60
Ford, **1976** 13-26; **1977** 45-56
Democratic responses to, **1976** 13-15, 26-35
Nixon, **1972** 73-113; **1973** 209-225, 303-329, 801-808; **1974** 41-53
accompanying messages, **1974** 42-43, 53-62
Democratic responses to, **1974** 41-42, 62-65

State of the Union addresses *Continued*
Reagan, **1980** 27-102; **1982** 73-85; **1983** 77-91; **1984** 81-95; **1985** 105-117; **1986** 39-48; **1987** 105-115; **1988** 57-68
States' budget crisis, **2002** 54-55; **2003** 72
budget shortfalls, **2003** 72
States' rights, Supreme Court on, **1999** 333-356
Statue of Liberty
centennial celebration, **1986** 697-703
reduced visitor hours, **1995** 124
Stearns, Cliff (R-Fla.), steroid use in baseball, **2005** 215
Steel industry
competition from imports, **1973** 437-438
labor-management agreement, **1973** 437-444
price increases of, Carter on, **1976** 878, 881-883
underfunded pensions, **2003** 708, 709
Steele, Shelby, **1992** 450-451
Steen, Alan, hostage, **1991** 751-753
Stehling, J. H., on discrimination in Medal of Honor award, **1989** 698, 700
Stein, Herbert, **1990** 253
Burns's inflation proposals, **1972** 962
CEA report, **1974** 70
Stein, Howard M., **1988** 11
Steinberg, Elan, **1997** 262
Steinbrenner, George M., **1975** 666; **1990** 483-485, 487-490; **1993** 168-169
Steinbruck, Peer, German finance minister, **2005** 877
Steinem, Gloria, **1987** 376
Steiner, Michael, UN Mission in Kosovo administrator, **2003** 1139, 1142
Steinfeld, Jesse L., on health dangers of smoking, **1972** 45-47
Steinhoff, Jeffrey C., District of Columbia financial crisis, **1995** 500-505
Steinmeier, Frank Walter, German foreign minister, **2005** 877, 879
Stello, Victor, Jr., appointment of at Energy Department, **1989** 357, 359-360
Stem cell research
See also Embryos
in adults vs. embryos, **2001** 478, 542
alternative sources, defined, **2005** 319
alternative sources of stem cells, president's council on bioethics on, **2005** 317-328
Bush opposition to, **2001** 127, 539-546; **2005** 79, 86, 317-318
California state funded research, **2004** 157
congressional action, **2005** 318-320, 322-323
ethics of, **2004** 157-158
federal funding controversy, **2004** 159-161
Kerry support for, **2004** 160, 842
as presidential campaign issue, **2004** 159-160
Reagan's son's remarks on, **2004** 483
Stempel, Robert C., **1983** 11; **1992** 14
Stenberg v. Carhart, **2000** 429-446; **2003** 995-996, 1002, 1003
Stennis, John C. (D-Miss.)
D.C. voting representation in Congress, **1978** 590
proposed review of White House tapes, **1973** 860-861, 870, 878-880
Senate confirmation of presidential appointments, **1974** 5
shooting of, **1973** 201-202
U.S. bombing of Cambodia, **1973** 730
Stephanides, Joseph, UN oil-for-food program scandal, **2005** 235
Stephanowicz, Steven, Abu Ghraib prison abuse scandal, **2004** 210
Stephens, Gene, **1995** 464
Stephenson, Arthur G., Mars *Climate Orbiter* investigations, **2000** 90
Sterilization, and minor's rights, judicial immunity for order, **1978** 159-168
Stern, Abraham, **1983** 832
Stern, Andrew L.
on hospital oversight, **1999** 414
on labor union rift, **2005** 487, 735
Stern, Carl, Haitian refugees, **1993** 374
Stern, David, **1986** 170
Stern, Edward J., mutual funds scandal, **2003** 694
Stern, Marc, school vouchers, **2002** 409-410
Stern, William, Baby M case, **1987** 373-387; **1988** 71-79
Stern gang, **1983** 832
Stethem, Robert D., **1985** 465
Stetson, Peter, age of universe, **1994** 462
Stevens, Bob, anthrax mailings victim, **2001** 674
Stevens, John Paul
abortion
anti-abortion demonstrations, **2000** 433
clinic protests, **1994** 312-321
family-planning clinic advice, **1991** 259, 266-272
partial-birth, **2000** 432, 440-441
public funding of, **1980** 515, 534-535
regulations, **1989** 367, 387-389
right to, **1986** 559
state regulations on, **1983** 544-545, 565-566, 569-572
affirmative action, **1986** 654; **1987** 332-333, 345-346; **2003** 362, 363
federal government plans, **1995** 308-309, 317-318, 320-323
medical school admissions, **1978** 468-469, 471, 491-492
and seniority protections, **1984** 366
age discrimination, **1983** 232
alimony payments to men, **1979** 193, 200
antitrust immunity of cities, **1982** 35
asset forfeiture
drug trafficking, **1993** 432-438
pornography seized, **1993** 432, 440-446
auto searches, **1982** 425, 427-439
passengers' rights in, **1978** 754, 761
ballot initiatives, **1999** 6
bankruptcy and labor contracts, **1984** 182
bankruptcy law, **1982** 597-610
broadcast of offensive material, **1978** 515-525
campaign finance reform, **2003** 1159, 1161-1169
child pornography, **1982** 677; **1990** 240, 245-249
church-state separation
church's objection to liquor license, **1982** 956-961
public display of Nativity scene, **1984** 219, 231, 239
religious organizations' use of campus buildings, **1981** 875

clean air regulations, **1984** 427, 429-437
coastal property rights, **1992** 616
coerced confessions, **1991** 175
congressional immunity, **1979** 467, 475-478
congressional term limits, **1995** 260, 262, 263-270
creation science, **1987** 566
damages for tobacco-related ills, **1992** 564-573
deaf parochial student, **1993** 400, 403-406
death penalty, **1976** 921; **1977** 517; **1983** 709-710
constitutionality of state laws on, **1976** 489-491, 503, 506
ex post facto, **1977** 519
and ICJ jurisdiction, **2005** 182
jurors opposed to, **1986** 454
for juvenile offenders, **2002** 358; **2004** 797; **2005** 179
mandatory for murder of police officer, **1977** 397
for the mentally retarded, **2002** 356, 360-365
mitigating factors, **1982** 51
racial discrimination in, **1987** 463, 473
state's misuse of, **1980** 455, 457
detentions in terrorism cases, **2004** 377, 378, 390-392, 392-395
disabilities in the workplace, **2002** 6
disability, definition of, **1999** 319, 320
drug testing of students, **1995** 339, 340, 346-349
education for children of aliens, **1982** 490
electronic surveillance
covert entry for, **1979** 269-271, 279-284
phone company ordered to assist, **1977** 884, 891-896
eminent domain, **2005** 363, 365-371
endangered species on private lands, **1995** 359-368
entrapment in child pornography case, **1992** 313-322
exclusionary rule, **1984** 507-508, 515-516
faculty tenure review disclosure, **1990** 23-34
federal minimum wage laws applied to state governments, **1976** 388-389
flag burning, **1989** 343-344, 354; **1990** 358, 363-365
free speech
child pornography and "community standards," **2002** 291
corporate, in referendum campaigns, **1978** 307
Internet and, **1997** 444-446, 446-454
Internet pornography filters in public libraries, **2003** 388, 389, 397-399
freedom of residential signs, **1992** 290-297
gay rights discrimination, **1996** 286
gay rights to march, **1995** 327-335
grandparents' rights, **2000** 289, 295-297
gun-free school zone, **1995** 184, 195, 196-200
Haitian refugees returned, **1993** 413-421
hate crimes, **1992** 544-551; **1993** 385-389
HIV as a disability, **1998** 379, 388-389
home video taping, **1984** 53-54, 56-69
impeachment, Senate's authority to remove judge, **1993** 81-87
intra-enterprise conspiracy doctrine, **1984** 414, 422-426
job discrimination
fetal protection, **1991** 144
involving African Americans, **1993** 424, 424-430
proof of, **1989** 322, 328
settlements, **1989** 322, 331-332
suit against member of Congress, **1979** 399
judicial immunity, **1978** 260
labor unions, freedom of members to resign, **1985** 415
legislative intent, **1993** 250-253
legislative veto, **1983** 619
libel, of private and public persons, **1986** 355-357, 364
libel award, appellate review of, **1984** 300-309
line-item veto, **1997** 612; **1998** 421, 422-430
medical use of marijuana, **2001** 327
Meese criticism of Court, **1985** 479, 653-655, 666-668
military draft, sex discrimination in, **1981** 521
minority set-aside programs, **1980** 539-541, 564-566; **1989** 324; **1990** 419-429
Miranda warnings, **1984** 388, 395; **1985** 226, 250-253; **2000** 389
definition of interrogation, **1980** 431, 433, 441-444
rule upheld, **1990** 785-790
NAACP boycott, **1982** 656-674
Nixon papers and tapes, custody of, **1977** 467, 492-493
Noriega phone calls dispute, **1990** 721-724
obscenity
harmless error in case, **1987** 479, 481, 485-487
tests for, **1987** 487-490
open political primaries, **1986** 1065
OSHA safety inspections, **1978** 340-341, 346-353
PAC spending limits, **1985** 279
parental consent for abortions, **1990** 387-407
parental leave
reemployment rights after, **1987** 17
seniority rights after, **1977** 872, 880-881
parental rights in child custody, **1982** 260
parochial school aid, **1997** 363
patenting of living organisms, **1980** 493
physician-assisted suicide, **1997** 461, 473-476
political asylum, **1987** 253-262
political firings from public jobs, **1980** 259-266
pregnancy coverage in company disability plans, **1976** 892, 905
presidential elections recount, **2000** 1000, 1002, 1003-1004, 1019-1024
presidential immunity, **1982** 539; **1997** 291-298
press
access to pretrial hearings, **1979** 511
gag orders, **1976** 464, 479
libel of public figure, **1979** 285
newsroom searches, **1978** 355, 357, 370-372
preventive detention, **1987** 491-492
on prison inmates, beaten by guards, **1992** 176-182
prisoners' rights
appeals, **1991** 205, 215-218
from death row, **1993** 142, 149-152
prison crowding, **1981** 478, 484
in searches, **1984** 480-481, 485-488, 491
property takings
in historic preservation, **1978** 453, 462

Stevens, John Paul *Continued*
uncompensated, **1987** 532-533, 541-546
public aid to nonpublic schools, **1977** 431-432, 444-445; **1985** 433
public broadcasting editorials, **1984** 450-451, 461
public lands and developers, **1994** 299, 306-309
punitive damages, for consumer product liability, **1996** 274, 276-282
racial discrimination, in private school admission, **1976** 392, 400-401
redistricting
political, **1986** 632
race-based, **1993** 461, 474-481; **1995** 371, 380-384; **1996** 370, 381-383
racial criteria in, **1977** 151-152
religious clubs in public schools, **2001** 422, 429-430
religious freedom, **1997** 408, 417
religious publications, **1995** 386, 393-395
retirement, mandatory, **1985** 397-407
right to counsel, **1979** 207, 211
and police procedure, **1977** 220, 229
right to die, **1990** 375, 386
school book banning, **1982** 567-578
school desegregation, **1977** 457; **1991** 24, 29-33
restrictions on busing, **1982** 620
school prayer, **1985** 379-380, 382-387; **1992** 553-562; **2000** 366-367, 369-376
school vouchers, **2002** 409, 416-423
searches, and home arrests, **1980** 281-291
sentencing
and double jeopardy, **1980** 978, 986, 988
excessive prison, **1983** 659-674
in murder cases, **1991** 381-382
sentencing laws, **2003** 984; **2004** 360
separation of powers, Gramm-Rudman-Hollings, **1986** 707-708, 718-723
sex discrimination
in education programs, **1984** 202-203, 212-213
in pension plans, **1978** 293-301; **1983** 691, 694-701
by private clubs, **1984** 468
in Social Security survivors' benefits, **1977** 169-170, 174-177
sex offenders, right to confine, **1997** 384, 392-394
sexual harassment, **1998** 442; **1999** 215
at school, **1992** 188-197
in workplace, **1993** 939-944
snail darter protection from dam project, **1978** 433
sodomy and privacy right, **1986** 601, 608
sodomy laws, **2003** 403
state utilities, federal regulation of, **1982** 448
states' rights, **1999** 333, 345-349
statutory rape laws, sex discrimination in, **1981** 340, 348
student drug testing, **2002** 426-427, 433-436
students' rights
corporal punishment, **1977** 293, 303, 309
free speech, **1986** 731, 733, 740-742
in searches, **1985** 15
tax increase for school desegregation, **1990** 227-228, 229-232
Ten Commandments displays, **2005** 378
therapist-patient privilege, **1996** 388-389, 390-395
treatment of severely handicapped infants, **1986** 543, 545-554
treaty termination, **1979** 917, 933
tuition tax credit, **1983** 676, 684-688
unreasonable searches, **2001** 408-409, 410, 416-419
use of school facilities by religious groups, **1993** 363-369
water export, state regulation of, **1982** 689-699
welfare reform, **1999** 260
women's right to choose abortion, **1992** 589-611
worker health protection, **1981** 492
Stevens, L. Nye, **1990** 171
Stevens, Ted (R-Alaska)
Alaska federal lands, **1978** 733
Alaskan bridges projects, **2005** 125
Arctic National Wildlife Refuge oil exploration, **2005** 784
energy prices and oil company profits, congressional hearings on, **2005** 781, 784-785
wartime relocation of Aleuts, **1988** 291-292, 388
Stevens, William K., on ecological restoration, **1993** 886
Stewart, David O., **1993** 81-82
Stewart, Martha
indictment and conviction of, **2004** 420-421
insider trading scandal, **2002** 399; **2004** 415
Stewart, Payne, death of, **1999** 424
Stewart, Potter
abortion
and privacy right, **1973** 102
public funding of, **1980** 515-525
advertising prescription drug prices, **1976** 352, 361
affirmative action
in employment, **1979** 494
medical school admissions, **1978** 468-469, 471, 491
alimony payments to men, **1979** 193
auto searches, passengers' rights in, **1978** 753
broadcast of offensive material, **1978** 515, 517, 530-531
congressional immunity, **1979** 467, 475
from job bias suit, **1979** 399, 401, 409-410
from libel suits, **1979** 479, 481, 491
death penalty
constitutionality of, **1972** 499-502
constitutionality of state laws on, **1976** 489-491, 503, 506
mandatory for murder of police officer, **1977** 397
for rape, **1977** 517
state's misuse of, **1980** 455-462
electronic surveillance
covert entry for, **1979** 269, 278
phone company ordered to assist, **1977** 883, 891
employees' rights in dangerous workplaces, **1980** 199-207
federal minimum wage laws applied to state governments, **1976** 378
free speech, corporate, in referendum campaigns, **1978** 307
immunity of municipalities, **1980** 299, 308
job discrimination, and seniority systems, **1977** 383-391
judicial immunity, **1978** 260-261, 266-268

jury size and unanimous verdict, **1979** 264, 268
jury trials, split verdicts in, **1972** 423, 425-426
mental patients, confinement of, **1975** 469-476
military draft, sex discrimination in, **1981** 521
minority set-asides, **1980** 539-540, 560-564
Miranda warnings
and definition of interrogation, **1980** 431-439
and right to counsel, **1981** 433
obscenity
and community standards, **1974** 516, 519, 522
tests for, **1973** 612, 622
OSHA safety inspections, **1978** 340
patenting of living organisms, **1980** 493
political firings from public jobs, **1980** 259-261, 266
pregnancy coverage in company disability plans, **1976** 892
press
access to pretrial hearings, **1979** 511-512, 514-521
confidentiality of sources, **1972** 508, 518-519
gag orders, **1976** 464, 473
libel of public figure, **1979** 285, 287, 306-307
newsroom searches, **1978** 355, 357, 367-370
property takings, in historic preservation, **1978** 453
public aid for nonpublic schools, **1977** 431-432
public housing in suburbs, **1976** 224-232
racial discrimination, in private school admissions, **1976** 391-398
Reagan inaugural, **1985** 40
redistricting
one-man, one-vote rule, **1973** 278
racial criteria in, **1977** 152, 163-164
retirement of, **1981** 575
right to counsel and police procedure, **1977** 220-227
school desegregation, **1979** 536
cross-district remedies for, **1974** 639, 648-649
school financing based on property tax, **1973** 363
sentencing and double jeopardy, **1980** 977
sex discrimination
in employer pension plans, **1978** 293
in Social Security survivors' benefits, **1977** 170, 177
snail darter protection from dam project, **1978** 433
statutory rape laws, sex discrimination in, **1981** 339-340, 344, 348
students' rights, corporal punishment, **1977** 293
televised trials, **1981** 164, 170, 175
wiretapping authorization by attorney general, **1974** 393, 403
worker health protection, **1981** 492, 501
Stickney, Wallace E., **1992** 534, 844
Stiglitz, Joseph E.
on AIDS epidemic, **1997** 83
Argentine financial crisis, **2002** 86
economic crisis and the poor, **1998** 725
on economic growth, **1996** 51
on income inequality, **1997** 52
Indonesian economic crisis, **1998** 724
Stimson, Henry L., **1988** 289
Stimson (Henry L.) Center, **2000** 281
Stine, Robert J., Jr., Iraq reconstruction contracts, bribery allegations, **2005** 723
Stock market
See also Insider trading
auto industry debt ratings, **2005** 140
buying on margin, **1999** 210
"circuit-breaker" mechanism, **1988** 11, 15, 33, 35
corporate scandals and bankruptcies, **2002** 54, 392-393
crash of 1987, **1997** 724
day-trading, **1999** 206-207, 208-209
decline, CEA report on, **2003** 76-77, 87
digital economy (dot-com), **2000** 299-307
dividend tax, proposal to eliminate, **2003** 70
Dow Jones industrial average, **2004** 57
Federal Reserve Board restraints, reaction to, **1979** 771-772
illegal manipulations in, as reflection of values, **1987** 45-47
Jiang Zemin visit to NYSE, **1997** 730
late trading of securities, **2003** 694, 697, 700, 701-703
leveraged buyouts (LBOs), growth of, **1988** 921-924
limit orders, **1999** 209-210
margin requirements regulation, **1988** 11, 15, 32-33, 35
market timing of securities, **2003** 694, 697, 700-701, 703-706
mutual funds industry scandal, **2003** 693-706
NASDAQ composite index, **2004** 57, 63, 64
New York Stock Exchange scandal, **2003** 332, 693, 697-698; **2004** 422
online investing, **1999** 203-214
overhaul of trading system, **1987** 835
ownership of stocks, **1999** 86
performance of the, **2003** 71; **2004** 57
price fluctuations, **2005** 151
reforms, congressional legislation, **2003** 697
regulation, **1984** 143-144
retirement fund loses, **2002** 101
September 11 aftermath, **2001** 664
slowdown, signs of, **2000** 45-46
Standard and Poor's 500 Index, **2004** 57
stock analysts and conflicts of interest, **2002** 1036; **2003** 698-699
stock prices falling, **2002** 693
suitability rule, **1999** 205
volatility, **1997** 721-727, 834
Wall Street brokerages, **2002** 397-398
Stock market crash (1929), **1987** 834
Stock market crash (1987)
Brady commission report on, **1988** 9-12, 13-34
causes and reactions, **1987** 833-842
Reagan economic advisers on, **1988** 117-118, 132-135
Working Group report on, **1988** 9-10, 12, 34-36
Stockdale, James B.
Perot campaign, **1992** 719-722
vice presidential debates, **1992** 909, 977-1001
Stockholm Conference on the Human Environment, **1972** 636
Declaration of, **1972** 475-479
Stockman, David A. (R-Mich.)
Reagan budget revisions, **1981** 326
resignation from OMB, **1985** 73
on supply-side economics, **1981** 642

Stockman, Steve, **1994** 514
Stoddard, Thomas B., on military homosexual ban, **1993** 154-155
Stoessel, Walter J., Jr.
Sinai return to Egypt, **1982** 338
Soviet chemical warfare, **1981** 681, 685-686; **1982** 235
Stohr, Klaus, bird flu pandemic preparations, **2004** 925, 926
Stoiber, Edmund
chief minister in Bavaria, **2005** 877
German parliamentary elections, **2005** 875
Stojilkovic, Vlajko, war criminal, **1999** 803
Stokes, John, Jr., **1977** 626, 655
Stokes, Louis (D-Ohio)
COA reform, **1992** 10
House censure of Crane and Studds, **1983** 726
House inquiry on assassinations, **1978** 912-913
Stolz, Richard, Ames espionage case, **1994** 488
Stone, John P., Columbine High School shooting incident, **2001** 349, 353
Stone, Marvin, in presidential debate, **1980** 920, 922-923, 936-937
Stone, Michael P. W., **1989** 700
Stone, Richard (D-Fla.), **1983** 441
Stone, Wendy, **1991** 259
Stone v. Graham, **2005** 376
Stone v. Powell, **1976** 521-536; **1991** 212
Stonecutters Island, return of to China, **1984** 1045
Storer v. Brown, **1999** 7
Stotts, Carl, in affirmative action case, **1984** 365, 368
Strachan, Gordon C., Watergate indictment of, **1974** 157, 159-161, 165-167, 180-184
Strategic Arms Limitation Talks/Treaty (SALT I)
See also Anti-Ballistic Missile (ABM) Treaty
agreement on declaration of principles for, **1973** 588, 590-591, 603-604
agreement on verification of compliance with, **1973** 588, 591
agreements reviewed, **1978** 549-550, 556-558; **1979** 413-414, 455; **2000** 205; **2002** 278
Democratic Party platform on, **1972** 577-578
interim agreement, **1972** 436-439, 446, 453-454; **1978** 556-558
expiration of, **1977** 243-245, 249-250, 253-254
means of verification, **1978** 557-558
signing of
agreements, **1972** 431-463
Nixon on, **1973** 525, 527
Soviet compliance with, Schlesinger on, **1975** 499-502
strategic balance in, **1972** 765-774
Strategic Arms Limitation Talks/Treaty (SALT II)
assurances to Soviets, summit leaders on, **1979** 3-8
and Carter's human rights stand, **1978** 224-225, 549
Democratic Party platform on, **1976** 546, 587-588; **1980** 759-760
final provisions explained, **1979** 413-418, 463, 465-466
history of, **1985** 750-751
means of verification of compliance, Carter on, **1978** 549-550, 560-562, 567, 573-574
negotiations, rejection of U.S. proposals, **1977** 243-268
Nitze report on, **1978** 551, 567-582
nonaligned nations on, **1979** 686, 689
progress in, **1974** 535-537, 561
Brezhnev on, **1976** 144, 150-151
Carter on, **1977** 190, 193, 737, 740; **1978** 9, 16, 19, 49, 235
Ford-Carter debate on, **1976** 734, 747-749
NATO concern about, **1976** 345-346, 348
ratification of
Carter call for, **1979** 19-21, 26-27, 73
deferred, **1979** 967, 982
stalled, **1979** 763-765, 769-770; **1986** 781, 783-784, 788-789
Vance on, **1980** 476-477, 481-482
renegotiation of, Carter-Reagan debate on, **1980** 921, 936-939
Republican Party platform on, **1980** 569, 635, 638
State Department report on, **1978** 551-567
strategic balance in, Carter on, **1978** 223-224, 230, 238
text, **1979** 419-453
and U.S. and Soviet defense buildup, **1980** 126-127, 132-133, 142, 148
and U.S. defense posture, **1980** 153
U.S. opponents of administration strategy, **1978** 550
verifying compliance with, Carter on, **1978** 224, 230
Vladivostok agreement on resumption of, **1974** 957, 968
Vladivostok preparation for, **1977** 244, 248-253, 257-259, 265; **1978** 558-559
Strategic Arms Limitation Talks/Treaty (SALT III)
guidelines for negotiations, **1979** 414, 452-453, 459, 466
preparation for, **1978** 559-561, 566
Strategic Arms Reduction Talks/Treaty (START)
Bush press conference, **1990** 809, 810
Bush-Gorbachev agreement, **1991** 451, 475-490
Bush-Gorbachev summit, **1990** 332, 348-349
Bush-Yeltsin agreement, **1992** 52, 520-521, 523-524, 528-529
Malta summit progress in, **1989** 645, 648, 652-653
Moscow summit progress in, **1988** 353-355, 357, 369-373
MX missile's role in, **1983** 365, 367-369, 373-374
prospect of agreement, Reagan on, **1988** 58, 67
and Reagan INF proposal, **1983** 791-793, 795-797
Reagan proposal for opening, **1981** 823-824, 828-829; **1982** 385-393
Ukrainian ratification requirement, **1993** 19-20, 714
Washington summit progress in, **1987** 991, 995-997, 1003, 1006
Strategic Arms Reduction Treaty (START II)
analysis of text, **1993** 28-61
Bush statements, **1993** 20-23, 60-61
congressional actions on, **1995** 234, 236
Eagleburger letter of submittal, **1993** 23-27
ratification of, **2002** 278-279
Russian support for, **1995** 234, 236

UN Nuclear Nonproliferation conference and, **2000** 209-210
and U.S. security needs, **1993** 714-715
U.S.-Russian pact, **1993** 17-61
Yeltsin statement, **1993** 59-60
Strategic Arms Reduction Treaty (START III)
agreements reviewed, **1999** 53; **2000** 205; **2002** 279
UN Nuclear Nonproliferation conference and, **2000** 210
Strategic balance, U.S.-Soviet
defense posture report, **1980** 151-157
and PRC power, **1972** 179-182
Ford on maintaining, **1977** 46, 54-55
and global stability, Reagan administration on, **1982** 312-313, 388-389
in SALT I agreements, **1972** 765-774
in SALT II negotiations, **1978** 549-556, 567-568, 581-582
and U.S. defense strategy, Carter reassessment of, **1978** 223, 225, 228-232, 237-238
Strategic Defense Initiative (SDI)
and ABM Treaty, **1986** 877-882, 884-885; **1987** 289-317
Bush support for, **1989** 80; **1992** 61
changing focus of, **1988** 323-331
costs of, **1984** 258-259, 261-262
critics of, **2000** 678
critiques of science in, **1984** 257-272
as defense policy component, **1983** 305-316
defense spending for, **1998** 484
economic summit on cooperation on, **1985** 349, 355
funding and strategy for, **1986** 782, 784, 786-788
and Geneva summit, **1985** 750, 758
and Geneva talks, **1985** 709, 714-715
Gorbachev on arms control, **1986** 9, 14, 17
and INF treaty, **1987** 947
Japan in, **1987** 429
Milestone Panel study of, **1988** 323-331
national security needs review, **1993** 697
Phase I of, **1988** 324-326, 331
political and strategic implications, **1984** 264-266, 269-272
presidential debates on, **1984** 847, 893-895; **1988** 745-746
in Reagan budget, **1986** 51; **1987** 4
Reagan commitment to, **1985** 107, 115; **1986** 7, 40, 46; **1987** 106, 109; **1988** 58, 67; **2001** 283, 928; **2004** 318
Reagan proposal of, **1983** 305-316
Republican Party platform on, **1984** 726; **1988** 615, 690; **1992** 839; **1996** 541
Sakharov criticism of, **1986** 1093-1094
and Soviet buildup, Reagan on, **1985** 40, 45
Soviet position on, **1984** 812-813, 824, 918, 920; **1986** 4, 6
as START obstacle, **1984** 813, 824; **1988** 355
and Washington summit, **1987** 992, 1006
Strategic energy reserves
development of
Democrats on, **1975** 38
FEA on, **1974** 910, 914
Ford CEA on, **1975** 103; **1977** 65-66, 71
Ford energy program, **1975** 22, 24, 92
Nixon on, **1973** 918; **1974** 105
Reagan administration on, **1983** 828-829
expansion of, Carter on, **1977** 128
Strategic weapons
B-2 bomber, **1992** 56, 60
distinguished from tactical, Schlesinger on, **1975** 495-496, 498-499, 501
Gorbachev on, **1992** 437
Patriot Missile Performance report, **1992** 865-874
Seawolf nuclear submarine, **1992** 56
Stratton, Samuel S. (D-N.Y.), **1976** 684
Strauss, Annette, **1992** 67
Strauss, Joseph, **1989** 334
Strauss, Lewis L., **1989** 107
Strauss, Robert S.
at Democratic convention, **1976** 595, 597
in multilateral trade negotiations, **1979** 637-638, 643
Straw, Jack
Iran nuclear program, **2004** 869
secret detainees allegations, **2005** 906
Srebrenica massacre, **2005** 854
war in Afghanistan, **2001** 628
Strawn, Julie, **1991** 828
Streptokinase, effectiveness of, **1987** 875-876
Strickland v. Washington, **1990** 312
Strickler, Tommy David, death sentence, **1999** 829
Striking workers
coal miners' strike, **1978** 113, 115-118, 121, 124
on federal contracts, **1995** 129-133
Pittston coal strike settled, **1990** 19-22
steelworkers strike, **1997** 291
UAW General Motors strike, **1998** 320-325
UPS strike, **1997** 628-635; **1998** 320
Stringer, Howard, **1993** 487-488
Stringfellow Acid Pits, and investigation by EPA, **1983** 749, 753
Strip mining. *See* Mining industry
Stromberg v. California, **1995** 331
Strong, Curtis, **1986** 169, 172
Strong, Maurice, **1972** 475-476; **1992** 500-501
Strong, Richard S., mutual funds financial penalty, **2004** 419
Strong Capital Management Inc., mutual funds scandal, **2003** 695; **2004** 419
Stroud v. Swope, **1992** 183
Structural Impediments Initiative (SII), **1992** 21
Strügib, Heinrich, hostage, **1991** 751
Stuart, Carole, **1990** 35-40
Stuart, Hugh, **1976** 463
Stuart, Matthew, **1990** 36-40
Stuart, United States v., **1992** 465
Studds, Gerry E. (D-Mass.)
House censure of, **1983** 725-734
protection of endangered species, **1995** 360
Student aid
See also Pell grant scholarships
Clinton program, **1995** 82
Community Service Incentive Program, **1993** 177
Hope scholarship program, **1998** 43, 78, 87; **1999** 46; **2001** 58
Republican Party platform on, **1984** 692
restructuring of programs for, **1985** 585, 590-591; **1993** 171-179

Student aid *Continued*
Student's Total Education Package (STEP), **1993** 172, 175-176
tax-related incentives, **1993** 178-179
tuition tax credit proposal, **1997** 30, 36
Student Press Law Center, **1988** 39
Students
activism of, working for change within system, **1972** 419
AIDS risks for high school students, **1992** 339-343
assaults on in public schools, Senate report on, **1975** 207-208, 211, 219
deaf parochial student, **1993** 399-406
drug testing, Supreme Court on, **2002** 424-436
drug testing in schools, **2004** 21, 28
foreign student surveillance in U.S., **2000** 280-282
international math and science test, **1992** 85-96
PRIDE drug abuse report, **1992** 1013-1016
random drug testing of, **1995** 339-349
religious publications, **1995** 385-395
report on gender learning differences, **1992** 141-154
report on national standards, **1992** 45-54
undergraduate exchanges with Soviet Union, **1990** 341
Students' rights
See also Academic freedom
and corporal punishment, **1977** 293-309
and discipline in schools, **1975** 208-209, 219-221
freedom of speech and press, **1986** 731-742; **1988** 37-46
hazing and other practices at military academies, **1992** 481-487
searches, privacy vs. discipline, **1985** 13-26
suspensions in public schools, **1975** 67-80, 208, 217-218
Study to Understand Prognoses and Preferences for Outcomes and Risks of Treatment (SUPPORT), **1997** 329, 330
Stukey, R. John, Iraqi abuse of prisoners, **2005** 663
Stump, Harold D., **1978** 259-268
Stump v. Sparkman, **1978** 259-268
Sturckow, Rick, **1998** 932
Sturgis, Frank A.
offers of clemency and cash to, **1974** 158-160
Watergate sentencing, **1973** 415, 419-423
Submerged Lands Act (1953), control of offshore seabed resources, **1975** 169, 173-175
Sub-Saharan Africa. *See under* Africa
Substance abuse
See also Alcohol use; Alcoholism; Drug use
disorders in U.S. adult population, **1984** 833-836, 838, 840-841
rehabilitation for drug addicts, **1992** 220
teen attitudes survey, **2002** 177-178
Substance Abuse and Mental Health Services Administration (SAMHSA)
drug use survey, **1999** 461
suicide prevention report, **2001** 290-303
youth violence prevention, **2001** 74
Sudan
African Union peacekeeping mission, **2004** 588, 592, 594, 595
conflict in, **1999** 431; **2002** 447; **2003** 452; **2004** 931
Darfur region conflict, **2004** 115, 116, 588-601, 890, 891; **2005** 514-518
genocidal war investigations, **2005** 514-516
janjaweed militia violence, **2005** 515, 517-518
drought and famine in, **1984** 978-979
expels Osama bin Laden, **2001** 688, 803; **2003** 452, 840
human rights, **1990** 133
human rights violations, **2003** 839-840; **2004** 890; **2005** 514-525
human trafficking, **2002** 349; **2004** 125
Lord's Resistance Army (Uganda guerrillas) supporter, **2003** 471, 840
peace agreement, **2003** 835-845; **2005** 519-520
refugees in Egypt, **2005** 169-170
religious persecution, **1997** 564
sexual violence, **2005** 514-525
Uganda relations, **2003** 476-477
UN Mission in Sudan (UNMIS), **2005** 520
UN peacekeeping mission, **2003** 450; **2004** 115
U.S. air strikes against terrorists, **1998** 555, 586-591
U.S. economic and political sanctions, **2004** 125
U.S. relations, **2003** 840-841
willingness to accept PLO, **1982** 744
Sudan People's Liberation Movement and Army (SPLA), **2003** 836, 839; **2004** 589
Sudanese Liberation Army (SLA), **2004** 589
Sudanese Liberation Movement, **2005** 519
Sudarsono, Juwono, **1999** 720
Suez Canal
opening of to Israel, **1975** 574, 577, 583
reopening of, **1974** 20, 277, 280, 282
al-Suhail, Safia Taleb, Iraqi human rights advocate, **2005** 88-89
Suharto
corruption charges, **2002** 706
corruption charges, pardon for, **1999** 721
Indonesian president resignation, **1998** 284-288, 722; **2001** 562-563
and Islamic extremism, **2002** 704
ousted as president, **1999** 512, 718; **2002** 256
Suicide
in children, and antidepressant drugs, **2004** 640, 745-752
physician-assisted
end-of-life care and, **1997** 326
federal appeals court on, **1996** 121-132
House bar on, **1999** 441-442
legalization of, **1997** 329
Oregon ballot measure on, **1994** 501-512; **1997** 461-463
Oregon legislation, **2001** 290-293
Supreme Court on, **1997** 459-479
prevention, surgeon general on, **1999** 439-455, 836; **2001** 290-303; **2002** 268
protective factors, **1999** 450-451
rate, for Native Americans, **2001** 576
risk factors, **1999** 449-450
Suicide bombings
Iraq, UN compound in Baghdad, **2003** 109, 614, 808-809; **2004** 876

Israel
by Hamas of Palestinian *Intifada,* **2001** 363-365, 367; **2002** 927, 929-931, 933; **2003** 191, 192, 195, 196
by Islamic Jihad, **2005** 29, 31
Palestinian suicide bombings, **2003** 197; **2004** 302, 535, 811-812
London subway and bus systems, **2005** 393-404
Saudi Arabia, bombings in Riyadh, **2003** 227-244
Sri Lanka, by Tamil Tigers, **2002** 93
Uzbekistan, bombings in Tashkent, **2005** 429
Sukarnoputri, Megawati
East Timor independence, **2001** 595
presidential address on challenges in Indonesia, **2001** 562-574
presidential elections defeat, **2004** 753-755
terrorist bombings in Indonesia, **2002** 702-712
Suleiman, Bahjat, Hariri assassination, UN investigation, **2005** 691
Sullivan, Brendan, Microsoft antitrust case, **2001** 779
Sullivan, Gordon, on women in combat, **1993** 334
Sullivan, Joseph P., America's Cup ruling, **1989** 184, 188-193
Sullivan, Kathleen
family-planning clinic advice, **1991** 259
Florida recount case, **2000** 1004
Sullivan, Leon, **1985** 532, 535
Sullivan, Louis W.
abortion issue, **1991** 257-273
Bush committee on health care, **1990** 56
on damage for tobacco-related ills, **1992** 564-565
food labeling rules, **1990** 175-181
Sullivan, Scott D.
WorldCom collapse, **2002** 395; **2003** 334, 342-348
WorldCom fraud indictment, **2004** 417
Sullivan, Thomas P., death penalty, **2002** 354
Sullivan v. Little Hunting Park, Inc., **1992** 193, 195
Sullivan v. New York Times, **1990** 616
Sullivan principles, on labor practices in South Africa, **1985** 532, 535
Sulmasy, Daniel P., end-of-life care, **1997** 327, 328-330
Sultan bin Abdul Aziz (prince of Saudi Arabia), **2003** 233
Sultygov, Abdul-Khakim, Chechen war human rights investigations, **2002** 766
Sumbeiywo, Lazaro K., Sudanese peace negotiations, **2003** 837
Sumita, Satoshi, **1985** 624
Sumitomo Shoji America, Inc. v. Avagliano, **1992** 465
Summers, Laura, **1991** 828
Summers, Lawrence, economic summit (Tokyo), **1993** 543
Summit conferences
Bush-Gorbachev Summit Meetings, (Moscow), **1991** 475-484
Bush-Yeltsin Summit Meetings, (Washington), **1992** 519-531
Earth Summit (Rio), **1992** 499-506, 641-642
Economic Summit (London), **1991** 451-473; **1992** 520, 637-638
Economic Summit (Munich), **1992** 637-648
Economic Summit (Tokyo), **1993** 541-557
European Security Summit, **1994** 583-591
Summit of the Americas, **1994** 595-601; **2005** 766-767
Declaration of Principles, **1994** 595-601
Sun Microsystems, and Microsoft Corp. antitrust case, **1999** 659; **2000** 106-107, 110, 113, 118
Sunni Baathists, **1984** 748
Sununu, John E. (R-N.H.), warrantles domestic surveillance, **2005** 960
Sununu, John H.
appointment to chief of staff, **1988** 892
Bush's chief of staff, **1992** 534
resignation as, **1991** 769-773
criticism of banking regulation, **1990** 819
at education summit, **1989** 562, 563
endorses Souter, **1990** 615
ethics report, **1992** 293-299
Federal Emergency Management Agency, **1992** 534
greenhouse effect, **1990** 468
national education goals, **1990** 154-163
Seabrook nuclear plant, **1990** 196
Super collider, superconducting (SSC), in Reagan budget, **1988** 155
Superfund
See also Hazardous waste; Resource Conservation and Recovery Act
Bush administration, **2002** 900-901
Clinton reforms, **1994** 40
enactment of, **1980** 452; **1981** 84; **1983** 479-480; **1995** 113
House investigation of EPA enforcement of, **1982** 965-970
renewal of, Reagan call for, **1984** 83, 90
Supersonic transport (SST) plane
environmental effects of, **1973** 235-244
impact on ozone layer, **1975** 437
Supplemental Security Income (SSI)
in Carter welfare reform proposal, **1979** 391, 394
and Medicare and Medicaid benefits, **1999** 320
Supply-side economics. *See* Economics, supply-side
Support Center for School-Based Clinics, **1986** 1058
Supreme Council for the Islamic Revolution in Iraq (SCIRI), **2005** 663, 673
Supreme Court appointments, **1981** 575-590; **1986** 591-599; **1987** 720-721; **1990** 615-628; **1993** 391-398; **2005** 41, 77, 376, 379, 551, 814-815
Alito confirmation, **2005** 79, 551, 558, 563, 815
Bork nomination rejected, **1991** 551; **2005** 558-559
Burger retirement, **1986** 591, 594-595, 597
Ginsburg nomination, **1993** 391-398
Marshall resignation, **1991** 377-379
Miers nomination withdrawn, **2005** 79, 551, 562-563
as presidential campaign issue, **1976** 814-815; **1988** 723, 772-773
Roberts confirmation as chief justice, **2005** 79, 551, 558-565
Thomas nomination, **1991** 551-615; **2005** 559
open letter from Judge Higginbotham Jr., **1992** 33-43
Supreme Court cases
Abington Township School District v. Schempp, **1985** 379, 386, 390, 395; **1992** 559, 561, 562; **1995** 547

Supreme Court cases *Continued*
Adams v. Richardson, **1995** 245
Adarand Constructors, Inc. v. Peña, **1995** 307-326, 485-486; **1997** 190, 191, 193, 194; **1998** 855-856; **2003** 370
Addington v. Texas, **1979** 335-344
Agostini v. Felton, **1997** 361-381
Aguilar v. Felton, **1985** 433-436, 449-461, 480, 487; **1997** 361-381
Ake v. Oklahoma, **1985** 207-219
Akron v. Akron Center for Reproductive Health, Inc., **1983** 543-564; **1986** 559-560; **1990** 400, 401, 402
Al Odah, et al. v. United States, **2003** 114-117
A.L.A. Schechter Poultry Corp. v. United States, **1995** 187, 192
Albemarle Paper Co. v. Moody, **1998** 450
Alden v. Maine, **1999** 334-349
Alexander v. United States, **1993** 432, 437, 438-446
Allegheny County v. Greater Pittsburgh ACLU, **1995** 399, 401, 402
Allen v. Illinois, **1997** 393
American Iron and Steel Institute v. Natural Resources Defense Council, **1984** 427-437
American National Red Cross v. S.G., **1992** 462
American Newspaper Publishers Association v. National Citizens Committee for Broadcasting, **1978** 419-432
American Textile Manufacturers Institute v. Donovan, **1981** 491-505
Anderson v. Liberty Lobby, **1986** 357-358
Apodaca v. Oregon, **1972** 423, 426-429
Apprendi v. New Jersey, **2002** 357; **2004** 358, 360, 363-374; **2005** 680
Argersinger v. Hamlin, **1979** 208-214
Arizona Governing Committee for Annuity and Compensation Plans v. Norris, **1983** 691-705; **1990** 429
Arizona v. Fulminante, **1991** 175-184
Arizona v. Robertson, **1990** 789, 791; **2000** 393
Arkansas Ed. Television Comm'n v. Forbes, **2003** 395
Arkansas v. Sanders, **1991** 382
Arkansas Writers' Project, Inc. v. Ragland, **1991** 262, 819-822
Arlington Heights v. Metropolitan Housing Development Corp., **1976** 225; **1977** 35-44
Ashcroft v. Planned Parenthood Association of Kansas City, Missouri, **1983** 545, 565-572
Associated Press v. NLRB, **1991** 328
Associated Press v. United States, **1990** 426
Astroline Communications Co. v. Shurberg Broadcasting of Hartford, Inc., **1990** 419-435
Atkins v. Virginia, **2002** 353-368; **2005** 178-179, 187, 188, 190, 193
Atwater v. City of Lago Vista, **2001** 407-408
Austin v. United States, **1993** 431-438
Automobile Workers v. Johnson Controls, Inc., **1991** 143-153; **1993** 945
Ayotte v. Planned Parenthood of Northern New England, **2005** 818
Babbitt v. Sweet Home Chapter of Communities for a Greater Oregon, **1995** 359-368
Baker v. Carr, **1972** 935, 937-938
Baker v. Los Angeles Examiner, **1991** 322
Baldrige v. Shapiro, **1982** 171-178
Banks v. Dretke, **2004** 795-796
Barefoot v. Estelle, **1983** 707-723
Batson v. Kentucky, **1986** 409-433
Beal v. Doe, **1977** 407-409, 411-419
Bell v. Ohio, **1978** 495-498, 511-514
Bergna and Brown v. Stanford Daily, **1978** 355-372
Berkemer v. McCarty, **2000** 394
Berman v. Parker, **2005** 368-371, 373-375
Bertrand v. Sava, **1992** 460
Bethel School District v. Fraser, **1986** 731-742
Blackburn v. Alabama, **1991** 179
Blakely v. Washington, **2004** 358-374; **2005** 680
Block v. Rutherford, **1984** 481, 488-491
BMW of North America, Inc. v. Ira Gore Jr., **1996** 274-283
Board of Ed. v. Dowell, **1991** 23-33
Board of Ed. of Central School District No. 1 v. Ball, **1995** 395
Board of Ed. of Kiryas Joel School v. Grumet, **1997** 362, 366
Board of Ed. of Westside Community Schools (Dist.66) v. Mergens, **1995** 392-393, 398
Board of Education of Independent School District No. 92 of Pottawatomie County v. Earls, **2002** 424-436
Bob Jones University v. United States, **1983** 489-505
Bolling v. Sharpe, **1990** 430; **1995** 313
Boos v. Barry, **1990** 360
Booth v. Maryland, **1991** 382-396
Bose Corp. v. Consumers Union of the United States, **1984** 299-312
Bouie v. City of Columbia, **1990** 243
Bowen v. American Hospital Association, **1986** 541-558
Bowers v. Hardwick, **1986** 601-614; **1996** 285; **2003** 402-404, 407-413
Bowsher v. Synar, **1986** 705-730
Brady v. Maryland, **1991** 208-209
Bragdon v. Abbott, **1998** 378-392
Bram v. United States, **1991** 179
Branch v. Texas, **1972** 499-505
Branti v. Finkel, **1980** 259-271
Branzburg v. Hayes, **1972** 507-519; **1998** 401
Bray v. Alexandria Women's Health Clinic, **1993** 93-112
Brewer v. Williams, **1977** 219-235
Browder v. Gayle, **2005** 357
Brown v. Bd. of Education of Topeka, **1972** 935-937; **1979** 535-537; **1990** 230, 237, 430, 434, 616; **1991** 23, 27, 29; **1992** 577, 578, 579, 581, 585, 599; **1995** 456, 458; **2000** 771
Brown v. Thomson, **1983** 601
Buckley v. American Constitutional Law Foundation (ACLF), **1999** 5-14
Buckley v. Valeo, **1976** 71-111; **1998** 435; **1999** 11; **2003** 1157, 1159
Burch v. Louisiana, **1979** 263-268

Burlington Industries, Inc. v. Ellerth, **1998** 439-442, 453-465
Burnet v. Colorado Oil & Gas Co., **1991** 389
Bush v. Gore, **2000** 999-1024
Bush v. Vera, **1996** 368-387
Butler v. Michigan, **1997** 454
Byrd v. Raines, **1997** 612
Cable News Network, Inc. v. Noriega, **1990** 721-725
Calder v. Bull, **2005** 371
Calder v. Jones, **1984** 247-248, 253-256
Califano v. Goldfarb, **1977** 169-181
California Federal Savings and Loan v. Guerra, **1987** 17-27
California v. Ramos, **1983** 710
Callins v. Collins, **1994** 161-171
Capitol Square Review v. Pinette, **1995** 385, 387, 396-404
Carpenter v. United States, **1987** 881-889
Carroll v. President and Commissioners of Princess Anne, **1994** 316, 317
Carroll v. United States, **1982** 425-426
Central Intelligence Agency v. Sims and Wolfe, **1985** 333-344
Chabad-Lubavitch v. Burlington, **1995** 397
Chabad-Lubavitch v. Miller, **1995** 397
Chandler v. Florida, **1981** 163-176
Channel Two Television Company v. National Citizens Committee for Broadcasting, **1978** 419-432
Chapel v. Center Moriches Union Free School, **2001** 421, 425-432
Chaplinsky v. New Hampshire, **1990** 361
Chapman v. California, **1991** 175-176, 179-180, 183, 382
Chevron U.S.A. Inc. v. Echazabal, **2002** 5-6
Chevron v. Natural Resources Defense Council, **1984** 427-437; **1991** 258, 261
Chicago, B.&Q.R. Co. v. Chicago, **1994** 302
Chisholm v. Georgia, **1999** 338, 345
Church of Lukumi Babalu Aye, Inc. v. Hialeah, **1997** 421
Cipollone v. Liggett Group, Inc., **1992** 563-573
City of Boerne v. Flores, Archbishop of San Antonio, **1997** 406-421
City of Cleburne v. Cleburne Living Ctr., **1997** 191
City of Ladue v. Gilleo, **1994** 289-297
City of Richmond v. J. A. Croson Co., **1995** 308, 315-316, 322, 323; **1997** 193; **1998** 862, 867
Clark v. Arizona, **2005** 182
Clinton v. City of New York, **1998** 419-437
Clinton v. Jones, **1997** 290-298
Cohen v. Cowles Media Co., **1991** 317-318, 326-330
Cohen v. Jenkintown Cab Co., **1998** 398, 402, 404
Coker v. Georgia, **1977** 517-528
Coleman v. Thompson, **1991** 382-383
College Savings Bank v. Florida Prepaid Postsecondary Ed. Expense Bd., **1999** 334, 340
Columbus Board of Education v. Penick, **1979** 535-546
Committee for Public Education and Religious Liberty v. Nyquist, **1973** 641-643, 646-656
Community Communications Co., Inc. v. City of Boulder, Colorado, **1982** 35-49
Conroy v. Aniskoff, **1993** 249-258
Consolidated Edison Co. v. NLRB, **1995** 198
Container Corp. of America v. Franchise Tax Board, **1983** 645-658
Copperweld Corp. v. Independence Trade Corp., **1984** 413-426
Crawford v. Los Angeles Bd. of Education, **1982** 619-652
Cruzan v. Director, Missouri Dept. of Health, **1990** 373-386; **1996** 122, 127, 130; **1997** 465, 471
Dalia v. United States, **1979** 269-284
Dames & Moore v. Regan, **1981** 559-573
Davis v. Bandemer, **1986** 615-635
Davis v. Monroe County Board of Education, **1999** 216-234
Davis v. Passman, **1979** 399-411
Dayton Board of Education v. Brinkman, **1977** 447-457; **1979** 535-536, 546-552
Democratic Party and Democratic National Committee v. NCPAC, **1985** 277-294
DeShaney v. Winnebago County Dept. of Social Services, **1991** 265
Detroit Bank v. United States, **1995** 313
Diamond v. Chakrabarty, **1980** 493-502; **1987** 352, 358
Dickerson v. United States, **2000** 385-395
Dobbert v. Florida, **1977** 519
Doe v. Bolton, **1973** 101-102, 111-114
Dolan v. City of Tigard, **1994** 298-310
Dothard v. Rawlinson, **1991** 149
Doyle v. Ohio, **2000** 393
DuPont et al. v. Train, **1977** 131-141
Eastman Kodak v. Image Technical Services Inc., **2000** 109, 121-126
Eddings v. Oklahoma, **1982** 51-63
Edwards v. Aguillard, **1987** 565-576; **2005** 1011
Edwards v. Arizona, **1981** 431-433, 441-445; **1990** 786-793
Edwards v. South Carolina, **1995** 331
Eisen v. Carlisle & Jacquelin, **1974** 427-433
Elrod v. Burns (1976), **1980** 259-260, 262-267
Employment Division v. Smith, **1997** 406-407, 410, 411, 416, 418-420, 421
Engle v. Vitale, **1985** 379, 389-390; **1995** 547
Enmund v. Florida, **1991** 385
Environmental Protection Agency v. Natural Resources Defense Council, **1984** 427-437
Epperson v. Arkansas, **2005** 1011
Equal Employment Opportunity Commission v. Wyoming, **1983** 231-240
Estelle v. Smith, **1981** 431-441
Estes v. Texas (1965), **1981** 164
Faragher v. City of Boca Raton, **1998** 439-442, 443-452
FCC v. League of Women Voters of Calif., **1984** 449-463; **1987** 626-627, 633-636; **1991** 263-264
FCC v. National Citizens Committee for Broadcasting, **1978** 419-432

Supreme Court cases *Continued*
FCC v. Pacifica Foundation, **1978** 515-531; **1986** 732, 738, 742; **1991** 821; **1997** 447-448, 451
Federal Election Commission v. National Conservative Political Action Committee, **1985** 277-294
Ferguson v. City of Charleston, **2001** 407
Field v. Clark, **1998** 428-429
Firefighters Local Union No. 1784 v. Stotts, **1984** 365-385; **1986** 653, 662-663, 672-677
First English Evangelical Lutheran Church of Glendale v. Los Angeles County, **1987** 531-546
First National Bank of Boston v. Bellotti, **1978** 307-324
Fisher v. United States, **1998** 402
Florida v. College Savings Bank, **1999** 334
Ford Motor Co. v. EEOC, **1998** 450
Franklin v. Gwinnett County Public Schools, **1992** 187-199
Frontiero v. Richardson, **1995** 313
Fullilove v. Klutznick, **1980** 539-566; **1995** 312, 314, 321, 323-324
Funk v. United States, **1998** 398, 402
Furman v. Georgia, **1972** 499-505; **1976** 490-502; **1978** 495-497, 503-510, 513-514; **1980** 455-456, 460, 464-466, 471
Gannett Co., Inc. v. DePasquale, **1979** 317-318, 511-533
Garcia v. San Antonio Metropolitan Transit Authority, **1985** 167-187, 480, 484; **1999** 334, 347
Garrison v. Louisiana, **1991** 321
Gebser v. Lago Vista Independent School District, **1998** 442; **1999** 222, 228, 229
General Electric Co. v. Gilbert, **1976** 891-905
Gherebi v. Bush; Rumsfeld, **2003** 118-120
Gibbons v. Ogden, **1995** 186-187
Gideon v. Wainwright (1963), **1979** 207-208, 211-212
Giglio v. United States, **1991** 208-209
Gilmore v. Utah, **1976** 917-923
Ginsberg v. New York, **1997** 447-448, 451, 454-457
Glover v. Patten, **1998** 399
Godfrey v. Georgia, **1980** 455-472
Goldsboro Christian Schools, Inc. v. United States, **1983** 489-505
Goldwater v. Carter, **1979** 917-918, 920, 932-938
Good News Club v. Milford Central School, **2001** 420-432
Goss v. Lopez, **1975** 67-80; **1995** 348
Grand Rapids School District v. Ball, **1985** 433-449, 451-452, 457, 459, 480, 486-487; **1997** 361, 368-371, 375-379
Gratz v. Bollinger, **2003** 362-363, 381-386
Green v. New Kent County School Bd., **1991** 27, 29; **1992** 582
Gregg v. Georgia, **1976** 489-503; **1980** 455-465, 468, 472
Gregory v. Ashcroft, **1995** 186
Gregory v. Chicago, **1995** 331
Griffin v. Wisconsin, **1995** 342
Griggs v. Duke Power Co. (1971), **1989** 321-322, 325, 328
Grove City College v. Bell, **1984** 201-214
Grutter v. Bollinger, **2003** 362, 364-381, 383
Habib v. Bush, **2003** 115
Hague v. Committee for Industrial Organization, **1995** 334
Haig v. Agee, **1981** 541-555
Hamdi v. Rumsfeld, **2004** 377, 381-392; **2005** 555, 962
Hamling v. United States, **1974** 515-517, 520-522
Hans v. Louisiana, **1999** 339
Harris v. Forklift Systems, Inc., **1993** 939-945; **1998** 462
Harris v. McRae, **1980** 515-535
Harris v. New York, **2000** 393
Hawaii Housing Authority v. Midkiff, **2005** 369-371, 373-374
Hazelwood School District v. Kuhlmeier, **1988** 37-46
Heffron v. International Soc. for Krishna Consciousness, Inc., **1995** 398
Herbert v. Lando, **1979** 285-311, 315-318; **1998** 402
Herrera v. Collins, **1993** 141-152
Hill v. Colorado, **2000** 433
Hills v. Gautreaux, **1976** 223-233
Hirabyashi v. United States, **1995** 313; **1997** 190
Hodgson v. Minnesota, **1990** 387-398; **2005** 194
Hoffman Estates v. Flipside, **1982** 215-223
Honig v. Doe, **1988** 47-56
Hopwood v. State of Texas, **2003** 361
House v. Bell, **2005** 182
Hudson v. MacMillian et al., **1992** 175-185
Hudson v. Palmer, **1984** 480-488
Hunt v. Blackburn, **1998** 398
Hunt v. McNair, **1973** 643-644
Hunter v. Erickson, **1997** 188, 192
Hurley v. Irish-American Gay, Lesbian and Bisexual Group of Boston, **1995** 327-335
Hustler Magazine and Larry C. Flynt v. Falwell, **1988** 175-182
Hutchinson v. Proxmire, **1979** 479-491
Idaho v. Coeur d'Alene Tribe of Idaho, **1999** 348
Illinois v. Krull, **1995** 346
Illinois v. McArthur, **2001** 407
Illinois Broadcasting Co. v. National Citizens Committee for Broadcasting, **1978** 419-432
Immigration and Naturalization Service v. Cardoza-Fonseca, **1987** 253-265
Immigration and Naturalization Service v. Chadha, **1983** 617-644; **1998** 427
Immigration and Naturalization Service v. Lopez-Mendoza, **1984** 508
Ingraham v. Wright, **1977** 293-309; **1995** 348
International Association of Firefighters v. Cleveland, **1986** 652-653, 667-678
International Brotherhood of Teamsters v. United States, **1977** 383-393
Island Trees Union Free School District v. Pico, **1982** 567-585
Jackson v. Georgia, **1972** 499-505
Jacobson v. United States, **1992** 313-327
Jacoby v. Arkansas Dept. of Ed., **1999** 336
Jaffee v. Redmond, **1996** 388-395

J.E.B. v. Alabama, **1994** 223-236
Jefferson Parish Hospital District No. 2 v. Hyde, **1984** 415; **2000** 109, 121-126
Jenkins v. Georgia, **1974** 515-522
Jett v. Dallas Independent School District, **1989** 323
Johnson v. Eisentrager, **2003** 108, 115-117, 119-120; **2004** 378, 392-398
Johnson v. Louisiana, **1972** 423-429
Johnson v. Transportation Agency, Santa Clara, California, **1987** 331-349
Jones v. Alfred H. Mayer Co. (1968), **1976** 392-403
J. W. Hampton, Jr. & Co. v. United States, **1998** 436
Kaiser Aluminum & Chemical Corp. v. Weber, **1979** 493-507
Kansas v. Hendricks, **1997** 382-394
Kansas v. Marsh, **2005** 182
Kaplan v. Burlington, **1995** 397
Karcher v. Daggett, **1983** 599-616
Katzenbach v. Morgan, **1997** 415
Keeton v. Hustler Magazine, **1984** 247-253
Kelo v. City of New London, **2005** 362-375
Keyishian v. Board of Regents, **1991** 265
Kirkingburg v. Albertson's, **1999** 319
Korematsu v. United States, **1995** 313
Krause v. Rhodes, **1974** 265-270
Kyllo v. United States, **2001** 407-419
Lamb's Chapel v. Center Moriches Union Free School District, **1995** 390-391, 393, 398, 399
Larkin v. Grendel's Den, **1982** 955-963
Lau v. Nichols, **1986** 961; **1998** 313
Lawrence v. Texas, **2003** 403, 406-413; **2004** 42
Lee v. Weisman, **1992** 553-562; **1995** 547; **2005** 382
Lemon v. Kurtzman, **1983** 677, 680-681; **1985** 380-381, 385-388, 394, 435, 439-449, 452-455; **1987** 567-569, 572, 575-576; **1997** 372; **2005** 381
Levitt v. Committee for Public Education and Religious Liberty, **1973** 641-642, 644-646
Linmark Associations, Inc. v. Willingboro, **1977** 313-320
Lockett v. Ohio, **1978** 495-511
Lockhart v. McCree, **1986** 445-456
Los Angeles v. Manhart, **1978** 293-306
Loving v. United States, **1997** 296
Loving v. Virginia, **1995** 313
Lucas v. South Carolina Coastal Council, **1992** 615-620
Lynch v. Donnelly, **1984** 213-239; **1995** 399; **2005** 381
Madsen v. Women's Health Center, **1994** 311-326
Mahan v. Howell, **1973** 277-289
Maher v. Roe, **1977** 407-409, 419-427
Malloy v. Hogan, **2000** 390
Marbury v. Madison, **1997** 417
March v. Chambers, **2002** 385
Marshall v. Barlow's, Inc., **1978** 339-353
Martin v. Wilks, **1989** 322, 324, 329-332
Maryland v. Wirtz, **1976** 377, 380-381, 385, 388
Massachusetts v. Sheppard, **1984** 508
Massiah v. United States, **1991** 207, 209-211, 214-215
Masson v. New Yorker Magazine, **1991** 317-326
McCleskey v. Kemp, **1987** 463-476
McCleskey v. Zant, **1991** 205-218
McConnell v. Federal Election Commission, **2003** 1155-1172
McCreary County v. ACLU of Kentucky, **2005** 376-380, 384-389
McCulloch v. Maryland, **1999** 347
McDonald and Laird v. Santa Fe Trail Transportation Co., **1976** 405-411
McKelvey v. Turnage, **1988** 277-285
McLaughlin v. Florida, **1995** 313
McNichols v. Baldrige, **1982** 171-178
Medellin v. Dretke, **2004** 798
Meek v. Pittenger, **1997** 366, 377
Memoirs v. Massachusetts, **1973** 611, 614-617, 626
Meritor Savings Bank v. Vinson, **1998** 438, 445-446, 449, 455-457, 460, 463
Metro Broadcasting, Inc. v. Federal Communications Commission, **1990** 419-435; **1995** 308, 312, 315-316, 322-323
Meyer v. Grant, **1999** 5
Meyer v. Nebraska, **2000** 292
Miami Herald Publishing Company v. Tornillo, **1974** 523-528
Michael M. v. Superior Court of Sonoma County, **1981** 339-349
Michigan Dept. of State Police v. Stitz, **1995** 342
Michigan v. Tucker, **1974** 473-485; **2000** 392
Miller v. California, **1973** 611-621; **1974** 515-521; **1987** 480-485, 487; **1997** 449-450
Miller v. Johnson, **1995** 369-384; **1996** 369
Miller-El v. Cockrell, **2002** 359; **2004** 796; **2005** 182
Milliken v. Bradley, **1974** 639-654; **1976** 223-233; **1977** 447-448, 457-464
Minneapolis Star & Tribune Co. v. Minnesota Commissioner of Revenue, **1991** 820, 822
Minnick v. Mississippi, **1990** 785-793
Miranda v. Arizona, **1980** 431-444; **1985** 223-253; **2000** 385-395
  interrogation after right to counsel invoked, **1981** 431, 433, 441-445
  pre-Miranda right to counsel, **1974** 473-485
  psychiatric interview, **1981** 431-441
Mississippi University for Women v. Hogan, **1991** 309
Missouri v. Jenkins, **1990** 227-238
Morrison v. Olson, **1988** 465-478
Mueller v. Allen, **1983** 675-687
Murphy v. United Parcel Service, **1999** 319
NAACP v. Claiborne Hardware Co., **1982** 655-674
Nashville Gas Co. v. Satty, **1977** 871-881
Nassau County, Florida, School Board v. Arline, **1987** 245-252, 828-829
National Association of Broadcasters v. Federal Communications Commission, **1978** 419-432
National Collegiate Athletic Association v. University of Oklahoma, **1984** 415
National Cotton Council v. Donovan, **1981** 491
National Endowment for the Arts v. Finley, **1998** 405-418; **2003** 395

Supreme Court cases *Continued*
National League of Cities v. Usery, **1976** 377-389; **1983** 231-232
National Organization for Women v. Joseph Scheidler et al., **1994** 26-33
Nebraska Press Association v. Stuart, **1976** 463-479
New Jersey v. T.L.O., **1985** 13-26; **1995** 342, 347, 348
New York v. Ferber, **1982** 675-688
New York v. Quarles, **1984** 387-397; **2000** 392, 393
New York State Club Association v. City of New York, **1988** 399-403
New York Times v. Sullivan, **1979** 286, 289-310, 315-317; **1986** 355-356, 359-368; **1988** 176-182; **1991** 321, 325-326
Newport News Shipbuilding & Dry Dock Co. v. EEOC, **1991** 149
Nix v. Williams, **1984** 505-506
Nixon v. Administrator of General Services, **1977** 465-516
Nixon v. Fitzgerald, **1982** 539-559; **1997** 294, 295
Nixon v. United States, **1974** 621-638
NLRB v. Bildisco & Bildisco, **1984** 181-199
NLRB v. Jones & Laughlin Steel Corp., **1995** 187, 188, 191, 191-192
NLRB v. Mackay Radio and Telegraph, **1995** 129
Nollan v. California Coastal Commission, **1987** 531, 533, 547-553
Northern Pipeline Construction Co. v. Marathon Pipe Line Co., **1982** 597-610
Norwood v. Harrison, **1973** 643
O'Connor v. Donaldson, **1975** 469-480
Ohio v. Akron Center for Reproductive Health, **1990** 387, 395, 398-407
Olmstead v. L.C., **1999** 319, 320, 325-332
Oncale v. Sundowner Offshore Services, Inc., **1998** 441-442
Oregon v. Elstad, **1985** 223-253, 481, 486
Oregon v. Guzek, **2005** 182
Oregon v. Mitchell, **1997** 413-414, 415
Orr v. Orr, **1979** 193-206
Osborne v. Ohio, **1990** 239-249
Owen v. City of Independence, Missouri, **1980** 299-316
Pacific Gas & Electric Co. v. Public Utilities Commission of Calif., **1995** 333
Padilla v. Rumsfeld, **2004** 378
Palila v. Hawaii Dept. of Land and Natural Resources, **1995** 366
Panama Refining Co. v. Ryan, **1998** 436
Pappas, In the Matter of, **1972** 507-512, 514-519
Parden v. Terminal R. Co. of Ala. Docks Dept., **1999** 340
Parham v. J. R., **1990** 377, 380
Paris Adult Theatre I v. Slaton, **1973** 611-613, 621-628
Pasadena City Board of Education v. Spangler, **1976** 413-423
Pattern Makers' League v. National Labor Relations Board, **1985** 415-429
Patterson v. McLean Credit Union, **1989** 322-324
Payne v. Tennessee, **1991** 381-395; **1993** 142-143
Payton v. New York, **1980** 281-297
Penn Central Transportation Co. v. City of New York, **1978** 453-465
Penry v. Johnson, Texas Dept. of Criminal Justice, **2001** 387-394; **2004** 796
Penry v. Lynaugh, **2005** 187, 188
Perez v. United States, **1995** 198
Perry v. Sindermann, **1991** 263; **1994** 309
Philadelphia Newspapers, Inc. v. Hepps, **1986** 355-368
Pierce v. Society of Sisters, **2000** 292
Planned Parenthood Association of Kansas City, Missouri, Inc. v. Ashcroft, **1983** 545, 565-572
Planned Parenthood of Central Missouri v. Danforth, **1976** 483-488
Planned Parenthood of Southeastern Pa. v. Casey, **1992** 589-613; **1996** 125-127; **1997** 373, 465-466; **2000** 429-446
Plessy v. Ferguson, **1991** 31; **1992** 37-38, 42; **1995** 456
Plyler v. Doe, **1982** 489-506
Poe v. Ullman, **1997** 189, 476
Poelker v. Doe, **1977** 407-409, 427-430
Pope v. Blue, **1993** 463
Pope v. Illinois, **1987** 479-490
Post Co. v. National Citizens Committee for Broadcasting, **1978** 419-432
Powell v. McCormack, **1995** 262, 264, 267
R. A. V. v. City of St. Paul, **1992** 543-551
Raines v. Byrd, **1998** 423
Rakas v. Illinois, **1978** 753-764
Rasul v. Bush, **2003** 114-115; **2004** 378-379, 392-398; **2005** 448
Red Lion Broadcasting Co. v. Federal Communications Commission (1969), **1987** 629-630, 632-635
Reed v. Reed, **1995** 313
Regan v. Taxation with Representation of Wash., **1991** 262, 264
Regan v. Time, Inc., **1991** 820
Regents of the University of California v. Bakke, **1978** 467-492; **1995** 313-314
Reno v. American Civil Liberties Union, **1997** 444-458
Renton v. Playtime Theatres, Inc., **1986** 131-144; **1997** 447-448
Rhode Island v. Innis, **1980** 431-444
Rhodes v. Chapman, **1981** 477-490
Richmond v. J. A. Croson Co., **1989** 323-324; **1995** 308, 315-316, 322, 323
Riddick v. New York, **1980** 281-297
Riddick v. School Bd. of City of Norfolk, **1991** 27
Ring v. Arizona, **2002** 353, 357; **2004** 360, 797
R. M. J., In re, **1982** 65-71
Roberts v. Louisiana, **1976** 489-490, 505-507; **1977** 397-405
Roberts v. United States Jaycees, **1984** 465-478
Rodriquez de Quijas v. Shearson/American Express, Inc., **1997** 374
Roe v. Wade, **1973** 101-111; **1977** 408, 413-429; **1980** 515-521, 524-529, 532-534; **1986** 559-580; **1989** 365-387; **1991** 257, 272; **1992** 589-613;

1993 339, 935; **1994** 317; **2000** 429-430, 434; **2001** 128; **2003** 995-1000; **2005** 554, 561, 563, 815, 819
Rogers v. EEOC, **1998** 462
Romer v. Evans, **1996** 284-295
Rompilla v. Beard, **2005** 182
Roper v. Simmons, **2004** 797; **2005** 177-196
Rosenberger v. Rector and Visitors of the University of Virginia, **1995** 385-395; **1997** 368, 376
Rostker v. Goldberg, **1981** 521-540
Roth v. United States, **1973** 611, 614-618, 622-623, 626-627
Ruckelshaus v. Monsanto, Co., **2005** 369
Rufo v. Inmates of Suffolks County Jail, **1997** 366
Runyon v. McCrary, **1976** 391-404; **1989** 323
Rust v. Sullivan, **1991** 257-273
Sable Communications of Cal., Inc. v. FCC, **1997** 450
Saenz v. Roe, **1999** 261
Sale v. Haitian Centers Council, **1993** 413-421
San Antonio Independent School District v. Rodriguez, **1973** 361-377
Sanders v. United States, **1991** 215-217
Santa Fe Independent School District v. Doe, **2000** 365-378; **2001** 423
Santosky v. Kramer, **1982** 259-280
Schechter Poultry Corp. v. U.S., **1998** 436
Scheuer v. Rhodes, **1974** 265-270
Schiro v. Summerlin, **2004** 360, 797
Scott v. Illinois, **1979** 207-214
Selective Service System v. Minnesota Public Interest Research Group, **1984** 493-503
Seminole Tribe of Fla. v. Florida, **1999** 334, 336, 340, 345-346
Shaw v. Hunt, **1996** 368; **1998** 866-867
Shaw v. Reno, **1993** 459-481; **1995** 370, 373-376, 380-382, 384; **1996** 368; **1997** 190, 193
Sheet Metal Workers' Local 28 v. Equal Employment Opportunity Commission, **1986** 651-667
Sherbert v. Verne, **1997** 410, 411
Simon & Schuster v. Crime Victims Board, **1991** 813-825; **1992** 546, 548
Simopoulos v. Virginia, **1983** 545, 573-576
Sims and Wolfe v. Central Intelligence Agency, **1985** 333-338, 342-344
Skinner v. Railway Labor Executives' Assn., **1995** 342, 343, 344, 345
Sloan v. Lemon, **1973** 641-643, 656-658
Smith v. Allwright, **1991** 389
Smith v. County of Albemarle, **1995** 397
Smith v. Daily Mail Publishing Co., **1991** 328
Smith v. Reeves, **1999** 339
Smith v. Texas, **2004** 797
Solem v. Helm, **1983** 659-674
Sony Corp. of America v. Universal City Studios, **1984** 53-80
South Carolina v. Gathers, **1991** 382-396
South Carolina v. Katzenbach, **1997** 412, 413
Spangler v. Pasadena City Bd. of Education, **1991** 27
Sporhase v. Nebraska, **1982** 689-701
St. Amant v. Thompson, **1991** 321
St. Mary's Honor Center v. Hicks, **1993** 423-430
Stanford v. Kentucky, **2005** 179, 186-187, 188, 193-194
Stenberg v. Carhart, **2000** 429-446; **2003** 995-996, 1002, 1003
Stone v. Graham, **2005** 376
Stone v. Powell, **1976** 521-536; **1991** 212
Storer v. Brown, **1999** 7
Stromberg v. California, **1995** 331
Stump v. Sparkman, **1978** 259-268
Sutton v. United Air Lines, **1999** 318, 320-325
Swain v. Alabama (1965), **1986** 409-433
Swann v. Charlotte-Mecklenburg Bd. of Education, **1976** 413-414, 418-422; **1991** 29
Swidler & Berlin v. U.S., **1998** 393-404
Tashjian v. Republican Party of Connecticut, **1986** 1065-1073
Taylor v. Louisiana, **1975** 55-66
Teamsters, International Brotherhood of, v. National Labor Relations Board, **1984** 181-199
Tennard v. Dretke, **2004** 796-797
Tennessee v. Blumstein, **1972** 283-290
Tennessee v. Garner, **1985** 303-315
Tennessee Valley Authority v. Hill, **1978** 433-452
Texas v. Johnson, **1989** 343-354
Thompson v. Oklahoma, **2005** 186, 189
Thornburg v. Gingles, **1995** 370
Thornburgh v. American College of Obstetricians and Gynecologists, **1986** 559-580
T.I.M.E.-D.C., Inc. v. United States, **1977** 383-393
Tinker v. Des Moines Independent Community School District, **1986** 732-740; **1988** 38, 41, 45-46; **1995** 331; **1999** 223
Toyota Motor Manufacturing, Kentucky, Inc. v. Williams, **2002** 4, 7-14
Train v. City of New York, **1975** 135-140; **1998** 433
Train v. duPont et al., **1977** 131-141
Trammel v. U.S., **1998** 402
Traynor v. Turnage, **1988** 277-285
Treasury Employees v. Von Raab, **1995** 342, 344, 345
Trop v. Dulles, **2005** 191
Troxel v. Granville, **2000** 287-298
TVA v. Hill, **1995** 363-364
United Jewish Organizations of Williamsburgh, Inc. v. Carey, **1977** 151-167; **1995** 376
United States Term Limits, Inc. v. Hill, **1995** 263
United States Term Limits, Inc. v. Thornton, **1995** 259-275
United Steelworkers of America v. Weber, **1979** 493-507
University of California Regents v. Bakke, **2003** 358, 360-363, 383-386
University of Pennsylvania v. Equal Employment Opportunity Commission, **1990** 23-34
Upjohn Co. v. United States, **1998** 398, 402
U.S. v. Bass, **1995** 189
U.S. v. Caldwell, **1972** 507-509, 512-519
U.S. v. Chavez, **1974** 392-393, 400-405
U.S. v. Curtiss-Wright Export Corp., **1998** 429
U.S. v. Darby, **1995** 188
U.S. v. DiFrancesco, **1980** 977-988

Supreme Court cases *Continued*
U.S. v. Eichman, **1990** 357-365
U.S. v. Emerson, **2001** 726-737; **2002** 963
U.S. v. Fordice, **1992** 575-587; **1995** 239, 242, 245-247
U.S. v. Giordano, **1974** 392-399
U.S. v. Haggerty, **1990** 357-365
U.S. v. Hays, **1995** 370
U.S. v. Helstoski, **1979** 467-478
U.S. v. Kokinda, **1991** 265
U.S. v. Leon, **1984** 505-519; **1985** 480-481, 485
U.S. v. Lopez, **1995** 183-200, 260
U.S. v. Maine et al., **1975** 167-175
U.S. v. Martinez-Fuerte, **1995** 342
U.S. v. Microsoft, **2001** 780-792
U.S. v. Miller, **2001** 728-730; **2002** 964-968
U.S. v. Morrison, **2000** 328
U.S. v. New York Telephone Co., **1977** 883-896
U.S. v. Nixon, **1974** 621-638; **1997** 297; **1998** 401, 402
U.S. v. Oakland Cannabis Buyers' Cooperative, **2001** 325-330
U.S. v. Osborn, **1998** 399
U.S. v. Ptasynski, **1983** 517-523
U.S. v. Ross, **1982** 425-446
U.S. v. Salerno, **1987** 491-508; **1991** 20.260
U.S. v. Swift and Co., **1991** 28
U.S. v. Tucker, **1991** 386
U.S. v. United Shoe Machinery Corp., **1991** 28
U.S. v. Weber, **1979** 493-507
U.S. v. Zolin, **1998** 403
U.S. Airways v. Barnett, **2002** 6
U.S. House of Representatives v. Immigration and Naturalization Service, **1983** 617-644
U.S. Senate v. Immigration and Naturalization Service, **1983** 617-644
Vacco, Attorney General of N.Y. v. Quill, **1997** 459-479
Van Orden v. Perry, **2005** 376-384
Vernonia School District 47J v. Acton, **1995** 339-349; **1999** 223; **2002** 425-435
Virginia Beach v. Howell, **1973** 277-289
Virginia State Board of Pharmacy v. Virginia Citizens Consumer Council, **1976** 351-363
Wainwright v. Sykes, **1991** 215-216
Wallace v. Jaffree, **1985** 379-395, 480, 487-488
Walz v. Tax Commission of City of New York, **1993** 406; **1997** 372
Wards Cove Packing Co. v. Antonio, **1989** 321-322, 324-329; **1991** 148-149, 761
Washington v. Davis, **1977** 35-36, 40-44; **1997** 190
Washington v. Glucksberg, **1997** 459-479; **2000** 291
Washington v. Seattle School District no. 1, **1982** 619-652; **1997** 188
Watchtower Bible & Tract Soc. N.Y. Inc. v. Village of Stratton, **2003** 398
Webster v. Reproductive Health Services, **1989** 365-389; **1993** 339
Weinberg v. Prichard, **1973** 277-289
Weinberger v. Wiesenfeld, **1975** 177-185
Wesberry v. Sanders, **1995** 265
West Virginia Bd. of Education v. Barnette, **1995** 331
Western Air Lines v. Criswell, **1985** 397-407
Whirlpool Corp. v. Marshall, **1980** 199-207
Wickard v. Filburn, **1995** 188
Widmar v. Vincent, **1981** 869-879; **1995** 391, 392, 393, 398, 399
Williams v. Taylor, **2000** 991-992
Wisconsin v. Mitchell, **1993** 385-389
Wisconsin v. Yoder, **1997** 411
Witherspoon v. Illinois, **1986** 446-456
Witte v. United States, **1997** 391
Witters v. Washington Dept. of Services for the Blind, **1997** 362, 368-371, 378-379
Wolff v. Rice, **1976** 521-536
Wolman v. Walter, **1977** 431-445; **1997** 366
Woodson v. North Carolina, **1976** 489-490, 503-505; **1991** 385
Wygant v. Jackson Bd. of Education, **1995** 314-315; **1997** 191
Yee v. City of Escondido, **1992** 615; **1993** 436
Youngberg v. Romeo, **1982** 521-530
Youngstown Sheet and Tube Co. v. Sawyer, **2004** 342
Zant v. Stephens, **1991** 385
Zauderer v. Office of Disciplinary Counsel of Supreme Court of Ohio, **1995** 333
Zelman v. Simmons-Harris, **2002** 406-423
Zobrest v. Catalina Foothills School District, **1993** 399-406; **1997** 362, 368-371, 377-378
Zurcher v. Stanford Daily, **1978** 355-372
Supreme Court opinions
abortion
clinic blockades, **1993** 93-112; **1994** 311-326
family-planning clinic advice, **1991** 257-273
parental consent, **1990** 387-407; **2005** 817-818
partial-birth abortion, **2005** 818
protesters and RICO law, **1994** 26-33
public funding for, **1977** 407-430; **1980** 515-535
right to, **1973** 101-114; **1983** 543-576
state restrictions on, **1976** 483-488; **1983** 543-547, 552-553, 562-565, 568-569, 573; **1989** 365-389
women's right to choose, **1992** 589-613
affirmative action, **2003** 358-386
federal government plans, **1995** 307-326, 484-485
promotion of women, **1987** 331-349
racial hiring goals, **1989** 322, 324, 329-332
and reverse discrimination, **1978** 467-492; **1979** 493-507
age discrimination, **1983** 231-240
mandatory retirement, **1985** 397-407
antitrust
immunity of cities, **1982** 35-49
intra-enterprise conspiracy doctrine, **1984** 413-426
asset forfeiture
drug trafficking, **1993** 431-438
pornography seized, **1993** 431, 432, 433-438
attorney-client privilege, **1998** 393-404
auto searches
passengers' rights, **1978** 753-764
probable cause for, **1982** 425-446

ballot initiatives, **1999** 3-14
bankruptcy, collective bargaining agreements and, **1984** 181-199
bankruptcy law, **1982** 597-610
Bork confirmation hearings, **1987** 717-744
broadcasting, public, editorials on, **1984** 449-463
campaign finance, **2003** 1155-1172
campaigns and elections
  campaign financing, **1976** 71-111
  corporate free speech and spending in, **1978** 307-324
  PAC spending limits, **1985** 277-294
  political party's right to hold open primaries, **1986** 1065-1073
census data confidentiality, **1982** 171-178
child pornography, **1982** 675-688; **1990** 239-249
church and state, deaf parochial student, **1993** 399-406
church-state separation
  church's objection to liquor license, **1982** 955-963
  public display of Nativity scene, **1984** 217-239
  religious organizations' meetings on campus, **1981** 869-879
civil rights cases under Warren, **1972** 935-938
class action suits, **1974** 427-433
coerced confessions, **1991** 175-184
compensation law, **1991** 813-825
congressional immunity
  in job bias suit, **1979** 399-411
  for legislative acts, **1979** 467-478
  in libel suits, **1979** 479-491
congressional term limits, **1995** 259-275
creation science, **1987** 565-576
death penalty
  appeals by death row prisoners, **1993** 141-152
  consideration of mitigating factors, **1978** 495-514; **1982** 51-63
  constitutionality of state laws on, **1976** 489-507
  fairness of, **2001** 387-394; **2005** 182
  and *habeas corpus* appeals, **1983** 707-723
  for juveniles, **2002** 357-358; **2005** 177-196
  mandatory for murder of police officer, **1977** 397-405
  for mentally retarded, **2002** 353-368; **2005** 177-178
  racial discrimination in, **1987** 463-476
  for rape, **1977** 517-528
  renunciation of, **1994** 161-171
  state's misuse of statute on, **1980** 455-472
detainees, Guantanamo Bay , **2003** 109-111
detainees, indefinite detention of suspects, **2004** 342
disabilities in the workplace, **2002** 3-14
disability, definition of, **1999** 317-332; **2002** 3-4
drug paraphernalia sales, **1982** 215-223
drug testing of students, **1995** 339-349
education
  for children of illegal aliens, **1982** 489-506
  discriminatory public financing of, **1973** 361-377
  disruptive handicapped students, **1988** 47-56
  public aid to nonpublic schools, **1977** 431-445; **1985** 433-461
  remedial courses for victims of bias, **1977** 447-448, 457-464
  school book banning, **1982** 567-585
  tax exemptions for discriminatory schools, **1983** 489-505
  teaching about religion, **1987** 597-598, 602-605
  tuition tax credit, **1983** 675-687
electronic surveillance
  covert entry for, **1979** 269-284
  by government enforcement agencies without warrant, **1972** 485-489
  phone company ordered to help, **1977** 883-896
  wiretap approval by attorney general, **1974** 391-405
eminent domain, **2005** 362-375
employees' rights in dangerous workplaces, **1980** 199-207
endangered species
  on private lands, **1995** 359-368
  protection from dam project, **1978** 433-452
entrapment in child pornography case, **1992** 313-327
exclusionary rule, **1984** 505-519
executive immunity, and Kent State parents' right to sue, **1974** 265-270
federal laws applied to state governments, **1976** 377-389; **1985** 167-187
fetal protection, **1991** 143-153
flag burning, **1990** 357-365
free speech
  flag burning, **1989** 343-354
  on the Internet, **1997** 444-458
  residential signs, **1994** 289-297
  in satire, **1988** 175-182
  in student newspapers, **1988** 37-46
  use of school facilities by religious groups, **1993** 363-370
gay rights, **1995** 327-335; **1996** 284-295
grandparents' rights, **2000** 287-298
gun-free school zones, **1995** 183-200; **1999** 335
hate crimes
  cross-burning, **1992** 543-551
  racially motivated assault, **1993** 385-389
HIV infection, as a disability, **1998** 378-392
home video taping, **1984** 53-80
immigration act, Haitian refugees returned, **1993** 413-421
immunity of municipalities, **1980** 299-316
impeachment, Senate's authority to remove judge, **1993** 81-91
Internet pornography filters in public libraries, **2003** 387-400
Iranian claims, executive power to block, **1981** 559-573
Japanese-American and Aleut native wartime internment, **1983** 213-214
job discrimination
  adverse effect on minorities, **1989** 321-322, 325, 328
  against African Americans, **1993** 423-430
  proof of, **1989** 321-322, 324-329
judicial activism, **1981** 541
judicial immunity, **1978** 259-268

Supreme Court opinions *Continued*
- jury selection, **1994** 225-236
  - racially motivated, **1986** 409
- jury service for women, **1975** 55-66
- jury size and unanimous verdicts, **1979** 263-268
- jury trials, split verdicts in, **1972** 423-429
- justices, ages of, **1986** 560
- labor unions, freedom of members to resign, **1985** 415-429
- lawyer advertising, **1982** 65-71
- legislative intent, **1993** 249-258
- legislative redistricting, **1983** 599-616
  - one-man, one-vote rule, **1973** 277-289
  - political gerrymandering, **1986** 615-635
  - racial criteria for, **1977** 151-167
- legislative veto, **1983** 617-644
- liability, punitive damages, **1996** 274-283
- libel
  - appellate review of awards, **1984** 299-312
  - of private persons and burden of proof, **1986** 355-368
- libel from misquotation, **1991** 317-329
- liquor advertising, **1996** 771-772
- marijuana legalization for medical use, **2001** 325-330
- media ownership in same community, **1978** 419-432
- Meese criticism of, **1985** 653-668
- Meese on role of, **1985** 479-484, 488-489
- mental patients
  - confinement of, **1975** 469-480
  - standard of proof for involuntary commitment, **1979** 335-344
- mentally retarded, rights of, **1982** 521-530
- military draft, sex discrimination in, **1981** 521-540
- minority broadcasting, **1990** 419-435
- minority set-asides, **1980** 539-566; **1989** 323-324
- Miranda warnings, **1990** 785-793
  - interrogation definition, **1977** 219-235; **1980** 431-444
  - police interrogation after right to counsel invoked, **1981** 431, 433, 441-445
  - psychiatric interview, **1981** 431-433, 434-441
- NAACP boycott damages, **1982** 655-674
- Nixon tapes
  - custody of, **1977** 465-516
  - executive privilege for, **1974** 289, 302, 621-638; **1975** 665-666
  - release of, **1973** 859-863, 870-871, 878
- obscenity standards, **1973** 611-618; **1974** 515-522; **1987** 479-490
- offshore oil resources, federal control of, **1975** 167-175
- OSHA safety inspections, warrants for, **1978** 339-353
- parental leave
  - job reinstatement after, **1987** 17-27
  - seniority rights after, **1977** 871-881
- parental rights in child custody, **1982** 259-280
- passport revocation and national security, **1981** 541-555
- patenting of living organisms, **1980** 493-502
- patient-therapist privilege, **1996** 388-395
- Pentagon Papers publication, **1973** 537
- physician-assisted suicide, **1997** 459-479
- police use of deadly force, **1985** 303-315
- political asylum, **1987** 253-265
- political dismissals from public jobs, **1980** 259-271
- Powell's retirement, **1987** 577-581
- pregnancy coverage in company disability plans, **1976** 891-905
- presidential immunity, **1982** 539-559; **1997** 290-298
- presidential impoundment of appropriated funds, **1975** 135-140
- press
  - access to pretrial hearings, **1979** 511-533
  - attitudes toward Court rulings, **1979** 311-318
  - candidate's right of reply, **1974** 523-528
  - confidentiality of sources, **1972** 507-519
  - editorial process, protection of in libel suit, **1979** 285-311, 315-316
  - gag orders in criminal trials, **1976** 463-479
  - newsroom searches, **1978** 355-372
- preventive detention of felony suspects, **1987** 491-508
- prison crowding, **1981** 477-490
- prison inmates, beaten by guards, **1992** 175-185
- prisoner appeals, **1991** 205-218
- prisoners' rights, searches and visits, **1984** 479-491
- property rights
  - on coastal land, **1992** 615-620
  - developers and public land, **1994** 298-310
- property taking, for historic preservation, **1978** 453-465
- psychiatric aid, criminal indigents' right to, **1985** 207-219
- public use of audiotaped court cases, **1993** 935-937
- race-based redistricting, **1993** 459-481; **1995** 369-384
- racial barriers in state-supported universities, **1992** 575-587
- racial gerrymandering, **1996** 368-387
- racial integration
  - promoting by prohibiting "for sale" signs, **1977** 313-320
  - public housing in suburbs, **1976** 223-233
- railroad reorganization, **1975** 530
- religious clubs in public schools, **2001** 420-432
- religious symbols and publications, **1995** 385-404
- residential signs, **1995** 289-297
- right to counsel
  - pre-Miranda self-incrimination, **1974** 473-485
  - in trial for offense punishable by prison, **1979** 207-214
- right to die, **1990** 373-386
- role of
  - Brennan on, **1985** 656-661
  - study group on, **1972** 953-954
- school desegregation, **1979** 535-552; **1991** 23-33
  - court-ordered citywide busing, **1977** 447-457
  - court-ordered cross-district busing, **1974** 639-654
  - state restrictions on busing, **1982** 619-652
- school prayer, **1985** 379-395; **1992** 553-562
- school vouchers, **2002** 406-423
- searches
  - exclusionary rule and *habeas corpus* claims, **1976** 521-536
  - and home arrests without warrant, **1980** 281-297

secrecy of CIA sources, **1985** 333-344
seniority systems, and racial discrimination, **1977** 383-393
sentences, excessive prison, **1983** 659-674
sentencing
double jeopardy in prosecution's appeal, **1980** 977-988
guidelines, **2004** 358-374
murder case, **1991** 381-395
separation of powers, and Gramm-Rudman-Hollings, **1986** 705-730
sex discrimination
alimony payments to men, **1979** 193-206
in commercial organizations, **1984** 465-478
in educational programs, **1984** 201-214
harassment in workplace, **1993** 439-945
in pension plans, **1978** 293-306; **1983** 691-705
in Social Security survivors' benefits, **1975** 177-185; **1977** 169-181
sex offenders, confining, **1997** 382-394
sexual harassment, **1998** 438-465; **1999** 215-234
monetary relief for, **1992** 187-199
sodomy and privacy right, **1986** 601-614
state utility, federal regulation of, **1982** 447-467
states' rights, **1999** 333-356
statutory rape laws, sex discrimination in, **1981** 339-349
students' rights
and corporal punishment, **1977** 293-309
in disciplinary procedure, **1975** 67-80
free speech, **1986** 731-742
searches, **1985** 13-26
supremacy of federal law in tobacco cases, **1992** 563-573
suspects' rights and public safety, **1984** 387-397
tax increase for school desegregation, **1990** 227-238
televised trials, **1981** 163-176
Ten Commandments displays, **2005** 376-389
tenure review, **1990** 23-34
terrorism case detentions, **2004** 375-398
treaty termination power, **1979** 917-918, 920, 932-938
unitary taxation, **1983** 645-658
unreasonable searches, **2001** 407-419
vagrancy laws, **1972** 207-211
veterans' education benefits and alcoholism, **1988** 277-285
water export, state regulation of, **1982** 689-701
water pollution regulation, **1977** 131-141
welfare reform, double-tier benefits, **1999** 260-261
windfall profits tax on oil, **1983** 517-523
worker health protection, **1981** 491-505
workload of, **1972** 639-640, 642, 953-954; **1982** 705-727
and proposed appeals court, **1972** 953-959; **1975** 455-467
zoning regulations
for adult theaters, **1986** 131-144
barring public housing, **1976** 224-225; **1977** 35-44
Surgeon general
AIDS education, **1986** 889; **1987** 320
Elders resignation, **1994** 592-594; **1995** 61
Infant Health Objectives (1990), **1987** 149, 158-161, 164
mental health, **1999** 836-849; **2001** 575, 868
minority mental health, **2001** 575-592
nomination of Dr. Henry W. Foster, Jr., **1995** 61-68
nutrition and health report, **1990** 177; **1997** 167
obesity, **2001** 935-954; **2003** 480-491
oral health in America, **2000** 222-239
physical exercise, benefits of, **1996** 418-429
sexual health and responsible sexual behavior, **2001** 456-471
smoking
and cancer, **1982** 163-169
health consequences of, **1972** 45-54; **2004** 280-298
involuntary, **1986** 1079-1090
in Latin America, **1992** 267-275
low-tar cigarettes, and cancer, **1981** 3-12
nicotine addiction, **1988** 309-322
reports, history of, **1988** 310, 312, 318-319; **1989** 31-40
risks of, **1992** 565
by women, **1980** 17-26
and young people, **1994** 172-184
suicide prevention, **1999** 439-455; **2001** 290-303
tobacco reduction, **2000** 555-580
TV violence, **1972** 61-66
women and smoking, **2001** 222-244
Workshop on Violence and Public Health, **1992** 495
youth violence, **2001** 73-85
Suro, Roberto, Hispanic research studies, **2003** 349, 352
Surrogate motherhood
legality of contract, **1987** 373-387; **1988** 71-79
state laws prohibiting, **1988** 72-73
Vatican teaching on, **1987** 267-268, 279, 286
Surrogate Parenting, Center for, **1987** 376
Surrogate Parenting Practitioners, American Organization of, **1988** 73
Surveillance
domestic
by CIA, Rockefeller commission on, **1975** 401-402, 409, 426-427
FBI, for national security leaks, **1974** 488-495
government wiretaps
Democratic Party platform on, **1972** 529, 566
on dissident groups without warrant, **1972** 485-489
and rights of U.S. citizens, **1976** 237, 264-265
electronic
court-ordered aid by phone companies, **1977** 883-896
covert entry to install, with warrant, **1979** 269-284
by executive branch
political uses of FBI, **1973** 538-541, 544-545; **1975** 873-874, 876, 880-882
standards governing, **1975** 653-654, 680-681
for foreign intelligence, with warrant, **1976** 125-126, 129, 137
government wiretaps, attorney general's authorization procedure, **1974** 391-405

Surveillance *Continued*
for national security reasons
in Johnson administration, **1973** 738, 748
in Kennedy administration, **1973** 738, 748, 750-751
Nixon on, **1973** 566-567, 572
in Nixon White House, **1974** 449-450, 487-495; **1976** 159-168
of news media, by Nixon administration, **1973** 14
of Nixon's brother, **1973** 949, 959
by White House aides in Watergate break-in, **1974** 600-601, 608-610
Surveillance of terrorist suspects, **2002** 559, 561-564; **2005** 958-969
Survivors Network of Those Abused by Priests (SNAP), **2002** 870; **2004** 83, 86; **2005** 866
Suss, Herbert, **1974** 802-803
Susser, Asher, on Israeli Jewish state, **2004** 308
Sustainable Development, United Nations World Summit on, **2002** 593-604
Sutherland, John H., and King assassination, **1979** 595, 618-619
Sutherland, Thomas, hostage released, **1991** 752, 754-756
Sutton v. United Air Lines, **1999** 318, 320-325
Suzuki, Zenko, **1981** 591
Swain v. Alabama (1965), **1986** 409-433
Swann v. Charlotte-Mecklenburg Bd. of Education, **1972** 16; **1976** 413-414, 418-422; **1991** 29
SWAPO. *See* South West African People's Organization
Swartz, Mark H., Tyco International scandal, **2004** 422
Sweatshop Watch, **1997** 208
Sweden
aid to Nazi Germany, **1997** 259, 262, 263; **1998** 291, 292
allied relations and negotiations with, **1998** 304-307
assassination of UN representative (1948), **1983** 832
and Chernobyl nuclear accident, **1986** 383
EU membership, **2004** 197
farm-animal rights law, **1988** 347-351
liquidation of German assets, **1997** 267
at poverty summit, **1981** 770
Stockholm environment conference, **1972** 475
Swedish International Development Authority, on disaster relief, **1984** 974
Sweeney, John J.
AFL-CIO leader on labor split, **2005** 485, 487-488, 490-494
labor movement advances, **1999** 630-638
new AFL-CIO president, election remarks, **1995** 680-685
U.S.-China trade agreement opponent, **1999** 728
WTO talks in Seattle, **1999** 800
Swidler & Berlin v. United States, **1998** 393-404
Swift, Jane, birth of children while in office, **2001** 549
Swift and Co., United States v., **1991** 28
Swift Boat Veterans for Truth, **2004** 481
Swing, William Lacy, Congo UN peacekeeping mission, **2004** 508; **2005** 1030
Swinton, David, **1987** 44
Swiss Foundation for Solidarity, **1997** 259
Switzerland
aid to Nazi Germany, **1997** 257-272; **1998** 293-294
John Paul II visit, **1984** 399-406
military service in, **1988** 883
refugee policy, **1997** 264-265
student test scores, **1992** 91
Sylvester, Kathleen, working women, **2001** 548-549
Symbionese Liberation Army (SLA), Hearst kidnapping by, **1974** 247-253
Symington, Fife, and tax cuts, **1995** 43
Symms, Steve (R-Idaho)
bipartisan accord on Nicaraguan contras, **1989** 163
fire-management policy, **1988** 942
Genocide Convention, **1986** 116-117
Synar, Mike (D-Okla.)
antitobacco legislation, **1988** 310
budget reduction, **1985** 804
Synthetic fuels
development of
economic feasibility of, **1974** 910, 912
economic summit on, **1980** 503-504, 509
in Ford energy program, **1975** 17, 24, 103
Schlesinger on, **1979** 660, 665-666
government corporation on, in Carter energy program, **1979** 323, 568
Syracuse Peace Council, complaint with FCC, **1987** 626, 628
Syria
Arab-Israeli (October) War
cease-fire with Israel, **1973** 932
disengagement agreement with Israel, **1974** 435-439
Soviet supplies to, **1973** 883-884
Beirut hijacking negotiation, **1985** 464-465
British diplomatic break with, **1986** 832
chemical weapons stockpiles, **1993** 72
Egypt, breaking of diplomatic relations with, **1977** 829
French cooperation with to free hostages, **1986** 831, 833
on Golan Heights annexation by Israel, **1981** 788, 899-909
Hamas taking refuge in, **2003** 1202; **2004** 559
Hezbollah, support for, **2004** 558-559
Iran, support for, **1987** 869, 871
Islamic Jihad, **2003** 1202; **2004** 559
and Israel peace process, **1994** 329-330
Israel relations, **1999** 362; **2003** 1201-1203; **2004** 559
Israeli air strikes, **2003** 1201-1202
Israeli attack on guerrilla bases in, **1972** 751-753
Israeli-Lebanese conflict, role in, **1982** 742-744
Israeli-Lebanese security agreement, **1983** 471-473
Lebanon, troop withdrawal from, **2004** 557-563; **2005** 80, 271, 686, 688-689
Muslim Brotherhood, **2004** 558
oil embargo against U.S., objection to lifting, **1974** 221, 224
peace negotiations, U.S. role, **1995** 622-624
peace negotiations with Israel, **1999** 890-897
political reform, **2003** 961

on Sadat after Camp David accords, **1978** 607
Sinai accord between Egypt and Israel, **1975** 575
terrorism by, CIA on, **1981** 463, 465, 468-469
UN Oil for Food Program, **2004** 717
U.S. aid to, **1974** 278, 280-281, 436
U.S. diplomatic relations with, **1974** 449, 451, 462-464
U.S. economic sanctions, **1994** 330
U.S. relations, **2002** 717; **2004** 557-560; **2005** 80-81
Syria Accountability and Lebanese Sovereignty Restoration Act (2003), **2004** 558
Syverud, Kent, affirmative action case, **2003** 367-368
Szasz, Thomas, **1975** 470
Szilagyi, Jozsef, **1989** 341

T

Tadic, Boris
assassination attempt, **2004** 956
Kosovo independence, opposition to, **2005** 855-856
Serbia presidential candidate victory, **2004** 956
Tadzhikistan. *See also* Tajikistan
Alma-Ata Declaration, **1991** 804-806
Commonwealth Pact, **1991** 803-804
Soviet Union restructuring plans, **1991** 532-533
Taft, Robert, Jr. (R-Ohio), **1974** 813
Taft, Robert A., presidential nomination, **2000** 519
Taft, William Howard, press conferences of, **1988** 840
Taft-Hartley Act (1947), and coal miners' strike, **1978** 111-123
Taguba, Antonio M., Iraqi detainee abuse investigations, **2004** 208, 209-210, 217-234
Taguba Report, on Abu Ghraib prison abuse investigation, **2004** 217-234
Taha, Ali Osman Mohammed, Sudan peace talks, **2003** 838, 839; **2005** 520-521
Tahir, Buhari Sayed Abu, nuclear weapons-smuggling network, **2004** 328; **2005** 934
Tailhook scandal
court-martial decisions, **1994** 107-115
Defense Department report on, **1993** 315-325
sexual harassment, **1992** 190, 482-483; **2003** 791
Taiwan (Republic of China)
Chen presidential inauguration, **2000** 190-200; **2004** 258-267
China relations, **2000** 190-200; **2002** 856; **2003** 1173, 1180-1181; **2004** 937; **2005** 17, 622-623
Chinese sovereignty claims, **2005** 612
democratic political system, Bush comments on, **2005** 613
earthquake relief, **1999** 465, 467-468
elections, **2003** 1180; **2004** 262-263
expulsion from UN (1971), **1972** 183
Haiti diplomatic relations, **2005** 332
independence referendum, **2003** 1180-1181; **2004** 259, 261
Japan, lapsing of diplomatic relations with, **1972** 827-829
on Nixon trip to PRC, **1972** 183-184
one China policy, Clinton and Jiang on, **1997** 735, 738
and PRC constitution, **1975** 43; **1978** 158, 159
on PRC invasion of Vietnam, **1979** 185
pro-independence movement, **2004** 942-943; **2005** 622
Republican Party platform on, **1996** 544
reunification with China, **1984** 1047; **2005** 622-623
Shanghai communiqué on, **1972** 189-190
student test scores, **1992** 86-87, 91, 92, 94, 95
U.S. arms sales, **2001** 250-251, 739
U.S. diplomatic ties with, severing of, **1979** 135-137
U.S. mutual defense treaty, **1976** 733, 744-745
termination of, **1978** 781-783, 787; **1979** 917-938
U.S. recognition of, **2004** 258
U.S. relations with
arms sales, **1984** 23-24, 289-290
Republican Party platform on, **1972** 661; **1980** 643-645
U.S. support for, American Party platform on, **1972** 615, 622
U.S. withdrawal of recognition of, **1978** 781-787
and U.S.-PRC relations, **1973** 291-293, 297; **1978** 585; **1979** 672
Tajikistan. *See also* Tadzhikistan
debt relief program, **2005** 407
human trafficking, **2002** 350
U.S. base, **2005** 433
Takeovers, corporate. *See* Corporate takeovers
Takeshita, Ben, **1988** 290
Takeshita, Noboru, **1985** 624; **1988** 392
Takings clause. *See under* Constitutional amendments (U.S.), Fifth Amendment, property takings
Talabani, Jalal, Kurdish leader, **1996** 680; **2003** 946
Talalay, Paul, **1992** 277-281
Talbott, Strobe
Armenian negotiations, **1999** 640
European defense force, **1999** 819
Georgian parliamentary elections, **2003** 1040
Russian elections speech, **1996** 431, 432-437
Talent, Jim, **2002** 821
Taliaferro, Capt. Jeff, **1999** 53
Taliban regime
Pakistan relations, **2005** 473
in postwar Afghanistan, **2003** 1090-1092
refuge in Pakistan, **2002** 170
U.S. attacks on in Afghanistan, **2002** 20, 33; **2004** 23
Talley, J. Ernest, sex discrimination in hiring, **2001** 549-550
Tallgrass Prairie Reserve, ecological restoration of, **1993** 885-891
Talmadge, Herman E. (D-Ga.)
denouncing of by Senate, **1979** 623, 625, 631-636
on Panama Canal treaties, **1978** 179
Tambo, Oliver N.
ANC leader in exile, **1999** 299
illness of, **1990** 66
South Africa study group meeting with, **1986** 582, 588
Tamil Tigers (Liberation Tigers of Tamil Eelam)
cease-fire in Sri Lanka, **2002** 92-100
insurgency in Sri Lanka, **1987** 615-622
tsunami relief efforts, **2005** 996
unlawful support for, **2003** 612
Tamm, Edward A., on treaty termination, **1979** 919, 931

Tamposi, Elizabeth M., Clinton's passport search, **1992** 1046, 1049-1052
Tan, C. J., chess victory for IBM computer, **1997** 275
Tanaka, Kakuei
diplomatic relations with PRC, **1972** 827-830
Ford meeting with in Japan, **1974** 955-956, 962-965
Nixon meetings with, **1972** 745-749; **1973** 717-722
Tanaka, Kenneth L., water on Mars, reaction to possibility of, **2000** 381
Taney, Roger B., **1989** 107
Tang, Kainan, **1993** 271
Tang Jiaxuan
American spy plane incident, **2001** 248, 249
U.S. bombing of Chinese embassy, **1999** 305-306, 307
war on terrorism, **2001** 626
Tanner, Michael, retirement fund savings, **2002** 104
Tanweer, Shahzad, London terrorist bombing suspect, **2005** 396, 474
Tanzania
Burundi peace negotiations, **2003** 924
Burundi refugees in, **1999** 435
criticism of Rhodesian settlement plan, **1976** 721-722, 728-729
economic sanctions against Rhodesia, lifting of, **1979** 941
embassy bombings, **1998** 555-563; **1999** 53, 524, 690; **2000** 277, 278; **2001** 3, 617, 688; **2003** 841; **2004** 520
at poverty summit, **1981** 770
rejection of Rhodesian internal agreement, **1978** 150
tsunami relief effort, **2005** 1005
U.S. consultation with on Zimbabwe-Rhodesia, **1976** 292
Taraki, Nur Mohammad, **1980** 190
Tariffs. *See* Trade barriers, tariff reduction
Tarleton, Donald G., in Lance investigation, **1977** 626, 652-655
Tarr, Curtis W., **1972** 247
Tashjian v. Republican Party of Connecticut, **1986** 1065-1073
Task Force Report on Greater CIA Openness, **1992** 4, 5-10
Tass, on espionage at UN, **1986** 268-269
Tatel, David S., September 11 detainees' names secret, **2003** 316
Tatum, Wilbert A., on criminal justice system, **1995** 611-612
Taubman, Philip, **1986** 386
Tax credits
for domestic oil exploration, **1973** 466, 477
earned income, for low-income families, **1976** 39; **1977** 59, 553-554, 556, 558, 560-561; **1979** 391, 394
to employers hiring CETA workers, **1978** 242, 244, 246, 250
for residential energy conservation, **1974** 910, 915; **1975** 104
in Carter energy plan, **1977** 279, 284, 286, 288, 291
tuition
constitutionality of, **1973** 642-643, 648-649, 654; **1983** 675-687
Joint Committee on Taxation on, **1983** 678
Moral Majority on, **1983** 818
Nixon support for, **1973** 304, 310, 641
Reagan on, **1983** 78, 85, 109, 111
Republican Party platform on, **1980** 584-585
for urban business, **1978** 252
Tax cuts
business
in Carter budget, **1978** 95, 97, 98
to create jobs, **1976** 13-14, 19, 30, 697
as investment incentive, **1978** 8, 13, 20; **1979** 217
Carter administration position on, **1976** 849; **1980** 112, 216
corporate
Carter on, **1976** 696, 699
CBO analysis of, **1976** 188-189
Ford economic report on, **1977** 65, 67-70, 76-79
Ford on, **1975** 88
as investment incentive, in Ford budget, **1976** 39, 41
as economic stimulus, **1999** 93-94
impact on economy
Ford CEA on, **1976** 52
Reagan on, **1983** 104-106; **1989** 3, 5, 9, 16, 19-20
impact on federal revenues, CBO on, **1982** 191-192, 194
impact on inflation, Reagan-Anderson debate on, **1980** 848, 850-852, 861-864
impact on social programs, **1983** 768-769
individual
Carter plan for, **1977** 107-108; **1978** 8, 12, 20, 95, 97-98
CBO analysis of, **1976** 188-189
to end recession, **1976** 13, 18-19, 49
in Ford budget, **1976** 39, 41; **1977** 57-58, 61
Ford CEA on, **1977** 65, 68-70, 76-79
in Ford program, **1975** 16, 20, 25, 30, 33
to stimulate economy, **1975** 84, 87-89, 102-104, 109
Kemp-Roth proposal, Democrats' attack on, **1980** 772, 781, 785-786, 788
law signed by Reagan, **1981** 639-646
legislation, **1999** 352
for lower- and middle-income persons, Democratic plan for, **1975** 17, 33
and "marriage penalty" issue, **2000** 17, 18, 25
paying for, Ford on, **1976** 698, 706
phased-in, three-year proposal of Reagan, **1980** 848, 851-852
plan for, Democrats on Joint Economic Committee, **1981** 295-297, 302-304
postponement of by Carter, **1978** 688-689, 693; **1979** 96-97, 110
Reagan proposal, **1980** 920, 926, 928; **1981** 213-214, 220-221, 294, 325, 327, 639-642
effects of (CEA report), **1984** 134-136
Republican Party platform on, **1976** 649-650; **1980** 567-568, 573-574
to stimulate economy, **1975** 15-17, 20, 25, 30, 33
Carter plan for, **1978** 65-67, 70, 72-74
congressional proposal, **1980** 209-210, 216, 219-223

Reagan on, **1980** 652, 659-660
supply-side
Carter CEA warning on, **1981** 105-106, 133-134, 214
in Reagan economic plan, **1981** 214, 639-640, 642
Republicans on Joint Economic Committee on, **1981** 294, 299, 313, 321
targeted, Democratic Party platform on, **1980** 712, 718
Thatcher government on, **1979** 379, 382, 384
Tax evasion, charges against Agnew, **1973** 827-836
Tax increases
Bentsen-Quayle debate on, **1988** 800, 803-804
Bush on in acceptance speech, **1984** 741-742
Bush pledge on, **1988** 610; **1989** 43, 73
Bush-Dukakis debate on, **1988** 756-758, 769-770
corporate, in McGovern's economic program, **1972** 737, 740
Mondale on, **1984** 653, 661-662
Mondale-Reagan debate on, **1984** 846, 849-852, 865-866
to pay for Democratic programs, Nixon on, **1972** 711, 719-720
Reagan on, **1984** 732-733; **1986** 39-40, 43, 50, 53
rejection of for wage earners, in McGovern's economic program, **1972** 737, 740
Republican Party platform on, **1984** 661-662; **1988** 615-616, 623-626
Tax reform
See also Capital gains taxes; Tax cuts
Alternative Minimum Tax (AMT), **2005** 123
behavioral effects of, **1988** 129-130; **1989** 9
and blacks in U.S., **1987** 44, 52-55
Bush proposals for tax cuts, **2005** 78
Bush Tax Code reform, bipartisan panel on, **2005** 83, 143
Bush tax relief plan, **2001** 54, 171, 400-406, 666; **2002** 43; **2003** 23-24, 25-26, 69-70; **2004** 19-20
Carter support for, **1976** 597, 601, 711-713; **1977** 110; **1978** 67, 70, 98
child tax credit, **1998** 90; **2004** 20, 26
comptroller general report on, **2005** 134-135
and corporate accountability, Darman on, **1986** 972-981
and deficit reduction, **1996** 67
Democratic Party platform on, **1972** 535-537; **1976** 545, 553-554; **1980** 712, 718, 745-746; **1984** 555, 566-567; **1996** 628-629; **2000** 613
Democratic tax relief plan, **2003** 37
Dole-Mondale debate on, **1976** 782-784, 792
Earned Income Tax Credit (EITC), **1993** 183-184; **1994** 145; **1995** 78; **1996** 28
Ford pledge to accomplish, **1976** 672
and human needs, Urban League on, **1985** 29, 35-36
incentive-based policy of Reagan, **1982** 126, 143, 148-149
inflation relief for individuals and industries, domestic summit on, **1974** 861-863, 865, 871, 873, 879
interest rates and, **2003** 88-90
in McGovern's economic program, **1972** 595, 737-742
Nixon proposals on, **1973** 224; **1974** 43, 53, 57, 96, 102
Perot Reform Party nomination speech on, **1996** 558-559
of rates, Ford on, **1976** 701, 713
Reagan on need for simplified system, **1983** 79, 84; **1984** 82, 88; **1985** 39, 43-44, 105-106, 110
Reagan on progress in, **1983** 105; **1985** 74-76; **1986** 65-67
Reagan proposals on, **1984** 101, 106, 119, 125-126; **1985** 86
Republican Party platform on, **1972** 669-670; **1976** 623, 650; **1984** 667-669; **1992** 819-821; **1996** 503-505; **2000** 512
stock dividend tax, proposal to eliminate, **2003** 70
tax cuts
and budget deficit, **2004** 236; **2005** 122
as economic stimulus for long-term growth, **2002** 36-37; **2003** 69-70, 442, 752; **2004** 68-69
legislation, **2002** 53; **2004** 68-69
and "marriage penalty" issue, **2004** 20, 26
rebate checks, **2003** 85-86
U.S. Catholic bishops on need for, **1986** 992, 1001, 1005, 1010
Tax Reform Act (1986), **1987** 121, 125-126, 131, 134-135
Bush on, **1990** 85, 89
Reagan and CEA on, **1987** 121, 124-126, 133-135
Taxes
See also Capital gains taxes; Gasoline tax; Investment, business capital, tax incentives for
bankruptcy filing of Bridgeport (Conn.), **1991** 304, 306
Bush on tax increases, **1990** 409-417
corporate
Carter on unfairness of, **1976** 712
loopholes in, Democrats on Ford economic plan, **1975** 17-18, 33
delinquent
civil penalties imposed by IRS, **1975** 844-848
IRS procedures for collection of, **1975** 829, 836-844
exemptions
for discriminatory schools, **1983** 489-505
for medical care, **1983** 319, 334
income bracket rise due to inflation, **1977** 732
individual returns, executive branch access to, **1975** 829-830, 849-857
payroll, as income for Social Security system, **1975** 115-119, 121-122
presidential authority to vary rates, OECD recommendation, **1973** 684, 693-694
property
and equalizing school spending, **1972** 537, 562
and local government needs, **1972** 551-552
passage of Proposition 13 in California, **1978** 397-402
public school financing based on, **1972** 74, 106-107, 221, 232, 676; **1973** 361-377
standard deduction increase, **1977** 104, 108, 110, 127, 129
stand-by limited, Reagan support for, **1983** 78, 83-84, 103, 109

Taxes *Continued*
tax policy, **1991** 833-834
TIP incentives proposed by Carter, **1981** 62, 105-106, 112-113, 131-133
unitary taxation by states, **1983** 645-658
value-added, for federal aid to schools, **1972** 221, 232
windfall profits on oil
Carter proposal, **1979** 258, 319-329, 332-333, 568, 570-571, 577
constitutionality of, **1983** 517-523
Ford CEA on, **1975** 103, 111
Nixon proposal, **1974** 42, 47, 54, 81, 96, 101, 104
Republican Party platform on, **1984** 662
Taxman, Sharon, affirmative action case, **1997** 185
Taxpayer Relief Act (1997), **1998** 90
Tayara, Adnan Wajih, **1974** 436
Taylor, Bruce, Internet pornography filters, **2003** 390
Taylor, Charles
exile in Nigeria, **2003** 770, 771; **2005** 800-801
jailing of "illegal combatants," **2002** 560
Liberia civil war, **2002** 251; **2003** 767
Liberian president's relations with Congo, **2000** 1072-1075
ousted/resigned from presidency, **2003** 767, 769-771
war crimes, **2005** 803-804
Taylor, Gene (D-Miss.), on vote for Speaker of the House, **1995** 3
Taylor, John B.
CEA member, **1990** 82; **1992** 99
economic crisis in Argentina, **2002** 80-91
national energy policy, **2001** 337
Taylor, Maxwell, **1985** 161
Taylor, Michael R.
ground beef ban, **1994** 404
meat safety inspections, **1996** 415
Taylor, Myron D., **1984** 20
Taylor, Richard E., Nobel in physics, **1990** 796
Taylor, William M., **1989** 335
Taylor v. Louisiana, **1975** 55-66
Taylor-Kamara, Ahmed Mohammed, **1989** 154
Teachers
assaults on, in U.S. public schools, **1975** 207, 211-213, 219
certification of, **1986** 458-459, 468-472, 804, 806, 815
effectiveness of, **1986** 222-232
expectations for urban students, **1988** 196, 200-201
merit pay for, **1986** 805; **1988** 299, 301
pay and working conditions of, **1986** 458, 465-469; **1988** 202, 212-213
quality initiative, **1999** 64-71; **2000** 23
relieving of nonteaching duties, **1987** 692-693, 695-696
shortages of, **1986** 815; **1999** 64-65
tenure decision, Supreme Court on, **1990** 23-34
testing of, **1998** 57
training of
emphasis on subject knowledge, **1987** 683, 692-695, 696
in teaching about religion, **1987** 604-606, 608
Teaching
preparation for, **1986** 458-476
research vs., **1988** 517, 520-522
in science, quality and quantity of, **1988** 378-379, 385-390
in undergraduate colleges, **1986** 941, 944, 951-953
upgrading of profession, **1983** 414, 428-429
Teamsters, International Brotherhood of
AFL-CIO split, **2005** 488
corruption in, **1986** 180, 206-207
labor contracts of bankrupt companies, **1984** 181, 184-199
organization of farm workers, **1975** 377-379
Teamsters, International Brotherhood of v. National Labor Relations Board, **1984** 181-199
Teamsters Union, UPS strike, **1997** 628-635
Technology. *See* Military technology; Science and technology
Technology and Literacy Challenge initiative, **1997** 65
Technology transfer
ban on exports for Soviet pipeline, **1981** 884; **1982** 879-884
China from Western nations, **1984** 25
China's role in, **1998** 467, 976-982
to developing countries
Kissinger proposal, **1975** 589, 594-595; **1976** 300-301, 304-307, 311-312
processing of own commodities, **1975** 326, 331
UN resolution on, **1975** 608-609
and export controls, **1987** 29-42
and government-supported scientific research, **1982** 813-819
to Soviet bloc, Republican Party platform on, **1980** 636-637; **1984** 724-725
Soviet espionage program, **1985** 603-614
Teenagers
See also Youth
adult attitudes toward, **1997** 422-443
antidepressant drugs and risk of suicide in, **2004** 746-752
antismoking campaigns, **2004** 281-282
drinking, CASA study on, **2002** 175-176, 178
murder rate, **1999** 615
pregnancy
abstinence as prevention of, **1986** 1060
among African Americans, **1985** 28-29, 35-36
declining, **1999** 384, 385-386
Democratic Party platform, **1996** 638-639
and low birth weight and infant mortality, **1987** 148, 150-151, 153, 156-158
National Center for Health Statistics report on, **1998** 260-267
and parental notification of birth control use, **1983** 269, 272
and poverty, **1983** 47, 53
prevention programs, **1995** 61, 65-67
recommendations for action against, **1986** 1057-1064
school drop-out rate and, **1992** 149
sports participation and prevention of, **1997** 170
and statutory rape law, **1981** 340-343, 346-347
student newspaper discussion of, **1988** 37-41, 44-46

smoking, **1997** 332, 335, 336; **1998** 47, 89, 845-846; **1999** 49, 384
substance abuse, CASA study on attitudes toward, **2002** 177-178
Teitelbaum, Michael S., **1986** 965-966
Teixeira, Paulo, AIDS drug treatment plan ("3 by 5" plan), **2003** 785
Tejada, Miguel, steroid use in baseball, **2005** 216
Tejeda, Frank (D-Texas), death of, **1997** 43, 44
Tekoah, Yosef, **1974** 920
Tela declaration, on demobilization and repatriation of Nicaraguan contras, **1989** 161-162, 168-172
Telecommunications
access to electronic services, **1999** 368-383
AT&T deregulation, **1982** 17-33
cable TV, FCC rules on, **1972** 137
Democratic Party platform commitment to, **1984** 578-579
E-rate program, **1999** 371; **2000** 48
industry, and Meese ethics investigation, **1988** 496-497, 505-506
industry mergers, **1998** 339, 340-341
technology, and public broadcasting, **1979** 125, 129
telephone penetration, **1999** 373-374
Telecommunications Act (1996), **1999** 371; **2002** 69, 287; **2003** 387; **2004** 63
Telecommunications Policy, White House Office of, FCC rules on cable TV, **1972** 137
Telegraph companies, cooperation in U.S. government cable interception, **1975** 799-803
Telescopes. *See* Hubble space telescope
Television broadcasting
See also Broadcasting
cable TV
city regulation of, **1982** 35-49
FCC rules on, **1972** 137-142
as catalyst in Egyptian-Israeli peace initiative, **1977** 828
CBS documentary on Vietnam, Westmoreland suit, **1983** 401-412; **1985** 159-165
docudrama on nuclear war, **1983** 859
family values and "Murphy Brown" controversy, **1992** 443-452
and humanities in U.S., **1988** 518, 523-525
marketing violent entertainment to children, **2000** 729-739
network coverage of Watergate, **1973** 897-899, 903-909
network decline in news programming, **1973** 57
program rating system, **2000** 27-28
public
government control of content, **1973** 58
proposed reorganization of, **1979** 119-121, 124-131, 133-134
rating system, **1996** 831-837; **1997** 527-533
station license renewal, proposed changes in, **1973** 55-62
tobacco advertising on, **1972** 46; **1973** 64
trials on, fairness of, **1981** 163-176
U.S. Arab language station (Al Hurra), **2005** 581
V-chips for blocking programs, **1997** 527, 529
viewing, student test scores and, **1992** 87, 92, 94, 95
violence on
effect on social behavior, **1972** 61-66
link to aggressive behavior, **1982** 365-383
network agreement on parent advisory, **1993** 487-492
Television Violence Act (1990), **1993** 488
Tellico Dam, project halted by endangered species, **1978** 433-452
Temple, Robert, on risk of suicide, **2004** 748
Temporary Assistance to Needy Families (TANF), **1996** 452; **1997** 618; **1998** 354, 357, 358, 362, 363; **1999** 258, 261-271; **2001** 134
Temporary worker program/temporary visas (T visas), **2004** 20, 27, 124-125
Tenet, George J.
Afghanistan detainees interrogations, **2004** 339
bin Laden and al Qaeda terrorist network, **2002** 1017; **2003** 550, 886
Chinese nuclear-espionage matter, **1999** 238
CIA director
appointment, **2001** 97
resignation, **2004** 711, 965
CIA intelligence gathering, congressional panel investigations, **2002** 992, 995; **2003** 546, 550, 552
Hanssen espionage investigation, **2001** 157
Iraq War, prewar intelligence gathering, **2003** 883, 886
Iraq weapons of mass destruction intelligence, **2003** 45, 137, 882; **2004** 711, 712, 718
Iraq-Niger uranium sales allegations, **2003** 20-21, 876; **2005** 700
Middle East peace talks, **2001** 366
missile threat to U.S., **1998** 483
Russia-U.S. relations, **2001** 892
terrorist threat assessments, **2002** 741-742; **2003** 1051; **2004** 269, 456, 537-538
terrorist "Tip-off" watch list, **2003** 157
Teng Hsiao-ping. *See* Deng Xiaoping
Tennard v. Dretke, **2004** 796-797
Tennessee
See also Memphis (Tennessee)
welfare reform, **1999** 258
Tennessee v. Blumstein, **1972** 283-290
Tennessee v. Garner, **1985** 303-315
Tennessee Valley Authority (TVA)
dam project halted by endangered species, **1978** 433-452
programs of, **1978** 387, 389
Tennessee Valley Authority v. Hill, **1978** 433-452
Tenney, Charles, **1977** 884
Tereby, Susan, **1998** 115
TerHorst, Jerald F., **1974** 814
Term limits
California state legislature, federal appeals court on, **1997** 886-891
congressional, **1995** 259-275; **1996** 696-697
Terminally ill patients
See also Bioethics; Death and dying; End-of-life care; Physician-assisted suicide
physicians' responsibility toward, **1984** 275-285
Ter-Petrosian, Levon, **1999** 641
TerriPAC, **2005** 159

Terrorism
See also Counterterrorism; Oklahoma City bombing incident; September 11 (9/11) terrorist attacks; War on terrorism; World Trade Center bombing
agroterrorism, **2002** 582-583
air hijacking, industrialized countries' cooperation in combating, **1978** 533, 535, 541-542; **1981** 594-595
antiterrorism. *See* Counterterrorism
antiterrorism bill, **1995** 178-179; **1996** 231-236
in Argentina, **1977** 5-7; **1984** 789-793
aviation safety report and, **1990** 301-310
aviation security requirements, **1996** 666-667
bargaining with terrorists, in Iran-contra scandal, **1987** 106, 109
biological or chemical weapons threat, **1999** 502, 503; **2000** 278, 281-282, 285
bioterrorism
anthrax mailings in U.S., **2001** 3, 615, 672, 674-676; **2004** 442-443
preparations against, GAO report on, **2001** 672-685
Project BioShield, **2003** 30; **2004** 442-449
ricin discovery, Senate Office Building, **2004** 268, 442-443
bombings, **1997** 714; **2005** 393
Afghanistan
of humanitarian workers, **2003** 1091
post U.S.-led invasion, **2003** 1053
African embassies in Kenya and Tanzania, **1998** 555-563; **1999** 53, 524, 690; **2000** 277, 278; **2001** 3, 617, 688; **2003** 453, 841; **2004** 520
Argentina, Israeli embassy in Buenos Aires, **2003** 829
Berlin disco, **2004** 172
Chechen rebels. *See* Chechen rebels
Colombia, car bombing at nightclub in Bogota, **2003** 426
Egypt, Red Sea resorts, **2004** 535, 812; **2005** 165, 168, 399
Indonesia, Bali resorts and Jakarta, **2002** 702-712, 1014, 1016; **2003** 1052; **2004** 754-756; **2005** 399-400
Iraq
postwar attacks, **2003** 939-943, 1052
UN headquarters in Baghdad, **2003** 109, 614, 808-809, 939, 1091
Israel
suicide bombings by Islamic Jihad, **2005** 29, 31
U.S. diplomatic convoy in Gaza Strip, **2003** 1202-1203
Japan, Tokyo subway (Aum Shinrikyo group), **1999** 502, 503; **2000** 278, 282
Jerusalem, by Palestinian militants, **2004** 302
Jordan, hotels in Amman, **2005** 400-401
Kenya hotel bombing, **2002** 1014-1015, 1046; **2003** 453
Lebanon, **1998** 555-556; **2001** 3
Lockerbie Pan Am flight 103, **2003** 1218, 1223-1224; **2004** 171
London subway and bus systems, **2005** 393-404
Los Angeles International Airport attempt, **2001** 804
Middle East
Hamas suicide bombings, **2001** 363-365, 367; **2002** 927, 929-931, 933; **2003** 191, 192, 195, 196
Palestinian *Intifada*, **2002** 927, 929-931
Morocco, in Casablanca, **2003** 1052
Niger, French airliner (1989), **2004** 171
Northern Ireland, **1998** 206
Olympic Park bombing, **1996** 445-449
Pakistan, in Islamabad and Karachi, **2002** 166-167
Pakistani guerrilla groups, **2002** 326-327; **2003** 210-211, 212
Russia
by Chechen rebels, **2003** 249-250; **2004** 565-566
Moscow subway, **2004** 565
Russian airliners, **2004** 566
in Saudi Arabia, **1996** 672-679
bombings in Riyadh (2003), **2003** 227-244, 1052
Khobar Towers apartment complex (1996), **2000** 280, 861; **2001** 3, 796-797, 807
Spain, in Madrid linked to al Qaeda, **2004** 105-114, 137, 268, 535, 540; **2005** 393
Sri Lankan Tamil Tigers suicide bombings, **2002** 93
Turkey, bombings linked to al Qaeda, **2003** 1052-1053
USS *Cole* (Aden, Yemen), **2000** 27, 861-865; **2001** 3-16
Uzbekistan, suicide bombings in Tashkent, **2005** 429
World Trade Center (New York City, 1993), **1999** 502; **2000** 278; **2001** 804
border arrests of potential terrorists, **1999** 499, 763
border security
arrests of potential terrorists, **2003** 38
radiation detectors, **2003** 221-222
tracking foreign visitors, **2003** 218-226
visa application process, **2003** 218, 219, 222-223
watch list consolidation, **2003** 155-172, 221
confronting an "axis of evil," Bush on, **2002** 33-34, 40-41, 612, 614, 635, 714; **2003** 19, 875, 1025, 1219
control of
as human rights issue, **1981** 179, 462
international cooperation, **1973** 519, 523
counterfeit documents/identification, **2003** 219-220, 223-226
countering, **1997** 351; **1999** 502-503
presidential debates on, **1980** 932-936; **1984** 885-886
counterterrorism. *See* Counterterrorism
cyberterrorism (computer security), **2002** 746
definition of, **2004** 889
and drug trafficking, **1986** 181, 187-189
FBI antiterrorism guidelines, **2000** 279
foreign student surveillance in U.S., **2000** 280-282
GAO report, **1997** 711
groups networking with organized crime, **2000** 1051
hostages
Afghanistan, UN election workers, **2004** 917

Americans in Iran, **2003** 1033
in Russian school in Beslan, by Chechen rebels, **2004** 535, 564-576; **2005** 299, 300, 303
in Russian theater in Moscow, by Chechen rebels, **2002** 763-773
industrialized countries' cooperation on, **1984** 357, 363-364; **1986** 437-439, 443-444; **1987** 525-530
Iranian support of, **1979** 867-871, 877-881; **2001** 796-797
John Paul II on, **1986** 640, 643-645
kidnapping of Hearst by SLA, **1974** 247-253
Libya as "state sponsor" of major attacks, **2004** 171-173
Libyan support for, **1986** 348-350
major attacks
in 2003, **2003** 1051-1053
in 2004, **2004** 534-536
military response to
Bush administration plans for, **1989** 317, 320
hostage rescue attempt, **1980** 351, 353, 357-358
Shultz on, **1984** 933-935, 940-944
in Northern Ireland conflict
British power-sharing plan, **1973** 353-354, 356, 359
by IRA, **1981** 463, 471
Oklahoma City bombing, prayer service for, **1995** 176-182, 183
in Palestinian struggle
Arafat on at UN, **1974** 919-920, 924-925, 930-931, 934-937
Israeli hostages at Entebbe, **1976** 517-520
PLO renunciation of, **1988** 905-911
Pan America Flight 103 (Lockerbie, Scotland), **1995** 176
Paris bombings, security measures to combat, **1986** 829-838
prevention of
NSA monitoring of cable traffic, **1975** 711
U.S.-sponsored resolution and draft treaty on, **1972** 752, 756-763
Republican Party platform on, **1980** 571, 634; **1984** 711, 716, 725; **1988** 617, 687-688
retaliation for
Reagan on, **1985** 464, 466-469, 473-477
U.S. air strike against Libya, **1986** 347-354
Soviet view of, Gorbachev on, **1986** 146-147, 166-167
by Soviets, CIA on, **1981** 462, 467
spread of, **1981** 862; **1985** 463-473
CIA on, **1981** 461-475
UN condemnation of, **1972** 751-752
state-supported, Gromyko on, **1984** 828-829
Syrian, Begin on, **1981** 904
threat levels, **2005** 896-897
threats
during presidential campaign, **2004** 270-272
financial centers on alert, **2004** 268, 270-271, 538
Hart-Rudman task force report, **2002** 740-763
National Intelligence Council forecasts, **2005** 15-16
news conference on, **2004** 268-279
possible scenarios, National Intelligence Council report on, **2005** 15-16, 24-25
prevention efforts, **2004** 142
U.S. financial centers, **2004** 268
threats in the next century, **1999** 499-510; **2000** 277-286
UN monitoring of al Qaeda and related terrorist networks, **2004** 534-547
Unabomber manifesto on society's ills, **1995** 600-610
Unabomber sentencing memorandum, **1998** 233-252
U.S. air strikes against terrorists, **1998** 586-591
U.S. policy on
and Iran-contra affair, **1986** 1013-1024; **1987** 206, 208-209, 219-221
Soviet propaganda on, **1981** 754, 760
war on terrorism
Bush plans for, **2001** 637-649; **2002** 41-42
costs of, **2002** 41
and weapons of mass destruction, **1996** 223-224
World Trade Center Building (New York City), **1995** 176
Terrorism, National Commission on, **2000** 277-286; **2001** 765
Terrorism Information and Prevention System (TIPS), **2002** 564; **2003** 613
Terrorist Attacks Upon the United States, U.S. National Commission on. *See* National Commission on Terrorist Attacks Upon the United States
Terrorist organizations
See also al Qaeda terrorist network; Hamas (Islamic resistance movement)
Abu Sayyaf (Father of the Sword) guerillas, **2001** 105-106; **2004** 536
al Aksa Martyrs Brigade (Palestinian), **2002** 370; **2003** 196, 1053
Ansar al-Islam (Islamic group), **2004** 539
Arum Shinrikyo (Japanese), **1999** 502, 503; **2000** 278, 282
al Fatah (Palestinian), **2002** 370, 372, 1040, 1045; **2004** 807
al-Haramain Islamic Foundation (HIF), **2003** 231, 1058; **2004** 520-521, 522-533
Hezbollah (Shi'ite militant group), **2001** 796-797, 807; **2003** 159, 942; **2004** 558-559
Hizb-ut-Tahrir, Andijon killings, **2005** 429-431
Islamic Jihad, **2001** 363-365; **2002** 930, 933; **2003** 196, 841, 1202; **2004** 559, 809; **2005** 29
Jaish-e-Muhammad (Pakistan), **2002** 166, 167, 326; **2003** 210, 212
Jemaah Islamiyah (Southeast Asia), **2002** 705-706; **2003** 1052; **2004** 539, 754-755, 756
Lashkar-e-Jhangvi (Kashmiri guerrillas), **2002** 167
Lashkar-e-Taiaba (Kashmiri guerrillas), **2002** 326; **2003** 210, 212; **2004** 539
al Qaeda and Islamic terrorists in Pankisi Valley (Georgia), **2003** 1045
Salafist Group for Call and Combat (GSCP), **2004** 539
Tamil Tigers (Sri Lanka), **1987** 615-622; **2002** 93
Xinjian terrorists in China, **2001** 740
Terrorist Threat Integration Center (TTIC)
creation of, **2003** 30, 156-157
Terrorist Screening Center, **2003** 155, 157-158
Terrorists
See also Abu Ghraib prison abuse scandal; Guantanamo Bay detainees

Terrorists *Continued*
convictions thrown out, **2004** 273
detentions of terrorism suspects
secret detentions, **2004** 339; **2005** 582
Supreme Court on, **2004** 375-398
U.S. court of appeals rulings on, **2003** 105-120
financing, **2003** 1057-1058; **2004** 540
in Saudi Arabia, **2004** 522-533
Foreign Terrorist Tracking Task Force, **2001** 765-766, 768
foreign visitors, tracking in U.S., **2003** 218-226
interrogations
abuses of detainees, **2005** 913-914
Bush administration policy, **2004** 212-213, 336-337
DOD policy directive, **2005** 910
FBI reports on, **2004** 380-381
"renditions" or transfers of detainees to foreign security services, **2004** 339; **2005** 906
use of torture
Justice Department legal memorandum, **2004** 207, 336-347, 375, 778; **2005** 906
McCain amendment on treatment of detainees, **2005** 80, 909-910
Rice statements on U.S. policy, **2003** 905-918
UN convention against torture, **2004** 338, 340; **2005** 582, 908
Uzbek security torture of detainees, **2005** 429
training camps, **2002** 40
watch lists
CIA lists, **2003** 158, 566-567
FBI consolidation, **2005** 157-158, 897-898
GAO report on, **2003** 155-172
"no-fly" lists; **2003** 157-158; **2004** 145; **2005** 898
Terry, Luther L., smoking report (1964), **1988** 310; **1989** 31-34
Terry, Randall, Schiavo end-of-life care case, **2005** 158
Terzi, Zehdi Labib, **1979** 647-657
Tesoro Beach accords (1989), **1989** 162
Texaco, Inc.
antitrust probe of Aramco, **1983** 921-922
racial slurs by executives, **1996** 764-769
Texans for a Republican Majority (TRMPAC), campaign contributions, **2005** 632-634
Texas
abortion restrictions, **1973** 101-111
bank failures, **1988** 914-915, 917
bird flu outbreak, **2004** 924
death penalty, **2004** 795-797; **2005** 181-182
death penalty executions, **2005** 178, 179
education for children of illegal aliens, **1982** 489-506
public school financing, **1973** 361-377
redistricting controversy, **2005** 632, 634-635
Texas v. Johnson, **1989** 343-354; **1990** 358, 359, 360, 362, 363-365; **1992** 546
Texas & New Orleans R. Co. v. Railway & Steamship Clerks, **1992** 193
Texas & Pacific R. Co. v. Rigsby, **1992** 193
Texas A & M University, Bush speech on changes in Soviet Union, **1989** 175-176, 179-181
Texas Dept. of Community Affairs v. Burdine, **1993** 425, 426, 427, 429-430
Textbook Publishers' Association, **1987** 599
Textbooks
coverage of religion's influence, **1987** 597-608
creation science in California textbooks, **1972** 843-844
for humanities education, **1987** 688-691, 696
multicultural, **1991** 31-347
sex discrimination in, **1974** 507
Textile industry
effect of OSHA regulations on industry, **1981** 492
EU Chinese textile import quotas, **2005** 617
exports of, U.S.-PRC agreement on, **1980** 829, 832, 844-845
labor union and, **1999** 632
restriction of foreign imports, **1988** 339, 341, 344-346
U.S. footwear and textile industries, **1988** 339-341, 344-346
Thaci, Hashim
Kosovo conflict, **1999** 288; **2000** 145
Kosovo elections, **2001** 822
Thagard, Norman, **1995** 419-425
Thailand
bird flu outbreak, **2004** 924-925
financial crisis, **1997** 833-834, 838; **1998** 722, 723
IMF aid package, **1997** 836
John Paul II visit, **1984** 327-329, 334-338
opium growing in, **1972** 646-649
SARS (severe acute respiratory syndrome) outbreak, **2003** 132
sex trade in children, **2001** 956; **2004** 126
tsunami disaster, **2004** 995
tsunami relief effort, **2005** 1004-1005
unemployment, **1998** 726
Thatcher, Margaret, **1985** 709
on Blunt as Soviet spy, **1979** 905-914
EC, British contribution to, **1984** 439-441
economic summits, **1980** 504; **1981** 591; **1984** 357-358; **1986** 438; **1987** 525; **1988** 392-393
election to prime minister, **1979** 379-387
EU "rebate" for Britain, **2005** 343
Falklands War, **1982** 284-287, 292-303; **1983** 3-23
on German reunification, **1989** 626
Hong Kong agreement, **1984** 1045-1050
Hong Kong transfer ceremony, **1997** 502
IRA prison hunger strike, **1981** 401-402, 404, 409-412
Northern Ireland, accord on, **1985** 723-732
as prime minister, **1997** 277-278
privatization policy, **1988** 230, 238
resignation from prime ministership, **1990** 747-752
Soviet pipeline sanctions, **1982** 880
tribute to Ronald Reagan, **2004** 320
U.S. air strike against Libya, **1986** 351
Zimbabwe independence, **1979** 939, 941
Theoneste, Bagosora, Rwanda war crimes tribunal defendant, **2004** 117
Thernstrom, Abigail, **1995** 372; **1997** 316
Thi, Dinh Ba, on PRG domestic policy after takeover of South Vietnam, **1975** 301-307
Thiessen, March, UN death penalty, **1998** 185
Thieu, Nguyen Van
meeting with Nixon, **1973** 193, 195, 447-451

resignation, **1975** 279-299
support for Paris peace accords, **1973** 115-118
and surrender of South Vietnam, **1975** 251, 274
on U.S. bombing objectives in North Vietnam, **1972** 611-614
on Vietnam peace negotiations, **1972** 868
Third World countries. *See* Developing countries
Thomas, Bill (R-Calif.), tobacco buyout program, **2004** 283
Thomas, Bob, race relations panel, **1998** 668
Thomas, Cassandra, **1992** 386
Thomas, Clarence
abortion, **2000** 430
anti-abortion demonstrations, **2000** 433
partial-birth, **2000** 432, 444-446
clinic protests, **1994** 312, 322-326
affirmative action, **2003** 362, 363, 376-381
affirmative action, federal government plans, **1995** 308, 320
asset forfeiture
drug trafficking, **1993** 432-438
pornography seized, **1993** 432, 438-440
attorney-client privilege, **1998** 395, 401-404
campaign finance reform, **2003** 1160
child pornography, and "community standards," **2002** 291
coastal property rights, **1992** 616-620
confirmation hearings, **1998** 439
congressional term limits, **1995** 260, 271-275
damages for tobacco-related ills, **1992** 546-573
deaf parochial student, **1993** 399-403
death penalty
fairness of, **2001** 389; **2004** 796
for juvenile offenders, **2002** 358; **2004** 797; **2005** 180, 192-196
for the mentally retarded, **2002** 356, 365-368
death row, appeals from death row prisoners, **1993** 141-147
detentions in terrorism cases, **2004** 378, 392, 397-398
disabilities in the workplace, **2002** 6
disability, definition of, **1999** 319
drug testing of students, **1995** 339-346
eminent domain, **2005** 363, 371-375
endangered species on private lands, **1995** 360, 366-368
entrapment in child pornography case, **1992** 313-322
free speech
ballot initiatives, **1999** 6
decency in the arts, **1998** 405, 415-417
and the Internet, **1997** 445
Internet pornography filters in public libraries, **2003** 388
freedom of residential signs, **1994** 290-297
gay rights discrimination, **1996** 286, 291-295
gay rights to march, **1995** 327-335
grandparents' rights, **2000** 289, 295
gun-free school zone, **1995** 184, 194-195
Haitian refugee interdiction, **1992** 453, 459-468; **1993** 413-421
hate crimes, **1992** 543-551; **1993** 385-389
HIV as a disability, **1998** 380, 389-392
impeachment, Senate's authority to remove judge, **1992** 81-87
job discrimination involving African Americans, **1993** 423-429
legislative intent, **1993** 250-258
medical use of marijuana, **2001** 327, 328-330
Miranda warnings, **2000** 389, 394-396
monetary damages for sexual harassment, **1992** 188-199
nomination hearings, **1991** 551-615
open letter from African American judge to, **1992** 33-43
parochial school aid, **1997** 363
physician-assisted suicide, **1997** 461
presidential elections recount, **2000** 1002, 1003
prison inmates, beaten by guards, **1992** 176-177, 182-185
public lands and developers, **1994** 299, 300-306
punitive damages, for consumer product liability, **1996** 275
race-based redistricting, **1993** 459-474; **1995** 369, 371, 373-380; **1996** 369, 381
religious clubs in public schools, **2001** 421, 424-429
religious freedom, **1997** 408
religious publications, **1995** 385-395
religious symbols, **1995** 387, 396-400
school facilities use, by religious groups, **1993** 363-370
school prayer, **1992** 555; **2000** 367, 376-378
school vouchers, **2002** 408
sentencing laws, **2003** 984; **2004** 360
sex offenders, right to confine, **1997** 383, 385-392
sexual harassment, **1998** 439, 441, 452, 461-465; **1999** 215, 227-234
issue, **1993** 354
at school, **1992** 187-188
in workplace, **1993** 939-944
states' rights, **1999** 333
student drug testing, **2002** 426, 428-433
Supreme Court nomination, **2005** 559
Ten Commandments displays, **2005** 377, 380-383
unreasonable searches, **2001** 409, 410
women's right to choose, **1992** 35, 589, 611-613
Thomas, Derrel, **1986** 171
Thomas, Dorothy, on women's rights, **1995** 581
Thomas, E. Donnall, Nobel in medicine, **1990** 796
Thomas, Frank, steroid use in baseball, congressional testimony on, **2005** 214, 224
Thomas, Lee M., **1988** 223
Thomas, Oliver, religious freedom, **1997** 408
Thomas, Peter, *NEAR Shoemaker* mission, **2001** 135
Thomas, Robert, race relations panel, **1997** 316-317
Thomas Jefferson Center for the Protection of Free Expression, on hate crimes, **1992** 545
Thomas-Keprta, Kathie, **1996** 474, 476
Thomason, Harry, **1992** 669
Thompkins, George, **1989** 184
Thompson, David R., California term limits, **1997** 887, 889-891
Thompson, Frank, Jr. (D-N.J.), conviction of, **1980** 900-902

Thompson, Frank, Jr. (D-N.J.) *Continued*
Butterfield testimony to Watergate committee, **1973** 698-701
campaign finance investigations, **1998** 891
Middle Class Bill of Rights, response to, **1994** 615-616
U.S. sanctions for Chinese companies, **2000** 217
Thompson, James R. (Illinois governor), **1981** 647
national commission on terrorist attacks hearings, **2004** 453
Thompson, Larry
Enron Corp. collapse, **2002** 396
September 11 detainees treatment, **2003** 314
Thompson, Linda Chavez, race relations, **1998** 668
Thompson, Meldrim, **1990** 615
Thompson, Robert, race relations panel, **1997** 322
Thompson, Tommy G.
AIDS drugs, FDA approval process, **2004** 432
AIDS prevention program, **2002** 469-470, 473-474
and balanced budgets, **1995** 11, 43
biomedical research, security issues, **2004** 443
bioterrorism attacks, **2001** 676
flu vaccine shortage, response to, **2004** 642, 644
food supply, and bioterrorism, **2004** 446
government-funded propaganda, **2005** 646
Health and Human Services Department secretary nomination, **2001** 127, 128
medical records privacy, **2001** 487-488
Medicare cost estimates withheld from Congress, investigation of, **2004** 579
Medicare financial situation, **2004** 582-583
nursing home staffing standards, **2002** 121
obesity, combating, **2002** 627; **2003** 483
prescription drug importation, opposition to, **2004** 985-986
prescription drug plan, **2001** 713; **2002** 950
"quit smoking" telephone help line, **2004** 281
Republican Party platform, **2000** 509
sex education, **2001** 458
smoking and health report, **2001** 223, 226-227
stem cell research, **2001** 542
worldwide tobacco regulation treaty, **2003** 262
Thompson v. Oklahoma, **2005** 186, 189
Thompson v. Thompson, **1992** 198
Thomson, James A., on embryonic research, **1998** 66
Thomson, Scott, **1989** 563
Thomson, Suzi Park, in Korean influence-buying scheme, **1978** 846, 849, 852, 891-895
Thonier, Jean Paul, UN French-led peacekeeping mission in Congo, **2003** 292
Thorn, Gaston
EC-British agreement, **1984** 441
at economic summit, **1981** 591
Thornburg v. Gingles, **1993** 472-473; **1995** 370
Thornburgh, Richard L., **1991** 310
abortion, state restrictions on, **1986** 163; **1989** 367
appointment to attorney general, **1988** 496, 892
evacuation from Three Mile Island area, **1979** 826, 836
on flag protection, **1989** 345
Keating inquiry, **1990** 817
Oliver North Iran-contra conviction, **1990** 493
on racketeering by Marcoses, **1988** 868
and secrecy of government documents, **1989** 393
Supreme Court nominees, **1990** 615
WorldCom collapse, **2002** 395; **2003** 334, 341-348
Thornburgh v. American College of Obstetricians and Gynecologists, **1986** 559-580; **1991** 265-266; **1992** 597, 601, 605-606
Three Mile Island (Pennsylvania), nuclear accident, **1979** 823-863; **1990** 196
3M, affirmative action, **2003** 362
Threshold Test Ban Treaty (1974), **1995** 553-554
U.S. strategy on, **1986** 781, 783, 790
Thrifts. *See* Savings and loan institutions
Thurber, James A., Frist insider trader allegations, **2005** 636
Thurmond, Strom (R-S.C.)
100th birthday party celebration, **2002** 970
D.C. representation in Congress, **1978** 590
party switch, **2001** 377
retirement, **2002** 823
Souter nomination, **1990** 619-620
Thomas confirmation hearings, **1991** 561-562, 583, 603-604
transfer of presidential power, **1985** 493
Thyroid cancer, from nuclear testing fallout, **1997** 591-601
Tiananmen Square (Beijing), repression of prodemocracy demonstrations, **1989** 275-278, 281-288
Tianyuan, Li, **1992** 137
Tibet
Chinese immigration to, **1989** 574-575, 578-579
Chinese policies, **1997** 570, 739
PRC occupation of, **1989** 573-581
Tien, Lee, on Pentagon database proposal, **2002** 561
Tierney, John T., **1989** 43
Tigue, John J., Jr., **1988** 869
Tihic, Sulejman, Bosnia-Herzegovina constitutional reform, **2005** 858-859
Till, Emmett, trial for murder of, **2005** 353
Timber industry
Clinton logging decision, **1993** 495-499
ecosystem management approach, **1992** 489-492
effect of Mount St. Helens eruption, **1980** 812-816
endangered species and, **1995** 359-368
multiple-use management of national forests, **1973** 21-26
spotted-owl ruling, **1993** 496-497
Timberlake, Lloyd, **1984** 974-995
Time magazine
CIA influence on Chile cover story, **1975** 875, 897
"Murphy Brown" cover, **1992** 445
Sharon libel suit, **1985** 47-52
Time Warner, merger with America OnLine (AOL), **2000** 1034-1046
T.I.M.E.-D.C., Inc. v. United States, **1977** 383-393
Timerman, Jacobo, Argentine repression reported by, **1981** 180
Times Mirror Center for People and the Press, radio talk show survey, **1993** 585-598
Tinker v. Des Moines Independent Community School District, **1986** 732-740; **1988** 38, 41, 45-46; **1995** 331; **1999** 223

Tinsley, Nikki L.
  air quality at ground zero, **2003** 548
  mercury emissions, EPA regulations on, **2005** 97-98
  new source review rules, **2004** 665-666
TIPOFF terrorist watchlist, **2003** 157, 169; **2004** 469
TIPS. *See* Terrorism Information and Prevention System
Tire safety. *See* Automobile safety
Tissues
  and cells, ownership of human, **1987** 351-372
  irritation of from involuntary smoking, **1986** 1086, 1089-1090
Titan, *Voyager I* photo mission, **1980** 990, 993
Tito, Josip Broz, **1991** 367
  communist leader of Yugoslavia, **2003** 56
  on foreign domination, at nonaligned nations conference, **1979** 681-682, 688-691
  on independence of Yugoslavia, **1976** 869-873
  relations with Hoxha, **1985** 327
  on Yugoslav Communist Party, **1976** 434-435, 459-461
Titone, Vito, **1990** 269, 273
Tizzard, Bob, **1989** 101
Tlatelolco Treaty (1967), on nuclear-free zone, **1979** 173-174, 717
Toaff, Elio, John Paul II visit to synagogue, **1986** 339-342
Tobacco
  See also Cigarettes; Smoking
  consumption in the Americas, **1992** 267-275; **1996** 578
  and nicotine addiction, **1988** 309-317, 319-322; **1994** 205-217
  related ills, **1992** 563-573
  sales to children, **1996** 589-599
  smoke, allergy to, **1972** 53
  use reduction, surgeon general on, **2000** 555-580
  use survey, **1999** 462-463
  warning labels on, **1988** 310-311, 314
Tobacco control, surgeon general's report on, **2004** 298
Tobacco industry
  accountability for smoking-related illnesses, **1999** 49-50
  advertising, FTC report on, **2003** 265
  on cigarette additives as trade secret, **1981** 4
  cigarette advertising restrictions and mandatory labeling, **1972** 46
  cigarette regulations, resistance of, **1995** 670-679
  claims settlement, **1997** 331-339
  expanding to Latin America, **1992** 268-269, 272, 273, 274-275
  FDA tobacco products regulation authority, **2000** 555, 556-557
  federal lawsuit, **2004** 283-284
  health risks fraud accusations, **1999** 536-661
  Justice Department lawsuit, **2003** 261, 263-264
  lawsuits on cigarette smoking, **2003** 484
  nicotine addiction controversy, **1995** 670-679; **1999** 546-548; **2001** 222-223
  nicotine levels in cigarettes and, **1994** 205-217
  regulation, World Health Assembly treaty, **2000** 537-538
  state attorneys general claims settlement, **1998** 842-854; **1999** 536-537; **2000** 131; **2001** 223
  World Health Organization, conspiracy against, **2000** 536-554
Tobacco Institute
  health care costs of smoking, **1985** 616
  health consequences of smoking, **1972** 46
  involuntary smoking, **1986** 1080
  on nicotine addiction, **1988** 310-311
  PHS report on changing cigarette, **1981** 4
  secondhand smoke report, criticism of, **1993** 63-64
  on smoking prevention legislation, **1982** 165
  women, smoking by, **1980** 19
  workplace, smoking in, **1985** 810
Tobias, Randall
  Bush AIDS initiative chairman, **2003** 783
  Bush AIDS relief emergency plan, **2004** 432, 433-441; **2005** 53
Tobin, James, **1995** 135
Tocqueville, Alexis de, on Congress, **1995** 6-7
Todhunter, John A., **1983** 751
Toffler, Alvin, **1992** 494-495
Togo, John Paul II visit, **1985** 500-504
Tokyo Declaration, **1992** 16, 21
Tolba, Mustaka K., **1989** 154
Tolbert, William R., Jr.
  Liberian president assassination, **2003** 768
  meeting with Carter, **1978** 271
  ouster and execution of, **1980** 275-280
Toledo, Alejandro, Venezuela coup attempt, **2002** 204
Tomenko, Mykola, Ukrainian cabinet resignation, **2005** 68
Tomura, Masahiro, **1989** 101
Toner, Robin, **1988** 723
Tongass National Forest (Alaska), protection of roadless lands, **2001** 216-217; **2002** 899; **2004** 669
Tonkin, Gulf of, resolution (1964), repeal of, **1973** 923
Toohey, William D., **1981** 4
Tools, Robert, artificial heart implant patient, **2001** 476
Toon, Malcolm, **1992** 521, 525
Toon, O. B., on nuclear winter, **1983** 857, 860-870; **1985** 542
Töopfer, Klaus, global warming, **2001** 111
Torres, Art, **1986** 960
Torrey, Barbara Boyle, **1988** 877
Torricelli, Robert G. (D-N.J.)
  balanced budget amendment and, **1997** 30-31
  on human rights in El Salvador, **1993** 238
  on independent counsel, **1999** 167
  senatorial election, withdrawal from, **2002** 821
  U.S. sanctions for Chinese companies, **2000** 217
Torrijos Herrera, Omar
  death of, **1989** 704; **1992** 651
  Panama Canal treaties, **1977** 591, 593-594; **1978** 177, 179-181, 186, 188-189; **1999** 851
  Soviet propaganda about, **1981** 754
Torry, E. Fuller, **1990** 573-598
Tort reform
  ABA recommendations on, **1987** 165
  Reagan advisers on, **1987** 142
Torture. *See* Abu Ghraib prison abuse scandal; Guantanamo Bay detainees; Terrorists, interrogations

Toshiba Corp., sales of military technology to Soviets, **1987** 427, 429
Total Information Awareness (TIA) project, **2003** 613
Touche Ross & Co. v. Redington, **1992** 192, 198
Tourism, and Mount St. Helens eruption, **1980** 811-813, 823-824
Tov, Emanuel, Dead Sea scrolls, **1991** 638
Tower, John G. (R-Texas)
on chemical warfare, **1994** 271
defense secretary nomination defeated, **1998** 696
on Reagan budget message, **1983** 103
on report on intelligence agencies, **1976** 236
review of NSC operations in Iran-contra affair, **1986** 1017; **1987** 205
Senate rejection of nomination, **1989** 105-120
Tower Commission, report, **1987** 205-242
Townsend, Frances Fragos, terrorist threat to U.S. financial centers, **2004** 271
Townsend v. Sain, **1993** 145
Toxic chemicals
See also Chemical weapons; Hazardous waste
Bhopal accident, **1984** 1023-1026; **1985** 295-302
control of, in Nixon environmental program, **1972** 147-148
exposure to, interaction with smoking, **1985** 820
Great Lakes water quality report, **1994** 147-152
Love Canal dumpsite for, **1980** 445-447, 452-454
Mississippi River water quality report, **1994** 147-148, 152-160
OSHA protection of workers from, **1981** 491-505
release of from nuclear explosions, **1985** 542, 548-549
standards for testing, Nixon call for, **1973** 216-217
Toyota Motor Manufacturing, Kentucky, Inc. v. Williams, **2002** 4, 7-14
TPA (tissue plasminogen activator), FDA approval of, **1987** 875-879
Tracy, Edward, **1991** 753
Trade
See also Commodities; Economic sanctions; North American Free Trade Agreement; Protectionism
agricultural subsidies and, **2005** 409-412
Bush remarks on free and fair trade, **2005** 144
Caribbean Basin initiative benefits for, **1982** 179-180, 185; **1983** 440, 443, 450
China's trading practices, **2004** 937-948
credit guarantees to Central America, Kissinger commission on, **1984** 32, 37
developing countries, bias against, **1972** 329-336
"dumping" on world markets by Japan, **1987** 427-433
EC
ban on Argentine imports, **1982** 284, 298
goals of common policies and open borders, **1984** 439-441
economic summit (London), **1991** 462-463
expansion of between developing and industrialized countries, McNamara on, **1977** 688, 704-707
export expansion
gains in Carter administration, **1981** 63-64
plan of Republicans on Joint Economic Committee, **1981** 313
in U.S., **2003** 80-81
exports and imports, **2005** 148-149
free
case for, Reagan and CEA on, **1983** 84-85, 87-88, 121-122, 133-135, 137; **1985** 81, 96-99; **1986** 68-69; **1987** 138-140
Summit of the Americas, **1994** 595-601
G-8 summit on, **2000** 486-487; **2005** 409-411
in hazardous wastes, treaty on, **1989** 153-160
legislation, Reagan vetoes of, **1988** 339-346
liberalization of, economic summit on, **1984** 356, 361
open markets
CEA report on, **1997** 61-62, 68; **1998** 83-84, 91-92; **1999** 91
Clinton administration and, **1995** 85; **1997** 51; **1998** 45, 78; **1999** 51-52; **2000** 29, 47
within industrialized countries, and Brady debt relief plan, **1989** 144
reform, G-8 summit meeting, **2005** 409-411
Republican Party platform, **1996** 510-511
tariffs on steel imports, **2003** 445-446
U.S. competitiveness
Reagan on, **1988** 339-341, 344-346
Republican platform on, **1972** 671
U.S. exports
ban on equipment for Soviet gas pipeline, **1982** 471, 879-884
to Latin America, and debt crisis, **1983** 379-381
new markets for, Carter on multilateral trade agreement, **1979** 639-644
opening markets for, Reagan CEA on, **1987** 126, 137-140
U.S. market expansion, **1996** 61; **1997** 53-54, 58
U.S. policy, and dependence of developing countries, Catholic bishops on, **1986** 1007-1008
U.S. privileges
denied to OPEC members, **1975** 224, 233
linked to Soviet emigration policy, **1973** 587-588; **1974** 42, 55, 538, 901-906; **1975** 224-225, 235
U.S. sanctions
against Poland, **1982** 879, 949
lifting of, **1987** 183-188
against Soviets for Polish martial law, **1982** 563, 879-880, 882, 949
against Vietnam, lifting of, **1994** 95-99
U.S.-African trade bill, **2000** 65-66
U.S.-Japan relations
Bush's mission to, **1992** 11-22
improvement in, **1972** 41-43; **1973** 717-720
and open trade, **1983** 894, 897-900, 903-904
sanctions for unfair practices, **1987** 427-437
U.S.-Mexican, Carter and López Portillo on expanding, **1979** 160-171, 175-176, 181
U.S.-PRC relations, history of, **1984** 24
U.S.-Soviet agricultural trade, and foreign policy, **1982** 823-835
U.S.-Soviet cooperation in, Moscow summit joint communiqué, **1974** 565-566
world recession and high oil prices, effect of on, **1983** 801-802, 806-808, 810, 812
Trade, multilateral negotiations
economic summit on new round, **1984** 356, 361
on tariff treatment of tropical products, **1976** 309-310

Trade Act (1974)
denial of trade preferences
link to Soviet emigration policies, **1975** 224-225, 235
to OPEC members, **1975** 224, 233
Nixon proposals for, **1973** 379-382, 389
provisions of, **1974** 116-117
and Soviet assurances on emigration policy, **1974** 901-906
Soviet rejection of conditions for trade agreement (1972), **1975** 5, 12-13
Trade agreements
See also Central America Free Trade Agreement; Free Trade Area of the Americas; General Agreement on Tariffs and Trade; North American Free Trade Agreement
Canada-U.S., transmittal to Congress and implementation, **1988** 571-578
Israeli-U.S., **1983** 834
preferential, between industrialized and developing countries, **1975** 589, 597-600
presidential power to negotiate, **1973** 379-381, 389
U.S.-Central American countries, **2003** 8
U.S.-China trade agreements, **2001** 738; **2005** 617
U.S.-Polish, on double taxation, **1974** 883-885
U.S.-PRC, **1979** 670-671, 675-676; **1984** 23-30
on textiles and grain, **1980** 829-832, 844-846
U.S.-Soviet
1972, **1972** 845-858
linked to Soviet emigration policy, **1973** 792-793, 797-798, 800; **1975** 5, 12-13; **1976** 143, 149
1973, on elimination of double taxation, **1973** 589, 606-607
1974, **1974** 536, 538, 546-548
proposed, linked to Soviet emigration policy, **1989** 645
Trade Agreements Act (1979), signing of, **1979** 637-644
Trade barriers
See also Protectionism
Chinese import tariffs, **2005** 617
costs of to economy, Nixon on, **1973** 382
import restrictions
effect on U.S. economy, **1973** 386, 388
relaxation of in certain industries, **1978** 684, 692, 696
reduction of
for developing countries' exports, **1975** 597-598; **1976** 301, 309-310
and economic integration, Nixon report on, **1973** 386-389
economic summits on, **1976** 430; **1977** 368-370, 372-373; **1981** 591, 598; **1982** 469-470, 474; **1983** 507, 509, 511-512; **1985** 348, 351, 354; **1988** 396
by industrialized countries, UN resolution on, **1975** 605
by international agreements
Carter on, **1978** 14, 45-46
Nixon call for, **1974** 113, 115-116
by multilateral negotiations, **1974** 90; **1979** 33, 637-644
Reagan and CEA on, **1989** 6-8, 10, 13-14
Republican Party platform on, **1988** 616, 630-632; **1992** 823-824
and U.S. workers, **1980** 568, 598, 648-649
tariff reduction
presidential power to negotiate, **1973** 379-381, 389, 428, 434
U.S. proposal for, **1973** 389
U.S.-Japan, **1985** 319-323
World Bank study, **2005** 411-412
WTO negotiations, **2005** 409-411
Trade deficit
for 2004 and 2005, **2005** 137
of developing countries, IMF help for, **1976** 4, 6; **1977** 368, 372
evolution of, **1973** 384-385
expansion of, **2005** 148
factors affecting
Nixon economic report on, **1973** 186, 191
Reagan CEA on, **1987** 125-126, 135-137
Greenspan remarks on, **2004** 237-238
and international monetary crisis, **1973** 344-346, 348-349
link to budget deficit, Reagan and CEA on, **1987** 117-118, 122-123, 125-126
oil price impact on, **1973** 186; **1978** 70, 790; **1979** 92-93
Perot Reform Party nomination speech, **1996** 556-557
protectionist legislation, **1986** 69
reduction of imbalance
economic summit on, **1978** 533-536, 539
Japan's pledge to economic summit, **1978** 533-534, 539
and stock market crash, **1987** 835-836
strong dollar as cause of, Reagan economic report on, **1984** 119-120, 124, 130, 140-141; **1985** 84
U.S. with Japan, **1985** 319-322, 624-625, 627-629; **1986** 971-972, 975; **1987** 427-429, 434-436; **1992** 11-22; **1996** 729-730
causes and remedies, **1983** 135-137
efforts to correct, **1972** 745, 747-749
U.S. with major partners, IMF concern about, **1978** 659-665
Trade embargos. *See* Trade, U.S. sanctions
Trade negotiations
See also World Trade Organization
China-U.S. relations, **2003** 1179-1180
labor standards as part of, Clinton administration, **1999** 799-800
multilateral
and barrier reductions, Ford on, **1977** 50
Carter support for, **1977** 195
Doha Round, **2003** 742, 746, 766; **2005** 410, 411
economic summit support for, **1976** 430; **1980** 512
Millennium Round (Seattle meeting), **1999** 797-801; **2000** 476; **2003** 742; **2005** 409
Summit of the Americas, Declaration of Principles, **1994** 595-601
Tokyo Round, **1979** 26, 33
progress in, **1978** 538-539
reducing barriers to agricultural trade, **1979** 67
and trading system rules, **1979** 92

Trade negotiations *Continued*
U.S. implementing legislation, **1979** 637-644
Uruguay Round, **1995** 74, 85; **1997** 53, 61-62; **1998** 83; **2001** 59; **2003** 742
progress in, **1987** 122; **1988** 123; **1989** 425, 431; **1994** 142
presidential "fast-track" negotiations, **1997** 612; **1998** 75, 95; **1999** 43
U.S.-China agreement, **1999** 724-734, 797; **2000** 19, 192
U.S.-Vietnam agreements, **1999** 477-478; **2000** 913-915
World Trade Organization
Cancún meeting, **2003** 8, 740-750, 755
and negotiations with Brazil, **2003** 8
Trade Representative (U.S.)
Special, and trade sanctions against Japan, **1987** 431-433
World Trade Organization talks, **1999** 797-801
Trade unions. *See* Labor unions
Traditional Values Coalition, **1989** 305-306
Trafficante, Santos, **1979** 595, 611
Trafficking Act (2000), **2004** 125
Trafficking in Persons, Interagency Task Force to Monitor and Combat, **2002** 335
Train, Russell E.
ocean dumping agreement, **1972** 907
at Stockholm environment conference, **1972** 476
U.S.-Soviet environment agreement, **1972** 806
Train v. City of New York, **1975** 135-140; **1998** 433
Train v. duPont et al., **1977** 131-141
Trainor, Bernard, No Gun Ri (Korean War) incident, **2001** 37
Trains. *See* Railroad industry
Trammel v. United States, **1990** 28; **1998** 402
Trans World Airlines, hijacking at Beirut, **1985** 463-466, 469, 474
TransAfrica, **1989** 547
Transamerica Mortgage Advisors, Inc. v. Lewis, **1992** 198
Transparency International, **1997** 801
Transportation
See also Airline industry; Railroad industry; Trucking industry
deregulation of
Carter on progress in, **1981** 59, 74
Carter proposals for, **1979** 24, 36-37, 39-40; **1980** 64, 72-73
Democratic Party platform on, **1980** 735-736; **1984** 580
Ford on, **1976** 50
Reagan CEA on progress in, **1986** 60, 85-88
Republican Party platform on, **1976** 644; **1980** 568, 612-613; **1984** 687-688; **1988** 671-673
efficiency and safety of, U.S.-Soviet agreement on cooperation in, **1973** 588, 609
highway repair program consolidation, **1981** 73
rebuilding infrastructure of, **1983** 113; **1984** 110
regulation of, inefficiency of, **1974** 87-89
revenue sharing for, Republican Party platform on, **1972** 687-688
safety of, **1986** 87
strikes in
and compulsory arbitration legislation, **1972** 385, 389
costs of, **1972** 102-103
technological progress in, impact on railroads, **1975** 529-532
user fees for, **1983** 112-113; **1984** 110
Transportation Department
on Alaska oil spill, **1989** 230-233
removing FAA from, **1988** 267, 269-271, 275-276
shipment of hazardous wastes, **1980** 449
Transportation Security Administration (TSA)
See also Aviation security
air cargo security, **2004** 153
airport screening, **2002** 531-532; **2003** 726; **2005** 896
Computer Assisted Passenger Prescreening System (CAPPS II) program, **2003** 722, 726-727, 731; **2004** 144-145, 148-149
costs of, **2003** 724-725
creation of, **2004** 142, 147
established, **2002** 530, 740, 746-747; **2003** 720
GAO progress report, **2003** 725-739
"no-fly" terror suspect watch list, **2003** 157
screener workforce
hiring and deploying, **2004** 150
training programs, **2004** 150-151
Secure Flight system, **2005** 898
Transportation Workers Identification Card (TWIC) program, **2003** 726, 730-731
Travel, freedom of
and four-power Berlin agreement, **1972** 467-470
and Helsinki Final Act, **1975** 559-561, 568-570
passport revocation power, **1981** 541-555
Sakharov on, **1975** 915-918, 925
Travis Air Force Base, California, U.S. POWs' return to, **1973** 246
Traynor v. Turnage, **1988** 277-285
Treasury Department
Office of Thrift Supervision (OTS) creation, **1989** 464-466
O'Neill resignation, **2002** 880
role in budget information controls, **1974** 589-590
on Secret Service performance during Reagan shooting, **1981** 353, 359-367
Waco incident report, **1993** 819-820, 821-829
Treasury Employees v. Von Raab, **1995** 342, 344, 345
Treaty of Friendship, Cooperation and Mutual Assistance. *See* Warsaw Pact
Treaty of Peace and Friendship (Japan-China), **1998** 540-541
Treaty ratification, and ABM treaty reinterpretation, **1987** 290, 292-304
Treaty termination, presidential vs. congressional power, **1979** 917-938
Treurnicht, Andries, **1992** 285
Trewhitt, Henry L., at presidential debates, **1976** 735; **1984** 877, 886-888, 899-900
Trial
right to fair
dismissal of Pentagon Papers case, **1973** 537-542
gag orders on press coverage, **1976** 463-479

pretrial publicity and reversal of Calley's conviction, **1974** 857-859
right to public, and closed pretrial hearings, **1979** 511-533
Tribe, Laurence H., **1986** 412
on congressional authority and commerce clause, **1995** 185
on Constitutional law, **1995** 259-260
Trichet, Jean-Claude, **1998** 273
Trietley v. Bd. of Education of Buffalo, **1993** 365
Trilateral Commission, on Gorbachev initiatives, **1989** 298-299
Trimble, David
Northern Ireland election defeats, **2005** 508, 510
Northern Ireland peace negotiations, **1998** 203-206; **1999** 754, 755-756, 757-758; **2001** 759-761; **2005** 508
Trinidad and Tobago, Republic of, John Paul II visit, **1985** 57, 59
Trinity Institute, **1992** 381
Tripp, Linda R., Lewinsky confidante, **1998** 565, 634; **1999** 22
Tritt, United States v., **1994** 109-115
Trop v. Dulles, **2005** 191
Trost, Carlisle A. H., **1989** 519-521
Trotter Institute for the Study of Black Cultures, **1989** 447
Troutt, William E., National Commission on the Cost of Higher Education, **1998** 3
Troxel v. Granville, **2000** 287-298
Trucking industry
in Chile, CIA support for truck owners' strike, **1975** 903-904
deregulation of
Carter on, **1978** 32, 690; **1979** 24, 36-37, 40; **1980** 948; **1981** 59
Reagan CEA on, **1986** 60, 87
regulation of, inefficiency of, **1974** 89
Trudeau, Pierre Elliott
and constitutional reform, **1981** 813-814; **1982** 317-320
economic summits, **1977** 367; **1978** 533; **1980** 504; **1981** 591
farewell address, **1984** 407-412
on Lévesque election victory, **1976** 855-857, 859-862
at poverty summit, **1981** 770, 775-778
on separatist vote in Quebec, **1980** 401-408
Truitt, Kendall, **1989** 518-519
Trujillo, Chadwick, planetary studies, **2002** 215
Trujillo, Rafael
as target of CIA
Ford on, **1975** 401
Senate investigation of, **1975** 710, 715-716, 759-763, 770-772, 777, 785-787
Truly, Richard H., **1981** 419; **1990** 755
Truman, Harry S.
administration
cable traffic interception by, **1975** 709, 800-803
on political uses of FBI, **1975** 873, 876-877
atomic bomb controversy, **1995** 56
division of Germany, **1986** 792
equality for all Americans, **1997** 762
Genocide Convention, **1986** 115
press conferences of, **1988** 841
and steelworkers' strike, **1997** 291
and Swiss relations with Nazi Germany, **1997** 259
U.S. acceptance of ICJ jurisdiction, **1985** 638, 640
and "Verona" project, **1997** 104
on world peace, **1997** 42
Trumka, Richard L., **1990** 19-22; **1995** 681, 683
Trunk, Anne D., **1979** 825
Trust for America's Health, bioterrorism readiness study, **2004** 444
TSA. *See* Transportation Security Administration
Tsang, Donald, Hong Kong prodemocracy dissenters, **2005** 623
Tsongas, Paul E., at Democratic Party convention, **1992** 669, 686-687
Tsunami disaster in Indian Ocean region, **2004** 348
Aceh province (Indonesia) devastation, **2004** 753
"core group" for rescue and recovery efforts, Bush on, **2004** 891
death toll estimates, **2004** 991
recovery and reconstruction, UN report on, **2005** 990-1009
UN relief efforts, **2004** 887, 891, 992-993
UN report on, **2004** 991-1000
U.S. response, **2004** 891, 993-995
warning system, **2004** 995
Tsvangirai, Morgan
trial for treason, **2003** 1110, 1112
Zimbabwe presidential elections, **2002** 134; **2003** 1110, 1112-1113
TTIC. *See* Terrorist Threat Integration Center
Tuberculosis
and drug-resistant bacteria, **1999** 192-193
and job discrimination, **1987** 245-252
OTA report on, **1993** 851-869
resurgence of, **1992** 1007-1011
Tubman, William V. S., **1980** 276
Tuck, John, Russian nuclear weapons panel, **2001** 20
Tucker, C. DeLores, **1995** 455
Tucker, Jim Guy, Whitewater indictment, **1998** 633; **1999** 22; **2000** 764
Tucker, Marc, education reform, **1986** 459
Tucker, Robert W., on Bush's "freedom crusade," **2005** 44
Tucker, United States v., **1991** 386
Tucker, Willard, anthrax mailings victim, **2001** 676
Tudjman, Franjo
anti-Semitic statements, **1993** 307
Bosnia accord, **1995** 719
Croatian president, **2005** 857
Croatian war crimes, **2003** 465
death of, **2000** 141
Tueni, Tueni, Lebanese car bombing victim, **2005** 692
Tung, Rosalie, **1990** 23-34
Tung Chee-hwa
Chinese chief executive of Hong Kong appointment, **1997** 501
Clinton endorsement of democracy in Hong Kong, **1998** 468
Hong Kong security and prodemocracy dissenters, **2003** 1181-1182; **2005** 623
Tunisia, PLO forces relocated in, **1982** 744

Tunney, John V. (D-Calif.)
  and endangered species act, **1995** 365
  on Kleindienst confirmation, **1972** 396, 404-406
Tunney Act. *See* Antitrust Procedures and Penalties Act
Turbay, Jorge Gechem, kidnapping of, **2002** 570-571
Turco, R. P., on nuclear winter, **1983** 857, 860-870
Turk, Rifat, on Middle East violence, **2000** 932
Turkey
  aid to Nazi Germany, **1997** 259, 262, 263; **1998** 291
  allied relations and negotiations with, **1998** 307-310
  arms sales to, and use of in Cyprus, **1975** 224-225, 232-233
  conflict with Greece over Cyprus, **1975** 354-355; **1982** 420
  Cyprus peace negotiations, **2004** 977
  earthquakes, U.S. aid, **1999** 465-471
  economic situation, **2002** 909
  elections, **2002** 906, 907
  European Union membership invitation, **2004** 973-980
  European Union membership issue, **1999** 158, 466-467; **2002** 906, 909-910; **2004** 197; **2005** 338, 340
  German assets, **1997** 267
  human rights, and torture issue, **2002** 910
  human rights in, **1985** 156-157; **1988** 108-110, 884, 887-888; **1990** 137
  human trafficking, **2002** 350
  Iraq and the U.S.-led war, **2002** 910-911; **2003** 43, 139
  Iraq Kurdistan relations, **2003** 139
  Islamist Welfare Party, **2002** 908
  Justice and Development Party (AKP), **2002** 906, 907-908
  Kurdish refugee crisis, **2002** 911
  on Law of the Sea Treaty, **1982** 345-361
  military takeover in, **1980** 807-810
  NATO
    defense participation of, **1982** 420
    membership, **2004** 973
    threatened withdrawal from, **1975** 353-354
  NATO ally, **1997** 269
  opium growing in, ban on, **1972** 646, 648-650
  political situation, **2002** 906-915
  Republican People's Party, **2002** 907
  return of Nazi valuables, **1998** 292-293
  right-wing groups in, Agca link to, **1981** 428
  terrorist bombings linked to al Qaeda, **2003** 1052-1053
  UN Oil for Food Program, **2004** 717
  U.S. relations, **2004** 977-978
Turkmenia
  Alma-Ata Declaration, **1991** 804-806
  Commonwealth Pact, **1991** 803-804
  Soviet Union restructuring plans, **1991** 532-533
Turner, Jesse, hostage release, **1991** 753-754
Turner, Jim
  bioterrorism assessment, **2004** 444
  color-coded threat alert system, **2004** 269
Turner, John
  on Canada-U.S. trade agreement, **1988** 572
  on international monetary reform, **1972** 817
  as successor to Trudeau, **1984** 407-409
Turner, Stansfield, on B. Carter's Libyan contacts, **1980** 914-916
Turner, Ted
  baseball owner suspension, **1993** 169
  United Nations, U.S. dues payment, **2000** 182
Turow, Scott, death penalty panel, **2000** 989
Tuskegee Syphillis Study, **1995** 62
Tutsi (ethnic group)
  See also Burundi; Rwanda
  Rwanda war crimes tribunal, **2002** 607; **2004** 117-118
Tutu, Desmond
  AIDS prevention in South Africa, **2002** 473
  on apartheid, **1993** 878, 880
  on Botha speech, **1985** 518
  Commonwealth study group meeting with, **1986** 582
  de Klerk meeting, **1989** 546
  on death penalty, **1995** 283
  on ending of pass laws, **1986** 371
  Nobel Peace Prize recipient, **1984** 1027-1037; **1993** 878; **2002** 982
  South African elections, **1994** 248
  Truth and Reconciliation Commission, **1998** 755-756
Tutwiler, Margaret
  Clinton's passport search, **1992** 1046, 1059-1060
  on Iraq invasion of Kuwait, **1991** 157, 158
al-Tuwaiji, Saleh, terrorist bombings in Saudi Arabia, **2003** 230
TVA. *See* Tennessee Valley Authority
TVA v. Hill, **1995** 363-364
Twagiramungu, Faustin, Rwanda presidential candidate, **2003** 1070-1071
Twain, Mark, lynchings, opposition to, **2005** 356
Twentieth Century Fund, education reform task force, **1983** 415
Twin City Bank v. Nebeker, **1990** 377
Tyco International, corporate scandal, **2002** 392, 398-399; **2003** 332, 340-341; **2004** 422
Tydings, Joseph D. (D-Md.), **1974** 444
Tymon, Philip, **1984** 451
Tymoshenko, Yulia V.
  dismissal as prime minister, **2005** 68-69
  political relationship with Yushchenko, **2005** 64-70
  Ukraine parliamentary elections, **2004** 1006
  as Ukrainian prime minister, **2005** 64-69
Tyrie, Andrew, U.S. policy on torture, Rice statements on, **2005** 908
Tyson, Don, Espy resignation, **1994** 407-408
Tyson, Laura D'Andrea, CEA report, **1994** 124
Tyson, Mike, date rape, **1992** 388, 395
Tyson Foods, Inc., **1994** 403-408

U

UAW. *See* United Auto Workers
Udall, Morris K. (D-Ariz.)
  on Ford cuts in social programs, **1975** 85
  presidential nomination of, **1976** 597
Ueberroth, Peter V.
  California gubernatorial recall election, **2003** 1008
  on drug use in baseball, **1986** 169-175

UFW. *See* United Farm Workers Union
Uganda
AIDS infection rate dropping, **2000** 412
AIDS prevention, ABC plan—Abstain, Be Faithful, Use a Condom, **2003** 782; **2005** 52
Clinton state visit, **1998** 159
conflict in, **2003** 470-479
human rights abuses, **2001** 505; **2003** 470-479
human rights in
Amin message to Carter on, **1977** 143-148
state department on, **1988** 97-98
Israeli raid on Entebbe, **1976** 517-520
Lord's Resistance Army (LRA), **2003** 470-479, 840
Operation Iron Fist, **2003** 471-472, 473, 475, 479
silencing of political opponents in, **1975** 645-646, 649
troop withdrawal from Congo, **2002** 550; **2003** 290-291
Uhl, Jeff, prescription drug imports, **2004** 984
Ukraine
Alma-Ata Declaration, **1991** 804-806
Commonwealth Pact, **1991** 786-791, 787-791, 803-804
CSCE, **1994** 583
effect of Chernobyl on soil, **1986** 384
European Union membership proposals, **2004** 1002; **2005** 66
foreign aid, **1994** 364
health problems, **1994** 415-430
independence, **1991** 785, 786-787
Kuchma presidential term, **2004** 1001, 1002
NATO cooperation, **1997** 518, 522
Nixon's speech on Russian aid, **1992** 255, 260
Nuclear Arms Pact, **1991** 806-808
nuclear weapons, **1991** 787; **1993** 554; **1994** 363-373; **1996** 219-221
dismantling of, **2001** 18; **2004** 169
Orange Revolution, **2005** 64, 65, 272, 300, 342
political protests, **2005** 43, 64-65
presidential elections, **2004** 569, 1001-1008; **2005** 299, 300
Soviet Union restructuring plans, **1991** 532-533
START I ratification, **1993** 19-20, 714
START II, **1993** 19-20
U.S. expulsion of UN mission personnel, **1986** 267, 271
Yushchenko presidential inauguration speech, **2005** 64-74
Ulasewicz, Anthony T., political investigations by, **1974** 338-339, 354, 601, 611
Ullman, Al (D-Ore.), **1975** 17
Ulrich, Eugene, Dead Sea scrolls, **1991** 638
Ultraviolet (UV) radiation, **1992** 75-83
Ulusu, Bulent, **1980** 808
Umarov, Sanjar, Uzbekistan opposition group leader imprisoned, **2005** 432
Umbach, Frank, German political situation, **2005** 878
UN. *See* United Nations
Unabomber
See also Kaczynski, Theodore J.
manifesto on society's ills, **1995** 600-610
sentencing memorandum, **1998** 233-252
UNAIDS. *See* United Nations Programme on HIV/AIDS
Unanian, Nairi, **1999** 639
UNCTAD. *See* United Nations Conference on Trade and Development
Underwood, Julie, on sexual harassment of students, **1999** 215
Underworld. *See* Organized crime
UNDOF. *See* United Nations Disengagement Observer Force
UNDP. *See* United Nations Development Programme
UNEF. *See* United Nations Emergency Force
Unemployment
See also Job creation
adult, Democratic Party platform on, **1976** 544, 547-550
among blacks, **1983** 41-44, 48-51; **1985** 28, 31, 34-37; **1987** 43-44, 48, 58-59
among minorities and women, **1982** 919-944
among urban minorities, **1988** 185-188, 191-193
among youth
Carter proposals for, **1980** 165, 167-168
economic summit on, **1977** 368, 371
benefits, **1992** 63
Bush on, **1990** 83
and Carter anti-inflation program, **1978** 686-687
in coal strike, **1978** 111, 115, 119
combating through flexibility of Nixon budget, **1974** 97-101
cyclical, Reagan plans to combat, **1983** 132-133
decline in, Ford on in campaign statement, **1976** 797, 816-817
in developing countries, **1983** 263-265
economic advisers' report, **1990** 98-101; **1991** 82
economic summits on, **1976** 426, 428-429; **1981** 591, 596; **1982** 470-471, 473-474
and Ford economic policies, Democrats' election-year attacks on, **1976** 14, 29, 693-694, 711, 797; **1978** 817
and hunger in U.S., **1985** 191, 200-202, 204
increase in
Democratic opposition on countering, **1975** 16, 32, 34-35
Ford on countering, **1975** 15-16, 19-20, 28, 30
and inflation fight, **1974** 861-862, 869, 872
and passage of Reagan economic plan, **1981** 642
and inflation, tradeoff between, **1975** 635-642; **1976** 45, 48; **1977** 718, 720-722, 727-728; **1982** 122, 134-137, 144, 152
and inflation fight, Democratic Party platform on, **1972** 530-531
job programs to combat
Carter on, **1976** 693-694, 696
Muskie on, **1976** 14, 29
in Reagan budget, **1983** 85, 115-116, 124; **1985** 88-89
and Reagan budget cuts, **1983** 772
jobless recovery, causes of, **2003** 441, 443-444
long-term trends, **1992** 167
minimum and youth wage effects on, **1983** 785-790
of minority youth, **1982** 920, 941-943
outsourcing/offshoring impact on, **2004** 58-59
politics of, **2003** 444-446
as priority problem, Mondale on, **1976** 773, 775, 778, 781, 792-793

Unemployment *Continued*
projections of
by Carter CEA, **1981** 106
by Ford CEA, **1975** 83, 85, 87-89, 99-101
in Reagan budget, **1984** 101, 107-108; **1985** 81
by Reagan CEA on, **1982** 122
reduction of
Carter on progress in, **1978** 66, 77-78, 84-85, 92; **1981** 57, 63
Reagan CEA on progress in, **1985** 79, 81-84
Reagan economic plan for, **1981** 214-215, 326; **1983** 84, 121, 123
reduction of in economic recovery
and Ford budget, **1976** 37, 39, 41
Joint Economic Committee on, **1977** 718-722
Reagan CEA on, **1984** 122-123, 128-129
and revision of economic order, John Paul II on, **1982** 838, 850-853
and social responsibility of economic policies, **1984** 957-958, 960, 963-964, 967
structural
and investment in jobs, **1981** 295, 297
National Agenda for the '80s on combating, **1981** 45-46
private sector role in correcting, **1978** 65-67, 74, 92
Reagan plans to combat, **1983** 77-78, 131-133
underemployment, **1992** 168
Unemployment insurance
benefit increases, in Ford budget, **1975** 88-89, 91, 95, 106-107
liberalization of, Burns on effect of, **1975** 639, 642
Nixon proposal to raise standards and extend coverage, **1974** 96-97, 101
for people affected by energy crisis, **1974** 42, 54, 57-58
Unemployment rate
of foreign-born, **1997** 180
in Indonesia, **1998** 726
job statistics, **2004** 57-58
for minorities in U.S., **2003** 447
in South Korea, **1998** 726
in Thailand, **1998** 726
in U.S., **1992** 98, 109, 118; **1997** 50, 53, 59, 70; **1998** 73-74, 75, 79, 85, 364; **1999** 86; **2001** 55-56, 57; **2003** 441-443, 447; **2005** 140, 143
for 1995, **1996** 51, 55, 69
for minorities, **1999** 87
UNEP. *See* United Nations Environmental Program
UNESCO. *See* United Nations Educational, Scientific, and Cultural Organization
UNGA. *See* United Nations General Assembly
Unger, Laura, on online investing, **1999** 206
UNICEF. *See* United Nations Children's Emergency Fund
Unidentified flying objects (UFOs), Roswell incident, Air Force report, **1997** 395-405
Uniform Anatomical Gift Act (1968), **1987** 354
Uniform Child Custody Jurisdiction Act, **1993** 515-529
Uniform Determination of Death Act, model code, **1983** 282, 290-291
Uniforms, in public schools, **1996** 84-92
Union Carbide, Bhopal gas poisoning, **1984** 1023-1026; **1985** 295-302
Union of Concerned Scientists
advisory panel appointments, **2004** 843
endorsement of Kerry, **2004** 842
ethics of cloning, **2004** 159
global warming, **2002** 301
on SDI, **1984** 257-258, 260-266; **1988** 324
Union of Needletrades, Industrial and Textile Employees (UNITE), **1999** 632
Union of Soviet Socialist Republics (USSR). *See* Soviet Union
Unions. *See* Labor unions
UNITA. *See* National Union for the Total Independence of Angola
Unite Here (labor union), **2005** 487, 488
United Airlines
bankruptcy and labor unions, **2005** 486
bankruptcy and pension plans, **2004** 734, 736; **2005** 197, 199, 201, 206-207
bankruptcy protection, **2002** 53; **2003** 709
Boeing 737 crash, **1999** 116
jobs for welfare recipients, **1997** 34, 622
United Arab Emirates
funding of terrorist activities, **2001** 619
human trafficking, **2002** 350-351
oil price cut, **1981** 799
oil price increases, **1979** 252-254
split from OPEC on, **1976** 937-939
UN Oil for Food Program, **2004** 717
United Auto Workers (UAW), **2005** 486
General Motors strike, **1998** 320-325
and national health insurance plan, **1978** 545
wage hike concessions to Chrysler, **1979** 695, 710-711
United Democratic Front
demands for lifting of ban on, **1989** 546
and state of emergency in South Africa, **1986** 372
United Farm Workers Union (UFW), organization of California farm workers, **1975** 377-379
United Food and Commercial Workers (UFCW) International Union, **2005** 487, 488, 735, 739
United Iraqi Alliance, **2004** 404
United Jewish Organizations of Williamsburgh, Inc. v. Carey, **1977** 151-167; **1993** 464-465, 467, 470-471, 473, 474, 475-477; **1995** 376
United Kingdom. *See* Great Britain
United Mine Workers of America, coal strikes, **1978** 111-124; **1990** 19-22
United Nations
See also Food and Agriculture Organization (FAO); International Criminal Tribunal for Rwanda; Peacekeeping; United Nations conventions
abuse of older persons report, **2002** 194
AIDS initiatives
Bush administration policy on, **2003** 21-22, 29, 453-454, 780, 781-783
HIV/AIDS epidemic, campaign against, **2004** 429, 430
anniversary commemorations
fiftieth, **1995** 350-358
fortieth, **1985** 707, 709-712
antidrug efforts, **1992** 208

charter
fortieth anniversary, **1985** 709-712
goals of organization, **1984** 815, 822
reform, **2005** 245
chemical warfare
investigation of use of, **1989** 25, 27, 29-30
report on, **1981** 682, 688, 693; **1982** 235, 237
chemical weapons convention, **1996** 740-743; **1997** 195-201; **2004** 169
"Dialogue Among Civilizations" address, **2001** 793-801
disaster relief, Earthscan report on, **1984** 973-995
Drug Control Program (UNDCP), **1992** 217
economic cooperation, restructuring for, **1975** 325-351, 588; **1976** 611
effectiveness in conflict resolution, **1973** 753-765; **1982** 769-779
environment conference, U.S. delegation at, **1972** 476
Environment Program, **1992** 78
expenses of, cuts in U.S. contributions to, **1972** 337, 339-342
global warming treaty, **1997** 859-876
Gorbachev advocates restructuring, **1992** 432, 438
HIV infection worldwide estimates, **1997** 83-84
HIV/AIDS epidemic, **1998** 878-889; **2000** 410-428
Holocaust statement by, during World War II, **1983** 150
human embryonic cloning ban, **2004** 160-161
human rights activities
Carter support for, **1972** 189-190; **1977** 195-197
State Department on, **1981** 182-183
Hurricane Mitch damage report, **1998** 789-798
ICJ
establishment of, **1985** 638, 640
John Paul II speech to, **1985** 369-371
International Women's Year, Mexico City conference, **1975** 507-522
Jewish homeland, **1988** 581
Law of the Sea Treaty, **1982** 345-361
multilateral diplomacy in, Waldheim on, **1972** 631-634
national policies pursued in, Waldheim on, **1973** 753, 760
nondemocratic developing countries in, Moynihan on, **1975** 645-651
nuclear freeze demonstration at missions, **1982** 886
ozone depletion report, **1992** 75, 77, 81-83
peacekeeping missions
forces in Sinai, **1978** 614-615; **1979** 229, 234-235, 238-241
GAO report on, **1997** 150-157
improving effectiveness of, **1972** 337-338, 340-341; **1973** 809, 814
UN panel on reforms, **2000** 642-666, 702-703
purposes of, John Paul II on, **1979** 729, 748-753
al Qaeda terrorist network
sanctions against, **2003** 1050-1068
UN report on, **2004** 518, 534-547
reform efforts, **1997** 351-352
GAO report on, **2000** 179-189
secretary general Annan on, **2003** 808-816; **2004** 887-911; **2005** 228-245
restructuring of secretariat, **1975** 341-345
role of, **2003** 808-810
Schevardnadze address, **1990** 629, 635-646
secretary general appointment, **1996** 824-830
sexual abuse scandals, by UN peacekeepers, **2004** 509, 893-894; **2005** 237-238
sexual harassment of staff, **2005** 238
staff overhaul by Annan, **2005** 235-236
strengthening, **2000** 710-711
terrorist networks, monitoring of, **2004** 534-547
Transition Assistance Group (UNTAG), **1990** 202-203
tsunami relief effort, **2005** 990-1009
Vatican representation in, **1979** 748; **1984** 21
violence on the Temple Mount, **1990** 695-711
women's rights, **2000** 325-336
work of, Waldheim report on, **1972** 631-637
World Food Conference (Rome), **1974** 939-953
worldwide population, **1999** 584-591
United Nations (by country)
Afghanistan
humanitarian aid and reconstruction, **2002** 15-32
interim government peace agreement, **2001** 881-882
interim government, role in, **2001** 890-891
International Security Assistance Force (ISAF), **2002** 16, 18
peacekeeping forces, **2001** 690-691, 882-883
political situation, UN report on, **2002** 15-32
postwar reconstruction fund, **2001** 741, 880, 884
Afghanistan agreements, mediation of, **1988** 257-266
African conflict
peacekeeping missions, **2001** 507-508
secretary general on, **1998** 220-232
Angola
Arab Human Development Report, **2002** 484-487; **2003** 489-502, 956-957, 962-978
charter reform recommendations, **2004** 910-911
membership in UN, **2002** 152
peacekeeping force withdrawal, **2002** 151, 153
Bosnia
peacekeeping operation, **1995** 351-352
resolution condemning aggression in, **1994** 550-554
UN peacekeeping mission, **2003** 460-469, 811; **2004** 785, 953, 954
Cambodian peace plan, **1990** 561-569
Central American peace role, **1989** 163, 168-169
Congo
peacekeeping mission, secretary general report, **2004** 505-516
resource exploitation, panel on, **2002** 551-552
Congo war
secretary general report, **2000** 978-987; **2001** 159-170
UN peacekeeping mission, **2002** 547
East and West Germany
membership for, four-power declaration on, **1972** 897-898, 900
treaty declaring allegiance to principles of, **1972** 897, 899
East Timor
independence, **2001** 593-599

United Nations (by country) *Continued*
membership as Timor-Leste, **2002** 256, 259
Transitional Administration in East Timor (UNTAET), **1999** 514; **2002** 258-259
UN Mission of Support in East Timor (UNMISET), **2002** 259
El Salvador, human rights mission, **1992** 25
Haiti
peacekeeping mission, **2001** 396; **2004** 94
post-Aristide era, **2004** 94-102
India, nuclear testing, **1998** 326-332
India-Pakistan conflict
Kashmir dispute, **2003** 213
U.S. actions in regarding, **1972** 23-33
Iran, nuclear weapons program, **2004** 868
Iraq
air strikes against, **1998** 934-944
detainees abuse scandal, **2004** 208
human rights, **2000** 581-595
interim government and elections, **2004** 401-402
postwar report, **1991** 165-174
postwar situation, **2003** 933-954
sanctions against, **1995** 355-356; **1997** 767, 769-770; **2000** 581, 583-585; **2001** 849-850
second resolution authorizing war fails, **2003** 47-49
weapons inspections (biological, chemical, and nuclear), **1998** 934-944; **1999** 147-148; **2000** 585; **2003** 41, 45-46, 136-137, 874-875
Ivory Coast peacekeeping mission, **2003** 239-240; **2004** 819-820
Kosovo
UN mission, **2003** 1138-1154; **2004** 949-964; **2005** 855-856
war crimes tribunal, **1998** 831; **2001** 826-848
Lebanon, Hariri assassination investigations, **2005** 690-692
Liberia, UN Mission in Liberia (UNMIL), **2003** 450, 767-779, 772; **2005** 801-803
Namibian independence and UN membership, **1990** 200
North Korea, humanitarian aid, **1999** 572
Pakistan, nuclear testing, **1998** 326-332
Persian Gulf War
Baker remarks, **1990** 769-771
Iraqi invasion of Kuwait, **1990** 545-550
Kuwaiti emir's address, **1990** 655-660
UN resolutions, **1990** 769-771
PLO observer mission
U.S. attempt to close, **1988** 479-485
Young meeting with, **1979** 647-657
Rwanda
genocidal war, report on, **1999** 860-889
peacekeeping missions, **2003** 450; **2004** 115-116
refugee camps, **1994** 541-549
Sierra Leone, UN peacekeeping mission, **2002** 247-248, 250, 547
Somalian aid, **1992** 1067-1072
Srebrenica massacre, UN role, **1999** 735-752; **2001** 899
Sudan
humanitarian aid, **2004** 590
peacekeeping mission, **2004** 115; **2005** 520-521
United States
Bolton UN ambassador appointment, **2005** 236-237
Clinton address, **1993** 805-817
death penalty, **1998** 183-193
dues payment, **1997** 152-153; **1998** 50; **1999** 54, 700-701; **2000** 181-182; **2001** 12, 901
expulsion of Soviet personnel, **1986** 267-272, 820
role in the UN, **1993** 805-817; **2002** 606
withdrawal from, American Party platform on, **1972** 615, 621
Vietnam, U.S. veto of membership for, **1977** 208, 211
Yugoslavia, UN membership, **1992** 875-878
United Nations, General Convention of Privileges and Immunities (1946), on size of UN missions, **1986** 268
United Nations Children's Emergency Fund (UNICEF)
AIDS in Africa, **1999** 489-498
child soldiers, **2002** 917
child welfare reports, **1996** 776, 777-778; **1999** 386-387; **2002** 222
Clinton praises, **1995** 351, 356
education worldwide, **1998** 920-928
health care crisis in Eastern Europe, **1994** 415-430
history of, **1996** 777
malnutrition of children, **2002** 222
maternal deaths, report on, **1996** 343-352
on poverty of children, **1981** 911-921; **1988** 878-879
sexual exploitation of children, **2001** 955-962
United Nations Conference on New and Renewable Sources of Energy, **1981** 14, 22
United Nations Conference on Trade and Development (UNCTAD), **1972** 636
Allende speech to, **1972** 329-336
commodities resolution, **1976** 299-300, 315-319, 427, 431
history of, **1976** 299-300
nonaligned nations on strategy at, **1983** 265
restructuring of, **1975** 335-336
role in redressing economic imbalances, UN resolution on, **1975** 604, 607-608, 611
United Nations conferences
Against Illicit Traffic in Narcotic Drugs and Psychotropic Substances, **1992** 210, 211, 212
Against Racism, Racial Discrimination, Xenophobia, and Related Tolerance, **2001** 603-613
Civil and Political Rights, **1993** 455
Climate Change (Montreal), **2005** 922-924, 927-930
Environment and Development (New York City), **1997** 488
Environment and Development (Rio de Janeiro), **1992** 641-642; **1999** 403; **2002** 593
Financing for Development (Monterey, Mexico), **2002** 448-449
Human Environment (Stockholm, 1972), **2002** 593
Illicit Trade in Small Arms and Light Weapons in All Its Aspects, **2001** 516-521
Nuclear Nonproliferation (New York City), **2000** 201-212; **2005** 933-934
Nuclear Non-Proliferation Treaty Review and Extension Conference, **1995** 233-238

Population and Development, International Conference on (Cairo, 1994), **1994** 351-359; **1995** 136, 583
Status of Refugees, **1992** 455, 456, 465, 466; **1993** 414, 420-421
Straddling Fish Stocks and Highly Migratory Fish Stocks, International Conference on, **1995** 524-531
World Assembly on Aging (Second), **2002** 193-200
World Conference on Women (4th, Beijing), **1995** 136, 581-587; **1996** 138
World Summit for Social Development, **1995** 134-140
World Summit on Sustainable Development (Johannesburg, 2002), **2002** 593-604
United Nations conventions
Biological Diversity, **1999** 403
Biological Weapons, **1972** 323-328; **1981** 682, 685-686; **1998** 50; **2001** 676-677
Chemical Weapons, **1996** 740-743; **1997** 195-201; **2004** 169
Climate Change (UNFCCC, Rio Treaty), **2000** 337; **2002** 300, 305-321, 593-594; **2004** 829
Genocide, **2002** 605
Physical Protection of Nuclear Material, **2005** 935
Safety of United Nations and Associated Personnel, **1998** 541
Suppression of Acts of Nuclear Terrorism, **2005** 935
Tobacco Control, **2000** 537-538, 552; **2003** 260-278; **2004** 280, 284
Torture and Other Cruel, Inhuman, and Degrading Treatment, **2004** 338; **2005** 582, 908
Transnational Organized Crime, **2004** 132-133
United Nations Decade for Women (1976-1985), Nairobi Conference, **1985** 555-570
United Nations Development Programme (UNDP), **1996** 438-444; **1999** 393
Arab human development reports, **2002** 483-502; **2003** 489-502, 956-957; **2004** 628; **2005** 269-289
China's economic growth, **2005** 618
on food self-sufficiency, **1984** 981
Haiti economic situation, **2004** 94
human development and poverty, **2002** 689-690
Kosovo security issues, **2003** 1141
Malloch appointed head of, **2004** 893
U.S. contributions to, **1972** 341
United Nations Disarmament Committee, Nuclear Nonproliferation Treaty (NPT) debates, **2004** 325-326
United Nations Disengagement Observer Force (UNDOF), peacekeeping between Israel and Syria, **1974** 435-439
United Nations Economic and Social Affairs Department, global economic outlook, **2002** 689-701
United Nations Economic and Social Council
McNamara speech on developing countries' poverty, **1972** 859-865
reform recommendations, **2004** 909-910; **2005** 244
restructuring of, **1975** 338-341
tobacco industry regulation, **2000** 549-550
United Nations Educational, Scientific, and Cultural Organization (UNESCO)
Israel's exclusion from, **1975** 326
John Paul II speech to, **1980** 968-969
on study of limits to world growth, **1972** 215
U.S. membership in, **2003** 810
U.S. protest of anti-Israel actions, **1975** 826
U.S. withdrawal from, **1983** 967-971; **1995** 351
United Nations Emergency Force (UNEF)
in Sinai
after Egyptian-Israeli cease-fire, **1973** 931-934
role in Egyptian-Israeli disengagement, **1974** 29-32
United Nations Environmental Program (UNEP)
control of chlorofluorocarbon emissions, **1987** 747
environmental degradation and drought, **1984** 978
Global Environment Outlook, **2002** 594-595, 855
greenhouse effect, **1988** 862
hazardous waste shipments, **1989** 154
mercury emissions treaty, **2005** 97
ozone depletion, **1988** 221, 223
United Nations Food and Agriculture Organization. *See* Food and Agriculture Organization (FAO)
United Nations Fund for Population Activities (UNFPA), **1987** 454-458
United Nations General Assembly
Ahmadinejad (Iranian president) speech on "nuclear issue," **2005** 593, 595, 596-603
AIDS declaration, **2001** 438-455
Arafat speech to
Geneva, **1988** 905, 907-908
New York, **1974** 919-937
arms control
Carter speech on, **1977** 737-745
Reagan speech on, **1983** 791-800
Barco speech on drug cartel war in Colombia, **1989** 499-501, 511-515
Bush address on terrorist threat, **2003** 19-20
human cloning resolution, **2005** 323
human rights commitment, Carter speech on, **1977** 189-197
Israeli security wall in West Bank, **2004** 309
Korean observers to, **1988** 853
oil consumers and producers meeting, **1974** 124
PLO observer invitation from (1974), **1988** 479-482
Protocol to Prevent, Suppress, and Punish Trafficking in Persons, Especially Women and Children, **2002** 333
raw materials and developing countries, special session on, **1974** 255-264
reform recommendations, **2004** 906; **2005** 230-231, 243
resolutions
2852, on napalm study, **1972** 837-841
3236, and Arab-Israeli peace talks, **1977** 830
3362, on economic cooperation between developing and industrialized countries, **1975** 587-589, 603-611
Second World Assembly on Aging, **2002** 193-200
Soviet invasion of Afghanistan, **1979** 966, 971-972; **1980** 3
Sustainable Development Commission, **1992** 642
troop reductions, Gorbachev speech on, *perestroika,* **1988** 927-940
U.S. foreign policy, Gromyko speech on, **1984** 813, 821-829

United Nations General Assembly *Continued*
U.S. invasion of Panama, **1989** 703
U.S.-Soviet relations, Reagan speech on, **1984** 811-812, 814-821
Zionism resolution, **1975** 825-827, 923
United Nations Global Fund to Fight AIDS, Tuberculosis, and Malaria, **2002** 473, 476; **2005** 51-53
United Nations Headquarters Agreement (1947)
and closing of PLO observer mission, **1988** 479-485
and denial of U.S. visa to Arafat, **1988** 907
on size of UN missions, **1986** 268, 270-271
United Nations High Commissioner for Refugees (UNHCR)
Afghanistan conflict refugees, **2002** 21-22; **2003** 1098-1099; **2004** 918
Afghanistan humanitarian aid, **2001** 883-884
Afghanistan relief worker Bettina Goislard killed, **2003** 1091
asylum for victims of religious persecution, **1998** 28
Bosnia returnees, **2004** 954
child abuse in refugee camps, **2002** 919
child soldiers, **2002** 918
Kosovo conflict refugees, **1999** 289, 804
Liberian refugees, **2005** 801
promoting peace in Africa, **1999** 428-438
refugee settlement, **1991** 671-678; **1992** 466
Rwandan refugees, **2004** 119
West Timor incident, **2001** 594
United Nations Human Rights Commission, **1980** 194
Carter's call for more active role of, **1977** 189-190, 196
on Central America, **1985** 146
Chechen war violations, **2000** 175-176
Cuban dissidents, **2004** 250
death penalty in U.S., **1998** 183-193
East Timor independence, **1999** 511-523
on human rights in Iran, **1978** 14
on human rights in Uganda, **1977** 143-145, 147
Iraq human rights, **1999** 144-152
Ivory Coast civil war, **2004** 819
membership, **2004** 890
Middle East violence, **2000** 930-951
reform recommendations, **2004** 910; **2005** 230
religious freedom in multilateral institutions, **1998** 29
report to on Afghanistan, **1986** 919-936
Sudan genocidal war, **2004** 116, 591
Sudan sexual violence, **2005** 514-525
tsunami disaster relief, **2005** 994
Uzbekistan, killings in Andijon, **2005** 429-433, 436-445
United Nations Intergovernmental Panel on Climate Change (IPCC), report, **2001** 109-126
United Nations Interim Force in Lebanon (UNIFIL), terrorist attack against French in, **1986** 838
United Nations International Children's Emergency Fund. *See* United Nations Children's Emergency Fund
United Nations International Conference on Population
Bucharest (1974), **1987** 449
Mexico City (1984), **1984** 521-522, 544-547; **1987** 450, 454, 457
United Nations Military Observer Group, **1997** 152
United Nations Millennium Summit, **2000** 179, 326, 477
AIDS epidemic, **2002** 476, 478
Millennium Development Goals, **2002** 446; **2003** 755-757, 766, 813-814; **2004** 888
UN Declaration, **2000** 700-711; **2001** 900; **2002** 595
United Nations Monitoring, Verification, and Inspection Commission (UNMOVIC), **2002** 718
United Nations Office for the Coordination of Humanitarian Assistance, Sudan conflict, humanitarian aid, **2004** 590
United Nations Oil for Food Program, corruption scandals, **2004** 717, 887, 891-893; **2005** 228, 233-235
United Nations Organization Mission in the Democratic Republic of Congo (MONUC), **2003** 293, 296-297; **2004** 508-509, 510-516; **2005** 1029-1030
United Nations Peacebuilding Commission, proposal, **2004** 908
United Nations Population Fund
estimates for year 2150, **1992** 500
world population, **2001** 314, 318-319
United Nations Programme on HIV/AIDS (UNAIDS), **1998** 878-889; **1999** 489; **2000** 410-428; **2002** 469-482; **2003** 781; **2005** 50-51
United Nations Protocol Relating to the Status of Refugees, **1992** 455, 456; **1993** 417, 420
United Nations Relief and Works Agency (UNRWA) for Palestinian Refugees, **2002** 933, 936; **2003** 1212; **2004** 310
United Nations Secretary General. *See* Annan, Kofi
United Nations Security Council (UNSC)
Arab-Israeli conflict, debate on terrorism, **1972** 751-753
Arab-Israeli War
cease-fire resolutions, **1973** 881-895
Egyptian-Israeli cease-fire resolution, **1974** 30-31
peacekeeping force, resolution on, **1973** 898-900
Cuban attack on civilian aircraft, **1996** 93-94
economic sanctions. *See* Economic sanctions
Falkland Islands sovereignty, **1982** 284-285, 300
Gorbachev advocates restructuring, **1992** 432, 438
Gorbachev on, **1992** 437
Iran hostages, resolutions on, **1979** 870, 875-876, 880-881
Iran-Iraq War
ban on arms sales, **1987** 527
cease-fire resolutions, **1984** 750
Iraq, weapons inspection in, **1997** 767-773
Israeli settlements
resolution on dismantling of, **1980** 235-242
U.S. criticism of, **1976** 191-196
Israeli-Lebanese conflict, **1982** 742, 745
Khomeini message to, **1979** 870, 875-876
membership
for India, **2005** 465
for Japan, **2003** 811-812; **2005** 465, 622
membership expansion, **2003** 811; **2004** 888-889; **2005** 229-230
Namibia, resolution on South African promise of free elections, **1976** 611-612

Nicaraguan protest against U.S., **1985** 256
peacekeeping mission mandate, **1997** 153-154
PRC invasion of Vietnam, **1979** 184
reform recommendations, **2004** 906-908; **2005** 229-230, 243-244
Rhodesia
economic sanctions against, lifting of, **1979** 941-942
UN participation in settlement, **1977** 585
South Africa
arms embargo against, **1977** 823-825
economic sanctions against, **1985** 533
Soviet downing of Korean plane, **1983** 777, 781-782
U.S. invasion of Grenada, **1983** 850
use of force guidelines, **2004** 889-890, 904-905; **2005** 230
United Nations Security Council (UNSC) resolutions
242
as basis for Middle East peace, **1977** 830, 834, 846, 849; **1978** 608-609, 612-613; **1991** 125
"land for peace" formula, **1989** 289, 295
PLO acceptance of, **1988** 905-908; **1989** 291
Saudi peace plan's consistency with, **1981** 632, 635
and U.S. policy on PLO, **1976** 192; **1979** 647-657
on withdrawal of Israeli occupation forces, **1976** 194, 196
338
as basis for Middle East peace, **1977** 830, 834, 849; **1978** 609, 613; **1979** 846; **1991** 125
on Egyptian-Israeli cease-fire, **1973** 931-933
PLO acceptance of, **1988** 905
Saudi peace plan's consistency with, **1981** 632, 635
U.S. commitment to, **1976** 194, 196
and U.S. policy on PLO, **1976** 192
339, Egyptian-Israeli cease-fire, **1973** 931, 933
435, Angola and Namibia, basis for cease-fire, **1988** 948-949
487, Israeli raid on Iraqi nuclear plant, **1981** 507-519
497, Israeli annexation of Golan Heights, **1981** 899, 904-905
598, Iran-Iraq truce, **1987** 527, 530, 609-613, 869, 873; **1988** 529-532, 704
678, Iraq weapons, **1991** 15, 17-18
687, Iraq weapons, **1991** 191-203; **2003** 147
959, Bosnia, **1994** 550-554
1199, Kosovo conflict, **1998** 829, 830
1203, Kosovo war crimes tribunal, **1998** 831
1244, Kosovo conflict, NATO-led peacekeeping forces, **1999** 138-139, 285-296; **2000** 145; **2003** 61
1258, Congo, UN peacekeeping forces, **1999** 647
1272, East Timor, UN administration of, **1999** 514
1334, Sierra Leone peacekeeping forces, **2000** 1072-1077
1341, Congo conflict, **2001** 166-170
1368, condemning terrorist group activities, **2001** 625, 631-632
1441, Iraq disarmament and weapons inspections, **2002** 35, 713, 715-717, 724-728, 819; **2003** 19, 32-34, 40-52, 147, 945, 1179; **2004** 558
1479, Ivory Coast peace agreement, **2003** 237-244
1483, Iraq sanctions lifted/Iraqi oil money, **2003** 943; **2005** 721-723
1484, Congo peacekeeping mission, **2003** 288-297
1491, Bosnia peacekeeping mission, **2003** 460-469
1493, Congo, peacekeeping mission (MONUC), **2004** 513
1509, Haiti, UN international peacekeeping force, **2004** 100
1510, Afghanistan, International Security Assistance Force (ISAF) authorization, **2003** 1094
1511, Iraq, UN multinational force authorized, **2003** 945, 950-954
1526, Analytical Support and Sanctions Monitoring Team (monitoring al Qaeda terrorist network), **2004** 540-547
1529, Haiti, peacekeeping forces, **2004** 96, 100-102
1541, Haiti, UN Stabilization Mission (MINUSTAH), **2004** 97
1546, Iraq interim government and elections, **2004** 401-402
1556, Sudan conflict, **2004** 592
1559, Lebanon, withdrawal of Syrian troops, **2004** 557-563; **2005** 687, 688
1564, Sudan genocidal war, **2004** 594
1572, Ivory Coast arms embargo, **2004** 822-826
1574, Sudan conflicts, **2004** 595
1575, NATO peacekeeping mission transferred to European Union Force (EUFOR), **2004** 954
1593, Darfur human rights crimes referred to ICC, **2005** 516
United Nations Special Commission (UNSCOM), air strikes against Iraq, **1998** 934-944
United Nations special sessions
on children, **2002** 221-231, 917
on HIV/AIDS, **2000** 413; **2002** 476, 477-478
on Women's Rights, **2000** 325-336
United Nations Truce Supervisory Organization, **1997** 152
United Nations Truth Commission, violence in El Salvador, **1993** 237-248
United Nations War Crimes Commission
uses for files of, **1987** 519
Waldheim investigation, **1986** 744-745, 746
United Nations World Conference on Women's Rights (Beijing), **2000** 325
United Nations World Food Programme (WFP)
Afghanistan humanitarian aid, **2001** 884
Darfur region refugees, **2005** 515
on famine relief, **1984** 974
North Korea aid, **2005** 609
Sudan genocidal war, **2004** 591, 595
worldwide famine and, **2002** 157
Zimbabwe food shortages, **2002** 136; **2003** 1111
United Nations World Summit on Sustainable Development, **2002** 593-604
United Parcel Service (UPS)
jobs for welfare recipients, **1997** 34, 622
Teamsters union strike, **1997** 628-635; **1998** 320
United Press International (UPI), on refugee flight from Da Nang, **1975** 201-204
United Shoe Machinery Corp., United States v., **1991** 28

United Space Alliance, and space shuttle program safety, **2000** 93-94
United States Agency for International Development (USAID). *See* Agency for International Development
United States Commission on Immigration Reform, **1994** 387-400; **1995** 564-565
United States Commission on National Security/21st Century, **1999** 499-510
United States Conference of Catholic Bishops (USCCB)
and Catholic Church, **2005** 293
gay seminarians prohibition, **2005** 864
sexual abuse by priests, **2002** 867-876; **2003** 523, 526-528; **2004** 82, 88; **2005** 866
United States Conference of Mayors, **1994** 290
United States Railway Association, on railroad reorganization, **1975** 529-542
United Steelworkers of America, **1973** 437-444; **2005** 488
United Steelworkers of America v. Weber, **1979** 493-507
United Way of America (UWA), **1992** 303-311
Uniting and Strengthening America by Providing Appropriate Tools Required to Intercept and Obstruct Terrorism Act. *See* USA Patriot Act
Universal Declaration of Human Rights, **1980** 192; **1984** 815; **1987** 555-556; **1988** 885-887
Universal Employment and Training System, Urban League proposal, **1983** 41
Universities. *See* Colleges and universities
University of Arizona, return of skeletal remains by, **1989** 541
University of California (Davis), affirmative action in medical school admissions, **1978** 467-492
University of California (San Francisco), Institute for Health and Aging, on Medicare costs, **1986** 274
University of California Regents v. Bakke, **2003** 358, 360-363, 383-386
University of Chicago, National Opinion Research Center, **1992** 87
University of Georgia, Burns speech on inflation and unemployment, **1975** 635
University of Kentucky, Rehnquist speech on Court workload, **1982** 706, 723-724
University of Michigan, return of skeletal remains by, **1989** 541
University of Minnesota, return of skeletal remains by, **1989** 541
University of Mississippi, **1992** 576, 578-587
University of Pennsylvania Law Review, **1992** 33, 35-43
University of Pennsylvania v. Equal Employment Opportunity Commission, **1990** 23-34
University of South Carolina, Medical School, rape study, **1992** 385-395
University of Southern Mississippi, **1992** 576, 578-587
University of Texas, affirmative action program, **1996** 762-763
University of Virginia, religious publications, **1995** 388-395
University of Wisconsin, on hate crimes, **1992** 545
UNSC. *See* United Nations Security Council
UPI. *See* United Press International
Upjohn Co. v. United States, **1998** 398, 402
Uranium enrichment
See also Nuclear weapons
highly enriched uranium supplies in former Soviet Union, **1996** 140, 142-143
increased production of, **1977** 271-272, 274, 279, 290
reactor leaks, **1994** 340
Uranus, *Voyager* mission to collect data about, **1981** 836
Urban, Jerzy, **1983** 579
Urban enterprise zones. *See* Enterprise zones
Urban Institute, The
Coleman report on school desegregation, **1975** 613-633
poor children and elderly in U.S., **1988** 877-880
welfare reform report, **1999** 258, 259-260, 269
Urban League. *See* National Urban League
Urban policy
See also Cities
Carter proposals for development and renewal, **1978** 241-258
in developing countries, and population pressure, **1987** 440, 444-445
federal aid to states and localities, **1976** 641-643
inner cities, Eisenhower Foundation report on, **1993** 211-233
and Sun Belt migration, **1981** 39-40, 49-54
Urbanek, Karel, **1989** 636
Urcuyo Maleanos, Francisco, **1979** 582
Uribe, Alvaro
Colombia presidential elections, **2005** 771
Colombia presidential inauguration speech, **2002** 569-578
democratic security and defense policy, **2003** 425-438
Urquhart, Brian, UN "rapid reaction force," **2003** 809
Uruguay
and Contadora Group, **1987** 638
political situation, **2005** 772
presidential elections, **2004** 548
role in Falklands War, **1983** 23
smoking in the Americas, **1992** 269
Uruguay Round. *See under* General Agreement on Tariffs and Trade; Trade negotiations, multilateral
U.S. v., See name of opposing party
U.S. Airways
bankruptcy and pension plans, **2005** 199, 206, 486
bankruptcy protection, **2002** 53
pilots' pension plan, defaulting on, **2003** 709; **2004** 734, 736
U.S. Airways v. Barnett, **2002** 6
U.S. Bancorp, online stock trading study, **1999** 203
U.S. Conference of Catholic Bishops. *See* United States Conference of Catholic Bishops
U.S. Conference of Mayors
AIDS, **1983** 533-541
budget cutbacks affecting cities, **1973** 454
distortion of national priorities, **1972** 481
homeless families, **1989** 672, 675
hunger in large cities report, **2003** 73
job shortages in cities, **1998** 365

U.S. Council for Energy Awareness, **1990** 197
U.S. Election Assistance Commission, voting results, **2004** 778
U.S. News and World Report, arrest of Daniloff, **1986** 819
U.S. Preventive Services Task Force (USPSTF)
  depression screenings report, **2002** 265-274
  hormone replacement therapy, **2002** 503
U.S. Steel Corp., labor-management agreement, **1973** 437-438
U.S. Term Limits, Inc. v. Thornton, **1995** 259-275
USA Freedom Corps
  Bush proposal, **2002** 37, 44
  Bush statement on, **2003** 28
USA Patriot Act (2001), **2001** 641; **2002** 559, 562, 833; **2003** 166, 167
  Ashcroft speeches, **2003** 607-611, 613-619
  Bush State of the Union address on, **2004** 23
  congressional oversight and response to, **2003** 608, 612-613
  extension, opposition to, **2005** 80, 958
  Gore speech, **2003** 608, 619-630
USA Today, Arthur Ashe story, **1992** 335, 336, 338
U.S.-Canada Power System Outage Task Force, investigation report, **2003** 1015, 1018-1024
USCCB. *See* United States Conference of Catholic Bishops
USDA. *See* Agriculture Department
User fees
  in federal budget, **1987** 3, 4, 10-11
  for government services, **1986** 57
  to recover government costs, in Reagan budget revisions, **1981** 334
Usery, William J., Jr.
  coal strike settlement, **1990** 19-22
  Commission on the Future of Worker-Management Relations member, **1995** 15
Ushakov, Yuri, U.S.-Russian relations, **2001** 153
Ushuilidze, Nona, Georgian presidential elections, **2003** 1043
US-VISIT (United States Visitors and Immigrant Status Technology) program, **2003** 218, 220-221
Utilities
  acid rain and, **1983** 198
    environmental restrictions on, **1981** 277
  phone company's aid in government electronic surveillance, **1977** 883-896
  rate structure revision, **1975** 18, 36; **1977** 283, 288-289, 291
  state, federal regulation of, **1982** 447-467
Utley, Garrick, **1990** 818-823
Uwilingiyimana, Agathe, assassination of, **1994** 542; **1998** 614
Uzbekistan
  Alma-Ata Declaration, **1991** 804-806
  Andijon uprising, UN Human Rights Commission Mission on, **2005** 429-433, 436-445
  Commonwealth Pact, **1991** 803-804
  presidential elections, **2005** 428-429
  refugees, **2004** 431-432
  Soviet Union restructuring plans, **1991** 532-533
  "Sunshine Coalition" (opposition group), **2005** 432
  U.S. base "Camp Stronghold Freedom," **2005** 429, 433
  U.S. "Strategic Partnership" agreement, **2005** 429
  war on terrorism, support for U.S., **2001** 627, 894

V

VA. *See* Veterans Administration; Veterans Affairs Department
Vacco, Attorney General of N.Y. v. Quill, **1997** 459-479
Vacco, Dennis, apparel industry sweatshops, **1997** 206
Vagrancy laws, municipal and state, constitutionality of, **1972** 207-211
Vajpayee, Atai Bihari
  India nuclear testing, **1998** 326, 329-330
  India-Pakistan relations, **2002** 326-328; **2003** 209-213, 215; **2004** 352
  Kashmir dispute, **2001** 964-965; **2003** 209; **2004** 1010
  state visit to Pakistan, **1999** 624
  term as prime minister, **2004** 348-349; **2005** 467
Valde, Juan Gabriel, UN mission to Haiti, **2004** 98
Valdiserri, Ronald A., on antiretroviral drug therapy for HIV prevention, **2005** 56
Valenti, Jack, **1984** 55
  marketing violent entertainment to children, **2000** 731
  television rating system, **1996** 831, 834, 836-837
  on TV violence, **1993** 487
Valeriani, Richard, **1976** 735
Valley Forge (Pennsylvania) Declaration of Independence bicentennial celebration, **1976** 509-510
Valley of the Drums (Kentucky), hazardous waste disposal at, **1979** 782, 785, 787, 792
Value added taxes (VAT), and EC budget problems, **1984** 440-443
Values
  and adult attitudes toward children survey, **1997** 422-443
  Bush State of the Union address on, **2004** 20-21
  Dole social issues speech, **1995** 573-580
  family, John Paul II on, **1982** 837
  moral and religious, Carter inaugural on, **1977** 90, 91-92
  of Reagan administration, and state of black America, **1987** 46-47
  return to family and religious, Reagan on, **1985** 105, 107, 113-114
  and social involvement in colleges, **1986** 940-941, 945, 958
  teaching of in schools, **1987** 599, 603, 606-607; **1988** 299, 305-306
    colleges, **1985** 599-600
    elementary school, **1986** 804-805, 808-809
ValuJet crash, **1996** 237-240; **1997** 113
Van Amburg, George, **1978** 654
Van der Stoel, Max, human rights in Iraq, **1999** 144-152; **2000** 582
Van Gogh, Theo, murdered by Islamic extremist, **2005** 340
Van Orden, Thomas, **2005** 377

Van Orden v. Perry, **2005** 376-384
Vance, Cyrus R.
Agee passport revocation, **1981** 541-555
appointment to secretary of state, **1976** 877-878, 880-881, 884, 886-889
Carter world trip, **1977** 897
on flag protection amendment, **1989** 345
foreign policy goals, **1980** 476-483
Iran, UN effort against, **1979** 970
Israel, assurances to, **1979** 225
Latin America policy, **1979** 713-721
national security strategy, **1986** 781
Nicaraguan change of government, **1979** 581-582, 585-588
Panama Canal treaties, **1977** 592
PRC's use of force to regain Taiwan, **1978** 158
resignation, **1980** 475-476
sales of warplanes in Middle East, **1978** 125-126, 128-129
SALT II negotiations, **1977** 243-250; **1979** 414
Soviet presence in Cuba, **1979** 763-764
Uganda's treatment of Americans, **1977** 144
UN vote on Israeli settlements, **1980** 235-237, 242
U.S.-PRC relations
assurances to Soviets on, **1979** 137
consular exchange, **1979** 151
Young's resignation from UN, **1979** 648, 654, 656
Vandalism, school, costs of, **1975** 207-208, 214-216
Vander Schaaf, Derek J., Tailhook courts-martial, **1994** 487
Vanderbilt University, **1992** 88
Vanocur, Sander, presidential debate, **1992** 910, 918, 927-928
Varela Project (anti-Castro democratic movement), **2002** 234; **2004** 249
Vargas, Getulio, **1985** 5
Vargas Llosa, Mario, **2000** 923
Varmus, Harold, on embryonic research funding ban, **1998** 66
Vasquez, Efrain, on Chavez resignation, **2002** 203
VAT. *See* Value added taxes
Vatican
as a city-state, **1984** 20-21
diplomatic relations
with Israel, **1988** 411, 413
with Poland, **1987** 555
with U.S., **1984** 19-22
disciplining of Father Curran, **1986** 757-765
dissent among U.S. clergy, **1986** 985
Evangelium Vitae (Gospel of Life), **1995** 145-161
excommunication of Lefebvre, **1988** 489-491
female priests ban, papal letter reaffirming, **1994** 276-280
funeral mass for John Paul II, **2005** 290-298
gay seminarians prohibition, **2005** 863-872
on homosexuals, pastoral care of, **1986** 909-918
Israeli accord on diplomatic relations, **1993** 1033-1040
John Paul II apology for errors of the church, **2005** 293
jurisdiction for Agca trial, **1981** 428
on liberation theology, **1984** 759-775; **1986** 317-338
Papal Nunciature of, Noriega refuge in Panama, **1989** 701-702
on reproductive technologies and bioethics, **1987** 267-287
selection of new pope, **2005** 294-295
sexual abuse by priests, **2002** 867-877; **2005** 294
Synod Secretariat, U.S. bishops' report to, **1985** 571-581
twenty-fifth anniversary of John Paul II's reign, **2003** 524
UN Conference on Women, objections to plan of action, **1995** 583
on women, role of, **1983** 95; **1988** 785-792
Vatican Council I (1869–1870), **1983** 93-94
Vatican Council II (1962–1965)
celebration and renewal of, **1985** 765-780
changes brought by, Lefebvre's rebellion against, **1988** 489-494
creation of World Synod of Bishops, **1980** 871-872
and dissent among clergy, **1986** 757, 759, 761, 765
effects of in U.S., **1985** 571-581
on family life, **1980** 874-875
and Netherlands Catholic Church, **1985** 363-364
on the poor, **1984** 760, 763, 770
rejection of anti-Semitism, **1986** 340, 343-344
VaxGen Inc., anthrax vaccine, **2004** 446
Vazquez, Tabare
as president of Uruguay, **2005** 772
Uruguay presidential elections, **2004** 548
Vedrine, Hubert
European defense force, **1999** 819
on war in Iraq, **2002** 614
Veneman, Ann M.
agriculture secretary confirmation, **2001** 97
mad cow disease, **2003** 1234-1244
obesity, combating, **2002** 627
roadless initiative for forest preservation, **2001** 216; **2004** 669
Venereal Disease, National Commission on, recommendations of, **1972** 343-350
Venereal disease, research on and control of in U.S., **1972** 343-350
Venezuela
Caribbean economic aid from, **1982** 180, 186
Carter visit, **1978** 269-270
and Contadora Group, **1987** 638
Coordinadora Democrática (Democratic Coordinator), **2003** 279, 283-287
debt problem of, **1982** 972; **1989** 137-138
drug summit, **1992** 201-221
economic recovery, **2003** 755
failed coup attempt, **2002** 201-211
flood, **1999** 469
foreign trade, **1994** 596
general strike, **2003** 280-281
human trafficking, **2004** 125, 552-553
John Paul II visit, **1985** 57-61
Law of the Sea Treaty, **1982** 345-361
national referendum on presidency of Hugo Chavez, **2003** 279-287
negotiations with Jimmy Carter, **2002** 201, 983
oil industry, **2004** 188
OPEC oil price cut, **1981** 799

OPEC oil price increase, **1976** 938
political situation, **2002** 775
at poverty summit, **1981** 770
recall vote, OAS resolution on, **2004** 548-554
smoking in the Americas, **1992** 269
U.S. relations, **2005** 770-771
U.S. trade preferences denied to, **1975** 224, 233
Ventner, J. Craig, Human Genome Project, **2000** 398, 399, 407-409
Vento, Bruce F. (D-Minn.), BCCI banking scandal, **1991** 635
Ventura (California), air quality of, **1981** 275
Ventura, Stephanie, on teenage pregnancy, **1999** 385
Ver, Fabian C., and B. Aquino assassination, **1984** 926-927, 929-931; **1986** 98, 307-309
Vergès, Jacques, **1987** 518
Verheugen, Gunter, EU membership expansion, **2004** 975
Verhofstadt, Guy
African economic development, **2001** 504
European Commission presidential candidate, **2004** 201
Rwanda genocidal war remembrance, **2004** 116
Vermont, same-sex civil unions legislation, **2000** 158-167; **2004** 37
Verner, Liipfert, Bernhard, McPherson, and Hand (law firm), United Way ethics case, **1992** 303-311
Vernonia School District 47J v. Acton, **1995** 339-349; **1999** 223; **2002** 425-435
Vershbow, Alexander, North Korea-South Korea relations, **2005** 609
Vesco, Robert L., SEC investigation, and Nixon campaign contributions, **1973** 564; **1975** 143
Vessey, John W., Jr. (Gen.)
Vietnam POW/MIAs investigations, **1993** 124-125; **1995** 473, 475
Vietnam trade embargo, **1994** 98
Vessey, John W., terrorist threats, task force on, **2002** 743
Vest, William T., Jr., Tailhook courts-martial, **1994** 107-115
Veterans
British Gulf War veterans with illness, **2001** 910
Democratic Party platform on, **1972** 546-547
on draft evader pardon, **1977** 96
education and employment for, **1972** 97-98, 108-109
Gulf War syndrome report, **1994** 264-275; **1997** 740-745
Gulf War veterans with ALS, **2001** 907-912
homeless report, **1994** 254, 257
Pearl Harbor anniversary, **1991** 775-784
preference in federal employment, **1978** 138, 140, 145-146
programs for under Carter, **1981** 77
and Reagan budget cuts, **1981** 217, 326
Republican Party platform on, **1972** 707-708; **1984** 723-724
Tomb of the Unknowns (Arlington National Cemetery), disinterment remarks, **1998** 281-283
Vietnam, employment rate of, **1973** 220-221
Vietnam War, Agent Orange exposure, **2001** 908
Vietnam War memorial, **1993** 347-349
Veterans Administration (VA)
Cleland appointment to, **1977** 184
extension of education benefits, **1988** 277-285
history of, **1988** 873-875
Veterans Affairs Department (DVA)
creation of, **1988** 873-876
disability programs, **2005** 132
Gulf War syndrome report, **1994** 265-266; **1995** 275; **1997** 742
Gulf War veterans with ALS, **2001** 907-912
human radiation experiments, **1993** 988
racial disparity in care, **1993** 672
Veterans of Foreign Wars (VFW)
on draft evader pardon, **1977** 96
Ford announcement of amnesty for draft evaders, **1974** 819, 821
Nixon speech on bombing of Cambodia, **1973** 731-735
Veto, line-item
Bush on, **1989** 74
Clinton's use of, **1997** 611-616
congressional passage of, **1995** 169-170; **1996** 149, 696
Reagan call for, **1984** 82, 89, 101, 105, 127, 170; **1985** 85; **1986** 40, 44; **1987** 106, 111, 122; **1988** 58, 62-63, 161; **1989** 11
unconstitutional, Supreme Court on, **1998** 419-437, 909
Vetoes
by Ford, **1975** 18; **1976** 709-713, 780
of government appropriations bill by Reagan, **1981** 642, 831-834
VFW. *See* Veterans of Foreign Wars
Vice president
See also under individual names of vice presidents
Agnew case
immunity of from indictment, **1973** 828-829, 832-833
investigation of charges against, **1975** 881-882
resignation, **1974** 696, 987
debates, **1992** 977-1001
Ferraro nomination, **1984** 647, 649
Gore nomination acceptance speech, **1996** 602, 603-608
Quayle nomination acceptance speech, **1992** 783, 794-798
resignation of and filling vacancy, **1973** 827
Rockefeller
nomination and confirmation, **1974** 707-711, 988-989
swearing-in, **1974** 987-990
role of
Cheney on, **2001** 171-172
Dole-Mondale debate on, **1976** 776-777
Ford on for Rockefeller, **1974** 766-767, 770
selection procedure for, reform of, **1972** 598-599
transfer of power to, **1985** 491-495
Vice presidential debates
Bentsen-Quayle, **1988** 799-829
Cheney-Edwards, **2004** 678
Cheney-Lieberman, **2000** 797, 800, 810-817
Dole-Mondale, **1976** 773-796

Vice presidential debates *Continued*
Gore-Kemp, **1996** 707-709, 718-724
Vice presidential papers
Nixon donation and tax deduction on, **1973** 947, 957; **1974** 235, 237, 239-240, 243-245
subpoena of in Agnew case, **1973** 829-831
Vichy government, complicity with Nazis, **1995** 478-479
Victims of Pan Am Flight 103 (group), **1990** 303
Victims of Trafficking and Violence Protection Act, **2004** 123
Victims Rights Amendment, **1997** 39
Videla, Jorge Rafael, and human rights in Argentina, **1977** 5, 8
Video news releases (VNRs), as government propaganda, **2005** 644-655
Videotape recorders, fair use of, **1984** 53-80
Vienna (Austria), airport attack, **1985** 463, 468
Vienna Convention for the Protection of the Ozone Layer (1985), **1987** 747-748; **1992** 76
Vienna Convention on Consular Rights (1963), **2004** 797; **2005** 181
Vietcong, military activity of, Kissinger report on (1969), **1972** 362, 369-371
Vietnam
AIDS epidemic, **2004** 430
bird flu outbreak, **2004** 924-925
Clinton state visit, **2000** 913-922
reunification
Paris peace accords on, **1973** 123-124, 138
peace negotiations on, **1972** 868-869, 875
SARS (severe acute respiratory syndrome) outbreak, **2003** 131
trade agreement, **2000** 913-915
U.S. consulate, secretary of state on, **1997** 489-492; **1999** 475-479; **2000** 913
U.S. diplomatic relations, **1995** 472-477; **1997** 489-492; **1999** 475-479
U.S. economic sanctions against, **1995** 474; **1997** 489; **1999** 476
U.S. trade embargo, **1994** 95-99; **1995** 474
Vietnam, Democratic Republic of (North Vietnam)
cease-fire violations by, **1973** 247, 332, 447, 450
and U.S. aid to South, **1975** 279-281, 285-288, 298-299
control of South Vietnam territory, **1975** 201-202
military activity of, Kissinger report (1969) on, **1972** 362, 368-371
military offensive of, **1972** 361, 612-613
U.S. response to, **1972** 407-408
Paris peace accords, **1973** 115-167
Paris peace negotiations
Hanoi Radio on settlement provisions, **1972** 867-870
presence of forces in South, **1972** 943-944, 950
reneging on agreed provisions, **1972** 941-951
peace plan of, **1972** 133-134
POWs
negotiations on tied to U.S. withdrawal, **1972** 3, 5-7
stalling on release of, **1973** 331
torture and mistreatment of, **1973** 247
takeover of South Vietnam, **1975** 201-202, 225, 353, 356, 496, 502
violation of Paris peace accords, **1975** 251-253, 266-277
troops in South, as cease-fire provision, **1975** 280, 284, 287-288, 296, 299
U.S. bombing of
congressional reaction, **1973** 3-4, 6-7, 9-13, 15, 17
objectives, **1972** 611-614
and peace negotiations, **1972** 491-497; **1973** 116
and protection of withdrawing troops, **1972** 57
renewed, **1972** 4-5, 351, 355-359, 361, 385-388, 942
U.S. mining of harbors of
and peace negotiations, **1973** 116
and stepped-up bombing, **1972** 407-412
U.S. relations
and reconstruction aid, **1972** 870, 875; **1973** 193, 195-196, 198, 246
and removal of mines, **1973** 144-145, 331-332
Vietnam, North. *See* Vietnam, Democratic Republic of
Vietnam, Provisional Revolutionary Government of the Republic of South (PRG, Vietcong)
on American MIAs, **1977** 208
domestic policy announcement, **1975** 301-307
negotiations with South Vietnam after peace accords, **1975** 279
Paris peace accords, signing of, **1973** 115-167
peace proposal of, **1972** 143-145
on rights of South Vietnamese, **1975** 202
role in peace settlement, **1972** 869-870, 877
Vietnam, Republic of (South Vietnam)
cease-fire violations by, North Vietnam on, **1973** 332
CIA support for coup in, Senate investigation of, **1975** 710, 715, 770, 776
Communist victory in, **1975** 201-202, 225, 251-253, 266-277, 353, 356
and U.S. foreign commitments, **1975** 496, 502
Da Nang
evacuation of refugees from, **1975** 201-204
retreat of South Vietnamese army from, **1975** 288-289
elections in, as peace settlement provision on, **1972** 868-869, 874
improvement of forces of, Kissinger's 1969 report on, **1972** 363-364, 371-373
internal politics and attitudes toward U.S. policies, **1972** 365-366, 375-376
North Vietnamese invasion of, **1972** 351, 355-357
Paris peace accords, signing of, **1973** 115-167
Paris peace negotiations, objections to proposals, **1972** 942-944, 947, 949-950
peace plan, U.S.-South Vietnamese, **1972** 126-127
self-determination for
in Paris international conference act, **1973** 331-334
Paris peace accords on, **1973** 115-118, 120, 122-123, 136-138
in peace proposals, **1972** 125-129, 133-134, 144-145, 407-409
troop morale, impact of renewed U.S. bombing of North, **1972** 407
U.S. aid requested for, **1974** 278, 281-283; **1975** 223-225, 227-230, 252, 254

U.S. assurances of continued aid, **1973** 447, 450-451; **1975** 279-281, 285-299
U.S. consultations with on peace settlement, **1972** 867, 873, 877-878
U.S. withdrawal, **1972** 3-6, 55-59; **1973** 247; **1975** 280, 287
delays in, **1973** 331
meaning of to North Vietnamese, **1972** 128-129
Vietcong proposal on, **1972** 144
Vietnam, Socialist Republic of
Chinese invasion of, **1979** 137, 183-190
human rights in, **1981** 180, 188-189; **1983** 193-195
negotiations with U.S. on normalization of relations, **1977** 207, 209, 211-212, 218
population growth in, **1987** 440, 443
presidential commission on MIAs, trip to Southeast Asia, **1977** 207-218
U.S. aid for in exchange for POW-MIA information, **1976** 926, 930; **1977** 208-212, 217-218
Vietnam Veterans of America, on discrimination in Medal of Honor award, **1989** 697
Vietnam War
See also Prisoners of war (POWs)
Agent Orange exposure, **2001** 908
Bush service record, **2004** 480
Clinton's letter on draft, **1992** 155-161
congressional vs. executive power in conduct of, **1973** 3-4, 6-7, 9-13, 15, 17, 923-925; **1975** 227-228, 231
controversies about in U.S. government, Kissinger's 1969 report on, **1972** 361-379
disappointments and lessons of, Muskie on, **1976** 33
dissent
demonstrations against, **1972** 407, 711; **1973** 79, 81, 428, 430
Nixon on, **1973** 80-81, 84; **1977** 347-348
divisiveness of in U.S., **1984** 347-350
draft evaders
amnesty for, **1972** 12-13, 528, 576, 722; **1973** 193-194, 197-198; **1974** 768, 813, 819-831; **1976** 701-703
pardon of, **1977** 95-99
ending
Nixon and Agnew on Democrats' solution for, **1972** 711, 715, 722
Nixon on, **1972** 721-722
enemy troop count and CBS documentary, **1983** 401-412; **1985** 159-165
Garwood conviction for enemy collaboration, **1981** 197-201
Gulf of Tonkin resolution, **1991** 4-5
incendiary weapons in, **1972** 838-839
Johnson's handling of, **1972** 789-790
Kent State protesters commemorated, **1990** 289-294
Kerry service record, **2004** 481-482
land mine warfare, **1995** 50
memorial, Clinton remarks on Memorial Day, **1993** 347-349
MIAs in
commission investigating, **1977** 207-218
House report on, **1976** 925-936
Senate report on, **1993** 113-127
My Lai incident, and reversal of Calley's conviction, **1974** 857-860
Navy ships in combat zone, racial unrest aboard, **1972** 901
Nixon policies as election issue, **1972** 589, 593-594
pacification program, Kissinger's 1969 report on, **1972** 364-365, 373-375
Paris peace accords
cease-fire agreement, **1973** 115-167
implementation of, **1973** 125-128, 193, 195-196; **1975** 292-294
International Commission of Control and Supervision, **1973** 126-127, 130, 138-142, 147-149, 160-167, 332, 334; **1975** 280, 297
international conference, **1973** 142, 247, 292, 296, 331-336
Joint Military Commissions, **1973** 127-128, 138-141, 146-155, 157-158
on MIAs, **1977** 208
negotiation and meaning of, Kissinger on, **1973** 116-117, 120-133
Nixon announcement of, **1973** 115, 117-120
Nixon on, **1973** 269-276, 515-516, 518-520, 522, 525-526
North Vietnamese violation of, **1973** 516; **1975** 227-230, 251-253, 259-260, 270-272, 275; **1976** 930
Nixon and Thieu on, **1973** 447, 450
and POW release, **1973** 245-247
self-determination for South Vietnam, **1973** 449
Thieu's objections to, **1975** 279-299
Paris peace negotiations
cease-fire provisions, **1972** 868-869, 874, 876
deadlock in, **1972** 941-951
effects of congressional action on, **1973** 4
linguistic problems, **1972** 941, 945-947
Nixon on, **1972** 355, 357; **1977** 323, 347-348
North Vietnamese motivation in, **1972** 362, 367-369
secret negotiations
North Vietnamese version of, **1972** 351-355
U.S. revelation of, **1972** 121-134
settlement provisions, Kissinger and Radio Hanoi on, **1972** 867-878
on South Vietnam elections, **1972** 868-869, 874
on supervisory commissions, **1972** 870, 874-875
U.S. proposals and Vietnamese rejection of, **1972** 407-409
on U.S. withdrawal, **1972** 868-869, 874
U.S.-PRC communiqué on, **1972** 189
Vietcong proposal, **1972** 143-145
on Vietnamese reunification, **1972** 868-869, 875
peace negotiations
U.S. bombing of North to encourage, **1972** 491-497, 611-614
U.S. search for intermediaries, **1972** 491, 494-496
Pentagon Papers on, **1972** 491-497; **1974** 33-37
political and military situation, Kissinger's 1969 report on, **1972** 361-379
unknown serviceman interment, **1984** 347-352
U.S. and South Vietnamese disagreements on conduct of, **1972** 611-614
U.S. bombing
of Cambodia, **1973** 729-735
of North Vietnam

Vietnam War *Continued*
Nixon explanation of, **1972** 351, 355-359
Thieu on objectives of, **1972** 611-614
U.S. domestic reconciliation after, **1975** 251-263
U.S. evacuation of Da Nang, **1975** 201-204
U.S. failure to understand, Solzhenitsyn on, **1978** 405, 413-414
U.S. policy in, Wallace on, **1975** 156-159
U.S. troop withdrawal
Democratic Party platform on, **1972** 529, 575-576
Nixon on, **1972** 3-6
Republican Party platform on, **1972** 653, 656-657
stages of, **1972** 74, 76
Vietnamization of, **1972** 55-59, 122, 356-357, 574-575
war powers debate, **1990** 663-664
Vigil-Muniz, Claudia, on BIA apology to Indians, **2000** 725
Viguerie, Richard, direct mail for conservative causes, **2005** 562
Vike-Freiberga, Vaira, Latvian membership in NATO, **2002** 887
Viking Penguin (publisher), and death threat against Rushdie, **1989** 86-87
Viktora, Robert, **1992** 543-551
Village Voice, leak of House draft report on intelligence community, **1976** 683-686
Villalobos, Joaquin, **1993** 239
Villepin, Dominique, on Qaddafi decision to dismantle nuclear weapons, **2003** 1222
Vilsack, Tom (Iowa governor), vice presidential candidate, **2004** 480
Vincennes (USS), downing of Iranian airliner by, **1988** 703-717
Vincent, Francis T. "Fay," Jr.
resignation as baseball commissioner, **1992** 855-858
Steinbrenner's gambling, **1990** 483, 487-490
Vincent, Jean-Marie, **1994** 439
Vinicor, Frank, on diabetes and obesity, **2000** 243
Violence
See also Domestic violence; School violence
against children, **1999** 617
against women, **1999** 527; **2000** 327-328
Justice Department report, **1994** 62-72
aggressive driving, **1997** 550-561
crimes of, Attorney General's Task Force on, **1981** 647-670
crimes of, DOJ reports on, **1992** 375-378
in El Salvador, **1993** 237-248
FBI crime report, **1994** 574-582; **1995** 710-716; **1997** 681-689; **1998** 869-877; **1999** 614-622, 618-619; **2000** 856-857; **2002** 788-789; **2003** 979-992; **2004** 765; **2005** 681-683
gun-related deaths, **2001** 723
honor killings of women, **2000** 327
marketing entertainment to children, **2000** 722-729
media and, **2001** 73, 75-76
report on gun violence, **1992** 493-498
school safety report, **1998** 735-741
shooting of Capitol policemen, **1998** 510-517
shootings in Armenian parliament, **1999** 639-642
shootings in schools, **1998** 735-737
sniper attacks, **2003** 992
sniper shootings in D.C. metropolitan area, **2002** 959-960, 961; **2005** 180
surgeon general's report on, **2001** 73-85
on television
effect on social behavior, **1972** 61-66; **1982** 365-383
parent advisory, **1993** 487-492
television voluntary rating system, **2000** 27-28
youth violence
myths about, **2001** 79
prevention programs, **2001** 84
Violence Against Women Act (1994), **1995** 277; **2000** 35; **2001** 725
Violent Crime Control and Law Enforcement Act (1994), **1997** 247
Vioxx
drug safety, **2004** 640, 747, 850-866
heart attacks or stroke risk and, **2004** 856-857
withdrawal, **2004** 850-851
Virgin Islands
Hurricane Hugo in, **1989** 668
trade status with U.S., **1982** 180, 186
Virginia
See also Richmond (Virginia)
first African American governor, **1990** 41-47
legislative apportionment, and one-man, one-vote rule, **1973** 277-289
Virginia Beach v. Howell, **1973** 277-289
Virginia Military Institute (VMI), all-male policy, **1991** 309-316
Virginia State Board of Pharmacy v. Virginia Citizens Consumer Council, **1976** 351-363
Vishnevskaya, Galina, voluntary exile of, **1975** 161-165; **1981** 376
Vivanco, José Miguel, amnesty for Colombian guerillas, opposition to, **2003** 428
Vladivostok accord (1974)
Ford on accomplishments of his term, **1977** 49
hopefulness of, Brezhnev on, **1976** 143, 148
as preparation for SALT II, **1975** 93; **1978** 558-559; **1979** 413-414, 455
on strategic nuclear weapons and MIRVs, **1974** 955-958, 967-968
U.S.-Soviet interpretations of, **1977** 243-268
Vlazny, John G. (archbishop of Portland), sexual abuse of priests, **2004** 87
VOA. *See* Voice of America
Vocational education, definition of in urban schools, **1988** 210-211
Vogle, Paul, on refugee flight from Da Nang, **1975** 201-204
Voice of America (VOA)
China broadcasts, **1994** 83
independence of from White House, **1981** 754
Voice of the Faithful, **2005** 867
Voinovich, George V. (R-Ohio), on Bolton UN ambassador nomination, **2005** 237
Volcanoes, eruption of Mount St. Helens, **1980** 811-824
Volcker, Paul A.
appointment to Fed, **1979** 562, 575, 578
Arthur Andersen collapse, **2002** 397

on Burns's speech on international monetary reform, **1972** 413
commission on neutral aid to Nazi Germany, **1997** 260
credit restraint to fight inflation, **1979** 771-774, 776-780
Group of Five meeting, **1985** 623
head of commission on public service, **1989** 196
reappointment, **1983** 595-597
resignation, **1987** 511-516
restraint on money supply, **1980** 244
UN oil-for-food program investigative panel, **2004** 892; **2005** 234-235
Volcker commission. *See* National Commission on the Public Service
Volkogonov, Dimitri, **1992** 525
Volodski, Lev, **1974** 779
Volokh, Eugene
pledge of allegiance, constitutionality of, **2002** 385
on Supreme Court justice O'Connor, **2005** 553-554
Voloshin, Alexander (Russian chief of staff), resignation, **2003** 247
Voluntary organizations
in Carter urban proposals, **1978** 241-245, 247, 256-257
USA Freedom Corps, Bush administration proposals for, **2002** 37, 44
Vondra, Alexandr, Iraq War supporter, **2003** 44
Vorster, John
apartheid policies of, black leaders on, **1976** 677-680
and Namibian interim government proposal, **1976** 612
Rhodesian settlement, **1976** 289, 721-723
Soweto riots, **1984** 1027
Voter participation
by African Americans, **1983** 47-48, 50, 54
expectations for 1976 election, **1976** 778-779, 797, 800-802
report on, **1990** 295-299
residence requirements, constitutionality of, **1972** 283-290
rules to encourage, Democratic Party platform on, **1972** 587-588
by young first-time voters, in 1972 election, **1973** 35-38
Voter registration
election-day, proposed, **1977** 199-203
Farrakhan on minority drive, **1995** 656, 666-667
NAACP campaign, **1995** 454, 462
Voting districts, minority-dominated, **1995** 369-384
Voting rights
Democratic Party platform on, **1976** 545, 562; **1984** 609-611
Texas redistricting controversy, **2005** 632, 634-635
for women
in Kuwait, **2005** 272
in Saudi Arabia denied, **2005** 271
Voting Rights Act (1965), **2001** 523-524; **2005** 353
provisions of, Warren on, **1972** 939
race-based redistricting, **1993** 459-481; **1995** 369-384
Voting Rights Act (1970), amendments, and racial criteria in redistricting, **1977** 151-167
Voucher systems
as privatization technique, **1988** 230, 233, 237
in public schools, **1997** 363-364
Voyager missions, **1980** 989-993; **1981** 835-844
Voyaguers National Park (Minnesota), snowmobile regulation, **2001** 216
Vrooman, Robert S., Chinese nuclear-espionage matter, **1999** 241

W

Waagner, Clayton Lee, anthrax threat, **2001** 130
Wachtler, Sol, **1990** 269, 273
Waco (Texas) incident
Branch Davidian mass suicide, **1997** 123
Clinton's defense of attack on, **1993** 293-301
cult compound attack, **1995** 177; **1996** 362
Justice Department report, **1993** 819-821, 829-840
NRA criticism of ATF role, **1995** 209
and Oklahoma City bombing, **1997** 623-624
special counsel investigations, **1999** 165, 480-488
Treasury dept. report, **1993** 819-820, 821-829
Wade, Abdoulaye
New African Initiative, **2001** 507; **2002** 447
NEPAD, **2002** 447-448, 450
Wade, Richard H., medical mistakes, **1999** 781
Wadsworth, Deborah, adult attitudes toward children, **1997** 423-424
Wage and price controls
Burns on, **1972** 961-965, 969; **1974** 421
Carter on as president-elect, **1976** 878, 882-884, 886
Democratic Party platform on, **1972** 528, 531, 533-534; **1976** 544, 552, 619
domestic summit endorsement of, **1974** 862, 865-866, 868-869, 873, 875
Ford opposition to, **1974** 765-766, 769-770
gradual loosening of, Nixon and CEA on, **1974** 42-43, 55, 82
Kennedy support for, **1980** 702, 706, 711
in Nixon economic stabilization program, **1972** 82-84; **1973** 703-713
impact on inflation, **1973** 186, 188-190
OECD on, **1973** 683, 685, 688-689, 692, 695
Nixon's termination of, **1973** 43-54, 186, 189
Republican Party platform on, **1972** 652, 667-668; **1976** 619, 622
standby authority for, JEC on, **1981** 295, 309-310
Wage and price standards
in Carter anti-inflation program, **1980** 163, 166-167, 174, 180-181, 183, 250-251, 255
Democratic alternative to Ford plan, **1975** 18, 37
tax credit for not exceeding, Carter CEA on, **1981** 106, 112-113, 129-133
voluntary
Burns recommendation, **1975** 635, 642
in Carter anti-inflation program, **1978** 14, 20, 66, 76-77, 684, 690-693, 695-697; **1979** 22, 32, 83-85, 89
JEC on, **1979** 217, 219
in Nixon economic stabilization program, **1973** 43, 47-48, 50, 221-222, 577-579

Wages
See also Minimum wage
insurance, real, Carter anti-inflation program, **1978** 684, 692, 696; **1979** 11, 31-32, 83-84
just, John Paul II on, **1981** 695, 712-713
and prices
behavior of in U.S. economy, Carter CEA on, **1981** 123-125
CEA report on, **2005** 150
freeze on, in Nixon economic stabilization program, **1973** 703-713
increases in, and inflation, Ford and CEA on, **1976** 46, 53, 62-65
inflation in, Burns' explanation of, **1975** 636-640
and salaries, **1999** 87-88, 98-99
Wagie, David A., sexual misconduct at the Air Force Academy investigations, **2003** 794
Wagner, Judith, drug pricing, **1993** 199
Wagner, Robert (D-N.Y.), national health insurance, **1993** 782
Wagner, Thomas, genetic engineering, **1983** 525, 529
Wahid, Abdurraham
president of Indonesia, **1999** 514, 718-723; **2001** 563-564
protection for UN relief workers, **2000** 702
Wainwright v. Sykes, **1991** 215-216
Waite, Terry, hostage released, **1991** 752-753, 756
Wake Forest University, Carter speech on Soviet policy, **1978** 223-233
Wake Up Wal-Mart, **2005** 735-737
Waksal, Samuel D., IMClone Systems insider trading scandal, **2002** 399-400; **2004** 420
Walchholz, Bruce, **1997** 592
Wald, Charles, al Qaeda affiliated terrorist groups, **2004** 539
Wald, Patricia M., **1979** 919
DOJ nomination withdrawal, **1993** 136-137
Oliver North conviction, **1990** 492, 504-505
Waldheim, Kurt
counter-terrorism, **1972** 751-752
meetings with John Paul II, **1987** 699-700; **1988** 405-407
PRC invasion of Vietnam, **1979** 184
selection as secretary-general, **1972** 631-632
South Africa, UN arms embargo against, **1977** 823
UN effectiveness, **1973** 753-765
UN restructuring, **1975** 325
UN role in settling disputes and solving global problems, **1972** 631-637
U.S. hostages in Iran, negotiations on, **1979** 871, 892-893
war service and Austrian election, **1986** 743-750
at Zimbabwe independence, **1980** 318
Waldie, Jerome (D-Calif.), **1974** 988
Wales, John Paul II trip to, **1982** 409
Walesa, Lech
anti-Semitism, apology for, **1991** 253-256
Bush on, **1990** 52
Bush visit to Poland, **1989** 412-416, 420-421, 423
Geneva Accord for Middle East peace, **2003** 1204
John Paul II meetings in Poland, **1983** 579-580; **1987** 556
Katyn massacre by Stalin, **1990** 224
lifting of U.S. trade sanctions, **1987** 185
martial law, **1981** 882, 884, 892; **1982** 947-948
Nobel Peace Prize, **1983** 925-932
Partnership for Peace, **1994** 46
Polish priest's killing, **1985** 120-121
solidarity, establishment of, **1980** 793-795; **1987** 184
U.S. Congress, speech in, **1989** 523-525, 534-538
Warsaw Pact dissolution, **1991** 400
Wali, Abduli, prison abuse death scandal, **2005** 914
Walke, John
air pollution clean up, **2003** 180
on mercury emission regulations, **2005** 97
Walker, Alice, **1990** 354, 355; **1993** 978
Walker, Arthur, **1985** 603
Walker, David M.
bankruptcy and pension plans, **2004** 736
federal budget, reexamining the base of, **2005** 121-136
government-funded propaganda, **2005** 646-647
private pension funds, **2002** 102, 105-113
SEC failures, **2002** 1035
spending and tax policies, **2005** 124
Walker, John, **1994** 480
Walker, John Anthony, Jr., **1985** 603-604, 606
Walker, John M., Jr., **1992** 455, 459
Walker, Mary L.
Guantanamo Bay interrogations, review panel, **2004** 338
sexual misconduct at the Air Force Academy investigations, **2003** 793, 794, 799
Walker, Michael, **1985** 603
Walker, Robert S. (R-Pa.), Bush's no taxes pledge, **1990** 409
Walker, William, **1999** 135
Wall, M. Danny, **1989** 465
Wall Street Journal
on Boskin, **1990** 81-82
on Earth Summit in Rio, **1992** 500
insider trading case, **1987** 881-889
junk bonds, **1990** 252, 253
right to die case, **1990** 376
Souter nomination, **1990** 616, 617
Wallace, George C.
on foreign policy, **1975** 155-160
as presidential candidate, **1972** 201, 590, 592, 615; **1974** 854
proposals for Democratic Party platform, **1972** 527-528
Wallace, Mike
Krogh interview, **1974** 34
Westmoreland libel suit against CBS, **1979** 286, 289; **1983** 401; **1985** 159, 161-162, 164
Wallace, William, commander in Iraq War, **2003** 141
Wallace v. Jaffree, **1985** 379-395, 480, 487-488; **1992** 556
Wallach, E. Robert, in Meese investigation, **1988** 497-516
Wallenberg, Raul, **1989** 496
Wallis, W. Allen, **1975** 116
Wallop, Malcolm (R-Wyo.)
and CIA manual, **1984** 904
on fire-management policy, **1988** 942
on SDI, **1983** 306-307

Wallstrom, Margot, environmental policy, **2002** 595
Wal-Mart Stores, Inc.
benefits, meal breaks for employees, **2005** 740
child labor agreement, **2005** 738-739, 740-744
health benefits, **2005** 737-738
history of, **2005** 734-735
labor agreement, inspector general's report on, **2005** 734-744
labor union campaigns, **2005** 487, 488, 735-737
Wal-Mart Watch, **2005** 735-736
Wal-Mart Workers of America, **2005** 736
Walpole, Robert, Chinese nuclear-espionage matter, **1999** 238-239
Walsh, Frank E., Tyco International scandal, **2002** 398
Walsh, Jim (R-N.Y.), on legal immigrants rights, **1995** 565
Walsh, Lawrence E.
appointment as independent counsel, **1986** 1052
and independent counsel law, **1988** 466, 468
on independent counsel legislation, **1999** 168
Iran-contra affair, **1991** 429; **1998** 905-906; **1999** 165
limited immunity for North and Poindexter, **1987** 892
Oliver North charges dismissed, **1991** 618-620
Oliver North involvement, **1990** 492
pardons denounced, **1992** 1074-1075
Reagan involvement in, **1994** 8
and Tower Commission, **1987** 205
Walsh, Seana, IRA militant call to "dump arms," **2005** 509
Walsum, Peter Van, on Kosovo conflict, **1999** 287
Walt, Lewis, **1972** 647
Walt Disney Productions, and home video taping, **1984** 54, 57
Walter, Norbert, German economic situation, **2002** 692
Walters, Barbara
Carter interview on Iran, **1978** 713-714
Haig interview, **1982** 561
in presidential debates, **1980** 920, 933-935, 946; **1984** 848-876
Walters, Vernon A., and CIA in Watergate investigation, **1974** 675-676, 679, 682
Walz v. Tax Commission of City of New York, **1993** 406; **1997** 372
Wang Bingquian, **1980** 884
Wang Hung-wen, in Chinese leadership, **1973** 768-770
Wang Wei, Chinese pilot hit by U.S. spy plane, **2001** 248
Wanga, Jeronimo, UNITA leader, **2002** 155
War crimes
See also International Criminal Court (ICC)
Argentina "dirty war," **2003** 828-829
Balkan wars, **2005** 851
Barbie extradition and trial, **1983** 737-747; **1987** 517-524
Demjanjuk acquittal, **1993** 617-623
East and West German responsibility for Holocaust, **1990** 105-112
East Timor human rights violations, **2002** 260-261; **2004** 756-757
Hussein trial, **2003** 1195-1196; **2005** 941, 949-951
Israel invasion of West Bank, **2002** 931
Kosovo conflict, **1995** 718; **1998** 381; **1999** 738, 739, 802-804; **2003** 58-59
Slobodan Milosevic indictment, **2001** 826-848; **2003** 58, 463-464
Liberia conflict, UN tribunal, Charles Taylor indictment, **2003** 769
Mengele, discovery of in Brazil, **1985** 409-414
Rwanda tribunal, **1998** 614-625; **1999** 866; **2000** 454-455; **2002** 607; **2004** 117-118
Sierra Leone tribunal, **2002** 250; **2005** 803-804
Slobodan Milosevic trial, **2001** 826-848; **2002** 984; **2003** 99, 463-464, 1072-1073, 1144, 1195; **2004** 956; **2005** 851, 950
Srebrenica massacre. *See* Srebrenica massacre
Yuglosav civil war, **1992** 767
Yugoslav "Ethnic Cleansing" report, **1992** 771-779
Yugoslav tribunal, **2002** 607, 984
War on terrorism
Afghanistan war against Taliban regime, **2001** 686-697
Bush "Plan for Victory" speeches, **2005** 838-839, 842-850
Bush plans for, **2001** 637-649
Bush State of the Union address, **2004** 22-23, 537
Guantanamo Bay detentions, **2002** 830-841, 1016
military tribunals, **2001** 642-643
U.S. costs of war in Afghanistan, **2001** 687
War powers debate, **1990** 663-679
War Powers Resolution (1973), **1973** 923-930
and Grenada military operation, **1983** 850
and *Mayaguez* incident, **1975** 311-314
use of U.S. military, **1984** 1006, 1008-1009
War Relocation Authority, **1988** 288-289
Ward, William, Israel Gaza Strip withdrawal, **2005** 531
Ward v. Rock Against Racism, **1994** 316
Wards Cove Packing Co. v. Antonio, **1989** 321-322, 324-329; **1991** 148-149, 761
Warner, Frederick, **1985** 542-543
Warner, John W. (R-Va.)
Air Force Academy sexual misconduct investigations, **2003** 795
Cuban foreign policy, **1998** 33
House vote on impeachment, **1998** 958
Inman nomination, **1994** 24
on Iran-contra affair, **1994** 8-21
Iraq
call for troop withdrawal timetable, **2005** 837
prewar intelligence gathering, **2003** 881
Lott resignation, **2002** 972
McCain amendment on detainees treatment, **2005** 909-910
and navy racial unrest, **1972** 901-902
Oliver North Senate campaign, **1994** 9
nuclear test ban treaty, **1999** 602, 604, 608
on test ban treaty, **1995** 56
on Tower rejection, **1989** 106
USS *Cole* bombing, **2001** 6
women in combat, **1991** 492, 495, 508-509
Warner, Kenneth E., **1981** 4
Warner, Margaret, in presidential debates, **1988** 723, 758-760, 766-768, 774, 776
Warner, Mark R., commuted Robin Lovitt's death sentence to life in prison, **2005** 178
Warnke, Paul C.
on Gorbachev arms control proposal, **1986** 10

Warnke, Paul C. *Continued*
on SALT II progress, **1977** 245
Warren, Earl
civil rights, **1972** 935-940
Court of, **1990** 616
Bork on, **1987** 718-719
and racially motivated jury selection, **1986** 409
internment of Japanese-Americans, **1988** 289
Miranda ruling, **1981** 432; **1990** 785
Miranda warning, **2000** 385
Warren, Gerald L.
on aid to Syria, **1974** 278
on White House tape erasure, **1974** 24
Warren, Shields, human radiation experiments, **1993** 988-989
Warren Commission, shortcomings of in Kennedy assassination inquiry, House committee on, **1978** 910-911, 915-916; **1979** 593-596, 604, 613, 615
Warsaw Pact
challenge of for NATO, **1978** 373-374, 377-378, 380
in changing Europe, **1989** 646, 654-655, 665
condemnation of Czech suppression, **1989** 400
conventional forces in, Reagan on limiting, **1982** 478-479
dissolution of, **1990** 455-456, 463; **1991** 399-401
and INF treaty, **1987** 946-947
military buildup of, **1980** 124, 126, 129-131, 141, 153-155
as NATO concern, **1975** 354, 357; **1976** 345-348
military interests of, Gorbachev on eliminating, **1989** 400, 403-405
military maneuvers in Poland, **1981** 881
Wartime Relocation and Internment of Civilians, Commission on, **1988** 288-292
Washington (D.C.)
Mayor Barry sentencing, **1990** 707-711
summit, Reagan-Gorbachev, **1987** 945, 991-1006
Washington (state)
discrimination against homosexuals, legislation banning, **2005** 869
morning-after pill, without prescription for, **2003** 999
physician-assisted suicide, **1994** 502
welfare reform, **1999** 258
Washington, Claudell, **1986** 170
Washington, George
Capitol Bicentennial and, **1993** 893, 896, 901
inaugural of, **1989** 123-125, 133-135
Washington, Paul, **1989** 52
Washington, Thomas L., on NRA fund-raising letter, **1995** 209
Washington, Walter E., mayor of D.C., **1995** 498
Washington v. Davis, **1977** 35-36, 40-44; **1993** 467; **1997** 190
Washington v. Glucksberg, **1997** 459-479; **2000** 291
Washington v. Harper, **1990** 377, 383
Washington v. Seattle, **1982** 619-652
Washington v. Seattle School District No. 1, **1997** 188
Washington Council of Lawyers, **1983** 46
Washington Declaration, **1994** 329-335
Washington Dept. of Services for Blind, **1993** 401, 402-403, 406
Washington Energy Conference
communiqué, **1974** 123-127
follow-up actions, **1974** 185-186
Washington Journalism Review, **1992** 336
Washington Policy Group, Inc. (WPG), **1997** 8
Washington Post
abortion legislation, **1990** 216
"Big Bang" theory, **1992** 379
Clarence Thomas, **1992** 39
Economic Summit (Munich), **1992** 638
junk bonds, **1990** 253
National Park Service, **1992** 330
new Saudi constitution, **1992** 227
prison inmates beaten by guards, **1992** 177
Quayle-"Murphy Brown" controversy, **1992** 443-444
silicone breast implants, **1993** 369
Washington Special Action Group (WSAG), secret documents on Indo-Pakistani conflict, **1972** 23-40
Washington Star-News, Horner interview with Nixon, **1972** 881-892
Waste
See also Hazardous waste
ocean dumping of
international agreement on, **1972** 907-919
northeast Atlantic agreement on, **1972** 173-177
solid waste combustion, and lung cancer from air pollution, **1972** 777
Watchtower Bible and Tract Soc. N.Y. Inc. v. Village of Stratton, **2003** 398
Water management
assistance for developing countries, **1974** 940, 947-948
conservation, as component of national policy, **1978** 385, 387-390, 392-393
global problems of, U.S. strategies for, **1981** 14, 25-26
shortages of water linked to deforestation, **1980** 95, 666, 669, 682, 686
water projects, guidelines for federal planning and coordination, **1978** 385-395
Water pollution
from agricultural chemicals, **1980** 666, 688-689, 695
contribution of deforestation to, **1980** 95, 666, 669, 682
control of, Nixon's impoundment of funds for, **1973** 13
dredging the Hudson River, **2001** 218
and EPA regulation of chemical discharge, **1977** 131-141
study of, U.S.-Soviet agreement on, **1972** 806-807
and vessel safety, **2004** 618
Water Pollution Control Act Amendments (1972), presidential impoundment of funds for, **1975** 135-140
Water quality
acid rain effects on, **1983** 198, 200-207
arsenic levels in water, **2001** 212-221, 541
Clinton administration proposals, **2001** 217-218
control of sediment from soil erosion, Nixon on, **1972** 148; **1973** 217
drinking water, **1993** 261-270; **1994** 153-154
standards for, **1973** 217
and ecosystem health, **2004** 617-618
Great Lakes, **1994** 147-152
Mississippi River, **1994** 147-148, 152-160
nuclear war effects on, **1983** 859, 881

Water Resources Council, and control of water projects, in Carter plan, **1978** 385, 387, 389-390, 393
Water rights, state regulation and conservation, **1982** 689-701
Watergate
break-in
background of, White House tapes on, **1974** 340-346
CIA response to investigations of, **1974** 675-680, 682; **1975** 428-429
criminal liability of Nixon aides, White House conversations on, **1974** 305, 307, 321, 358-361
cover-up
conviction of, **1974** 991-1002
criminal liability of Nixon aides, White House conversations on, **1974** 305, 307, 321, 358-361
Ford involvement investigated, **1976** 760-764, 802-803
White House taped conversations on, **1974** 301-387
defendants
Ellsberg break-in involvement, **1973** 537-548
fairness to of Nixon pardon, **1974** 812-813
grand jury testimony by, **1973** 500
indictment of, **1973** 659, 662-663; **1974** 157-184, 309
pardon requests, Ford on, **1974** 895
payments and clemency for
Dean testimony on, **1973** 667-671, 674
Nixon on, **1973** 572, 952; **1974** 189-196, 200-201
White House conversations on, **1974** 306-308, 321, 340, 348-353, 356, 359, 361, 362-364, 369-373, 375, 378, 992, 994-1002
sentencing of, **1975** 141-151
trial of, **1973** 415-423; **1974** 309-310, 317-319
Nixon tapes and papers as evidence, **1977** 465-469
White House conversations on, **1974** 317-319
White House tapes as evidence, **1973** 842, 847, 851
White House commitments to, Hunt memo on, **1974** 992-994
emerging scandal, **1973** 413-415, 423-425
FBI investigation of, **1973** 337-338
grand jury
access to White House tapes, federal court rulings on, **1973** 839-857
cover-up indictments, **1974** 157-184
Ellsberg break-in indictments, **1974** 205-214
investigation by, **1973** 413-414
report on Nixon involvement, Sirica decision to release, **1974** 225-232
testimony of break-in defendants, **1973** 500
White House strategy for, **1974** 305-306, 373-381
White House tapes, nonexistent, **1973** 948-950
Nixon's knowledge of, **1973** 563-565, 571-572
Watergate committee. *See* Senate Select Committee on Presidential Campaign Activities
Watergate scandal
See also Saturday night massacre
abuses of, Mansfield on, **1974** 62-63
climate at White House and CRP, Nixon on responsibility for, **1973** 737-738, 744
effect on U.S.-Soviet summit in Moscow, **1974** 535-536
executive branch responsiveness program of White House, **1974** 602-603, 611-613
Ford on end of nightmare, **1974** 695, 698
and government ethics
Blackmun on, **1973** 723-727
effect on young people, **1974** 190-191, 197
investigations of, Nixon on concluding, **1974** 41, 52
news media coverage of, Nixon attacks on, **1973** 897-899, 903-905, 907-909
news media role in, **1973** 488, 495-498, 629, 631-633, 637
Nixon administration resignations, **1973** 499-512
Nixon involvement
House Judiciary Committee on, **1974** 715-724
impeachment articles on, **1974** 655-659
public opinion on, **1973** 564
release of June 23, 1972, tapes, **1974** 673-682
Nixon on, in Frost interviews, **1977** 321-322, 324-335, 357-359, 362-365
Nixon presidential campaign, **2003** 1157
and Nixon's credibility, **1973** 947-948, 953-955, 959
and public confidence in government, **1973** 550, 555; **1976** 14-15, 17, 26-27, 778-779, 790-791
Mondale and Carter on, **1976** 597-598, 600, 603, 606
special prosecutor firing, **1987** 718, 720, 725, 739-740; **1988** 466
White House investigation of, **1973** 500-501, 503, 572, 666, 743
Watergate special prosecutor
access to presidential tapes
Court ruling on, **1974** 621-638
and erasure, **1974** 23-25
federal court rulings on, **1973** 839-857
Nixon on refusal to release, **1973** 737, 741-742
Nixon's cooperation with, **1974** 189, 196, 202, 287, 289-290, 302-303, 675, 680-681
appointment of second, **1973** 898, 901
charge and independence of, **1975** 660-662, 665
Colson plea bargain, **1974** 443-446
continuing work of, Ford on, **1974** 766, 769
final report, **1975** 653-689
firing of, **1973** 698, 859-880; **1988** 466
and immunity of congressional witnesses, **1975** 656-657
Nixon on written response to interrogatories, **1974** 146, 150
Nixon pardon and tape agreement, effect of on investigation, **1974** 813-814, 892-895, 897-900
recommendations of, **1975** 653-654, 670-689
Waters, Joe, ozone depletion, **1992** 77, 80
Waters, Maxine (D-Calif.)
cocaine possession sentencing, **1997** 247
Elian Gonzalez political asylum case, **2000** 269
House Judiciary Committee impeachment inquiry, **1998** 708
minority business competition, **1998** 856
Watkins, David, White House Travel Office, **1993** 532, 536-537
Watkins, James D.
AIDS commission, **1988** 416-417

Watkins, James D. *Continued*
environmental plan for Energy Department, **1989** 355-362
ocean protection policy, **2004** 602, 605
Watkins, Sherron S., Enron Corp. collapse, **2002** 396
Watson, Arthur K., **1973** 293
Watson, Chuck, Dynegy Inc.-Enron merger, **2001** 860-861
Watson, Dwight, sentencing of, **2004** 361
Watson, Henry L., climate change, U.S. delegate, **2004** 830; **2005** 923
Watson, James, **1975** 319
DNA discovery, **2000** 398
Watson, Robert, on global warming, **2001** 111
Watson, Robert T., ozone depletion, **1988** 221
Watson, Thomas, on Humvee vehicle protection in Iraq, **2004** 875
Watson, Thomas J., **1979** 966
Watson Wyatt Worldwide, retiree benefits, **2002** 667
Watt, James
controversial remark on minorities, **1983** 827-829
environmental position, **1983** 828
influence peddling for HUD contractor, **1989** 333-337
resignation, **1983** 827-830
Watt, Melvin (D-N.C.)
on affirmative action, **1995** 309
House Judiciary Committee impeachment inquiry, **1998** 706
"racial gerrymandering," **1993** 460
Wattleton, Faye, **1991** 259
Watts, J. C. (R-Okla.)
affirmative action programs, **1998** 859
Clinton State of the Union address, Republican response, **1997** 31, 44-49
Republican senior leader, **1998** 952
retirement, **2002** 822
Watts, William, **1972** 215-216
Waxman, Henry A. (D-Calif.)
on AIDS, **1987** 320; **1988** 417
Clean Air Act revisions, **1990** 716, 717
drug pricing, **1993** 198-199; **1994** 87-88
flu vaccine shortage, and FDA responsibility, **2004** 643
food labeling proposal, **1990** 176
mercury emissions from power plants, **2004** 842-843
Nursing Home Compare Web site, **2002** 120
on public broadcasting editorials, **1984** 449
Schiavo end-of-life care case, **2005** 158
steroid use in baseball, **2005** 215
terrorist watch list, **2003** 157
tobacco control, **2001** 226
tobacco industry, **1994** 207
tuberculosis report, **1993** 852
Waco incident, **1999** 482
Waxman, Matthew, Guantanamo Bay detainees, **2005** 450
Waxman, Seth P.
campaign finance reform, **2003** 1159
FDA cigarette regulation, **1999** 539
jury selection and racial bias, **2002** 359; **2004** 796
medical use of marijuana, **2001** 327
Miranda warning, **2000** 385
Weah, George, Liberian presidential elections, **2005** 802-803
Weakland, Rembert G.
pastoral letters on economic policies, **1984** 957; **1986** 983
on Vatican enforcement of orthodoxy, **1986** 758
Weapons
*See also*Chemical weapons; Gun control; Nuclear nonproliferation; Nuclear testing; Nuclear weapons; Strategic weapons
destruction by IRA, **2001** 758-763
incendiary, effects of in war, UN report on, **1972** 837-841
land mine crisis, **1995** 46-54
security for materials for producing, **2003** 902
small arms trade, **2001** 516-521
smart bombs used in Iraq War, **2003** 140
"smart" weapons effectiveness, GAO report, **1997** 493-500
"smart" weapons performance report, **1996** 403-413
Weapons of mass destruction (WMD), **1996** 210-230; **1998** 935
See also Biological weapons; Chemical weapons; Nuclear Nonproliferation; Nuclear weapons
and the "axis of evil" in Iran, Iraq, and North Korea, **2002** 33-34, 40-41, 612, 614, 635, 714; **2003** 19; **2004** 867
Bush position on, **2003** 19-20, 874; **2004** 19
combatting, **2002** 639-640
commission on intelligence capabilities of the U.S. and, **2005** 246-266
congressional investigations, UN weapons inspector testimony, **2003** 874-900
definition of term, **2003** 901
"dirty bomb" threat, **2002** 441-442; **2003** 106, 222
G-8 summit on, **2002** 437-445
Hussein development of, Bush statement on, **2003** 32-34
Iraq
UN weapons inspections, **2003** 136-137, 878-880
U.S. weapons search, **2003** 880-881
Iraq Survey Group (weapons inspectors), **2003** 880-881; **2004** 712
Libya dismantling weapons, **2003** 1218-1233; **2004** 169-171, 173-175
National Intelligence Estimate report, **2003** 874, 875; **2005** 247
national strategy report on combatting, **2002** 534
pre-Iraq War allegations, **2003** 874-877
preventing the spread of, **2002** 284-285
Proliferation Security Initiative, **2004** 323, 324
Russia, storage and security for, **2003** 906-907
terrorist threat preparedness, **2005** 894-895
U.S. inspector on Iraq's "missing," **2004** 711-733
U.S. weapons inspector testimony on, **2003** 880, 881-883, 886-900
Weather
early-warning system for world agriculture, **1974** 940, 950-951
nuclear war effects on, **1983** 857-859, 871-878
Weather Underground, warrantless FBI break-ins against, **1981** 371-372
Weaver, Rander, and Ruby Ridge incident, **1995** 178

Weaver, Warren, Jr., **1973** 613
Webb, James H., Jr., **1987** 672
Webber, Alan, on government reform, **1993** 719
Weber, Brian F., and reverse discrimination in job program, **1979** 493-494, 505
Weber, United States v., **1979** 493-507
Webster, William G., Jr., training Iraqi military, **2005** 662
Webster, William H.
  Ames espionage case, **1994** 488
  appointment to CIA, **1987** 208; **1988** 892
  on Donovan investigation, **1982** 588
  FBI internal security review, **2001** 154, 157
  Freeh, FBI Director, appointment, **1993** 611-612
  Los Angeles riots, **1992** 409-410, 413-429
  Persian Gulf crisis, **1990** 776-779
  SEC accounting board nomination controversy, **2002** 1032-1035; **2003** 338
  terrorist threats, task force on, **2002** 743
Webster v. Reproductive Health Services, **1989** 365-389; **1990** 215, 216, 287-388, 374, 395, 404; **1992** 590, 591, 597, 611, 612; **1993** 339
Wedtech Corp., and Meese investigation, **1988** 496-503
Weed, Steven, and Hearst kidnapping, **1974** 247, 251
Wehlehan, Harry, Irish abortion case, **1992** 249-254
Wei Jingsheng, Chinese dissident released, **1997** 730-731
Weicker, Lowell P., Jr. (R-Conn.)
  bioterrorism readiness study, **2004** 444
  Bridgeport bankruptcy, **1991** 304
  and ERA, **1988** 617
  press protections, **1972** 509
  school prayer, **1984** 241, 243
  on Watergate abuses, **1974** 605
Weiler, Edward
  on Hubble Space telescope repairs, **2002** 213
  NASA space programs, **2000** 92
  space mission failures, **1999** 713, 715
Weiming, Zhang, **1993** 565
Weinberg, Daniel, income inequality report, **1996** 397, 398-400
Weinberg, Jeshajahu, at Holocaust Museum, **1993** 308
Weinberg v. Prichard, **1973** 277-289
Weinberger, Caspar W.
  defense department, reorganization of, **1985** 671-672
  defense department security clearances, **1985** 606
  fetal research regulations, **1975** 543-556
  Haig disputes with, **1982** 562
  Iran-contra affair, **1986** 1016; **1987** 232-233, 893, 899, 922
    pardon, **1992** 1073-1079; **1994** 9, 11-17, 19
  Libya, air strike against, **1986** 350
  military force, use of, **1984** 1005-1015
  missile basing plan, **1982** 907
  nuclear arms reduction, **1982** 386-397, 403-407
  Packard commission, **1986** 681
  Persian Gulf, U.S. presence in, **1988** 705
  as presidential counselor, **1973** 338
  presidential pardon, **2001** 90
  SDI, **1984** 259-260
    and ABM treaty, **1987** 292-293, 306-307
  sex discrimination in schools, HEW rules prohibiting, **1974** 508
  Social Security's financial condition, **1975** 117
  Soviet power, DOD report on, **1981** 717
  terrorist attack on U.S. Marines in Beirut, **1983** 935
  women in military, **1987** 672
Weinberger v. Wiesenfeld, **1975** 177-185
Weingarten, Reid, Espy resignation remarks, **1994** 407-408
Weir, Benjamin
  as hostage in Lebanon, **1985** 466
  release of, **1986** 1015
Weis, Joseph F., Jr., **1989** 197
Weisgan, Asher, Gaza Strip withdrawal protest, **2005** 532
Weiss, Mark, acoustical analysis of Kennedy assassination, **1978** 910; **1979** 594, 602-603
Weiss, Ted (D-N.Y.), **1989** 337
Weissglas, Dov, Gaza Strip disengagement policy, **2004** 308
Weissman, Irving L., stem cell research, **2002** 516
Weizäcker, Richard von
  contrition to Czechoslovakia, **1990** 4
  dedication of Holocaust Museum, **1993** 309
  German unity day speech, **1990** 681-693
Weizman, Ezer, state visit of John Paul II, **2000** 80
Welch, Jack, General Electric CEO and corporate scandals, **2002** 400
Welch, Ron, privacy of medical records, **2000** 1065
Welch, Tom, Salt Lake Olympics committee, **1999** 106, 107
Weld, William F.
  abortion issue, **1996** 497
  antistalking bill, **1993** 288
  and balanced budgets, **1995** 11
Welfare policy
  See also Social service programs
  Democratic Party platform on, **1992** 696; **1996** 637-639
  dependency on, debate about, **1988** 847-852
  Dole Republican convention speech on, **1996** 490-492
  faith-based and community initiatives, **2001** 132-140; **2002** 37; **2003** 27-28; **2004** 29
  and illegal aliens, **1986** 964
  immigrant benefits, **1997** 177-178
  impact of cuts on young families, **1992** 354
  programs, HEW definition of, **1977** 552
  as women's issue, **1977** 866-867
Welfare reform
  Carter plan, **1977** 551-565; **1978** 27, 71, 97; **1979** 389-395; **1981** 58, 71-72
    women's opposition to, **1977** 866-867
  Catholic bishops on, **1984** 969-970; **1986** 983-984, 992-994, 998-1000, 1002
  CEA report on, **1995** 87-88; **1997** 70-72; **1998** 85, 89-90
  Clinton plan, **1994** 35, 40-42; **1995** 74-75; **1996** 65; **1997** 33-34, 617-622; **1998** 46; **2000** 21
  Democratic Party platform on, **1976** 561; **1980** 730-731
  double-tier benefits, Supreme Court on, **1999** 260-261
  Eisenhower Foundation inner-city report, **1993** 223
  federalizing, Urban League on, **1985** 29, 35
  Ford call for, **1975** 95-96; **1977** 62

Welfare reform *Continued*
GAO report on, **1998** 354-363; **1999** 257-271
Gingrich comments on, **1995** 4-5, 11-13
Nixon proposals, **1972** 87, 881, 891-892; **1973** 304, 310-312; **1974** 41, 49, 54, 58, 99, 110
passage of legislation, **1988** 847-852
Quayle on, **1992** 449
Reagan call for, **1986** 45-46; **1987** 107, 112
Republican bill, **1996** 450-463
Republican Party platform on, **1972** 651, 678-679; **1976** 639-640; **1980** 574-576; **1984** 682-683; **1988** 657-659
support for mothers, **1988** 847-849, 851-852
tightening eligibility and benefits, Ford on, **1976** 14, 22
and uninsured, **2000** 788
Welfare-to-work programs, **1997** 619, 622; **1998** 90, 356, 357, 362; **1999** 50
Welfshofer, Lewis, Abu Ghraib prison abuse scandal, **2005** 913
Well Head Protection program (WHP), **1993** 267-270
Wellesley College, **1992** 141
Wells, John Calhoun, **1997** 629
Wellstone, Paul D.
mental health legislation, **2002** 268
plane crash and death of, **2002** 821
Wen Jiabao
on AIDS epidemic in China, **2003** 784, 1175
Chinese economic growth, **2004** 940
Chinese social distress, **2004** 937
political reforms in China, **2003** 1173-1188
prime minister of China, **2003** 1174
Taiwan independence referendum, **2003** 1181
visit to U.S., **2003** 1173; **2004** 939; **2005** 612
Wennberg, John E., end-of-life care, **1997** 326
Wertheimer, Fred, campaign finance reform, **2003** 1160-1161
Wesberry v. Sanders, **1995** 265
Wesley, Cynthia, church bombing victim, **2002** 240, 244
Wessinger, Catherine, on cults, **1997** 124
Wessmann v. Gittens, **1998** 855-868
West, Togo D., Jr.
extremists groups in the military, **1996** 178, 179
sexual harassment in the military, **1997** 654
West Bank settlements
See also Israel, occupied territories; Palestinians
agreement, **1995** 622-630
Jordan's legal and administrative links to, **1988** 579-585
peace plan for West Bank and Gaza Strip, **1977** 855-857
unrest, UN debate on, **1976** 191-192
West Germany. *See* Germany, Federal Republic of
West Timor, attack on UN relief workers, **2000** 702; **2001** 594
West Virginia Bd. of Education v. Barnette, **1995** 331
West Virginia Univ. Hospitals, Inc. v. Casey, **1992** 463
Western Air Lines v. Criswell, **1985** 397-407
Western Electric and AT&T, United States v., **1982** 17-33
Western Electric Co., and AT&T divestiture, **1982** 19, 21-27
Western Europe
See also Economic summits; Europe; European Community; North Atlantic Treaty Organization
and Chernobyl nuclear accident, **1986** 384-385
economic coordination in oil crisis, Kissinger on need for, **1975** 4, 7, 11
integration of, **1973** 487-495
and EC budget arrangements, **1984** 439-445
Soviet pipeline to, and use of forced labor, **1982** 857-858, 860
Soviet trade
and U.S. credit restrictions, **1982** 469-471, 474
and U.S. economic sanctions on pipeline equipment, **1982** 879-883
terrorism in, CIA on, **1981** 465-466
U.S. defense capability in, **1980** 129-134, 153-157
U.S. deployment of missiles in, **1981** 717-718, 824; **1982** 225-226, 232-233, 305-306, 308-310, 983-988
Reagan and Gromyko UN speeches, **1984** 811-813, 822-823, 827
U.S. relations
and hard line on Soviets, **1982** 386-389
revitalization of, **1973** 487-495, 515-516, 518, 522, 525
Westmoreland, William C.
libel suit against CBS, **1983** 401-412; **1985** 159-165
as potential witness in Calley trial, **1974** 858-859
Weston, Russell Eugene, Jr., slaying of Capitol policemen, **1998** 510-517
Wetherbee, James, NASA safety issues, **2005** 499
Wetlands preservation, **2001** 219; **2002** 902; **2003** 182-183; **2004** 670
Wexler, Robert (D-Fla.), House Judiciary Committee impeachment inquiry, **1998** 710
Weyrich, Paul M., **1989** 106
WFP. *See* United Nations World Food Programme
Wheeler, Earl G., **1973** 729
Whelehan, Harry, **1992** 249
Whip Inflation Now (WIN) campaign, **1974** 979
Whirlpool Corp. v. Marshall, **1980** 199-207
Whistleblowing
executive privilege, Nixon on Fitzgerald case, **1973** 194-195, 202-204
presidential immunity in Fitzgerald suit, **1972** 539-559
rights of federal employees, **1978** 139, 141-142
Whitaker, Ridley, **1973** 36
White, Byron R.
abortion
parental consent for, **1990** 387-407
and privacy right, **1973** 102, 114
public funding of, **1980** 515
right to, **1986** 559-562, 571-579
state restrictions on, **1983** 544-545, 557-564, 572; **1989** 366-367
techniques, state restrictions on, **1976** 483-484
woman's right to choose, **1992** 589, 611-613
affirmative action, **1986** 654, 667, 676-677; **1987** 332-333, 346
in job program, **1979** 494
and seniority protections, **1984** 366, 368-376

age discrimination, **1983** 232
alcoholism and veterans' benefits, **1988** 279-284
alimony payments to men, **1979** 193
arrests in suspects' homes without warrant, **1980** 282-283, 291-297
asset forfeiture
drug trafficking, **1993** 432-438
pornography seized, **1993** 432, 438-440
auto searches, **1982** 425
passengers' rights, **1978** 754, 761-764
bankruptcy and labor contracts, **1984** 182, 193
bankruptcy law, **1982** 597-598
broadcast of offensive material, **1978** 515, 517, 531
child pornography, **1982** 676-688; **1990** 239-249
church-state separation
church's objection to liquor license, **1982** 956-961
public display of Nativity scene, **1984** 218
religious organizations' use of buildings on campus, **1981** 870, 877
clean air regulations, **1984** 427
coastal property rights, **1992** 616-620
coerced confessions, **1991** 175-176, 177-182
congressional immunity, **1979** 467
in job discrimination suit, **1979** 399
counsel, right to, and police procedure, **1977** 219, 234-235
Court workload, **1982** 706, 715-718
damages for tobacco-related ills, **1992** 564-573
deaf parochial student, **1993** 399-403
death penalty
consideration of mitigating factors, **1978** 497, 508-510; **1982** 51, 60
constitutionality of state laws on, **1972** 499-500, 502; **1976** 921-922
and expedited appeals, **1983** 707-708, 711-716
mandatory for murder of police officer, **1977** 397, 400-401
racial discrimination in, **1987** 463
for rape, **1977** 517, 519-525
state's misuse of, **1980** 455, 457, 467-472
discrimination, by private clubs, **1988** 401-403
drug paraphernalia sales, **1982** 223
education
for children of illegal aliens, **1982** 490, 501
school financing based on property tax, **1973** 363
teaching of creation science, **1987** 566
tuition tax credit, **1983** 676, 684-688
election campaigns
financing, **1976** 107-110
open political primaries, **1986** 1065
PAC spending limits, **1985** 279, 290-294
electronic surveillance, phone company ordered to assist, **1977** 883-891
entrapment in child pornography case, **1992** 313-322
exclusionary rule, **1976** 523, 535-536; **1984** 506-514
faculty tenure review disclosure, **1990** 23-34
flag burning, **1989** 343, 351; **1990** 358, 363-365
free speech
corporate, in referendum campaigns, **1978** 307, 309, 318-322
in satire, **1988** 177, 182
freedom for residential signs, **1994** 290-297
gay rights to march, **1995** 327-335
Haitian refugee interdiction, **1992** 453, 459-468; **1993** 413-421
hate crimes, **1992** 544-551; **1993** 385-389
home video taping, **1984** 53
impeachment, Senate's authority to remove judge, **1993** 82-91
insider trading, **1987** 882, 884-889
job discrimination
fetal protection, **1991** 144, 151-153
involving African Americans, **1993** 424, 424-430
proof of, **1989** 322, 325-327
judicial immunity, **1978** 260-266
jury service for women, **1975** 55-63
jury trials, split verdicts in, **1972** 423-428
labor unions, freedom of members to resign, **1985** 415-416
legislative intent, **1993** 250-253
legislative redistricting, **1983** 600, 612-615
gerrymandering, **1986** 616-629
one-man, one-vote rule, **1973** 278
racial criteria in, **1977** 151-159
legislative veto, **1983** 617-618, 620, 634-644
libel
from misquotation, **1991** 317
of private and public persons, **1986** 355, 357-358, 364
libel awards, appellate review of, **1984** 300-301, 309
minimum wage laws applied to state governments, **1976** 378, 385
minority set-aside programs, **1980** 539, 541; **1990** 419-428
Miranda warnings
interrogation definition, **1980** 431
and pre-Miranda right to counsel, **1974** 483-484
and right to counsel, **1981** 431-433, 441-445
rule affirmed, **1990** 785-790
murder case sentencing, **1991** 389-390
NAACP boycott damages, **1982** 656
Nixon papers and tapes, custody of, **1977** 487
Noriega phone calls dispute, **1990** 721-724
obscenity, legal tests for, **1987** 479-484
offshore oil resources, federal control of, **1975** 167, 169-175
OSHA inspections, warrants for, **1978** 339-346
parental leave, and job discrimination, **1987** 17, 19, 25-27
parental rights in child custody, **1982** 260, 271
patenting of living organisms, **1980** 494, 500
police use of deadly force, **1985** 303-311
political asylum, **1987** 254, 262
political firings from public jobs, **1980** 259
pregnancy coverage in company disability plans, **1976** 892
presidential immunity, **1982** 539, 552
presidential impoundment of funds, **1975** 135-140
press
access to pretrial hearings, **1979** 511, 513, 525
confidentiality of sources, **1972** 507-517
gag orders, **1976** 464, 478
libel of public figure, **1979** 285-297
newsroom searches, **1978** 355-356, 358-367

White, Byron R. *Continued*
political candidate's right of reply, **1974** 524, 527-528
preventive detention, **1987** 491
prison crowding, **1981** 487
prison inmates, beaten by guards, **1992** 175-182
prisoner appeals, from death row, **1993** 141-147, 148
prisoners' rights in searches, **1984** 480
property takings, in historic preservation, **1978** 453
public aid to nonpublic schools, **1973** 642; **1977** 432, 440-441; **1985** 433, 449
public broadcasting editorials, **1984** 450, 461
racial discrimination, in private school admission, **1976** 392, 401-404
"racial gerrymandering," **1993** 461, 474-481
racial segregation, public housing in suburbs, **1976** 233
retirement from Supreme Court, **1993** 391
reverse discrimination
in firing employees, **1976** 406
in medical school admissions, **1978** 468-471, 478, 485-487
right to die, **1990** 373-382
school desegregation, **1979** 535-542, 546-551; **1991** 24
cross-district remedies for, **1974** 639, 649-651
restrictions on busing, **1982** 620
schools
book banning, **1982** 568-569
prayer in, **1985** 380-381; **1992** 555
segregated colleges, **1992** 575-587
use of facilities by religious groups, **1993** 363-369
sentencing
and double jeopardy, **1980** 978, 986
excessive prison, **1983** 660, 670-674
separation of powers, and Gramm-Rudman-Hollings, **1986** 707-708, 724-728
sex discrimination
in education, **1984** 202, 204-210
by Jaycees, **1984** 468
in military draft, **1981** 521-522
in pension plans, **1978** 293; **1983** 691, 694-701
in Social Security survivors' benefits, **1977** 169
sexual harassment
monetary damages for, **1992** 188-197
in workplace, **1993** 939-944
snail darter protection from dam project, **1978** 433
sodomy and privacy right, **1986** 601-607
state utilities, and federal regulation, **1982** 448
statutory rape laws, sex discrimination in, **1981** 346
students' rights
corporal punishment, **1977** 293-295, 303-309
in disciplinary procedure, **1975** 67-75
free speech, **1986** 731
newspaper censorship, **1988** 37-44
searches, **1985** 14-24
suspects' rights and public safety, **1984** 388
tax increase to promote desegregation, **1990** 227-228, 229-232
televised trials, **1981** 164, 170, 176
treatment of severely handicapped infants, **1986** 543-544, 554-558
treaty termination, **1979** 918, 933, 937
unitary taxation, **1983** 645
water export, federal vs. state regulation of, **1982** 689
wiretaps, authorization procedures of attorney general, **1974** 392-403
worker health protection, **1981** 492
zoning regulations barring low-income and minority housing, **1977** 36, 43-44
White, Frank, **1982** 3-16
White, Mary Jo, and Marc Rich pardon, **2001** 90
White, Robert E., **1981** 242
White, Ronnie, federal district court nomination, **2001** 97
White, Ryan, **1992** 709
White, Thomas E., Iraq postwar planning, **2003** 948
White v. Regester, **1993** 466
White House
See also names of individual U.S. presidents
FBI files, mishandling of, **2000** 765
Office of Domestic Preparedness for Terrorism Management proposed, **2000** 281
Office of Faith-Based and Community Initiatives (OFBCI), **2001** 132, 133, 136-138
Office of Homeland Security, **2001** 637, 639-640, 673-674, 765
creation of, **2002** 36, 531
national strategy report, **2002** 535-545
Office of National Drug Control Policy, video news services as government propaganda, **2005** 646
Office of Science and Technology Policy (OSTP), **2004** 846
Pennsylvania Avenue closing, **1995** 254-258
plane crash on White House lawn, **1995** 255
security against terrorist attacks, **1983** 934
shooting incidents, **1995** 256
Sununu resignation as chief of staff, **1991** 769-773
Travel Office probe (Travelgate), **1993** 531-539; **1997** 21; **1998** 394, 565, 633; **2000** 763, 765
White House Commission on Aviation Safety and Security (Gore Commission), report, GAO on, **1997** 113-121; **1998** 170-171
White House Conferences
on Child Care, **1998** 47
on Early Learning and the Brain, **1997** 36
on Mental Health, **1999** 49, 836-837; **2000** 25
on Social Security, **1998** 40, 43, 98-99
White House Council on Environmental Quality, Ocean Policy Committee, **2004** 605
White House Millennium Program, **1998** 52-53; **1999** 57
White House National Economic Council, **2002** 880
White House tapes
conversations of June 23, 1972, released by Nixon, **1974** 673-682
conversations released by Judiciary Committee, **1974** 303-387
delivery of to Sirica, Nixon on, **1973** 901-903
edited transcripts of
compared with Judiciary Committee's versions, **1974** 301-381
released by Nixon, **1974** 287-299, 622
federal court orders on executive privilege, **1973** 839-857

introduced in cover-up trial, **1974** 991-1002
missing portions of, **1973** 840
Nixon's refusal to release, **1973** 737, 741-742
nonexistent, Nixon's explanation of, **1973** 948-953
Watergate special prosecutor's access to, compromise plans for, **1973** 859-872, 878-879
White House taping system
Butterfield testimony on, **1973** 697-701
Nixon on, **1973** 739-740, 948, 951-953
White Panther Party, warrantless wiretapping of, **1972** 486
White supremacy, Farrakhan's remarks on evils of, **1995** 663-665
Whitehead, Clay T.
broadcast regulations, changes in, **1973** 55-62, 899
network news, **1973** 55-57
Whitehead, John C., **1987** 185
Whitehead, Mary Beth, surrogate motherhood contract, **1987** 373-387; **1988** 71-79
Whitehead v. Shattuck, **1992** 197
Whitehurst, Frederick
FBI crime lab complaints, **1997** 222-224, 225-227
FBI crime lab evidence in Oklahoma City bombing case, **1997** 625
Whitelaw, William, **1973** 354
Whitewater investigations, **1996** 22; **1997** 21; **1998** 393-394, 565, 633; **1999** 22; **2000** 907
closing of, **2000** 762-770; **2001** 88
costs of, **2000** 764
Whitewater scandal, **1994** 36
Whitley v. Albers, **1992** 176-178
Whitman, Christine Todd
arsenic levels in water, EPA regulations on, **2001** 214-215, 219-221
and balanced budgets, **1995** 11
Cabinet appointment, **2000** 1027-1028
Cabinet resignation, **2002** 897; **2003** 173-174
Clinton State of the Union address [response to], **1995** 25, 43-45
EPA new source review regulations, **2002** 896-897
federal advisory panels, NAS study on, **2004** 844
Whitman-Walker Clinic, **1992** 709
Whittemore, James D., Schiavo case, **2005** 157
Whitworth, Jerry A., **1985** 603
WHO. *See* World Health Organization
Whoie, United States v., **1992** 320
Wick, Charles Z., **1981** 753-754
Wickard v. Filburn, **1995** 188
Wicker, Tom, **1972** 419
Wickham, John A., **1985** 671
Wickremesinghe (Sri Lanka prime minister), **2002** 95
Widera, Siegfried, priest sexual offender, suicide of, **2005** 866
Widmar v. Vincent, **1981** 869-879; **1993** 368-369; **1995** 391, 392, 393, 398, 399
Widnall, Sheila, **1997** 656
Widnall, William B. (R-N.J.), **1973** 802
Widowers, Social Security benefits for, **1975** 56, 177-185; **1977** 169-181
Wieghart, James C., in presidential debates, **1984** 848-851, 858-860, 868-870
Wiesel, Elie
on Genocide Convention, **1986** 116
at Holocaust commemoration, **1981** 382-386
and Holocaust Museum, **1993** 307-308
Nobel Peace Prize, **1986** 1075-1078
testimony at Barbie trial, **1987** 517-524
Wiesenthal Center, discovery of Mengele, **1985** 410, 413
Wigand, Jeffrey, nicotine addiction, **1997** 333
Wiggins, Alan, **1986** 171
Wiggins, Charles E. (R-Calif.)
Judiciary Committee impeachment report, **1974** 714
Nixon impeachment, **1974** 674
Nixon's White House tapes, **1974** 288
Wiggins, Kevin, death row inmate, **2002** 359
Wilcox, Kenneth, **1978** 654
Wilder, L. Douglas, **1989** 368; **1990** 41-47
Wilderness areas, protection of, **1972** 151; **1973** 218-219
Wilderness Society
land use permit for Alaska pipeline, **1972** 271
U.S. fire-management policy, **1988** 942
Wildfires, forest fire prevention guidelines, **2000** 712-722
Wildlife
Alaskan oil spill impact on, **1989** 227-230
protection, and management of national forests, **1973** 21-26
Wilentz, C. J., on surrogate motherhood contract, **1988** 72-79
Wilken, Claudia, California term limits, **1997** 887
Wilkerson, Lawrence, on Bush administration distortion of intelligence information, **2005** 251-252
Wilkerson, S. Jeffrey K., **1992** 137
Wilkerson v. Utah, **1992** 180
Wilkey, Malcolm R.
on treaty termination, **1979** 919
on White House tapes, **1973** 842, 854-857
Wilkins, Roger, **1988** 186; **1995** 658
Wilkins, Roy, **1995** 455, 459
on busing moratorium, **1972** 259
on Coleman report on desegregation, **1975** 614
Wilkinson, Beth, death penalty, **2001** 390
Will, George F.
on death penalty, **2000** 989
interview of Sakharov, **1986** 1093-1095
on sexual harassment in schools, **1999** 217-218
Willadsen, Steen M., cloning research, **1997** 212, 215
Willard, Richard K., **1988** 468
Willemssen, Joel C., Y2K computer crisis, **1998** 545, 547-554
Willey, Kathleen, Clinton sexual misconduct charges, **1998** 698
William J. Clinton Foundation. *See* Clinton Foundation
Williams, Anthony, on eminent domain and economic development, **2005** 364
Williams, Anthony A., **1996** 784
Williams, Armstrong, **2005** 644-645, 653-655
Williams, David, FBI crime laboratory reports, **1997** 222-223
Williams, Debra, affirmative action case, **1997** 185
Williams, Eddie N., **1990** 295-299
Williams, Harrison A., Jr. (D-N.J.)
Abscam scandal, **1995** 594

Williams, Harrison A., Jr. (D-N.J.) *Continued*
conviction and Senate recommendation for expulsion, **1981** 673-679
on disclosure by municipal bond issuers, **1977** 568
on dismantling of OEO, **1973** 454
indictment of, **1980** 900
on Nixon's social program cutbacks, **1973** 171
Williams, Hubert, **1991** 405
Williams, Jody, land mines ban, **1997** 845-846
Williams, Joe, Tallgrass Prairie Reserve, **1993** 888-889
Williams, Juan, on Marshall's papers, **1993** 340-341
Williams, Leroy, **1982** 730
Williams, Pete, Patriot missile performance report, **1992** 866
Williams, Richard S., U.S. peacekeepers protection from prosecution, **2002** 608
Williams, Robin M., Jr., **1989** 446
Williams, Stanley "Tookie," death penalty execution, **2005** 178
Williams, Stephen F., Hamdan detainee case, **2005** 447, 460-461
Williams, Terry, death sentencing of, **2000** 992
Williams, United States v., **1992** 324
Williams, Willie L., **1992** 409
Williams v. Taylor, **2000** 991-992
Williamson, Richard, **1988** 490, 492
Williamson, Thomas, Jr., **1992** 158
Williemssen, Joel C., on Y2K computer conversion, **1997** 535
Willingboro, New Jersey, promoting integration by prohibiting lawn signs, **1977** 313-320
Willis, Daniel K., violent aggressive driving study, **1997** 551
Willis, Kent, **1996** 85
Wilmon, Donald E., **1990** 511
Wilmut, Ian, cloning research, **1997** 212-220
Wilner, Thomas, Guantanamo Bay detentions, **2003** 108
Wilson, August, death of, **2005** 357
Wilson, Bob (R-Calif.), and ITT campaign contributions, **1972** 396-397, 404, 406
Wilson, Carroll L., **1980** 417
Wilson, Charles H. (D-Calif.)
House censure of, **1980** 485-491; **1983** 727
House reprimand of, **1978** 845-846, 879-880
Wilson, Don W., constitutional amendment (27th), **1992** 439-442
Wilson, Harold, **1975** 354
Wilson, James Q., **1983** 358
violent crime, **1997** 682
Wilson, John J.
at Haldeman sentencing, **1975** 142, 144-146
on release of Watergate grand jury report, **1974** 225, 227-228
Wilson, Joseph C., IV
on disclosure of wife as covert intelligence operative, **2003** 20, 21
Iraq-Niger uranium sales investigations, **2003** 20; **2005** 249, 699-700
Wilson, Pete (R-Calif.)
abortion issue, **1996** 497
on affirmative action, **1996** 759-760, 762
and balanced budgets, **1995** 11
energy crisis in California, **2001** 332
gubernatorial elections, **2003** 1006
and health care reform, **1995** 43
on Japanese-American internment, **1988** 287, 288
on Los Angeles earthquake, **1994** 4, 5, 7
on Los Angeles riots, **1992** 410
Wilson, Robert
Cosmic Background Explorer (COBE) satellite, **1992** 380, 381
hormone replacement therapy, **2002** 504
Wilson, Valerie Plame. *See* Plame, Valerie
Wilson, Will, **1984** 19
and wiretap approval by attorney general, **1974** 392-395
Wilson, Woodrow
democracy and, **2005** 43
illness of, **1985** 492
press conferences of, **1988** 839-840
Wilson v. Seiter, **1992** 179, 180-181, 183-184
Winans, R. Foster, insider trading case, **1987** 881-889; **1991** 814
Winchell, Barry L., beating death of, **1999** 900; **2000** 160-161
Wind, Timothy E., King case acquittal, **1992** 409; **1993** 633-642, 647, 650
Windham, Thomas, **1991** 405
Windom, Robert E.
on AIDS spending, **1986** 887
on approval of AZT, **1987** 327-330
Wines, Michael, **1992** 520
Winfield, Dave, **1993** 169
Winkenwerder, Bill, Jr., military service health risks, **2001** 909, 910
Winn, Larry (R-Kan.), **1977** 778-781
Winnick, Gary, Global Crossing collapse, **2002** 399
Winograd, Morley A., **1978** 767
Winter, William F., race relations panel, **1997** 316, 322; **1998** 668
Wiranto, General
East Timor war crimes arrest and conviction, **2004** 756
Indonesian presidential candidate, **2004** 753-754
Wiretaps. *See* Surveillance, electronic
Wirth, Timothy, **1995** 126
Wisconsin, welfare reform, **1999** 258
Wisconsin v. Mitchell, **1993** 385-389
Wisconsin v. Yoder, **1997** 411
Wise, Robert E., Jr. (D-W.Va.), **1992** 295
Wisenberg, Solomon L., Lewinsky scandal investigations, **1998** 567, 576-585
Witcomb v. Chavis, **1990** 230
Witherspoon v. Illinois, **1986** 446-456
Witt, James Lee
Los Angeles earthquake and, **1994** 5, 6
midwest floods, **1993** 485, 486
Red River floods, **1997** 232
Witte v. United States, **1997** 391
Witters v. Washington Dept. of Services for the Blind, **1997** 362, 368-371, 378-379
Witteveen, H. Johannes, on international recession, **1977** 692-698
WMD. *See* Weapons of mass destruction
WMO. *See* World Meteorological Organization
Wojtyla, Cardinal Karol. *See* John Paul II (pope)

Wolf, Frank (R-Va.), comments at bipartisan prayer service, **1995** 8
Wolf, Milton A., **1979** 649
Wolfe, Leslie, on sexual harassment, **1993** 355
Wolfe, Sidney M., **1990** 573-598; **1993** 369
Wolfensohn, James D.
  aid on Africa, **2002** 449
  Asian economic crisis, **1998** 725, 726-734
  economic aftermath of September 11, **2001** 668
  Israel Gaza Strip withdrawal and international aid, **2005** 531
  U.S. representative for "Quartet" Middle East peace process team, **2005** 415
  World Bank president resignation, **2005** 414
  WTO trade negotiations, **2003** 744
Wolff, Sidney C., **1990** 754
Wolff v. Rice, **1976** 521-536
Wolfowitz, Paul D.
  defense secretary resignation, **2005** 45
  financing of Iraq reconstruction, **2003** 949
  in Iraq hotel during bombing, **2003** 940
  Iraq-U.S. relations, **2001** 851
  Middle East peace process, **2003** 1203
  missile threat, **1998** 481
  national security strategy, **2002** 634
  relationship with Colin Powell, **2004** 630
  Russian-U.S. relations, **2001** 893
  U.S. defense policy, **2004** 626
  as World Bank president, **2005** 45, 414-415
Wolfson, Lewis W., on Nixon administration and the press, **1973** 630-637
Wolman v. Walter, **1977** 431-445; **1993** 405; **1997** 366
Wolpe, Howard (D-Mich.), **1989** 547
Wolper, David, **1986** 698-699
Wolter, Kirk, presidential election and Florida recount, **2001** 525
Women
  See also Abortion; Discrimination, sex; Minorities; Pregnancy
  advancement of
    Bush on, **1988** 607
    during Carter administration, **1981** 58, 62, 75
    Republican Party platform on, **1984** 698-700
  alcoholism among, **1983** 344
  attitudes toward, and high public office, **1989** 106, 109-110, 115-118
  Barbara Bush's speech at Wellesley commencement, **1990** 353-356
  blacks as heads of household, **1983** 43, 47
  in business, assistance for, **1980** 52
  in Catholic Church
    John Paul II on, **1987** 701, 712-713, 715; **1988** 785-792; **1994** 276-280
    revised canon law on, **1983** 93, 95
    U.S. bishops on, **1985** 573, 577, 579, 766, 777; **1986** 985
  in Congress, **2000** 906-907
  discrimination against
    in federal programs, **1976** 545, 562
    Reagan on, **1980** 652, 654
  domestic violence, **1983** 357-364; **1994** 62-72
  earnings comparison with men, **2001** 547-553
  economic integration of, **1974** 779, 783-785
  economic rights of mothers, John Paul II on, **1981** 697, 713
  education of in developing countries, **1980** 889-890
    and birth rates, **1984** 523, 538
  equality for
    in athletic programs, HEW rules on, **1974** 507-508, 510-511
    Democratic Party platform on, **1984** 550, 598-608, 612
    national women's conference on, **1977** 861-867
    Republican Party platform on, **1972** 698-700
    UN conference on, **1985** 556-563
  ERA debate
    Carter on passage of, **1979** 55-56
    Democratic Party platform support for, **1984** 603-604, 607
    expiration, **1982** 611-617
    at national women's conference, **1977** 861-864
  and the family, Southern Baptist Convention statement on, **1998** 333-337
  Ferraro nomination, **1984** 647, 649
  gender learning differences, **1992** 141-154
  infant formula vs. breast-feeding, **1981** 447-458, 917
  job discrimination, Nixon on, **1972** 97; **1973** 187
  jury service, exclusion from, **1975** 55-66
  in labor force, **1987** 127, 143-144
  and mental health services, **1984** 833-834, 840-841, 843
  in the military, **1997** 654-660; **1998** 335-336
    combat assignments, **1981** 521; **1987** 671, 673, 675-676; **1989** 704; **1991** 491-512; **1992** 1029-1044; **1993** 333-336
    professional opportunity for, **1972** 627-629
    treatment in draft, **1981** 521-540
  in modern world, U.S. Catholic bishops on, **1988** 785-786
  national conference, Houston, **1977** 861-867
  ordination of
    dispute between Vatican and Dutch Catholics, **1985** 363-364, 373
    as Episcopal and Anglican bishops, **1989** 49-54
    John Paul II on, **1979** 725, 729, 755; **1994** 276-280
  parental leave
    and reemployment rights, **1987** 17-27
    seniority rights after, **1977** 871-881
  rape report, **1992** 385-395
  as Reagan appointees, **1981** 575-579; **1982** 965-970; **1983** 756, 914
  representation at Democratic convention, **1972** 590; **1976** 596
  rights for
    in Chinese constitution, **1978** 174
    Democratic Party platform on, **1972** 543; **1980** 723
    Reagan administration positions on, **1983** 755-763; **1984** 83-84, 92
    Republican Party platform on, **1980** 568, 580; **1988** 617, 634, 643
    UN conference on, **1975** 507-522
  rights of, UN Conference on, **1995** 581-587
  science skills among, **1988** 385
  smoking by
    health consequences of, **1982** 163

Women *Continued*
trends in, **1981** 4; **1989** 36-38
Social Security reform, effect of on, **1983** 74
in space exploration, **1996** 691-694
status of in developing countries, **1984** 545; **1994** 351-359
and population growth, **1987** 441, 450-452, 458, 461
TV watched by, **1982** 366
UN World Conference on, **1995** 136, 581-587; **1996** 138
violence against, **1999** 527; **2000** 327-328
wage discrimination, Reagan on, **1983** 78, 85-86
as wage earners, Social Security discrimination against survivors of, **1975** 56, 177-185; **1977** 169-181
on welfare, education and support for, **1988** 847-852
working conditions for in Poland, John Paul II on, **1987** 556, 560-564
working women, attitudes about, **2001** 548-549
workplace segregation and stereotypical roles, **1985** 789-790, 792-794, 799
Women, Infants, and Children (WIC)
program cuts, **1987** 151, 163-164
Supplemental Program for, **1985** 202-203
Women, World Conference on (Nairobi), **1985** 555-570
Women's Department, proposed, **1977** 861
Women's health
drug testing for pregnant women, **2001** 409-410
health care, **1993** 653-658
hormone replacement therapy, **2002** 503-511
mammogram screenings, **1997** 38, 142-149; **2001** 869-870; **2002** 265, 510
Republican Party platform on, **2000** 514-515
and smoking, **2001** 222-244
Women's Health Initiative (WHI), hormone replacement therapy study, **2002** 503, 505-506, 507-511
Women's Republican Leadership Forum, Reagan speech on alternative to ERA, **1983** 757
Women's rights
Afghanistan
new freedoms, **2002** 23-24, 39
suppression under Taliban, **2002** 17
AIDS epidemic, feminization of, **2004** 430-431
Arab world
status of women in, **2002** 485, 487
UN human development report on, **2005** 279-280
honor killings of women, **2000** 327
trafficking in humans, State Department report on, **2002** 332-352
UN special session on, **2000** 325-336
UN World Conference on, **2000** 325
voting rights denied in Saudi Arabia, **2005** 271
voting rights in Kuwait, **2005** 271
Wong, Alfred, **1993** 935-937
Wong Sun v. United States, **1985** 224
Wonnacott, Paul, **1992** 99
Woo Suk Hwang, human cloning, **2004** 158
Wood, Gordon, **1994** 523
Wood, Kimba M., Justice Department nomination withdrawal, **1993** 137
Wood, Susan F.
FDA assistant commissioner resignation, **2005** 817
morning-after pill, FDA ruling, **2005** 816-817
Wood, Tom, on racial preferences, **1997** 184
Woodcock, Leonard
ambassadorial appointment to PRC, **1979** 137
MIA commission, **1977** 207, 209
on Mondale's China visit, **1979** 671
negotiations with PRC on normalization, **1978** 783
Woodham, Luke, **1998** 736
Woodpecker, red cockaded, **1995** 359-368
Woodrow Wilson International Center for Scholars
AIDS in Russia study, **2005** 54
as sponsor of inter-American dialogue, **1983** 375-390
Woodruff, Judy, **1988** 801-802
Woods, Marvin, **1992** 175-185
Woods, Rose Mary, and White House tape erasure, **1974** 23-24; **1977** 324, 358-359
Woodson v. North Carolina, **1976** 489-490, 503-505; **1991** 385
Woodward, Bob, **1994** 239
CIA leak case, **2005** 702, 704
Woolsey, James R.
Ames espionage case, **1994** 476-480, 484
CIA counterterrorism recruitment restrictions, **2000** 278
missile threat, **1998** 481
Woolsey, Lynn (D-Calif.), Iraq War troop withdrawal, calling for, **2005** 836
Wootan, Margo
on federal dietary guidelines, **2005** 5
obesity, **2001** 935-936; **2002** 624
Work, dignity of, John Paul II on, **1981** 204, 207-208, 695-698, 703-705, 714; **1985** 59-61; **1987** 557-560
Work force
growth forecast by Carter CEA, **1981** 106, 109
women in, trends, **1987** 127, 143-144
Work teams, role in future of labor-management relations, **1995** 16-17
Workers
alien legalization, **1981** 265-266, 270-272, 605, 611-612
blue-collar and white-collar, smoking by, **1985** 810-811, 814-816; **1989** 32, 37-38
Democratic Party platform on, **1992** 692-693, 697
dignity for, John Paul II on, **1986** 640, 642, 644-646
guarantees to in Soviet constitution, **1977** 748, 753-754, 762
immigration control, law enforcement for, **1981** 265, 271-272, 605-606, 610
Japanese view of U.S., **1992** 13
labor markets report, **1992** 123-127
layoff and plant closing notice, **1988** 340-341, 343
literacy and basic skills among U.S., **1988** 298, 379-380, 383-384
minimum wage, federal law applied to state and local governments, **1976** 377-389; **1985** 167-187
Pittston coal strike settled, **1990** 19-22
poor, benefits to in Carter's welfare plan, **1977** 551, 553-554, 556, 558, 560-561
productivity of, and smoking, **1985** 615, 617-619, 622, 811
protection of, Democratic Party platform on, **1976** 554-555; **1980** 720-721
quality of, **1992** 127

retraining for displaced, **1988** 343, 345
rights of, in PRC constitution, **1975** 44, 46-47
social justice for
John Paul II on, **1985** 365, 374-376
Vatican on, **1986** 319, 321-324, 327-328, 333-338
unfair treatment of
ILO assessment of, **1982** 857; **1983** 969
in Soviet labor camps, **1982** 857-869
union political activity, **1992** 345-351
work and leisure report, **1992** 163-173
Working Group on Financial Markets, on stock market crash, **1988** 9-10, 12, 34-36
Workplace
AIDS in, **1985** 733-747; **1986** 888-889; **1988** 437-439
apparel industry sweatshops, **1997** 206-211
cancer-causing substances in, **1978** 633-651
contagious disease in, **1987** 245-252
disabilities in the, Supreme Court on, **2002** 3-14
discrimination against African Americans, **1993** 423-430
drug testing in, **1986** 839-846
ergonomics, OSHA standards, **1999** 769-778
exposure to toxic substances in
OSHA protection from, **1981** 491-505
and smoking, **1985** 810-811, 813-814, 817-821
future of, **1995** 15-23
genetic testing in the, **1998** 63-72
hazardous, and employee rights, **1980** 199-207
involuntary smoking in, **1986** 1079-1082, 1086-1087, 1090
sex segregation and discrimination in, **1985** 789-801
sexual discrimination, **1993** 939-945
smoking in
and other hazards, **1985** 809-822
segregated areas, **1972** 46-47
World Affairs Council
Enders on El Salvador civil war, **1981** 242, 257-261
Reagan on aid to developing countries, **1981** 770
Smith speech on counterintelligence, **1981** 862
World Anti-Doping Agency, **2005** 213
World Bank
African debt-relief program, **2000** 450, 479
aid to Russia, **1992** 257
and AIDS prevention programs, **1997** 83
Asian financial crisis, **1998** 722-734
Bosnia economic situation, **2005** 852
capitalization increase, U.S. support for, **1977** 689, 691, 707-709, 715
China economic situation, **2002** 854
and debt crisis
Baker plan for relief of, **1985** 643-652
Brady plan for relief of, **1989** 138, 141-143
economic summit on, **1984** 356, 359-360
Reagan and Larosière on, **1983** 801-814
debt reduction, **1999** 702
development aid
economic summit on, **1982** 470, 475
McNamara on goals of, **1972** 859-865
development loans, increased funding for, Kissinger on, **1975** 589, 593-594, 600-603
economic aftermath of September 11, **2001** 663-671
economic aid, **1991** 452, 464-466
economic development report, **2003** 756
establishment of, **1972** 815; **1985** 624
fuelwood-forestry lending program, **1981** 14, 21
health problems in Eastern Europe, **1994** 416
income inequality, **2002** 690
Indonesian transmigration project, impact on rain forests, **1986** 859-873
Iraq reconstruction, **2005** 717-718
Latin America economic growth, **2005** 765
McNamara farewell address to, **1980** 883-893
meeting with IMF
Belgrade, **1979** 771-776
Seoul, **1985** 643-652
Washington, **1972** 815-826; **1977** 687-716; **1978** 659-666; **1980** 883-896; **1983** 801-814; **1984** 795-802
Multilateral Debt Relief Initiative, **2005** 407
Munich economic summit on, **1992** 648
Palestinian economic aid, **2005** 34-35
poverty report, **2000** 478-479
proposed economic organization, effect on position of, **1981** 769, 773
proposed energy affiliate of, **1981** 773
Shultz on U.S. proposals for international monetary reform, **1972** 815, 820-826
Sierra Leone debt relief, **2002** 249
Soviet Union status, **1990** 808, 809-810
trade barriers and subsidies study, **2005** 411-412
U.S. debt, **1997** 42
on world economy, **1984** 795-796, 800-802
world population and development report, **1984** 521-543
WTO trade talks, and economic expansion, **2003** 740
World Coal Study, on energy resources, **1980** 417-430
World Conference on Tobacco or Health, **2000** 551
World Council of Churches
John Paul II speech to in Geneva, **1984** 399-402
on South Africa, **1984** 1028
World Court. *See* International Court of Justice
World Food Conference (Rome, 1974)
cooperation on food shortages, **1975** 10, 189, 190, 195, 197, 599
as Kissinger proposal, **1973** 809, 814
resolutions adopted, **1974** 939-953
U.S. proposals at, **1975** 236
World Food Council, UN, establishment of, **1974** 939-940
World Food Programme. *See* United Nations World Food Programme (WFP)
World Health Assembly (WHA), **2000** 537, 549
World Health Organization (WHO)
acupuncture treatment, **1997** 750
AIDS drug treatment, **2003** 780, 781
antiretroviral drugs (ARVs), **2003** 785-786; **2004** 432-433; **2005** 51
AIDS prevention, **2002** 472
avian flu outbreaks, **2005** 747
cigarette advertising and warning labels, **1988** 312
cigarette advertising ban, **2001** 226
Clinton praises, **1995** 351, 356
flu pandemic
global action plan conference, **2005** 750
preparing for, **2004** 923-928; **2005** 750

World Health Organization (WHO) *Continued*
flu vaccine shortages, **2004** 643, 925
global dietary guidelines, **2003** 481, 484-485
health problems in Eastern Europe, **1994** 416
infant formula code, U.S. vote on, **1981** 447-458
infectious diseases, **1996** 302-311
mad cow disease, **2000** 880-881
minority mental health, **2001** 575, 578
obesity guidelines, **2002** 628-629
pain management guidelines, **1997** 328
pharmaceutical quality control, **1997** 348
SARS (severe acute respiratory syndrome) outbreak, **2003** 121-134; **2004** 924
smoking and health, **2001** 222; **2004** 280
smoking in developed countries, **1989** 32, 37
spread of AIDS, **1985** 735; **1986** 888, 904-905, 908
suicide prevention, **1999** 440, 443
tobacco control, framework convention on, **2003** 260-278; **2004** 280, 284
tobacco industry conspiracy, **2000** 536-554
tsunami disaster assessment, **2004** 994
tuberculosis report, **1992** 1009
UN postwar report on Iraq, **1991** 165
World Jewish Congress
German confiscations of gold, **1997** 258
neutral aid to Nazi Germany, **1997** 257, 260, 262
on U.S. Jews and the Holocaust, **1983** 145
on Waldheim's war service, **1986** 744; **1988** 405-406
World Jewish Restitution Organization, **1997** 260
World Meteorological Organization (WMO)
global warming, **1988** 862
global warming report, **1998** 945-950; **2004** 833; **2005** 926
World Population Conference (Bucharest, 1974), **1974** 777-797; **1984** 521, 544, 547
World Stem Cell Hub, **2005** 321
World Summit for Social Development, **1995** 134-140
World Synod of Bishops, on the family, **1980** 871-882
World Tamil Coordinating Committee (New York), **2003** 612
World Trade Center bombing (1993), **1999** 502; **2000** 278
See also September 11 (9/11) terrorist attacks
convictions, **2001** 804
FBI crime report, **1997** 221, 223, 225-226
World Trade Organization (WTO)
AIDS drugs patents, **2002** 472-473
antimonopoly powers, **1999** 393
Cancún trade talks collapse, **2003** 740-750, 755; **2005** 409
China's compliance, **2004** 943-948
Clinton administration negotiations, **1997** 543
creation of **1994** 556-557; **1997** 53; **1999** 798; **2000** 47
Doha Round (Development Agenda), **2003** 742, 746, 766; **2005** 410, 411
generic drug trade, **1999** 492; **2003** 783
Hong Kong talks, **2005** 411
intellectual property rules, **2004** 939
labor standards and, **1999** 800-801
market vs. nonmarket economy rules, **2004** 938
membership
for China, **1999** 724; **2000** 19, 30, 50, 213, 217-218, 1049; **2001** 738; **2002** 851-852; **2003** 1179-1180
for Iran, U.S. objections, **2005** 593
membership request
for China, **1997** 730
for Russia, **1997** 341
negotiations with Brazil, **2003** 8
organized labor, **1999** 630
role of, **1997** 58, 61, 68
Seattle meeting (Millennium Round), **1999** 797-801; **2000** 476; **2003** 742; **2005** 409
U.S. tariffs on steel imports, **2003** 446
World War I
chemical weapons in, **1989** 25
incendiary weapons in, **1972** 838
World War II
anniversary of Allied victory in Europe, Reagan visit to Bitburg, **1985** 347, 357-362
Austria under Nazism, papal visit, **1988** 405-414
Barbie war crimes, **1983** 737-747; **1987** 517-524
causes of and alliances in, Wallace on, **1975** 155-156, 160
declassification of documents, **1997** 271
European devastation and basis for EC, **1984** 439-440
fiftieth anniversary commemoration, **1995** 216-221
German guilt and remorse for, **1989** 487-497
Germany, division of, **1986** 792, 795-796
heroism in, and Medal of Honor award, **1989** 697-700
Hirohito in, **1989** 99-101
and Hitler-Stalin nonaggression pact (1939), **1989** 469, 472
Holocaust, and U.S. Jews, **1983** 143-161
Holocaust, Catholic Church repentance for, **1998** 121-130
Holocaust Museum, **1993** 307-313
Holocaust victims restitution, **1997** 270-271
incendiary weapons in, **1972** 838
Japanese apology for suffering, **1995** 302-306
Japanese-Americans, U.S. internment of, **1988** 287-295
Japan's responsibility for damages to China in, **1972** 827-829
land mine warfare, **1995** 50
Nazi confiscated art, return of, **1998** 294-295
neutral nations aid to Nazi Germany, **1997** 257-272; **1998** 291-312
Pearl Harbor fiftieth anniversary, **1991** 775-784
Polish suffering in, **1977** 898, 909, 912; **1989** 524-525, 536
Soviet-West German relations, **1973** 558-559
Stalin's leadership in, Gorbachev on, **1987** 857, 862-863
Tripartite Gold Commission (TGC), **1997** 266, 271
U.S. postwar policy, **1997** 268-270
U.S.-Soviet lend-lease settlement, **1972** 845, 855-858
Waldheim service in, **1986** 743-750
war crimes, Demjanjuk acquittal, **1993** 617-623
World Youth Day, and John Paul II's visit to Denver, **1993** 659-669
WorldCom
bankruptcy, **2004** 417-418

fraud investigation, **2003** 332-348
retirement fund losses, **2002** 102; **2005** 201
SEC civil action complaint, **2002** 391-405
Worldwatch Institute
on drought, **1988** 863
on Soviet farming and agricultural trade, **1982** 823-831
Wörner, Manfred, **1990** 456, 458
Wounded Knee (South Dakota), AIM occupation of, **1973** 531-535
Wrangell-St. Elias National Monument, **1978** 731, 738-739
Wright, Betty, in Wright ethics investigation, **1989** 240, 248, 251-257, 259-263
Wright, Charles Alan, on White House tapes, **1973** 698, 840-841, 860-863, 867-869
Wright, Edward, **1992** 382
Wright, J. Skelly
on treaty termination, **1979** 919, 931
on White House tapes, **1973** 842
Wright, Jim (D-Texas)
appointment of Iran-contra committee, **1986** 1052
bipartisan accord on Nicaraguan contras, **1989** 164
at Bush inauguration, **1989** 42
and Central American peace plan, **1987** 638
at congressional bicentennial, **1989** 127-129
ethics charges, **1995** 746; **1996** 839; **1997** 5
ethics investigation and resignation, **1989** 239-271
House Speaker resignation, **1997** 5; **1998** 800
Nicaraguan officials, meetings with, **1987** 1008; **1989** 241
on Reagan State of the Union, **1985** 108; **1987** 107; **1988** 59
Wright, Susan Webber
Clinton contempt ruling, **1999** 21-22
Clinton sexual harassment suit, **1998** 566; **1999** 21-22
Wright v. Rockefeller, **1993** 468, 471, 477
Wriston, Walter B.
on Carter anti-inflation program, **1980** 245
on Citibank and New York City's fiscal crisis, **1977** 569
on privatization commission, **1988** 229
Writers and writing
response to death threat against Rushdie, **1989** 95-97
teaching of, **1986** 220-221, 225-226
Writer's Guild of America, **1989** 86
WTO. *See* World Trade Organization
Wu, David (R-Ore.), physician-assisted suicide, **1999** 442
Wu Bangguo, Chinese leadership, **2003** 1174
Wuerl, Donald, **1986** 985
Wurst, Andrew, **1998** 736
Wyandotte Transp. Co. v. United States, **1992** 194, 195
Wyatt, Watson, retirement plans study, **2005** 202
Wyden, Ron (D-Ore.)
Clinton's health care plan, **1993** 783
elected to Senate, **1995** 592
on Negroponte national intelligence director nomination, **2005** 253
physician-assisted suicide, **1997** 462-463; **2001** 293
timber cutting and wildfires, **2000** 714
tobacco claims settlement, **1998** 845
Wygant v. Jackson Bd. of Education, **1993** 467; **1995** 314-315; **1997** 191
Wylie, Chalmers P. (R-Ohio)
BCCI House hearings, **1991** 632
House censure of Crane and Studds, **1983** 728
Wyman, Louis P. (R-N.H.), **1972** 500
Wyoming
See also Yellowstone National Park
Bridger-Teton National Forest, oil and gas drilling, **2004** 670

X

X and Others v. The Attorney General (Supreme Court of Ireland), **1992** 249-254
Xerox, and corporate scandals, **2002** 400

Y

Y2K (Year 2000) conversion, **1997** 534-540; **1998** 543-554; **1999** 51, 760-768
and leap year rollover problems, **2000** 4, 12
President's Council on, **1998** 543-544; **2000** 3-15
and related investments, **2004** 63
success of, **2000** 3-15
Yaalon, Moshe, on Israeli-Palestinian conflict, **2003** 1205-1206
Yach, Derek, weight loss advertising, **2002** 628
Yachting, international, court action on America's Cup race, **1990** 267-273
Yakovlev, Alexander
Gorbachev's ally, **1990** 440
UN oil-for-food program scandal, **2005** 235
Yamani, Ahmed Zaki
on OPEC oil prices, **1978** 791; **1979** 253; **1980** 995; **1983** 922
on Saudi oil output, **1974** 222; **1981** 800
on Saudi oil price increase, **1976** 938, 940-942
Yanayev, Gennadi I.
appointment as Soviet vice president, **1990** 826
Soviet coup attempt, **1991** 400, 515-517
Yang, Zhou, **1994** 79
Yang Doo Wan, influence buying in Congress by, **1977** 769, 775-776, 786, 799
Yang Lwei, first Chinese astronaut, **2003** 1173, 1178
Yanukovich, Viktor F., Ukrainian presidential candidate, **2004** 1001-1007; **2005** 65
Yao Tiansheng, **1994** 80
Yarkas, Imad Eddin Barakat (*aka* Abu Dadah), al Qaeda leader, **2004** 108
Yaron, Amos, and Palestinian refugee camp massacre, **1983** 166, 179
Yassin, Ali Mohamed Osman, Darfur human rights violations, **2005** 516
Yassin, Sheikh Ahmed (Hamas leader), **2002** 933
assassination, **2004** 301, 302
funeral, **2004** 810
Yastrzemski, Carl, **1994** 361
Yates, Buford, Jr., WorldCom collapse fraud case, **2002** 39; **2003** 335
Yavlinsky, Grigory Y., Putin challenger in Russian elections, **2000** 172

al-Yawar, Ghazi, Iraq interim government, **2005** 944-945
Yazov, Dmitri T., **1991** 515, 517
Ye Jianying, **1978** 157
Yee v. City of Escondido, **1992** 615; **1993** 436
Yekhanurov, Yuri, as Ukrainian acting prime minister, **2005** 68-69
Yellowstone National Park
  centennial of, **1972** 795
  fire-management policy in, **1988** 941-942, 946
  snowmobile regulation, **2001** 218; **2002** 902
Yeltsin, Boris N.
  address to Congress, **1992** 526-531
  address to new Russian parliament, **1994** 185-194
  arms reduction, **1992** 60
  Bush aid package, **1992** 257
  Bush on, **1992** 19
  Bush-Yeltsin summit meeting, **1992** 519-526
  challenges Gorbachev, **1990** 333, 441
  Chechnya war, **1999** 909-910, 913
  collapse of Soviet Union, **1991** 785-787
  coup attempt
    eulogy for casualties, **1991** 524-525
    postcoup dominance, **1991** 786
    statement on, **1991** 516, 517-520
  crises in Russia of 1993, **1993** 769-779
  economic summits
    Denver, **1997** 340-342
    Munich, **1992** 637
    Tokyo, **1993** 541, 543, 552-555; **1995** 93
  election victory, **1996** 139, 430-437; **1997** 515
  European Security Summit, **1994** 583-584, 588-591
  Gorbachev's resignation and, **1991** 527-528
  Israeli-Palestinian Peace Accord, **1993** 768
  NATO expansion, **1999** 120
  NATO summit meeting, **1997** 515
  Nixon on, **1992** 256, 261
  presidential election, **1989** 173, 175, 177; **1991** 527-528
  priorities for 1995, **1995** 100-101
  progressive supporters, **1989** 827
  relationship with Putin, **2003** 245
  religious freedom legislation, **1997** 564
  resignation as Russian president, **1999** 917-923; **2001** 254-255
  Russian economic crisis, **1998** 601-613
  Soviet economic reforms, **1987** 858; **1995** 93, 96-98
  Soviet Party Congress, **1990** 439, 448-449
  START II agreement, **1993** 17-20, 60-61
  state of the nation speech, **1995** 92-101
Yemen
  U.S. relations, **2001** 7
  USS *Cole* attack, **2000** 277, 861-865; **2001** 3-16
Yemen, South
  breaking of diplomatic relations with Egypt, **1977** 829
  chemical weapons treaty, **1993** 72
  and Israeli-Lebanese security agreement, **1983** 473
  on Sadat and Camp David accords, **1978** 607
  terrorism by, CIA on, **1981** 468
  willingness to accept PLO, **1982** 744
Yen, European competition with, with European Monetary System, **1978** 741-743, 749-750
Yeo, Tim, mad cow disease, **2000** 882
Yeutter, Clayton
  on environmental law exemptions, **1991** 275
  food aid to Soviets, **1990** 809
Yokich, Stephen P., **1995** 682
Yom Kippur War. *See* Arab-Israeli War (October War, 1973)
Yoo, John C., Afghanistan detainees, and prisoner-of-war status, **2004** 337-338
Yosemite National Park, **1995** 126
Yost, Charles W.
  and MIA commission, **1977** 207-208
  on Middle East peace, **1979** 226-227
Young, Andrew J. (D-Ga.)
  on Centennial Olympic Park bombing, **1996** 448-449
  resignation as UN ambassador, **1979** 647-657
  Rhodesian settlement plan, **1977** 583, 585
  UN arms embargo against South Africa, **1977** 823
  at Zimbabwe independence, **1980** 318
Young, Brigham, **1981** 337-338
Young, David R., Jr., **1974** 662-664
Young, Frank E.
  on interferon, **1986** 481-482, 484-485
  on TPA, **1987** 876-879
Young, John W., space shuttle pilot, **1981** 417, 420
Young, Thomas, Mars mission failures investigations, **2000** 90-92
Young, W. Dale, ruling on frozen embryo, **1989** 551-559
Young Voters for the President, **1973** 36
Youngberg v. Romeo, **1982** 521-530; **1990** 377-378
Youngstown Sheet and Tube Co. v. Sawyer, **1992** 460, 467, 468; **2004** 342
Yousef, Ramzi, World Trade Center bombing, **2001** 804; **2002** 705; **2003** 1055
Youth
  See also Children; Education; Teenagers
  adult attitudes toward, **1997** 422-433
  alcoholism in, **1983** 342-344
  in Arab countries, **2002** 486
  black, problems of, **1983** 43, 47-48
  breaking cycle of violence, John Paul II's message to, **1983** 241, 243-244
  in Catholic Church, **1985** 573, 578, 777
  contraceptive services for, **1972** 301, 311
    and parental notification, **1983** 269, 271-272
  death penalty, age as mitigating factor in, **1982** 51-55, 58-63
  educated, vision of for America, **1972** 789-793
  employment for
    effect of subminimum wage on, **1983** 785-786, 788, 790
    Reagan-Anderson debate on, **1980** 860-861
  first-time voters, participation in 1972 election, **1973** 35-38
  HIV epidemic and, **1998** 888-889
  job training for
    Carter on, **1980** 28, 41, 49-50, 165, 167-168; **1981** 58, 62-63
    Reagan on, **1981** 326; **1983** 77, 84, 115-116
  juvenile curfew laws, **1996** 325-333
  marijuana use among, **1982** 203, 205, 210-211
  myths about youth violence, **2001** 79
  pages, and congressional misconduct, **1983** 725-734

rape trial, age as factor in, **1981** 340, 344
represented at Democratic convention, **1972** 590
and sexuality, **1986** 1057, 1059
smoking by, **1989** 31-32, 35-36, 38-39
FDA regulations of tobacco sales, **1996** 589-599
health consequences, **1982** 164, 169
women, **1980** 17-19, 25
suicide prevention, **1999** 453-454
TV's effect on behavior of, **1982** 365-383
unemployment among
economic summits on, **1977** 368, 371; **1983** 508, 513-514
minorities, **1977** 722; **1978** 68, 74, 84, 92; **1982** 920, 941-943
venereal disease treatment, and parental consent, **1972** 343, 347-348
Youth Citizenship Fund, **1973** 36
Youth Crime Watch of America, **1999** 385
Yucca Mountain (Nevada), and nuclear plant wastes, **1989** 357
Yudhoyono, Susilo Bambang, Indonesian presidential inauguration, **2004** 753-760
Yugoslavia, **1981** 770
See also Bosnia
CSCE, **1994** 583
economic summit (Munich), **1992** 637
human rights report, **1993** 559, 561-564
independence from Soviet Union, **1975** 869-873; **1976** 434-435, 459-461
independence of Republics, **1991** 367-376
Kostunica presidential inauguration, **2000** 833-839
and nonaligned nations strategy, **1979** 681-862
presidential elections, **2000** 141, 833-839
relations with Albania, **1985** 327
Senate "Ethnic Cleansing" report, **1992** 771-779
UN membership, **1992** 875-878
U.S. bombing of Chinese embassy in Belgrade, **1999** 304-316, 726
U.S. diplomatic relations with, **2000** 837
U.S. use of force in, Carter on, **1976** 798, 803
war in Kosovo, **1998** 827-841; **1999** 119, 134-143
wartime atrocities in, **1986** 743-745
Yugoslavia (former)
dissolution of, **2003** 55-57
human trafficking, **2002** 351-352
political protests, **2005** 43
political situation, **2001** 831; **2005** 64
U.S. bombing of Chinese embassy in Belgrade, **2001** 247
U.S. economic aid, **2001** 827, 829
war crimes tribunal, **2002** 607
Yukon Flats National Monument, **1978** 732, 740
Yukon-Charley National Monument, **1978** 731, 738
Yukos (Russian oil company), seizure and dismantling of, **2004** 569; **2005** 301, 302-303
Yurchenko, Vitaly, **1985** 604
Yurek, Stephen R., on sexual harassment in schools, **1999** 218
Yuschenko, Viktor A.
dioxin poisoning during campaign, **2004** 1002-1003, 1006; **2005** 64
news conference with Rice, **2005** 908
Ukrainian political dissension, **2005** 64-70
Ukrainian presidential election victor, **2004** 1001-1008
Ukrainian presidential inauguration speech, **2005** 70-74
visit to U.S., **2005** 66

Z

Zablocki, Clement J. (D-Wis.)
Caribbean Basin Initiative, **1982** 181
nuclear freeze, **1982** 887
WHO infant formula code, **1981** 448, 457-458
Zadok, Haim, and Sharon libel suit, **1985** 48, 51
Zadornov, Mikhail, Beslan school crisis, **2004** 568
Zahir Shah (king of Afghanistan), **2003** 1097
Zaire
See also under its later name Congo, Republic of
CIA activity in, **1975** 710, 720-724, 769-772, 778
John Paul II visit, **1985** 501
Mobutu ousted from, **1997** 877-879; **1998** 161, 220, 615; **1999** 428
Rwandan refugee camps, **1994** 541-549; **1996** 809-815
U.S. aid to, **1976** 288, 292
Zakharov, Gennadi F., espionage charges against, **1986** 269, 819-821, 826-827
Zambia
AIDS prevention programs, **2002** 475
economic sanctions against Rhodesia, **1979** 941
presidential elections, **2001** 504
on Rhodesian internal agreement, **1978** 150
on Rhodesian settlement plan, **1976** 721-722, 728-729
South Africa's attack on ANC in, **1986** 583
U.S. aid to, **1976** 287-288, 291-292
Zamir Commission on Temple Mount Violence Report, **1991** 696-697, 699-705
Zant v. Stephens, **1991** 385
Zapatero, José Luis Rodriguez, Spanish election for prime minister, **2004** 105, 108-109
Zare, Richard, **1996** 474
al-Zarqawi, Abu Musab
attempted assassinations of, **2005** 661
audiotape broadcasts, **2005** 943
audiotape on bombings in Amman, **2005** 501
Fallujah as headquarters for insurgent attacks, **2004** 880
Foley murder conviction, **2005** 400
insurgency against U.S. in Iraq, **2004** 877; **2005** 660
terrorist leader linked to al Qaeda, **2003** 47, 1056; **2004** 539, 877; **2005** 401
Zauderer v. Office of Disciplinary Counsel of Supreme Court of Ohio, **1995** 333
al-Zawahiri, Ayman
at-large status, **2004** 1012; **2005** 970
audiotape broadcasts, **2004** 269, 271-272, 536
linked to September 11 terrorist attacks, **2001** 620
opposition to Musharraf, **2003** 214
al Qaeda leader, **2002** 1017; **2003** 1052, 1054
videotapes on London bombings, **2005** 398
ZDV (zidovudine). *See* AZT (azidothymidine)
Zedillo, Ernesto, inaugural address, **1994** 563-573
Zeevi, Rehavam, assassination of, **2001** 364

Zeid Al Hussein (prince of Jordan), on sexual abuse by peacekeepers, **2005** 237
Zeitz, Paul
on AIDS epidemic and drug therapy, **2005** 52
Bush AIDS initiative, **2003** 782, 783
Zelikow, Philip D., national commission on terrorist attacks, **2004** 452
Zelman v. Simmons-Harris, **2002** 406-423
Zeltner, Thomas, tobacco industry conspiracy, **2000** 538
Zeman, Milos, **1999** 702
Zemlykov, Yevgeny, **1986** 93
Zenawi, Meles (Ethiopian president), **2000** 754
Zerhouni, Elias A., stem cell research, **2004** 160
Zero option, Reagan proposal for nuclear force reduction, **1981** 823, 827; **1983** 792, 796
Zhang Chunquiao, trial of, **1980** 955-958
Zhang Jinfu, **1984** 25
Zhao Ziyang
death of, **2005** 620
Hong Kong agreement, **1984** 1045-1050
as premier, **1980** 834, 956
prodemocracy demonstrations, **1989** 276-277
Reagan trip to PRC, **1984** 287-294
Tiananmen Square protests, **2005** 620
U.S.-PRC trade and technology agreements, **1984** 23-28
warning to two superpowers, **1985** 710
Zhelev, Zhelyu, **1991** 400
Zheng Bijian, U.S.-China relations, **2005** 613
Zhironovsky, Vladimir, **1995** 94
Zhou Enlai, **1997** 95
Zhou Xiaochuan, Chinese monetary policy, **2004** 239
Zhu Bangzao, U.S.-China relations, **1999** 236
Zhu Chenghu, Chinese nuclear weapons threat to U.S., **2005** 614
Zhu Rongji
China-Taiwan relations, **2000** 192
Chinese leadership, **2002** 850; **2003** 1174
U.S.-China trade negotiations, **1998** 468; **1999** 726
Zhvania, Zurb, Shevardnadze resignation, **2003** 1042
Zia ul-Haq, Mohammad
as leader of coup in Pakistan, **1977** 537-541
on Soviet intervention in Afghanistan, **1980** 4
Ziegler, Ronald L.
Burns-Nixon disagreement on economy, **1974** 419
executive privilege claims, **1973** 338
Fitzgerald case, **1973** 194-195
impeachment inquiry, **1974** 304
Kissinger's threatened resignation, **1974** 488
performance of, National Press Club on, **1973** 629-630, 638
Vietnam peace negotiations, **1973** 4
Ziglar, James W., INS reorganization, **2001** 767
Zijlstra, Jelle, **1972** 413
Zimbabwe
See also Rhodesia
AIDS pandemic, **2002** 136-137, 470; **2003** 1112
creation of, U.S.-British plan for, **1977** 583-590
drought in, **1984** 978-979
elections, **2002** 133-137, 447, 448
famine/food crisis, **2002** 156-157; **2003** 1110-1112
independence for, **1980** 317-336
land reform, **2002** 135-137; **2003** 1111
Libya relations, **2003** 1227
majority rule in, Carter on progress toward, **1977** 738, 743; **1978** 270, 282-283
national strikes against government, **2003** 1113
political situation, **2001** 508; **2003** 1110-1118
preparation for independence, **1979** 939-948
settlement in, front-line presidents on, **1976** 721-722, 728-729
South Africa's attack on ANC in, **1986** 582-583
suspension of membership in British Commonwealth, **2003** 1114-1118
Zimbabwe African National Union-Patriotic Front (ZANU-PF), **2002** 133-134, 136, 138-144
Zimbabwe Human Rights Forum, **2003** 1112
Zimring, Franklin, prison populations, **1998** 871
Zinchenko, Olieksandr, Ukrainian political situation, **2005** 68
Zinni, Anthony C.
Aceh province cease-fire agreement, **2002** 708
Middle East peace talks, **2001** 367; **2002** 370
Zionism
Arafat on at UN, **1974** 919, 922-933, 936-937
issue at women's conferences, **1975** 507, 521; **1985** 555-556
as racism, UN resolution on, **1975** 646, 649, 825-827
Zivkovic, Zoran, prime minister of Serbia, **2003** 59-60
al-Zobeidi, Muhammad, "mayor" of Baghdad, **2003** 936
Zobrest, James, **1993** 399-406
Zobrest v. Catalina Foothills School District, **1993** 399-406; **1997** 362, 368-371, 377-378
Zoellick, Robert B.
China's military buildup, **2005** 613
Sudan peace talks, **2005** 519
WTO trade talks collapse, **2003** 741, 744
Zogby, James J., **1989** 58
Zolin, United States v., **1998** 403
Zon, Leonard, stem cell research, **2005** 320
Zoning regulations
for adult movie theaters, **1986** 131-144
barring low-income housing, **1977** 35-44
Zougam, Jamal, al Qaeda terrorist suspect arrested, **2004** 108
Zubaydah, Abu, al Qaeda leader captured and detained, **2002** 1016; **2003** 106
Zuma, Jacob
Burundi peacekeeping mission, **2003** 925
Congo peace negotiations, **2002** 549
Zuma, Nkosazana, sanctions against Zimbabwe, **2002** 137
Zumwalt, Elmo R., Jr.
assigning women to warships, **1972** 627-629
Navy race relations, **1972** 901-906
Zurcher v. Stanford Daily, **1978** 355-372
Zvania, Zhurab, Georgian presidential candidate, **2004** 72
Zyuganov, Gennady, opposes Yeltsin, **1995**